MW01446328

History of western Maryland. Being a history of Frederick, Montgomery, Carroll, Washington, Allegany, and Garrett counties from the earliest period to the present day; including biographical sketches of their representative men Volume 2, pt.1

Scharf, J. Thomas (John Thomas), 1843-1898. 1n, Long, Helen

Nabu Public Domain Reprints:

You are holding a reproduction of an original work published before 1923 that is in the public domain in the United States of America, and possibly other countries. You may freely copy and distribute this work as no entity (individual or corporate) has a copyright on the body of the work. This book may contain prior copyright references, and library stamps (as most of these works were scanned from library copies). These have been scanned and retained as part of the historical artifact.

This book may have occasional imperfections such as missing or blurred pages, poor pictures, errant marks, etc. that were either part of the original artifact, or were introduced by the scanning process. We believe this work is culturally important, and despite the imperfections, have elected to bring it back into print as part of our continuing commitment to the preservation of printed works worldwide. We appreciate your understanding of the imperfections in the preservation process, and hope you enjoy this valuable book.

HISTORY

OF

WESTERN MARYLAND

BEING A HISTORY OF

FREDERICK, MONTGOMERY, CARROLL, WASHINGTON, ALLEGANY, AND GARRETT

COUNTIES

FROM THE EARLIEST PERIOD TO THE PRESENT DAY;

INCLUDING

BIOGRAPHICAL SKETCHES

OF THEIR

REPRESENTATIVE MEN.

BY

J. THOMAS SCHARF, A.M.,

AUTHOR OF "CHRONICLES OF BALTIMORE," "HISTORY OF BALTIMORE CITY AND COUNTY," [illegible] MARYLAND HISTORICAL SOCIETY AND ACADEMY OF SCIENCES; MEMBER OF THE HISTORICAL [illegible] HONORARY MEMBER OF THE GEORGIA HISTORICAL SOCIETY; CORRESPONDING MEMBER OF [illegible] OF NEW YORK, WISCONSIN, MINNESOTA, SOUTH CAROLINA, AND VIRGINIA, OF THE [illegible] SOPHICAL SOCIETY OF [illegible], OF THE NEW ENGLAND HISTORIC [illegible]

IN TWO VOLUMES, ILLUSTRATED.

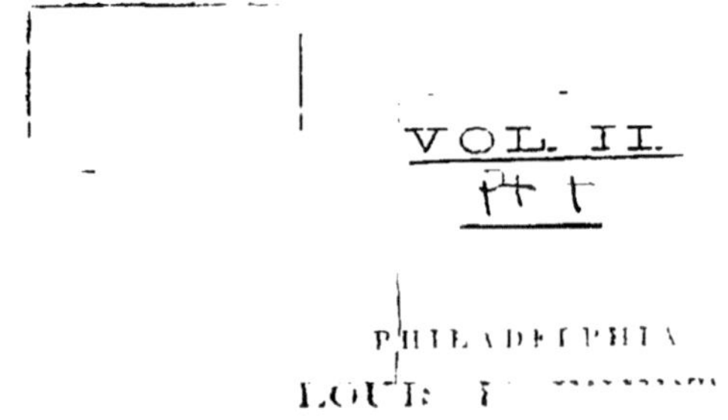

VOL. II.

Pt I

PHILADELPHIA:

LOUIS [illegible]

1533582

pyright, 1882, by Louis H Everts

L0486

CONTENTS OF VOLUME II.

ILLUSTRATIONS IN VOLUME II.

HISTORY

OF

WESTERN MARYLAND.

CARROLL COUNTY.

CHAPTER XXXVIII.

INTRODUCTORY.

First Settlers—Land Grants—Erection of Carroll County—Elections—Bench and Bar—Distinguished Men—County Officers—School Statistics.

THE territory embraced within the limits of Carroll County was settled at an early period in the history of Maryland. The first settlers were Scotch-Irish, Germans, and the descendants of the English from Southern Maryland. The Indians, before the advent of the whites, had retired across the South Mountain into the Cumberland Valley. A remnant of the "Susquehannocks," numbering between sixty and seventy, lived within less than a mile of Manchester (then a part of Baltimore County) until 1750 or 1751, and were probably the last aborigines residing in the county. About that period, without any stir or apparent preparation, with the exception of two, they all disappeared in a single night. The exceptions were a chief named Macanappy and his wife, both old and infirm, and they survived the departure of their race but a few days. The similarity of names has given rise to the impression that this tribe found its way to Florida, and that Miconopy, the celebrated chief, who afterwards gave the United States so much trouble, was one of the descendants of the old Indian left to die near Manchester. In the Land Office at Annapolis patents are recorded for land grants in this portion of the State as early as 1727. In that year "Park Hall," a tract of land containing two thousand six hundred and eighty acres, was surveyed for James Carroll. This land was then situated in Prince George's County, between New Windsor and Sam's Creek. In 172[illegible] [illegible]

Fredone and subsequently sold to Allan Farquhar. It now embraces a part of the town of Union Bridge and the farm of E. J. Penrose. "Brierwood" was surveyed for Dr. Charles Carroll in 1731. "White's Level," on which the original town of Westminster was built, was granted to John White in 1733. "Fanny's Meadow," embracing the "West End" of the present town of Westminster, was granted to James Wells in 1741. "Fell's Retirement," lying on Pipe Creek, and containing 475 acres, was granted to Edward Fell in 174[illegible]. "Arnold's Chance," 600 acres, was granted to Arnold Levers in 1743. "Brown's Delight," 350 acres, situated on Cobb's Branch, near Westminster, was granted to George Brown in 1743. "Neighborly Kindness," 100 acres, to Charles Carroll in 1746. "Cornwell," 666 acres, on Little Pipe Creek, was patented in 1749, and afterwards purchased by Joseph Haines and his brother. "Terra Rubra" was patented to Philip Key in 1752, for 1865 acres; "Ross' Range" to John Ross in 1752, for 3100 acres; "Spring Garden," on part of which Hampstead is built, to Dunstan Dane in 1748; "Brothers' Agreement," near Taneytown, to Edward Diggs and Raphael Taney in 1754, for 7900 acres; "Foster's Hunting Ground" to John Foster, 1139 acres; "German Church" to Jacob Schilling and others in 1758, for a German Reformed and Lutheran church at Manchester; "Five Daughters" to Carroll's daughter, 1759, for 1500 acres; "New Market," on which Manchester is built, to Richard Richards in 1754; "Rattlesnake Ridge" to Edward Richards in 1738; "Caledonia" to William Lux and others in 1761, for 11,638 acres; "Bond's Meadow" to John Ridgely in 175[illegible], for 1915 acres (Westminster is partly situated on this tract); "[illegible] Inheritance" to Michael Swope in 1761, for [illegible] acres; "Ohio," north of Union [illegible], to S[illegible] in 1763, for 9270 acres; "New Holland" near Mid[illegible]

h[illegible] [illegible]

1762 for 5801 acres, "Gilbea" to Thomas Rutland, 1762 for 2772 acres; "Runnymeade," between Uniontown and Taneytown, to Francis Key and Upton Scott in 1767, for 3677 acres, "Hale's Venture" to Nicholas Hale in 1770, for 2886 acres, "Windsor Forest" to John Dorsey in 1772 for 2886 acres, "Rochester" to Charles Carroll of Carrollton in 1773, for 1706 acres and "Lookabout," near Roop's mill, to Leigh Master in 1774, for 1443 acres.

Among the earliest settlers in this section of Maryland was William Farquhar, whose energy, thrift, and wisdom aided materially in the development of the country. His ancestors emigrated from Scotland to Ireland, where he was born July 29, 1705. When sixteen years of age he left Ireland with his father, Allen Farquhar, and settled in Pennsylvania. Allen Farquhar, as was mentioned above, acquired from John Tredane a large tract of land on Little Pipe Creek, but there is no evidence that he actually resided there. In 1735 he conveyed this tract, known as "Kilfadda," to his son William, one of the conditions of the gift being that he should remove from Pennsylvania to "ye" province of Maryland. In compliance with the terms of the deed, William Farquhar, with his wife Ann, came to Maryland and entered into possession of his estate. The country was then a wilderness and destitute of roads, except such paths as were made by wild beasts and Indians, and no little intrepidity was required for such a journey, clogged with a helpless family. Farquhar had learned the trade of a tailor, and by his skill and industry in making buckskin breeches, the garments then most in vogue, he prospered. He invested his savings in land, and in 1768 he was the possessor of two thousand acres, in which was included all the ground upon which the present town of Union Bridge is built. He was a counselor and peace-maker, and it is related of him that upon one occasion he rode home in the evening and found his house surrounded with emigrant-wagons belonging to settlers who had been driven from their homes by the Indians and had fled to him for protection. They had their stock and movable property with them, and were afraid to go back to their lands. Farquhar visited the Indians and soon pacified them, and the settlers returned to their homes and were never afterwards molested.

Between the years 1730 and 1740 great advances were made in the settlement of what is now known as Carroll County. "The Marsh Creek settlement" in the western section of York County, Pa., including the region around Gettysburg, composed almost exclusively of Scotch-Irish, [illegible] Hanover and Conewago in the same county, settled entirely by Germans, provided a large contingent. The latter located principally in the Manchester and Myers Districts, where many of their descendants now live.

Many were attracted thither also from St. Mary's, Prince George's, Anne Arundel and Baltimore Counties, on the Western Shore of Maryland. The dispute concerning the boundary line between the provinces of Pennsylvania and Maryland was a fruitful source of trouble to those who possessed interests in the debatable ground. A strip of land six or eight miles wide was claimed both by the province of Pennsylvania and the proprietary of Maryland. John Digges obtained a Maryland grant of six thousand eight hundred acres in the vicinity of Hanover, and Charles Carroll procured a similar grant in the neighborhood of Fairfield or Millerstown, and the latter now goes by the name of the Carroll Tract. Hanover, at that time known as McAllisterstown or Kallisterstown, was within the disputed territory, and became a refuge for disorderly characters and hence was called "Rogues' Harbor."

This vexatious boundary question, which had agitated the two colonies since the arrival of William Penn in America in 1682, was decided, as we have shown elsewhere in favor of the province of Pennsylvania in 1769 by Mason and Dixon, two surveyors sent out from London for that purpose, and Mason and Dixon's line has ever since remained the unquestioned boundary between the two commonwealths. The dispute having reached a definite conclusion, an impetus was given to development. Settlers multiplied, the country was cleared up, and convenient farm-buildings were erected. The inhabitants soon learned to appreciate the fine water-power so abundant in this portion of Maryland, and in 1760 David Shriver, the grandfather of the older members of the family of that name now living in Western Maryland purchased a tract of land on Little Pipe Creek and erected a mill and tannery. Mr. Shriver was a prominent and useful citizen. He represented Frederick County in the convention called in 1776 to frame a constitution for the State of Maryland, and for a number of years he was the representative of that county in the Senate and House of Delegates. In May, 1765, a bateau loaded with iron was successfully navigated from the Hampton Furnace on Pipe Creek to the mouth of the Monocacy, [illegible] Frederick County. There is no record of the establishment of this furnace, but that it must have been in operation for [illegible] the [illegible] is evident [illegible] 28, 1767,

in which Benedict Calvert, Edward Digges, Normand Bruce, William Digges, Jr, and James Caudy offer for sale the "Hampton Furnace, in Frederick County, together with upwards of three thousand acres of land The furnace (with casting-bellows) and bridge-houses were built of stone, also grist-mill and two stores, the whole situated on a branch of Monocacy River"

The entire stock of negroes, servants, horses, wagons, and implements belonging to the works were offered for sale There was on hand at the time coal for six months, fourteen hundred cords of wood five hundred tons of ore at the side of the furnace and four hundred tons raised at the banks The advertisement concludes with the announcement that Normand Bruce lived near the works

Solomon Shepherd, grandfather of Thomas, Solomon, and James F Shepherd, married Susanna Farquhar, the youngest child of William Farquhar, Oct 27, 1779, and settled on a portion of the Farquhar estate, about three quarters of a mile east of Union Bridge Mr Shepherd was a wool comber and fuller, and established a fulling mill where the factory now stands For some time after the construction of his mill he was without a house of his own and boarded with his father-in-law, at some distance down Pipe's Creek, and it is related of him that in walking back and forth along the banks of the stream from the mill to the house at night he was wont to burn the ends of a bunch of hickory sticks before he would set out on his hazardous journey, and when the wolves (which were savage and ravenous) approached too near he would whirl his firebrand about him to drive them away He afterwards moved into a log house, which is still standing, and in 1790 built the brick house in which Shepherd Wood now resides The latter was at that time considered a palatial extravagance, and the neighbors dubbed it "Solomon's Folly" In 1810 he built the present factory, and put in carding and spinning-machines and looms for the manufacture of cloths, blankets, and other fabrics In 1815 he purchased land of Peter Benedune, and removed to the place now owned and occupied by E G Penrose, where he lived until his death in 1834

In 1783, David Rhinehart and Martin Wolfe walked from Lancaster County, Pa, to Sam's Creek, where they purchased a tract of land and soon afterwards settled on it Wolfe was the grandfather of Joseph, Samuel, and Daniel Wolfe He was somewhat eccentric after a very unusual fashion, and is said to have been unwilling to dispose of property for a price which he believed to exceed its real value David Rhinehart was the grandfather of David, Daniel, William H, E Thomas, J C, and E F Rhinehart William H Rhinehart, the great American sculptor, received his first lessons on the farm now owned and occupied by Daniel Rhinehart, twelve miles southeast of Union Bridge

Joel Wright, of Pennsylvania, married Elizabeth Farquhar, daughter of William Farquhar, and settled on a part of the land acquired by his father-in-law He was a surveyor and school teacher, and superintended a school under the care of Pipe Creek Monthly Meeting, at that time one of the best educational institutions in the State His pupils came from all parts of the surrounding country and many were sent to him from Frederick City and its vicinity It was common in those days for ladies to make long journeys on horseback to attend religious meetings or to visit friends Mrs Wright traveled in this way to Brownsville, then called "Red Stone," in Pennsylvania, to attend meeting and to visit her relatives She brought back with her, on her return, two small sugar-trees and planted them, and from these have sprung the many beautiful shade-trees of that species which adorn the vicinity of Union Bridge

Francis Scott Key, whose name the "Star-Spangled Banner" has made immortal was born at Terra Rubra, near the Monocacy, in what is now the Middleburg District of Carroll County, Aug 9, 1780 In his day he was well known as an able lawyer and Christian gentleman, but with the lapse of time his reputation as a poet has overshadowed his many other excellent qualities

Col Joshua Gist was an early settler in the section of Maryland now embraced within the limits of Carroll County He was an active partisan in the Revolutionary war, and during the administration of President John Adams, near the close of the last century, was marked in his disapproval of the riotous and insurrectionary proceedings of those opposed to the excise duty laid upon stills The disturbance, known in history as the "Whisky Insurrection," became so formidable, especially in Western Pennsylvania, that Mr Adams appointed Gen Washington commander of the forces raised to suppress it The excitement extended to this region, and the Whisky Boys in a band marched into Westminster and set up a liberty-pole The inhabitants of the town becoming alarmed sent out for Col Gist, who then commanded a militia regiment The colonel, a very courageous man, mounted his horse, rode into town, drew his sword, and ordered the pole to be cut down, which was at once done, and placing his foot on it, he thus remained until it was hewn in pieces The Boys, concluding discretion to be the better part of valor, stole out [illegible] th [illegible] was stayed

by the coolness and judgment of a single individual In 1748, Frederick County was created by the Colonial Legislature, and that portion of the present county of Carroll which had previously belonged to Prince George's was embraced within its limits, as was almost the whole of Western Maryland Col Gist and Henry Warfield were elected to the House of Delegates of Maryland towards the close of the eighteenth century, for the express purpose of securing a division of the county into election districts for the convenience of the inhabitants, who were at that time compelled to cross the Monocacy and go all the way to Frederick City to vote

Joseph Elgar, in the latter part of the last century, established a factory at Union Bridge for the manufacture of wrought nails,—that is, the nails were so designated, but in reality they were cut from the bar of iron, lengthwise with the fibre of the bar, which gave them ductility and clinching qualities equivalent to wrought nails Elgar subsequently removed to Washington and entered the service of the United States, where his genius was duly appreciated About the year 1809, Jacob R Thomas, a neighbor of Elgar, conceived the idea that the very hard labor of cutting grain in the harvest-field could be done by machinery driven by horse-power Prior to this time, and for some years afterwards, the old system of cradling grain was the only process generally known for harvesting, and the reaping-machine may be truthfully said to have been invented by him Thomas worked at his machine with great assiduity, and added to it an automatic attachment to gather the cut grain into sheaves, it being substantially the self-raker of the present day During the harvest in the summer of 1811 his machine was so far perfected as to admit of a trial It had not been furnished with a tongue and other appurtenances for attaching horses, and was therefore pushed into the harvest field and over the grain by a sufficient number of men Thomas Shepherd, recently deceased, and William Shepherd, his brother, and father of Thomas F Shepherd and Solomon Shepherd, and Rudolph Stern, father of Reuben W Stern, of Westminster, were three of the men who aided in the trial, and their testimony is unanimous that it cut the grain well and perfectly, but that its delivery was defective and did not make a good sheaf There is no evidence on record as to the manner in which the gathering attachment was constructed, whether it was like or unlike any of the automatic rakes of the present day, but the cutting apparatus was the same in principle as those now in use on the best reapers, mowing in the same shears-like manner, which has been universally approved and adopted as the best method of cutting grain, and differing only in the manner of attaching the knives to the sickle bar In modern machines the knives are short and broad and riveted fast to the sickle bar, while in Thomas' machine the knives were longer and pivoted in the middle, and attached to the sickle bar by a pivot at the rear end Thomas was extremely sensitive, and unable to bear up against and overcome the incredulity and ridicule consequent upon the partial failure of the machine and it was never finished by him He afterwards built a factory for the manufacture of flax into linen, but it did not prove remunerative He subsequently removed to Baltimore, where he kept the Globe Inn, on Market Street, and then to Frederick City, where he kept the City Hotel, and afterwards to Point of Rocks, on the Potomac River, where at the time of his death he was engaged in the construction of a steam canal-boat invented by himself Obed Hussey, the pioneer in the manufacture of practical reaping-machines, was a cousin of Jacob R Thomas They were intimately acquainted, and Hussey afterwards perfected Thomas' invention, and from that McCormick's, and all others cutting on the same principle, were framed The pathetic story of Jacob R Thomas is the same so often repeated in the lives of inventors and discoverers The spark of genius went out amid the vapors of poverty, while his quick-witted imitators reaped the golden showers which should have been poured into his own lap The region of country afterwards known as Carroll County now grew apace The lands were cleared of their dense forests, the magnificent water-courses were utilized for mills and manufactures, towns sprang into existence, and the inhabitants, following the motto of the commonwealth, increased and multiplied Taneytown, Westminster, Manchester, Hampstead, Union Bridge, Middleburg, and New Windsor became prosperous villages At the close of the last war between Great Britain and the United States agricultural products commanded excellent prices Wheat flour was sold in the Baltimore markets for fourteen dollars per barrel, and other commodities realized proportionate prices The value of land had greatly appreciated In April, 1814, Peter Benedune sold out all his land in the vicinity of Union Bridge at prices ranging from one hundred to one hundred and twenty dollars per acre and removed to the Valley of Virginia About this time also the spirit of progress was abroad The Westminster Fire-Engine and Church Lottery [illegible] drawn in Frederick City, July 10, 1813 A [illegible]k was established [illegible] Westminster [illegible] om the [illegible] of th[illegible] day th[illegible] [illegible] spirit,

fanned into a flame during the Revolution, and rekindled in 1812 by the invasion of the British, was still active and vigorous. Under date of Oct. 13, 1821, the Frederick *Herald* says, "At a meeting of the Columbian Independent Company, commanded by Capt. Nicholas Snider, of Taneytown, and the Independent Pipe Creek Company, commanded by Capt. Thomas Hook, at Middleburg, in Frederick County, . . . information of the death of Gen. John Ross Key was received."

The people were virtuous and God-fearing. The corner-stone of the German Reformed and English Presbyterian church was laid in Taneytown, Sept. 5, 1821. It was about this date also that the inhabitants awakened to a sense of the value of regular postal communication, and a postal service on horseback was established from Frederick City to Westminster *via* Union Bridge and back once a week. The people were gradually becoming sensible of the overgrown bulk and unmanageable interests of the immense counties of Frederick and Baltimore, and the leading men residing in either county in the vicinity of Westminster began to take an active interest in politics. Joshua Cockey became a prominent politician in this end of Frederick County, and represented his constituents in the Senate and House of Delegates. Isaac Shriver also represented the county several times. William P. Farquhar and John Fisher were also members of the House of Delegates. Peter Little and Elias Brown, of Freedom District, represented the Baltimore District in Congress between the years 1818 and 1828. In 1832 the feeling, which had been gaining strength for years, that a new county was absolutely needed for the convenience and prosperity of those dwelling in the eastern portion of Frederick and the western portion of Baltimore Counties culminated in a memorial to the Legislature of Maryland petitioning for a division of these counties and the establishment of a new one to be called "Westminster."

When the area and population of Frederick and Baltimore Counties are considered it seems extraordinary that this movement should have been so long delayed or that it should have met with such decided opposition when inaugurated. The two counties contained nearly one-fifth of the territorial area of the State, and, exclusive of the city of Baltimore, they possessed a population of upwards of eighty-five thousand inhabitants, or very nearly one-fifth of the whole number of inhabitants in the State. The bounds of the new county, as proposed by the memorialists, were as follows: "Beginning at Parr's Spring, at the head of the western branch of the Patapsco River, and running with said branch, binding on Anne Arundel County, to the north branch of said river; thence running up said north branch, excluding the same, to the old mill on Dr. Moore Falls' land, including said mill; thence north seventeen degrees east to the Pennsylvania line; thence, binding on said line, westwardly to Rock Creek, one of the head-waters of the Monocacy River; thence with said creek and river, excluding the same, to Double Pipe Creek; thence with said creek, and with Little Pipe Creek and Sam's Creek, including their waters, to Maurois' mill, excluding said mill, and thence with a straight line to Parr's Spring, the beginning."

It was estimated that the new county would contain about twenty-five thousand inhabitants. The town of Westminster, beautifully situated in the valley between the head-waters of Little Pipe Creek and those of the north branch of the Patapsco, on the road leading from Baltimore to Pittsburgh, generally known as the Reisterstown turnpike road, and containing a population of seven hundred souls, was to be the county-seat. The people in some of the districts were now thoroughly aroused. Complaints were frequent and vehement of the distance to be traversed to reach the seats of justice in Baltimore and Frederick Counties respectively, and the difficulties and delays encountered because of the overcrowded dockets of the courts. The *Star of Federalism*, a newspaper, was established at Uniontown, and at different periods three papers were published at Westminster by George Keating, Mr. Burke, and George W. Sharpe, all strenuously advocating a division. The latter afterwards removed to Frederick and established the Frederick *Citizen*. The support of these papers was small, and they were soon discontinued. Although the sentiment in favor of a division was general, the people were very much divided in opinion as to how it should be done. Some favored a division of Frederick County alone, some were in favor of separating Baltimore County from the city and locating the seat of justice at a central point, while the inhabitants of Westminster and its vicinity, which was on the dividing line between the two counties, were anxious to take a portion of each of those counties and form a new one with Westminster as the county-seat. The memorial mentioned above was presented to the Legislature of Maryland in 1833, and referred to a committee of which William Cost Johnson, of Frederick, was chairman. Mr. Johnson was a man of great ability and popularity. He introduced a bill into the Legislature which created a county with the metes and bounds prayed for by the memorialists, and it was mainly through his efforts th[illegible] been the [illegible]

intention of the petitioners to give the name of Westminster to the new county, but the bill as passed named it "Carroll," in honor of Charles Carroll of Carrollton, then recently deceased, a man who in character, ability, patriotism, and usefulness has never been surpassed in Maryland

The act of Assembly was clogged with a provision requiring its submission to the vote of the people who lived in the sections of the two counties proposed to be cut off, and further exacting a majority of the voters in its favor in each segment The vote was to be taken *viva voce*, at the October election in 1833 The people were now fully alive to the importance of the question, and the issue was fairly joined Col John K Longwell established the *Carrolltonian* at Westminster, June 28, 1833, a journal whose aim was to advocate the division and educate the people up to a full knowledge of the advantages likely to accrue from the creation of the new county The paper was conducted with marked ability and zeal, and the division, which occurred four years later, was measurably due to its unflagging energy and fidelity As the fall election approached public meetings were held in the districts interested and the merits of the proposed division very thoroughly discussed A very large meeting was held at Westminster and an able address issued, which was published in pamphlet form in the English and German languages and very freely circulated in the counties A committee composed of the following-named gentlemen was appointed to further the object of the meeting C Birnie, Sr, William Murray, Edward Dorsey, Joshua C Gist, Thomas Hook, John McKaleb, Archibald Dorsey, William Sheppard, Mordecai G Cockey, John McKellip, Joseph Steele, John Baumgartner, Nicholas Algire, William Shaw, of H, George Richards, William Roberts, Frederick Ritter, Samuel Galt, Nicholas Kelley, James C Atlee, Washington Van Bibber, Evan L Crawford, Peter Hull, Philip G Jones, Peter Erb, Jacob Shriver, William Brown, Evan McKinstry, Basil D Stevenson, Philip Englar, Abraham Bixler, Jacob Landes, William Caples, David Kephart, Sr, Joshua Sellman, William B Hebbard, John Malehorn, J Henry Hoppe, Michael Miller, John Swope, George Warfield, William Jordan, George Crabbs, Sebastian Sultzer, John C Kelley, David Foutz, Jesse Slingluff, Nathan Gorsuch, Joseph Keifer, Abraham Null, Jesse L Warfield George Cassell

It would seem that with such an array of citizens of worth and excellence in its favor there should have been no difficulty in securing the passage of the bill, but a strong opposition was developed in the districts which belonged to Baltimore County Their attachment to the county clouded their judgments, and they refused to listen to reason or to consult their own interests The campaign in behalf of the new county was one of the most memorable and exciting that had ever taken place in Western Maryland, and after a canvass which embraced every nook and corner of the districts in Frederick and Baltimore Counties to be segregated the election took place, and the new county failed to receive a majority of the votes in the Baltimore County segment, and the division was consequently defeated, as the following vote by districts will show

FREDERICK COUNTY

Districts	For	Against
Westminster	610	139
Taneytown	398	187
Liberty	4	101
New Market	0	22
	1012	449

BALTIMORE COUNTY

Districts	For	Against
Dug Hill	150	304
Freedom	141	208
Woolery's	250	53
Wise's	0	11
Reisterstown	13	17
	554	593

The election was a severe blow to the friends of the new county They had not anticipated defeat indeed, they thought that the measure would be approved by a large majority of the voters They did not make sufficient allowance for county attachments and the influence of tradition, nor did they properly estimate the jealousy of other villages and the prejudice and fear of increased taxation, but they were not dismayed by the disaster They now knew both their weakness and strength, and they went manfully to work to retrieve their mistakes More meetings were called, the people were reasoned with, and a public sentiment created in favor of the measure in places where the stoutest opposition had been developed In 1835 the Whigs nominated Dr William Willis as a member of the House of Delegates from Frederick County, and the Democrats nominated Isaac Shriver They were both elected, many of the friends of the new county voting for them Willis and Shriver, with their colleagues, Robert Annan and Daniel Duvall, originated and boldly pressed another bill on the attention of the Legislature By this act a large portion of the Liberty District in Frederick County and all of the New Market District were excluded from the limits of the new county by making the Buffalo road the line from Sam's Creek to Parr's Spring, and thus were removed the objections of the people residing in those districts, who were almost unanimously opposed to separation from the old county The delegates

were supported in their action by a petition containing 1800 names, and after laboring diligently during the whole session they had the satisfaction of procuring the passage of the bill by both branches of the Legislature

A confirmatory act by the next Legislature was necessary before the bill could become a law, and it was expected that the measure would have to encounter determined opposition, especially from the representatives of Baltimore County, as the project was strongly opposed there and her representatives considered themselves under obligations, if possible, to defeat it

The political campaign of 1836 was one of the most exciting and closely-contested struggles that has ever taken place in the State, and resulted in important changes of the organic law Senatorial electors were to be chosen, two from each county, who were to meet in Annapolis and select the Senate, then consisting of fifteen members The Whigs of Frederick County nominated Evan McKinstry and Gideon Bantz, and the Democrats, John Fisher and Casper Quynn A strong party in favor of reform in the State Constitution caused the election of Fisher and Quynn Of the whole number of electors the Whigs elected twenty-one and the Democrats nineteen The constitution prescribed that twenty-four electors should constitute a quorum The electors met in Annapolis, but the nineteen Democrats claimed a majority of the senators as Reformers, inasmuch as they represented a large majority of the popular vote of the State, and declined to enter the electoral college until their proposition was granted The Whigs indignantly refused to accede to their demand, and the Democrats left for their homes in a body, receiving from their friends the appellation of the "Glorious Nineteen"

The withdrawal of the Democrats from Annapolis produced a profound sensation in Maryland By the Whigs it was considered revolutionary, and many persons became alarmed The Whig friends of the new county were afraid that it would cause the rejection of their favorite scheme

When the Whig and Democratic senatorial electors were nominated in Frederick County a ticket was named by each party for the House of Delegates The Whig ticket was composed of Jacob Matthias, Francis Brengle, Joshua Doub, and George Bowlus Isaac Shriver was again placed on the Democratic ticket Francis Thomas, afterwards Governor of Maryland, was at that time the leader of the Democracy in the western portion of the State The action of the Democratic electors, and the feeling in the party consequent thereupon, led him to believe that the time was ripe for a change in the constitution He therefore advised the withdrawal of the Democratic legislative ticket, and proposed instead the selection of delegates to a Constitutional Convention at the regular election This was done, and the Whig delegates in Frederick County were elected without opposition In other portions of the State the secession of the "Glorious Nineteen" was not regarded with favor, and the reaction in public sentiment gave the Whigs a large majority in the House of Delegates, a number of counties in which they had been defeated at the September elections sending solid Whig delegations to Annapolis

Five of the Democratic senatorial electors considered themselves instructed by this decisive manifestation of the will of the people, and agreed to unite with the twenty-one Whigs and elect a Senate William Schley, of Frederick, and Elias Brown, of Baltimore County, were chosen as two of the fifteen senators. The proposition to hold a Constitutional Convention was abandoned It was conceded, however, that some reform was needed, and accordingly, upon the assembling of the Legislature, Governor Veazy, in his annual message, recommended that the election of Governor and senators should be given to the people, and that Carroll County be created, so as to diminish the size of the largest two counties and give an addition of four members to the popular branch of the Legislature These measures received the sanction of public approval, the constitution was amended to meet the views of the Governor, and the confirmatory act creating Carroll County passed the House of Delegates by a majority of twenty-eight, and every senator, with the exception of Elias Brown, cast his vote in favor of it It was signed by the Governor, and became a law Jan 19, 1837, so that in all probability the course pursued by the "Glorious Nineteen," instead of proving adverse to the creation of the new county, had the tendency to bring to its support, as a conciliatory measure, many of the representatives from the smaller counties of the State This long-deferred victory was hailed with demonstrations of delight by the citizens of Westminster and the surrounding country It was celebrated by a procession, with arches, banners, and an illumination, and an address was delivered in the Old Union church by James Raymond

The following is the act of Assembly, passed March 25, 1836 for the creation of Carroll County

"WHEREAS, a considerable body of the inhabitants of Baltimore and Frederick Counties, by their petition to this General Assembly [illegible] sed for a division of [illegible] at of parts thereo-

of, and whereas, it appears to this General Assembly that the erecting of a new county out of such parts of Baltimore and Frederick Counties will greatly conduce to the ease and convenience of the people thereof, therefore

SEC 1 *Be it enacted by the General Assembly of Maryland*, That after the confirmation of this act such parts of the aforesaid counties of Baltimore and Frederick as are contained within the bounds and limits following, to wit beginning at the Pennsylvania line where Rock Creek crosses said line, thence with the course of said creek until it merges in the Monocacy river, thence with the Monocacy to the point where Double Pipe Creek empties into Monocacy, thence with the course of Pipe Creek to the point of junction of Little Pipe Creek and Big Pipe Creek, thence with the course of Little Pipe Creek to the point where Sam's Creek empties into Little Pipe Creek, thence with Sam's Creek to Warfield's mill, thence with the road called the Buffalo road, and to a point called Parr's Spring, thence with the western branch of the Patapsco Falls to the point of its junction with the northern branch of the Patapsco Falls, thence with the northern branch of said falls to the bridge erected over said falls on the turnpike road leading from Reisterstown to Westminster, thence with a straight course to the Pennsylvania line, running north seventeen degrees east, thence with the Pennsylvania line to the place of beginning, shall be erected into a new county by the name of Carroll County and that the seat of justice thereof be established at Westminster

"SEC 2 *And be it enacted*, That the inhabitants of Carroll County shall have, hold, and enjoy all the immunities, rights, and privileges enjoyed by the inhabitants of any other county in this State

"SEC 3 *And be it enacted*, That the taxes which shall be levied by the commissioners of Baltimore County, prior to the confirmation of this act, on such parts of Baltimore County as are to constitute a part of Carroll County shall be collected and paid to the treasurer of Baltimore County, and the same be applied precisely as if this act had not passed and that the taxes which shall be levied by the justices of the Levy Court of Frederick County, prior to the confirmation of this act, on the parts of Frederick County as are to constitute Carroll County shall be applied precisely as if this act had not passed

"SEC 4 *And be it enacted*, That all causes, processes, and pleadings which shall be depending in Frederick County Court and Baltimore County Court when this act shall be confirmed shall and may be prosecuted as effectually in the courts where the same be depending as if this act had not been made

"SEC 5 *And be it enacted*, That the county of Carroll shall be a part of the Third Judicial District of this State, and the justices of the said district for the time being shall be the judges of the County Court of Carroll County, and the said County Court shall be held as may be directed by law, and shall have and exercise the same powers and jurisdiction, both at law and in equity, as other County Courts of this State

"SEC 6 *And be it enacted*, That the election districts in Carroll County shall be nine in number, and their limits, as well as the limits of the election districts in Baltimore and Frederick Counties, shall be established after the confirmation of this act as shall be directed by law

"SEC 7 *And be it enacted*, That after the confirmation of this act by the next General Assembly, a writ of election shall issue for holding an election in said county for four delegates to represent said county in the General Assembly which shall then be in session

"SEC 8 *And be it enacted*, That if this act shall be confirmed by the General Assembly, after the next election of delegates at the first session after such new election, according to the constitution and form of government, that in such case this alteration and amendment of the constitution and form of government shall constitute and be valid as part thereof, and everything therein contained repugnant to or inconsistent with this act be repealed and abolished"

The county was created, but much remained to be done Carroll was in an embryotic condition She was as helpless as a newly born babe Public buildings were to be erected, courts of justice established, officers chosen, and the county must be districted Mr Matthias, who had labored zealously for the creation of the new county, now applied himself to bringing order out of chaos Bills were introduced into the Legislature for the working machinery and to set it in motion At that time the register of wills was chosen by the Legislature After a sharp contest between a number of candidates, John Baumgartner, of Taneytown District, was elected Acts of Assembly were introduced and passed providing for the appointment of county commissioners, for the assessment of real and personal property, for the meeting of the County Court, for the establishment of the Orphans' Court, for the opening of public roads, for the purchase of sites and the erection of public buildings thereon, for the election of a sheriff and the appointment of subordinate officers, and for the election of four delegates to the General Assembly, and at the end of the session of 1837 Carroll County was fairly on its legs and provided with the necessary legislation for the career of prosperity and progress upon which it was about to enter

The following named gentlemen were appointed to lay off the election districts Samuel Galt, James C. Atlee, Thomas Hook, Samuel W Myers, Joshua Smith, Abraham Wampler, Daniel Stull, Mordecai G Cockey, Stephen Gorsuch, Joseph Steele, George W Warfield, Frederick Ritter, and William McIlvain They divided the county into nine districts as follows Taneytown, Uniontown, Myers', Woolery's, Freedom, Manchester, Westminster, and Franklin Since then the districts of Middleburg, New Windsor, and Union Bridge have been added The districts were marked out Feb 15, 1837, and the report of the commission was filed with the county clerk June 20, 1837, but not recorded until May 18, 1846 In March, 1837, an election was held for sheriff, the first that had taken place in Carroll County, and as a matter of interest the judges and clerks of election are given

District No 1, John Clabaugh, Jacob Correll, John Thomson, Jacob Wickert, James McKellip

District No 2, Moses Shaw, Sr, Israel Norris, David Fontz, John Hyder, Wm C Wright

District No 3, Wm C [illegible], Peter Pank[illegible], David B Earhart, John F [illegible]

District No 4, Wm Jameson, Edward E Hall, George Jacobs, Wm Jordan, Wm Sainsberry
District No 5, Robert Hudson, Nicholas Dorsey, Benjamin Bennett, Wm Whalen Otho Shipley
District No 6, Henry N Brinkman, Frederick Ritter, Jarrett Garner, John Kerlinger, Joseph M Parke
District No 7, Joshua Smith, David Uhler, Lewis Wampler, Jonathan Norris, Charles W Webster
District No 8, Wm McIlvaine, George Richards, John Lamotte, John Fowble, George Richards, Jr
District No 9, James Douty, Thomas Barnes, Robert Bennett, Joshua C Gist, Thomas E D Poole

A number of candidates sought the suffrages of the citizens, and the contest between Nicholas Kelley, Isaac Dern, and Basil Root, the leading aspirants, was very close, resulting in the election of Nicholas Kelley as the first sheriff of the county The inauguration of the county government took place the first Monday in April 1837 On that day the Circuit Court, the Orphans' Court, and the county commissioners all met in Westminster

The Circuit Court met in the dwelling of Dr Willis, now owned by Mr Boyle, Judges Dorsey and Kilgour on the bench After an appropriate introductory address, Judge Dorsey announced the appoint- of Dr William Willis as county clerk, which was received with unqualified approval by those present The court then appointed James Keiffer court crier, and accepted the bonds of the clerk and sheriff William P Maulsby, James Raymond, James M Shellman, A F Shriver, and T Parkin Scott were admitted as attorneys of the Carroll County bar Mr Maulsby was appointed and qualified as State's attorney for the county The court then adjourned to meet in the old Union church, where its sessions were afterwards held until a court-house was built

The Orphans' Court of Carroll County convened for the first time April 10, 1837, in the Wampler mansion, on the corner of Church Street, which building it occupied until the erection of a court-house The commissions of Judges Abraham Wampler, William Jameson, and Robert Hudson were received from Theodore Bland, chancellor of the State of Maryland, and read and recorded, after which the judges qualified and proceeded to business John Baumgartner was qualified as register of wills, and appointed George B Shriver assistant register The first business of a general nature transacted by the court was the appointment of Peter Gettier and Peter Utz to view and estimate the annual value of the real estate of Julia, Mary, George, Joseph, Peter, and Amos Sauble, minors, in the hands of Dr Jacob Shower, their guardian A notice was filed from Elizabeth, widow of Peter Sauble, refusing to administer on decedent's estate, also a similar notice from John and Michael, brothers of the deceased

April 17th The court directed Nelly Demmitt to dispose of the personal property of William Demmitt as administratrix

May 1st James Raymond was admitted as an attorney in this court, the first mentioned in the proceedings, and William P Maulsby was admitted at the same time

May 8th Nancy Koutz was appointed guardian to Joshua Koutz

June 5th In the case of Jacob Sellers, administrator of Philip Sellers, deceased, *vs* George Wareham, a citation was issued, the first citation going out of this court

June 12th On application of Jesse Lee, John Barney, a colored boy, aged six years, was bound to said Lee until the said boy arrived at twenty-one years of age

The first administrators mentioned at the April term were Dr Jacob Shower, of Peter Sauble's estate, Nelly Demmitt, of her husband, William Demmitt, Adam Feeser, of Elizabeth Feeser

The first executors were Joseph Cookson, of the estate of Samuel Cookson, deceased, Karahappuck Towson, of James Towson, and Peter Nace, of Peter Nace, Sr

The first petition filed in any suit was that of George Wareham *vs* Jacob Sellers, administrator of Philip Sellers, deceased The first suit was indorsed "No 1"

The following is a list of the wills admitted to probate during the first two years subsequent to the organization of the county

1 Elizabeth Tawney, April 10, 1837 Witnesses, David Roop, John Schweigart, John Roop, Jr Before John Baumgartner, register and the judges of the Orphans Court

2 Samuel Cookson, April 17th Witnesses, Joseph, Samuel, and John Weaver

3 James Towson April 17th Witnesses, John Philip and Jacob Franc

4 Peter Nace, the elder (dated 1827), and admitted to probate in Baltimore County, Dec 27, 1831 Certified copy recorded in Carroll County, April 17, 1837

5 Lauranty Freed, of Baltimore County Certified copy of its probate there Recorded April 17, 1837

6 Lydia Hatton, April 17th

7 Jacob Hoffman, May 1, 1837

8 Solomon McHanney, June 5th

9 Elizabeth Ann Howard, July 25th Witnesses, Samuel Greenhalt, Asbury O Whitfield, D W Null

10 Henry Wareham, July 22d Witnesses, J Henry Hoppe, Jacob Matthias, of George, Daniel Stowsifer, John Baumgartner

11. David Gorman, August 9th Witnesses, David Lister, of J[illegible] [illegible] Myerly

12 Ann Brown, August 30th Witnesses, N Dorsey, Abel Scrivener, Geo. W Warfield

13 Eliza C Dorsey, August 30th Witnesses, Edward Frizzell, Joseph Black, Thomas Beasman

14 Aquila Garretson, September 5th Witnesses, George Bramwell, Mordecai G Cockey, John Malehorn

15 Jonathan Parrish, September 11th

16 John Menche, October 17th Witnesses, Peter Sauble, Michael Gettier, Jacob Kerlinger

17 John Feltze, November 6th Witnesses, Jacob Gitt, George Weaver, of H, James Marshall

18 John Kramine, November 27th Witnesses, Jacob Baumgartner, Philip Wentz, Jonathan Steiner

19 Adam Frankforter, Jan 1, 1838 Witnesses, Henry N. Brinckman, Jacob Gitt, Jacob W Boesing

20 Mary Ann Engel, January 2d Witnesses, John Baumgartner, George Hawk

21 John Gilliss, January 13th Witnesses, Augustus Riggs, Wm Curlhen, James L Riggs

22 Archibald Barnes, January 22d Witnesses, Joshua C Gist, Joshua Franklin, Benjamin Bennett

23 Joseph Arnold, February 12th Witnesses, David Leister, George Croul, John Baumgartner

24 Richard Manning, Sr, February 19th Witnesses, Wm Jameson, David Tawney, Peter Flater

25 Catharine Manro, February 20th Witnesses, Joshua C Gist, Joseph Harden, Jacob Hiltabeidel

26 John Lambert, March 26th Witnesses, John Smelser, David Smelser, David Gorsuch

27 James Steele, April 2d Witnesses, N Browne, Beale Buckingham, Vachel Buckingham

28 Ezekiel Baring, May 7th

29 Rachel Wentz, May 14th

30 Mary Hooker, June 25th

31 Baltzor Hesson, July 9th Witnesses, Sterling Galt, Josiah Baumgartner, F J Baumgartner

32 Nicholas H Brown, July 13th

33 George Teuer, July 30th

34 Jacob Brown, September 3d Witnesses, Michael Sholl, Jr, John Streavig, George Koons

35 Peter Shriner, September 4th Witnesses, Evan McKinstry, David Engler, John P Shriner

36 Patrick Hinds, October 8th

37 Margaret Reid, October 8th Witnesses, A B R McLine, Samuel Naill, James Maloney

38 Veronica Peters, October 8th

39 Margaret Durbin, October 8th

40 Hannah Wampler, October 15th Witnesses, Jacob Yingling, Wm Yingling, Wm Zeppe

41 Peter Arbaugh, October 29th Witnesses, Solomon Wooley, William Lockard, Stephen Ourslers

42 Jacob Reid, October 29th

43. Elizabeth Keys, October 29th

44 Mary Lamport, November 19th Witnesses, James H Gorsuch, Henry Long, Jacob Frine

45 Susannah Loveall, Jan 14, 1839 Witnesses, Henry Ebaugh, of George, George Ebaugh, John Rinehart

46 Peter Shoemaker, Dec 31, 1838 Witnesses, John Nusbaum, Abraham Hesson, Jacob Sell, Peter Dehoff

47 Solomon Foutz, Feb 11, 1839 Witnesses, Abraham Myers, John Flegle, Philip Poyle

48 Michael Wagner, March 4th Witnesses, John Hyder, John Smith, John Nusbaum

The first death was recorded April 1, 1837. It was that of Basil D Stevenson, surviving executor of Samuel Stevenson, deceased, to Hannah Shipley for four hundred and sixty nine acres, adjoining "Fell's Dale," consideration, $2665 Dated April 1, 1837

The first mortgage was recorded April 5th, and was from John Knox to James Knox *et al*, and dated March 2, 1837

The second deed was from J Mason Campbell, trustee, to the president and directors of the Union Bank of Maryland, and was recorded April 8th Dated April 1, 1837, consideration, one dollar The land conveyed was Lot No 6, of ninety acres, and was called "Legh Castle," being part of the late Legh Master's estate. It adjoined tracts called "Bond's Meadow Enlarged," "Long Valley," and "Brown's Delight" It was a part of the tract issued to the late William Winchester and his heirs by James Clark and Joseph G J Bend, surviving trustees of Rev Legh H Master, by an indenture of March 11, 1812

The third deed was recorded April 8th, and was from Basil D Stevenson, surviving executor of Samuel Stevenson, deceased Its date of execution and record were the same It conveyed one hundred and forty seven acres, three roods, and twelve perches, and was parts of tracts called "The Resurvey on Father's Gift," "Rich Meadows," and "Pigeon's Hill" Consideration, $1034 76

The second mortgage was recorded April 11th, and was from William Jordan to Richard Johns It was on one hundred and thirty-nine and a half acres called "Curgafergus," and two hundred and fifty acres called "Mount Pisgah"

The fourth deed was recorded April 11th, from Jacob Reese and wife to Jacob Roop, dated March 25, 1837 It was for one-half acre of "Bond's Meadow" Consideration, $600

The following are the first marriage licenses issued by the clerk of the court for a period of two years after the creation of the county of Carroll

1837		
April	8	John Kroh and Julia Weaver
May	1	Thomas Bosley and Elizabeth Wheeler
"	9	Samuel Dayhoffe and Nancy Wheeler
"	14	Silas M Hurner and Elizabeth McAlister
"	17	Samuel L Linah and Maria Six
June	5	Shadrach Bosley and Serepta Sater
"	6	Joseph Bowers and Elizabeth Cullison
"	6	Wm F Smyth and Elizabeth Bixler
"	8	Jeremiah Robinson and Ann Smith
"	16	Geo B Shipley and Ann Shipley
"	20	Wm Naill, Jr, and Mary A Rudisel
July	8	Abraham Reaver and Catharine Jones
"	15	Jacob Michael and Eve Grogg
"	26	Wm W Warfield and Jemima Formwalt
"	26	Daniel [illegible] (Rev E Keller)

Sept 1 Conrad Koons and Mary E Zunbunn
" 1[illegible] Porcius Gilleys and Rachel Evans (Rev. Lloyd Selby)
" 23 David Haines and Sarah W Durbin
" 25 Thos C Thomson and Mary Shunk (Rev E Keller)
Oct. 2. James Snaeffer and Margaret Cottrider
" 7 George Pixler and Mary Gritter
" 9 Andrew C Powble and Elizabeth Murray.
" 16 Nicholas Dorsey and Rachel Clemson (Rev Dr Reese)
" 16 Peter Rinamon and Margaret Strickling (Rev J Geiger)
" 2[illegible] George W Mauro and Elizabeth Kelly (Rev Samuel Gore)
Nov 11 John Sweeden and Charlotte Weaver
" 28. Josiah Roop and Elizabeth Shafer (Rev William Prettyman)
Dec 6 Elisha Shreeve and Minerva Bennett
" 20 D W. Houck and Rachel F Allgire
" 22 Aaron Goswell and Ann Leatherwood
" 26 Elisha Wheeler and Sarah Shamberger
" 27 Beall Sellman and Mary B Weaver
" 29 Thomas Rudisell and Ann M Snyder (Rev E Keller)

1838

Jan 15 John Weist and Elizabeth Mouse (Rev Jacob Geiger)
Feb 1 Jacob Lynn and Louisa Crabbs (Rev D Zollickoffer)
" 3 George W Grimes and Eliza Bufington (Rev E Keller)
" 8 George W Litzenger and Martha A Keefer
" 10 Samuel Myers and Liza C Dagen (Rev Daniel Zollickoffer)
" 12 Jacob Gieman and Julian Haines (Rev Jacob Geiger)
" 28. Joseph Kelly and Naomi Ross (Rev N Harden)
March 3 William E Shipley and Mary A Dorsey (Rev Hood)
" 6 Samuel Price and Catharine Ripple
" 7. James Smith and Catharine Diffenbaugh (Rev Israel Haines)
" 8 Jacob Flatter and Elizabeth Bush
" 12 Jacob Smith and Angeline Christ (Rev Miller)
" 18. Thomas Loveall and Jane A Cushing (Rev Jonathan Forrest)
" 19 John Myerly and Emmaline Little (Rev Israel Haines)
" 22 George Richards, Jr, and Lucinda Allgire
" 26 Henry S Black and Rachel Maring (Rev E Keller)
" 30 N B Stocksdale and Elizabeth Cover (Rev Lloyd Selby)
April 3 Noah Brown and Bartholow Richards (Rev Aaron Richards)
" 3. Christopher Weisman and Mary A Guthing (Rev Jacob Geiger)
" 5 Peter Nace and Susanna Meyselman
" 14 Lewis J Grove and Carrilla Barnes (Rev Hunt)
May 9 Alexander H Senceny and Lavinia Fuglar (Rev David Englar)
" 14 John Roberts and Catharine A Boyle (Rev N Zocchi)
" 21 Jos[illegible] Wilson and Sar[illegible]h E [illegible] (Rev. Samuel Grove)
May 21 Elisha Bennett and Rachel Prugh (Rev Jonathan Forrest)
" 25 John Warner and Susanna Fisher
" 30 Ephraim Lindsey and Eliza Fringer (Rev Samuel Gore)
" 31 Benjamin W Bennett and Margaret Clemson (Rev Daniel Zollickoffer)
June 11 John Loveall and Elizabeth Houck
" 23 Aaron Wheeler and Matilda Barnes
" 26 Washington Wilson and Margaret Smith (Rev Daniel Zollickoffer)
" 30 Robert Collins and Honor Elder (Rev William Hunt)
July 2[illegible] David Shipley and Mary A Wheeler
Aug 13 Jacob Ocker and Barbara Fleegle
" 13 John W Ogborn and Eliza Pole (Rev Daniel Zollickoffer)
" 21 Larkin Shipley and Rebecca Shipley. (Rev S Gore)
" 31 Giles Cole and Mary Merryman (Rev William Hunt)
Sept 12 John Bixle and Sarah L Eby (Rev Boyle)
" 15 Obadiah Buckingham and Mary A Barlow
" 17 Dones Groff and Mary S Biggs (Rev William Prettyman)
" 20 Ephraim Shultz and Jane Crawford
" 22 John M Blizzard and Ann Welsh
" 2[illegible] John Slyder and Catharine Wentz
Oct 6 Thomas Wright and Caroline Frizzell
" 11 Dr David Diller and Ann E Matthias (Rev N Zocchi)
" 15. Washington Senceney and Mary A Grimes (Rev Daniel Zollickoffer)
" 18 Henry Nicodemus and Margaret McCreery (Rev William Prettyman)
" 18 William S Brown and Carrilla Manning
" 27 Samuel B Shipley and Leah Shipley
" 27 William Otter and Elizabeth Lathem
" 30 John Reigle and Catharine Reaver (Rev E Keller)
Nov 6 John Obergoast and Barbara Leister
" 20 John Elder and Rebecca Selby (Rev Samuel Gore)
" 20 Jacob Ecker and Sarah Dudderar (Rev Webster)
" 22 Dennis Grimes and Sarah A Pool (Rev Nicholas Harden)
" 27 Levin Williams and Susan Haines (Rev N Harden)
" 28 John Walker and Mary A Tucker (Rev Lloyd Selby)
Dec. 5 Michael Smith and Maria Haines
" 14 W. W. Garner and Harriet Murray
" 19 Joseph Marriott and Sarah Shipley
" 22 Benjamin Davis and Mary Ward
" 24 Wm Warner and Rebecca Warner (Rev Daniel Zollickofter)
" 28 Abraham Wilson and Delilah Hervey

1839

Jan 17. Jesse Baker and Eliza E Bailey (Rev S Gore)
" 23 John T Fisher and Sophia Stansbury (Rev Harple)
Feb 8 Jonas Engler and Hannah St[illegible]
" 14 Geo Croft and Anne Ruby (Rev Richard[illegible])
" [illegible] J[illegible] H[illegible] [illegible] (Rev Daniel Zollick[illegible]

Feb 26 James Thompson and Mary A Hitterbridle (Rev Robert S Grier)
" 28 Conrad Moul and Lydia A Kesselring (Rev Josiah Varden)
March 2 Michael Bartholow, Jr, and Elizabeth A Platten
" 9 Hanson Carmack and Harriet Clabaugh
" 11 Josiah Baugher and Mary Babylon (Rev Daniel Zollickoffer)
" 13 Levi Davis and Julian Shriver (Rev Josiah Varden)
" 13 James Parrish and Ruth Creswell
" 15 Samuel Shriner and Mary A Merring
April 1 Isaac Magee and Margaret Dayhoffe
" 1 Henry E Beltz and Julian A Mottor
May 4 Michael Hubbard and Rachel Durbin (Rev D Zollickoffer)
" 15 John Roop, Jr, and Lydia Engle

On Oct 5, 1840, at Annapolis, Hon James G Berrett, of Carroll County, was married by Rev Mr McIlheney to Miss Julia W, only daughter of the late John W Bordley, of the former place

The following is the first marriage license issued in the new county

"*Whereas*, application has been made to me by John Kroh, of Carroll County and Julia Weaver, of Carroll County, for License to be joined in Holy Matrimony

"These are therefore to authorize and license you to solemnize the Rites of Matrimony between said persons according to law, there appearing to you no lawful cause or just impediment by reason of any Consanguinity or Affinity to hinder the same

"Given under my hand and the seal of my office this 8th of April, in the year 1837

[SEAL] "GEORGE MACKUBIN,
"*Treasurer Western Shore*

"To the REV. JACOB GEIGER or any other person authorized by law to celebrate the marriage in the State of Maryland

"WILLIAM WILLIS,
"*Clerk C C, Md*"

Sheriff Kelley converted a portion of the brick mansion in Westminster now owned by William Reese into a jail, and used it as such until the present prison was built There was but one prisoner confined in it, and he is said to have made his escape by sliding down the spouting The county commissioners met in a room of the Wampler tavern, and organized with Otho Shipley as clerk, and Thomas Hook county collector A number of places were suggested as sites for the public buildings, including the land on which they now stand, the lot at present occupied by the Dallas mansion, and the ground on which the Reformed church is built The advantages of all were fairly considered by the commissioners, and on May 25, 1837, they accepted for the site of the court-house an acre of ground from Isaac Shriver, immediately in rear of his tavern stand, and about three hundred yards from Main Street, with ground for streets on three sides of it For the jail they accepted an acre of land a short distance northeast of the court-house site, and about four hundred yards from Main Street This was donated by the heirs of David Fisher

The jail was built in 1837, by B F Forester and Johnzee Selby, at a cost of four thousand dollars, and since that time the jail-yard and other improvements have been added

The second term of the Circuit Court was held Sept 4, 1837 Chief Justice Thomas B Dorsey presided, with Thomas H Wilkinson as associate judge The grand jury, the first in the new county, appeared, and was sworn as follows William Brown (foreman), Jonathan Dorsey, Charles Devilbiss, Daniel Stull, John T Mathias, William McIlvain, David Z Buchen, Jacob Kerlinger, Daniel Horner, Nathaniel Sykes, Frederick Ritter, William Caples, William Fisher John Jones, Jacob Grove, Michael Sullivan, Andrew C Fowble, Thomas Sater, Samuel L Swarmstead, Edward Dorsey, Joseph Shafler, Isaac Dern, and John Henry Hopper

Nicholas Kelley was sheriff, William Willis, clerk, and Emmanuel Gernand and Henry Geatty, bailiffs The grand jury returned true bills against George Ramsbery for resisting an officer, Jacob Boring, breach of the peace, Whitfield Gainer, the same, Charlotte White, colored, larceny, Michael Wagner, assault, B Eck, maltreatment to his slave "Poll," William Coghlan and Peter Baukert, misdemeanor in office, William Grimes, Benjamin Davis Resin Franklin, Jacob Graviel, Nimrod Booby, Jacob Sanders, selling liquor without a license The presentments against the last four were withdrawn by the grand jury and not returned It will be observed from the perusal of the above that the offenses committed in 1837 did not differ materially from those of which the county courts take cognizance nowadays, though there was a commendable absence of the higher crimes, such as murder, arson, burglary, and robbery, which too frequently deface the present records of judicial tribunals. James Keifer was appointed court crier James Mybrea filed a declaration of his intention to become a citizen of the United States and renounce his allegiance to the King of Great Britain Henry Short, a native of Holland, also appeared and gave notice of his intention to become a naturalized citizen of this country The following was the petit jury, the first in the county John Cover, Jacob Gitt, John Kuhn, Sr, Basil Root, Evan L Crawford William Shaw, Joshua F Copp, Robert Crawford, Isaiah Pearce, Nicholas H Brown, Elijah Bond, Henry H Harbaugh, Benjamin Bennett, Daniel Yeiser, Evan Garner, Thom[illegible] Barth[illegible]w, Nimrod Frizell, [illegible] [illegible] Cockey,

Hezekiah Crout The first case tried was that of an appeal of William Null vs Jesse Reifsnider The witnesses for appellant were Elias Grimes and Elias Null, and for appellee, Samuel Reindollar and Israel Hiteshue The jury found for the appellant without leaving the box The next cause was that of James Smith vs Samuel Gatt, William Shaw, Silas Hauer Washington Hauer, and Jacob Shoemaker, trustees of the church, an appeal The witnesses were John W. McAlister for appellant, and James Birr, David Kephart, John Thompson for appellee Judgment was affirmed with costs Godfried Guyser, a native of Wurtemberg, Germany, John Reisly, of the same place, and Jacob Lewis and Philip Yoost, natives of Darmstadt, Germany, all filed their intentions to become American citizens Fifty-six witnesses testified before the grand jury, among whom were the following constables John Shockney, Jacob Frankfortder, Thomas Brummel, Andrew P Barnes, George Ogg, Emanuel Gernand, Warren P Little, Evan Black, John Krantz, William Grumbine, Abraham England William Stansbury, Samuel Lammott, John Clabaugh, David Kephart, George Willott, Frederick Yingling, Joseph Smith On the petition of John S Murray to inquire whether George Ecklar was an insane person and a pauper the jury refused an inquisition The first criminal case tried was that of the State of Maryland vs Charlotte White (colored), indicted for larceny, and the jury found a verdict of not guilty The second State case was that of George Ramsbery for resisting a constable, in which a verdict of guilty was returned The defendant was ordered to pay a fine of five dollars and be imprisoned sixty days The third session of the County Court met Sept 3, 1838, when the following grand jury was sworn Jacob Landes (foreman), John A Byers, John Adlsperger, Josiah Shilling, Peter Lippy, George W Munro, Eli Hewitt, George Miller, Thomas Shepherd, Nimrod Woolery, Robert J Jameson, Richard Smith, Samuel W Myers, Robert B Shipley, Joseph Poole, William Lockert, Solomon Myerly, Lewis Shuey, Benjamin B Forrester, Henry Cover, Martin Krole, Adam Beiser The petit jury were John McCollum, David Weaver, Julius Bennett, Nelson Norris, David Buffington, Isaac Powder, John Fowble, Francis Haines, David P Deal, Henry W Ports, Daniel Hoover, Micajah Rogers, Richard Owings, Denton Shipley, Horatio Price, Beal Buckingham, David Fowble, John Krouse, John Gornell, Michael Sullivan John H Hoppe, Francis Shriver, George Bramwell, Jacob Null

The corner stone of the present court-house of Carroll County was laid in June, 1838 with appropriate military and civic ceremonies It was an occasion of general rejoicing, and a large concourse of people assembled to mark the event Four military companies marched in the procession, commanded by Capts Skinner of Hanover, Swope, of Taneytown, Bramwell, of Finksburg, and Longwell, of Westminster The stone was laid by Andrew Shriver, assisted by Col Joshua Gist, then in his ninety fourth year, a brother of Gen Mordecai Gist, of Maryland, who won an imperishable name during the Revolution as a soldier and patriot, he having especially distinguished himself in the battles of Long Island and Camden An address was delivered by Samuel D Lecompte, and a number of impromptu speeches were made by prominent citizens Conrad Moul was the contractor for the building, and the masonry of both the court-house and jail was done by Ephraim Swope and Thomas W Durbin The court-house was built at a cost of eighteen thousand dollars, and notwithstanding it was erected more than forty years ago it is now a substantial and durable edifice, and a credit to the commissioners under whose administration it was constructed

In 1838 the county government was perfected, all necessary subordinate officers had been elected or appointed, those who had opposed the creation of a new county had become reconciled to the situation, and thenceforward Carroll took its proper place among the older organizations as one of the most vigorous, progressive, and influential counties of Maryland

Carroll County is bounded on the north by Pennsylvania, on the south by the Patapsco River, which separates it from Howard County, on the east by Baltimore County, and on the west by Frederick County Its natural advantages are great The surface is undulating, the gently sloping hills like the billows of the ocean, swelling gradually in the direction of the Catoctin range, a spur of the Blue Ridge The tributaries of the Patapsco and Monocacy Rivers permeate the soil in every direction, not only supplying abundant water for farming purposes, but affording to the miller and manufacturer unlimited power for their handicrafts The soils comprise all the varieties of the Blue Ridge division of the State, as white and red isinglass, slate, mica, limestone, and the "Red Lands" They are for the most part exceedingly fertile, the county possessing probably a smaller proportion of poor land than almost any other in Maryland, and where impoverished they are readily susceptible of improvement by careful cultivation and the use of lime, which exists in such abundance beneath the surface The county is well wooded, and the scenery picturesque and beautiful, abounding in charming valleys [illegible] hills [illegible] which the growth of

the heaviest forest-trees gives the necessary shading to the landscape, and where a view of the distant Blue Ridge can be obtained, which is the case in many portions of the county, very happy effects are produced The inhabitants have always been thrifty and energetic, and agriculture has received here its most perfect development Fine farms abound Wheat, rye, oats and corn, the various grasses, fruits, and vegetables are grown, and magnificent herds of cattle and improved breeds of horses, sheep, and hogs are the principal productions of the farmers, while much attention is paid to the dairy business, the proximity to the city of Baltimore by means of the railroads and turnpikes insuring profitable returns to those engaged in it Tobacco has been grown to some extent, and small crops are still raised in parts of the county, but the expense and uncertainty attending its production have been so great as to render it unpopular with the majority of farmers Well-tilled farms and fine residences are confined to no particular district, but are freely distributed through the county There are numerous mills and manufacturing establishments, and a large number of tanneries in the county, the last induced, doubtless, by the heavy growth of oak timber, which forms the body of the woods in that section of country Large supplies of granite, marble, limestone, and brick clay are to be had for building purposes

1523582

There are also large quarries of the best variety of soapstone near Marriottsville, adjacent to the Baltimore and Ohio Railroad The stone is of the purest quality, and at the factory is sawed into every imaginable shape, and used for many varied purposes, its uses having multiplied greatly of late years Even the refuse stone and dust are valuable in various ways

Some of the finest hematitic iron ore in the United States, and also some excellent specimens of oxide of manganese have been found in Carroll The climate is salubrious, and the lay of the land and purity of the water favorable to health, so much so as to make many portions of the county favorite places of resort for the citizens of Baltimore during the summer months The county is rapidly increasing in population, wealth, and enterprise, and the public-spirited citizens who have managed its affairs have adopted all judicious means for social and material advancement The Baltimore and Ohio Railroad on its southern border, the Western Maryland Railroad which passes almost directly through the centre of the county, the Frederick and Pennsylvania Line Railroad which runs across the northwestern portion, and numerous fine turnpikes, as well [illegible] of public roads, constitut[illegible] of transportation, and few sections of the country possess greater conveniences in this regard Through these channels it is placed in direct communication with the city of Baltimore, where a ready market is found for its productions, and the rapid transportation furnished by the railroads has enabled its citizens to build up a trade in the products of the dairy unsurpassed probably elsewhere in Maryland The prices of land vary of course with the quality of the soil and its proximity or remoteness to the highways of travel, but one hundred and fifty dollars per acre is not unusual, and many who have purchased land at that rate have had no cause to regret it As far back as April, 1814, Peter Benedune, who was a restless speculator, sold out all his land in the vicinity of Union Bridge at from one hundred to one hundred and twenty dollars per acre, and removed to the Valley of Virginia The accessibility of the lands in Carroll County, their healthfulness, and the social advantages in many of the neighborhoods, render them desirable either as residences or safe investments The brown sandstone, so highly valued for building purposes, is found in the western part of Carroll, and will compare very favorably with the Connecticut sandstone, so generally in use in the construction of the finer class of edifices in large cities In Emmittsburg, among the upper layers of brown sandstone are found strata of flagging Some of it separates into flags from two to four inches thick, with smooth surfaces ready dressed for paving The boundaries of Carroll County were made for political convenience and not as divisions between distinct varieties of soil or different geological formations The "Red Lands," beginning in the northwestern part of the county and extending through the Taneytown and Middleburg Districts into portions of the Union Town District, are similar in geological formation to those found in Frederick County, differing only in their agricultural value, the former being more decomposed, thereby insuring a deeper soil These lands are underlaid by compact shales, among which red sandstone is frequently found sufficiently durable for building purposes The value of these lands is materially influenced by the proximity of these shales or sandstones to the surface When they are immediately beneath it the soil is unproductive, being easily affected by droughts, as there is not sufficient depth to retain the necessary supply of water for the crops When this is the case the remedy is always at hand The land should be subsoiled and heavily manured with lime

Slate soils are a continuation of those found in Fr[illegible] from the red [illegible] which the

soils overlying them are formed are mica slate, talc slate, chlorite slate, and blue, or roofing slate, the composition of all of which is, in an agricultural point of view, so nearly allied as to render any separate description of them unnecessary, and they are so intimately mixed that it would require almost an innumerable number of analyses to determine the special composition of each

The lands drained by the waters of the Little Pipe Creek and its tributary branches are composed mainly from the disintegrated particles of these rocks or slates They have by various influences become thoroughly decomposed, have been well manured and well cultivated, and are equal in productive value to the average of the best in the State These lands are formed from the same rocks, and have the same composition in every particular, as all the lands in this section of the State are underlaid by the slates above spoken of, and the question naturally arises, why should some of them be so barren and some so productive? Why should the soils of the same formation on Parr's Ridge, running through the county to Manchester and the Pennsylvania line, be generally unproductive? Their mechanical texture must be examined for an explanation of their different degrees of fertility Most of the soil in this part of the county, as it has been formed, has been washed off, and there has not been enough of it left to meet the wants of plants by retaining a sufficiency of moisture for their support or a proper quantity of nutrient materials to develop their growth and structure To obviate these difficulties the soil must be deepened, decomposed, and the mineral set free which it has in a crude state

There are also the light red sandy loams of this county, at the foot of Parr's Ridge, represented by the lands which extend over the whole county in a line more or less directly parallel with Parr's Ridge They are famous for producing a variety of tobacco known as the Bay Tobacco, which sells at a very high price

The red clay loam begins at the eastern border of the above-described lands, and extends eastward to where they meet the granite or isinglass soil The next varieties met after going eastward from these are the white isinglass, soils formed from the disintegration of granite rocks These are easily recognized, the bright shining spangles of mica, or isinglass, glistening everywhere They are exceedingly light and dry, and are occasionally very barren These comprise the chief soils of Carroll, they follow each other in regular succession, from west to east, in the order in which they are named, and can be readily recognized by their location as well as by their description

The limestones of Carroll are fully equal to those found in any other portion of Western Maryland Many of them are used only in the neighborhood where they are located, but there are many excellent limestone-quarries both for agricultural and building purposes The principal limestones in the upper part of the county are as follows

No 2, a white limestone of fine crystalline texture, Uniontown, Maryland.

No 2, a dark gray variety, slatish, with crystals of calc spar imbedded

No 3, a dark gray and homogeneous mass of fine crystalline texture, and small white veins of calc spar traversing They were found to be composed as follows

	No 1	No 2	No. 3
Carbonate of lime	99 5	68 3	98 8
Carbonate of magnesia		11 5	0 5
Sand slate, etc . .	0 5	20 2	0 7
	100	100	100

and will, therefore, produce, when burnt, of

Caustic lime .	56 0	38 3	55
Caustic magnesia		5 5	0 2

and when water-slacked, of

Water-slacked lime	73 7	50 6	73 10
Water slacked magnesia		8 0	0 3

The second series are those of the western flank of Parr's Ridge They usually have a fine grain resembling that of Carrara marble, and they vary in color from white to grayish blue They contain little silicious matter, and in general but small proportions of magnesia or other impurities They have sometimes a slaty structure Near the southern limits of the formation the proportion of magnesia is somewhat larger

Iron ores occur in immense quantities in connection with the limestones before mentioned They range from the Pennsylvania line (north of Westminster) southwesterly for ten or twelve miles Westminster lies on the eastern edge of the range There are the ruins of an iron-furnace about two and a half miles southwest of Westminster, on the property of Mr Vanbibber, where these ores were smelted many years ago The Western Maryland Railroad reaches this range of ore at Westminster, and passes through it for several miles This affords every facility for transporting the ore or the iron that may be made therefrom

The magnetic oxide of iron is the richest of iron ores, and when pure (as is sometimes the case in Sweden) contains seventy-two per cent of metal It is usually, however, more or less mixed up with earth matters, and sometimes contains the oxides of titanium and manganese

It has a metallic lustre and a dark gray or almost black color, the latter being also the color of its powder It strongly attracts the magnetic needle, and when in small grains it is attracted by the magnet Some of its varieties are sufficiently magnetic to attract iron filings and needles, hence the name of loadstone, which was formerly applied to it These characters distinguish it from all other ores of iron

It occurs in small quantities about seven miles west northwest from Baltimore, near the Bare Hill's Copper-Mine, and again near Scott's mills, about eighteen miles north-northwest of Baltimore It is found in massive as well as in octahedral crystals and grains An iron-furnace at Sykesville is in part supplied by ore which is mined in that vicinity

When the northwestern edge of the mica slates is reached, there is found what may be termed a metalliferous range, extending from the northern part of Cecil County through Harford, Baltimore, Carroll, Howard, and Montgomery Counties

In addition to the magnetic iron ores of this range already referred to, there are ores of copper, chrome, and gold Indications of copper may be seen at various points, and several mines have been opened in this county, one of which, at Springfield, near Sykesville, continues to be profitably worked Near Finksburg a copper mine was successfully worked during several years, and, if proper skill and sufficient capital are applied, it will probably prove productive The ore consists of yellow or pyritous copper and still richer quartz, called purple copper ore

Sulphuret of cobalt was discovered among the products of this mine, but this rare and valuable material occurred in very small quantity, and has not been found elsewhere in this State Other mines have been opened in this range, between Finksburg and Sykesville, and at one of them native gold was discovered.

Northeastward from Finksburg there are indications of copper at many points, especially near the forks of the Gunpowder River, about twenty-two miles north of Baltimore. Some explorations and diggings have been made without discovering the ore in quantity It appears to be associated with the magnetic oxide of iron of this formation

There are also abundant traces of copper in the northwest part of the county, in the red shales They give so little promise of profitable mines, however, that it is almost useless to expend money in digging for the ore

Copper ore accompanies (in very small proportion) the magneti[...] steatite in [...]

certain parties caused a shaft to be sunk on one of these veins with the hope that copper might be obtained in available quantities beneath, but they were disappointed The Springfield mine was a success, and a similar result might happen at the Gunpowder veins, but the cost of sinking deep shafts is too great for the chances of a favorable result In following this metalliferous range southwestward no indications of either chrome or copper are encountered until the vicinity of Finksburg is reached From this point for about seven miles, to Springfield (one mile and a half north of Sykesville, on the Baltimore and Ohio Railroad), there are numerous indications of copper ores A mine was opened near Finksburg about thirty years ago, and for some time was worked with success The ore was found in a true vein, and consisted at first principally of carbonate of copper, which, as usual, was succeeded by a sulphuret of copper ore, containing sixty per cent of metal when free from gangue, or about thirty per cent after being prepared for sale At depths of from fifty to one hundred feet the ore was abundant, and it was usual for them to mine thirty tons a week

Subsequently the vein became thinner, or pinched off, to use a mining term, but there is every reason to believe that with more knowledge of such matters on the part of the owners the vein might have been reached at a lower depth as rich as it was above. Veins of this kind are irregular in thickness, but mining to depths of two to three thousand feet has never yet reached the bottom of one of them Another vein was slightly explored a short distance from this opening, but the owners became discouraged and suspended operations

Another mine was opened at Mineral Hill, about seven miles southwest of Finksburg, in the same range It was penetrated to a considerable depth Cobalt ore has been found at Mineral Hill in small quantity, and native gold in the outcrop in inappreciable amount The veins were opened and some work done about two miles southwest of this point In the Springfield mine the main shaft has been carried down on the large vein to a distance of seven hundred feet, with much better indications at the greatest depth penetrated than near the surface, where there was little copper, but a considerable thickness of magnetic oxide of iron In fact, this mine was originally worked for iron but as it progressed in depth the proportion of copper continued to increase, so that for several years it was worked as a copper-mine, and turned out better than any other in the State

[...] r, which, when [...] ree per cent of

the metal, but owing to the mixture of vein-stone, or gangue, the proportion of metal was about thirteen per cent The ore sold for about fifty dollars per ton to the copper-smelting works of Baltimore Chrome ores occur at many points in a serpentine formation which stretches from New Lisbon four miles west to Rockville, Montgomery Co, and nearly to the Potomac River The ore has been worked at several points, and is found to vary considerably in quality

The range of limestone, useful as marble is on the western flank of Parr's Ridge, extending southwestward from a little northwest of Manchester, passing near and west of Westminster, and extending into Frederick County They are usually stratified, and consist of very small crystalline grains, and are generally white or some light shade of blue It is found, however, towards the southern limits of this range more variegated, with shades of red less pure, and the stratification more disturbed The different layers of this vary considerably, and even in the same quarry there are strata of pure white and light blue, and sometimes variegated with light and dark shades of red They take a fine polish, and are free from the grains or masses of quartz and other minerals which sometimes exist in the older limestones The quarries, with cheap transportation, will increase their depths The effect of this will be to bring to light the marble, less acted upon by the weather, at less cost than when large quantities of stone have to be quarried and thrown aside in order to get unaltered blocks of marble of large size

Carroll County is well supplied with railroad facilities The Western Maryland Railroad was chartered in January, 1852, and work was commenced on it in July, 1857 It was completed to Union Bridge in 1861, and to Williamsport, on the Potomac River, in 1873 In its inception it was a Carroll County enterprise, the inhabitants of that section subscribing for nearly all of the original stock of the company William Roberts, the president, and William W Dallas, John Smith, Samuel McKinstry, J Henry Hoppe, and John K Longwell, directors, contracted with Messrs Irwin, Taylor & Norris to build the road to Union Bridge, the contractors to receive the stock subscription, amounting to one hundred and sixty thousand dollars, and six hundred thousand dollars in first mortgage bonds It was subsequently completed to its present terminus on the Potomac River by Baltimore capitalists, who were very materially aided by Baltimore City The presidents of the company have been Robert Magraw, Nathan Haines, William Roberts, A[illegible] Robert Ir[illegible] Smith, John [illegible] M Bokee, Robert T Banks, James L McLane, Alexander Reiman, and the present very able and efficient executive, J. M Hood The value of this road to Carroll County can scarcely be overestimated It passes directly through the centre of the county, entering Woolery District on its eastern border, and passing up through the northern corner, it skirts the southern extremity of Hampstead, thence through the centre of Westminster District, and taking in the county seat, it crosses the New Windsor District passing through the town of New Windsor, thence across the Union Bridge District, embracing the town of that name, and then along the southwestern portion of Middleburg District into Frederick County At Bruceville, in Middleburg District, it intersects the Frederick and Pennsylvania Line Railroad, through which Frederick City, Taneytown, and points in Pennsylvania are reached The scenery along the line of the road in Carroll County is exquisitely beautiful, and affords to the tourist in the summer months abundant opportunities for the study of nature in her loveliest and most varied forms The land through which it passes is fertile, productive, highly cultivated, and teeming with the fruits of the earth The road is intersected at many points by rapid, sparkling and limpid streams, which promise in the near future to furnish power for innumerable mills and factories Already the spirit of progress has manifested itself Many mills have been erected along the course of the road and the tanneries and ore-mines show that the confidence of the projectors of the enterprise was not misplaced Property of every description in the vicinity of the railroad has greatly appreciated in value, and an unmistakable impetus has been given to all industries which the county is capable of sustaining The stations in Carroll County are Carrollton, Gorsuch Road, Westminster, Avondale, Wayside, New Windsor, Linwood, Union Bridge, Middleburg, Frederick Junction, York Road (Bruceville), and Double Pipe Creek

The Bachman's Valley Railroad begins at the Chestnut Hill iron ore mines, about the centre of the Manchester District, and runs almost due north across the line into Pennsylvania until it intersects the Hanover Branch Railroad Immense quantities of iron ore are transported over this road to furnaces in Pennsylvania The officers for 1881 were President, Capt. A W Eichelberger Directors Stephen Keifer, H C Shriver, Joseph Dellone, Joseph Althoff, C L Johnson, J W. Gitt, Levi Dubbs, Perry Wine, Edwin Thomas, Samuel Thomas, E W Hendele, and [illegible] road was built [illegible] Maryland Rail-

road, to Hanover in 1879 It passes through Hampstead and Manchester Districts Its officers are President, Capt A W Eichelberger, Directors, Stephen Keifer, Mr Meltheimer, W H Hoffman, William Slagle, Calvin C Wooden, and J W Gitt

The Frederick and Pennsylvania Line Railroad runs from Frederick City, Md, through Middleburg and Taneytown Districts, in Carroll County, taking in the extreme western corner of Myers District, to Hanover, in Pennsylvania It intersects the Western Maryland Railroad at Bruceville, in Middleburg District, and furnishes several outlets for the produce of the remarkably fertile grain-growing and grazing country through which it passes

Prior to the building of railroads turnpikes were the readiest means of commercial intercourse between the great centres of trade and the outlying districts So important were they considered that the policy of a great party in this country was to some extent based upon the advisability of their construction by the national government, and many severe contests were waged over this question in Congress

At an early period in the history of the section now known as Carroll County the increase in population and trade made it necessary to secure greater facilities for transportation, and in 1805 the Baltimore and Reisterstown Turnpike Company was chartered The capital needed for its construction, six hundred thousand dollars, was subscribed for by the merchants and capitalists of Baltimore, and in 1807 the road was constructed through this county It entered Woolery District near Finksburg, and passing through Westminster, connected with the Hanover Branch It is sixty miles in length, including the latter The goods and produce carried over this road in early days was immense The large Conestoga wagons, so familiar to denizens of the West as "schooners of the desert," passed each other, hundreds in a day, on their way to and from Pittsburgh and Baltimore, and the jingling of bells, the cracking of whips, the horses gayly caparisoned, and the drivers in picturesque costumes constituted an animating and enlivening spectacle, the recollection of which occasionally excites regret in the bosoms of the old-timers, and arouses a fleeting wish for the populous roads and the good old country inns which have been so effectually superseded by the trailing smoke and lightning dash of the steam-engine

The Westminster and Hagerstown turnpike was begun about 1824, but before much progress had been made railroads had become a question of absorbing interest to enlighten [illegible] people all over the world, and doubtless occasioned a [illegible] with reference to pikes which materially interfered with the completion of the enterprise At many points on the line sections of road were made, but the only portion finished was between Westminster and Uniontown

The Liberty turnpike passes through the southern portion of the county, and there are short turnpikes at Union Bridge, New Windsor, and Finksburg In 1851, about the time that the mania for plank-roads was at its height in the United States, it was determined to build one from Westminster to Emmittsburg, but, fortunately perhaps, it was never completed

The following is a correct list of the judges, county clerks, sheriffs, State's attorneys, registers and subordinate officers of Carroll County since its creation in 1837 to this present writing

Judges of the Circuit Court

1837-52, Thomas B Dorsey, Thomas H Wilkinson, Nicholas Brewer [1] 1851-64, Madison Nelson, 1864-67, John E Smith, 1867-81, Oliver Miller, Edward Hammond, Wm N Hayden

County Clerks

1837-41, Dr William Willis 1841-49, Dr Jacob Shower, 1849-57, John B Boyle 1857-62, George E Wampler, 1862-67, William A Mckellip, 1867-73, John B Boyle, 1873-81, Dr Frank J Shaw

Sheriffs

1837-39, Nicholas Kelly, 1839-42, Jacob Grove, 1842-45, J Henry Hoppe, 1845-48, Lewis Trumbo, 1848-51, Hanson T Webb, 1851-53, William S Brown 1853-55, John M Yingling, 1855-57, Joseph Shaeffer, 1857-59, William Wilson, 1859-61, William Segafoose, 1861-63, Jeremiah Babylon, 1863-65, Joseph Ebaugh, 1865-67, Jacob D. Hoppe, 1867-69, Thomas B Gist, 1869-71, John Tracey, 1871-73, George N Fringer, 1873-75, Edward Devilbiss, 1875-77, James W White, 1877-79, Peter Wood, 1879-81, George N Fringer

Court Criers

1837-57, James Kiefler, 1857-68, Benjamin Yingling, 1868-81, William S Brown

State's Attorneys

1837-46, William P Maulsby, 1846, James Raymond, 1847-49, William N Hayden 1849-51, Charles W Webster, 1851, A N Hobbs, 1852-56, Daniel L Hoover, 1856-67, Charles W Webster, 1867-71, Charles T Reifsnider, 1871-75, Richard B Norment, 1875-81, David N Henning

Registers of Wills

1837-53, John Baumgartner, 1853-65, Joseph M Parke, 1865-67, Henry H Herbaugh, 1867-73, Joseph M Parke, 1873-79, Henry E Beltz, 1879-81, J Oliver Wadlow

Judges of the Orphans' Court

1837-39, Abraham Wampler, William Jameson, Robert Hudson, 1839-42, Nimrod Frizell Michael Sullivan, Michael Barnitz, 1842-45, Michael Sullivan, Jesse Manning, John

---

[1] Judge Charles [illegible] attended the first court, but was [illegible] ceeded by Judge [illegible]

B Boyle 1846-48, Jacob Matthias William Shepherd, Mordecai G Cockey, 1848-51, Basil Hayden, William Fisher, George W Manro, 1851-55, George W Manro, Levi Buffington, Michael Sullivan, 1855-59 Michael Sullivan, Horatio Price, Thomas S Brown, 1859-63 Horatio Price, John Thomson, Joshua C Gist, 1863-67, John Thomson, Joseph Schaeffer, Thomas S Brown, Michael Baughman (part of 1863), 1867-70, Jacob Powder, 1867-71, Levi Buffington, Hanson T Webb 1870-71, Ira E Crouse, 1871-79, Adam Shower, Isaac C Baile, 1871-72, Upton Roop, 1872-79, L P Slingluff, Granville I Hering (chief justice), William Frizell, Melchour F Allgire

And tors to the Circuit Court as a Court of Equity

September term, 1837, James M Shellman, April term, 1851, Abner Neal, April term, 1862, Charles I Reifsnider, Jan 1, 1867, Augustus D Shaefler, Nov 29, 1867, John J Baumgartner

County Surveyors

Charles W Hood, Jacob Kerlinger, James Kelly, J Henry Hoppe, J William Everhart, Francis Warner, J Henry Hoppe (deceased in 1881)

County School Commissioners

Aug 7, 1865 to April 27, 1868, Jacob H Christ, Washington Senseney, Zachariah Ebaugh, Andrew K Shriver, Joshua Yingling Andrew J Wilhelm, James V Cresswell, Peter Engel, Secretary, William A Wampler April 27, 1868, to Jan 3, 1870 (appointed by county commissioners), Sterling Galt, Reuben Saylor, Isaac Winchester, L A J Lamotte, Dr J W Steele, George A Shower, John K Longwell, Lewis Green, W P Anderson, Jacob Sharrets, Peter Shriner, Joseph Davis, counsel, Joseph M Newson, secretary, treasurer, and examiner Jan 3, 1870, to Jan 3, 1872 (elected by the people), Daniel H Rudolph Robert C McKinney, Charles H Gilbert, Jacob H Crummer, W N Matthews, Dr J W Steele David T Schaefler, Isaac Winchester, Joseph B Boyle, W P Anderson, Solomon Shepherd, Job Hibberd, Counsel, R B Norment, Secretary, Treasurer, and Examiner, J M Newson Jan 3, 1872, to 1881 (appointed by the court), Dr William Reindollar vice R C McKinney, Alfred Zollickofler, Francis H Hering, David Prugh, William Reese, Counsel, John E Smith, Secretary, Treasurer, and Examiner, Joseph M Newson

County Commissioners

1837-39, William Shepherd, Sterling Galt, John Erb, Joshua C Gist, Joseph Steele, Jacob Reese, John Lamotte, Nimrod Gardner, Henry N Brinkman, 1839 to 1843, William Shaw, John Roop, of Joseph, Daniel Stull, Peter Hull, Eli Hewitt, Frederick Ritter, Jacob Shaeffer, William Houck, Joshua Barbager, 1843-45, William Shaw, John Adelsperger, John Roop, Lewis Shue, Peter Hull, George Bramwell, Eli Hewitt, James Morgan, Frederick Ritter, Jacob Shaffer, William Houck, Larkin Buckingham, 1845-48, Henry Carter, Samuel Evans, Peter Geiger, Richard Richards, David B Earhart, David Cassell, Frederick Badchman, Elias Grimes G W Gorsuch, 1848-51, James Crouse, Cornelius [illegible] David Feever, Daniel Bush, John H Lindsey, George Crouse, Joseph Orendorff, George Richards, Jr Bennett Spurrier, 1851-54, James Crouse, Thomas Smith, George L Little, Jacob Wickert, Julius B Berrett, George Crouse, Jacob Grove George Richards, Jr, Bennett Spurrier, [illegible] (now elected by the people), John Cover, [illegible] Dorsey, Michael Baughman, 1856-58, [illegible] [illegible] Christ, John [illegible]

60, Andrew K Shriver, Jacob Morelock, G W Gorsuch, 1860-62, A K Shriver, H W Dell, Zachariah Ebaugh, 1862-64, Benjamin Shunk, Thomas F Shepherd, John H Chew, 1864-66, same board, 1866-68, Thomas Pamter, John H Chew, Thomas F Shepherd, 1868-70, Josiah Adelsperger, Upton Roop, Jabez A Bush, 1870-72, Jacob Sharretts, Josiah Adelsperger, Upton Roop, 1872-74, Josephus H Hoppe, G K Frank, Joseph Spurrier 1874-76, M C McKinstry, John W Murray, John O Devries, 1876-78, same board, 1878-80, Jonas S Harner, John J Abbott, David Fowble, 1880-82, J K Longwell, W C Polk, Francis Warner

Clerks to Commissioners

1837-39, Otho Shipley, 1839-45, Basil Root vice Andrew Grammer resigned, 1845-48, Otho Shipley, 1848-56, Jacob Myerly, 1856-64, James Blizzard, 1864-68, Levi Valentine, 1868-72, James Blizzard 1872-78, James A Bush, 1878-80, L C Trumbo, 1880-82, Joseph A Waesche

Collectors of Taxes

1837-39, Thomas Hook 1839-45, Tobias Cover, 1845-48, Josiah Baumgartner, 1848-51, Richard Manning, 1851-54, Tobias Cover, 1856-58, S R Gore, 1858-60 John T Diffenbaugh, 1860-62, James Campbell,[1] 1874-78, Jabez Bush, 1878-80, L C Trumbo, 1880-82, Joseph A. Waesche

Attorneys to Commissioners

1837-39 James Raymond, 1843-45, William P Maulsby, 1845-48, C Birnie, Jr, 1848-51, Joseph M Parke 1851-56, E F Crout, 1856-60, C W Webster, 1868-76, Charles B Roberts, 1876-81, Richard B Norment

Members of Congress

Peter Little, Elias Brown, Dr Jacob Shower, Charles B Roberts

Members of Constitutional Conventions

1851, Elias Brown, Dr Jacob Shower, Joseph M Parke, A G Ege, Mordecai G Cockey, 1864, Dr John Swope, John E Smith, Jonas Ecker, William S Wooden, 1867, William N Hayden, George W Manro, Thomas J Cover, Sterling Galt, Benjamin W Bennett, John K Longwell

State Senators

1838-44, William P Maulsby, 1844-50, William Roberts, 1850-55, John K Longwell 1855-57, Dr Francis T Davis, 1857-62, John E Smith 1862-64 Jacob Campbell, 1864-67, Dr James L Billingslea, 1867-70, Dr Nathan Brown, 1870-74, John K Longwell, 1874-78 James Fenner Lee, 1878-82, Henry Vanderford

Members of the House of Delegates

1837-38, Dr Jacob Shower, James G Berrett, John B Boyle, Jacob Powder 1839, Joseph M Parker, George Bramwell, George Crabbs, Thomas Hook, 1840, John B Boyle, Dr Jacob Shower, Samuel D Lecompte, Daniel Stull, 1841, John B Boyle, Jacob Powder, Dr Francis T Davis, Daniel Stull, 1842, Elias Brown, Samuel D Lecompte, Jacob Powder, William Shaw, 1843, Samuel Ecker, Jacob Powder, William Shaw, Daniel Stull, 1844, James Raymond, John Thomson, Micajah Rogers, Joseph Ebaugh, 1845, Thomas Hook, James M Shellman, Abraham Wampler, 1846, A G Ege James M Shellman, Upton Scott, Charles Devilbiss 1847, John B Boyle, Nicholas Kelly,

[1] [illegible] appointed, which system [illegible]

Tobias Cover, Jacob Powder, 1849 Elias Brown, Samuel A Lauver George Motter, Lewis Trumbo, 1851, Elijah F Crout, Dr J E H Ligget, Daniel Stull, 1854, Thomas Smith, Robert F Dade, Josiah Baugher, 1856, Stephen T C Brown, David Buffington, John E Smith, 1858, Samuel McKinstry, Milton Day Samuel Reindollar, 1860, Dr B Mills, John W Gorsuch, David Roop, 1861, Somerset R Waters, George Everhart, Warren L Little (December session), 1862, Jonas Ecker, John N Starr, Somerset R Waters, 1864, Moses Shaw, George Everhart, John W Angel, William S Wooden, N D Norris, 1865, William A Wampler, Benjamin Poole, James V Criswell, E T Benton, S L Gore, 1868, Henry S Davis John H Jordon, John W Hardin, Benjamin Worthington 1870, William H Crouse, Airhart Winters, George A Shower, John H Jordon, 1872, James H Steele, Lewis A J Lamotte, Trusten Polk, H H Lamotte, 1874, Henry Vanderford, Henry Galt, Dr S R Waters, Thomas C Brown, 1876, Frank Brown, H H Lamotte, Dr Jacob Rinehart, Dr. S R Waters, 1878, Frank T Newbelle, T Herbert Shriver, Robert Sellman, Sr, Frank Brown, 1880, William T Smith, T Herbert Shriver, Robert Sellman, Sr, Benjamin F Crouse, 1882, Henry Galt, Edward W Leeds, David A C Webster, Joseph W Berret

Miscellaneous Officials in 1881

Assistant School Examiner, Orlando Reese, Deputy County Clerks, George A Miller, N Bruce Boyle, James A Difenbaugh, Deputy Register of Wills, George M Parke

Justices of the Peace in Carroll County since its Organization as a County—When Appointed or Elected

1839, John Manning Basil Root, James Keefer, John C Kelly, Adam Feeser Michael Smith, Josiah Shilling, Henry Drach, Jonathan Dorsey, Jacob Wickert, Thomas B Owings, Wilson Burdett, John Jones, of John Michael Lynch, John Kerlinger, John F Reese, Charles Denning, Jacob Farver, Thomas Ingels, George W Manro, 1840, J Henry Hoppe, 1841, Jabez Gore, Jesse Brown, John Lockard, 1842, Benjamin Williams, Samuel Moffitt, Jabez Gore, Thomas J Carter, J Henry Hoppe, John Potherer, Jacob Grove, Abraham Lamott Josiah Shilling, George Williams, 1843, Thomas Grisley, John Malehorn, Jacob Kerlinger, John Rinehart, Samuel Lamott, James Hood, David Roop, Basil Hayden 1844, Jacob Myerly, Julius B Berret, Elijah Woolery, Michael Smith, 1845, Otho Shipley, James Smith, Benjamin Shunk, John Loebitz, Washington Van Bibber, Isaac Dern, Jeremiah Bartholow, Daniel Stonesifer, William Ecker, James Kelly, David C Frankforter, George D Klinefelter, Abraham Bixler, Henry H Herbaugh, Stephen Oursler, Nimrod Stevenson, Charles Devilbiss, Abraham England, James McKellip, John K Longwell, Henry V Buchen, Richard A Kirkwood, Jacob Stone, Archibald Dorsey, Frank Yingling, Joshua H Shipley, Zachariah Ebaugh, James Douty, John Hood Jr, Solomon Stocksdale, Geo E Wampler, Richard Owings, Charles Stevenson, William Shaw, Washington Barnes, Samuel Swarmstedt, Warren L Little, Alexander Gilliss, Nicholas Dorsey, Thomas Hook, Horatio F Bardwell, David B Earhart, Moses Myers, Joshua Smith, G Ogg, Henry Stumf, 1846, John Leatherwood, James Rodgers, Jonathan Morris, David Kephart Wm Jordan, John Delaplane, Peter E Myers, Thomas W Durbin Israel Banker, Joshua Stansbury, Jacob Zumbrun, Franklin J Smith 1847, Geo W Wilson, Stephen Gorsuch [illegible]

Myerly, Joseph Gernand George Everhart, James Baker, J Henry Hoppe, Geo W Manro, Jonathan Dorsey, Eli Hewitt, George Foster, William Fisher, Thomas Hook, George Miller, Daniel L Hoover, Samuel A Lauver, Daniel J Geiman, D F Lamott, Thos S Brown, John Mauss, Geo L Little, Michael Sullivan, David Bussard, Samuel Messinger, Michael Smith, Kelpher Crawmer, Julius B Berret, Francis J Crawford, D W Houck, John C Price, Charles Denning, Jacob Kerlinger, Joseph Spurrier, George Bramwell, William Lockard, George P Albaugh, Joseph Creiger, John Rinehard, Thos B Buckingham, George Williams, Jesse Manning, David Bussard, James Rodgers, William Tagg, Samuel Messinger, Geo W Daniel, Peter B Mikesell, David Hope, Richard Harris, Larkin Buckingham, 1849, Michael Sullivan, Joseph Stonesifer, 1850, David Wolf, Geo L Little, Jacob Wickert, Michael Smith, D F Lamott, John Rinehart, Charles Dunning, David Bossard, Elijah Woolery, D W Houck, George Foster, 1851, John W McAllister, 1852, Jacob Myers, Jesse Manning J Henry Hoppe, David Wolf, Wm Jordan, David Feeser James Rodgers, John Mauss, Eli Hewitt, George Miller, William Tagg, James Baker, Jacob Kerlinger, Larkin Buckingham, George Foster, Basil Hayden, William Fisher, George Everhart, Thos B Owings, George Ogg, Joseph Spurrier, John W McAlister, George Bramwell, D F Lamott Thos S Brown, Kelpher Crawmer, Joshua Lamott, Peter B Mikesell, Henry W Deel, Henry H Herbaugh, L L Crawford, David Hape, Richard Harris, John C Price, 1853, Jesse Hollingsworth, D W Houck, Richard Deel, Mordecai G Cockey Benj Shunk, J Henry Hoppe, David B Earhart, Wm Gonsfrihe Jesse Manning, Wm A Wampler, Charles Denning James McKellip, Wm Haugh, Wm R Curley, Wm Walter, Jacob Kerlinger, Richard Harris, John C Price, F O Franklin, H H Herbaugh, John Koontz, Isaac Dern, David Otto, Joshua Switzer, John Hood, Thomas B Owings, Alex Gilliss, Abraham Lamott, 1854 Bennett Spurrier, 1855, Wm Walter, Henry Flegle, George Miller, Jacob Kerlinger, Henry Motter, John Fowble, of Jacob, Edwin A Atlee, W A Wampler, Jacob Shorve, Abraham Albaugh, H H Herbaugh, Reuben Conaway, Mordecai G Cockey, Aquila Pickett, J Henry Hoppe, A H Jenkins, Geo Richards, John T Lowe, Joseph Matthias, David Otto, Nathan Gorsuch, Nicholas D Norris, M B L Bussard, John Delaplane, Wm Crouse Elijah Woolery, Daniel Stonesifer, Geo L Little, 1856, Daniel I Hoover, John C Price, 1857, J Henry Hoppe, F O Franklin, Wm Crouse, David E Flegal M G Cockey, Hanson M Drach, Joseph Matthias, Reuben Conaway, Aquila Pickett, Benjamin W Bennett, N D Norris, W G Shipley, Peter B Mikesell, Daniel Stonesifer, Henry Glaze, Jesse B Christ, F A Switzer, Elijah Woolery, Benj Shunk, Geo Miller, Frederick H Crabbs, John C Price, Wm Haugh, Geo Richards, Jr., Wm Walter, Abraham Albaugh, John Delaplane, Nathan Gorsuch, D Otto, H H Herbaugh, H Geatty, 1859, E A Atlee, Joseph Mathias, A S Yentz W A Wampler James Lockard, J Henry Hoppe, Wm Walter H M Drach, D B Flegal, John T Young, Henry Motter, John Mauss, P B Mikesell Jacob Zumbrun, Jacob Shriver, Benjamin Shunk, John Delaplane Samuel A Lauver, Aquila Pickett, W G Shipley, John C Price, William Crouse, Joshua Switzer, F A Switzer, M G Cockey, H H Herbaugh, Jesse Brown, Israel Norris Evan Thomp[illegible] Mathias W A [illegible] John Mauss, [illegible] Lockard, H

H Herbaugh, John G Ways, M G Cockey, William Lensfeld J William Everhart, Nathan Gorsuch, L A Atlee, George P Albaugh, George Miller, John Fultz, Jacob Zumbrun Joshua Switzer, John I Young William Haugh, Henry Motter, A Pickett, Eli Hewitt, John C Price, Jetson L Gill D B Flegal, Thomas Tipton, Solomon S Ecker, William Fisher 1863, William Fensfield, W J Mitten, Joseph Mathias William E Shriner, Richard Harris George Miller William Haugh, Amos Brice, Aquila Pickett, John Hesson, Joseph Brummel, Joseph H Gilliss, J C Price, Henry Frael, H H Herbaugh J W Cochran, Nathan Gorsuch, S B Stocksdale, Thomas Tipton, Levi B Frock, Eli Hewitt George E Buckingham, John Delaplane, William Fisher, Henry Motter, Francis Warner, Joshua Switzer, Solomon S Ecker, John Mauss, 1864, William Lockard George E Buckingham, 1865, John S Wampler William Lockard, Benjamin Shunk, James Kelly, William Haugh George Miller John T Ways, J Williams, D E Fulhart, David Otto, J William Everhart, Thomas Tipton, Henry Glaze, Aquila Pickett, George E Wampler Joshua Switzer, Joshua Cain, T L Gill Peter A Shipley, John Hesson, Solomon S Ecker, John Fultz, John W Cochran, Nicholas S F Harden, Eli Hewitt, Michael Babylon 1866, George L Wampler, J L Gill, Thomas Demoss Michael Babylon, Joshua Cain, Peter Ritter 1867 John W McAlister, John Lamott, Cornelius Jenkins, William Fisher, Henry Galt, W H Stocksdale, Levi Yingling, Joshua Cain, Francis Warner, John Mauss, Nathan Gorsuch Azariah Oursler A Neal, Stephen Gorsuch, W J Mitten, J Henry Hoppe, Eli Hewitt, John W Jones, D H Hoffacker J B Summers, William I Smith, J Oliver Wadlow, Henry Bussard, Henry Motter, David Otto, Michael Babylon 1868, Peter B Mikesell, William Fisher, W L Tracey, Henry Galt, Simon Bange, Charles Denning, Joshua Switzer Joshua Cain, W H Stocksdale, W T Smith, Levi Yingling, C W Hood, Henry Bussard, J W McAlister Charles Sykes, David Otto, John Lamott, J Henry Hoppe, J B Summers, W J Mitten, John Mauss, J Oliver Wadlow C Jenkins, Henry Motter, J W Jones, A Neal Nathan Gorsuch, Thomas B Buckingham, G W Gilbert, 1870, W L Tracey, G A Flicking, G W Gilbert C W Hood, A Oursler, N Gorsuch, Henry Bussard, William Fisher, T C Jenkins, W G Byers, J Henry Hoppe, J Oliver Wadlow, Stephen Gorsuch, William T Smith W H Stocksdale, Henry Motter, John W Jones, Henry Galt, Thomas B Buckingham, George L Stocksdale T B Deboff, John W McAlister, A J Houck, P B Mikesell, Charles Denning, E Legore, W J Mitten, A Neal, Joshua Switzer, Andrew Grammer, 1872, Ezra Legore, Stephen Gorsuch, Henry Galt, William Fisher, J William Everhart, C Jenkins, William J Mitten Abner Neal, Joshua Switzer, J Oliver Wadlow, William T Smith, William L Tracy, Azariah Oursler, George A Flickinger, Henry Motter, A J Houck, Henry Bussard, Charles W Hood, James Morgan, William Stocksdale, Nathan Gorsuch, Peter B Mikesell, Thomas B Buckingham, George L Stocksdale, George W Gilbert, Samuel Shunk 1873, John W Abbott 1874 Charles W Hood, James Morgan, S B Stocksdale Henry Galt, Joel Brown, J Henry Hoppe, J I Wateborn J Oliver Wadlow Charles Denning, Lewis Dielman, William P Smith, Henry Motter, Joshua Switzer, Ezra Legore William J Mitten, William L Tracey, G A Flickinger, A Oursler Jacob P Baltozer, J W Abbott, Elijah Vance Brown, G W Gilbert C W Hood J B Summers [illegible] Buckingham Abner Neal Stephen Gorsuch Peter [illegible] Mikesell, William H Crouse Samuel Shunk, Henry A McAtee, 1875, Francis Warner, 1876, J P Baltozer, Francis Warner, Louis Dielman, G A Flickinger Joab Brown, John B Summers, W T Smith, Joshua Switzer, W H Fogle, G W Matthews, Jesse A Legore, Samuel Messinger J K Kearney, Thomas Tipton, W J Mitten, J Henry Hoppe, G W Crapster, T E Ward, A Oursler James Morgan, J W Abbott, J Oliver Wadlow Charles Denning, Henry Galt Stephen Gorsuch, Henry Motter, William Fisher, Dr H M Drach, J E Christ, John Elgen, Howard McGill, Isaiah Hann C W Hood, G F Yingling, Thomas Jones, Charles B Favour, 1877, Richard Dell, 1878, Jacob P Baltozer, Samuel S Spalding Dr H M Drach Peter B Mikesell, Azariah Oursler J Henry Hoppe, J U Legore, J H Knipple, G A Flickinger, Henry Galt, Louis Dielman, W J Mitten, Joab Brown John W Abbott, P Bennett, William Fisher, Gustavus W Crapster, H McGill, Thomas Jones, Thomas B Buckingham, J B Summers, Francis Warner, John Elgen, James Morgan, J K Kearney, T Bowman, Isaiah Hann, Daniel E Christ William F Smith, J Oliver Wadlow, W H Stocksdale, Richard Dell, Henry Motter, Thomas Tipton, Nathan Gorsuch, John P Fowler, Charles B Favour, D Calvin Warner, T Frank Shipley, 1880, Joab Brown, Henry Galt Azariah Oursler, J P Baltozer, William Fisher, James C Davis, S S Spalding, Richard Dell, Thomas Tipton John W Abbott, Dr Hanson, M Drach, Louis Dielman Thomas Jones, William J Mitten, S H Hoffacker, G W Crapster, John Burgoon, T E Lovell, John Elgen, Ira F Crouse John P Fowler, Thomas P Buckingham, Peter B Mikesell, Henry Motter, John Bowman, D Calvin Warner, W H Stocksdale J Henry Knipple, Charles B Favour, Nathan Gorsuch, T F Shipley, J K Kearney, John L Summers, David H Reindollar, Jesse F Billmyer, Henry Crook, 1881, Joseph Arnold, Andrew J Dougherty

Registers of Voters

1866–67—1st District, W A Hiteshue, Washington Galt, 2d, J H Jordan, 3d, Peter E Myers, Abraham Long, 4th, Thomas Gorsuch, 5th, Jesse Hollingsworth, 6th, Jacob Linaweaver, 7th, Benjamin Williams, George W Shriver, 8th, Richard Harris, 9th, Abraham Albaugh 10th, David Otts, 11th, Jesse Lambert

1868—R B Warden, W H Lamott, John M Yingling, Abraham Albaugh, George Shower, S G Harden, W A Hiteshue, Peter L Myers, Jeremiah Malehorn, Jesse Lambert, William Valentine G W Crapster

1869—Uriah B Mikesell

1870—Jesse Lambert, G W Crapster, W H Lamott, Abraham Albaugh, George Shower, William H Hull, Uriah B Mikesell, John R Haines, William Valentine, Samuel G Harden, Jeremiah Malehorn

1871—8th District, Jacob Coltrider

1872—1st District, G W Crapster 2d, John R Haines, 3d, Eli Erb, 4th, William H Lamott, 5th, S D Warfield, 6th, George Shower, 7th, Uriah B Mikesell, 8th, Jacob Coltrider 9th, Abraham Albaugh, 10th William Valentine, 11th, Jesse Lambert, 12th, John Hartsock

1873—7th District, Lee McElroy

1874—1st District, William Fisher, 2d, John R Haines, 3d, Jonas Frock, 4th Daniel Ebaugh 5th, Surratt D Warfield 6th, George Shower, 7th, Lee McElroy, 8th, Jacob Coltrider, 9th, Abraham Albaugh, 10th Levi Buffington, 11th, Jesse Lambert 12th John Hartsock

1876—1st District William L Rudisel 2d John R Haines, [illegible] b, Samuel S Spalding [illegible] McElroy, 8th,

Francis L Haon, 9th, Abraham Albaugh, 10th John Shunk, 11th, Jesse Lambert, 12th, John Hartsock

1877 —4th District, Noah Stockdale

1878 —1st District, W L Rudisel, 2d, John R Haines, 3d, Jonas Frock 4th, Noah Stockdale, 5th Dr Joseph W Steele 6th, George Shower, 7th, Lee McElroy, G W Matthews, 8th, Francis L Hann, 9th, Abraham Albaugh, 10th, John Shunk, 11th, Jesse Lambert, 12th, John Hartsock

1880 —1st District, Charles A Waesche, 2d, John R Haines, 3d, William G Byers, 4th, John Frick, 5th, Dr J W Steele, 6th, George Shower, 7th, George W Matthews, 8th, James W Hann, 9th, Lewis C Franklin, 10th, John Shunk, 11th, Jesse Lambert, 12th, John Hartsock

Tax Collectors

1866 —1st District, Samuel T Clingan, 2d, T H Routson, 3d, Benjamin Hesson, 4th, Stephen Oursler 5th, William D Frizzell, 7th, Henry Shreve, 8th, David Grogg, 9th, John Hood, 10th, John Root, 11th, Mordecai Engler

1867 —1st District, S T Clingan, 2d, T H Routson, 3d, Benjamin Hesson, 4th, Stephen Oursler, 5th, W T Frizzell, 6th, Jesse Schultz, 7th, Henry Shreve, 8th, David Grogg, 10th, Jacob Shriner, 11th, Mordecai Engler

1868 —7th District, Jacob Holmes, 8th, Benjamin Jackson, 9th, Joseph Spurrier, Edward Spalding, Henry T Eck, Nathan Hanna, G K Frank, Samuel A Lauver, James Gilbert, James White, Freeborn Gardner, Edward Spalding

1869 —Henry T Eck, James Gilbert, Freeborn Gardner, Nathan Hanna, Samuel A Lauver, Benjamin Jackson, James W White, George K Frank, Jacob Holmes, Edward Spalding, Joseph Spurrier

1870.—1st District, A F Arndorff, 2d, James Gilbert 3d, W T Feeser, 4th, Samuel A Lauver, 5th, Freeborn Gardner, 6th, George K Frank, 7th, Jacob Holmes, 8th, Benjamin Jackson, 9th, Joseph Spurrier, 10th, William A Grimes, 11th, D W Snader

1871 —Same, excepting Isaiah Hann in 10th and John N Selby in 9th, *vice* Grimes and Spurrier

1872 —1st District, Edward Spalding, 2d, Dennis Cookson, 4th, Jesse Long, 6th, John J Abbott, 7th, George P Albaugh, 8th, Benjamin Jackson, 9th, John N Selby, 10th, Isaiah Hann

1873 —1st District, Edward Spalding, 2d, Dennis Cookson, 3d, Daniel Myers, 4th, Jesse Long, 5th, Freeborn Gardner, 6th, John J Abbott, 8th, Benjamin Jackson, 9th, Henry S Davis, 10th, Isaiah Hann, 11th, D W Snader

1874 —1st District, Edward Spalding, 2d, J Hamilton Singer, 3d, Daniel Myers, 4th, Jesse Long 5th, Freeborn Gardner, 6th, Joseph Weimer, 7th, George P Albaugh, 8th, W H Armacost, 10th, Jacob Sharretts, 11th, D W Snader

1875 —1st District, Edward Spalding, 2d, J H Singer, 3d, Daniel Myers, 4th, Jesse Long, 6th, Joseph Weimer, 7th, G P Albaugh, 8th, J Thomas Green, 9th, Byron S Dorsey, 10th, Jacob Sharretts, 11th, D W Snader

1876 —1st District, Edward Spalding, 2d, J H Singer, 3d, Daniel Myers, 5th, Freeborn Gardner, 6th, Joseph Weimer, 7th, G P Albaugh, 8th, J Thomas Green, 9th, Byron S Dorsey, 11th, Joseph A Waesche

1877 —1st District, Washington Reaver, 2d, J H Singer, 3d, Daniel Myers, 4th, Jesse Long, 5th, R H Widlow, 6th, Joseph Weimer, 7th, G P Albaugh, 8th, Isaac T Green, 9th, B S Dorsey, 10th, Jacob Sharretts, 11th, J A Waesche

1878 —1st District, W Reaver, 2d, Benjamin Reaver, 5th, G W Manro, 6th, G K Frank, 7th, W G Rinehart, 8th, Isaac T Green, 9th, B S Dorsey, 10th, J H Diffendal, 11th, J A Waesche, 12th, George P Buckley

1879 —1st District, W Reaver, 2d, Benjamin Reaver, 3d, Daniel Myers, 4th, Jesse Long, 5th G W Manro, 6th, G K Frank, 7th, W G Rinehart, 8th, J T Green, 9th, B S Dorsey, 10th, J H Diffendal, 11th, J A Waesche, 12th, G P Buckley

1880-81 —Same, save D P Smelzer in 11th

It is sometimes interesting to glance over the results of successive elections held during a given period and to note the gradual changes effected in public sentiment by the lapse of time, the march of enlightenment, or the happening of exciting events which exert an influence on the minds of electors A philosophic study of such statistics will enable a careful student to evolve the outline of the history of a people, the bent of their minds, and even their character and habits

The names of the principal candidates for office at every prominent election held in Carroll County since 1847 to the present time (1881) is given below, together with the number of votes cast for each candidate

Gubernatorial Vote, 1847

Districts	Francis Thomas (Democrat)	Goldsborough (Whig)
Taneytown	203	296
Uniontown	261	358
Myers'	205	79
Woolery's	195	94
Freedom	106	208
Manchester	352	72
Westminster	262	203
Hampstead	159	64
Franklin	109	150
Total	1854	1524

Vote for Delegates, 1847

Boyle	1831	Kelly	1785
Ege	1493	Hood	1105
Powder	1791	Cover	1512
Ecker	1038	Wampler	1513

Third Congressional District

	Ligon	Philpot
Baltimore County	2401	1902
Five Wards of Baltimore	2509	1612
Howard District	726	661
Carroll County	1801	1531
Total	7447	5706

Vote for Sheriff, 1848

Districts	Sullivan (Democrat)	Gore (Dem)	Webb (Whig)	Fulhart (Whig)	Bishop (Ind)
Taneytown	132	173	261	186	5
Uniontown	148	166	324	114	11
Myers'	117	109	79	124	5
Finksburg	122	163	131	28	19
Freedom	37	95	249	103	7
Manchester	286	216	60	28	5
Westminster	222	237	200	70	10
Hampstead	119	115	73	10	29
Franklin	[illegible]		[illegible]	59	2
Total	[illegible]	[illegible]	[illegible]	722	96

Vote for President, 1848

Districts	Lewis Cass	Zachary Taylor
Taneytown	195	318
Uniontown	208	373
Myers'	181	100
Woolery's	112	134
Freedom	88	258
Manchester	362	75
Westminster	245	262
Hampstead	154	73
Franklin	97	170
Total	1672	1763

Gubernatorial and Senatorial Vote, 1850

Districts	Governor		Senator	
	Clark (Whig)	Lowe (Democrat)	Langwell (Whig)	Liggett (Democrat)
Taneytown	321	162	293	189
Uniontown	358	218	357	217
Myers'	80	157	82	155
Woolery's	116	155	120	149
Freedom	215	88	221	80
Manchester	79	361	80	359
Westminster	261	250	288	226
Hampstead	77	146	81	140
Franklin	157	74	160	71
Total	1664	1611	1682	1586

Vote for Delegates to Constitutional Convention, 1850

Democratic Ticket

Districts	Cockey	Brown	Edge	Parke	Shower
Taneytown	273	268	328	288	283
Uniontown	171	135	190	185	180
Myers'	114	100	116	115	113
Woolery's	153	126	135	133	134
Freedom	74	61	65	66	70
Manchester	273	271	275	280	282
Westminster	225	197	220	232	217
Hampstead	117	112	115	116	119
Franklin	51	41	31	61	68
Total	1431	1309	1473	1479	1466

Whig Ticket

Districts	Wampler	Ecker	Swope	Frankforter	Grimes
Taneytown	96	98	134	79	91
Uniontown	230	287	236	239	232
Myers'	48	54	45	50	48
Woolery's	97	93	90	85	90
Freedom	154	161	161	156	166
Manchester	61	59	60	81	56
Westminster	236	222	221	218	225
Hampstead	50	48	45	46	45
Franklin	114	142	128	127	157
Total	1086	1164	1117	1081	1110

Vote on the Adoption of the New Constitution, June 4, 1851

Districts	For	Against
Taneytown	227	124
Uniontown	115	274
Myers	90	97
Woolery's	205	39
Freedom	73	201
Manchester	287	37
Westminster	227	162
Hampstead	151	40
Franklin	66	121
Total	1071	1095

Vote for Congressman, Oct 1, 1851

Districts	Hammond (Democrat)	Lynch (Whig)
Taneytown	185	100
Uniontown	112	80
Myers'	158	27
Woolery's	94	6
Freedom	59	89
Manchester	253	33
Westminster	191	131
Hampstead	211	
Franklin	115	86
Total	1378	552

Vote for State Comptroller, November, 1851

Districts	P F Thomas (Democrat)	G C Morgan (Whig)
Taneytown	246	277
Uniontown	250	376
Myers	204	89
Woolery's	170	128
Freedom	82	206
Manchester	317	90
Westminster	269	269
Hampstead	170	73
Franklin	87	146
Total	1795	1654

For Court of Appeals, John T Mason 1604, Fred k A Schley 1672

For Circuit Judge, Madison Nelson 1732, R H Marshall 865, W M Merrick 153, J M Palmer 721

For Clerk of Court, John B Boyle 1882, John McCollum 1596

For Sheriff, W S Brown 2193, S J Jordan 1191, Otho Shipley 973

For Register of Wills, Joseph M Parke 1607, J J Baumgardner 1902

For State's Attorney, D L Hoover 1807, C W Webster 1543

For Orphans Court, M Sullivan 1707 G W Manro 1800, Levi Buffington 1784, J C Gist 1598, H Price 1493, John Thomson 1562, D B Earhart 214, L Hayden 378

For Assembly, E F Crout 1730, D Stull 1702, J L H Ligget 1793, Thos Hood 1505, E G Cox 1346, G E Wampler 1665, R R Booth 234, A Lamott 300

For Surveyor, J Henry Hoppe 1582, James Kelly 1828

Vote for President, 1852

Districts	Pierce	Scott
Taneytown	153	236
Uniontown	244	341
Myers'	201	79
Woolery's	182	103
Freedom	94	236
Manchester	423	89
Westminster	279	252
Hampstead	166	83
Franklin	108	153
Middleburg	69	120
Total	1919	1702

Vote for School Commissioners, Nov. 3, 1852

Districts.	Shriver	Holmes	Cookson	Hiteshue	Horbaugh	Earhart	Nat Mon
Taneytown	62	59	63	101	59	60	$8 62
Uniontown	54	17	51	37	73	71	5 00
Myers'	85	40	52	9	8	72	20
Woolery's	56	59	54	2	3	1	1 75
Freedom	25	30	25	28	28	27	1 78
Manchester	102	104	104	14	13	14	5 00
Westminster	96	99	100	73	79	74	13 [illegible]
Hampstead	25	24	24	20	8	7	6 [illegible]
Franklin	28	29	29	17	19	19	1 32
Middleburg	19	14	21	30	27	18	2 05
Total	[illegible]	[illegible]	[illegible]	[illegible]	[illegible]	323	$48 07

Average D[illegible]

Gubernatorial Vote, 1853

Districts	T W Ligon (Democrat)	E J Bowie (Whig)
Taneytown	136	221
Uniontown	289	329
Myers'	216	91
Woolery's	202	121
Freedom	100	202
Manchester	410	88
Westminster	300	282
Hampstead	180	81
Franklin	134	184
Middleburg	79	103
Total	2016	1702

For Congress, Dr Jacob Shower 2055, John Wethered 1651

For Delegates, Josiah L Baughei 1882, Thomas Smith 1909, Robert Dade 1918, George E Wampler 1859, Joseph Ebaugh 1714, Stephen Oursler 1618

For Register of Wills, J J Baumgardner 1782, J M Parke 1903

For Sheriff, J M Yingling 2077, S J Jordan 1751

For School Commissioners, Samuel Eckei 1669, J H Shipley 1498, J W Earhart 1730, J C Cookson 2009, A K Shriver 2061 Jacob Holmes 2011

For County Commissioners, J B Chenowith 1731, J C Gist 1780, John Coier 1593, Michael Baughman 2038, Jonathan Dorsey 1927, Isaac Applei 1726

Vote for State Comptroller, 1855

Districts	W H Purnell (American)	W W W Bowie (Democrat)
Taneytown	249	134
Uniontown	487	180
Myers	110	183
Woolery's	216	119
Freedom	306	85
Manchester	103	444
Westminster	303	313
Hampstead	123	146
Franklin	221	134
Middleburg	134	73
Total	2252	1811

Presidential Vote, 1856

Districts	Buchanan	Fillmore
Taneytown	147	270
Uniontown	154	343
Myers'	227	113
Woolery's	175	207
Freedom	105	314
Manchester	494	122
Westminster	334	274
Hampstead	171	133
Franklin	99	195
Middleburg	71	156
New Windsor	122	221
Total	2099	2348

Gubernatorial Vote, 1857

Districts	J C. Groome (Democrat)	T H Hicks (American)
Taneytown	161	260
Uniontown	165	343
Myers'	230	105
Finksburg	186	207
Freedom	118	294
Manchester	502	135
Westminster	336	270
Hampstead	186	126
Franklin	107	204
Middleburg	74	145
New Windsor	114	224
Total	2179	[illegible]

Vote for State Comptroller, 1859

Districts	A L Jarrett (Democrat)	W H Purnell (American)
Taneytown	157	279
Uniontown	176	351
Myers'	252	106
Finksburg	220	208
Freedom	139	290
Manchester	501	139
Westminster	373	324
Hampstead	181	132
Franklin	122	186
Middleburg	73	165
New Windsor	128	228
Total	2325	2408

For County Officers

Sheriff, William Leg fooso 2417, M F Shilling 2319

State's Attorney, Edmund O'Brien 2322, C W Webster 2333

Register of Wills, J M Parke 2435, Jacob Campbell 2293

Judges of Orphans' Court, D S Herring 2401, G W Manro 2314, Jonas Ecker 2361, John Thompson 2593, J C Gist 2376, Horatio Price 2401

Presidential Vote, 1860

Districts	Breckenridge	Bell	Douglas	Lincoln
Taneytown	126	289	18	7
Uniontown	155	292	6	36
Myers'	209	100	7	1
Woolery's	110	189	59	
Freedom	95	323	26	1
Manchester	131	177	49	
Westminster	247	295	85	9
Hampstead	133	133	47	
Franklin	109	171	18	
Middleburg	60	152	11	4
New Windsor	122	214	8	1
Total	1797	2295	334	59

Gubernatorial Vote, 1861

Districts	A W Bradford (Republican Union)	B C Howard (Democrat)
Taneytown	375	94
Uniontown	452	86
Myers'	195	172
Woolery's	268	184
Freedom	398	98
Manchester	319	323
Westminster	478	245
Hampstead	215	113
Franklin	250	68
Middleburg	185	45
New Windsor	260	94
Total	3105	1522

Vote for County Commissioners

Benjamin Shunk 3371, Thomas F Shepherd 3348, John H Chew 3376, H S Davis 1531, Samuel A Lanier 1568, George K Frank 1522

Vote for Comptroller of State, 1863

Districts	H H Goldsborough (Independent.)	S S Maffit (Unionist.)
Taneytown	268	147
Uniontown	294	86
Myers	10	275
Finksburg	61	299
Freedom	[illegible]	13
Manchester	97	257
Westminster	105	501
Hampstead	[illegible]	134
Franklin	106	83
Middleburg	[illegible]	37
New Windsor	[illegible]	80
Total	[illegible]	1912

Vote for Sheriff

Joseph Ebaugh 2051 J M Yingling 1406, R W Stern 1138, H P Albaugh 161.

Presidential Vote, 1864

Districts	Lincoln	McClellan
Taneytown	303	119
Uniontown	287	173
Myers'	90	243
Finksburg	124	180
Freedom	211	121
Manchester	156	375
Westminster	325	315
Hampstead	107	169
Franklin	136	67
Middleburg	119	62
New Windsor	169	61
Total	2057	1885

Vote for Sheriff, 1865

Districts	Jacob D Hoppe. (Republican)	J A Bush (Independent)
Taneytown	237	14
Uniontown	252	17
Myers'	86	19
Finksburg	90	47
Freedom	151	13
Manchester	97	30
Westminster	289	51
Hampstead	77	22
Franklin	75	16
Middleburg	69	9
New Windsor	106	8
Total	1529	250

For Commissioners

T F Shepherd 1421, Thomas Paynter 1471, John H Chew 1728, Israel Norris 372, John H Jordan 268

Surveyor

James Kelley 1749

Register

H H Harbaugh 1800

Vote for State Comptroller, 1866

Districts	Robt Bruce (Republican)	W J Leonard (Democrat)
Taneytown	322	55
Uniontown	339	145
Myers'	123	127
Finksburg	166	201
Freedom	223	135
Manchester	153	78
Westminster	371	309
Hampstead	129	138
Franklin	131	88
Middleburg	159	66
New Windsor	143	149
Total	2259	1494

Vote on the Adoption of the Constitution, Sept 18, 1867

Districts	For	Against
Taneytown	103	293
Uniontown	145	269
Myers'	251	91
Finksburg	217	157
Freedom	156	195
Manchester	441	124
Westminster	383	334
Hampstead	166	102
Franklin	111	115
Middleburg	66	105
New Windsor	148	13[illegible]
Total	2187	1920

Vote for Calling Constitutional Convention, April 10, 1867

Districts	For	Against
Taneytown	80	275
Uniontown	96	238
Myers'	245	85
Finksburg	166	137
Freedom	116	164
Manchester	373	142
Westminster	307	308
Hampstead	123	99
Franklin	69	96
Middleburg	39	94
New Windsor	107	117
Total	1721	1755

Vote for Delegates

Districts	Longwell	Manro	Galt	Bennett	Cover	Hayden
Taneytown	79	79	79	79	79	79
Uniontown	96	96	96	96	96	96
Myers	245	215	213	245	244	245
Finksburg	166	166	166	166	166	166
Freedom	115	116	115	115	115	114
Manchester	378	372	372	372	372	373
Westminster	310	309	309	309	309	309
Hampstead	123	123	123	123	123	123
Franklin	69	68	69	70	69	69
Middleburg	39	39	39	39	39	39
New Windsor	108	104	109	109	109	108
Total	1723	1717	1720	1723	1721	1721

The Republicans voted against calling a convention, and placed no candidates for delegates in the field

Gubernatorial Vote, 1867

Districts	Oden Bowie (Democrat)	Hugh L Bond (Republican)
Taneytown	143	336
Uniontown	245	316
Myers'	283	106
Finksburg	290	173
Freedom	243	222
Manchester	483	167
Westminster	475	366
Hampstead	204	144
Franklin	160	145
Middleburg	95	150
New Windsor	195	166
Total	2815	2291

For Senator, Nathan Browne 2789, D H Swope 2352

For Delegates, H S Davis 2806 J H Jordan 2786, Benjamin Worthington 2799, John W Harden 2777, Robert Russell 2334, W W Naill 2324, Jesse Andrews 2352, Jacob C Turner 2327

For Clerk, John B Boyle 2716, William A McKellip 2406

For Register of Wills, Joseph M Parke 2710, H W Herbaugh 2358

For State's Attorney, C T Reifsnyder 2780, A D Schaeffer 2350

For Sheriff, Thomas B Gist 2804, Washington Galt 2327

For Surveyor, Francis Warner 2707, James Kelley 2340

For Orphans' Court, H T Webb 2786, Jacob Powder 2719, Levi Buffington 2770, Joseph Shaeffer, 2370, Jacob Campbell 2378, David Pugh 23[illegible]0

Presidential Vote, 1868

Districts	Seymour	Grant
Taneytown	122	328
Uniontown	216	306
Myers	272	108
Finksburg	241	174
Freedom	215	216
Manchester	463	173
Westminster	469	375
Hampstead	201	136
Franklin	140	158
Middleburg	81	149
New Windsor	187	177
Total	26[illegible]	2300

Vote for State Comptroller, 1869

	Levin Walford	Wm A McKillip.
Taneytown	119	302
Uniontown	235	278
Myers'	248	105
Finksburg	221	169
Freedom	160	180
Manchester	459	144
Westminster	419	394
Hampstead	208	138
Franklin	150	132
Middleburg	77	134
New Windsor	162	174
Total	2458	2150

Vote for Sheriff, 1869

John Tracey (Democrat) 2522, Michael Baughman (Republican) 2073, John M [illegible]ingling (Independent) 42

Congressional Vote, 1870

Districts.	John Ritchie	John E Smith
Taneytown	138	309
Uniontown	266	349
Myers	280	104
Finksburg	307	159
Freedom	251	268
Manchester	473	164
Westminster Precinct No 1	288	285
" " No. 2	262	228
Hampstead	218	119
Franklin	192	193
Middleburg	86	160
New Windsor	205	220
Total	2966	2558

Gubernatorial Vote, 1871

Districts.	W P Whyte (Democrat.)	Jacob Tome. (Republican)
Taneytown	144	322
Uniontown	236	354
Myers'	256	92
Finksburg	284	169
Freedom	256	266
Manchester	486	172
Westminster Precinct No 1	278	285
" " No. 2	255	229
Hampstead	211	123
Franklin	180	185
Middleburg	71	157
New Windsor	195	234
Total	2858	2583

Presidential Vote, 1872

Districts.	Greeley	Grant.
Taneytown	127	325
Uniontown	177	295
Myers'	249	105
Woolery's	245	154
Freedom	162	276
Manchester	474	156
Westminster Precinct No 1	260	269
" " No 2	247	231
Hampstead	192	128
Franklin	117	193
Middleburg	43	141
New Windsor	162	195
Union B[illegible]	[illegible]	[illegible]
Total	2505	[illegible]

Vote for State Comptroller, 1873.

Districts	Levin Wolford (Democrat)	H H Goldsborough (Republican)
Taneytown	155	315
Uniontown	213	289
Myers'	278	108
Finksburg	296	178
Freedom	249	272
Manchester	493	180
Westminster Precinct No 1	302	295
" " No 2	257	241
Hampstead	200	131
Franklin	181	177
Middleburg	62	132
New Windsor	207	274
Union Bridge	71	134
Total	2964	2666

Congressional Vote, 1874

Districts.	Charles B Roberts (Democrat.)	John T Ensor (Republican)
Taneytown	123	299
Uniontown	188	250
Myers'	239	81
Woolery's	252	138
Freedom	183	210
Manchester	490	141
Westminster Precinct No 1	259	181
" " No 2	264	256
Hampstead	167	117
Franklin	141	137
Middleburg	61	93
New Windsor	185	170
Union Bridge	82	102
Total	2664	2155

Gubernatorial Vote, 1875

Districts	John Lee Carroll (Democrat)	J Morrison Harris (Republican)
Taneytown	124	355
Uniontown	197	292
Myers'	267	135
Finksburg	291	182
Freedom	222	295
Manchester	464	191
Westminster Precinct No 1	267	237
" " No 2	260	325
Hampstead	195	162
Franklin	153	222
Middleburg	66	138
New Windsor	171	250
Union Bridge	76	130
Total	2753	2914

Presidential Vote, 1876

Districts	Tilden	Hayes
Taneytown	148	370
Uniontown	213	309
Myers'	294	143
Woolery's	346	218
Freedom	304	270
Manchester	544	175
Westminster Precinct No 1	307	245
" " No 2	303	331
Hampstead	247	145
Franklin	215	196
Middleburg	86	116
New Windsor	204	228
[illegible]	[illegible]	136
[illegible]	[illegible]	2902

Vote for State Comptroller, 1877

Districts		T J Keating	Dr G Ellis Porter
Taneytown		148	338
Uniontown		184	275
Myers'		265	108
Finksburg		280	172
Freedom		272	215
Manchester		477	168
Westminster	Precinct No 1	280	237
"	" No 2	257	293
Hampstead		216	135
Franklin		179	164
Middleburg		62	114
New Windsor		178	209
Union Bridge		75	121
Total		2873	2549

Vote for Sheriff, 1877

Peter Woods 2725, Edmund A Ganter 2563, Abraham Greider 101

Congressional Vote, 1878

Districts		J Fred C Talbott (Democrat)	G B Milligan (Independent)
Taneytown		104	94
Uniontown		120	49
Myers'		221	27
Finksburg		178	45
Freedom		163	112
Manchester		393	92
Westminster	Precinct No 1	213	170
"	" No 2	205	197
Hampstead		147	54
Franklin		160	4
Middleburg		56	36
New Windsor		147	104
Union Bridge		68	66
Total		2175	1050

The vote was 2000 short McCombs also received 89 votes, Vorling 27, and Miller 11

Gubernatorial Vote, 1879

Districts		W T Hamilton (Democrat)	J A Gary (Republican)
Taneytown		179	399
Uniontown		241	348
Myers'		295	124
Finksburg		327	253
Freedom		322	290
Manchester		545	186
Westminster	Precinct No 1	329	276
"	" No 2	304	348
Hampstead		253	147
Franklin		229	227
Middleburg		98	144
New Windsor		188	230
Union Bridge		107	149
Total		3417	3121

Presidential Vote, 1880

Districts		Hancock	Garfield
Taneytown		190	375
Uniontown		234	348
Myers'		297	127
Finksburg		335	229
Freedom		307	326
Manchester		570	194
Westminster	Precinct No 1	339	249
"	" No 2	298	348
Hampstead		281	160
Franklin		228	238
Middleburg		91	147
New Windsor		206	248
Union Bridge		116	149
Total		3492	3138

Weaver (Greenback candidate) received 42 votes.

Vote For or Against Liquor License, 1880

Districts		For	Against
Taneytown		182	336
Uniontown		224	310
Myers'		321	77
Finksburg		286	242
Freedom		286	288
Manchester		591	138
Westminster	Precinct No 1	301	238
"	" No 2	335	269
Hampstead		262	148
Franklin		239	189
Middleburg		103	123
New Windsor		133	165
Union Bridge		102	146
Total		3375	2688

Bench and Bar—The bar of Maryland since the days of Luther Martin has enjoyed a national reputation for the ability, eloquence, and sound opinions of its members It has been mainly recruited from the counties of the State, and some of its most eloquent advocates have been reared amid rural surroundings and their pure influences The local bars at the smaller county-seats are seldom heard of beyond the circumscribed area of their practice, and yet men frequently pass their lives at these provincial points whose energies and abilities, exerted in wider fields, would have commanded fame and wealth They are useful in their day and generation, and perhaps, after all, the approval of their own consciences, and the esteem of those who know them best, is a more enduring reward than the fleeting praises of the multitude, or the honors which leave canker and corrosion behind

At the first meeting of the Circuit Court of Carroll County in 1837, William P Maulsby, James Raymond, James M Shellman, Arthur F Shriver, and T Parkin Scott were admitted to practice Of these but one now remains

Col William P Maulsby, in the fullness of years, but with unabated vigor, still represents the interests of his clients in the leading courts of the State, and many a more youthful attorney envies the elasticity of mind and knowledge of law which he displays Col Maulsby was born in Harford County, Md, and after careful training selected law as a profession He removed to Frederick, where he practiced until the creation of the county of Carroll, when he removed to Westminster, and was appointed by the court the first State's attorney of the new county He filled this position with great credit until 1846 He was also the first State senator from Carroll, and was an active and influential member of the higher branch of the State Legislature for eight years At the breaking out of the civil war Col Maulsby's convictions were decidedly in favor of the Union and he gave practical direction to his opinions by taking command of a

Maryland regiment in the Army of the Potomac, where he saw much active service Upon his retirement from the army he resumed the practice of his profession in Frederick City, and he was appointed by the Governor, Jan 20, 1870, chief judge of the Sixth Judicial District of Maryland, composed of the counties of Frederick and Montgomery, to fill the vacancy occasioned by the death of Judge Madison Nelson He filled this position acceptably until his successor was chosen at the November election He is now the senior member of the bar in Carroll County has an extensive practice, and stands deservedly high in the legal profession

Thomas Parkin Scott, one of the pioneers of the Carroll County bar, was born in Baltimore in 1804, and educated at St Mary's College He studied law with an elder brother, and was admitted to the bar in Baltimore, where he soon acquired a large practice He was the auditor of the Equity Court for many years He was at one time a member of the City Council of Baltimore, and served several terms in the Maryland Legislature, of which body he was a member at the breaking out of the war in 1861 He was arrested by the military because of his sympathies with the South, and confined successively in Forts McHenry, Lafayette, and Warren during a period of fourteen months It is related of him that while confined in Fort Warren a Northern preacher requested to be allowed to preach to the Southern prisoners, which was acceded to provided the latter were permitted to select the text Judge Scott selected Acts xxv 27 "It seemeth to me unreasonable to send a prisoner and not withal to signify the crimes laid against him" The prisoners did not receive the benefit of the clergyman's ministrations on that occasion Judge Scott was elected judge of the Circuit Court of Baltimore City in 1867, and was made chief judge of the Supreme Bench in the following year, both of which positions he held until his death, Oct 13, 1873 In politics he was a stern, uncompromising Democrat, and in religion a sincere convert to the Catholic faith As a judge, he was upright, impartial, and wise, and as a man, he was beloved and lamented by the community in which he had lived

Col James M Shellman was born in Louisville, Ga., Sept 8, 1801 His wife was a daughter of Philip Jones, of the "Gallipot" farm, in Baltimore County, who was a soldier in the war of 1812 The grandfather of Mrs Shellman was the first register of wills for Baltimore County, and her great-grandfather was Philip Jones [illegible] surveyor who laid out the town of Baltimore in [illegible] Col Shellman was the auditor of the court of Carroll County from its organization in 1837 until his death, which occurred Jan 14, 1851. His long service is sufficient evidence of the faithful performance of the duties appertaining to the position He was an active and influential member of the House of Delegates of Maryland in 1845 and 1846

James Raymond was State's attorney from 1846 to 1847, and a member of the House of Delegates of Maryland in 1844

Samuel D Lecompte was a member of the House of Delegates in 1842

Charles W Webster was a son of Rev Isaac Webster, a pioneer preacher, and served several years as deputy attorney-general

John E Smith was judge of the Circuit Court from 1864 to 1867, and his law-partner, Col William A McKellip, was clerk of the court from 1862 to 1867

Hon John E Smith was born at Westminster, on the 19th of January, 1830, and received his education at Pennsylvania College, Gettysburg where he graduated in 1849 Returning home he determined to study law, and entered the office of the distinguished lawyer, J M Palmer, at Frederick City After a thorough course of study he was admitted to the bar at Westminster, on the 2d of September, 1851, and at once secured the respect and esteem of the profession and the confidence of his fellow-citizens His success at the bar was rapid and pronounced, and he soon acquired an extensive popularity and influence in politics In 1856 he was elected to the State Legislature, and took a very active and prominent part, with Hon Anthony Kennedy, William M Travers, William T Merrick, and others, in securing the repeal of the stamp tax and in effecting other reforms

In 1857 he was elected to the Senate of Maryland, and in 1859 re elected to the same body In 1864 he was elected a member of the Constitutional Convention which abolished slavery in this State Upon the adoption of the constitution of 1864, Judge Smith was elected judge of the Fourth Judicial Circuit, comprising the counties of Carroll and Howard During the three years he occupied a position on the bench he discharged his duties in so careful and impartial a manner that when the State was redistricted under the constitution of 1867, he retired with the confidence and respect of the people of the two counties without reference to party In 1870 he was the Republican candidate for Congress in the Fourth, now the Sixth, Congressional District, but was defeated During the session of the Legislature of that year, upon th[illegible] Wave[illegible] to the United State[illegible] unan[illegible]ously selected

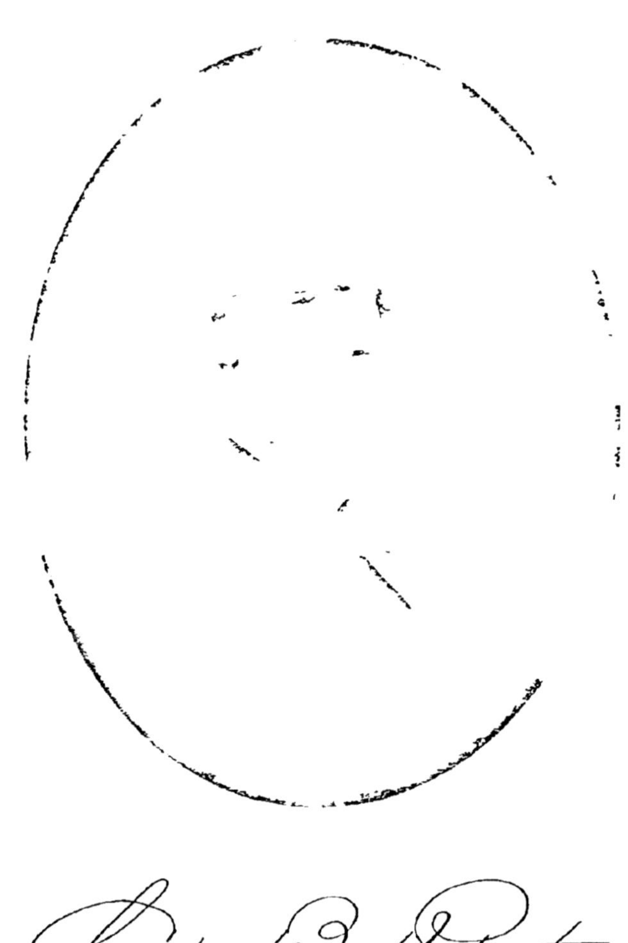

Charles G. D. Roberts.

by the Republican members and voted for as Governor of the State, but was defeated by Governor Groome. Judge Smith has repeatedly served as elector at large upon the Republican Presidential ticket, and as delegate to various district, State, and National Conventions. On the death of Judge Giles he was prominently mentioned for United States District Judge of Maryland, and again in 1879 as Republican candidate for Governor of Maryland. On the latter occasion he publicly announced that he was not an aspirant for any office, and that he intended thenceforth to devote himself exclusively to the pursuit of his profession. This declaration was received with regret by the general public, as well as by his many friends of all shades of political opinion throughout the State, as Judge Smith had always borne, and still bears, the highest reputation as a lawyer and a man. He is now in the prime of life, and in the active practice of his profession, which is very large and lucrative. Judge Smith is regarded as being one of the soundest and ablest lawyers in the State, and enjoys a personal influence in his community which is the legitimate fruit of a life of the strictest rectitude in all his relations, and of scrupulous fidelity in discharging every trust that has been confided to him. He has never sought office, and all the nominations bestowed upon him were entirely without any solicitation on his part. In fact, it was only after repeated and urgent requests that he ever consented to serve the people. He has never been a bitter partisan, but at the same time has always been a zealous and consistent member of the Republican party, and to his uniformly conservative and temperate course is to be ascribed much of the well-earned popularity which he enjoys.

Hon Charles Boyle Roberts, ex-congressman and one of Carroll County's leading lawyers, was born in Uniontown, Carroll Co, April 19, 1842. His father (John Roberts) and his mother (Catharine A Boyle) were natives of Uniontown, and his ancestors were among the earliest settlers of the vicinity. Charles B. Roberts was educated at Calvert College, New Windsor, where he graduated in 1861. Directly thereafter he began the study of the law with Hon William N Hayden (now one of the associate judges of the Circuit Court for the Fifth Judicial Circuit), and in 1864, being admitted to the bar, made his residence in Westminster, where he has lived and practiced his profession ever since. In 1868 he was chosen on the Democratic ticket as one of the Presidential electors from Maryland, and six years later (in 1874) was elected to Congress from the Second District of Maryland, composed of the counties of Cecil, Harford, and Carroll, and all of Baltimore County save the First and Thirteenth Election Districts. His majority over John T Ensor, the Republican candidate, was 2414 in a total vote of 18,920. During his term he served on the Committee of the Levees of the Mississippi River and on the Committee of Accounts, of which latter he became the chairman upon the transfer of the former chairman (James D Williams) to the Governorship of Indiana. Mr Roberts introduced a bill providing for the equalization of the tax on State and national banks, and supported his measure in a speech that attracted marked attention. His record in the Forty-fourth Congress was so creditable that he was nominated by acclamation for a seat in the Forty-fifth, and out of a total vote of 27,017, gained over J Morrison Harris, the Republican candidate, a majority of 3149. His earlier experience and the generous development of his capacity as a statesman rendered his service in the Forty-fifth Congress singularly useful not only to his own district but to the State of Maryland. He served as chairman of the Committee on Accounts, and discharged his duties with rare discrimination and judgment. He was likewise a member of the Committee on Commerce, and in that capacity accomplished much beneficial work for the State. He secured liberal appropriations for the improvement of Baltimore Harbor, and was chiefly instrumental in the passage of the bill granting a portion of the Fort McHenry reservation as the site of the new dry-dock. He bent his best energies to effect a revision of the tariff law, under which Baltimore has suffered the loss of her sugar and coffee trade, and opposed with earnestness and vigor the proposed subsidy to John Roach's line of Brazilian steamers. In a strong speech against that measure he concluded as follows:

"In conclusion, Mr Speaker, permit me to say that while the pending amendment may possess attractions for some because of the supposed advantages which are expected to accrue to the localities named in it, and while the prosperity of a thrifty and enterprising city may be destroyed by the exercise of an unjust, arbitrary, and doubtful power of the Federal government in seeking to build up and foster a trade which private enterprise has failed to develop, I yet sincerely question whether the victory thus gained will commend itself to the plain, sober second thought of those who are its advocates to-day. The wrong thus accomplished will not fail to seek a compensation. Time will furnish the opportunity, and circumstances will shape the occasion. We are not here to legislate for any particular locality, but we come here under the provisions of the Constitution, which in plain terms declares that 'no preference shall be given by any regulation of commerce or revenue to the ports of one State over those of another.' It is but a few weeks since we passed the inter-State commerce bill, [illegible] which demanded that unjust [illegible] should not be imposed upon

the citizens of one State or locality in favor of those of another, and if this amendment is to become a law it will very manifestly appear that we do not object to the general government's crushing the prosperity of a great and flourishing city, but we will not permit the corporations of the country to exercise any such right, that being a special reservation of Congress How different was Mr Webster's view of this subject, as presented in his speech in the Senate, March 7, 1850, when he said,—

"'If there be any matter pending in this body, while I am a member of it, in which Massachusetts has an interest of her own not averse to the general interests of the country, I shall pursue her instructions with gladness of heart and with all the efficiency which I can bring to the occasion But if the question be one which affects her interest, and at the same time equally affects the interests of all the other States, I shall no more regard her particular wishes or instructions than I should regard the wishes of a man who might appoint me an arbitrator or referee to decide some question of important private right between him and his neighbor and then instruct me to decide in his favor If ever there was a government upon earth it is this government, if ever there was a body upon earth it is this body, which should consider itself as composed by agreement of all, each member appointed by some, but organized by the general consent of all sitting here, under the solemn obligations of oath and conscience, to do that which they think to be best for the good of the whole'

"Sir, when we shall have reached the conclusion that the highest obligations we owe to the government is to make it subserve the wants of one State, utterly disregarding the rights of the others, when we shall resort to combinations of doubtful propriety to purchase successful legislative action when we can afford to ignore past friendly relations, and upon mercenary motives seek new alliances, personal and political, it will not be long ere we shall realize—

> 'How nations sink, by darling schemes oppressed,
> When Vengeance listens to the fool's request'"

As chairman of the Committee on Commerce, Mr Roberts perfected a measure for a thorough reorganization of the United States Life Saving Service, and enjoyed the gratification not only of securing the passage of the act, but of receiving the warmest approval of his work abroad as well as at home At the close of his term in the Forty-fifth Congress he decided to resume the practice of the law and to retire from public life In recognition of his valuable services in Congress he was tendered, in the spring of 1879, by leading citizens of Baltimore, a complimentary banquet at the Mount Vernon Hotel The following is the letter of invitation

"BALTIMORE, March 7, 1879

"HON CHARLES B ROBERTS, Westminster, Md.

"DEAR SIR,—A number of your friends here among our business men have been desiring for some time to make you some acknowledgment of the earnestness and ability with which you have dedicated yourself in the House of Representatives to the furtherance of the business interests of this community There has been no measure of importance to the prosperity of Baltimore in the promotion of which you have not taken an active and useful part, or in which we have not had occasion to be grateful to you for your accessibility and courtesy, as well as for the [illegible] and great efficiency of your labors The [illegible] of Congress affords us the desired opportunity, and we beg that you will do us the favor to meet us at dinner on Thursday, the 13th of March, at 7 P M, or at such other time as may better suit your convenience

"It will be agreeable to you, we are sure, to know that while the gentlemen whom you will oblige by accepting this invitation represent all shades of political opinion, they are of hearty accord in their estimate of your impartial fidelity as a public servant, and in their high personal respect and esteem for you

"We are, dear sir, with great regard,

"Truly yours,

"S T Wallis — William H Perot
John W Garrett — Henry C Smith
Decatur H Miller — Christian Ax
Enoch Pratt — Daniel J Foley
James Hodges — J D Kremelberg
Washington Booth — S P Thompson
Robert A Fisher — James A Gary
John J Middleton — John S Gilman
Israel M Parr — Robert Garrett
Stephen Bonsal — Walter B Brooks
C W Humrickhouse — Charles D Fisher
Richard D Fisher — Charles A Councilman
James Carey Coale — James E Tate
Robert T Baldwin — William Keyser
John E Hurst — Louis Muller
William H Graham — F C Latrobe
R W Cator — H M Warfield
George B Coale — Basil Wagner
John L Thomas, Jr — P H MacGill
George P Frick — S E Hoogewerff"
James Sloan, Jr

Although he has not been a candidate for public office since the close of his last congressional term, Mr Roberts has nevertheless been frequently called to occupy positions of prominence in connection with public and private enterprises In June, 1880, he was sent as a delegate to the National Convention at Cincinnati that nominated Gen Hancock to the Presidency, and as a member of the Democratic State Convention of 1881, was appointed one of the committee selected to draft a new registration bill for the State He is one of the managers of the Maryland House of Correction, and in his own town and county occupies a prominent place in connection with projects devoted to the public welfare He is a director of the Union National Bank of Westminster, as well as of the Westminster Gaslight Company, and of the Mutual Fire Insurance Company, and president of the recently organized Westminster Water-Works Company In 1875 Mount St Mary's College, of Emmittsburg, Md, conferred upon him the degree of Doctor of Laws His chosen profession has ever found in him an ardent devotee, and to its pursuit he gives his warmest efforts and most zealous ambition, encouraged by the knowledge that his labors find ample reward and bear abundant fruit He was married Nov 10, 1863, to Annie E, daughter of Col John T Mathias of Maryland At his home in Westminster [illegible] that is widely

known and warmly esteemed among the many who have from time to time been privileged to share it

Politically, Mr Roberts has always been a zealous but conservative Democrat, and while he has steadily adhered to the regular organization of that party, he has exhibited on all occasions an independence and conscientiousness in the discharge of his duties, both as a member of the Democratic party and as a public official, which have secured him the highest confidence and respect of the best elements in both parties He has frequently been mentioned in various quarters as the Democratic candidate for Governor With exceptional abilities as a lawyer Mr Roberts combines the qualities of a sound and practical judgment and remarkable business energy and tact, qualities which, together with his attractive personal characteristics, have secured him an enviable popularity throughout the State as well as in his own immediate community, where he is best known and most thoroughly appreciated In fact, he is one of the most enterprising, progressive, and influential gentlemen in the State, not only as a public man of the best and most honorable type, but also as a sound and well-read lawyer and a highly successful and prosperous business man

The three attorneys who have been longest at the bar of Carroll County are Judge Maulsby, C W Webster, Joseph M Parke, the last having been register of wills from 1869 to 1873

The list given below includes all the attorneys who have been regular practitioners at the Carroll County bar, together with the names of eminent lawyers from other parts of the State who have been specially admitted for the trial of particular causes

1837
April 3 William P Maulsby
" 3 James M Shellman
" 3 James Raymond
" 3 Arthur F Shriver
" 3 T Parkin Scott
Sept 7. Samuel D Lecompte
" 7. Isaac Van Bibber
1838
Madison Nelson
Edward Shriver
George Schley
Joseph Breck
R J Bowie
1839.
Sept 6 Charles W Webster
" 6 James M Coale
" 6 B S Forrest
" 6 Wm Cost Johnson
1840
Sept 7 Joseph M Parke
1842
Sept W H G Dorsey,
John T B Dorsey.

1844
Sept 2 William N Hayden
" 4 John H Ing
" 4 Nathaniel Williams
" 4 G Eichelberger
1845
April 7 W T Palmer
" 7 John J McCullough
" 9. Elijah F Crout
July 1 Clothworthy Birnie
1846
April 7. Elbridge G Kilbourn
" 7 R Willson, Jr.
" 7 Wm McSherry
" 7 James McSherry.
" 8 Covington D Barnitz
" 15 Wm G Matthias
Sept 9 J J Baumgardner
" 9 Michael G Webster
1847
April 6 Geo K Shellman
Sept 7 Joseph C Boyd
" 7 Will Motter

1848
April 4 H F Bardwell
Sept 5 James Cooper
1849
April 7 Daniel L Hoover
Sept 4 Edmund L Rogers
" 4 Wm C Sappington
" 5 Thomas Whelan, Jr.
" 5 G W Nabb
Dec 3 R G McCreary
1850
April 1 E Holloway
" 1 E G Day
1851
April 7 A H Hobbs
Sept 1 Robert Lyon Rogers
" 2 Wm M Merrick
" 2 John E Smith
1852
April 5 M B Luckett
" 6 James Hungerford
" 7 Ephraim Carmack
" 15 Dennis H Poole
" 15 John S Tyson
Sept 7 Worthington Ross
" 7 Bradley T Johnson
" 7 Frederick Nelson
1854
April 5 Isaac E Pearson
Sept 6 Thomas Donaldson
" 8 J T M Wharton
1855
April 2 Oscar Baugher
" 3 W H Dallam
" 5 M P Gallagher
" 10 John Ritchie
1856
Sept 1 Wm G Reid
1858
April 6 Wm A Fisher
" 8 John A Lynch
Sept 8 E O'Brien
" 8 W Scott Roberts
" 9 James T Smith
1859
April 4 John T Ensor
" 6 E Louis Lowe
Sept 5 T S Alexander
" 8 S Morris Cochran
1860
Sept 4 Samuel L Kuch
" 4 J S Yellott
1861
April 1. C C Raymond
" 4 Wm Schley
Sept 4 R R Boarman
" 4 W P Preston
" 9 C H Busby
1862
July 15 David Wills
" 16 D McConnaughy
1863
S J Frank
1864
April 5 Charles J [illegible]
Sept 1 Milton G [illegible]

1865
May 10 W C. Griffith
" 10 C T Reifsnider
" 10 Milton Whitney
" 10 Abner Neal
" 31 H Winter Davis
" 31 A Sterling, Jr
" 31 W L McLaughlin
Nov 14 Peter W Crain
" 14 Joseph Davis
1866
Nov 12 Isaac E Pearson, Jr
" 28 W Fernandis, Jr
1867
May 13 S D Webster
" 13 James A C Bond
" 14 Wm Price
Aug 1 James W McElroy
Oct 28 R B Norment
Nov 13 B F M Hurley
" 13 Wm A McKellip
1868
June 11 Wm Reynolds, Jr
" 11 W W Sullivan
Sept Wm Waterman
" D W Zepp
Dec 1 F C Latrobe
" 4 D H Roberts
" 4 J A C Bond
" 4 A D Schaeffer
1869
Nov 8 D G Wright
" 29 R G Keene
Dec 11 John W Breaver
1870
Feb 14 W W Dallas
May 17 Orville Horwitz
" 17 R J Gittings
" 31 Thos R Clendinen
Nov 14 Wm Rowland
1871
May 13 A K Syester
" 16 A H Norris
Nov 7 A S Diller
" 28 T Sturgis Davis
" 28 W H Cowan
1872
May 13 D N Henning
Aug 12 Harris J Chilton
Nov 23. W J Jones
1873
May 12 Z S Claggett
" 24 Henry A McAtee
Nov 10 E J. D Cross
" 17 George Freaner
1874
May 14 James Fenner Lee
" 14 J Q A Jones
" 18 T H Edwards
" 18 T Q Kennedy
" 18 Wm T Hamilton
" 18 H K Douglas
Aug 13 J E K Wood
1875
May 11 A H Robertson
" [illegible] Richard Stake

May 25 K Chumfours
July 15 L L Conard
" 20 J J Alexander
Aug 9 M E Settle
Nov 17 B Frank Crouse
1876
May 31 Trueman Smith
June 1 James W Pearre
Aug 15 Thos W Brundige
Nov 15 S L Stockbridge
Dec 11 W M Busey
" 14 W A Hammond
1877
May 25 William Grason
" 25 D G McIntosh
" 30 O F Mack
June 2 John S Shillson
Nov 27 O P Macgill
Dec 12 J T Mason
1878
May 13 S F Miller
" 14 John R Buchanan
" 17 T W Hall
" 20 W C N Carr
June 17 Frank X Ward
Aug 13 Jas A Diffenbaugh
Nov 12 George E Cramer
" 30 W H Washington
1879
May 12 John Berry
May 12 Charles I Fink
" 19 Benj F Cohen
June 6 Wm L Seabrook
" 10 L L Billingslea
" 17 G W Pearce
Nov 10 Charles L Wilson
" 19 Frank L Webb
" 28 —— Shull
Dec 8 John Sterrat
" 15 John McCleu
" 23 William Walsh
" 23 D D Blackeilton
" 23 James E Ellegood
1880
May 10 W. J Keech
" 10 John F Conrep
" 10 N W Watkins
June 3 Douglas B Smith
Aug 9 H W Crowl
Nov 8 C P Meredith
" 9 H M Clabaugh
" 10 George Whitelock
" 16 A Hinton Boyd
1881
May 20 John S Donaldson
" 20 Thos K Bradford
" 20 Joseph C Puyd
" 20 John H Handy
" 30 Frederick E Cook

Literature and art are essentially the products of life in the country The freedom of the woods and fields, the rippling streams, the hills and valleys, and the health giving atmosphere uncontaminated by the thousand impurities of large cities, seem necessary for the nurture and development of genius Nature in her simplest and grandest forms there excites the imagination and fosters the creative faculty in man However great may be the influence of culture and accumulated experience and example, only to be obtained in great cities, the narrow ruts of life in a metropolis and the concentration of all the powers of body and mind in one direction are unfavorable to the production or early development of genius, and hence it is found that a very large proportion of the really great poets, painters, and sculptors of the world have been born in the country, and very many have passed their early years there Carroll County in this regard has been no exception to the rule Artists and poets have been born within her borders whom the world will not willingly let die, some whose works have received the approval of distant lands and whose names are spoken with homage in all cultivated households The aggregations of books and master-pieces in large cities and the splendid advantages which wealth has extended through the instrumentality of schools of design, conservatories, and colleges make it of the first importance that the devotees of art and literature should seek the great centres of civilization and avail themselves of the resources so lavishly supplied True genius is never appalled by obstacles, and so it generally happens that those who recognize its promptings sooner or later work their way to the attainment of their wishes, and the city rather than the country is a gainer by their reputation Few counties can present nature to the inspired student of art in more beautiful or more varied aspects than are to be found in Carroll County Almost every phase of natural scenery is illustrated within her borders, from the landscapes of simple pastoral beauty to the rugged and sublime outlines of the lofty peaks of the Blue Ridge, and some of these scenes have been faithfully reflected in the works of her sons, who have sought the distinction elsewhere that they could not expect at home

In 1850 there was to be seen at the Chesapeake Bank a sculptured bust of Andrew Jackson which had been presented to Col J S Gittings by the Messrs F M & H F Baughman It was the work of an apprentice to the Messrs Baughman, named Reinhart It was executed chiefly at night, after the hours of labor, and was the first effort of his chisel "The excellence of the work gives promise of high attainment in this beautiful art, and leads us to hope that Maryland may yet be able to give to the world some enduring memento of the age in one of the most admirable departments of human genius" Such was the greetings of encouragement which the first work of young Reinhart received, and the contemporaneous description of the first work of his chisel

William H Reinhart was born in Carroll County, Md, about the year 1826, his father was a well to-do farmer of German descent, living near Westminster, in that county, and characterized by thrift, perseverance, and economy All the children were actively employed about the farm, and received the rudiments of an English education at a school in Westminster When a mere boy young Reinhart evinced very great interest in the working of the marble quarries that abounded in the neighborhood, and in this particular he found opportunity for the bent of his genius in the quarry and stone-cutting yard on his father's farm At the age of sixteen, with his father's consent, he came to Baltimore, and presented himself at the store of Andrew Gregg, on Franklin Street, to whom his father was in the habit of consigning produce of his farm He told Mr Gregg that he desired to apprentice himself to some useful trade, and preferred that of marble-working, with which he already had some familiarity He was immediately taken to the [illegible] nent of Baugh [illegible] rentice by that

He proved himself to be a steady and industrious youth, with a taste for reading and study which he gratified at night by regular attendance at the Maryland Institute and School of Design, where his favorite studies were mythology, ancient history, anatomy, architecture, and books on art and artists He continued the improving studies for several years and before his majority his chisel and proficiency obtained for him the execution of all the fine work on mantles of the establishment of the Messrs Baughman When twenty three years of age he was made foreman of the establishment and gave full satisfaction to his employers In 1855 he left Baltimore for Italy to prosecute the higher studies of his art with a full knowledge of practical marble-working He prosecuted his studies with great diligence at Florence, where he went to reside, working with other young artists on trial for wages He returned to Baltimore in 1857, bringing with him two beautiful *basso relievos* in panel of "Night and Morning," which were purchased by Augustus J Albert He returned to Italy in 1858, and made his residence at Rome, where he remained, with the exception of short trips to Baltimore, until his death in 1874

Probably the greatest event in the life of the young artist was the unveiling of the Taney statue at Annapolis, Dec 10, 1872 This heroic statue of Chief Justice Roger B Taney in bronze had been ordered by the Legislature of Maryland and was erected in front of the State-House On that occasion there were assembled in the Senate chamber the leading representatives of the State in politics, at the bar, in literature and art, to hear the addresses of S Teackle Wallis and Governor William Pinkney Whyte Mr Wallis alluded to the fact that the appropriation by the State had not been sufficient compensation to the artist for such a work, and recognized the liberality and public spirit of the artist in accepting and executing the work notwithstanding "The figure,' Mr Wallis said, "had been treated in the spirit of that noble and absolute simplicity which is the type of the highest order of greatness, and is therefore its grandest, though its most difficult, expression in art" In 1872 the statue of Clytie, which is Reinhart's masterpiece in marble, was exhibited in Baltimore, attracting the admiration of thousands of her people It was purchased by John W McCoy, and placed in the Peabody Gallery of Art as a gift to the citizens of Baltimore Among the other works of this artist are the bronze doors of the Capitol at Washington, begun by Crawford, and completed after four years of labor by Reinhart, the statuettes on the clock of the House of Representatives as well as the statue on the fountain in the General Post-office at Washington, Endymion, now owned by J W Garrett, Antigone, owned by Mr Hall, of New York, Hero, for A J Albert, of Baltimore, Leander, owned by Mr Riggs, of Washington, the Woman of Samaria, for W T Walters, of Baltimore, the bronze monumental figure at the tomb of Mrs W T Walters, in Greenmount Cemetery, and the "Sleeping Children," in marble, in the lot of Hugh Sisson, as well as many other works in Mount Auburn Cemetery, Boston, Loudon Park Cemetery, Baltimore, and many busts of citizens of Baltimore

William H Reinhart died in Rome on Wednesday, Oct 28, 1874, in the forty-eighth year of his age, having fully enabled his native State, Maryland, "to give to the world" not only "some," but many "enduring mementoes of the age in one of the most admirable departments of human genius" By his will he attested further his great love for art, after amply providing for relatives he directed that his executors, W T Walters and B F Newcomer, of Baltimore, should apply the residue of his estate, according to their best judgment, to the promotion of interest in and cultivation of taste for art, by the following clause of his will

"Third, Being desirous of aiding in the promotion of a more highly cultivated taste for art among the people of my native State, and of assisting young men in the study of the art of sculpture who may desire to make it a profession, but having at the present time no definite plan in view for the accomplishment of these objects, I give, devise, and bequeath all the rest and residue of my estate, real, personal, and mixed, and wheresoever situated, unto my two personal friends, William T Walters and Benjamin F Newcomer, of the city of Baltimore, or the survivor of them, or the heirs, executor, or administrator of such survivor, in trust and confidence, with the injunction that the whole of said residue of my estate or the proceeds thereof shall be devoted and appropriated by them, according to their best judgment and discretion, to the promotion of the objects and purposes named above, and if in the opinion of my said trustees this can be best accomplished by any concert of action with the trustees of the Peabody Institute, or by the establishment of a professorship in connection with the Gallery of Art, which at some future time is to be provided for by that corporation, or by the investment of any portion of the funds so held by them in trust, and aiding from the income derived from such investments deserving young men who are desirous of pursuing their studies abroad, but are without the means of doing so, they, my said trustees, are at liberty to adopt any or all or none of these methods, or to transfer the trust or the estate so held by them in trust to any corporation which in their judgment would best serve the purpose indicated"

Willie T Hoppe was the second son of Hannah and the late Jacob D Hoppe, of Carroll County His life in some important features resembled that of Chatterton, the boy-poet of England At an age when most children make their highest pleasure in a game of marbles or hide and seek, his mind was at

work like the piston rod of a steam-engine, grinding out tales, editorials, and local histories in a ceaseless flow. His mental faculties and energy far outstripped his weak and sickly body, and absolutely wore it out before he arrived at man's estate. His first essay in literature was as the editor and publisher of an amateur journal entitled *The Boys' Rights*, which astounded the neighbors and friends of his family by the extraordinary precocity exhibited in its contents. He subsequently conducted the *Amphion Journal* and *Cupid's Messenger*, and, as president of the Amateur Press Association, still surprised his friends and the public not only by the marvelous maturity of his intellect, but by a display of executive ability which his years and experience did not appear to justify. In 1878 he entered the office of Charles Poe, of Baltimore, as a law-student, but it soon became painfully evident that while his mind was ripening and brightening with study and training, his body was gradually wasting away before the inroads of some insidious malady, and he died July 24, 1880, in the twentieth year of his age. In his literary efforts and on his papers he was frequently assisted by Miss Mary Shellman, a lady of rare literary attainments, whose historical contributions to the press have earned for her a merited reputation as a writer.

Dr Washington Chew Van Bibber was born in Frederick, now Carroll, Co, Md, July 24, 1821. His family settled in that section very early in the history of the State and soon acquired influence and prominence. After a thorough course of study at a number of colleges, Dr Van Bibber entered the office of Prof Nathan R Smith, of Baltimore, and matriculated at the University of Maryland, from whence he graduated in 1845. After some years spent in the South, where he had an opportunity to familiarize himself with the yellow fever in all its phases,—that dread pest of Southern cities,—he returned to Baltimore and began the practice of his profession. His practice rapidly increased, and with it his reputation as a skillful and excellent physician, and to-day he is fully the equal of any of the galaxy of physicians who have made Baltimore famous as a centre of instruction in the healing art. As a writer, Dr Van Bibber deserves especial mention. Few have recently added more to the literature of medicine. From 1856 to 1859 he was associate editor of the *Virginia Medical Journal*, and from 1859 to 1861 he was associate editor of the *Maryland and Virginia Medical Journal*, and he has contributed a large number of papers to the various medical periodicals of the day, replete with interest and valuable scientific information.

Thomas E Van Bibber, a relative of Dr Van Bibber, is a native of Carroll County, but is now a resident of California. He early developed a taste for literature, and many of his youthful efforts will compare favorably with those of more pretentious poets and authors. He is best known by his poem, "The Flight into Egypt," a work exhibiting considerable power, a beautiful fancy, and a true conception of the poet's vocation. It was very favorably received by American critics, and has stood the test of time remarkably well. His many miscellaneous prose efforts have added to his reputation as a cultured and popular writer.

For many years the meetings of the "Addison Reunion Association" constituted a delightful feature of society in Westminster. The organization was literary in character, and a number of the most cultivated and influential citizens were members and contributors. The intention was to combine social with literary recreation, and for a longer time than usually occurs to such associations the effort was successful. The papers read before it took a wide range, embracing poetry, history, art, science, and the various branches of polite literature. In 1871, Dr Charles Billingslea compiled "The Addison Reunion Papers," a neat volume of three hundred pages, containing the choicest of the papers delivered before the society during its existence, and embracing selections from the writings of Emma Alice Browne, the poetess, and authoress of "Ariadne," Rev Josiah Varden, Rev James T Ward, D D, Mrs Albert Billingslea, Rev David Wilson, D D, Dr Charles Billingslea, Isaac E Pearson, Mrs Carrie Brockett Anderson, Miss Ada Billingslea, and Thomas E Van Bibber. The "Addison Reunion Association" gave its closing entertainment June 9, 1871, at the "Montour House," a noted hostelry, which derived its name from the famous Indian chief of that name who flourished in colonial times.

The religious denominations of Carroll County recognizing the paramount value of religious instruction through the instrumentality of Sabbath-schools, and anxious to extend their influence and usefulness, consulted together as to the best method of accomplishing this desirable result. Their deliberations culminated in 1867 in a county Sabbath school association to be composed of delegates from all the Protestant denominations in the county. The second annual convention of the society was held in the Lutheran church at Westminster, Sept 8, 1868. Rev J T Ward, of the Methodist Protestant Church, was called to the chair, and [illegible] C Grammer appointed secretary. [illegible] and the follow-

ing delegates enrolled Finksburg, John H Chew, D Ebaugh, A Gersley, R A Smith, Wm Cruse, Rev W T Dunn, Hampstead, S Roby, Joseph Lippy, New Windsor, Clinton Hanna, Wm A Norris, Isaac C Baile, Rev Mr Scarborough, Manchester, Rev R Weiser, Jacob Campbell, Edmund Gouder, D Frankforter, Jos Shearer, H B Lippy, D W. Danner, J T Myers, Misses F Crummine, S Trump, Ellen Trump, V C Weizer, Lizzie Earle, Myers, Jacob Wolfe, T T Tagg, J Baukard, Middleburg, Thos Newman, Wm H Boust, John W Angell, Jacob Koons, A E Null, Albert Koons, John Feezer, Eli Hahn, Taneytown, Peter Mark, G Stover, J T Clay, Uniontown, Revs P A Strobel, J T Ward, J T Hedges, Van Meter, E H Smith, J Monroe, W C Creamer, H B Grammer, Wm H Cunningham, G W Cecil, F Herr, M Baughman, H L Norris, E Koons, R Gorsuch, Josh Sellman N Pennington, J N Williams, Mrs M A Wagner, Mrs M Cunningham, Misses Sanford, Sue Cassell, Annie Ocker The committee appointed to select permanent officers reported the following nominations, which were unanimously confirmed

President, Hon John E Smith, Vice Presidents, J W Angell, David H Webster, —— Debough, Jacob Campbell, Alfred Zollicoffer, A McKinney, C D Frieze, Joseph Ebaugh, Secretaries, H. B Grammer and Wm A Baker

The convention continued their interesting exercises until Thursday, June 10th, when they adjourned until their annual meeting in 1869

The German Baptists sought the region embraced in Carroll County very soon after its settlement by white people, conceiving it to be a favorable field for their ministrations Congregations have been established at Pipe Creek, Meadow Branch, Sam's Creek, New Windsor, Union Bridge, and Westminster They are all under the charge of an ordained elder, who has five or six assistants Philip Englar was the first elder in charge of whom there is any record, and served in this position from 1780 to 1810, when he was succeeded by David Englar, who had been his assistant for some years The latter served from 1810 to 1833, and was followed by Philip Boyle, who occupied the position for thirty-five years, having been assisted by Michael Petry, Jesse Royer, Jesse Roop, David Miller, Howard Hillery, Hanson Senseny, and Solomon Stoner Rev Mr Boyle was succeeded by Hanson Senseny as ordained elder He served in that capacity until 1880, and was assisted by Solomon Stoner, E W Stoner, William Franklin, Amos Caylor, Joel Roop, and Uriah Bixley The denomination in the county numbers between four and five hundred members

Pipe Creek congregation, the mother of all the other German Baptist organizations in the county, and one of the oldest in Western Maryland, was established prior to the year 1780, and worshiped in a log building which stood at Pipe Creek In 1806 their present church edifice was erected, since when it has been used constantly by the congregation The church was repaired in 1866, having been enlarged and remodeled It is now a plain brick structure, thirty five by seventy-one feet, with a seating capacity for six hundred persons The congregation numbers about one hundred members, who are very active in the interests of their church

Meadow Branch church is situated about two miles from Westminster, on the plank road and was erected in 1850 It is a stone structure, and was originally built thirty-five by fifty-five feet in dimensions, but was recently enlarged to the size of thirty-five by eighty feet The congregation numbers about ninety members

Sam's Creek German Baptist church was erected in 1860 It is situated on the old Liberty road, about two miles from Naill's Mill, up Sam's Creek, in New Windsor District It is a frame building, very neat in appearance, about thirty by forty feet in size, and capable of holding one hundred and fifty people About fifty members worship here

New Windsor church was built and the congregation formed about the year 1873 It is a fine brick building, erected at a cost of sixteen hundred dollars, and is conveniently located on Church Street, in the town of New Windsor The building in size is thirty by forty feet About fifty members constitute the congregation at the present time, which is steadily increasing

Union Bridge church, a beautiful little edifice, was erected in the town of Union Bridge in 1877 It is a brick building, situated on Broadway Street, thirty by forty-five feet in size, and cost eighteen hundred dollars The seats are so arranged as to comfortably seat about four hundred persons Fifty members comprise the congregation

Westminster church was purchased by the German Baptist denomination from the Baptist Church in 1879, at a cost of two thousand two hundred dollars

It has been several times attempted to divide the church in this county into three congregations or charges, viz Pipe Creek, to be composed of Pipe Creek and Union Bridge, Meadow Branch, to embrace Meadow Branch Church and Westminster, and Sam's Creek, composed of S[illegible] Creek and New

Windsor Although the efforts have thus far proved unsuccessful, doubtless this division will occur sooner or later

A short distance from the German Baptist church at Pipe Creek, and one and a quarter miles from Uniontown, is the large German Baptist Cemetery, the first grave in which was dug in the year 1825 Among the names of those buried are the following

Catharine Garber, died Dec 30, 1847, aged 73 years, 10 months, 5 days

Lydia A Garber, died May 4, 1861, aged 38 years, 10 months, 10 days

Johannes Garber, born April 4, 1769, died Oct 4, 1839

Christian Roop, Jr, died Aug 14, 1825, aged 20 years, 9 months, 13 days

Esther Roop, born Feb 11, 1776, died July 2, 1850

Christian Roop, born Nov 4, 1764, in Lancaster County, Pa He removed in 1784 to the precinct in which he died, March 18, 1855.

Abraham Roop, died Sept 11, 1871, aged 74 years, 7 months, 12 days, Lydia, his wife, died Oct 6, 1858, aged 56 years, 6 months, 10 days

Isaac Slingluff, born Aug 5, 1807, died April 30, 1852

Elizabeth Foutz, died July 1, 1860, aged 67 years, 11 months, 12 days

John Stoner, born Feb 21, 1796, died March 14, 1874

Mary Stoner, died May 19, 1853, aged 57 years, 11 months, 1 day

Sarah, wife of John Stoner, died June 6, 1835, aged 58

Betsey, wife of William Warner, died Nov 15, 1830, aged 58

Ann, wife of Otho Warner, died Oct 1, 1836, aged 42 years, 6 months, 22 days

Joseph Roop, Sr, died May 3, 1829, aged 69 years, 9 months, 6 days, Mary Roop, his wife, born Feb 15, 1767, died July 25, 1853

Margaret Snader, born Aug 7, 1794, died Aug 27, 1877

Mary Snader, died Feb 4, 1835, aged 65

Jacob Snader, died Dec 2, 1847, aged 85 years, 3 months, 13 days

Michael Garber, died Jan 4, 1847, aged 53 years, 7 days

Hetty Garber, born Feb 5, 1778, died March 2, 1857

Samuel Bare, born March 29, 1793, died Jan 22, 1845

Jacob Rhodes, died July 26, 1846, aged 77 years, 7 months, 9 days

Sarah Rhodes, born Oct 15, 1763, died Jan 8, 1854

Lydia Bare, died Aug 16, 1858, aged 59 years, 11 months, 13 days

Daniel Harman, born Jan 1, 1821, died Aug 20, 1862

William Plaine, died May 1, 1847, aged 65 years, 8 months, 7 days, and Margaret, his wife, Jan 15, 1849, aged 65 years, 4 months, 20 days

Daniel Plaine, born June 19, 1783, died July 2, 1872, and Penelope, his wife, Aug 24, 1853, aged 76 years, 4 months, 17 days

Catharine Wantz, died Aug 14, 1866, aged 51 years, 6 months, 20 days

Philip Boyle, died Aug 15, 1872, aged 65 years, 6 months, 4 days, Rachel, his wife, and daughter of Jacob and C Zimmerman, died Sept 15, 185[illegible], aged 74 years 10 days

William H Shriner, died Feb 14, 1856, aged 32 years, 3 months, 16 days

John P Shriner, died April 18, 1849, aged 32 years, 7 months, 3 days

Eliza, wife of Joseph Stoufler, died June 20, 18[illegible], aged 48

Jacob Roop, born Sept 4, 1785, died Jan 19, 1860, Sarah, his wife, died June 20, 1866, aged 79 years, 2 months, 22 days

Jacob Shriner, died Dec 28, 1869, aged 76 years, 10 days, Elizabeth, his wife, died Feb 1, 1851, aged 85 years, 4 months, 11 days

Isaac W Shriner, born Dec 13, 1818, died Dec 5, 1873, Rachel Ann, his wife, died Aug 2, 1875, aged 55 years, 11 months, 23 days

Benjamin Bond, died Sept 12, 1863, aged 72

Matilda Bond, died Dec 17, 1860, aged 58 years, 11 months.

Joseph Englar, died July 4, 1872, aged 72 years, 4 months, Susannah, his wife, died May 20, 1861, aged 59 years, 3 months, 10 days

Elizabeth, consort of John Englar, died Feb 2, 1879, aged 54 years, 2 months, 6 days

Tobias Cover, died March 26, 1865, aged 65, Elizabeth, his wife, died Feb 14, 1869, aged 69

David Gilbert, born Nov 22, 1798, died Sept 5, 1865

William Ecker, born Aug 10, 1809, died Oct 7, 1861, Mary A, his wife, born Sept 6, 1813, died Oct 2, 1869

Mary A, wife of William Bloxsten, born Nov 11, 1804, died Sept 5 1879

William Bloxsten, born Sept 2 1802, died March 11, 1876

Henry Rinel, died Dec 4, 1867, aged 85, Mary, his wife, died July 10, 1869, aged 75

Eliza A, wife of Thomas A Franklin, born April 15, 1812, died April 3, 1876

Ezra Stoner, born July 19, 1830, died June 4, 1867

Elizabeth, wife of William Gilbert, died March 22, 1870, aged 49 years, 7 months, 1 day

Josiah Englar, died Oct 25, 1878, aged 69 years, 7 months, 1 day

Elizabeth, wife of Daniel S Diehl, died Aug 6, 1879, aged 30 years, 4 months, 6 days

Lucretia, wife of Levi N Snider, died June 13, 1876, aged 49 years, 1 month, 16 days

Nathan Crumbacker, born Aug 27, 18[illegible]1, died Aug 31, 1880

David Crumbacker, born Aug 12, 1808, died Feb 5, 1881

Ezra O Englar, born Aug 10, 184[illegible], died Oct 31, 18[illegible]

Robert M Jenkins, born May 1[illegible] 181[illegible], died April 19, 1879

William Segafoose, died Aug 29, 1876, aged 69 years, 9 months, 22 days

David Engel, of D, born Jan 1[illegible], 1784, March 31, 1854

David Engel, born Oct 23, 1754, died July, 1802, Elizabeth Engel, his wife, died Oct 2, 1841, aged 90 years, 10 months, 2 days

Elizabeth, wife of Jacob Stem, died Sept 19, 1836, aged 32 years, 2 days

Hannah Ecker, died May 13, 1862, aged 71 years, 1 month, 4 days

Elizabeth, daughter of P and H Myers, died Dec 16, 1845, aged 20 years, 11 months, 23 days

Daniel Engel, died Jan 16, 1874, aged 76 years, Thirza A, his wife, died July 14, 1878, aged 64 years, 8 months, 22 days

Eleanor M, wife of George Ebb, born Oct 28, 1820, died Jan 6, 1873

Anna M, consort of Daniel Engel, died March 12, 1859, aged 53 years, 4 months, 27 days

William Hoffman, died March 7, 18[illegible]8, aged 60 years

Peter Engel, died April 5 18[illegible] aged [illegible] years, 5 months 17 days, Hannah, his wife, died Feb 8, 1867, aged 84 years, 10 months, 2[illegible] days

John Engel, born Sept 13, 1785, died June 21, 1870, Nancy, his wife, died May 11 1871, aged 71 years, 8 months, 15 days

Jacob Smith, died Feb [illegible], 18[illegible], aged [illegible] years, 5 months, 2 days

Jacob Highmiller, of Company F, Seventh Regiment Maryland Volunteer Infantry, born Jan 11, 1839, "died in the service of his country," Jan 30, 1864

Daves Lightner, died Sept 11, 1867, aged 67 years, 10 months, 2 days

Joseph Roop, born July 21, 1810, died Oct 3, 1877

Mary, wife of Daniel Petry, died June 16, 1865, aged 63 years, 1 month

Jacob Fib, died April 1, 1862, aged 65 years, 3 months, 13 days

Nathan W Stem died Dec 29 1862, aged 46 years, 4 months, 6 days, Eliza, his wife, died Dec 18, 1854, aged 38

John Roop, died March 14, 1872, aged 76 years, 5 months, 8 days

Upton Stoner, born March 24, 1796, died May 30, 1876

Joseph Myers, born July 7, 1801, died April 8, 1880, Elizabeth, his wife, born Feb 11, 1801, died Nov 1, 1864

Mary Roop, died Nov 10, 1847, aged 49 years, 6 months, 27 days

Conrad Englar, born Oct 13, 1804, died Sept 3, 1842

Margaret Brown, born Sept 1, 1800, died May 2, 1862

Mary Englar, died Jan 1, 1851, aged 81 years, 8 months, 22 days

Abraham Englar, died March 13, 1879, aged 67 years, 7 months, 12 days

Jacob Diehl, died Dec 28, 1848, aged 49 years, 6 months, 5 days

Rachel Warner, died Dec 11, 1853, aged 47 years, 8 months, 10 days

Samuel Leaming, died May 25, 1837, aged 48 years, 9 months, 14 days

Alfred F Mering, born Dec 6, 1835, died Feb 21, 1879

Lewis G Lindsay, died Nov 9, 1870, aged 65 years, 7 months, 25 days

Deborah Weaver, died Dec 25, 1871, aged 76 years, 9 months, 22 days

John K Weaver, died Dec 13, 1878, aged 88 years, 26 days

Joseph Weaver, born Sept 16, 1779, died Oct 14, 1866

John Weaver, born 1753, died 1829

Susannah Weaver, born 1753, died 1833

Samuel Weaver, born May 25, 1786, died May 21, 1863

Elizabeth Weaver, born Oct 14, 1803, died June 15, 1856

Philip Weaver, died Jan 10, 1873, aged 74

Ann Weaver, born June 24, 1827, died Aug 23, 1847

Susie Weaver, born Oct 10, 1844, died July 19, 1866

McKendrie Weaver, died May 29, 1870, aged 22 years, 10 months

Jesse Weaver, died July 24, 1878, aged 18 years, 11 months, 7 days

Frederick Englar, born May 10, 1811, died Nov 17, 1875

Ann, consort of M Smith, died Feb 21, 1849, aged 37 years, 7 months, 10 days

Catharine, wife of Jacob Zimmerman, died May 30, 1827, aged 64 years, 5 months, 19 days

Jacob Zimmerman, died Sept 30, 1834, aged 28 years, 4 months, 5 days

David Johnson, born Oct 19, 1800, died April 20, 1879, Susanna, his wife, died Jan 21, 1861, aged 64 years, 9 months, 22 days.

Anna, wife of William Zimmerman, and only daughter of William and Anna Shirk, born Nov 17, 1831, died Nov 17, 1860

Catharine Martin died Nov [illegible], 1864, aged 91

John Hess, died Oct 5, 1861, aged 76, Mary, his wife, died April 24, 1865, aged 67 years, 8 months, 25 days

Jacob Bower, born Nov 19, 1771 died April 11, 1825

Margaret Bower, died March 25, 1835, aged [illegible] years, 4 months, 11 days

Catharine wife of J P Haines and daughter of Christopher and S Johnson, died Jan 30, 1871, aged 77 years, 4 months, 26 days

Jacob Switzer, died June 20, 1854, aged 84 years, 3 months, 13 days, Susanna, his first wife, died Nov 25, 1827, aged 52 years, 6 months, 19 days Elizabeth, his second wife, died Jan 1, 1865, aged 76 years, 1 month, 19 days

Samuel Switzer, died March 1, 1829, aged 27 years, 7 months, 24 days

Esther, wife of Jos Bower, died Oct 31, 1834, aged 40 years, 3 months, 28 days

Barbara, wife of John Hess, died Feb 11, 1829, aged 46 years, 1 month, 26 days

George Umer, died Oct 7, 1830, aged 25 years, 8 months, 19 days

Margaret Walter, born Dec 29, 1780, died Oct 4, 1876, aged 95 years, 5 months, 9 days

Elizabeth Umer, died Oct 8, 1828, aged 26 years, 9 months, 15 days

Jonathan Plaine, died April 27 1855, aged 48 years, 6 months 26 days, Lydia, his wife, died Oct 3, 1866, aged 85 years, 1 month, 14 days

George Harris, Sr, died April 14, 1833, aged 40 years, 5 months, 17 days

Margaret Harris, died July 24, 1870, aged 75

Samuel Plaine, born Dec 10, 1778, died Oct 5, 1865

Catharine, wife of David Plaine, died 26th of 9th mo, 1826, aged 76

Elizabeth Nusbaum, died April 17, 1851, aged 85 years, 8 months

John Nusbaum, died Aug 8, 1825, aged 70

Isaac Hiltabidle, died Sept 4, 1827, aged 27 years, 3 months, 12 days, Mary Ann, his wife, died Sept 19, 1845, aged 44 years, 10 days

Joseph Englar, died Feb 2[illegible], 1845, aged 64 years, 8 months, 25 days, Esther, his wife, died June 27, 1867, aged 82 years, 9 months, 9 days

David Englar, died Aug 9, 1839, aged 66 years, 6 months, Elizabeth, his wife, died Nov 12, 1849, aged 79 years, 4 months, 22 days

Deborah, wife of Henry Cover, died Feb 2, 1858, aged 74 years, 9 months, 25 days

Henry Cover, died Nov 20, 1857, aged 76 years, 1 month, 20 days

Deborah, wife of Joseph McKinstry, died Dec 14 1845, aged 32 years, 18 days

Elizabeth Stoner, died Oct 24, 1851, aged 85 years, 11 days

Margaret Stoner, died April 19, 1849, aged 17 years, 2 months, 17 days

Margaret Crumback, died Aug 14, 1844, aged 67

Hannah Nicodemus, died Aug 10, 1852, aged 18 years, 3 months, 26 days

Philip Englar, born May 13, 1778, died Dec 19, 1852

Hannah Englar, born Nov 22, 1799, died Jan 20, 1873

John Stoner, died Sept 2, 1852, aged 64 years, 1 month, 10 days

Samuel Leightel, died Dec 13, 1840, aged 43 years, 11 months, 8 days

Ephraim Englar, born June 4, 1806, died Nov 8, 1857, Agnes, his relict, and wife of Jos Stouffer, died Jan 19, 1863, aged 52 years 9 months, 14 days

Samuel Johnson, born June 15, 1804, died March 13, 1869

Jacob Plowman, born Feb 4, 1816, died Feb 7, 1870

Rufus K Bowers, born Feb 1, 1830, died April 30, 1875

Samuel Hohman, died June [illegible], [illegible], aged [illegible] years, 9 months, 13 days

Daniel Ogle, born Aug 16, 1805, died Dec 8, 1865

Philip Snade, born Jan 2, 1802 died Feb 4, 1864, aged 62 years, 1 month 2 days

David W Snader, died April 4, 1877, aged 47 years, 4 months, 16 days, Sophia, his wife, died April 7, 1875, aged 42 years, 8 months, 14 days

Abraham Wolfe, born Dec 21, 1782, died Oct 22, 1863, Sarah, his wife, born Oct 24, 1786, died July 11, 1880

Israel Rinehart, born June 25, 1792, died Nov 21, 1871, Mary, his wife, died Dec 15, 1865 aged 68 years, 1 month, 26 days

John M Wolfe, died March 15, 1876, aged 54

Mary A, wife of Hiram Davis, died Oct 9, 1878, aged 58 years, 7 months, 5 days

Joseph Foutz, born Oct 5, 1793, died Jan 13, 1878, Margaret, his wife, born July 10, 1801, died May 26, 1869

Mary A, wife of Richard B Foutz, died Sept 8, 1857, aged 55

Maria Null wife of Jacob Snader, born Sept 26, 1806, died Dec 21, 1875

Martha A, wife of J T Devilbiss, died Jan 26, 1875, aged 34 years, 9 months, 19 days

Eve E, wife of Jacob Sooble, died Aug 4, 1877, aged 70 years, 25 days

Louisa, wife of Asa Zent, died Aug 21, 1877, aged 77 years, 2 months, 21 days

Hannah Little, born May 20, 1804, died Oct 10, 1877

Jacob Harman, died Aug 13, 1871, aged 76 years, 2 months, 18 days, Mary, his wife, died June 28, 1875, aged 80 years, 11 months, 19 days

Hannah, wife of John Warebime, born April 11, 1801, died March 2, 1873

Peter Utz, born Sept 4, 1796, died July 27, 1878

Jacob Rider, died May 31, 1871, aged 58 years, 6 months, 5 days

George Hess, died Dec 20, 1863, aged 80 years, 5 days

Susanna Hess, died Feb 24, 1870, aged 88 years, 5 days

George Kelly, born Dec 21, 1834, died Sept 24, 1874, Sarah, his wife, died April 24, 1868, aged 37 years, 1 month, 1 day

John Banker, born Feb 4, 1790, died Aug 23, 1870

Catharine Banker, born Dec. 8, 1793, died Feb 20, 1873

Mary, wife of S Hamilton Snouser, born Jan 30, 1828, died Dec 4, 1869

David S Golly, died Dec 27, 1863, aged 50 years, 7 months, 4 days

Eliza Golly, died Aug 6, 1878, aged 67 years, 6 months, 23 days

Samuel Bower, died January, 1867, aged 60 years, 5 months, 13 days, Nancy Ann, his wife, died April 22, 1866, aged 54 years, 6 months, 8 days

Ephraim Powell, died March 2, 1872, aged 52

Peter M Calwith, died June 10, 1866, aged 74 years, 5 months

Rachel Calwith, died Feb 26, 1860, aged 35 years, 5 months, 6 days

Washington Wilson, born Jan 12, 1815, died Jan 17, 1856

John M Romspert, born May 7, 1838, and "was instantly killed while on duty by the explosion of No 4 engine on W M R R," Oct 24, 1876

Ulrick Messler, born June 30, 1811, died March 9, 1870

Martha Messler, died Dec 27, 1858, aged 40

Julia Ann Shriver, died Oct 29, 1861, aged 48 years, 5 months, 18 days

Martin Billmyer, born March 2[illegible], 177[illegible], died Sept [illegible] 18[illegible]

Salome, relict of Jacob Yon, born Dec 10, 1769, died Nov 22, 1855

Hannah Yon, born April 3, 1793, died Oct 11, 1868

Samuel Moyers, died Sept 11, 1856, aged [illegible] years, 5 months, 7 days, Eliza C, his wife, died Dec 30, 1875, aged 68 years, 6 months, 3 days

Stephen Bower, died March 12, 1856, aged 76 years, 7 months

Mary Bower, died Feb 5, 1855, aged 71 years, 10 months

John Rheam, died June 25, 1858, aged 67 years, 6 months, 18 days

Elizabeth Rheam, died Jan 12, 1871, aged 81 years, 8 months

Eliza, consort of Abraham Myers, born Dec 12 1801, died Nov 21, 185[illegible]

Anna Myers, died March 6, 1817, aged 78 years, 6 months, 6 days

Jacob Myers, died April 25, 1876, aged 69 years, 8 months, 15 days, Lydia, his wife, died Sept 5, 1866, aged 49 years, 1 month, 13 days

John Englar, born March 11, 1812, died July 29, 1860

Daniel Englar, died June 12, 1840, aged 63

Mary A Englar, died Oct 6, 1867, aged 50 years, 4 months, 27 days

David Englar, died Jan 21, 1841, aged 64 years, 6 months

Ann Singer, born July 31, 1811, died Oct 28, 1876, Jacob, her husband, born April 9, 1813, died Feb 2[illegible], 1877

Magdalena Sherbig, died July 23, 182[illegible], aged 87 years, 10 days

Jacob Cowell, died March 23, 1841, aged [illegible] years, 5 months, 27 days

Elizabeth Cowell, died Oct 17, 1849, aged 74 years, 2 months, 18 days

G M Jordan, died Aug 20, 1841, aged 81 years, 5 months, 27 days

Anna M Jordan, born March 19, 1758, died July 17, 1825

Abraham Caylor, died May 25, 1857, aged 64 years, 5 months, Anna, his wife, died March 24, 1841, aged 46 years, 9 months, 5 days

Dorothy Wildermute, born Jan 10, 1750, died Sept 9, 1823

"M R," died 1827

Henry Fulkerth, died July 2, 1848, aged 84

Margaret Fulkerth, died Dec 21, 1847, aged 69 years, 6 months

Ebenezer Carlyle, died July 27, 1840, aged 66 years, 1 month

Margaret, his wife, died April 26, 1839, aged 53 years, 9 months 18 days

Anna Carlyle, died Aug 1, 1880, aged 68 years, 3 months, 23 days

Rachel O Brien, died Dec 25, 1870, aged 70

Sarah Boman, died July [illegible], 1857, aged 71

Jacob Zimmerman, born Dec 30, 1787, died Feb 5 1859

Peter Little, died Dec 11, 1839, aged 37 years, 3 months, 1[illegible] days

Sophia Little, died March 11, 1852, aged [illegible]0

John Moore, died Aug 1, 1860, aged 86 years, 5 months, 19 days

Rachel Smith, died July 28, 1840, aged 52 years, 1 month, 24 days

Barbara Kemn, born Sept 15, 1786, died Aug [illegible]0, 1852

Jacob Kemne, died March 16, 1849, aged [illegible]

Priscilla, wife of William Stoner, died March 2[illegible], 1864, aged 38 years, 4 months 10 days

Henry Row, born Dec 10, 1812, died Dec 10, 1871

George Row, died May 5, 1857, aged 84 years, 7 months, 10 days Margaret, his wife, born Aug 1, 17[illegible], died Feb 11, 1870

Carroll County w[illegible] free from the vicissitude[illegible] between the

th and the South At the beginning of the unfortunate struggle there was the same diversity of sentiment which existed in the other counties of Maryland, but those who favored the South were far inferior in numbers to the supporters of the Union The young men volunteered freely in defense of their opinions, and it is estimated that the Federal army was supplied with eight hundred recruits from this region, while two hundred enthusiastic young men of Southern sympathies made their way through the Union lines into the camps of the Southern army The contingents of Carroll in both armies fully maintained the character of her people for gallantry and true manhood In June, 1863, the soil of Carroll echoed the tread of large bodies of armed men from both armies A portion of the cavalry force belonging to the army of Northern Virginia passed through Westminster on its way to Gettysburg, and encountered a battalion of cavalry, which it dispersed or captured after a slight skirmish The troops rested in the city during the night and proceeded on their way with the dawn They had scarcely emerged from the city when the Sixth Corps of the Army of the Potomac entered from the opposite side Much excitement prevailed among the citizens, who had seen but little of either army, but their fears were groundless, as both detachments behaved with exemplary courtesy and evidenced thorough discipline For some days the transportation wagons of the Union army were parked around the town and the streets presented an animated appearance, but they were moved to the front prior to the battle of Gettysburg The booming of the cannon on that fatal field was heard with conflicting emotions by the friends of the combatants, and as the echoes died away the town relapsed into its wonted quiet It was roused again in the succeeding year for a brief period by a raid of the Confederate forces under Gen Bradley T Johnson and Maj Harry Gilmor, but as they had learned by experience that the presence of troops was not such a serious infliction as their fears had painted, the short visit of the Confederates was made rather an occasion of rejoicing than sorrow

The ex-Federal soldiers from Carroll County met in Westminster, March 13, 1880, and formed a post of the Grand Army of the Republic, to be known as Burns' Post, after W H Burns, of the Sixth Maryland Regiment Col William A McKellip was elected Commander, Capt A Billingslea, Senior Vice-Commander, Capt Charles Kuhns, Junior Vice-Commander, Dr William H Rippard, Surgeon, Lee McElroy, Quartermaster, Sylvester Mathias, Adjutant, and John Matthews, Chaplain The officers were installed March 27th by department commander Gen William Ross and staff, of Baltimore

The Carroll County Agricultural Society was incorporated March 8, 1869, by John E Smith, Jeremiah Rinehart, William A McKellip, Richard Manning, David Fowble, Hashabiah Haines, George W Matthews, and John L Reifsnider The object of the association was "to improve agriculture by attracting the attention, eliciting the views, and combining the efforts of the individuals composing the agricultural community of Carroll County, and aiming at the development of the resources of the soil so as to promote the prosperity of all concerned in its culture" Grounds containing thirty acres of land were purchased on the Baltimore turnpike at the east end of Westminster, just outside of the corporation limits They were inclosed with a substantial fence, and stabling was erected for the accommodation of five hundred head of stock A race-track, half a mile in length, was made from a diagram furnished by George W Wilkes, of the *Spirit of the Times*, and all the necessary preparations completed for the annual exhibitions of the association The constitution of the society requires the members to meet three times a year, and Article III of that instrument defines the aims of the association to be, in addition to others, "to procure and improve the implements of husbandry, to improve the breed of domestic animals" The first officers of the society were John E Smith, president, Jeremiah Rinehart, vice-president, William A McKellip, secretary, Richard Manning, treasurer, David Fowble, George W Matthews, Edward Lynch, Hashabiah Haines, and John F Reifsnider, directors At a meeting of the board of directors in 1869, the following committees were appointed to solicit subscriptions to the capital stock of the society

District No 1, Samuel Swope, Jno McKellip, Samuel Smith, No 2, Reuben Saylor, Thomas F Shepherd, Jeremiah Rinehart, No 3, H Wirt Shriver, Geo W Shull, Samuel Cover, No 4, James Lee, Jeremiah Babylon, P A Gorsuch, No 5, S T C Brown, David Prugh, J Oliver Wadlow, No 6, George A Shower, Edwin J Crumrine, P H L Meyers, No 7, Wm A McKellip, Richard Manning Hashabiah Haines, Augustus Shriver, No 8, David W Houck, Wm Houck, John W Murray, No 9, Dr F J Crawford, Col J C Gist, Robert D Gorsuch, No 10, Geo Harris, Joseph Davis, John Wincmiller, No 11, L P Slingluff, Wm A Norris, Sol S Fisher, Jos A Stouffer

Preparations having all been completed, and the society having fully realized their anticipations of support from the people of the county, on the 3d of July, 1869, the grounds of the association were opened with much ceremony and with a fine exhibition,

which embraced the varied productions of the county and admirable specimens of improved stock and horses A grand tournament attracted a large concourse of people, after which some interesting trotting races took place Among the cattle exhibited were beautiful selections from Durham Devon, Ayrshire, and Alderney breeds The exhibition of horses was worthy of careful inspection, the large majority of the animals having been raised by the enterprising farmers of Carroll County

The following is a list of the officers of the society during each year, including 1881

1870 —President, John E Smith Vice President, Jeremiah Rinehart, Secretary, Wm A McKellip, Treasurer, Richard Manning, Directors, David Fowble, Edward Lynch, H Haines, W G Rinehart, Joseph H Hoppe

1871 —President Augustus Shriver, Vice-President, Jeremiah Rinehart, Secretary, Wm A McKellip, Treasurer, Richard Manning Directors, Edward Lynch, David H Byers, Geo W Matthews, David Fowble, Josephus H Hoppe

1872 —President, Augustus Shriver, Vice President, Jeremiah Rinehart, Secretary, Wm A McKellip, Treasurer, Richard Manning, Directors, David Fowble, Edward Lynch, H E Morelock, Joseph Shaeffer, Louis P Slingluff

1873 —President, Granville S Haines, Vice-President, Jeremiah Rinehart, Secretary, Wm A McKellip, Treasurer, Richard Manning, Directors, Edward Lynch, David Fowble, Joseph Shaeffer, Dr C Billingslea, Noah Shaeffer, E O Grimes, Louis P Slingluff, Lewis H Cole

1874 —President, Granville S Haines, Vice President, George W Matthews, Secretary, C V Wantz, Treasurer, Richard Manning, Directors, F H Orendorff, H E Morelock, Joseph Hibberd, Thomas F Shepherd, E J Crumrine

1875 —President, Granville S Haines, Vice President, Joseph Shaeffer, Secretary, C V Wantz, Treasurer, Richard Manning, Directors, H E Morelock, F H Orendorff, David Fowble, Thos F Shepherd, Samuel Roop

1876 —President, Jeremiah Rinehart, Vice President, Noah Shaeffer, Secretary, George W Matthews, Treasurer, Richard Manning, Directors, David H Byers, Samuel Lawyer, Henry B Albaugh, John Sellman, David Stoner

1877 —President, Col William A McKellip, Vice-President, David Fowble, Secretary, G W Matthews, Treasurer, Richard Manning, Directors, Dr Jacob Rinehart, Granville S Haines, L P Slingluff, Edward Lynch, Orlando Reese

1878 —(Same board)

1879 —Same board, save Francis H Orendorff, secretary, vice G W Matthews

1880 —Same board, Assistant Secretary, Frank W Shriver, Chief Marshal, Joseph W Berret, Assistant Marshals, Robert M Hewitt, Wesley A Steele, G Edwin Hoppe, William N Sellman, Committee on Grounds and Side Shows, David Fowble, Granville S Haines, Edward Lynch, Superintendents of Departments, Henry E Morelock, Wm J Morelock, D H Byers, Thomas L Gist, Elias Yingling Charles N Kuhn, Francis Shriver Lee McElroy, W G Rinehart, Vice Presidents, Dr Samuel Swope, Frank Brown, J C Brubaker, A G Houck, Emanuel Myers, Geo W Manro, P H L Myers, John W Murray, Solomon Shepherd, Lewis Dielman, Benj Poole, David Rinehart, Committee of Reception, Hon Charles L Roberts, Hon John E Smith Henry Galt Thomas F Shepherd, Samuel Cover, John H Chew, E J Crumrine, R D Gorsuch L A J Lamotte, A Augustus Roop J H Steele, F H Clabaugh The fair this year was held September 28th to October 1st, and in the trials for speed there were six trots, in which $775 were given as awards

1881 —President, Col William A McKellip, Vice President, David Fowble, Secretary, Francis H Orendorff Treasurer, Richard Manning, Directors, Edward Lynch, Dr Jacob Rinehart, Jeremiah Rinehart, John B Boyle, William J Morelock

The Agricultural Hall, for the productions requiring shelter, is eighty-five by forty feet, and two stories high The pavilion seats over two thousand persons, and a music-stand, octagonal in form, is erected in the centre of the track This society has a capital of nearly thirty thousand dollars invested in its properties The quality of horses, cattle, hogs, sheep, and mules in the county, as annually exhibited, is superb, and makes a good return in profits to the growers and owners It is universally admitted that the generous rivalry in their exhibitions has stimulated the farmers to more active exertions, and the machinists have been aroused to the necessity of producing implements of superior quality

As has been before observed in these pages, the inhabitants of Carroll County have always been a peaceful and law-abiding people The records of the court have seldom been defaced by the more heinous offenses which sometimes mar the moral symmetry of other communities There have been but two executions in the county since its creation in 1837 Rebecca McCormick, a colored woman, was tried at the April term of the Circuit Court for 1859 for the murder of a colored boy, fourteen years of age She was convicted of murder in the first degree, and executed in the month of June following

On the 5th of April, 1872, Abraham L Lynn, a miller near Lynwood Station, was found dead in his grain-bin with his skull fractured in several places It was at first supposed that he had accidentally fallen into the bin, but the suspicious movements of a young man named Joseph W Davis, employed in the mill, attracted attention, and he was arrested and charged with the murder Hamilton Shue, a shoemaker in the village, was also arrested as an accomplice The trial of Davis before the Circuit Court of Carroll County, in June, 1872, resulted in a disagreement of the jury His case was then removed to Washington County, where he was tried in September, 1872, and convicted of murder in the first degree There succeeded a series of delays almost unexampled in the history of jurisprudence The evidence was entirely circumstantial and his counsel, Col Maulsby and J A C Bond believed implicitly in his innocence

The case was taken on a bill of exceptions to the Court of Appeals, and the decision of the lower court affirmed Subsequently, in deference to the appeals of counsel, the case was reopened by the highest court in the State and reargued, with the same result as before An appeal was now made to the Governor for pardon, and the case elaborately argued before him, but he declined to interfere Again, on the supposed discovery of new evidence, it was argued before the Governor with a like result Some mistakes were then discovered in the court papers and a writ of error was sued out by the counsel of Davis, which was heard by the Court of Appeals, and decided adversely to Davis As a last resort an application for interference was made to the Legislature, which was then in session, but while the proceedings were pending before this body Davis made a full confession, acknowledging his guilt and exonerating Shue, who had already been acquitted Davis was executed in the jail yard at Westminster, Feb 6, 1874 A fearful storm of wind and snow prevailed during the day, but the case had become so generally known through the extraordinary efforts of counsel in his behalf, that thousands of people were drawn thither to witness the last act in the tragedy He broke down utterly at the last, and had to be borne up the steps of the gallows His confession was sold to the spectators while he was delivering his farewell to the populace, and appeared the next day in the morning papers

The financial exhibit of Carroll County for the year ending June 30, 1881, was very gratifying to the taxpayers There was a reduction of $10,641 61 in the public debt over the previous year, and an increase of $5172.41 in assets, making a general improvement of $15,787 02 The liabilities over assets were $12,532 82, which was about the actual debt of the county The tax levied was fifty cents on a hundred dollars, the lowest in the State The expenses of the Circuit Court for August and November, 1880, and for February and May, 1881, were $8303 46, for sundry attorneys, $1[illegible] 33, for the Orphans' Court, $1573 81, for county commissioners, $1868 50, for county jail, $2390 59, for public schools, $21,000, for registers of voters, $825, for collection of taxes, $2635, for justices of the peace, $157 68, for constables, $464 79, for public printing, $722 83, for taxes refunded, $14 10, for State witnesses, $41 58, for laying out and opening public roads, $109, for inquests, $166 94, for sundry minor expenses, $970 55, for county roads, small bridges, and culverts, $9369 90, for bridges, $3732-88, for county indebtedness, $14 230 31, for judges and clerks of election $[illegible]286, for out-door pensioners, $2803, for special pensions by order, $619 60, for miscellaneous accounts, $2364 36, for the almshouse, $3822 70 The liabilities of the county on June 30, 1881, were given by Joseph A Waesche, the treasurer, as follows County certificates outstanding, $47,495, note due Union National Bank, $5000, Daniel Bush estate, $1200, George W Armacost, $400, total, $54,095 The amount of liabilities June 30, 1880, $64,709 61 The assets were stated as follows Outstanding taxes in hands of collectors for former years, $38 230 71, cash in bank, $2396 97, due from Baltimore City and Allegany County, $935 50, total, $41,563,18 Amount of assets July 30, 1880, $36,390 77 The commissioners were John K Longwell, president, Francis Warner, William C Polk

The following statistics in regard to Carroll County are furnished from the census bureau Total value of real estate assessed for the year ended June 30, 1880, $11,215,334, personal property, $5 030,142, aggregate value of real and personal property assessed, $16,245,476 Receipts from taxes for all purposes except schools, $90,687 65, for school purposes, $37,245 47, total receipts from State taxes for all purposes except schools, $14,214 79, total receipts from State taxes (or apportionment) for schools, $16,245 47 Expenditures for schools, $37,245 47, State roads or bridges, $11,996 71, poor, $7590, all other purposes, $24,337 95 Total, $81,170 13 The bonded indebtedness is based on the issue of bonds bearing 6 per cent interest in 1864 and 1865, as bounties for volunteer soldiers, which matured in 1866 and 1867 The amount paid is $16,675, outstanding, $48,325 Assets, par value outstanding taxes in the hands of collectors, $36,390 17, almshouse property, containing 175 acres of land, $15,000 Total, $51,390 17, estimated value, $51,390 17

The total population of the county in 1880 was 30,992, of which the males numbered 15,495, and the females 15,497

The population of Carroll County, according to previous census returns, has been as follows

	1870	1860	1850	1840
White	26,444	22,525	18,667	15,221
Colored	2,175	1,225	974	898
Slave		783	975	1,122
Total	28,619	24,533	20,616	17,241

The cereal production of Carroll County, as returned by the census of 1880, was as follows

	Acres	Bushels
Barley	143	3,724
Buckwheat	972	12 [illegible]13
Indian corn	31,983	1,003,986
Oats	11,972	262,[illegible]8
Rye	5 209	54,879
Wheat	[illegible]	379,[illegible]
Tobacco	[illegible]	137,171

Summary of School Statistics for 1880

Number of school-houses (frame 32, brick 63, log 18, stone 12)	125
Number male teachers (principals)	82
" female " "	49
" " " assistants	1
" fenced lots	9
" schools having outbuildings	105
" " " good blackboards	110
" " " " furniture	112
Different pupils for the year (white)	6152
" " " " (colored)	307

Receipts

Balance on hand Sept 30, 1880	$180 30
State school tax	12 662 30
" free school fund	1,[illegible] 02
County school tax at 18 cents on the $100	20,000 00
Book fees	7,811 60
State appropriation to colored schools	2,171 88
License	201 33
Rent	25 00
Total	$44,991 43

The total disbursements were $44,994 43, of which $36,991 40 were teachers' salaries, $1579 96 for fuel, $1902 89 for stationery, $4033 12 for colored schools (included in the above disbursements), and the balance (save $3146 07 cash on hand) for various incidental and contingent expenses.

According to the United States census of 1880, the total number of persons in Carroll County who cannot read is 1419, and of those who cannot write 2125 Of the latter, 1209 are native white, 66 foreign white, and 850 colored Of the white population who cannot write, 95 males and 61 females, total, 156, are between 10 and 14 years of age, 43 males and 49 females, total, 92, are from 15 to 20 years of age, and 383 males and 644 females, total, 1027, are 21 years and over Of the colored population who cannot write, 43 males and 51 females, total, 94, are from 10 to 14 years old, 42 males and 58 females, total, 100, are from 15 to 20 years, and 320 males and 336 females, total, 656, are 21 years and over

CARROLL COUNTY DISTRICTS.

CHAPTER XXXIX

TANEYTOWN DISTRICT, No 1

THE metes and bounds of this district are as follows

"Beginning at the Pennsylvania line where Rock Creek crosses said line, thence with the course of said creek until it empties into the Monocacy River, thence with the Monocacy to the point where Double Pipe Creek enters the river, thence with the course [illegible] Pipe to the point of junction with Little Pipe Creek and [illegible] Pipe Creek, thence with the course of Little Pipe Creek to Eckait's Ford, thence with a straight line to Sack's Ford on Big Pipe Creek, thence up Big Pipe Creek to Grove's Mill, thence with the stone road to Littlestown turnpike thence with the turnpike to the Pennsylvania line, thence to the place of beginning"

The district is bounded on the north by Pennsylvania, on the east by the Myers' and Uniontown Districts, on the south by the Uniontown and Middleburg Districts, and on the west by Frederick County Its western boundary line is the Monocacy River, and Big Pipe Creek separates it from the Uniontown District Alloway's Creek, which rises in Pennsylvania, passes through the northwest corner of the district and empties into the Monocacy River, and Piney Creek, which takes its rise in the same State, passes diagonally through the district, dividing it into two nearly equal parts, and finds its outlet in the Monocacy Upon the tributaries of these stream many mills have been erected, some of them prior to the Revolutionary war Taneytown District was first settled by the Scotch Irish Presbyterian Covenanter stock, who were either natives of the north of Ireland or the descendants of those who came to Pennsylvania very early in the history of the colonies Among them were the Gwynns, McKalebs, McKellips, Galts, Birnies, Knoxes, and Rudesils The Goods, Crouses, Swopes, Hesses, Nalls, Hecks, Reindollars, Thompsons, and Shunks are names intimately associated also with the first settlement of the district Frederick Taney was the earliest settler of whom any record is preserved He took up a tract of land in the vicinity of Taneytown at present the business centre of the district, in 1740, and in 1754 "Brothers Agreement," a tract of seven thousand nine hundred acres, was patented to Edward Digges and Raphael Taney About 1750 a heavy tide of immigration set in from Pennsylvania John McKellip, Sr, a sea-captain was born in the County Antrim Ireland, where his parents had removed from the neighborhood of Castle Stirling, England He married, Nov 9, 1780, Mary Drips, his first wife, and after her death Ann Adams, of Maryland He settled in the Taneytown District in 1780, whither he had come from Ireland in company with Rogers Birnie He died March 10 1834, aged eighty years His first wife died Feb 15, 1799, and his second, Dec 14, 1827, she being sixty-four years of age Three of his brothers William, Hugh, and David, settled in America John McKellip's son James by his second wife was born Nov 5, 1805, and died May 4, 1859 He was the father of Col William A McKellip, a prominent lawyer of Westminster The early settlers were all staunch Whigs during [illegible] largely in

troops and treasure to its success "Brother's Inheritance," a grant of three thousand one hundred and twenty-four acres, was patented to Michael Swope in 1761

If longevity be an indication of the salubriousness of a climate, Taneytown District has reason to be proud of its record in this regard John Welty was born in Eppingen, Germany, Sept 4, 1722 He came to this country and settled in the Taneytown District, and died near Emmittsburg, Jan 16, 1817, aged ninety-four years, four months, and two days His son, Frederick Welty, was born on Piney Creek, near Taneytown, March 12 1779, and afterwards removed to Dellsburg, York Co, Pa, where he died April 28, 1877, aged ninety-eight years, one month, and sixteen days, Elizabeth Kuntz, a daughter of John Welty, lived to be one hundred and three years of age, Susanna Hornaker died in March, 1855, aged eighty-four years, four months, and two days, Casper Welty, a son of John, died Feb 27, 1856, aged eighty-eight years, nine months, and twenty one days, Bernard Welty, another son, died April 1, 1856, aged eighty-two years, eight months, and eleven days, Mary Hoovs, another daughter, died Sept 17, 1866, aged ninety-one years, Abraham Welty, died May 2, 1874, aged ninety-seven years, eleven months, and twenty-two days Their aggregate ages amounted to six hundred and fifty seven years, giving an average of ninety-four years to each member of the family, probably the most remarkable instance of longevity since the days of the patriarchs

Piney Creek Presbyterian Church.—"April 13, 1763, Tom's Creek and Pipe Creek Churches ask leave to apply to the Presbytery of New Brunswick for a young man to supply them" The answer to this request is not recorded, but the Rev. Samuel Thompson was appointed to preach at Tom's Creek, and the Rev Robert McMardil was at the same time appointed to preach at Pine Creek, on the fourth Sabbath of April At this point in the history the name of Pipe Creek disappears from the record, and that of Pine, then Piney Creek, is substituted, showing that the congregation now adopted a new name, if it did not also change its place of worship The church was supplied during the next autumn and winter by William Edmeston and John Slemons, licentiates of the Donegal Presbytery, by William Magin, a licentiate of the Presbytery of Philadelphia, and by the Rev Robert Smith For the summer of 1761, Mr Slemons had three appointments at Piney Creek During the next five years Tom's Creek and Piney Creek had occasional supplies, appointed chiefly at the stated meetings of the Presbytery in April and October Andrew Bay, John Slemons, John Craighead, Hezekiah James Balch, Samuel Thompson, and Robert Cooper were among their preachers Rev John Slemons was born in Chester County, Pa His parents were emigrants from Ireland He was a graduate of Princeton College, and was licensed by the Presbytery of Donegal in 1762 or 1763 He was unanimously called to Lower Marsh Creek on the third Saturday of November, 1764 He also received calls from Tom's Creek and Piney Creek about the same time At Philadelphia, May 8, 1765, the Presbytery desired his answer respecting the calls under consideration, when "he gave up that from Piney Creek and Tom's Creek" Not being "clear" with respect to the call from Lower Marsh Creek, the Presbytery "recommend him to come to a determination as soon as he can in that matter"

On the 23d of May he declared his acceptance of the call to Lower Marsh Creek, and was ordained and installed by the Presbytery of Carlisle Oct 30, 1765, Mr Slemons frequently supplied Tom's Creek and Piney Creek, both before and after his settlement at Marsh Creek His relation to this church had dissolved in 1774 He was pastor of Slate Ridge and Chanceford from their organization until his death June, 1814 in the eightieth year of his age His remains, and those of his wife Sarah, who died June 2, 1823, are interred in the Piney Creek burying-ground Mrs Slemons was the daughter of the Rev Joseph Dean, a co laborer of the Tennents, who was buried in the Neshaminy Church graveyard Two brothers and a sister of Mr Slemons, and the children of one of the brothers, are buried in the Lower Marsh Creek burying-ground Piney Creek had meanwhile asked for the appointment of the Rev Joseph Rhea "in particular" as supply, and had also requested that some member of the Presbytery be deputized to assist in the preparation of a call to Mr Rhea He had already been before the congregation, having become a member of the Presbytery, October, 1770 That Mr Rhea's ministrations were highly acceptable is evinced by the fact that not only Piney Creek, but also Upper Marsh Creek (now Gettysburg) and the united churches of Tuscarora and Cedar Springs, all presented calls to him in April, 1771 Hanover, in Dauphin County, likewise asked for him as supply at the same time The call from Tuscarora and Cedar Spring was withheld for correction That from Upper Marsh was presented to Mr Rhea, and taken into consideration by him

The commissioners from Piney Creek were Patrick Watson and Matthew Galt They stated that subscriptions amounting to £110 or £112 had been

secured for Mr Rhea's support, that if he became pastor they proposed to maintain his family for the first year in addition to the salary, and that this agreement had been entered of record in their "Book of Congregational Affairs"

The Presbytery found the call to be regular and the people unanimous, but an existing difficulty between Tom's Creek and Piney Creek was an impediment in the way of placing it in Mr Rhea's hands Another committee was now raised to hear and determine the matters now in dispute This committee consisted of the Rev Messrs Thompson, Roan, Duffield, and Cooper, and was directed to put the call in Mr Rhea's hands, if no sufficient objections arose out of the questions submitted for their decision

The committee was directed to meet on the Monday following their appointment, but in this they failed, and so reported to the Presbytery in June, when the reasons assigned for the failure were sustained During the delay occasioned by these efforts of conciliation Mr Rhea declared his acceptance of the call to Upper Marsh Creek, but afterwards declined it under circumstances which led the Presbytery to disapprove of his conduct "as having too great an appearance of inadvertency and instability," and recommending him to be "more cautious in the future with respect to such matters"

Piney Creek now urged the Presbytery to put their call into Mr Rhea's hands, and in case of his acceptance to have him installed as soon as convenient The same obstacle being still in the way as at the April meeting, action upon this request was again deferred

But, in order to expedite the business, a new committee, consisting of the Rev Messrs Cooper, Craighead, and Duffield, with Robert Dill and Robert McPherson as elders, was appointed to determine the matter in debate, and if the way should be clear, put the call into Mr Rhea's hands and receive his answer

The committee met at Tom's Creek on the fourth Tuesday of June, 1771, all the members being present except Mr Craighead and Elder Dill Mr Cooper was chosen moderator, and Mr Duffield clerk The commissioners from Piney Creek were Patrick Watson, Abraham Heyter, Benjamin McKinley, James Galt, and James Hunter, from Tom's Creek a committee of four

When the committee and the parties came together, there were two subjects of dispute to be considered The first was that Piney Creek desired a separation from Tom's Creek and the settlement of a pastor of their own, whereas Tom's Creek favored the continuance of the former union and a joint settlement of a pastor After a full and patient hearing of the arguments on both sides, the committee decided this first question in favor of Piney Creek, and dissolved the union

The second subject of controversy was that of the boundary line between the two congregations It will be remembered that in April, 1765, this question was considered and apparently settled The following is the concluding part of the committee's decision .

"The committee therefore determine that although Monocacy does appear to be a just and natural boundary to Tom's Creek, yet for the present such persons as live between the above-mentioned Stony Ridge and Marsh Creek, or Monocacy, and choose to join with Piney Creek, shall be at liberty so to do But that in case of Tom's Creek obtaining a minister, it shall be deemed more regular in them to join with Tom's Creek (within whose reasonable bounds they are to be esteemed residing), as being more conducive to the general good of the church, even though they should still continue a connection with Piney Creek as being nearer to them as that house is now seated"

In the judgment and determination of the committee the commissioners of both congregations acquiesced, and thus disposed of questions which had been sources of controversy and distraction The way was now clear for presenting the call to Mr Rhea It was accordingly placed in his hand by the committee After due deliberation he accepted it The record omits the arrangements for his installation, but this doubtless soon followed, as from this time he discharged the duties of the pastorate Thus after depending upon the Presbytery for supplies for nearly ten years, Piney Creek had, for the first time, a settled minister At what precise time the first house of worship was erected at Piney Creek is unknown It was, however, prior to the settlement of Mr Rhea, as is shown by the deed conveying the lot of ground, and the house built upon it, to the trustees The original Piney Creek church, as stated above, erected prior to Mr Rhea's settlement in 1771, was a very plain log structure. Its pews were

"—— Straight backed and tall,
Its pulpit, goblet formed
Half-way up the wall,
The sounding-board above"

It was removed about the year 1818, when the present brick church was built upon the same site, and much after the same fashion It was remodeled and modernized in 1869, during the pastorate of Mr Patterson The number of pews in the second church before the last improvements were made were fifty-eight

The deed of the old church is dated Feb 15, 1771, and was given [illegible] shillings, by

Abraham Heyter, of Frederick County, province of Maryland, to Patrick Watson, James Galt, and John McCorkle, of the same county and province, and James Barr and James Hunter, of York County, province of Pennsylvania, in trust for a church and burying-ground. The grant contained two acres of land, and the use of a spring of water contiguous thereto, on the southeast side of the land, and was situated in Piney Creek Hundred, Frederick Co. In shape it was a parallelogram, with lines running north and south twenty perches, and east and west sixteen perches. The grantor restricted the use and privilege of the land to "a congregation of people called Presbyterians, who shall hold or continue to hold that system of doctrine contained in the Westminster confession of faith, catechisms, and directory as the same principles are now professed and embraced by the Synod of New York and Philadelphia, to which they are now united."

While Piney Creek was enjoying the regular ministrations of a settled pastor, Tom's Creek was dependent upon the Presbytery for supplies. In 1772 subscriptions to the amount of fourteen pounds were taken up in Piney Creek for the benefit of Nassau Hall College, New Jersey. In June, 1775, Mr Rhea informed the Presbytery that he desired to visit some parts of Virginia, and that his people had given consent to his absence. The Presbytery permitted him to carry out his purpose, and furnished him with the usual traveling credentials.

Mr Rhea tendered his resignation as pastor of the Piney Creek Church in April, 1776. His reasons for doing so are not upon record, but subsequent proceedings show that his salary was in arrears. The commissioners of the congregation were Robert Bigham and Adam Hoop. Upon their acceding to Mr Rhea's request, the Presbytery, after due deliberation, dissolved the pastoral relation. An agreement was, however, previously entered into whereby Mr Rhea engaged to receipt in full for his salary upon the payment of one hundred and fifty pounds. He also agreed that if upon examination of accounts it should appear that any moneys had been received for which due credit had not been given, the proper deductions should be made. The date of these transactions was April 11, 1776.

Mr Rhea obtained leave to spend the following summer in Virginia, and was furnished with the usual Presbyterial certificate.

Being unable to effect a settlement with Mr Rhea, the congregation applied to the Presbytery in October of the same year for a committee to adjudicate the matter. The Rev Messrs. Balch and Black, with Elders William Blair and David McConaughy, were appointed said committee, and directed to meet at Piney Creek, when Mr Rhea could be present. But as he had gone to Virginia the meeting was necessarily delayed, and before it could be arranged for his convenience he died. This event occurred Sept 20, 1777. Mr Rhea was a native of Ireland. Piney Creek was his only pastorate in this country. His remains lie in the burying ground attached to this church. His tombstone bears the following inscription:

"Sacred to the memory of the Rev Joseph Rhea, who died in 1777, aged about sixty two years. Erected at the request and the expense of a grandson of the deceased, in 1859, by the elders of the Piney Creek Church, where he preached seven years."

In October, 1778, a paper signed by Patrick Watson, Robert Bigham, Samuel McCune, James Watson, and William Linn showed that the arrears due to the heirs of Mr Rhea had been collected, and all the obligations of the congregation to him honorably discharged. Supplies were appointed for Piney Creek at this meeting, and from time to time for the next two years.

On the 22d of May, 1777, the Rev James Martin, a member of the Associate Presbytery of Pennsylvania, was received by the Synod and assigned to the Presbytery of Donegal. He was enrolled as a member of this latter body June 18th. In 1780 he accepted a call to Piney Creek Church. The support promised was "four hundred bushels of wheat per year, or the current price thereof in money, and as much more as the circumstances of the congregation would admit." He was installed Nov 9, 1780, by a committee consisting of the Rev Messrs James Hunt, John Slemons, and John Black. The pastorate of Mr Martin was continued eight and a half years. In October, 1788, he applied to the Presbytery of Carlisle for a relief from his charge. The commissioners of the congregation had not been instructed to acquiesce in this application, but they presented a memorial showing that their financial affairs were not in a healthy condition. The church was cited to appear at the next meeting and show cause why Mr Martin's request should not be granted, and a committee consisting of Rev Messrs Black, McKnight, and Henderson, with Elders John Linn, Robert McPherson, and James McKnight, was directed to meet at Piney Creek on the first Tuesday of December and inquire into the condition of affairs.

The committee reported, April 15, 1789, that the whole amount paid Mr Martin in nine years was £612 12s 8d, that £297 7s 4d were still due, that for his fut[illegible] [illegible], raise seventy

pounds per annum, and will only be responsible for forty pounds of the said sum The pastoral relation was therefore unanimously dissolved, and the congregation was directed to use every honorable effort to liquidate their indebtedness to Mr Martin At the same meeting Mr Martin accepted a call to East and West Penn's Valley Warrior Mark, and Half-Moon, in Pennsylvania within the present bounds of the Presbytery of Huntingdon Here he labored until his death, J[illegible] 20, 1795 He was a native of the County Down of Ireland He came to this country before its independence was declared, and labored for a season in South Carolina Piney Creek was his first settlement here, though he had preached for some years in his native land He was one of the original members of the Presbytery of Huntingdon, which was constituted April 14, 1795 He died at the age of sixty-seven, and was buried in Penn's Valley, where he resided after he moved to Maryland Tradition speaks of him as an able and popular preacher He is said to have been a very earnest and animated speaker Like all the preachers of that day, and those especially of the denomination from which he originally came, his sermons were long, perhaps seldom less than an hour and a half and sometimes considerably longer On a warm summer day it was not unusual for him to take off his coat and preach in his shirt-sleeves In the pulpit he was very forgetful of himself and his personal appearance, so intensely was he taken up in his subject He would first take off his coat, then begin to loosen his cravat, and conclude by taking off his wig, holding it in his hand and shaking it in the face of the congregation, and sometimes during the course of his sermon his wig would become awry, the back part turned to the front, and he utterly unconscious of the metamorphosis Surely a man of such earnestness was above and beyond the ridicule of the profane Mr Martin was twice married His first wife was Annie McCullough, his second, Ellen Davidson, of York County After his death she returned to her home She had no children Mr Martin had four sons,—James, Samuel, John, and Robert

The pulpit remained vacant for several years after Mr Martin's resignation, and depended upon the Presbytery for preaching and the administration of the sacraments The process of liquidating their indebtedness went on slowly

In October, 1792, a statement of accounts between the congregation and their late pastor showed a remaining indebtedness of £96 17s 11*d* The only other reference to the subject is in April, 1793, when the people are [illegible] directed to take all proper means to secure a speedy discharge of their obligations to Mr Martin

In August, 1793, the advice of the Presbytery was sought in the following case "A certain widow of Piney Creek, with her husband in his lifetime, applied to a certain man who passed under the name of a gospel minister and had the ordinance of baptism in appearance administered to her two children, but it was afterwards discovered that the said administrator had never been authorized by any regular church of Christ to act as a gospel minister" The Presbytery decided the act of the impostor to be invalid, and advised that the children be baptized by a regularly ordained minister

In October, 1801, the Piney Creek Church, which had been vacant since the resignation of Mr Martin, April 15, 1789, extended a call to Mr Davidson, offering him £87 10s for one-half of his ministerial and pastoral services A commissioner informed the Presbytery that Tom's Creek had been consulted, and had agreed that Mr Davidson's services should be divided between the two congregations The call was accordingly presented to Mr Davidson, and upon his acceptance of it the arrangement was consummated

Tom's Creek and Piney Creek were now for the first time in a period of forty years united under the same pastor The union then established has, however, been continued with entire harmony through successive pastorates for three-quarters of a century Mr Davidson's labors were continued in the two congregations until the autumn of 1809

At the Presbytery meeting at Carlisle, Sept 26 1810, charges of a serious nature were made against Mr Davidson by Mr Emmit Only six were deemed relevant 1 A charge of fraud and falsehood in a business transaction with said Emmit 2 Of fraud towards the purchasers of certain lots of ground in the above transaction 3 Of falsehood in renting to Anthony Troxel a brick house only and afterwards giving him possession of orchard clover, and garden, though said property was claimed by said Emmit according to contract 4 Of fraud and falsehood (1) in settling an account with Robert Holmes, and (2) in his dealings with Lewis Weaver, wherein he promised to settle with said Weaver before he (Davidson) removed to Frederick, but violated said promise 5 Of cruel and unchristian conduct in ejecting George Hockensmith, wife, and children, with beds and furniture, during a heavy rain, despite all said Hockensmith's entreaties to give him two or three days, for which he would pay him two dollars, and in ref[illegible] to give him time [illegible] his children to [illegible] was provided

for them and already on the table 6 Of a breach of the Sabbath, in June, 1805, in dealing with Solomon Kephart for harvest liquors "

A committee consisting of the Rev John McKnight, D D, chairman, and the Rev Messrs William Paxton and David McConaughy, with Elders Alexander Russel, Walter Smith, and John Eadie, appointed to hear and take testimony in the case, met at the house of Patrick Reed, in Emmittsburg, on the first Tuesday of November, 1810, and entered upon an examination of the charges Mr Davidson declined to make any defense The committee reported to the Presbytery April 11, 1811 The charges were taken up seriatim, and after mature consideration it was decided that none of them had been sustained It was thereupon

"*Resolved*, That the Presbytery declare their high disapprobation of the conduct of William Emmit, in instituting and prosecuting charges evidently unjust, slanderous, and vexatious "

It was also ordered that an attested copy of this resolution be read from the pulpit of the churches

Of the internal and spiritual condition of Piney Creek during Mr Davidson's pastorate little is known In 1806 the total membership was 124, in 1807, 113, in 1808, 108 In 1805 the additions to the church were 10, in 1807, 8, in 1808, 7, in 1809, 9 The baptisms in 1806 were 14, in 1807, 8, in 1808, 24, in 1809, 10, in 1810, 14

The next pastor of the united congregations was the Rev Robert Smith Grier A complete roll of the membership of Piney Creek was prepared in January, 1824, from which it appears that there were then one hundred and forty-four communicants, of these eighty-nine were females Piney Creek had at that date thirty-seven members more than Tom's Creek, and was most probably as strong as at any period of its history Emigration westward by which it has been greatly depleted of late, had not then fairly set in The elders were Alexander Horner, John McAllister, Samuel Thompson, and John Barr Many names then on the list of members have since disappeared The Adairs, the Baldwins, the Blacks, the Darbys, the Fergusons, the Heagys, the McCrearys, the Reids, the Wilsons, and others familiar doubtless to many now living are no longer upon the register

In May, 1825, Catharine Harris, Susan Jamison, Sarah and William Thompson, Rebecca Wilson, Henry Dinwiddie, Amelia Rhinedoller, and Sophia Deukart were received, and in September Robert Flemming and Miss Eliza Graham In 1830 the Session received Jacob Shoemaker, who became a useful member of the church, and was ordained to the eldership in 1838 He died Feb 4, 1869 Mrs Margaret Shoemaker, wife of Jacob, was received at the same time, she was a diffident though a sincere and humble Christian woman At her death, which occurred Oct 26, 1875, it was discovered that she had bequeathed two thousand dollars to the board of the church

John Adair was treasurer of Piney Creek Church from 1814 to 1822, James Barr, from 1822 to 1836 The position of doorkeeper was held by Abraham Shoemaker from 1815 to 1819, James Ross, from 1819 to 1822, Elijah Curren, from 1823 to 1837 The number of persons subscribing to the pastor's salary in 1806 were 95, in 1810, 75, in 1816 and 1817, 100, which appears to be the maximum number so far as can be ascertained The subscriptions ranged from one to ten dollars, the average being about three, and were paid semi-annually

The pastorate of Mr Grier, though covering more than half a century, was quiet and uneventful He lived during a large part of his ministry upon his farm, three miles north of Emmittsburg, and over the line separating Maryland and Pennsylvania After the decease of Mr Grier both churches were supplied for a few months by Rev Daniel B Jackson, then a licentiate, but now pastor of the Black River Falls Church, Wis Early in the summer of 1866 they were visited by the Rev Isaac M Patterson, pastor of the Annapolis Church, and a member of the Presbytery of Baltimore This visit resulted in a call to the pastorate of both churches Mr Patterson commenced his labors early in August, and was installed at Piney Creek November 13th, and on the next day at Emmittsburg Mr Patterson's ministry lasted seven years In the summer of 1873 he resigned his pastoral charge with a view to accept a call to Milford, N J, which is his present field of labor The relations of the present pastor to the united churches of Emmittsburg, Piney Creek, and Taneytown were constituted in December, 1873, by a committee of the Presbytery of Baltimore

In January, 1824, there were in the church at Piney Creek four elders,—Alexander Horner John McAllister, Samuel Thompson, and James Barr —and the following are the names of the communicants

Alexander Horner, Sarah Horner, Eli Horner, Ann Walker, John Horner Ann Thompson, Robert McCreary, Robert Thompson Eleanor Thompson, Ann McCreary, Mary Thompson, Andrew Walker, Maria McCreary, Sarah Horner, James Horner, James Black Jane Black Philip Heagy, Esther Heagy, Jesse Quinn, Margaret Lane, William Walker, William Stevenson, Peggy Stevenson, John McCallister, J W McCallister, Betsy McCallister, Mary McC[illegible] W[illegible], Jane Cor-

nell, Margaret Paxton, William Paxton, Caroline Harris, Jane McCrea, Elijah Baldwin, Matthew Galt, Mary Galt, Elizabeth Galt, Susan Galt, Rebecca Galt, Abraham Linor, Sterling Galt, Margaret Galt, Samuel Galt, Mary Galt, Mary Jones, Elizabeth McCrea, Thompson McCrea, Samuel Thompson, Archibald Clingan, Ann Clingan, William Clingan, Elizabeth Clingan Hugh Thompson, Margaret Snyder, Elijah Baldwin, Elizabeth Baldwin, Mary Baldwin, Kizeah Baldwin, Rachel Miller, Sarah Drummond, James Smith, Sarah Smith, —— Alison, Martha Alison, Mary Ann Alison, Isabella Barr, James Barr, Margaret Barr, Sally Barr, Mary Cornell, Esther Cornell, Sarah Galt, Martha Breckenridge, Margaret Birnie, Hester Birnie Charles Birnie, Hester Birnie, Jr, Rose Birnie, John McKaleb, Mary Jane A[illegible]n, John McKillip, Ann McKillip, Mary Gillelan, Sarah Clanbach, Catherine Musgrove, John Ferguson, Sr, John Ferguson, Rebecca Ferguson, John Adair, Esther Adair, Sarah Adair, Samuel Adair, Hannah Adair, Frances Alison, Margaret Reid, Margaret Reid, Jr, Mary Reid, Weemes Black, Elizabeth Larimore, Lucind McCalister, Thomas McCune Thomas McCune, Jr, Mary McCune, John Thompson, Andrew Guin, Margaret Hunter, Susanna Hunter, Jane Hunter, Elizabeth Hunter, John Hunter, Andrew Horner, Margaret Horner, William Horner, Elizabeth Horner, Nancy Bentley, John Darby, Catharine Darby, Elizabeth Smith, Mary Wilson, Jane Wilson, John Wilson Betsy Larimore, George Guin, Elizabeth Baldwin, John McClanahan, Ann McClanahan, James McCalester, James McCalister, Jr, Mary McCalister, Alexander McCalister, James McIlhenny, Maria McIlhenny, Sally McIlhenny, Robert McKinney, Susanna McKinney, Esther McKinney, James Smith, Jane Longwell, Sally Jamison, Miss Jamison, Kitty (colored), Jack (colored)

The following is a list of the persons subscribing to the pastor's salary in the year 1817

Adair, John
Adair, Samuel
Alison, Francis
Alexander, William
Armstrong, Isaac
Barr, James
Breckinridge William
Black, James
Birnie, Clotworthy
Baldwin, Daniel
Beard, William
Breckinridge, Widow
Brannon, Margaret
Cornall, Thomas
Cornall, William
Crabbs, John
Currens, Elijah
Currens, William
Cornall, Jesse
Cornall, Smith
Clingan, Archibald
Clingan, William
Crabster, John
Crabster, John, Jr
Darby, John
Dorborrow Isaac
Drummond, James
Ferguson, John
Ferguson, William
Galt, John
Galt, Matthew
Guin, George
Galt, Moses
Gilliland, John
Guin, Andrew
Gurdin, Mary
Horner, Alexander
Hill, Hannah
Hunter, Joseph
Horner, William
Horner, Andrew
Horner, John
Hunter, John
Heagy, Philip
Hays, Joseph
Hunter, Susanna
Heagy, George
Jamison, Widow
Jamison, John
Jones, John
Lion, James
Linn, Samuel
Love Robert
Leech, Robert
Linah, Abraham.
Larimore, Thomas
Linn, Samuel, Jr
Little, Susanna
McCreary, Robert
McAlister, John
McAlister, James
McKaleb, John
McKillip, John
McCune Thomas
McIlvane, Moses
Major, Robert
McKinney, John
McCune, Thomas
McIlhenny, John
McCrea, Elizabeth
McCrea, Thomson
Musgrove, Samuel
McIlhenny, James
Paxton, William
Paxton, Thomas
Paxton, Margaret
Ross, James
Robinson, Robert
Reed, Francis
Smith, Samuel
Smith, James
Stevenson, William
Shoemaker, William
Snyder, Nicholas
Shaw, Hugh
Six, George
Sink, George
Smith, Obadiah
Shoemaker, Abraham
Stevenson, James
Thomson, John
Thomson, Samuel
Thomson, Robert
Thomson, Hugh
Wilson, William
Walker, Mary.
Walker, William
Wilson, Charles, Jr
Wharton, James
Weems, Fanny
Walker, Andrew

Rev Sterling M Galt was born in Taneytown District, Carroll Co, Md, Feb 28, 1837 He was the son of Sterling Galt, a wealthy and influential citizen of the county and a descendant of one of the oldest settlers He entered Princeton College, and pursued a thorough course of study both in the academic and theological departments He was licensed to preach by the Presbytery of New Brunswick in 1861 He began his ministrations at Newark and Red Clay Creek, Del, within the bounds of the Presbytery of New Castle, where he was ordained in 1862 and installed pastor of these churches After three years of incessant labor in this his only charge, he fell a victim to typhoid fever, Oct 24, 1865

Piney Creek has done her share to replenish the ministerial ranks John W Smith was the only son of Stephen and Frances Smith He entered himself as a student of Pennsylvania College, at Gettysburg, and studied at the same time for the Presbyterian ministry He was a young man of talent and gave promise of eminent usefulness, but was taken off by disease, May 26, 1872, in the twentieth year of his year The inscription upon his tombstone in Piney Creek graveyard tells that "he was a candidate for the ministry"

Rev James Grier Breckinridge, son of Robert and Mary Grier Breckinridge, and brother of Mrs Matilda Allison, of Emmittsburg, was born in Carroll County, Md, May 30, 1808 His parents were members of the Piney Creek Church His mother was a daughter of Rev James Grier, a convert of Whitefield, and pastor of the Deep Run Church, Bucks County, Pa, from 1776 to 1791 Mr Breckinridge received his collegiate education at Dickinson College, studied theology at Princeton, and was licensed by the Presbytery [illegible] of 1831 he

assisted in protracted services held at Bedford, Pa., after which he supplied the Bedford Church for some months. In May, 1833, a colony of thirty members from this congregation formed a new church at Schellsburg, of which Mr. Breckinridge became the first pastor. Accompanied by his wife he attended the sessions of the Carlisle Presbytery, at Chambersburg, in October, 1833. After the adjournment they visited their relatives in Carroll County, Md., and while there were prostrated by an attack of typhoid fever, from which neither of them recovered. Mr. Breckinridge died Nov. 1, 1833, when but twenty-six years of age, and Mrs. Breckinridge on the 19th of the same month, aged thirty years. They were both buried in the graveyard of Piney Creek Church.

John Motter Annan, the son of Dr. Andrew and Elizabeth Motter Annan, was born in Emmittsburg, Md., March 17, 1841. Early in life he exhibited a decided predilection for the church, and with a view to prepare for the ministry entered Lafayette College Sept. 7, 1859. At the breaking out of the civil war he left school and joined the Union army, enlisting in Company C, First Regiment of the Potomac Home Brigade, Maryland Cavalry, Capt. John Horner, of which company he was chosen first lieutenant. While at Camp Thomas, Frederick, Md., before the company had been in active service, he was accidentally killed by the discharge of a carbine in the hands of a soldier with whom he was conversing, Nov. 13, 1861. He was a young man of some talent, and possessed of moral qualities which would have made themselves felt in the community had he lived and carried out his original intentions.

The pastors of the Piney Creek Church have been:

1763-70, vacant, with occasional supplies; 1771-76, Rev. Joseph Rhea; 1776-80, vacant, with occasional supplies; 1780-89, Rev. James Martin; 1789-1800, vacant, with occasional supplies; 1801-10, Rev. Patrick Davidson; 1811-13, vacant, with occasional supplies; 1814-66, Rev. Robert S. Grier; 1866-73, Rev. Isaac M. Patterson; 1873, Rev. William Simonton.

Taneytown is the oldest village in Carroll County. It was laid out about the year 1750 by Frederick Taney, who came from Calvert County, Md. It is situated on the main road from Frederick to York, Pa., and prior to the Revolutionary war, and for many years afterwards, was the principal thoroughfare between the North and South. Frederick Taney, the founder of the town, was a member of the family of Roger B. Taney, the late eminent chief justice of the Supreme Court of the United States, whose remains now repose in a cemetery in Frederick after a grand but stormy career, in which heroic devotion to duty and extraordinary judicial acumen were so faithfully illustrated that his bitterest enemies have united to do justice to his memory. The ancestors of Frederick Taney were among the earliest settlers in the province of Maryland, and were large landed proprietors in Calvert County for many generations before his birth. Raphael Taney, in conjunction with Edward Digges, patented a tract of seven thousand nine hundred acres of land in this vicinity in 1754, but the Taney estate passed into other hands many years ago. The Good family succeeded by purchase to Taneytown. The land eventually fell into the hands of an old bachelor named Taney, who was a hard drinker. When not in his cups he was crusty and disagreeable, and could not be brought to entertain a proposition for the disposal of his property. Certain parties familiar with his habits, and anxious to secure the land, probably for speculative purposes, plied him with liquor, and when reduced to the convenient state of intoxication induced him to sign the papers which conveyed away his property. From the Good family the property descended by inheritance to the Gwinns, and from them, by sale and otherwise to John McCaleb, the most extensive owner, Crouse, McKellip, Swope, Knox, Birnie, Rudisel, Hess, Null, Galt, and other families, until to-day there are but few acres within a radius of several miles around the town owned by parties bearing the names of those who were the proprietors sixscore years ago. Exception must be noted in the case of Sterling Galt. His estate has been the homestead of the family for one hundred and thirty-five years. In the original plan of Taneytown it was intended that a public square should be placed at the intersection of York Street and the Emmittsburg pike, now known as Bunker Hill, but the idea, an excellent one, was never carried out.

On a lot at the southeast angle of the intersection above mentioned, and directly opposite the residence of John Reindollar, stood the oldest house in the village, supposed to have been built one hundred and forty-five years ago. When Peter Heck was a boy, in 1790, it was a very old house. It was owned by Mrs. Margaret Angel, and in 1876 it was taken down.

In the latter part of the eighteenth century there stood on or near what is now the lime-kiln in Taneytown a long, low frame building, in which were manufactured, by a Mr. Sroyer, such implements as fire-shovels, tongs, hoes, nails, and guns. The venerable Mrs. Elizabeth Thompson has in her possession a heavy pair of tongs made at this primitive factory, on which is inscribed the date of manufacture, 1796. The establishment was under the supervision of the

government, or at least that portion which embraced the manufacture of firearms, and was annually visited and inspected by government officials. The machinery was very crude and simple. Instead of the belts, pulleys, emery-wheels, and ordinary appurtenances of a modern factory, regulated by steam, and by means of which a gun barrel or other iron implements can be polished in a few moments, the only contrivance then known and used was a huge grindstone turned by an old horse. With these limited facilities, however, many guns were made for the government. The factory burned down early in the present century, and was never rebuilt, the government factory having been subsequently transferred to Harper's Ferry, Va.

Taneytown, situated on the great highway of travel between the North and South, doubtless witnessed more of the conflict between Tory and Federal partisans than has been recorded or remembered. On more than one occasion the British and their allies rendezvoused at the head-waters of the Elk, in Cecil County, and sent out marauding parties, who ravaged the country and committed many outrages which time has suffered to lapse into oblivion. It would be strange, indeed, if in some of their raids they had not directed their energies against the rich country now forming Carroll County, and the road passing through Taneytown offered inducements of no ordinary nature to the baser class of army followers. The most annoying feature of these raids must have been the idiotic search made for prominent patriots. Houses were entered, the inmates insulted, and the furniture ransacked and broken to pieces. The late Mrs. Elizabeth Galt, whose death occurred some thirty-five years ago, was wont to exhibit with pride to interested visitors several bed-quilts which in "the days that tried men's souls" had been perforated by the swords or bayonets of the soldiers in search of some victim. The fires of patriotism burned very brightly in the vicinity of Taneytown, and Tories were seldom rash enough to brave the anger of the people by an open expression of their sentiments. The martial spirit pervaded the neighborhood. A company of light horse was organized here, of which the father of Mrs. Elizabeth Thompson, an old and highly esteemed resident, was a member. They were accustomed to assemble for drill at stated times in full regimentals in what is now known as "the race-ground field," a short distance east of the village. As the country had need of every soldier that could be spared from the ordinary avocations of life, it is probable that this company took the field early in the struggle and combated gallantly for the rights of the people. On one occas[illegible] the Revolution Gen. Washington, accompanied by his wife, halted in Taneytown on his way North to join the army, and remained there overnight. The log house, since then covered in with a casement of brick, still stands where the general and his wife passed the night. It is the building on Frederick Street now owned and occupied by Ephraim Hackensmith, but at that time kept as a tavern by Adam Good. Many old citizens remember the quaint sign which hung above the door, and whose creaking of a chill winter's night, accompanied by the shrill blasts of wind, filled the souls of the small fry with awe and dread, suggesting ghosts and hobgoblins to their impressionable minds. It is related of Washington that when asked what he would have for supper he replied "mush and milk," and Mrs. Washington having some leisure moments during the evening, drew from her reticule an unfinished stocking and began to knit. After the death of Adam Good, the proprietor of the inn where the distinguished guests were entertained, his furniture was sold at auction, and Matthew Galt, the father of Sterling Galt, purchased the table upon which the very modest supper was served to Gen. Washington and his wife. It has since then passed through a number of hands in the same family, and is now the property of John McKellip.

As far as is known there are no other existing relics or vestiges of colonial times, save the almost undistinguishable remains of an old burial-ground about a mile and a half southwest of the village, in the woods, on the farm of William Brubaker. The only stone remaining upon which characters can be traced is one bearing the date 1764. Mr. Brubaker has a stone taken from there on which is inscribed the date 1701. Inasmuch as the oldest inhabitants have no knowledge of those buried there, and that there has been no mention made of the spot for several successive generations, it is inferred that the pioneers of this section, persons who penetrated the wilderness before the advent of Taney or the building of Taneytown, were laid to rest in this spot of ground, and that many friendly Indians are peacefully sleeping their last sleep in company with their white brethren. The tribes of Indians scattered through this region in early days were on the most friendly terms with the whites, and tradition tells of a friendly contest in marksmanship which took place many years before the Revolution between the whites and Indians in the vicinity of Taneytown. There were excellent marksmen on both sides, and the struggle was prolonged until all the lead was used up. An Indian offered to bring them within an hour an abundance of lead if they would [illegible] furnished with

a fleet horse and the hour had scarcely expired when he returned bringing with him a huge lump of crude lead Where he got it has always been a mystery At the time efforts were made to induce the Indians to reveal the whereabouts of this lead mine, but the red men were too wary for the whites, and no expedient could draw from them a disclosure of their secret This vein of lead is popularly supposed to be somewhere near Monocacy Creek, but repeated attempts have been made to discover it without success

During the war of 1812 a company of volunteers was organized in Taneytown, and commanded by Capt Knox and Lieut Galt, and forty men responded to the call of the United States government during the war between the North and South, some of whom laid down their lives in defense of the Union

In 1836 an act was passed by the General Assembly of Maryland incorporating the inhabitants of Taneytown, and prescribing the following metes and bounds for the municipality Beginning at the southwest corner of lot number one, at the public square of the town, thence in a straight line to a stone planted at the fork of the road leading from Taneytown to Westminster and Uniontown, thence a straight line to a branch where it crosses the main road leading from Taneytown to Frederick town, at Ludwick Rudisel's tan-yard, and down the bed of said branch to its intersection with Spark's Run, thence in a straight line to Piney Run, where said run crosses the main road leading from Taneytown to Gettysburg, thence by a straight line to a spring run, where said run crosses the main road leading from Taneytown to Littlestown, where said run passes into John McKaleb's meadow, thence in a straight line to a stone planted at the fork of the roads leading from Taneytown to Westminster and Uniontown, thence in a straight line to the place of beginning And that the taxable limits of the said town shall be as follows including all that part of the town now improved, or which the citizens may at any time hereafter improve

In 1838 another act of Assembly was passed supplementary to the above, and changing somewhat the boundaries of the town, but as both of the acts were allowed to expire by limitation it is not necessary to give the latter here The village is accredited by the census of 1880 with a population of five hundred and nineteen

The Reformed Church was among the first places of worship established in Taneytown There are no records preserved of a date prior to 1770 In that year Rev W Faber accepted the pastorate, and remained in charge of the church until 1785 The next pastor was old Mr N[illegible] lemius, who was deaf as a post He ministered to the spiritual wants of the congregation between 1790 and 1800 His successor was Rev W Rahauser, a young man who remained but a short time He was followed by Rev W Runkle who came from Germantown, Pa, and is reputed to have been an excellent preacher He did not stay longer than one year The congregation at that time numbered about six hundred members Father Greeves succeeded Mr Runkle He remained several years, and was then called to Woodstock, Va Jacob Helfenstein succeeded him, and was noted for his zeal and anxious-bench system Rev W Aurand followed, and created some difficulty about his salary, which is still remembered in the neighborhood Father Greeves was recalled, and remained in charge of the congregation until his death leaving a good name behind him The church was now vacant for some time Rev N Hibbert, of the Presbyterian denomination, was subsequently called, and promised to connect himself with the German Reformed Church, but never did At this time Rev W Leidy officiated, and preached in the German language He is said to have been very eccentric During this period the congregation thinned out considerably After the departure of Mr Leidy the charge was vacant until Rev W Heiner settled in Emmittsburg and took the church under his pastoral charge In 1838, Rev Daniel Felte took charge of the congregation, and served until June, 1841 He was followed by Rev J G Wolf, who retired from the charge June 1, 1850, and was succeeded by Rev Charles M Jameson in February, 1851 Mr Jameson remained only a year, when Rev John G Fritchey was called He entered upon his duties April 1, 1852, and was installed pastor of the charge June 7, 1852, by a committee consisting of the following divines William F Colliflower, M Shuford, and George Hughenbaugh Rev W F Colliflower preached the installation sermon At a meeting in June, 1854, the number of elders was increased to four

At a joint consistorial meeting, held at Mount Union church on Nov 28, 1864, Rev John G Fritchey tendered his resignation, which after some consideration was accepted with a great deal of reluctance A call was then extended to the Rev N E Gibbs, of St Clairsville, Bedford Co, Pa who accepted the same, and entered upon the pastoral work in May, 1865 After two years he resigned the charge to accept a call to Mechanicstown In September, 1873, Rev P D Long of Navarre, Ohio, was called to the charge by a unanimous vote of the congregation He took charge of the church Nov 14, 187[illegible], and [illegible] 1-71

This congregation worshiped in the "Old Yellow" Union church until 1822 On Sept 6, 1821, the corner stone of their present edifice was laid, the sermon and services being delivered by Rev J B Winebrenner The estimated cost of their church was about three thousand five hundred dollars, the members numbering about two hundred at that time The church has since been remodeled and repaired, and now presents a handsome appearance Their parsonage, which is occupied by the present pastor, was built in 1848 The congregation numbers about two hundred members and the officers are David Buffington, Wm Hough, Joshua Houtz, Abraham Shriner, elders, Thomas Shriner, Jonas Harner, James Shriner, Michael N Fringer, deacons, Abraham Hess, Wm Fisher, Americus Shoemaker, and Toba Fringer, trustees

Among the persons buried in the German Reformed Cemetery are the following

Elizabeth Blum, died Nov 30, 1831, aged 11 years

John Shriner, born March 18, 1796, died July 24, 1874 and Susanna, his wife March 12, 1818, aged 40 years

Rachel Newcomer, wife of Samuel, died Jan 29, 1849, aged 38 years, 10 months, 2 days

Lydia, daughter of J Shriner, born Dec 26, 1837, died July 6, 1865

Sarah Clabaugh, aged 64

Jacob Clabaugh, aged 48

John J, son of J Hann, died Nov 6, 1830, aged 2

Henry Hann, died Sept 12, 1812, aged 71

Elizabeth Hann, died June 10, 1821, aged 71

John Hann died June 10, 1830, aged 34

William Hann, son of J Hann, died Oct 3, 1835, aged 20

Naumary A Lindau, died Sept 11, 1787, aged 27

A Bigail Land, died June 23, 1819, aged 29

Nicholas Lind, died Feb 21, 1823, aged 73 years, 3 months, 4 days

Harmon Hersh, died November, 1818, aged 75

Susan E Baemer, born January, 1731, died September, 1804

Philip Baemer, born 1729, died 1806

Elizabeth Baemer, born Sept 2, 1779, died Nov 1, 1805

Elizabeth Baemer, born Oct 26, 1806, died Dec 20, 1806

Catharine, wife of Jacob Hape, died Sept 29, 1838

George Koons, born Jan 21, 1790, died March 12, 1815

Matthias Hann, died Feb 17, 1831, aged 92 years, 9 months

Mary Hann, died March 29, 1829, aged 72 years

Elizabeth Koons, died April 19, 1830, aged 35

John Fuss, died Feb 4, 1826, aged 29 years, 2 months, 22 days

Daniel Fuss, died July 29, 1834, aged 47 years, 2 months, 9 days

John Fuss, born May 20, 1754, died Jan 25, 1836

John Crubb, died Feb 11, 1829, aged 62

Mary A Fuss, died June 14, 1831, aged 38 years, 9 months, 12 days

Catharine Fuss died Sept 20, 1849, aged 62 years, 5 months, 12 days

Mary, wife of John Fuss, died May 27, 1840, aged 80 years

Elizabeth, consort of J H Hays died Jan 4, 1846, aged 30

James Slick, died Dec 22, 1814, aged 33 years, 10 days

Nicholas Fringer born Aug 27, 1751, died July 12, 1810

Margaret Fringer, died Aug 12, 1850, aged 86

George Fringer, died Oct 20, 1846, aged 43 years, 10 months, 20 days

Wilhelm Slick, died March 20, 1804, aged 49 years

Rebecca Homer, died 1806

W Hiner, died April 8, 1801 aged 32

Mary Hiner, died Dec 15 1808, aged 61

Herbert Hiner, died Oct 16, 1806, aged 65

Henry Koontz, of John, died July 30, 1825, aged 50 years 6 months, 8 days, and Margaret, his wife, Jan 27, 1835, aged 52 years, 7 months

Peter Shriner, born Oct 25, 1767, died Aug 5, 1861

Mary Shriner, born Aug 6, 1773, died March 17, 1811

Cot Munshower, born March, 1737, died in 1792

Nicholas Munshower, born 1743 died Oct 1, 1814

Conrad Orndorff, born Sept 10, 1722, died Nov 26, 1795

Mary B Shriner, born Aug 9, 1770, died Sept 1, 1825

Henry Shriner, born Feb 15, 1765, died April 11, 1835

William Otto, died Dec 26, 1806, aged 61 years, 2 months

E Burke, 1866

John Kehn, died March 9, 1868, aged 80 years, 6 months 27 days

Louis Reindollar, died Jan 10, 1848, aged 67 years, 8 months

Henry Reindollar, died July 7, 1830, aged 51 years

Rebecca Starr, died May 8, 1851, aged 21 years, 3 months, 1 day

Elizabeth McKellip, wife of James, and daughter of H Reindollar, Sept 2, 1851, aged 24

James Reindollar, died April 8, 1825, aged 22

John Kraus, born 1737, died 1777

Joseph Crouse, died May 1, 1850, aged 52 years 11 months, Elizabeth, his wife, died Oct 26, 1850, aged 52 years, 2 months

George Krabbs, died March 27, 1810, aged 65

John Six, died May 15, 1865, aged 79 years, 9 days, and Sarah A, his wife, born March 11, 1809, died March 26, 1874

Catharine Heagy, died March 8, 1852, aged 42 years, 6 months, 7 days

Samuel Heagy, died Oct 15, 1837, aged 56 years, 9 months, 6 days

George Keefer, died Jan 25, 1831, aged 55 years 4 months, 26 days

Joseph Shanor, died Aug 24, 1880, aged 79

David Fleagle, died Jan 4, 1865, aged 79 years, 7 months, 15 days

Margaret, his wife, died Sept 12, 1844, aged 45 years, 5 months, 22 days

Benjamin Koons, died May 14, 1851, aged 41 years, 1 month 10 days

Polly Frock, born Oct 9, 1817, died March 15, 18[illegible]

Philip Frock, born June 14, 1813, died April 16, 1863

Daniel Frock, born June 30, 1777, died May 30, 1857

Elizabeth, his wife, born Feb 9, 1779, died May 22, 1857

John Frock, born Dec 18, 1801, died May 14, 1858 and Mary, his wife, Aug 5, 1875, aged 68 years

Ann, wife of J Shaner, born Oct 25, 1805, died March 20, 1874

Abraham Haugh, died Oct 17, 1835, aged 18 years, 5 months, 18 days

Paul Haugh, Jr, died June 15, 1819, aged 1 year

Josiah Haugh, died March 13, 1820, aged 18

Susannah, consort of John Crapster, born July 1, 1766, died June 23, 1855

Walter O'Neal, died June 27, 1827, aged 31 years, 6 months

Margaret Wilt, died Nov 25, 1869, aged 45 years, 6 months, 25 days

John Weant, died Sept 11 1858, aged 81 years
Catharine his wife, died Aug 26, 1833, aged 71 years
Jacob Weant died July 2, 1850, aged 44 years
Peter Ondorff, died Jan 16, 1847, aged 58 years, 5 months, 11 days and Elizabeth, his wife, died Nov 20, 1851, aged 60 years, months 20 days
Henry Kiser, died June 30, 1850, aged 47 years, 19 days
Phoebe, his wife, died Oct 27, 1870, aged 65 years, 8 months, 11 days
Mary Heiner, born May 28, 1793, died May 17, 1837
John Cover born 1798, died 1864 and Susan, his wife, Oct 3, 1876, aged 78
Peter Ridinger, born Oct 28, 1793, died May 11, 1812
Henry Keefer, died Aug 10, 18 aged years, 8 months, 2 days
Christiana Koons, died June 23, 1841, aged 33 years, 4 months, 23 days
Jacob Koons, died May 22, 1879, aged 68 years, 5 months, 21 days, and Elizabeth, his wife, March 28, 1861, aged 47 years, 4 months
Catharine wife of Jacob Koons Sr, died Feb 15, 1846, aged 60 years 11 months, 19 days
Jacob Koons, Sr, died Dec 31, 1844, aged 68 years, 1 month, 28 days
Margaret, wife of Jacob Koons, Jr, died June 8 1848, aged 39
Thomas Keefer, born Jan 8, 1797, died aged 53 years, 4 months, 29 days
Ephriam Koons, died Oct 14, 1856, aged 42 years
Rev John Lantz, pastor of the German Reformed Church, died Jan 26, 1877, aged 62
Daniel Sell, died Nov 19, 1874 aged 90 years, 10 months, 10 days
Mary, his wife, died Feb 28, 1874, aged 85 years, 20 days
Samuel Longwell Sr, died Aug 21, 1854 aged 86 years, 6 months, 15 days, and Margaret, his wife, Jan 1, 1845, aged 65 years, 3 months
Joseph Bergan Sr, died June 17, 1842, aged 65
Robert Arthur, died Feb 23, 1860, aged 88
Agnes Arthur, died March 11, 1816, aged 64
Paul Haugh, Sr, died March 5, 1847, aged 67 years, 1 month, 16 days
Elizabeth Rech, died Dec 25, 1845, aged 55 years, 6 months, 17 days
Abraham Hitesbew, born March 28, 1789, died Aug 1, 1875
Catharine, his wife, died April 3, 1858, aged 69
Henry Koons born Jan 18, 1789, died Dec 25 1853
Emily Koons, died April 2, 1867, aged 39 years, 11 months, 18 days
Jacob Keefer, born March 28, 1780, died Sept 28, 1855
Catharine Keefer, died March 29, 1859, aged 68 years, 6 months 15 days
Isaac Newcomer, died April 10, 1870, aged 55 years, 5 months, 23 days
Jacob Newcomer, died Jan 5, 1869, aged 61 years, 8 months, 5 days
George Crabbs, Sr, died Jan 6, 1859, aged 65 years, 10 months, 16 days
Hugh Thomson, died Dec 18 1852, aged 68
Nicholas Snider, born May 9, 1786, died June 11, 1856
Margaret, his wife, died July 20, 1865, aged 86 years
Ann, wife of George Shriner, died July 16, 1853, aged 72 years
Elizabeth, wife of John Slogenhaupt, died March 18, 1865, aged 48 years, 2 months, 2 days
Elizabeth Fleagle, died March 19, 1871, aged 50 years, 4 months, 20 days

Mary A, his second wife, died Oct 17, 1854, aged 27 years, 1 month, 11 days
Francis Shick, died Feb 8, 1857, aged 63
Magdalena Shick, born Nov 26, 1790, died April 6, 1853
John Fleagle, died Dec 24, 187, aged 93 years, 2 months, 15 days
Susanna Fleagle, died April 23, 1851, aged 76 years, 2 months, 11 days
Samuel Newcomer, died July 4, 1848, aged 75 years, 7 months, 1 day
Barbara Newcomer, died March 6, 1853, aged 7 years
John Henry, son of J and B Ocker, born Feb 10, 1841, died April 30, 1862, "of typhoid fever, whilst a volunteer in the defense of his country's honor"
Jacob, son of J and B Ocker, "killed on Maryland Heights by an explosion, June 30, 1863," aged 21 years, 10 months, 28 days "He was beloved by his officers and companions, and was a faithful and obedient son to a widowed mother"
Mary Wilson, died May 16, 1861, aged 78
Michael Ott, born Oct 16, 1793, died May 20, 1872
Mary, his wife, born Dec 12 1796, died Oct 10, 1871
Isabella G Keaver, died March 11, 1880, aged 45 years, 7 months
Lewis Mins, born Nov 8, 1777, died Sept 26, 1826
"D M" died 1817
Daniel Hawn, born Sept 9, 1802, died Jan 30, 1877, Magdalena, his wife, born Oct 9, 1801, died March 25, 1877
Wm Shaner, born Feb 2, 1798, died June 16, 1850, Rosanna Shaner, died Feb 12, 1868, aged 67 years, 10 months, 18 days
Henry Hiner, born Jan 28, 1836, died Oct 23, 1875
Eleanor Fleagal, died March 31, 1839, aged 43 years, 2 months, 15 days Sarah wife of John Stockslayer, born July 22, 1795, died June 15, 1865
Mary Hawn, died Dec 19, 1872, at an old age
Henry Hawn, born Dec 10, 1781, died Jan 25, 1857, Anna M, his wife, died Aug 9, 1859, aged 64 years, 7 months, 6 days
Matthias Hawn, born Feb 20, 1794, died April 1, 1858
Jacob Hawn, born Nov 6, 1785, died May 25, 1878
Elizabeth, wife of Samuel Hough, died March 26, 1877, aged 50 years, 9 months, 27 days
Reuben Stonesifer, died Dec 1, 1876, aged 52 years, 8 months, 16 days
Elizabeth Tracy, died Aug 7, 1878, aged 90
John Angel, died April 16, 1872, aged 72 years, 5 months, 9 days
Magdalena Angel, died Feb 18, 1880, aged 42 years, 3 months, 21 days
Elizabeth Angel, wife of John A Sr, died Jan 18, 1861, aged 61 years, 7 months, 22 days
Elizabeth, wife of Samuel Hough, died March 26, 1877, aged 50 years, 9 months, 27 days
Harvey T, son of S and M Null, who fell at Loudon Heights, Jan 10, 1864 aged 21 years months, 25 days
"Sweet be the slumbers of him who fell for his country fighting for liberty and law"
Jacob Shriner, born Jan 5, 1800, died April 13, 1874, Catharine, his wife, died Feb 6, 1865, aged 63 years, 9 mos, 23 days
Mary Ann Stultz, died Aug 4, 1879, aged 55 years, 1 months, 19 days
Ann Stultz, born Jan 31, 1804, died Jan 28, 1875
Samuel F Stultz, born Sept 20, 1835, died Aug 10 1870
Maria Smith, died Feb 13, 1871, aged 37 years
Eli Sowers, born Jan 6, 1805, died Nov 3, 1878 Elizabeth, his wife, and daughter of Peter Shriner, died Sept 16, 1838, aged 61 years [illegible]

Wm Newcomer, died Jan 10, 1872, aged 40

Henry Peters, died Dec 4, 1872, aged 63 years 1 month, 28 days

Samuel Newcomer, born Oct 30, 1807, died April 19, 1877, Frances, his wife, born July 16, 1807, died Feb 14, 1878

Philip Hann, born Oct 22, 1777, died Dec 31, 1863, Elizabeth, his wife, died March 10, 1860, aged 78 years, 10 days

Philip W Hann, died April 8, 1867, aged 67 years, Susannah, his wife, died March 29, 1864, aged 78 years

Frederick Dotteren, died Aug 25, 1851, aged 66 years, 1 month, 5 days

Lydia, wife of John Shoemaker, born Aug 14, 1798, died Feb 15, 1867

Esther Shoemaker, died Nov 20, 1861, aged 86 years, 1 month, 15 days

Joseph Shoemaker, died March 28, 1863, aged 57 years, 2 months, 1 day

John Davidson, born May 12, 1795, died Dec 23, 1873, Margaret, his wife, born July 11, 1793, died March 30, 1872

Mary E, wife of George Baird, died Nov 5, 1867, aged 72 years, 12 days

Frederick Crabbs, died Oct 3, 1861, aged 62 years, 4 months, 23 days, Matilda, his wife, died Jan 13, 1878, aged 79 years, 7 months, 8 days

George W McConkey, born Sept 20, 1799, died June 30, 1880, Eliza, his wife, died Dec 27, 1876, aged 71

Jesse Heck, born March 3, 1807, died Sept 4, 1866

James Crouse, died March 27, 1868, aged 68

Elizabeth Crouse, died Feb 11, 1877, aged 68

Barbara, wife of George Crise, died Nov 5, 1873, aged 82 years, 4 months, 12 days

Sarah, wife of James Heck, died March 28, 1872, aged 63 years, 3 months, 3 days

Susanna, wife of Philip Shriner, died Aug 10, 1863, aged 83 years, 10 months, 27 days

John Koons, died March 6, 1869, aged 51 years, 11 months, 15 days

John Kuhns, died May 12, 1875, aged 58 years, 7 months, 2 days, Lovey, his wife, died Feb 8, 1868, aged 39 years, 11 months, 22 days

Michael Fringer, died July 12, 1879, aged 72 years, 6 months, 16 days

Nicholas Fringer, born Dec 20, 1798, died Sept 2, 1869

Israel Hiteshue, born Dec 1, 1803, died Sept 13, 1856

Gideon Hiteshue, died April 9, 1865, aged 71 years, Mary Ann, his wife, died June 26, 1879, aged 76 years, 8 months, 19 days

Margaret Arthur, died July 22, 1870, aged 50 years, 4 months, 10 days

Adam Tobias Hokensmith, died Oct 27, 1865, aged 35 years, 7 months, 11 days

George Crabbs, died Jan 6, 1859, aged 65 years, 10 months, 16 days

John Shoemaker, born March 11, 1822, died Feb 2, 1878

Catharine Buffington, aged 44 years, 5 months, 11 days

John M Cover, died Jan 9, 1877, aged 46 years, 3 months, 14 days

J R Harmish, died Feb 23, 1879, aged 49 years, 6 months, 26 days

Lutheran Church—This congregation was organized about the year 1780 They worshiped in the "Old Yellow" church, a structure weather-boarded and painted yellow which was situated on the graveyard lot No regular pastor was employed, but Dr Melsheimer and Dr Runkel, from Gettysburg, delivered sermons to the congregation occasionally in German About the year 1800 the congregation removed to the church they now occupy Rev John Grubb was the regular pastor in 1815 and for some time before, and it was he that first introduced English preaching About the year 1817 he nearly made a failure, owing to his not being familiar with the language He would open his sermon in English, and in his efforts to convey an idea in that language would become confused and finish his expression in German Rev John N Hoffman succeeded Mr Grubb, and was the first regular English pastor He continued in this charge for some years, and was followed by Rev Ezra Keller, who upon resigning his position after some years' services was appointed a professor of the Wittenburg College, Springfield, Ohio Rev Solomon Sentmen was then next pastor, and continued for seventeen years and a half to attend to the duties of the church He was succeeded by Rev Levi T Williams, who occupied the pulpit about seven years Rev Bertgresser followed him, and was succeeded by Rev Williams, whose failing health compelled his resignation, and Rev W H Luckenbach was his successor In 1878 their present pastor, Samuel G Finckel, was called to the church The salary of the pastors was always paid by voluntary subscriptions up to the new organization of the congregation and the remodeling of the church, since when the salary has been raised by assessment, each member paying according to his wealth or worth The present officers are Samuel Shriner, Jacob Sherratts, elders, Charles Hess, Daniel Null, Jacob Mehring, William Crutz, deacons, Dr George T Motter, John Reindollar, David Mehring, John Renner, Elijah Currans, Dr Samuel Swope, trustees The congregation numbers between four and five hundred members, and possesses a fine and substantial parsonage

The following names of persons buried in the Lutheran Cemetery are given

Jacob Snider, born Oct 15, 1796 died Aug 29, 1868, Hester, his wife, died Nov 9, 1871, aged 60 years, 6 months, 22 days

George Snider, died Aug 29, 1871, aged 74 years, 7 months, 14 days

Levi Snider, died May 24, 1874, aged 39 years, 6 months, 10 days

Sarah, wife of J Angell, died Feb 22, 1871, aged 62 years, 1 month, 25 days

Elizabeth Norris, born Aug 20, 1820, died July 1, 1870

Jacob Clutts, died Sept 4, 1870, aged 66 years 7 months, 12 days, Rosanna, his wife, died Dec 21, 1870, aged 63 years, 8 months, 13 days

Wm Reaver, died March 31 1871, aged 58 years 11 months, 12 days

Mary A, wife of Daniel Null, died Feb 1, 1877, aged 43 years, 4 months, 25 days

David Kephart, died Jan 22, 1874, aged 77 years, 0 months, 27 days

Susan his wife, died April 15, 1872, aged 70 years, 8 months

Samuel Crouse, died May 31, 1871, aged 61 years, 3 months, 12 days

George Leifsnider, born April 22, 1803, died May 14, 1869, Catharine his wife, born Sept 21, 1807, died Dec 1, 1846

Daniel H Rudolph, born Oct 5, 1821, died Jan 9, 1871

Amelia Jean, wife of Elijah Currens died April 20, 1880, aged 71 years, 9 months, 7 days

Samuel B Hess, born March 17, 1823, died Sept 12, 1871

John Hess, born Dec 21, 1802, died March 22 1875, Barbara, consort of John Hess, born Aug 30, 1803, died April 3, 1877

John Baumgardner, born Dec 6, 1797, died Feb 15, 1874

Dr John Swope, died Sept 5, 1871, aged 74 years, 1 month

Daniel H Swope, died April 19, 1873, aged 64 years, 7 months

Catharine, wife of John Renner, died Jan 14, 1879, aged 59 years, 10 months, 21 days

Andrew Harner, born Jan 2, 1788, died March 12, 1873, Sarah, his wife born May, 1801, died Oct 1, 1872

Jacob Sheets, died Jan 27, 1826, aged 65 years, 5 months, 26 days "A soldier of the war of 1776 Enlisted under Washington as he passed through Taneytown"

Hannah Sheets, died May 5, 1852, aged 85 years, 4 months, 11 days

Jacob Sheets, died Nov 11, 1866, aged 76 years, 4 months, 6 days

Elizabeth, wife of Wm Koons, died June 5, 1867, aged 74 years, 3 months, 15 days

Mary Null, died Jan 7, 1812, aged 71

Regina Noel, born 1745, died Dec 5, 1812

Valentine Null, died Nov 21, 1815, aged 79

Michael Null, died Feb 15, 1817, aged 70, Anna Maria, his wife, died May 25 1818, aged 80

Michael Null, born Nov 5, 1770, died Dec 11, 1850

Elizabeth Null, born May 7, 1778, died Oct 19, 1856

Abraham Null, born Jan 12, 1799, died April 26, 1851, Mary, his wife, died April 6, 1849, aged 49

Ulrich Richer, aged 79

Margaret Wolf, born Aug 4, 1799, died Dec 5, 1821

Elizabeth Kephart, died June 20, 1814, aged 80 years, 4 months, 12 days

David Kephart, born Nov 17, 1729, died June 5, 1792

Margaret Kephart, died Oct 15, 1852, aged 73

David Kephart, died Nov 24, 1836, aged 74

Joseph Davidson, died Aug 15, 1801, aged 30 years, 6 months

Phinehas Davidson, died March 16, 1798, aged 72 years, 11 months, 20 days

Susan Davidson, died June 12, 1845, aged 64 years, 3 months

James Matthews, died Jan 4, 1872, aged 74

Adam Black, died Dec 18, 1818, aged 74 years, 6 months

Margaret Black, born in 1752, died in 1773

John, son of Lawrence and Hannah Bowers, died Oct 29, 1816 aged 11 days

Frederick Black, died Nov 3, 1826, aged 85

[illegible] Black, daughter of Frederick Black, "who came into this world in the year of our Lord 1785, the 29th day of January, at 9 o clock in the morning," and wife of George [illegible], died Aug 12, 1834, aged 49 years, 6 months, 12 days

Elizabeth Bernhart 1791

Philip Rever, died Nov 2 1845, aged 78

Gritzena Rever, died August, 1841, aged 81

Elizabeth, wife of John B Grobp died April 15, 1835, aged 69

Jacob Buffington, born Aug 10, 1756, died Aug 7, 1831; Mary Magdalena, his wife, died Dec 15, 1840, aged 81 years, 16 days

Peter Schener, died Dec 13, 1790, aged 52

Joshua Delaplane, died Oct 14, 1830, aged 42

Hannah Delaplane, died Aug 4, 1879, aged 93 years, 6 months, 12 days

Wm Cover, born July 1, 1814, died Oct 4, 1824

Wm Jones, born Aug 20, 1796, died Jan 12, 1818

Wm Jones, died Sept 25, 1824, aged 76

James Ielces, died March 4, 1852, aged 57 years, 2 months, 24 days

M M Hess, died April 26, 1841

H A Hess, died April, 18[illegible]

Mary Hess, born May 1, 1797, died March 5, 1850

Samuel Hess, born Nov 11, 1796, died Dec 24, 1873

George Ott, died July 23, 1854, aged 77

John Baumgardner, born Nov 10, 1781, died Sept 6, 1828

Margaret Ott, consort of George, born Sept 8, 1761, died Sept 5, 1828 Her maiden name was Margaret Slothm

Nicholas Ott, died Dec 16, 1853, aged 25 years, 4 months, 21 days

Abraham Herner, born 1803, died 18[illegible]

Susan Neher, born 1802, died ——.

Amanda E Ott, died April 7, 1854, aged 18

Mary E, wife of Wm L Crapster, died April 17, 1818, aged 45 years, 11 months, 7 days, and five of her children, from one to ten years of age

Catharine Swope, daughter of H and E, died Nov 16, 1865, aged 1 year, 5 days

Jesse Swope, son of the same, died Sept 21, 180[illegible], aged 4 years, 6 months, 21 days

Henry Swope, born April 5, 1767, died Feb 13, 1812, Elizabeth, his consort, died June 13, 184[illegible], aged 66 years, 8 months, 18 days

Jacob Sheetz, died Oct 27, 1806, aged 81

Catharine Sheetz, died May 5, 180[illegible] aged 75 years, 4 months, 11 days

Henry Clutz, died Sept 10, 1851, aged 67 years, 14 days

Elizabeth Clutz, born March 12, 1762 died Oct 5, 1821

John D Miller, son of George and Eliza Miller, "who fell in the defense of his country near Petersburg, Va, June 22, 1864," aged 24 years, 2 months, 16 days

Susanna Cover, born Nov 26, 1775, died Feb 7, 1821

Jacob Cover, died Sept 29, 187[illegible], aged 64 years, 9 months

Philip Rudisel, born March 20, 1785, died Nov 21, 1810

Elizabeth Koberger, born 1763, July 23d, died Aug 21, 1801

Lewis Rudisil, born Feb 27, 1783, died Aug 11, 1805

G Rudisil, born March 15, 1770, died March 13, 1795

Maria Rudisil, born Feb 15, 1765, died April 23, 1784

Tobias Rudisil, born April 1, 1736, died March 26, 1816

T Louis Rudisil, born April 7, 1743, died December, 1821

Magdalena Weiwell, died Aug 25, 1796, aged 25 years, 5 months, and 26 days

Michael Sawyer, died Nov 25, 1825, aged 63

Ann Mary, his wife, died Aug 8, 1829, aged 65 years, 1 month, and 16 days

John Feirc, died Dec 13, 1827, aged 42 years, 11 months, and 13 days

Anna B, his wife, died May 25, 1867, aged 75 years, 7 months, and 27 days

Peter Slyder, born July 25, 1759, died May 25, 1840 On his left are his two wives, Mary, born Sept 8, 1763, and died Jan 11, 1796, [illegible] Sept 22, 1830

Jacob Cornell, died July 9, 1863, aged 66 years, 11 months, and 10 days.

Mary Cornell, died Nov 27, 1815, aged 59 years, 8 months, and 6 days

Conrad Shorb, died Oct 16, 1803, aged 77

John Hartman born Sept 8, 1792, died Aug 7, 1870

Hezekiah Harman born Feb 1 1831, died Aug 15, 1866

Elizabeth, wife of John Good, died Sept 29, 1865, aged 56 years 1 month, and 6 days

John Good, born Feb 28, 1802, died May 11, 1879

Samuel Naill, died Oct 19, 1869, aged 8[illegible]

Elizabeth Naill died Jan 27, 1878, aged 76

Elizabeth Naill, wife of Samuel, died Aug 28, 1826, aged 34 years, 9 months, and 25 days

Anna Naill, wife of Jacob Mering, born Feb 8, 1805, died February, 1824

Mary Naill, born Feb 28, 1778, died Nov 17, 1815

Dr Wm B Hibbard, died March 11, 1839, aged 61 Ann, his first wife, died Feb 18, 1835, aged 44

Christian Naill, born Jan 5, 1747, died June 15, 1815

William Naill, died April 6, 1846, aged 67 years 9 months, and 25 days Elizabeth, his wife, died Feb 26, 1853, aged 75

William Naill died June 28, 1868, aged 54 years, 9 months, and 16 days Mary Ann, his wife, died July 11, 1869, aged 54 years, 3 months, and 20 days

John Raitt, died Feb 14, 1833, aged 31

Basil Raitt, died July 10, 1839, aged 32 years and 7 months

John Rudisel, born Aug 25, 1772, died March 25, 1810

Barbary Shunk born 1757, died 1826

Peter Shunk, died June 19, 18[illegible] aged 87 years, 10 months, and 14 days

Joseph Shunk died May 28 1840, aged 66 years, 7 months, and 5 days, Aberrilla Shunk, his wife, died June 6, 1852, aged 67

Elizabeth S Sawyer, died Sept 29, 1854, aged 45 years, 7 months, and 29 days

Abram Buffington died Aug 5, 1872, aged 85 years, 7 months, and 28 days, Anna his wife, died April 19, 1854, aged 61 years, 6 months, and 21 days

Hammond Raitt, died Feb 1, 1858, aged 82

Harriet Raitt, died Jan 22, 1852, aged 52

Eleanor, consort of Hammond Raitt, died June 9, 1847, aged 69

Jacob Zumbrum, died Sept 13, 1868, aged 74 years and 2 months, Margaret his wife, died Jan 16, 1852, aged 57 years and 8 months

David Harper, died Feb 28, 1844, aged 43 years, 5 months, and 15 days

Rachel, wife of Tobias Haines, died Feb 1, 1852, aged 40 years, 1 month, and 17 days

John K Hilterbrick, born Sept 27, 1796, died Nov 18, 1869

Anna M Slyder, born Dec 21, 1800, died April 29, 1877

Sarah Reaver, died March 29, 1867, aged 66 years, 11 months, and 29 days

Maria Apolonia Hoeffner, born May 8, 1776, died May 2, 1841

Magdalena Mock, died Feb 24, 1852, aged 66 years, 2 months, and 8 days

Daniel Harman Sr, died Aug 10, 1864, aged 64 years, 5 months, and 15 days

Thomas Mathias Greaves, born Aug 22, 1825, died Feb 7, 1853

Sophia Kregelo died Aug 30, 1872, aged 81 years, 11 months, and 15 days

Jacob Kregelo, born Oct 28, 1865, aged 80 years, 6 months, and 26 days

Rev. J M Kr[illegible] died Nov 11, 18[illegible] aged 27

Isaac McGee, born Dec 24, 1795, died Jan 9, 1881

Dorothy McGee, died Jan 2, 1836, aged 34 years, 2 months, and 6 days

John Kregelo, Sr, died Nov 30 1871, aged 87 years, 7 months, and 27 days

John Kregelo, died May 29, 1837, aged 55 years, 8 months, and 5 days

John Kregelo, died Sept 14, 1880, aged 70 years, 9 months, and 1 day

Margaret, wife of Isaac McGee, died Aug 20, 1860, aged 52 years, 3 months, and 13 days

Dorothy Harner, died May 27, 1851, aged 93

Christian Harner, died June 24, 1840, aged 91

Catharine, wife of Frederick Harner, died June 7, 1859, aged 7[illegible] years, 6 months, and 9 days

Frederick Harner, died Sept 18, 1862, aged 79 years, 9 months, and 12 days

Samuel Harner, died May 13, 1867, aged 60 years, 2 months, and 8 days

Susannah Null, born March 11, 1797, died Feb 11, 1868

Samuel Null, born Feb 15, 1793, died Feb 4, 1853

Abraham Null, died Feb 27, 1850, aged 48 years, 11 months, and 19 days

Catharine Null, died April 3, 1860, aged 88 years, 4 months, and 19 days

Tobias Rudisel, died Dec 24, 1863, aged 50 years 3 months, and 11 days Mary T, his wife, died Jan 21, 18[illegible], aged 54 years, 4 months, and 17 days

Nancy Rudisel, born Sept 7, 1787, died Sept 9, 1861

Ludwick Rudisel, born Feb 25, 1778, died June 28, 1812

Susanna, wife of Samuel Babylon, died Dec 6, 1861, aged 52 years, 9 months, and 21 days

Elizabeth, consort of David Reifsnider, born July 2[illegible], 1783, died Oct 19 1811

David Reifsnider, Sr, died Feb 26, 1811, aged 66

Joseph Reever, died Aug 11, 1853, aged 65 years, 11 months, and 11 days, Margaret, his second wife, died January, 185[illegible], aged 48, Mary, his first wife, died April 25, 1845, aged 19 years, 2 months, and 13 days

Hanna Reven, died Feb 11, 1848, aged 41 years, 2 months, and 25 days

Amelia, wife of Henry Picking, died Oct 27, 1865, aged 51 years 1 month, and 3 days

Eliza L, consort of Rev Solomon Sentman, born Sept 28, 1811, died Dec 4, 1855

George Lambert, died Oct 25 1875, aged 89, Elizabeth, his wife, died Oct 1, 1859, aged 64 years, 1 months, and 16 days

Anna M, wife of Jacob Lambert, died March 27, 1852, aged 49 years, 2 months, and 4 days

Elizabeth N Clabaugh, died May 25, 1852, aged 75 years, 10 months, and 25 days

Margaret, wife of Henry Black, born May 24, 1799, died Dec 14, 1868

Elizabeth, wife of Henry Hess, died Oct 13, 1860, aged 67 years, 1 month, and 19 days

Henry Hess, born Feb 20 1794, died Aug 20, 1874

Thomas Obler, died Dec 8, 1843, aged 63 years

Margaret Fair, wife of George H, died April 8, 1866, aged 52 years, 11 months, and 5 days

Eliza, wife of John Cownover, born Jan 26, 1812, died Dec 16, 1871

John Cownover, died March 24, 1851, aged 42

Christian Naill, died July 13, 1869 aged 6[illegible] years, 8 months, and 3 days, Lydia Naill, his wife died Aug 14, 18[illegible], aged 5[illegible] years 8 months and 3 days

Ma[illegible] [illegible] 6, 1879

George Hawk, born Oct. 17, 1776, died Dec. 29, 1855.

Sophia, wife of Nicholas Heck, born April 27, 1818, died May [illegible], 1868.

Mary A. Bower, died Dec. 14, 1880, aged 70 years, 7 months, 10 days.

John Shoemaker, born Aug. 19, 1803, died June 18, 1864.

Lawrence Bower, died Nov. 30, 1842, aged 69 years, 9 months, [illegible] days.

Hannah Bower, died April 11, 1855, aged 76 years, 5 months, [illegible] days.

Susanna Stoner, died March 24, 1843, aged 57 years, 7 months, [illegible] days.

Wm. Mering, died March 16, 1856, aged 50.

Rebecca, wife of Jacob Snider, born Feb. 4, 1812, died Jan. [illegible], 1863.

Jacob Snider, died Jan. 30, 1850, aged 81 years, 6 months, 5 days.

Thomas Rudisel, died Jan. 18, 1880, aged 68 years, 3 months, [illegible] days.

Anna Rudisel, died March 22, 1874, aged 50 years, 9 days.

Anna M., wife of Thomas Rudisel, died June 7, 1857, aged 44.

William Rudisel, died Oct. 16, 1866, aged 56 years, 8 months, 10 days.

John Moring, born Dec. 4, 1795, died March 24, 1857.

Henry Baumgardner, born Dec. 11, 1810, died Nov. 16, 1880.

Jacob Null, died March 20, 1873, aged 68 years, 6 months, 17 days.

Wm. Shoemaker, born Dec. 24, 1817, died Jan. 11, 1864.

Mary A., wife of James McKellip, born Oct. 11, 1811, died Jan. 25, 1854.

Mary A., consort of Samuel Shriner, died Nov. 13, 1866, aged 42 years, 6 months, 10 days.

Michael Mentzer, born Sept. 11, 1775, died Dec. 23, 1848; Magdalena, his wife, and daughter of John and Ann Diller, born Sept. 28, 1787, died Oct. 29, 1846.

Elizabeth, wife of John D. Woods, born Nov. 1, 1781, died Dec. 18, 1860.

John D. Woods, born Dec. 23, 1786, died Jan. 29, 1869.

Daniel Shunk, born Jan. 15, 1788, died April 5, 1860.

Euphemia Shunk, died Nov. 31, 1861, aged 76 years, 6 months, 21 days.

Benjamin Shunk, died Oct. 30, 1876, aged 70 years, 8 months, 15 days; Rebecca, his wife, died Dec. 20, 1863, aged 61 years, 7 days.

John White, born Aug. 18, 1796, died March 31, 1863; Mary White, his wife, died Aug. 4, 1850, aged 57 years, 6 months, 26 days.

John Ott, died Dec. 14, 1857, aged 52 years, 2 months, 21 days; Mary, his wife, died May 10, 1856, aged 47 years, 9 months, 28 days.

Catharine Ott, died July 26, 1851, aged 64 years, 6 months, 11 days.

Elizabeth Baumgardner, died June 10, 1851, aged 66 years, 1 month, 10 days.

George Reed, born July 12, 1782, died Nov. 3, 1857. Mary, his wife, died Sept. 29, 1856, aged 73 years, 3 months, 12 days.

James Aring, born Dec. 29, 1866, aged 67 years, 9 months, 23 days.

Jacob Valentine, born May 18, 1790, died Aug. 15, 1863.

David Reifsnider, died July 28, 1858, aged 50 years, 6 months, 2 days.

Anna M. Mering, died April 29, 1867, aged 55 years, 5 months, 18 days.

Jacob Heltibridle, died March 21, 1866, aged 79 years, 6 days; Barbara, his wife, died July 21, 1863, aged 74 years.

Jacob Slagenhaupt, died [illegible] 1863, aged 73.

Elizabeth Slagenhaupt, died 1844, aged 52.

Philip M. Smith, died Dec. 4, 1860, aged 43 years, 6 months, 9 days; Rebecca Smith, died Dec. 14, 1865, aged 46 years, 7 months.

Jacob Bushey, died Aug. 31, 1861, aged 75 years, 8 months, 12 days.

Mary Bushey, died Feb. 8, 1862, aged 72 years, 21 days.

Susanna, consort of David Buffington, born in 1802, died in 1859, aged 57 years, married in 1822.

Magdalena Wolf, died March 10, 1869, aged 58 years, 3 months, 10 days.

The founder of Taneytown was a Catholic, and it is reasonable to suppose there were others of the same faith living in the vicinity of the town at an early period. As far back as 1790 there are records of mass having been said at private dwellings by Fathers Frambaugh, Pellentz, Brosuis, and Cefremont. In 1804, Prince Geliven visited the village, and built St. Joseph's church. Father Zocchi, an Italian priest of great learning and remarkable executive ability, was the first pastor of St. Joseph's, and remained in charge of the parish during the extraordinary period of forty-one years. He died in 1845, regretted by all who knew him, and there was no priest regularly assigned to the charge until 1851. From the latter date until 1862 the parish was under the control of Father Thomas O'Neill, who was succeeded by Father J. Gloyd, who remained in charge until Jan. 1, 1879. Father Gloyd's first assistant was Rev. Richard Haseman, from May, 1871, to January, 1873; his second, Rev. Casper Schmidt, from 1873 to 1874; and his third, Rev. John T. Dulaney, from 1874 to Jan. 1, 1879. At this date the mission was divided, Father Dulaney retaining charge of St. Joseph's, and St. Thomas', at New Windsor, while Father Gloyd took charge of St. John's, Westminster, and St. Bartholomew's, Manchester. Father Dulaney is a native of Baltimore, and was educated in that city. Though comparatively a young man he is a thorough classical scholar, and while scrupulously discharging the onerous duties of his pastorate is also a laborious student. His many engaging qualities and his unflagging zeal in the cause of religion and charity have not only endeared him to the people of his parish, but have won for him the confidence and respect of the entire community without reference to denominational lines. Taneytown was the headquarters of the mission until 1869, when the residence of Father Gloyd was changed to Westminster by Archbishop Spalding.

The following persons are buried in the Catholic cemetery:

Rev. Nicholas Zocchi, late pastor of Taneytown Catholic Church, died Dec. 17, 1845, aged 72 years.

Mary J., daughter of Dr. John Swope, died July 30, 1846, aged 13 years, 10 months.

Robert McGinnis born Jan 17, 1817, died Oct 12, 1871, Catharine, his wife, born Jan 8, 1815, died June 24, 1874

Samuel P Chase, born March 30, 1831, died Nov. 10, 1872

Susan McAllister, daughter of Lewis Eliot, born Nov 23, 1853, died Feb 4, 1879

Lucinda, daughter of J and M Orndoff, died April 22, 1877, aged 23 years, 8 months

Anna, wife of Anthony Wivell, died June 12, 1876, aged 68 years, 10 months, 14 days

Margaret, wife of Samuel J Wivell, born Aug 26, 1819, died May 22, 1872

Joseph Hawk, born Jan 31, 1811, died May 28, 1871

Margaret Hawk, born Oct 20, 1809, died September, 1875

Honora Donnelly, died Oct 29, 1874, aged 79

Wilhemina, wife of Joseph Ries, born May 14, 1814, died Feb 25, 1878

Catherine Sebald, born in Berks County, Pa, July 11, 1786, died Dec 27, 1827

Joseph Wivel, born Dec 12, 1790, died Jan 10, 1853

Christena Wivel, his wife, died March 23, 1818, aged 55

George Spalding, born Oct 4, 1792, died Aug 9, 1854, Mary, his wife, born Aug. 10, 1797, died Feb 22, 1875, Edward P, their son, died Feb 16, 1878, aged 53 years, 1 months, 8 days

Mary Diffendall, born Sept 11, 1808, died Sept 26, 1878

John Diffendall, born Aug 14, 1788, died May 4, 1876

Andrew Kuhns, died July 8, 1874, aged 81, Rachel, his wife, died July 18, 1861, aged 64 years

Paul Kuhns, died March 15, 1815, aged 55 years, 18 days

Mary A Kuhns, born March 24 1758 died June 23, 1814

Elizabeth Baumgardner, died June 23, 1819, aged 27 years, 11 months, 29 days

Peter Diffendal, died March 19, 1849, aged 51 years, 19 days, Mary, his wife, died April 20, 1863, aged 67 years, 6 months, 9 days

Samuel Diffendall, born March 14, 1781, died July 11, 1855

Christiana Diffendall, died June 12, 1859, aged 88

John Cline, died Jan 30, 1846 aged 83, Catharine, his wife, died Sept 11, 1848, aged 56 years, 5 months, 4 days

Juliana, daughter of John Adlesperger, died Oct 8, 1854, aged 40 years, 10 months, 13 days.

John Adlesperger, born Jan 17, 1785, died June 22, 1859, Margaret Adlesperger, born April 30, 1784, died Aug 16, 1861, Mary their daughter, born March 15, 1812, died Aug 12, 1867

Magdalena, wife of Jacob Yingling, died September 1855, aged 42

John Althoff, died Jan 13, 1873, aged 85 years, 6 months, 28 days; Mary C, his wife, died July 26, 1867, aged 86

Daniel Rose, died Nov 9, 1815, aged 13 years

Peter Hamburg, died Jan 24, 1869, aged 73 years, 2 months, 29 days, Mary, his wife, died July 26, 1870, aged 71 years, 11 months, 21 days

Mary Hamburg, died Oct 6, 1863, aged 31 years, 11 months, 15 days

James Taney, died Oct 2, 1817, aged 19

Dorothy Taney, wife of Joseph, died April 17, 1817, aged 61

Catherine Boyle, died April 12, 1814, aged 97 years

Ann Boyle, died Sept 16, 1811, aged 22 months

Roger Joseph Boyle, died Jan 14, 1841, aged 25

Henry Boyle, died Feb 14, 1805, aged 37 years

Mary H Boyle died May 2, 1821, aged 41 years

Daniel Boyle, died Dec 5, 1830, aged 66 years

Jane, wife of Raphael Brooke, died Nov 19, 1818, aged 67 years

Raphael Brooke, died July 7, 1816, aged 69 years

Ann, wife of [illegible] Jamison, died [illegible] 11, 1792, aged [illegible]

Catherine Wilson, died Dec 20 1815, infant

Joseph C Clements, died March, 1807

Francis Elder, died Oct 1, 1809, aged 54, Catherine, his wife, died April 12, 1834, aged 67

Mary Mourie, born 1743, died Jan 30, 1810

James Clabaugh, died March 16, 1867, aged 80 years, 4 months, 16 days, Monica, his wife, born July 22, 1787, died Nov 30, 1851

Ann M, wife of John Classon, born Dec 3, 1802, died Sept 4, 1864

Rebecca, wife of Levi Murrin, died July 22, 1844, aged 23 years, 5 months, 8 days

Caroline, wife of David S Smith, died Jan 3, 1857, aged 30 years, 7 months

Barbara, wife of Joseph Gartner, died June 5, 1852, aged 27

Mary Gardner, died March 23, 1816, aged 25 years, 15 days

Joseph Gardner, died March 4, 1879, aged 69 years, 9 months, 24 days

Jacob Eckenrode, died July 22, 1865, aged 81 years, 9 months, Mary, his wife, died Feb 10, 1859, aged 71 years

Mary Ann, consort of Christopher Storm, died Jan 3, 1863, aged 88 years, 11 months, 13 days

John Burk, died Dec 6, 1839, aged 16 years, Catharine, his wife, died Sept 7, 1819, aged 22 years

Joseph Welty, born Aug 8, 1810, died Jan 24, 1864

Peter A S Noveel, died Jan 2[illegible], 1837, aged 21

Elizabeth, wife of Basil Brooke, died Aug 27, 1827 aged 34 years

John Spalding, died Dec 23, 1807, aged 28 years

Henry Spalding, died Feb 19, 1816, aged 69 years, Ann, his wife, died Jan 17, 1800, aged 54 years

Cecilia, daughter of Geo and Mary Spalding, born Sept 30, 1836, died Feb 25, 1856

Margaret Adams, died Sept 8, 180[illegible]

Henry O'Hara, died June 14, 1815, aged 8[illegible] years

Elizabeth Stigers, died Feb 17, 1828, aged 31 years, 11 months 11 days

Thomas Adams, died Jan 18, 1826, aged 64 years

Magdalena Adams, wife of Thomas, who died at the age of 104, "loaded with years and virtuous deeds," Jan 21, 1826

Margaret, wife of John Dougherty, died Oct 17, 1860, aged 79 years

Margaret A, daughter of James and Rebecca Adlesperger, born Aug 16, 1862, died May 12, 1880

"This stone laid by Capt John Gwinn, U S N, and Dr Wm Gwinn," for their mother, Mary, who died April 8, 1837, aged 60

P Hinds, died Sept 23, 1828, aged 79 years

Easter Hinds, died May 28, 1835, aged 65 years

John Eckenrode, born April 2, 1780, died Nov 2[illegible], 1849, Elizabeth, his wife, born July 6, 1788, died Sept 20, 1850

Lydia E, their daughter, and wife of Samuel B Horner, died May 13, 1871, aged 58 years, 10 months, 11 days

Ann Louisa wife of Jos A Orendorff, died Aug 15, 1872, aged 38 years, 2 months, 27 days

Elizabeth Eline, died July 14, 1873, aged 68 years, 10 months, 25 days Wm Eline, her husband, died Dec 11, 1879, aged 79 years, 4 months, 29 days

Louisa C, wife of John M McCarty, born Oct 9, 1813, died April 3, 1880

John Gonker, died Dec 4, 1811, aged 71 years

Barbara Gonker, died Dec 27, 1827, aged 77 years

Eliza Gonker, died Oct 16, 18[illegible], aged 75 years

Hannah Gonker, died April 21, 1878, aged 81 years

Mary Gonker died Oct 26 1861 aged 86 years

J [illegible]

Jacob Welty, died March 7, 1816, aged 26 years

John son of John and Eliza Welty, died March 25, 1816, aged 12 years

John Welty, died Sept 15, 1816, aged 54 years

Mary Welty, died Dec 20, 1816, aged 24 years

Elizabeth, consort of John Welty, died Nov 22, 1843, aged 7- years, 3 months, 18 days

Alexander Frazier, died Oct 9, 1872 aged 60 years, 5 months, 26 days; Polly, his wife, died June 30, 1854, aged 39 years

Ann C, wife of Henry Althoff, died Oct 11, 1845, aged 92 years

Frederick Shoemaker, died March 31, 1864, aged 48 years, 11 months, 28 days

Wm Clabaugh died Nov 7, 1855, aged 34

Sylvester N Orndorff, died August, 1854, aged 19 years, 5 months, 20 days

Joseph Eck, died Jan 15, 1856, aged 62

Margaret Eck, born July 7, 1816, died July 15, 1853

Paul Eck, died Sept 12 1860, aged 63 years

Wm Staubb, died Oct 23, 1842 aged 43 years, 22 days

Peter Mathias, died Feb 4 1824, aged 37 years

Klara, wife of Francis J Albrecht, born Dec 2, 1819, died May 4, 1858

Catherine Snovell died Oct 17, 1761, aged 79

Elizabeth, wife of Daniel Snovell, died Feb 11, 1852, aged 37 years, 5 months Elizabeth, his second wife, died Sept 21, 1853, aged 27 years, 2 months

Isaac T Stonesifer, died Aug 21, 1867, aged 26 years, 3 months, 17 days

Elizabeth F Watson, died Aug 19, 1854 aged 24 years, 1 month, 24 days

Wm Watson, born November, 1798, died Feb 16, 1861

Mary A Sewell, died March 16, 1871 aged 39 years

John Hopkins, died June 20, 1833, aged 58

Wm Cash, born Dec 21, 1800, died April 3, 1872

Ann E Cash, died Feb 12, 1858, aged 22 years

Anthony Arnold, died April 3, 1854, aged 78 years, 7 months, 11 days

Ann, wife of Augustine Arnold, died Dec 30, 1863, aged 62 years

Taneytown Presbyterian Church.—Prior to 1820 German preaching was the rule in Taneytown, English the exception Indeed, a strong prejudice existed against preaching in the English language It is related that when the corner stone of what is the original part of the present Lutheran church was laid, in 1812, the Rev John Grope, pastor at that time, remarked to the bystanders, "This corner-stone is laid on a German foundation, and there is to be no English preaching here only when there must be"

But the world moves, and men must move with it Some of the persons who heard the remark to which reference has been made lived to hear the same minister preach in the English language About the year 1820 the younger portion of the German speaking part of the community began to manifest a desire to have preaching in the English language This desire was strenuously opposed by the older persons

The house in which the German Reformed congregation worshiped at that time, known as the "Yellow Church," was in a very dilapidated condition This, together with the desire of many members of the German Reformed congregation to have service in the English language, opened the way for the formation of certain "articles of association" between the members of the latter church at Taneytown and the members of the Presbyterian Church of the same place, to unite for the purpose of building a Union church

In virtue of the seventh of these "articles of association," the parties concerned, in March 1821, elected five persons as a building committee, and vested in them full power to purchase a lot or lots in such locality as they might think would best suit the different congregations, and to build thereon said church

This committee, the members of which were Nicholas Snider, William B Hilberd, George Shriner, Abraham Linn, and Samuel S Forney, bought of Elizabeth Hughs, the widow of John Hughs, lots Nos 78 and 80, situated in Taneytown, for the sum of eighty-nine dollars sixty-eight and a half cents ($89 68½) These lots were conveyed to the persons composing said committee, to be held by them in trust for the German Reformed and Presbyterian congregations until such time when said congregations may become corporate bodies, and thus by law be authorized to have and to hold the same by their trustees

The corner-stone was laid on the 5th or 6th of September, 1821 Rev John Winebrenner preached on the occasion from Zachariah iv 7 Rev Mr Reilly also preached at the same time from Isaiah lxvi 1

The erection of the building progressed slowly In the autumn of 1822 the church was dedicated The Presbyterian element, during the interval between 1822 and 1828, worshiped with the German Reformed congregation, which was during that time served by the following-named pastors Rev Jacob Helffenstein, Rev Mr Aurand, a short time, and Rev Deatrick Graves

In the year 1828 the "Presbyterian Church of Taneytown" was organized

The Presbytery of Baltimore met in Taneytown on the 24th of February, 1828, and ordained Rev Austin O Hubbard, who had been licensed in 1826 On the 30th of March, 1828, Rev Mr Hubbard ordained Philip Hann and William Cormack ruling elders, and administered the communion On Sabbath, June 22, 1828, the church was regularly organized by the admission of the following-named persons as members Mrs Elizabeth Hann, Mrs Alih Clabaugh (probably Alice) Miss Mary Ann McCollough Miss Mary Musgrove on confession of their faith and Miss Margaret Burne Miss Hester Burne, Miss Margaret Ried Miss Mary Ried [illegible]

Mr Hubbard's pastorate extended from his ordination, Feb 24, 1828, until the 18th of November, 1829, during which three persons were received into the church, two on confession of their faith and one by certificate From the close of Mr Hubbard's pastorate to Jan 13, 1838, a period of eight years, the church was ministered to by Rev George W Kennedy, Rev Nathan Harnad, Rev Mr Ammerman, and Rev Jaleel Woolbridge

Rev George W Kennedy was licensed, received, and ordained by the Presbytery of Baltimore in 1831, and dismissed in 1833 From Sessional records he appears to have been in Taneytown Church during the year 1831, and may have been pastor Of the others, they served here a short time as supplies During these eight years twelve persons were received as members of the church On Sunday, May 13, 1838, Rev John P Carter, appointed by the "General Assembly's Board of Missions," commenced preaching in Taneytown church Mr Carter was installed pastor Oct 29, 1838 His pastorate extended five years, to Dec 17, 1843 After his resignation the church was vacant until the 1st of September, 1844, when Rev Jacob Belville, a licentiate, was unanimously elected pastor, and soon afterwards ordained and installed a pastor of the church by the Presbytery of Baltimore He was pastor four years His pastorate closed about the 1st of September, 1848 The pulpit was then supplied between September, 1848, and June 2, 1849, by Rev Mr Connell

In a Sessional record Rev James Williamson, pastor elect, is spoken of as being present He was soon after installed as pastor, and served the church as such until some time during the year 1854 He was dismissed from the Presbytery of Baltimore in 1854 It appears that the church was vacant from the close of Mr Williams' pastorate to April 13, 1857, during which time the pulpit was supplied for a few months by Rev Mr Dodder, a licentiate April, 1857, Rev William B Scarborough was ordained and installed pastor Mr Scarborough was pastor until the latter part of December, 1868, making a pastorate of eleven years and seven months He handed his resignation to the Session 22d of November, 1868, to take effect in December The Presbytery having granted the congregation the privilege of supplying their own pulpit, Rev Isaac M Patterson was unanimously elected stated supply, and entered upon his duties on the first Sabbath of January, 1869 In October, 1871, Mr Patterson was installed pastor by a committee of the Presbytery of Baltimore He resigned July, 1873, and preached his last sermon on the 27th of the same month

After the union between the Old and the New School branches of the church, changes in the bounds of Synods and Presbyteries threw Emmittsburg and Piney Creek into the Presbytery of Baltimore, thus opening the way for Mr Patterson to become pastor of Taneytown, in connection with Emmittsburg and Piney Creek Since Mr Patterson's installation, October, 1871, Emmittsburg, Piney Creek, and Taneytown have constituted, and at this time constitute, a pastoral charge When the church became vacant by Mr Patterson's resignation it united with the other churches of the charge in unanimously calling Rev William Simonton, of Williamsport, Pa Mr Simonton accepted and soon entered upon his duties His pastorate dates from Oct 1, 1873 and still continues

Philip Hann and William Cormack were ordained ruling elders at the organization of the church Mr Hann died Dec 31, 1863, having served as an elder for a period of thirty five years Of Mr Cormack it is recorded, "Did not apply for a certificate—joined the Methodists" Clotworthy Birnie, Sr, united with the church by certificate Sept 8, 1832, and was ordained a ruling elder Aug 8, 1838 He died June 2, 1845 He was a member of this church almost thirteen years, and a ruling elder seven years, four of which he was clerk of the Session The members of the Session at present are Rogers Birnie, ordained Aug 1, 1844, Andrew McKinney and Clotworthy Birnie, M D, ordained Nov 27, 1864 John W Davidson and Andrew Arthur, ordained May 5, 1872 Rogers Birnie, the senior member, was clerk twenty-three years Andrew McKinney has been clerk since 22d of November, 1868 Clotworthy Birnie, M D, is a grandson of Clotworthy Birnie, Sr, who was a member of the Session during the earlier history of the church

Taneytown Church was organized with ten members In 1840 it had increased to twenty-six, in 1850 to thirty five, and at present has a membership in full communion of forty-two The whole number of persons who have been members of the church is about two hundred, and while the number in communion at any given time has always been small, the fact may be noted that it was never less at any period than it had been at an earlier date in the church's history Two of the original members still survive

In 1853, during Mr Williamson's pastorate, the congregation bought a house and lot in Taneytown for the sum of nine hundred dollars, this was conveyed by deed, executed by John K Longwell and Sarah Longwell to Rogers Birnie and Philip Hann elders and their successors in trust, to be held for th[illegible] The property

was used most of the time as a parsonage, except the latter part of Mr Scarborough's pastorate, during which he resided in New Windsor After the congregation became part of the pastoral charge of Emmittsburg and Piney Creek it was deemed best to dispose of the parsonage, which was accordingly done on the 29th of October, 1870, and on the 1st of April, 1871, it was conveyed to Thomas Rudisel by Rogers Birnie, Clotworthy Birnie, and Andrew McKinney, elders, for the sum of $3126 The congregation was incorporated by the laws of the State of Maryland, January, 1871, previous to that time the members of the Session attended to the secular interests of the church, and since then it has been governed by a board of trustees

The pastors and stated supplies have been

1828-29, Rev Austin O Hubbard, 1829-38, vacant, with supplies, 1838-43, Rev. John P Carter, 1843-44, vacant, with occasional appointments, 1844-48, Rev Jacob Bellville, D D, 1848-49, vacant, with supplies, 1849-54, Rev James Williamson 1854-57, vacant, with occasional supplies, 1857-68, Rev William B Scarborough, 1868-73, Rev Isaac M Patterson, S S and P, 1873, Rev William Simonton

Taneytown Academy —This institution was incorporated Jan 25, 1844, with the following trustees Solomon Sentman, Israel Hiteshue, Thomas Rudisel, John B Boyle, John Thompson

The Church of the United Brethren in Christ was incorporated March 10, 1858, with the following trustees Henry Shriner, Daniel Frock, Joseph Witherow, John Ridinger, and Peter Mark

A lodge of Knights of Pythias was organized in Taneytown Sept 17, 1877 Their charter and paraphernalia were purchased from the Frederick City Lodge, and were issued to them in 1871 The first officers of the lodge were as follows

C C, C C Steiner, Master at Arms, G T Crouse, Dr C Birnie, Prelate, David Fogle, V C, L. D Reed, K of R and S, J E Davidson, M of E Ezekiah Hawk, O G, Elwood Burns, I G, E K Weaver, M of F The present officers are S E Reindollar, V C, D R Fogle, C C, J E Davidson, M of E, E K Weaver, M of F, C C Stuller, K of R and S, W T Hawk, P, L D. Reed, O G, J Hahn, I G, B B Miller, P C

They have twenty-one members in good standing, and hold their meetings in Reindollar's Hall The lodge is in a very prosperous condition, and is steadily increasing in numbers

The Regulator and Taneytown Herald was published by Samuel P Davidson, who was also the editor, "in Church Street, adjoining Mr Sebastian Sultzer's tavern, Taneytown, Md" The eighteenth issue, dated Sept 7, 1830, contains among its news the names of Isaac Shriner, John Kinzer, Madison Nelson, and Daniel Kemp, of Henry, who are published as candidates on the Jackson Republican ticket for members of the Assembly from Frederick County, and the candidates on the National Republican ticket were David Kemp, Jno H Melford, Evan McKinstry, and David Richardson

From the market reports, copied from the Baltimore *American*, we learn that wheat was worth 98 cents to $1 00 per bushel, rye, 47 and 50 cents, corn, 45 and 47 cents, whisky, 22 and 24 cents per gallon, plaster, $3 80 per ton

But two marriages are published, one of which is that of Mr Adam Bowers and Miss Mary Ann Currans

A Reck, secretary, gives notice that the Evangelical Lutheran Synod of Maryland and Virginia will assemble at Taneytown on the third Sunday of October (1830)

Michael Wagner advertises a stray heifer Nathan Hendricks announces a barbecue at Bruceville on the 23d of September Samuel Thompson, Sterling Galt, and David Martin, trustees, advertised for "a man of good moral character, who is well qualified to teach reading, writing, arithmetic, and mathematics in a school house lately erected within one mile of Taneytown" The teacher secured was J M Newson, the present superintendent of public schools Mathias E Bartgis Wm H Cannon, Abner Campbell, and Peter Brengle published cards announcing themselves as candidates for sheriff of Frederick County John N Hoffman, agent, gives notice to the subscribers to the theological seminary at Gettysburg that three installments are due. David H Fries, seven miles from Taneytown, near Smith's tavern, advertises public sale of personal property James Raymond trustee, advertises sale of land of Abraham Derr, near Taneytown Nathan Hendricks, "desirous of leaving Frederick County," advertises Bruceville Mills at public sale Louisa Rinedollar and Abraham Lichtenwalter, executors, give notice to the creditors of Peter Micksell James Heird advertises the Fairview races to come off on the 6th, 7th, and 8th of September, and offers three purses,—$25, $15, $20 John Hughes nominates himself for the Assembly as the Workingmen's independent candidate, "who is a friend to railroads, canals, and turnpikes," etc "A valuable family of negroes" is offered for sale, "but not to traders," and another negro is also advertised for sale, those desiring to buy are requested to inquire at the office of the *Regulator* C Birnie offers Merino rams for sale Israel Hiteshew and James Kindler announce [illegible] and tailoring"

The *American Sentinel*, published in Westminster, is a combination of *The Regulator* The paper was bought from Mr Davidson by Col John K Longwell, who moved the office to Westminster in May, 1833, and changed its name to *The Carrolltonian* The paper was moved there solely to advocate the formation of Carroll County In 1838 a Democratic journal called *The Democrat* was established here by Wm Shipley, Jr, when *The Carrolltonian* was announced as a Whig journal Col Longwell continued the publication of the paper until 1844, when Francis T Kerr, a brother-in-law to the late John J Baumgartner, Esq, succeeded to its proprietorship Upon the death of Mr Kerr in 1846 or 1847, George D Miller, of Frederick, took charge of the paper, and was shortly after succeeded by W H Grammer, in 1850 In 1854, upon the rise of Know Nothingism, the name of the paper was changed to the *American Sentinel*, its present title

Among the early physicians were Dr Joseph Sim Smith, a patriot in the Revolution and a brave soldier He died Sept 6, 1822 William Hubbert and Dr Boyle were also among the first physicians in Taneytown The latter and Henry Swope were among the earliest merchants John White and Joseph Lambert were the blacksmiths of the village in the olden time A tavern was kept by Mary Crouse in the house now occupied by Mr Stonesifer as a hotel, and the Crabsters kept the inn just opposite and across the street The following advertisement appeared in a newspaper of Dec 16, 1801

"For sale, the tavern 'American Coat of Arms,' in Taneytown Apply to James McSherry, Littlestown, Pennsylvania, or Richard Coale, Libertytown, Maryland"

Harney is a small hamlet about four and a half miles from Taneytown and near the Monocacy River, which is at this point a small stream It was named in honor of the late Gen Harney, of the United States army The United Brethren, a religious denomination, have built a church in the village recently, of which Rev J Whitlock is pastor D L Shoemaker is the village postmaster A number of mills are located here, under the charge of William Starner, John Unger, and Peter Selt There is a hotel in the village, kept by W F Eckenrode, and John Eckenrode keeps an assortment of general merchandise There are also two excellent physicians, John C Bush and E B Simpson The population of the Taneytown District, according to the census of 1880, is 2596

For many years the old free-school system, which obtained so extensively in the rural districts of Maryland, was in vogue in Carroll County At the public schools the children were taught the three R's,—"reading, 'riting, and 'rithmetic,"—and if they desired further education, they either had to teach themselves or attend one of the many excellent private schools within reach During the civil war there was an awakening of the public mind to the advantages of general education, and a cumbersome system, expensive in character, resulted from inexperienced legislation This was superseded by the present system, now general throughout all the counties of the State, which gives all necessary advantages, and has the additional recommendation of simplicity The following is a list of public school trustees for 1881 and 1882 in the Taneytown District

1 Pine Hill —William Clutz, Michael Humbert, Charles M Hess
2 Piney Creek —Franklin Keppert, Daniel Hesson, Richard Hill
3 Walnut Grove —Samuel Brown, Upton Harney, David W Bowers
4 Washington —No appointments
5 Oak Grove —Samuel P Baumgartner, Henry Eck, Hezekiah Hahn
6, 7, and 8 Taneytown, Nos 1, 2, and 3 —William S Rudisell, Jesse Haugh, Ezra K Reaver
9 Oregon —Gabriel Stover, William W Koontz, Ezra Stull
10 Martin's —Valentine Harman, Jacob Shriner, Martin L Luffington
11 Shaw s —Daniel Harman, Edward Shorb, William Smith

The teachers for the term ending April 15, 1881, were

1, H C Wilt, 53 pupils, 2, S F Hess, 48 pupils, 3, J H Lambert, 51 pupils, 4, J Ross Galt, 44 pupils, 5, Calvin T Fringer, 51 pupils, 6, Levi D Reid, 55 pupils, 7, Mrs Emma L Forrest, 54 pupils 8, James F Fringer, 47 pupils, 9, John T Rock, 68 pupils, 10, George W Hess, 51 pupils, 11, C A Waesche, 29 pupils, 1 (colored school), C H Studer, 20 pupils

The following is the vote for local officers from 1851 to 1861, inclusive

1851 —Vote for Primary School Commissioners Israel Hiteshue 190, Benjamin Shunk 155, Israel Hiteshue 159, John H Clabaugh 8[illegible], Benjamin Zumbrum 41

1853 —For Justices William Haugh 227, George Miller 17[illegible], Benjamin Shunk 216, James McKellip 242, Constables Thomas Jones, Jr, 250, James Burke 64, John Reindollar 248 David Kephart 87, Road Supervisor Patrick Burke 103, James Thompson 243

1855 —For Justices George Miller 240, William Haugh 245 Jacob Shriner 249, George Crabbs 132, James Crouse 1[illegible]2, L Buffington 137, Constables Thomas Jones, Jr, 2[illegible]6, Henry Rinaman 242, Michael Fogle 127, James Rodgers 135, Road Supervisor James Thompson 220, I Newcomer 131

1857 —For Justices B Shunk 216, William Haugh 2[illegible]0, George Miller 245, Constables H Rinaman 13[illegible], A Shoemaker 238, W States 240, Road Supervisor William Hener 20[illegible]

1859 —For Justices William Fisher 157 Jacob Zumbrum 2[illegible] [illegible], Constables

James Burke 152, Wendell Slates 270, J E Delaplane 2[illegible]9, Road Supervisor William Hess 27[illegible]

1861 — For Justices William Haugh 377, William Fisher 191, J Zumbrum 207, George Miller 356, Constables W Slates 217, Joel Bowers 284, David Kephart 206, Road Supervisor Gabriel Stover 266, John Reindollar 105, W Shoemaker 82, William Hess 2

UNIONTOWN DISTRICT, No 2

The metes and bounds of Uniontown District are as follows

"Beginning at Grove's Ford, on Big Pipe Creek, thence down Big Pipe Creek to Sick's Ford, thence with a straight line to Eckert's Ford on Little Pipe Creek, thence up Little Pipe Creek to Sam's Creek to Landis' mill thence with a road leading between the farms of Jacob Sneader and the late Henry Nicodemus to a stone on the Buffalo road, thence near Levi Devilbiss' house, now occupied by Jacob Nusbaum, leaving said house in District No 9 (thence near John Myers' house, leaving the same in District No 9), thence to Philip Nicodemus' mill, thence down Turkeyfoot Branch to where it intersects Little Pipe Creek, thence up said creek to Haines' mill, running through Widow Haines' farm, leaving her house in District No 2, thence through Joseph Haines' farm, leaving his house in No 7, thence through Michael Morelock, Sr 's farm, leaving his house in No 2, thence to Morelock s tavern, on the Uniontown turnpike leaving his house in No 7, thence through Shaffer s farm, leaving his house and factory in District No 7, thence with a straight line to Smith s old tavern on the Taneytown turnpike, leaving said house in District No 7, thence to H[illegible] s house, leaving his house in No 2, thence to Messing's mill, leaving his dwelling in No 7, thence to the stone road near Stonesifer s house, thence with the stone road to place of beginning "

This district is bounded on the north by Myers', northwest and west by Taneytown, east by Westminster, south by New Windsor, and west by Union Bridge and Middleburg Big Pipe Creek divides it from Taneytown District, and Little Pipe Creek skirts its southwestern corner, forming for a short distance the boundary line with New Windsor Bear and Meadow Branches flow westerly through its centre and empty into Big Pipe Creek Wolf Pit Branch flows southwest, and Log Cabin Branch northwest, emptying respectively into Little and Big Pipe Creeks The population of the district, according to the census of 1880, is two thousand six hundred and three

The district was settled before 1745, and about 1760 the population increased rapidly Among the pioneers were the Herbaughs, Norrises, Eckerds, Nicodemuses, Harrises, Babylons, Roops, Shepherds, Zollickoffers, Senseneys, Hibberds, Farmwalts, Brubakers, Hiteshews Roberts, McFaddens, Stonesifers, Erbs, Markers, Zepps, and Myerlys The early settlers were largely Germans, with a sprinkling of English and Scotch-Irish The Barnharts were the original owners of the land on which A Zollicoffer now lives, and the land n[illegible] by Capt [illegible]ker was formerly in the possession of the Cover family Mrs Mehring owns the land upon which the Grammers lived The Stouffers also took up a large tract south of Uniontown

Uniontown is situated in an undulating and healthy country, two and a half miles from Linwood, seven from Westminster, and forty-three from Baltimore Before there was any town here, more than a hundred years ago, Peter Moser kept a tavern, which is marked on the old Maryland maps, on the road from Baltimore through Westminster and Moravian Town (Graceham) to Hagerstown

The first house built in the village was situated at the forks of the Hagerstown and Taneytown road, a log building one and a half stories high, containing three rooms It was used as a hotel and store, and was kept first by Peter Moser, before the Revolution, and afterwards by Mr McKenzie, and then by Mr Hiteshew, who conducted it until 1809 It was built on the lot now occupied by Nathan Heck, and was torn down in 1831 The second house, a low structure, was built by Stephen Ford, and is now occupied by Mr Segafoose Mrs Green's hotel was built in 1802 by Conrad Stem, and was first kept by John Myers The next house was built in 1804, and is now occupied by Charles Devilbiss It was first occupied by a family named Myers That in which Reuben Matthias lives was erected in 1805 Its first occupant was John Kuntz, who kept a store The town was then called "The Forks," and its name was changed in 1813 to Uniontown, when the people were trying to secure a new county, which it was proposed to call "Union County," with this town as the county seat The project failed, but the village retained the name of Uniontown The first physician was Dr Hobbs, and he was succeeded by Dr Boyer, who lived outside of the town His successor was Dr. Hibberd The first blacksmith was Nicholas Hiteshew, whose shop was at the foot of the hill leading to the Stouffer residence His shop was there in 1800 Wm Richmacker and George Attick were the pioneer carpenters of the hamlet The first schoolmaster was Thomas Harris, who taught in 1807 in the house now occupied by Mr Segafoose Moses Shaw came here in 1816 and kept a tavern on the property now owned by Charles Devilbiss In 1817, Jacob Appler was a wealthy citizen living near town Charles Devilbiss, David Stouffer, Isaac Hiteshew, Upton Norris, Capt Henry Anders, Mr Harris, Samuel Shriner, Thomas Metcalf, and many others from Uniontown and its vicinity volunteered for the defense of Baltimore during the war of 1812 The first school house was erected in 1810, in the lower part of the town It has been removed

several times and is still standing Cardinal McCloskey, of New York City, was born in Uniontown, in a log house opposite the cemetery In 1818 St. Lucas' church was built, under the pastorate of Rev Winebrenner Subsequent pastors were Revs Helfenstein and Graves It is now occupied by the Church of God In those days it was customary to raise funds for the erection of churches and other public enterprises by means of lotteries Below is given the scheme by which the money was obtained to build St Lucas' church

UNIONTOWN DISTRICT

Stationary Prizes

1	prize of $1200 is		$1200
1	"	500 is	500
1	"	200 is	200
4	"	100 is	400
10	"	50 is	500
60	"	10 is	600
250	"	8 is	2000
800	"	7 is	5600
1127	prizes		
1073	blanks		
2200	tickets at $5 is		$11,000

"1st drawn 300 tickets, each $7

"1st drawn ticket after 1000, $500

"1st drawn ticket after 2000, $1200

"Part of the above prizes will be paid in part as follows prize of $1200 by 100 tickets in 2d class, Nos 1 and 100 inclusive, prize of $500 by 50 tickets in 2d class, Nos 101 and 150 inclusive, prize of $200 by 15 tickets in 2d class, Nos 151 and 166 inclusive, prizes of $10, $8, and $7 by 1 ticket in 2d class, commencing with first drawn of ten dollar prizes with No 167, and so upwards in regular succession with said prizes of $10, $8, and $7 Ticket in 2d class valued at $5 each

"SECOND CLASS

1	prize of $1000 is		$1000
1	"	400 is	400
1	"	200 is	200
2	"	100 is	200
6	"	50 is	300
20	"	20 is	400
122	"	10 is	1220
155	"	8 is	1240
720	"	7 is	5040
1028	prizes		
972	blanks		
2000	tickets at $5 is		$10,000

"*Stationary Prizes*

"1st drawn 200 tickets, each $7

"1st drawn ticket after 1500, $1000

"Part of the above prizes will be paid in part as follows prize of $1000 by 80 tickets in 3d class, Nos 1 and 80 inclusive, prize of $400 by 40 tickets, Nos 81 and 121 inclusive, prize of $200 by 15 tickets, No 122 and 137 inclusive, prizes of $10, $8, and $7 by 1 ticket each, commencing with No 138 to the first drawn ten dollar prize, and continuing regularly up with said prizes Tickets valued in 3d class at $ each

"THIRD CLASS

1	prize of $1500 is		$1500
1	"	600 is	600
1	"	300 is	300
2	"	100 is	200
20	"	50 is	1000
26	"	15 is	390
261	"	10 is	2610
400	"	8 is	3200
600	"	7 is	4200
1312	prizes		
1488	blanks		
2800	tickets at $5 each is		$14,000

"*Stationary Prizes*

"1st drawn 250 tickets, each $7

"1st drawn ticket after 1000, $300

"1st drawn ticket after 2400, $1500

"Prizes subject to a deduction of 20 per cent in each class, and payable ninety days after the completion thereof The managers in offering the above scheme to the public, for the purpose of appropriating the proceeds to a church, feel confident that they will meet with a general support Perhaps no scheme has been offered heretofore that affords so great a chance to adventurers, there being more prizes than blanks, and only few tickets in each class

"Those persons who purchased tickets in the original scheme will please to exchange them for tickets in the first class as soon as possible, as the managers are very reluctantly obliged to abandon it, as a duty they owe to the church and the public, in consequence of the magnitude of the original scheme As a number of tickets are already held in the first class, the managers pledge themselves to commence the drawing as soon as possible

"MANAGERS

"Jacob Appler, Sr[1]	Thomas Boyer
Nicholas Snider	John Hager
Moses Shaw	Jacob Shriver
John Crabb	John Shates
William B Hubbard	

"UNIONTOWN, MD, April, 1817"

In 1807, Mr Cover established a tan-yard The tan yard now operated by Mr Hoffman was opened in 1842 by Charles Devilbiss The Methodist church was built in 1822 In 1813 the Masonic Temple was erected where the house of the Misses Yingling now stands It was torn down between 1825 and 1830, and its brick used in building a house on Mr Zollikoffer's farm The town has been several times incorporated, but its charters expired for want of elections or failure to conform to them In 1807 the house now used as a dry-house in the tannery was removed from Westminster by Frederick Stem It had been a Catholic church, and its brick was brought from England The post-office was established here about 1813, and the first postmaster was John Hyder, who laid out the town after a few houses had been

[1] On Thursday, Aug 28, 1817, Jacob Christ was married to Miss Elizabeth Appler daughter of Jacob Appler, by Rev Curtis Walls.

built In 1817 Jonas Crumbacker advertised the "Bournavean Lotion" for sale at his store as a grand anti-rheumatic tincture In 1817 the Frederick County Court, at its October term, ordered a public road to be laid out from Liberty Town through Union Town to Andrew Shriver's mill Dr Clement Hubbs in 1817 lived on his farm called "Valley Farm"

Moses Shaw and John Gibbony advertised that races would be run over a handsome course near Uniontown, Wednesday, Sept 10, 1817, and a purse of ninety dollars was free for any horse, mare, or gelding running four miles and repeat, carrying weight agreeable to the rules of racing And on the Thursday following a purse of forty dollars was offered, free as the above, the winning horse of the preceding day excepted, two miles and repeat carrying a feather, and on Friday a purse of seventy dollars, free as above, the winning horses the preceding days excepted, running three miles and repeat, carrying a feather Four horses to be entered each day or no race, to be entered the day previous to running or pay double entrance, entrance to pay one shilling in the pound No jostling or foul riding to be countenanced

Uniontown is one of the most enterprising villages in Carroll County According to the last census it contained three hundred and eighteen inhabitants It is the commercial centre of the district, the polling-place for the voters, and a popular resort for the energetic and intelligent population by which it is surrounded A number of charitable, social, and business organizations have been formed in the town, or have moved thither from other portions of the county, and are all in a flourishing condition

Door to Virtue Lodge, No 46, of Ancient Free and Accepted Masons, moved Nov 7, 1813, to Uniontown from Pipe Creek, where the members met uninterruptedly until 1824

At the communication of November 21st, "Brothers William P Farquhar, J Cloud, and Jacob R Thomas were appointed a committee to prepare a petition to the Legislature for a lottery to defray the expense of building the Uniontown Masonic Lodge Hall," but the committee never reported, the lottery was never granted, and the hall was never built

The officers from December, 1813, to June, 1814, were William P Farquhar, W M, J R Thomas, S W; C Ogborn, J W, and Jesse Cloud, Sec, J Wright, Treas From June to December, 1814, William P Farquhar, W M, J R Thomas, S W, Joseph Wright, J W., Henry Gassaway, Sec, and Enoch Taylor, Treas From December, 1814, to June, 1815, Jesse Cloud, W. M, J R Thomas, S W, J Wright, J W, William Bontz, Sec, and John Richnecker, Treas From June to December, 1815, Jacob R Thomas, W M, William P Farquhar, S W, Henry Gassaway, J W, William Bontz, Sec, and Isaac Lyon, Treas From December, 1815, to June, 1816, Joseph Wright, W M, Isaac P Thomas, S W, John C Cockey, J W, William P Farquhar, Sec, and Charles Devilbiss, Treas

During this term, at a meeting held Feb 25, 1816, the lodge manifested its appreciation of the importance of "proficiency" by passing the following resolution "That every member shall make himself well acquainted with such degrees of Masonry as have been conferred upon him before he can be permitted to advance further into Masonry," thus anticipating by forty-four years the standing resolution of the Grand Lodge of May, 1860 The officers from June to December, 1816, were Wm P Farquhar, W M, J R Thomas, S W, Isaac Lyon, J W, John C Cockey, Sec From June, 1817, to June, 1818, Wm P Farquhar, W M, Isaac Lyon, S W, Joseph Wright, J W, J C Cockey, Sec, and John Richnecker, Treas

The lodge, from the beginning, had always held its stated meetings on Sunday, but on the 28th of December, 1817 it was resolved, "That the meetings shall for the winter season be on the Saturday evening preceding the fourth Sunday, at 6 o'clock P M" In the following spring we find the brethren again assembling as usual on the first day of the week The officers from June to December, 1818, were Wm P Farquhar, W M, Joseph Wright, S W, Israel Lyon, J W, J C Cockey, Sec, and George W Gist, Treas On the 18th June, this same year, the lodge had its first funeral procession It was at Libertytown, and in honor of Enoch Taylor, who was one of the original or charter members the first senior deacon, and afterwards junior warden, senior warden, and treasurer

The first junior warden, William Slaymaker, it appears, also died during this term, as the lodge, on the 13th of September, appointed a committee "to take in subscriptions to be applied to the erection of a tombstone over his remains, and to wait on the widow and trustees of the church on this subject to obtain their consent," etc

The officers from December, 1818, to June, 1819, were Wm P Farquhar, W M, Alexander McIlhenny, S W, Charles Devilbiss, J W, J C Cockey, Sec, and George W Gist, Treas At the meeting of Feb 22, 1819, "a memorial was presented from Wm H McCannon, Thomas Gist, and others, Master Mason [illegible] for [illegible]ation to the

Grand Lodge for a charter for new lodge, to be established in Westminster On motion, the further consideration thereof was postponed until the fourth Sunday in March," and the postponement seems to have been indefinite, as nothing more is heard of the memorial "The craft then moved in procession down to the lodge-hall, where an oration was delivered in honor of the day by Upton Scott Reid, in the presence of the lodge and the public, after which the craft returned to the lodge room, and the honors of the lodge were conferred on Bro Reid for his oration" On the 25th of April it was

"*Resolved*, That hereafter the stated meetings of this lodge shall be on the evening of the day of every full moon at two o'clock P M, except from the first of November until the first day of April, during which time the lodge shall meet at ten o'clock A M, unless the moon shall be full on Sunday, in which case the meeting shall be held at the same hour on the Friday preceding"

The officers from June to December, 1819, were Alexander McIlhenny, W M, George W Gist, S W, Benjamin Yingling, J W, Upton S Reid, Sec, and Dr William B Hebbard, Treas The festival of St John the Baptist (June 24th) was kept this year in true Masonic style The number of brethren present, including visitors, was over one hundred, and after conferring the third degree "a procession was formed and the craft proceeded to St Lucas' church, where divine service was performed and a discourse delivered by the Rev Bro John Armstrong" By a resolution passed July 7th the fee for each of the three degrees was fixed at ten dollars, and it was also "*Resolved*, That if a candidate for initiation be elected, and does not attend at the first or second meetings after such an election, having been duly notified thereof his petition shall be returned, and his deposit retained for the benefit of the institution" The officers from December, 1819, to June, 1820, were Alexander McIlhenny, W M, Upton S Reid, S W, Benjamin Yingling, J W., John Hyder, Sec, and Dr William B Hebbard, Treas, from June to December, 1820, Upton S Reid, W M, Benjamin Yingling, S W, John W Dorsey, J. W, John Hyder, Sec, and W B Hebbard, Treas On St John's day (June 24th) "a discourse was delivered by the W M, highly gratifying to all the brethren present" Soon after, on the 25th of July, the lodge, for the first time, was compelled to visit upon an unworthy member the severest penalty known to their laws The offender was an unaffiliated Master Mason, formerly a member of Mechanics' Lodge, No 153, New York, whose application for membership in this lodge had been twice rejected He was tried on the charge of "unmasonic conduct Specification 1st Using profane language at Uniontown, on or about the 1st of May 1820' To which the accused pleaded "guilty" "Specification 2d Being intoxicated on the evening of the said day at Uniontown" Pleaded "guilty" "Specification 3d Giving the G—— and S——, etc, to persons, or in the presence of persons who were not Masons, at New Windsor, some time in the spring of 1819" Pleaded "not guilty" "The testimony being closed,' says the record, "the accused made his defense and then retired" The lodge then proceeded to consider the case, and after mature consideration did find the accused guilty of the charge, and sentenced him to be expelled from all the rights and benefits of Masonry" The officers from December, 1820, to June, 1821, were U S Reid, W M, W H McCannon, S W, Joshua W Owings, J W, John Hyder, Sec, and W B Hebbard, Treas, from June to December, 1821, Alexander McIlhenny, W. M, Benjamin Yingling, S W, James Blanchford, J W, William Curry, Sec, and W B Hebbard, Treas

On the 24th of June, "it was unanimously resolved, in conformity with the recommendation of the Grand Lodge at its last Grand Annual Communication, that this lodge in future abandon and desist from the practice of using spirituous liquors at their refreshments in and about the lodge'

On the 11th of October there was a solemn procession and commemorative services in honor of the Grand Master of the State, Charles Wirgman who had recently died The sermon was preached in St Lucas' Reformed Church, by the Rev R Elliott, P M of Columbia Lodge, No 58, Frederick, who generously returned the fee of ten dollars offered him "into the charity fund, with his hearty and most sincere thanks and prayers for their welfare in this world and eternal happiness hereafter' The officers from December, 1821, to June, 1822, were A McIlhenny, W M, B Yingling, S W, James Blanchford, J W, William Curry, Sec; and W B Hebbard, Treas

On the 7th of January, 1822, it was unanimously resolved, "that hereafter our stated meetings shall be held on the fourth Sunday in the month, as originally printed in the by-laws of 1813" Soon after, on the 28th of the same month, at Taneytown, the lodge buried with Masonic honors its late Past Master, Upton Scott Reid The chaplain on this mournful occasion was the Rev Daniel Zollikoffer

The officers from June to December, 1822, were W [illegible] W M, William H McCan-

non, S W., Nicholas Snider, J W, Alexander McIlhenny, Sec, and W B Hebbard, Treas From December, 1822, to June, 1823, Benjamin Yingling, W. M; John Giboney, S W, James Blanchford, S W, William Curry, J W, A McIlhenny, Sec, and W B Hebbard, Treas From June, 1823, to December, 1823, W P Farquhar, W M, N Snider, S W, William Curry, J W, A McIlhenny, Sec, and W B Hebbard, Treas On the 24th of February, 1823, the fee for the three degrees was reduced to twenty dollars, viz, seven for the first, five for the second and eight for the third From December, 1823, to June, 1824, W P Farquhar, W M, N Snider, S W, Jacob Glazer, J W, A McIlhenny, Sec, and Israel Bentley, Treas

From June 4, 1815, there had been connected with this lodge a "Mark Lodge," for the purpose of conferring the degree of Mark Master, which is now given only in Royal Arch Chapters, but at the meeting held Feb 22, 1824, "Door to Virtue Mark Lodge" was declared to be defunct and its books closed

On the 13th of April, 1824 there was a special meeting at "Shriver's Inn," Westminster, the object of which was to pa proper Masonic respect to the memory of a deceased brother, John Holmes, of No 1, Ohio

On the 13th of June the lodge went into mourning for sixty days for the death of the Grand Master, Gen W H Winder The officers from June to December, 1824, were W P Farquhar, W M, John C Cockey, S W, Joshua W Owings, J W, W H McCannon, Sec, and Michael Bornetz, Treas

Wyoming Tribe, No. 37, I O. R. M, was instituted March 18, 1860, and the charter was granted April 23, 1860, to the following members, who then composed the lodge Frank E Roberts, John S Devilbiss Jr, George H Routson, B Mills, C S Devilbiss, and C A Gosnell, all residing within Uniontown The first officers of the lodge were, viz Prophet, F E Roberts, Sachem, Dr B Mills, Senior Sagamore, John S Devilbiss, Junior Sagamore, George H Routson, Chief of Records, Charles Gosnell, Keeper of Wampum, C S Devilbiss

The tribe numbers sixty-eight members in good standing, and the present officers are as follows Prophet John A Brown, Sachem, B L Waltz, Senior Sagamore J Hamilton Singer, Junior Sagamore, William Strimme, Chief of Records, H P [illegible], Keeper of Wampum, Jesse T H Davis, Guard of Wigwam, G A Davis, Guard of the Forest, William H Baker

Brothers' [illegible] Division, No. 136, Sons of Temperance, was incorporated by the General Assembly, Feb 24, 1860 The incorporators were Alfred Zollickoffer, S Hope, E Bankerd, J Bankerd, E Adams, Samuel Anders, D Stultz, J H Christ, T H Adams, M Jenkins, J Bean, J H Gordon, J Zepp J McHenry, T Welling, A Bitesell, R Sharpley, A Hurley, W S Lantz, J E Starr, William Eckard, D Seller, Charles Myers, Lewis Byers, N N Meredith, T H Routson, F A Devilbiss, J A Eckard, J N Galwith, G H Brown, William H Bankerd, G Kugle, G Winter, T A Eckard, John W Kinney, J Little, P Smith, T Eckard, G Hamburg, G. W Gilbert, A Eckard, A Little, P Little

The Uniontown Academy was incorporated by the General Assembly by an act passed March 26, 1839, making Samuel Cox, Dr James L Billingslea, John Smith, Henry Harbaugh and William Roberts trustees, and making them and their successors a body politic

The Carroll County Savings Institution was organized in Uniontown Feb 27, 1871, by an act of the General Assembly, with the following gentlemen as incorporators Robert B Varden, William H Starr, Levi Caylor, David Foutz, Dennis Cookson, John Gore, Daniel S Diehl, Emanuel Formwalt, J Hamilton Singer, and Levi Engler, all citizens of Carroll County The amount of capital of the corporation was twenty thousand dollars, and the above gentlemen were appointed a board of directors

The present officers of the institution are D Stoner, president, W H Starr, treasurer, Levi Caylor secretary, and T H Davis assistant secretary Board of trustees, D N Stoner, D Foutz, Levi Caylor, Edwin J Gilbert, Daniel S Diehl, T H Davis, W H Stoner, Dr J J Weaver

The institution is in a very prosperous condition, and has been successful since its formation

The Maryland Mutual Benefit Association of Carroll County for Unmarried Persons was incorporated under the laws of Maryland with its home-office in Uniontown The officers are President, Thomas H Routson, Vice President, Philip H Babylon, Secretary, Jesse T H. Davis, Treasurer, Edwin G Gilbert, Agent, John A Brown, Attorney, Charles T Reifsnider The board of trustees are Thomas H Routson, Edwin G Gilbert, Jacob J Weaver, Jr, M.D, P H Babylon, John A. Brown, Thomas F Shepherd, Jesse T H Davis

A copy of the *Engine of Liberty and Uniontown Advertiser*, No 22 of Volume I, dated Feb 3, 1814, a newspaper published by Charles Shower, at two dollars per annum, [illegible] matters the

proceedings of the Legislature of Maryland, Louis Gassaway, clerk, and a short extract of the proceedings of the Massachusetts Legislature

The editor advertises for subscriptions to a novel entitled "The Storm," in two volumes, price seventy-five cents, also that the office of the *Engine of Liberty* is removed "to the new brick building of Mr Henry Meyers nearly opposite to where it was formerly kept" Some news is given from New York, January 29th, and Richmond, January 27th, with an account of the camp at New Point Comfort, and describing the enemy's fleet An account of an earthquake at Showanoetown, Illinois Territory, Dec 13, 1813 is published, also a resolution passed by the New York Legislature, January 29th, appropriating fifty thousand dollars for the relief of the sufferers of the Niagara frontier

Among the advertisements Morris Meredith advertises for sale a lot of twenty-five acres of valuable land adjoining Uniontown, on the road leading from Baltimore to Hagerstown

Joshua Gist offers for sale his dwelling-house and plantation, containing six hundred acres, within two miles of Westminster The said Westminster is expected to be the county town of a new county that is to be made out of Baltimore and Frederick Counties Also two hundred and eighty acres about three or four miles from Westminster

Israel Rinehart and Ulrich Switzer, executors of David Rinehart, deceased, and Hannah Urner and John Rinehart, administrators of Jonas Urner, give notice to creditors

On the fourth page is given a column of foreign news, embracing England, France, and Germany Jacob Appler, Sr, advertises three lots of land in Libertytown, also seven and a half acres of woodland adjoining the lands of Abraham Albaugh

Ann Willis offers her farm of two hundred and eighty-two and a half acres, on Sam's Creek, on the road leading from Libertytown to Baltimore, for sale

Beal Dorsey near Freedom Town, advertises one hundred and fifteen acres of land, near McMurray's tavern

John Shriver offers for sale a dwelling-house, wheelwright-shop, and two lots in Uniontown

Samuel Lookingpeale, at Capt John Williams', desires to sell sixty five acres of land within half a mile of Ph[illegible] p Cromer s tavern

Edward Stevenson, within four or five miles of the Sulphur Springs, Frederick County, advertises his farm of two hundred and ten acres

Henry C [illegible] offers his mill seat and farm, on the waters of [illegible] Creek, three-quarter of a mile below Mr Londes' mill, also two hundred and twenty-three acres in Hampshire County, Va, for sale

John Williams, desiring to move to the Western country, wishes to sell his farm of two hundred and thirty-eight acres, situate on the waters of Sam's Creek

This copy was about one fourth the size of the *Democratic Advocate*, is well printed and seems to have been well sustained, judging from its advertising patronage

A copy of the *Engine of Liberty*, bearing date Nov 25, 1813, which was published at Uniontown, contains nine columns and a half of Judge Luther Martin's charge to the grand jury of Baltimore County and the grand jury's reply

The marriages of Philip Bishop, of Adams County, Pa, and Miss Mary Senseney of Frederick County, on the 23d of November, 1813, and Daniel Stoner and Miss Ann Roop, both of Frederick County, on the 25th of the same month, are published, also the death, on the 12th of November, of Philoman Barnes aged about ninety years

A meeting of the citizens of Uniontown and vicinity is called to meet on December 7th, at the house of George Herbach, to petition Congress for a post-route from Westminster to Fredericktown, also to petition the next Legislature to grant them a lottery to raise money to purchase a fire engine

Some war news is reported, including an account of his victory over the Creek Indians on November 4th by Gen Jackson One or two articles published showed that the editor, like most Federalists, was opposed to the war of 1812-14

Among the advertisements are the sale of farming utensils and household goods by Francis Hollingsworth, Little Pipe Creek, auction sale of dry goods, etc, by John Kurtz, at Uniontown, the sale of one hundred and twenty acres of land on Meadow Branch, one mile from Uniontown, by Christian Stouffler, also notices of two petitions to the General Assembly of Maryland, one of which, signed by citizens of Baltimore and Frederick Counties, is a prayer for a new county The metes and bounds asked for are substantially the same as those granted twenty four years later, when the bill was passed creating the county of Carroll

The other petition was for a law "to open a road from New Windsor to intersect the old Liberty road, on the line between Eli Dorsey and James Pearre, about a quarter of a mile below Conrad Dudderar's tavern"

The *Star of Federalism*, a small newspaper of four pages [illegible] published March,

1816, by Charles Sower with the motto, "Nothing extenuate, nor aught set down in malice" Its terms were two dollars per annum, and it was printed in the building now occupied by R J Matthias Its agents were

Liberty Town, Nathan England, Sam's Creek, Jacob Landis, New Windsor, William Brawner, Chr Ecker, Baltimore County, Thomas Pole, Westminster, Thomas Gist, Nicholas Kelson, New Market, William Hodgkiss, Taneytown, Nicholas Snider, Middleburg, J C and G W Gist, Pipe Creek, W P Farquhar, Union Bridge, Moses B Farquhar, Emmitsburg, P Reid, of Alexander, Baltimore, Edward J Coale, Cumberland, Francis Reid, Mount Pleasant, David Stem Norristown, Christopher Sower, Nathan Potts, Trindelphia, Andrew Graff, Daines Town, Robert Groomes, John Candler, Hyatt's Town, William Hyatt, Pickneysville, D Holliday

It was in size thirteen by twenty inches, and after its publication in Uniontown for a year was removed to Frederick Town, and there published by Mr Sower as late as December, 1819

The Enterprise was established in 1856 by William Sedwick and Dr Mills It was a small sheet, and was published until the close of the year, when it was merged into a larger paper called *The Weekly Press* The latter was first issued in January, 1857, with J H Christ as editor, its publishers being those of its predecessor, Dr Mills and William Sedwick It was published as late as July 26, 1861

Church of God—Religion appears to have taken firm hold of the people of Uniontown and its vicinity at an early date Allusion has already been made to the building of St Lucas' church by a lottery, under the auspices of the Presbyterian denomination The congregation of the Church of God was organized in 1833, numbering at that time about fifty members, and the Presbyterian faith not having proved as popular in the community as was expected, St Lucas' was transferred to the new organization Abraham Appler was the elder of the church, and Isaac Appler, deacon Edward West was the first regular pastor, and was succeeded by Rev Maxwell, Rev Jacob Linninger, Rev Joseph Adams, Rev William McFadden, Joseph Bomberger, R C Price, Rev I L Richmond, Rev Seltzmer, and several others The congregation now numbers about fifty members, and is under the care of Rev Mr Lugenbeel This church is the mother of the churches at Middletown, Mayberry, Frizzelburg, and Greenwoods, which are all now in this charge The Warfield, Winfield, and Carlton churches at one time belonged to the same charge, and were under the supervision of this church Their annual camp-meeting is held a few miles from Uniontown

The Church of God Cemetery is situated immediately in rear of the church The remains of the following persons are buried within its limits

M M Currey, died July 5, 1830, aged 35
Martha Currey, died May 16, 1852 aged 56
Eleanor Banks, died Dec 31, 1839, aged 81
John M Ferguson, born Sept 8, 1786, died Oct 20, 1861
Rebecca, his wife, died Sept 16, 1843, aged 60
James Currie, died Aug 26, 1827, aged 64
Rebecca Eckard, died Feb 6, 1842, aged 39 years, 3 months, 9 days
John W Davis, born March 22, 1813, died Aug 9, 1877
Mary Davis, born March 5, 1792, died Jan 8, 1865
Jonathan G Davis, born March 28, 1779, died Jan 4, 1842
Edward Davis, died Aug 2, 1825, aged 8
John S Shriver, born Aug 26, 1791, died Dec 6, 1814
Elizabeth Ann Mary Martha Grammar, died April 26, 1833
Andrew Werble, died April 29, 1849, aged 65 years, 6 months, 4 days
Rachael Metcalf, died April 12, 1826, aged 51 years
Solomon Beam, born July 11, 1798, died June 20, 1819
Isaac Hiteshew, died March 19, 1829, aged 34 years, 2 months, 15 months
Sybilla Reck, died March 15, 1826, aged 27 years, 1 month, 13 days
Ezra Metcalfe, died Jan 1, 1841, aged 29 years, 2 months, 25 days
Conrad Stuller, born June 8, 1823, died July 3, 1876
Henry Hiner, born March 9, 1770, died Sept 12, 1847
Hannah Hiner, died Dec 11, 1817, aged 62 years, 3 months
Samuel Hiner, born April 5, 1817, died Nov 8, 1876
Esther Hiteshow, died Oct 31, 1844, aged 72 years, 14 days
David Yingling born Oct 20, 1804, died April 2?, 1874
William H Christ, born April 25, 1831, died Nov 9, 1862
Morgan A Christ, died Jan 2, 1870, aged 31 years, 3 months, 25 days
Jacob Appler, died April 23, 1823, aged 34 years, 4 months, 1 day
Abraham Appler, born Dec 10, 1790, died Feb 1, 1878
Rebecca, his wife, and daughter of Jacob Hoffman, of Bainbridge, Lancaster Co, Pa, died Aug 28, 1866, aged 70, and who was a member of the church for 50 years
Mary J, wife of D R Carlyle, died Feb 19, 1875, aged 50 years, 5 months
Jacob Christ, born Sept 22, 1789, died Nov 30, 1872
Elizabeth, his wife, died May 16, 1867, aged 68 years, 10 months, 12 days
Abraham Garner, died Aug 2, 1789, aged 63 years, 10 months, 25 days
Mary Cover, born Dec 20, 1754, died March 17, 1828
Sarah, wife of Dan Smith, died July 4, 1844, aged 66 years, 3 months, 14 days
Barbara, relict of Barton Bean, died May 12, 1858, aged 74 years, 1 month, 5 days
Sophia Yingling, aged 70
William Wilson, died Nov 12, 1849, aged 73 years, 9 months, 28 days
Elizabeth, his wife, died Dec 25, 1869, aged 84 years, 4 months, 7 days
Margaret, wife of Ephraim Garner, died Aug 12, 1855, aged 54 years, 2 months 6 days
Oliver, son of William and Elizabeth Hiteshew Enlisted in Co E, 203d Regiment P V, Aug 31, 1864, and was killed Jan 15, 1865, whilst in the act of planting the flag on Fort Fisher, aged 1[illegible] years, 3 months, 1[illegible] days

James Hiteshew, died Nov 21, 1874, aged 24 years
Anna, wife of John Gore, died March 10, 1874, aged 63 years, 6 months, 16 days
Rebecca Grammar, born Sept 10, 1793, died June 8, 1864
Sarah C Grammar, born June 22, 1824, died April, 1864
Mary D C, wife of John Grammar, died Aug 23, 1856, aged 57 years, 8 months
Elizabeth, wife of A Koons, died Aug 2, 1874, aged 82
Angeline, wife of John T Wilson, died Feb 5, 1878, aged 62 years, 3 months, 26 days
Annie Clay, died Feb 19, 1877, aged 69 years, 10 months
Mary Ann Hollenberger, died Jan 4, 1865, aged 37 years, 0 months, 10 days
Peter Hollenberger, died March 22, 1860, aged 70 years, 4 months, 22 days
Magdalena, his wife, died Feb 23, 1862, aged 76
Rachel Yingling, born Jan 28, 1801, died July 30, 1865
Jacob Bloom, born July 20, 1794, died Sept 19, 1862
Mary, his wife, born Jan 20, 1800, died March 24, 1877
Samuel Anders, died April 26, 1865, aged 61 years, 10 months, 5 days
Lydia, his wife, died Dec 12, 1876, aged 74 years, 8 months, 28 days
John Garner, died Sept 13, 1860, aged 57 years
Hannah Hetshue, died March 1, 1876, aged 74
Ary, wife of James Few, died April 30, 1861, aged 69 years, 3 months, 19 days
Thomas Metcalf, born Dec 5, 1783, died March 17, 1862
George Warner, died June 18, 1862, aged 79
Elender A Warner, born Dec 22, 1786, died Feb 26, 1867
Catharine Hollenberger, born July 4, 1825, died April 7, 1874
John P Glass, a member of Co G, 6th Md Potomac Home Brigade, who died at Frederick Hospital, Sept 12, 1863, aged 29 years, 4 months, 6 days
Lieut Peter Wolfe, Co G, Md P H B, died Aug 1, 1862, aged 54 years, 4 months, 3 days
Mary Smith, died Jan 11, 1865, aged 54
Sarah Burgoon, died Nov 20, 1878, aged 71 years, 11 months, 20 days
John Eckard, born Jan 21, 1795, died Sept 8, 1872
Elizabeth Eckard, born Jan 12, 1799, died Dec 30, 1865
John A Eckard, born Aug 29, 1831, died Aug 21, 1870
Anna Fuss, died Dec 1, 1863, aged 88
Elizabeth Bare, born Oct 15, 1777, died Feb 12, 1865
Lydia Senseney, died Oct 20, 1869, aged 64 years, 6 months, 19 days
Washington Senseney, born May 28, 1810, died Dec 18, 1868
Mary A, his wife, born July 27, 1815, died June 20, 1875
Joanna Gilbert, died March 8, 1873, aged 37 years, 5 months, 6 days
Sarah Herbach, born Oct. 16, 1801, died April 12, 1872
Mary Eeotley, died Sept 27, 1821, aged 21 years, 6 months, 15 days
Rebecca Steele, died April 6, 1879, aged 65 years, 6 months, 16 days
William Hollenberry, born Nov 13, 1817, died Feb 23, 1870
Peter Christ, born July 19, 1786, died March 2, 1876
Elizabeth his wife, died Oct 17 1868, aged 81
James Gilbert died July 15, 1877, aged 73 years, 5 months, 6 days
Alumanda Eckard, died July 13, 1879, aged 43 years, 8 months, 12 days
Henry Eckard, died April 21, 1876, aged 45
Edward Arntz died Oct. 16, 1867, aged 26 years 1 month, 3 days

St Paul's Evangelical Lutheran congregation was formed Dec 29, 1869 It was then under the charge of Rev J F Deiner, and numbered eight members The elders were Dr J J Weaver and Jacob Ecker, the deacons, O M Hitshew, W H Hoffman, and J Routson Mr Deiner held the position as pastor of the charge until 1872, when he was succeeded by Rev G W. Anderson, the membership at this time was steadily increasing They held their services in a hall until the erection of their present edifice The church, which was built by a general contribution, cost about two thousand dollars The corner stone was laid Oct 24, 1874 and the building was dedicated in December of the same year, under the supervision of Rev D Morris, of Baltimore After three years of untiring services Mr Anderson resigned his charge, in May, 1876, when the Rev David B Floyd was called to occupy the pulpit The estimated cost of their handsome parsonage, which is now under erection, is two thousand dollars The present officers of the church are Elders, Dr Weaver and Jacob Ecker, Deacons, O M Hitshew and J Routser, who have occupied those respective positions since the organization of the church The congregation now numbers forty members, and the amount of contributions for 1881 was about four hundred dollars This church has in its charge three other congregations, viz, "Winter's Church," "Baust Church," and "Mount Union," it has also a Sunday school attached to it which is in a very flourishing condition Rev Mr Floyd has been the pastor for five years and gives entire satisfaction, and is untiring in his efforts to promote the interests of his church

The Pipe Creek Circuit of the Methodist Protestant Church was organized in 1820, and has steadily increased in power and influence Below is given the names of the pastors who have successively ministered to the various congregations under their charge in Uniontown and its vicinity

1829, D F Reese 1830, F Stier, J Hanson, 1831, F Stier, I Ibbertson, 1832, Isaac Webster, C W Jacobs 18 [illegible] Isaac Webster, W Sexsmith, 1834, Josiah Varden, H Doyle, 1835, H Doyle, J W Everest, A A Lipscomb 1836-37, J S Reese, J W Porter, 1838, Eli Henkle, J W Porter 1839, G D Hamilton, F Henkle, 1840, G D Hamilton, B Appleby, 1841, J S Reese, J T Ward 1842, L R Reese, P L Wilson, J Elderdice, 1843, J S Reese, S L Rawleigh, W T Eva 1844, W Collier, J [illegible] McLean, J D Brooks, 1845, W Collier, P L Wilson, J K Nichols, 1846, W Collier, J K Nichols 1847 [illegible] Morgan, T D Valiant 1848, J Morgan, W [illegible] 18[illegible] D L Reese, T L McLean, 1851, H P Jordan, J Roberts, 1852, H P Jordan, H J Day, 185[illegible], I M Wil[illegible] H I Day, 1854, J A McFadden, 1855, J A McFadden F Swentzell 1856 [illegible] Gr[illegible] F Swentzell, [illegible], J T [illegible] P [illegible] Reese, J

B Jones 1861, D E Reese, 1862-65, P L Wilson, 1865-68, R S Norris, 1868-71, D Wilson 1871, J R Nichols, 1872-74, H C Cushing, 1874-77, J W Charter, 1877-80, C H. Littleton

The following are the names of some of the persons buried in Uniontown cemetery

Washington, son of Moses and S B Brown, died March 1?, 1874 aged 39 years, 3 months, 2 days He was a member of Co 1, 4th Regiment Md Vols

Anna Carlyle, died Aug 1, 1860, aged 80 years, 3 months, [illegible] days

Isabel O'Brien, died Dec 25, 1870, aged 70

Sarah Bohain, died July 7, 1857, aged 71

Jacob Zimmerman, born Dec 30, 1787, died Feb 5, 1859

Mary, wife of John Babylon, died March 2, 1859, aged 45 years, 9 months, 11 days

William Roberts, died March 29, 1860, aged 61, and his wife, Eleanor R, May 13, 1875, aged 70

Philip Babylon, born Oct 6, 1776 died Jan 10, 1842

Elizabeth Babylon, born Oct 12, 1782, died July 19, 1857

Rachel Hammond, died July 23, 1846, aged 82 years, 5 months, 6 days

Eleanor Roberts, died Feb 28, 1816, aged 77

Rachel Brooks, born Dec 18, 1818, died Jan 31, 1851

Caroline Zollickoffer, died Dec 20, 1850, aged 84

John M A Zollickoffer died May 20, 1836, aged 51 years, 4 months, 10 days

William Wright died Jan 25, 1838, aged 36

Rev Daniel Zollickoffer, died Nov 1 1862, aged 72, and Elizabeth, his wife, died July 5, 1851, aged 57

Rev Dr William Zollickoffer, died April 6, 1853, 59 years, 5 months, and Sarah, his wife, died May 24, 1843, aged 44 years, 10 months, 20 days

Richard Brown, born Dec 2?, 1793 died March 14, 1850, and Susan, his wife, born June 10, 1787, died Sept 24, 1872

Samuel Roberts, died June 15, 1838, aged 32 years, 5 months, [illegible] days

Charles Stephenson, died Sept. 10, 1832, aged 91 years, 8 months, 26 days

John D Norris, died Feb 4, 1829, aged 23

Elizabeth Norris, died April 11, 1841, aged 57

Nicholas Stevenson, born May 18, 1750, died Aug 8, 1838

Nancy Stevenson died May 21, 1848, aged 70

Sarah Stevenson, died April 10, 1844, aged 60

William Devilbiss, born April 30, 1790, died Sept 1, 1854

Jemima Stevenson, died May 7, 1852, aged 70

Peter Senseney, born Feb 3, 1789, died March 21, 1855

Keturah Senseney, died June 11, 1858, aged 70

Richard Parrish, born May 10, 1822, died Dec 2, 1851

Rachel Rebecca Senseney, died March 19, 1862, aged 36

Michael Spousler, died Oct 25, 1832

George Herbach, died April 28, 1836, aged 69 years, 4 months, and Elizabeth, his wife, born Dec 21, 1771, died July 28, 1858

Zachariah Weeling, died Sept 16, 1870, aged 65

Abraham Shriver, died Aug 24, 1855, aged 80 years, 5 months, 29 days

[illegible] Shriver, died April 25, 1864, aged [illegible]

[illegible] Dungan, born March 28, 1818, died April 18, 1858

[illegible] Dungan, born Jan 16, 1811, died April 28, 1863

Elizabeth Wright, died July 14, 1867, aged 8? years, 7 months, [illegible]

[illegible] Francis G Wright [illegible] of M P Charles, died Feb 2? [illegible] aged 3? years, 7 [illegible]

Norris Meredith, died Sept 12, 1860, aged 90 years, 10 months, 15 days

Lydia Meredith, died Jan 23, 1867, aged 70 years, 11 months, 10 days

Catharine Meredith, died Feb 21, 1867, aged 75 years, 9 months, 5 days

William N Meredith, died Jan 14, 1868, aged 53 years, 9 months, 20 days

Mary G Meredith, died Jan aged 16, 1868, aged 61 years, 2 months, 29 days

Elizabeth B Meredith, born Feb 22, 1802, died Nov 20, 1875

Nathaniel N Meredith, born April 5, 1798, died Dec 25, 1874

Nathan Roop born May 3, 1835, died April 10, 1874

Michael Nusbaum, died March 8, 1877, aged 66 years, 2 months 8 days and Catharine, his wife, Jan 19, 1873, aged 77 years, 7 months, 3 days

William Shaw, died April 18, 1869, aged 68 years, 3 months

Ann Maria, wife of Rev David Wilson, died May 29, 1870, aged 41 years 4 months, 11 days

Dennis Cookson, died July 22, 1879, aged 44 years, 1 months, 10 days

Joseph Cookson, born Aug 21 1793 died June 1, 1846

Rachel Cookson, born Feb 1, 1800, died Jan 24, 1875

Samuel Cookson, born Sept 17, 1762, died Dec 22, 1836, and Rachel, his wife, born 1779, died 1853, aged 74

John W Babylon, died Nov 19, 1866, aged 21 years, 8 months 18 days

John N Starr, born March 24, 1808, died May 26, 1880, and Mary, his wife born March 10, 1810 died Aug 27, 1878

Hannah M wife of Milton S Starr, died Jan 13, 1874, aged 29 years, 5 months, 27 days

Mordecai Haines, died Jan 19, 1861, aged 40

Louisa Babylon, died Dec 6, 1854, aged 38 years, 9 months, 17 days

Deborah, wife of David Foutz, died Sept 25, 1842, aged 41

Charles Devilbiss, born Aug 15, 1786, died Sept 29, 1862 and Elizabeth, his wife, died Feb 27, 1864, aged 76 years, 1 month, 21 days

Ann Eliza, consort of John S Devilbiss died April 4, 1869, aged 34 years, 6 days

Martha Devilbiss, died Jan 19, 1868, aged 37 years 15 days

Mary E Devilbiss, died Oct 17, 1870, aged 40 years, 1 month, 4 days

Wm H Devilbiss, born Jan 13, 1821, died April 3 1880

Edward Devilbiss born Oct 5, 1822, died Jan 1, 1880, and Louisa C, his wife, born Sept 11, 1825, died Feb 2, 1879

John B Williams, died July 23 1861, aged 66, and Temperance his wife, died Nov 19, 1872, aged 69 years, 7 days

John Smith died Aug 7, 1868 aged 70 years, 4 months, 9 days, and Mary, his wife, died Nov 6, 1878, aged 77 years, 7 months, 16 days

William Goswell, died July 20, 1839, aged 56

Matilda Morelock, died April 15, 1851, aged 53 years, 6 months

Nancy Wilson, wife of George Harris, died March 1, 1858, aged 65

Mary Brisco died Aug 17, 1869, aged 75

John Hyder, born Aug 22, 1787, died March 20, 1878, and Catharine, his wife born April 16, 1788, died March 13, 1863, Enghd Hyder, their son, born Aug 31, 1814, died Feb 12, 1853

"Sydney Hyder Johnson, aged 23"

Below are given the votes polled for district officers since June [illegible] 1851

1851 —Vote for Primary School Commissioners Isaac Shingluft 253, Wm Hughes 117, Henry H Herbaugh 157, William Ecker 44

1853 —For Justices Richard Dell 280, Helpher Crawmer 55, John Smelzer 33, H W Dell 17, H H Herbaugh 351, Samuel Shunk 259, W R Currey 292, Joshua Switzer 321, Constables Wm Segafoose 384, Wm Brown 225, Wm Wilson 311, Wm Delphy 197, Road Supervisor Frederick Tawney 240, Thos P Shepherd, 302

1855 —For Justices Henry Fleagle 476, H H Herbaugh 486, E A Adee 481, John T Lowe 180, John Smelzer 147, Constables Wm Delphy 465, Wm Wilson 160, W Segafoose, 232, Road Supervisor Hiram Englar, 458

1857 —For Justices H H Herbaugh 378 D B Fleagle 359, J B Christ 301, S Anders 340, Constables Wm Brown 166, J T Myers 328, Isaac B Wright 338, Road Supervisor J B Williams 312

1859 —For Justices W H Haines 153, Caleb Baring 138, W H Herbaugh 311, D B Fleagle 334, Joshua Switzer 345, John Hesson 355, Constables Frederick Tawney 137, J R Haines 361, Levi Haifley 351, Road Supervisor Samuel Beck 330

1861 —For Justices H H Herbaugh 454, John Hesson 117, Levi Fleagle 145, Joshua Switzer 419, Constables A S Warner 346, Wm Singer 412, J W Segafoose 202, Road Supervisor Wm Bock 361, W S Jantz 91, Noah Plowman 74

The public school trustees for 1881 and 1882 have been

1 and 2 Uniontown —T C Brubaker, Jesse J H Davis, Wm H McCollum

3 Dunker Meeting house —George H Brown, Levi Caylor, John H Jordan

4 Moredock's —David Roop, John Royer, Henry Brunner

5 and 6 Frizellsburg —Dr Jacob Rinehart, Alfred Warner, Leonard Zile

7 Pleasant Valley —Wm Bowers, Noah Powell, Uriah Feeser

8 Baust Church —Jesse Unger, Wm Neusbaum, Wm Farmwalt

9 Fairview —Davis Myers, Daniel Diehl, David Stoner

10 Bear Mount —Samuel Wantz, David E Morelock, George W Hull

1. Middletown African School —John Thompson, Summerfield Roberts, Lloyd Coats (colored)

The teachers and number of pupils for the term ending April 15, 1881, were

1, H P Engler, 49, 2, Ella Beam, 42, 3, T H Adams, 30, 4, S P Weaver, 54, 5, Thomas Tipton, 11, 6, J J Reindollar, 18, 7 J P Earnest, 42, 8, Francis L Delaplane, 51, 9, A H Diffenbaugh, 17, 10, Sue L Lingly, 34, 1 (colored school), T F McCann, 20

Frizzellburg.—The village of Frizzellburg is five miles from Westminster, and pleasantly situated near Meadow Branch It was named in honor of the Frizzell family, early identified with the settlement

Among the first families located in the immediate vicinity of the town were the Smiths, Haifleys, Harmans Blacks, Roops, and Warners

The house now owned by Jeremiah Rinehart was the first erected in the village, and was occupied by Daniel Smith, one of the first residents of the town, in 1814, and was built probably prior to the year 1800 In the year 1814, Nimrod Frizzell, accompanied by his family, settled in the neighborhood and worked at his trade, that of a blacksmith At that time there were but few houses within the village limits The Haifleys lived in the house now occupied by Larry Freeman George Harman built and resided in the present residence of Edward Six Jacob Black lived in the house which is now the home of Mrs Vance In 1818, Nimrod Frizzell built the house which is now owned and occupied by Judge Frizzell He lived there and kept a hotel, together with a small store which was conducted in his name after his death until 1860 Frank Lytle was the first school teacher in the village, and was followed by Samuel Moffat and Francis Matthias Dr Cook was the first regular physician, and located here about the year 1847 He remained but a short time, and was followed by Dr Baker, Dr Shipley, Dr Roberts, Dr Kennedy, and Dr Price respectively In 1864, Dr J E Rinehart located here He was a native of Carroll County, and was born in Hampstead District He came to the vicinity of Frizzellburg in 1836, attended the public schools at this point, and in 1849 entered the Gettysburg Academy, Pa, where he graduated in 1855 He attended lectures in Philadelphia, and graduated at the Medical College in 1858 After locating and remaining in Pennsylvania during the war, he permanently located in Frizzellburg He was married to Maggie, a daughter of Peter Greeble, of Emmittsburg, Frederick Co, Md Mr Rinehart represented his county in the Maryland Legislature in 1876 Richard Brown was the earliest merchant, and was succeeded by Darius Brown who opened his place of business in the front room of the house now occupied by Ephraim Cover In 1849 he built himself a store-room and removed his goods to that building Campbell & Everheart succeeded to his business in 1851 Mr Brown having died the previous year, they built themselves a larger store house to accommodate the rapidly-increasing trade of the village A gentleman by the name of Richard Dell, and also a Mr Hollibery, were the successors of Messrs Campbell & Everheart, and were themselves succeeded, in 1881, by Mr Kerster

In 1842, Isaac Appler built the dwelling and store house now owned and occupied by Mr Warner Mr Appler sold it to Mr Gilbert, who kept a grocery-store, and who subsequently sold it to Valentine Vance A dry-goods and grocery-store has since been established here, Mr Warner having purchased the property from Mr Vance in 1860

Mr Frizzell the son of Nimrod Frizzell, from whom the village received its title, was born in the year 1818, and has always been a resident of the place For three years he held the position of leather inspector of the city of Baltimore He married, in 1841, Miss Barbara N, daughter of John and Mary Swigart Mr Frizzell is at present one of the judges of the Orphans' Court

Church of God—This congregation was formed under the auspices of Rev William McFadden The church was erected and dedicated in the year 1842, at a cost of seven hundred and fifty dollars Rev Joseph Bombarger delivered the dedicatory sermon The following gentlemen composed the building committee, and were authorized to collect all the subscriptions Benjamin Fleagle, Levi Fleagle, James Gilbert, Caleb Boring, and Henry Fleagle The congregation at that time numbered forty members

Rev Mr Lugenbeel is the present pastor, and Levi Fleagle the elder The latter has held that position since the organization of the church The trustees for the year 1881 are Levi Fleagle, Wm L Fleagle, Benjamin Fleagle, and John T Baust, and the number of members fifteen In the rear of the church is the Church of God cemetery, in which are buried several children, and there are also many unmarked graves Among the names recorded are Eliza Jabe[illegible], died Jan 22, 1862, aged sixty-five years, four months, four days, and Thomas Jones, died Aug 11, 1873, aged fifty-two years

The building in which are held the sessions of the Frizzellburg Academy is commodious and amply provided with all the necessary paraphernalia for proper training and education The school is graded to suit the ages and development of scholars and is supplied with an excellent corps of teachers

Within four miles of the village, on the banks of the Big Pipe Creek, there stood until recently an old stone mill and dwelling, erected in 1776 by two Tories named Graffs They were driven from Philadelphia because of the intemperate expression of their unpopular opinions and sympathies, and fled to Carroll County (at that time Frederick) for refuge They settled upon this stream and prospered, their calamities having taught them the wisdom of moderation and taciturnity

Tyrone.—The village of Tyrone is situated thirty-two miles west of Baltimore and six miles west of Westminster, on what is generally known as "the [illegible] road" leading from Westminster to Taneytown It contains a handsome church, a mill, a store for general merchandise, and a number of dwelling-houses The Farmwalt [illegible], early settlers in the neighborhood, founded the town William L Fleagle is the postmaster and principal merchant, and W H Rider superintends the mill

Emmanuel Church, or Baust's church, in which the Lutheran and Reformed congregations jointly worship, was built many years ago, but was thoroughly repaired and almost completely remodeled, Oct 18, 1868 The congregations were originally organized prior to the year 1794, and worshiped in an old log school-house which stood upon the site of the present church, the land having been deeded Jan 10, 1791, by Valentine and Maria Baust, to build a church and school house, and it was from the donors that the church derived its former name

The two congregations were incorporated by an act of the General Assembly of Maryland passed Jan 12, 1835 The incorporators were John Fleagle, Sr, John Derr, Michael Morelock, and Peter Halfley At a meeting of the two congregations in 1838 there were present John Derr, Peter Dayhoff, Peter Golle, George Maxwell John Fleagle, Jr, Valentine Wentz, and Jacob Valentine

The officers of the church at this time were as follows

German Reformed Congregation Elders, John Fleagle, Peter Golle, Deacons, Peter Dayhoff, John Fleagle Trustees, George Maxwell, John Derr Lutheran Congregation Elders M Morelock, Andrew Babylon, Deacons, Henry Hahn, Jacob Valentine, Trustees, Valentine Wentz, Peter Halfleigh

The ministers who have served the Lutheran congregation, as far as can be ascertained, are as follows John Grupp was the first, and was at the time also the pastor of Taneytown, Kinder's, Winter's, and Silver Run Lutheran Churches He was followed in 1819 by Henry Graver, Rev John N Hoffman, 1833, Samuel Finckle 1834, Ezra Keller, 1835, Solomon Sentman, 1840, Rev Philip Willard, 1845, Cornelius Reimensnider, John Winters, 1850, Samuel Henry, 1855 to 1868, Mr Deiner, 1872, Rev G W Anderson, and the present pastor, Rev David B Floyd

This church was in the Emmittsburg and Taneytown charge until 1840, when it was transferred to the Westminster Circuit Again, about the year 1870, it was transferred to the Uniontown Circuit, to which it now belongs The present officers of the two congregations are

Lutheran Elders, William Nusbaum and Jacob Myers, Deacons, Dr J F Rinehart, Lewis Myers, Trustees, Jeremiah Rinehart, Ephraim Winter This congregation numbers ninety members German Reformed Elders, Jesse Unger, Joshua [illegible] Trustees Jacob Sell, Wm Farr [illegible] William Nus-

baum, Secretary, Dr J E Rinehart Jacob Myers, joint treasurer, Jacob Myers, treasurer Lutheran Congregation, Jesse Unger, treasurer Reformed Congregation

As was said above, in 1868 the church was thoroughly remodeled and rededicated, the services being interesting and impressive The preparatory exercises were conducted by Rev Griffith Owen, of Baltimore, and the sermon was preached by Rev P A Strobel, of Westminster The dedicatory services were performed by Rev J Stemer The debt of the church was liquidated by subscriptions raised during the services The name of the church was also changed at that time, and it has since been known as Emmanuel The following persons are buried in Baust Church Cemetery

Abraham Hann, died Oct 5, 1862, aged 80 years, 11 months, 25 days

Josiah Hafley, died Nov 29, 1855, aged 36 years, 5 months, 13 days

Margaret Fluegal, born Jan 3, 1770, died Dec 4, 1842

John Fluegal, born Nov 17, 1762, died Sept 3, 1845

Uriah Baust, born Nov 23, 1822, died Nov 16, 1849

Abraham Hann, born May 4, 1817, died March 16, 1841

Jacob Keefer, died July 13, 1837, aged 34 years, 6 months, 21 days

Lydia Hesson, wife of John Hesson, and daughter of John Yaley, died Aug 27, 1842, aged 17.

Peter Haiffle, born April 11, 1786, died Jan 11, 1869

Levi Haifley, died July 3, 1830, aged 17

Margaret, wife of Peter Hafley, died Dec 23, 183–, aged 43 years, 1 month, 23 days

Sophia Wagner, died Aug 13, 1836, aged 62 years, 7 months

Mary Wantz, died March 25, 1842, aged 24 years, 9 months, 28 days

Catharine Shoemaker, died 1834

Peter Shoemaker, died Dec 24, 1838, aged 61 years, 8 months, 21 days

Mary E Wentz, died 1833, aged 40

George Warner, died April 30, 1836, aged 77 years, 10 months, 10 days

Johannes Bischoff, born 1740, died July 9, 1813, aged 73 years, 4 months

Maria Bischoff, died Dec 21, 1824, aged 80

Jacob Bishop, died Aug 31, 1852, aged 59 years, 9 months, 7 days, and Elizabeth, his wife, died Dec 4, 1824, aged 35 years, 9 months, 18 days

Margaret Mock, died Jan 2, 1815, aged 64

Peter Mock, died April 3, 1812, aged 85

Jacob Honer, died 1798

Frederick Wentz, Jr, died Sept 27, 1824, aged 63

Geo Frederick Wentz, died Feb 3, 1833, aged 78 years, 1 month, 15 days

Frederick Keefer, born Dec 2, 1795, died Aug 4, 1855

Elizabeth Shriemer, born in 1771, died in 1773

Sarah Swigart, died March 28, 1813, aged 25 years, 10 months, 2 days

"Wagner, born 17[illegible]5, died 1801"

Michael Wagner, born Nov 6, 1752, died Feb 21, 1829

Barbara Yar, born Dec 4, 1784, died Dec 2, 1806

Ulrich Stollern, born April 15, 1737, died September, 1816

John Marker, died Aug 16, 18[illegible]4, aged 65, and Susannah, his wife, born Fe[illegible] 12, 1[illegible]74, died March 3, 18[illegible]

Elizabeth Molor, born Nov 14, 1776 Feb 18, 1813

Magdalena Derr, died July 19, 1822, [illegible] 25.

Abraham Derr, died May 11, 1829, aged 62

Elizabeth Derr, died Nov. 13, 1822, aged [illegible]

Jacob Derr, born Nov 12, 1788, died Dec 23, 1819

Valentine Wentz, died Feb 19, 1843, aged 56 years, 1 months, 20 days

Catherine Bishop, born Oct 13, 1783, died June 13, 1845

John F Haifley, died Sept 14, 1845, aged 55 years, 5 months, 13 days

George Eckard, died Nov 9, 1822 aged 55 years, 11 months, 20 days

Aaron P Erviesse, died Aug 24, 1829, aged 6

Mary Seel, died Aug 27, 1813, aged 80

Sarah Worley, born March 6, 1799, died Sept 13, 1857

Lydia Worley, born June 18, 1803, died Feb 17, 1858

Lydia, wife of Daniel Myers, died July 16, 1856, aged [illegible] years, 11 months

Elizabeth Hann, died March 20, 18[illegible], aged 69 years, 2 months, 1 day

Peter Hesson, born July 21, 1783, died Dec 16, 1865, and Susannah, his wife, born Dec 15, 1797, died Jan 25, 1857

Catherine, wife of John Fleet, died Dec 11, 1856, aged 72

Peter Zepp, died Aug 21, 1879, aged 71 years, 1 month, 14 days, and Catherine, his wife, born April 28, 1810, died Jan 23, 1855

Abraham Hesson, died Feb 19, 1855, aged 8[illegible] years, 1[illegible] months, 21 days

Louisa Hesson, died Jan 11, 1859, aged 70 years, 11 months, 27 days

Eli Hesson, died Sept 9, 1859, aged 17 years, 6 months 1[illegible] days

John L Powell, born June 23, 1779, died April 15, 1855, and Elizabeth, his wife, born April 12, 1782, died May, 1861

Peter Gatle, died July 7, 1855, aged 76 years, 10 months, 1 days and Catherine, his wife, Feb 25, 1862, aged 65 years, [illegible] months, 3 days

Josiah Bankard, born Oct 25, 1830 died July 17, 1873

Abraham Bankard, died Oct. 30, 1879, aged 80 years, [illegible] days

Ezra Haifley, "Co A, 6th Md Regt Vols," born Sept 27 1840, died Oct 14, 1864

Wm Gregg, born April, 1818, died April, 1866

Lydia, wife of Josiah Babylon, died Aug 10, 1867, aged 4[illegible] years, 10 months, 9 days

Joseph Cox, born Aug 10, 1801, died Oct 29, 1879, and Rachel, his wife, born Nov 8, 1811, died May 24, 1872

"John Mathew, honest and faithful servant to Abraham Hesson, died Sept 9, 1855 aged 61"

Valentine Wantz, died June 25, 1876, aged 65 years, months, 23 days, and Susannah, his wife, born July 8, 18[illegible] died March 5, 1870

Mathias Copenhover, died Jan 8, 1877, aged 68 years [illegible] months, 22 days, and Mary, his wife, died May 4, 1875, aged 72 years, 8 months, 8 days

Sarah, their daughter born Dec 5, 1830, died March 1[illegible] 1864, and Elizabeth, another daughter, born Dec 3, 1[illegible] died August, 1863

John Fleagle, a soldier of 1812, born June 25, 1793, [illegible] March 15, 1879 and Rachel, his wife, born Jan 22, 179[illegible], [illegible] May 8, 1855

Uriah Fleagle, of "Co G, 1st Regt Md Vols" (P H B) born Feb 21, 1843, fell at the battle of Gettysburg, Jul 1863, aged 20 years, 4 months, 9 days

[illegible] Fleagle [illegible] killed at the battle of Murfreesboro', [illegible]

George Fleagle, died Feb 27, 1880, aged 81 years, 7 months, 4 days

Iona Louisa, wife of Amos Hull, died Dec 22, 1876, aged 2[illegible]

Margaret Rinehart, died June 5, 1863, aged 49

Samuel Fitze, died Nov 30, 1871, aged 49 years, 2 months, 27 days

Valentine Wantz, born Jan 27, 1820, died March 11, 1860

Anna Maria Meyers, born Dec. 21, 1777, died Oct 3, 1863

Susan, wife of Jacob Eckard, died Jan 9, 1861, aged 51

John Lampert, died June 20, 1874, aged 76, and Louisa, his wife, Feb 17, 1877, aged 78 years, 11 days

Hezekiah Lambert, born Oct 24, 1825, died April 7, 1860

George Warner, born July 15, 1811, died Feb 6, 1872

Sarah Warner, born May 24, 1795, died May 16, 1872

Elizabeth Warner, born May 26 1776, died Oct 1, 1857

William Warner, died Dec 30, 1853, aged 36 years, 7 months, 15 days

Michael Dotzour, died March 19, 1858, aged 35 years, 5 months 10 days

Margaret Dotzour, died May 6, 1872, aged 68

John Babylon, born May 10, 1803, died March 1, 1862

John Dell, born Dec 17, 1773, died Oct 23, 1871

Mary Dell, born July 26, 1777, died Sept 28, 1851

Michael Babylon, died Dec 12, 1870, aged 70 years, 8 months, 24 days

Andrew Babylon, born Aug 20, 1779, died Oct 21, 1851

Susanna Babylon, died Feb 8, 1870, aged 91 years, 9 months, 17 days

David Babylon, born Dec 21, 1820, died July 15, 1857, and Mary, his wife, born Feb 13, 1821, died Feb 4, 1857

George Rodkey, born Dec 8, 1790, died Nov 25, 1851

Mary Eckard, born Dec 13, 1765, died Jan 31, 1856

Solomon Farmwalt, born Sept 4, 1793, died Feb 22, 1881, and Elizabeth, his wife, born April 28, 1800, died March 22, 1852

Ellenoore Froinfelter, died Feb 15, 1870, aged 76 years, 3 months 4 days

John Nusbaum, born March 25, 1793, died June 1, 1866, and Elizabeth, his wife, born July 28, 1799, died Dec 6, 1864

Henry Beard, died Aug 4, 1861, aged 41 years, 6 months, 5 days

Cornelius Baust, born Feb 10, 1785, died April 26, 1868, and Elizabeth, his wife, born Sept 6, 1791, died March 1, 1865

Charles Crawford, died Dec 11, 1871, born May 23, 1805

Fred Wantz, born March 3, 1778, died Jan 24, 1857, and Mary his wife, died Feb 8, 1857, aged 61 years, 2 months, 8 days

George Wantz, died May 6, 1866, aged 36 years, 1 month, 11 days

Eliza Hunger, died May 2, 1877, aged 63 years, 25 days

Catharine, wife of Jesse Babylon, died April 5, 1878, aged 62

Elizabeth, wife of Joshua Stansbury, born Aug 13, 1813, died Feb 1, 1874.

Wm Lampert, born Sept 1, 1826, died April 7, 1878

Dr David B Fleagle, died Feb 26, 1878, aged 35 years, 9 months 6 days

Jacob Englesong, born Jan 12, 1807, died Nov 27, 1880

Nusbaum's Cemetery

Peter Babylon, born Nov 14, 1751, died Jan 28, 1850

Hannah Foutz, born Nov 26, 1770, died Aug. 28, 1815

Elizabeth Foutz, died Sept 27, 1860, aged 43

Solomon Foutz, died [illegible] 1[illegible], 18[illegible], aged 78 years 10 months, 25 days

Jacob Youn, died January, 1830, aged 60

Mary Youn, died March 15, 1824, aged 37 years, 2 months, 13 days

Mary, infant daughter of Wm Youn, died May 4, 1825

John Yon, born April 1 1829, died Jan 1, 1851

Catherine Yon, born 1785, died 1797

Elizabeth Babylon, born Dec 22, 1790, died April 26, 1813

Samuel Farnhord, born Oct 9, 1817, died June, 1818

Leonard Kitzmiller, born April 27, 1732, died March 1, 1820

David Stouffer, died Dec 15, 1867, aged 76 years, 11 months, 14 days, and Mary, his wife, died March 26, 1841, aged 48 years, 4 months, and 12 days

Emma Kate, daughter of N and C Heck, died Aug 30, 1869, aged 7 months, 21 days

Susannah Holloway, daughter of Samuel and Elizabeth Holloway, died 1809

"P W, died 1785"

Alexander McIlheny, died Jan 25, 183[illegible], aged 56 years, 10 months, 20 days, and Elizabeth, his wife, born Aug 1, 1779, died May 2, 1853

Mayberry is a small village five miles from Taneytown, near Bear Branch N H Fleagle is the postmaster and merchant of the place, and William Stonesifer and Henry Eck are the millers

Pleasant Valley, another small village, is five miles from Westminster Samuel Lawyer is the postmaster, H B Albaugh, merchant, and F L Yingling & Son, mill-owners St Matthew's Reformed church was built at a cost of $2400, and dedicated Nov 30, 1879

MYERS DISTRICT, No 3

Myers District, or the Third District of Carroll County, is bounded on the north by Pennsylvania, on the east by Manchester District, on the south by the districts of Uniontown and Westminster, and on the west by Taneytown District Big Pipe Creek, Silver Run, and their tributaries flow through the district in many directions, and Piney Creek forms the boundary line on the northwestern border, these fine streams furnishing excellent power for mills, which has been utilized to a considerable extent by the inhabitants Union Mills, Myersville, Silver Run, and Piney Creek Station, on the Frederick and Pennsylvania Line Railroad, are flourishing villages The metes and bounds of the district, as laid out by commission appointed in 1837, are as follows

"Beginning at the end of Royer's and Guyman's lane, on Baughman's county road, thence with said road to Lawyer's Branch, thence down said branch to Big Pipe Creek, thence with a straight line through Peter Bixler's farm, leaving said Bixler in District No 6, thence with a straight line to a branch known by the name of Ohio, where said branch crosses Trump's county road, thence up said branch through to Wm [illegible]s farm, up said branch to its head, thence with a straight line to the nearest point on Rinehart's county road, thence on said road to the Pennsylvania line, thence with Pennsylvania line to Littlestown and Westminster turnpike, thence down said turnpike to the [illegible] with [illegible] stone road to [illegible] said road to the

aforesaid turnpike at the 33d mile stone, thence with said turnpike to Rinehart's county road, thence with said road to Rinehart's mill, thence up the road by Rinehart's dam, thence with said road, between Frederick Baughman's farm and Jacob Snyders, to Andrew Angel's, leaving said Angel in District No 7, thence to Bixler's tan-yard, leaving said Bixler in District No 7, thence with a straight line to the beginning"

By an act of the General Assembly of Maryland, passed April 2, 1841, the division line between the Third (Myers) and Seventh (Westminster) Districts was altered and made as follows "Beginning at the natural boundary at the intersection of Big Pipe Creek, in Peter Bixler's meadow, and running thence by a direct line to Jacob Frock's dwelling house, leaving the same in the Seventh Election District, thence by a direct line to Adam and William Bishe's dwelling-house, leaving the same in the Seventh Election District, and thence to the Westminster and Littlestown turnpike road at the intersection of the stone road, which was then the boundary line between the Third and Seventh Election Districts" The district in 1880 had a population of 1959

Union Mills was made the place for holding the polls The district was named in honor of the Myers family, one of the first to settle in this portion of Carroll County one of whose descendants, Samuel W Myers, assisted in laying out the nine districts into which Carroll was originally divided in 1837

A tract of land known as "Ohio," containing nine thousand seven hundred and fifty acres, was patented to Samuel Owings in 1763

The early settlers were almost entirely Germans from York and Lancaster Counties, in Pennsylvania, or directly from the Palatinate, and to this day there are in its limits but few families not of German extraction

For the first half-century of its history and settlement the German was the only tongue spoken, and after that, for a generation, the German and English languages were spoken indiscriminately, but since 1835 the English only has been used These settlers were a hardy and thrifty race, of strong religious sentiments, and rapidly increased in numbers and wealth Among the pioneers were Joseph Leaman, Nicholas Deal, George Michael Derr, Charles Angel, the Erbs, Myerses, Bankerds, Nails, Krouses, Yinglings, Farmwalts, Hessons, Flickingers, Koontz', Frocks, Bixlers, Bachmans, Groffs, Hahns, Wisels, Kesselrings, Leppoes, and afterwards there came the Burgoons, Joneses, Morelocks, Gearharts, Fishers, and others

Over a century ago "Bankerd's mill" was in operation on the site of the present Union Mills and "Groff's mill" was located where now James F Bud-[illegible] has a saw [illegible] both on Big Pipe Creek [illegible]

The Shriver Family and Union Mills.—Andrew Shriver, son of David and Rebecca (Ferree) Shriver, was born on Little Pipe Creek (Westminster District), Nov. 7, 1762, and was the eldest of nine children His parents were among the first settlers in this section of country He was married Dec 31, 1786, to Miss Elizabeth Shultz, daughter of John Shultz, at his house in Baltimore, by Rev William Otterbein, a distinguished clergyman of that day His wife was born Aug 15, 1767, and died Sept 27, 1839 Their children were John Shultz, born March 1, 1788, Thomas, born Sept 2, 1789, Rebecca, born Dec 29, 1790, Matilda, born Oct 3, 1792, James, born at Littlestown, Pa, April 4, 1794, William, born at same place, Dec 23, 1796, and died June 11, 1879, Elizabeth, born at Union Mills, March 14, 1799, and Andrew Keyser, born at the same place, March 25, 1802, Ann Maria, born March 13, 1804, Joseph, born Jan 11, 1806, and Catharine, born May 27, 1808

All of these children grew up and married respectably, and left surviving children to perpetuate their name and lineage

After the death of his wife, Elizabeth, in 1839, Andrew Shriver continued to live at the old homestead at Union Mills until his death, Sept 20, 1847 aged nearly eighty five years In the fall of 1784, when twenty years of age, with a capital of four hundred and sixty pounds, having been assisted to this extent, perhaps, by his father, who had accumulated considerable means, Andrew Shriver engaged in the mercantile business on Little Pipe Creek, and subsequently in Baltimore After his marriage in 1786 he continued to make his home with his wife on Little Pipe Creek until 1791, when he removed to Littlestown, Pa, where he kept a store and tavern until 1797 On June 26th of that year he removed with his family, then comprising six children, to the Union Mills property which he bought, in partnership with his brother David, of the heirs of Jacob Bankerd, deceased This property is located on the northern branch of Pipe Creek, in what was then Frederick, now Carroll, County, five miles southeast of the Pennsylvania State line Andrew and David Shriver experienced great difficulty in gaining possession of their property David Shriver, Sr [illegible] then, and for some thirty years afterwards, employed by them to get a chancery decree for the sale of the land of the Bankerd estate He was at length successful, and was appointed trustee for the sale of the property Andrew Shriver became the purchaser [illegible] the mill, [illegible] by the pres-

ent structure They got possession of the property with difficulty, even after its sale, some of the heirs not being willing to yield By arrangement of the above partners with John Mung, a millwright, work on the mill was completed satisfactorily for the sum of four hundred and thirty dollars This agreement was witnessed by James McSherry, Dr. S Duncan, and Susannah Showers (sister of Andrew and David Shriver), and dated Jan 26, 1797. An agreement of the same parties, of the same date, with Henry Kohlstock, carpenter,—

"Witnesseth that for and in consideration of one hundred pounds to be paid by the said Andrew and David Shriver to the said Henry Kohlstock, he, the said Kohlstock, agrees to finish two small houses fourteen by seventeen feet each, to be connected by a porch and passage about ten feet wide,—that is to say, he is to do all the joiner work so as to complete said houses, passage, porch, and stairways, agreeably to a plan thereof now produced, also to do all the carpenter work of a mill house forty by fifty feet, and to complete the whole thereof in a sufficient and neat, workmanlike manner, as expeditiously as possible, and farther, finally to complete the whole, he is to paint the work, both dwelling and mill house, in a proper and sufficient manner, they, Andrew and David Shriver, to find all the materials, paint oil etc

"R McILHENNY, JOHN MONG, *Witnesses*"

This house was completed according to the agreement and occupied, and one of the rooms on the ground-floor was used for a store The partnership between the brothers suggested the name of the "Union Mills" to their homes, which was subsequently extended to embrace the whole village The date of the dissolution of the firm is not exactly known —David was afterwards employed in locating and constructing the National road from Baltimore through Fredericktown, Hagerstown, and Cumberland to Wheeling, on the Ohio River He displayed great skill in working iron, having made some of the most difficult parts of the mill-machinery (the appliances at hand being embraced in an ordinary blacksmith-shop at this place), some of which are still about the premises, and will compare favorably with the productions of the best workmen of the present day A couple of pair of steelyards, with his name stamped upon them, are now in use, and are perfectly reliable, the State inspector of weights and measures having certified to their accuracy some twenty years since The Shriver family developed great skill in working iron At a very early date they had a shop at Little Pipe Creek, in which they all worked at times for different purposes, and Isaac Shriver took a contract from the government to furnish a large quantity of gun barrels, to be delivered at a stated time Although the designated time was short for that day, he finished the contract according to the terms and to the satisfaction of the authorities Andrew Shriver after the removal of his brother David from the mills, continued to keep a store for the sale of general merchandise, and secured for the village a post-office of which he took charge He also held the office of magistrate for a long time, and it was chiefly owing to his influence that the public road was opened from Union Mills to Hanover, Pa He was afterwards instrumental in getting the turnpike from Baltimore to Chambersburg through the village With a growing family and continued prosperity in business, Mr Shriver required more house-room, and wings were added at different periods to the original building Architectural beauty was not much studied, but the mansion is quaint and picturesque It still stands with but little alteration, and is now occupied by Andrew K Shriver, one of the sons, born under its ancient roof Andrew Shriver, although an active politician as was also his father, never held any public office other than magistrate, which position he filled during the greater part of his life, having been retained through all the political changes which occurred in the State His magisterial services were highly appreciated, and were characterized by moderation and dignity Very few appeals from his decisions to the higher court were made, thus saving expense to the county, as well as to individuals In his judicial business, which extended over a wide region he exerted a large personal influence, often acted as peacemaker between litigants and brought about amicable settlements where a continued appeal to law tended only to make matters worse Elizabeth Shriver, wife of Andrew Shriver as mistress of a large household and mother in the family, was an admirable Christian woman, and her influence had much to do in moulding the character and shaping the future of her children The children of Andrew and Elizabeth Shriver were married thus John Shultz to Henrietta Myers, of Baltimore, Thomas, three times,—first, to Ann Sharp, of York, Pa , and the third time to Miss Sherrard, Rebecca Ferree to James Renshaw, of York, Pa , Matilda to Michael H Spangler, of York, Pa , James to Elizabeth B Miller, of Uniontown, Pa , William to Mary Owings, of Littlestown, Pa , Elizabeth (Eliza) to Lawrence J Brengle, of Frederick (after the decease of Catharine Shriver, his first wife), Andrew Keyser, on Feb 16, 1837, to Catharine Wirt, of Hanover, Pa (who died Aug 24, 1872), Ann Maria to William Tell Steiger, of Washington, D C , Joseph to Henrietta Coston, of Washington, D C , Catharine to Lawrence J Brengle, of Frederick The children of these several family unions form a large connection [illegible] a wide ex-

tent of country, though the majority of them are living in the vicinity of the old homestead Andrew K and William, two of the sons, with parts of their families, retain the mill property in their possession at this date, 1881 This place is on the Baltimore and Reisterstown turnpike,—the old road to Pittsburgh,—over which noted thoroughfare in the days of stage-coaches there was an immense deal of travel. Among the many eminent men who tarried overnight or stopped for meals at the old Shriver mansion was Washington Irving who spent the Sabbath there, and a chapter of the recollections of his stay is found in his writings, but the scene is laid in England The first postmaster was Andrew Shriver, the present efficient officer Andrew K Shriver, and William Shriver once held the office For nearly fourscore years, save a brief space of time, this office has always been in the Shriver family B F Shriver & Co now operate the flouring-mill, and run a large canning factory, while the tannery is run by A K Shriver & Sons on the same site where the first enterprise of that character was located in 1795

William Shriver was born at Littlestown, Pa, Dec 23, 1796, and at the time of his death, which occurred in 1879, was one of the proprietors of the flour mills, and of the old estate there, which had been in the family many years He was a brother to the late John S Shriver, so well known as the president of the Ericsson line of steamboats between Baltimore and Philadelphia He had several brothers, one of them, Thomas Shriver, living in New York City, ninety years old Mr Shriver's father was a very old man when he died, and the family is generally long lived He left an aged wife and a large number of children and great-grandchildren He celebrated the fiftieth anniversary of his wedding several years ago Few persons had a larger personal acquaintance or more friends than the deceased

The following is a list of persons living within a radius of four or five miles of Union Mills, and all, with a few exceptions, in Myers District, who were seventy years old and upwards in 1879

	Years.		Years
Christina Yingling	80	Samuel Lookingbill	77
William Shriver	83	Isaac Beal	76
Mrs Mary Shriver	72	George Stegner	88
Andrew K Shriver	77	Mrs Rebecca Leppo	80
Peter Yingling	82	Mrs Catharine Meyers	84
Mrs Yingling	74	Mrs Mary Yeiser	91
Mrs Willet	73	Mrs Sarah Little	7[illegible]
Jacob Snyder.	84	John Stonesifer	84
John Koontz	76	Mrs Rachel Warner	85
Philip Arter	75	Mrs Margaret Duce	71
John Frock, of J	72	Henry Dutteror	73
Isaac Bankert	77	Mrs Mary Kelly	79
John Flickinger	73	John Study	74
Jacob Leister	77	[illegible]	[illegible]
Mrs Elizabeth Kemp	9[illegible]	[illegible]	7[illegible]
Jacob Hahn	76	John Snyder	76
Samuel Hahn	7[illegible]	Mrs Elizabeth Myers	77
Mrs Sarah Shull	79	George Fleagle, Sr	82
George Bowman	77	Mrs Lydia Fleagle	76
Andrew Stonesifer	77	Mrs Judith Cumarine	81
Mrs Mary Stonesifer	74		

Directly across Big Pipe Creek is a village laid out by Peter E Myers and called Myersville, but as the post-office is called Union Mills, the latter is the name by which the mills and the village are generally known The Methodist Episcopal church was erected in 1880, and has a flourishing Sunday-school attached to it, of which William Yingling is superintendent

Carroll Academy was organized in 1838, and a stone building was erected by stock subscriptions The first trustees were William Shriver, William N. Burgoon, John Erb, Peter E Myers and Isaac Bankerd, secretary of the board, A K Shriver The first principal was James Burns, an Irishman, the second, James Small, and among their successors were Bushrod Poole, Christian Erb Samuel S Shriver, John G Wolf, John A Renshaw, Bernard McManus, and Mr Bardwell Upon the creation of the public school system, the academy passed under the control of the school authorities Mr Burns, the first teacher of the academy, organized the first Sunday-school in the district,—a union school and not denominational Dr William R Cushing is the physician of the town F M Hall is a prominent merchant in Union Mills. William Bankerd, Joseph Erb, Samuel Stonesifer are coopers, John Beemiller, Jesse Koontz, shoemakers, W G Byers, undertaker, J William Everhart, surveyor, Jesse Legare is a justice of the peace, Jeremiah Myers carries on a saw mill, Jesse Myers and P Wolf are millers, John Myers is a manufacturer of brick The blacksmiths are Samuel Stansbury, Samuel Orem, William Tagg & Sons, William Rennaker is a carpenter, Ephraim and Ezra J Yingling are tinners, and Martin Yingling, a cabinet maker

Silver Run is on the turnpike from Westminster to Littlestown, Pa, nine miles from the former and five from the latter Its postmaster is John N Mark, and assistant, Augusta J Mark The village is near the stream, Silver Run, from which it takes its name The village store is kept by Albaugh & Haines, and the hotel by Andrew Wisner J Henry Knipple is justice of the peace, and Dr James M Marshall, the physician The various industries are represented by Elias Bankerd, wheelwright, Joseph Beemiller, T W Little, shoemakers, Mis T Kesselring, millinery and confectionery, Henry and Jacob Koontz, blacksmiths, George L Little, cabinet-maker, and Rufus Strouse, constable

[illegible] m," and is the

joint place of worship of the German Reformed and Lutheran congregations The present church edifice is of stone, and was erected in 1822 It is on a tract of land called "Dyer's Mill Forest," adjoining a survey called "Lewis' Luck" It occupies the site of the first church, a rude log structure, built in 1768 The deed for the fifteen acres on which it is located was made by Joseph Dyer in 1768 to John Leaman, Nicholas Deal, George Michael Derr, Charles Angel, of the "Dutch Congregation of Silver Run," a committee of the Lutheran and Reformed Calvinists The consideration named in the conveyance is £4 3s 9d The witnesses to its execution were William Blair and Abraham Hayton It was duly acknowledged March 21, 1769, before "His Lordship's Justices of the Peace," William Blair and Thomas Price On the back of this instrument is a receipt from Christopher Edelin acknowledging to have received "7 pence half-penny stirling," as alienation fee on the said fifteen acres, from Daniel, of St Thomas Jenifer, his lordship's agent This was ground-rent money due the Lord Proprietor, and payable semi-annually at the two annual feasts at St Mary's, but which had to be paid before a good conveyance could be obtained This deed was recorded March 27, 1769 Rev J G. Noss is the present Reformed pastor, and Rev J M Alleman the Lutheran, and H W Shriver the superintendent of the Reformed Sunday-school.

Immediately above the junction of Silver Run with Big Pipe Creek, on the latter, John Wiest has large flouring-mills, and David B Earhart has a fulling-mill

West of Union Mills, on Big Pipe Creek, James E Dodrer has flouring-mills, once called "Old Graves' mills," but put down on the old maps, made a century ago, as "Groff's mill"

Piney Creek Station is on the Frederick and Pennsylvania Line Railroad, in the northwestern part of the district C Shere is the postmaster and merchant, and P M Wiest has charge of a mill on the Westminster turnpike At the boundary line dividing Myers from Westminster District is "Mount Pleasant Academy," built in 1854, and a store kept by John Crouse There is a saw- and grist-mill on the estate of the late Dr Study, on Big Pipe Creek Near the Hanover road, in the north of the district, are large beds of iron ore. In the eastern part, on Big Pipe Creek, A Fush has a store and flour-mill

The first physicians who practiced in the district were Dr Wampler, of Hanover, Dr Shorb, of Littlestown, and the Taneytown doctors There were no resident physician [illegible] years after the first settlement Dr Study, long ago deceased, was the pioneer in his profession, and he was succeeded by his son, Dr John Study, who still practices in the neighborhood

The following is a list of public school trustees and teachers for Myers District for 1881 and 1882

1 Mount Pleasant —J Crouse, Frank Burgoon, John C Baukert

2 and 3 Carroll Academy —Jacob Humbert, H W Shriver, John Bemiller

4 Wisner's —Jacob Feever, Larkin Belt, John H Baum

5 Bishe s —Emanuel Yeizer, Samuel Getting, Josiah Steiner

6 Humbert's —Ezra M Lawyer, Lewis Morelock, George Humbert

7 Mauss' —John Maus, Cyrus Feever, Absalom Koontz

8 Green Mount —Jacob P Hull, John Starr John Boose

9 Erb s —Jesse Lemon, S Keefer, Jacob Marker

10 Good Hope —George Bowers, William Yingling, John Leister

11 Cover's —Samuel Cover, Solomon Boose, Joseph Mathias

12 Cherry Grove —Peter Kump, David Shull, William A. Lippo

The teachers for the term ending April 13, 1881, were

1, C H Bixler, 43 pupils 2, John Burgoon, 20 pupils, 3, Isaac Wright, 44 pupils, 4, G W Yeizer, 50 pupils 5, J H Stonesifer, 40 pupils, 6, G F Morelock, 30 pupils, 7, John N Mark, 49 pupils, 8, A F Galt, 45 pupils, 9, George Fleagle 63 pupils, 10, N H Kester, [illegible] pupils, 11, Richard Dell, 41 pupils, 12, A S Morelock, 35 pupils.

Below are given the votes cast for local officers in Myers District from 1851 to 1861 inclusive

1851 —Vote for Primary School Commissioners William Earhart 89, A K Shriver 59, Samuel Bowers 37, J William Earhart 131 P B Mikesell 19

1853 —For Justices William Tagg 135, John Koontz 196, D B Earhart 157, Daniel Stonesifer 153, Constables Perry Rumler 125, Peter Wolf 204 Samuel Bowers 92, Peter Lingenfelter 88 John Hornberger 56 Road Supervisor David Circle 77, James F Dodrer 146, Peter E Myers 17

1855 —For Justices Samuel Bowers 12, J W Earhart 99, D B Earhart 72 Eli Erb 28, Henry Shuler 122, Peter Kump 117, D Stonesifer 68 Constables D E Leister 79, W H Lippy 56, Peter Rumler 102, Daniel Shull 167, J H Wimert 122 Road Supervisor Peter E Myers 98, Abraham Koontz 19[illegible]

1857 —For Justices D Stonesifer 177, P B Mikesell 223, William Tagg 108, D F Earhart 71, Constables J H Knipple 203, J L Farmwalt 185, P Rumler 150 B J Matthias 51 Road Supervisor Daniel Lippo 232

1859 —For Justices John Maus 257, P B Mikesell 262, Constable J H Knipple 219, Gershom Huff 2[illegible], W N Burgoon 134, Road Supervisor Daniel Lippo 18[illegible], Emanuel Yeiser 132

1861 —For Justices J W Earhart 183, D H Rudolph 150, D B Earhart 55, John Maus 191, Eli Erb 123 Constables D L Feeser 170, Levi Fish 127, Joshua Wisner 53, G Huff [illegible] Road Supervisor Moses [illegible]

WOOLERY DISTRICT, No 4

Woolery District, or District No 4, of Carroll County, is bounded on the north by Hampstead, on the west by Baltimore County, on the south by Freedom District, and on the west by the district of Westminster

Deep Run, Middle Run, Beaver Run, and the Patapsco River, with their tributaries, furnish abundant water-power for manufacturing and milling purposes In addition to the numerous excellent public roads and the Chambersburg turnpike, the Western Maryland Railroad passes through the northeastern portion of the district, and furnishes admirable facilities for travel and transportation The metes and bounds of the district, as originally laid down by the commission of 1837, were as follows

"Beginning at the twenty sixth milestone on the Reisters town turnpike road, thence with a straight line to the late Richard Gorsuch's house, leaving said house in No 4, thence to the Patapsco Falls, thence down said Falls to Stansbury's house, leaving said house in District No 4, thence with the county road to Brown's meeting house thence to Brown's mill, thence to Williams' school house binding on the road leading past John Kelly's, thence to Edward Bond's, thence with the county line to the bridge over the Patapsco Falls, near John Ely's mill, thence with the Patapsco Falls to Bentman's bridge, thence with the Deer Park road to the road leading from Philip Nicodemus's mill to the Calico House, thence with said road to Pool's school-house, thence to Morgan's Run, near Thomas Bensman's barn thence up Morgan's Run to Hawkins' Branch, thence up Hawkins' Branch to the county road leading past Benjamin Gorsuch's, thence with said road until it intersects a county road leading from the 'Stone Chapel' to the Washington road, thence with said road to the Washington road, thence with a straight line to the place of beginning"

Daniel Weaver's was made the place for holding the polls

By an act of the General Assembly of Maryland, passed May 23, 1853, it was provided that "so much of the Fourth Election District lying north and west of the Washington road should thereafter be deemed and taken as part of the Seventh Election District, and that the division line between Election Districts Five and Nine should be so far altered and changed as to commence at a point where the then division line crossed the new Liberty road, and running thence with a straight line to the dwelling house then occupied by James McQuay, leaving said McQuay's in district number nine, thence with a straight line to the dwelling-house then occupied by John Hess, leaving said Hess in district number nine, thence to the Washington road, thence with said road to Morgan's Run, and up said run to the original division line" Woolery District had 274[illegible] inhabitants in 1880.

The German element [illegible]

tent in the first settlement of this district, which was part of Baltimore County until the creation of Carroll in 1836 Among the early settlers were the Woolerys (from whom the district received its name), Stockdales, Garners, Jacobs, Gorsuches Shipleys, Barneses, Cockeys, Finks, Leisters, Zepps, Armacosts, Prughs, Conaways, and Flaters

Finksburg, the most prominent town in the district, is twenty miles from Baltimore and about one mile from the Western Maryland Railroad It was laid out in 1813 by a Mr Quigly, a contractor on the Chambersburg turnpike, then being built through it It is situated on a survey called "Hooker's Meadow," and was named Finksburg in honor of Adam Fink, who built the first house Mr Fink lived and kept tavern on the land now owned by Daniel Frazier, and was succeeded by William Horner, Sr, who kept the inn for twenty years Mr Fink had fifteen acres of land, eleven of which Daniel Frazier now owns, but the house (tavern) built by the former was long ago taken down Mr Quigly laid out the town for Mr Fink on the latter's land The oldest house is that of Thomas Demoss Thomas Ward kept the first store, Samuel Hughes was the first blacksmith, and his shop was that now occupied and carried on by Thomas Demoss The first physician was Dr Forrest, and the first teacher Charles W Webster, an attorney at-law of Westminster, son of Rev Isaac Webster, who taught the school in Finksburg in 1831 in a log school-house on the site of the present school building The oldest man in the village is John Nelson Whittle, aged seventy-three years, who married, June 11, 1830, Miss Cynthia Ann, daughter of Thomas Ward, an old settler and the first merchant of the place The merchants are George W Horner and H S Thompson,—the latter being the postmaster Dr S L Morris is the resident physician, and the venerable Samuel Stansbury keeps the toll-gate at the east end of the village

Zion Methodist Protestant church was erected in 1856, under the auspices of Rev Scott Norris Frank Hering is superintendent of the Sunday-school

The pastors of Zion Methodist Protestant Church have been

1856, R S Norris, A Anderson, 1857, R S Norris, C H Littleton, 1858, J A McFadden, N S Greenaway, 1859, J A McFadden, C M Whiteside, 1860, J Elderdice C H Littleton, 1861, C H Littleton, G W Wells, 1862 J F Whiteside, G W Wells, 1863, J T Whiteside, J W Gray, 1864, T M Bryan, G D Edmondston, 1865, T M Bryan, C T Cochel, 1866, C T Cochel, F M Hawkins 1867, C T Cochel, 1868–70, W T Dunn 1870–72, J H Littlewood 1872, A D Dick, J G Sullivan 187[illegible], A D [illegible] 875, G D Ia[illegible] tler, 1877, S [illegible]

T Ferguson, G F Farring, 1878, S S T Ferguson J M Brown, 1879-81, J W Charlton, 1881, W D Litsinger

The church building of the Methodist Episcopal Church South was erected in 1856 by the Methodist Episcopal Church, but shortly after the late war the church organization became so feeble and so reduced in numbers that the building was sold to the Methodist Episcopal Church South Its first pastor under the Church South was Rev William Etchison, and the present incumbent is Rev Mr Brown, of Reisterstown

In the rear of the church is a graveyard, with only a few interments, among which are William L Crawford, born December, 1834, died January, 1879

The two most prominent burials are those of Judge Mordecai G Cockey who died July 29, 1872, aged 70, and his wife Eurith, who died Dec 27, 1843, aged 42

In a field adjoining are the graves of the following-named persons Ann E Corbin, wife of William Corbin born Sept 12, 1800, died April 30 1829, and Keturah Wheeler, died June 15, 1829, aged 2 years and 20 days

The Independent Order of Mechanics was instituted in 1872, in which year it built its hall, which was sold recently to George W Horner He has enlarged and beautified it, and the order continues to hold its meetings there Its officers are

W M, Frank Stocksdale, S M, John Simmons, J M, Conrad Mann, Sec, Alfred Williams, F S, John W Barrett, Treas, L A J Lamott

The Excelsior Literary Society, an association for entertainment and instruction, is in a flourishing condition Its officers for 1881 were

Pres, B L Fair, Sec, Dixon Leister, Treas, Miss Alverdie Lamott, Vice Pres, F L Hering

Samuel Shoemaker the wealthy and distinguished Baltimore railroad and express man, was raised in this village, and Lewis H Cole lives near the town, on his elegant farm known as "Clover Hill" Abraham Leister owns part of the old Leister estate, among the first located in the district That portion of this farm near the railroad is owned by William Zepp Thomas Gorsuch came to this section of country at an early day from Baltimore County, and settled where Elias Gorsuch now lives, before whose time George W, son of Thomas Gorsuch owned it

The Garner Graveyard is on the road from Finksburg to the railroad station and is a private burial-lot, in which only three of the tombstones have inscriptions, as follows

"In memory of Flinn Garner, who departed this life Feb 20 1839, aged 93 years He was a member of the Methodist Church 60 years"

"In memory of Cary Garner, wife of Flinn Garner, the mother of 13 children"

"Sarah Fresh, died Sept 19, 1822, aged 28"

Carrollton is a romantic and pretty village on the Western Maryland Railroad, seven miles from Westminster and twenty-six from Baltimore The North Branch of the Patapsco River passes by the hamlet, and furnishes an abundance of water for manufacturing and other purposes Thomas Chapel, Pleasant Grove, and Bethel churches are near Edward H Bash is a merchant, railroad agent, and postmaster J A Bush, a surveyor, lives here, as does also W J Houck, the undertaker

Patapsco —This village lies on the Western Maryland Railroad, twenty-seven miles from Baltimore and six from Westminster Ezra Chew is postmaster J H Chew & Co, J W Sanders, and John S Martin are merchants in the village P Lingenfelter keeps the hotel, and E E Koons, a miller and lumberman, resides there

Bird Hill is on the "Nicodemus road," six miles from Westminster, and near Morgan's Run John W Nelson is the postmaster of the village and keeps a store

Louisville is also on the "Nicodemus road," six miles from Finksburg, ten from Westminster, and twenty from Baltimore There are copper-mines situated on Morgan's Run, within a half mile of the town, containing large deposits of copper, and operated by John Vial S H Patterson is postmaster, and John Reed and Nicholas Benson, merchants The village has two churches,—Mount Pleasant Methodist Episcopal and Providence Methodist Protestant The millers are G W McComas and George F Brauning The town is partly in Woolery's and partly in Freedom District,—the "Mineral Hill Copper-Mine" being in the latter

Mechanicsville —This pleasant village, rapidly growing in business and population, lies on the Nicodemus road, midway between Bird Hill and Louisville It has a Methodist church and cemetery, two stores, several shops, and is the home of an industrious people

Shamberger's Station, on the Western Maryland Railroad, is an important shipping-point, and has large and excellent flouring-mills

The following is a list of persons seventy years old and over living in the district in 1879

Mrs Margaret Wickert aged 9[illegible] years, her son, Jacob Wickert, 77, her daughter, Mrs Margaret Crapster, 75 Mrs Rachel Roache, 79, her sister, Mrs Mary Criswell, 71 Samuel Stansbury, 75, his wife, Rachel, 7[illegible], John Whittle, 7[illegible], Mrs Lavina Crumbine 7[illegible] her sister Mrs Eliza Stocksdale 71, [illegible] 71, her brother,

Benjamin Haines, 82, Cornelius Cole, 82, his wife, Maria 73, Cornelius Buckley, 80, his wife, Annie Buckley, 74, Mrs Henrietta Williams, 74, John Uhler, 81, Cyrus Shilling, 79, his wife, Annie, 71, Mrs Elizabeth Shilling, 80, Lloyd Shipley, 85, Joshua Murray, 71, his wife, Mary, 76, Abraham Prugh, 80 his wife, 72, Rich Manning, 80, his wife, 79 Mrs Lydia Crawford, 74, Stephen Oursler, 83, his wife, 75, her brother, Edward Gardner, 78, Elias Brothers 70, Mrs Mary Haines, —, George Ward, 74, his wife, 70 Mrs Catherine Hedges, 79 Miss Mary Caple, 83, Mrs Augustus Galloway, 75, Lewis Hobb, 85, Daniel Bush, 73, Mrs Mary Gorsuch, 82, Mrs Mary Ogg, 73, Lovelace Gorsuch 76, his wife, 71 Nathan Gorsuch, 70, Mary Gorsuch, 72 Philip Smith, colored, 79, his wife, 76 The list comprises 26 females, whose combined ages are 2040 years, averaging 7[illegible] years, 22 males whose united ages are 1703 years, averaging 77 9/22 years Total average, 76⅓ years

Some of the finest estates and most beautiful residences in the State are situated in this district, among which may be noted "Wilton," the present country-place of Thomas C Brown Mr Brown was born at Elkridge Landing, Md, where his father, an emigrant from England, had settled prior to 1760 He married Nancy Cockey, of the well known Baltimore County family of that name, and removed to the neighborhood of Sykesville, in Freedom District, towards the last decade of the eighteenth century His son William served with distinction in the war of 1812, and was adjutant of Col Beall Randall's battalion when only eighteen years of age He participated in the battle of North Point, where he acquitted himself with credit William Brown married Miss Ann Waters Perry, by whom he had twelve children He was a brother of Hon Elias Brown, a former Congressman of the Baltimore District, and, like his brother, an active and prominent politician, he was a Presidential elector for Gen Jackson in the campaign of 1824 He was born in 1796, and died in 1836, aged sixty years His mother, Nancy (Cockey) Brown, was an aunt of the late Judge Mordecai Gist Cockey, who died in 1872 Thomas Cockey Brown was the third child of his parents, and was born in Freedom District, April 5, 1822 He was raised on his father's large estate and educated in the neighboring schools He was early inured to farm work, which he thoroughly understood and at which he continued until his twenty-sixth year

In 1848 he went to the State of Louisiana, where he remained until 1869, as agent and general manager of a large sugar plantation He worked three hundred and sixty negroes and eighty other hands, averaging an annual yield of eighteen hundred hogsheads of sugar He returned to Maryland in 1869, and bought his present splendid farm, "Wilton," of Dutell and Humphreys It consisted of 185¾ acres, and was originally owned by the Gaither family He erected an elegant mansion on the place, and since then has greatly improved his farm, which is now one of the best in the county and in the highest state of cultivation It lies near Finksburg, and is a mile from the Western Maryland Railroad He received the three symbolical degrees in Masonry in 1851, in Lodge A F and A M "True Friends," at Grand Island, in the Gulf of Mexico He was elected a member of the Maryland House of Delegates in 1874 from Carroll County, and served two years in the Legislature, in which he was a zealous advocate of reform and economy in all public expenditures of the people's funds Mr Brown has ever been an active public man, and a warm adherent of the Democratic party He has never married By his own industry, integrity, and prudent management he has arisen to be one of the leading farmers and most public-spirited citizens and business men of the county, and largely enjoys the esteem and confidence of his fellow-citizens

The following are the public school trustees and teachers, with the number of pupils under each, for this district in 1851

1 Carrollton —William Arbaugh C W Brown, Isaac Green
2 Browns Meeting-House —S A Martin, George Taylor, Noah Bucher
3 Patapsco —John H Taylor, Edmond Koontz, David Abbott
4 Sandy Mount —Peter Woods, H H Caple, William A Bush
5 and 6 Finksburg —William H Stocksdale, G W Horner, Stephen B Stocksdale
7 Fairmount — Nicholas Benson, Hanson Davis, D E Hoff
8 Deer Park —H F Smith, E N Davis, Henry Vardenfelt
9 Morgan's Run —George Freemar, John Owings, George Caple
10 Louisville —Joshua Baesman, Eli F Bennett, William Roberts

The teachers for the term ending April 15, 1881, were

1, Laura S Poole, 58 pupils, 2, John W Abbott, [illegible] pupils 3, Joel Ebaugh, 53 pupils, 4, Ida F Fox, 40 pupils, 5, D I Farrar, 20 pupils, 6, Mary E Johnson, 29 pupils, 7 S G Harden, 53 pupils, 8, Aquilla McGee, 46 pupils, 9, G J Shipley, 42 pupils, 10, M F Ebaugh, 43 pupils 11. J C Nutting, 38 pupils, 1 (colored school), E H [illegible], 23 pupils

The justices are William Stocksdale, Nathan Gorsuch, Azariah Oursler

The following is the vote of the district for local officers from 1851 to 1861 inclusive

1851 —Vote for Primary School Commissioners John W Gorsuch 136, E D Paine 105, John W Gorsuch 99

1853 —For Justices Mordecai G Cockey 187, Jacob Wink[illegible] 130, Abraham Lamott 149, Thomas S Brow 120, James Baker 12, Josse Frizzell 2[illegible], George Ogg 13[illegible], Samuel Wilderson 67 Constables J F Gardner 1[illegible], J M Flater [illegible] ale 148 Road

Thos. C. Brown

Supervisor John D Powdor 176, Elijah Wooden 113, A Taylor 12

1 ,—For Justices M G Cockey 2?8, N Gorsuch 190, E Woolery 184 J D Powder 121, S Wilderson 38, Constables S Flater 165, Jesse Magee 146, D D Byers 198, Road Supervisor Lewis Taylor 200, Amon Allgire 123

.7—For Justices S. A. Lauver 188, Daniel Stoll 184, L Lamott 186, M G Cockey 208, Nathan Gorsuch 206, Elijah Woolery 191, Constables J Shilling 178, J H Uhler 172, Samuel Flater 204, D D Byers 201, Road Supervisor G Mommaugh 193, H T Barthulow 198

9—For Justices Joseph Poole 187, James Lockard 208, S A Lauver 198, M G Cockey 203, Azariah Oursler 188, Nathan Gorsuch 186, Constables William Crusey 192, Lewis Taylor 170, Jesse Magee 203, William Gorsuch 212 Road Supervisors Henry Taylor 203, Joseph Bromwell 214

1861—For Justices William Lockard 240, M G Cockey 232, N Gorsuch 213, N Burgett 48, Azariah Oursler 166, J W Steele 182, L A J Lamott 187 Constables P Gorsuch 271, Jesse Magee 272, Ier Taylor 161, D D Byers 163, Road Supervisor Peter Flater 268, John Uhler 180

One of the best known farmers in this district is Col James Fenner Lee, who was born in Providence, R I, July 9, 1843 He is the eldest living son of Stephen S and Sarah F (Mallett) Lee, who removed to Baltimore the year of his birth In that city he was placed under the instruction of the best masters, and in 1855 sent to Europe, where he was for several years in one of the first schools of Switzerland He completed his collegiate studies in Paris, at the Lycée St Louis, and after having traveled over the continent returned to Baltimore There he entered as a law student the office of Brown & Brune, and before applying for admission to the bar spent a term at the Law School of Harvard University In 18?? he married Mrs Albert Carroll, daughter of Hon William George Read, and granddaughter of Col John Eager Howard On this occasion his parents presented him with a farm in this district, and he decided to devote himself to agricultural pursuits as soon as he could dispose of his law business and complete the third volume of the "Maryland Digest," which he had, in conjunction with his friend, Jacob I Cohen, undertaken to publish Having in time accomplished this and settled upon his farm, he soon became identified with, and earnest in the promotion of, every material interest of the county In a short time, such was his popularity, he was constantly chosen to represent the interests of his district in the Democratic County Conventions, and frequently in the State councils of that party In 1874 he was appointed by Governor Groome one of his aide de camps, with the rank of colonel He was nominated in 1875 for State senator by the Democratic party, and elected after a most active and exciting campaign In the Senate he was chairman of the joint Committee on Printing, and did good service to the State by reducing the expenditures of the same twenty thousand dollars This position he retained in the second session of the Legislature, in which he was equally successful in his efforts to secure economy in that department At the assembling of the Senate he was unanimously chosen president of the temporary organization and was very often called to the chair during the absence of Col Lloyd, the permanent president It was mainly through the efforts of Col Lee that the endowment of twenty six free scholarships was obtained from the State for the Western Maryland College at Westminster His children are Arthur F, Sarah J Fenner, and Stephen Howard Lee

FREEDOM DISTRICT, No 5

Freedom District, or District No 5, of Carroll County, is bounded on the north by Woolery District, on the east by Baltimore County, on the south by Howard County, and on the west by Franklin District It is intersected by Piney Run, Big and Little Morgan's Runs, Owings' Run, and their tributaries, and the North and West Branches of the Patapsco form the eastern and southern boundary lines of the district respectively In addition to a number of turnpikes and excellent public roads, the Baltimore and Ohio Railroad skirts the southern portion of the district, affording the most ample facilities for traffic with points of commercial importance Freedom District in 1880 had a population of 3154 The following are the metes and bounds of the district as originally laid out by the commission appointed in 1837:

"Beginning at the mouth of Gill s' Falls where it enters in the Western Falls, thence running with said falls to its junction with the Northern Branch, thence with the Northern Branch to Beasman s bridge, thence with the Deer Park road to the road leading from Philip Nicodemus's mill to the Calico House, thence with said road at Pool's school-house, thence to Morgan s Run, near Thomas Beasman's barn, thence up Morgan's Run to District No 9, thence with District No 9 to the place of beginning "

Freedom was made the place for holding the polls The above lines were somewhat changed by an act passed May 3, 1853, readjusting the bounds of the Fifth, Ninth and Fourth Districts This is the largest district in the county in area, and was the first settled Its pioneers were mostly of English descent, with some of Welsh and Scotch-Irish extraction Among the first to make their homes in the district were John Welch, Abel Brown, Robert Twis, Edward Dorsey, John Elder, Joshua Glover, Samuel Sewell, Grove Shipley, the Littles, Mr O Donald, the Steeles, Dorseys, Wadlows, Scriveners, Gores, Lees, Binghams, Ritters, Parishes, Bennetts, Gardners Buckinghams, Enoch Baker, Joseph Willis, John Beard, Lindsays, and Hoods. The [illegible] several

branches, was the most numerous, and is to the present day.

The founder of the Ritter family in Maryland was Elias Ritter, who settled on the Western Shore of the province in 1650

He was a native of Bedingen, Hesse-Darmstadt, Germany, where, it is said, he possessed an estate covering twenty-four square miles of land, embracing three towns within its bounds Bedingen, the main town, was fortified, and contained the "Ritter Castle," the walls of which were still standing in 1848 The family furnished men and munitions to the Protestant cause during the "Thirty Years' War," and at the close of that struggle was sent into exile and their property confiscated Elias Ritter went to England during the protectorate of Oliver Cromwell there joined one of the expeditions sent by Lord Baltimore to Maryland, and settled in the western part of Anne Arundel County

At the time of the formation of Frederick County the family was located on the banks of the Monocacy River The names of the principal members of the family at that time were Elias, John, William, Tobias, Michael, and Ludwig, or Lewis

John, a son of the founder of the family, assisted William Penn in surveying the province of Pennsylvania in 1682, for which service he received five thousand acres of land in Berks County, Pa A descendant of this Ritter occupied a seat in the Twenty-eighth and Twenty ninth Congresses William and Elias Ritter were members of Capt William Keeport's company, Stricker's battalion, Maryland line of 1776

Tobias Ritter, another brother, was a member of the third company of Col Armand's Pennsylvania Legion

Lewis Ritter, born Oct 20, 1778, in Frederick County, Md married Margaret Stall in 1803 This lady was the daughter of John Stall, of Franklin County, Pa, whose wife had been made a prisoner of war by the French and Indians after Braddock's defeat, and taken to France, where she remained until 1770, when she was restored to her family The husband had been with Braddock's army

Jacob Ritter, born Nov 20, 1804, near Fayetteville, Franklin Co, Pa, married, December, 1829, Elizabeth, eldest daughter of Philip J Neff, a soldier in the war of 1812, and eldest son of Col Michael Neff, a drill officer under Washington during the American Revolution Col Neff served under Frederick the Great during his "Seven Years' War" as one of the "Light Horse" and the king's body guard At the commencement of the Revolutionary war Col. Neff resided in Tyrone township, Adams Co, Pa, where Philip J Neff, his eldest son, was born At the time of the marriage of Jacob Ritter and Elizabeth Neff, Philip J Neff resided near Fayetteville, Franklin Co, Pa

In 1830 Jacob Ritter was commissioned as first lieutenant of Company A, One Hundred and Fifty-fifth Regiment of State Militia, by Governor Joseph Ritner, of Pennsylvania and served in that capacity six years

In August, 1847, he removed to Finksburg, Carroll Co, Md, and in 1850 to Eldersburg, Freedom District, same county, where he died in 1870

William L Ritter, the son of Jacob Ritter, was born near Fayetteville, Franklin Co, Pa, on the 11th of August, 1835 He began his career with only a common-school education, which by diligence and perseverance he supplemented in after-years with all that was needed for the part he was called upon to play in life

At the age of twenty two he was appointed mail agent under the Buchanan administration, and held this position until the breaking out of the war When hostilities began his convictions led him to embrace the cause of the South, and without a moment's delay he resolved to cast his lot with the Confederate army Accordingly, on the 24th of October, 1861 in connection with Capt Henry B Latrobe and Lieuts F O Claiborne, John B Rowan, and William T Patton, he recruited and organized the Third Battery Maryland Artillery When the company was mustered into service he was appointed orderly sergeant

Soon afterwards the battery was ordered to [illegible] Tennessee, where it remained until Gen E Kirby Smith marched into Kentucky, in August, 1862 when it accompanied his army to Covington, opposite Cincinnati, Ohio After the army returned to Tennessee the battery was ordered to Vicksburg, Miss Capt Latrobe there retired from service, and Lieut Claiborne was placed in command On the 17th of March, 1863, Sergt Ritter was elected second lieutenant to fill the vacancy caused by the promotion of his superior officer Not long after his promotion he was sent to Gen Ferguson's command, on Deer Creek Miss, above Vicksburg, to take charge of a section of light artillery of the Third Maryland Battery, then operating on the river in connection with a section of Capt Bledsoe's Missouri Artillery Lieut Ritter distinguished himself during this service for bravery and skill and when during the long siege of Vicksburg Capt Claiborne was killed, he was promoted to the rank of first lieutenant In the seven days' [illegible] Lieut [illegible] was wounded

and Ritter took command In the October following he rejoined his old battery at Decatur, Ga At the battle of Resaca, in May, 1864, he was wounded, but refused to retire from the field He dressed his own wound, and although urged by the battalion surgeon to go to the hospital, kept his post, and in the absence of Capt Rowan, withdrew the guns from one of the most exposed positions on the line At the siege of Atlanta, Lieut Ritter took command of the battery, Capt Rowan having been called to the command of the battalion At the death of Capt Rowan, who was killed at the battle of Nashville, in December, 1864, he assumed command of the battery, and worked the guns until the enemy drove his men from the pieces at the point of the bayonet At Columbus, Miss, Lieut Ritter was promoted to captain to fill the vacancy caused by the death of Capt Rowan, his commission dating from the 16th of December, 1864

He remained in active service until the troops were surrendered and paroled at Meridian, Miss, never having taken a furlough nor spent a day in the hospital during the entire term of his service

In February, 1866, he returned to Maryland, and on the 20th of November, 1867, married Mrs Sarah Howard Rowan, widow of Capt John B Rowan, his late companion in arms, and daughter of Col Thomas Howard, of Elkton, Md

The Springfield Estate—George Patterson was the youngest son of William Patterson, well known in Baltimore, who was possessed of a large amount of real estate in that city He was also the brother of Mrs Elizabeth Patterson, the first wife of the late Jerome Bonaparte He took possession of his estate in Carroll County, containing about three thousand acres of land, in 1824, and made it his home until the time of his death, which occurred Nov 19, 1869, in his seventy-fourth year He was possessed of considerable wealth, and was largely engaged in importing and raising improved stock He was an extensive exhibitor at the agricultural fairs held in the State before the beginning of the late war, but never competed for premiums, taking pride only in adding to the interest of the show by the presence of his fine animals His immense farm was called "Springfield," and was situated near Sykesville He was an esteemed citizen, and his death was lamented by a large circle of friends and acquaintances

Springfield is one of the most admirable and complete farming establishments in Maryland It is situated a short distance from the Sykesville Station on the Baltimore and Ohio Railroad, and contains about [illegible] thousand acres of land, fifteen hundred of which in 1870 were under cultivation It is furnished with a flour mill, saw mill, and a comfortable country-house, with room enough for the uses of home and the claims of a generous hospitality, with lawns, orchards and outhouses of every description and variety It is high, healthy, rich, well watered and wooded

More than forty years of Mr Patterson's life were spent in changing this excellent homestead from "a naked surface, incapable almost of cultivation," to a rich, highly cultivated farm "Time and grass were at the bottom of all" his achievements in this respect Every field has had two hundred bushels of lime to the acre, and each "passed six years of nine in grass" The great pasture, in full view from the front door of the dwelling, has not been broken for many years and being constantly pastured by the beautiful Devons, has grown richer and richer, and grasses native and exotic strive there for the mastery

His system of farming was first corn, manured on sod broken deeply, and yielding an average of twelve barrels to the acre This was followed by a crop of oats, and then two years of clover Next a crop of wheat on which ammoniated phosphate was used for the purpose of ripening the crop At the time the wheat was sown the field was set to grass for hay, and for three years after the wheat crop was taken off mown, and the next year grazed Manure was applied during the last year and the sod again broken for corn, beginning the regular nine years' course

Mr Patterson raised Berkshire hogs instead of Chester, Southdown, and Shropshire sheep, and game chickens instead of fancy fowls His stock of horses was unsurpassed Many Marylanders will long remember Mr Patterson's stout well proportioned powerful and active horses at the State fairs

Under the cultivation of Mr Patterson Springfield became the most celebrated, and was truly what he designed it should be, the *model* farm of Maryland He erected his mansion on an eminence overlooking the farm and surrounding country It is one hundred and seventy five feet front by fifty feet deep The front has a two story porch supported by pillars The house, which is somewhat classical in style, is unique in its arrangements and a perfect country home The iron and copper-mines upon this property, discovered in 1850, were profitably worked until 1861 and more recently leased to Graff, Bennett & Co of Pittsburg, and Read, Stickney & Co, of Baltimore, who have begun operations with indications of valuable results "Springfield Farm" is distinctively noted for its *Devon* cattle, Mr Patterson having made, in 1817 the [illegible] libred Devons

into the United States, through his brother Robert, and as a present from Mr Coke, afterwards Earl of Leicester[1] The following were his importations in order, as recorded in the "Devon Herd Book" Bulls, Anchises, No 140, Eclipse, No 191, Herod, No 214, Norfolk, No 266, Chatsworth, No 182, Dick Taylor, No 486, the President, Nos 639 and 904 From these most of the Devon herds of this country are descended

George Patterson married Prudence A Brown, the daughter of Thomas C and sister of Stephen T C Brown, who survives him and lives in Baltimore Their only child, Florence, married James Carroll, of Charles She died in 1878, much lamented After Mrs Carroll's death, Mrs Patterson and Mr Carroll decided to sell "Springfield" to Frank Brown, which was done in 1880 Mr Brown inherited the estate known as "Brown's Inheritance" from his father, Stephen T C Brown The land had been brought to the highest state of cultivation by Mr Brown's father and his grandfather, Thomas C Brown, and is one of the best farms in the State He combined the two farms, and has since been actively engaged in cultivating and improving the whole estate As consolidated, his farm now contains two thousand five hundred acres, and is not surpassed in point of cultivation by any in the State Mr Brown has not only maintained the reputation of Devon cattle, but has even improved it

It will be seen that these two farms have been blended together from their origin in the close alliance of the families of their respective owners

Frank Brown, proprietor of the one farm by inheritance and of the other by purchase, is the only son and heir of the late Stephen T C and Susan Bennett Brown He was born Aug 8, 1846, on "Brown's Inheritance" The ancestor of the family in this country was Abel Brown, who emigrated from Dumfries, Scotland, to near Annapolis, Md, in 1730, he removed later to this part of Carroll (then Baltimore County), and purchased a large tract of land adjoining Springfield This he brought to a high state of cultivation, it came into the possession of Elias Brown, Sr, who erected a stone saw and flour-mill, the corner-stone of which bears the date of 1798 He was a prominent citizen, and actively participated in civil affairs He had four sons,—Thomas Cockey, Elias, Jr, William, and Stephen,—all of whom served in the war of 1812 Elias Brown, Jr, became prominent in the State, was a member of the United States Congress, and a Democratic Presidential elector a number of times Thomas C Brown inherited the estate, a division of which having been made, William Patterson, of Baltimore (the distinguished merchant and citizen, one of the organizers of the Baltimore and Ohio Railroad, the father of Robert, George, Joseph Edward, Henry, and Elizabeth Patterson,—Madam Bonaparte), purchased a portion which contributed largely to make up his "Springfield" estate Thomas C Brown married Susan Snowden, a descendant of Baptiste Snowden, of St Mary's County, Md, who had removed to the vicinity on a farm which he called Branton, on which he built a house of cut straw and clay, still standing in a good state of preservation Col Francis Snowden, the son of Baptiste, married Miss Miles, of St Mary's, and these are the maternal great grandparents of the subject of this sketch The children of Thomas C Brown were Lewis, Prudence A, the widow of George Patterson, and Stephen T C, the father of Frank Brown

Stephen T C was born in 1820, reared on the "Inheritance," and in 1842 married Susan Bennett, was a member of the State Legislature, one of the original subscribers to the Maryland Agricultural College, a most useful citizen, a representative man and agriculturist of the county He was an official and leading member of the Springfield Presbyterian Church, which was established and supported by him and George Patterson, and whose edifice and parsonage were erected by their combined efforts Mr Brown was a man of decided character, strong convictions, benevolent spirit and works Christian consistency and activity, and universally esteemed He died in December, 1876

Frank Brown is the only son of the last mentioned At the age of eighteen his father gave him a farm well stocked and furnished, adjoining the homestead which he successfully managed for several years He entered the agricultural implement and seed house of R Sinclair & Co, of Baltimore, where he received valuable training, of practical use in his after-years He was later placed in charge of the Patterson estates in Baltimore, which he managed to the satisfaction of the heirs He was subsequently appointed by Governor Bowie to a responsible place in one of the State tobacco warehouses, which position he held for six years In 1875 he was elected to the House of Delegates, Maryland Assembly, and in 1878 re-elected His success was a gratifying proof of the public confidence in him At the close of his second term he withdrew from political affairs, the care of "Springfield" and the Patterson interests having devolved [illegible] who for six

[1] "American Devon Herd-Book," vol iii, and old *American Farmer*, vol ix [illegible]

Frank Brown

years subsequent to George Patterson's demise had the management of them This was a task requiring the exercise of financial wisdom and good executive ability, but Mr Frank Brown has been equal to these great responsibilities Naturally endowed with business capacity, his early experience fitted him for the management of his trusts Like his father, he, too, takes a lively interest in the affairs of the county and his vicinity, and in many respects supplies his place He was elected a trustee of Springfield Presbyterian Church, to fill the vacancy caused by his father's death He was also made trustee under Mrs James Carroll's (*née* Florence Patterson) will, for her legacy to the church of five thousand dollars He is one of the executive committee of the Maryland State Agricultural Association, and a director of the Maryland Live Stock Breeders' Association At the late tenth annual meeting of the Maryland Agricultural and Mechanical Association, held Oct 27, 1881, he was elected its president

Mr F Brown married (December, 1879) Mary R Preston, *née* Miss Ridgely, daughter of David Ridgely, of Baltimore They reside on the farm during summer and in Baltimore during the winter

Below is given a list of persons in Freedom District in 1879 who had reached the age of eighty years The names of twenty-two persons are given, whose ages amount to 1881 years, or an average of eighty-five and a half years

Mrs Jane C Smith, 83, Joshua Hipsley, 81, Mrs Rebecca H Lithicote, 81, Daniel Gassaway (colored) 85, Mrs P Wilson, 84 Samuel Jordan, 84, Mrs E Ware, 85, Nathaniel Richardson, 86, Jacob Beem, 86, Rev Dr Piggot, 84 J Linton, 85 Mrs Matilda Phillips, 84, George Haywrath, 82, Nathan Porter, 85, Mrs Susanna Warfield, 83, Sebastian Bowers, Sr, 86 Ruth Shipley, 99, James Morgan, 85, Ruth Frizzle, 94, P Dicus (colored), 90, Kate Philips, 85, Susan Dixon (colored), 85

Defiance, a small village, is situated on the western edge of the district Horace L Shipley here has a store, formerly kept by his father, Larkin Shipley, a son of John Shipley, one of the oldest settlers

St. Stephen's Lodge, No 95, I O O F, located at Defiance, was instituted in May, 1857 Its charter members were Jesse Leatherwood, Larkin Shipley, Dr Francis J Crawford, Abraham Greenwood, Hanson Leatherwood Its first officers were

N G, Jesse Leatherwood, V G, Larkin Shipley, Sec, Dr F J Crawford, Treas, Hanson Leatherwood

Its present officers (second term, 1881) are

N G, John W Pickett, V G, F L Criswell, Sec, Augustus Brown, Per Sec, Thomas L Shipley, Treas, C R Pickett, Con, J N Shipley, Chapl, Dr D F Shipley, Marshal, A Brown, Warden, David H Haines Dist Dep, Horace L Shipley

Its neat frame hall, forty-four by twenty-two feet, was built in 1880 The trustees are John H Conoway, William H Pickett, F L Criswell Number of members, seventy

Bethesda Methodist Episcopal church is situated north of the hamlet of "Pleasant Gap" It is a substantial brick structure, erected in 1880 Immediately in its rear is the old log church, in which services were held from 1810, the date of its erection, until the completion of the new church in 1880. The graveyard adjoining contains the following interments

Ruth, wife of James Parish, died July 21, 1875, aged 60
Vachel Buckingham, died Sept 4, 1866, aged 76, and his wife, Eleanor, Feb 8, 1871, aged 71
Prudence A Lindsay, died Jan 3, 1879, aged 63, John A Lindsay, died Jan 10, 1877, aged 61
Eliza J, wife of Andrew Wheeler, died Jan 5, 1878, aged 19.
Henry S Buckingham, died March 26, 1872, aged 13
Ellen Nora Elizabeth, wife of Richard M Chenoweth, died Nov 13, 1863, aged 22
Ann, wife of Joseph Willis, died Sept 7, 1865, aged 88
Elizabeth, wife of Grove Shipley, born Sept 11, 1776, and died July 8, 1854, and her husband, born April 4, 1776, died Oct 20, 1819
Louisa, wife of Grove Shipley, Jr, died June 21, 1816, aged 42
James Parish, born April 15, 1773, died March 29, 1853.
Kiturah Parish, died June 1, 1818, aged 76
Thomas Barnes, died Feb 29 1860, aged 13
Array Parish, wife of Moses Parish, and daughter of Richard and Array Condon, died Nov 29, 1861, aged 62 Moses Parish, born Sept 6 1795, died April 27, 1862, and his wife, Michal, daughter of Grove and Elizabeth Shipley, died Sept 21, 1839, aged 43
Nicholas Shipley, born Jan 28, 1805, died Jan 15, 1837
Sarah Shipley, born Nov 20, 1797, died Jan 22, 1873
Sarah, wife of William A Gibson, died March 12, 1873, aged 39
William Baker, born April 27, 1806 died July 20, 1876
Enoch Baker, died June 27, 1864, aged 97, and Mary, his wife, July 8, 1863, aged 87
Elizabeth wife of Samuel Hughes, died May 1, 1854, aged 31
Hannah, wife of Reese Brown, born Sept 10, 1789, died Sept 29, 1861
John Beard, born Aug 21, 1780, died Aug 28, 1850
James W Parish, died June 17, 1871, aged 50
Elizabeth, wife of John W Parish, born March 25, 1830, died April 21, 1878

The Methodist Protestant church, built about 1840, is just south of "Pleasant Gap" It is a frame structure, originally built of logs, and then weather boarded It has one gallery, and is two stories high In the graveyard adjoining are only a few graves, among which is that of Abraham, son of Nicholas and Mary J Wilson, born April 12, 1867, died Jan. 2, 1872 Most of them have no tombstones

Nathan Manro was born in the State of Rhode Island, Sept 2?, 17?0, and was married, Nov 21,

1750, to Miss Hannah Allen, of that State. She was born April 14, 1733. Their children were Hannah, Sarah, Elizabeth, Squire, Lydia, Nathan, Mary, Jonathan, David, Allen, and Thomas. Of these, Jonathan, the eighth child, was born Nov. 28, 1766, and came to Maryland from near Providence, R. I., with his brother Nathan, who died in 1827. Jonathan settled in Baltimore, and became a rich and prosperous merchant. He owned several ships that were engaged in the London and West India trade. He was married, Jan. 15, 1795, to Sarah Conner, daughter of James Conner, and died Jan. 22, 1848. They had thirteen children, of whom two survive, Mrs. Dr. Turnbull, of Baltimore, and Judge George W. Manro. The latter was born in Baltimore March 22, 1810, and was liberally educated in the schools of that city. He followed the high seas for ten years on merchant vessels owned by his father, and served as second mate under Capt. James Beard. Before he quit the seas he had command of the ship "Ocean," owned by the Osgoods. In 1837 he removed to the farm on which he now resid[illegible] [illegible]nd wh[illegible]h w[illegible] a part of the lands purchased at an early date by his mother's father, James Conner. Mr. Conner owned six hundred and three acres, made up of tracts surveyed and patented to Samuel Sewell and Joshua Glover. One of these, "Buck's Park," was surveyed for Samuel Sewell April 16, 1739, for fifty acres. Another, "Sewell's Park," of twenty acres, was surveyed March 17, 1745, and another of one hundred and twenty-one acres, "Buck's Park," at another date. "William's Neglect," of thirteen and three-fourths acres, was surveyed for Joshua Glover, Dec. 9, 1795. Judge Manro was married, Oct. 26, 1837, to Elizabeth Kelly, daughter of William and Martha (Loveall) Kelly, by Rev. Samuel Gore. Her brother, Nicholas Kelly, was the first sheriff of Carroll County. Judge Manro was one of the first magistrates appointed in the new county of Carroll, and held this office for a long term of years. He was appointed one of the judges of the Orphans' Court in 1848, and served three years, and was elected in 1851 for the term of four years according to the provisions of the new constitution adopted that year. He was elected in 1867 one of the six members from this county to the Constitutional Convention, and aided in framing the organic law under which Maryland is now governed. In 1868 he was appointed by Governor Oden Bowie inspector of tobacco, which position he held several years. At present he is collector of taxes. Both on the bench and in all other public positions held by Judge Manro, his administration of affairs has been characterized by the ability, purity, and suavity of manner that has ever distinguished his life, and has made him a popular and valued public servant. He is a zealous member of the Masonic order, in which, over thirty years ago, he received its first three degrees. He has been a lifelong Democrat, devoted to the interests of his party, to which, under all vicissitudes, he has strongly adhered, and to whose counsels he ever gave his voice, and for the success of which his vote was always freely given. He is connected with the Methodist Episcopal Church South at Freedom, in the erection of whose church edifice in 18[illegible] he liberally contributed, and was chairman of the building committee. The judge resides on a splendid farm of three hundred and one acres, located a mile north of Eldersburg, where he and his accomplished lady dispense old-fashioned Maryland hospitality. The name of his estate is "Buck's Park," called after two of the original surveys of the grant.

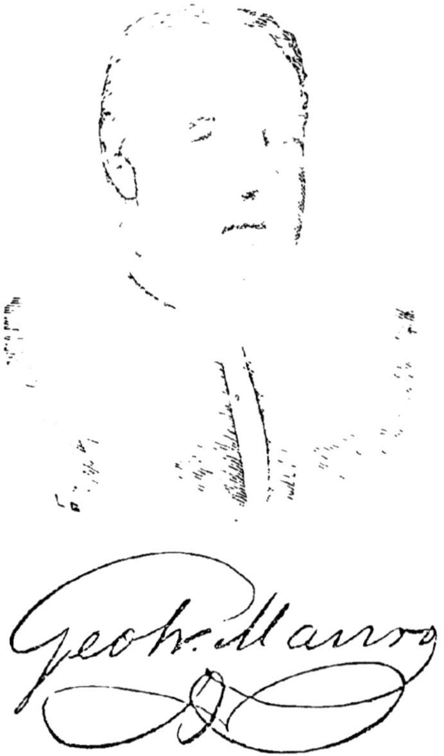

Freedom.—The village of Freedom is four miles from Sykesville, and adjacent to Morgan's Run. [illegible]

O'Donald, a very large landed proprietor in this district at an early date O'Donald, in laying out the village gave the alternate lots to those who purchased lots, and his liberality and *freedom* in his transactions gave the name to the village, and when the district was organized, in 1837, it took its name from the village, which was founded shortly after the Revolution The residence of Dr Joseph W Steele, a log structure weather boarded, was built about 1769, and during the Revolution and until a few years ago was occupied as a tavern John Little kept it for many years The village is on the old Liberty road, built in olden times by convicts, but before its construction there was an older road, which ran back of Dr Steele's residence (the old tavern) The Berret family is an old one in this region, and its first head here was a Hayti refugee, who married a daughter of O'Donald, the great land owner Mary E Wadlow is postmistress, and J Wadlow & Sons, merchants J Oliver Wadlow, the popular and efficient register of wills of Carroll County, resides here

The physician of the town is Dr Joseph W Steele, who has been engaged in the practice of his profession at this point since 1856 He was born near the village, March 6, 1831 (also the day of the birth of J Oliver Wadlow), and is, on his father's side of Irish extraction His grandfather was John Steele, who taught school and kept store at an early date a few miles distant (now in Franklin District) John Steele met for the first time his future wife, Mary Hays, during the Revolution, at the tavern in Freedom at a social party The doctor's grandmother on his maternal side was a Gore, one of the oldest settlers, and his wife was Margaret J Smith, a descendant of the earliest settlers of Baltimore Town Where the village stands the only house for many years was the old tavern, whose high mantels and unique hand carving betoken its great age Dr Nathan Browne, who lived near here and died in 1873, was a celebrated physician He was born on the Eastern Shore of Maryland, and was distinguished for his philanthropy He never married, and lived with his beloved nieces He was a State senator from 1867 to 1871, and held other positions of great trust He practiced here forty-five years

Dr W M Hines resides just west of the village Dr Hines has steadily practiced medicine in Carroll County since 1846, save for a period of three years and it may therefore be easily understood that he is pretty well known all over the county as well as in adjacent sections He was born July 23 1825 in the town of Liberty, Frederick County There also his father David, was born David

57

Hines was educated at Georgetown, D C, and passed a busy life as farmer and merchant He owned and farmed in early life the valuable tract known as "Glade Garden" As a merchant he was prominent in Liberty, Frederick, and Baltimore, in which latter city he ended his days His wife was Jane C,

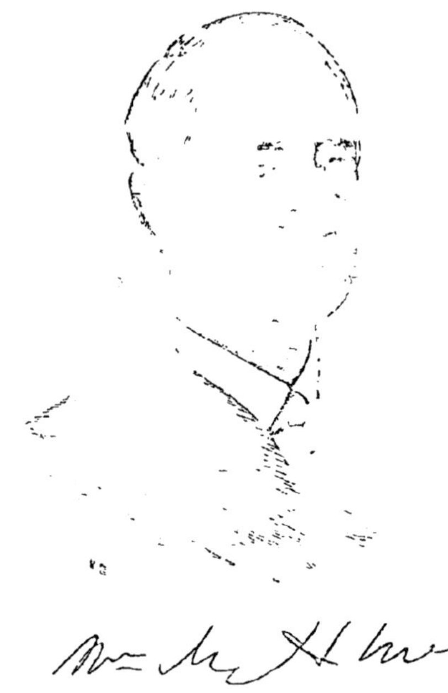

daughter of Samuel Marshall His father, Philip Hines, served with considerable distinction in the war of the Revolution The living sons and daughters of David Hines are Mrs Augustus Webster and Mrs Ignatius Gore, of Baltimore, and Dr Hines of Carroll County Dr Hines passed his early youth at Glade Garden farm, and at the age of fifteen was sent to Dickinson College, at Carlisle At the end of four years of study he occupied a place in the junior class, from which he was forced to retire by reason of ill health A brief rest recuperated his energies, and in 1844 he began the study of medicine under Dr Nathan R Smith, one of Baltimore's most distinguished surgeons Young Hines attended lectures at the University of Maryland, and graduated at that institution in March, 1846 Very soon thereafter he located in Carroll County, near his present home, and gave himself with such energy and vigorous determination to the practice of his profession that he found himself in due time in active demand in all the country roundabout His field was a large one, and his call [illegible] in his early experi-

ence he almost literally lived in the saddle For a period of three years he was connected with the United States custom house at Baltimore, and for three months during the war of 1861-65 was a surgeon in the Federal army, with his station at Convent Hospital, Baltimore Excepting these absences Dr Hines has been regularly, in season and out of season, one of Carroll County's leading physicians, and now, after a practice of thirty six years, is hale, hearty, and vigorous, and still rides a large circuit and attends upon his numerous patients with wellnigh as much briskness and ambitious spirit as marked the younger portions of his career Like his father before him, he was an Old Line Whig Later he became and remains a Republican Although alive to the progress of political events and deeply interested therein, he has steadily from the outset of his manhood's experience held consistently aloof from the business of office-seeking or office holding In 1855 he married Frances H, daughter of Rev Augustus Webster, of Baltimore Mrs Hines died Oct 3, 1877 There are three living children, two of them being sons, Augustus W and William M

Freedom Lodge, A F and A M, No 112, was chartered in 1862, with the following charter members

W M, Warren N Little, S W, Dr Joseph W Steele, J W, Nicholas L Rogers, Sec, J Oliver Wadlow, Treas, John Deckabaugh

The lodge built its hall before obtaining its charter It is a two story frame building, twenty four by forty-five feet, the lower part being used for a public school Of the fourteen charter members the following are living John Deckabaugh, Thomas Paynter, Lewis Ohler, J Oliver Wadlow, Dr J W Steele John L Nicholas, and Robert Clark Its Worshipful Masters have been John Deckabaugh, J Oliver Wadlow, Dr J W Steele, Lewis Ohler, and Warren N Little

Officers for 1881

W M, John Deckabaugh, S W, Thomas Paynter, J W, Samuel W Barnet Sec, Dr J W Steele, Treas, J Oliver Wadlow

It numbers forty-seven Master Masons, two Fellow Crafts, and one Entered Apprentice Dr J W Steele has served as Grand Standard Bearer in the Grand Lodge At a single festival this lodge took in fourteen hundred dollars, which cleared it of all debts, and left a surplus for charitable purposes

The Methodist Episcopal church, built in 1822, is between Freedom and Eldersburg It is a handsome edifice, displaying considerable architectural taste

In its cemetery are the graves of the following persons.

Nicholas Dorsey, died Sept 9, 1876, aged 60

Elizabeth Dorsey, died March 2, 1881, aged 76

Samuel Bingham, died Aug 17, 1876, aged 66

Ruth Bingham, died Aug 27, 1880 aged 72

Caroline Brown, born April 15, 1815, died July 17, 1878

Jesse W Brandenburg born Dec 15, 1838, died Jan 9, 18[illegible]

Caroline, wife of William Cooley, died March 3 1877, aged 49

Sarah, wife of David Slack, died Feb 20, 1878, aged 91

Rebecca, wife of William D Frizzell, born March 17, 18[illegible], died Feb 25, 1866, and her husband, born March 7, 1829 died March 24, 1875

John Frizzell, died March 31, 1870, aged 69

John Wadlow, died Sept 10, 1854 aged 50, and Jemima his wife, April 8, 1872, aged 67

Anna Maria Shipley, born Feb 2[illegible] 1775, died Jan 1[illegible], 18[illegible]

Frances Hollis, wife of Dr William M Hines, died Oct 3, 1877.

Achsa, wife of William Serivenor, died April 8, 1872, aged 82

Israel Frizzell, born March 23, 1807, died Aug 6, 1870

Stephen R Gore, born April 1, 1818, died Feb 25, 1872

Jabez Gore, died Jan 7, 1851, aged 39

Rev Samuel Gore died Sept 4, 1858, aged 75 (a local preacher of Methodist Episcopal Church for 50 years), and Theresa, his wife, born Nov 20, 1789, died Feb 29, 1864

Nathan Clark, died Sept 22, 1852, aged 68

Joseph Steele, died Aug 2[illegible], 1855 aged 61 and his wife Charlotte, April 22, 18[illegible] aged 58

John T Steele (a Freemason), died Aug 9, 1863, aged 4[illegible]

Cecilia, wife of William Beam, and third daughter of Matthew and Catharine Chambers, born Jan 21, 1806, died Dec 18, 1870

Matthew Chambers died Aug 1[illegible], 182[illegible], aged 52

Col Peter Little, died Feb 5, 1850, aged 54, and his wife, Catharine, July 18, 1867, aged 79

Sophia Lovely, died Sept 17, 1845, aged 55

Warren Little (a Freemason), born Feb 29, 1811, died [illegible] 21, 1863

John Little, died Sept 5, 1853, aged 50

Mrs Catharine Steele, eldest daughter of John and Anne Little, died April 11, 1865, aged 55

David Little, died Aug 23, 1857, aged 62

George Clift, died Feb 9, 1852, aged 75

Elizabeth Clift, died Dec 30, 1858, aged 94

Elizabeth Hines died May 3, 1867, aged 58

Hannah Lindsey, died Aug 31, 1862, aged 7[illegible]

Joshua Lee, died March 4, 1871, aged 88, and his wife, Susannah, Nov 21, 1869, aged 83

Jesse Lee, died March 23, 1866, aged 68

Thomas Lucy, died July 16, 1853, aged 92

Margaret, wife of John Elder, born Jan 16, 1774, died May 8, 1849

Thomas Bingham, died May 5, 18[illegible], aged 80.

Mary, wife of John Twemmy, born Aug 9, 1812, died Jan 21, 1855

Julia, wife of William C Lindsey, died Aug 6, 1874, aged 49

Honor Lee, wife of Thomas Lee, died June 30, 1853, aged 64, and her husband, Nov 5, 18[illegible], aged 7[illegible]

Larkin Fisher, died Feb 21, 1870 aged 71

The corner-stone of the Methodist Episcopal Church South, a handsome brick structure, lying between Freedom and Eldersburg was laid April 13, 1868, when Rev Wm F [illegible] was p[illegible] [illegible] George W

Manro was chairman of the building committee Its present pastors are Revs Watters and Martin

In the churchyard are buried the following persons

John W Brown, born Oct 9, 1811, and died March 7, 1877

Jemima E, wife of John G Pearce, born Sept 14, 1827, died Jan 12, 1875

Their son, Elias J, born Feb 2, 1856, died Aug 23, 1876

Jacob Ritter, born Nov 20, 1801, died Dec 26, 1870,—descendant of the earliest Ritter of 1650,—and Elizabeth, his wife, born Feb 17, 1806, died March 23, 1879

Juliet Welsh, wife of Luther Welsh, died June 1, 1869, aged 63

Ruth, wife of Freeborn Gardner, died March 29, 1870, aged 62

Elizabeth, wife of Samuel W Barnett, died July 7, 1871, aged 4[illegible]

Cornelius Shipley, died Feb 3, 1862, aged 61

Eldersburg —The town of Eldersburg, three and a half miles from Sykesville and thirty two from Baltimore, was named in honor of John Elder, who laid it out before 1800 and who was an early settler, owning large tracts of land in the vicinity It has a lodge of I O Good Templars, and Grange No 139 of Patrons of Husbandry, of which N D Norris is Master, and George M Prugh, secretary Among the business men of the town are T A. Barnes, postmaster and merchant, Dr H C Shipley, physician, L. H W Selby, undertaker, J & L H Selby, millers, and J Collins, shoemaker

Holy Trinity Parish, Protestant Episcopal Church, originated on March 8, 1771, when John Welch entered into a bond in the penal sum of two hundred pounds, English sterling, to convey to Abel Brown, Robert Twis, Edward Dorsey, and John Elder two acres of land, provided the said persons would build a "Chappell of Ease" for the benefit of "Delaware Hundred," the name of then election district The church was built (a stone structure), and became a part of St Thomas' Parish, Baltimore County In the lapse of time the congregation thinned out, Episcopal services were no longer held, and the Baptists for some years occupied the edifice After a time the Baptists were unable to maintain their congregation, and the building was not used for religious services, but became the abode of cattle and horses

On June 1, 1843, Holy Trinity Parish was formed out of St Thomas', and this ancient building repaired, rebuilt, and refurnished, and on Oct 31, 1843, consecrated anew The vestrymen then chosen were George F Warfield, Wm H Warfield, James Sykes, [illegible] Hollingsworth, George W Manro, John Col[illegible]n, Nicholas Dorsey, and Warner W Warfield, and the Register, Washington L Bromley Its pastors and rectors have been

1[illegible]7, Rev D Hillhouse Buell, 1847, Rev Wm E Snowden, 1[illegible]-51 Rev [illegible] [illegible]-6[illegible], Rev Thomas J Wyatt, 1869, Rev J Worrall Larmour, Dec 6, 1869, Rev Robert Pigott, D D, present rector

The officers for 1881 were Vestrymen L W W Selby, Dr C C Moorehead, Thomas B Jones, Capt J W Bennett, John Grimes, W B Shipley, A Voorhees, John Barnes, Sr, Wm P Grimes, and George W Holmes, Wardens, George W Holmes, John Grimes, Register Charles R Favour, Esq

In the churchyard the following persons are buried

Kate, wife of Z Hollingsworth, died Sept 21, 1858

Their son, Zebulon, died April 4, 1861 aged 31

Elizabeth, wife of Edward Ireland, Jr, died Jan 19, 1862, aged 32

Emma E Lucy, died Nov 14, 1861, aged 41

Barbara, daughter of Andrew and Martha [illegible], born July 16, 1831, died April 7, 1865

Jesse Hollingsworth, born March 19, 1800, died April 8 1872

Anna Baker, daughter of Jesse and Sophia Hollingsworth, born April 21 1829, died April 10, 1870

George Fraser Warfield, born March 20, 1769, died Dec 11, 1849, and his wife Rebecca (daughter of Abel Brown), born Dec 24, 1771, died March 4, 1852

William Warfield, born Aug 3, 1807, died March 26 1857

Augustus Edward Dorsey, died Dec 9, 1869, aged 60

James Soper, died Oct 10, 1811, aged 15

Springfield Presbyterian church, a fine three-story structure, was erected in 1836 by George Patterson and Stephen T C Brown A few years later the parsonage, adjoining, was built The building has been used both as a church and school The school was incorporated as "*Springfield Academy*" by an act of the Legislature passed Jan 6, 1838 The first trustees designated in this act were Dr Hawes Goldsborough, Dr R D Hewitt, Dr Nathan Browne, Eli Hewitt, Nathan Gorsuch, Joseph Steele, and Cornelius Shipley The last pastor of the church was Rev Charles Beach, who had charge of the academy now conducted by his daughters The present trustees of the academy are Frank Brown, Wm C Polk, Lewis Shultz, Richard J Baker, Johner Wadlow, J O Devries, Joshua D Warfield, P W Webb, and Robert C McKinney Miss Florence Patterson, who died in 1878, left to the church and academy a bequest of five thousand dollars, which is held by Frank Brown in trust for the interests of the church

In the graveyard in the rear of the church and academy the following persons are buried

George Devries, over whom there is erected an elegant Scotch granite monument with simply his name.

Sarah L, his wife, died Aug 26, 1877

Stephen T C Brown, born Nov 12, 1820, died Dec 6, 1876

Mary, daughter of Stephen T C and Susan A Brown, born Aug 29, 1843, died May 30, 1863

Susan, wife of Thomas C Brown, born Feb 1, 1791, died Sept 19, 1861

[illegible] and daughter of George and

Prudence A Patterson, born June 13, 1817, died Oct 15, 1878 (resting on her breast was the body of her infant son)

George Patterson born Aug 26, 1796, died Nov 26, 1869

George, son of George and Prudence A Patterson, born Sept 9, 1841, died Dec 21, 1849

Eli Hewitt, died April 10, 1868, aged 62, and Ann E, his wife, Jan 18, 1859, aged 52

Susanna, wife of John L Nicholas, died July 14, 1862, aged 38

Nicholas Harry, born in parish Tywardreath, County Cornwall, England, May 1809, died Feb 5, 1862

Catharine Buckingham, died Nov 1, 1875, aged 71

Augustus Smith, died June 15, 1862, aged 42

Jane, wife of Henry Nicholas, died Aug 2[illegible] 1858, aged 37

Sykesville is on the Baltimore and Ohio Railroad thirty-two miles from Baltimore, and by turnpike twenty two, and seventeen from Westminster It is pleasantly located on the West Branch of the Patapsco River, which supplies abundance of water for milling and other purposes It is a flourishing town, and a large business is done here in lumber, lime, coal, fertilizers, and general merchandise It has become a favorite resort for the families of Baltimoreans, many of whom board at the farm-houses in the neighborhood during the summer The town was named after James Sykes, son of John Sykes, a famous Baltimore merchant He came here in 1825, and bought a thousand acres of land in different tracts, including the site of the town, on which at that time the only building was a saw- and grist-mill He replaced the old mill by a new and substantial structure in 1830–31, and erected a five story stone hotel to meet the requirements of the railroad then built to this place, and for a summer resort It was fifty by seventy-four feet in dimensions, and the finest hotel in Maryland outside of Baltimore at that date In 1837, when John Grimes (the present hotel-keeper) came here, there were but four or five houses, and John Garrett kept the big hotel In 1845, Mr Sykes enlarged his stone mill and converted it into the "Howard Cotton-Factory," and also built large houses for his operatives He carried it on until 1857, employing over two hundred hands, when the monetary crisis caused his suspension This factory has not been in operation since, except for a short time, when run by L A Purennet and Miller for a year or so, and for a brief period during the war by James A Gary on certain lines of manufactured goods Mr Sykes died in the spring of 1881, universally esteemed and respected The oldest house standing is a log hut occupied by George Collins The first house built on the site of the town was carried off by the flood of 1868, which did immense damage, sweeping away many buildings, including the large hotel then kept by John [illegible] and the store of Zimmerman & Shultz This firm lost all their goods, and also their iron safe with its contents of money books, etc The safe was never found The first physician to settle here was Dr Array Owings in 1846 J M Zimmerman is postmaster, railroad and express agent, and Dr C C Moorhead, the physician of the neighborhood Messrs Zimmerman & Shultz, merchants came here from Frederick in 1858, and have built up an immense trade, having been very successful in business After being washed out by the great freshet in 1868 they built another fine stone house across the street and opposite their old place of business John McDonald & Co erected their elegant stone store in 1865, and have an extensive trade Samuel R Duvall has just completed a large building, where he carries on a big business in agricultural implements, hardware, etc Messrs Zimmerman & Shultz own the mill property and factory formerly belonging to Mr Sykes All these houses, together with the Methodist Episcopal and Episcopal churches, are on the Howard County side of the river E M Mellor is also engaged in the merchandise business When Mr Sykes came to this spot in 1825 there were only three houses or buildings, including the mill, but to-day the population is over four hundred

The Methodist Episcopal church, a handsome stone edifice, was erected in 1878 on a very high eminence overlooking the town It has stained windows and a well-toned bell It was built under the pastorate of Rev C W Baldwin, who was in charge from 1875 to 1879 His successor, Rev T M West, remained from 1879 to 1881, when the present incumbent Rev A J Gill, entered upon the discharge of his duties as pastor The Sunday-school superintendent is J E Gaither

Previous to the erection of the church building in 1878 the congregation held its services in a large frame building opposite the cotton factory

St Joseph's Catholic church, a handsome structure, is near the depot, and on a beautiful site It was begun before the war, and completed in 1867 Its pastor is Father Loague of Woodstock College, and the congregation is large and zealous

The Protestant Episcopal church in Holy Trinity Parish was built in 1850, on June 11th of which year the corner stone was laid Its rector then was Rev S Chalmers Davis, who, in 1851, was succeeded by Rev Thomas J Wyatt, who continued to 1869 during which year Rev J Worrall Larmour officiated a few months The present rector, the learned and venerable Robert Pigot, D D came to the parish [illegible] a substantial

stone structure of imposing architecture, and located on the Howard County side, with a fine view of the whole town The list of its officers is given above, being the same as those in charge of the Eldersburg Church, which with this forms Holy Trinity Parish, made out of St Thomas' in 1843 Its rector, Rev Dr Pigot, was born May 20, 1795, in New York City His father was a native of Chester, England, came to America a soldier in the king's army, and was present, Sept 13, 1759, at the battle of Quebec, under Gen Wolfe, where he witnessed that famous commander's victory and death He located after the close of the French and Indian war in New York City, where before and after the Revolution he was a successful school-teacher During the French and Indian war he was one of the secretaries of Lord Amherst, the commander of all the king's forces in America

The doctor's family was founded in England by Pigot, Baron of Boorne, in Normandy, one of the forty knights who accompanied William the Conqueror An elder branch settled at Chetwynd Park and Edgemont, in Shropshire, where it yet continues, another possessed Doddeshall Park, in Bucks, and the third removed to Ireland Its arms were—sanguine—three pickaxes—argent crest—a greyhound, *passant*, sable, mottoes, *labore et virtute*, and *commuti debitum*, seats, Archer Lodge, Sheffield upon Lodden Hants, and Banbury, Oxfordshire On the maternal line, Dr Pigot is descended from Cerdic a Saxon prince, who invaded England 495 and 519 B C He was brought up in the church, and ordained Nov 23, 1823, by Bishop White He came to Maryland from Pennsylvania in 1837, and was made rector of North Sassafras, Cecil Co In 1840 he became rector of Grace Church, Elkridge Landing, and Ellicott Chapel, Anne Arundel County In 1842 he was chosen principal of Darlington Academy, and in 1844, missionary and rector of Redemption Church, in Baltimore, to which, in 1845, was added Cranmer Chapel In 1847 he was made professor in Newton University of Baltimore, in 1850 was city missionary In 1855 he was an assistant in the University of Maryland, and chancellor of the Protestant University His first rectorship was St Mark's, Lewistown, Pa, from 1825 to 1828 In 1869 he came to Holy Trinity Parish, and on March 30, 1870, his house burned down, and he lost by the fire the church register, all his literary labors for fifty three years, and all his sermons for forty-seven This venerable divine is one of the oldest Freemasons in America, having received the three first degrees in Masonry in 1824. Since then he has taken all the degrees to and including the thirty second He belongs to the Maryland Commandery, No 1, of Baltimore, from which he was the recipient of a splendid sword, presented to him as a Sir Knight A handsome Masonic medal, bearing date of his initiation into the order (1824), was also presented to him, with the Latin inscription, "*Tolle crucem et coronam*" He has repeatedly, and for many years, served as chaplain in various Masonic organizations and bodies, both in Pennsylvania and Maryland

Another noted family connected with Holy Trinity Parish since its establishment in 1843 is that of the Warfields Richard Warfield, a native of Wales, came to this country in 1638, and pitched his tent nine miles from Annapolis, Md, at a place now known as the "Black Horse Tavern" His second son was Alexander, whose third son was Hazel Warfield The latter was twice married By his first wife were born Henry Warfield, a member of Congress, Dr Charles Alexander Warfield, Dr Peregrine Warfield, Dr Gustavus Warfield and by his second wife, George Frazer Warfield and Sally Waters, of Tennessee, whose daughter married Dr Robinson, who was the father of the wife of Judge Henning, of New Orleans, whose daughter married Gen Hood, of the Confederate army Dr Charles A Warfield was a stanch patriot (as were all the Warfields) in the Revolution, and was a lieutenant in the Continental army He was with the party which boarded the British vessel "Peggy Stewart" and burned her with her cargo of tea at Annapolis George Frazer Warfield was born March 20, 1769 in Baltimore, and became a noted merchant of that city In 1834 he removed to his country-seat, "Groveland," in the vicinity of Sykesville, where he died Dec 11, 1869 His wife was Rebecca Brown, daughter of Abel Brown, and a sister of ex-Congressman Elias Brown She was born near Sykesville, Dec 24, 1774, and died March 4, 1852 The Warfield family was largely instrumental in creating the parish of Holy Trinity, rebuilding the church edifice at Eldersburg, and building the one at Sykesville, and three of its members, William H, George F, and Warner W, were members of the first vestry in 1843 George Frazer Warfield's children were Lewis, George F, Warner W, William H (of United States army), Susanna, Rebecca, married to Richard Holmes, and Elizabeth, married to Mr Wade, a lawyer of Massachusetts Miss Susanna Warfield lives at "Groveland" with her nephew, George W Holmes She was born in 1794, and is a well preserved lady of the old school,—dignified and courtly paying great attention to current [illegible] and [illegible] interested in the

church George Frazer Warfield was one of the defenders of Baltimore, and named his country seat "Groveland" at the suggestion of Miss Bentley, a sister of his son George's wife "Aunt Harvey," a sister of Abel Brown, and aunt to Mrs George Frazer Warfield, was murdered by the Indians near Harper's Ferry, while on her way to the West, about 1775, and one of Abel Brown's brothers was killed under Braddock at this unfortunate general s defeat

In the Protestant Episcopal graveyard there are a few interments among which are the following

James Berry died Sept 13, 1865, aged 78

Mamie F, daughter of John K and Rachel A Mellor, born Oct 17, 1869, died Feb 26, 1872

Ida Helena, daughter of William L and Ann E Long, born Oct 20, 1867 died Jan 1, 1869

Margaret, wife of William Dean, died Feb 14, 1858, aged 68

Catharine H, wife of William H Hooper, died Feb 3, 18[illegible]4, aged 31

Mary Gill, died March 26, 1863, aged 57

Fanny Isabel, born July 27, 1811, died Oct 24, 1870

Marcellus Warfield died June 3, 18[illegible], aged 35

Warner W Warfield, born March 20, 1788, died July 28, 1867

Elba furnace lies just below Sykesville, but has not been worked since the flood of 1868 It was opened and operated years ago by the Tysons

Elias Brown, a son of Abel Brown, one of the first settlers and largest landed proprietors of the district, died July 3, 1857 He was a Presidential elector for Monroe in 1820, and for Gen Jackson in 1828, and in 1824 his brother, William Brown, was also a Presidential elector for Jackson in the great quadruple contest Elias Brown was for several years a member of Congress He was a delegate to the State Constitutional Convention of 1851, and a member of the House of Delegates from Carroll County in 1849 He had frequently represented Baltimore County in the Legislature before the creation of Carroll County in 1837

Col Peter Little was born in 1776, and died Feb 5, 1830 He was of a family that settled in the district before 1765 He was at one time a member of Congress from the Baltimore district, and an active and zealous officer in the militia He served with honor in the war of 1812

Porter's is a small village on the Liberty road, six miles from Sykesville, and near Piney Run, and derives its name from an old family which settled in the vicinity many years ago. Branchburg's Methodist Protestant church is near the hamlet Mrs M E Trenwith is postmistress, and keeps the only store in the place

Hood's M[illegible] the B[illegible] and O[illegible] road, thirty four miles from Baltimore, and fifteen from Westminster It was named after the Hood family, as one of them, James Hood, and John Grimes erected the famous mills in 1845 Winfield S Robb is postmaster, railroad and express agent, and keeps the only store Watson Methodist Episcopal chapel is near here Gen J M Hood, the estimable president of the Western Maryland Railroad, was born and raised here, and Charles W Hood, a successful land surveyor in his early life, died in the vicinity, Jan 19, 1877, aged sixty years

Morgan is on the Baltimore and Ohio Railroad thirty four miles from Baltimore, and near the Patapsco River John A Dushane, of Baltimore, has an extensive paper mill here, giving employment to a number of persons, and manufacturing all grades of paper George F Jones is the superintendent of the paper-mill, postmaster, and railroad agent

Woodbine.—This station is on the Baltimore and Ohio Railroad thirty-seven miles from Baltimore, and near the Patapsco River Morgan chapel (Methodist Episcopal) is near the village A Owings is postmaster and railroad agent E A Owings and Mrs H A Ways are the store keepers J A Albaugh keeps the hotel, and J M Baker has charge of the mill The Warfield family in America is of Welsh descent The first representative was Richard Warfield, an emigrant from Wales, who came to this country in 1637 and settled nine miles from Annapolis, at a place now called "Black Horse Tavern" A descendant of this emigrant was Charles A Warfield, of Howard County, whose son, Charles A, married Julianna Owings and resided near Lisbon, in that county Of their six children,—five sons and one daughter,—the next to the youngest was Charles A, born Oct 16, 1836, in Howard County, near Sykesville He was raised on his father's farm, a mile and a half from the Carroll County line, and was early inured to labor by tilling the soil and taking care of the stock on the farm He received a good education in the English branches at the public schools of the neighborhood In December, 1862, he removed to Freedom District, and purchased one hundred and sixty-two acres of land of George Wethered This is the splendid farm he now owns, and to which the previous owner, Mr Wethered, a soldier in the Mexican war, gave the romantic name of "Chihuahua," a name it still retains Mr Warfield was married, Nov 16, 1864, to Caroline A Devries, daughter of Christian and Jemima Devries near Marriottsville Their son, Wade Hampton Devries Warfield, was born Oct 7, 1865 Mr Warfield's farm is three fourths of a mile [illegible] al country sur-

rounded by picturesque scenery His mansion is an elegant three story frame building delightfully located on an eminence, with pleasant surroundings of lofty trees and beautiful shrubbery In the heated term during the summer months he entertains summer boarders from the cities, who find his place a delightful resort He is specially engaged in dairying, and sends a daily average of forty five gallons of milk to "Olive Dairy," Pennsylvania Avenue, Baltimore He was one of the first in this section to embark in this business, and his dairy is the largest in this region, save that on the Frank Brown estate His family and himself are attendants on the Springfield Presbyterian Church He is a Democrat in politics, but has never held or sought office His farm is in an excellent state of cultivation, and its buildings, fences, and general improvements indicate the best qualities of a thorough and successful farmer, while the tidiness and order of the house betoken rare domestic graces in his estimable wife

Below is given the vote for local officers in the district from 1851 to 1861, inclusive

1851 —Vote for Primary School Commissioner John Warden 182, L Gardner 91, John W Wadlow 110

1853.—For Justices Jesse Hollingsworth 201, Alex Gillis 200, William Tensfield 215, Constables L H Boring 200, Aaron Gosnell 199 Road Supervisor, Reuben Conoway 221

1855 —For Justices R Conoway 310, N D Norris 312, N H Jenkins 312, Constables W C Lindsay 310, J H Conoway 310, Road Supervisor, J Hollingsworth 310

1857 —For Justices J Morgan 73, J Dorsey 13, R Conoway 299, W G Shipley 293, N D Norris 303 Constables P Welsh 12, A Gosnell 303, W C Lindsay 294, Road Supervisor A Evans 12, Joshua Lee 297

1859 —For Justices C W Hood 75, James Morgan 61, N D Norris 285, Larkin Shipley 262, W G Shipley 2?1, Constables J H Hood 121, W C Lindsay 2?0, Aaron Gosnell 243, Road Supervisor W H Harden 160, Brice Shipley 249

1861 —For Justices Eli Hewitt, Sr, 397, John T Ways 396, William Tensfield 378, E Thompson 97, James Morgan 98, Abel Scrivnor 97, Constables Aaron Gosnell 397, W C Lindsay 389 Road Supervisor Wesley Day 373, O Buckingham 112

The public school trustees for 1881 and 1882 were

1 Oakland —Joseph Gist, John Melvin, William Bachman

2 Stony Ridge —John O Devries, John Pearce, Austin Arrington

3 Mechanicsville —No trustees

4 Sykesville —Lewis H Shultz, S P Duvall, Charles R Ijnar

5 Hood's Mills —Solomon Shoemaker, Zachariah Wolfe, R C McKinney

6 Brandenburg's —J M Dorsey, Henry Cook, Joseph Barnes

7 Pleasant Gap —James H Shipley, Brice Shipley, Cornelius Shipley.

8 Farver's —Thomas L W Condon, Joseph Wilson, David McQuay

9 Jenkins —No appointments

10 Woodbine —George L Buckingham, Elisha Young, R H Harrison

11 Freedom —Joseph W Berret, J Doekabaugh, Thomas Painter

1 White Rock (African) —Isaac Dorsey, Wesley Costly, Aaron Austin (all colored)

The teachers for the term ending April 15, 1881, were

1, Celie E Goldsmith, 41 pupils, 2, Lizzie A Bennett, 35 pupils 3, C L Hughes 22 pupils 4, Isabel N Hale, 51 pupils, 5, S Spalding, 26 pupils, 6, Sue M Matthews, 41 pupils 7, Libbie Shipley, 27 pupils, 8, L A Koontz, 50 pupils, 10, M I Hoffman, 46 pupils 11, Minta Shipley, 33 pupils, 1 (colored school), Emma V Randolph, 70 pupils

MANCHESTER DISTRICT, No 6

Manchester District, the Sixth District of Carroll County, is bounded on the north by Pennsylvania, on the east by Baltimore County and Hampstead District, on the south by the districts of Hampstead and Westminster, and on the west by Westminster and Myers Districts The principal stream in the district is the Gunpowder Falls Creek, which passes through the northeastern portion and flows into Baltimore County and which has several small tributaries Big Grave Run has its source in the centre, and flows southeast into Baltimore County, and the head waters of Big Pipe Creek and the North Branch of the Patapsco take their rise in the district The population of Manchester District was in 1880 three thousand five hundred and one The metes and bounds of Manchester District, as laid out by the commission of 1837, are as follows

"Beginning at the forks of the county road leading from Westminster to the town of Hampstead and George Richards' mill, thence to the falls of Aspin Run and Long Glade Branch, thence up said branch to the spring near the house of Joseph Bowser, deceased, thence to the spring near the house of John Orendorff, thence to the forks of the most northern branch of Patapsco Falls and Bosley's Spring Branch, where they unite in Wm Albaugh's meadow, thence through the farms of John Reed and Joshua Bosley, Sr, leaving said Reed and Bosley in District No 6, thence to Michael Baker's tavern on the Hanover and Baltimore turnpike road, leaving said Baker in District No 6, thence across said turnpike east of Shriver's tan-yard, thence through the lands of Daniel Caltuder, leaving said Caltuder in District No 6, thence through the lands of (Gist's, thence through the land of) George Caltuder, deceased, and John Wareham, leaving said Caltuder and Wareham in District No 8, thence to Michael Miller's well on the middle road, thence to Joshua Stansbury's spring, near the house on the Falls road, thence through the lands of Hair, leaving said Hair in District No 8, thence to Henry Zimmerman's county road, where said road crosses Carroll and Baltimore county line at a blazed hickory-tree thence on said county line to the Pennsylvania line thence with said line to Pinchart's county road, thence [illegible] head spring of

Ohio Branch, thence down said branch to where it crosses Trump's county road, thence through Peter Bixler's farm to Big Pipe Creek, where Lawer's Branch unites with Big Pipe Creek, leaving said Bixler in District No 6, thence up said branch to Baughman's county road thence with said road to the mouth of a line between Royer and German, thence through the farm of Abraham Shiffer leaving said Shiffer in District No 7, thence to the forks of Manchester and Hampstead road, thence to the place of beginning "

Manchester was made the place of holding the polls

Among the earliest surveys were "Rattlesnake Ridge," of 50 acres, surveyed July 18, 1738, for Edward Richards, and patented in 1739, "Three Brothers," of 300 acres, surveyed Aug 2, 1746, "Easenburg," Aug 26, 1761, "Shilling's Lot," of 40 acres, Oct 3, 1751, "Heidelburgh," Aug 10, 1752, and resurveyed Feb 22 1762, for Elias Harange, "Frankford," surveyed Jan 27, 1761, for Conrad Barst, 'Motter's Choice," resurveyed December, 1751, for 162 acres, "Potter's Lot," of 40 acres, for John Pilack, Oct 30, 1760, "Richard's Chance," of 50 acres, Jan 1 1749 for Richard Richards, "Pomerania," near Whistler's Mill, now Bixler's, for 50 acres, to William Winchester, Jan 8, 1755, 'Johnsburg," of 130 acres, resurveyed for John Shrempling, May 20, 1761, "Mount Hendrick," of 48 acres, to James Hendrick, March 3, 1768, "McGill's Choice," of 50 acres, to Andrew McGill, June 12, 1744, 'Winchester's Lot," Oct 23, 1751, "Everything Needful,' to Richard Richards, May 16, 1763, and for 1646 acres, same afterwards resurveyed, Nov 14, 1786, as "Everything Needful Corrected," to Samuel Owings, in three parts, one of 1573 acres and one of 58½, Ulrich Freeland getting the latter, "Warms," 'Bridgeland,' Feb 28, 1751, "California," of 490 acres, March 26, 1765, and "Dey's Chance," June 10, 1755

The earliest actual settlers were Germans, mostly from Pennsylvania, and some from the Fatherland Among these may be mentioned the Showers, Ritters, Jacob Shilling, Philip Edleman, Jacob Utz, Michael Burn, Kerlingers, Faess, Gethiers, Motters, Werheims, Weavers, Steffers, Everharts, Bowers, Warners, Bachmans, Ebaughs Paul Everhart, an emigrant from Germany settled first at Germantown, Pa, and in 1761 removed to this district His son George, then seven years old, died in 1851 Paul settled where are now the iron ore works His great-grandson, George Everhart, born in 1800 is still living

Manchester, the commercial centre of the district, is the second town in size and importance in Carroll County, containing in 1880 six hundred and forty inhabitants It is situated on the Hanover turnpike, and contains a population of about nine hundred inhabitants, with a number of churches, a Masonic Hall, an Odd-Fellows' Hall, an academy, and a number of stores and manufactories The people, as a rule, are educated and enterprising A number of railroads have been projected, which if completed will make the town a centre for business second to none in Maryland outside of Baltimore Of late years an æsthetic taste has been manifested by the inhabitants, which has given rise to associations for the culture of literature and music, and the town now possesses all the elements for enlightened existence in the country remote from the temptations and embarrassments of a large city

From 1760 to 1790 a few houses stood where the site of the present thriving village is situated In 1790, Capt Richard Richards, an Englishman, living in the Hampstead settlement, laid out the town and called it "Manchester," after that city in England, from which he had emigrated many years before It was part of a survey of fifty acres, called "New Market," patented to him in 1754, but which was surveyed for him March 5, 1765, and thirty-three of which he laid out in lots These lots were sold subject to an annual ground-rent, and to this day on one and one-fourth acres of land George Everhart pays a yearly rent of five dollars to Judge John E Smith, of Westminster, the representative of or successor to the Richard rights The ground rents on all the other lots have expired "The German Church Lands," of twenty-five acres, adjoining the above and a part of the town, were surveyed Dec 20, 1758, to Jacob Shilling, Philip Edleman, Jacob Utz, and Michael Burns, as trustees. The church at the present time receives from its ground-rents on these lands or lots an annual sum of more than one hundred and fifty dollars The town is designated on the old maps as "on the original road leading to Baltimore and near Dug Hill" The oldest man in the town is George Everhart, aged eighty two, who came here from the country in 1826, and was nearly half a century in the mercantile business The oldest house in the village is an old log building now owned by Edward Oursler It was formerly kept as a tavern by Christian Heibly On the lot now owned by Mr Brinkman, the jeweler, a tavern once stood before any other house had been built in the town The first physician was Dr Urnbaugh, who was followed by Dr Turner and Dr Jacob Shower The last began practice in 1825 Among the first schoolmasters was a Mr Keller who taught part of his pupils in the German, and the others in the English language. About the first storekeeper was [illegible] Motter, and in 1826, George

Everhart bought out Mark Spencer (an Eastern man from the State of New York), and continued in business until 1877 George Linawcaver was the earliest blacksmith George Gettier, born here in 1791, was a soldier in the war of 1812, and died in Cincinnati, Ohio

The town was incorporated in 1833, and a supplementary act of 1836 revived the incorporation, confining the limits of the town to the lots on the several tracts of land known as "New Market" and "German Town" The corporation was reorganized by an act of 1870 before which the records are mislaid or lost Since that time the officers have been

1871[1]—Mayor, F A Genter, Councilmen, George Everhart, Adam Shower John Weaver, James Kelly, Henry Reagle, Secretary L C Myerly, Treasurer, John Weaver, Bailiff, James Greenholtz

1872—Mayor, John C Danner, Councilmen, Wm Walter, Geo Everhart, John Weaver, James Kelly, Henry Reagle

1873—Mayor, John Carl, Councilmen, James Kelly, Henry Reagle, Simon J Grammer, Henry E Masenheimer, D Hoffacker

1874—Mayor, John Carl, Councilmen, John Fritz, W L Fries, S J Grammer H Masenheimer D Hoffacker

1875—Mayor, John Carl Councilmen, Henry Reaglo, H E Masenheimer, D Shultz, Edward Ouisler, S J Grammer

1876—Mayor, Jacob Campbell, Councilmen, Emanuel Shaffer, Henry Reaglo, Edward Ouisler, Luther Trump, Oliver Lipper, Secretary, Ferdinand A Dieffenbach

1877—Mayor, Jacob Campbell, Councilmen, John J Lynerd, Henry Reagle, Luther Trump, John Bentz, Edward Ouisler, Secretary, G W J Everhart

1878—Mayor, H W Fi[illegible], who resigned, and George M [illegible] took his place Councilmen, Cornelius Miller, E A Ganter, F Shaffer Geo M Stein, Dr J F B Weaver, Secretary G W J Everhart

1879—Mayor, John H Lamott, Councilmen, E A Ganter, N W Sellers, P Goher, Emanuel Shaffer, Cornelius Miller, Secretary, G W J Everhart

1880—Mayor, John H Lamott, Councilmen, Edward A Ganter, N W Sellers, P G Ober, Emanuel Shaffer, Cornelius Miller

1881—Mayor, Henry H Keller, Councilmen, E A Ganter, F Shaffer, Oliver Lippy, John J Lynerd, Edward J Sellers, Secretary, G W J Everhart, Treasurer, E A Ganter, Bailiff, Wm J Lisenbrown

In 1878 the first crossings were laid to the streets, in 1879 the town was supplied with street lamps, and in 1881 the streets were all graded

Zion Church, with two exceptions, was the oldest congregation in Baltimore County (in which Manchester was located until 1836) It was organized Feb 12, 1760, by a union of the Lutheran and German Reformed congregations During that year was [illegible] the first meeting house, a log structure, which [illegible] until 1798, when a brick edifice was built It was repaired in 1836, and a steeple built from the ground up in November of that year. During these repairs Rev Jacob Albert was chief manager, and Philip Grove and Charles Miller, assistants Jacob Houck was the contractor for making the repairs, John Matthias was the contractor for building the steeple, Michael Gettier did the masonry, John M Miller was the gilder and painter, and Jarret Garner furnished the materials, Jacob Weyant, Peter Shultz, Joshua F Copp, Jesse Shultz H and W Brinkman, Jacob Garrett, and Philip Crumrine were the under workmen, Rev Jacob Albert (Lutheran) and Rev Jacob Geiger (German Reformed) were the pastors In June, 1862, this church was taken down, and each of the two congregations erected a separate church building, that of the Lutherans being on part of the old church tract The first church (log) of 1760 and the second (brick) of 1790 stood in the graveyard lot This church was popularly known as the "Union Church," from the fact that two congregations worshiped peacefully therein The Lutheran pastors who preached in it were

1760–83, Rev Newburg, 1783–90, Johan Daniel Schroeder, 1791–96, Rev Meltzheimer (the elder), 1797–1825, John Herbst, 1826 (six months), Emanuel Keller, 1827–37, Jacob Albert 1837–38, Jeremiah Harpel 1838–42, Philip Willard, 1842–44, Frank Ruthrauff, 1844–48, Elias Swartz, 1848–53, Jacob Kaempfer 1853–62, Daniel J Hauer, D D

The German Reformed pastors to 1862 were from 1823 to 1848, Rev Jacob Geiger, C F Colliflower, and Henry Wissler The names of subsequent pastors are not accessible

Emanuel Lutheran Church, after the old "Zion Church" was torn down in 1862, erected in that and the following year its present edifice Its pastors have been

1862–65, Peter Kiver, 1866–69, R Weiser, 1870–81, G Sill, 1881 (April 1), E Manges

The superintendent of Sunday-school is D H Hoffacker

After the taking down of the "Zion church" in 1862, the Trinity Reformed Church congregation erected its present building, which was completed in 1863 The German Reformed pastors of Zion and Trinity Churches from 1760 to 1881, as far as ascertainable, were 1823 to 1848, Jacob Geiger, C F. Colliflower, Henry Wisler, J W Hoffmeier, D W Kelley, and William Rupp, the latter the present pastor, who came July 2, 1877 The superintendent of the Sunday-school is J P Baltozer, elders, J. P Baltozer, George Bixler, deacons, Emanuel Shaffer, Chal Brillhart

[1] The total valuation this year of the real estate was $232,-7

The corner stone of the Methodist Episcopal church edifice was laid in 1839, before which there was a mission here with occasional preaching At the erection of the building Rev E G Ege was the pastor, and the present incumbent is D Benton Winstead

The erection of the Manchester Bethel church (United Brethren in Christ) was begun in 1870, and was completed in the same year The building is a handsome brick structure It was dedicated on Sunday, Jan 1, 1871 At its dedication Bishop J Weaver, of Baltimore, was present, and preached morning and night to a large congregation Rev John Shaeffer, of Baltimore, preached in the afternoon in the German language The spire is forty feet above the roof, and presents a fine appearance The first pastor, under whose auspices the building was erected, was Rev Mr Hutchinson, the next one, Rev J B Jones, and the present incumbent, Rev Mr Quigly, who took charge in 1881 In the rear of the church is a neat graveyard, in which are buried

Mary M Baring, born July 25, 1752, died Jan 29, 1830, and her husband, Ezekiel who died March 30 1838, aged 87

Rev Ezekiel Baring, born Jan 16, 1780, died Feb 14, 1861

John Baring, died Dec 17, 1869, aged 85

Villet Baring, wife of Jacob Swartzbaugh, born Jan 17, 1796, died March 2, 1857

Margaret A Stultz, born April 1, 1780, died April 23, 1861

Elizabeth, wife of John Young, died Nov 18, 1873, aged 76

Catherine Lyncrd, died Nov 5, 1873, aged 73

Martha Burkett, died July 17, 1866, aged 83

Levi Fecher, died Oct 11, 1866, aged 52, and his wife, Eve, Nov 22, 1865 aged 53

This church organization had a log church prior to 1870, on the same lot where the brick building now stands Its trustees in 1877 were Samuel Dehoff, Joseph H Little, Jacob W Baring, Amos Williams, and Henry W Stefly

St Bartholomew's Catholic church was built by the Redemptorist Fathers of Baltimore, who had charge of it until 1876, when it was placed under the pastorate of Father John Gloyd, pastor of St John's Church, Westminster It was erected under the supervision of Mr Frederick, an eminent architect and builder of Baltimore

The Manchester United Academy was incorporated March 3, 1829 The first trustees were Rev Joseph Geiger, Rev Jacob Albert, Dr Jacob Shower, Solomon Myerly, George Motter, John Weaver, George Everhart, Peter Sable, Martin Kroh, George Shower and Frederick Ritter The building was erected in 1831, and its first teacher was Hon Joseph M Parke

Irving College was incorporated by the Legislature Feb 1, 1858 with the following trustees Ferdinand Dieffenbach, John H Falconer, John W Horn and Henry B Roemer Mr Dieffenbach was a refugee of the Revolution of 1848, and a fine scholar and educator This institution opened with two pupils, and soon became flourishing and noted Its able head died in March, 1861, when it was for some time carried on under the auspices of his widow Subsequently Lewis C Myerly was at its head, and in 1880 Prof D Deulinger took charge, under whose management it yet remains He changed its name to Irving Institute, and has made it a boarding school for students of both sexes Its aims are to prepare students for business, for teaching advanced classes in college, or the study of a profession The course of study embraces Latin, Greek, French German, mathematics, the sciences, music, painting, and drawing Since the abandonment of the old "academy" this institution receives all the advanced scholars of the town and neighborhood

The Thespian Society was incorporated in 1835 and the Manchester Band in 1836 The latter was reorganized in 1855 Its first leader for a few months was Dr Charles Geiger, and since then it has been under the direction of Edward A Ganter The following are its present members Edward A Ganter (leader), C J H Ganter, C Frankforter, D Frankforter, Jesse Leese, Nelson Warheim, Jeremiah Yingling, John Stump, Ephraim Freyman Aaron Hoffman, J D Lotz N W Sellers, Jacob Hoffman, William Hoffman, R L Simpers, S F Frankforter

The first Sunday-school was organized in 1828

The first newspaper was issued Nov 14 1870, by W R Watson as editor, and J A Bartley, assistant It was called the *Manchester Gazette*, an independent journal, and was published up to March, 1872, when it was sold to Messrs Smith & Sites, who removed the paper and presses to Glen Rock, Pa, where they established a new journal The next paper was the *Manchester Enterprise*, established in November, 1880 It is a sprightly four page sheet of twenty eight columns, devoted to general and local news, "independent in all things, neutral in nothing" Joseph S Cartman, late of Carlisle, Pa, is its editor, a journalist of ability and experience

The Lutheran and Reformed cemetery was set apart for burial purposes in 1760, and interments began to be made in that year Among the persons buried there are the following

Frederick Ritter, died Feb 9, 1864, aged 76

George Motter, born Nov 27, 1751, died Oct 1, 1800

Erwar Conrad Kerlinger, born 1731, died October, 1798

Henry N Frankman died Oct 22 1867, aged 76

[illegible]

[illegible]

[illegible] Menche, born March 19, 1771, died Sept 11, 1837
Catharine Faess, died March, 1850, aged 86
[illegible] Faess, born 1752, died 18[illegible]
Catharine Gettier, born Oct 27, 1822, died 1826
Anthony Hines, died Nov 29, 1825
Hannes Motter, born April 10, 1771, died March 28, 1819
Jacob Motter, died 1798
John Peter Gettier, died Dec 2, 1837, aged 80, and Elizabeth, first wife, Aug [illegible], 1791, and his second, Mary F, Oct 14, [illegible]
George Kerlinger, born Nov 18, 1795, died Oct 6, 1797
Catharine Motter, born 1782, died 1790
Daniel Bowman, born Feb 27, 1783, died May 21, 1854
[illegible] Swartzbaugh, died Feb 7, 1825, aged 85
Heinrich Werheim, born 17[illegible], died 1828
Elizabeth Kantz, died Oct 28, 1854, aged 86
Joseph Kopp, died Jan 26, 1852, aged 75, was in all the Napoleonic wars
John Ritter, died March 17, 18[illegible], aged 73
[illegible] Ports, Sr, died July 19, 1854, aged 82
Henry Glase, died Feb 24, 1879
George Warner, born Jan 17, 1791, died Aug 24, 1874
George Yingling, died May 14, 1879, aged 85
Michael Ritter, died Oct 1, 1878, aged 81
Henry Beltz, born June 27, 1783, died March 19, 18[illegible]
Johannes Schaurer (now Shower) born 1730, died 1810, married in 1764, Anna Maria Eine who was born in 1740, and died Aug 10, 1833
John Adam Shower, died Aug 27, 185[illegible], aged 59, and his wife, [illegible] E, Feb 13, 1854, aged 81
George Weaver, born Jan 27, 1776, died Jan 15, 1852, and wife, Mary Magdalene, March 23, 1850, aged 69
Elizabeth Utz, born 1742, married 1766, to Peter Utz, and [illegible] 1797
Margaret, second wife of Peter Utz, died Jan 3, 1826, aged [illegible]
Peter Utz, born 1740, died 1820
Martin Kro[illegible], died May 23, 1866, aged 83
Elizabeth, wife of John Sellers, born Feb 5, 1[illegible]68, died Sept 2[illegible] 1860
George Utz, born Oct 7, 1774, died 1842
Henry Lamott, died Feb 15, 1845, aged 75
Daniel Hoover, born Sept 9, 1792, died Aug 16, 1864
Louisa, wife of Jacob Bear, born Aug 30, 1761, died March 18[illegible]6
Jacob Sherman, born Jan 19, 1779, died April 8, 1861
Michael Miller, died Jan 10, 1845, aged 80
George Lineweaver, died April 12, 1844, aged 75
Michael Steffee, born Dec 16, 1769, died May 15, 1850, and his wife, Christina, born April 8, 1760, died June 16, 1851
George Everhart, died July 4, 1857, aged 86, and his wife, Elizabeth, March 7, 1868, aged 90
Rev Jacob Geiger (31 years and 6 months pastor), died Oct 1[illegible], 1848, aged 55 years and 2 days, and his first wife, daughter of Jacob and Mary Seltzer, born June 1, 1801, died March 12, [illegible]

The Union Fire Company was incorporated by act of the General Assembly, March 26, 1839 The incorporators were Solomon Myerly, Jacob Sellers, Lewis [illegible], George Messamore, David Lippy, Elias Buck[illegible], Jacob Houck, George E Weaver, George [illegible]hart, George Trump, William Crummine, Jacob Weaver, Henry Krantz, Henry Brinkman, John [illegible]tz, Jesse Sh[illegible], Andrew Pfeifer, Ezekiel Baring, James Davis, Jacob Frankforter, David Frankforter, Joseph Gouter, George Baker, Joseph Gardner, Jacob Wentz, Frederick Hamburg, Jacob Kerlinger, Jacob Miller, Charles Miller, S B Fuhrman, George Matter, David Houck, Amos Gauman, Jacob Campbell, Adam Shower, J F Kopp, John Kuhn, Michael Gettier, George Lineweaver, Levi Maxfield, Michael Matter, Garret Garner, Richard Jones, James Stansbury, Henry E Beltz, Joseph M Parke, Philip Crummine, Frederick Smith, John N Steffy, Levi Mansfield, Henry Lippy, John Krantz, John Everhart, David Whiteleather

The Carroll Literary Society was organized Feb 12, 1881, with J P Baltover, president, Dr J W Bechtel, vice-president, Joseph S Carman, secretary, P G Ober, treasurer. The object of the association is general improvement and the development of a taste for belles lettres

The school house for the pupils of the public schools is a fine brick building, seventy-five by forty five feet, erected in 1878

The dispensation of the Knights of Pythias, Manchester Lodge, No 78, was dated Sept 14, 1872, and the lodge was instituted on the 17th of that month The first officers were

C C, J W Dehoff, Prel, Aaron Miller, V C, J S Kerlinger, M of E, Cornelius Miller, M of F, E A Ganter

The charter was dated January, 1878, and the charter members were John W Dehoff, Aaron Miller, J S Kerlinger, E A Ganter, H Falkenstine, Jr, C J H Ganter, James Cross, M D, G W J Everhart, Daniel Dubbs, C Miller, George Pfeiffer, Luther Trump The officers for the second term, 1881, were

P C Emanuel Sherrick, C C, John W Burns, Vice C, Charles F Bergman, Prel, D M Brillhart, M of F, Jacob Wink, M of E, Cornelius Miller, K of R and S, J P Baltover, M at A, Aaron Hoffman, I G, D F Boose, O G, J C Hoffman, Rep to Grand Lodge, J E Menschenheimer, Dist Dep, R Lee Simpers, Trustees, Christian Buchanan, A Appold, Charles Brillhart.

Number of members, 40

Lebanon Lodge, A F and A M, No 175, was instituted Oct 9, 1856, as No 104, and its first officers were

W M, William L Nace, S W, Ferdinand Dieffenbach, J W, John H Lamott, Sec, Dr Jacob Shower, Treas, George Shower, S J, Amos L Wolfing, Tyler, John Bentz

It lost its charter, but on May 14, 1879, it was rechartered as No 175 Its officers then were Dr Theodore A Shower, W M, E G Sellers, S W, John M [illegible], J W [illegible]

W M, Lewis C Myerly, S W, Wm C Murray, J W, E T Sellers Sec, Adam Shower, Treas, Samuel Miller, S D, John Fultz, J D, Jacob Fink, Tyler, John H Lamott

Number of members, 25

The present secretary, Adam Shower, was initiated in 1859, and became secretary in 1861

Daniel and Jacob Lodge, I O. O F, No 23 A petition was sent to the Maryland Grand Lodge of I O O F in 1834 for a lodge to be located here, the two first petitioners on the list being Daniel Hoover and Jacob Shower The petitioners designating no name for the proposed lodge, the Grand Lodge named Daniel and Jacob, in honor of Daniel Hoover and Jacob Shower The charter was dated Oct 17, 1834, and signed by James L Ridgely, G M, and Robert Neilson, G S Its first officers were N G, Dr Jacob Shower, V G, Daniel Hoover, Sec and Treas, Jacob Keilinger

At the first meeting the following were the initiates Samuel Lamott, Wm Crumrine, Henry Brinkman, John Lamott The second set of officers were N G, Daniel Hoover, V G, William Crumrine, Sec and Treas, Jacob Keilinger The officers for 1881 were

S P G John Fultz, N G, Henry Boose, V G, Nimrod Armstrong, Rec Sec, G W J Everhart, Per Sec, E A Ganter, Treas, Edward Oursler, Marshal, Wm A Wolf, R S N G, N W Sellers, L S N G, Henry Reagle, R S V G, John Wink L S V G, George L Beltzer, I G, John Emmel, O G, A Pfeiffer

The lodge owns a fine hall, and has 74 members Its accumulated funds are $1500 The district deputy is William A Wolf

The charter of Carroll Encampment, No 17, I O O F, dated Oct 26, 1866, was granted by J L Baugher, G P, and John M Jones, G S The charter members were Wm Crumrine, Henry Falkenstine, Henry Zimmerman, Samuel Wilhelm, C Frankforter, Adam Barns The first officers were W C P, Conrad Frankforter, H P, Henry E Beltz, J W, Samuel Wilhelm, Scribe, Henry Falkenstine

The following were the initiates at the first meeting, Oct 26, 1866 Theo J Kopp, J Alfred Kopp, E A Ganter, G W J Everhart, E H Croutch The officers for 1881 were

W C P, John C Danner, H P, Wm J Eisenbrown, S W, D H Hofacker, J W, Samuel Miller, Rec Sec, G W J Everhart, Per Sec, A N Ganter, Treas, N W Sellers, Dist Dep, Samuel Miller

Number of members, 39

Bachman's Mills is a small village on the road leading to Hanover turnpike seven miles from Westminster, five from Manchester, and at the head Big Pipe Creek This was formerly Bower's m erected about 1780 William and A C Bachm own the mills, and the latter is postmaster The v lage lies in a beautiful and productive valley, wh was settled early in the eighteenth century

Jerusalem Church was organized in 1799 by Lutheran and Reformed congregations, who h jointly used the same building in their worship T first edifice was a log structure, but the present i substantial brick building, and was erected b a few years ago Since 1825 its pastors have b the Lutheran and Reformed preachers living i Manchester

Lazarus Church is also a union church of t Lutheran and Reformed congregations It was erec in 1853 The building committee were V B Wa John Kroh, and George Weaver The Lutheran c gregation organized Sept 5, 1853, and held its f communion June 4, 1854 Since 1863 the Luther and Reformed pastors have been the Manches preachers Its flourishing Sunday school is u the charge of Francis Warner as superintendent

On Feb 27, 1770, Jonathan Plowman conveyed John Davis (pastor), John Whitaker, and Sa Lane fifteen acres of land "for the sole use of meeting-house for the worship of God forever I 1828, the Particular Baptist Gunpowder Church incorporated by the General Assembly, and Th Layman, John Pergoy, and Benjamin Buckingh were designated in the act as its trustees Of th two died, and one removed from the neighborh The meeting-house fell into decay, and the con tion was broken up The Particular Baptist Chur of Black Rock Baltimore County, being the m church of the same faith and order, appointed J B Ensar, Joshua Plowman, and James Blizzard trustees, who began erecting thereon a suitable h of worship To cure all existing and supposed l disabilities of the trustees, and to ratify their p ceedings, the Legislature incorporated this chur again, March 1, 1858, retaining the trustees ab named

St John's church is used jointly by the Reform and Lutheran congregations, and was built in 18 It is a log structure weather-boarded It is five m from Westminster, which supplies it with pastors

The Baltimore and Hanover Railroad Comp was organized under the general railroad act pass the General Assembly of Maryland in 1876 southern terminus is at Emory Grove, nineteen m from Baltimore City, on the Western Maryland R road Th [illegible] Baltimore

Carroll Counties to Black Rock Station, where it connects with the Bachman Valley Road, the latter forming a connecting link with the Hanover Junction, Hanover and Gettysburg Railroad The Baltimore and Hanover road forms a most valuable and important connection of the Western Maryland company, by which it is enabled to drain the rich and fertile territory of Southern Pennsylvania The officers of the company are A W. Eichelberger, president, William H Vickery vice-president, L T Melsheimer, secretary, R M Wirt, treasurer, Directors, Stephen Keefer, Hanover, Pa, William H Hoffman, Baltimore County, Md, Charles W Slagle, William H Vickery, Baltimore, C C Wooden, Carroll County, Md, L F Melsheimer, Hanover, Pa

Bachman's Valley Railroad runs from the iron-ore banks and intersects the Hanover Railroad Its present officers are. President, Capt A W Eichelberger, Directors Stephen Keefer, H C Shriver, Joseph Dellone, Joseph Althoff, C L Johnson, J W Gitt, Levi Dubbs, Perry Wine, Edwin Thomas, Samuel Thomas, E W Heindel, and Adam Newcomer

Pair Ridge Gold and Silver Mining Company.—Many years ago gold was discovered in various places on a ridge extending through Manchester town from Cranberry Valley In 1879 Messrs Keeport and Lafeber, of Littlestown, made a thorough examination of the gold region, and found by assays that it was in sufficient quantities to pay for digging In the summer of 1881 this company was organized with Daniel Beckley as president, and C J H Ganter as secretary On Aug 13, 1881, the stockholders at a called meeting voted to purchase the necessary machinery to proceed to work, and the work is being pushed to an apparently successful conclusion The largest quantities of gold have been found right in the town, or on farms close to the corporation limits The company has leased several farms, and is actively engaged now in searching for the treasure

The Dug Hill Mutual Fire Insurance Company has been in operation several years, insuring buildings and general farm property against loss by fire Its president is P H L Myers, and secretary, John Strevig Its main and home office is in Manchester Its former secretary was Francis Warner

The Shower Foundry a large manufactory, was established in 1851 by Jacob Shower, who used to employ some thirty hands in the manufacture of different kinds of machinery, of which the larger part was agricultural implements It is now operated by his son, William H Shower, and employs some fifteen persons in its various departments The foundry cast a cannon which was successfully used on the Fourth of July, 1881.

The following are the district officers serving at this date (1881) Justices of the Peace, Henry Motter, J P Boltoser, Samuel Hofflicker, Constables, George P Burns, Geo Reagle

Ebbvale is a village on the Bachman's Valley Railroad, nine miles from Westminster and near to Big Pipe Creek C Wentz is postmaster Of the iron ore mines located here C L Johnson is superintendent, Martin Hugenborn and F Schenck, engineers, and F Tragesser, mine boss

Melrose is on the same railroad, and thirty miles from Baltimore C B Wentz is postmaster Dr J S Ziegler, physician C B Wentz & Sons, merchants, and Levi Hoff, hotel keeper

Springfield Grange, No 158, is located near Bahn's Mill, and has seventy members Officers for 1881

Master, Francis Warner, Sec, J D Sharer, Treas Joseph Miller, Lecturer, John Hinkle, Door keeper D Resh, Steward, J H Hoffman, Pomona, Mrs J A Bahn, Flora, Mrs Francis Warner, Ceres, Mrs E Shriver, Lady Assistant Steward, Mrs Lydia Sharer

This is the best conducted grange in the county, and is well officered

The names of the following persons, residents of the district, aged seventy years and upwards in 1879, are given as a matter of local interest

Josiah Dehoff, 78, Mrs Nancy Dehoff, 88, George Yingling, 85, Mrs Yingling, 82, Mrs Catherine Ganter, 78 Mrs Mary Frankforter, 76, Henry Stefly, 84 George Leese, 79, Mrs Susannah Leese, 80, John Sellers, 84, Mrs Sellers, 71 Mrs Elizabeth Martin, 83, Mrs Sarah Bixler, 83, Mrs Mary Gettier, 89, Henry Glize, 79 David Lippy, 73, Geo Everheart, 79 Dr Jacob Shower, 76, Mrs Mary Shower, 71, George Shower, 74, Mrs Rachel Shower, 76, Mrs Barbara Warner, 78, Mrs Elizabeth Shaffer, 8[illegible] Mrs Lydia Black, 75 Mrs Catherine Zepp, 75, Henry Lucabaugh, 85, Mrs Mary Yingling, 85, Mrs Anna M Wolfgang, 77, Ephraim Tracy, 76, John Redding, 76, John Everheart, 76, George Trump, 71 George Warehime, 89 Stephen Reys, 78, Christian Kexel, 78, Adam Markel, 83, Mrs Martha Stansbury, 76, John Bentz, 72, Mrs Maria Bentz, 75, Mrs Mary Stansbury, 79 Sarah Butler (colored), 81, Nicholas Warner, 81, John H Bordleman, 76, Benjamin Lippy, 71, Elizabeth Gettier, 73 Females, 22, aggregate ages, 1711, average, 79 Males, 23, aggregate ages, 1803, average, 78

Mr John Sellers, one of the soldiers of the war of 1812, and a member of Capt Adam Shower's company, died at his residence, in Manchester District, on Feb 27, 1879, aged 84 years, 4 months, and 11 days

Dr Jacob Shower, a prominent citizen of this county, and well known in former years throughout the State as a Democratic leader, died at his residence in Manchester on Sunday, May 25, 1879, aged seventy-seven years He was the son of Col Adam Shower, who represented Baltimore County in the

House of Delegates for many years during the early part of this century. Dr. Shower entered politics when quite young, and served in the House of Delegates from Baltimore County several years prior to the organization of Carroll County in 1837, and was in the Legislature when the bill for its formation was passed. He was upon the first ticket nominated in this county for the House of Delegates, and was elected. He was elected for a second, and declined a nomination for the third term. In 1841 he was appointed to the position of clerk of the court, made vacant by the death of Dr. Willis, and served about seven years. In 1851 he was elected a member of the Constitutional Convention, but declined the position. Since his term in Congress, from 1854 to 1856, he had not been in public life, but had ever evinced a great interest in State and national politics. He was a member of the first Andrew Jackson Club in this State, which was formed at the Washington Hotel, on Gay Street, Baltimore, in the year 1821, and which adopted the die for the figure-head, "Jackson and Liberty." Dr. Shower was possessed of a strong mind. His genial disposition and general fund of information endeared him to all who knew him, and his society was much sought by the politicians of the State. As a politician he was a link between the past and the present. He saw the rise of the Democratic party, was a participator in all its contests, saw its overthrow, and again witnessed its triumph. He left a large circle of relatives and friends to mourn his death. His was one of the most familiar faces in all the State Democratic conventions from the time of his first connection with politics until his death. He was arrested by the United States provost-marshal in 1863 upon some trivial charges, and imprisoned for some months.

The following is a list of school trustees and teachers for this district for 1881 and 1882, with number of pupils:

1 and 2. Grammar School and Primary No. 1.—J. H. La Motte, D. H. Hoffacker, John M. Gettier.

3 and 4. Primary Nos. 2 and 3.—G. W. Everhart, Jacob Wink, H. K. Grove.

5. Miller's.—George K. Frank, George P. Miller, John P. Frank.

6. Zimmerman's.—Benjamin Bowser, J. David Shearer, John Hilker.

7. Kroh's or Lippy's.—Joseph Price, Francis Warner, C. R. Wentz.

8. Tracey's.—Jonas Warner, Wm. Zepp, A. J. P. Rhoads.

9. Wentz's.—Peter Gettier, Daniel Wentz, G. Bixler.

10. Kridler's.—Edward Kridler, Philip Yoatz, Samuel Shaeffer.

11. Bachman's Mill.—D. S. Palmer, Jacob Shaeffer, Samuel Wine.

12. Royer's.—Daniel Reese, Christian Royer, Jeremiah Mathias.

13. Union.—J. J. Abbott, H. B. Houck, Nathaniel Leister.

14. Old Fort (Nace's).—Charles Grove, Jacob Boring, L. Kreitzer.

15. Bosley's.—H. M. Menshey, D. Burns, D. Garrett.

16. Ebbvale.—Oliver Hoover, C. Wentz, Edward Garrett.

The teachers for the term ending April 15, 1881, were:

1, Nellie R. Lilley, 10 pupils; 2, J. P. Baltzer, 41 pupils; 3, Willie Cox, 45 pupils; 4, Lizzie Trump, 39 pupils; 5, E. S. Miller, 55 pupils; 6, Emma Lorringer, 38 pupils; 7, V. B. Wentz, 58 pupils; 8, Noah Peterman, 42 pupils; 9, I. R. Streving, 58 pupils; 10, J. F. Peterman, 47 pupils; 11, G. T. Palmer, 42 pupils; 12, Mary C. Bixler, 17 pupils; 13, J. A. Abbott, 65 pupils; 14, G. W. J. Everhart, 54 pupils; 15, Laura M. Burnee, 27 pupils; 16, T. R. Streving, 53 pupils.

The following were the votes cast from 1851 to 1861, inclusive, for local officers:

1851.—Vote for Primary School Commissioner: George Crouse 229, Philip H. L. Myers 76, David Bachman 56, John C. Price 30.

1853.—For Justices: George Everhart 234, Jacob Keilinger 386, John C. Price 324, Wm. Walter 358; Constables: John Shultz 455, Anthony Hines 358; Road Supervisor: Frederick Litter 488.

1855.—For Justices: J. Keilinger 415, W. Walter 145, Henry Motter 423, Geo. Bixler 104; Constables: J. A. Hines 435, Henry Krantz 125, Emanuel Trine 61, John Shultz 113; Road Supervisor: Frederick Ritter 437, Samuel Witter 102.

1857.—For Justices: John C. Price 479, Wm. Walter 174, Henry Motter 134, Henry Glaze 401; Constables: J. A. Hines 501, Henry Krantz 501; Road Supervisor, Michael Ritter 497.

1859.—For Justices: Henry Motter 176, John C. Price 480, Wm. Walter 490, Michael Sullivan 134; Constables: Henry Krantz 491, Eli Myers 474, John Shultz 151; Road Supervisor: Michael Ritter 491.

1861.—For Justices: Henry Motter 326, John C. Price 318, D. T. Shaeffer 311, Henry Glaze 299, Geo. Huntley 309, John Fultz 318; Constables: Henry Krantz 330, John Lockard 281, Henry Reagle 308, Henry Cramer 264; Road Supervisor: D. H. Hoffacker 329, Henry Fair 307.

Among the thrifty and industrious German emigrants to Pennsylvania in 1720 was Jacob Warner, a young man from the kingdom of Bavaria, who settled in York County of that State. His son, Melchior Warner, removed, about 1780, to that part of Baltimore County now forming a part of Manchester District, in Carroll County. His son, Jacob H. Warner, was the father of Francis Warner, who was born July 28, 1826, three miles east of Manchester. He lived on a farm until the twenty-first year of his age. He was liberally educated at the noted "White Hall Academy," near Harrisburg, Pa. He was elected magistrate by the voters of his district during the late civil war (1863), and was subsequently repeatedly appointed to the office, which he held with complete

satisfaction to the public for eight successive years He was twice elected surveyor of Carroll County, and in 1879 was chosen county commissioner, which position he now most acceptably fills, having for his colleagues Col John K Longwell, of Westminster, and William C Polk, of Freedom District He was for nine consecutive years a director of the "Farmers' Mutual Insurance Company of Dug Hill," and its secretary and treasurer for five years He resides on Dug Hill," an historical part of the district, situated on the Pennsylvania State line, and settled about the middle of the past century He takes great interest in educational matters, having been engaged in teaching fourteen years, and is one of the trustees of School No 7 He is superintendent of the Sunday school of Lazarus Church, jointly erected and occupied by the Reform and Lutheran congregations A practical farmer, and thoroughly conversant with agriculture in all its minutiæ, he has ever zealously labored for the material interests of the tillers of the soil He is Master of Springfield Grange, No 158, located near Bahn's Mill,—the most flourishing organization of the kind in the county,—formed and chiefly built up under his management He was married, Nov 8, 1859, to Adaline C Wolfgang, daughter of Jacob Wolfgang, by whom he has three children,—two daughters and a son Besides having served two terms as county surveyor, he has for many years been engaged in private surveying, in which profession he stands deservedly high because of his proficiency and skill He has filled all public positions intrusted to him with credit, and the board of county commissioners has rarely had a member who paid closer attention to the wants and interests of the public than Mr Warner

HAMPSTEAD DISTRICT, OR DISTRICT No 8,

of Carroll County, is bounded on the north by Manchester District, on the east by Baltimore County, on the south by Woolery's, and on the west by the districts of Westminster and Manchester The east branch of the Patapsco Falls flows south through the centre of the district, and Aspen and White Oak Runs intersect the western portion, and empty into the Patapsco In addition to the turnpikes and private roads the Hanover Railroad furnishes an outlet for the products of the district in a northern direction, and the Western Maryland Railroad passes along its southwestern edge In 1880 it had a population of 1983 The metes and bounds of the district as determined by the commission of 1837 are as follows

"Beginning at the forks of the county roads leading from Westminster to Hampstead [illegible] George [illegible]'s mill, thence to the forks of Aspen Run and Long Glade Branch, thence up said branch to the spring near the house of Joseph Bowser, deceased, thence to the spring near the house of John Orendorff, thence to the forks of the most northern branch of Patapsco Falls and Bosley's spring branch where they unite in William Albaugh's meadow thence through the farms of John Reed and Joshua Bosley, Sr, leaving said Reed and Bosley in District No 6, thence to Michael Becker's tavern, on the Hanover and Baltimore turnpike road, leaving said Becker in District No 6 thence across said turnpike east of Shriver's tan-yard, thence through the lands of Daniel Caltuder, leaving said Caltuder in District No 6, thence through the lands of —— Gist, thence through the lands of George Caltuder, deceased, and John Wareham, leaving said Wareham and Caltuder in District No 5, thence to Michael Miller's mill, on the middle road, thence to Joshua Stansbury's spring, near the house on the Falls road, thence through the lands of Hair leaving said Hair in District No 8, thence to Henry Zimmerman's county road where said road crosses the Carroll and Baltimore County line at a blazed hickory-tree, thence on Baltimore County line to Edward Bond's, thence with the lines of District No 4 to Richard Gorsuch's farm on Patapsco Falls thence with a straight line to the place of beginning"

Hampstead was made the place for holding the polls The tract of land known as "Transylvania" was originally surveyed for Thomas White, Aug 8 1716, but resurveyed and patented to Capt Richard Richards, June 10, 1751

The district took its name from Hampstead in England, a town from which Capt Richard Richards emigrated about 1735 The early settlers were Capt Richard Richards and his brother in law, Christopher Vaughn, the Coxes, Stansburys, Henry Lamott, the Fowbles, Houcks, Snyders, Ebaughs, Murrays, Browns, Leisters, Rubys, Lovealls, Cullisons, Gardners, Hammonds, and Armacosts The first settlers were generally English, but afterwards the Germans came into the district in large numbers

Hampstead, a village containing upwards of three hundred inhabitants, is located on surveys called "Spring Garden," patented to Dustane Dane in 1748, and "Landorff" It was called "Coxville" for over fifty years in honor of John Cox, its first settler, but finally took the name of Hampstead from the district About a century ago, Col Johns, of Baltimore County (in which this district was then situated), built a warehouse of logs to receive and store wheat for his mills, near Dover That house was afterwards weather-boarded and sold by Col Johns to John Cox, the first actual settler, who kept a tavern in it Cox subsequently sold it to Henry Lamott It is the oldest house in the town, and is now owned by Micajah Stansbury The town was laid out about 1786 by Christopher Vaughan, a brother-in-law of Capt Richard Richards They were both Englishmen, and during the Revolution Richards sympathized with the British, but Vaughan was an active Whig Henry

Lamott came to the village in 1798 from Havre de Grace, when there were only a few houses in it He was the son of John Lamott, a French nobleman, who settled in Maryland about 1760, and was the first of this family in America The first physician of the town was Dr Urnbaugh, who had been a Hessian soldier, and lived a short time in nearly all the villages of the county The first schoolmaster was a Mr Parks After Dr Urnbaugh, Dr Hall, who lived several miles distant, attended patients here, and the next resident physician was Dr Richard C Wells, with whom Drs Roberts Bartholow and Hanson M Drach studied in 1850–51 and '52 The last two married daughters of John Lamott John Fowble kept the first store Peter Frank kept the first tavern, and was succeeded by John Cox. Capt Richard Richards owned fifteen hundred acres of land near the town

The village is on the Hanover pike, and is one of the best stations on the Hanover Railroad Its oldest citizens are Col John Lamott and William Tall Hammond, who both served in the war of 1812, the latter being now (1881) eighty seven years old Col Lamott was born in 1795, and was three years old when his father Henry Lamott, moved to Hampstead In the war of 1812 he was in Capt Adam Shower's company of Col Shultz' regiment, of which Conrad Kerlinger was major He was in the battle of North Point, and draws a pension for his services His father, Henry Lamott, kept a tavern here forty-five years, and died in 1851 Since the completion of the railroad in 1879 the town has rapidly increased in population, and the value of real estate has doubled The physicians are Drs Richard C Wells and his sons, Edward and Constant Wells, Hanson M Drach, John W Stansbury, and W W Warehem C M Murray is postmaster, and Lewis C Myerly, attorney-at law The latter was admitted to the bar during his residence in Indiana He was born Jan 24, 1829, in Westminster District, and was a son of Jacob, and grandson of George, Myerly The latter was one of two brothers who came from Germany before 1775 The Myerly family is of German and French extraction Jacob Myerly married Eve Bishop, by whom he had the following children Rachel, Benjamin, Reuben C (wounded in the Mexican war, and died in Lima, La) Jacob, Mary J, Lewis Cass, and Susanna It was owing largely to the efforts of Lewis C Myerly that the Hanover Railroad was located and built on its present road-bed John Armacost, aged ninety-two years lives near town with his wife, to whom he has been married seventy years, and during all of that time he has been a member of the M E Church Shane Cullison, living near, died in 187[illegible] aged ninety-six years

The first edifice of the Methodist Episcopal Church was a log structure, built about 1800, which is now occupied by Charles Roat It was used also as a school house The present stone church was erected in 1815 by Richard Richards as contractor The parsonage was built in 1878 Rev D Benton Winstead is the pastor The graveyard ground in its rear was a donation from John Lamott Interred there are

Maria, wife of Jackson Belt, who died June [illegible], 1880, aged 6[illegible]
Elizabeth, wife of John Cox, died Aug 20, 1872, aged 77
Nicholas Gardner, died Nov 3, 1874, aged 65
Jeremiah Malchorn, died Feb 28, 1871, aged 17
Anna, wife of Christian Wisner, died March 28, 1869
Leonard Belt, died Nov 7 1871, aged 59
Mary, wife of Caleb Blizzard, died July 7, 1866, aged 56
Susan, wife of Elisha Gorsuch, died July 1, 1863, aged 62
Keziah Caltrider, died Oct 3, 1876, aged 71, and her husband, John Caltrider, born March 5 1795, died Feb 28, 18[illegible]
Elizabeth, wife of Richard D Armacost died July 16, 18[illegible], aged 68
Moses Myers, died Nov 18, 18[illegible], aged 58, and his wife Jane, March 18, 1863, aged 67
Llender wife of Dr Henson L Drach (U S Army), died Oct 3, 1861 aged 32, and Susan, wife of Dr Roberts Bartholow (U S Army), died July 6 1862, aged 28, both daughters of John and Rachel Lamott The latter (Rachel) died Jan 11 1850, aged 46
George Ports, died April 18, 1872, aged 70
Joshua Tipton, born Aug 11, 1800, died Sept 20, 1853
Dr J Haugh, died Oct 1[illegible], 1818, aged 24
Absalom Null, died Feb 24, 1862, aged 10

Rev Amon Richards was the first preacher of this church, and died but a few years ago nearly one hundred years old

The United Brethren church is situated one mile from town, at Greenmount, on the Hanover pike Its pastor is Rev J R Snake

The Lutheran congregation has no church edifice but holds its services in the hall of the Independent Order of Red Men Rev H Burk is pastor

Dehoff's church, not now standing, was near Greenmount, and was built over seventy years ago by John Dehoff, who preached himself, although a plain farmer with limited education

Red Jacket Tribe, No 24, of the Independent Order of Red Men, was instituted about 1845 It owns a fine hall and is in a flourishing condition William A Murray is its Chief of Records and Keeper of Seal

Snydersburg is on the east branch of the Patapsco three and a half miles from Manchester, seven and a half miles from Westminster, and twenty nine miles from Baltimore The merchants are E Snyder [illegible] J H [illegible] the latter [illegible] the postmaster

St Mark's church was erected in 1878 by the Lutheran and Reformed congregations, who jointly use it in worship. The building committee were Michael Brillhart (Reformed), Jacob Yingling, and Mr Ruby (Lutheran). The house was consecrated Sept 29, 1878. The Lutheran organization was perfected March 9, 1879, when Jacob Yingling and Elisha Snyder were elected elders, Edmund Reed and Daniel S Hann, deacons.

Houcksville is three miles from Patapsco, near the Patapsco River, thirty-four miles from Baltimore, and fifteen from Westminster. The merchants are S A Lauver & Son, G W Keller, and A J Houck. The latter is postmaster, and it is from his family that the place takes its name. Geo W Keller has an extensive paper manufactory here. Dr C S Davis is the physician of the town, and Dr George Rupp the dentist. Mr Keller's paper-factory gives employment to many mechanics and laborers. The water power of the Patapsco at this point is magnificent, and numerous mills and factories are successfully operated.

The Bartholow family is one of the oldest in this district, and has given to the country a man distinguished at home and in Europe for his great medical learning and attainments. Dr Roberts Bartholow was born and raised near Hampstead, and educated at Calvert College, after which he graduated at the University of Maryland. During the war of 1861–65 he was brigade surgeon on the staff of Gen McClellan. After his resignation he took a professorship in the University of Maryland, and from there he removed to Cincinnati, Ohio, at which place he was chosen Professor of Materia Medica of the Ohio Medical College. He is the author of several meritorious medical works. In March, 1879, this most skillful and scientific physician was appointed Professor of Materia Medica and Therapeutics in the Jefferson Medical College of Philadelphia. Dr Bartholow, within the past ten years, has attracted the attention of his profession, both in Europe and America, by the freshness and vigor of his writings and the variety of his contributions to science. In the literature of his profession he is now an acknowledged authority, and the fact that Jefferson Medical College chose him for the responsible position named is an evidence that this standard institution is determined to keep abreast of the age. He studied medicine with Dr Thomas W Webb, graduated on March 9, 1852, and practiced his profession at New Windsor until his removal to Cincinnati, Ohio. He married Susan, daughter of John and Rachel Lamott.

The following is a list of public school trustees in this district for 1881 and 1882, together with the names of teachers and number of pupils in each school:

1 Jesse Brown's —Leven Wright, John E Houck, Adam Shaffer

2 and 3 Snydersburg (Nos 1 and 2) —J Switzer, Wm H Ruby, John F Reed

4 Eberg —John Strickland, George Gross, George Shaffer

5 and 6 —Hampstead (Nos. 1 and 2) —James Sugars, William Houck, Jacob Caltrider

7 Houcksville —Michael Buchman, Joseph Brummel, A J Houck

8 Emory Chapel —Appointments deferred

9 Lowe's — Miles Long, D Lester, Lewis Green

10. Salem —J M Bush, John P Murray, John A Armacost

11 Mount Union Mills —Thomas J Gorsuch, Casper Mullinder, William Engle

The teachers for the term ending April 15, 1881, were:

1 F S Martin, 39 pupils; 2, A Eugenia Foltz, 36 pupils; 3, J H L Boyer 30 pupils; 4, G A Lester, 46 pupils; 5, Mettie Miller 11 pupils; 6, W A Abbott, 42 pupils; 7, Joel Sykes, 58 pupils; 8, Anna M Buckingham, 27 pupils; 9, J Thomas Green, 27 pupils; 10, Sadie L Myers, 34 pupils; 11, John W Rabb, 48 pupils.

The justices are Dr Hanson T Drach, John W Abbott; Constable, Benjamin Croft.

Below are given the votes cast for local officers in this district from 1851 to 1861, inclusive:

1851 —Vote for Primary School Commissioner: F J Smith 101, Daniel Hoover 89, F J Smith 126, Daniel Hoover 88

1853 —For Justices: D W Houck 181, Richard Harris 160, H Jordan 68. Constables: John Marsh 67, Jetson L Gill 179; Road Supervisor: Joseph Armacost 174, Jacob Lippo 72

1855.—For Justices: Richard Harris 122, Jesse Brown 103, John Fowble 111, George Richards 150; Constables: J L Gill 137, J Campbell 191; Road Supervisor: E Ebaugh 110, Leonard Belt 154

1857 —For Justices: Dr H M Drach 183, George Richards 189, J L Gill 120, Daniel Richards 116; Constables: H W Potts 177, Jerome Ebaugh 121. Road Supervisor: L Belt 172, C P Frick 121, William Corbin 8

1859 —For Justices: H M Drach 162, Jesse Brown 110, John Lamotte 62, R Harris 137; Constables: J G Gittinger 175, Jerome Ebaugh 134; Road Supervisor: Leonard Belt 179, Henry Stansbury 130

1861 —For Justices: W S Wooden 209, Jacob Miller 194, Jesse Brown 116, Richard Harris 131; Constables: Elisha Bromwell 216, Alfred Ruby 108; Road Supervisor: William Houck 199, Leonard Belt 132

The reputation of Hampstead District for good order has been uniformly excellent, and there has seldom happened anything of an exciting character to arouse the feelings of the inhabitants. On the night of Feb 12, 1870, however, at a place known as Houck & Hoffman's fulling-mill, and about one mile from the store of D W Houck, Edward Woolman, a German, stabbed Samuel P Linkinholer to the heart with a shoe-maker's knife, killing him instantly. At

the subsequent investigation Woolman was discharged from custody, it having been shown that the homicide was committed in self-defense

FRANKLIN DISTRICT, No 9

The Ninth District of Carroll County, known as Franklin, is bounded on the north by the districts of New Windsor and Westminster, on the west by Freedom, on the south by Howard County, and on the west by Frederick County Morgan's Run waters the northern portion of the district, Gillis' Falls the centre and south, and a number of small streams pass through the western part of Franklin The southern extremity of Franklin District is traversed by the Baltimore and Ohio Railroad, which offers unlimited facilities for the disposal of produce, and the Western Maryland passes through New Windsor, not very far from the northern boundary The following are the metes and bounds prescribed by the commission of 1837, which were afterwards slightly altered by an act of Assembly passed May 23, 1853 and already given

"Beginning at Parr's Spring, thence with the Western Branch of Patapsco Falls to the junction of Gillis's Falls, thence with Gillis's Falls to Times Steel's, leaving him in District No 5, thence with a straight line to a branch crossing the new Liberty road near Conway's, thence with a straight line to Crawford's road at the old Liberty, thence up the old Liberty road to Larfer's old fields, thence with the road running near Gideon Mitchel's, leaving him in District No 9, thence with said road to Morgan's Run, thence up Morgan's Run to Hawkins' Branch, to a road leading from Benjamin Gorsuch to George Warfield's store, thence with the road leading to the 'Stone Chapel,' thence with Howard's road to Turkey Foot Branch, thence down said branch to Philip Nicodemuses mill, thence with the lines of District No 2 to Sandis Mill, thence with the county line to the place of beginning"

Franklinville was made the place for holding the polls The district contained 2225 inhabitants in 1880

The district was settled by the English and emigrants from the southern counties of the province of Maryland Among the first settlers were the Franklins, from whom the district took its name, Charles and Alexander Warfield, John and David Evans, Rawlingses, Beaches, Samuel Kitzmiller, the Waterses, Brashearses, Spurriers, Gosnells, Barneses, Ingelses, Buckinghams, Lindsays, Dorseys, Bennetts (Samuel, Benjamin, and Lloyd), Selbys, Hoods, and Elgins

Ebenezer church (M E), a frame building, is situated in the eastern part of the district, on the road from Winfield to Defiance, and was built in 1851 For the past six years it has been a part of the New Windsor Circuit and before that was connected with Westminster Its pastors for 1881 were Revs James Cadden and Howard Downs In the graveyard adjoining the church are buried

Perry C Harp, died April 26, 1879, aged 80

Eliza Ann, wife of R L Farver, died Oct 17, 1872, aged 40

Nicholas H Jenkins, died Jan 31, 1877, aged 61

Airey, wife of Warner Pickett, born June 20, 1821, died Jan 28, 1871

Marsha, wife of J T Jenkins, born Oct 16, 1848, died Aug 2, 1872

Joseph Atkins, of First Massachusetts Cavalry, died July 8, 1863, aged 34

Catharine Harp, died Nov 16, 1874, aged 73

John Day, died March 5, 1871, aged 60, and his wife, Emily, born Jan 29, 1818, died April 30, 1876

Joshua Grimes, died April 12, 1867, aged 61

David A Hiltabridel born Aug 2, 1818, died Nov 21, 1862, and Temperance, his wife, died Dec 31, 1866, aged 51

Samuel Choate, born Jan 23, 1822, died Nov 1, 1[illegible]2

Hamilton P Skidmore, died March 17, 1878, aged 51

Ruth Ann, wife of Basil Shipley, died Feb 24 1859, aged 27

Cordelia, wife of Perry G Purdett, died April 28 18[illegible]7, aged 28

Catharine wife of Joseph Frizzell, died Jan 16, 1871, aged 63

John W Criswell, died Nov 18, 1808, aged 42, and Ruth, his wife, Dec 28, 1879 aged 66

Sarah A Rawlings, born Nov 3, 1809, died May 29, 1878

Catharine, wife of Dr J Rinehart, died Dec 19, 1879, aged 29

Cornelia wife of John A Snider, died Jan 23, 1872, aged 30

Taylorsville was named in honor of Gen Zachary Taylor, and the first house was built in it in May, 1846, by Henry D Franklin Mr Franklin still resides therein, and has adjoining a wagon-making shop which he carries on The second settler in the place was David Buckingham, who keeps a store and is the postmaster

The Methodist Episcopal church is a neat frame edifice erected in 1878, before which services were held in a building constructed in 1850, and now used as a band hall The present pastor is Rev Mr Shriner, and the Sunday-school superintendent is Thomas Shipley In the cemetery attached to the church are buried James Beach, born Aug 19, 1816, died Oct 29, 1880, Charles G Franklin died Dec 24, 1878 aged seventy, N Harvey Shipley, died Feb 1, 1881 aged eighteen, Louisa, wife of David Buckingham died July 22, 1849, aged forty-two

Franklinville is seven and a half miles from Mount Airy and near Parr's Falls, a small stream which drains the neighborhood It was settled in the beginning of the century, and named for the Franklin family one of the first to settle in the district, about 1745 R Dorsey is merchant and postmaster, and Dr R O D Warfield, the physician of the village William Long, John Elgin, and John T Derr have shoe shops, and George Pickett and Jesse Wilson are the millers It is the voting-place of the district and is pleasantly situated on the old Liberty road

Th[illegible] (Bethany

was organized in 1871, under the auspices of Rev A Q Flaherty, and its neat frame edifice was built in the same year Its pastors have been

1871-73, Rev A Q Flaherty, 1873-76, Rev David Bush, 1876-79, Rev W R Stringer, 1879-82, Rev M G Balthis

In the graveyard in its rear are, among others, the following interments

Levin Gosnell, died Dec 21, 1879, aged 86

Bennett Spurrier died Nov 9, 1879, aged 75, and his wife, Rachel died Dec 25, 1879, aged 77

Lizzie M, wife of Samuel Elgin, died March 1, 1875, aged 68

Lewis Lindsay, died Nov 21, 1878, aged 57

Casadora Lindsay, died June 18, 1876, aged 28

Charles W Franklin, died March 1, 1874, aged 53

Samuel Kurtzmiller, died Sept 15, 1854, and born May 10, 1790 and his wife, Catharine, born June 8, 1799, died June .. 1865

Thomas B Franklin, died Oct 30, 1878, aged 65

Winfield is six miles from the Baltimore and Ohio Railroad at Woodbine, and was named in honor of Gen Winfield Scott The Bethel Church of God, Rev Mr Palmer, is located here The village was established about 1851 and 1852 Franklin Grange, No 117, of Patrons of Husbandry, of which Dr F J Crawford was for a long time Master, holds its meetings in Winfield H M Zile is a merchant in the village and James Easton postmaster Dr F J Crawford is the physician Its schools, Pine Orchard and Jenkins', are among the best in the county

Mount Airy, so named from its elevated and healthy location, is on the Baltimore and Ohio Railroad J C Duvall is postmaster and track foreman The store keepers are J B Runkles, S E Grove, A Anderson, and Cochran & Harrington The hotels are kept by R A Nelson and C A Smith Drs B H Todd and J E Bromwell are the physicians, and T P Mullinix, railroad and express agent The Mount Airy Coal and Iron Company was incorporated March 9, 1854, with F A Schley, J M Schley, Thomas Hammond, George Schley, and John G Lynn as incorporators

Newport, a small hamlet, lies near the Frederick County line

Parrsville and **Ridgeville**, small villages, lie south of the Baltimore and Ohio Railroad In the former is a Methodist Episcopal church, and between it and Mount Airy is the Presbyterian church

Hooper's Delight, a neat brick school-house, a mile [illegible] Sam's Creek was built in 1875

Bethel Methodist Episcopal church, a brick building of two stories and a basement, was erected in 1[illegible] on the site where the old log structure stood [illegible] 1815 It be[illegible] to the New Wind[illegible] Circuit, and its pastors for 1881 were Rev Howard Downs and J A Fadden The beautiful cemetery adjoining the church contains the graves of the following persons

Thomas Devilbiss, died July 12, 1878, aged 77

Benjamin Bennett, born Aug 21, 1809, died Dec 23 1863

Robert Bennett, died March 26, 1856, aged 78, and Elizabeth Bennett, died Jan 4, 1840, aged 78

Nathan L Stocksdale born Feb 2, 1806, died Jan 20, 1865

Jesse M Zile, born July 26, 1831, died June 11, 1875

Lewis Keefer, born July 31, 1803, died Sept 7, 1850, and Rachel, his wife, died July 26, 1873, aged 63

Mahlon, son of Casper and A E Devilbiss, died Nov 8, 1878, aged 11

Casper Devilbiss, died March 4, 1868, aged 73

Mary Hiteshew, died Dec 10, 1871, aged 83

Sarah T Sebier, died Nov 21, 1871, aged 55

Mary Nusbaum, died Jan 1, 1864, aged 44

David Nusbaum, died Sept 21, 1861, aged 60

Benjamin Sharrets, born Feb 19, 1808, died Aug 24, 1873

Mary M Sharrets, born April , 1812, died March 26, 1874

John T Reigler, born July 5, 1805, died April 12, 1879, and Annie, his wife, died March 24, 1862, aged 58

Ursala Patbain Reigler, born Dec 14, 1811, died March 5, 1874

John Greenwood, born Feb 25, 1817, died Feb 12, 1878

Ellen Chase, died June 19 1874, aged 62

Mary E wife of R Dorsey, born Oct 20, 1829, died April 17, 1875

Urland Greenwood, died Dec 3, 1875, aged 57

Stephen Gorsuch, died June 9, 1880, aged 80

Jane Gorsuch, born June 19, 1786, died Sept 3, 1858

Nathan, son of Stephen and Jane Gorsuch, born Jan 26, 1826, died April 6, 1849

Thomas Poole, died Aug 31, 1821, aged 37

Dr Lewis Kelly, died April 13, 1872, aged 30

Alexander Warfield, died Jan 6, 1835, aged 70, and his wife, Jemima, died Nov 20, 1847, aged 72

Elizabeth Worthington, born Oct 22, 1826, died July 6, 1851

Rev Joshua Jones, died Sept 19, 1836 aged 70, and his wife, Annie, March 12, 1811, aged 53

Horatio J Warfield, died Aug 5, 1877, aged 53

Rev Geo W Johnson, born Oct 10, 1841, died May 28, 1874

Francis A Davis, died Dec 7, 1850, aged 50, and his wife, Cecilia died Aug 28, 1819, aged 40

Rev John Davis, died April 28, 1817, aged 85

Joshua Warfield, died April 1, 1880, aged 79

Evelina C Warfield, died May 24, 1877, aged 47

David Warfield, died March 1, 1871, aged 13

Virginia S, wife of J P Naill, died July 22, 1874, aged 28

Near this church—but a few yards away—is the old Alexander Warfield homestead It is now occupied by Rev Charles A Reid, a native of Virginia, who began preaching in the Methodist Episcopal Church in 1842 He married Elizabeth, daughter of Joshua Warfield, and granddaughter of Alexander Warfield The latter's father was one of the earliest settlers in the district, and owned all the land around the Bethel church Alexander Warfield was first married to Elizabeth Woodward, Dec 30, 1788, by whom he had four children He was again married March 11, 1[illegible] [illegible] His house,

built over a hundred years ago and now occupied by Rev Dr Reid, was the early stopping place of Bishop Asbury and all the circuit riders and preachers Bishop Asbury visited it last in 1816 Mr Warfield was church steward in 1801, and active in the church services until his death, Jan 6, 1835 At John Evan's old house, now owned by Jesse Stern, was likewise a home for preachers, and preaching held there as late as 1809, when services were transferred to the house of Benjamin Bennett The Evan's house was a log structure one and a half stories high Samuel and Lloyd Bennett were early converted to Methodism, and became noted in the church

Creameries—Pinkney J Bennett owns two creameries, both of which are in successful operation, one of which is located in the Franklin District and the other in New Windsor He is the largest butter producer in Maryland His establishments are fitted up with the best of machinery, and together have a capacity of ten thousand pounds of butter daily His varied appliances include five horse engines At present he is making about five thousand pounds daily, while the average daily yield throughout the year is six thousand pounds The lands in the vicinity are finely adapted to the business, producing the best of blue grass and clover, and are free from noxious weeds Mr Bennett gets his milk from thirty-five farmers, and the amount used is the product of a herd of four hundred cows all healthy and vigorous animals The butter is made by machinery, and is never touched by the employés during its manufacture He also makes ice-cream and ships milk, but makes no cheese He does not think that the increased value of the product is equivalent to the extra labor, and believes his butter will keep longer The yield per hundred pounds of milk he also thinks to be greater than cheese-makers realize, and by returning the sour milk to the farmers for their pigs, he can buy for less than if it were retained for cheese-making

The price the farmers get for the milk is equivalent, if they made it into butter, to about twenty-five cents per pound of butter

The creameries are two stories high, thirty-five by forty feet, with engine-houses ten by twelve feet, and are erected over streams of running water

The farmers of the county are awakening to the importance of creameries, and at their solicitation Mr Bennett is considering the establishment of two more

He has been in the business since 1876, and since the first difficulties were overcome, of the educating of the farmers of his vicinity to keeping pastures and the necessity of cleanliness, he has been quite successful in his [illegible] He [illegible] and energetic gentleman, and has ample means to back him

Harrisville, a small hamlet, is in the western part of Franklin District and on the Frederick County line

Hood & Clary have a store here, and the place has a mill and several shops

Watersville is a village situated in the Franklin District, on the Baltimore and Ohio Railroad, about forty miles from Baltimore The Methodist Episcopal and Baptist congregations have a place of worship England & Kenly are the merchants of the town, and the former is postmaster Dr S R Waters is the practicing physician for the village and the surrounding country, and it is from his family, one of the oldest in the district, that the town derives its name Joshua Hall is the railroad foreman stationed at this point, and D L Kenly is the railroad and express agent The country in the vicinity of the village is noted as a tobacco-growing region

David Crawford, one of the first settlers in New Windsor District, where in early days he was a leading man in public affairs, was a native of Pennsylvania He married Miss Lloyd, from which union were born seven sons and two daughters Of these, Evan Lloyd Crawford married Isabella Smith, a daughter of Duncan Smith She was born at Inverness, Scotland, near the city of Edinburgh, and came to America with her parents when a little girl Evan Lloyd Crawford was the father of one son and four girls, who grew up to maturity and of the latter three yet survive The son, Francis Jesse Crawford, was born on the farm on which he now resides, then in Baltimore County Nov. 1, 1819 Until twenty-one years of age he worked on the farm, and attended the neighborhood schools during the winter months He then attended for three years the academy at Johnsville, Frederick Co, of which that eminent instructor, Prof John S Sandbatch, was principal Among his classmates was Judge William N Hayden, of Westminster He taught school for several winters near home, in both Baltimore and Frederick Counties, to acquire funds sufficient to enable him to prosecute his studies for the medical profession He then read medicine with Dr James H Claggett, of Washington County, one of the most distinguished physicians of his day, after which he attended the lectures of Washington University, in Baltimore, where he graduated in the class of 1843 and '44 In that institution he was under the tutelage of such eminent and learned men as Drs Baxley, Vaughan, Jennings, Monroe and Webster great lights in the medical [illegible] ned to his

Francis J. Crawford, M.D.

home in Franklin District and began the practice of his profession, in which he has been successfully engaged for thirty eight years In that period of time he has not been excelled as a practitioner, and before the war his practice extended over a field now filled by some eight physicians In one year he paid two thousand two hundred medical visits, of which sixty five were in obstetrical cases The doctor is a strong Democrat in politics and active in the counsels of his party, and, although often solicited by his friends, has ever firmly refused to be an aspirant for office Some thirty years ago he became a member of Salem Lodge, No 60, I O O F, at Westminster, and subsequently of Columbia Encampment, No 14, of the same place On the institution of St Stephen's Lodge, No 95, I O O F, at Defiance, in May, 1857, he was one of its charter members, and since then has passed all the chairs, and has been a representative to the Grand Lodge He is Master of Franklin Grange, Patrons of Husbandry, No 117, and was largely instrumental in its organization Although connected with no denomination, he is a liberal giver to all the churches in his neighborhood He was married in May, 1853, to Ruth Elizabeth Bennett, daughter of Benjamin Bennett, of Franklin District, by which union he has five children Fannie Belle, married to Dr R O D Warfield, Kate Emma, married to Henry S Davis, Francis Albert, William Lloyd, and Charles Clement, besides two daughters who died young Dr Crawford's fine farm of three hundred and seventy acres, known as Waterloo, is within some sixty yards of the Frederick County line He is a self-made man, who, with no resources with which to begin life but a firm will and energy, has by his ability and industry reached an eminent place in his profession, and has been otherwise very successful in life He is the most noted fox-hunter in the county, and has a pack of eighteen hounds unsurpassed in this part of Maryland He is also a fine horseman, and in breeding horses has made the Morgan stock a specialty, having years ago purchased from Col Carroll a pure-blooded Morgan mare His horses are among the first in Carroll County In cattle he prefers Alderneys or Jerseys, and his herds take rank with the best and purest in the State

Below are given the votes cast for local officers in this district from 1851 to 1861, inclusive

1851 —Vote for Primary School Commissioner Charles Denning 87, Stephen Gorsuch 86, Charles Denning 136, Lyan I Crawford 11

1853 —For Justices Thos B Owings 145, Charles Denning 164, E L Crawford 52, John Hood 171, David Buckingham 117, Aquila Pickett 179, Constables Joshua Shuster 175, Lewis Lin[illegible] Buckingham 118, Road Supervisor F J Crawford 118, A P Barnes 160

1855 —For Justices Milton Bussard 209, Aquila Pickett 263, A Albaugh 215, T B Owings 135, C Denning 127, G W Chase 87, Constables John Hood 222, J Criswell 233, Henry Lida 117, Road Supervisor Wm Gosnell 223, J Nausbaum 127

1857 —For Justices T B Owings 105, A Pickett 106, Abraham Albaugh 172, F A Switzer 188, John Hood 83, Constables Vachel Hammond 199, J V Criswell 212, Road Supervisor G. H Davis 121, W Gosnell 177.

1859 —For Justices T B Owings 116, John Hood 174, F A. Switzer 163, Aquila Pickett 164, J Thomas Young 185, Constables W W Pickett 184, J B Runkles 173, Road Supervisor Jesse Jarrett 98, Kanan Sprinkle 67

1861 —For Justices I W Cochran 256, John T Young 255, Aquila Pickett 247, Constables W W Pickett 248 W P. Davis 264, Road Supervisor W H Barnes 261

The following is a list of public school trustees for 1881 and 1882, together with the names of teachers and number of scholars

1 Parr's Ridge —No appointments

2 Chestnut Grove —James H Steele, Wesley P Gosnel, Dr. S R Waters

3 Cabbage Spring —J N Selby, S Hood, N Davis

4 Franklinville — Ambrose G Franklin, W H Barnes, G W Baker

5 Pine Orchard —Augustus Brown, David Zile, David Cover

6 Salem —Wm Y Frizzell, John B T Sellman, Vincent Cresswell

7 Hooper's Delight —No appointments

8 Ridge —Richard J Brashears, Wesley Harrison, James Hood

1 Fairview (African) —No appointments

The teachers for the term ending April 15, 1881, were

1, Ettie Shipley, 41 pupils, 2, Sallie N Waters, 25 pupils, 3, Clara Selby, 40 pupils 4, Jacob Farver, 41 pupils, 5, A W Buckingham, 41 pupils, 6, Louisa A Hoffman, 41 pupils, 7, C W Reagan, 32 pupils, 8, Geo A Davis, 41 pupils, 1 (colored school) John H Henderson, 38 pupils

MIDDLEBURG DISTRICT, No 10

The Tenth District of Carroll County, generally known as Middleburg is bounded on the north by the Taneytown District, on the west by the districts of Uniontown and Union Bridge and by Frederick County, on the south by Frederick County The Monocacy River, Double Pipe Creek, and Little Pipe Creek separate the district from Frederick County, while Big Pipe Creek flows through the centre of the district These streams and their tributaries supply an abundance of water for all purposes The Western Maryland Railroad passes through the southern portion of the district, and the Frederick and Pennsylvania Line Railroad divides it very nearly into equal p[illegible] facilities

for outside communication, trade, and traffic The district in 1880 had a population of 1221

Middleburg District was created by an act of the General Assembly of Maryland, passed March 24, 1852, in which William Shepperd, William Shaw, and John Clabaugh were named as commissioners to ascertain and fix the boundaries The town of Middleburg was chosen as the place for holding the polls The first settlers in the district were Scotch-Irish They entered upon and cleared up a large amount of land between 1750 and 1770

Among the pioneers in this portion of the State were Normand Bruce, Philip and Francis Key, Upton Scott, the Delaplanes, Dernses, and Landises "Terra Rubra," a tract of eighteen hundred and sixty-five acres, was patented in 1752 to Philip Key, and "Runnymeade," of three thousand six hundred and seventy-seven acres, to Francis Key and Upton Scott in 1767

Normand Bruce was sheriff of Frederick County before the Revolution under the proprietary government, and the most important personage in this part of the county "New Bedford," of five thousand three hundred and one acres, was patented in 1762 to Daniel McKenzie and John Logsden

John Ross Key, son of Philip Key, the owner of "Terra Rubra," was born in 1754 He was a lieutenant in the First Artillery, which went from Maryland at the outbreak of the Revolutionary war, and owned a large estate in Middleburg District, then a part of Taneytown, in Frederick County His wife, Anne Phebe Key, was born in 1775 Their mansion was of brick, with centre and wings and long porches It was situated in the centre of a large lawn, shaded by trees, and had attached to it an extensive terraced garden adorned with shrubbery and flowers Near by flowed Pipe Creek through a dense woods A copious spring of the purest water was at the foot of the hill A meadow of waving grass spread out towards the Catoctin Mountain, which could often be seen at sunset curtained in clouds of crimson and gold When the labors of the farm were over, in the evening, the negroes were summoned to prayers with the family, which were usually conducted by Francis Scott Key when he was there, and by his mother when he was away After prayers, almost every night, as was common on plantations in Maryland, music and dancing might be heard at the quarters of the negroes until a late hour It was at this happy home that Roger Brooke Taney, then a young attorney, and subsequently chief justice of the United States, married, Jan 7 1806, Anne Phebe Charlton Key daughter of the proprietor of the estate John R[illegible] d[illegible] Oct [illegible] 1[illegible]21, and his wife, Anne Phebe, July 8, 1850 Both are buried in Frederick City, in Mount Olivet Cemetery Their daughter, the wife of Judge Taney died of yellow fever at Point Comfort Va, Sept 29 1855, and is buried near her parents in the same lot, by the side of her daughters, Ellen M and Alice Carroll

No man in Frederick County took a more active part in the Revolutionary struggle than John Ross Key, who fought on the field, and was of great service to the patriot cause in committees and as a counselor As early as 1770, when a mere boy, he attended the preliminary meetings of the pioneers held at Taneytown to consult as to the odious stamp measures then oppressing the colonies He was the father of the wife of Chief Justice Taney and of the author of "The Star Spangled Banner,"—one a woman of rare virtues and graces, and the other the favorite national poet

Francis Scott Key, the author of the "Star-Spangled Banner," was a native of Middleburg District, where he was born Aug 1, 1779 A graduate of St John's College, Annapolis, he adopted the law as his profession, began his practice at Frederick, and thence removed to Georgetown, D C He was for many years district attorney for the District of Columbia His only sister was the wife of Roger B Taney, chief justice of the United States Hon George H Pendleton, of Ohio, is one of his sons in law.[1]

In personal appearance Mr Key was tall and thin, cleanly shaven, with a head of heavy brown hair, disposed to curl slightly He had a face of marked beauty, of peculiar oval form, and a notable sweetness of expression He had large, dreamy, poetic eyes, and a genuinely sympathetic and mobile countenance A portrait in possession of his daughter, Mrs Turner, who with some of her descendants lives in California, has been copied for the statue to adorn the monument which is to be erected to him in accordance with the $150 000 bequest for that purpose of James Lick the millionaire

Mr Key died in Baltimore, Jan 11, 1843 while on a visit to his son-in-law, Charles Howard, and was buried in the Monumental City At the death of his wife, in 1857, his remains were removed and placed by the side of her remains in Mount Olivet Cemetery, Frederick City, under the direction of his son in-law, Hon George Hunt Pendleton, United States senator from Ohio, who married his daughter Alice, the favorite niece of Chief Justice Roger Brooke Taney

Daniel Turner, who graduated at the head of th

[1] [illegible] History of Fred[illegible]

first class which went out from West Point Military Academy, was a nephew of Jacob Turner, one of three commissioned officers who, with six soldiers, were killed in the battle of Germantown

After the war of 1812, Turner retired from the army and became a member of Congress from North Carolina John Randolph, then in Congress, an intimate friend of John Ross Key, and a frequent visitor at his hospitable home, took Mr Turner there and introduced him into the Key family, one of whose daughters he married

The Scott family was an old one in the district, and one of its most noted members, Hon Upton Scott, was born in Annapolis in 1810, when his mother was on a visit to her relatives He was a delegate to the General Assembly in 1846, and in 1866 removed to Baltimore County, and later to Baltimore City Governor Whyte appointed him a justice of the peace for the city and he was reappointed by Governor Carroll Mr Scott died in Baltimore, Aug 3, 1881 He was the father of Mrs Judge William N Hayden, and brother-in-law of Hon John B Boyle both of Westminster His father, John Scott, married a daughter of Normand Bruce

Middleburg, the largest village in the district, is situated on the Frederick road The land on the south side of that road was originally owned by the Brooks family, and it was a dense woods in 1800 The town in 1817 comprised the following houses The old stone house now occupied by William Dukart was then kept as a tavern by William Neil An old stone house also stood upon the site of J H Winebrenner's dwelling, a part of which was, in 1817, used by Mr Clapsaddle as a black-smith shop Mr Fulwiler, a tailor, lived in the house now occupied by Dr Thompson, which was built about the year 1800 by John Dust, and is the oldest house in the village The stone house now owned by Arnold was built in 1815, or thereabouts, and was then owned by Dickey Brooks The tavern now owned by Lewis Lynn was also built about the year 1815 The building now occupied by Mr Williams, and which belongs to Mary Koontz, was built in 1816, and was intended to be used as a bank, as at that time there was talk of organizing a county, and Middleburg was to be the county-seat. Dr William Zollicoffer was the physician, and moved here in 1817, and lived in a shed-house which was attached to the Williams property Mr Steiner kept a store in the house where Mr Thompson now lives, there being then an additional building attached to it, which has since been removed Mr Zultzer kept a store in the Williams property The old well which is situated on the pike south of Mr Arnold's residence was dug by an Irishman, named Elick Fulton, in 1808 It is supposed that the town received its name from the fact that it is situated about middle way between Westminster and Frederick It did not improve much until after the war of 1812–14, when, under the lead of Mr Winemiller, several fine houses were erected The house now occupied by Susanna Dehoff was standing in 1817, and was owned by her mother

At a meeting of the "Columbian Independent Company," commanded by Capt Nicholas Snider, of Taneytown, and the "Independent Pipe Creek Company," under the command of Capt Thomas Hook, held at Middleburg, Oct 13, 1821, information of the death of Gen John Ross Key was first received Middleburg is on the Western Maryland Railroad, forty-eight miles from Baltimore and fifteen from Westminster, in a fertile and thriving section of country The merchants are Ferdinand Warner and H D Fuss, the physician, Dr Charles Thompson, and the hotel keeper, Lewis F Lynn A large pottery establishment is conducted by U T Winemiller

The congregation of the Methodist Episcopal Church, which is quite old, held its services in the old log school-house until 1850, when the church was built Rev William Keith was the pastor in 1866, and was succeeded by Rev Mr Haslet, who was followed by Rev J D Moore, Rev William Ferguson, Rev George Madewell, Rev Charles West, Rev Mr Smith, and others E O Eldridge is the present pastor The officers of the church are C Brooks, Mr Buffington, J A Miller, E C Utter Attached to this church is a neat cemetery, and the following persons are buried there

Isaac Dern, died March 9, 1861, aged 75

Mary, wife of Joshua Delaplane, died Aug 11, 1862, aged 87 years, 4 months, 20 days

John Delaplane, born Aug 10, 179 , died Feb 10, 1868

Abraham L Lynn, born Aug 13, 1844 died April 5 1872

Anna E, wife of D H Lynn, died Aug 17, 1873, aged 20 years 7 months, 7 days

Anna R, wife of C W Winemiller, died April 7, 1876, aged 52 years, 5 months, 19 days

Michael Magaley, born April 16, 1799, died Dec 19 1878

Joshua Parrish, died March 27, 1862, aged 59 years, 7 months, 24 days

John Wesley Wilson, born April 7, 1818, died Oct 11, 1856

Mary Dayhoof, died Jan 1, 1858, aged 47 years, 1 month, 13 days

Joseph Dayhoof, died Feb 16, 1862, aged 57 years, 18 days

William Koons, born July 2, 1794, died Dec 18, 1852

John Nipple born Jan 27, 1815, died Dec 31, 1877

Margaret Souder, wife of Joshua S, died June 18, 1850, aged 30 years, 7 months, 14 days

Henrietta, wife of Evan C Otts, died March 24, 1856, aged 35 years, 9 days

Catharine [illegible] died Jan 2?, 1853, aged 86

Frederick Dern, Jr., died May 20, 186 aged 5[illegible] years, 11 months, 23 days

Mary J., his wife, died May 31, 1861, aged 36 years, 4 months, 1[illegible] days

Frederick, Sophia, John W., their three children

Ann P., daughter of J and M Winemiller, died Dec 11, 18[illegible]9, aged 1[illegible] years, 2 months, 25 days

John H Winemiller, died March 14, 1879, aged 59 years, 8 months, 12 days

Susan Alice, their daughter, died Dec 2, 1859, aged 11 years, 10 months, 7 days

John N 1 Winemiller, died Dec 8, 18[illegible]9, aged 8 years, 1 day

Thomas Hook, died May 12, 1869, aged 77 years, 23 days

Sarah Hook, died May 17, 1868, aged 83 years, 4 months, 23 days

Elizabeth C Hook, died June 13, 18[illegible]8, aged 53 years, 14 days

Regina L., daughter of J M and Agnes McAllister, died Jan 4, 186[illegible], aged 16 years, 10 months, 1 day

Lavina Margaret, wife of Abendago Flick, died Nov 8, 1855, aged 27 years, 23 days

John W McAllister, died Nov 10, 1880, aged 82 years, 8 months, 12 days

Agnes McAllister, died Oct 23, 1880, aged 75 years, 9 months, 13 days

David Hope died Nov 1, 18[illegible]9, aged 57 years, 4 months, 22 days

Keysville, a small village, received its title from the fact that the land upon which the old school-house and church were built was presented to the inhabitants by Francis Scott Key

Though the house in which Mr Key was born has disappeared a large barn and spring house, which he built not long before he died, are still standing on the farm now owned by John Winemiller, and occupied by Jacob Wentz

Double Pipe Creek is on the Western Maryland Railroad, fifty one miles from Baltimore Double Pipe Creek, from which it takes its name, is near, and furnishes water sufficient for milling and other purposes The improvements recently made indicate the zeal and energy of the people Of the Dunker Church, here located, Revs D Panel and Daniel R Sayler are the preachers The merchants are John T Ott, J W Weant, and J H Angell, the latter is also postmaster The physician is Dr Charles H Diller William T Miller has a cooper's factory, and C B Anders runs the flouring mill There are several shops and local industries that give considerable business to the place

The old stone mill at Double Pipe Creek, now owned and operated by C B Anders, has stood since 1794, in which year it was founded by Joshua Delaplaine, although it was not completed until 1800, as an inscription upon a stone in the "fire arch" bears witness Joshua Delaplaine was a manufacturer of some note in his day, and carried on not only the grist-mill, but a woolen mill on the opposite side of the creek The last-named structure still stands, but no looms have made music within its walls for these many years In 1836, Henry Waspe built an addition to the grist-mill, making it what it now is In 1878, C B Anders bought the mill and other property of Thomas Cover Mr Anders was born at Double Pipe Creek in 1830, and in the old Delaplaine mill his father, Aaron, was a miller many years ago Aaron Anders removed to Linganore, and in the mill at that place followed his calling upwards of twenty-five years C B Anders was placed in the Linganore mill when sixteen years of age, and has ever since followed the occupation of a miller His mill, three stories in height, is furnished with four pairs of burrs, has a capacity of one hundred barrels of flour daily, and is devoted almost exclusively to merchant-work The motive power is supplied by two turbine-wheels measuring, respectively, fifty four and thirty-six inches in diameter, with a head of nine feet The manufacturing apparatus includes all the latest devised mill improvements All the barrels used are manufactured in the mill The total number of employés is seven Choice Red Longberry wheat is chiefly used in the production of flour for shipment, and in Baltimore the "Double Pipe Creek" brand ranks high Mr Anders owns also the old Delaplaine woolen-mill property, a brick residence on the Frederick County side of the creek, and two residences on the Carroll County side, besides the railroad warehouse His home, near the railway depot, is a handsome two-story structure of imposing appearance He built it in 1878, and spared no expense to make it a model of its kind It is a striking object in the architecture of the village, and is conceded to be one of the most completely appointed homes in Carroll County

Bruceville is a small village about the centre of the district Long before the Revolutionary war Normand Bruce, a Scotchman, emigrated to this country and settled in the Middleburg District, in the locality now known as Keysville At that time the land in and about Bruceville was owned by John Ross Key Bruce desiring the Key property for the purpose of building a mill on Big Pipe Creek entered into negotiations with Key, which resulted in an exchange of their estates Bruce erected a large stone mill, which stood until February, 1881, when it was partially destroyed by fire He also built a dwelling-house, the same which is now occupied by Frederick Mehring The town was laid out by Bruce and named about the close of the eighteenth century Bruce had three children,—Betsey, who married John Scott, the parents of the late Upton Scott, Mrs Daniel Swope, a[illegible] John B[illegible], Hugh [illegible] Charles Bruce.

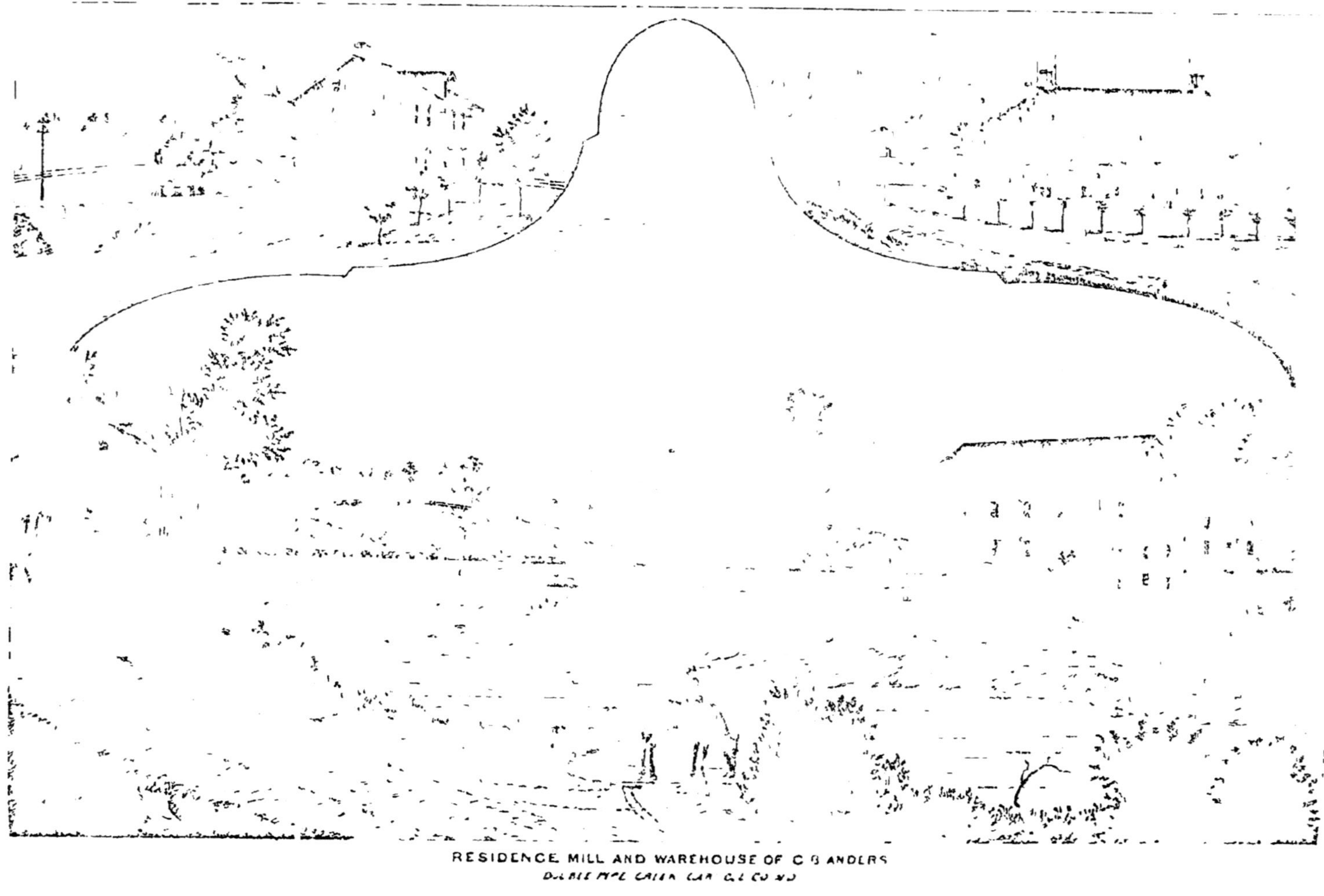

RESIDENCE MILL AND WAREHOUSE OF C B ANDERS
DOUBLE PIPE CREEK CARROLL CO MD

one of his sons, was born in Middleburg District, but in early life left this country and resided in the West Indies While on a visit to his birthplace he first saw his sister, she then being a wife with a large family Bruce was the third son The Landis family came from Scotland in 1812, and located on a part of the Key estate John Landis, one of the sons, who is still living, was in Washington in the year 1814, learning his trade, and was among the first who saw the British fleet sailing up the Potomac

Nicholas Kuhen was the earliest blacksmith in the town, and Jesse Cloud kept the hotel Dr Leggett was the physician, and Mr Trego the merchant Hudson and Brooks were prominent farmers who resided near the mill at the time of its erection

What was at one time quite an extensive cemetery is at present a thick growth of underbrush, and contains only five graves the inscriptions upon which can be deciphered

Basil Brooks, eldest son of Raphael and Jane, died Jan 24, 1829, aged 56

Robert T Dodds, died April 17, 1806, aged 74, "a native of East Lothian County, Scotland, of Haddington, of Aberlady" Selkirk Dodds, his wife, "a native of Edinburgh, Scotland," died April 21, 1825, aged 73

John Dodds, their son, died Oct 17, 1816, aged 42

John Scott, died Feb 28, 1814, aged 71

It is stated that the body of Normand Bruce lies in this yard, but should the same be true, it is unmarked by even a grave

Double Pipe Creek Division, No 36, of Sons of Temperance, was incorporated by an act of the Legislature, passed March 3, 1847 The incorporators were John E H Ligget, George H Wareche, Isaac Dern, Eli Otto, Noah Pennington, Benjamin Poole, Martin Grimes, Nicholas Stansbury, Hiram Fogle, George Lauders, James Thomas, William Carmack, Abednego Shek, Francis Carmack, Joseph Fogle, Jesse Anders, William Miller, Edward Carmack, Samuel Buely

York Road is the station and post-office for Bruceville It is a small village, at the junction of the Western Maryland Railroad with the Frederick Division of the Pennsylvania Line Railroad, and is sixteen miles from Westminster by rail David Hiltabidle is the railroad and express agent and postmaster Dr M A Lanver is the physician

The following is the vote for local officers in this district from 1853 to 1861, inclusive

1853 —Vote for Justices Isaac Dern 113, David Otto 73, David Rupe 67, J W McAllister 57, Constable John Six 105, Road Supervisor J W Wilson 13, Thomas Hook 90, Philip W Hann 47

1855 —For Justices J Delaplane 123, David Otto 128, Thomas Hook 71, J W M[illegible] 71, Constable John Six 11[illegible] A Slick 91, Road Supervisor John Angell 109, H Clabaugh 98

1857 —For Justices David Otto 174, John Delaplane 114, Constables John Six 160, J S Shriner 149, Road Supervisor Jacob Sayler 177

1859 —For Justices Thomas Hook 93, John Delaplane 130, A S Zentz 146, Constables John Six 158, John A Mackley 148, Road Supervisor Ephraim Hiteshue 163

1861 —For Justices Samuel Angell 182, John Delaplane 181, Constables John Six 188 Samuel T Linn 178, Road Supervisor Nicholas Koons 149, A S Zentz 81

The following are the public school trustees for 1881 and 1882, together with the names of teachers and number of pupils

1 Mount Union —John Shunk, J Thaddeus Starr, Henry Williams

2 Middleburg —Dr C Thomson, Lewis Lynn, Moses Seabrook

3 Bruceville —Jacob Buffington, John Biehl, M Fringer

4 Franklin —Samuel Waybright, Joshua Dutterer, Sylvester Valentine

5 Keysville —Aaron Weant, Peter Writter, Benjamin Poole

6 Double Pipe Creek —J W Weant, A N Forney, Lewis Cash

The teachers for the term ending April 15, 1881, were

1, W J Crabbs, 30 pupils. 2, S Jeanette Dutterer, 39 pupils, 3, C F Reindollar, 36 pupils, 4, S Linn Norris, 41 pupils, 5, James B Galt, 46 pupils, 6, Luther Kemp, 27 pupils

The justices of the peace are Calvin Warner, Joseph Arnold, Constable, Moses Seabrook

NEW WINDSOR DISTRICT, No 11

The Eleventh District of Carroll County, generally known as New Windsor, is bounded on the north by Uniontown District, on the east by Westminster, on the south by Franklin, and on the west by Frederick County and Union Bridge Sam's Creek separates the district from Frederick County, and Little Pipe Creek flows east from Westminster through the northern portion The Western Maryland Railroad passes directly through the district, and furnishes excellent facilities for trade and travel In 1880 it contained 2199 inhabitants

This district was created by an act of the General Assembly of Maryland, passed March 10, 1856, out of parts of the Second, Seventh, and Ninth Districts Its boundaries were defined as follows.

"Beginning at the intersection of the county line with the Buffalo road at Sam's Creek, and running up a branch of said creek to a spring near the dwelling of Abraham Albaugh, Esq, thence by a straight line to a point on the road leading from Mount Airy to Westminster, directly opposite the dwelling of Maj Benjamin Gorsuch, thence with said road to the Nicodemus road, thence with said Nicodemus road westwardly to the house of A Brown (colored), thence by a straight line to Cassell's mill, on Little Pipe Creek thence down said creek to the [illegible] on Roop's saw-

LIBRARY

mill, and down the branch thence to said Pipe Creek, and with it to the bridge on the road leading from McKinstry's mills to Uniontown thence by a straight line to the bridge over Sam's Creek, near Rinehart's marble quarries, thence up said creek, the county line, to the place of beginning"

The same act established the following primary school districts Priestland, No 1, Greenwood, No 2, Snader's, No 3, Bailes', No. 4, Carroll, No 5, Wakefield, No 6, Springdale, No 7, and New Windsor, No 8

Early Settlers.—"Park Hall," a tract of 2680 acres, was surveyed for James Carroll in 1727 It lies between New Windsor and Sam's Creek, and was the first survey recorded in this portion of Maryland Among the early settlers were Rev. Robert Strawbridge, John Maynard, Henry Willis, David Evans, Hezekiah Bonham, John and Paul Hagarty, the Poulsons, Baxters, Durbins, Wakefields, Joshua Smith, Richard Stevenson, the Devilbisses, Nails, Nausbaums, Peatres, Nicodemuses, Buckinghams, Englars, Lamberts, Roops, Michael Barthołow The tract of land known as "Cornwall," for 666 acres, patented in 1749, lies on Little Pipe Creek, and was purchased by Joseph Haines and his brother "Windsor Forest," of 2880 acres, was patented to John Dorsey in 1772

Rev David Englar, a preacher in the Society of Dunkers, died August, 1839, aged sixty seven years

The Strawbridge Pipe Creek, or Sam's Creek, Methodist Episcopal Church was established in 1760, in Frederick County (now Carroll), the birthplace of American Methodism At that time Frederick embraced the counties of Montgomery, Washington, Allegany, Carroll, and Garrett, and in 1774 appeared the first record of the Frederick Circuit, which was in less than a hundred years to expand until it encircled with its Briarean arms every State and Territory within the limits of the United States. For years it was a frontier circuit, extending as far as Fairfax County, Va, and the pioneer preachers who traveled it came prepared to endure hardships and encounter dangers from which the advance of civilization has happily freed them Its first appointments were Pipe Creek, Frederick-Town, Westminster, Durbin's, Saxon's, Seneca, Sugar-Loaf, Rocky Creek, Georgetown (District of Columbia), and Adams

Rev Robert Strawbridge, the *first* Methodist preacher in America, was a native of Drummer's Nave, near Carrick-on-Shannon, County Leitrim, Ireland Upon his arrival in this country with his wife and children he settled on Sam's Creek As soon as he had arranged his house he began to preach in it, as early as 1760, and besides his appointment in his own house he had another, in 1762 at the house of John Maynard, who was a Methodist, where he baptized his brother, Henry Maynard, aged six years, at a spring in the same year,—the *first* Methodist baptism in America Henry Maynard died in 1837, aged eighty-one years The society formed by Mr Strawbridge consisted of about fifteen persons, among whom were David Evans, his wife and sister, and Mrs Bennett The latter, who was living in 1856, aged eighty-nine years, described Mr Strawbridge as of medium size, dark complexion, black hair, and possessing a very sweet voice When Mr Asbury first visited the society, in 1772, he found there such names as Hagarty, Bonham, Walker, and Warfield Hezekiah Bonham had been a Baptist until influenced by Mr Strawbridge's preaching when he became a Methodist, and was much persecuted by his former sect At this time Mr Asbury heard him speak in public, and seeing that he had gifts as a speaker he gave him license to exhort He afterwards became a preacher, and in 1785 his name is in the minutes of the Conference among the itinerants His son, Robert Bonham, was also a traveling preacher Paul Hagarty was a member of the Pipe Creek Society as was also his brother, John Hagarty, who became a traveling preacher, and could hold service in both German and English Robert Walker had been converted by Mr Whitefield at Fagg's Manor, Chester Co, Pa He afterwards removed to this county and joined the Pipe Creek Society He subsequently removed to Sandy River, S C, where he entertained Bishops Asbury and Whatcoat in 1800 Dr Alexander Warfield was a kind and useful friend to the organization Mr Asbury dined with him on his first visit to Pipe Creek, and Dr Warfield's wife was a member of Mr Strawbridge's first society Rev Lott Warfield, formerly of the Philadelphia Conference, was of this family

Not far from Pipe Creek lived William Durbin, who with his wife joined the Methodists in 1768 Their house was an early stand for preaching, and their son, John Durbin, was a traveling preacher in the beginning of this century In the same region lived George Saxton, whose house was a preaching place at that early date Mr Strawbridge also extended his labors to Baltimore and Harford Counties Samuel Merryman visited Pipe Creek, and was converted by the remarkable preacher who could pray without a book and preach without a manuscript sermon, which was regarded by many in that age and place as an impossibility From that day the old and noted Merryman family of Baltimore County were Methodists [illegible] first intro

duced into Frederick Town by Mr Strawbridge, on an invitation from Edward Drumgole, who, when he came from Ireland in 1770 bore a letter to Mr. Strawbridge, and heard him preach at Pipe Creek Mr Strawbridge was the first of Mr Wesley's followers to preach on the Eastern Shore, in 1769, at the house of John Randle in Weston, Kent Co He built up the *first society* of Methodists, and built the first Methodist chapel in America, which was on Pipe Creek In 1764 a log meeting-house was erected, about a mile from Mr Strawbridge's house It was twenty-two feet square, on one side the logs were sawed out for a door, on the other three sides there were holes for windows, but it does not appear that it ever was finished It stood without windows door, or floor until 1844 when it was demolished and hundreds of canes manufactured out of its logs William Fort sent one to each of the bishops, then in New York, and one to Dr Bond

STRAWBRIDGE'S LOG MEETING-HOUSE

Mr Strawbridge continued to reside at Sam's Creek about sixteen years, and then removed to the upper part of Long Green, Baltimore Co, to a farm given him for life by the wealthy Capt Charles Ridgely by whom he was greatly esteemed, and who often attended his preaching It was while living here, under the shadow of "Hampton" (Capt Ridgely's beautiful seat), that in one of his visiting rounds he was taken sick at the house of Joseph Wheeler and died, in the summer of 1781 His funeral sermon was preached by Rev Richard Owings, to a vast concourse of people, under a large walnut-tree His grave and that of Mrs Strawbridge (who died in Baltimore) were in the small burying-ground, about eight miles from Baltimore, in the orchard south of the house, and a large poplar-tree has grown up between them as a living monument

Mr Strawbridge had six children,—Robert, George, Theophilus, Jesse, Betsey, and Jane Two of his sons, George and Jesse, grew up and became carpenters Bishop Asbury on Sunday, Nov 22, 1772, preached in the log meeting-house on Pipe Creek, and in 1801 at the residence of Henry Willis, held his Conference During the session of that Conference he made the significant entry in his journal, "Here Mr Strawbridge founded the first society in Maryland or *America*" underscoring the latter word The home of [illegible] on the farm [illegible] owned by Charles Devilbiss, and the log chapel was on that now owned by Peter Cover, but when torn down was owned by Peter Engle The site of this first American chapel is a few yards from Mr Cover's barn, and is now a part of a corn field, and is unmarked David Engle is the only living man who has a personal knowledge of the exact site, and he assisted in removing the logs of the rude fabric to another place During 1866, the centennial year of American Methodism, denominational relic hunters removed these logs, and thus every vestige of the building disappeared The last log was presented by the Rev Charles A Reid to the Rev Frank S DeHass, D D, to be placed in the Metropolitan Methodist Episcopal church at Washington, D C, where it was converted into an ornament Before they were taken away they were measured, and from their length it was inferred that this primitive structure was about twenty-four feet in length and breadth A part of one of the logs was sawed out by Charles Devilbiss, who presented it to Rev S V Leech, D D, of Frederick Methodist Episcopal Church He had the remnant made into canes and mallets, which were presented to various parties as mementos

About twelve years ago the remains of Mr Strawbridge were removed to the "Preachers' Lot" in Mount Olivet Cemetery, Baltimore, and the beautiful monument that marks his grave was presented to the National Local Preachers' Association, through its president, Rev Isaac P Cook, by the late Rev Geo C M Roberts, M D

Mr Strawbridge did not own any land until March 8, 1773, when, according to the county records, he purchased the fifty acres on which he had resided for thirteen years from John England The property was known as "Brothers' Inheritance" and "England's Chance," nor did he ever sell it Nearly six years after his decease his only heir, Robert Strawbridge, conveyed it to Richard Stevenson This deed is dated Jan 23, 1787 The log church of Strawbridge, on Sam's, or Pipe Creek, was built two years before the chapel erected by Philip Embury in New York City in 1766, and was the first church building erected by the Methodists on the American continent When Rev Thomas S Rankin, Mr Wesley's envoy, met the preachers in Philadelphia in 1773, that first Conference in America ordered that no local preacher should administer baptism or the Lord's Supper, Robert Strawbridge only excepted and by name, and permission was given him to administer these rites under direction of the regular Wesleyan missionaries Mr Strawbridge was a brave self-denying, and successful [illegible] log chapel

is the Mecca to which annually hundreds of Methodists repair to view the cradle of their faith in this country Four miles north of the site of the old Pipe, or Sam's Creek church of Robert Strawbridge stands the building known as "Stone Chapel" When Mr Strawbridge's log structure was abandoned a small log chapel known as "Poulson's" was erected, which was torn down in 1783, and "Stone Chapel" built on the site It was the Pharos of Western Maryland Methodism during several decades Memorable revivals have marked its history, and distinguished men of early Methodism have preached from its pulpit

Stone Chapel antedates the organization of the Methodist Episcopal Church in America It is a two story edifice, with small windows and galleries on three sides There is on the front, high up, next to the apex, a tablet, on which are first three stars, then the initials "J D" (Jesse Durbin), below there is an eagle with the initials "B B" (Benjamin Bennett) to its left, and beneath the inscription

"Bt 1783
Rebt 1800"

Jesse Durbin and Benjamin Bennett were very active in their efforts for its erection

This church is only a few feet from the Westminster District line Right opposite to it on the other side of the road, is a small graveyard in which are interred

Abraham Koontz, died Jan 18, 1873, aged 83
John N Koontz, died Nov 21, 1873, aged 32
Eliza, wife of James Robertson, and daughter of Thomas and Mary Stevenson, died Feb 11, 1879 aged 39
Joseph Cushing, died Jan 20, 1873, aged 83, and his wife, Susan, died Feb 14, 1871, aged 78
Mary, wife of Mahlon Bowers, died April 13, 1874, aged 42
Jeremiah H Smith, born Oct 23, 1835, died Dec 8, 1874
Ann Poulson died Dec 21, 1875, aged 78
Elizabeth Nicodemus, died July 10, 1870, aged 71
Maranda, wife of Joshua Sellman, died July 7, 1871, aged 68
William Wagner, born Aug 9, 183[illegible], died April 18, 1875
Sarah Hooper, born Jan 10, 1793, died Feb 8, 1875 (daughter of Michael and Ann Bartholow)
Washington Barnes, son of Elisha and Amelia Barnes, born July 10, 1801, died Oct. 2[illegible], 1873

The neighborhood of the old Strawbridge farm is dotted with venerable houses rich in early associations. Near it is the old mansion of Alexander Warfield, Asbury's friend and host The room where the great bishop slept is there, as is the table upon which he wrote his journals For twenty years that mansion was a circuit preaching appointment, and Bishop Asbury visited it for the last time in 1816 two years before his death It is now occupied by Rev C A Reid, whose wife is Alexander Warfield's gran[illegible]

Near to it is the Willis house, where the Rev. Henry Willis died Here Bishop Asbury held a Conference in 1801, attended by forty preachers Willis preached as far north as New York and as far south as Charleston, S C Within a circuit of six miles are the residences of William, Jesse, and John Durbin, Joshua Smith, Adam Poulson, William Poulson, the Wakefields Baxters, Joseph, Jacob, and Leonard Cassell Mrs Henry Willis was the daughter of Jesse Hollingsworth, and was born Feb 9, 1769 Her six children were William Jesse, Mary Yellott, Jeremiah, and Francis Asbury Henry Maynard was born Aug 17, 1759, and died in 1839 Henry Willis died in 1808

Among the old settlers in this district is Judge Louis Philip Slingluff Judge Slingluff was born in Uniontown District (now New Windsor), Frederick County (now Carroll), March 15, 1831 the eldest child of Isaac and Julianna (Englar) Slingluff The family is of German origin His grandfather, Jesse Slingluff, was born in Springfield township, Philadelphia Co, Pa, Jan 1, 1775 When a boy he removed to Baltimore, and eventually, under the firm-name of Bohn & Slingluff, carried on an extensive grocery trade for many years in that city He married Elizabeth Deardoff, of Adams County Pa, by whom he had ten children, viz Charles D, Sarah Ann, Isaac, George W, Joseph, Esther Ann Catharine, Elizabeth, Jesse, and Upton Except Catharine and Elizabeth, who died when young, all were married and raised families Charles D was a prominent merchant in Baltimore, and left a large family George W was a merchant and farmer in Canal Dover, Ohio He left one son, now living there Joseph was a prominent physician in Canal Dover Two sons survive him and are still living there Esther Ann was wife of Joseph Poole, eight children survive her Upton was a merchant in Baltimore He left five children Sarah Ann is the widow of Thomas E Hambleton, residing in Baltimore She has seven children Jesse is president of the Commercial and Farmers' Bank, of Baltimore and has eight children Isaac, father of Judge L P, was born in Baltimore, Aug 5 1807 At the time Baltimore was threatened by the British in the war of 1812-14, Jesse Slingluff moved his family from the city and settled on what was known as the "Avalon farm, in New Windsor Having secured the safety of his family he returned to give his services in the defense of the city He became the owner of a large tract of land in New Windsor, and the latter years of his life were spent upon his estate He died June 30 [illegible] buried in Green-

mount Cemetery, Baltimore. Upon the death of his father Isaac came into possession of the "Avalon" farm. He married Julianna, daughter of Philip Englar, of New Windsor. Their children were Louis

Philip, subject of this sketch; Mary Elizabeth, born Jan. 27, 1833, widow of Jesse Weaver; four children; Jesse, born April 14, 1835, died Oct. 9, 1836; Frances Hannah, born April 7, 1838, widow of Ezra Stouffer, living in New Windsor; six children. Isaac Slingluff died April 30, 1852; his wife, Dec. 14, 1848.

Upon the death of his father Louis Philip became the possessor of the "Avalon" farm, by purchase from the heirs. He was educated in Calvert College, New Windsor, under President A. H. Baker. Though thoroughly devoted to his occupation as a farmer, Judge Slingluff has always taken a lively interest in the political questions of the day. He has been identified actively with the Democratic party since he became a voter. In 1872 he was appointed by Governor William P. Whyte to fill the unexpired term of Judge Upton Roop as judge of the Orphans' Court, and upon the expiration of that term was elected for another term of four years. For the last six or seven years he has been one of the board of directors and the board of trustees of "New Windsor," formerly "Calvert," Coll

Though not a member of any church, the judge is a liberal contributor to the support of all churches and benevolent institutions of his neighborhood. He married, Oct. 18, 1855, Ellen, daughter of George W. Slingluff, of Canal Dover, Ohio. Mrs. Slingluff died Sept. 8, 1856. He married for his second wife Margaret Alverda, daughter of Thomas and Catharine (Stouffer) Cromwell, March 19, 1861. The latter was born Aug. 24, 1839, in Walkersville, Frederick Co., Md. Her grandfather, Philemon Cromwell, who was a descendant of Oliver Cromwell, came from Baltimore County, and settled in Frederick County, Md. Her father, after the death of his first wife, married again, moved to Tiffin, Ohio, and died there.

Judge and Mrs. Slingluff have five children, viz.: Isaac Jackson, born Dec. 17, 1861; Thomas Cromwell, born Dec. 21, 1862; Nellie, born June 24, 1866; Catharine Cromwell, born Dec. 22, 1867; Robert Lee, born Jan. 14, 1877; all living at home.

Many Germans from the old country and Pennsylvania settled in this part of New Windsor District as early as the year 1750. They worshiped at their homes until the increase in their numbers necessitated the building of a church. George F. Winter, one of the prominent men at that time, generously donated an acre of ground, upon which, in the year 1766, under the direction of the building committee,—Jacob Haines, Adam Swigart, John Engleman, and Mr. Prugh,—the church was erected. It is one and a half miles from New Windsor, on the road to Uniontown. It was built by the Lutheran congregation, assisted slightly by the German Reformed congregation, who were allowed to use the church for their worship.

The first pastor of whom there is any record was the Rev. Mr. Grubb, who occupied this position in 1800. He was followed by the Reverends Mr. Wachter, Reuben Weiser, and Mr. Kiler. After Mr. Kiler the congregation had no regular minister for some years, but was supplied with occasional preaching by ministers from Baltimore. Rev. Solomon Sentman, fearing the congregation would lose many of its members by this mode of ministering, organized a church council, and Rev. Philip Willard was appointed to the charge. The church at this time was in the Taneytown charge, but was subsequently joined to the Westminster charge. Rev. Mr. Reinsnider was the next pastor, and was followed by Rev. John Winter, who began his duties about the year 1848. He was succeeded in the year 1853 by Rev. Samuel Henry. Rev. Dr. Martin, Rev. H. C. Holloway, Rev. J. F. Deiner, Rev. A. Strobel, Rev. G. W. Anderson, and Rev. David B. Floy

About the year 1870 the church was again changed, and put in the Uniontown Circuit, where it now stands About eighty members worship at this church, and it is in a very prosperous condition The present trustees are Elmer Hyde, Ephraim Haines, Levi Winter, Wm Winter, Samuel Gilbert, Jonas Effert, Elders, Elmer Hyde, Levi Bankart, Deacons, Robert Davidson, John Wilhelm

In the Winters Cemetery, which is attached to the church, the following persons are buried

John Lambert, died March 1 1838, aged 80 years, 1 month, 23 days, Ellen, his wife, died April 1, 1829, aged 68 years, 17 days

Jacob Haynes, died July 2, 1820, aged 73 years, 4 months, 10 days

Peter Hens, born March 6, 1756, died March 9 1804

Mary M Greenwood, died Dec 2, 1812, aged 63

Jacob Mormin, born 1786, died 1801

Rosanna Shuey, died April 10, 1839, aged 83

Anna M Greenholtz, died June 19, 181[illegible], aged 53

Jacob Greenholtz, died aged 85

Catharine Greenholtz, died aged 4[illegible]

Rachel Greenholtz, died aged 75

John Greenholtz, died Dec 29, 1870, aged 81

Isaac B Norris, died March 19, 1819, aged 64

Jacob Smelser, died May 19, 1819, aged 31 years, 9 months, 27 days

Henry Haines, died Feb 25, 1873, aged 83 years, 12 days, Magdalena, his wife, died Sept 2, 1868, aged 75 years, 9 months, 25 days

Sarah, relict of John Lantz, died Dec 2, 1874, aged 77 years, 10 months, 22 days

Andrew Myers, died July 12, 1823, aged 30 years, 5 months

Mary Myers, died Aug 27, 1817, aged 21 years, 7 months, 3 days

Peter Myers, died Feb 22, 1814, aged 54 years, 21 days

Magdalena Myers, died Jan 14, 1829, aged 68 years, 5 months, 16 days

Noah Worman, died Oct 9, 1868, aged 83 years, 5 months, 4 days, Catharine, his wife, born July 26, 1787, died Aug 2, 1853

Rebecca Myers, died Jan 11, 1867, aged 66 years, 11 months, 11 days

John Engleman, died April 18, 1841, aged 52 years, 7 months, 4 days

Julia A Sellman, died July 19, 1880, aged 82

Mary Engleman, died Dec 15, 1822, aged 57 years, 6 months

John Engleman, Sr, died Dec 25, 1855, aged 75 years, 9 months

Henry Shriner, died Sept 25 1823, aged 7 months

Mary Myers, born April 16, 1826, died Oct 9, 1858

Jacob Myers, born July 29, 1787, died May 1[illegible], 1833, Mary, his wife, died Jan 4, 1822, aged 51 years, 4 months 18 days

Martin Winter, died July 7, 1876, aged 72 years, 6 months, 6 days

Catharine Winter, died Aug 20, 1851 aged 77 years, 10 days

Jacob Winter, died Dec 1, 1815, aged 58 years, 1 month, 18 days

Elizabeth, wife of Geo Winter, died Jan 16, 1866, aged 73 years, 1 month, 20 days

Geo Winter, Sr, died Aug 6, 18[illegible]1, aged 45 years, 11 months, 7 days

Catharine Garner, died Aug 22, 1831, aged 47 years, [illegible] months, 19 days

George Garner, died Aug 5, 1840, aged 68 years, 8 months, 15 days

James Crawford, died Feb 2, 1839, aged 77 years, [illegible] months, 14 days

Catharine, his wife, died May 7, 1848, aged 60 years, [illegible] months, 13 days

Charlotte Boblets, daughter of Geo Lambert, died March 1, 1830, aged 33 years, 5 days

Wm Brawner, died Aug 1, 1828, aged 76, Catharine, his wife, died Oct 25, 1824, aged 69

Elizabeth Crawford, died Dec 21, 1872, aged 86 years, [illegible] months, 5 days

Elizabeth Randel, died Oct 6, 1849, aged 67 years, 8 months, 27 days

Mary Lamberd, born Sept 21, 1822, died March 30, 187[illegible]

Abraham Lambert, died Sept 3, 1862, aged 76 years, 1 months

Joshua Metcalf, born June 30, 1787, died April 10, 186[illegible]

Eleanor, his wife, born Feb 21, 1799, died June 8, 1861

David Shuey died June 5, 1845, aged 15

Catharine Shuey, born Aug 2, 1778, died May 10, 185[illegible]

Margaret Kiler, died April 23, 185[illegible], aged 51 years, 7 months, 12 days

Rachel Blizzard born Sept 12, 1807, died May 31, 187[illegible]

Mary Traxell, died April 10, 1870, aged 95

Jacob Kiler, died Nov 15, 1844, aged 82 years, 9 months, [illegible] days

Simon Kiler, died Oct 1, 1839, aged 73 years, 9 months

Elizabeth, wife of Jacob Kiler, died April 2 183[illegible], aged 7[illegible]

Fred Buser, died June 21, 1871, aged 16

Josiah Prugh, died Aug 7, 181[illegible], aged 16

Lucia M Prugh, died July 19, 1816, aged 67 years, [illegible] month, 3 days

Geo Dugen, died Dec 17, 1810, aged 72

Elizabeth Dugen, died March 19, 1821, aged 82 years, [illegible] months, 9 days

Henry Cook, died Jan 11, 1820, aged 71

Mary Swigart, died March 5, 183[illegible], aged 81

Michael Smelser, died Nov 10, 1831, aged 71 years, [illegible] months

Adam Swigart, born 1724, died 1796

Adam Swigart, born Oct 25, 178[illegible], died March 17, 182[illegible]

Adam Swigart, died Jan 9, 1852, aged 82 years, 8 months, 22 days

Elizabeth Swigard, died Jan 15, 1812, aged 59 years, 4 days

Elizabeth Hanes, died March 1[illegible], 1822, aged 37 years, 11 months, 9 days

Geo Smelser, born Nov 1, 1811, died April 2[illegible], 1872

Mary, wife of Michael Smelser, died July 25, 1836, aged 77 years, 7 months, 11 days

David Smelser, died Feb 22, 1861, aged 63 years, 7 months, 11 days

Mary Magdalena Hanna, died Jan 25, 1841

Barbara Long, died April 18, 1811, aged [illegible] years, 6 months, 25 days

Michael S Norris, died April 3, 186[illegible] aged 7[illegible]

Isaac N Smelser, born May 1821, died May, 1850

Elizabeth Lambert, born Oct 6, 17[illegible], died Feb 3, 1862

John Lambert, died March 30, 18[illegible], aged 58 years, [illegible] months, 1 day

Esther, his wife, died Oct 16, 1876, aged 74 years, 11 months, 9 days

Joshua Yingling, born Oct 5, 1801, died Dec 9, 18[illegible]

[illegible] Aug 1[illegible], 1[illegible]

Mary A, wife of Samuel Lamberd died Jan 24, 1836, aged 35

Peter Geiger, born May 10, 1781, died Aug 7, 1835, Charlotte, his wife, born April 26, 1790, died Sept 6, 1863

Magdalen Cook, died June 1, 1849, aged 96 years, 4 days

Catharine Bayar, died Oct 1, 1811, aged 48 years, 1 months

J Lasler, born 1781

Tobias Gerner, born 1754, died 1793

Margaret Gerner, born 1750, died 1807

Israel Cook and Ephraim, infants, died 1820

David Brower, died Jan 7, 1823, aged 19

Rebecca Lehman, died 1820, aged 11 months

Michael, wife of John Brower, died June 22, 1849, aged 80 year, 7 months 15 days

Richard Adams, died April 9, 1867, aged 68

Hannah Adams, died Jan 29 1852, aged 52

Lewis Doublets, born 1802, died April 20, 1867

Elizabeth Frownfelter, died Nov 26, 1879, aged 39 years, 6 months, 7 days

Jacob Z Buchan, died May 24, 1813, died July 15, 1877

Michael Bagner, born 1723, died 1795

M Bagner, born 1725, died 1789

J Winter, died Oct 15, 1771, aged 61

John Winter, died June 3, 1827, aged 43 years, 5 months, 26 days

Christina Winter, died March 9, 1810, aged 25 years, 3 months

Fred Mihns, born in Etzdorf, kingdom of Saxony, Germany, Sept 15, 1767, died Oct 28, 1852, Mary E, his wife, born Dec 10, 1785, died Nov 21, 1874

John Shannon, died March 28, 1853, aged 65, Sarah, his wife, died April 21, 1859 aged 75

Samuel Townsend, died June 11, 1895, aged 21 years, 10 months

David Townsend, died May 16, 1835, aged 20 years, 3 months, 4 days

Thomas Townsend, died Nov 10, 1851, aged 73 years, 3 months, Elizabeth, his wife, born Aug 28, 1776, died April 27, 1850

Joseph Winter, born Feb 9, 1797, died Dec 2, 1865

Elizabeth Engleman, died Dec 16, 1879, aged 89 years, 8 months 14 days

Mary Engleman, died April 20, 1879, aged 85 years, 6 months, 18 days

Lewis Engleman, died Nov 19, 1870, aged 78 years, 11 months, 8 days

Josiah Pearce, died Dec 5, 1830, aged 53 years, 3 months, 5 days

Elizabeth Pearce, died Oct 10, 1852, aged 72 years, 10 months, 22 days

Sarah A, wife of Elmer Hyde, born March 6, 1829, died April 1, 1875

Isaac Hyde born Jan 9, 1798, died March 3, 1872, Mary, his wife, died May 14, 1876, aged 74 years, 1 month, 29 days

Jonathan Hyde, died July 31, 1802, aged 75

Ann Hyde, born June 16, 1725, died July 8, 1812

Elizabeth Hyde, born June 3, 1765, died Dec 11, 1814

Ann Hyde, died March 22, 1805, aged 87 years, 3 months, 23 days

[illegible] Engleman, died March 27, 1877, aged 39 years, 5 [illegible] 11 days

[illegible] Mering, died Oct 24, 1868, aged 67 years, 2 months, [illegible] days

[illegible] Frownfelter, born Aug 22, 1824, died Sept 15, [illegible]

Magdalena [illegible] born [illegible], 1790, died March 1[illegible], 1861

Thomas King, died July 26, 1879, aged 65

George Fishman died June 19, 1878, aged 84 years 1 month, 18 days, Regina, his wife, died Dec 5, 1876, aged 80 years, 7 months, 28 days

Francis Wagner, died Oct 7, 1869, aged 34 years, 4 months, 4 days

Peter Nace, died June 15, 1866, aged 73

George Wilhelm, died Feb 17, 1872, aged 34 years, 10 months, 16 days

Sophia L Wilhelm, born April 27, 1805, died Feb 7, 1875

Helper Grammer, born April 14, 1790, died April 17, 1869, Margaret Grammer, his wife, died Oct 5, 1868, aged 83 years, 5 months

Adam Fuss died Aug 28, 1879, aged 60 years, 9 months, 17 days

Louisa Muller, died Jan 21, 1880, aged 61 years, 9 months, 26 days

New Windsor.—This town is twenty-eight miles from Baltimore, and is the commercial centre of the district It is in an exceedingly fertile section of the county, and a branch of Little Pipe Creek passes along its outer edge It is one of the important stations on the Western Maryland Railroad, has a bank, two institutions of learning, a number of churches, a warehouse, some well stocked stores, and contains a population of more than 400 inhabitants In the immediate vicinity there are a number of lime and stone-quarries, and some valuable mills The town was incorporated by an act of the General Assembly of Maryland, passed Jan 25, 1844

On March 15, 1817, Joshua Metcalfe took charge of the Merino factory, a valuable property, formerly carried on by Silas Hibberd, near New Windsor Mr Metcalfe had been foreman in the factory for many years Aug 22, 1817, Charles W Pearre, who had been in business for a number of years, notified all those in debt to him to call and settle at Lemuel Pearre's store their accounts by September 20th

The following advertisement appeared in the *Star of Federalism* of Nov 19, 1819

"GERMAN REDEMPTIONERS —About one hundred and sixty German Redemptioners, who are principally young people, and among whom are farmers and tradesmen of every kind, have just arrived in the Dutch ship 'Batavia,' Capt B Ellers Apply to the captain on board at the Cove, Spring Garden, or to Chas W Karthaus & Co, 50 South Gay Street, Baltimore

Of these redemptioners, several who were bought came to this region and settled in the rear of the town of New Windsor

The first physician in New Windsor was Dr Robert Dodds, a native of Scotland, who died July 27, 1833

New Windsor was formerly called "Sulphur Springs," in consequence of an excellent mineral spring on the farm of Isaac Atlee, now owned by Dennis H Maynard The first officers of the town, who [illegible] 1845, were

Henry W Dell, burgess, Samuel Ecker, Jesse Lambert, Isaac Blizzard, commissioners, Samuel Hoffman, collector
1845-46 —H W Dell, burgess, Samuel Hoffman, Jesse Lambert, Samuel Ecker, commissioners
1846-47 —Samuel Ecker, burgess, H W Dell, Jesse Lambert, Jonas Ecker, commissioners
1847-48 —Jonas Ecker, burgess, Jesse Lambert, Andrew Baker, Samuel Ecker, commissioners
1848-49 —Jonas Ecker, burgess, Thomas Bartlow, Andrew Baker, Lewis Fowler, commissioners
1849-50 —H W Dell, burgess, Jesse Lambert, Jonas Ecker, Lewis Fowler, commissioners Dell resigned, and Samuel Hoffman was appointed in his place
1850-51 —Jonas Ecker, burgess, H W Dell, Nathan Hanna, Jesse Lambert, commissioners
1851-52 —Jonas Ecker, burgess, Henry Geaty, N Hanna, Jesse Lambert, commissioners
1852-53 —Jonas Ecker, burgess, Jesse Lambert, William R Curry, William Delphey, commissioners
1853-54 —The same re elected
1854-55 —Jonas Ecker, burgess, Jesse Lambert, Elijah Enfor, Henry W Dell, commissioners[1]
1861-62 —Henry Geaty, burgess, Ezra Stouffer, Levi N Snader, Jesse Lambert, commissioners
1862-63 —Jacob Roop, burgess, Levi N Snader, Ezra Stouffer, N Hanna, commissioners
1863-64 —James Earhart, burgess, Dr Buffington, Joseph A Stouffer, Jesse Lambert, commissioners
1864-65 —Levi N Snader, burgess, Jesse Lambert, Lewis Shully, Daniel Stouffer, commissioners

By an act of the March session of the General Assembly of Maryland the charter of the corporation was revived, and the limits extended as follows

"Beginning at a sycamore tree on Dickinson's branch, opposite the foot of Main Street southeast of said branch to the mouth of Ray's branch, thence with the northeast side of the mill dam to Chew's bridge, leaving the dam and bridge outside of the corporation, thence northeast on the west side of the road to the division line between Jesse Lambert and E W Englar, leaving said road outside of said corporation, thence with said line to a point directly opposite the line between Andrew H Baker and Josiah Hibbert, on the east side of Calvert College, thence from this point northerly through the lands of A H Baker, and the division line between the said Baker and Hibbert, to the northeast corner of the lands of said Baker, to a ten pin alley, and westwardly with the lines between said Baker and Hibbert, Frownfelter, and others to the lands of D H Maynard, then with a straight line parallel with said Maynard's garden fence, and with it to said Maynard's outer gate, thence with a straight line to a sycamore-tree, the place of beginning"

1867 —Joseph A Stouffer, burgess, A H Baker, Dr J F Buffington, E S Stouffer, commissioners
1868-69 —A H Baker, burgess, Dr J F Buffington, E S Stouffer, Joseph Stouffer, commissioners
1869 —Jesse Lambert, burgess, Jacob Frownfelter, Jesse Haines, Charles P Baile, commissioners
1870-71 —Jesse Lambert, burgess, Charles P Baile, Jacob Frownfelter, Jesse Haines, commissioners
1871-72 —Peter Baile, burgess, Lewis Dielman, William Vansant, James Devilbiss
1872-73 —The same re elected
1873-74 —The same re elected
1874-75 —Peter Baile, burgess, Lewis Dielman, Jacob Frownfelter, James Devilbiss, commissioners
1875-76 —P Baile, burgess, Lewis Dielman, C P Baile, Jacob Frownfelter, commissioners
1876-77 —P Baile, burgess, William Vansant, W A Norris, Dr J F Buffington, commissioners
1877-78 —Charles P Baile, burgess, W A Norris, William Vansant, Jeremiah Bailey, commissioners
1878-79 —Peter Baile, burgess, Lewis Dielman, Samuel Hoffman, Jacob Frownfelter, commissioners
1879 —Peter Baile, burgess, Jacob Frownfelter, George S Gitt, C P Baile, commissioners
1880-81 —Peter Baile, burgess, George A Gitt, F J Devilbiss, James Lambert, commissioners
1881 —Peter Baile, burgess, Jacob Frownfelter, Charles E Norris, C C Engel, commissioners

Prior to 1871 one of the commissioners served as a clerk to that body, but since that date Lewis Dielman has occupied that position

A correct list is given of thirty-one persons, living within a radius of five miles of New Windsor in 1879, who had lived to the age of seventy years and upwards

Males —William Engleman, 82, Jacob Sauble, 88 Israel Switzer, 74, Abner Baile, 71, Israel Norris, 80, Samuel McKinstry, 71, Samuel Winter, 79, Jacob Snader 74 Joseph Stouffer, 73, Daniel Lambert, 72, Esau Randall, 90, D Woodegard (colored), 88, David Crumbacker, 77, David W Naill, 84, Joshua Warfield, 82 Josiah Hibberd, 70, Thomas King, 70, David Engel, 77 *Females* —Mrs Sallie Wolfe, 92, Elizabeth Eckman, 88, Elizabeth Shriner, 83, Elizabeth Crumbacker, 84, Elizabeth Engleman, 89, Mary Diehl 90 Julia Earhard, 76, Polly Engleman, 86, Nelly Engleman, 71, Honor Williams, 82, Nancy Sanders[2] (colored), 110, Rebecca Crowl, 86, Sally Baile, 76

The First National Bank of New Windsor was chartered in 1860 Its officers have been President, Thomas F Shepperd, Cashiers, Joseph A Stouffer, Nathan H Baile, Directors, Job Hibberd, Solomon

---

[1] During the year 1855 the corporation died out, but in 1860 Jacob Roop was elected mayor or burgess, Dr. John Buffington, Daniel Stouffer, and William Brown, commissioner

[2] Nancy Sanders, a colored woman residing at Landis Mill in an interview, states "I belonged to Mr George Robeson, way down in 'Gomery County, and about the time the first war with the English closed I came to Carroll County, on Sam's Creek Then I was sixteen years old In a few years there was another war with the English, and just as Mr Peter Naill, Lud Greenwood, and Massa Clemson Skyles were about to start to jine the army, the English captain was killed down near Baltimore, and then the war stopped" Judging from her account, she was born in 1767, was sixteen years of age when the Revolutionary war ended (in 1783), and is consequently one hundred and fourteen years old now She says if she was not in such a bad state of health she could do more work than any woman in the county She claims that her age does not hurt her, for she can thread a needle, and laughs at her youngest son, George, who is sixty because he wears spectacles Her mind seems clear on all subjects except she thinks some one [illegible]

S Ecker, Samuel Hoffman, Upton Root, Peter Engle, and Joseph H Hibberd

New Windsor was thrown into a state of intense excitement Saturday morning, Jan 23, 1868, by the discovery that the bank had been robbed For some days previous two strangers had been in the neighborhood, who represented themselves as drummers for Baltimore houses About two o'clock on Saturday morning a physician who was called up to see a patient saw a man standing near the bank building, and although it was unusual to see any person on the street at that hour, he suspected nothing wrong Saturday morning the officers of the bank went as usual to their place of business, but discovered that the safe could not be opened One of them immediately started for the city of Baltimore, and called on the independent police firm of Smith, Pierson & West The detectives went immediately to New Windsor, and found that the lock had been successfully picked, and that important portions of it had been removed Upon opening the safe it was apparent that the whole contents had been removed

Ninety-nine thousand dollars in all had been taken Of this amount ninety thousand dollars were in the following securities which were the property of private parties, and had been deposited with the bank for safe keeping

United States five-twenties of 1862, Nos 3260, 7650, of five hundred dollars each, United States five twenties of 1864, Nos 39,663, 20,152, 20,153, 20,154, one thousand dollars each, United States five-twenty bonds of 1865 January and July, Nos B, 64,031, A, 2881, E, 177,342, B, 70,191, B, 57 982, of five hundred dollars each, United States ten forties, No. 19,747, of five hundred dollars, Central Pacific Railroad bonds, first mortgage, Nos. F, 7648, F, 4561, F, 4562, G, 8978, G, 8981, G, 8982, G, 8971, G, 8972, F, 4571, F, 4572, F 4569, F, 7648, Union Pacific Railroad, Nos [illegible]52, 9417, 9419, 9416, 8487, 8491, 7258, 7259, [illegible]486, amounting to $13,931 56, Western Maryland Railroad first mortgage bonds, Nos 93, 125, 107, of one thousand dollars each, Nos 447, 444, 449, 555, 44[illegible], 564, 525, 559, 526, 566, 441, of five hundred dollars each, Western Maryland Railroad second mortgage bonds, indorsed by Washington County, Nos 11, 13, 78, 81, 7 47, 43, 44, of one thousand [illegible]ars each, 7, 67, 68, 670, of five hundred dollars [illegible], 761, 696, of one hundred dollars each, Washington County bonds, Nos 65 66, 91, 39, 7, 55, of [illegible] thousand dollars each, 33, 30, 64, 65, 66, 67, 31, [illegible] [illegible]6, 37 53 of five hundred dollars each 53, 51, [illegible] of one hundred [illegible] each, New Orleans and Opelousas Railroad first mortgage, Nos 962, 963, 967, 968, 1805, 999, 128, 216, 127, 998, 1806, 1592, 1610, 1593 1599, 1479, 188, 1807, 966, 1804, 972, 1803, 474, 209, 997, 906, 475, of one thousand dollars each, and others

The remaining nine thousand dollars were in greenbacks, of the denominations of one thousand dollars and five hundred dollars and were the property of the bank

An examination of the premises disclosed that the burglars had but little difficulty in gaining access to the bank The upper part of the house was not occupied, and the entrance was effected through a second-story window, after which, with the aid of burglar's tools, the doors were easily opened One of the tools, a jimmy, made with a screw-thread on one end, by which it could be converted into a brace, was found on the premises, where it had been left The robbery was done by expert burglars, and it is supposed the arrangements for its consummation had been perfected for some time, so easily and thoroughly was it accomplished Messrs Smith, Pierson & West took charge of the matter at once

A new and elegant light jagger-wagon, badly mashed, was found beyond the limekiln, close to Lawrence Zepp's entrance, near Westminster William S Brown found tied to his garden fence a very fine horse with a set of silver mounted harness on him The harness and blankets were new and of costly make The impression was at the time that the robbers had intended to meet an accomplice here The burglars left New Windsor in a hand-car and ran down to within a mile of Westminster, at Hollow Rock limestone-quarries Here they threw the car off the track, and walked to Westminster, where they took the early train for Baltimore A reward of ten thousand dollars was offered for the apprehension of the robbers The detective learned that several persons, whose description he had with him, had registered at the hotels in Baltimore at different times previous to the robbery, and no doubt remained on his mind that these were the robbers The police in prosecuting the search visited Philadelphia, and gave the detective force there a description of a man whose identity could be established more readily that that of the others, and asked the co-operation of the Philadelphia officers The latter recognized in him Mark Schunbourn, a notorious New York burglar, who was then in New York, and for whose apprehension the New Hampshire authorities were offering a reward of one thousand dollars, he being an escaped convict from that State An additional reward was also offered for hi[illegible] [illegible] Navigation

Company, from whose office at White Plains he had stolen fifty-six thousand dollars' worth of bonds The Baltimore detective officers in continuation of their investigation, went to New York, and applied for assistance to the chief of police, relating the circumstances and their suspicion of Schunbourn Nothing further was heard of the robbers or their booty for about two weeks, at which time a man appeared at the New Windsor Bank with ninety thousand dollars of the missing securities, which he paid over, with a deduction of twenty per cent (nineteen thousand dollars) for his trouble and expense It then leaked out that Schunbourn and an associate named McQuade had been arrested, and were confined in the New York Police Central Office for about a week, and it is said when they turned over the securities they were allowed to depart in peace

New Windsor College, situated in the heart of one of the healthiest and most picturesque sections of Maryland, was chartered in 1843 by the Presbyterians In 1852 it was reorganized by Andrew J Baker and others, and though still under the auspices of the Presbyterian Church is not a sectarian institution the pupils being allowed to worship in accordance with their religious convictions The buildings are commodious, and fitted with all the modern appliances for health and comfort The institution has preparatory and collegiate departments, to which both sexes are admitted, with such restrictions only as the nature of the case demands Rev J P Carter was the first president He was succeeded in 1852 by Andrew J Baker, who presided until 1877, when Rev A M Jelly, D D, the present excellent principal, took charge

The college suffered greatly during the war, and for some years afterwards from financial embarrassments, but through the able management of Dr Jelly it weathered the storm and entered upon a career of prosperity and usefulness The college is essentially two separate institutions with two boards of instructors, located on the same ground and under the same general management, and thus parents are enabled to educate both their sons and daughters without separating them The students enjoy the advantages of a large and well-selected library and the "William Andrews" cabinet of geology, containing twenty thousand specimens

There are three literary societies,—the Alexandrian, in the academical department, the Minnehaha, in the Ladies' Seminary, and the Union Society, composed of the other two, which meets once a week for mental culture The faculty is composed of graduates from Yale, Princeton, W[illegible] [illegible] University of Maryland, and Washington and Jefferson College as well as from the best female schools

During the college year Joseph T Smith, M D, of the University of Maryland, delivers twice a week lectures upon anatomy, physiology, and hygiene, and there is a course of lectures during the session on general topics The institution has also a printing department, under the management of W. R A Kohl, of Baltimore, where the college printing is done

The curators are

Rev John C Backus, D D, LL D, Baltimore, Rev Joseph T Smith, D D, Baltimore, Rev John Leyburn, D D Baltimore, Rev J A Lefevre, D D, Baltimore Rev H Fulton, Rev J P Carter, Baltimore, Rev J I Leftwitch, Rev J S Jones, D D, Rev W T Brantl D D, Rev D J Beale, Rev W H Gill, Rev G[illegible] E Jones, Rev Joseph F Jennison, W W Spence, [illegible] W S Carroll, Esq, W B Canfield, Esq, E M Cole, Esq, C Dodd McFarland Esq, John I Reed, Esq, P H Perkins, M D, all of Baltimore, Rev Byron Sunderland D D Washington, D C, Rev John R Paxton, D D, Washington, D C, Rev Wm Simonton, Emmittsburg Md, Robert L Annon, M D, Emmittsburg Md L H Richardson M D, Bel Air, Md Rev R H Williams Arlington, Md Hon Alexander H Stephens, Georgia Rev J A Rondthaler, Hagerstown, Md, Rev George M[illegible] son, Aberdeen, Md, Rev Joseph Nesbitt, Lock Haven, Pa, Rev John Ewing, Clinton, N J, S D Bull, Esq Lock Haven, Pa, J D Shilling, M D, Lonaconing, Md T W Simpson, M D, Liberty, Md, Hon Thos C [illegible] New York City, Rev Wm H Cooke, Havre de Grace Md, Rev Thos Nelson, Madonna, Md, Rev Wm T I Kieffer, Churchville, Md, Rev W H Hoitzell G[illegible] ville, Md

Trustees—Hon L P Slingluff, president, Rev A M Jelly D D, vice-president, New Windsor, D P Smelser J[illegible] Erhard, Joseph A Stouffer, Job H Hibberd Jeremiah [illegible] Levi N Snader, Solomon S Ecker Rev Wm Louis Woodruff secretary all of New Windsor

Faculty and Instructors—Rev A M Jelly, D D president Professor of Mental and Moral Philosophy, Rev W Louis Woodruff A M, vice president Professor of Physical Science and Greek, James B Green, A B, Prof of Latin and Mathematics, J I B Woodruff, Instructor Mathematics, Joseph T Smith, M D, Professor of Anatomy, Physiology, Hygiene, and Chemistry, W L Woodruff, Instructor in Book-keeping Banking, Commercial Forms, Type-writing, Charles [illegible] Professor of M[illegible] J B Greene, Instructor in German Language The president and vice president, Instructors in Rhetoric and [illegible]tion. The vice president, Custodian of the Library [illegible] C Bond, Attorney-at-Law, Resident Counselor, [illegible] Buffington, M D, Resident Physician

Board of Instructors—Ladies' Seminary—Rev A M [illegible] D D, president, Rev Wm Louis Woodruff, A M [illegible] president, Mrs A M Jelly, principal of the sem[illegible] Mrs J I B Woodruff, Kindergartner, associate pri[illegible] James B Greene A B, Professor of Mathematics [illegible] man, Miss Nannie W McVeigh Teacher of [illegible] Branches, French, and Music Joseph T Smith [illegible] [illegible] Physiology, Hygiene, and [illegible] [illegible] [illegible], Instructor

NEW WINDSOR COLLEGE,

NEW WINDSOR, CARROLL CO., MD.

Physical Development Calisthenics, and Gymnastics, Charles Gold Professor of Music Special instructors in normal and Kindergarten training type-writing, telegraphy phonography, book keeping and penmanship Special artists in drawing painting wax flowers and fancy work Miss Kate L Miller, matron, J F Lufington resident physician

Calvert College, in the town of New Windsor, for many years one of the finest classical schools in the State, was under the auspices of the Catholic Church, and was noted for the thoroughness of its academic departments Many of the leading men of the State and county were here educated, among whom were Hon Charles B Roberts, of Westminster, Dr Roberts Bartholow, of Jefferson Medical College, Philadelphia, and Dr Hanson M Drach

Sulphur Spring Lodge, No 130, I O O F, was instituted in August, 1878, by the following charter members Gustavus Barnes, Chas F Myers, John W Myers, P J Bennett, Samuel Harris, Lewis H Greenwood, David Nusbaum The first officers were N G, Gustavus Barnes, V G, C F Myers, Sec, J W Myers The lodge then numbered nine members The officers from January to July, 1879, were

Chas F Myers N G, J Myers, V G, C C Ingle, Sec, Lewis H Greenwood, Treas July 1879, to January, 1880 N G, J H Myers, V G, L H Greenwood, Sec, C C Ingle, Treas, L Greenwood January to July, 1880, N G, Lewis H Greenwood, V G, C C Ingle, Sec, D C Ingle, Treas, Jesse Crawner July, 1880, to January, 1881, N G, C C Ingle, V G, W B Bowersox, Sec, C C Repp, Treas, Eph Haines January to July, 1881, N G., W C Bowersox, V G, Jesse Crawner, Sec, J W Myers, Treas, H Geatty

The lodge now numbers thirty members in good standing, which is a showing of an increase of twenty-one members in three years They hold their meetings in the Town Hall, on Bath Street The present officers are N G, Jesse Crawner, V G, Chas T Repp, Sec, C C Ingle, Treas, D O Bankard

The Methodist Episcopal Church was incorporated Feb 17, 1844, by the General Assembly of Maryland The first trustees were Andrew Nicodemus, David Cassell, Jeremiah Bartholomew, Dr J L Warfield, H W Dell, Thomas Devilbiss, Cooper Devilbiss, Daniel Danner, and H A Davis The pastors for 1881 were Revs J A Fadden, Howard Downs

St Thomas' Catholic church was built by Rev Thomas O'Neill about 1861 He was the priest then in charge of the Carroll County mission From November, 1862, to 1879, Father John Gloyd had charge of this church, and since then Father John T [illegible]mey, of Taneytown, under whose ministrations the [illegible] churches have formed one mission since 1879

The Presbyterian cemetery surrounds the Presbyterian church, and the following, among others, are buried there

Joshua C Gist, born Sept 15, 1792, died March 27, 1878

Samuel J Atlee, died Aug 10, 1861, aged 69 years, 1 month, 15 days

Augusta A Atlee, born March 22, 1840, died Dec 11, 1862

Isaac Richardson Atlee, son of Col Samuel John Atlee, of the Revolutionary war of 1775, born 1767, died 1842, aged 82

Mary Clemson, wife of Isaac R Atlee, born 1769, died 1834 aged 61

Wm Richardson Atlee, attorney at law, brother of Isaac R. Atlee, and son in law of Maj -Gen Anthony Wayne, of the Revolutionary war, born 1764, died 1844, aged 80

James C Atlee, born Aug 11, 1798, died May 3, 1855, Sarah S, his wife, born May 8, 1809, died Nov 1, 1876

Ellhanan Stouffer, died Dec 27, 1877, aged 34

John Lambert, born Sept 10, 1836, died June 1 1869

Jacob Hull, born June 12, 1782, died May 1, 1853

Anna M, wife of Jacob Wikert, died March 29, 1871, aged 83 years, 10 months, 7 days

William Hull, born Dec 13, 1824, died Sept 20, 1853

Mary A H, wife of Wm Mitten, died Dec 14, 1874, aged 61.

B I Bartholow, died at Henderson, N C May 18, 1873, aged 39

Jeremiah Bartholow, died in Baltimore, July 19, 1854, aged 67, Pleasant, his wife died Jan 28, 1876, aged 80

Wesley Bartholow, M D, died in New Windsor July 31, 1848, aged 29

Wm H Clay, died April 4, 1870, aged 33

Sarah E Smith, died May 4, 1879, aged 18 years, 4 months, 12 days

Thomas Bond, born April 26 1768, died Sept 27, 1827

James B Bond born Oct 8, 1782, died Oct 20, 1827

Elijah Bond, died Sept 15 1853 aged 61 years, 3 months

Mary A born Jan 21, 1801 died Feb 25, 1843

George Lebard, died July 28, 1868 aged 85, Julia A, his wife, died April 16 1880, aged 83 years, 5 days

Robert Dods M D "born at Prova, county of Haddington, Scotland" died at New Windsor, July 27, 1833, aged 48

Margaret Dods died June 11 1862, aged 82

Sarah Dods, died June 1, 1849 aged 62

Anna wife of H W Geatty born Sept 28, 1828 died Sept 15, 1879

Jonas Ecker, died Aug 22, 1870, aged 57

Francis Ecker, died May 19 1880 aged 61

Jeremiah Currey born April 1, 1801, died June 11, 1835, Sarah S, his wife, born June 18, 1805, died Oct 18, 1874

Jacob Repp died Feb 21, 1871, aged 84 years, 6 months, 13 days.

Ann Mumford born Dec 15, 1798, died Dec 25, 1867

Jacob Wilt, died Oct 27, 1873 aged 82, Elizabeth, his wife, died Oct 2, 1866, aged 61 years, 1 month 2 days

Ferdinand Matthes, a native of Germany, died Jan 16, 1876, aged 70 years 4 months, 8 days

Jacob Nusbaum, died Dec 11, 1876, aged 69 years, 11 months 10 days, Mary, his wife, died April 2, 1865, aged 54 years, 7 months 25 days

Jacob Stem, born April 10, 1793, died Nov 23, 1855, Mary A, his wife, died Jan 29, 1864 aged 42 years, 3 months, 25 days

John W Durbin, born Nov 5, 1821 died Nov 30 1859

Nancy Durbin born 1789 died Feb 20, 1865

Abraham Albaugh born Aug 29 1780, died Feb 27, 1851, Mary C, his wife, died Oct 17, 1851, aged 57 years 1 month, 19 days

John Haines, died July 6, 1859, aged 76, Susannah, his wife, died May 2, 1857, aged 63

Jos Ingham, born Feb 22, 1818, died April 5, 1860, aged 42 years, 1 month, 11 days

John Haines born Sept 1 1806, died March 23, 1870, Mary, his wife, born Dec 23, 1800, died July 23, 1855

Honor Williams, born Nov 29, 1803, died Oct 2, 1879

Francis Smith died April 4, 1861, aged 32

Henry Townsend, of Co C, First U S Sharpshooters killed in battle at Kelly s Ford Va, Nov 7, 1863 aged 23

Levi Picking died Jan 14, 1862, aged 50

Anna M Condon, died Aug 14, 1870, aged 38 years, 6 months, 8 days

Elizabeth Baines died Nov 10, 1858, aged 39

Thos Wm Baines died May 5 1858, aged 19 years 7 days

Richard Smith, born Dec 13 1768, died Dec 22 1783

Mary Leppo, died May 21, 1880, aged 80 years, 4 months 11 days

Ludwick Baile, born Sept 28, 1803 aged 69

Catharine, wife of Peter Baile born May 5, 1820 died June 27, 1859

Christiana A Diehl died Jan 5, 1866, aged 40 years, 3 months, 4 days

Nimrod T Bennett, died Sept 17, 1870, aged 27 years, 8 months, 19 days

Levi T Bennett died Dec 9 1865, aged 56 years 1 month, 14 days

Edwin G Shipley, died Nov 5, 1865, aged 40 years, 8 months, 10 days

Ann Shipley, died Sept 3, 1867 aged 85 years, 9 months, 5 days

Dr Joseph Shuey an alumnus of Calvert College, and a graduate of the University of Maryland, died Jan 10, 1865, aged 25 years, 10 months, 16 days

Mary L wife of J L Shuey, died Jan 22, 1863, aged 32 years, 4 months 18 days

Hester Brawner, died April 8, 1844 aged 55

Wm Thoburn born Oct 11, 1800 died Dec 28 1870 Eliza McRea his wife died Jan 11, 1870, aged 60 years, 7 months

Joseph Pool, born Oct 4 1802 died Jan 23, 1850, Esther, his wife, died April 2, 1864 aged 61

Washington M Null, born Feb 20 1826, died Feb 21, 1876

The *New Windsor Herald* was established in 1881, and is issued semi-monthly F J Devilbiss is associated with Mr Koehl in its publication

My Maryland was established in August, 1881, and is the fifth newspaper now published in the county.

The New Windsor Library Company was incorporated by the Legislature Jan 13, 1841 The incorporators were Rev John P Carter, Dr J L Warfield, Isaac Slingluff, Samuel Ecker, Michael Smith, J H Hibberd, William A Norris, William Pole, Jr, Ephraim Bowersox, Jesse Lambert, Jonas Ecker, William Kelley, Theodore Hibberd, James C Atlee, G W Willson, Nathan Haines, of Joseph, William Ecker, Josiah Hibberd, Isaac Blizzard, Silas Hibberd, Jacob Nasbaum, Catherine M Brawner, Lewis Shull

Mount Vernon is a pretty little village situated a mile northeast of Sam's Creek, and is on the road to Stone Chapel It has a store and several small shops

Denning's is four and a half miles from New Windsor, near Sam's Creek It has a Dunker Church Joseph T Stern is the merchant and postmaster, and Dr L A Aldridge is the physician of the village and the surrounding country

St James' Chapel (M E Church South), a substantial and commodious structure, was erected in 1879, under the auspices of Rev W R Stringer, who was its pastor that year Since then it has been under the pastorate of Rev M G Balthis

Wakefield is on the Western Maryland Railroad forty miles from Baltimore, and near Little Pipe Creek It is in the midst of a fertile portion of the county known as "Wakefield Valley" "The Wakefield Valley Creamery," a stock company composed of farmers of that vicinity, is an important business enterprise, consuming six hundred gallons of milk daily in the manufacture of butter and cheese Joseph Hoover is postmaster, H S Roberts, merchant, and Joseph A Waesche, florist

McKinstry's Mills is two miles from Linwood twelve from Westminster, and is situated near Sam's Creek The postmaster, Samuel McKinstry, from whom the post office derives its name, is the oldest officer in official servitude in the State He received his appointment from Amos Kendall, postmaster-general under Andrew Jackson, and has held it continuously from that time to the present M C McKinstry and Jacob Zumbrum & Sons operate the mills John McKinstry keeps the store, and Benjamin Jones the blacksmith shop

Sam's Creek Post-Office is three and a half miles from New Windsor, near Sam's Creek, a small but historical stream, from which it derives its name Rev Charles A Reid is pastor or local preacher of the M E Church D E Stem is merchant and postmaster, John W and William Yingling and Jesse T Wilson are blacksmiths

Linwood is on the Western Maryland Railroad ten miles from Westminster, and forty-three from Baltimore John Q Senseney was the original proprietor of the land, and Reuben Haines laid off the town The merchants are Josiah Englar and sons Josiah Englar is railroad and express agent and postmaster J & J Englar operate the mills, and Dr L Roser is the resident physician

Pipe Creek Beneficial Society was incorporated by the Legislature on Feb 28, 1844 The trustees were Abraham Jones, Francis Jones, Dr Thomas Sim, Jesse Wright, Israel Norris, Robert Nelson, and E S Reese

"Door to Virtue" Lodge No 46 of Ancient Free and [illegible] meeting (under

dispensation from the Most Worshipful the Grand Master of Masons in Maryland) on Sunday, June 23, 1811, at Pipe Creek, Frederick (now Carroll) County The members present on this memorable occasion were Jesse Cloud, Worshipful Master, William P Farquhar, Senior Warden, William Slaymaker, Junior Warden, Enoch Taylor, Senior Deacon, Daniel Slaymaker, Junior Deacon, Moses Wright, Secretary and Treasurer, William McCollum, Tyler, and Moses B Farquhar, an Entered Apprentice The visiting brethren were William Knox, John Crapster, Israel Wright, and Isaac Lightner, of Philadelphos Lodge, No 39, Taneytown, and John Cook, of Ireland "An Entered Apprentice's Lodge was formed, a charge was read, and a prayer made to the Divinity for a blessing" Petitions were presented from Caleb Ogborn, Joel Pusey, and Thomas B Franklin, "praying to be initiated into the mysteries of Masonry," which were referred to a committee appointed "to inquire into their characters, and to report the result of their inquiries" These the first applicants for initiation in this lodge, received the degrees at subsequent meetings, and became, as the old record shows, active craftsmen "A Fellow Craft's Lodge was then opened in due form, and Moses B Farquhar was permitted to take the second degree of Masonry, and returned thanks accordingly" Where and when this brother was initiated there are no means of knowing, but his advancement to the degree of Fellow Craft was the first "work" performed in Door to Virtue Lodge While working under a dispensation there were held eleven meetings, the last being on the 31st of October, when Jesse Cloud and Moses Wright were appointed the first representatives of this lodge to the Grand Lodge of Maryland, and during this period seven brethren were "raised" to the degree of Master Mason, among whom was the late venerable Thomas Shepherd, of Union Bridge

On Sunday, November 10th, at a special communication, "the representatives appointed to the Grand Lodge, with the proceedings of this lodge, report that they have performed that service and obtained a warrant" The warrant was presented to the lodge and, by virtue of the authority therein conferred, the officers already mentioned as acting during the period of dispensation were duly installed and Door to Virtue took the rank and number (46) which it still holds among the Maryland lodges

The charter or warrant referred to in the proceedings of Nov 10, 1811, is the one under which the lodge is now working, and as a matter of interest to the membership an exact and literal copy of it is printed

"JOHN CRAWFORD, M D AND G M [L S]

"*To all whom it may concern*

"We the grand Lodge of the State of Maryland of the most ancient and honorable Fraternity of Free and Accepted Masons, according to the Old Institution, duly established, constituted and organized for the said State by resolutions and authority of a Grand Convention held at Talbot Court House on the seventeenth day of April in the year of Masonry Five thousand Seven Hundred and eighty seven, Do hereby constitute and appoint our trusty and well beloved brethren, Jesse Cloud, Master, William P Farquhar, Senior Warden and William Slaymaker Junior Warden of a new Lodge to be held in the neighborhood of Little Pipe Creek in Frederick County by the name of Door to Virtue Lodge, No 46, and we do hereby authorize and empower our said trusty and well beloved Brethren to hold their Lodge at the place hereby appointed and directed at such times as they shall think necessary and convenient, and according to the constitution of Masonry, and to admit and to make Free Masons according to the most Honorable Custom of the Royal Craft in all ages and nations through out the known world and not to contrariwise And we do further authorize and empower said Brethren and their successors to hear and determine all and singular matters and things relating to the Craft within the jurisdiction of the said Lodge No 46 And lastly we do hereby authorize and empower our said trusty and well-beloved Brethren Jesse Cloud, William P Farquhar and William Slaymaker to nominate, choose and install their successors to whom they shall deliver this Warrant, and invest them with all their powers and dignities as Free Masons and such successors shall in like manner install their successors, etc, such installations to be upon or near St John's the Evangelist day Provided always, that the Master, Wardens and Brethren and their successors pay due respect to the Right Worshipful Grand Master, otherwise this Warrant to be of no force or Virtue Given under our hands, and the seal of the Grand Lodge, this 4th day of November, A D 1811, A L 5811, at the City of Baltimore

"GEORGE [illegible], *G J W*

"JOHN WALES, *G S*"

The lodge continued to hold its meetings at Pipe Creek until the autumn of 1813, the last recorded communication at that place being on the 25th of September of that year The officers to whom was intrusted the management of the lodge during this period of its history were as follows From December, 1811, to June, 1812, Jesse Cloud, W M, William P Farquhar, S W, William Slaymaker, J W, Moses Wright, Sec, and Moses B Farquhar, Treas From June, 1812, to December, 1812, Jesse Cloud W M, William P Farquhar, S W, Moses B Farquhar, J W, Jacob R Thomas, Sec, and Joseph Wright, Treas From December, 1812, to June, 1813, William P Farquhar, W M, Enoch Taylor, S W, Daniel Slaymaker, J W, Jacob R Thomas, Sec, and Joseph Wright Treas

This lodge was located in the loft of a spring house on Beaver Dam stream, a mile or two from Sam's Creek, on the property then owned by Alexander Slaymaker, but now owned by Nathan Englar

The following is a list of persons aged seventy years and upward in 187[illegible] in New Windsor District:

Nancy Sanders (colored), 110, Katie Moore, 94 Daniel Coke, 85, D W Naill, 81, Moses Hayes (colored), 92, Mrs D W Naill, 81, Jacob Shuster, 86, Boss Hammond (colored), 83, Moses Hammond (colored), 81, Joshua Warfield, 79, Stephen Gorsuch, 79, Miss H Williams, 78, Thomas Horton, 73, David Engle, of P, 74 William Lewis (colored), 80, Jacob Loolingoill, 72, Mrs Peter Naill 90, John Riggler, 75, Abraham Nusbaum, 76, Lewis Kiefler, 79 Jacob Nusbaum, 73, Michael Zepp, 74 Mrs Mary Devilbiss, 70, Mrs Casper Devilbiss, 75, Daniel Wagner, 75, Peter Long, 82, T Beal Porter, 80 Daniel and [illegible] Bowyer (colored), 72 and 76, Masheck Baker, 75 Peggy Porter, 79 Mrs Emerata Franklin, 75, Mrs Philip Snader, 71 Philip Nausbaum, 72, Daniel Nausbaum, 70, Michael Riggler, 75, Mrs Nancy Chippey, 70, Nathan Franklin, 75 Lewis Green, 95, Perry Green, 70, Caleb Pike (colored), 70, Mrs Mary Zepp, 78, Mrs Sellman, 85, Mrs Elizabeth Gillis, 90, Mrs Elizabeth Doety, 88, Mrs Mary Naille, 87, Singleton W Harn, 77 Mrs Maria Harn, 77 Mrs Elizabeth Stocksdale, 75, Mrs Susannah Parnes, 73, Rev James Peirre, 70, Mrs Sarah Lindsay, 70, Mrs Rachel Buckingham, 76, Mrs Annie Devilbiss, 75, Mrs Sarah Miller, 78, Abraham Cole (colored), 79, Samuel Brown (colored), 80, Moses Haines (colored), 80 Total, 4643, average, 80 There are numerous others between 60 and 70

The following is the vote for local officers from 1857 to 1861, inclusive

1857 —Vote for Justices Charles Denning 115, J Smelzer 23, B W Bennett 225, F H Crabbs 221, Constables P M Baile 47, Wm Delphy 228, Road Supervisor Moses Haines 237

1859 —For Justices Edwin A Atlee 264, Israel Norris 298, Constable Wm Delphy 241, Road Supervisor Wm Leker 269

1861 —For Justices Edwin A Atlee 266, George P Albaugh 257, Constable Simon Bange 258, Road Supervisor Wm Leker 243

Below are given the public school trustees for 1881 and 1882, together with the teachers and number of pupils in each school

1 and 2 New Windsor (Nos 1 and 2) —Elkanan Engler, J W Engler, Jacob Frownfelter

3 Park Hall —Solomon Leker, John W Myers, Abraham Koop

4 Baile's —W W Naille, Henry Drummitt, Abram Albaugh

5 Spring Dale —Theodore Hibberd, John Geiger, Gustavus Barnes

6 Wakefield —David Baille, Jesse Eckard, Isaac C Forrest

7 Mount Vernon —Jesse Haines, Jesse Baile, Dr B G Franklin

The teachers for the term ending April 13, 1881, were

1, A H Zimmerman, 40 pupils, 2, Annie R Yingling 40 pupils 3, G T Yingling, 36 pupils 4, A P Albaugh, 57 pupils, 5 Laura I Hooker, 41 pupils, 6, M R Lord, 43 pupils, 7, F E Lovell, 44 pupils

The justices are Lewis Dielman, Wm T Smith, Ellsworth Lovell, Constable Simon Bange, Notary Public, Dr [illegible]

WESTMINSTER DISTRICT, No 7

The Seventh District of Carroll County, generally known as Westminster, is bounded on the north by Myers District, on the east by the districts of Manchester, Hampstead, and Woolery, on the south by Woolery and Franklin, and on the west by New Windsor and Uniontown Districts Westminster is geographically the central district of Carroll County, and it is also the wealthiest, most prominent, and contains the largest number of inhabitants, the census of 1880 giving it a population of 5573 It is intersected by numerous streams, which furnish water power for milling purposes, and the pure limpid element for farming and grazing lands, among which are the Patapsco Falls, Bear Branch, Morgan's Run, Pipe Creek, Cranberry Run, and Copp's Branch It is bountifully supplied with turnpikes and excellent public roads, and the Western Maryland Railroad passes almost directly through the centre, furnishing admirable facilities for communication with Baltimore City and other commercial points The people are intelligent, industrious, and enterprising and it was in this district that the movement for the creation of a new county crystallized, and was moulded into such a shape as made its accomplishment a possibility The commission appointed by the act of Assembly passed in 1837 to divide the county into election districts prescribed the following metes and bounds for the district of Westminster

"Beginning at the 26th mile-stone, on the Reisterstown turnpike, thence to Richard Gorsuch's house, thence to the Patapsco Falls, thence to the forks of Hampstead and Richards roads, thence with said road to the forks of Manchester and Hampstead, thence to the farm of Abraham Schaffer, leaving him in District No 7, thence with the lane between Rover and Guyman's farm, on Baughman's county road, to Bixler's tan yard, leaving said Bixler in District No 7, thence with the road to Andrew Angel's, leaving him in District No 7, thence with the aforesaid road, thence on said road between the [illegible] of Baughman's and Jacob Snyder, thence to Kinehart's mill dam, thence to Kinehart's county road, thence to Rinehart's mill, thence on said road to Littlestown turnpike to the [illegible] mile-stone, thence with the stone road to Jacob Stonesifer's thence to Messing's mill, thence to Hesson's house, leaving said Hesson in District No 2 thence with a straight line Smith's old tavern, on the Taneytown and Westminster turnpike, leaving said house in District No 7, thence to Morelock's tavern, leaving his house in District No 7, thence through Michael Morelock's, Sen, farm, leaving him in No 7, thence through Widow Haines' farm, leaving her house in District No 2, thence to Haines' mill, thence down Pipe Creek to [illegible] foot Branch, thence up said branch to where the Howard r[illegible] crosses said branch thence with said road to the stone [illegible] thence with the county road leading to the Washington r[illegible] to its point of intersection, thence with a straight line to the beginning"

Westminster was made the place for holding the p[illegible] [illegible] of Maryland

passed April 2, 1841, the substance of which is given in the history of Myers District, the boundary lines were altered to some extent

The first settlers in the district were principally Germans from Pennsylvania or the Palatinate As early as 1763 the following heads of families, all land-owners, are recorded among the numerous settlers Daniel Kober, John Greyder (Kreider), Peter Kraul, Valentine Fleigel, F T Dreyer, Valentine Bast, Henry Warman The Everlys Fleckingers, Sullivans, Rineharts, Reifsnyders, Jacob Heldenbridel, Henry Neff, Jacob Cassell, Peter Bender, David Shriver (then spelt Devault Schreiber), Daniel Zacharias, Benedict Schwob (now Swope), Valentine Maurrer, Jost Runkel, Andrew Ruse the Gists, Roops, Jacob Schaeffer, the Trizzells, Hoppes, Wentzs. Myerlys There were also the Winchesters, Van Bibbers Leigh Master, and Fishers

The old Winchester mansion was on the land now owned by Judge John E Smith, and the fine residence and seat of Col William A McKillip is a part of the original Winchester tracts This mansion was built about 1800, and is still one of the finest in the county In 1816, David Fisher bought it, with ten acres, of the Winchester heirs, and soon after it became the property of Jacob Fisher, and subsequently of John C Trizzell Col McKillip purchased it in 1880

The tract of land known as "Brown's Delight," situated on Cobb's Branch, was patented for 350 acres in 1743 to George Brown

"On Aug 16 1698, John Young, of Frankelbach, and single state, was, after being regularly proclaimed, joined in wedlock with Anna Margarethe, the legitimate daughter of Hans Theobald Hess, of Altensborn, in the Electorate Palatine, Oberant Lantern The above-named Margaretha was baptized in the church of Altensborn, Oct 22, 1674, her father being Theobald Hess and mother Margaretha, citizens and wedded persons of that place, and during her marriage with her before-mentioned husband (John Young) she had the following two children Hans Theobald Young, baptized Feb 21, 1699, sponsors, Hans Theobald Hess and Anna, the legitimate daughter of the late Sebastian Hess, citizens and inhabitants of said place, and Anna Magdalena, baptized Oct 25, 1702, sponsors, Nicholas Speck and his wife Catharine"

After the death of the father (John Young) of these two children, the mother, Anna Margaretha, entered into wedlock as follows "August, 1706, *Andrew Schreiber*, legitimate son of *Jost Schreiber*, citizens of Altensborn, was, after being regularly proclaimed joined in wedlock with Anna Margaretha, the legitimate [illegible] the late John Young [illegible] was a citizen of that place of the aforementioned Schreiber's birth" A protocol obtained from the said church certifies that Andrew Schreiber was born and baptized Sept 7, 1673, the sponsors at the baptism being Andrew Fisher and his wife

The protocol further shows that this Andrew Schreiber begat during his marriage with Anna Margaretha the following children.

1 Ludwig, born and baptized Oct 14, 1709, sponsors, Ludwig Vollweiler and his wife, Anna Christiana

2 Andrew (2), born and baptized Sept 6, 1712, sponsors, Andrew Schram and Anna Barbara, legitimate wife of Nicholas Speck, citizens of that place.

3 Anna Margaretha, born and baptized July 25, 1715, sponsors, Jacob Gruger, legitimate son of Jacob Gruger, and Anna Margaretha, in the single state, citizens of the place The following certificate shows the standing and character at home of Andrew Schreiber and his wife, Anna Margaretha

"ALTENSBORN, May 13th, 1721, being in the Electorate Palatine Oberant Lantern

[SEAL] John Mueller, preacher of the word of God in the Reformed Congregation, Altensborn Circle

That the bearer of (or person showing) this, Andw Shriver, citizen and inhabitant of this place, and his wife Anna Margaretha, whom he has with him, confess themselves to be conformable to the pure word of God, of the Reform Church, and have until now assiduously observed the outward duties of Christianity in attending our public Worship receiving the Holy Sacrament, and otherwise, as far as is known, have been irreproachable in their conduct, I attest And whereas the said man and wife and their children, after having borne adversities, and about to turn their backs upon their country (God knows where), I would therefore recommend them to a willing reception by the preachers and elders of the said Reformed Church, wherever they may show this Altensborn, obeiant lantern, in the Electorate palatine, 13th May, 1721 [SEAL]

"JOHN MUELLER, *Pastor*"

Andrew Schreiber (2),—now Shriver,—son of Andrew Schreiber and his wife, Anna Margaretha, who had been the widow of John Young (*i e* Jung), came to America in the fall of 1721 with his parents, and landed at Philadelphia, after which they moved into the country, to the neighborhood of Goshehappen, near "The Trap," on the Schuylkill, where his father soon died, having supported himself and family by labor After his death his widow married John Herger, who lived in the same place Andrew Shriver there learned the trade of tanner and shoemaker He freed himself from his apprenticeship about 1732, and worked for one year, in which he received £18 ($78) in hand In the spring of 1733 he married Ann Maria Keyser, and the following spring moved to Conewago, where, after paying for sundry articles [illegible] left ten shil-

lings Ann Maria Keyser was a daughter of Ulrick Keyser and Fornica, his wife, who were both natives of Pfaltz, Germany Fornica's father was a tanner, who lived five hours from Heidelberg (long 48° E, lat 49° 20′ N), in a small village named Reuche Her eldest brother lived in a village called Schulughten, three hours from her father, and two from Holbron Her father and mother came with her to America about the fall of 1721 They arrived at Philadelphia and moved into the country where Andrew Shriver lived, and her father soon dying she married Andrew Shriver Andrew Shriver's step-brother, David Young, journeyed with him to Conewago and helped to clear three acres of ground, which they planted in corn, after which Young then returned home During this clearing they lived under Young's wagon-cover, after which Andrew Shriver peeled elm bark and made a temporary hut to keep off the weather, and by fall prepared a cabin The wagon that brought him to this place passed through what is now known as "Wills' Bottom" and in the grass, which was as high as the wagon, left marks of its passage which were visible for several years There was no opportunity of obtaining supplies for the first year short of "Steamer Mill," adjoining Lancaster Shriver settled one hundred acres of land where he lived, but whether he squatted upon it or shortly after purchased is not known It, however, cost him one hundred pair of negro shoes, this being the price agreed upon with Mr Digges, the owner, of whom he soon after purchased more land, which was paid for in money At the time of his settlement in Conewago the nearest neighbor Andrew Shriver had was a family of the name of Forney, living where the town of Hanover now is For a long time the public road from the south came by Andrew Shriver's house, and at the time of his settlement Indians surrounded him in every direction About this period and for several years after, the Delaware and Catawba nations were at war, and each spring many warriors passed by after stopping at Andrew Shriver's water spring, a large flush limestone drinking-place, when they would display in triumph the scalps, hooped, painted, and suspended from a pole, which they had been able to obtain from the enemy They demanded free quarters, but were very sociable, and smoked the pipe of friendship freely without any attempt at wanton injury His brother Ludwig Shriver, David Young, Middlekauf the Wills, and others followed in a few years and established a settlement Ludwig Shriver's settlement must have been early, as he burned coal out of hickory-bark, and made the knife with which Andrew Shriver carried his [illegible] father, which was [illegible] in troughs cut out of large logs Andrew Shriver's wife occasionally helped her husband in the tan-yard and dressed deer skins by night Their son, David Shriver, wore deer skin dressed as clothing, shirts excepted, until fifteen years old Having but little cleared ground at this time, the stock was left to run at large in the woods, such as were wanted David, being the oldest child, had to collect every morning regularly, much to his discomfort, as the pea-vines and grass were nearly as high as himself, and covered with dew, they soon made his deer-skin dress so wet as to render it like unto his skin, adherent to his body Deer and other game were at this time so abundant and destructive to grain-fields that hunting was necessary for self protection

About 1685, John Ferree (or Verree) resided in the town of Lindau, not far from the Rhine, in the kingdom of France His family consisted of himself, his wife, and six children,—three sons and three daughters The names of the sons were Daniel, Philip and John, and of the daughters, Catharine, Mary, and Jane John Ferree, the father, was a silk weaver by trade, his religion Calvinistic, consequently he became one of the sufferers under the edict of Nantes The Ferrees had no other resource left but flight leaving behind them all their property except some trifling articles and some cash They fled into Germany, not far from Strasburg, where they resided two years On leaving France they were accompanied by a young man named Isaac Lefever, who stated to them that his family were nearly all or all put to death by the soldiers, but that he had escaped unhurt He continued as one of the family until they arrived in America and then married Catharine Ferree, one of the daughters, and from whom, as far as is known, all of the name of Lefever in this country have sprung During their residence in Germany, John Ferree, the father, died, and it is singular that Mary Ferree, the widow, after she came to America, was not pleased to be called by any other name than that of Mary Warrinbuer, her maiden name Whilst residing at Strasburg, hearing of a fine province called Pennsylvania in North America, and that the proprietor, William Penn, lived in London, she set out for that city, determined if she should receive sufficient encouragement from Penn, she would try to get to America On her arrival in London she employed a person to conduct her to Penn's residence, and on their way her conductor pointed out to her Penn's carriage which was just meeting them, and she being of a determined and persevering disposition, called to Penn, who stopped his carriage, and, being well acquainted with the [illegible] her feelings

Penn having learned the nature and object of her call, invited her into his carriage, as he was then on his way home. Penn told her he had an agent in Pennsylvania; that he would give her a recommendation to him, so that her business, he hoped, might be done to her satisfaction. They remained in London about six months, when a vessel sailed for North River (New York was then a small town), in which they took passage. On their arrival they moved up the river to a place called Esopus, where they remained about two years, and then moved to Philadelphia, and from thence to Piquea settlement, previous to which they had taken up three thousand acres of land. Before they sailed from London a variety of implements of husbandry were presented to them by Queen Anne, which they found to be of great use to them in cultivating and improving their lands. Philip, their oldest son, was now about twenty-one years of age, and evinced a desire to earn something for himself. Having formed acquaintance with several families of Esopus, he pushed for that place, where he lived for one year with a respectable farmer of the name of Abraham DuBois, and while in his service formed an attachment for Leah, the daughter of Mr. DuBois, whom at the expiration of the year he married and brought to his people in the Piquea settlement. There Philip and his wife commenced improving land on the north side of Piquea Creek, that had been previously taken up by his mother and family. Abraham DuBois, on May 17, 1717, took out a patent for one thousand acres in Lancaster County, Pa., which he subsequently gave to his daughter Leah. Their first labor was cutting grass in the woods for the purpose of making hay, no land having been cleared on that part allotted to them. They placed timbers in the ground, forked at the top, laid poles across them, and built their hay upon the [illegible], which served as a roof to their house, under which they lived for several months. During their stay in this rude shelter their son Abraham was born. They lived to raise eight children,—five sons and three daughters,—the names of the sons being Abraham, Isaac, Jacob, Philip, and Joel, and of the daughters, [illegible], married to William Buffington; Leah, to Peter [illegible]; and Elizabeth, to Isaac Ferree. Abraham was married about 1735 or 1736 to a woman by the name of Elizabeth Eltinge, from Esopus, whose parents were Low Dutch. He lived on a part of the [illegible] taken up by his grandmother (Mary Ferree, or [illegible]buer) and her children. Their children were [illegible], Israel, Rebecca, Rachel, Elizabeth, and [illegible]. Israel married a Miss Dickey, Cornelius [illegible] in Virginia, and Rebecca married David Shriver. Abraham Ferree died at an advanced age, and was buried in a place now called Carpenter's graveyard, about one mile north of where he was born. This burial-place, near Paradise, was vested in trustees for the use of the settlement by Mary Ferree (Warrinbuer), who died in 1716, and was with several of her family interred in this graveyard. After Abraham's death his widow married one Curgus, and moved up the Susquehanna.

Sarah, daughter of Abraham Dubois, married Roeloff Ellsting, or Eltinge, who was therefore a brother-in-law to Philip Ferree.

It appears from a certain deed of partition (on record in Frederick County, Md.) made by sundry persons as devisees of Isaac Eltinge, dated April 18, 1771, that Isaac Eltinge was a resident of Frederick (now Montgomery) County anterior to March 13, 1756, the date of his last will and testament, and that he died without leaving issue, in which case he disposed of his estate in fee-simple to his sister Elizabeth (Eltinge) Ferree and the children of his sister Zechamintye Thompson. The will ordered it to be divided with three several parts, one of them to descend to his first-named sister, and the other two-thirds to the children of the last-named sister, namely, to William Thompson, Cornelius Thompson, John T. Thompson, and Ann McDonald. These appear to be the exclusive objects of the testator's bounty, but it is nevertheless known that he had one other sister, who married Isaac Hite, of Virginia. Of these sisters there are many descendants residing in Virginia.

Elizabeth Ferree had two sons and four daughters, viz.: Israel, Cornelius, Rebecca, Rachel, Elizabeth, and Mary. Israel married a Miss Dickey, by whom he had one son, who died without descendants. Cornelius married twice, and had a numerous family, who with himself emigrated to the Western country. Rachel resided near Bath, in Virginia, and was married to David Muskimmins. Elizabeth married William Miller. Mary first married a Mr. Graff, and on his decease Griffith Willett; and Rebecca married David Shriver. The latter couple continued to reside on their estate on Little Pipe Creek, in Carroll County, until their decease. They had nine children:

1. Andrew, born Nov. 7, 1762, married Dec. 31, 1786, to Elizabeth Shultz, of Baltimore, and died Sept. 20, 1847.
2. Elizabeth, born Nov. 23, 1764, died Feb. 18, 1766.
3. Rachel, born Jan. 7, 1767, married Adam Forney, of Hanover, Pa., and died Dec. 6, 1841.
4. David, born April 14, 1769, married Feb. 28, 1803.
5. Abraham, born May 5, 1771, married Feb. 18, 1893, and was for many years a judge of Frederick County Circuit Court.
6. Mary (Anna Maria?), born Nov. 29, 1773, and married John Schley, of Frederick City.
7. [illegible] April 22, 1862, and

died Dec 22, 1856 His wife, Polly, born 1781, died March 1, 1859

8 Jacob, born Dec 13, 1779, died Oct 15, 1841

9 Susan (Susanna?), born Jan 6, 1782, and married Samuel Frey, of Baltimore, Aug 22, 1809

In regard to Jacob Eltinge, it is not known whether he was father, brother, or son of the Eltinge family at the time of its settlement in Frederick County, or who the persons of the family were, further than is given in the deed above referred to But it is evident that the settlement was at a very early date, and it is known to have adjoined the Potomac River at a time when much land along its banks was vacant, of which they secured considerable bodies by grants from the proprietary government And from the manner in which the surveys were made, it would seem to have been anticipated that the navigation of that river would become highly improved, and that it would be controlled by running the lines of the tracts across the river, many of the tracts being thus located It is known that the Eltinges migrated from New York, and that a number of the males fell victims to the bilious disease that prevailed with great malignity upon the banks of the Potomac There were two branches of the Eltinge family in New York, one located with the New Paltz patentees in Ulster County, about sixteen miles from Kingston, the other at Kingston County Of the latter, or Esopus family, some removed to New York City, some to Red Hook, in Dutchess County, and the others continued at Kingston

The following is the history of the New Paltz branch: Two brothers, Josiah the elder and Noah the younger, were the patentees in the New Paltz patent, and had one sister, Zacamintye, who married in the Bivier family Noah had no son, but one daughter, who married Dench Wynkoop and had two daughters The eldest, Guityou Gitty was married in the Colden family and left heirs The youngest, Cornelia, was married to Isaac Eltinge, of the Kingston family, and left heirs Zacamintye bore several sons and daughters Josiah was married to Magdalena Dubois, and had four sons—Abraham, Ralph, Solomon, and Cornelius—and one daughter,—Catrientye (Catharine) The latter married Jacobus Hardenbaugh, at Hurley, two miles from Kingston, and had one son—Jacobus—and three daughters,—Magdalena, Catrientye, and Ann,—all of whom married and had heirs Abraham was married in the Dubois family, and had five sons, viz Josiah, Noah, Philip, Henry, and Jacobus (who all had heirs), and two daughters, Jane and Magdalena, who left numerous progeny Ralph m[illegible] the [illegible] family and had five sons, viz Josiah, Solomon, Ez[illegible] John, and Ralph, and four daughters, viz M[illegible] lena, Sarah, Catherine, and Mary, who all left [illegible] scendants The descendants of Ralph and Abrah[illegible] lived about the New Paltz Solomon married in t[illegible] Vanderson family at Hurley, and had no heirs C[illegible] nelius married in the Elmendorf family at Hurley [illegible] had three sons, viz Wilhelms, Solomon, and C[illegible] nelius, and five daughters, viz Magdalena, J[illegible] Maria, Blandina, and Catharine, all of whom [illegible] Blandina married and left numerous offspring T[illegible] descendants of Cornelius and Catrientye are sett[illegible] at Hurley and Marbletown, near Kingston, except [illegible] Cornelius and Wilhelms (descended from Cornelius) who were ministers and lived in New Jersey,—Cor[illegible] lius in Sussex County, and Wilhelms at a point f[illegible] miles from New York City called Patterson Land[illegible] whose Indian name was Uncloquachinwick W[illegible] helms had three children,—Cornelius Housman, M[illegible] Blandina, and Jane Van Winkle The eldest w[illegible] married to Cornelius Van Winkle and had a [illegible] Wilhelms Eltinge The New Paltz branch [illegible] probably more nearly related to the branch that set[illegible] on the Potomac in Frederick County, Md, and Virginia Abraham, the eldest son of Josiah Eltin[illegible] had land in an unsustained claim upon some of tracts upon the Potomac as legal heir, and hence [illegible] inference is that Josiah, Noah, and Zacamintye w[illegible] brothers and sister, either to Isaac Eltinge, resi[illegible] of Frederick County (now Montgomery) and [illegible] sisters, Elizabeth Ferris, Zacamintye Thompson, [illegible] Mrs John Hite, of Virginia, or they, Noah, et[illegible] were brothers and sister to Abraham Eltinge, [illegible] father of Isaac and his sister

Andrew Shriver, who came to America in 17[illegible] when a boy nine years of age, with his parents [illegible] drew and Anna Margaretha Shriver died Aug [illegible] 1797, and was the grandson of Jost Shriver

David Shriver, son of Andrew and Ann M[illegible] (Keyser) Shriver, was born in York County, Pa[illegible] Conewago, south of Hanover His parents had [illegible] but a few years from Germany, and were rec[illegible] married when they settled at that place in the w[illegible] surrounded by Indians On account of his fat[illegible] settlement on the frontier, remote from the centre[illegible] civilization, David Shriver, the first-born, grew with scarcely any education, the opportunity [illegible] means being both wanting The time of his mi[illegible] was employed in aiding his father in his busin[illegible] tanning and cultivating the soil When h[illegible] twenty one years of age he attracted the attenti[illegible] Andrew Steiger, an enterprising business ma[illegible] [illegible] ployed hi[illegible]

store-keeper in a country store, located not far from David's father. Here the want of education was immediately felt, and he so applied himself that in a short time he acquired a pretty good knowledge of figures. He also learned to write a fair hand, and otherwise improved himself in knowledge and address. At this time Lancaster, Pa., had become considerable of a town, and it was a custom there (continued to this day) to hold semi-annual fairs, which drew together vast numbers of people. At one of these fairs David Shriver first saw Rebecca Ferree, who had been sent to Lancaster to acquire a knowledge of ornamental needlework. He undertook to accompany her home, and was received with becoming respect by her father, but with much displeasure and indignity by her mother, who had imbibed high notions in consequence of the opulence and distinction enjoyed by her family in New York. Standing well, however, with the daughter and father, he persevered and succeeded in his suit. About 1759 or 1760, and previous to his marriage, which was in 1761, he had settled upon a tract of land provided for him at Little Pipe Creek, in Frederick County, Md. (now in Westminster District, Carroll County). The place of his location is the old "Shriver Homestead," some two miles southwest of Westminster, on Little Pipe Creek, where Copp's Branch joins it, now occupied by Mrs. Augustus Shriver, widow of a grandson of David. Here David had erected buildings and cleared land, and to this place he brought his wife. He then built a mill, which was of great importance to himself and neighbors at that early period when the settlement was in its infancy. Having experienced the want of education, he early sought to have his children taught, and for this purpose sent his eldest son abroad for some time, there being no school within reach of his home. His efforts were unceasing to promote education in the neighborhood, and he so far succeeded as to obtain for all his children a good English education. The community was much indebted to him for his exertions in this respect, and many persons afterwards enjoyed the receipt of useful knowledge which but for him they would not have acquired. Possessing an inquiring and discriminating mind, he added rapidly to his stock of information. As a self-taught mathematician, he made considerable advances, and was instructor to all his [illegible] in the art of surveying, the compass and other instruments used being of his own manufacture. His mechanical talents were no less remarkable. He was carpenter, joiner, cooper, blacksmith, silversmith, [illegible]maker, wheelwright; in short, he made everything that was wanting on the place, as well as the tools which occasion called for. He was, moreover, the umpire of the neighborhood in the settlement of controversies. Having a great aversion to lawsuits and litigation, he did much to preserve peace and harmony. His house was the resort of much company and the place where travelers regularly sought shelter and repose, and they were always received with kindness and hospitality.

The disputes between the colonies and the mother-country early attracted his attention, and he became an active and devoted Whig. So warm was he in the support of the rights of his country that his friends were alarmed for his safety, and his pastor emphatically warned him to beware, as the powers placed over him were of God, and that he would be hung for treason to Great Britain and his family made beggars. He treated the admonition with marked contempt, and persevered in taking an active part on the Committees of Vigilance and Public Safety and rousing his countrymen to vindicate their rights. He was in consequence elected a member of the Convention of 1776 to frame a constitution for the State of Maryland, and was afterwards continued, with the exception of a year or two, a member of one or the other branches of the Legislature for about thirty years, until the infirmities of age admonished him of the propriety of retirement. At the time of his death he had an estate valued at seventy thousand dollars. When he was married his wife's parents gave her a negro girl, from whom sprang a numerous progeny, more than forty in number, of whom about thirty remained in his possession at the time of his death, and whom he liberated by will. In the same instrument he divided his estate equitably among his children and provided for the inclosure of a family burial-ground, where his remains, those of his wife, and some of his children repose. He had two brothers and four sisters,—the former were Andrew and Jacob, of whom Andrew continued to reside on the home plantation and raised a large family. Jacob removed to Littlestown, Pa., and had one son, who died young, and his father passed away shortly afterwards. The four sisters married Henry and George Koontz, John Kitzmiller, and Jacob Will. They all lived to an old age within a few miles of their father and reared large families, except the wife of George Koontz, who had but three or four children and died in early life. David Shriver died Jan. 29 (or 30), 1826, aged ninety years and nine months. He was the oldest of his brothers and sisters, and survived them all.

His wife, Rebecca (Ferree) Shriver, was a noble Christian woman, of rare domestic qualities and withal finely educated for the [illegible] days in which

she grew up to womanhood. She was the oldest of her family. The home plantation being large enough for two places was divided between her brothers, Cornelius and Israel. The latter with his family having died, the former afterwards sold the places and went West. Rebecca Shriver died Nov. 24, 1812, aged seventy years, ten months, and three days.

Mordecai Gist, so distinguished in the Revolutionary struggle, was a son of Capt. Thomas Gist and Susan Cockey, and was born in Baltimore Town, Feb. 22, 1742. He was educated at St. Paul's Parish School, Baltimore City, and at the breaking out of the Revolution was a merchant doing business on Gay Street. The Gists were early emigrants to Maryland, and took an active part in the affairs of the province. Christopher Gist was of English descent, and died in Baltimore County in 1691. His wife was Edith Cromwell, who died in 1694. They had one child, Richard, who was surveyor of the Western Shore, and was one of the commissioners in 1729 for laying off Baltimore Town, and was presiding magistrate in 1736. In 1705 he married Zipporah Murray. Christopher Gist, one of his sons, because of his knowledge of the country on the Ohio and his skill in dealing with the Indians, was chosen to accompany Washington on his mission in 1753, and it was from his journal that all subsequent historians derive their account of that expedition. Christopher Gist, the son of Richard, married Sarah Howard, the second daughter of Joshua and Joanna O'Carroll Howard, and had four children,—Nancy, who died unmarried, and Thomas, Nathaniel, and Richard. Christopher, with his sons Nathaniel and Richard, was with Braddock on the fatal field of Monongahela, and for his services received a grant of twelve thousand acres of land from the King of England. It is said that Thomas Gist was taken prisoner at Braddock's defeat, and lived sixteen years with the Indians in Canada. Richard married and settled in South Carolina, and was killed at the battle of King's Mountain. He has descendants yet living in that State. Thomas, after his release from captivity, lived with his father on the grants in Kentucky, and became a man of note, presiding in the courts till his death, about 1786. Gen. Nathaniel Gist married Judith Carey Bell, of Buckingham Coun[illegible] Va., a [illegible]

GEN. MORDECAI GIST

Carey, the mover of the Bill of Rights in the Virginia House of Burgesses. Nathaniel was a colonel in the Virginia Line during the Revolutionary war, and died early in the present century at an old age. He left two sons,—Henry Carey and Thomas Cecil Gist. His eldest daughter, Sarah Howard, married the Hon. Jesse Bledsoe, a United States senator from Kentucky, and a distinguished jurist, whose grandson, B. Gratz Brown, was the Democratic candidate for Vice-President in 1872. The second daughter of Gen. Nathaniel Gist, Anne (Nancy), married Col. Nathaniel Hart, a brother of Mrs. Henry Clay. The third daughter married Dr. Boswell, of Lexington, Ky. The fourth daughter, Eliza Violetta Howard Gist, married Hon. Francis P. Blair, and they were the parents of Hon. Montgomery Blair, ex-Postmaster-General, and Gen. Francis P. Blair, Jr. The fifth daughter married Benjamin Gratz, of Lexington, Ky. Mordecai Gist was a member of the Baltimore Town non-importation committee in 1774, and in December of the same year was captain of the first company raised in Maryland. He was three times married. His first wife was a Miss Carman, of Baltimore County, who died shortly after marriage. His second was Miss Sterrett, of Baltimore, who died in giving birth to a son. His third was Mrs. Cattell, of South Carolina. She also bore him a son. One of the boys was named "Independent," the other "States." Gen. Mordecai Gist died at Charleston, S. C., Aug. 2, 1792.

On Jan. 1, 1776, the Maryland Convention appointed Mordecai Gist second major of Col. Smallwood's First Maryland Battalion. In the battle on Long Island, in August, 1776, the Maryland regiment, not numbering more than four hundred and fifty, was commanded by Maj. Gist, as Col. Smallwood and Lieut.-Col. Ware were in New York attending the court-martial of Lieut.-Col. Zedwitz. On Washington's retreat through New Jersey Maj. Gist's Marylanders were reduced to one hundred and ninety effective men, who with Lord Stirling's and Gen. Adam Stephen's brigades covered the retreat. Maj. Gist's (formerly Smallwood's) regiment, on Dec. 1, 1776, re-enlisted for three years. In February, 1777, Gen. Smallwood sent Col. Mordecai Gist with a detachment against the Somerset and Worcester County Tories and insurgents, who were put to flight, many captured, and the others forced into obedience by stern measures, and the disaffection quieted by overawing and quelling the insurgents. The battle of Brandywine was fought Sept. 11, 1777, when Col. Gist was at home attending his sick wife, but on learning of its disastrous termination, by a special [illegible] ith reinforc[illegible]

ments collected at home In May, 1779, when Maryland was threatened with British invasion, on the application of its Governor, Col Gist was ordered to that State, and assumed command of its defenses Gen DeKalb, who died on the third day after he was wounded, near Camden, S C (Aug 16, 1780), in his last moments dictated letters to Gens Gist and Smallwood expressive of his affection for them and their men, who had so nobly stood by him in that deadly battle In this battle DeKalb led a bayonet charge with Col Gist's Second Maryland Brigade, drove the division under Rawdon, took fifty prisoners but fell exhausted after receiving eleven wounds Congress voted thanks to Gens Gist and Smallwood and their men In June, 1781, Gen Gist joined Lafayette's army on the march to Yorktown with the Maryland levies On Nov 21, 1783, at a meeting of the officers of the Maryland Line to form a State Society of the Cincinnati, Gen Otho H Williams presided, and Lieut Col Eccleston was secretary Maj Gen Wm Smallwood was made permanent president, Brig-Gen Mordecai Gist, vice-president, Col Nathaniel Ramsey, treasurer, and Brig Gen Otho H Williams, secretary

Joshua Gist, one of the early settlers in Carroll County was a brother of Gen Mordecai Gist, and was born in Baltimore Town, Oct 16, 1743 His parents were Capt Thomas and Susan (Cockey) Gist His grandfather was Richard Gist, son of Christopher, the emigrant During the administration of John Adams, near the close of the last century (1794), an excise duty was laid on stills This created what was then known as the "Whisky Insurrection" by those opposed to the tax The rebellion became so formidable, particularly in Western Pennsylvania, that Washington, at the request of President Adams, took the field in person as commander of the forces raised to suppress it The excitement extended to what is now Carroll County, and the "Whisky Boys" marched in a band into Westminster and set up a liberty-pole The people of the town became alarmed and sent out for Col Joshua Gist, who then commanded a regiment of the militia The colonel, who was known to be a brave man, mounted his horse, rode into town, drew his sword, ordered the pole to be cut down, and placing his foot on it it was cut to pieces, when the Boys left He died Nov 17, 1839, aged ninety-one years, one month, and one day*

The Gist family graveyard in Carroll County contains the graves of the following members of the family

Harriet Dorsey, wife of Nicholas Dorsey, and daughter of Col Joshua Gist died June 25, 1804, aged 74 years and 18 days

Sarah (Harvey) Gist wife of Col Joshua Gist, died June 6, 1827, aged 72 years, 7 months and 1 days

Sarah (Gist) wife of Lewis A Beatty, died March 30th, in her 27th year

Rachel, wife of Independent Gist died May 2, 1830 aged 50 years, 1 month and 15 days

Independent son of Gen Mordecai Gist died Sept 16 1821

Richard Gist died Aug 6, 1811 aged 23 years

Mary G, wife of States Langan Gist and daughter of States Gist of Charleston S C, died Feb 8 1817 aged 30 years

Bradford Porcher Gist born May 28 1842, died Jan 2, 1865 He was a soldier of the Union and died from disease contracted while a prisoner

Richard Milton infant son of Mordecai and Elizabeth (Orndorff) Gist died Sept 13 1871

Maggie, only child of George W and Mary Owings died Sept 21, 1862 aged 3 years, 1 month and 8 days

Elizabeth (Gist) wife of Joseph Woods, born June 8 1844 died Dec , 1873, and her daughter Mary died Oct 15 1877, aged 3 years, 4 months, and 26 days

Rachel, infant daughter of Mordecai and Elizabeth (Orndorff) Gist died 1873

The Gists were of English descent, and took an active part in the affairs of the province Christopher Gist married Edith Cromwell, sister of Richard Cromwell, a son or brother of Oliver Cromwell Christopher Gist died in Baltimore County in 1691, and his wife, Edith, in 1694 Their only child, Richard Gist, married Zipporah Murray, by whom he had three sons—Christopher, Nathaniel, and Thomas—and four daughters,—Edith, Ruth, Sarah, and Jemima Christopher married Sarah Howard, Edith was married to Abraham Vaughan, Ruth to William Lewis, Sarah to John Kennedy, and Jemima to Mr Seabrook Thomas Gist married, July 2, 1735 Miss Susannah Cockey, daughter of John and Elizabeth Cockey, by whom the following children were born

1, Elizabeth born Dec 24, 1736 2 John Nov 22 1738, 3, Thomas March 30 1741, 4, Gen Mordecai Gist Feb 22, 1742, 5 Richard, Nov 1, 1745 6, Joshua, Oct 16, 1746, 7, Rachel, Sept 17, 1750, and, 8 David, April 29, 1753

Thomas Gist died May 24, 1787, aged seventy-four years and nine months, and his children died as follows Elizabeth, March 6, 1826, John, July 16, 1800, Thomas, Nov 22, 1813, Gen Mordecai Gist, Sept 12, 1792, Richard, Nov 1746 (an infant), Rachel, Sept 8, 1825, Joshua, Nov 17, 1839, and David, Aug 3, 1820 Of these, as we have stated, Gen Mordecai Gist first married a Mrs Carman, of Baltimore County, who died shortly after marriage, his second wife was Miss Sterrett, of Baltimore, who died Jan 8, 1779 in giving birth to a son (Independent), and his third wife was Mrs Cattell, of South Carolina, who bore him a son named States These were his only children

* Joshua Gist died Nov 17, 1839, aged 91 years, 1 month, and 1 day

Col Joshua Gist, son of Thomas and Susannah (Cockey) Gist, and brother of Gen Mordecai Gist, married, March 21, 1772, Sarah Harvey, who was born Nov 2, 1755, and died June 2, 1827 Their children were

1 Anna, born Feb 24, 1774, died Aug 26 1790
2 James Harvey, born Dec 29 1775, died Dec 7, 1823
3 Susannah, born March 21, 1778, married Joshua Jones, and died Oct 8, 1817
4 Rachel, born March 17, 1780, died May 2, 1830
5 Mordecai born June 20, 1782
6 Polly Julia, born June 3, 1784
7 Thomas born April 1, 1786
8 Sarah, born June 17, 1788, married Lewis A Beatty, and died March 31, 1815
9 Harriet born June 7, 1790, married Nicholas Darsey, and died June 25, 1864
10 Joshua Cockey, born Sept 15, 1792, died March 27, 1878
11 George Washington, born Dec 18, 1795, died Nov 20, 1851
12 Federal Ann Bonaparte, born Aug 14 1791 and is the only one surviving of the above twelve children

Independent Gist, eldest son of Gen Mordecai Gist, married, Jan 8, 1807, Rachel Gist, daughter of Col Joshua Gist, his own cousin He died Sept 16, 1821, and his wife May 2, 1830 Their children were

1 Mary Sterrett born Sept 1 1808, and living
2 Joshua Thomas born Sept 15, 1810, and living
3 States Lingan born July 31, 1812, died Nov 9, 1879.
4 Mordecai, born Oct 16, 1814 and living
5 Independent born Aug 15, 1816, died June 29, 1839
6 George Washington, born July 10, 1819, fought in the Union army under Gen Sheridan in late war and still living
7 Richard, born Sept 1, 1821, died Aug 6, 1844

Of the above children, States Lingan married Mary G Gist, June 13, 1836, who died Feb 8, 1847 Their children were

1 Mary, born April 7, 1837
2 Mordecai Joseph born May 29 1838
3 Independent, born June 10, 1840
4 Bradford Porcher, born May 28, 1842, died Jan 2, 1860
5 Elizabeth Sarah, born June 8, 1844, married Joseph Woods, and died Dec 3, 1873
6 Richard Joshua, born Sept 14, 1845, died July 21 1864

States Gist, second and youngest son of Gen Mordecai Gist, married Sarah Branford Porcher and lived in Charleston, S C

The subject of this sketch, Mordecai Gist, son of Independent Gist, and grandson of Gen Mordecai Gist was born Oct 16, 1814, in Frederick County, four miles from Taneytown After his father's death, when but two years of age, his mother removed to Western Run, in Carroll County, and when he was about sixteen years old his mother moved to the farm on which he now resides, then the property of her father, Col Joshua Cockey Col Cockey before the Revolution, about 1765, had removed from Baltimore Town and entered or purchased two tracts of land containing about four hundred acres He built a house which burned down in 1795, when he erected

MORDECAI GIST

house which burned down in 1795, when he erected part of the present mansion He subsequently made an addition to it, as did afterwards Mordecai Gist, the present owner Part of these lands belonged to the tract known as "Fell's Dale," patented to Edward Fell in 1712 Mordecai Gist was educated in the old brick school-house still standing in Westminster in the cemetery near the 'Old Union Meeting House Among his teachers were Mr White and Charles W Webster His place now consists of one hundred and eighty acres of land lying a mile and a half south of Westminster, on which he has resided for the past sixteen years

He was married Nov 7, 1848, to Elizabeth, daughter of Joseph and Mary (Byers) Orndorff by whom he has had the following children

Joseph Independent, born Nov 18, 1850, and married, M[illegible] 5, 1878, to Debbie F Nelson
Rachel, born Dec 28, 1852, died Jan 2 1853
Harriet Ann, born April 27, 1854, and married to Silas B Gaitskill Oct 4, 1876
Joshua, born Nov 22, 1856, and married to Susie E [illegible] Nov 7 1878
William Mordecai born Aug 10 18[illegible]
Mary Alverda, born March, 186[illegible]
George Washington, born Sept 27, 1861
Robert born July 21 1868
[illegible] Sept 13, 1871

Mr Gist is one of the best practical farmers in the county, and pays special attention to dairying, selling his milk, save in the winter, when it is made into butter He belongs to the Methodist Episcopal Church, and for thirty-five years has been a member of Carroll Division, No 42, Sons of Temperance During the late civil war he was a strong supporter of the Union In his spacious parlor hang elegant oil portraits of his paternal and maternal grandfathers, Gen Mordecai Gist and Col Joshua Gist, with their wives While Gen Gist, of the Maryland line was fighting the British in many battles, his brother, Col Joshua Gist, was effectively sustaining the Continental cause at home, holding the Tories in check by his bold measures, which made him the terror of the disaffected and the idol of the Revolutionary Whigs

The Van Bibbers were an ancient Holland family, its progenitor in this country being Capt Isaac Van Bibber, a native of Amsterdam, who came to America in command of a vessel belonging to Lord Baltimore's fleet and settled in Cecil County, Md From him descended Isaac Van Bibber, a native of Bohemia Manor in that county who very early located in what is now Baltimore County, and was a famous sea captain and voyageur, owning the ship he commanded He married a Chew, of Philadelphia His son, Washington Van Bibber, born in Baltimore, was one of the defenders of that city in 1814 He became an extensive farmer in Westminster District, and owned part of the old Leigh Master estate, Avondale, where the Master furnace was established in 1762 to 1765 The Van Bibbers were members of the Protestant Episcopal Church, and "Ascension church" in Westminster was largely built by their contributions and active support His son, Dr Washington Chew Van Bibber, was born near Avondale, July 24, 1824, and married, in 1848, Josephine, youngest daughter of Dr Peter Chatard, an eminent physician of Baltimore His success and ability in the medical profession of Baltimore, where over a third of a century he has been in practice, places him alongside of the most honored of its members

St Benjamin's (Kreiger's) Union Lutheran and Reformed Church, the joint place of worship of the Lutheran and Reformed congregations, was organized in 1763 On April 14, 1763, the members of each congregation entered into articles of agreement to build a church Those signing it on the part of the Reformed denomination were Jost Runkel, Valentine Maurer, Benedict Schwob, Daniel Zacharias (the four elders), David Shriver (there signed as *Devault Schreiber*), Peter Bender, Jacob Cassel, Henry Neff, Jacob Helden[illegible] Henry Warman, Valentine B[illegible] F T Dieyer, Valentine Fleigel, Peter Kraul, John Greyder (afterwards corrupted into *Kreider*), Daniel Kober

In 1763 was erected the first church, a story and a half log structure, which stood until 1807, when the present building, a two story brick structure of ancient architecture, was erected on the same site It was built on a tract of land called "Brown's Delight" The first four baptisms were in 1763, by Rev William Otterbein, a German Reformed missionary of Baltimore, who for six years previous had been traveling through Frederick County (of which this section was then a part) preaching and holding religious services The four children baptized were those of John Greyder (Kreider) viz John Peter (born May 25, 1754), John, Jacob and Elizabeth On May 8, 1766, this pioneer church had thirty-six communicants, nearly all heads of families It is located on the Gettysburg turnpike, on the left side going from Westminster, and a mile and a half from that town Its first Reformed preacher was the Rev Jacob Lischey, and Rev Jacob Wiestling was pastor before 1813. Since 1819 its pastors have been

1819–41, Jacob Geiger, 1842–44, William Philips, 1844——, John G Wolf, William I Cellflower, W Wissler, John W Hoffmeier, 1868–76, William C Cremer, 1876–82, J G Noss

Adjoining the church is perhaps the oldest burying-ground in the county, which is still in an excellent state of preservation It was laid out in 1763, in which year the first interments were made in its grounds The inscriptions on the earliest stones are in German, and for about the first thirty years are illegible, owing to the corrosion of time The dates of the births and deaths of many here buried are given

John Schweigart born in Berks County, Pa, Dec 2, 1785, died Jan 30, 1853

Christian Schweigart, born in March, 1762, died June 1846, and his wife, Dorothy, born Dec 6, 1763, died Dec 10 1838

Jacob Marker, born March 11, 1786, died Dec 8, 1879, and his wife, Catharine, born Dec 26, 1797 died Feb 5, 1859

Mary Myerly, born June 1 1792, died Jan 8, 1817

Jacob Grammer, died March 13 1815, aged 66

Johannes Schnauffer born Nov 13, 1752, died Sept 3, 1776, and his wife, Christina, born in 1756, died Oct 15, 1818

John Diffenbough, born Nov 24, 1766, died April 16, 1814, and his wife, Eve Catharine, born Sept 22, 1766, died April 26, 1842

Catharine Klein, born Dec 1, 1760, died May 19, 1819

Eurnice Farmwalt, born March 9, 1713, died July 8, 1807

Susanna, wife of George Z[illegible], and daughter of Conrad Sherman born April 2, 1786 died Feb 5, 1852

William H Editor (editor of *American Sentinel* many years), died Jan 11, 1862, aged 39

Jacob Schaeffer, died Feb. 2, 1851, aged 70, and Susan, his wife, born March 24 1781, died March 25, 1852

John Schaeffer, born June 11, 1755, died March 11, 1828, and his wife [illegible] 12, 1831

Mary Magdalene, wife of Abraham Kurtz, born Nov 5, 1783, died Dec 8, 1827

Jacob Utz, Sr, died Nov 5 1826, aged 61

Jacob Utz, Jr died Aug 1, 1826 aged 27

Jacob Henry born March 15, 1791, died May 22, 1861

George Henry, born Feb 2[illegible], 1791, died Sept 30, 1860, and his wife, Margaret, born Jan 20, 1781, died Feb 5, 1858

George Crowl, born Oct 26, 1795, died Feb 4, 1865, and his wife, Rebecca, born Jan 1, 1798 died July 29, 1862

Hannah, wife of Michael Sullivan, born July 23, 1790, died Nov 5 1840

Peter Lantz, died Nov 22, 1840, aged 70

Anna Maria Keller, wife of Jacob Keller, died Aug 1, 1841, aged 79

Elizabeth Krise, born July 20, 1781, died Oct 24, 1850

Mic[illegible]ah Strausb[illegible]y, died July 14, 1858, aged 85 and his wife, Mary M Nov 18, 1861, aged 78

James Beggs, born in County Antrim, and Parish Carulla, Ireland, 1752, died Feb 12, 1829

John Beggs (native of same place), died Feb 28, 1875, aged 71

Andrew Reese, died April 11 1794, aged 61, and his wife, Barbara, Sept 15 1791, aged 71

Frederick Boyers, born Oct 10, 1781, died Feb 26, 1815

Barbara Angel, daughter of John Schaeffer, born March 10 1786 (married to Frederick Boyers, 1807, by whom she had three sons and two daughters, married to Andrew Angel, 1816, by whom she had six children) died Jan 18, 1832

Jacob Flickinger, born July 25, 1712, died June 17, 1807, and his wife, B[illegible]ra, born July 25, 1745, died aged 73 years

John Reese, born Jan 26 1793, died March 5, 1858, and his wife Susan, died Nov 30, 1875, aged 67

Cornelius Sullivan, died 1816, aged 67, and his wife, Catherine, born 1753, died 1824

David Sullivan, born June 1, 1788, died aged 25

Margaret E[illegible]el, born 174[illegible], died March 3, 1811

Daniel Zacharias, born April 6, 1777, died April 24, 1815

George Peter Rinehart, born Oct 17, 1787, died May 1, 1845

Mary Kuhn, died July 18 1811

George Daniel Zacharias, died Aug 24, 1807, aged 61

Jacob Schaeffer, born Feb 6, 1723, died February, 1800

Wesleyan Methodist Episcopal Church (colored) is one and a half miles from Westminster, due west, and its pastor in 1881 was Rev. R J Williams In the cemetery adjoining are buried

Jesse Cromwell, died Feb 28, 1874, aged 74

Ann Hays, died July 2, 1880, aged 78

D Woodward, aged 85

Rebecca Cross, born Sept 5, 1818, died Feb 15, 1858

Maria Buchanan, died Dec 31, 1869, aged 75

Dinah Smith, aged 78

The following graves, among others, are found in the German Baptist cemetery situated in Westminster District, between Westminster and Frizzelberg

Polly Roop born M[illegible], 1808, died Feb 1, 1811

Sarah, wife of Israel P Haines died July 11, 1835, aged 35 years [illegible] months

Catharine, wife of John Roop, Sr, died Dec 17, 1837, aged 61 years 4 months, 10 days

John Roop, born Nov 1[illegible] 1770, died June 21, 1852

Ann R, wife of Jacob Petry, born Nov 4, 1829, died Feb 5, 18[illegible]

John Roop, died Sept 1, 1868, aged 58 years, 2 month[illegible] days

Lydia, his wife, died Feb 4, 1879 aged 61 years, 6 months 21 days

Rebecca Reese, died Oct 16 1872 aged 68 years, 11 mo[illegible] 18 days

Chas B Stoner, died Oct 26, 1878, aged 22 years, 8 months 11 days

Lovina his wife, died, aged 17 years 11 months, 9 days

David Roop born Dec 21 1795 died Nov 19 1878

Mary, wife of Abraham Cassell born April 5, 1822, died Jan 28 1879

Abraham Cassell died Aug 30, 1877, aged 60 years, 1 month, 3 days

David Petry born Feb 25, 1821 died Aug 16, 1878

Peter Benedict born May 1, 1797, died Feb 19, 1859

John Hoffman, died April 25 1823 aged 80 years

Dolly, his wife born May 23 1765 died Sept 4, 1818

Isaac Kurtz, born Sept 27 1811 died March 22, 1831

Richard Belt, died March 28, 1865, aged 57 years 2 month[illegible] 21 days

Anna C Miller, died Sept 2 1862, aged 32 years, 8 months 15 days

John P Kauffman, born May 31, 1818 died Jan 10 1872

Margaret wife of George Kauffman, born March 13 17[illegible] died Sept [illegible] 1858

Louisa wife of Peter Myers, born April 5, 1769, died A[illegible] 20 1858

Anna A Miller died Jan 3, 1857 aged 22

J G Miller died Feb 28 1863 aged 29 years 1 month, [illegible] days

Mary, wife of John N Harman, died April 13, 1865, aged 50 years, 3 days

Elizabeth Diffenbough died April 18 1866 aged 66 ye[illegible] 11 months, 14 days

George Deeler, born Jan 11, 1794, died Dec 30 1872

Eli G Butler, died April 1, 1880, aged 53 years

Sarah Routson, died March 19 1878, aged 88 years, 7 mont[illegible] 19 days

Frederick Tawney, died Dec 29 1871, aged 53 ye[illegible] months, 23 days

Catherine wife of R Beggs, died Nov 5, 1877, aged [illegible] years 2 months, 24 days

Rebecca wife of Samuel Myers, born June 12, 1793, [illegible] March 19 1863

Elmira F Tawney born May 5, 181[illegible], died Oct 9, 1861

George Harman born May 28, 17[illegible], died March 11 18[illegible]

Eliza Harman born April 8 1811 died Nov 11 1860

Lucinda Royer born May 5 1820 died May 28, 1840

Peter Royer born Aug 17, 1775, died July 22 1842

Anna, his wife, died Jan 7, 1858, aged 83 years 6 months [illegible] days

Anna Weybright died Dec 17 1855, aged 52 years 1 m[illegible] 2 days

Mary daughter of Peter and Ann Royer, wife and [illegible] respectively of Jacob Mering and John Burgord died Jan [illegible] 1879, aged 73 years

John Royer died Oct 22, 1865, aged 52 years 9 month[illegible] days

Amos M Royer died Oct 27 1865 aged 27 years 7 m[illegible] 21 days

Christian Royer died March 11, 1870 aged 70 years 11 [illegible]

Louisa wife of David Engler died Sept 29 18[illegible] years 9 months 2 days

Polly Schaeffer born Sept 27, 1792 died Jan 2 18[illegible]

[illegible] March 15, 1[illegible]

Catharine Schaeffer, died December, 1878, aged 81 years, 6 months 10 days

David son of John and Margaret Royer, "who was wounded [in] the battle of the Wilderness, Virginia, May 5, 1864, and died the morning of the following day," aged 20 years, 7 months, [illegible] days

Catharine, wife of John Wentz born Sept 28, 1818, died March 9, 1880

Jessie Myers, born Aug 20, 1797, died Jan 2, 1880

David Myers born Dec 27, 1802, died Jan 23, 1879

Lewis Myers, died Aug 2 1876, aged 66 years, 3 months, 28 [days]

Mary A, his wife, died Dec 2, 1875, aged 53 years, 11 months, [illegible] days

Michael Petry Sr, died April 25, 1837, aged 59 years, 6 [months] 20 days

Mary, wife of C Albert Sproudon, died Nov 19, 1865, aged [illegible] years, 2 months, 8 days

John Towney died Jan 18, 1862, aged 76

Elizabeth, his wife born Jan 11, 1781 died May 1, 1863

Nancy wife of Francis Matthias, born Aug 19, 1796, died M[illegible] 10, 1866

Mary Piper died Dec 31, 1866, aged 10

Larkin McGomis, died May 10, 1848, aged 40

Louisa Gearing died March 6 1878, aged 55 years, 9 months, [illegible] days

Henry Williams, born Dec 20, 1824, died Dec 22, 1853

Mary L Jones, died May 30, 1871, aged 79

That portion of Western Maryland now known as Carroll County is filled with legends and romances, [but] none is remembered so well by the oldest inhabitant, or believed in so firmly by the superstitious, as "The Ghost of Furnace Hills" Leigh Master came [to] this country from New Hall, Lancashire, England, in the early part of the eighteenth century He was [then] quite a young man, full of enterprise and energy, and had come to "the new country" for the purpose [of] unearthing the hidden treasures and making a fortune therefrom No place presented more promising inducements than that portion of Maryland situated [a] few miles west of Westminster When Leigh Master took possession of the Furnace Hill property, [then] known as "Avondale," and owned by Thomas E [illegible] Bibber, he set to work to build furnaces and dig [for] the ore which he found in such profusion Hence [the] name of "Furnace Hills" He not only owned a furnace, but also large tracts of land, some five or [six] thousand acres, about Avondale, New Windsor, L[illegible]wood, and Pipe Creek He owned at one time [the] following tracts of land

	Acres.
[illegible] Valley containing	101
[illegible] of Arnold's Chance	306
[illegible] Delight	19
[illegible] War	100
[illegible] Purchase	50
[illegible] of Cobb's Choice	50
[illegible] Spot	30
[illegible] Edward's Fancy	21
[illegible]	21
[illegible]	21
[illegible]	11[illegible]
[illegible]	

	Acres
Part of Bottom and Top	50
Part of Content	
Part of Wilson's Chance and Mistake	18¾
Part of Gaither's Choice	80
Part of York Company's Defense	1000
Lincloch	11
Part of Brown's Plague and Mine Bank	11¾
Neglect	6¾
Cold [illegible]ing's Stone Quarry	25
The Increase	5¼
Hug me Snug	10¾
Discovery	50
The Parish	[illegible]
Strawberry Mead	12¼
The Oblique Angled Triangle	1½
Leigh Castle	2686
The Resurvey on Look About	1413¾
Stoney Hollow	

He was a man of means and an enterprising citizen, and also aspired at one time, in 1786, to represent Frederick County in the State Legislature, but he was not successful as a politician He was rather "inclinable" to use the expressive word of that day, to the British side of public affairs, which was not the popular side at that time He owned considerable mountain land, and old Ben Biggs used to tell a queer story about his wrapping himself up in a white sheet and going through the woods at night crying, "Stuck, stuck," which scared a great many timid people, and secured for him an unsavory reputation He was a great wag One poor fellow, a little superstitious, in going through a woods from a neighbor's house, with a long pole balanced over his shoulders and hung full of shad and herring, ran against Master's ghost and hearing his voice shouting "Stuck, stuck," was so frightened at the strange apparition that he took to his heels, and dropped all his fish on the ground in his rapid flight, hallooing to his old woman, as he came in sight of the house, for God's sake to open the door, as Leigh Master's ghost was after him

Much of his land was surveyed and recorded in the old books of Frederick County Court in the days before the Revolution, and during the reign of George III when John Darnall was clerk and George Scott sheriff

He employed a number of hands, bought negroes to work the furnaces and plantation, and in a short time the mines were in a promising condition, and the name of Leigh Master was known throughout the country Among the slaves who worked the furnaces at "Furnace Hills" was one "Sam," an object of special dislike to his master, the owner of the property From what cause his violent dislike sprang tradition does not tell, but Sam disappeared very mysteriously one dark night, when the furnaces were in full blast, and from that time Leigh Master was never known to mention his name Years rolled by, and after a long life he died [illegible] the [illegible] of the 2[illegible] day of March,

1796, in the eightieth year of his age In all probability his name would have perished also but for the vague rumors concerning the sudden and mysterious disappearance of the ill-fated negro, and the strange scenes and extraordinary sounds which followed so closely upon his death, accounts of which have been handed down from father to son through all these years, and have probably gathered strength in their travels Suspicions of a desperate deed committed by Leigh Master during his lifetime began to be whispered about, and old men remembered, or thought they did, a scared and haunted look in his eyes, which they attributed to the constant dread of the discovery of his miserable secret And thus the rumor spread, gathering as it went, until it was told that Leigh Master had taken the life of his despised slave, and had cast him into the furnace, that he might hide all traces of his crime

To show that people were at least as superstitious in those days as at the present time the following unique fable is given One dark night as a workman was returning home from a neighbor's house, he heard a rustling, hurried sound at the edge of the woods skirting the Furnace Hill, and in an instant Leigh Master rode past him, crying and begging for mercy upon his miserable soul The terror-stricken man was rooted to the spot, and stood trembling like a leaf, when suddenly the vision appeared the second time, urging his horse to its utmost speed, while the rattling of chains and horrible groans were heard in the distance A third time the spirit of Leigh Master appeared with agony on its face, and a third time the noises were heard Thus night after night strange sounds and scenes were witnessed in the furnace woods Sometimes the spirit was followed by three little imps carrying lanterns, and creeping stealthily along as if in search of some object Sometimes Leigh Master would appear at one portion of the hill, as if he was seeking to hide something, but always on a gray horse, emitting flames and smoke from his nostrils

And thus the story passed from mouth to mouth, till at length the sound of human footsteps in the haunted woods was a thing unknown after nightfall, and the ghosts held undisputed possession

Whether Leigh Master got tired of roaming around, or whether the three little imps found what they were seeking, is not known, but the ghosts of Furnace Hill disappeared with the furnaces and the superstition of the people, and nothing is left now but an old gray stone, marking the resting-place of the once famous owner of Furnace Hill, and bearing the following inscription

"Leigh Master, Esquire,
late of
New Hall, Lancashire,
England,
Died the 22d day of March,
1796
Aged 79 years"

In 1876, Rev Isaac L Nicholson, Jr, of the P E Church (Ascension), had the remains of Mr Master removed to the parish cemetery at Westminster He was a member of a notable English family, but a roving disposition forced him to leave his native home in early life and migrate to America The ruins of the furnace are still standing To Master is attributed the unfortunate introduction of the white blossom, or daisy, into this country, the bane of farmers to this day It is related that he sent to the old country for English clover-seed, and that this daisy-seed was sent him by mistake, and that he sowed the seed far and wide before the irretrievable error was discovered They are known as "Caroline pinks," or "Leigh Master's clover," in the neighborhood where he lived Some of the descendants of the Master family are still living in England among them Rev Charles Shrewsham, Vicar of Wiltshire, Salisbury

The tradition as to Leigh Master's slave and his imagined untimely taking off only obtained credence with the ignorant and superstitious, for careful investigation shows that while Leigh Master was a rough man in manners,—no uncommon thing in early days,—he was an honest, charitable, and public-spirited citizen, and the very soul of honor and manliness He left by will all his Carroll County real estate to his son Charles, living in England (where his mother had died before her husband, Leigh Master, came to America), with this condition precedent, that he became a naturalized citizen of the United States Charles came to Maryland, sold this realty, and returned to England without ever becoming a naturalized citizen of this country Though often threatened, the will of Leigh Master has never as yet been disturbed by litigation

The death of August Shriver, which occurred July 28, 1872, was quite sudden, and a severe shock to his numerous relatives and friends Mr Shriver occupied the position of president of the Western Maryland Railroad in the early stages of its history and contributed much to the building of the road by his efficient management At the time of his death he was president of the First National Bank of Westminster, which office he had filled with great credit since its establishment He dispensed unbounded hospitality at his mansion in Carroll County, and his heartfelt courtesy and suavity made him many friends

He was well known in Baltimore by reason of his [illegible] connections He was president of the Carroll County Agricultural Society, and a successful farmer on a large scale The news of his death [illegible] much regret, not only in the community in which he lived, but also in other portions of the State, where he was well known His public spirit and usefulness were exhibited in many undertakings in which he was concerned, and his death caused a loss in this respect which was widely felt In all his acts he elicited the confidence and esteem of those who were brought into association with him, and he enjoyed the reputation of a worthy gentleman and a faithful and efficient officer At various periods of his life he filled a number of positions of importance, in all of which he gave entire satisfaction to those whose interests were in his charge Faithfulness in the discharge of duty and an unswerving adherence to correct principles were the leading characteristics of a more than ordinarily successful life

The Hon Jacob Pouder died Sunday, Feb 13, 1870 at his residence near Westminster, in the seventy-eighth year of his age Mr Pouder had filled many prominent positions in his native county, and was much respected for his gentlemanly demeanor and courtesy towards all with whom he had business transactions At the time of his death he was the chief judge of the Orphans' Court of Carroll County, a position which he filled with great satisfaction to the people He was on several occasions a member of the State Legislature

The Spring Mills Lead-Mine is on the property of John T Hill, one mile south of Westminster, on the Western Maryland Railroad Mr Hill discovered the deposits in March, 1878 The ore is said to be very rich, assaying about eighty five to ninety per cent Upon the same property has also been discovered a good quality of iron ore, the vein being from twenty to thirty feet in width Gilberg & Lilly, of Philadelphia, in 1879, leased the mineral right to this property, and explored it to learn its real value in lead and iron An engine from the Taylor Manufacturing Company was taken to the scene of operations and is used in hoisting out ore and draining the mines

John C Frizell, of Westminster, had several springs on his estate which he supposed contained medicinal properties, as a number of his friends had derived considerable benefit from the use of the water, and at their suggestion he had it analyzed The water has also been highly recommended by physicians as anti-dyspeptic During the first part of July, 1870, he placed some of the water in the hands of Prof William E Aiken, of the University of Maryland, Baltimore, who sent him the following analysis

UNIVERSITY OF MARYLAND,
"July 7, 1870

"JOHN C FRIZELL

'*My dear Sir*,—I have just completed the qualitative analysis of the sample of mineral water you sent me, and herewith send results a gallon of water contains 15 76 grains of saline matter This quantity, taken in connection with the character of salts present will fully entitle the water to the name of a mineral water The contents of the water are

"Hydrochloric acid
Sulphuric acid
Carbonic acid
Silicic acid of the last a trace
Lime
Magnesia
Soda
Iron
Alumina a trace
Organic vegetable matter

"The above substances, arranged in their order of the well-known combinations, may be considered as representing the following compounds, which give the mineral character and medicinal value of the water

Bicarbonate of lime
Bicarbonate of magnesia
Bicarbonate of iron
Sulphate of lime
Sulphate of soda
Sulphate of magnesia
Chloride of sodium
Alumina, }
Silicic acid, } of each a trace
Organic vegetable matter, }

'Respectfully etc,
"WILLIAM E AIKEN

"P S —The copious deposit that falls when the matter stands for a time consists almost wholly of oxide of iron'

Westminster, the commercial centre of the district, is the county seat of Carroll County, and contained in 1880 a population of 2507 inhabitants Though not the oldest it is the largest and most important town in the county It is situated on Parr's Ridge, at the head waters of the Patapsco, about thirty three miles from Baltimore The town was laid out in 1764 by William Winchester, and the principal street was called King Street, showing that at the time it was founded its proprietor was loyal to the mother-country William Winchester was born in London, England, Dec 22, 1710 He came to America and settled in Maryland, March 6, 1729, and married Lydia Richards, July 22, 1747 He died Sept 2, 1790 The town was first named Winchester in honor of its founder but the name was subsequently changed by an act of the General Assembly to Westminster because of the number of towns bearing the same name, notably Winchester in Virginia, which was a source of [illegible] Westminster

is built on six different tracts of land The east end or original Winchester, is on the tract known as "White's Level," granted to John White in 1733, for 1692 acres The west end is on the tract called "Fanny's Meadow," granted to James Walls in 1711 A portion of the town is on "Bond's Meadow," granted to John Ridgley in 1753 for 1915 acres "Timber Ridge" and "Bedford," the latter Winter's addition, form the site of a part of Westminster, "Kelley's Range" takes in the Western Maryland College grounds, and "Bond's Meadow Enlarged" covers the ground upon which the court house stands Its situation on the main turnpike from Baltimore to the West gave the town great advantages in early days Long trains of wagons were constantly passing back and forth, all of which selected Westminster as a favorite halting-place for rest and refreshment, and the town, what there was of it, probably presented a more animated and business-like appearance then than now Business methods have undergone such a complete transformation since then that no just comparison can be instituted

The Westminster of to day is very interesting It is perhaps the longest city for its width in America, which is mainly due to its early location along the pike, the great highway of travel, and the anxiety of those who had business interests to place themselves in direct communication with the unceasing trade and travel encountered at that point The surroundings of the city are exceedingly picturesque The view from College Hill is very fine A beautiful, undulating country spreads out for many miles, and on very clear days the eye can take in an expanse of territory stretching from the Potomac to the Susquehanna The population of the town is now 2507, with a number of handsome church edifices, at least forty stores, three banks, a college, and several large manufactories and warehouses Some of the older residences in Westminster, handsome in themselves, possess that mellow tint so attractive to persons of taste, and which time alone can give, while those recently built are embodiments of the culture and refinement of their owners The country in the vicinity is well watered by the Patapsco and other streams, which furnish abundant power for manufacturing purposes It is a very healthy, rich, and productive agricultural region The Western Maryland Railroad passes directly through the centre of the town, and the numerous trains passing over the road leave nothing to be desired in the way of communication with distant points

Iron and copper ore abound in large deposits and are successfu[illegible] and shipped to Pennsylvania and New York. Quarries containing the finest varieties of marble have been opened, and are worked in the vicinity. The town contains the usual number of county buildings, commodious, and well adapted to the purposes for which they were erected

The Western Maryland College, a fine four-story brick building, is located upon the highest site around the town, and is admirably arranged for educational purposes The *Democratic Advocate* building, corner of Main and Centre Streets, forty by eighty feet, is a fair exhibit of the enterprise and energy of the conductor of this sterling journal

The I O O F Hall is an imposing structure, and on its first floor is the large and elegantly-arranged office of *The American Sentinel*, the Republican organ of the county

Among the earliest settlers up to the year 1800 were the Winchesters (William and his sons), the Fishers (John and David), McHaffies, Wamplers, Haines, Stansburys (Caleb, Sr and Jr, and Joshua), John Miller, Andrew Reese, Sr, Ulerick Eckler, Mordecai Price, Jacob Feterling, Jacob Pouder, John McComb, Jacob Sherman, Isaac Shriver, Nimrod Frizzell, Jacob Crouse, Jacob Righter, Thomas Ward, Joseph Shreeve, Jacob Fringer, the Yinglings, the Neffs, Adelspergers, Lockards, Smiths, Dells The oldest house standing in town is that occupied by Peggy Adelsperger It is a log structure on Main Street, nearly opposite the "City Hotel," and was erected between 1777 and 1780 It is yet a substantial dwelling, comfortable and neat Her sister Elizabeth died a few years ago Their parents, Thomas and Betsey went to this old house to live after their marriage, about a century ago

The oldest living person in town is William Crouse, who was born in Myers District in 1792, but came to Westminster in 1794 with his parents, and has resided here ever since He and his wife (Catharine Shaeffer, aged eighty-three years) have lived in happy wedlock sixty three years, since Feb 15, 1818 His father, Jacob Crouse, was one of the first blacksmiths here, succeeding a Mr Myers, whom he bought out in 1791 He was born Oct 30, 1766, and died Jan 1, 1846, and his wife, Elizabeth, born in 1773, died Sept 12, 1820 About the first storekeeper was David Fisher, and after him Mr Yingling, and then a Mr Utz The earliest schoolmaster remembered was Mr Gynn, who held forth with an iron rule on the plat where Charles T Reifsnider now resides Jacob Sherman, who was born in Lancaster County, Pa, March 7, 1756, and married Elizabeth Wagner Feb 23 1779 kept the first hotel or tavern, where the [illegible] in 1807 [illegible] he was suc

ceeded by Isaac Shriver He died July 7, 1822, but his widow survived till June 28, 1812 Afterwards, taverns were kept by Mr Winterow and Mr Wampler Jacob Wolf at an early period manufactured clocks, many of which are still in use over the country When Westminster was made the county-seat of the new (Carroll) county in 1837, the town had about five hundred inhabitants, but immediately thereafter it began to increase in population and business It received its greatest impetus, however, upon the completion of the Western Maryland Railroad to its limits New additions were made and new streets laid out to accommodate the increasing population and the wants of trade and awakened enterprise

The following legend of early days in Westminster is well authenticated "Many years ago, in the northwestern part of Maryland, there stood a little village bearing the proud English name of Winchester, now the beautiful city of Westminster For a long time peace and plenty had smiled upon its inhabitants, and they dreamed not of coming evil It was in the midst of summer when God saw fit to send a mighty drought upon the land For many days the scorching rays of the sun looked down upon the earth, burning and blighting the vegetation, and threatening to bring famine upon its track Flowers drooped and died, and water—one of God's best and most necessary gifts to man—began to fail In vain the people prayed and cried for rain The citizens of Winchester became alarmed, and many of them locked their pumps, and refused even a cooling drink to the thirsty traveler or the famished beast, lest they should not have enough for themselves Near the eastern end of the village dwelt two maiden ladies, aged and respected, who believed God would not forsake them in their time of need Unlike their neighbors they did not refuse water to any, but unlocking their gate, placed a placard near the well bearing the following words, 'Free admittance to all,—water belongs to God!' In those ancient days railroads were unknown, and all traveling was done by stages or wagons Emigrants were seen passing daily on their road to the great West, and the demand for water was constant The doubting citizens advised these two Christian ladies to tear down their notice and close the entrance to prevent the water being carried away, or they would be left without, but their answer was always the same, 'The Lord is our Shepherd, we shall not want We have no right to refuse, for water belongs to God' Soon all the wells and springs in the village began to fail, and only two remained to supply the demands of the famishing citizens One of these was the well which had been free to all The other belonged to an [illegible] old gentleman, who, as soon as he saw how great was the demand for water, guarded it and refused even a drop All flocked to 'God's Well,' as it was now called, and its old fashioned moss covered bucket was never idle And still the sky was cloudless, and the unrelenting rays of a July sun scorched and burned the earth A few more days passed, and he who had so cruelly refused to give a cup of cold water from his plenteous store was obliged to go and beg for himself from the unfailing fountain of 'God's Well' The demand on this well became greater day by day, but still its sparkling waters refreshed the thirsty traveler and the famishing beast At length a small dark cloud was seen in the sky, and how eagerly it was watched! Larger and larger it grew, till at last the whole sky was overcast The thunder pealed the lightning flashed through the heavens, and the floodgates were opened The clouds rolled away, and once more the whole face of nature smiled, and the grateful citizens of Winchester thanked God for the glorious rain, which had come just in time to save them from perishing Time has passed rapidly, leaving many traces of its flight Little Winchester is now a promising and thriving city, bearing the name of Westminster The two noble hearted Christian ladies, who in the time of need trusted in the Lord and shared with their suffering neighbors, have long since found their reward in heaven Their old home has been torn down, but the 'well' still remains on the old lot of Mrs Col James M Shellman, and though now covered over and out of repair, has never been known to fail, but to this day is filled with excellent, pure water"

The elegant mansion of Mrs James M Shellman on Main Street, opposite the City Hotel, was built in 1807 by Col Jacob Sherman He gave it to his daughter, the wife of David H Shriver, who subsequently removed to Wheeling, W Va Col Sherman was a native of Lancaster County, Pa He was born March 7, 1756, and married Elizabeth Wagner, Feb 23, 1779 He died July 7, 1822, and his wife, June 28, 1812 His son in law, David H Shriver, who occupied the house in Westminster, was born April 14, 1769, and married Miss Sherman, Feb 28, 1803

Mrs Shellman the owner of this mansion and the old well to which reference is made, is a great granddaughter of Philip Jones, Jr, who surveyed and, with three commissioners, laid out Baltimore Town in 1730 He was born in Wales, Oct 25, 1701, and came to this country about 1720 Oct 2, 1727, he married Annie Rattcenbury, whose ancestors came from the Isle of Wight in 1621 and settled in Virginia They had [illegible] children, [illegible] except Thomas

and Hannah Hannah married William Worthington, of Maryland Philip Jones, Jr died Dec 22, 1761, aged sixty years, three months, and six days His widow became the second wife of John Eager, and died shortly after her marriage Thomas, the only surviving son of Philip Jones, Jr, was the first register of wills of Baltimore, and afterwards became judge of the Court of Appeals He married Elizabeth McClure, widow of David McClure, of Carlisle, Pa He had three sons and three daughters. The oldest daughter married Maj Beall, of the United States army, the second married Mr Dallam, of Harford County, and the third Mr Schley, of Baltimore While on a visit to his daughter, Mrs Beall, at Fort McHenry, Judge Jones was taken ill and died, Sept 27, 1812, aged seventy-seven years Of his three sons, Harry, the youngest, remained a bachelor Thomas married and lived in Patapsco Neck He had ten children, one daughter being Mrs William Fenby, living near Westminster

Philip also married, and lived for some time on his farm, "Gallipot," Baltimore County He was one of the Old Defenders of Baltimore in the war of 1812 He came to Westminster in 1818, where he lived until within a few days of his death, and where he was one of the first merchants He had ten children, one of whom is Mrs James M Shellman The old Jones homestead in Patapsco Neck is still standing in a state of good preservation, has broad halls, large rooms, and very high ceilings It is surrounded by magnificent walnut-trees, which gives the name of "Walnut Grove" to the place, and has a lawn running to the bank of the Patapsco River It has always been in the possession of the Jones family, having been granted by royal patent through Lord Baltimore This patent is still held by the family at "Walnut Grove," which is at present occupied by John T Jones, two sisters and a brother, children of Thomas, and great grandchildren of Philip Jones, Jr, surveyor of Baltimore Town

When the Confederates under Maj Harry Gilmor and Gen Bradley T Johnson made a raid into Westminster in 1864, they occupied Mrs Shellman's mansion as their headquarters, and when Gen J E B Stuart was here with his command he caught up and carried in his front through town, on the saddle, Miss Mary M Shellman then a little lass, but the bravest Union girl of the place

About the first year of this century Dr Umbaugh practiced his profession in Westminster He was a German physician of note and rode over a vast territory to see his patients After his location here Dr Berrigheit came and remained [illegible] Dr George Colgate died May 1, 1822, in the prime of life and a martyr to the noble profession he adorned Dr William Willis was, on the organization of the county, made the first clerk of the court in April 1837, and was succeeded by Dr William A Matthias The oldest physician here (if not in the county) is Dr James L Billingslea He was born in Abingdon, Harford Co, in 1801 He was first educated in the common schools, then attended the Belair Academy and afterwards St Mary's College, Baltimore, where he completed his classical studies He graduated in medicine at the University of Maryland in 1827, and located the same year in the practice of his profession at Uniontown, in Carroll County He remained there twenty years, and then removed to Baltimore He subsequently settled at Long Green in Baltimore County, where he practiced for ten years and in 1860 he came to Westminster and continued the practice of his profession for many years, but has now retired He was in the State Senate from 1861 to 1867 He married Susan Harris, of Frederick County, in 1832, of the Society of Friends, for his first wife, and in 1867, Elizabeth Cove for his second wife When he came to Westminster, in 1860, the physicians here were Drs J L Warfield (now of Baltimore), Matthias, and J W Herring The latter is still in practice, and is also cashier of Union National Bank Dr Frank T Shaw has been clerk of the court since 1873

The Corporation and Officers.—The General Assembly incorporated the town of Westminster by an act passed April 6, 1839, supplementary to the first act of Feb 11, 1830, enacting that the adjoining towns, then called and known by the names of Westminster, New London, Winter's Addition, and New Elenburgh, together with Pigman's Addition, and all that space lying between Winter's Addition and Pigman's Addition, should forever thereafter be called and known by the name of Westminster This act provided for the election on the first Monday in May of a burgess and five commissioners, and for annual elections of said officers thereafter The act designated Andrew Pouder, Jacob Yingling, and Michael Barnitz as the judges to hold the first election

By the act of Feb 28, 1850, the town was erected into a city, and Michael Barnitz, Horatio Price, and Otho Shipley appointed judges to hold the first election under the city charter The city limits were thus established

* Beginning on the southeast at a stone planted near the Baltimore and Reisterstown turnpike, formerly a boundary [illegible] es and running [illegible] the four hundred [illegible]

yards, thence westerly and northerly, and running parallel with the course of said turnpike and four hundred yards therefrom to the line of Adam Gilbert's land, located at or near a public road leading from said turnpike to Abraham Wampler's mill, thence westerly and southerly with the outlines of said Gilbert's lands to a point four hundred yards southwest of the turnpike leading from Westminster to Uniontown, thence easterly and southerly and parallel with the last turnpike and the aforesaid Baltimore and Reisterstown turnpike, and four hundred yards from each, to the line formerly dividing Baltimore and Frederick Counties, and thence with the last line to the place of beginning"

The following persons have been elected to the office of burgess and mayor

Burgess —1839, James M Shellman, 1840 William Shipley, Jr, 1841-44, George Trumbo, 1844 David Keiffer

Mayor —1850, Dr Elisha D Payne 1851, Abner Neal 1852, Jacob Grove, 1854-58, R K Booth 1859 John M Yingling, 1860, Samuel L Swanstead, 1861-64, Michael Baughman 1864, Jacob Grove, 1865 Emanuel Gernand, 1866, Hashabiah Haines, 1867, A Reese Durbin 1868, David Fowble, 1869-71 Jacob Knipple, 1871, David H Leister, 1872, Henry H Herbaugh, 1873 E K Gernand 1874-76, David Fowble, 1876-82, P H Irwin

The other officers are given as far as the corporation records show them

1860 —Jacob Shaffer, Levi Evans, Michael Baughman (president), Reuben Cassell, Joshua W Hering, Clerk, Otho Shipley

1861 —Joshua Yingling, Henry Warner, William Reese Samuel Myers, Wm H Grammer, Clerk, Otho Shipley

1862 —George F Webster Joshua Yingling, Henry Warner Samuel Myers, Benton Gehr, Clerk Thomas J Lockard

1863 —Samuel L Myers, Henry Warner Edwin K Gernand Asbury Sharer, Joshua Yingling, Clerk, Thomas J Lockard

1864 —E K Gernand, S L Myers, J Yingling, Jeremiah Yingling, Ira E Crouse, Clerk, Thomas J Lockard

1865 —George Webster, Wm H Harman, F R Buell, John W Gorsuch, David Fowble Clerk, Thomas J Lockard

1866 —F A Shearer, E K Gernand A R Durbin, W A Cunningham, Clerk, Albert Billingslea

1867 —John H Yingling, W A Cunningham, F K Gernand, J H Bowers F A Shearer, Clerk C J Yingling, Bailiff and Collector, G W Sullivan, Counselor, J F Pearson, Sr

1868 —J W Perkins, M B Mikesell, G W Matthews, George S Fouke, S P Everhart, Clerks, J A Dillar, P B Mikesell, Treasurer, Dr George S Fouke, Counselor, E F Crout

1869 —George L Wampler David Wentz John Bernstine Elias Yingling, W H Harman, Clerk, W L W Seabrook, Collectors William Baker, George Stouel

1870 —John Bernstine, G W Matthews, J W Perkins, D H Leister, Joseph Woods, Clerks, W L W Seabrook, W H Bilenhover

1871 —J W Perkins, Samuel Everhart Jeremiah Yingling, William Yingling, Dr Francis Butler

1872 —H F Morelock, Reuben Cassell, A Shearer, Jesse Yingling, W H Harman, Clerk, L F Byers

1873 —Henry Vanderford, Joshua Yingling Edward Lynch, Elias Yingling, J W Hering, Clerk, George M Parke

1874 —[illegible]

1875 —Henry E Morelock, F O Grimes, William Lawyer James Rippard, George M Parke, Clerk, W H Rippard, Treasurer, E O Grimes, Counsel, J M Parke, Bailiff, Israel Zieber

1876 —N J Gorsuch, William B Thomas, Jesse Yingling G W Sullivan, J W Perkins, Clerk John Matthews

1877 —N J Gorsuch, J W Perkins W B Thomas G W Sullivan, Jesse Yingling, Clerk, John Matthews

1878 —Same board as for two previous years, Clerk, John Matthews

1879 —W B Thomas, E J Lawyer, G W Sullivan, Orlando Reese, N J Gorsuch, Clerk John Matthews

1880 —Same board and clerk

1881 —Same board, Clerk, C H Baughman, Bailiff, Street Commissioner, and Collector Israel Zieber, Counsel, Joseph M Parke Council Committees Streets, W B Thomas O Reese, Gas, G W Sullivan, N J Gorsuch, Finance, W B Thomas, N J Gorsuch

Western Maryland College is located in the city of Westminster, on the line of the Western Maryland Railroad, about midway between the cities of Baltimore and Hagerstown

The buildings stand on a commanding eminence at the "West End," overlooking the city and many miles of the surrounding country The main building is five stories high, and affords ample accommodations for chapel, recitation-rooms, halls for the societies, professors' apartments, and dormitories The grounds belonging to the college contain eight acres, allowing sufficient range for the exercise of students during the time not allotted to study The institution is conducted on a modern basis Young men and women are entered under the same corps of professors and instructors, enjoying all the advantages extended by the college The course of study, however, is not precisely the same for both sexes, the young ladies completing theirs in three years, and the gentlemen graduating in four, although both sexes have the same instructors, the two departments are kept entirely separate, the sexes meeting only at chapel service and in the dining-room with members of the faculty

The Western Maryland College was established under the auspices of the Maryland Annual Conference of the Methodist Protestant Church A charter was obtained for the institution from the Legislature of Maryland in 1861, which contemplated its establishment in the city of Baltimore, but subsequent events led to the selection of Westminster as the site of the new college, and a more favorable location could scarcely have been chosen In 1866, Rev James Thomas Ward purchased a homestead in Westminster, which being made known to Rev Rhesa Scott Norris, negotiations were entered into which resulted in a meeting between Fayette R B[illegible] J T Ward The

Conference of that year gave in its adhesion to the plan for making Westminster the place for the establishment of the enterprise and an appeal was made to friends for money to erect suitable buildings The responses were neither numerous nor large, and a loan was obtained from John Smith and Isaac C Pade, which enabled F R Buell to commence building on the site he had purchased The first stone of the building was laid Aug 27, 1866, and the cornerstone was laid Sept 6, 1866, by Door to Virtue Lodge, No 46 A F A M, in the presence of a large number of citizens of Westminster and friends from other places At the session of the Maryland Annual Conference in March, 1867, an advisory board of directors was appointed, as follows Revs J T Ward, J J Murray, D Bowers, P L Wilson and R Scott Norris, and on the part of the laity, J W Herring, John Smith, M Baughman, A Zollickoffer, John S Repp, and Samuel McKinstry This board in July announced F R Buell as proprietor of the college, and J T Ward principal of the faculty College exercises were begun Sept 4, 1867, and continued regularly thereafter Some difficulty of a financial character was experienced in 1868, but the friends of the institution came forward and relieved the embarrassment, and a second charter was obtained from the Legislature, placing the college under the direction of a board of trustees John Smith was elected president of the board, J T Ward, secretary, and J W Herring, treasurer It was determined at their first meeting to purchase the property from F R Buell for twenty thousand dollars The Conference in March, 1869, at the suggestion of J T Ward, appointed Rev P Light Wilson agent of the association on behalf of the college During this year the female students formed the "Browning Literary Society," whose first anniversary was celebrated during commencement week, June 14, 1869 The career of the college since then has been prosperous and useful In June, 1871, the first college degrees were conferred upon a class of four young men and three young girls On the 19th of July, 1871, the first stone of the foundation of an additional building was laid, rendered necessary by the increased patronage of the college In January, 1870, the State Legislature granted an appropriation out of the academic fund for Carroll County for the free tuition of one student from each election district in the county, and in 1878 an appropriation was made by the General Assembly of Maryland, enabling the college to furnish board, fuel, lights, washing, tuition, and the use of books free to one student, male or female from each senatorial district of the State This appropriation was continued by the Legislature of 1880 During the twelve years of its existence the college has had an average attendance of 11[illegible] pupils, 73 of whom were males and 43 females There have been altogether under its care and training 15[illegible] pupils, of whom 950 were males and 559 females They have pursued the various branches of an English and classical education Of this number 94 have been graduated with the degree of A B, and 45 have studied with a view to the Christian ministry The faculty of the male department is as follows

Rev J T Ward, D D, President Professor of Mental and Moral Science, Rev H C Cushing A M Vice-President, Professor of Belles-Lettres, T L Broelcker [illegible] Professor of Physical Science and the French Language, Rev James W Reese, A M, Ph D, Professor of Ancient Languages and Literature, G W Devilbiss, A M, Professor of Belles-Lettres, D W Herring, C E, Professor of Mathematics, Charles T Wright, Principal of Preparatory Department, and Professor of German Language [illegible] Augustus Webster, D D, Professor of Theology, [illegible] Herring, M D, Lecturer on Anatomy, Physiology, and Hygiene, R B Norment, Esq Lecturer on Civil Law and Political Economy, DeWitt C Ingle, A B, [illegible] Latin, Greek, and Mathematics

Female Faculty—Rev J T Ward, D D, President, Professor of Moral and Mental Science Rev H C Cushing [illegible] Vice President, Professor of Belles Lettres [illegible] Miss Lottie A Owings, Preceptress of Female Department and Teacher of Ornamental Branches, R L B[illegible] A M, Professor of Physical Science and the French Language, Rev James W Reese, A M, Ph D, Professor of Ancient Languages and Literature, G W Devilbiss [illegible] Professor of Belles-Lettres, D W Herring, C E [illegible] sor of Mathematics, J W Herring, M D Lecturer [illegible] Anatomy, Physiology and Hygiene, Charles T [illegible] Professor of the German Language Mrs S [illegible] Teacher of Vocal and Instrumental Music

List of Graduates

Class of 1871 Mrs Imogene L Mitten Ensor Charles [illegible] man, Mrs Mary M Ward Lewis, Rev. Thomas [illegible] A M, Anna R Yingling, William S Crouse, A M, Henry E Norris A M, M D

Class of 1872 Lizzie B Adams, Mary E Johnson, Mrs Annie Price Ilot, Annie G Ridgely, H Dorsey Newson, William P Wright

Class of 1873 Alice A Fenby, Mary N Nichols, Mrs [illegible] Smith Billingslea, Ida F Williams, B Franklin [illegible] A M, Joseph B Galloway, A M, M D Frank W [illegible] Frann n C Smith, LL B, Thomas B Ward

Class of 1874 Annie W Buckhead, Jennie M Pratt, A M, Mary Brockett, A M, Mrs Louisa D Hooper James, [illegible] M Emma Jones Willis, Mollie F Jones, Mrs [illegible] Lewis Fowler, Sarah L Whiteside, Rev Charles S [illegible] A M, James A Diffenbaugh, A M, Rev Philip [illegible] A M, George B Harris, Samuel R Harris, Philemon B Hopper A M, William Hogg, Rev Walter W White, A M

Class of 1875 [illegible] Armstrong, George W Devilbiss, A M, [illegible] Thomas H Lewis

Class of 1876 Drucilla Billard, Mrs Laura A Fdie [illegible] Laura K Matthews, Mrs Mary A Miller Hering, [illegible] E Rinehart Martha Smith, Louis L Billingslea, [illegible] [illegible] M D

J. T. Ward

Class of 1877 Florence M Devilbiss, Alice I Ernest, M Ada Starr, M Virginia Starr, Maggie I Woods, Edwin N Young, Winfield S Amoss, A M, LL B, C Berry Cushing, A M, LL B, Wilson R Cushing, Thomas J Wilson

Class of 1878 Lulu E Fleming, Minnie V Swornstedt, Alice V Wilson, De Witt Clinton Ingle, T Weldon Miles, Frank H Peterson

Class of 1879 Mollie T Lankford, Mamie M McKinstry, Mary Rinehart, Clara L Smith, Lizzie Trump, Lou B Wampler

Class of 1880 Lizzie L Hodges, Linnie C Kilmer, M Emma Selby, Florence F Wilson, Edward S Pole, William H DeFord, Lewis A Jarman, Rev Frederick C Klein, William R McDaniel, Joseph W Smith

Class of 1881 Hattie Ballinger, Bettie Bratt, Louise Cunningham, M Kate Goodhand, Hattie V Holliday, Bessie Miller, H Clay Nicodemus, Katie M Smith, Laura F Stalnaker, George V Everhart, J Fletcher Somers, George W Todd

James Thomas Ward the president of the Western Maryland College, was born in Georgetown, D C, Aug 21, 1820 His father, Ulysses Ward, born near Rockville, Montgomery Co, Md April 3, 1792, being the youngest of eight children of John Ward (born in London, England, Aug 1, O S, 1747) and Mary Ann Eustatia (maiden name Forbes), born in London, Jan 1, 1752, who came to America in 1770, and settled first in Prince George's Co Md, whence they removed to Montgomery County in 1776 The ancestors of John Ward had resided during the sixteenth and seventeenth centuries in Yorkshire, England, being farmers by occupation About the beginning of the eighteenth century the branch of the family from which he more immediately descended removed to London On the mother's side the ancestors of Mr Ward were of Scottish origin Ulysses Ward, his father, was married Sept 26 1816, to Susan Valinda Beall, daughter of James Beall, died 1821), son of James Beall, of the same family with George Beall, one of the first settlers of Georgetown, D C, and son of Ninian Beall, who emigrated from Scotland towards the close of the eighteenth century, and died in Maryland at the great age of one hundred and seven years Of the seven children of Ulysses and Susan Valinda Ward, James Thomas was the second At the time of his birth his mother was a member of the Protestant Episcopal, and his father of the Methodist Episcopal, Church, which latter his mother also subsequently [illegible] and by a minister of which (the Rev John Davis) he was baptized His parents then resided in Georgetown, as before intimated, and continued there till the spring of 1822, when they removed to Prince George's County and thence, after a brief stay in Georgetown, to Washington City, April, 1826, which became their permanent place of residence until the death of the f[illegible], [illegible] 1, [illegible] in the seventy-sixth year of his age Ulysses Ward was a most industrious, enterprising, and useful man As a local preacher in the Methodist Church he became quite popular because of his earnest labors He was extensively known as a business man first as a master-workman in his trade, and afterwards as a merchant, and, when he had acquired wealth, as a benefactor in church and city by the judicious and liberal bestowment of his means In the schools of Washington Mr Ward received his first lessons in the common branches of an English education, his principal instructors being the well-known John McLeod and Joseph H Wheat The advantages thus afforded during the week-days were supplemented by excellent home training, and on the Sabbath by the teachings imparted in the Sabbath school Thomas from his infancy had been feeble physically He gained knowledge rapidly, and was scarcely beyond the period of childhood when he made a public profession of his faith in Christ, and developed a fondness for learning and usefulness At the age of sixteen he entered the Classical Academy of Brookville, in Montgomery County, Md, at that time under the superintendence of Elisha J Hall, where he had fine opportunities, which were so well improved that when he left for home, in 1838, he bore with him the classical prize He returned to Washington, and for a time was employed in business with his father, in the mean time devoting much of his time to study, and taking a deep interest in the Sabbath-school work Still, he had no definite purpose of a professional career

In the summer of 1840 he decided to consecrate his life to the work of the gospel ministry In his preparations for this work he studied under the advice and counsel of Rev A A Lipscomb and Rev A Webster His parents were now, and had been since 1832, connected with the then recently organized church known as the Methodist Protestant In this church he began his career as a preacher of the gospel, being licensed Aug 30, 1840, by the Ninth Street Methodist Protestant Church, of Washington City After preaching in various places for many months, he was called to serve a church in the eastern part of the city until the meeting of the Maryland Annual Conference in the spring of 1841 The session of that Conference was held in the city of Philadelphia, in the Methodist Protestant church there which had been organized by the Rev Thomas H Stockton, and of which Mr Ward became years after the pastor, succeeding that distinguished and eloquent divine

Mr Ward's first regular appointment was to Pipe Creek Circuit, embracing part of Frederick County, Md [illegible] He was

associated with an elder minister, the Rev Dr John S Reese, a man of great wisdom, learning, eloquence, and piety Mr Ward became very popular in all the churches of the circuit, embracing parts of Washington County, Md, and Berkeley County, Va He had signal success in his work there, and during his term built a new house of worship and organized the church at Little Georgetown, Va, besides being instrumental in adding largely to the membership of the churches which had been established During these years he also traveled very extensively in other portions of the Conference territory, preaching to large congregations, especially at various camp-meetings on the Eastern as well as the Western Shore of Maryland His next appointment was the city of Cumberland, 1854, in the spring of which year he married Miss Catharine A Light, of Beddington, Va, a lady of great piety and Christian devotion, who was held in the highest respect and esteem by her husband's parishioners This year Mr Ward's health, always feeble, gave way, and, by advice of his friends, he asked the Conference to leave him without an appointment His request was complied with, and he spent three months in suitable recreation, a portion of the time in leisurely travel northward

He returned to his father's house in Washington so much renewed in health as to warrant him in applying to the president of the Conference for an appointment for the remainder of the year, and being informed by the president that there was then no suitable field for him until the next meeting of the Conference, he accepted a position offered him by his father, who was then engaged in publishing a temperance journal called the *Columbian Fountain*, to assist in editing the same Thus he became linked with an enterprise from which he found no opportunity to disconnect himself until the close of the year 1847, at which time also the regular close of the volume of the journal expired He then received a unanimous invitation to take charge of the church in Philadelphia which Rev Thomas H Stockton had served nine years, but which he had recently left to take charge of a church in Cincinnati, Ohio He accordingly obtained a transfer from the president of the Maryland Annual Conference, which was accepted by the president of the Philadelphia Conference, who appointed him to the pastorate of the church referred to A condition of affairs arose by which the subsequent sessions of the Philadelphia Conference were broken up and the church he served caused to assume a position of independence, and he, not having any reasons for abandoning [illegible] charge [illegible] case, to remain and serve it so long as pleasant relations existed between it and himself

This was the case until the close of 1856, when feeling it his duty to sever his connection with the charge, he returned to the Conference in Maryland was received by his brethren and associates of former years, and was again appointed to Pipe Creek Circuit which he had served sixteen years before, embracing however, not so large a field as when he was first appointed to it His colleague was the Rev J Thomas Murray, and they were both continued on the circuit for three successive years During these years more than four hundred members were added to these churches Mr Ward's next appointment was Alexandria, Va in the spring of 1860 During this year he visited Fredericksburg, Va, by request and organized a Methodist Protestant Church in that city, where he continued for two years The Conference of 186[illegible] sent him to the Liberty Circuit, where he labored with success From Liberty he was sent by his Conference to the church in Washington City from which he had first received his license to preach, and of which his parents, grown old by this time, were still members His pastorate there continued for two years, when, on account of failing health, he asked the Conference to relieve him from pastoral charge, and retired in the spring of 1866 to a little suburban home which had been provided for him by his parents at Westminster, which had been one of his regular preaching places in the years when he traveled Pipe Creek Circuit the second time His health being restored he became a teacher in the Westminster Academy, and afterwards president of Western Maryland College, to which position he has been re-elected from year to year since by the board of trustees, the appointment being confirmed by the Maryland Annual Conference, under whose auspices the college was founded and under whose patronage it has been from the time of its incorporation by the General Assembly of Maryland in 1868 Western Maryland College was organized in September, 1867, and incorporated by an act of the General Assembly of Maryland approved March, 1868 There have been about [illegible] students, of which one-tenth of the number have graduated, besides a score of young men educated with the view to entering the sacred office of the ministry and others who are now in positions of prominence and usefulness About the time of his entrance upon the duties of the presidency of the college Mr Ward inherited from his father some considerable means the available portion of which he devoted to the college enterprise, fulfilling the duties of his office at a [illegible] [illegible] expenses in [illegible]

[illegible]ition Mr Ward has great reason to rejoice at the success that has crowned his pastoral services, and deserves the heartfelt sympathies and aid of his church in his efforts to promote the success and prosperity of the college over which he presides

Westminster Academy was incorporated by an act of the General Assembly of Maryland, passed Feb 6, 1839 The incorporators were

Jacob Reese, Isaac Shriver, Jesse Reifsnider, Nicholas Kelly, John McCollum, Joshua Smith, Jr, Hezekiah Crout, Francis Shriver, John Baumgartner, Basil Hayden, John S Murray, Otho Shipley, John Fisher, Charles W Webster, Wm P Maulsby, A H Busby, George Shriver, Conrad Moul, James Keefer, Samuel Orendorff, Michael Baruits, Emanuel Gernand, S D Lecompte, Wm Sheev, Joshua Yingling, Wm Yingling, Benjamin Yingling, Elias Yingling, Levi Evans, David Keefer, John Fringwalt, John Swigart, Wm Shipley, Jr, Wm Zepp, Jacob Hartzhell, John M Yingling, Jacob Grove, Samuel I Dell, Lawrence Zepp, David Burns, George Sheets, George Kimby, Wm Grumbine John Baurgett Nelson Manning, Jesse Manning, John A Kelly Nimrod Beck, Jacob Jease, Henry Geatty, N H Thayer, R F Fowler, Mordecai Price, David Hedidebridler Amos Lightner, Ephraim Crumbicker Joseph Shafer, John F Reese, John K Longwell, James M Shellman

The "Old Union Meeting-house" was erected in 1818 Rev Charles G McLean preached the dedicatory sermon It is a two-story brick structure, and is now fast falling into decay Its windows are shattered, its steeple tumbling to pieces, and its interior crumbling away Here the Rev Lorenzo Dow the famous and eccentric revivalist and exhorter, preached eleven different times, once beginning his services at four o'clock in the morning This edifice stands on an elevated site in the centre of the Westminster Cemetery The pulpit, with a high stairway leading to it, and the old-fashioned galleries are all that is left of its interior For the last third of a century it has not been used for religious services It was built as a union church by contributions from various Protestant denominations, and was open for all Protestant sects For nearly a quarter of a century it was the only Protestant meeting-house in the town, and in that period many of the ablest clergymen of the State or country have preached from its old-fashioned pulpit Before its erection a log structure, built about 1790, was used, and at the entrance to the cemetery, on the right, is the old brick school-house

The first burial ground in Westminster was on the land now owned by George E Crouse, where interments were made from about 1761 to 1790, in which year the ground adjoining that on which the "Old Union Meeting-house" was built was used as a graveyard [illegible] It was occupied as an ordinary burying-place until 1864, when the Westminster Cemetery was organized and incorporated This corporation has added to the grounds, making about thirteen acres, and has greatly beautified them by walks, terraces, and other valuable improvements The officers of this corporation for 1881 are Joseph M Parke, president, and John K. Longwell, John E Smith, H L Norris (treasurer), Ira E Crouse, and Edward K Gernand (secretary), directors In this cemetery the graves of soldiers in the late war are numerous, and it is also the last resting-place of many prominent citizens of Westminster There is one old stone, about a foot high, on which the only inscription is 1707, but whether it refers to some person who died that year or to some one born at that date cannot be determined The oldest interment is that of Christian Yingling, born Oct 13, 1788, and who died Jan 24, 1790, the year the meeting-house was built and the graveyard first laid out The most prominent grave is that of the colonial proprietor of the town, who laid it out in 1764 and called it Winchester, which name it bore until superseded by the no less English name of Westminster By his remains lie those of his wife and descendants

The epitaphs on the tombstones are as follows

"In Memory of William Winchester,
who was born in London
on the 22d December, 1710
Arrived in Maryland
on the 6th March, 1729
Intermarried with Lydia Richards
on the 22d July, 1747,
And departed this life on the
2d September, 1790
In the 80th year of his age"

"In Memory of Lydia Winchester
(widow of William Winchester),
Who was born in Maryland on the
4th of August, 1727,
And departed this life on the
19th of February, 1809,
In the 82d year of her age"

There is still standing against the old church the first tombstone erected to Mr Winchester, but which was taken down from the head of his grave after his wife's death, when the two above mentioned were put up The old tombstone is somewhat different in phraseology, and makes a variance of two days in the time of his birth It is as follows

"In Memory of William Winchester, Born in the City of London on the 24th of December, Anno Domini 1710 (O S) Intermarried with Lydia Richards the 22d July, 1747, and Departed this Life 2d of September, 1790, aged 79 years, 8 months, [illegible]"

[illegible] ose of Lydia

Moore, eldest daughter of William Winchester the second and Mary his wife, born Feb 24 1771, died Dec 4, 1821, David Winchester, born April 18, 1769, and died Jan 13, 1835, Elizabeth Winchester, born April 19, 1763, and died June 17, 1814, and Lydia Winchester, born Dec 27, 1766, died April 19, 1849

Among other graves of old or distinguished people are the following

Catharine Fisher, born June 9, 1750, married David Fisher, June 5, 1776, and died Nov 15, 1793, and her husband, David Fisher, died Oct 15, 1815, aged 61 His second wife, Elizabeth, died April 16, 1849, aged 80

John Fisher, born in Westminster, Jan 7, 1780, died April 11, 1863

John C Cockey, born Feb 1, 1794, died Dec 16, 1826, and his wife, Ellen, born Oct 23, 1797, died July 21, 1858

James McHaffie born March 31, 1779, died Jan 3, 1818, and his wife Eleanor, born Jan 7, 1777, died April 6, 1815

Jacob Sherman born in Lancaster County, Pa, March 7, 1756 married Elizabeth Wagner, Feb 23, 1779, and died July 7, 1822, and his wife, Elizabeth, died June 28, 1842, aged 8?

Isaac Shriver, born March 6, 1777 died Dec 22, 1856, and Polly, his wife, born April 14, 1781, died March 6, 1859

Frederick Wagoner, born Feb 7, 1794, died Dec 22, 1855

Rev Isaac Webster, died Feb 4, 1851, aged 63

On one tomb are Sarah L Bennett, born April 12, 1841, died Oct 23, 1870, and Josephine I Bennett born July 4, 1843, died Feb 12, 1851

"Sacred to the memory of R H Clarke, Co B, Seventh Md Volunteers, who was sunstruck on the march from Virginia to victory at Gettysburg Brought in an ambulance to Westminster, and unable to proceed further, he here died June 30, 1863, aged 24 years

Toil worn and faithful to his country
And her service to the last"

William Frazier, Co F, 7th Md Vols, died 1864

William Horner, born Feb 1, 1778, died Aug 6, 1847, and Elizabeth, his wife, born March 18, 1793, died Jan 12, 1849

Sally Key, died Sept 14, 1855, aged 81

William Kung, born Dec 27, 1790, died Aug 6, 1851

Caleb Stansbury, Sr, died Nov 17, 1845, aged 90

Caleb Stansbury, Jr, died Aug 21, 1860, aged 66

Joshua Stansbury, died July 28, 1867 aged 75

John Powder, born April 6 1791 died Nov 10, 1844

Andrew Powder, of Jacob, born Dec 23 1798, married Elizabeth John, Jan 3 1822, and died Jan 28, 1830

Jacob Powder, died March 2 1842, aged 80

Jacob Powder, born Oct 20, 1794 died Feb 13 1870 and his wife, Elizabeth, died Aug 6, 1873, aged 74

Andrew Powder, born July 25 1793, died Oct 28, 1856

John Mitten died March 21, 1808, aged 72

Susanna Mitten, born Feb 29, 1789, died Aug 6, 1868

Henry Mourer, born Oct 17 1796 died Oct 20, 1862

Hannah Neff, died Jan 18 1826 aged 90

Andrew Reese, Sr, born Dec 12, 1759, died March 14, 1822

Andrew Reese, born May 18, 1791, died Sept 26, 1826

John Wampler, born Nov 19, 1773, died July 27, 1831, and his wife Elizabeth, born Jan 26 1780, died Nov 12, 1859

Abram Wampler, born Sept 22, 1791, died July 6, 1853

Dr S L Swormstedt born in Calvert County April 4, 1801, died March 1, 1872, and his wife, Margaret died Nov 8, 1848, aged 4?

"Sacred to the memory of J Thomas Manning, who served in the United States army against Mexico At peace he returned in ill health and after much suffering as a Christian he died His virtues end[illegible]

ions, to honor his patriotism and preserve his memory, h[illegible] erected to him this testimonial of their affectionate re[illegible] Requiescat in pace"

On the reverse side the monument reads "Died Feb 28, 1849, aged 23 years, 13 days," "Born February 1[illegible] 1826"

Jacob Righter, born July 2?, 1782, died March 21, 18?2, his wife, Rachel, born June 1 1788 died March 12, 1 4[illegible]

Dr George Colgate, died May 1 1862 aged 30

Elizabeth wife of John Winters, died Oct 15, 1858, aged [illegible]

Thomas Wood died Feb 10, 1852, aged 79

Martha, wife of Thomas Wood, died Aug 12, 1860, aged [illegible]

Dr Jesse J Utz, died July 4, 1849, aged 28

Joseph Shreeve, died Sept 10, 1858, aged 84, and his w[illegible] Comfort, died Nov 26, 1862, aged 82

Wm Shreeve, born Aug 16, 1805, died Feb 27, 1861, [illegible] his wife, Margaret, born May 16, 1802, died Jan 24 1863

Levi Shreeve, born March 6, 1807, died March 15, 1875

"Sacred to the memory of Charles W Oursler, a member [illegible] Co B, First Maryland Potomac Brigade, who fell in the [illegible] fence of his country on Maryland Heights, Sept 13, 1862, a[illegible] 21 years and 11 months"

Rachel Oursler, died Dec 5, 1841, aged 20

Catharine Keefer born March 5, 1776 married to Da[illegible] Keefer, May 18, 1795, died Sept 11, 1809

Polly Keefer, born Dec 26, 1796, died Oct 1 1862

Elerick Eckler, died Aug 27 1832, aged 67, and his wi[illegible] Elizabeth Eckler, died Sept 6, 1865, aged 100

Catharine, wife of Mordecai Price, died Feb 24, 1875, a[illegible] 80

"John W Grogg He was O S in Co A, 6th Md Vol In fantry Died in Washington Hospital, July 11, 1864, from effects of a wound received in the battle of the Wilderness A[illegible] aged 24 years, 9 months, 9 days"

Jacob Fetterling born Nov 2, 1745, died Jan 2 1830

John Grout, born April 7, 1788, died April 14, 1826

John McComb a native of Scotland, died Oct 2?, 18?0 [illegible] 74

Joshua Smith, born March 18, 1803, died July 24 18?8

Julia A, his wife, died April 24, 1880

David H Shriver, born Jan 8, 1807, died Sept 16 1[illegible] and his wife Mary, born March 17 1811, died Aug 2? 18[illegible]

Nimrod Frizzell, died Oct 13, 1842, and his wife, Anna, [illegible] 31, 1865, aged 72

Jacob Crouse, born Oct 30, 1766, died Jan 1, 1846, Elizabeth, his wife, died Sept 12, 1820, aged 47

Jacob Fringer, Sr, died June 22, 1874, aged 71, and M[illegible] garet his wife, April 12, 1841, aged 71

Catherine Yingling, born Nov 20 1790, died Dec 29, 18[illegible]

Mary Dell, died Aug 17, 1821, aged 55

Thomas Lockard born Jan 21, 1791, died April 2?, 1[illegible] and his wife, Sarah Feb 12, 1874, aged 80

Lewis Trumbo, born Oct 15, 1802, died Feb 11, 1860, [illegible] his wife, Sarah, Feb 18, 1870, aged 68

Jacob D Hoppe, died Feb 24, 1868, aged 31

Rev Jonathan Monroe 1801-1860, a Gospel Herald [illegible] years"

"Matilda Monroe 180?-1872, the Itinerant's Bride f[illegible] years"

Jacob Fisher born Aug 28 1783, died July 1, 1865

L F Grant, born Sept 5, 1818, died Nov 20, 1875

Ann Morthland, died Sept 16, 1868, aged 83

Michael Baughman, born Sept 23 1820 died Jan 2 1[illegible]

George Webster, born May 12, 1812, died Aug 22, 18[illegible]

Andrew W Durbin, died March 13, 1873 aged 50, and

Capt. George W. Shriver, born Aug. 7, 1835, died Feb. 5, 1879.

Margaret Shriver, wife of Joshua Yingling, born July 2, 18[illegible], died June 3, 1880.

Maria L. Wampler, born Jan. 29, 1811, died Sept. 11, 1875.

James L. Wampler, born March 26, 1815, died Dec. 4, 1876.

Moses Mitten, died Aug. 1, 1854, aged 67; and his wife, Rachel, Feb. 11, 1859, aged 65.

Sophia Shockey, born Jan. 10, 1808, died May 8, 1869.

Rebecca Catharine Sparklin, with her two little daughters, Eva and Lettie, instantly killed, Oct. 10, 1879, on the Michigan Central Railroad by a collision. She was born April 28, 1852.

Isaac Stansbury, died Jan. 23, 1873, aged 51.

Daniel P. Goodwin, died April 21, 1876, aged 61.

John Kuhn, died Aug. 13, 1870, aged 67.

Mahala Shue, wife of Daniel Shue, died Aug. 27, 1826, aged 22.

Dr. George Shriver, died Dec. 10, 1859, aged 31.

John Thomas Burns, born March 2, 1839, died from a kick by a horse, April 20, 1857.

Deborah D. Norris, died May 1, 1858, aged 14.

John M. Yingling, died July 19, 1873, aged 43.

Mary J., wife of H. L. Norris, died Oct. 21, 1852, aged 28.

William Metzger, born April 25, 1793, in Hanover, Pa., died Nov. 29, 1872.

William Yingling, born March 13, 1810, died March 13, 1876.

Annie L., daughter of Joshua and Julia A. Smith, and wife of Col. William A. McKellip, died May 1, 1880, aged 39.

Sarah J., wife of Wm. Reese, died Jan. 21, 1876, aged 47.

Gabriel Hannemann, died March 1, 1854, aged 65.

Abraham Shafer, died Dec. 13, 1872, aged 76; and his wife, Mary, Nov. 29, 1864, aged 65.

Mary Adrian, wife of John T. Diffenbaugh, born Jan. 22, 1828, died Feb. 6, 1877.

Miranda, wife of Richard Manning, died May 28, 1865, aged 31.

Jacob J. Leister, died Feb. 11, 1878, aged 67.

Alfred Troxel, born Nov. 25, 1816, died Feb. 27, 1867; and his wife, Louisa, Jan. 23, 1850, aged 30.

Absalom Kiell, born Jan. 1, 1795, died March 15, 1859.

Sallie H., wife of Dr. Charles M. Martin, died Jan. 26, 1872, aged 28.

Abraham H. Busby, born Sept. 4, 1865, died Aug. 5, 1867.

Rebecca M., wife of Solomon Zepp, died March 18, 1875, aged 58.

David Fisher, died April 10, 1827, aged 22.

Thomas Smith, born June 11, 1797, died Feb. 15, 1877; and his wife, Mary, born Oct. 25, 1807, died June 2, 1862.

Joshua Smith, died Dec. 13, 1841, aged 80; and his wife, Susanna, May 3, 1832, aged 63.

Joseph Smith, born March 10, 1801, died Nov. 6, 1866; and his wife, Elizabeth, born March 7, 1806, died Feb. 17, 1881.

Isaac E. Pearson, born November, 1811, died March 18, 1877; and his wife, Maria, born May 12, 1821, died Feb. 19, 1873.

Emanuel Herr, born December, 1799, died July, 1860.

George R. Rhodes, born in Nottingham, England, Nov. 5, 1805, died March 8, 1859.

Lodie Berry, wife of Rev. H. C. Cushing, born in Fauquier Co., Va., Oct. 18, 1826, died Sept. 7, 1874.

This cemetery corporation was organized June 17, 1864, under a charter passed by the Legislature of previous winter. The first officers were:

President, George E. Wampler; Secretary, E. K. Gernand; Treasurer, H. L. Norris; Directors, William Reese, Dr. J. L. Warfield, Joseph M. Parke, John K. Longwell, J. Henry Hoppe, Alfred Troxell.

After the Revolutionary war, John Logston gave four acres of ground in Westminster to the Catholic Church, and on it was erected the first church about 1785. It was a frame structure, which in 1805 made way for a neat brick edifice called "Christ Church." This stood until 1872, when it was taken down and part of the materials used in building that year St. John's Parochial School. The third, St. John's church, was dedicated on Wednesday, Nov. 22, 1866, according to the impressive and solemn rites of the Catholic Church. There were fifteen priests in attendance, among them Rev. John McCaffery, D.D., president of Mount St. Mary's College; Rev. John McClusky, D.D., vice-president of the same; and Rev. Thomas Foley, D.D., secretary to the archbishop. The dedicatory sermon, which was able and interesting, was delivered by the latter in a very chaste style. Solemn high mass was celebrated, Rev. John Dougherty being the celebrant, Rev. Henry McMurdie, deacon, Rev. Father Kronenberg, subdeacon. The music was grand, there being present thirteen members of the Cathedral choir of Baltimore, under Prof. Leinhardt, who presided at the organ. It is estimated that eleven hundred people were present in the church. Rev. John Gloyd was then and is now the pastor in charge.

The first pastor was Father Nicholas Zacchi, who came to Taneytown in 1804. Through his efforts the second church edifice was erected in 1805. He had charge of the church until his death in 1845. His successor was Father Thomas O'Neil, from 1851 to 1862, there having been an interregnum of six years. The next pastor was Father John Gloyd, who came in November, 1862, and is the present able and beloved pastor. He removed here from Taneytown in 1869, and this then became the headquarters of the mission until its division in 1879. Father Gloyd has charge of this church, St. Bartholomew's, at Manchester, and attends St. Mary's chapel, at Uniontown, at the residence of Mrs. William Shriver. St. John's school since its establishment, in 1872, has been under the charge of F. A. McGirr.

Many years ago Rajenia Grand Adams left thirty acres of land adjoining the town to the Catholic Church, which was leased, and its rents are applied, one-fourth to the church and the remainder to the priest in charge. John Orendorff, father of Francis H. and Josephus Orendorff, was mainly instrumental in rearing the present handsome church, having given five hundred thousand bricks, the quantity necessary for its construction. Father Gloyd's assistants on the

mission until its division, in 1879, were Richard Haseman, from 1871 to 1873; from 1873 to 1874, Casper Schmidt; and from 1874 to 1879, John T Delaney

The following persons are buried in the Catholic cemetery

Francis Anderson, died Oct 28, 1842, aged 44
Thomas Adelsparger, died Nov 28, 1822, aged 71; Eleanor, his wife, died Aug 1, 1846, aged 87
Mary A, wife of John H Logue, died June 2, 1865, aged 38
G W Fowler, died Dec 21, 18[illegible], aged 75; Rachel, his wife, died Jan 8, 18[illegible], aged 81
Mary Fowler, died Jan 30, 18[illegible], aged 77
Richard Fowler, died Dec 4, 1850, aged 87; Mary M, his wife, died June 15, 1866, aged 65
John A Hirsch, died Sept 1, 1872, aged 83 years, 4 months, 22 days; Anna M, his wife, born Sept 10, 1790, died May 15, 1868
Lydia C, wife of John Coker, died June 7, 1851, aged 34
Elias Weaver, born Feb 27, 1805, died Oct 3, 1828
John Keane, died Jan 2, 1815, aged 56
Frances Conly, died Nov 16, 1841, aged 79
Robina M Anderson, died Jan 2, 1869, aged 75 years, 3 months, 12 days
Ellen Weaver, born 1778, died April 28, 1851
Christian Orendorff, died Jan 21, 1816, aged 55
Polly, wife of John W Coker, died April 20, 1861, aged 70
Kate Orendorff, died Aug 13, 1869, aged 31
Elizabeth Wells, died Sept 3, 18[illegible], aged 58
Wm Orendorff, born July 6, 182[illegible], died Aug 9, 1847
John Orendorff, died Feb 18, 1829, aged 74
Joseph Orendorff, died April 6, 1821, aged 16 years, 7 months, 24 days
Hannah Williams, died Oct 21, 1831, aged 62
Hannah Fowler, died 1824
John Fowler, died 1825
Catharine F, wife of Jeremiah Lockard, born May 8, 1824, died Dec 25, 18[illegible]
John Feltz, died April 11, 1862, aged 1 year, 4 months
Joseph Arnold, died April 10, 1815, aged 70
Mary Arnold, died March 20, 18[illegible], aged 71
Joseph Arnold, died Feb 8, 18[illegible], aged 76
Wm Hayden, died June 4, 1862, aged 48
Honor Fowler, died May 7, 1862, aged 59 years, 1 month, 14 days
Rebecca Fowler, died Nov 8, 1863, aged 75 years, 10 days
Comfort Durbin, died June 4, 1855, aged 83
Benjamin Durbin, died Aug 6, 1811, aged 30 years, 1 month
Benjamin Durbin, born March 30, 1748, died Nov 20, 1815
Susannah Durbin, died Dec 24, 1836, aged 84
Catherine Durbin, died Dec 9, 1849, aged 58
Dr Wm Matthias, born March 8, 1821, died April 17, 1864; Adelaide E, his wife, born May 10, 1832, died Nov 10, 1865
Rebecca Orendorff, born Oct 26, 1818, died Dec 24, 1868
Eleanor Hayden, died April 19, 1841, aged 37
Catharine Hayden, died Oct 10, 1857, aged 85
Anna, wife of Patrick Hamitt, died May 3, 1817, aged 50
Wm Hayden, Jr, died March 12, 1817, aged 35 years, 6 months, 24 days
Thomas Durbin, died April 3, 1816, aged 77 years, 9 months
Daniel Arter, born Aug 4, 1742, died Feb 13, 1813
Wm Arnold, born Oct 6, 1758, died Feb 20, 1832
Henrietta Arn[illegible]

Mary Logsdon, died April 17, 1829, aged —
Elizabeth A, consort of W Loyd, died June 22, 18[illegible], aged 74
Philip Cleary, born Oct 18, 1797, died Oct 20, 1860
Dr W S Shipley, died June 21, 1870, aged 27
John Matthias, died Aug 6, 1817, aged 67
Catharine, his wife, died Nov 7, 1818, aged 59
Regina Grenadam, died May 2[illegible], 1817, aged 80
Francis Grenadam, born Feb 15, 1728, married to Regina Brechbeal, 1754, died Feb 18, 1806
Catharine Matthias, born Nov 22, 1785, died Sept 4, 1807
Margaret Matthias, born June 20, 1796, died Sept 7, 1807
Anthony Arnold, died Aug 19, 1824, aged 17 years, 4 months, 5 days
John Lockard, died May 8, 1874, aged 80 years, 5 months, [illegible] days; Elizabeth, his wife, died May 5, 1843, aged 55
Edward Fowler, died Nov 21, 1863, aged 86 years, 1 month, 21 days
Catharine Corban, died Sept 6, 1841, aged 47
Basil Hayden, died Feb 2, 1865, aged 79, and Apprillah, his wife, Feb 6, 1861, aged 79
John Matthias, wife of Jacob, born Nov 15, 1791, died June 8, 1872
Michael Lynch, died Nov 20, 1860, aged 67
Mary Lynch, died Oct 5, 1868, aged 65
Mary Ann Snider, died Sept 20, 1862, aged 12
Chryostom Burke, born Feb 29, 18[illegible]7, died Dec 18, 1863
Mary E, wife of Wm H Grumbine, born Feb 10, 1825, died Sept 11, 1863
Anna Doyle, died Nov 28, 1859, aged 50
John A Matthias, born June 18, 1821, died Dec 2, 1860
Cornelius Buckley, died May 12, 1877, aged 59 years, 2 months, 2 days
Eliza J Buckley, died Nov 3, 1876, aged 11 years, 10 months, 6 days
Joseph Eckenrode, died Sept 15, 1865, aged 54 years, 8 months
Regina Frankhouser, died August, 1853, aged 74
Christina Obold, died Feb 6, 1851, aged 89
John Wise, died July 27, 1860, aged 68 years, 7 months, 4 days
Susan, his wife, died April 19, 1861, aged 68
Benjamin Fowler, died Jan 7, 1862, aged 58 years, 9 months
Charlotte, wife of Bernard Kean, born Oct 21, 1801, died July 17, 1845
Sephero N Awald, died Jan 31, 18[illegible]5, aged 39
Geo Strawheaffer, died April 2, 185[illegible], aged 43
Catharine Keele, died Feb 16, 18[illegible], aged 62
Eve Awald, died April 4, 1856, aged 76
Henry Hilzkamp, died Jan 5, 18[illegible], aged 54
John Ore, died June 17, 186[illegible], aged 63
Anthony McConwell, a native of County Armagh, Ireland, died July 11, 1865, aged 50
Adam Bowers, died Nov 2, 1861, aged 72 years, 11 months, 25 days; Catharine, his wife, died Jan 6, 1874, aged 84 years, 11 months, 8 days
Anastace A, wife of John Ore, died March 4, 1876, aged [illegible]
Catharine, wife of Aquilla Bowers, died June 26, 1869, aged 70 years, 11 months, 11 days
John Yingling, died Jan 15, 18[illegible]0, aged 9[illegible]
Eliza Lovell, died Jan 10, 1870, aged [illegible] years, 6 months, [illegible] days
Theresa, wife of J W Zentgraf, born in Larbeck, Germany, Aug 7, 1767, died in Westminster, Dec 6, 1818
John Powers, died Aug 7, 1876, aged 40
[illegible]

Patrick O Brien, "a native of the parish of Castletownroche, County Cork Ireland," died Oct 7, 1873, aged 80

Margaret his wife born in Ireland died Oct 1, 1868 aged 72

Helen M, wife of William J Case, died Feb 22, 1878, aged [illegible] years, 10 months, 15 days

Sarah Haase, died June 27, 1876 aged 76

John Roberts born Aug 12 1804, died Oct 25, 1870

Ann wife of William Roberts, died June 27, 1860, aged 85

Daniel H Roberts, born Sept 18 1840, died July 19, 1871

Catharine G Roberts died April 26, 1805, aged 52

Catharine Hook, died Oct 27, 1873, aged 74

John Sinnott, died May 12 1880 aged 75

Andrew J Beaver, died May 8 1879, aged 53 years, 5 months, 15 days

Paul Case, born May 8, 1806, died Sept 5, 1875, Helen, his wife born Sept 5, 1810, died Nov 4, 1875

Rose F Neal, born July 8, 1867, died March 4 1875

Elizabeth Manydier, wife of John Brook Boyle, died Feb 6, 1876, aged 64 years 6 months

Mary A wife of Joshua Corbin, died April 6, 1880, aged 70

Michael O'Brien a native of Cork County, Ireland, died Dec 12, 1862, aged 40, Rebecca, his wife, died March 9, 1881, aged 60 years

John Everheart died Dec 7, 1876, aged 81 years, 11 months, 24 days

Anne Smith, born March, 1829, died February, 1877

Mary Myers, died Nov 8 1878, aged 76 years

Philip Keller, died July 15, 1867, aged 70 years 9 months, 20 days

John Koontz, died Sept 27, 1872, aged 70 years 6 months, 27 days

Thomas Hurley, died April 22, 1869, aged 67 years

Morris Hurley, died Oct 21, 1878, aged 32 years, 9 months, 9 days

Christopher Rooney, died Oct 23, 1865, aged 46 "Served in the U S Navy for fifteen years When the Rebellion broke out enlisted as a private in Company C, Sixth Regiment Md Vol U S Army and served as chief musician of the regiment until the close of the war receiving an honorable discharge Oct 5, 1865"

Elizabeth Buchman, a native of France, born March 16, 1771, died March 24, 1855

Elizabeth Koons died March 26 1851 aged 56

Matthew Denning, died Feb 4, 1865, aged 93, and Hannah, his wife, March 14, 1858, aged 78

"Jim," "as a recognition of his services and fidelity to the family" J T Mathias

Martin Whiteleather died Nov 29, 1876, aged 63 years, 1 month, 16 days

Joseph Hawn, died Feb 16, 1875, aged 81 years, 1 month, 27 days Catharine, his wife died March 23, 1861, aged 66 years, 5 months, 2 days

Nicholas Zentgraf, born in Larbach, Germany, Jan 10, 1810, died Oct 12, 1872

Joseph Shanaborough, died June 2, 1872 aged 75 years, 5 months, Patience, his wife, born Oct 26, 1797, died July 26, 1851

William Coghlan, born Dec 31, 1774, died March 27 1854

Grace Lutheran Church was organized in 1816, and on August 5th of that year the corner stone of its church edifice was laid with imposing ceremonies Before that time the members of this new congregation had worshiped at St Benjamin's church (Kreiger's), about a mile and a half from town Occasionally Lutheran services were held in the "Old Union Meeting-house" The first preaching in this section of the country was by Lutheran and German Reformed preachers and missionaries, as far back as 1747 and 1748 Its pastors have been

1842–53 Rev Philip Willard (preaching before the building of the church at Kreiger's), 1853–60 Rev Samuel Henry, 1860–63, Rev J Martin 1863–67 Rev H C Holloway, 1867–69, Rev P A Strobel, 1870–78, Rev John A Earnest, Aug 28, 1878 to the present time, Rev Henry W Kuhns

It has a flourishing Sunday school, of which Henry B Grammer is superintendent, and William Seabrook, assistant This church, an outgrowth of St Benjamin's, forms with it and St John's (Leister's), near Mexico, a charge under Rev Mr Kuhns From 1816 to about 1857 Boust and Winters' churches were united with these three in one charge

Adjoining the fine church is a neat parsonage owned by the congregation

St Paul's Reformed Church is a child of the old mother church, St Benjamin's (or Kreiger's), a mile and a half distant in the country Its separate church organization was formed in 1868, when was laid the corner-stone of its elegant edifice which was completed in 1869 Before that time its members worshiped at Kreiger's, though occasional Reformed preaching was heard in the "Old Union Meeting house" from 1790 to 1840 The church was organized and its building erected under the auspices of Rev W C Cremer, who continued as pastor until 1876 His successor was Rev J G Noss, who is the present incumbent, and was installed in December, 1876 The Consistory is composed of Peter B Mikesell, John H Bowers, John L Reifsnider, Andrew N Stephan, elders, and J Brinkerhoff, J T Orndorff, Theodore A Evans, William H H Zepp, deacons The superintendent of the Sunday school is William B Thomas The elegant parsonage adjoining the church was built after the latter's erection The site of this church, on the corner of Green and Broad Streets, is one of the most beautiful and desirable in the city The main building is forty six by seventy feet on the flank wall, with a pulpit recess of six by eighteen feet, making the entire length of the building, from the outside wall of the tower to that of the pulpit-recess, eighty-three feet The building has a basement ten feet high, and an audience-chamber eighteen feet deep on the flank wall and thirty-one and a half in the centre. The style of architecture is modern Gothic with traces of a composite nature The front and tower are supported by pilasters, capped with the Gettysburg granite The brick-work is adorned with pin-

nacles, and a spire sixty feet in height making the entire height of tower and spire one hundred and twenty six feet The windows are Gothic, with stained and frosted glass The audience-chamber has a chancel, with a beautifully designed pulpit, reading desk, and baptismal font The pews are scroll, front and back, and the ceiling is ornamented with panel, stucco, and fresco work The building committee were David H Shriver, Augustus Shriver S L Myers, A Long Jesse Crowl, Josiah Crowl, and Rev W C Creamer The architects were Shaib & Leister, master-carpenter George Lease, master-mason and bricklayer, Christian Awalt

The Westminster Society of the Methodist Protestant Church was organized in 1829 It was originally included in the association of churches constituting Pipe Creek Circuit In 1837 it was made a separate charge, and so continued until 1840, when it became a part of Baltimore Circuit In 1844 it was again united with Pipe Creek Circuit, and continued to hold that relation until 1871, at which time it became again a district church under the title of Westminster Station

Its pastors have been

1829, D E Reese Sr , 1830, F Stier, J Hanson, 1831, I Stier, J Ibberston 1832, Isaac Webster, C Jacobs, 1833, Isaac Webster, W Sexsmith 1834, Josiah Varden H Doyle, 1835, J W Everest, H Doyle, A A Lipscomb, 1836, John S Reese, J W Porter, 1837, I G Clayton, 1838, Josiah Varden, 1839, J W Porter, 1840 Eli Henkle, James Elderdice, 1841, J Keller, J Hisore, 1842, J Whitworth, J Hisore, 1843, Eli Henkle, 1844, W Collier, T L McLean, I D Brooks, 1845–46, W Collier, P L Brooks, J K Nichols, 1847, F Morgan, F D Valiant, 1848, J Morgan, W Roby 1849, D E Reese, W Roby, 1850, D E Reese, F L McLean, 1851, H P Jordan, J Roberts, 1852, H P Jordan, H J Day, 1853, I M Wilson, H J Day, 1854, I M Wilson, J A McFadden, 1855, F Swentzell, J A McFadden, 1856, F Swentzell, K S Greenaway, 1857–59, J T Ward, J T Murray, 1860, D I Reese, J B Jones 1861, D L Reese, 1862–64, P L Wilson, 1865–68 R S Norris 1868–71 D Wilson, 1871–74, W S Hammond, 1874–77, H C Cushing, 1877–81, S B Southerland, 1881, March, J T Murray, present incumbent

The present church edifice was built upon the site of the former, and was dedicated August, 1868, Rev Daniel Wilson being the pastor, when the dedicatory sermon was preached by Rev J J Murray, D D

The superintendent of the Sunday-school is Dr Charles Billingslea The church trustees are E O Grimes, Joshua Yingling, Dr J W Hering, and the stewards, Dr C Billingslea, R S Nairment, Isaac Baile, Jesse Shreeve, Elias Yingling, Dr W H Rippard, and M L Lantz

The church edifice owned and occupied by the German Baptists or Brethren (Dunkers), is situated on Bond Street, fronting Belle Park It was erected by the Baptists, assisted by friends of its pastor, Rev Dr Cole The congregation was small, and the sale of the building became advisable It was purchased by the Brethren they paying therefor the sum of two thousand two hundred dollars They were materially assisted therein by the citizens of Westminster not connected with their denomination The building is a handsome brick structure The congregation is a part of that very considerable body known as the "Pipe Creek Congregation" Its bishop or elder is Solomon Stoner, who resides at Uniontown The associate ministers are William H Franklin, Ephraim W Stoner, Joel Roop, Amos Caylor, and Uriah Bixler

The original trustees were Henry Warner, John Englar, D D Bonsack, Uriah Bixler, and Dr Lewis Woodward To these, in trust for the use of the Brethren, were conveyed the buildings by Rev Isaac Cole, Julia J Cole, George W Matthews, Charles L Morgan, Isabella M Matthews, trustees of the Westminster Baptist Church, by deed dated May 9, 1879

In November, 1880, a Sunday-school was organized numbering at present about one hundred and fifty scholars Its superintendent is Dr Lewis Woodward

The Protestant Episcopal Church (Ascension) was organized in 1842 by Revs David Hillhouse Buell and C C Austin, but Episcopal services had been held at various times previously The corner-stone of the church edifice was laid Aug 27, 1844, with appropriate ceremonies, by the Rt Rev Bishop Whittingham, assisted by other clergymen It was erected on one of the court-house lots It was built of stone, under the superintendence of R Carey Long, an eminent architect of Baltimore It was consecrated by Bishop Whittingham, May 19, 1846 The first record of baptism is that of Fannie C Shellman, now the wife of Isaac E Pearson, Oct 16, 1842, by Rev Charles C Austin Its rectors have been

1842 or '43 to 1847 or '48, David Hillhouse Buell, 1848–51, Samuel Chalmers Davis, 1851–53, Thomas James Wyatt, Feb 26, 1854, to 1857, Oliver Sherman Prescott 1857 to Sept 27, 1861, Edward H C Goodwin, April 20, 1862, to Jan 20 1864 James Chrystal, Jan 20, 1864, to March 8, 1870, James W Reese, A M , April 10, 1870, to July 10, 1871, John H Converse, A M , Aug 1, 1871, to April 1, 1875, Julian L Inge, Oct 1, 1875, to Dec 1, 1879 Isaac Leo Nicholson, Jr A M , Jan 7, 1880 James Stuart Smith, D D

The church officers in 1881 were Wardens, Henry Vanderford, Charles T Reifsnider, Vestrymen, Dr C … E … H … P … , George Shaffer,

Chapman Johnson, Dr. Columbus M Brown Rev Mr Smith the rector, is superintendent of the Sunday school, and has also a colored congregation in connection with his parish "The Guild of the Holy Child" has been in successful operation for several years The new chapel was begun June, 1876, and completed in September of that year, and was opened September 29th, on the festival of St Michael's The new communion plate was procured at Easter, 1876 and consecrated in August succeeding The commodious parsonage was commenced in October 1879, and completed the ensuing year, and occupied on St Barnabas' day, June 11th An English ivy covers the entire façade of the church, which is a pure model of Gothic architecture In the rear is the parish burying-ground, where lie at rest many who were prominently connected with the church An interesting tomb in this cemetery is that of Leigh Master, the inscription on which is as follows

"Leigh Master, Esquire,
Late of New Hall, in
Lancashire, England
Died the 22d day of March, 1796,
Aged 79 years"

In the corner of the yard lies the body of Capt William Murray, who fell in a skirmish at Westminster, June 29, 1863, during the civil war, between a company of Delaware Federal cavalry and the advance-guard of Gen J E B Stuart's Confederate command, where six or seven others were killed The names of all other persons in this cemetery to whom stones are erected are here given

Betty G Van Bibber, born May 18, 1816, died Oct 21, 1858 Sally F Van Bibber died Sept 21, 1852, aged 16

Isaac Van Bibber, born Jan 27, 1810, died Sept 28, 1847

Washington Van Bibber born Feb 15, 1778, died April 8, 1848, and Lucretia Van Bibber, died May 10, 1867, aged 80

Abraham Van Bibber, died Feb 12, 1861, aged 39 George L Van Bibber

Isaac Van Bibber, Ann Neilson (both on one stone) Marcher, son of G L and H C Van Bibber Mary Emory, died June 7, 1874, aged 82

Elizabeth S Perry, born March 31, 1817, died Oct 7, 1861

James M Shellman, born in Louisville, Ga, Sept 8, 1801, died Jan 14, 1851

Jacob Reese, born Jan 31, 1798, died April 19, 1872, and his wife, Eleanor, born Oct 5 1798, died Nov 20, 1871

John F Reese, born Feb 17, 1808, died April 15, 1859

Catherine F, wife of Edwin F Reese, born Jan 23, 1834, died Sept 7 1860, Fannie, her daughter aged 3 months, and Ella, another daughter, died July 11, 1863, aged nearly 1

Dr Elisha D Payne, born Nov 11 1796, died Jan 19, 1865

Grizelle daughter of Joseph M. and Margaret Newson, died July 11 1872, aged 16

Anna Mary, daughter of D W and Mary A Hunter, died Sept 3, 1870, aged 8 months Samuel Lantz

Samuel Butler, of Company C, Thirty second Regiment, U S C T, died A[illegible] aged 4[illegible]

61

George Ann Buyer, aged 13

Dr Bernard Mills, died May 19, 1869 aged 38

Eliza, wife of Francis Dorsey born April 16 1801, died March 14 1865

Clara V, daughter of George S and Mary J Fouke, died May 29 1863, nearly 3 years of age

Fannie, daughter of William and Mary A Moore, aged 1 year

R T D Rosan died Feb 25, 1852, aged 1 year

The Centenary Methodist Episcopal church was built in 1869 Methodist preaching was held at private dwellings in Westminster as early as 1769, and among the local or traveling preachers who held services were Hezekiah Bonham and his son Robert, Robert Strawbridge, Paul Hagarty John Hagarty, Robert Walker, and Freeborn Garrettson, who came at irregular intervals and preached in this new settlement After the building of the "Old Union Meeting-house" service was occasionally held until 1839, when the regular church organization took place In this year was erected the first Methodist Episcopal church, a brick structure, on the site of the present edifice In 1865 the parsonage was built The present church building was begun in April, 1868 Its corner-stone was laid in August following, and the edifice was completed and occupied in March, 1869 It is a Gothic structure, twenty nine feet high in the clear on the inside, and is thirty by eighty feet in size. It has an audience-room and basement, the latter one of the finest in the State outside of Baltimore The building, with its furnishings, cost nearly sixteen thousand dollars It has three organs Its site was formerly owned by John Fisher When erected its pastor was Rev J Edwin Amos, who was admitted to the Conference in 1859 Since it was made a station, in 1869, its pastors, with dates of their admission into the Conference, have been

1869, John W Hedges, adm 1845, 1870–72, C P Baldwin, adm 1866, 1872–74, C H Richardson, adm 1869 1874–76, George V Leech, adm 1856, 1876–78, E E Shipley, adm 1862, 1878–81 J D Still, adm 1859, 1881, John Edwards, adm 1871

Its Sunday school superintendent is H L Norris, and the assistant is Miss Sue Castle The number of scholars is 100

The Union National Bank of Westminster (usually styled the "Old Bank") was removed in April, 1868, from the building it had occupied as a banking institution for more than half a century to the fine building erected by Dr Hering in the central part of the town, which was fitted up in handsome style with all the necessary appurtenances for banking This is one of the oldest institutions in the State

The Union [illegible] Farmers' [illegible] of Baltimore

established a branch in Westminster in 1814 At that time the cities on the Chesapeake were threatened by the British army It was located in the building then owned by Jacob Krouse, where the vaults were prepared and the specie and the other funds of the Commercial and Farmers' Bank were removed for greater security The branch was under the management of Mr Thomal, one of the clerks of the parent bank

As this was intended merely as a temporary arrangement, after the war was over the branch was withdrawn

An act of incorporation was obtained for the Bank of Westminster in 1816, with a capital of three hundred thousand dollars The books of subscription for stock were opened in Westminster and Middleburg by commissioners, one of whom was Joshua C Gist The first election for directors was held in March, 1816, when the following-named gentlemen were elected, viz James McHaffie, John Fisher, Jesse Slingluff, Isaac Shriver, Joshua Delaplane Jacob Shriver, John Wampler, Dr George Colegate, Joshua Cockey, and Francis Hollingsworth Mr Hollingsworth declined serving, when Wm Durbin, Sr, was chosen

At the first meeting of the board, in April, 1816, James McHaffie was elected president, and at a subsequent meeting John Walsh (a clerk in the Union Bank of Baltimore) was elected cashier, and John Wampler appointed clerk

A considerable amount of the stock of the bank having been subscribed at "Frederick Town," the stockholders then asked for a branch, styled the "Office of Pay and Receipt," which was granted in 1817, under control of a board of managers, with the venerable Dr William Tyler at its head

This was the origin of what afterwards became and is now known as the Farmers and Mechanics' Bank of Frederick County

In 1818, Jesse Slingluff was elected president in place of James McHaffie, deceased

In 1819 the directors elected were as follows Jesse Slingluff, president, William Durbin, Ludwick Wampler, Henry Kuhn, George Colegate, Benjamin Rutherford, John C Cockey, Gideon Bantz, Thomas Boyer, John Fisher, Joseph Swearingen

In 1820, John Wampler was chosen cashier in place of Mr Walsh

In 1821, Mr Slingluff resigned the presidency and was succeeded by John C Cockey, Mr Slingluff continued as director until his death

In 1828, Mr Cockey died, Joshua Jones acted as president *pro tem.* until April 1827 [illegible] Shriver was elected president, and at the same time John Fisher was elected cashier in place of Mr Wampler

In 1827 the stockholders at Frederick demanded change, and the Legislature granted their request, changing the title from the "Bank of Westminster" to that of the "Farmers' and Mechanics' Bank of Frederick County," with the parent bank at Frederick and the branch at Westminster Dr William Tyler as president, and William M Beale as cashier, were the officers at Frederick, and Isaac Shriver as president, and John Fisher as cashier, were continued at the branch

In 1829 the Frederick stockholders attempted to abolish the branch, which was resisted, and finally resulted in a separation in 1830 of the two institutions, the bank here resuming its original title of "Bank of Westminster," with a capital of $100,000 one third of the original stock remaining here and two thirds in the Farmers' and Mechanics' Bank of Frederick County

In 1857, John K Longwell was elected president in place of Isaac Shriver, deceased, who had served in that capacity for thirty years

In 1863, John Fisher died, after having been cashier of the bank for thirty-six years, and having served as director or cashier from the creation of the bank in 1816 to the period of his death and was succeeded by the election of John C Frizzell as cashier

On April 27, 1865, the bank was robbed, as the following account of the same will show

"About two o'clock on Thursday evening the cry of fire was raised in the town John Frizzel the cashier and the clerk were both in the bank at the time Mr Frizzel locked the door of the building, leaving the vault open, and proceeded to the scene of the conflagration, which proved to be the barn of Mr Frizzel, which had been set on fire, and which the citizens succeeded in extinguishing On returning to the bank it was discovered that the front door had been forced, and the institution robbed of eleven thousand dollars in greenbacks and ten thousand dollars in the issues of the bank consisting of twenty and fifty-dollar notes A large package of ten dollar notes was dropped on the floor of the vault in the hurry of the thieves to get away The whole affair was executed in a few minutes and was remarkably well planned"

In 1866 the institution was changed from the State Bank of Westminster to that of the Union National Bank of Westminster, when John J Baumgartner was elected cashier in place of Mr Frizzell, resigned

In 1867, Mr Baumgartner resigned and Dr J W Hering was elected cashier

In 1869 the officers of the bank were as follows

Directors, John K Longwell president, Jacob Powder, James J Gorman Abraham Shaffer, William Reese John Roop J Henry Hoppe, Lawrence Zepp David Roop, [illegible] Hugo P [illegible]

In 1881 the directors were

[illegible] Longwell president Daniel J Gieman William Reese, David Gieman Lawrence Zepp, Charles B Roberts, Francis R Orendorff William P Maulsby, Dr Frank T Shaw Dr J Howard Billingslea, Cashier, Dr J W Hering

The committee of directors of the Farmers' and Mechanics' Bank appointed to secure an eligible location for the erection of a banking-house reported, Oct 25, 1850, that they had purchased the house and lot of ground then in the occupancy of Capt John McCollum This property was situated in the central part of the town and was bought for $2300 The stockholders connected a banking-house with the main building, eighteen feet front, and running back thirty feet, on the side next to A W Dorsey's drug store This building was erected by Wampler & Evans, and completed in January, 1851 In November, 1850, the president, Jacob Matthias, selected the plates for printing notes of the denominations of 1's, 5's, 10's, 20's, and 50's The third installment of five dollars on each share of subscribed stock was called for to be paid in by Jan 1, 1851

This bank has from the beginning done a large amount of business and is under judicious management The office of president has been filled by Jacob Matthias, John Smith, Dr J L Warfield Joseph Shaeffer, and that of cashier by Jacob Reese and A D Schaeffer In 1876 the directors were William Bachman, Andrew K Shriver, John Babylon, Benjamin W Bennett, George Schaeffer, William A McKellip In 1881 they were Joseph Schaeffer, Benjamin W Bennett, George Schaeffer, William Bachman, William A McKellip

The First National Bank of Westminster was established in 1860, under the new national system of banking and the result of its operations is considered a decided success by its stockholders and customers Up to 1881 its officers have been Presidents, Alfred Troxel, Augustus Shriver, Granville S Haines, Cashiers, William A Cunningham, George R Gehr, Directors, Joshua Yingling, David Englar, William Lawyer, David Cassell, Samuel McKinstry, Philip H L Myers, David J Roop, Henry Baile

The Mutual Fire Insurance Company of Carroll County was chartered and began business in 1869 Its first directors were Augustus Shriver (president), Richard Manning (secretary and treasurer), John E Roberts, Alfred Zollickoffer, Dr Henry E Beltz Edward Lynch, Dr J W Hering, Dr Samuel Swope Granville S Haines, David Prugh The directors in 1881 were

Dr J W Hering (president) Richard Manning (secretary and treasurer), Granville S Haines Edward Lynch David Fowble, Dr Samuel Swope Charles B Roberts David Prugh, Granville T Hering Alfred Zollickoffer

The above comprises all who have been directors from its organization save Daniel H Roberts, deceased

The Westminster Savings Institution was organized in 1869 In 1876 its officers were

President, Jesse Reifsnider Treasurer B W Bennett, Secretary J T Diffenbaugh, Directors Dr Charles Billingslea, Luther H Norris Nathan I Gorsuch, James W Beacham Ezra S Stouffer Charles T Reifsnider

Its officers in 1881 were

President, B W Bennett, Secretary, John T Diffenbaugh, Treasurer, Jesse Reifsnider, Directors H L Norris, Dr Charles Billingslea, J L Lawyer E O Grimes Mordecai McKinstry Charles T Reifsnider

It was incorporated Oct 4, 1869 Its incorporators and first officers were

President, Jesse Reifsnider, Secretary, John T Diffenbaugh, Treasurer Nathan I Gorsuch, Directors, Benjamin W Bennett John Englar, Josephus H Hoppe H L Norris, James W Beacham, Chas T Reifsnider, Wm L Legg

A mass-meeting of the citizens of Westminster was held April 27 1876, to consider the advisability of an additional water supply for the municipality An act of Assembly had been passed authorizing the levy of a tax for this purpose, coupled with a proviso that it should not be levied unless approved by a vote of the next city council of the town The meeting was enthusiastically in favor of the improvement Mayor David Fowble presided, and Dr William H Rippard and W H Vanderford acted as secretaries A ticket ignoring politics and in favor of the waterworks was chosen, as follows for mayor, P H Irwin, for councilmen, Jesse Yingling, Nathan Y Gorsuch, and M B Grammer The ticket was elected at the subsequent election to carry out the necessary measures to furnish the city with a supply of pure water

There was a meeting March 24, 1870, of the stockholders of the Westminster Gaslight Company, and the following officers were chosen to direct the affairs of the company President, John L Reifsnider, Directors, C Oliver O'Donnell, C Hart Smith, George C Hicks, Joshua Yingling, Charles B Roberts, and Edward Lynch Dr James L Billingslea was chairman of the meeting and W A Cunningham, secretary The progress of the company from this time was rapid The necessary buildings were begun and hurried to completion, and in September the city was lighted with gas The work of [illegible] A Holmes,

of Baltimore The officers of the company in 1876 were President, John L Reifsnider, Directors, Charles B Roberts, Edward Lynch, Joshua Yingling, C Hart Smith, George C Hicks, Charles E Savage, Secretary and Treasurer, William A Cunningham

Joseph M Parke, one of the most estimable citizens of Westminster, and the subject of this sketch, was born Feb 6, 1810, in Sadsbury township, Chester Co, Pa, about one mile north of Parkesburg His

Jos. M. Parke

father, George W Parke, was born Oct 18, 1780, and died Feb 25, 1860 His mother was Mary, daughter of John Fleming of the neighborhood of Coatesville She died in February, 1817 His maternal grandmother was a Slaymaker, of Pequea, Lancaster Co, Pa, and his paternal grandfather was Joseph Parke, who was born in Chester County, Pa, Dec 21, 1737, and died near Parkesburg, July 2, 1823 His paternal grandmother was Ann Maxwell, of Lancaster County, Pa His great-grandfather was John Parke, who died July 28, 1787, and his great-great grandfather was Arthur Parke, who came to this country with his family from Donegal County, Ireland, some time prior to 1724 and settled in West Fallowfield township, Chester Co, Pa, and died there in February, 1740, as stated in Everts' "History of Chester County, Pa," published in Jul [illegible] The Parke family is of the Scotch-Irish Presbyterian stock, and went to North Ireland at an early period from Scotland or England Joseph Maxwell Parke has several brothers and a sister still surviving, viz Samuel S, George W, Jr, and Dr Charles R Parke, all of Bloomington, Ill,—the latter a half-brother by his father's second marriage,—and Caroline, wife of Evan Jones, now residing near Winchester, Va In 1823, at the age of thirteen years he left home to attend a classical school started by his uncle, Rev Samuel Parke, a Presbyterian clergyman, at Slate Ridge, now the town of Delta York Co Pa, near the Maryland line After a few years spent in studying the Latin and Greek languages and other studies, preparatory to entering college, he was employed by his uncle as a teacher in the same academy He had a number of pupils of about his own age some from Harford County, Md, and among them was Dr F Butler, now of Westminster In 1829 he left Slate Ridge to attend college at Canonsburg, Washington Co, Pa, then in considerable repute, under the management of Rev Matthew Brown, and graduated in 1831, at the age of twenty one, in a class of thirty-one students Having his mind fixed on the profession of the law, and with a view of assisting himself thereto, as well as improving his education, he determined to engage for a time in teaching Seeing an advertisement in the Philadelphia *Saturday Evening Post* that a classical teacher was wanted at Manchester (then Baltimore), Carroll Co, he visited that place, and became the *first* principal of Manchester Academy, about Dec 1, 1831 He continued as such until 1839, with an intermission of a year In April, 1835, he was married to Amanda, second daughter of George Motter, of Manchester They have had a large family of children, of whom five survive, viz Frances H, wife of Edwin K Gernand, merchant, George Motter Parke, the present deputy register of wills, Mary Letitia widow of the late Prof J Mortimer Hurley, Josephine Amanda, wife of J Edwin Taylor, of the Taylor Manufacturing Company, and John Fleming, in the employ of said company,—all now of Westminster, Md

As we have stated, in 1837 the new county of Carroll was established and embraced Manchester within its limits Dr Jacob Shower, of that town, was one of the representatives of the new county for the first two sessions of 1837 and 1838, and having declined a re-election Mr Parke was nominated on the Democratic ticket, and elected in 1839 to the House of Delegates of Maryland For some years he had devoted his spare time to the study of law under the direction of the [illegible] and after the

adjournment of the Legislature in the spring of 1840 he was admitted to the bar in Baltimore City by the Baltimore County Court. In April, 1840, he removed to Westminster, Md., the new county-seat, where he has ever since resided. About the same time he purchased the *Democrat and Carroll County Republican*, which had been started at Westminster by William Shipley in February, 1838, and had been conducted by him for about six weeks more than two years. The editing of that paper, with some practice of the law, occupied his attention for about eight years, until 1848, when he disposed of his interest in it to J. T. H. Bringman, who had purchased a half-interest in it two years before.

During the eight years of his editorial control there were three memorable Presidential campaigns: in 1840, between Harrison and Van Buren; in 1844, between Clay and Polk; and in 1848, between Taylor and Cass. Though an ardent politician and devoted to his party, his course was always fair and honorable, and commanded the respect of his political opponents. With him patriotism was superior to party, and there were occasions on which he did not hesitate to rise above mere party influences when he conceived its objects did not correspond with the public good. For many years he strenuously supported the cause of reform in Maryland. The present generation has but little idea of the difficulties encountered by Reformers in breaking the hold of the minority upon the legislative power of the State. The constitution was the mere creature of the Legislature, and as each county had four delegates and the cities of Annapolis and Baltimore two each, without regard to size or population, the smaller counties had entire control of the government, and the minority was naturally inclined to hold to power with a firm grip. After the fright caused by the refusal of the "glorious nineteen" senatorial electors to enter the college and elect State senators, thus leaving the other twenty-one without a constitutional quorum, it was perceived that the State was on the verge of a revolution, and the Legislature undertook to make the changes of 1836 in the constitution, conceding the right of the people to elect their Governor and State senators by a direct vote, and a moderate increase to Baltimore City and the larger counties in legislative influence. Still it was far from satisfactory, and the Reformers continued to press the call of a convention. In the western counties, especially in Carroll and Frederick, very many Reformers, both of the Democratic and Whig parties, perceiving that party feeling tended to defeat reform measures, agreed to combine without distinction of party, and accordingly when the call for the convention of 1851 was obtained from the Legislature, a ticket was made up for the convention and triumphantly elected in Carroll County composed of three Democrats—Dr. Jacob Shower, Hon. Elias Brown, and Joseph M. Parke—and two Whigs,—Mordecai G. Cockey and Andrew G. Ege. In Frederick County three of each party were elected. In the convention Mr. Parke supported the most advanced measures of reform, including representation strictly according to population and the election of nearly all officers by the people.

John Baumgartner, the first register of wills of Carroll County, and the first elected under the constitution of 1851, died early in 1853, and Mr. Parke was appointed by the Orphans' Court to fill that vacancy. He held the office from Jan. 31, 1853, until the next election in the fall, when he was nominated by his party and elected for six years. In 1859 he was re-elected and served another term of six years. In 1865 he declined to be a candidate for that office, because, as he conceived, the Union party, with which he had acted during the civil war, had become merged into the Republican party, and he had supported Gen. McClellan, the Democratic nominee for President in 1864. In 1866 he purchased the *Democratic Advocate*, a newspaper started in November, 1865, by William H. Davis in the place of the old *Carroll County Democrat*, destroyed by a mob in April, 1865, and by its aid contributed to the success of the Democratic and Conservative party in the county and State. Under the constitution adopted by the convention of 1867, a new election of register of wills became necessary, and he was again nominated and elected to that office for another term of six years. On his election he sold the *Democratic Advocate* to W. H. Davis, who soon afterwards sold it to Henry Vanderford and his son, William H. Vanderford. He held the office of register of wills for nearly nineteen years, retiring therefrom in December, 1873, since which time he has not aspired to political station, but has quietly devoted himself to the practice of his profession. In 1860 he was a strenuous supporter of the late Stephen A. Douglas for the Presidency, and of the compromises introduced into Congress to heal the breach between the North and South. When the war broke out he adhered to the Northern Democracy, and warmly supported the cause of the Union, carefully discriminating between the government and the party conducting it; believing, in fact, that the South, by its factious rejection of Senator Douglas, one of its truest friends, and its secession from the Northern Democrats, had caused Mr. Lincoln's election.

When the war was over, Mr Parke favored the policy of President Andrew Johnson, to restore the era of good feeling between the sections, and to admit the Southern States at once to their rights in the Union He believed that there were mutual errors, and that the North was not so clear of blame as to entitle her to demand humiliating terms of the South He has always maintained and expressed an exalted idea of the future of our great republic, and of its providential mission, and predicts that as soon as the sore places caused by the late war shall have been healed our entire people will combine to make the country what Providence designed it to be,—an illustration of the ability of the people to govern themselves, allowing the maximum amount of freedom, and securing the greatest prosperity to all

The Farmers' and Planters' Live Stock Mutual Aid Association of Carroll County was incorporated May 9, 1881, with the home-office in Westminster, for the sole insurance of live-stock Its officers are Samuel Roop president, Theodore F Englar, vice president, Charles H Baughman, secretary, Charles Schaeffer, treasurer, B F Crouse, attorney Board of Trustees, Samuel Roop, Theodore F Englar, Milton Schaeffer, Charles H Baughman, Dr George S Yingling, Charles Schaeffer, B F Crouse

The State Mutual Benefit Association of Carroll County was incorporated in 1879 Its officers are: President Jesse Reifsnider, Vice President, Granville S Haines, Secretary, Dr George S Yingling, Treasurer George R Gehr, Counselor, Charles T Reifsnider, Medical Director, J G Keller, M D The board of trustees are Jesse Reifsnider, Granville S Haines Joshua Yingling, Philip H L Myers, Andrew N Stephan, George R Gehr, Charles T Reifsnider, Joseph G Keller, George S Yingling, M D

The corner-stone of the engine house of the Westminster Fire Department was laid Monday, April 14, 1879, in the presence of a large number of people Members of Door to Virtue Lodge and George Washington Masonic Lodge met at the Odd Fellows' Hall, and preceded by the Silver Run Band marched to the lot opposite the Catholic church, formed a square, and at once performed the ceremonies Dr William H Rippard, W M, called the brethren to order Prayer was offered by Rev J D Still, pastor of Centenary Methodist Episcopal Church The Master of the lodge, assisted by I H Miller, S W, and Edward Ziegler J W, then laid the corner-stone, the members making the necessary responses Hon John E Smith, the orator of the occasion, was absent, owing to indisposition Dr Rippard, president of the fire company, read a statement giving in brief a history of the fire department, what they had accomplished, and what they had every reason to expect from the citizens The customary box was placed in the stone It contains two copies each of the *Democratic Advocate* and *American Sentinel*, fractional currency, constitution, by-laws, and names of the members of the fire company, letters from Charles T Holloway, fire inspector, and from the fire commissioners of Baltimore, and an autograph album containing the names of the business men of Westminster and others to the number of about one hundred and fifty, and an account of the "Walking Match" The stone was made by A J Beaver, marble-cutter, of Westminster, and is seven by twelve inches It has inscribed on it, A D 1879 The officers for 1881 were

President Dr William H Rippard, First Vice President, Chas V Mantz Second Vice President E T Lawyer, Secretary and Treasurer, Denton S Gehr, Assistant Secretary and Treasurer, Frank W Shriver, Chief Foreman, Frank K Herr, Assistant Chief Foreman, J C Mobley, Foreman of Truck, Wm H Shaeffer, Assistant Foreman of Truck, A M Warner, Foreman of Engine J Frank Brinkerhoff, Assistant Foreman of Engine Edward L Smith, Marshal John H Mitten, Librarian, W I Seabrook, Janitor, Charles Hill

At a very early date in the history of Carroll County a decided interest was manifested in the organization and development of branches of the noted secret societies for the encouragement of brotherhood and benevolence among the people, and especially was this noticeable among the Masons, and doubtless much of the vigorous growth of sound principles and reciprocity of feelings and sentiments which characterize the people of that county in a marked degree are due to the benign influences of these orders

Door to Virtue Lodge, No 46, of Ancient Free and Accepted Masons, was chartered Nov 4, 1811, to hold its meetings at Pipe Creek, where it had held its first meeting on Sunday, June 23, 1811, under a dispensation from the Most Worshipful the Grand Master of Maryland Its last meeting at Pipe Creek was held Sept 25, 1813, when it was removed to Uniontown, where, Nov 7, 1813, the first meeting at that place was held The question of the removal of the lodge from Uniontown to Westminster had occupied the attention of the brethren for several months, and it was finally resolved, on the 11th of July, 1824, "that Door to Virtue Lodge, No 46, be removed, so that the lodge may be opened and held at Westminster on the fourth Sunday in this month (the 25th inst), at ten o'clock A M, and thereafter forever" A committee, previously appointed (June 20th) for that purpose, had entered into an agreement with Jacob Powder whereby the use of suitable rooms in

his house was obtained for the meetings of the lodge at the rent of thirty dollars per annum. The first communication of the lodge at Westminster was accordingly held on the 25th of July, 1824, and the record shows it to have been a very busy one indeed First the honorary degree of Past Master was conferred upon Jacob Pouder and John C Cockey, the latter of whom was then duly installed senior warden, after which John Gilbert and Joseph Arthur were raised to the degree of Master Mason Petitions for initiation also were received from George Warner and Henry Geatty The officers from December, 1824, to December, 1825, were John C. Cockey, W M, Benjamin Yingling, S W, Jacob Pouder, J W, W H McCannon, Sec, and M Barnitz, Treas On the 19th June, 1825, a resolution was adopted, changing the time of meeting to the third Saturday of each month "at early candlelight" The officers for December, 1825, to June, 1826, were J C Cockey, W M, B Yingling, S W, Joshua Sundergill, J W, A McIlhenny, Sec, and Jacob Pouder, Treas For the term ending December, 1826, no election appears to have been held, but on the 19th of November the following officers were selected to serve from St John the Evangelist's day until June, 1827, viz J C Cockey, W M, Dr William Zollickoffer S W, J Sundergill, J W, A McIlhenny, Sec, and J Pouder, Treas Mr Cockey died, however before the new term began, and his funeral, Dec 12, 1826 was long remembered, not only for the unusually imposing Masonic solemnities with which it was attended, but also for the expressions of respectful sorrow which it elicited from the entire community At the election held June 17, 1827, the officers chosen were Dr William Zollickoffer, W M, J Sundergill, S W, John S Murray J W, Dr James Fisher, Sec, and Joseph Arthur, Treas The lodge, however, seems at this time to have lost much of its original vigor, and to have succumbed to adverse influences, many of which are to-day merely conjectural

Prominent among them was doubtless the anti-Masonic excitement growing out of the alleged abduction of William Morgan, of Batavia, N Y, in the autumn of 1826, for his alleged exposure of the secrets of the craft, and the organization in the following year of a political party avowedly hostile to Freemasonry At all events, at the meeting held Oct 21 1827, it was resolved, "that Brothers Pouder and Murray settle and close the account of rent for the lodge," and the record of that date closes as follows "No further business appearing to claim the attention of this lodge, it was, in accordance with a previous resolution, in harmony and love, *closed forever* Signed, James Fisher, Sec"

Door to Virtue Lodge, it will be remembered, started with nine original or charter members, and held its first meeting on the 23d of June, 1811 In the course of the sixteen years and four months from that date till the surrender of its charter on the 21st of October, 1827, the number initiated was ninety-four, passed eighty, raised seventy-two, affiliated ten, while the honorary degree of Past Master was conferred upon forty-three members

For more than thirty eight years Door to Virtue's surrendered charter reposed in the archives of the Grand Lodge, and it seemed as if the old entry in the record was true, and that the lodge was in reality *closed forever* But it was not so As the result of a petition presented to the Grand Lodge at the November communication, 1865, and signed by twenty-five Master Masons, among whom were a due number of the old members of the lodge, the original charter was restored by Grand Master John Coates, Jan. 29, 1866, to Hon John E Smith as W M, Rev James W Reese, S W, and William H H Geatty as J W, on behalf of the petitioners The first meeting under the restored charter was held in Odd-Fellows' Hall, in the city of Westminster, on Tuesday evening, Feb 6, 1866, when the officers just named, as well as A D Schaeffer and William A McKellip, who had been elected respectively secretary and treasurer were duly installed by Daniel A Piper, P M, Concordia, No 13, Grand Tyler, proxy for the M W Grand Master, Bro E T Shultz, W M, Concordia, No. 13, and Grand Inspector for Baltimore City, as Senior Grand Warden, Bro William D Jones, P M, Warren, No 51, as Junior Grand Warden, John Van Tromp, W M, Mystic Circle, No 109, and Grand Inspector for Baltimore City, as Senior Grand Deacon, and David Martin, of Concordia, No 13, as Junior Grand Deacon On this occasion five petitions for initiation were received, and the first degree was conferred on William Hammett Jr Thus happily resuscitated, Door to Virtue Lodge became at once the centre of a vigorous and healthy Masonic activity, and applications from the best citizens were so numerous that for several years weekly communications were necessary in order to keep abreast of the "work" which came crowding in on the busy craft On the 7th of April the lodge accompanied to the grave the remains of their veteran brother, Henry Geatty, who was "entered" Aug 8, 1824, "passed" September 26th, and raised Jan 9, 1825 and who died April 5, 1866, aged seventy three year

The officers from June to December, 1866, were Rev James W Reese, W M, William H H Geatty, S W, William A McKellip, J W, A D Schaeffer, Sec, and William A Cunningham, Treas

On the afternoon of September 6th the Master, assisted by his wardens, and surrounded by seventy-five of the brethren, laid the corner stone of "Western Maryland College"

On Tuesday, November 20th, the lodge formed part of the immense procession which celebrated the laying of the corner stone of the new Masonic Temple in the city of Baltimore From December, 1866, to June, 1867 the officers were James W Reese, W M, Wm A McKellip, S W, A D Schaeffer, J W, E K Gernand, Sec, and W A Cunningham, Treas The festival of St John the Evangelist, Dec. 27, 1866, was appropriately observed by a banquet, a reunion of all the Masons of the county, and an oration by the Worshipful Master On the 6th of June, 1867, the "Committee of Southern Relief" reported that they had collected and forwarded to the Masonic authorities of Georgia the sum of one hundred dollars, "to relieve the distress of our suffering brethren in that State" The officers from June to December, 1867, were J W Reese, W M, A D Schaeffer, S W, J E Pierson Jr, J W, Joseph A McKellip, Sec, and W A Cunningham, Treas The lodge, August 22d, participated in a most enjoyable picnic, given by Freedom Lodge, No 112, during which, at the request of the latter the Master of Door to Virtue delivered an oration on the "characteristics of Freemasonry" From December, 1867, to June, 1868, the officers were J W Reese, W M, J E Pierson, Jr, S W, Michael W Sullivan, J W, Henry B Grammer, Sec, and W A Cunningham, Treas On Wednesday, Feb 26 1868, the remains of Jacob D Hoppe, an esteemed brother, ex-sheriff of the county, were consigned to the earth with Masonic ceremonies On the occasion of the marriage of Worshipful Master Reese to Miss Mary Pauline Perry, of Westminster, on the 12th of February, the members of the lodge had prepared a beautiful present for him, consisting of an ice-pitcher, a pair of goblets, and a waiter, all of silver and suitably inscribed On the evening of the 27th, says the record, "the Tyler was sent to summon the Master, who was unavoidably absent The Worshipful Master, on his entrance into the lodge, was received with the grand honors, and was at once presented by P M John E Smith, in the name of the lodge, with the gift above-named The Worshipful Master, as well as his surprise would permit, respon[illegible] with much fe[illegible]ling [illegible] cordial thanks" On the 6th of May a special communication was held at Union Bridge for the purpose of laying the corner-stone of the Methodist Episcopal church at that place The officers from June to December, 1868, were J W Reese, W M, C N Kuhn, S W, David H Zepp, J W, H B Grammer, Sec, and Michael Baughman, Treas From December, 1868, to June, 1869, J W Reese, W M, J W, S A Leister, Sec, and W A Cunningham, Treas The festival of the nativity of St John the Baptist, June 24, 1870, was observed in the afternoon by a procession and the solemn consecration of the burial lot belonging to the lodge in the Westminster Cemetery, and, at night, by the public installation of officers and an eloquent address by P M John E Smith on the principles and tenets of Freemasonry From June to December, 1871, the officers were J W Reese, W M, Wm Coon, S W, S A Leister, J W, Wm Moore, Sec, and W A Cunningham, Treas, who were publicly installed June 22d, in the presence of a large assembly, including many ladies The music, which was of a high order, was furnished by a volunteer choir and by the "Amphions," and the address, owing to the absence of Grand Master John H B Latrobe, who had been invited and expected to perform that duty, was delivered by the Worshipful Master of the lodge

At a special meeting held October 14th the sum of eighty-five dollars was contributed by the members present for the relief of sufferers by the great fire at Chicago

The officers from December, 1871, to June, 1872, were J W Reese, W M, S A Leister, S W, A D Schaeffer, J W, Wm Moore, Sec, and W A Cunningham, Treas, C N Kuhn, S W, George Leas, J W, Wm A McKellip, Sec, and M Baughman, Treas The festival of St John the Evangelist, December 27th, falling on Sunday in 1868, the lodge observed the day by proceeding in a body to Ascension (Protestant Episcopal) church, of which the W M was a rector, where they participated in divine service and listened to a sermon on the life and character of "that beloved Disciple"

On the 18th of February, 1869, by a unanimous vote, the lodge gave its recommendation to a petition of a number of Baltimore County brethren to the Grand Master for a dispensation to open the lodge at Reisterstown, now so well and favorably known as Ionic, No 115 June 8th was devoted by the lodge to the laying of the corner-stone of the Centenary (M E) church in Westminster From June to December, 1869, the officers were J W Reese, W M, C[illegible] [illegible] S W, William Coon, J W,

Francis D. Sanford, Sec.; and W. A. Cunningham, Treas. On September 27th the funeral of Michael W. Sullivan, a faithful and zealous brother, took place.

The officers from December, 1869, to June, 1870, were J. W. Reese, W. M.; George Leas, S. W.; William Coon, J. W.; S. A. Leister, Sec.; and W. A. Cunningham, Treas. From June, 1870, to June, 1871, J. W. Reese, W. M.; William Moore, S. W.; William Coon.

On Sunday, April 14, 1872, Dr. Lewis Kelley was buried with the honors usually paid by the fraternity to the memory of a deceased brother.

The officers from June to December, 1872, were J. W. Reese, W. M.; S. A. Leister, S. W.; L. F. Beyers, J. W.; William Moore, Sec.; W. A. Cunningham, Treas.

On the 3d of October the lodge received and accepted an invitation from Friendship Lodge, No. 84, Hagerstown, to participate in the laying of the corner-stone of the new court-house in that city.

From December, 1872, to June, 1873, the officers were J. W. Reese, W. M.; S. A. Leister, S. W.; F. D. Sanford, J. W.; William Moore, Sec.; and W. A. Cunningham, Treas.

At a special communication, June 18th, on the eve of the departure of the Master for Europe, the members of the lodge presented to him, through Brother John E. Smith, an envelope containing one hundred dollars, "as a tribute of love and respect." An elegant repast then followed, attended by toasts and speeches, and many expressions of good wishes for a happy termination to the European tour on which the Worthy Master and Brother William A. McKellip were to sail on the 21st.

The officers from June to December, 1873, were J. W. Reese, W. M.; W. A. Cunningham, S. W.; George R. Gehr, J. W.; William Moore, Sec.; and James Rippard, Treas. From December, 1873, to December, 1874, J. W. Reese, W. M.; George R. Gehr, S. W.; Wm. O. Liggett, J. W.; William Moore, Sec.; and James Rippard, Treas. On St. John's (the Baptist) day, June 24, 1874, the officers-elect were installed by Jacob H. Medairy, R. W. G. S. of the Grand Lodge of Maryland, after which a banquet was served in the Town-Hall, all the lodges of the county being present as guests. On September 2d the Master, assisted by the wardens and brethren, laid the corner-stone of the Baptist church in Westminster.

From December, 1874, to December, 1876, the officers were J. W. Reese, W. M.; G. R. Gehr, S. W.; E. J. Lawyer, J. W.; William Moore, Sec.; and James Rippard, Treas. On Jan. 4, 1876, the lodge consigned to the tomb with Masonic honors the body of Brother Michael Baughman, ex-treasurer, and on the 26th of the following month a special communication was held at New Windsor for the purpose of performing the same sad service for Brother Washington W. Naill.

At the meeting of Dec. 21, 1876, J. W. Reese, after expressing his high appreciation of the honor so repeatedly conferred upon him, respectfully but positively declined to be a candidate for re-election to the office of Worshipful Master. From that date to December, 1877, the officers were George R. Gehr, W. M.; E. J. Lawyer, S. W.; Dr. W. H. Rippard, J. W.; William Moore, Sec.; and James Rippard, Treas. At a special communication, Jan. 11, 1877, Past Master Rev. James W. Reese was presented by his successor, Worshipful Master George R. Gehr, on behalf of the members of the lodge, with a beautiful Past Master's jewel as a slight token of their appreciation of his continuous and valuable services as Master from June 21, 1866, to Dec. 21, 1876.

On Nov. 26, 1877, Brother James Rippard, the treasurer of the lodge, was buried with the customary Masonic solemnities. The officers from December, 1877, to June, 1878, were George R. Gehr, W. M.; E. J. Lawyer, S. W.; W. H. Rippard, J. W.; William Moore, Sec.; and J. W. Reese, Treas. From June to December, 1878, George R. Gehr, W. M.; W. H. Rippard, S. W.; I. A. Miller, J. W.; William Moore, Sec.; and J. W. Reese, Treas.

Aug. 23, 1878, a venerable brother, Joseph Hesson, was buried by the lodge. From December, 1878, to June, 1880, the officers were Dr. William H. Rippard, W. M.; I. Amos Miller, S. W.; H. E. Ziegler, J. W.; William Moore, Sec.; and J. W. Reese, Treas.

On April 17, 1879, Worshipful Master Dr. William H. Rippard officiated at the laying of the corner-stone of the new engine-house belonging to the Westminster Fire Department; and on December 26th following he read the solemn Masonic burial service for the burial of the dead at the grave of Brother Jeremiah Robertson.

Door to Virtue Lodge held its first meeting under the restored charter Feb. 6, 1866, with twenty-four members on its roll. From that date to June 1, 1880, fourteen were admitted to membership by affiliation, eighty-two candidates were initiated, seventy-two "passed" to the degree of Fellow Craft, and seventy-one "raised" to the degree of Master Mason; the number of deaths were eighteen, and of applicants rejected, eighteen. The lodge now (July, 1881) has on its register: Master Masons, sixty. From June to December, 1880, its officers were Dr. W. H. Rippard, W. M.; J. A. Miller, S. W.; George

Lease, J W, William Moore, Sec, E J Lawyer, S D, C V Wantz, J D From January to July, 1881, the officers were Dr W H Rippard, W M, J A Miller, S W, George Lease, J W, William Moore, Sec, J W Reese, Treas, E J Lawyer, S D, C V Wantz, J D From July to January, 1882, the officers were J Amos Miller, W M, George Lease, S W, E J Lawyer, J W, William Moore, Sec, J W Reese, Treas Of those members of the lodge when its charter was surrendered in 1827, Dr James Fisher was the last survivor, and he died at Springfield, Mo, in the spring of 1881

George Washington Lodge, No 94, A F and A M, was instituted some thirty years ago, but is not now in working order From 1866 to 1881, Dr Winfield K Fringer was Worshipful Master, and J W Perkins was the last secretary

The Independent Order of Odd Fellows, a much younger association, has in many instances made up in zeal and works for the lack of antiquity The attention of the order was directed to Carroll County soon after its formation, and some of its most active and flourishing branches are to be found there

Salem Lodge, No 60, I O O F, was instituted in May, 1848, by a charter bearing date of May 12th of that year, and signed by E P Holden, M W Grand Master, N T Durbin, R W Deputy Master, G D Tewsbury, R W G Sec, Wm Bayley, R W G Treas, and W Fitzsimmons, Grand Warden The charter members were C W Webster, Richard Manning, C A Smeltzer, Charles A Poole, John W Durbin, J Q Baugher, Joshua Yingling, D Mitten Its first officers were N G, J L Baugher, V G, Joshua Yingling, Sec, J W Durbin, Treas, Richard Manning In the first term of 1849, C W Webster was N G, William Wolf, V G, and George E Wampler, Sec The officers for the second term of 1849 were N G, William Wolf, V G, John Matthias, Sec, George E Wampler, Treas, Richard Manning, Per Sec, Joseph Shaeffer Its fine hall was dedicated on the second Thursday of November, 1858, the interesting ceremonies being performed by Hon Joshua Vansant, Grand Master of the Grand Lodge of Maryland William H Young, Esq, Deputy Grand Master, delivered the address on the occasion

The officers for the second term of 1881 were

N G, Samuel Hughes, V G, W L Brown, Rec Sec H L Norris (for 14 years), Per Sec, E K Fernand, Treas, F A Sharer, Marshal John Bernstine, R S to N G, F C Shuer, L S to N G John J Reese, Warden, John Bernstine Conductor W H Lappard, R S to V G, S P Everhart, L S to V G, S B Fowler, R S S, W J Beaver, L S S A F Fowler, O G, E L Zahn, I G, Geo A Zahn

Number of members, 145, value of real estate, $10,000

The charter of Columbia Encampment, No 14 was granted Dec 6, 1850, and signed by James P Merritt, Grand Patriarch The charter members were D Evans Reese, J L Baugher, James Brewster, William Shreev, Joshua Yingling, John Matthias, Joseph Shaeffer, Levi Shreev

The officers for 1881 were

C P, George P Albaugh H P H L Norris, S W, Lewis A Koontz, J W Charles H Henneman, Sec, Joshua Yingling Treas, H B Grammer, Trustees, H L Norris John Bernstein, G P Albaugh

The Independent Order of Red Men appears to have been a favorite association with the inhabitants of Carroll, as some of its lodges were instituted in the county at an early period, and have steadily grown in strength and influence

Conowaga Tribe, No 71, I O R M, was instituted in Westminster, Jan 11, 1881, with twenty four members

The officers are

P, Milton Schaeffer, S Charles H Baughman S S, E I Crouse, J S, James Humphreys, C of R, J W Shreev Ass't to C, George Batson K of W J Frank Lonkerhoff, Sannaps F S Wright John Keene, Warriors D Thomson John A Little, John Warner, Henry Hummer Braves O D Gilbert Milton Scept, John Mitten, D Cassell, G of W J P Barnes, G of F, James Short Rep. to Grand Council Milton Schaeffer

The tribe meets every Tuesday night in I O O F Hall

The dispensation for organizing Charity Lodge, No 58, Knights of Pythias, was granted June 11, 1870 Samuel Read Supreme Chancellor, and J M Butler Supreme Secretary and Corresponding Scribe The charter members were John W Yingling, J Webb Perkins, William Moore, Jacob Lister, J M Weller John T Ormsler, Charles J Yingling, Edward Bachman, Francis K Herr, Michael Baughman The regular charter was dated Nov 14, 1871, and signed by M. A Steiner, V G P, M Schmidt, G B G N. Dickinson, G C, John P Hudson, G G J. F. Lewis, V G C, Robert Sullapsey, G I S O H. Vaughan, G O S, Thomas S Upperco, G R S

The lodge officers for 1881 were

C C, John H Keene, V C, Milton Schaeffer, Prel I Matthews, K of R Clinton S Spurrier M of E G Shank, M of F Edwin J Lawyer, M at A John Mitten, Trustees, E J Lawyer John H Hilton John Shaffer J Wesley Pool John M Black Representative Grand Lodge, J H Mitten Number of members, 97

The officers of the lodge of Independent Order of Mechanics were in 1881:

W. M., Milton Shaeffer; J. M., James Humphreys; F. S., George Batson; R. S., C. H. Baughman; Chaplain, Benj. Franklin; Treas., Joseph Hunter; Conductor, Wm. J. Sheets; O. S., Fletcher A. Baile; I. S., Jesse Mitten; R. G. to W. M., F. A. Knight; L. G. to W. M., Harry Harman; R. G. to J. M., Philip Hunter; L. G. to J. M., Curtis A. Brown; Representative to Grand Lodge, Abraham Long.

J. Henry Hoppe was born near Bowers' church, now called Bachman's, in Bachman's Valley, Feb. 17, 1801. His father was Ferdinand Frederick Hoppe, and was born in Stuttgart, Germany. His mother was Catharine Snouffer, of Frederick County. Mr. Hoppe received a common-school education, after which he taught school for five years, studying surveying in the meanwhile, in which he became very proficient. On attaining his majority he united with the Democratic party, and always remained a stanch follower of "Old Hickory."

In 1825 he was appointed a magistrate, and, with the exception of a few years, he held the position until twelve months before his death. He became so thoroughly versed in testamentary law that he was frequently appointed to settle the estates of deceased persons, several of which were very large. In 1842 he was elected sheriff of this county, at which time there were fifteen candidates in the field. He received one hundred and forty-six votes more than Lewis Trumbo, Whig, who was the next highest. The incidents of that campaign he was fond of repeating.

Mr. Hoppe was a charter member of the Western Maryland Railroad, was elected secretary and treasurer, and was also a director in the road. He was for a number of years director of the Union National Bank of Westminster, and was also a charter member of George Washington Lodge, A. F. A. M., of that city. He was elected county surveyor for four consecutive terms. Mr. Hoppe always resided in Carroll County, though the place of his birth was then in Baltimore County. In 1829 he was united in marriage to Rachel Myerly, daughter of Jacob Myerly and Eve Bishop. They had only one child, Josephus H., who died Dec. 27, 1877. Squire Hoppe was a member of the Lutheran Church for over sixty years. No man in Carroll County was more generally or more favorably known. He died Jan. 5, 1881, after an active and busy career of nearly eighty years.

Carroll Division, No. 12, of the Sons of Temperance, was instituted Feb. 12, 1847, and has been in continuous and successful operation to the present time. The charter was signed by the State grand officers, William Young, Grand Worthy Patriarch, and W. H. Gobright, Grand Scribe. Its charter members were Isaac Shriver, Thomas W. Durbin, Rev. Theodore Gallaudet, Joshua Sundergill, Horatio Price, John Malchorn, Francis Shriver, William Zepp, Alfred Troxel, John Miller, James Keefer, Emanuel L. Kuns, Henry H. Wampler. It first met at Isaac Shriver's residence, and afterwards held its meetings over the *Sentinel* office, and later over Joshua Yingling's East End store. Since 1852 the society has met in its own elegant hall, completed in that year. Its officers for 1881 were:

W. P., F. K. Herr; W. A., George Lease; R. S., B. L. Norris (held this office for twenty-six years); A. R. S., C. H. Baughman; F. S., Dr. Charles Billingslea; Treas., Jesse F. Shreev; C., J. W. Pool; A. C., Thomas Bankert; I. S., George Arbaugh; O. S., George Litsinger.

Its motto is "Love, Purity, and Fidelity," which are the respective names of its three degrees, subsequently founded on this motto, adopted in 1847. It is a beneficiary association, and pays sixty dollars to the family of each deceased member. It also pays sick benefits of three and a half or four dollars per week. Its membership is forty-five. The corner-stone of the hall was laid July 4, 1850, and it was built by L. Evans and H. H. Wampler, at a cost of two thousand dollars.

The Taylor Manufacturing Company, of Westminster.—The property of a city is aptly illustrated by the number of its public buildings and its manufacturing establishments. "The Union Agricultural Works" of Westminster were opened in the summer of 1852, and were carried on under the management of William H. Harman & Co. The buildings, which had been from time to time enlarged and improved, consisted of a large two-story machine-shop, moulding-shop, blacksmith's shop, saw-mill, and sheds. They occupied nearly an acre and a half of ground. Their new mould-shop, which was finished in 1868, was one hundred feet long by fifty wide, and gave employment to fourteen hands. The machine-shop employed five iron and ten wood workers, and the blacksmith's shop and saw-mill four; a total force of thirty-three. These works turn out every season about three hundred plows, three hundred spring-tooth rakes, and sixty horse-powers, besides numerous other agricultural machines in less numbers. In 1872, in its place, was formed "The Taylor Manufacturing Company of Westminster," by J. A. Taylor, who was then president of the company. It was an incorporated company, composed of J. A. Taylor, G. A. Taylor, Edward Lynch, David Fowble, and O. B. Baile. It was a repair foundry, and manufactured agricultural implements

In January, 1879, it was reorganized under the name of "The Taylor Manufacturing Company of Westminster, Md" It is still a stock company, distributed among a few stockholders, with a capital stock paid in of twenty five thousand dollars Its members are

J A Taylor, president G A Taylor, secretary and treasurer, R N Beck, superintendent Directors, Michael Shaw, York, Pa, Thomas F Shephard, Union Bridge, and W N Wise, Baltimore

It is largely engaged in the manufacture of engines and other machinery, and employs one hundred and fifty hands

The people of Westminster have from the erection of the county manifested an enterprising disposition and a desire to keep abreast of the great practical discoveries of the century The question of railroad transportation engaged the attention of the inhabitants at an early date, and the extraordinary advantages to accrue to the county by rail and steam communication were thoroughly appreciated

The citizens of Carroll County convened at the court-house, April 7, 1847, to take into consideration the propriety of extending the Westminster Branch Railroad through Carroll County Mr Evan McKinstry was called to the chair, assisted by Mr Isaac Shriver, and John Switzer and William Reese as secretaries Col James M Shellman stated the object of the meeting, and introduced G Gordon Belt, Esq, of Baltimore, who addressed the meeting in favor of the contemplated road Cols Shellman and James C Atlee offered resolutions which were adopted, that a committee of ten be appointed to correspond with the president and directors of the Baltimore and Susquehanna Railroad, and urge upon them the necessity of early action under the act of 1845, so that the speedy building of the proposed road would follow

The committee selected were James C Atlee, William C Roberts, Samuel McKinstry, John Clemson Isaac Shriver, William N Hayden, David W Naille Augustus Shriver, John K Longwell, John B Boyle, and John McCollum

A town meeting was held at Westminster on the 16th of November, 1850, for the purpose of devising ways and means for connecting the Baltimore and Susquehanna Railroad with some point in the interior of Carroll County The meeting was addressed at some length by R M Magraw, Esq, president of that road, upon the advantages that might be expected to be derived from the road He was followed by Mr Taggart and Dr Cole A series of resolutions were adopted, one of which appointed an executive committee of [illegible] persons, whose duty it was to collect information in regard to the best probable route, cost of construction of said road, together with amount of revenue likely to accrue therefrom which information was to be submitted to an adjourned meeting to be held in Westminster on December 2 There were two projects entertained,—one to continue the road from Owings' Mills, and extend it into the county, instead of stopping at Westminster, and the other was to branch off at Cockeysville by way of Reisterstown to Westminster

On December 2d a large and enthusiastic meeting was held to further consider the project of building the proposed railroad Mr Magraw was again present and furnished abundant facts to prove the importance of the road, which he estimated would not cost more than two hundred and ten thousand dollars, pledging himself as one of two hundred to furnish the money to build it Four routes were proposed,—one from Cockeysville to Ely's Mill, one from Love's Switch to Black Rock, one from Cockeysville to Hampstead, and another from Owings' Mills, Reisterstown, etc Committees to examine and report as to right of way of each of these routes were appointed A committee was also appointed to secure a survey of the different routes

A convention was held for the same purpose at Westminster, Feb 26, 1851, and was composed of citizens from Frederick, Carroll, Washington, and Baltimore Counties The meeting was largely attended, but the surveys of the various routes not being complete but little was done Resolutions were adopted to appoint committees and take up subscriptions to make the road from some point on the Susquehanna Railroad through Westminster to Hagerstown which route was to be in the meanwhile surveyed The subscriptions and surveys completed they were to be forwarded to the executive committee who would then call a general meeting and consider the same

The engineers of the Baltimore and Susquehanna Railroad Company deputed to survey the route of the contemplated railroad arrived at Westminster Feb 22 1851 Their course was *via* Owings' Mills, Reisterstown, Ely's Mills, and up to the falls of Westminster

A large meeting of those interested in the construction of the Baltimore, Carroll and Frederick Railroad was held in the court house in Westminster on Sept 1, 1852 Delegates were in attendance from the whole line of the proposed road, as also from Washington and Frederick Counties, through which it was calculated to extend the road to Hagerstown where it would connect with the Franklin Road leading to Chambersburg The meeting was organized

J K Longwell

by the appointment of Col. Jacob Matthias, of Carroll, as president, Col. W. Fell Johnson, of Baltimore, vice-president, with Mr. Bradenbaugh, of Washington County, and Joseph M. Parker, as secretary. A resolution was offered by Jervis Spencer, looking to additional legislation in regard to the charter of the company. Among those in attendance at the meeting, and who participated in the discussion of the propositions submitted, were Jervis Spencer, Alexander Neill, and others, of Washington; Wm. P. Maulsby, A. G. Ege, W. Hayden, J. K. Longwell, and Jos. Raymond, of Carroll County. The citizens of Westminster seem to have been greatly elated on hearing that the mayor of Baltimore City had signed the ordinance passed by the City Council indorsing five hundred thousand dollars' worth of eight per cent. Western Maryland Railway bonds. On July 28th the event was celebrated by the firing of cannon, and at night a large meeting was held and speeches were made by John E. Smith, C. W. Webster, and Joseph M. Parker, attended with music by the Westminster Band. Another meeting of general rejoicing was held at New Windsor on July 31st.

Carroll County Lyceum was incorporated by an act of the Legislature, March 30, 1839. The incorporators were Jacob Mathias, John McCollum, A. H. Busby, John F. Reese, John K. Longwell, Dr. George Shriver, John Baumgartner, H. Crout, James M. Shellman, Nicholas Kelly, Dr. Wm. Willis, A. F. Shriver, Isaac Van Bibber, Thos. E. Van Bibber, N. H. Thayer, Thomas Hook, C. W. Webster, James Raymond, Jacob Grove, Horatio Price, James Keefer, Samuel Orendorff, Jacob Reese, S. D. Lecompte, George Webster, John S. Baurgelt.

Maj. A. G. Enge, formerly of this county, died at his residence in Kansas in December, 1876. He represented Carroll in the House of Delegates in 1851, and in the Constitutional Convention of 1851. During his residence here in Carroll County he was frequently and prominently spoken of as a Whig candidate for Governor of the State. He was a brother-in-law of Col. John K. Longwell, and emigrated to Kansas about twenty years prior to his death.

James Raymond, who was a well-known member of the Carroll County bar, and who was admitted to practice at the first term of the court in April, 1837, died at his home in Westminster in January, 1858, in the sixty-second year of his age. He was a native of Connecticut, a graduate of Yale College, and for twenty-one years a citizen of Westminster. Several years prior to his decease he represented Carroll County in the Legislature, and was the author of a work known as "Raymond's Digest of Chancery Cases."

In the past half-century no man has been more closely identified with the financial, political, and material history of Carroll County than Col. John K. Longwell. He was born in the historic town of Gettysburg, Pa., in October, 1810, and was the son of Matthew and Jane (Klinchoff) Longwell. His father, a reputable merchant in that town, was of Scotch-Irish descent, whose ancestors at a very early period emigrated from the north of Ireland and settled in Pennsylvania. His mother was of Hollandish extraction, and from a race noted for their thrift and rare domestic qualities. Col. Longwell was educated in the academy of his native town, and learned the printing business in the office of the *Adams Sentinel*, now the *Star and Sentinel*, of Gettysburg. In 1832 he removed to Taneytown, of this county, and established *The Recorder*, which paper was the successor of *The Regulator and Taneytown Herald*, a journal published for a year or two. He printed this paper about a year, and in the spring of 1833 came to Westminster and established *The Carrolltonian*. This journal was chiefly devoted to the interests of the formation of a new county with the county seat at Westminster. Its first issue appeared June 25, 1833, and even the opponents of the measure acknowledged the zeal, ability, and fidelity with which it was conducted, until in four years afterwards the efforts of its editor and friends were crowned with success. He edited, published, and was connected with this paper for about eighteen years, and it was finally merged into the *American Sentinel*. He was married in 1840 to the youngest daughter of Maj. John McCaleb, of Taneytown, who came when only nine years of age with his father, Joseph McCaleb, from the north of Ireland. The McCalebs were early settlers around Taneytown and large landed proprietors. By this union Col. Longwell has one surviving daughter. Originally a Whig in politics, he has acted with the Democratic party for over twenty years. He was elected a State senator in 1850, and served four years in the Senate. In 1867 he was elected one of the delegates to the Constitutional Convention, and assisted in the framing of the present organic law of Maryland. In 1871 he was again chosen State senator for a term of four years. In 1879 he was prevailed upon to accept a nomination for the office of county commissioner,—the most important office in the State to the farmers, business men, and tax-payers,—and was triumphantly elected and made president of the board. He was the author of the charter of the Western Maryland Railroad, and secured its passage by the Legislature, and when this railroad was put under contract he was one of its board of directors,

and is now a member of the board He became a director in the Westminster Bank (now Union National), and has been its president for twenty-five years Since 1858 he has been president of the Baltimore and Reisterstown turnpike, a road built in 1805, and for many years the great national thoroughfare from Baltimore to Pittsburgh for travel and freight At the centennial celebration of July 4, 1876, in Westminster, he prepared and read a history of the county, with which no person in its limits is more familiar He is a member of the Piney Creek Presbyterian Church, organized in 1763 His home, "Emerald Hill" at Westminster, is one of the most elegant private residences in the county Col Longwell contributed more than any single individual to the organization of Carroll County, and since its erection has been constantly associated with its progress, and the many public and fiduciary positions conferred upon him show the esteem in which he is held by the community

The Carroll Rifle Association, for recreation and improvement in marksmanship, was organized June 28, 1879, by the election of the following officers President, Dr W H Rippard, Secretary and Treasurer, J S Weavers, Captain of Team, John T Beard, Committee on Grounds, J A Miller, Joseph Puhs, and C W Knight The following is a list of members Col McKellip, William B Thomas, Dr Swarmstedt, Frank Shriver Ed W Shriver, Ed H Shriver, Denton Gehr, Henry Troutfelter, Michael Sluney, James Humphreys, Milton Wagoner, E J Lawyer, Samuel Roop, Willis R Zumbrum, John C Weaver, A H Wentz, B F Crouse, William Myerly, Jesse Smith, J E Crouse, J Shunk, P Callaghan, J Winfield Snoder, J J Baumgartner, Peter Woods, John T Anders

At the celebration of Easter Monday in 1879 the most prominent event of the day was the eight-hour go as you-please pedestrian contest on the grounds of the Carroll County Agricultural Society, which was nearly an all-day affair Large representations from every section of the county were present

The contest was for a purse of $50 $25 to the first, $15 to the second, and $10 to the third Half of the gate-money was also to be added in the same proportion The entrance fee was two dollars, and the following entered, drawing positions in the order named William Copenhover, John Groff, G H Walter, William H Bell, Benjamin Gist, R Palmer, Jacob Reinaman, Samuel Groff Henry Hinkler, S H Blakesly,—all residents of this city and vicinity, except Copenhover, who was from Silver Run, and Blakesly from Mexico

Below we give the distance made by each contestant in each of the eight hours

	1	2	3	4	5	6	7	8	Total
John Groff	7½	6¼	6	5½	6	6	4½	5	[illegible]
Copenhover	6	6	4½	5	off				[illegible]
Walter	5	4½	4½	off					15
Bell	6	6½	6	5½	5½	5½	5	5	[illegible]
Gist	6	7½	6	5	5	6	4½	4	[illegible]
Palmer	5½	5½	5	5½	4½	4½	5	4	[illegible]
Samuel Groff	6½	6	4	3½	off				20
Hinkler	6	5½	6	5½	6	5½	off		[illegible]
Blakesly	6	6	4½	4	off				21½
Reinaman	5½	6	5	5	4½	off			26

John Groff the winner, was a native of Westminster, and for nine years previous was engaged in a brickyard He was seventeen years of age, five feet four inches high, of slender build, and weighed one hundred and ten pounds

W. H Bell was also a native of the city of Westminster, twenty one years old, and weighed about one hundred and thirty pounds He was a blacksmith by trade

Benjamin Gist was a son of Samuel Gist, residing near this city, nineteen years old, and accustomed to farm-labor

The Fourth of July, 1876, the centenary of American independence, was universally and enthusiastically celebrated in the United States, and Westminster was no exception in this respect There were doubtless more imposing demonstrations at other points but few that were more sensible and useful, or that exhibited a profounder appreciation of the benefits derived from a hundred years of self-government, or a more grateful sense of the value of the inheritance bequeathed to their successors by the founders of the republic At an early hour the streets were thronged by an immense concourse of people, who were speedily formed into line by the chief marshal of the day, Hon Wm P Maulsby, and his aides

The order of the procession was as follows

Chief Marshal and Aides

Hanover Drum Corps

Capt A. D Kohler George Crumbine G K Metzer Kerwin Smith, Lewis J Renant Jacob Bonge, John A Cremer, W H Naill, Robert Stahl, Zachary Taylor Bonge, Franklin Kuhn

Surviving soldiers of the war of 1812, among them were Col Joshua C Gist Michael Pyers, Sterling Galt and J Ubler These were followed by the survivors of the first officers of the county invited guests, the reverend clergy the historian of the day, the readers of the Declaration Washington's Farewell Address and of the poem,—all in carriages

Thirteen young ladies in appropriate costumes on horseback each bearing a banneret representing one of the original thirteen States each horse led by a colored groom, dressed in white jacket and flowing pantaloons, with red cap of Nubian pattern each lady with an attendant guard of honor The names of the young ladies on horseback were Hattie Gist Maryland [illegible] Fringer, Pennsylvania, Alice Miller, New Jersey Alreta [illegible] North Carolina [illegible] Katie Miller [illegible] [illegible] Peachman, Del[illegible]

...shire Mollie Wheeler, South Carolina Jennie Wilson New Hampshire, Ella Shriever, Connecticut, Jennie Golden, Rhode Island, Cordelia Miller New York The place of honor was given to Miss Hattie Gist, the young lady who represented Maryland, who is a great granddaughter of Col Mordecai Gist, of the old Maryland Line

Mount Pleasant Band

Platoon of four Mounted Guards

Thirty seven young ladies, representing the different States of the Union, all dressed in white, with crimson caps, with the name of the State in gilt letters on the sash in a corner, appropriately festooned with flags and banners and decorated with a portrait of Washington in front The car was drawn by six [illegible] horses each horse was led by a colored groom in Nubian costume The car was driven by Mr John Tracey The names of the young ladies were Hattie Bollinger Louisa Zahn, [illegible] Ploom, Flora Buell, Sallie Gernand, Jennie Malehorn, [illegible] Lowble, Carrie McElroy, Estelle Marsh, Ida Fringer [illegible] Shriver, Ella Miller Katie Baumgartner, Nannie Miller Fannie Ebaugh Mattie Ebaugh, Maggie Horner Jennie Gist Mary C Wheeler Lizzie Buckingham Estelle White, Laura Smith, Ada Zepp Ida Koontz, [illegible] Amanda Poole, [illegible] Wagoner Mattie Hull, [illegible] Hull Grace Bowers, Hannah Bowers, Annie [illegible], Jennie Fowler Mollie Hoppe, Emma [illegible], Anna Haines, Emma Wright

There was a Guard of Honor composed of one hundred young men in rich and appropriate costumes mounted upon fine horses, and commanded by [illegible] Wheeler Some of these flanked the representatives of the States, and the remainder rode in solid column in the rear of the car Each guard had an eight-foot spear with streamer on the point

National Grays' Band

Representatives of Chili and Cuba, Arturo Leke and P M [illegible], mounted and bearing their national ensigns The first named was dressed in a rich Chilian uniform, prepared expressly for the occasion

Frizzelburg Band

[illegible] Lodge, No 60, I O O F, of Westminster Sons of Temperance Encampment Charity Lodge, No 58, Knights of Pythias, of Westminster in full uniform,—a very handsome display United Order of American Mechanics Trades, Granges, and Industries

Fairview Brass Band (Colored)

Sentinel Job Printing Press, on a wagon, driven by steam Handsome Portable Engine from the Taylor Manufacturing Company, Westminster Reaping Machines in motion, from the shops of Mr Elijah Wagoner Westminster Then followed a long line of visitors and citizens in carriages and on horseback which brought up the rear

The procession moved from the West End through Main Street to the Carroll County Agricultural Society's Fair Grounds, where a vast assemblage had already gathered The number present was variously estimated from three to five thousand The multitude were called to order by Col William A McKellip, chairman of the committee on exercises, who announced the following officers President Col William P Maulsby, Honorary Presidents, Hon William N Hayden, Nimrod Gardner J H Hoppe, Hon C B Roberts Col Joshua C Gist Col John Lamott, Hon John E Smith and [illegible] [illegible] John [illegible] [illegible] Daniel Stull, David Prugh, Hon J Shower, David Englar, Talbot Hammond, Henry Bussard, J H Wimemiller, Thomas Smith, Granville S Haines, Secretaries, William H Vanderford and William H Rippard The order of exercises at the stand was as follows

Singing of the "Star-Spangled Banner" by the chorus of Westminster, led by Mr Buell, Miss Fanny Buell, organist

Prayer by Rev J T Ward, president of Western Maryland College

Music by the Mount Pleasant Band

Reading of the Declaration of Independence by Dr F T Shaw

Music by Fairview Band

Reading of Washington's "Farewell Address," by Dr Charles Billingslea

Singing 'Hail Columbia' Choir

History of the County, prepared and read by Col John K Longwell

Music by the National Grays Band

Ode, by Emma Alice Browne (Mrs Capt J L Beaver), read by A H Huber Esq

Singing America, by choir

Prayer, by Rev William C Cremer

Doxology, by choir and audience and benediction, by Rev Dr Ward

The procession reformed and marched into the city, and was dismissed by the marshal

At the intersection of Main and Centre Streets, Messrs John Faber and J W Perkins erected an arch over Main Street, which was decorated with the national colors, Chinese lanterns, and a number of small flags The bells of the churches rang a merry peal in the morning, and again in the evening The "Centennial Bell," erected by Messrs Schenthall and Frank King was rung almost incessantly through the night of the 3d, and also on the 4th

Salutes were fired at morning, noon, and night by a detachment of artillery from Fort McHenry, under the charge of a sergeant and seven men As the evening salute was being fired a thunder-storm prevailed, and the booming of artillery upon terra firma was answered by the electric batteries of the skies with peal on peal which seemed to mock the impotence of man At night there was a grand illumination throughout the city which closed the observances of Centennial Day

Judge William Nicholas Hayden one of the presidents on this memorable occasion, is a lineal descendant of the Hayden family that came over with Lord Baltimore and settled in St Mary's County The family faithfully represented the Irish Catholic gentry, and took an active part in the first settlement of the province On March 17, 1768, John Hayden [illegible] [illegible] within a mile of [illegible] tract of land of

one hundred and sixty-four acres, called "Friendship Completed," from Isaac Dehaven for one hundred pounds The land was all in woods, but Mr Hayden cleared it up, together with other tracts he subse-

quently bought He had eight daughters and one son The latter, William, married Catherine Ensey He died in 1802, and his wife in 1838 They had three daughters and seven sons, most of whom emigrated West and South and settled in the new countries Of the sons Basil married Appanilla Buckingham daughter of Obadiah Buckingham, of a well-known Baltimore County family, by whom he had seven daughters and one son He removed from his father's farm to Westminster in 1807, about the year of his marriage He had learned the trade of hat-making with Mr Kuhn, and carried on this business many years He was a public spirited citizen, and held several positions of honor and trust, from constable up to the judgeship of the Orphans' Court, having occupied the latter from 1848 to 1851 He died in 1863, and his wife two years later, both aged seventy-nine years

Judge William N Hayden was born Sept 23, 1817, in Westminster, in the house his father had purchased ten years previously on his removal to this city, and in part of which his father had his hat manufactory His early education was obtained in the subscription schools of the city In 1[illegible] his father removed to Frederick County and engaged in farming for several years While there William N attended for a few months the school near Johnsville, after which he went to the Reisterstown (Baltimore County) Academy, then under the charge of his brother-in-law, Prof N H Thayer, at present (1881) librarian of Baltimore City College Here he pursued for a while his academic studies, and imbibed a great passion for historical literature, the reading of which induced him to turn his attention to the law As a preparatory measure to the study of the legal profession, and to obtain means for the prosecution of his studies, he taught school His first school was near McKinstry's Mills for three successive winters of six months each He then attended Prof Lanver's academy for four months at Uniontown, after which he taught school another winter

In 1842 he came to Westminster and began reading law with Hon James Raymond, then an eminent practitioner at the Carroll County bar He was admitted to practice as an attorney-at-law Sept 2, 1844, and on Dec 8, 1846, was appointed by Hon George R Richardson, attorney-general of Maryland, deputy attorney-general for the county, to conduct the criminal prosecutions He held this position for two years, until his increasing practice forced him to resign, to give his sole attention to other parts of his profession more congenial to his tastes He then formed a law partnership with John J Baumgardner, which continued until 1865, when the latter became connected with the old Westminster Bank (Union National)

In the spring of 1867, Judge Hayden was elected one of the members from Carroll County to the Constitutional Convention, in which he served on the judiciary and legislative committees, the most important in that body In the fall of the same year he was elected for the term of fifteen years as an associate judge of the Circuit Court for the Fifth Judicial District, composed of Carroll, Howard, and Anne Arundel Counties His term on the bench will expire Jan 1, 1883

He was married, May 31, 1859, to Eugenia Elizabeth Scott, daughter of Hon Upton Scott Her grandfather, John Scott, came from the north of Ireland at an early day and married a daughter of Normand Bruce, one of the first settlers near Bruceville, and sheriff of Frederick County before the Revolution Upton Scott was born in 1810, in Annapolis He represented Carroll County in the House of Delegates in 1846, and died in 1881 in Baltimore

Judge Hayden has one son and two daughters On [illegible] of [illegible] ection, and on

his mother's of English, while his wife is of Scotch-Irish descent. The Hayden homestead, where his great-grandfather, John Hayden, settled in 1768, remained in the family until 1838, when it was sold and subsequently divided.

Judge Hayden is a member of the Catholic Church, with which his ancestors were connected from time immemorial. Originally a Whig in politics, on the dissolution of that party in 1853 he attached himself to the Democratic organization, with which he has ever since affiliated. When engaged in a large and lucrative practice at the bar, he was noted for the ability and fidelity with which he conducted his causes, in which he won distinction and enjoyed the esteem of the court and community. On the bench he has made an able and upright judge, enjoying the respect of the bar and court officers and the confidence of the people, he being fearless in the discharge of his duties, but genial and affable in social life.

Jacob Marker, another prominent citizen of Westminster District, died Dec. 8, 1879, in the ninety-fourth year of his age. His father was a Hessian, and came over to this country during the Revolutionary war. He is believed to have been one of the fifteen hundred men stationed at Trenton, N. J., under the British Col. Rawle, when Washington crossed the Delaware amid floating ice to attack them, on the night of Dec. 25, 1776, nine hundred of whom were captured by him next day. Some of these Hessians, at the close of the war, returned to Europe with the British army, while others remained and settled in this country. The father of Mr. Marker was of the latter number. He settled at Littlestown, Pa., and married a Miss Reigel, of Myers District. Jacob Marker was born in Uniontown District, and was married when he was twenty-eight years of age. He was confirmed in the Lutheran Church when about fourteen years of age, and lived a consistent member of it for nearly eighty years. When a boy he helped to haul the stone to build the foundation of Kreider's church. His house was always open to ministers, and he was well known for his kindly disposition and charitable deeds.

The *Republican Citizen*, now published in Frederick City by the Baughman Brothers, was established in Westminster in March, 1821, under the auspices of the late Judge Abraham Shriver. A few years subsequently it was removed to Frederick. George W. Sharp was its first editor.

The *American Trumpet*, devoted to the promulgation of sentiments and news in the interest of the then called "Know-Nothing," or American, party, was established Nov. 16, 1854, by Hon. John E. Smith. After the [illegible] in [illegible] in 1855 it was sold to the Democrats. When sold its outside had been put to press, and the paper appeared with the outside zealous, as before, in its advocacy and support of the Know-Nothings, while the inside was a vigorous and uncompromising champion of the Democrats.

The Carrolltonian, a paper established and edited by Col. John K. Longwell, made its first appearance June 28, 1833. It was mainly devoted to the erection and organization of the new county, which followed in four years, and was largely due to its potent voice and influence. Before this paper was started three others had been published here by George Keating, a Mr. Burke, and George W. Sharp. The *Carrolltonian* was published up to Jan. 1, 1850, its last editor and publisher being George D. Miller. It was then merged into the *American Sentinel*, with William H. Grammer as editor, publisher, and proprietor. He conducted it several years and sold it to F. H. Kerr. The latter afterwards sold it to George H. Miller, who in turn sold it to William H. Grammer. After the latter's death, Jan. 11, 1862, it was edited by Harry J. Shellman, and published by Thomas J. Lockwood, for Mr. Grammer's estate. It was then, from Sept. 10, 1868, to 1874, owned, edited, and published by W. L. W. Seabrook & Co., who sold out the office to E. J. Rippard & Co., the present publishers and proprietors, under whom Dr. William H. Rippard is editor. Both the editorial and business management of this paper have been characterized by great ability and energy. It has a very large circulation, and enjoys a lucrative advertising business.

It is the organ of the Republican party of the county, and has great influence in the counsels of that party in the State, of which it is a fearless exponent.

William L. W. Seabrook, who edited this paper from 1868 to 1874, during the two important Presidential campaigns of 1868 and 1872, was born near Fairfield, Adams Co., Pa., Oct. 9, 1833. The death of his father when he was four years of age left his mother in rather straitened circumstances with three children, of whom the eldest was nine years of age. Six years afterwards she returned with her children to her native place, in Frederick County, Md., at which time Mr. Seabrook was ten years of age. During the succeeding ten years he resided with a maternal uncle, and was employed alternately in tilling the soil and selling miscellaneous merchandise in his uncle's store, varied by attendance at the village primary school during the winter months, where he obtained a fair education in the English branches, American hi[illegible] rudiments of [illegible] he entered

the office of the *Adams Sentinel*, at Gettysburg, Pa., where he continued about eighteen months and became a practical printer. On account of failing health he then abandoned the case for a period of six months, but at the age of nineteen resumed the occupation and became assistant foreman of the *Frederick Herald*, a newspaper published in Frederick City. At the age of twenty-one years he became one of the proprietors and leading editor of the paper referred to, a connection which continued about three years.

During this time, and subsequently, he has taken an active part in political movements, and has frequently discussed political issues on the public rostrum. In 1857, at the age of twenty-four, he was elected commissioner of the Land Office of the State of Maryland for the term of six years, having been a candidate on the American State ticket with Thomas Holliday Hicks, who was elected Governor at the same election. At the expiration of his term of office he was re-elected without opposition, having received the unanimous nomination of both radical and Conservative Union State conventions of that year, 1863. The adoption of the State constitution of 1867 cut short the tenure and vacated all the offices in the State except that of Governor. At the election of that year Mr. Seabrook was the Republican candidate for clerk of the Court of Appeals, but, with the other candidates on the ticket for State offices, was defeated. He was a delegate to the National Republican convention of 1864, at which Mr. Lincoln was renominated for the Presidency, and was a member of the committee which conveyed the action of the convention to the nominees. He was also elected a delegate to the National Convention of this party which renominated President Grant in 1872, but was unable to attend its sessions. Upon retiring from the Land Office in 1868 he became connected with the *American Sentinel* newspaper at Westminster, Md., as one of its proprietors, and as sole editor and manager, and so continued until Jan. 1, 1874.

In 1873 he was appointed superintendent of public stores in the Baltimore custom house, and filled that position until Dec. 1, 1876, when he became chief United States weigher at that port. He has been prominently connected with the order of Ancient Free and Accepted Masons, having been Senior Grand Warden from 1861 to 1862, and Deputy Grand Master of the Grand Lodge of the State of Maryland from 1862 to 1864. He was married Sept. 4, 1855, in Frederick, Md., to Miss Harriet P. Thomas, a native of that city. He has been a member of the Evangelical Lutheran Church since 1851, and later has been actively identified with the work of the Young Men's Christian Association.

The Democrat and Carroll County Republican was published by Joseph M. Parke, Jan. 1, 1844, at the rate of two dollars per annum. The first page was devoted to political and miscellaneous matter, and the fourth page had twelve insolvent debtors' notices, while Hance's patent medicines occupied nearly the remainder of the page. Michael Sullivan, Benjamin Yingling, Lewis Trumbo, Jesse Manning, and Samuel Moffet announced themselves as candidates for the sheriffalty. The inside pages were filled with editorial, foreign news, and advertisements. The paper contained the following information:

The semi-annual meeting of the Carroll County Temperance Convention was held on the 26th of December. Rev. Daniel Zollickhoffer was president, and Jacob H. Christ, secretary; Rev. Hezekiah Crout opened the convention with prayer. Reports were read from the societies of Uniontown, Warfieldsburg, Westminster, Franklin, Bethesda, and Salem. Resolutions were offered by C. Birnie, Jr., asking that a committee of three be appointed to wait upon the commissioners of tax and solicit their aid in forwarding the temperance cause. Messrs. Birnie, Willard, and McCollum were appointed. Capt. McCollum offered a resolution asking that petitions be sent to the Legislature asking that each election district be allowed to say, by ballot, whether or not it would have a license issued to taverns or grog-shops. At the afternoon session the resolution was adopted. Rev. W. Harden offered a resolution inquiring into the absence of the Freedom societies and why they were not present. He was appointed to inquire into the causes. On motion of Rev. E. Henkle, the following persons were appointed to address the several societies, viz.: Revs. W. Harden, T. Gallaudet, P. Willard, J. P. Carter, E. Henkle, and Jacob Holmes, and J. McCollum, Isaac Cox, J. H. Christ, C. Birnie, Jr., J. J. Baumgardner, O. Cox, J. Lindsay, A. Gorsuch, C. W. Webster, E. T. Curry, E. F. Crout, Jesse Malehorn, S. Murray, W. H. Grammer, F. H. Zollickhoffer, W. Zollickhoffer, I. N. Storr, and W. Holmes. The convention adjourned to meet at Westminster on Whit Monday, May 12th. The members of the Westminster choir attended and "gave conclusive demonstration of their proficiency in sacred music."

Mrs. Susanna Morelock, wife of Jacob Morelock, died on the 19th ultimo, in Uniontown District; Elizabeth, wife of Jacob Beam, died in Baltimore on the 7th ultimo.

List of Letters Remaining in the Post office at Westminster, Md Jan 1, 1844—Thomas Ashton, John Abbot, John Buel [illegible]ham, George Cox, J G Capito, J B Chenowith, Daniel [illegible], James Davis, Maria Frieling, John G Frick, [illegible] Green, John Gross Samuel Harding, Richard Harris, Francis Keiser [illegible]erouse Mr Michael Ludwig, John Mile, Adams [illegible] Pugh, Mrs Rachel Poulson Mr Stansifer, Michael [illegible]fler, Noah Stansbury Miss Mary Stevenson, Diana Smith, William Stonebraker, Elvira Sherfy, Samuel Shade, John or Jacob Seel, Peter Woods, Mr Wimpiper Nimrod Woolery, Peter Zeutz, Henry Zimmerman, Christiana Zimmerman — Joshua Yingling, Postmaster

Basil Rook was clerk to the county commissioners

Dr William A Mathias gave notice that he had located himself in Westminster opposite the store of Samuel Orendorff

Charles Rix advertised stoves and tinware

Samuel Bennett, trustee of the late William Beam, advertised two farms for sale, situated near Marriottsville

Elijah Wagner advertised cabinet-making and machine shops

Henry Saltzgiver advertised a price list of hats, which he said were the best and cheapest in the State

Joshua Smith, trustee, advertised a lot of ground and a brick brewery, occupied by Solomon Zepp, situated on the alley running from Court Street to Stone Alley

Basil Root offered at private sale a farm on the Washington road, adjoining lands of Jacob Groves and others, also two unimproved lots situated at the Forks, in Westminster, fronting on the Littlestown road

Joseph Stout advertised lime at nine cents per bushel His kiln was on the Joseph Orendorff farm, now occupied by S Meyerly, one and one-fourth mile from Westminster

Jesse Manning offered for sale or rent his tavern-stand, situated on the turnpike six miles below Westminster, also forty acres of land

The *Carroll County Democrat* of Oct 2, 1851, contained the valedictory of Josiah T H Bringman, who retired from the editorship, and also the salutatory of Augustus C Appler, who assumed control of the paper

At that time a warm political contest was going on, the Democratic ticket being

[illegible] Judicial District For Judge of the Court of Appeals W[illegible] P M[illegible], for Commissioner of Public Works, John [illegible] *Democratic State Nominations* For Comptroller of the Treasury Philip Francis Thomas for Commissioner of [illegible] Office, James Murray, for Lottery Commissioner, Thomas [illegible] Stewart *Democratic County Ticket* For House of Delegates [illegible] Daniel S[illegible] John [illegible] H Liggett, Elijah J Crout, for Judges of Orphans' [illegible] H [illegible] W M[illegible] [illegible] Buffington [illegible] for Register of Wills, Joseph M Parke, for State's Attorney, Daniel L Hoover, for County Surveyor J Henry Hoppe, for Commissioners of Tax James Crouse, Thomas Smith, George L Little, Jacob Wickert, Julius B Berrett, George Crouse, Jacob Grove George Richards, Jr, Bennett Spurrier

On the Thursday night previous a large meeting of voters of Hampstead was held at Scarff's tavern, and was addressed by Dr Liggett and Maj Ege Mr Crouse was absent, owing to ill health In behalf of the Whigs, Drs Booth and Cox spoke

On Saturday there was a large meeting at Union Bridge, which was addressed principally by Daniel L Hoover and Charles W Webster, candidates for prosecuting attorney, also by Messrs Hook, Crout, Booth, Liggett, Cox and Ege The Union Bridge Brass Band, under Prof Burke, enlivened the occasion

On the 1st of October an election for Congressmen and school commissioner was held The returns from only Westminster and Myers Districts were given For Congress, Edward Hammond received 60 majority in Westminster District over Dr A A Lynch In Myers District he received 131 over the doctor For school commissioner, John B Summers received 67 majority over William Baughman in Westminster District, and in Myers District, J William Earhart received 85 majority over Peter B Mikesell

The marriage of James W Lantz and Eleanor Hyde, of Uniontown District, by Rev J Winter, was announced

A political meeting was advertised to be held in Middleburg, October 11th, at which time all the candidates for the various offices were requested to attend

Robinson & Eldred's circus was advertised to exhibit on October 6th

Kettlewell & Cox advertised the Clover Hill farm, in Finksburg District, at public sale, October 25th

William P Maulsby and W C Van Bibber advertised the farm of George L Van Bibber part of the Avondale estate, two and one half miles from Westminster, for sale on the 10th of November

A statement of the expenditures of the county for the fiscal year ending July 6, 1851, is given, viz Outdoor pensioners, \$3202 60, public roads, \$3111 25, bridges and repairs to bridges, \$553 16, judges and clerks of election for September and October, 1850, and June 1851, \$320, county commissioners, \$625 50, colonization fund \$439 52, tax collector, \$340, printing \$101 75, public buildings, \$1000, clerk to commissioners, \$200, preparing book for collector of State taxes, \$50 counsel to commissioners, \$50, [illegible] of the [illegible] Court, \$379 50, janitor \$27 [illegible], [illegible] \$21 [illegible] [illegible] of wills, \$5,

stationery and postage, $18 50, wood for jail and commissioners' room $56 30, grand and petit jurors for September, 1851, and April, 1852, $867 62, bailiffs and talesmen for same terms, $103 50, prosecuting attorney, $146 66, crier of the court, $59 95, clerk of the court, $345 50, sheriff, for fees and board, $431, State witnesses, $300, costs in removed cases, $56, constables, $65 55, miscellaneous, $255 34 Total amount of expenditures, $13 535 27 The assessment was $6,777,636, on which there was a levy of 20 cents on the $100

Candidates were plentiful, as will be seen by the announcements

For Judge of the Circuit Court, Madison Nelson, William M Merrick, Richard H Marshall and Joseph M Palmer House of Delegates, Richard F Booth, L G Cox, Abraham Lamott and Thomas Hook, John McCollum as a candidate for clerk of the court, Register of Wills, John Baumgartner and John M Yingling, State's Attorney, Charles W Webster, Judges of the Orphans' Court, Jacob Mathias, Horatio Price, David B Earhart, and Basil Hayden, County Commissioners, William Reese and James Smith, County Surveyor, J Henry Hoppe and James Kerly, Sheriff, Wm S Brown Samuel J Jordan, and Otho Shipley

The issue of Oct 16, 1851, is lively and exciting The editorials are full of personal allusions, and the communications spicy It also contains a long article from Col William P Maulsby Political meetings are called for Uniontown District, at Crumrine's Hotel, four miles above Manchester, Finksburg, Franklinville, and at Little's Tavern, Freedom District

The issue dated Nov 6, 1851, was put in circulation on the 4th, two days before the election Some of the articles are more forcible than polite

The marriages of William Cornell and Elizabeth Kregelo, Emanuel Sell and Elizabeth Dotzour, George Gerhart and Lydia Black, William H Angel and Geronda C E Everhart, and Samuel Messinger and Miss Frownfeller are published

The issue of Jan 1, 1852, contains very little of interest It announces itself in favor of Stephen A Douglas for President By the census of 1850, Carroll takes rank as the fifth county in the State for the production of wheat

The Democratic Advocate, now owned and published by William H and Charles H Vanderford, under the firm-name of Vanderford Bros, is the regular successor or continuation of *The Democrat and Carroll County Republican*, which was established by William Shipley, in February, 1838 Mr Shipley continued its publication until April, 1840, when he sold out to Joseph M Parke Josiah T H Bringman bought a half-interest in it on March 12, 1846 The name was then changed to *The Carroll County Democrat*, and in 1848 Mr Bringman purchased the remaining half interest from Mr Parke Mr Bringman published the paper until Oct 2, 1851, when Augustus C Appler became its owner, and he sold it to George H Randall on May 15, 1855 In July, 1856, Joseph Shaw became its publisher and editor It was merged into a new paper called the *Western Maryland Democrat*, in May, 1861, of which W Scott Roberts was editor Joseph Shaw shortly afterwards again owned and controlled the paper On April 15, 1865, on the reception of the news of the assassination of President Lincoln the most intense excitement prevailed in Westminster A large mass meeting of its Republican citizens was held at the court-house in the evening, at which resolutions were adopted to notify Mr Shaw, of the *Democrat*, "that the publication of his paper would no longer be permitted," on account (as alleged) of its containing articles abusive of the late President and Andrew Johnson, the Vice-President At midnight, long after the meeting adjourned, the office of the *Democrat* was visited, and the type, cases, printing paper, and in fact all the material, were taken into the street and burned, and the presses, etc, in the building broken with axes, crowbars, and other items On Nov 22, 1865, *The Democratic Advocate* was established by W H Davis, who sold it to Joseph M Parke in 1866, and on Nov 28, 1867, Mr Parke sold it to Mr Davis again In March, 1868, W H Vanderford one of its present proprietors, purchased the establishment He assumed control on March 12th following, and in connection with his father, H Vanderford, published it until November, 1878, when he disposed of a half interest to his brother, Charles H Vanderford, H Vanderford then retiring almost entirely from editorial duties

In November, 1868, at the beginning of the fourth volume, W H Vanderford enlarged and otherwise improved the paper, and increased its subscription price from $1 50 to $2 00 per year Under the management of himself and father the *Advocate* began to prosper rapidly Its circulation increased, its advertising and job patronage expanded, and new material was added from time to time as necessity required

At the beginning of the eighth volume, in November, 1872, when Charles H Vanderford, who remained with the paper six months, became half owner, the paper was enlarged to its present size, a Cottrell & Babcock power-press and an entire outfit of new type was put in the office, including a large amount of [illegible]

The *Advocate* continued to prosper, and its patronage necessitated constant additions to its stock of material. The need of additional room became apparent, and its energetic proprietor purchased the lot on the corner of Main and Centre Streets, and erected the present *Advocate* building. It was finished in October, 1877, and the part occupied by the printing establishment is twenty by eighty feet, two stories high. The other part, twenty by forty feet, is occupied by James M. Shellman as a stationery store and news depot.

The building is of a very substantial character, well lighted and admirably adapted for the printing business. The first floor front is occupied as a business office, and the back room, fifty-six by eighteen feet, as a press and job room. In the second story is the editorial room, nicely carpeted and furnished and containing a library. It is connected with the office below by a dumb-waiter and speaking-tube. Back of the editorial room is the composing room, the same size as the press and job room. Under the latter room is a large cistern, from which, by means of a pump running up into the printing-office, water is obtained for the uses of the establishment.

The four presses—two new Universals, a Washington, and a Cottrell & Babcock—are run by steam, and the four rooms of the office are heated by steam.

The *Advocate* office in its appointments and equipments, and all the appurtenances necessary to a first-class establishment, is unequaled in Maryland outside of Baltimore, and the labors and enterprise of its proprietors have been generously appreciated by the people of Westminster and the county.

Henry Vanderford, editor and journalist, the father of the present editors and proprietors of the *Advocate*, was born at Hillsborough, Caroline Co., Md., Dec. 23, 1811. He is of Welsh descent, and was educated at Hillsborough Academy. He acquired a knowledge of the printing business in the office of the Easton *Star*, which he continued to publish after the death of Mr. Smith, the proprietor. He was subsequently employed on the Easton *Whig*. From 1835 to 1837 he published the *Caroline Advocate*, Denton, Md. The press and type he transferred in 1837 to Centreville, Queen Anne's Co., Md., and founded the *Sentinel*, which, though independent in politics, took a very decided part in the reform movement of 1836 and '37. He removed to Baltimore in 1842, and published *The Ray*, a weekly paper, and also the *Daily News* and the *Weekly Statesman*. In February, 1848, he bought the *Cecil Democrat*, enlarged the paper, quadrupled its circulation, and refitted it with new material. In 1868 he founded the *Middletown Transcript*, which was transferred in 1873 to his youngest son, Charles H. Vanderford. From 1870 to 1878 he was associated with his eldest son, William H. Vanderford, in the publication of the *Democratic Advocate* of Westminster. In 1870 he was elected to the House of Delegates from Carroll County, and re-elected in 1875, and in 1879 was elected a member of the State Senate, which office he still holds.

Mr. Vanderford married, June 6, 1839, Angeline Vanderford, a distant relative of his father. She is still living, being the mother of twelve children,—eight sons and four daughters. Only three of the sons are living, the eldest and youngest of whom are journalists, the former being William H. and the latter Charles H., late publisher of the *Old Commonwealth*, at Harrisonburg, Va. They are now the publishers of the *Advocate*. The second son, Dr. Julian J. Vanderford, is a dentist, and at present pursuing the practice of his profession in Stuttgart, Germany. Henry Vanderford and his wife are communicants of the Protestant Episcopal Church. He is a member of the Masonic order, and was formerly a member of the I. O. O. F.

The following is a list of persons living in Westminster in 1879, and within a radius of five miles thereof, who had attained to the age of seventy years and upwards. The list comprises one hundred and twenty-one persons, ranging from seventy to ninety-five years of age. There are omitted from the list the names of twenty-six persons above seventy years of age whose exact ages could not be obtained. The oldest inhabitant died at the almshouse, aged one hundred and twelve years.[1]

Jacob Stone, 95; Ruth Frizzell, 95; John Yingling, 94; Jacob Marker, 93; Joshua Biggs, 92; Henry Stonesifer, 90; Mrs. John Biggs, 89; James C. Graham, 89; William Crouse, 87; Miss Snider, 86; Mrs. D. Baumgartner, 85; Mary Beaver, 85; John Abbott, 84; James Williams, 84; Mrs. Jacob Snider, 84; John Crouse, 84; Mary Burke, 83; Mary Grammer, 83; Betsey Adelsperger, 83; James Hook, 82; Mrs. Wm. B. Crouse, 81;

[1] Becky McCormick, colored, familiarly known as "Old Becky," died on Sunday, March 9, 1879. It is impossible to give her exact age, but as far as can be ascertained, she was about one hundred and twelve years old. She had been an inmate of the almshouse for twelve or fourteen years prior to her death, and was a religious monomaniac. The most of her time was spent in singing and praying, intermingled with pleadings that her Good Master would take her home. She had been anxious to die for some years, saying that she wanted to go home to her people, and would sometimes get in paroxysms of excitement when any *one* would tell her that she would not die soon.

The "Beck" McCormick who was hanged in 1869, and who was the first to suffer death upon the scaffold in this county, was a granddaughter of this old woman. She was hanged for the murder of [illegible] William [illegible], [illegible] Westminster.

M Baumgartner, 80, Samuel Young 80, Joshua Sellman, 80 Joseph Keller, 79, Daniel Stultz 79, Andrew Reese, 79, Wm Stansbury, 79, John Gallandette, 79, Rev T Gallandette, 78, J Henry Hoppe, 78 Isaac Meyers, 78, Mrs Mary Beaver, 77, George Burbour, 77, Thomas Monahan, 77, Mrs Andrew Reese, 77, Samuel Snider, 76, James Blizzard, 76, Sarah Kuhns, 76, Rebecca Roop, 76, Nancy Blizzard, 76, Henry Dell, 76, H. H Harbaugh, 76 Jacob Babylon 75 David Wentz, 75, Dr J L Billingslea, 75, Thomas Williams, 75, Mr Brown, 75, Elizabeth Shaeffer, 75, Mrs Isaac Meyers, 75 Susan Gist, 75, John Babylon, 74, Sarah Leekins, 74, Henry Sneeve, 74 George Blizzard, 74, John Smith, 73, Catharine Stonesifer, 73, Mary Williams, 73, Mrs Sarah Fringer, 73, Peggy Adelsperger, 73, David Wentz 72 David Zepp, 72 Samuel Unger, 72, Mary Royer, 72, Catharine Meyers, 72 Daniel J Geiman, 72, Polly Shaeffer, 72, Margaret E Gerke, 72 Charles Meyers, 72, Joseph Newson, 72, Thomas Goodwin, 72, David H Shriver, 72, Mrs Horatio Price, 71, Daniel Shaeffer, 71 J W Swartzbaugh, 71, Henry Weiman, 71, Dr Francis Butler, 70 L W Bennett, 70, Mrs Mary Shriver, 70, Parry Laille, 70, Jesse Yingling, 70, Elizabeth Price, 70 *Colored People*—Samuel Robinson, 90, Philip Briscoe, 88, Philip Leman, 87, Robert Bell 85, Henry Anthony, 82 Serena Parker, 82, Samuel Thompson, 79, Wm Parker, 79, Rev J B Snowden, 77, Grace Paraway, 76, Elizabeth Hauden, 72, Charlotte Troupe, 71, Ellen Robinson, 70

John L Reifsnider, a prominent merchant in Westminster, Carroll Co, Md, was born in Taneytown, Oct 19, 1836 He has been twice married,—Dec 10, 1861, to the eldest daughter of Dr J L Billingslea, and Jan 12, 1871, to the eldest daughter of Augustus Shriver Mr Reifsnider began business at a very early age, and at the age of eighteen was a member of the well known firm of Reifsnider & Son, of Westminster He is the president of the Westminster Gas Company, the success of which is due more to him than any other man He has accumulated large wealth by his own industry, intelligence, and business judgment, and has retired from business, and lives in an elegant mansion in Westminster

The traveler along the Westminster and Meadow Branch turnpike will find his attention pleasantly invited, at a point about two miles from Westminster, to "Meadow Brook," the comfortable-looking and attractive home of Samuel Roop The house (a semi-Gothic structure) stands upon a gently-sloping eminence close to the highway, and is approached by a sweeping drive from either side A prettily kept lawn makes a charming foreground to the picture Mr Roop's great grandfather, Christian Roop, came from Switzerland to Lancaster County, Pa, during the eighteenth century Four of his sons (Joseph, Christian, David, and John) removed to Carroll County at different periods soon after the Revolution to find new homes John located upon the present Samuel Roop place, on which stood a small frame house when he purchased th[illegible] About 1[illegible]05 he built a brick house,—the one now occupied by Samuel Roop, who has by material improvements and tastefully-continued embellishments made it a bright, cheerful looking abode Of the large land tract owned by his grandfather John, Mr Roop is now the possessor of two hundred and fifty acres of as fine farming land as can be found in the county The barns, outbuildings, and general equipments are well constructed, and are kept with an eye to their appearance Since 1878, Mr Roop has devoted considerable attention to the breeding of short-horned cattle, with highly encouraging results The Westminster and Meadow Branch pike which passes his place, was built largely through his efforts Mr Roop's farm is one of the best managed and most inviting estates in this section of the county, and he is justly regarded as one of Carroll's most useful and substantial citizens He is an energetic and progressive agriculturist, and takes a keen interest in everything pertaining to his occupation

Stonersville is three and a half miles from Westminster, thirty two from Baltimore, and near the Patapsco Falls It takes its name from the Stoner family George W Stoner is postmaster The storekeepers are Noah Stansbury and D H Crouse

Cranberry is on the Sullivan road, five miles from Manchester and six from Westminster Samuel Snyder is postmaster, and Snyder & Gummell, storekeepers

Avondale is on the Western Maryland Railroad, three miles from Westminster, and thirty-four from Baltimore James W Beacham is postmaster

Tannery is on the Western Maryland Railroad, one mile from Westminster, and takes its name from the leather manufactory of A P Baer & Co, of Baltimore, which is here located James S Baer is postmaster The Methodist Episcopal Church has a neat chapel

Warfieldsburg is three miles from Avondale, and four from Westminster, and near Morgan's Run The merchants are J W Sellman and J B Allison, the latter is postmaster The resident physician is Dr J P Somers Of the Church of God located here, Rev Lewis Selby is pastor David Baile and Washington Nicodemus are millers The village takes its name from the Warfield family, one of the first to settle in the county

The following is the vote for local officers from 1851 to 1861 inclusive

1851 —Vote for Primary School Commissioner Jacob Matthias 225, Francis Shriver 137, William Lachman 12[illegible], John B Summers 189

1853 —For Justices Jesse Manning 317, J H Hoppe 287, James Keefer 217, F G Franklin 216, Otho Shipley 217, Wm [illegible] Bun[illegible] 169, Wm A Wam-

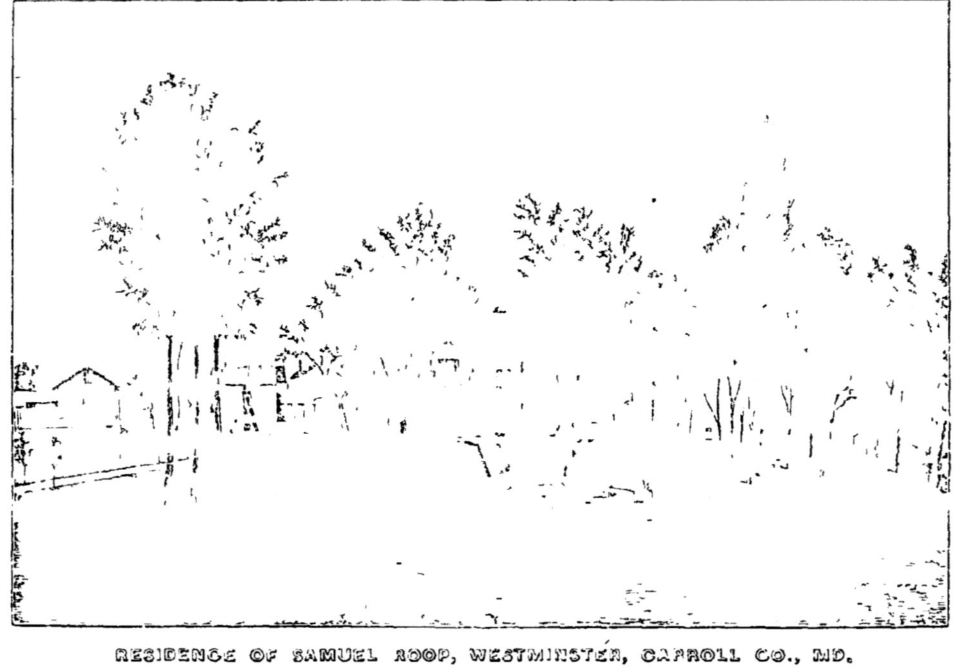

RESIDENCE OF SAMUEL ROOP, WESTMINSTER, CARROLL CO., MD.

plor 320, Constables Wm Ouisler 240, J T Diffenbaugh 294, Emanuel Gernand 355 Wm H Mourer 151 Road Supervisor Michael Lynch 266, Geo Shade 199 William Koontz 174

1855—For Justices H B Grammer 269, E Gernand 289, Jesse Manning 278, W A Wampler 295 Wm Crouse 336, J H Hoppe 312 Joseph Matthias 318, F O Franklin 291, Constables J Diffenbaugh 302, Geo Webster 287, Thos B Gist 299, John Blizzard 303, Road Supervisor Wm Miller 312, Wm Koontz 299

1857—For Justices W A Crouse 352, Joseph Matthias 371, F O Franklin 350 J H Hoppe 317, W A Wampler 289, Constables S M Gist 28? John Blizzard 330, J T Diffenbaugh 280, G Sheets 105 Road Supervisor M Lynch 344, Noah Mitten 249

1859—For Justices Joseph Matthias 128, Wm Crouse 369, Chas Denning 286 Jesse Manning 193, W A Wampler 350 James Keefer 178, Emanuel Funk 187, J Henry Hoppe 400 Constables J M Yingling 335, Levi Evans 275, R W Stem 366, David Kuhn 351, Road Supervisor Jacob Beaver 355, J Shambruch, Jr, 208

1861.—For Justices J Matthias 467, J H Hoppe 41?, F Gernand 421, W A Wampler 155, W J Mitten 53, William Crouse 256 Daniel Byers 259, Jesse Manning 224 J B Summers 213, Constables G W Plowman 116, R W Stem 459, Ira F Crouse 206, J M Yingling 219, David Kuhn 76, Road Supervisor J L Wampler 150, Philip Turfle 261

The public school trustees for 1881 and 1882 are given, together with the names of teachers and number of pupils

1 Grammar School—Elias Yingling, F A Sharrer, Geo W Miller

2 Primary No 1—David Fowble, Wm B Thomas, A H Huber

3 Primary, No 2—Elias Yingling, F A Sharrer George W Miller

4 Primary, No 3—Same as Primary, No 2

5 Primary No 4—David Fowble, Wm B Thomas, A H Huber

6 West End, No 1—B F Crouse, E J Lawyer, Milton Schaeffer

7 West End No 2—Same as No 1

8 West End, No 3—Same as No 1

9 Warfieldsburg, No 1—Joshua Sellman, David Owings, Albinus Poole

10 Warfieldsburg No 2—Same as No 1

11 Shades—Jesse Sullivan, A Gieman, Charles Schaeffer

12 Mexico—No trustees

13 Mountain View—David Warehime, Uriah Bixler, John Baust

14 Meadow Branch.—John D Koop, David Reese, Ezra Bisch

15 Cranberry—Noah Schaeffer, William H Reese, Lewis Schaeffer.

16 Friendship—William Fenby Frederick N Hook, Joshua Stevenson

17 Wm Bachman's—E Bixler, Wm Lease, William J Biggs

4 West End (African)—Alfred Bruce, J M Snowden, Reuben Woodyard (all colored)

The teachers for the term ending April 15, 1881, were

1, C H Baughman 32 pupils, 2, C H Spurrier, 31 pupils 3, Belle M Matthews 29 pupils, 4 F W Shriver, 36 pupils, 5, Maria Pearson, 37 pupils, 6, George Patson, 51 pupils, 7, Mattie W Beaver, 31 pupils, 8, Laura K Matthews, 37 pupils 9, Stanley R Still, 36 pupils, 10, C Belle Poole, 30 pupils, 11, Henry L Shriver, 29 pupils, 12 Geo H Gist, 19 pupils, 13, G. W Sullivan, 45 pupils 14, D L Meswiney 52 pupils, 15, Laura A Everhart, 21 pupils 16 F A Diffenbach, 55 pupils, 17 H B Burgoon, 12 pupils, 4 (African school), Fannie E Balls, 38 pupils

UNION BRIDGE DISTRICT, No 12

The Twelfth District of Carroll County, generally known as Union Bridge, is bounded on the north by Middleburg District, on the east by the districts of Uniontown and New Windsor, on the south by the latter and Frederick County, and on the west by Frederick County It is the youngest district in the county, having been created by an act of the General Assembly of Maryland, passed March 14, 1872, out of portions of the territory embraced by the districts of Middleburg, New Windsor, and Uniontown In area it is also smaller than the other districts, but it is by no means the least important It is magnificently watered by Sam's Creek, which forms the western boundary line between the district and Frederick County, and by Little Pipe Creek, which flows directly through the centre of the district from east to west, and by a number of smaller streams which are tributary to those just mentioned The soil is exceedingly fertile, and the Western Maryland Railroad, within easy reach from all parts of the district, furnishes ample facilities for the disposal of produce and communication with trade centres The population in 1880 was 1235 It contains within its limits one of the largest and most prosperous towns in the county, and a large share of the manufacturing establishments of this portion of Maryland The metes and bounds of the district, as prescribed by the act of Assembly which created it, are as follows

Beginning at Sam's Creek the boundary line between Carroll and Frederick Counties and at the point in said Sam's Creek where the tail race from McKinstry's mills empties therein and running thence by a straight line to intersect the middle of the public road from McKinstry's mills to Linwood, and at a point in said public road opposite the stone house now occupied by D J Albaugh and brother, thence by and with the centre of said public road to the bridge over Little Pipe Creek near Linwood being a corner of Election District No 2, thence through said district by a straight line to Reuben Haines' dwelling-house excluding said premises thence by a straight line to intersect the public road from Union Bridge to Union Town at a point in said road opposite the centre of a lane leading off therefrom towards the public school-house being between the house and premises of Abraham Harris and the premises of Abraham Stoner, thence by a straight line to the spring at the head of Log Cabin Branch being at a corner of Election District [illegible] to the centre of [illegible] g, thence [illegible]

the middle of said public road towards Middle[illegible] until opposite a lane known as Haines lane, being now be[illegible] the lands of Abraham Shirk and Joseph Roop, thence down said line to the south end thereof, thence by a straight line running by Lewis Haines' dwelling-house and including said premises to Pipe Creek, the boundary line between Carroll and Frederick Counties, thence up said creek and Sam's Creek to the place of beginning"

The first survey was that of "Kilfadda," for a large tract of land patented in 1729 to John Tredane, and afterwards to Allen Farquhar, being then in Prince George's County This land embraces a part of "Union Bridge" and the farm of E J Penrose

E G Penrose was born in the township of Washington, York Co, Pa, the 10th of the 9th month, 1817, the second in a family of four children of Josiah and Rachel (Garretson) Penrose The family in this country sprung from two brothers, who emigrated from England with Wm Penn at his second voyage They settled in Pennsylvania, and have scattered to different States, mainly Ohio, Illinois, Iowa, and Kansas The only one who settled in Maryland is the subject of this sketch

Thomas Penrose, his grandfather, born 4th day of the 1st month (old style), 1749, married Abigail Cadwalader, the latter was born the 18th of the 1st month, 1752 To this worthy couple were born seven children,—five sons and two daughters,—viz Amos, Thomas, William, Hannah, Ann Josiah, and Cyrus

Thomas moved to Illinois, and died there, William lived and died in Bedford County at the homestead, he raised a large family, Hannah married Jesse Kenworthy, a farmer near Brownsville, Washington Co Pa, she died there, leaving two daughters, Ann and Cyrus did not marry, lived and died at the homestead, Amos married and raised a family of eight children, he resided at the homestead and died there, Josiah, father of E G, was born in York County, Pa, 28th of 3d month, 1790, married Rachel, daughter of John and Mary Garretson, 18th of 5th month, 1815 Her father was born 5th of 4th month, 1741, his wife, Mary, 16th of 10th month, 1745 They were married 9th of 6th month, 1763, at a public meeting of Friends at Huntington He died 15th of 12th month, 1810, his wife, 3d of 7th month, 1827

Rachel G Penrose was born 8th of 12th month, 1788 When E G Penrose was seventeen years of age his father moved with his family to Menallen township, Adams Co, Pa, and settled on a farm, both himself and wife died in Adams County, the latter 25th of 12th month, 1824, the former 7th of 1st month, 1860

Elisha Garretson Penrose lived at home until he was nineteen years of [illegible] His education was limited to an attendance at a private school In 1836 he went to Baltimore, where he was employed as clerk in the grocery store of Isaiah B Price, with whom he remained four years He then engaged on his own account in the meat business on Hillen Street, near the Belair Market, and continued in it four years, making it a success

For the next three years he was engaged in the coal trade, in company with James Johnson, firm, Johnson & Penrose In 1847, in company with Jonathan Shoemaker,—firm, Penrose & Co,—he carried on a grocery on Pennsylvania Avenue, corner of St Mary Street At the end of three years the firm was dissolved He then engaged in his own name in the grocery and produce business corner of Franklin and Eutaw Streets, first renting and subsequently purchasing the store, remained there from 1850 to 1855 In the latter year he entered into partnership with Thomas Russell, and for three years, under the firm-name of Penrose & Russell, carried on a store at 153 North Howard Street At the end of that time he purchased Russell's interest, and took into partnership Wm A Simpson under the firm of E G Penrose & Co, which partnership continued for twelve years Upon its dissolution he took as partner John Russell, brother of former partner, the firm-name continuing as before In 1878, Russell withdrew, and a partnership under the firm name of Penrose, Nelker & Co, was formed, his associates in this partnership are J F Nelker and A H Nelker, which partnership still exists, the business being carried on in the old place From all his business transactions intoxicating liquors have been excluded

In politics he has been identified with the Whig and Republican parties He is a member of the Society of Friends, and although living in a slave State, has always been opposed to slavery During the late war he was a stanch friend of the Union cause He married, 24th of 2d month, 1853, Susan, daughter of Abel and Elizabeth (Roberts) Russell Mrs Penrose was born in Frederick County, Md, 7th of 1st month 1828. They have had three children, viz Lizzie, born 5th of 10th month, 1860, died 25th of 3d month 1866, William, born 16th of 6th month 1862, now engaged with the firm at Baltimore, Mary, born 22d of 1st month, 1869

In 1868, Mr Penrose purchased the well-known Shepherd farm, one hundred and eighty one acres, near Union Bridge, Carroll Co, Md, and moved there in 1869 Up to 1879 few men enjoyed better health or possessed a more vigorous constitution, and none who gave closer application to business At that time he withdrew from active participation in the

business of his house in Baltimore, retaining however, as a general partner his interest in the same

During the time he has been engaged in business in Baltimore his house has passed successfully through three severe panics, which sufficiently attests his prudence and excellent judgment as a business man

Many members of the Society of Friends settled in Union Bridge District prior to the war of the Revolution, and formed a "particular meeting," but the society never gained a strong foothold Some of the descendants of the first Friends who settled here are yet living in this region

Among the early settlers were the Farquhars, Wrights, Rinehards, Wolfes, Shepherds, Thomases, Husseys, and Beneduns These pioneers were men of unusual energy and intelligence, and they gave an impetus to this section which it has ever since maintained Their experiences, some of which will be found in the introductory chapter of the history of this county, were very interesting They evidently appreciated the natural advantages which the country offered and availed themselves of them without loss of time Mills, factories, and other necessary improvements were speedily erected, and many older settlements in Maryland might have profitably imitated their example The first nail-factory in the State, probably, was established in this district, and the first reaping-machine was invented by John B Thomas, in Union Bridge, the machine which Hussey used as his model, and from which all others generally in use on this side of the Rocky Mountains derived their origin

The first Farmers' Club in Carroll County of which there is any knowledge was formed in 1817, in the vicinity of Union Bridge, at that time a portion of Frederick County, by Thomas Shepherd, Daniel Haines, Ulrich Switzer, Samuel Haines, David Englar, Philip Englar, Henry Rial, and Israel Rinehart (whose son, Israel C, is still a member of the organization) It was a society of producers for their mutual benefit and protection against the middlemen, and was the germ of the organization now known as the Patrons of Husbandry, which has recently reached out with its Briarean arms and embraced the whole United States The plan of the club, or, as it was more generally styled, "the company," was to produce a first-rate article and deliver it directly to the consumer They made "gilt edged" butter, and got fancy prices for it A person who did not make a good article could not be a member of the club, and they established a first class reputation

The club ran a wagon, which conveyed the produce to the Baltimore m[illegible] every week The members took turns in going, the one accompanying the wagon furnished a horse his week, and acted as agent for the association in selling their produce and buying goods for them At their annual meetings they settled their financial business, and had no commissions to pay to agents at a distance

The club is still in existence, and is sending produce to Baltimore every week The excellent character established for its members enables them to command the highest prices for their produce

A second or Junior Club, was established in or about 1853, similar to the older company of 1817 It has been in successful operation ever since

In 1864 there was an association organized at Union Bridge, under the name and title of "The Union Bridge Agricultural and Scientific Club" The first permanent officers were elected Feb 20, 1861, as follows President, Granville S Haines, Recording Secretary, Joshua Switzer, Treasurer, Daniel Wolf, Librarian, Thomas W Russell, Executive Committee, Warrington Gillingham, Solomon Shepherd, and Pemberton Wood The meetings were held on the first and third Saturday of every month, at seven o'clock P M In 1868 there were other features introduced which materially enhanced the usefulness of the society The club now meets at a member's house every month, and half the membership are ladies The farmer's wife is as much a member of the club as he himself, with the same rights and privileges

The first duty after organization is usually to examine the farm, buildings, fencing, work, etc, criticising and answering questions, after which they return to the house, where essays are read and questions discussed, after which they repair to the table bountifully supplied with the products of the farm, nicely prepared to suit the palate The company having partaken of the feast, select the subject for their next meeting, and adjourn to meet again next month at the house of some other member The plan of holding circular meetings has been adopted by all the wide-awake neighborhoods in the country

The town of Union Bridge has a population of 576, and in both a commercial and social sense is the focal point of the district It was to this spot that the early settlers flocked, a hardy, energetic, and remarkably intelligent race of people, who have given a distinct character to the community The country in the vicinity of the town was very fertile, but in many places it was swampy, the woods and undergrowth were almost impenetrable, and ravenous wolves, made dangerous by hunger, were constantly prowling about [illegible] produce or the

stock, and even to attack the unwary passer by The remarkable fertility of the soil had evidently attracted the notice of man long before the settlement of the whites Upon the site of the present town large quantities of stone arrows, hatchets, and other implements referable to the stone age have been picked up, as well as numerous skulls and other human bones, indicating that sanguinary conflicts had taken place for the possession of this favored spot William Farquhar and his wife Ann, with their children, an interesting account of whose settlement in the district has already been given, were probably the pioneers of Union Bridge They settled upon a tract of land given them by Allen Farquhar, upon which much of the town now stands On Aug 7, 1747, a tract of land called "Forest in Need," containing one hundred and twenty acres, was granted to William Farquhar, in which is included all that part of the town south of Elgar Street That portion of the town west of Main Street and north of a line struck from the intersection of Elgar Street with Main Street to the intersection of Broadway and Canary Streets was Moses Farquhar's All that part south of the above line belonged to Samuel Farquhar The portion east of Main Street and north of Elgar Street was Allen Farquhar's The dividing line between the property of Samuel and William Farquhar became a road, which was subsequently placed on the county, and eventually became "Main" Street in the town of Union Bridge During the Revolution and for some time afterwards the neighborhood was known as the "Pipe Creek Settlement," the word Pipe Creek being a translation into English of the Indian name "Apoochkken" The inhabitants at that time were mainly Quakers, whose tenets were opposed to war, but their enthusiasm in many cases prevailed over their peaceful principles, and they contributed largely of their means in aid of the patriot cause, and not a few officers and soldiers were recruited from their number

Benjamin Farquhar, a grandson of William at the close of the last century, was the first to make use of the abundant water power of the town by building a saw-mill and an oil-mill to utilize the seed of the flax which was grown in the neighborhood This was on the site of what is now the Union Bridge Hotel, and is the same water power used by the Western Maryland Railroad Company in operating its machine shops Peter Benedam, an enterprising German from Lancaster County, Pa, came to Union Bridge at the beginning of the present century and purchased five hundred [illegible] of land, which included all of the town site [illegible] Elgar Street and [illegible] of Main Street, a large portion of which he cleared [illegible] drained, and brought under cultivation He app[illegible] to have been, from all accounts, a thoroughly [illegible] man in the community, and gave a healthy impetus [illegible] farming and other industries He constructed [illegible] own cost an elaborate, costly, and durable [illegible] across the creek, which remained as a monument [illegible] his judgment and skill and proof against the [illegible] of time and floods for more than half a century His residence was the premises now owned by Granville S Haines Joseph Elgar was the first merch[illegible] and manufacturer by machinery on the site of [illegible] town He also built the first brick house in the town in which Joseph Wilson now lives The pioneers [illegible] not pass away without leaving their "footprints on the sands of time" A well-paved wagon-road was [illegible] across the swampy ground northward from the town and a substantial bridge was built across the cr[illegible] done by the united labor of those who lived on [illegible] side of the stream After its completion, while [illegible] builders were still assembled, it was proposed that [illegible] bridge be called by some name to distinguish it f[illegible] other similar structures "Union Bridge" was suggested, and its peculiar appropriateness secured [illegible] unanimous adoption The bridge gave the name [illegible] both the town and the district Peter Benedam [illegible] out in 1814 and removed to the Valley of Virginia [illegible] and Jacob Switzer, the father of Joshua Switzer [illegible] very able centennial historian of the district, to wh[illegible] the author of this work is indebted for valuable [illegible]terial), purchased one hundred and thirty-eight [illegible] of his land, embracing that part of Union Br[illegible] west of Main Street and north of Elgar Street [illegible] war with Great Britain created a demand for agr[illegible]tural products, and Union Bridge and its vicinity [illegible]joyed a season of great prosperity All that p[illegible] the town west of Main Street was a clover-field, [illegible] plowed up and put in a crop of wheat and fol[illegible] with a crop of rye, would produce enough to p[illegible] the first cost of the land At this period the [illegible] contained but four houses,—one upon the [illegible] Hartsock's Hotel, which was taken down to [illegible] room for the hotel in 1870, one near the [illegible] Capt Isaiah Lightner's dwelling-house, which [illegible] removed in 1814, and is now the central part of [illegible] dwelling-house of William Stultz, one on the [illegible] site of William Wilson's store, afterwards for a time used as a shop and taken away about [illegible] years ago, and the brick house built by [illegible] Elgar All save the last were built of oak [illegible] though not strictly ornamental, were comfort[illegible] [illegible] shop [illegible] [illegible] Jacob R [illegible]

JOS MOORE

was subsequently converted into a dwelling-house George Cox succeeded Elgar as a merchant, and took butter, eggs, and other produce in exchange for goods He started a huckster wagon and created a local market, and from the quality or quantity of butter sold here the town was called "Buttersburg," a name which has clung to it and by which it is sometimes known to day There was no post-office nearer than Taneytown The growing condition of the "settlement" required better postal facilities, and in or about the year 1820 a post office, with a weekly mail, was established between this point and Frederick City In the selection of a name that might also designate its locality, the name of Union Bridge was chosen, after which time the village began to be called "Union Bridge Post-office," and then only "Union Bridge," and the name of Buttersburg was disused In 1821, Jacob Switzer removed the old oil-mill, and built upon its site a brick four story grist and merchant mill, forty by forty-two feet, the stone basement of which is now the basement of the "Union Bridge Hotel" A part of the brick dwelling house now the residence of Joseph Wolfe had also been built But very little progress was then made in buildings for the two succeeding decades In 1846, Joseph Moore having become the owner by purchase of all that part of the town site west of Main Street, laid out a series of lots along the whole length of said street, fronting thereon and running about fourteen and a quarter perches, which he afterwards sold from time to time, and building then first began on the west side of Main Street, the first dwelling-house being that now owned and inhabited by Reuben Sayler

Joseph Moore was born in Taneytown District (now New Windsor), Frederick Co (now Carroll), Md, Sept 26, 1802 His grandfather, John Moore, was a native of West Caln township, Chester Co, Pa He married Hannah Hollingsworth, of Birmingham township, same county, April 13, 1749 Their children were David, Joanna, Enoch, John, Jehu, Mary, and Abigail David married and settled and died in Petersburg, Va Enoch and John were neither married, both were soldiers in the war of the Revolution Enoch died at his father's residence, at Union Bridge John died at his father's residence, near Westminster Mary married a Mr Stephenson moved to Illinois, and died there Soon after his marriage John Moore moved to Baltimore, where he carried on milling About the time of the Revolution he moved to Westminster, and subsequently purchased a farm about two miles from that place, he died there Jehu Moore, fourth son of John [illegible] father of Joseph, was born in Baltimore, Oct [illegible] married [illegible] of Joseph and Jane Hibbard, of Pipe Creek, March 23, 1796 Mrs Moore was born in Willets township, Chester Co, Pa, March 3, 1768 Their children were Ann, born Feb 3, 1801, Joseph, and Mary, born Aug 9, 1804 Ann died June 22, 1822 Mary, widow of Isaac Dixon, is a resident of Baltimore

Jehu Moore settled in Union Bridge District (then Taneytown) in 1794, and engaged for several years in merchandising in company with Solomon Shepherd Selling out his interest in the store about 1808, he purchased a farm east of the village, which he carried on to the time of his death, which occurred Dec 11, 1841 His wife lived to the advanced age of ninety-six years, and died May 3, 1863 Both are buried in the Friends' burying-ground at Pipe Creek

Joseph Moore lived on the home-farm from his birth to 1865 His education was limited to an attendance in summers at the common school of his neighborhood In 1837 he purchased of David Switzer the tract of land known as the "Rich Indian Garden," consisting of forty one acres, a portion of which he allotted, and upon which all that portion of the village of Union Bridge lying west of Main Street has been built up The home-farm, which came into his possession by will, he sold in 1865, taking up his residence in the village of Union Bridge, where, with the exception of two years spent in Baltimore, he has since resided He built his present residence, a fine brick mansion, on a site commanding a fine view of the village and surrounding country, in 1879 and 1880 In religion Mr Moore belongs to the Society of Friends, in politics, first a Whig, then a Republican, and took an active interest in securing the construction of the Western Maryland Railroad, which has been the means mainly of building up the village of Union Bridge He married, June 8, 1871, at Troy N Y, Hannah P, daughter of Elias and Mary (Bryant) Lord Mrs Moore was born Oct 3, 1837, in Colchester, Chittenden Co, Vt She received her education at Burlington Female Seminary and Mrs Wooster's Ladies' School, Burlington, Vt They have had two children,—Mary Hannah, born July 3, 1873, and Archer Joseph, born July 20, 1876, died May 23, 1877

About this time the railroad which is now called the Western Maryland Railroad first began to be talked of (previous to which a connection with the Baltimore and Ohio Railroad had been supposed to be the most feasible after the unsuccessful attempt to secure the passage of its main stem through the place), but it was not until ten years afterwards, or in 1855–56, that [illegible] it, and in the [illegible] trains came

to Union Bridge During this period but little additional building had been done in the town, other than the brick depot and warehouse built by Moses Shaw and David Hiltabidle, and some buildings by the railroad company preparatory to the opening of the road On the completion of the railroad to this point, which remained its western terminus for six years, and the erection of the company's machine-shops here, an active demand sprang up for dwelling-houses for its employes and their families That part of the town nearest and most convenient to the depot and machine-shops, being east of Main Street and bounding on Elgar Street, could not be obtained either by purchase or lease for the purpose of building thereon by reason of the occupants having a life estate therein On Tuesday, June 30, and Wednesday, July 1, 1863, the Second and Fifth Army Corps, forming the central column of the Army of the Potomac, passed through the town on their march towards Gettysburg, being about the only local incident to recall the memories of the great civil war, and in this the town did not suffer, but rather prospered In 1864 a telegraph company located an office here, which has since been maintained In the same year Moses Shaw and Joseph Moore opened that part of the street since known as Broadway Street from Main Street westward, and this gave access to the remaining portion of Joseph Moore's premises a great part of which he has since sold by the acre or fractions of an acre, in such quantities as were desired by the purchaser About the same time the first public primary school house was built In 1865 all that part of the town south of Elgar Street and east of Main Street which could not heretofore be procured was brought into market, and it was laid out into lots and sold by the executor at public sale, Feb 3, 1866, and purchased by Jesse Anders, Jasper C Shriner, and Thomas T Norris, who have from time to time sold the lots upon which the dwelling-houses are built The town now made a more decided progress in improvement In 1868 the Methodist Episcopal church was built, and also Anders & Lightner's store and public hall On the 3d day of December, 1868, at eight o'clock P M, the machine-shop, carpenter-shop, blacksmith-shop, and all the other buildings and local improvements (except the engine house) of the Western Maryland Railroad Company took fire and were burned The fire originated in the oil-house, and so rapid was the conflagration that the tools of the workmen, the books of the railroad company, and all the finished and unfinished work, including a new locomotive engine in process of construction, therein were destroyed and lost, but by extraordinary labor and vigilance all other contiguous buildings in the town were saved This was the first experience of a loss by fire in the town, and was severely felt by the railroad company, then in its infancy, and was also felt as a public local calamity by the inhabitants of the town and vicinity, the mutual character of which being manifested by the local and substantial pecuniary aid contributed and the energy and enterprise of the railroad company, which being combined, all of the said shops and other buildings were forthwith rebuilt in a better and more substantial manner In the same year the railroad began to run its trains westward from Union Bridge, and about that time much of the building on Benedam and Farquhar Streets was done A "Building Association" was formed, by the aid of which twelve of the dwelling houses in the town were erected

An act of the General Assembly of Maryland passed in 1872, to incorporate the town of Union Bridge in Carroll County An election was held on the first Monday in April ensuing for a mayor and Common Council, and Reuben Saylor was elected the first mayor of the town, and John Hartsock, Philip B Meyers, Joseph Wolf, and J Calvin Wentz were the first elected councilmen, and John B Eppley was its first bailiff, and Joshua Switzer its first clerk, and also treasurer, and what had been prior to that time a "settlement," a "burg," and a "village," at once rose to the dignity of a town, clothed with a municipal government

At a session of the mayor and Common Council, held March 31 1874, the same mayor and Council mentioned above, except that John M Furney had been chosen in place of Joseph Wolf (who declined to serve), the following preamble and resolution were passed

"*Whereas*, The streets in the town of Union Bridge have heretofore had no legal name, and some of the said streets have been called by different names, causing much ambiguity and misunderstanding in their location and description.

"*Therefore Resolved*, That the principal thoroughfare through the said town, being the Liberty and Pipe Creek turnpike road, be called Main Street, and that the street next westward thereof and running parallel therewith from the county road No 80 at the southwest corner of the school house grounds past the premises of William H Rinehart (the American sculptor) and Thomas Russell, Philip B Meyers and others, be called Whyte Street, and that the street next eastward from Main Street and running nearly parallel therewith from the ground for the track of the Western Maryland Railroad past the premises of G F Grumbine, Margaret Spurrier, Joshua Switzer and others to intersect the said county road No 80 (the southern boundary of the town), be called Benedam Street and that the street near the eastern boundary of the said town, and running parallel with the said eastern boundary from the ground for the track of the Western Maryland Railroad, along [illegible] J Calvin Wentz,

[illegible]ward Kelly, and others, to intersect the said county road [illegible]n, be called Farquhar Street, and that the street running [illegible] Main Street eastward at the corners of the premises of [illegible] W Diehl and Howard D Hartsock, crossing Benedum [St]reet at the corner of G T Grumbine and others, and crossing [Far]quhar Street at the corner of J Calvin Wentz, Isaiah [Li]ghtner, and others to the eastern boundary of the town be called Elgar Street, and that the wide street crossing Main [St]reet at the residence and stores of Jesse Anders Anders & Lightner, William Wilson and John N Weaver, and running [th]rough the town from east to west be called Broadway, and that the street next southward from Broadway Street, and running parallel therewith from Main Street at the corner of the premises of Jesse Anders and E O Mannakee (now M C Kinstry), and crossing Benedum street to Farquhar Street, be called Thomas Street, and that the short street next westward [fr]om Whyte and running parallel therewith and connecting the [wes]t end of Broadway Street with the aforesaid county road No 80, as the same is marked and laid down on the plat, but not yet opened, be called Canary Street And that the clerk be and he is hereby directed and authorized to write, mark, and designate the names of the said streets on the plat of the said town and also cause the same to be written on the records of the said plat in the office of the clerk of the Circuit Court for Carroll County, in Liber J B B, No 42, folio 241, and the aforesaid names shall be the established names by which the aforesaid streets shall be respectively known, called, and described and the clerk is hereby directed and ordered to enter upon the records of the proceedings of the mayor and Council a brief synopsis of the meaning of the said names, or the reasons why the said local names were given or chosen and applied to the streets of the said town"

All of which has been duly done, and the general answer is, because they are historic and intended to perpetuate the local history of the town "Main" Street, because it is the oldest, and is the principal traveled thoroughfare through the town, "Broadway" fifty feet wide, although not wider than Benedum and Whyte Streets, because it was the first wide street opened through the town, "Farquhar," "Benedum," "Elgar," and "Thomas," for the obvious reasons given in the preceding pages, "Whyte," so called for the Hon William Pinkney Whyte, who was Governor of the State, and who approved of and signed the charter at the time of the incorporation of the town, whilst His Excellency vetoed all other town charters except one passed by the General Assembly of Maryland at the same session, "Canary," so called for the first railroad locomotive that came into the town of Union Bridge It was a small engine with only two driving-wheels, but did all the work in the construction of the railroad to this place It was called the "Canary" because of its diminutive size and its restless and constant activity, and while the town of Union Bridge is largely indebted to the railroad for her growth and prosperity, the railroad is also indebted to the town and country immediately surrounding it for the very large and liberal stock subscriptions which [illegible] and [illegible]

the construction of the road at that time a possibility

In 1873 a separate passenger-house and depot was built by the railroad company, the town contributing $100 as a corporation, and private individuals $500 additional In the same year another produce and freight depot was built by William Zimmerman and H D Hartsock, on the west side of Main Street

In September, 1875, Messrs Nock & Snyder introduced a printing-press and materials, and began the publication of the first newspaper in the town, called the *People's Voice*, which supplied a very important link in the chain connecting the town with the more advanced civilization of the age On the 4th of July, 1876, the centennial year of independence was celebrated with imposing ceremonies in the town of Union Bridge Hon Joshua Switzer delivered an address which embodied the history of the town It was admirably prepared, replete with valuable information, much of which has been utilized by the author of this history, and exceedingly interesting

In April, 1875, John Hartsock was elected mayor, and John W Furney, J C Wentz, P B Meyers, and Jesse Anders, members of the Council J Switzer, secretary and treasurer In 1876, D Rinehart was elected mayor, and M C McKinstry, Jesse Anders, P B Meyers, and Peter Hollenberger were chosen members of the Common Council, J Switzer secretary, John Hartsock, treasurer In 1877, John Hartsock was elected mayor, and Moses Shaw, Jo[seph] Wilson, D R Fogle, and William Kelley, councilmen, and John B Eppley, secretary and treasurer In 1878, John Hartsock was elected mayor, and Moses Shaw, Joseph Wilson, William Kelley, and D R Fogle, common councilmen, John B Eppley secretary and treasurer In 1879, John Hartsock was elected mayor, and Moses Shaw, Jesse Anders, William Kelley, and John N Weaver, Common Council, John B Eppley, secretary and treasurer In 1880, John Hartsock was elected mayor, and Moses Shaw, Jesse Anders, D Rinehart, and J C Wentz to the Common Council, John B Eppley, secretary and treasurer In April, 1880, a new act of incorporation was granted by the Legislature, to take effect June 1, 1880, when under its provisions John N Weaver was elected a member of the Common Council, making five in that body In 1881, D Rinehart was elected mayor and Jesse Anders, P B Meyers, J C Wentz, and E O Mannakee were chosen as the Common Council, John B Eppley secretary and treasurer Jesse Anders and P B Meyers refused to qualify and a new election w[as] call[ed] [illegible] C F Reck,

Thomas Grumbine and E W Leeds, who compose the present Council

Strawbridge Methodist Episcopal Church was formed under the supervision of Rev Thomas Sheer A few years prior to 1868 they held their services in the public school-house until the erection of their church, which occurred in 1868 The church was named in honor of Robert Strawbridge, one of the pioneer Methodists of the county, and is a very neat frame structure, capable of holding about four or five hundred people Rev Thomas Sheer was succeeded by Rev Montgomery, who was followed by Rev William Ferguson in the year 1870 Mr Ferguson occupied the pulpit only for one year, when the Rev C D Smith was chosen as pastor He remained in charge of the congregation until 1872, when he was succeeded by Rev Reuben Kolb, whose pastorate expired in 1874 Rev Edwin Koontz was the next pastor, and served in that position for three years, and was succeeded by Rev J J Sargent until 1881, when their present pastor, the Rev Wright, took charge

The present trustees of the church are Edward Kelly, A L Beard, Joseph F Snavely, E Ingleman, Jesse T Cleary, David Ogle, Dr J McK Norris

Steward, Edin Ingleman, Leader of Class and Exhorter Jos F Snavely

The church numbers about thirty eight members, and it formerly belonged to the New Windsor charge, but is now in the Linganore Circuit A very prosperous Sunday school, numbering about one hundred and sixty members, is under the control of the church

Through the united efforts of Capt Isaiah Lightner and James M Hollenberger, a dispensation was granted to Plymouth Lodge, No 143, A F A M, on Jan 12, 1869 On that date an organization was effected, the lodge working under the charge of A T Geatty, W M, Isaiah Lightner, S W, John J Derr, J W, and D E Buckey, S D *pro tem*, A L Beard, J D *pro tem*, J M Hollenberger Sec *pro tem*, J T Hedrick, Treas *pro tem*, John M Furney Tyler

At a meeting held Feb 12, 1869, the first application for membership was received, the applicant being Ephraim B Repp

February 10th, E B Repp was received in the lodge and initiated at this meeting

March 23d E B Repp was raised to the degree of Master Mason

On May 10th the charter was granted, empowering Isaiah Lightner, W M, J M Hollenberger, S W, John J Derr, J W D E Buckey was elected secretary, and J T Hedrick, treasurer These officers were publicly in[illegible] June 30 1869 by Brother William H Moore, of George Washington Lodge, Westminster

The officers from December, 1869 to July, 1870, were Isaac Lightner, W M John J Derr S W, A L Beard J W, D E Buckey, Sec, Abraham Stoner Treas During this term Mr Buckey removed from the town and A T Geatty was appointed to fill the vacancy From July to December, 1870 the officers were Isaiah Lightner W M John J Derr, S W, John M Furney J W, A Stoner, Treas, A Geatty Sec From December, 1870, to July, 1871, Isaac Lightner, W M, E O Mannakee S W, J M Furney, J W, A Stoner, Sec, John D Myers Treas From July to December, 1871 the officers were Isaiah Lightner, W M, E O Mannakee, S W, L Kimball J W A Stoner, Treas, J M Hollenberger Sec The officers from December, 1871, to July 1872, E O Mannakee, W M, J M Furney S W J D Myers S W, J M Hollenberger Sec From July to December, 1872, Isaiah Lightner, W M, E O Mannakee S W J M Furney J W, A Stoner, Treas A T Geatty, Sec From December 1872, to July, 1873, J M Furney, W M J M Hollenberger S W, L W Partridge, J W A T Geatty Sec, E O Mannakee, Treas From July to December, 1873, the officers of the lodge were J M Hollenberger, W M J D Meyers, S W, Isaiah Lightner Sec L W Partridge J W, and E O Mannakee, Treas From December, 1873 to July 1874, the officers were J D Meyers W M, L W Partridge S W, Wm J Crabbs, J W A L Beard Sec, E O Mannakee, Treas From July to December, 1874, John M Furney, W M, A L Beard, S W, George W Love J W J M Hollenberger, Sec John D Meyers, Treas From December, 1874, to July, 1875, J M Furney, W M, A L Beard, S W, Wm J Crabbs, J W, J M Hollenberger, Sec, J D Meyers, Treas From July to December, 1875, J M Furney, W M, J D Meyer, S W, W J Crabbs, J W, J M Hollenberger, Sec, A L Beard Treas From December, 1875, to July 1876 the officers were J M Furney, W M J D Meyers S W W J Crabbs J W, J M Hollenberger, Sec A L Beard Treas From July to December, 1876, J D Meyers W M, W J Crabbs, S W, A L Beard, J W, J M Hollenberger, Sec, J M Furney, Treas From December, 1876, to July, 1877, J D Meyers, W M Wm J Crabbs S W, W F Penrose, J W J M Hollenberger, Sec J M Furney, Treas From July to December, 1877, the officers were J D Meyers, W M A T Beard, S W, Wm J Crabbs, J W J M Hollenberger, Sec J M Furney, Treas From December, 1877, to July, 1878, J D Meyers W M Oscar Stoner, S W, Granville Crouse, J W J M Hollenberger, Sec, J M Furney, Treas From July to December, 1878 they were J D Meyers, W M, Oscar Stoner, S W, G Crouse J W, J M Hollenberger, Sec J M Furney, Treas From December, 1879 to July, 1880, the officers were J M Hollenberger W M G W Love, S W Henry Crook, J W M C Stoner, Treas J M Furney, Sec

The lodge holds its meetings in the Mechanics' Hall, and their members in good standing number sixteen The present officers, for 1881, are John D Meyers, W M, Henry Crook, S W, George W Love, J W, John M Hollenberger, Sec E O Mannakee, Treas

Olive Council, No 50, of United American Mechanics, was organized and received their charter on March 31, 1875

The charter was issued to W H Morningstar, John M Fur- [illegible], H [illegible] J H Hooker, J.

C Wentz, P B Meyers, David G Ogle, Clinton Maynard, Theodore Clay, Wm Kelly, Basil Metz, John Delaplane, Eli H Hiltbidle, John D Meyers, Edward Kelley, L L Walker, James W Ogle, S J Graber

Their first officers were elected in July and served to December, 1875, and were

Jr Ex C, P B Meyers C, W H Morningstar, V C, Eli Hiltbidle, R S, H Clay Devilbiss, Treas, J C Wentz From December, 1875, to July, 1876, Jr Ex C, W H Morningstar, C, R C Billmeyer, V C, E H Hooker R S, H Clay Devilbiss Treas, J C Wentz From 1876 to 1877, Jr Ex C, R C Billmeyer, C, E H Hooker V C, Basil Mentz, R S, H C Devilbiss January, 1877 to July, Jr Ex C, E H Hooker, C Basil Mentz, V C, D E Little, R S J M Hollenberger July 1877, to January, 1878, Jr Ex C, Basil Metz, C, D E Little, V C, M C Stoner R S J M Hollenberger From January to July, 1878, Jr Ex C, D E Little, C, M C Stoner, V C, Benjamin Philips R S, J M Hollenberger July, 1878, to January 1879, Jr Ex C, M C Stoner C, Benj Philips, V C, J M Turney R S J M Hollenberger From January to July 1879, Jr Ex C, Benj Philips, C, Basil Metz, V C, John Delaplane R S J M Hollenberger From July, 1879 to January 1880, Jr Ex C W H Morningstar, C, Basil Metz, V C, J M Turney, R S J M Hollenberger From January to July, 1880 Jr Ex C Benj Philips, C, Basil Mentz, V C, J M Turney R S J M Hollenberger From July, 1880 to January, 1881 Jr Ex C, W H Morningstar C Basil Mentz, V C M C Stoner R S, J M Hollenberger January, 1881, Jr Ex C, W H Morningstar, C, Basil Metz, V C, D E Little, R S, J M Hollenberger, who are the present officers

J M Hollenberger and W H Morningstar were two of the original members, and have been very active in its management since that time

The Union Bridge Brass Band and Orchestra is under the leadership of S R Garver, musical director, and has sixteen pieces It has a handsome band wagon, and is one of the best drilled organizations in the State

In the year 1735 the Friends, William Farquhar and Anna, his wife, removed from Pennsylvania and settled at Pike Creek In process of time other members of this denomination settled there, and held meetings for worship at the Farquhar residence by permission of Fairfax Monthly Meeting They were allowed to build a house for worship by Chester Quarterly Meeting, held at Concord in the 5th month, 1757, and a preparative by the Western Quarterly Meeting, held at London Grove on the 8th month, 1759, which continued and increased

In the 9th month, 1746, came the Friends, Thomas and Joseph Plummer, from Patuxent, in Prince George's County, and in 1750 and 1751, Richard Holland and William Ballenger, with their wives, Ruth and Casandra, who settled at Bush Creek, and for some time were members of Monocacy Meeting In 1755 they were allowed to hold meetings on First days for the [illegible] house, and in the year following week day meetings, which continued until a house was built and a meeting for worship allowed by the Western Quarterly Meeting, held at London Grove in the 11th month, 1764 This house was erected near the locality now called Muttontown, but has long ago been torn down They were then members of the above Preparative Meeting which was held Circular, answerable to Fairfax Monthly Meeting

After considerable time, the number at each meeting increasing, they petitioned for a Monthly Meeting in the 7th month, 1767, which was again renewed in the 5th month, 1768, and being sent to the Quarterly Meeting in the 8th month 1771 was granted accordingly at the 11th month Quarterly in the year following

About this time the meeting-house was erected, which is situated close to the town of Union Bridge

At a meeting on the 19th of the 12th month, 1772 the representatives present on behalf of the Preparative Meeting were William Farquhar, William Ballenger Richard Holland, and William Farquhar Allen Farquhar was chosen clerk

On the 16th of the 1st month 1773, Samuel Cookson, a widower and Mary Haines, a widow of Daniel Haines, were united in marriage being the first wedding in that old edifice Joseph Wright was appointed overseer of Pipe Creek

At Bush Creek, 20th of 2d month, 1773, Joseph Talbott (afterwards keeper of the "Washington Hotel" in Frederick) produced a certificate for himself and wife Anna, from West River, Md, Meeting

Ruth Holland was appointed a minister to the meeting of ministers and elders

In 1774, Joel Wright was chosen clerk

In 1777, William Matthews was chosen clerk, and Joseph Wright, Sarah Miller, elders for Pipe Creek Particular

Friends' cemetery is situated immediately in the rear of the meeting-house, and contains the graves of the following persons

Beulah, wife of Nathan Haines, died 6th of 11th month, 1869, aged 56 years

William Hughes, died 7th of 4th month, 1866, aged 67 years

Eliza H Moore, born in Petersburg, Va, Sept 25, 1787, died Oct 10, 1866

Susan S, wife of Granville S Haines, died Aug 4, 1873, aged 53 years

Elisha Janey, died 1876 aged 82

Lydia Hughes, died 10th of 7th month, 1867, aged 74

Harriet, wife of Thomas F Shepherd, died Feb 15, 1869, aged 47 years, 1 month, 9 days

Mary G Plummer, born 11th of 1st month, 1815, died 23d of 2d month 1880

Rebecca Russell, born 9th of 3d month 1817, died 22d of [illegible]

Mary Wood, born 29th of 1st month, 1791, died 7th of 10th month, 1875

Edith P Wood, born 12th of 1st month, 1853, died 17th of 5th month, 1870

Susanna S Russell, born 21st of 7th month, 1821, died 26th of 4th month, 1868

William Russell, born 22d of 10th month, 1812, died 17th of 12th month, 1877

Ephraim Haines, died 26th of 2d month, 1868, aged 71 years, 4 months, 10 days

Ann, wife of Moses Shaw, died July 16, 1866, aged [illegible]3

Stephen Haines died Feb 16, 1879, aged 79 years, 11 months, 14 days

Samuel Haines, born 25th of 4th month, 1763, died 15th of 2d month, 1833

Lydia Haines, born 29th of 6th month, 1768, died 22d of 11th month 1850

William Haines, died 1830, aged 67 years.

Joanna McKinstry, born 1788, died 1812

Esther, wife of Stephen Haines, died Dec 16, 1845, aged 33 years, [illegible] months, [illegible] days

Job C Haines, born 21st of 3d month, 1790, died 29th of 11th month, 185[illegible]

Sarah Cox, wife of George C, died 26th of 1st month, 1878, aged 82 years [illegible] months, 15 days

George Cox, born in Harford County, 17th of 6th month, 1789, died 2d of 6th month, 1857

Ann Shepherd, died 1858

Samuel Haines, died 1856, aged 77

Ruth Anna Hibberd died 1855

Lean McKinstry died 24th of 11th month, 1852, aged 73

Thomas Shepherd, died 12th of 11th month, 1875, aged 87

Portia H, wife of W J Smith, died 10th of 9th month, 1864, aged 27 years, 11 months, 2 days.

Rachel K Hibberd, and M Hibberd

Elias F Hibberd, died 1850

Esther Hibberd, died 1850

Hannah Moore, died 21 of 5th month, 1863, aged 96

John Moore, died 2d of 12th month, 1841, aged 86

William Shepherd, died 14th of 2d month, 1862, aged 76

Ruth Shepherd died 31st of 1st month, 1854, aged 65

Mary S, wife of Nathan Smith, died 22d of 9th month, 1879, aged 64 years

John A Shugh, born Oct 5, 1811, died Aug 9, 1877

Mary, wife of Samuel Haines, died 1852 aged 67

Esther Haines, died 1851, aged 84

Nathan Haines, died 3d of 2d month, 1862, aged 73

Sarah Haines, died 13th of 2d month, 186[illegible], aged 51

Elizabeth M Fisher, died July 22, 1860, aged 51

In the Union Bridge Cemetery the following persons are buried

John Davis Clemenson, born Jan 21, 1816, died July 10, 1880

John B Norris, died May 9, 1871, aged 54 years, 2 months, 24 days

Ephraim H Hoover, died April 6, 1880, aged 37 years, 7 months, 9 days

Clementine, wife of George W Cribbs, and daughter of R and S Hollenberger, born Nov 13, 1842, died June 2[illegible], 1863

George W Cribbs, born March 22, 18[illegible]6, died Dec 7 1865

Adam Willard, born Sept 26, 1790, died March 26, 1877

Catharine Anders died April 17, 18[illegible], aged 42 years, 9 months

John [illegible] Smit[illegible] [illegible] 16, 1[illegible] [illegible]

Thomas F Shepherd was born Oct 10, 1815 near Union Bridge, Frederick Co (now Carroll), Md, of Scotch-Irish ancestry His great-grandfather, William Farquhar, and his wife, Ann, moved from the province of Pennsylvania to the province of Maryland in 1735, and settled near the present town of Union Bridge, Carroll Co He was the first white settler in that part of the State, and there being no roads, except the paths made by the Indians and wild beasts, he was obliged to move his family and goods on pack-horses He was a tailor by trade, and made buckskin breeches and other clothing for the settlers when they came His father, Allen Farquhar, gave him two hundred acres of land, and he took up and patented from time to time, as he acquired means, different tracts of land until in January, 1865, he owned two thousand two hundred and fifty six acres, including all of the site of the town of Union Bridge, which he divided among his seven children, some of which is still owned by his descendants His grandfather, Solomon Shepherd, was the oldest son of William and Richmonda Shepherd, of Menallhen township, county of York, Pa He married Susannah Farquhar, daughter of William Farquhar, October, 1779 and built a fulling-mill upon a part of his wife's land He subsequently built a woolen-mill on the same site, which is still owned by some of his descendants Solomon Shepherd had four daughters and two sons His eldest son, William Shepherd, was born Feb 2, 1786 He married Ruth Fisher, daughter of Samuel Fisher, of Baltimore They had four sons and four daughters Thomas F Shepherd was the oldest son and second child Solomon, one of the brothers, and Mary Stultz, his sister, are living near Union Bridge James, the oldest brother, lives in Iowa City Thomas F., being the oldest son, in his youth was needed in the factory, and all the education he received was obtained at a district school and the business training he got by managing the factory and keeping its books His brothers were more highly favored in this particular William H studied medicine, practiced in Maryland and Wisconsin, went to Australia in 1857, and thence to California, where he practiced his profession until his death in 1864 Solomon carried on the woolen factory for a few years after Thomas left it, then moved to Wisconsin, where he engaged in farming for a few years, returned to Maryland and is now farming near Union Bridge James was farming in Iowa until his health failed, he then sold his farm and moved to Iowa City, where he now resides In October 1842, Thomas F Shepherd married Miss Harriet Haines, born Jan 6, 1822 [illegible] Joel C Haines,

farmer, and sister of G. S. Hol[illegible]
First National Bank of Westmi[illegible]
Shepherd withdrew from the [illegible]
his health, and removed to his f[illegible]
miles, containing about two h[illegible]
January, 1860, he was elected [illegible]
Mutual Fire Insurance Comp[illegible]
County, Md., which position he [illegible]
[illegible], he was appointed [illegible]
[illegible] still holds [illegible]
[illegible] to its [illegible]
His residence [illegible]
[illegible] was elected county commissi[illegible]
[illegible] six years, having been re[illegible]
[illegible] and was [illegible]
[illegible] of 1867. He [illegible]
the time.

The First National Bank of N[illegible]
[illegible] in 1865, and Mr. Shep[illegible]
[illegible] to which position he has [illegible]
[illegible]. His wife [illegible]
[illegible] daughters. [illegible]
[illegible] by burglars [illegible]
eight thousand [illegible]
which was recovered. The [illegible]
[illegible] confidence [illegible]
[illegible] the entire [illegible]
[illegible]. Mr. Sh[illegible]
[illegible] Whig. [illegible]
[illegible] appointed [illegible]
[illegible] in the Senate. He [illegible]
[illegible] of the Second County [illegible]
[illegible], also the Executive [illegible]
[illegible]
[illegible], March, 1874 [illegible]
executive committee, and [illegible]
[illegible]. Mr. Shepherd's parents [illegible]
Society of Friends, of which [illegible]
Rev. Thomas Shepherd, of [illegible]
of Baltimore, [illegible]
[illegible] Col. [illegible]
[illegible] of the same family [illegible]
[illegible]
[illegible]

[illegible] ad.—Peter [illegible], Jo[illegible]

[illegible]

thriving villages of Williamsport, Hancock, Clear Spring, Smithsburg, Leitersburg, Boonsboro', Funkstown, Keedysville, Sharpsburg, Cavetown, and others. Agriculturally, Washington ranks as one of the most flourishing counties of Maryland, and its population is remarkable for intelligence, prosperity, and thrift. Its area is five hundred and twenty five square miles, and its population, according to the census of 1880, is as follows:

First Election District (Sharpsburg), including town of Sharpsburg		2311
Sharpsburg	1260	
Second Election District (Williamsport), including town of Williamsport		2625
Williamsport	1503	
Third Election District (Hagerstown), including part of the town of Hagerstown		4031
Hagerstown (part of)	3188	
Fourth Election District (Clear Spring), including town of Clear Spring		2715
Clear Spring Town	721	
Fifth Election District (Hancock), including town of Hancock		2233
Hancock Town	931	
Sixth Election District (Boonsboro'), including the following places		2262
Boonsboro' Town	859	
Mount Pleasant Village	165	
Seventh Election District (Cavetown), including the following places		1665
Cavetown Village	221	
Smithsburg	433	
Eighth Election District (Pleasant Valley), including the following villages		1304
Brownsville Village	68	
Rohrersville Village	106	
Ninth Election District (Leitersburg), including village of Leitersburg		1546
Leitersburg	308	
Tenth Election District (Funkstown), including village of Funkstown		1531
Funkstown	600	
Eleventh Election District (Sandy Hook), including village of Sandy Hook		1585
Sandy Hook	373	
Twelfth Election District (Tilghmanton) including village of Tilghmanton		1580
Tilghmanton	171	
Thirteenth Election District (Conococheague), including village of Fairview		1630
Fairview Village	59	
Fourteenth Election District (Ringgold), including village of Ringgold		823
Ringgold	109	
Fifteenth Election District (Indian Spring), including hamlet of Millstone Point		1736
Millstone Point Hamlet	62	
Sixteenth Election District (Beaver Creek)		1199
Seventeenth Election District (Antietam), including part of the town of Hagerstown		4591
Hagerstown (part of)	3439	
Eighteenth Election District (Chewsville), including village of Chewsville		973
Chewsville Village	110	
Nineteenth Election District (Keedysville), including the town of Keedysville		1205
Keedysville	389	
Twentieth Election District (Downsville)		1013

The population of Hagerstown, situated partly in the Third and partly in the Seventeenth Election Districts, is 6627.

The total population is 38,561, of whom 19,068 are males, 19,493 females, 37,942 native, 619 foreign, 35,497 white, 3064 colored.

The population of the county since and including the census of 1790 has been as follows:

White		*Free Colored*	
1870	31,874	1870	[illegible]
1860	28,305	1860	1,677
1850	26,930	1850	[illegible]
1840	24,724	1840	1,580
1830	21,277	1830	1,082
1820	19,247	1820	627
1810	15,591	1810	[illegible]
1800	16,108	1800	342
1790	14,472	1790	64
Slave		*Aggregate*	
1860	1,435	1870	34,712
1850	2,090	1860	31,417
1840	2,546	1850	30,848
1830	2,909	1840	[illegible]
1820	3,201	1830	25,268
1810	2,656	1820	23,075
1800	2,200	1810	[illegible]
1790	1,286	1800	18,659
		1790	15,822

The agricultural products of the county, as reported in 1880, were: Buckwheat, 183 acres in cultivation, yielding 1506 bushels; Indian corn, 31,910 acres, 1,090,972 bushels; oats, 2874 acres, 52,497 bushels; rye, 1818 acres, 21,750 bushels; wheat, 56,923 acres, 1,024,769 bushels; tobacco, 5 acres, 7050 pounds.

The following interesting statistics give the figures of the yield of corn and wheat per acre in Maryland in 1879. It will be seen that Harford takes the lead in raising corn, the yield being 38¼ bushels per acre. Frederick follows with 34½, Washington 34, Baltimore 33¾, Cecil 33, the lowest being Worcester, 8½ bushels.

In the production of wheat, however, Washington is far above any of her sister counties, the average yield per acre being 25¾ bushels. Montgomery, next in order, with 17¼ bushels, is followed closely by Frederick with 17. Harford is fourth in the list, with 16½ bushels, Howard being the same. The average yield in Cecil 16, and in Baltimore County 13¾. Worcester shows the lowest average yield, namely, 7 bushels. The average yield of wheat in the State is about 14½ bushels.

The following is the yield of corn and wheat per acre in each county of the State:

Counties	Corn per Acre	Wheat per Acre
Allegany	28	9
Anne Arundel	23¼	9
Baltimore	33¾	13¾
Calvert	20	7½
Caroline	17	11
Carroll	31½	14½
Cecil	33	16
Charles	16	8
Dorchester	16½	7½
Frederick	34½	17
Garrett	21½	11
Harford	38¼	16½
Howard	29	16½
Kent	26¾	15
Montgomery	29	17¼
Prince George's	[illegible]	9
Queen Anne's	24½	13½
St Mary's	15¾	8¼
Somerset	17	10¾
Talbot	26½	11
Washington	34	25¾
Wicomico	11	7¼
Worcester	8½	7

Public Schools.—The public schools of Washington County have long enjoyed a high reputation for thoroughness and regularity of attendance. Following are the statistics for 1881, as returned by P. A. Witmer, county superintendent, for the term ending Nov. 15, 1881:

No. of Election District.	No. of School.	Teachers.	Fall Term, 1881. Pupils Enrolled.	Fall Term, 1881. Average Attendance.	Winter Term, 1881. Pupils Enrolled.	Winter Term, 1881. Average Attendance.
1	1	John E. Kelly	41	32	34	[illegible]
	"	Sue D. Johnson	59	42	62	45
	"	John P. Smith	68	57	63	50
	"	Alice V. Gower	75	40	72	50
	"	Lizzie Alder	49	29	109	61
	2	A. D. Warfield	34	25	49	22
	3	R. E. Borden	22	13	39	17
2	1	I. T. Beard	34	30	18	23
	"	E. W. Byers	38	25	61	33
	"	Cora Slowen	42	30	55	36
	"	Mamie Hawken	52	37	72	48
	"	Ella Hoffman	73	52	88	63
	2	F. L. King	45	32	64	35
	3	S. A. Poffenberger	42	23	50	34
	4	A. M. Lynch	34	29	42	31
High School.		George A. Harter	50	15	35	31
3	1	J. A. Zeigler	37	33	40	35
	"	F. J. Hahn	25	27	38	31
	"	Bettie Brady	54	44	58	25
	"	Annie Cook	52	44	48	36
	"	Nettie Baker	45	34	41	34
	"	Mary Buoiel	59	42	48	35
	"	Ella Taggart	60	29	52	40
	2	George B. Cummings	48	27	60	35
	3	D. F. Newcomer	44	23	37	24
	4	S. J. Baker	35	25	28	39
4	1	Isaac Sprecher	26	31	38	26
	"	W. S. Richardson	23	20	31	21
	"	Kate Slaughenhaupt	27	22	38	26
	"	A. E. Snyder	44	38	48	31
	2	John Q. Miller	25	20	35	20
	3	George S. Fockler	[illegible]	21	42	28
	4	John J. Kreps	54	30	63	32
	5	B. F. Angle	39	25	41	27
	6	Cora Seiss	24	17	28	13
	7	Wm. H. Angle	24	25	36	24
	8	Joshua Phillips	27	25	41	25
	9	John M. Smith	34	17	41	24
5	1	George C. Pearson	27	22	38	26
	"	Milton Spessard	24	12	31	26
	"	Pleasant Johnson	42	30	51	32
	"	Mary B. Stuart	76	60	70	41
	2	N. McKinney	29	18	51	23
	3	James S. Grant	24	16	34	14
	4	Annie Ambrose	32	21	29	20
	5	Clara Shepherd	25	14	20	13
	6	Sadie Carter	32	12	24	16
	7	George H. Seigman	[illegible]	15	25	18
	8	Scott Battenfield	[illegible]	15	23	17
6	1	D. B. Staley	23	25	29	22
	"	J. Harlan Smith	36	28	35	27
	"	Harry Davis	33	28	45	32
	"	Amanda Barr	37	31	38	30
	"	Effie Grossnickle	63	49	63	47
	2	G. A. Newton	44	30	55	42
	3	T. H. Smith	32	21	54	33
	4	George M. Stover	43	21	47	21
	5	L. L. Grossnickle	16	11	29	19
	6	S. B. Sheap	45	37	51	40
7	1	George Pearson	25	19	21	20
	"	J. D. Seigman	37	23	22	19
	"	Hattie Poe	56	32	41	35
	"	Maggie Bingham	[illegible]	54	58	41
	2	Dillon Wesley	24	18	49	37
	"	D. H. Garver	51	44	57	43
	3	Emma Bachtel	36	10	57	22
	4	L. A. R. Keller	40	19	41	15
8	1	Eugene Brown	57	43	49	36
	2	O. M. Snyder	21	16	20	13
	3	A. W. Leslie	22	24	48	32
	"	Thalia Bateler	42	24	45	23
	4	W. G. Zahn	49	29	55	43
	5	A. W. Kesler	30	17	39	27
	6	Jacob Smith	24	14	24	19
9	1	Frank [illegible]	[illegible]	23	23	26
	"	Em[illegible]	[illegible]	[illegible]	[illegible]	31
	1	Linna Bell	43	33	47	40
	2	Orville Long	29	22	40	29
	3	T. F. Dillendal	38	24	49	35
	4	Robert Lamar	18	35	46	31
	5	John F. Kayhoe	46	28	45	37
	6	T. Harry Davis	41	27	51	36
	7	Preston Vogle	30	21	33	27
	8	James P. Harter	48	41	44	37
10	1	M. Emmett Cullen	21	18	29	24
	"	Charles W. McDade	37	27	35	26
	"	Sallie Gower	44	37	45	40
	"	Martha D. Stuart	73	53	58	47
	2	M. L. Keedy	22	16	20	15
	3	Marene Lamar	37	25	44	24
	4	Ambrosia Reed	30	18	35	21
11	1	Anna Carter	43	25	47	30
	2	James Smith	38	21	36	16
	3	O. M. Younkins	40	22	45	39
	"	Emma M. Virtz	51	30	49	30
	4	Lend F. Currie	30	19	48	23
	5	D. P. Keedy	44	22	64	30
12	1	Amanda Sheap	41	29	45	30
	2	Laura Grossnickle	31	23	54	28
	3	M. L. Schmucker	45	25	61	34
	4	Peter Schnebel	25	19	41	31
	"	Alfred Betts	61	49	49	37
	5	T. J. Fahrney	39	21	44	28
13	1	George W. Hicks	66	38	57	43
	2	Samuel Hicks	39	25	33	35
	3	George H. Uhler	45	27	68	35
	4	Jos. M. Keeny	39	24	63	38
	5	Thos. B. Rice	50	37	64	51
	6	D. S. Pittinger	35	23	55	22
	7	J. E. S. Pryor	29	19	37	21
	8	Wilfred Rice	59	24	47	31
14	1	L. F. Bencholl	54	31	70	41
	2	J. V. Shank	30	21	39	27
	3	John Masters	36	22	38	24
	4	Maggie Bachtel	19	12	16	10
	5	A. F. Dillendal	42	28	45	32
15	1	W. F. Hamblett	24	12	47	30
	2	M. L. Bachtel	32	16	48	28
	3	A. W. Coller	26	17	32	15
	"	Rebecca Boyd	26	12	36	22
	5	A. Shaefer	52	47	41	32
	6	E. G. Kinsell	33	23	41	27
	7	George M. Draper	27	[illegible]	45	25
	8	H. S. Smith	30	14	36	27
	9	O. J. Zittle	26	15	38	19
	10	J. L. V. Cook	42	22	47	28
16	1	Cyrus D. Harp	53	29	49	28
	2	John Wagaman	22	15	30	20
	3	J. M. Kreidler	66	44	75	48
	4	A. G. Davis	44	30	32	29
	4	A. J. Harsh	19	15	38	21
	6	M. Newcomer	25	19	26	17
17	1	Wm. D. Piper	36	25	21	18
	"	Mary Rowland	41	30	35	26
	"	Mary Dunlap	30	23	31	25
	"	Mary Hurley	37	30	58	32
	"	Daniel A. Thomas	49	30	31	21
	"	Blanche Wagoner	50	45	50	30
	"	Mary Ronskulp	41	36	40	15
	"	Margaret Newcomer	57	46	52	42
	"	Emily Walsh	71	58	48	38
	2	Cyrus Simmons	48	35	56	35
	3	Wm. Anthony	30	19	33	24
	4	A. Huntsberger	34	24	32	14
	5	Thos. Palmer	36	25	43	34
18	1	Chas. A. Santee	47	34	49	24
	2	John P. Fockler	30	25	45	37
	"	R. E. Brown	50	43	49	25
	3	Fred. K. Sykes	46	31	47	34
	4	J. H. Brewer	19	15	25	15
	5	A. M. Wallinger	46	35	56	44
19	1	[illegible] Schildknecht	31	28	32	30
	"	E. G. Hetfrell	19	15	17	22
	"	Ella Kelsey	29	24	[illegible]	24
	"	Achen Stevenson	41	30	50	37
	2	D. W. Wyand	36	32	47	30
	3	C. W. Reichard	32	25	48	31
	4	Asa Lamar	45	29	38	24
20	1	C. A. Wayant	33	22	50	27
	"	Geary S. Betts	56	43	49	37
	2	D. F. Wolf	32	30	44	23
	3	O. V. Middlekauff	40	26	46	18
	4	W[illegible] F. E[illegible]	[illegible]	28	24	20

COLORED SCHOOLS

No of Election District	No of School	Teachers	Fall Term, 1880: Pupils Enrolled	Fall Term, 1880: Average Attendance	Winter Term, 1881: Pupils Enrolled	Winter Term, 1881: Average Attendance
1	4	T I Sansons	22	16	22	13
2	5	C W Trusty	46	26	51	29
4	10	W T Williams	39	41	57	38
5	9	John Truman	29	16	52	22
6	6	John Newman	18	14	17	12
10	5	Louisa Jacobs	17	16	16	12
11	6	Wm I Hill	23	19	30	18
12	6	Wm F Nelson	42	25	23	14
16	7	F V Williams	23	17	23	15
17	6	George W Bayo	50	30	67	47
"	"	Mary Russell	72	38	72	37
19	5	Truelove McDaniel	26	20	31	20

The following are the school district trustees for the year ending May, 1882

Election District 1—School District 1, J C Wilson, R E Hugg, J McGraw 2, J Frees, E Marker, E Easterday, 3, S J Piper, Moses Cox, D Coffman, 4, N Zimmerman, Levi Porter, S Wagoner, 5, H Watson, George Tyler, D B Sannons

Election District 2—School District 1, T Burrow J Hawken, A Schnebley 2, J D Byers J Hilbrick, G Bussard, 3, D Summer C D Sprecher, W Middlekauff, 4, Peter Kaufman, L Trone, Joseph Powland 5, T Barnum C Brown, Eli Hess

Election District 3—School District 1, J W Storr, Peter Gracey, W S Stover, 2, J E Johnson, Eli Summer, J Hebb, 3, P Wingert, J I Hershey, C McBride 4, J M Startzman, F Baker, M Startzman

Election District 4—School District 1, S Reitzell, J Bain, J I Snyder 2, John Woolford, Eli Heller, D Cowton 3, J C Brewer S Mitchell, J Lindsay 4, G Sprecher, L A Spickler, J A Miller, 5, John Strite, George Rusch, M Schnebley, 6, D Seibert, Israel Reiff, E McLaughlin, 7, J P Blair, D Clopper, Thomas Corbett 8, T Charlton, S Davis, W Cushwa, 9, J M Smith, Frank Ellis, A Snyder, 10, Israel Dorris, Henry Miles, T Dorsey

Election District 5—School District 1, Dr W H Perkins, S Crown, J W Baxter, 2, Emory Pelton J O Farrell, R Shives, 3, R Murray, Henry Stine, Samuel Dignan 4, S Summer, Harvey Taylor, Alfred Watts, 5, J Sheppard, John Henlin, C Harvey, 6, H Spicer, J McAvoy, Joseph Fahne, 7, T L Norris Charles Norris, M Yonker 8, William Poole, D Mann, Nathan Hartley, 9, N Proctor, L Robinson, John Thomas

Election District 6—School District 1, Dr H B Wilson, J L Nicodemus, M Bomberger, 2, D O Hammond, D Foltz, D F Stouffer, 3 E Miller, D Poffenberger, R Munford, 4, J W Smith, H St Clair, J P Summers 5, B F Brinham, G Wolleck, W Fahrney 6, J Gaylor, D Stull, Benjamin Foltz 7 Lloyd Kadont, J Shorter Guy Butler

Election District 7—School District 1 H Lyday, A C Hildebrand J D Slaughenhaupt 2 D W Blessing J Wegley, F Lutth, 3, S Smith John Grey, Daniel Burns, 4, J M Brown, Josiah Taggert, J Brown

Election District 8—School District 1 G H Brown, J H West, W J Kelley, 2, postponed, 3 J H Poffenberger, J H Mull J I Bean 4, George Stine, J D Keedy, J G Hines, 5, L Stine, G G Brane, John Shfer, 6, D Baker, Henry C Holmes D Gloss

Election District 9—School District 1, S Strite, Upton Bell, Solomon Hartle 2, J Trovinger, W Cramm, D Sheerer, 3, Peter Smith, Isaac Jacobs, Isaac Herks, 4, Abram Strite, Joseph Strite, S Martin, 5, J M Bell, Benjamin Newcomer, U Clopper, 6, D W Durburrow, H Martin, J Fahrney, 7, Abram Shank, Joseph Shank, D G Krouse, 8, D Shumaker, P B Harter, W M Lantz

Election District 10—School District 1, V Newcomer, R Cushen, Isaac Hanna, 2, J Keedy, William South, Peter Kesselring, 3, Abram Hamburg, J Young, J Hufler 4, D Doub, J W Murdock D Hershman, 5, Levi Grant, William Bell

Election District 11—School District 1, Warren Garrott, W McDuell, C W Fry, 2 J H Elgin, G E Stonebraker, C Virtz, 3 P Higgins, C Cole, John McCormick, 4, John Heskett, William Thompson, D Reed, 5, James Ingram, M T Holmes, John Best, 6, K Anderson, H Duckett, R Edemy

Election District 12—School District 1 T J Warfield S Reichard, C Bair, 2, D Wolf, N Mumma, Jacob Leatherman, 3, T Wolford, George Fahle, L Davis, 4, Simon Coffman, John Petre, E Yourtee 5, A Highberger, J Fahrney, A Hammond, 6, B Oldwine, E Whiting W Wade

Election District 13—School District 1, L R Schnebley, F T Spickler, Joseph Hershberger, 2, J Keller, J McDonald J Buchanan, H Strock, S Wolfensberger S Cearfoss, 4 J Maugans, S Weaver, H St Clair 5 John Strite, Henry Strite, S Foltz, 6, J F Neibert, G W Hamilton, Frank P Spickler 7, J Summer, J Emmert, E Clarkson, 8, D Ankeney, G W Kretzer, D Carl

Election District 14—School District 1, L Barkdoll, J Reecher, L Tesinger 2, J J Newcomer, J Martin, Jr, J W Cable, 3, E J Wade, John Gladhill, Henry Crider, 4 A Shrockey, J Rhinehart, H Socks, 5, T B Coyle, H V Schull, H M Stoufter

Election District 15—School District 1, T H Moore, J H Martin, Dennis Cain, 2, J Houck, J McCormick, S Weller 3, J Cameron, L Eichelberger, D Dick, 4, A Ditto, D G Holland, H Startliper, 5, S Penner, A J McAllister, J Sponseller 6, L Shank, William S Cook S Lauchbaum, 7, J D Tice, M Whitson David Myers, 8, A Flory, John Kuhn, J B Martin 9, G Eichelberger G W Bowers, William Gehr, Jr, 10, F S Zimmerman S Beckley, W Ernst

Election District 16—School District 1, Jonas Hufler William C Gray, J L Harp, 2, Benjamin Doyle, William Funk, Leonard Detrow, 3, H Funk, J Foutlers, F Stover, 4, J M Newcomer, J Funk, M Witmer, 5 G Adams, J Middlekauff, F Kaylor, 6, C Lamb, J R Adams, George Orrick, 7, F Williams, James Sewell, H Williams

Election District 17—School District 1, M L Byers, J F Bikle J F Bitner, 2, H C Loose, Joseph Itnyre, J Snyder 3, J Claic, D Downin, Abram Martin, 4, G Cressler, J Eshleman, D Martin, 5, J Walleck, A C Miller, D Bostetter, 6 William Russell, 7 J Hopkins, J F Wagoner

Election District 18—School District 1, J Houck, John Osler, Silas Alsup, 2, John H Harp, J D Betts, D Spessard 3, G L Harbaugh, D Stover, D F Spessard, 4, Jacob Stoufler, J H Mulnicl, D Snyder, 5 J B Brusman, S Bachtel William Lohrer

Election District 19—School District 1, J Thomas G W [illegible], W C Snavely,

J L Clopper, 3, G Line, C Snavely C M Poffenberger, 4 A C Huffer, N G Thomas, S Thomas, 5, G Fisher, Henry Keats, William Sommer

Election District 20 —School District 1, S Long B Hoffman L O Downs 2, I Cromer, Ezra Nally, A Middlekauff, 3, W Hagerman, E Jacobs, J Cunningham 4, T Bowman, William Barnhart, R Hurlighe

The educational statistics of the county for 1880 were

126 elementary schools, 12 schools for colored children, 129 school buildings of which 1 has more than one study room, 9 42 seats provided total seating capacity of schools 10,689, 1 8 schools reported in good condition, 21 reported in bad condition, 122 male teachers, 44 female ditto, total, 166, 9 male colored teachers, 4 female colored ditto, total, 13 whole number of teachers white and colored 179, of whom 73 were educated at high schools or academies 16 were educated at normal schools, 2 at colleges or universities, and 65 held certificates other than the preceding The average of teachers' salaries per month was $33 44, average number of months employed, 7 10

The county commissioners fixed the rate of taxation for 1881 at 83 cents on $100 for county tax, which, added to the State tax of 18⅜ cents, makes an aggregate taxation of 101⅜ cents on the $100, which rate of taxation produces $148,570 25

The following are the several appropriations

Condemnations, etc	$1,129 14
Constables	911 8
Printing	1,196 57
Collector	2,450 00
Court-house and jail	1,594 33
Coffins and graves	180 75
Magistrates	350 48
Registers and Orphans Court	1,542 65
Sheriff's office	5,191 60
Commissioners office	1,578 60
Bellevue	8,777 42
Attorneys	2,301 68
Clerk of court	1 662 76
Court house and school bonds and interest	12,384 00
Fire department	266 61
McCausland debt	240 00
Interest R R and bounty bonds	34,122 00
Jurors and State witnesses	8 000 00
Roads	9 000 00
Bridges	2,500 00
Fox-scalps	19 50
Miscellaneous	542 30
Judges and clerks of election	803 00
Inquisitions	296 14
Pensioners	5,691 00
Schools	34,000 00
Registers	1,020 90
	$138,411 11
Amount of levy	148,570 25
Surplus	$10,159 14

The rate of assessment on the $100 is as follows

For county purposes	27½ cts
Court house and school bonds and interest	7 "
Court expenses	4½ "
Bellevue Asylum	5 "
R R and bounty interest	19½ "
Schools	19½ "
	83 "
State tax	18⅜ "
	101⅜ "

The levy includes enough to pay off $9600 of court-house and school bonds

The taxable basis has been increased over half a million of dollars by the new assessment of the railroads The whole basis for 1881 was about $17,900,000, against $17,375,000 for 1880 The assessment of the Washington County Railroad, 24¼ miles, has been increased from $75,225 to $276,750 The Western Maryland road has been raised from $80,250 to $277,000 This includes $8000 for the portion of the Baltimore and Cumberland Valley road lying in this county The Cumberland Valley road has been increased from $50,879 to $131,000, and the Shenandoah Valley road has been assessed at $69,000

The schools get $2810 more for 1881 than 1880, which increases the rate 1½ cents on $100 The almshouse rate and rate for bonds is decreased, offsetting the increase for the schools, which makes the rate the same as for 1880, although, on account of the increase in the basis, the amount produced is increased $4100

The bonded indebtedness of the county in 1880 was $693,475, and its floating debt was $5450, making the gross debt $698,925 The net debt per capita was $18 13

Early History —The county was established by an act of the Provincial Convention, passed on Friday, Sept 6, 1776 Previous to that time from the organization of Frederick County in 1748, it had been a portion of that county The first mention we have of a separate representation of that portion of Frederick now called Washington County in the legislative proceedings of the province was on July 26, 1775, when the Provincial Convention, sitting at Annapolis, enacted the following

"That for the ease and convenience of the people of Frederick County there be three different places of election, that the said county be divided into three districts, to wit upper, middle and lower the upper district (now *Washington County*) to be divided by the South Mountain, and the lines of the county westward of the South Mountain, the middle district to be bounded from the mouth of Monocacy with Potowmack to the South Mountain, with that mountain to the temporary line with the lines of the county to the head waters of Patuxent, and with the lines of the lower district to Potowmack, the lower district to be bounded with Potowmack to the mouth of Monocacy, then with Monocacy to the mouth of Bennett's Creek and with the creek to the head-waters of the Patuxent, that there be elected in the lower district one delegate, two persons to act as a committee of correspondence, and seventeen as a committee of observation, that in each of the other districts there be elected two delegates and eighteen persons to act as a committee of observation, and that three persons be elected in the middle district to act as a committee of correspondence, that the elections for the upper district be held at [illegible] middle district [illegible] at Hunger-

ford's, and that no person residing or voting in one shall be admitted to vote in either of the other districts."

The convention proceedings further show that on Monday, Dec 18, 1775, William Baird, a member for the upper district of Frederick (now Washington County), appeared and took his seat in the convention On Jan 6, 1776, the convention elected the following officers for the militia in the upper district of Frederick County

"*First Battalion*—Mr John Stull, colonel, Mr Andrew Kench, lieutenant colonel Mr Henry Shyrock, first major, Mr George Woltz, second major, Mr Elie Williams, quartermaster *Second Battalion*—Mr Samuel Beall colonel, Mr Joseph Smith, lieutenant colonel, Mr Richard Davis, first major, Mr Charles Swearingen second major, Mr James Chapline, quartermaster"

On Friday, May 24 1776, the convention again met, with all the members present, "as on yesterday," except Mr Rumsey, Mr Baird Mr Handy, and Mr Stull, and transacted the following business

"On hearing Mr Daniel Hughes as to the execution of the contract made by Samuel Hughes, on the behalf of himself and the said Daniel Hughes, for the casting and furnishing cannon for the public,

"*Resolved*, That the inquiry be made what is the standing proof of cannon contracted for on account of the continent, and that the same proof be had of the cannon to be furnished by the said Hughes on their contract

"*Resolved*, That notwithstanding the said Hughes have not furnished the public with cannon within the time they contracted to do the same, that on their pursuing the work with diligence the council of safety for the time being take the whole number contracted for on the account and for the use of the public"

On Monday, July 1, 1776, the convention met and passed the following

"*Resolved* That for the encouragement of Daniel and Samuel Hughes to prosecute their cannon foundry with spirit and diligence, the council of safety be empowered, on their application, to lend and advance to them any sum not exceeding two thousand pounds common money out of the public treasury, they giving bond with good security to interest and apply the same in prosecuting the said cannon-foundry, and repaying the same into the public treasury by the 10th day of April next"

The Hugheses were residents of Washington County, and were among the earliest organizers of the new county

At a convention of delegates chosen by the several counties and districts, and by the city of Annapolis and town of Baltimore, of the province of Maryland, at the city of Annapolis, on Aug 14, 1776, there were present as delegates from the upper district of Frederick (now Washington County) Samuel Beall John Stull, and Henry Schnebly

On Thursday, Aug 15, 1776 the convention again met, and the [illegible] Election [illegible]ted

"That by the return for the upper district of Frederick County (now Washington County), Samuel Beall Samuel Hughes, John Stull, and Henry Schnebly Esqrs, were duly elected delegates to represent that district in the convention"

As originally constituted, Frederick County was a vast and sparsely settled tract, and the people living west of the South Mountain were put to great inconvenience in traveling to and from Frederick, the county-seat Consequently, in response to their petition, the Provincial Convention, at a session held at Annapolis on Saturday, Aug 31, 1776, granted leave for the introduction of an ordinance for the division of Frederick County Later on the same day Mr Wootton brought in and delivered to the president of the convention (Matthew Tilghman) an ordinance for the division of Frederick County into three distinct and separate counties, which was read and ordered to lie on the table

On Friday, Sept 6, 1776, the ordinance for the division of Frederick County was read the second time, and, on motion, the question was put, "That the consideration thereof be postponed till the next session of convention?" Carried in the negative" Those voting in the negative were Messrs Barnes, Semmes, Plowden, Fitzhugh, J Mackall Bowie, Hall, Sprigg Marbury Hammond, Paca, Wootton Bayly, Williams, Sheredine, Edelen, Beall, Hughes Stull, Schnebly, Ridgely, Deye, Stevenson, J Smith H Wilson, Love, Archer, Bevard, T Ringgold, and Johnson, those voting in the affirmative being Messrs Hooe, Dent, Carroll, W Ringgold Earle, T Smythe, Goldsborough, Murray, Gus Scott, J Wilson Fischer, Schriver, Bond, Ewing, T Wright, S Wright, Edmondson, Gibson, George Scott, Lowes, Mason, and Chaille The convention then proceeded to take the same into consideration, which was agreed to The bill, so far as it relates to Washington County, is as follows

"*Whereas*, It appears to this convention that the erecting two new counties out of Frederick County will conduce greatly to the ease and convenience of the people thereof,

"*Resolved*, That after the first day of October next such part of the said county of Frederick as is contained within the bounds and limits following, to wit beginning at the place where the temporary line crosses the South Mountain, and running thence by a line on the ridge of the said mountain to the river Potowmac and thence with the lines of the said county so as to include all the lands to the westward of the line running on the ridge of the South Mountain, as aforesaid, to the beginning, shall be and is hereby erected into a new county by the name of *Washington* County[1]

* * * * * * * * *

"*Resolved*, That the inhabitants of the said counties of Washington and Montgomery shall have, hold and enjoy all such rights and privileges as are held and enjoyed by the inhabitants of any county in this State

[1] The second [illegible] lines of the new [illegible] county

"*Resolved*, That Messrs. Joseph Sprigg, Joseph Smith, John Barnes, Andrew Rench, Daniel Hughes, William Yates, and Conrad Hogmire shall be and are hereby appointed commissioners for Washington County, and they, or the major part of them, shall be and are hereby authorized and required to buy and purchase in fee a quantity of land not exceeding four acres, at or adjoining such place as a majority of voters within the limits of the said county, qualified as this convention, shall hereafter direct, the election to be held at the place heretofore appointed for the choosing of delegates in this convention (the said commissioners giving ten days' notice of the place and time of voting) for the purpose of building thereon a court-house and prison for the said county; and shall cause the said land to be laid out by the surveyor of Frederick County with good and sufficient boundaries, and a certificate thereof to be returned and recorded in the records of the said county; and the said commissioners, or a major part of them, shall draw their order on the sheriff of Washington County to pay such sum as shall be agreed upon for the said land, and the sheriff is hereby directed and required to pay the said order out of the money hereafter mentioned, to be collected by him for that purpose, and such payment for the land shall invest the justices of Washington County and their successors with an estate in fee simple therein, for the use of the said county forever; and if the said commissioners, or the major part of them, and the owner of the said land shall differ about the value of the said land, in such case the commissioners, or the major part of them, shall be and they are hereby authorized and empowered to order the sheriff of Washington County to summon twelve freeholders upon the said land, who shall be empowered and sworn as a jury to inquire the value of the said land; and the said commissioners, or the major part of them, shall draw their order on the sheriff of Washington County to pay the said valuation, and the said sheriff is hereby directed to pay the said order out of the money hereafter mentioned to be by him collected for that purpose, and upon his payment of the said order the fee simple in the said land shall be invested, as aforesaid, in the justices of Washington County and their successors for the use of the said county forever.

* * * * * * * * *

"*Resolved*, That the justices of Washington and Montgomery Counties, or the major part of them, respectively be and they are hereby authorized to contract and agree for a convenient place in each of the said counties to hold the courts for the said counties, and to contract and agree for a convenient place in each of the said counties for their books, papers, and other records, and also for a fit building for the custody of the prisoners, and the said courts shall be held and records kept at such places respectively until the court house and prison for the said counties respectively shall be erected and built; and the charge and expense of such places shall be defrayed by the said counties respectively, and assessed with the public and county levy.

"*Resolved*, That the justices of the said counties respectively shall be and they are hereby authorized and required to assess and levy on the *taxable* inhabitants of the said counties respectively, with the public and county levy, as much money as will pay for the purchase or valuation of the land aforesaid, together with the sheriff's salary of such per centum as may be hereafter allowed for collection of the same, which said sum shall be collected by the sheriffs of the said counties respectively from the inhabitants of the said counties respectively, in the same manner as other public and county levies may be by law hereafter collected; and the said money, when collected, shall be paid by the sheriff to such person or persons as the commissioners aforesaid, or the major part of them, shall order and direct.

"*Resolved*, That the justices of Washington County shall be and they are hereby authorized and required to assess and levy by three equal assessments, in the years 1777, 1778, and 1779, with their public and county levy, any sum not exceeding thirteen hundred pounds common money in and upon the inhabitants of Washington County, together with the sheriff's salary, of such a per centum as may be hereafter allowed for collection of the same, which said sum, so to be assessed and levied, shall be collected by the sheriff of Washington County from the inhabitants thereof, *in the same manner as other public and* county levies shall be hereafter by law collected, and the said money, when collected, shall be paid by the said sheriff to the commissioners of Washington County aforesaid, and shall be by them applied towards building the court house and prison in the said county.

* * * * * * * * *

"*Resolved*, That the commissioners of the said counties respectively, or the major part of them, shall be and they are hereby authorized and required to contract and agree for the building of the said court house and prison on the land to be purchased as aforesaid.

"*Resolved*, That all causes, pleas, process, and pleadings which now are or shall be depending in Frederick County Court before the first day of December next shall and may be prosecuted as effectually as they might have been had these resolves never been made; and in case any deeds or conveyances of land in Washington County or Montgomery County have been, or shall be before the division aforesaid acknowledged according to law in Frederick County, the enrollment and recording thereof within the time limited by law, either in the County Court of Frederick County or in the County Court of Washington or Montgomery County, shall be good and available, the division aforesaid notwithstanding.

"*Resolved*, That executions or other legal process upon all judgments had and obtained, or to be had and obtained on actions already commenced, or to be commenced before the first day of December next in Frederick County Court, against any inhabitant of Washington or Montgomery County, be issued and enforced in the same manner as if these resolves had not been made, which said writs shall be directed to the sheriff of the said counties respectively, and the said sheriffs are hereby authorized and directed to serve and return the same to Frederick County Court, with the body or bodies of the person or persons, if taken, against whom such writ or writs shall issue for that purpose; and during the attendance of the sheriff of Washington or Montgomery County at Frederick County Court he shall have a power to confine in Frederick County jail, if he shall think it necessary, such persons as he shall have in execution, but after his attendance shall be dispensed with by the said court, he shall then, in a reasonable time, remove such persons as he shall have in execution to his county jail, there to be kept till legally discharged.

"That the public and county levy now assessed or levied, or *to be levied and assessed by the justices of Frederick County* Court, at their Levy Court for the present year shall and may be collected and received by the sheriff of Frederick County, as well of the inhabitants of Frederick as of Washington and Montgomery Counties aforesaid, and collected, accounted for, and applied in such manner as the said public and county levy would have been collected, accounted for, and applied had these resolves never been made.

"*Resolved*, That the County Court of Washington County shall begin and be held yearly on the fourth Tuesdays of those months in which other County Courts are held, and shall have equal power and jurisdiction with any County Court in this State."

The new county was named Washington, in honor of Gen Washington, then conspicuous before the country as commander in chief of the Continental forces. The men who passed the ordinance creating it were the sturdy patriots who drafted the Declaration of Rights and adopted the first constitution of Maryland.

On the 11th of September, 1776, on motion of Mr Hughes, it was

"*Resolved*, That the qualification of voters in Washington County for the purpose of fixing on the most convenient place for a court house and prison in said county be the same as of voters for representatives in this convention." A few days later it was resolved that the elections for Washington County be held at Hagerstown, and that "Joseph Smith, Noah Hart, and Elie Williams, Esquires, or any two of them, be judges of and hold the elections for Washington County."

The people residing west of Sidling Hill, however, were dissatisfied with the provisions of the resolution,—i e, naming Hagerstown as the place for holding the election,—and in consequence they immediately petitioned the convention to establish a voting precinct in the western part of the county. On Monday, Oct 21, 1776, the following action was taken by the convention

"On reading and considering the petition of sundry inhabitants of Washington County, setting forth that by a late resolve of convention the election for fixing the place for the court house of Washington County was to be held at Hagertown, which would be so distant from many of the inhabitants of the said county that it would be very inconvenient for them to attend, and praying that the election might be held for one or more days at Skiptoo or Oldtown, thereupon the question was put, That for the ease and convenience of the inhabitants of the upper part of Washington County the election for fixing the place for the court house of the said county shall be held two days at Skipton, beginning on the sixth day of November next, and that Andrew Bruce, Lemuel Barrett, and Thomas Warren, or any two of them, be judges of the said election, and give due notice to the inhabitants of the said county, and that the judges appointed to hold the election at Hagerstown and those appointed to hold the election at Skipton meet together as soon as conveniently may be at Hagerstown, and there examine the said polls and declare the said election according as the majority of voters may appear to be on both the said polls? Resolved in the affirmative."[1]

On Thursday, Nov 7, 1776, on motion of Mr Johnson, the convention

"*Resolved*, That all justices of the peace and other officers who were such of Frederick County shall continue and may exercise the same power and authority as if the resolutions of this convention for dividing Frederick County into three counties had not passed, and the justices of the County Court of Frederick, to be held in the month of November in this present year, or by adjournment, shall have cognizance of, and may proceed to hear and determine all causes, matters, and things, criminal and civil, although the same have arisen or shall arise in Washington or Montgomery County, in the same manner and as fully as the same court might or could have done if the said resolutions had never been made and the justices aforesaid may appoint constables and overseers of the highways [illegible] well in the said counties of Washington and Montgomery [illegible] in Frederick County.

"That the County Court for each of the said counties of Washington and Montgomery shall be first held as for separate and distinct counties, in the month of March next and where any defendant against whom any original writ or process shall, after the first day of December next, issue resides in Washington or Montgomery County, the writ or process shall issue out of Frederick County Court, directed to the sheriff of the county where the defendant resides, if such county shall then have a sheriff qualified to act in the county separately, and if not, to the sheriff of Frederick County, and shall be returnable and returned to the next March court to be held for the county where the defendant resides.

"That the justices of Frederick County Court aforesaid may, at their November court aforesaid, assess and levy on the taxable inhabitants of Washington and Montgomery Counties, separately and respectively, such money or tobacco as the justices of the same counties might respectively have assessed at their November courts in this year had the same been held."

In 1789 a new county, Allegany, was formed out of Washington County, which had become sufficiently populous even at that early day to make the division a matter of necessity. Joseph Scott the geographer writing about 1807, says that Washington

"is a rich, fertile county forty-nine miles long and twenty seven broad, but at Hancock on the Potomac, not more than two. It contains 317 126 acres. It is divided into the following hundreds, viz Upper Anti Etam Lower Anti Etam, Elizabeth, Marsh Manor, Sharpsburg Salisbury, Conococheague, First (Fort?), Frederick, and Linton. Washington County lies principally between the North and South Mountains, and includes the fertile and well cultivated valley extending on each side of Conococheague Creek. The lands are esteemed equal if not superior in fertility to any in the State. All that part of the county northwest of the South Mountain, extending in breadth about twenty miles to the Pennsylvania line is chiefly limestone land, interspersed with some slate land. That part of the county between the North Mountain and Allegany County is hilly and mountainous, and mostly slate and stony land, except the bottoms on the Potomac and the tributary streams which fall into that river. Many of these bottoms are exceedingly fertile in all kinds of productions peculiar to the climate. Wheat rye, Indian corn, oats, potatoes, hemp, flax, with a great variety of vegetables, are chiefly cultivated by the farmers. Large quantities of flour are manufactured particularly on the Anti Etam, and transported to Baltimore. In some seasons considerable quantities are sent down the Potomac to Georgetown and Alexandria. Large quantities of whisky are distilled latterly and sent to the different seaports. It contains mines of iron ore, for the manufacturing of which three furnaces and three forges have been erected, which manufacture pig, hollow-ware, bar iron, etc. There are about fifty grist mills in the county, several saw mills, fulling, hemp, and oil mills. The water of the Anti Etam turns fourteen mills. It is the largest and most constant stream in the county, and where the largest quantities of flour are manufactured. There are very few quarries of any other kind of stone than those of limestone which are very abundant. It is the [illegible] In the North

[1] All of the members present voted in the affirmative, except Messrs Stull and [illegible], who voted No

Mountain are quarries of freestone but so hard that they are not used for any purpose nor has any quarry been opened In the South Mountain is a remarkable cave "

The Valley of the Antietam or Hagerstown Valley, as it is sometimes called, is remarkable for its fertility, and the wheat grown here is of the finest quality, and is manufactured into superior brands of flour The valley was the scene of the military operations during the war which culminated in the great battle of Antietam The county is penetrated by the Washington County Branch of the Baltimore and Ohio, the Western Maryland, the Cumberland Valley, and the Shenandoah Valley Railroads and the Chesapeake and Ohio Canal extends along its entire southern and southwestern boundary It is thus abundantly supplied with transportation facilities The county roads are numerous and excellent and the general condition of the county is that of a high degree of prosperity The principal products are wheat, corn, oats, hay, potatoes, wool, rye, live stock butter, and honey

Lying at the foot of the Alleganies, Washington County has a pure, healthful, invigorating atmosphere, an industrious and numerous population of the most progressive American type, unusual facilities for manufactures, a fine soil, and, in fact, all the advantages necessary to enable it to maintain its position as one of the leading agricultural communities of the United States

A spur of the Blue Ridge, named Elk Mountain, extends through the southeastern part of the county between which and the South Mountain on the east is included a very charming and beautiful valley, whose qualities are but faintly expressed in the name of Pleasant Valley Looking westward from Hagerstown, the eye, after wandering over some twenty miles of hill and dale, rests upon the bold crest of the old North Mountain, and still farther beyond that other spurs of the Alleganies These mountains of Washington County do not need "distance" to "lend enchantment to the view," but afford, whether far or near, the most beautiful and picturesque scenery, and at the same time yield large returns for the skillful cultivation bestowed on them to their very summits The surface of the remainder of the county is rolling, and in many instances very charming to the eye The soils are very fertile being for the most part of the very best quality of clay and limestone lands, with occasional varieties of shaly soil, all susceptible of high and easy improvement Agriculture is conducted in a scientific manner, the implements in use are of the very best, and as a result unusually large crops are produced Live-stock has been improved with the best foreign breeds, and the care, skill and attention bestowed on this branch of husbandry has met with most gratifying rewards The abundance of clover and the other cultivated grasses affords a large supply of dairy products Quarries of excellent limestone, suitable for the manufacture of lime and for building purposes, are numerous in various parts of the county, and some also of the kind used for making hydraulic cement Good iron ore exists in considerable quantities, and superior brick clay is found in almost every locality This region has long been famous for the distillation of whisky the excellence of which has been attested by good judges in every section of the country The best fertilizers, paper, and iron are manufactured to a very large extent

The Potomac River, the Antietam and Conococheague Creeks, and their tributaries afford fine water-power privileges in almost every neighborhood These, since the first settlement of the county, have been utilized to a large extent, and their surplus waters have turned the wheels of many flour grist, paper, and saw mills, and various other manufactories

The original settlers of Washington County, were composed principally of Germans, English Scotch, Swiss, and French, the latter from the border provinces of Alsace and Lorraine

It is impossible to state exactly when and where the first settlement within the present boundaries of Washington County was made, but from the fact that the Lords Proprietary caused surveys to be made, and began granting lands (situated on the west side of the Blue Ridge or South Mountain, in Prince George's County) to individuals as early as 1732, it is safe to assume that a number of families were established in the present county of Washington as early as 1735 and that from about 1740 onward their numbers rapidly increased They were Germans chiefly the friends and relations of those who were then clearing away the forests of Frederick, Montgomery, Carroll, and the lower counties of Pennsylvania

A few families among the early settlers, however, usually of English origin, and the proprietors of "manors," or large tracts of land, lived in lordly style, and dispensed a generous hospitality But the hardy pioneers who settled the country were a simple, industrious people, who ate out of wooden trenchers and platters, sat upon three-legged stools or wooden blocks upon a dirt floor used bear's grease for lard and butter, and cut up their food with the same sheath knife which they used in dressing the deer killed by their rifles Westward of the Conococheague the country was in possession of the savages, with a few isolated exceptions for a number of years and not until th[illegible] the [illegible] Indian war

was it fully opened up to settlers. But when peace was declared there was a great influx from the North and East, and flourishing settlements were speedily established at numerous points west of South Mountain.

Washington County began the year 1800 with a population of 16,108 whites, 342 free colored, and 2200 slaves, being a gain of but 2828 over the total number reported in 1790.

Hagerstown and Williamsport were already commercial and manufacturing centres of considerable importance, many saw, grist, and woolen-mills dotted the banks of the Conococheague and Antietam, and besides those of the villages numerous taverns were established at short intervals along the route of the principal highways and almost invariably at the cross-roads.

Comparatively, the county at that early date was an old, settled region. Indeed, many considered it as already overstocked with human occupants, and a large number moving on to the westward sought homes in Kentucky.[1]

There has been no partition of the county since Allegany was taken off in 1789, though efforts have been made from time to time to procure a redivision. As late as the winter of 1851 there was a movement in favor of creating a new county out of the southwestern portion of Frederick and the southeastern portion of Washington County, and meetings were held at various places within the territory of the proposed new county both in favor of and in opposition to the project. The movement came to nothing. Allegany County was divided in 1872, and the new county of Garrett created from territory which had once belonged to Washington County.

Land Grants, Surveys, Etc.[2]—Prior to the Revolutionary war grants of land were made by the Governor of the province on behalf of the Lord Proprietary, and subsequently by the State government. Following is a list of the principal grants prior to 1800:

Name of Lot	To Whom Granted	Date	Acres
Addition	R. Prather	Oct. 25, 1738	20
Addition to Black Oak Land	Charles Carroll	May 11, 1750	22
Addition to [illegible] Bottom	D. David J[illegible]	Sept. 29, 1761	33[illegible]
Addition to Lawrence's Disappointment	Richard Barnes	April 3, 1794	10[illegible]½
Addition to Locust Swamp	F. Hersh		
Addition to Six [illegible]			50
" to Spear	John Hoover	April 14, 1794	1
" to Stoney Batter	Jonathan Hager	March 9, 1763	82
Agreed to leave it Stated	Benjamin Bowman	April 11, 1784	71
All Meadow	Henry [illegible]	Sept. 2, 1761	4½
All that's left	Peter Shesso	April 23, 1765	297
All[illegible]'s	"	Sept. 26, 1750	100
All w[illegible]	Surveyed	May 6, 1781	195
Ann[illegible]	Joseph Chapline	Feb. 21, 1761	50
Anything	Thomas Johnson	Feb. 23, 1765	84
Avey's Delight and Resurvey	John Avey	Aug. 19, 1751	4[illegible]0
Avey's Good Luck	" "	June 2, 1763	4[illegible]
Bashore's Misfortune	Christian Buckler		50
" Resurveyed	George French	Nov. 9, 17[illegible]	115
[illegible]'s Refuse	Joseph Chapline	May 12, 1759	50
Bald Friend	John B[illegible]	Feb. 8, 17[illegible]9	[illegible]
Bachelor's Delight	John [illegible]	Nov. 1, 1762	818½
Beall's Lot	Evan Shelby	Aug. [illegible], 1741	50
Beall's Neglect	Samuel [illegible]	Feb. 8, 17[illegible]	11
B[illegible]'s Purchase	[illegible]	Sept. 9, 17[illegible]	[illegible]¾
Belt's Bash	Benj. Belt	April 24, 1762	6[illegible]
Birkhead's Dispute	Jacob Hunter	Feb. 2, 17[illegible]	[illegible]
Bennett's Folly	George [illegible]	Nov. 9, 17[illegible]	[illegible]
[illegible]'s Delight	Samuel [illegible]	April 1[illegible], 17[illegible]	373
Big Spring	Evan Shelby	Nov. [illegible], 1741	1[illegible]
Black Oak Level	John [illegible]	July [illegible], 17[illegible]	[illegible]
Black Oak Land	Charles Carroll	April 10, 17[illegible]0	2[illegible]
Blind Man's Choice	Michael Miller	Oct. 31, 17[illegible]	1
Blue [illegible]	Isaac Baker	Sept. 29, 17[illegible]	[illegible]
Blue Rock	Lawrence Bombarger	July [illegible], 1758	25
B[illegible]'s Fancy	John Myers	Feb. 1[illegible], 1761	242
Bore Range	[illegible]	May 26, 17[illegible]	[illegible]
Br[illegible]well's Choice	Jonathan H[illegible]	March [illegible], 17[illegible]	50
Brooks Blunder	John [illegible]	Sept. 7, 17[illegible]	9
Brookfield	Daniel Hughes	May 1[illegible], 17[illegible]	4[illegible]½
[illegible]'s Request	[illegible]	May 1, 17[illegible]	[illegible]00
Burns Justice	Jonathan [illegible]	Aug. [illegible], 179[illegible]	[illegible]
[illegible]'s Quarry	[illegible]	Dec. [illegible], 17[illegible]	69
Chance	[illegible]	May 11, 17[illegible]	
"	Dr. Henry Schnebly	May 30, 17[illegible]	112
"	Isaac [illegible]	April 29, 17[illegible]	4
"	Joseph Chapline		142
Charlton's Victory			
" Resurveyed	John Scott	July 2[illegible], 17[illegible]	187
" Forest			[illegible]
Chapline's Neglect	John Cannon	Aug. 10, 17[illegible]	[illegible]½
Cheney's Delight	Ezekiel Cheney	Aug. [illegible], 17[illegible]	[illegible]5
" Choice	Zechariah Cheney	April 2, 17[illegible]	27
" Lot	Charles Cheney, Jr.	March 2[illegible], 17[illegible]	[illegible]8
Clear Spring	George [illegible]	Sept. 6, 17[illegible]	100

[1] After the close of the war of 1812 many Washington County people removed to Ohio, Indiana, Illinois, and Missouri, and in years quite recent the same restless spirit has carried large numbers of them to the Pacific Slope and to various Western States.

[2] The Hagerstown *Mail* of Sept. 9, 1870, gives the following description of one of the early land patents:

"Dropping into the sheriff's office a day or two since, we found Mr. Sol. B. Rohrer, of our place, overhauling some very memorable parchments belonging to his family, of which he is the only remaining representative, and which, along with the Hagers, were the pioneers of civilization in the valley of the Conococheague and Antietam. We selected a conveyance to which was dangling, as to a treaty between nations, a ponderous seal. It was, with the present coat of arms of our State impressed on one side and 'St. George and the Dragon' on the other. The document bore date Jan. 16, 1739, being, as was recited, 'the twenty-fifth year of our dominion,' and was issued by 'Charles, Absolute Lord and Proprietary of the Province of Maryland and Avalon, Lord Baron of Baltimore,' etc. It recites [illegible] Jacob Rohrer, of Prince George's County [how very few persons living here know that they occupy a portion of what was once Prince George's County!], by his humble petition to our agent for *management* of our land affairs within this province,' etc., 'did sell fifty acres of vacant land lying in and being in county aforesaid, about a mile from *Antietam* Creek and about three miles from Shirk's mill,' etc. The whole document, as well as the other deeds, are quite curious and interesting, and to future historians may prove valuable. It was issued by Samuel Ogle, Lieutenant Governor of the province.

"Rohrer's Addition to Hagerstown, of which the new academy is now the most conspicuous object, was made by a collateral branch of this family, which is still perpetuated in some of the Western States. The old family graveyard at the [illegible] of the family [illegible] the Potomac [illegible] of the Franklin [illegible] all that remains of that family, and [illegible] that [illegible] by the plow."

Name of Lot.	To Whom Granted.	Date.	Acres.
[illegible] Spring[1]	Nathan Bruce and Jno. Jones	April 20, 1787	
[illegible]dale	Joseph Chapline	Feb. 21, 1764	24[illegible]
[illegible]'s Amendment	Frederick Nicholson	Oct. 6, 1768	44[illegible]
" Original.			
Conquest	James Tedeford	July 11, 1789.	
[illegible]tentment	Joseph Chapline	Feb. 21, 1764	1155
Continuation of Friendship	Samuel Hepler	Jan. 9, 1771	51
[illegible] Hook	J. [illegible]	April 1, 1760	12
Cumberland	John Stone	Oct. 15, 1750	19[illegible]
[illegible]'s Defeat	Arthur Charlton	Aug. 2, 1775	60
[illegible]	John Charlton	July 24, 1745	450
[illegible] Bargain and Resurvey	Roger Dart	March 25, 1750	122
[illegible] Bargain	Charles Friend	Dec. 18, 1741	25
Discovery (Original)			100
" (Resurvey)	Thomas Beatty	Feb. 5, 1769	275
[illegible] (and Resurvey)	[illegible]	[illegible], 1764	102
[illegible] Little	John [illegible]	Nov. [illegible], 1748	30
[illegible]			25
[illegible] in haste	Henry [illegible]	April 24, 1752	50
[illegible]	[illegible]	[illegible] 16, 1767	119
[illegible]ney's Lott	Robert [illegible]	Dec. 2, 1741	100
" "	" "	July 13, 1742	50
[illegible] Plain	Daniel and Walter Dulany	Sept. 28, 1765	29[illegible]
[illegible] Spring	[illegible]	Aug. 26, 1762	1[illegible]
[illegible]	John [illegible]	March 12, 1744	2[illegible]
[illegible]'s Folly	[illegible]	[illegible] 11, 1774	2[illegible]
[illegible]man's Request	William Ma[illegible]	[illegible] 15, 1750	151
[illegible] Folly	Thomas [illegible]	[illegible] 2, 1749	100
[illegible]	[illegible]	[illegible], 1774.	
[illegible]	[illegible]	[illegible], 1762	50
[illegible]'s Lott	[illegible]	[illegible], 1747	113
[illegible]	[illegible]	[illegible]	1[illegible]
[illegible]ange	[illegible]	[illegible] 4, 1762	7[illegible]
"	Christopher Burkhead	[illegible]	1[illegible]
"	William [illegible]	[illegible], 1784	20
[illegible] Virgin	John [illegible]	[illegible] 11, 1755	[illegible]
[illegible]	William [illegible]	[illegible]	[illegible]
[illegible]'s Good Will	[illegible]	[illegible], 1767	[illegible]
Fellowship	[illegible]	[illegible]	10[illegible]
[illegible]	[illegible]	[illegible], 1765	1[illegible]
[illegible]	[illegible]	[illegible], 1753	[illegible]
[illegible] Choice	[illegible]	17[illegible]	[illegible]
[illegible]	[illegible]	[illegible], 1778	47[illegible]
[illegible]'s Purchase	[illegible]	[illegible], 1792	2[illegible]
[illegible] Out	Capt. [illegible]	[illegible] 11, 1753	[illegible]
[illegible] Springs	[illegible]	[illegible]	[illegible]
[illegible]	[illegible], Jr.	[illegible] 11, 1760	[illegible]
Friendship	[illegible]	[illegible], 1750	[illegible]
"	John [illegible]	[illegible] 11, 1768	10
"	[illegible]		10[illegible]
[illegible]'s [illegible]	[illegible]	[illegible], 1753	[illegible]
[illegible]	John [illegible]	[illegible]	1[illegible]
Garden Spot	William [illegible]		1[illegible]
[illegible]	Betty Doyle	[illegible] 1, 1738	1[illegible]
[illegible] Lambert's Land			200
" " Delight			1[illegible]
George's Discovery	George French	April 11, 1761	1[illegible]
" Venture	" "	Dec. 1, 1747	50
George the Second	Samuel Chase and Thos. Johnson	Feb. 8, 1764	7[illegible]
Germany	H. Waggoner	May 4, 1754	4[illegible]
Gillespie's Bargain	George Gillespie	June 8, 1767	9[illegible]
Good Friendship	Dr. Henry Schnebly	Feb. 26, 1765	7[illegible]
" Hope	" "	Feb. 21, 1766	4[illegible]
" Luck	Richard Lilley	April 7, 1767	2[illegible]
" Neighbor	Stephen Clark	Sept. 29, 1767	6[illegible]
" Will (Original)	Christopher Reeves	[illegible] 19, 1767	1[illegible]
" "	Chase & Johnson	Feb. [illegible], 1764	2[illegible]
Great Rock	Daniel Dulany	April [illegible], 1760	50
Greenwood	H. Toms	No date	50
Green Castle	James Sharp	Feb. 7, 1745	625
Hager's Defence	David Hager	May 17, 1760	22
Hampton Forrest			20
" Plains	Richard Lilley	March 23, 1764	200
Harrod's Profit	Michael Funk	Oct. 16, 1762	1[illegible]
Harry's Grave			140
" Last Shift	M. Ridenour	April 18, 1769	50
Hartel's Lott	Hartel	April 10, 1762	[illegible]
Help to Hall's Sale	George Cohet	Nov. [illegible], 1768	4[illegible]
Hempfield	Bartholomew Booth	June [illegible], 1776	2[illegible]
Hermit's Fancy	John Lilley	March 15, 1762	274
[illegible]	H. Stoltz	No date	5[illegible]
[illegible] Swamp	William Wil[illegible]	None	5[illegible]
[illegible]	John [illegible]	[illegible] 25, 1754	[illegible]
[illegible] More	David Stuttzman	[illegible] 16, 1765	1[illegible]
[illegible]'s Made Over	Conrad Hoenicke	[illegible] 21, 1767	1[illegible]
[illegible]	John [illegible]	July 4, 1761	[illegible]
[illegible]'s Last Chance	John [illegible]	Feb. 11, 1791	[illegible]
[illegible] Timber	George Kester	Nov. 4, 1755	1[illegible]
[illegible] it is no worse	Adam Ronghkoing	Nov. 24, 1776	[illegible]
[illegible]	James Marshall	March 31, 1755	[illegible]
[illegible] Well	Sebastian Sheap	June 24, 1761	12[illegible]
Ingram's Delight	John Ingram		1[illegible]
Israel's Lot			7[illegible]
Jack's Bottom	Jeremiah Jack	Dec. 12, 1779	175
Jacob's Delight	Jacob Shockey	Sept. 6, 176[illegible]	25
Jacob's Well	Jacob R[illegible]	Feb. [illegible], 17[illegible]	[illegible]½
Jerico	Cold. T[illegible]	Nov. 16, 17[illegible]	41
Jerico Hills	John Ribott	March 10, 177[illegible]	322
John's Lott	John Bond		241
Jones' Discovery	Mary Brooke	Dec. 11, 1752	6[illegible]
Jones' Delight	William Jones		1[illegible]
Joseph's Chance	Joseph Bet[illegible], Jr.	June 23, 1752	3[illegible]
Joseph's Last Ent[illegible]	Moses Chapline	Oct. 12, 1791	67
Kelly's Delight	Wm. Kelly	June 28, 17[illegible]	10[illegible]
Kent's Chance	Joseph Cheney		70
Ketmans	Charles Carroll	April 19, 17[illegible]	1[illegible]
Kindness	Dr. Charles Carroll	Aug. 10, 17[illegible]	3716
Kysser's Landing	John Summers	May 6, 17[illegible]	110
Kyser's Inheritance	Frederick Kyser	Nov. 28, 1792	100½
[illegible] and [illegible]	Simon [illegible]	Aug. 21, 1792	3[illegible]½
Lambert's Delight	Geo. Lambert	April 21, 17[illegible]	4[illegible]
Lambert's Park	" "	Feb. 17, 174[illegible]	[illegible]
Lambert's Strip	" "	June 9, 176[illegible]	2[illegible]
[illegible]'s Folly			100
Lawrence's Disappointment	John Johnson	Aug. 19, 17[illegible]	279
Leather Button	Chris. Everhardt	Feb. 11, 17[illegible]	20
Leese			50
Lilley's Discovery	Samuel Lilley	April 19, 1764	2[illegible]
Lilley's Discovery Resurveyed	" "		36[illegible]
Lilley's Industry	" "	Aug. 27, 1764	4[illegible]
Limestone Land	John Howard	Feb. 11, 175[illegible]	2[illegible]
Link's Fo[illegible]	Andrew Link	May 3, 1759	50
Linton	Thomas Cresap	Aug. 2, 1742	1[illegible]
Little Enlarged	Dr. H. Schnebly	June 12, 17[illegible]	1[illegible]
Little Friendship	Joseph Chapline	July 1, 17[illegible]	2[illegible]
Little Timber	Geo. Hartle	Nov. 6, 17[illegible]	[illegible]
Littleworth	[illegible]		[illegible]
Locust Swamp	Frederick Heis[illegible]	Sept. 29, 1779	10[illegible]
Locust Thicket	N. Nesbitt	May 5, 1764	93
Long Hill	Henry Schnebly	Feb. 18, 1766	8[illegible]
Long Life to Lord Calvert	Capt. George Beall	Oct. 16, 17[illegible]	1[illegible]
Long Bottom	Frederick Ba[illegible]		5[illegible]
Love in a Village	Joseph Chapline	Oct. 14, 178[illegible]	3[illegible]½
Lunafield (and Resurvey)	Peter John	April 24, 17[illegible]	1[illegible]
[illegible]'s Fancy	[illegible]	June [illegible], 17[illegible]	[illegible]
[illegible]'s Choice	Evan Shelby	Aug. 7, 17[illegible]	1[illegible]
[illegible] Fancy	Thomas Chapline	April 20, 1779	1[illegible]
Maidom	Henry Fra[illegible]	May 2, 1754	
Marlboro' Fields	C. Hoenicke	Nov. [illegible], 17[illegible]	2[illegible]
McCoy's Delight	Dr. C[illegible]	Nov. 6, 177[illegible]	[illegible]
McCoy's Discovery	Daniel McCoy	April 23, 17[illegible]	4[illegible]
McLaughlin's Chance	McLaughlin	June 16, 17[illegible]	[illegible]
Meadow Green	John [illegible]	June 2[illegible], 178[illegible]	[illegible]
[illegible]'s Neglect	[illegible]	June 3, 176[illegible]	1[illegible]
Meshack's Con[illegible]	Geo. Ro[illegible], Jr.	Feb. 13, 17[illegible]	[illegible]
Miller's Chance	Michael Miller	June 13, 17[illegible]	[illegible]
" Fancy	" "	March 9, 17[illegible]	[illegible]
" Range			[illegible]
Mine Bank	Richard [illegible]	Jan. [illegible], 17[illegible]	[illegible]
Monthlepone	Evan Shelby	Nov. 30, 1741	[illegible]
Mount Ætna	Daniel and Samuel Hughes	Resurveyed Nov. 30, 1787	41[illegible]
Mountain of Wales	Evan Shelby	Oct. 15, 17[illegible]	[illegible]
Mountain Foot	Conrad Hoenicke	Nov. 21, 17[illegible]	[illegible]
" Lott	Richard Fischer	Dec. 2[illegible], 176[illegible]	1[illegible]
Mount Misery	Fasnacht	Dec. 6, 17[illegible]	7[illegible]
" Pleasant	Hester		[illegible]
" "	Henry Darby	July 24, 1762	[illegible]
" "	John Darby	Oct. 6, 17[illegible]	2[illegible]
Mumma's Lott	Jacob Mumma	Jan. 7, 181[illegible]	1[illegible]
Nancy	Geo. Moore	April 7, 1768	2[illegible]
Neal's Bottom	Christopher Burkhead	Sept. 29, 17[illegible]	50
Near the Navel	Joseph Chapline	Dec. 20, 1761	1[illegible]
Need Not	Daniel Dulany	Surveyed Feb. 11, 1742	2[illegible]
Neglect	H. Keefer	Dec. 1, 1764	1[illegible]
"	John McCoy	Nov. 9, 1742	150
"	Geo. Miller	Oct. 5, 1761	7[illegible]
Neighbors' Neglect	Owen Da[illegible]	July 24, 1749	52
New Work	Jonathan Hager	May 6, 1765	114
Nicholas' Contrivance	Edward Nichols	Oct. 28, 1740	75
" "	Edward Nichols	No date	110
Nicholas' Contrivance Resurveyed	James Dowey	April 10, 17[illegible]	[illegible]
No More Left	Isaac Baker	Feb. 21, 17[illegible]	1[illegible]
None Left	Jacob Fr[illegible]	May 16, 178[illegible]	[illegible]½
None Such	James Davis	July 21, 17[illegible]	[illegible]
North Point	William Thomas	April 11, 17[illegible]	[illegible]
Not Much	William Good	Nov. 6, 178[illegible]	11
Nottingham	Isaac Brooke	July 26, 17[illegible]	
Obid	John Stull	Sept. [illegible]	1[illegible]
Old Plott	Christian Yost	April 30, 17[illegible]	[illegible]
Paradise Regained	Philip Key	Oct. 13, 17[illegible]	5[illegible]
Part of Chestnut Hill Resurvey	John Stull	Sept. 3, 17[illegible]	3[illegible]
Part of Dutch [illegible] Resurvey	[illegible]	[illegible] 18, 1746	11[illegible]

[1] This land was [illegible] Philip Kelly in Ja[illegible] [illegible] 17[illegible] and [illegible]

Name of Lot	To Whom Granted	Date	Acres
Part of Third Resurvey on Sarah's Delight	Dan and Sam Hughes	February, 1771	770
Part of Third Resurvey on Sarah's Delight	Dan and Sam Hughes	Feb 15, 1787	637
Pattison's Resurvey	James Pattison	April 10, 1755	411
Paul's Travels	Paul Rhodes	June 7, 1769	40
Pearce Well	[illegible] Pearce	Nov 13, 1769	21
Pelican		Oct 27, 1759	9[illegible]
Perry's Retirement			100
[illegible]	George Gillespie	July 6, 1768	28[illegible]
Pierpoint's Contest?			100
Pleasant Bottom			226
Pleasant Bottom and part of the resurvey on the Mountain of Wales	Isaac Baker	Aug 10, 1770	1130
Pleasant Hill	[illegible]	July 9, 1741	4[illegible]
Pleasant Spring	John [illegible]	March 10, 1760	100
Pleasant Valley	I. Houser	Sept 2, 1747	59
Poor Chance	[illegible]	Jan 7, 1811	1[illegible]
Poor Robin's Almanac?	Richard [illegible]	April 23, 1766	187
Prevention	James Walling, Jr	Dec 10, 1770	20
"	Thomas Lloyd	Sept 29, 1763	104
Purchase	Arthur Charlton	June 4, 174-	100
Ravine Spring	William Borland?	Sept 8, 1760	11[illegible]
Resurvey on [illegible] Misfortune	George French		115
Resurvey on Chester			388
" " Jericho Hills	John Ridout	March 10, 1775	62[illegible]
Resurvey on Joseph's Heritage	Henry Stultz	May 1, 1786	129
Resurvey on Lilley's Discovery	Samuel Lilley	Oct 29, 1776	45
Resurvey on Nicholas' Mistake		Sept 21, 1752	1025
Resurvey on part of [illegible] Lott	John Scott	April 4, 1770	293
Resurvey on part of [illegible] Lott	Christian Hyple?	April 1, 1785	208¾
Resurvey on part of [illegible]	[illegible] Cheny	Aug 5, 1766	16[illegible]¼
Resurvey on part of Well Taught	George Hartley?	June 16, 177[illegible]	183
Resurvey on Pleasant Valley	I. Houser	May 31, 1769	24[illegible]
Resurvey on Pete's Hill?		Dec 21, 1760	300
Resurvey on Saint Patrick	Isaac Houser	May 20, 1762	722
Resurvey on Saint Patrick's Lott	Isaac Houser	Dec 7, 1752	587
Resurvey on Smith's Lott	Mathias Otto	Sept 9, 1762	3[illegible]0
Resurvey on [illegible]	Samuel Hughes	Nov 14, 178[illegible]	852½
Resurvey on Webb's Discovery	Margaret Webb	Oct 24, 1788	451
Resurvey on White's Lott	James White	Nov 20, 1762	104
Rich Barrens	Paul Rhodes	Nov 25 1769	10[illegible]
Rich Barrens Resurvey	Peter [illegible]	June 1, 176[illegible]	115[illegible]
Richard's Choice	Thomas Prather	Oct 21, 1748	
Rocky Hill	Joseph Miller	March 29 1792	5
[illegible]	John [illegible]	Nov 28, 1792	40
Rocky Neck	Lancelot Jacques and Thomas Johnson	Feb 11 1764	548
Rutter's Delight	John Rutter	March 7, 1738	100
[illegible] Spring			26
Saint Patrick	Isaac Houser	Nov 1, 1743	50
Saint Patrick's Lott	Isaac Houser	Feb 1, 1737	127
Save All	Andrew Rench	Nov 29, 1759	50
" "	Philip Davis	July 12, 17[illegible]	50
Scant Timber	[illegible]	Feb 20, 176	210
Scared from Home	Nicholas Baird	Feb 7, 1760	13[illegible]
Scotch Lott Resurveyed	Henry Avey	March 19 1746	202
Scotch Lott Original	Evan McDonald	Dec 4, 1740	100
Scotch Lott and Resurvey	Henry Avey	March 19, 1746	202
Scott's Grief	William Douglass	Feb 12, 17[illegible]2	100
Scruple	Jacob Friend	May 26, 1764	40½
Search well and you will find	Anthony Bell	June 20, 1788	20¼
Second Addition	H. Toms	June 15, 1765	50
Settled in Time	Resurveyed for Joseph, John, and Andrew Rench	Dec 3, 1785	2227
Shoe Spring and Resurvey	James Spencer	Sept. 4, 1740	150
Shockey's Part of Third Resurvey of Sarah's Delight	Jacob Shockey	Oct 2, 1769	112
Shockey's Mistake	Jacob [illegible]	Dec 3, 1787	50
Sink Hole	Mathias Lizer	Dec 8, 1761	50
[illegible]	[illegible]	Nov 27, 1740	100
[illegible]	Francis Beatty	Dec 10, 1769	92
Sly Fox			42
Small Pit	John Snevely	Jan 31, 1761	10
Small Lot to David			40
Small Hope	Martin Rohrer	Aug 19, 1769	4
Small Spring	Andrew Rench	March 10, 1750	50
Smithfield	Patrick Murphy	Sept 29 1757	155
Smith's Choice	Peter Slusser	Jan 7 1761	50
[illegible] Friendship	George Moore	May 23 1739	84
Spring Garden	[illegible]	Sept [illegible], 17[illegible]7	1
[illegible]			[illegible]

Name of Lot	To Whom Granted	Date	Acres
Spring Head	Dr. Charles Carroll	May 20, 17[illegible]	
Stokes	Joseph Chapline	Feb 27, 1787	1[illegible]
Stone Walls	Lancelot Jacques and Thomas Johnson	Dec 6, 1767	4[illegible]
Steiner's Luck	John Steiner	Sept 11, 1764	
Stoney Choice	James Smith	Feb 2[illegible], 1761	4[illegible]
Stoney Hill	[illegible]	April 27 17[illegible]4	1[illegible]
Stoney Ridge	Peter [illegible]	Jan 7, 1764	[illegible]
Stoney Run	George [illegible]	May [illegible], 17[illegible]4	[illegible]
Stoney Valley	David Mong?	March 21, 1787	4
Strawberry Bottom	Richard Mackelfish	July 1, 176[illegible]	1
Strife	Edward Dawson	Aug 7, 17[illegible]	1[illegible]
Struggle	John Click	Aug 12, 1767	1[illegible]
Stull's Forest	John Stull	Feb 12 1764	1[illegible]
"	"	Feb 15 1761	[illegible]
Stoney Ridge	John Mcaster	July 18 176[illegible]	7[illegible]
Sugar Bottom	John Lloyd	1734	
Sweed's Delight	Charles Friend	Aug 15, 1738	[illegible]
The [illegible]	James Walling Sr	Nov 26, 1[illegible]	[illegible]
Tetrick's Folly	David Rose	May 23, 1766	2[illegible]
The Addition to Catherine's Part	Matthias Musselman	Feb 25, 1754	[illegible]
The Adventure	James Walling, Jr	Aug 15, 1762	1[illegible]
" Original			[illegible]
The Amendment of Dawson's Strife and Richman's Meadows	Peter Pench?	March 10, 1767	191[illegible]
The Barron Hills	Dr Charles Carroll	May 11, 17[illegible]	[illegible]
The Barrens	James [illegible]	May 11 1744	1[illegible]
The Chance	John Rowland?	Aug 11, 17[illegible]	110
The Conquest	James Bedford	July 11, 17[illegible]9	[illegible]7
The Forrest	Conveyed by [illegible] to Peter Hoover	Jan 17, 1774	1[illegible]
The Four Springs	Peter [illegible]		
The [illegible]	George Putman	March 1 1744	1[illegible]
The Hazzard	[illegible]	Oct 23, 1749	[illegible]
The Long Meadow	[illegible]	Feb 1, 1747	[illegible]
"	Thomas Cresap?	June 16 17[illegible]	[illegible]
The Mistake	Daniel Dulany	March 3, 1742-43	100
"	George French	Dec 4, 17[illegible]	1[illegible]
The Narrow Meadow	Henry [illegible]	Dec 2[illegible], 17[illegible]	[illegible]
The Notch	Dr. Charles Carroll	May 21, 17[illegible]	1[illegible]
The Old Fox Deceased	James Walling	Sept 9, 17[illegible]	1[illegible]
The [illegible]	—— [illegible]		[illegible]
The Saw Pitt	George [illegible]	Oct 22, 1754	1[illegible]
The Steeple	Walter [illegible]	Sept 29, 17[illegible]	10[illegible]
The Storm	Henry [illegible]	May 21, 1[illegible]	1[illegible]
The third time of asking	Charles Clune?	Sept 20 1797	6[illegible]
The Venture	Beverly [illegible]	Aug 11 17[illegible]	[illegible]
The White Oak Lick	Walter and Daniel Dulany	Sept 29 17[illegible]	2[illegible]
The Wife's Choice	Michael Hallam	May 1, 1767	[illegible]0
The Resurvey on Addition to [illegible]	Jacob Funk	Feb 17 17[illegible]	21[illegible]
The Barney's Venture	Barnabus Swope	Aug 24, 17[illegible]	[illegible]
The Castle Plains	William Boyd	Sept 29, 17[illegible]	4[illegible]0
The [illegible] Contrivance	Jacob Brumbaugh	Dec 10 17[illegible]	
The Dickson's Chance	Michael Kirkpatrick	Sept 1 1764	[illegible]
The Discontent	Matthew Clark	April 27, 17[illegible]	1[illegible]
The First Choice	Thomas Powell	Feb 15, 17[illegible]	[illegible]
The First Choice second resurvey	" "	Dec 1 1768	[illegible]
The French's Vineyard	Andrew Grim	Dec 10, 17[illegible]9	[illegible]
The Gaming Alley	John Rutter	Nov [illegible], 1752	1[illegible]
The [illegible] Loss	Daniel McCoy	June 25, 174[illegible]	[illegible]
The George's Mistake			
George's Venture, and the Barrens	George French	Dec 20 17[illegible]3	14[illegible]
The [illegible]	Michael Funk	March 2 1767	11
The Hartman Place		Feb. 19, 17[illegible]	[illegible]
The Hazzard	Hugh Gilliland	Oct 25, 174[illegible]	[illegible]
The Hazzard and Locust Thicket	Nathaniel Nesbitt	May 5 1761	[illegible]
The [illegible]	Robert Twiggs	Sept 20, 1753	[illegible]
The Lilley's Discovery, second resurvey	Samuel Lilley	Oct 29, 1776	[illegible]
The Locust Thicket	Nathaniel Nesbitt	May 5, 1761	[illegible]
The Ogle's Friendship			2[illegible]
The Resurvey on part of Bachelors' Delight	Joseph Chapline	Sept 19, 1763	41[illegible]
The Resurvey on part of Cadiz	Ezekiel [illegible]	Aug 5, 1766	1[illegible]9
The Resurvey on part of Kindness	Evan Shelby	March 12, 1771	424¾
The Resurvey on part of Simmons' Racket	I. Simmons		472
The Resurvey on part of Mountain of Wales	Evan Shelby	April 23, 1767	[illegible]
The Resurvey on part of Pleasant Bottom and part of Mountain of Wales	Isaac Baker	March 7, 17[illegible]	[illegible]
The Resurvey on part of Dawson's part of Well Taught	Jacob Lighter	April 1 17[illegible]	
The Resurvey on part of Sarah's Delight	Charles Carroll	March 10, 1753	[illegible]
The Resurvey on part of Sarah's Delight [illegible]		[illegible], 17[illegible]	[illegible]

Name of Lot	To Whom Granted	Date	Acres.
[illegible] survey on part of [illegible] Racket.	[illegible] Simmons	Oct 1, 1748	545
Resurvey on part of [illegible] Corner	Francis Rohrer	Dec 27, 1763	83
Resurvey on part of [illegible] of Wales	[illegible] Shelly	Feb 22 1763	9860
Resurvey on part of — Well Done	Moses Chaplin	Feb 1, 1764	1822
Resurvey on part of Well Taught	George Poe		1300
Resurvey on part of [illegible] Oak Grove	[illegible]	Feb 3, 17[illegible]	354
[illegible]	Henry Teims	Oct 16, 1[illegible]	18½
Three Friends and [illegible]	John Jones	Sept 9, 17[illegible]	9[illegible]
[illegible] Bottom	[illegible]	Sept [illegible], 17[illegible]	200
[illegible] Hills	Wm [illegible]	Jan 27 17[illegible]	20[illegible]
[illegible]	[illegible] Johnson	Feb 17, 1764	1417
[illegible] Lane	John Stull	[illegible] 9, 1767	41
[illegible]	[illegible], Jr	May 27, 17[illegible]	8½
[illegible] Good Will	[illegible]	[illegible]	
[illegible]	Jacob [illegible]	[illegible] 8 1781	224¾
[illegible]	[illegible] Hughes	April 15, 1770	24½
[illegible]	Joseph Chapline	Sept 21, 1759	75
[illegible]		Feb 21, 1763	42
[illegible]'s Lott	John Ulrich	April 18, 1765	50
[illegible]	Thomas Bowles	Oct 26, 1767	8[illegible]6
(Upper and Lower) In [illegible] Bottom	John Hamilton	Aug 10 1741	100
[illegible] Cold			50
[illegible]	Bumbarger		58
Walter's Welcome to An [illegible]	Samuel Hughes	April 1[illegible], 1770	4
Wall Neglect	William Dedings	July 9, 17[illegible]	197
Walnut Lott [illegible]	Jacob Bowman	[illegible] 1764	587
[illegible] Weather	John Snevely	Sept 5, 1769	313
Webb's Discovery (and resurvey)	Margaret Webb	Oct [illegible] 1769	451
[illegible] Home	[illegible]	Nov 22, 1756	11[illegible]
Well Done (Resurvey)	Moses Chapline	Feb 1, 1764	1822
Well Pleased	David [illegible]	June 19, 177[illegible]	600
Whisky (Original and First and Second Additions)	John Stull		
Whisky with First and Second Additions Resurveyed	John Stull	Oct 2[illegible] 1744	580
Whisky Alley	James Dickson	Nov 21 1752	115
White Oak Grove	Conrad Hogmire	April 16 1[illegible]	50
" Plains	[illegible] David, & George Peters	Nov 3 1812	6[illegible]4
" Stun[illegible]	[illegible]		50
[illegible] Hill	Bamb[illegible]		50
Wolf [illegible]	Thomas Wells	May 17, 1765	50
" Spring	Nicholas Beard	March 1 1762	50
Woodstock	Robert Owen	April 6, 1762	
Woolwich	Michael [illegible]		
Heister [illegible]	Daniel Heister	April 1[illegible], 1784	14[illegible]
Ash Swamp	Joseph Perry	Jan 12, 17[illegible]	200
[illegible]	[illegible]	Aug 20, 17[illegible]	1780
Green Bottom	Wm Williams	Nov 17 1741	250
[illegible]	[illegible] Hager	March 2[illegible] 1762	118
Williams Chance	George Williams	Feb 24, 1762	150
[illegible]	Thomas Gatterell	Dec 14, 1739	50
Plumb [illegible]	Charles Lucas	Oct 22, 1759	300
[illegible]	Col Thomas Cresap	May 1 17[illegible]	160
Little Thought	Joseph Chapline	Feb [illegible], 1763	[illegible]
Huckleberry Hall	Daniel [illegible]	Dec [illegible] 1742	100
The Three Springs	George Stewart	Oct 26, 1739	22[illegible]
Hagers Fancy	Jonathan Hager	Dec 1[illegible] 1739	200
Iron Mountain	Dr Charles Carroll	April [illegible], 1749	50
Sally's Misfortune	"	April 10, 1749	250
Hanover	"	June 10 17[illegible]	1010
Marie [illegible]	Nicholas Cr[illegible]	Sept 18 17[illegible]	50
Walnut Level	Richard Snowden	Dec [illegible]	50
The Hurry	Daniel Dulany	July 24 1744	100
[illegible]	Cornelius O Neal	Sept 7, 1741	50
Hills and Dales	Joseph Chapline	June 2[illegible] 1749	50
Perrin's Adventure	John Perrin	Nov 20 1739	100
Burrell's Bower	Francis Burrell	Aug 20, 1742	50
Elting's Right	Cornelius Elting	Oct 2[illegible] 1742	32[illegible]
Caledonia	Geo Frazier Hawkins	Oct 31 1765	3910
Park's Hall	William Parks	Nov 24, 1752	1550
Pile's Delight	Richard Sprigg	Dec 14, 1742	7[illegible]
The Addition to Pile's Delight	Col Edward Sprigg	Aug 9, 1743	117
The Resurvey of the Addition to Pile's Delight	Col Edward Sprigg	Jan [illegible] 1750	2617
[illegible]	Daniel Dulany	Oct 1[illegible] 17[illegible]	100
[illegible]	Andrew Stevenson	June [illegible] 17[illegible]	1[illegible]
The First S[illegible]	Peter R[illegible]	Aug 10 17[illegible]	1[illegible]
The White Oak Land	Robert Chel[illegible]	[illegible] 1777	47[illegible]
[illegible]	John Weit	Sept 24 17[illegible]	50
The Resurvey on part of Striking Hill	Richard Henderson	April 17, 1757	1[illegible]

Name of Lot	To Whom Granted	Date	Acres.
New Design	John Knox	Feb 1, 1791	1[illegible]
Hunting Ground	Joseph Chapline	May 19, 1[illegible]	[illegible]
Elwick's Dwelling	John Elwick	Aug 4 17[illegible]	1[illegible]0
"	Joseph Smith	Feb 1 1747	270[illegible]
Smith's Purchase	"	May 1 1747	[illegible]
Hopewell	Joseph Chapline	Aug 11 17[illegible]	1[illegible]
Porto Sancto	James Smith	July 1[illegible] 17[illegible]	[illegible]
Welch's Lott (resurvey)	Jacob Koontz	May 17, 17[illegible]	1[illegible]
" "	Wm Welch	Sept 2[illegible], 1760	2[illegible]
Conn's Lott	George Conn	March 5, 1762	2[illegible]
Dragon's Disappointment	J[illegible] Walling	March 8 1[illegible]	[illegible]
Walling's Mistake	Alex McCollum	"	2[illegible]½
Manlum	Henry Kendrick	Oct 17, 17[illegible]	
Funny Luck Pond	Peter Bench	March 1[illegible] 17[illegible]	[illegible]0
The Resurvey on Free Stone	Joseph Wolgamott	June 27, 17[illegible]	5[illegible]
The Adventure	James Walling	Nov 10 17[illegible]	[illegible]0
Long Meadow	Thos Cresap	June 1[illegible] 17[illegible]	[illegible]
Addition to Long Meadow	[illegible] Cresap	July [illegible], 17[illegible]	1[illegible]0
The west addition to Long Meadow	Thos Cresap	Aug 8 17[illegible]	1[illegible]
Long Meadow enlarged	Daniel Dulany, Jr	Nov [illegible] 1751	2[illegible]
" " "	Col Henry Boquett	Sept 1[illegible] 1[illegible]	4[illegible]
Whiteman's Prospect	Henry [illegible]	Feb [illegible] 17[illegible]	10[illegible]
The Resurvey on Deceit	Joseph Perry	Feb 17, 17[illegible]	[illegible]8
Darling Side	John Charlton	Oct 26 1752	4[illegible]0
Stiller's Home	Andrew, Nicholas, George, Michael, Peter, Catharine, Ann and Elizabeth Stiller	May 12 1801	3[illegible]
Sawers' Lodge	Jacob Mills	Aug 10 17[illegible]	[illegible]
Fiddle Stone	John Williams	July 1[illegible], 17[illegible]	50
Luck	Isaac Baker	Aug 11, 1[illegible]	12½
Painter's Range	Daniel Painter	Feb 1, 1787	[illegible]0
The Resurvey on Round Meadow	Henry Rhodes	July 17, 17[illegible]	[illegible]
The Resurvey on Timber Land	Dr Upton Scott	July 7, 17[illegible]	20[illegible]
Liberty	Francis Deakins	Dec [illegible] 17[illegible]	4[illegible]
Antietam Hills	John [illegible]	Sept 2[illegible], 17[illegible]	1[illegible]
Smallest Five	John M Jordan	Nov [illegible], 17[illegible]	17[illegible]
Garden of Eden	Leonard Marbury and Otho H Williams	June 3 1788	
Shippey's Neglect	Joseph [illegible]	Aug 21 1749	74
The Resurvey on Canoe Bottom	Robert Wells	Oct 1[illegible], 17[illegible]	2[illegible]
Aground in Peace	Jacob [illegible]	Jan 11 1[illegible]	[illegible]
Walnut Grove	Edmond Tolliar	Aug 31 1741	17[illegible]
Timber Wood	Jos Graybell	May 14, 17[illegible]	[illegible]
[illegible] Oak [illegible]	"		[illegible]
[illegible] Enough	Jacob [illegible]	July 13 17[illegible]	[illegible]
[illegible]	James Dickson	July 1[illegible] 17[illegible]	10[illegible]
[illegible] Delight	"	Jan 7 17[illegible]	20[illegible]
Salisbury	Hugh Parker	Feb 27 17[illegible]	1119
Hager's Fancy	Jacob Hager	March 19, 1747	7
The Resurvey on Walnut Point	Wm [illegible]	Aug 10 1753	3[illegible]
The Resurvey on Dawson's Stuff	Peter Rench	Jan 17, 17[illegible]	
Cousin's Obligement	Andrew Hoover	Feb 1[illegible] 17[illegible]	51
The Chance	Jacob Brumbaugh	May 11 17[illegible]	[illegible]
Brumbaugh's Lott	"	Feb 2[illegible], 17[illegible]	[illegible]
Joe's Lott	Joseph Chapline, Jr	Sept 7 1770	21[illegible]
Hunting the Hare	Joseph Chapline	Nov 1 17[illegible]	
Alston's Forest	Thos Alston	Nov 2[illegible] 17[illegible]	
Dorsey's Risque	Edward Dorsey	Dec 14 17[illegible]	[illegible]
Water Sink	Joseph Tomlinson	Aug 27, 17[illegible]	—
The Resurvey on Hopewell	Joseph Chapline	17[illegible]	717
Loss and Gain	"	April 11, 17[illegible]	11[illegible]
Addition to Loss and Gain	"	Oct 18 17[illegible]	1[illegible]
Long Sought	John Wilson	Aug 10 17[illegible]	12
[illegible]well	Philip Keywanghover	April 10 17[illegible]	90
Whisky Alley	Caleb Touchstone	March 18, 174[illegible]	67
The Resurvey on Whisky Alley	Philip Keywanghover	Sept 14 17[illegible]	[illegible]
Chews Farm	Samuel Chew, Jr	June 2 17[illegible]	[illegible]
Dear Bought	James Wardrobe	Oct 10, 17[illegible]	[illegible]
The Resurvey on Sprigg's Delight	Peter Rench	July 27, 17[illegible]	[illegible]
Hallum's Lookout	William Hallum	Nov 13 17[illegible]	2[illegible]
Hard Fortune	John Mackintire	April [illegible] 17[illegible]	50
Scotch Well	James Smith	Sept 29 17[illegible]	[illegible]
Mistaken Friend	Edward Ricketts	Oct 2 17[illegible]	11[illegible]
Content	Ralph Higginbottom	Jan 1[illegible] 17[illegible]	11[illegible]
Spring Hill	James Smith	Oct 12 17[illegible]	8[illegible]
Mill Fly	John House	Dec 1 17[illegible]	[illegible]
[illegible] Dutch Lo[illegible]	John Vandever	Sept [illegible] 17[illegible]	1[illegible]
Gaither's [illegible]	Henry Gaither	Oct 21, 17[illegible]	[illegible]
The Resurvey on Dry Land	Andrew [illegible]	July [illegible] 17[illegible]	1[illegible]
[illegible]	[illegible]	Aug 1 17[illegible]	[illegible]
Long Looked for	Robert [illegible]	July 2[illegible] 17[illegible]	1[illegible]
Grandfather's Gift	Henry Hollingsworth, Jr	Nov 1[illegible] 17[illegible]	
The Resurvey on part of Park's Hall	Andrew [illegible]	July 2[illegible] 17[illegible]	[illegible]
[illegible]	[illegible]	[illegible]	[illegible]

This lot began at a bounded white-oak standing on the side of a hill with[illegible] yards of the said Hager's dwelling house, which shows that he was first in [illegible]

Name of Lot	To Whom Granted	Date	Acres
Cheney's Neck	Charles Cheney	Sept 29 1754	[illegible]2
Sweed's Delight	Charles F[illegible]	July 11 1749	260
Addition to Fickel's Bottom	Dr David Ross	Sept 2[illegible] 1761	495
Keep Triste	John Sample	Sept 2[illegible] 1764	10 202
Smith's Hills[1]	James Smith	April 17 1[illegible]4[illegible]	205
Funk's Jum[illegible]	Michael Funk	Feb 19 17[illegible]	50
Shadrick's Lott	C Atkinson	May 6 17[illegible]1	21[illegible]
Nancy's Fancy	Joseph [illegible]	March 1[illegible] 1764	341
Draper's Chance	John Draper	Dec 24 17[illegible]4	20
The Shoe Spring	James Spencer	Sept 4, 1740	150
The Resurvey on the Shoe Spring	John Stull	Oct 3 17[illegible]	510
Rogue's Harbour	William Stroope	Aug 10 17[illegible]	110
Duckett's Misfortune	Richard Duckett	March 19 1744	200
Mill Place	William Yates	Dec 13 1764	[illegible]0
Chance	Dr Henry Schnebly	March 10 1770	112
"	Henry Shryock	June 10 1771	42[illegible]
Long Look'd For	John Perry	Nov 2, 17[illegible]4	1[illegible]0
Colmore's Ramble	Colmore Beanes	Feb. 28, 174[illegible]	6[illegible]
Darling's Delight	Thomas H[illegible]	Oct 23 17[illegible]	1[illegible]0
Conoloway's Neck	James Dickson	Aug 24, 1747	100
Pool's Meadow	Charles Beall	Jan 11, 1748	100
Boston	David Ross, Richard Henderson and Samuel Beall J	July 25 17[illegible]	8025
Johnson's Lott	Peter Johnson	April 7, 174[illegible]	139
Turkey Hill	Michael Mills	April 16 17[illegible]4	87
Skip Thorn	Col Thomas Cresap	June 16, 17[illegible]9	[illegible]70
Strife	William Chapline	July 20, 1740	100
Bachelors' Hall	Thomas Mills	April 1 1748	1[illegible]0
The Widow's Last Shift	Ann Keisher	July 31 1749	100
The Ash Swamp	John George Arnold	Jan 16 17[illegible]9	1[illegible]0
Pleasant Bottom	William Boyd	Nov 12, 1759	100

Indian Antiquities — The antiquities of the county are very interesting In the vicinity of Sharpsburg there are mounds and earthworks, some of which have been destroyed and others of which having been excavated were found to contain numerous interesting archæological specimens Tradition says that a most bloody affair occurred on the Antietam Creek near its mouth (which is distant three miles south of Sharpsburg) more than a century ago, between those hostile and warlike tribes, the Catawbas and Delawares, who, it is said, were engaged in a strife when this section of the country was first known, and so continued for a long period subsequent This event occurred some time between the years 1730 and 1736 The evidences of this conflict are still apparent in the skeletons which from time to time are exhumed

On the farms of the heirs of William Hebb distant two miles west of Sharpsburg, and near the Potomac River, vast quantities of arrow-heads, pestles, skinning-knives, and tomahawks of superior workmanship have been found

On the farm of Lafayette Miller, about a mile and a half from Sharpsburg and adjoining the lands of the last mentioned farm, an abundance of stone implements have been brought to light These implements were found in the fields, and were particularly numerous on the hills Some curiously-wrought stones, varying from three to six inches in diameter, and about two inches in thickness have been found from time to time on this farm They are perfectly flat on both sides, and polished A short distance from this farm, and bordering on the Potomac River, is the farm of Samuel Beeler, where two small stone mounds have been discovered, one of them [illegible]ut twel[illegible] in length and six in width The[illegible] [illegible]e comp[illegible] small stones One had been opened years ag[illegible] other was excavated recently After working f[illegible] eral hours in throwing off the loose stones, a [illegible] was found ingeniously constructed beneath it [illegible] bottom was laid with flat stone, the sides and [illegible] composed of the same set up in a slanting po[illegible] and the covering was of large flat stone, built [illegible] form of a comb roof of a house In this mound [illegible] found the remains of a skeleton, some broken [illegible] of pottery, and the part of a stone knife

On the farm of the heirs of the late Jacob M[illegible] two miles south of Sharpsburg, on a high bluff [illegible]dering on the Potomac River, are two extensive [illegible] mounds, which had been partly explored some tw[illegible] years ago, but on a more recent examination [illegible] found to contain bones, pottery flints, etc [illegible] mounds were about twelve feet long, six feet [illegible] and were composed entirely of stone The b[illegible] were so much decayed that they crumbled into [illegible] on being handled A few years ago a skeleton [illegible] found near this mound buried in a perpendicular [illegible]sition At the head was a small vessel of pott[illegible] holding about a quart, which fell to pieces on [illegible] handled

About a mile and a half from this point, on [illegible] farm of William Blackford, several articles of pott[illegible] have been unearthed Traces of some earth [illegible] still exist, and beautifully finished arrow-heads still to be found

On the lands of James Marker, three miles so[illegible] east of Sharpsburg, is a cave, which tradition s[illegible] was used both as a dwelling and a burial place Th[illegible] cave is about twenty feet in diameter and abo[illegible] feet in height, and contains two rooms The o[illegible] room has been partially explored The openi[illegible] the inner room is so small that it would be difficul[illegible] access In digging in this cave a year or two [illegible] quantity of ashes and burnt bones were found, l[illegible] underneath large flat stones There were also [illegible] ornaments, arrow heads, and flints and a pipe [illegible] quisite workmanship On a bluff of land opp[illegible] the Antietam Furnace building, on the left-hand s[illegible] of the creek, is a small stone mound While s[illegible] workmen were putting up a fence, which came d[illegible] over the mound they found a skeleton apparently [illegible] a good state of preservation In Cedar Grove [illegible] Rohrersville, are several small earth mounds wh[illegible] it is said are the burial places of the aborigine[illegible] every farm within a radius of three miles [illegible] Sharpsburg are to be found numerous specimen[illegible] imp[illegible] [illegible] [illegible]ale

[1] Originally [illegible] Dr [illegible] [illegible]art, D[illegible]

When the Chesapeake and Ohio Canal was being constructed, tomahawks, arrow-heads, and ornaments were found in its bed. On the canal, near a place called Mercerville, is an old burial-ground, containing half an acre, which no doubt belonged to the Indians. On this spot are found pottery, bones, ornaments, and stems of pipes, etc. About two feet below the surface the bodies were buried. Ashes and burnt bones were found in the graves.

At the coke-yard at the Antietam Furnace, bordering on the Chesapeake and Ohio Canal, three miles south of Sharpsburg, is an Indian burial-ground. At this point, tradition informs us, a fierce battle was fought between the Catawbas and Delawares, which resulted in the destruction of the Delawares.

At Reynolds' Dam, on the Potomac River, Maryland side, one mile south of Shepherdstown, W. Va., an abundance of fragments of pottery have been found from time to time, which plainly indicate that this point was the site of an ancient aboriginal pottery. At Eakles' Mills, one mile south of Keedysville, at what is known as the limestone quarries, belonging to the Baltimore and Ohio Railroad, some singular indentations are to be seen in the rocks, and no doubt were the work of the Indians. They are of the shape of a basin, varying from the size of a basin to that of a tea-cup. These might have been used for pounding hominy, mixing paint, etc., as several pestles were found near these rocks. In quarrying the workmen came upon several caves and fissures in the rocks, which led a considerable distance under the hill, and which, no doubt, were used by the aborigines. In a few of the rocks were impressions like footprints, and also singular characters like letters or hieroglyphics. In various other portions of the county are similar memorials of the original occupants of the soil.

CHAPTER XLI.

PUBLIC OFFICIALS.

As Washington County was part of Frederick until 1776, the names of many of the officers selected by the people of Washington from time to time or appointed by the executive are comprised in the list of Frederick County officials. The same is true of their representatives in the Continental army. At the session of the Provincial Convention held at Annapolis, Dec. 7, 1775, there was no delegate present from the upper district (now Washington County) of Frederick, but on the 18th of [illegible] "Mr. William Baird, a member of the upper district of Frederick County, appeared and took his seat in the House." About this time Charles and Thomas Beatty were prominent among the patriots of Frederick County, and their names are mentioned on several different occasions in the proceedings of the convention. On the 14th of August in the following year the convention again assembled at Annapolis, and among its members were Samuel Beall, Samuel Hughes, John Stull, and Henry Schnebly, as delegates from the upper district of Frederick. On the 6th of September the new county of Washington was formed by act of the convention, and since that date the following is a list of citizens of the county who have either been elected or appointed to office:

GOVERNOR OF MARYLAND.

Wm. T. Hamilton, elected 1879.

UNITED STATES SENATOR.

William T. Hamilton, term of service, 1869 to 1875.

CONGRESSMEN.

Thomas Sprigg, 1793–1809; Daniel Heister, 1809–4; Roger Nelson, 1805; Samuel Ringgold, 1810, 1812, 1816, 1818; John Thomson Mason, 1840; J. Dixon Roman, 1846; William T. Hamilton, 1848–54.

PRESIDENTIAL ELECTORS.

Samuel Hughes,[1] 1792; Martin Kershner, 1801; Frisby Tilghman, 1805; Nathaniel Rochester, 1809; Daniel Rentch, 1812; John Buchanan, 1817; William Gabby, 1821; William Fitzhugh, Jr., 1828; William Price, 18[illegible], 18[illegible], 1845; J. D. Roman, 1849; R. H. Alvey, 1853; J. D. Roman, 1857; Isaac Nesbit, 1865; J. Thomson Mason, 1869.

STATE SENATORS FROM WASHINGTON COUNTY.

1781–8[illegible], Samuel Hughes, May 9th, to fill the vacancy caused by the death of Charles Carroll, barrister; 1786–90, Samuel Hughes, December 2d, in place of Thomas Johnson, who did not accept; 1801–6, Samuel Ringgold; 1806, John Thomson Mason; 1811–14, Moses Tabbs; 1816–18, William T. Mason; 1821–24, William Price; 1836, William Price; 1838, Robert Wason; 1840–45, John Newcomer; 1846–50, William B. Clark; 1852–53, George French; 1854–57, George Schley; 1858–61, John G. Stone; 1862–64, Lewis T. Fiery; 1865–67, Elias Davis; 1868–70, James H. Grove; 1872–74, Z. S. Claggett; 1876–78, David H. Newcomer; 1880–82, Joseph H. Farrow.

MEMBERS OF THE HOUSE OF DELEGATES FROM WASHINGTON COUNTY.

1777.—Joseph Sprigg, John Barnes, Samuel Hughes, Henry Schnebely.

1779–82.—John Stull, John Barnes, Joseph Sprigg, James Chapline.

1783.—John Stull, James Chapline, Nicholas Swingle, John J. Jacob.

1784.—John Stull, John Cellars, Nicholas Swingle, Thomas Hart.

1785.—John Stull, John Cellars, Jacob Funk, Henry Snively.

[1] Mr. Hughes was not present at the election, and consequently did not cast his vote. George Washington was unanimously [illegible] Vice-President.

1786 —John Cellars, Jacob Funk, John Stull, Richard Cromwell
1787 —Jacob Funk, Andrew Bruce, John Cellers, Ignatius Taylor
1788 —Thomas Sprigg, Henry Shryock, Ignatius Taylor, John Lynn
1789 —Henry Shryock, John Stull, Adam Ott, John Lynn
1790 —Adam Ott, Nathaniel Rochester, John Cellars, Lancelot Jacques, Jr
1791 —Adam Ott, John Cellers William Clagett, Benoni Swearingen
1792 —Adam Ott, Benoni Swearingen, Richard Cromwell, Lancelot Jacques, Jr
1793 —Benoni Swearingen, Matthew Van Lear, Robert Hughes, William Clarke
1794 —Henry Schnebly, Martin Kershner, Robert Hughes, William Clarke
1795 —Samuel Ringgold, Richard Cromwell, John Barnes, Lancelot Jacques
1796 —John Celler, Thomas Bowles, James McClain, Robert Douglass
1797 —Martin Kershner, Cephas Beall, Ambrose Geohogan, John Buchanan
1798 —Martin Kershner, John Cellers, Ambrose Geohogan, John Buchanan
1799 —John Buchanan, Ambrose Geohogan, James McClaine, John Cellers
1800 —John Cellers Robert Smith, Ambrose Geohegan, Richard Cromwell
1801 —Robert Smith, John Cellers, Frisby Tilghman, Adam Ott
1802 —Martin Kershner, Richard Cromwell, Robert Smith, Frisby Tilghman
1803 —Martin Kershner, Jacob Zeller, Robert Smith, William Yates
1804 —John Bowles, William Yates, Tench Ringgold, Benjamin Clagett
1805 —John Bowles, Robert Smith, Tench Ringgold, William Yates
1806 —John Bowles, Tench Ringgold, Martin Kershner, David Schnebly
1807 —John Bowles, David Schnebly, Moses Tabbs, Upton Lawrence, William Gabby, *vice* Lawrence, resigned
1808 —Frisby Tilghman, William Gabby, William Downey John Bowles
1809 —John Bowles, George Celler, Moses Tabbs, William L Brent
1810 —John Bowles, Thomas B Hall, Dr William Downey, Dr William B Williams
1811 —John Bowles, Thomas B Hall, Dr William Downey, Charles G Boerstler
1812 —John Bowles, Henry Lewis, William B Williams, William O Sprigg
1813-14 —Frisby Tilghman, John T Mason Martin Kershner, William Gabby
1815 —Martin Kershner, Jacob Schnebly, John Bowles, Edward G Williams
1816 —Edward G Williams, John Bowles, Jacob Schnebly, Christian Hager
1817 —Henry Sweitzer, William Yates, Jacob Schnebly, Thomas Kennedy
1818 —William Yates, Thomas Keller, Thomas Kennedy, Jacob Schnebly
1819 —Jacob Schnebly, Thomas Keller, Joseph Gabby, Thomas Kennedy
1820 —Joseph Gabby Thomas Kennedy, Andrew Kershner, John Lead
1821 —John Bowles, Joseph Gabby, Andrew Kershner, Caspar W Weaver
1822 —Thomas Kennedy (author of the bill abolishing the religious test in Maryland), Ignatius Drury, Elie Williams (died before taking his seat), Thomas Keller Benjamin Galloway *vice* Williams
1823 —Andrew Kershner, Joseph Gabby, James H Bowles, Joseph I Merrick
1824 —James H Bowles Henry Fouke, Isaac S White, Joseph I Merrick
1825 —Joseph I Merrick, Andrew Kershner, Lancelot Jacques, Jr, Thomas Kennedy
1826 —Thomas B Hall, Robert M Tidball, Jonathan Newcomer William H Fitzhugh
1827 —William H Fitzhugh, John Wolgamot Daniel Reich William Yates
1828 —Jonathan Shafer, Benjamin F Yoe, Jacob Miller, Robert H Beatty
1829 —Benjamin F Yoe, David Brookhart, John Witmer, and Daniel Donnelly
1830 —Andrew Kershner, Benjamin F Yoe, David Brookhart, Joseph I Merrick
1831 —David Brookhart, Joseph Hollman, John Hall, William H Fitzhugh
1832 —John H Mann, Joseph Hollman, Thomas Kennedy, John D Grove, Joseph Weast *vice* Kennedy
1833 —John H Mann, John O Wharton, John D Grove, Frederick Humrickhouse
1834 —Joseph Weast, John O Wharton, Andrew Kershner, John Weltz
1835 —John V Wharton, Michael Newcomer, David Brookhart Jacob Fiery
1836 —John H Mann, Michael Swingley, Andrew Rench, Andrew Kershner
1837 —John H Mann, Michael Swingley, Andrew Rench, John Witmer, Jr
1838 —John O Wharton, John T Mason, Frederick Byers, John D Grove
1839 —John Thompson Mason, Michael Newcomer, Frederick Byer, William McK Kepler
1840 —David Claggett, Lewis Zeigler, Isaac Nesbit, Joseph Weast
1841 —Samuel Lyday, Jacob H Grove, Jervis Spencer, Joseph Hollman
1842 —Jonathan Nesbit Jr, Jacob H Grove, William Weber, Horatio N Hirne, Edward L Boteler
1843 —Warford Mann, William Weber, Henry Wade, Edward L Boerstler, Joseph Hollman
1844 —Wm B Clarke, Hezekiah Boerstler, Isaac Motter, John D Hart, Charles A Fletcher
1845 —George W Smith Elie Crampton, John Cushwa, of D, Lewis Tritle, Henry W Dellinger
1846 —Wm L Doyle George French, Joseph Fetter, Benjamin Reigle, Wm F Hamilton
1847 —George French, Hezekiah Boteler George L Zeigler, Robert Fowler, Times Brays
1849 —Thos Davis, Andrew K Stake, Jacob Smith, Elie Crampton Jeremiah S Besore
1852-53 —George Cushwa, John Wolf, George Strause, Edward M Mealey Wilfred D McCardell
1854 —Solomon Helser, T H Crampton Daniel J Grove Andrew K Syester Denton Jacques
1856 —Lewis P Fiery, Benjamin Witmer, David Lecher ? William Loughridge, John Corby
1858 —George C Rohrer John Wesley Summers, John I [illegible]

18[illegible].—James Coudy, Martin Eakle, John C. Brinning, George Freaner, Andrew K. Stake.

18[illegible].—December Session, George Pearson, Samuel Rohrer, John J. Thomas, F. Dorsey Herbert, John V. L. Findlay; April Session, Martin Eakle, John C. Brinning.

18[illegible].—Jno. V. L. Findley, Samuel Rohrer, George Pearson, Jno. J. Thomas, F. Dorsey Herbert.

1864.—Wm. Cushwa, Jacob B. Masters, Jacob A. Miller, Henry Gantz, Frederick Zeigler.

1865.—E. F. Anderson, Henry S. Eavey, Henry S. Miller, Frederick K. Ziegler, Benjamin F. Cromise.

1867.—R. C. Bamford, A. R. Appleman, Jonathan Toboy, Jacob Hoffhine, Joseph P. Bishop.

18[illegible].—A. K. Syester, James Coudy, F. Dorsey Herbert, Elias E. Rohrer, David Seibert.

1870.—Alex. Neill, John Welty, John Murdock, J. Monroe Sword, David Seibert.

1872.—Augustus H. Young, Moses Whitson, David H. Newcomer, Charles Ardinger.

1874.—Alonzo Berry, George Freaner, W. H. Grimes, A. K. Stake.

1876.—J. McPherson Scott, Lewis C. Smith, Joseph H. Farrow, Henry E. Ranger.

1878.—Joseph H. Farrow, Nathaniel Fiery, Joseph Harrison, Wm. H. Perkins.

1880.—Henry Funk, Thomas H. Crampton, Dr. J. E. Holmes, Dr. J. McPherson Scott.

1882.—Wm. D. Kelly, George A. Davis, George W. Pittman, Peter J. Mayberry.

MEMBERS OF THE CONVENTIONS OF MARYLAND.

Convention of 1776.—Samuel Beall, Samuel Hughes, John Stull, Henry Schnebly.

Convention to Ratify Constitution of the United States, 1788.—John Stull, Moses Rawlings, Thomas Sprigg, Henry Shryock.

Constitutional Convention of 1851.—George Schley, Lewis P. Fiery, Alexander Neill, Jr., John Newcomer, Thomas Harbine, Michael Newcomer.

Constitutional Convention of 1864.—Peter Negley, Henry W. Dellinger, James P. Mahugh, John R. Sneary, Lewis B. Nyman, Joseph F. Davis.

Constitutional Convention of 1867.—Andrew K. Syester, R. H. Alvey, Joseph Murray, S. S. Cunningham, William Motter, George Pole.

OFFICERS IN 1777.

Justices of the County Court, Samuel Beall, John Stull, Joseph Sprigg, Samuel Hughes, Henry Schnebly, Joseph Chapline, John Rainor, Richard Davis, Andrew Bruse, Andrew Rench, William Yates, Lemuel Barrett, Thomas Crompton, Christopher Crune, John Cellar; County Surveyor, Thomas Brook; Register of Wills, Thomas Sprigg; Coroners, James Waring, William Baird; Judge of the Court of Appeals, John Thomson Mason, appointed January, 1806; Richard Sprigg, appointed later in the same month, and John Buchanan, in place of Mr. Mason, who did not accept.

ATTORNEY-GENERAL.

John Thomson Mason, appointed July 12, 1806, to succeed William Pinkney; Mr. Mason resigned in October of the same year; Andrew K. Syester, elected November, 1871.

JUDGES OF THE CIRCUIT COURT.

John Buchanan, appointed for Fifth District, January, 1806; Thomas Buchanan, appointed for Fifth District, May 5, 1815; William [illegible], associate judge, appointed for Fifth District, May 5, 1815; Daniel Weisel, qualified as associate judge for Fourth District, November, 1861; Daniel Weisel, qualified as associate judge for Fifth District, November, 1864; George French, qualified as associate judge for Fifth District, January, 1865; R. H. Alvey, qualified as associate judge for Fourth District, November, 1867; W. Motter, qualified as associate judge for Fourth District, November, 1867.

STATE'S ATTORNEY FOR WASHINGTON COUNTY.

1859, W. Motter; 1863-64, T. M. Darby; 1869, H. H. Keedy; 1871, John C. Zeller; 1873, H. H. Keedy; 1875, Edward Stake; 1879, John F. A. Remley.

In 1838, Edward A. Lynch was appointed deputy to the attorney-general of Maryland for the counties of Washington and Allegany, to succeed James Dixon, deceased.

COUNTY COMMISSIONERS.

1830, David Claggett, Henry Firey, M. Van Lear, Jr., Henry Lyday; 1832, John Witmer, David Claggett, Robert Wason, Samuel M. Hill, Andrew Rench, Henry Firey; 1834, Thomas Hammond, Benjamin Oswald, Jonathan Shafer, David Rohrer, Nathaniel Swingley, David Claggett, John Sheppard, Andrew Rench; 1835, John Miller; 1836, W. H. Greve, George Sprecker, Frederick Dorsey, Henry Ankeney, John Sheppard, John Ringer, David Rohrer; 1838, W. H. Grove, Andrew Rentch, John C. Dorsey, Michael Smith, James Coudy; 1840, Horatio N. Harris, Eli Crampton, Samuel Lyday, Robert Fowler; 1842, John Otto, John Ash, Daniel South, Solomon Helser, James Coudy, John Horine, Jacob Adams, Emery Edwards, George Poe; 1844, Samuel Coss, John Ash, John C. Dorsey, Jereb Mason, J. Snively, John Horine, John Oswald, Wm. Easton, Wm. E. Doyle; 1846, John Newcomer, Michael Smith; 1847, John C. Dorsey; 1848, Lewis Watson; 1849, Wm. B. McClain; 1850, Jacob Funk, A. Leiter, John Shafer, Frederick Rohrer; 1853, Martin Eakle, Daniel Startzman, Jacob Newcomer, Joseph H. Piper, David Cushwa; 1855, J. J. Bowers, John Wachtel, Jonathan Schindel, Jacob Nicodemus, John Kretzer; 1857, Joseph Garver, Daniel Mentzer, John Kretzer, John Feidt, Jonathan Middlekauff; 1859, John Newcomer, David Cushwa, John Welty, Samuel Doub, A. Leiter; 1861, John Richard, Michael Newcomer, Daniel Startzman, William Rulett, Lancelot Jacques; 1863, John Reichard, William Rulett, Lancelot Jacques, John Zeller, Elias E. Rohrer; 1864, John Reichard, William Rulett, Lancelot Jacques, John Zeller, Elias E. Rohrer; 1865, John Zeller, John Reichard, George T. Heyser, Henry Adams, Frederick Bell; 1867, David Cushwa, David Hoover, Jr., B. F. Byers, John Shiffler, John Ash; 1869, J. G. Brown, Elias Eakle, J. J. Moore, F. T. Spickler, S. Bowles; 1871, Theo. Embry, Henry F. Neikirk, Samuel Strite, H. W. Lyday, John H. Harp; 1873, John Fessler, Joseph Seibert, Henry Funk, Elias Young, G. W. Brown; 1875, John Harp, J. W. Stonebraker, Isaac Aukeny, Jonas S. Deaner, P. R. Doub; 1877, J. W. Stonebraker, Isaac Ankeny, John J. Hersley, John M. Newcomer, Joseph Newcomer; 1879, J. W. Stonebraker, Joseph Newcomer, William T. Hassett, William Creager, John Helfelower.

CLERKS OF CIRCUIT COURT.

1845–64, Isaac Nesbitt; 1865, Lewis E. Nyman;[1] 1867, Wm. McK. Keppler; 1873–79, George B. Oswald.

The present deputy clerks are George I. Burkhart, O. B. Ridenour, P. J. Adams, and George T. Lolter.

[1] To fill vacancy [illegible] Isaac Nesbitt.

COUNTY SURVEYORS

Jonas Hogmire was appointed county surveyor by the Governor and Council, January, 1815, and was succeeded by Marmaduke W Boyd in June, 1818 Prior to Hogmire, Joseph Sprigg had held the office some twenty five or more years The succeeding surveyors have been

1848, S S Downin 1853, Thomas Taggart 1855, Isaac H ——, 1857, George W Bowers, 1859, Isaiah S Poe 1862-65, James Brown, 1867-73, S S Downin, 1875, Isaac H Durborow S S Downin, the present surveyor, qualified in November, 1877, and in November, 1879

JUDGES OF THE ORPHANS' COURT

1806, Ignatius Taylor, Elie Williams, Jacob Harry, Jacob Schnebly, 1807, Ignatius Taylor, Elie Williams, Jacob Schnebly, Frisby Tilghman, 1808-11, Elie Williams, Jacob Schnebly, Frisby Tilghman, 1812, Jacob Schnebly, Frisby Tilghman, Thomas B Hall, 1815-16, Matthew Van Lear, Alexander Neill, Richard Ragan, 1817-19, Alexander Ragan, Eli Beatty 1820, Jacob Schnebly, Frisby Tilghman, Thomas Kellar 1821-24, Jacob Schnebly, Thomas Kellar, William Gabby, 1855, Charles G Lane Michael H Miller, Charles Embrey, 1859, Peter B Small, Wm McK Keppler, Joseph Reneh, 1863-64, Peter B Small, A Shoop, Joseph Reneh, 1867, John W Brentbed, William H Knode, James I Hurley, 1870, James I Hurley Joseph F. Smith 1871, Joseph F Smith, William H Knode, John L Smith, 1875 John Reichard, John L Smith, Samuel Strite, 1879, William McK Keppler, A D Bennett, James Findlay

SHERIFFS

1801, Nathaniel Rochester, 1806, Isaac S White, 1809 Matthias Shaffner, 1812 Henry Sweitzer, 1815 Daniel Schnebly, 1818, Thomas Post 1821, John A Swearingen, 1822 Thomas Post, 1824 Alexander Neill, 1827, George Swearingen, 1828 Christian Newcomer, Jr, 1831, William H Fitzhugh, 1833, Daniel Malott, 1839, John Carr, 1842, Thomas Keller, David I Wilson, 1845, Thomas Martin 1848, Daniel South, 1851, Christopher Hilliard, 1853 William Logan 1855, Benj A Garlinger 1857, J M Hauck, 1859, E M Mobley, 1861, Henry Gantz, 1863-64, Samuel Oliver, 1865, Jonathan Newcomer, 1867, George W Grove, 1869, Daniel White, 1871, R C Bamford, 1873, Jacob Miller, 1875, Peter J Mayberry, 1877, B F Reichard, 1879, F K Zeigler

TAX COLLECTORS

1839, Christian Sheppard, 1841, George Shief, 1842, Joseph Weash, 1844, William Dellinger, 1845-46, Joseph P Mong 1847, William I Doyle, 1851, L R Martin (deputy), 1852-53, Horatio N Harne, 1854-55, Joseph O'Neal, 1856-57, Joseph G Pritzman, 1859, Henry Gantz, 1860, David Oswald, 1864, Samuel F Zeigler 1862-63, Benjamin A Garlinger, 1864-65, Samuel F Zeigler, 1866-67, Ed M Mobley, 1874, William N Keller 1876-77, W M Lantz, 1878-80, C W Miller

JUSTICES OF THE LEVY COURT

1806 —Thomas Sprigg Samuel Ringgold, Adam Ott, William Yates, Robert Smith Joseph Price, and Jacob Schnebly

1807 —Thomas Sprigg, Samuel Ringgold, Adam Ott, William Yates, Robert Smith, Josiah Price, and Nathaniel Rochester

1808-9 —The same were reappointed by the Governor

1810 —Samuel Ringgold, Adam Ott, William Yates, Robert Smith Josiah Price, Martin Kershner, and Jacob Reneh

1811 —Adam Ott, Robert Smith, Josiah Price, Martin Kershner, Jacob Reneh, William B Williams, and William Yates

1812 —Adam Ott, William Yates, Robert Smith, Josiah Price, Martin Kershner, William B Williams, and David Schnebly

1813 —William Fitzhugh, John Harry, Lancelot Jacques, John Wagoner, John Hershey, George Smith, and William Van Lear

1814 —John Harry, Lancelot Jacques, John Wagoner John Hershey, George Smith, William Van Lear

1815 —William Fitzhugh, John Harry, Lancelot Jacques, John Wagoner, John Hershey, George Smith, and Edmund H Turner

1816 —Those of 1815 reappointed

1817 —The same but in March of that year Matthew Van Lear was appointed, vice Col Wm Fitzhugh, resigned

1818 —Matthew Van Lear, John Harry, Lancelot Jacques, John Wagoner, John Hershey, George Smith, and Edmund H Turner

1819 —The same as previous year

1820 —William Gabby Frederick Dorsey, Daniel Reichard, John McClain, William Fitzhugh, Jr, Edward G Williams and Jacob Miller

1821 —Frederick Dorsey, Daniel Reichard, John McClain, William Fitzhugh Jr, Edward G Williams, Jacob Miller, and Jacob Zeller

1822 —Frederick Dorsey, Daniel Reichard, John McClain, William Fitzhugh, Jr, Samuel Ringgold, Jacob Zeller, and Jacob Miller

1823 —Frederick Dorsey, John McClain, William Fitzhugh, Jr, Samuel Ringgold Jacob Miller, David Schnebly, Joseph Gabby, Peter Seibert

1824 —Frederick Dorsey, John McClain William Fitzhugh, Jr, Samuel Ringgold, Jacob Miller, David Schnebly, and Peter Seibert

1825 —Frederick Dorsey, John McClain, William Fitzhugh, Samuel Ringgold, Jacob Miller, David Schnebly and Peter Seibert

1826 —John McClain, William Fitzhugh, Jr, Samuel Ringgold, Jacob Miller, David Schnebly, Peter Seibert, and Frederick Dorsey

1827 —Frederick Dorsey, John McClain, Peter Seibert, Jacob Miller, Daniel Pentch, and David Brookhart

1828 —Henry Firey, David Rohrer, Thomas C Brent

1829 —I S Swearingen, Thomas Hammond, Joseph Gabby

1830 —George Protzmbaugh James Grimes, John H Mann, Joseph West, Jacob Miller

COMMISSIONER STATE BOARD OF EDUCATION

1874-82, P A Witmer

SCHOOL COMMISSIONERS

1864, Thomas A Boullt, John A Miller, Joseph Garver, Jacob Funk, Isaac Garver, P S Newcomer, Samuel I Piper, William Davis, John J Hershey, Samuel Mason, Jonathan Tobey, F P Mayhugh, Samuel Baker, 1865, Thomas A Boullt, Joseph Garver, John Kretzer, Jacob Funk, John S Hedding Samuel Rohrer, John J Hershey, John A Miller Albert Small (secretary and treasurer), 1867 Edward Stake (secretary and treasurer), 1868, G W Smith, J A Ferry, G W Brown, John D Houck, Warren Garratt, A W Lakin Moses Poffenbarger, Edward Ingram Charles Hiteshew, Edward Smith, H T Spickler, William Jones, O W Johnson Warford Mann, Henry Fiekle, P W Witmer (secretary, treasurer, etc) James Cullen, 1869, W S W H [illegible] W [illegible] H Armstrong,

Henry Stroch, George F Leiter, David H Flory, 1870, J A Fiery, Moses Poffenbarger, Warren Garrett, G W Brown, Henry Fikle, Benjamin F Fiery, William H Armstrong, Samuel Knode, Isaac Garver, Henry Stroh, J Johnson, Denton G Gehr, Solomon Jenkins, J D Slaughenhaupt, W A Riddlemoser, P. A Witmer (secretary, treasurer, etc), 1872, William Ragan, Benjamin A Garlinger, H S Eavey, William B McClain, Thomas H Crampton 1874, William Ragan, William B McClain, Benjamin A Garlinger, Thomas H Crampton, H S Eavey, 1876, William Ragan, Thomas H Crampton, William B McClain B A Garlinger, H S Eavey, P A Witmer (examiner, treasurer, and secretary), 1878, William Ragan, William B McClain, B A Garlinger, H S Eavey, Thomas H Crampton 1879, William Ragan, 1880, B A Garlinger, William L Stonebraker, H S Eavey, William B McClain, P A Witmer (examiner and treasurer)

REGISTER OF WILLS

1777-64, William Logan, 1804, Thomas Bell, 1806, George C Smoot

JUSTICES OF THE PEACE

1802-6 — Thomas Crampton, Robert Douglass, George Nigh, Adam Ott, William Webb, John Hunter, William Van Lear, William Yates, John Good, John Langley, George Scott, Sr, Jacob Schnebly, William S Compton, Philip Mauns

January, 1806 — Thomas Crampton, Adam Ott, Samuel Ringgold, John Good, John Hunter Thomas Sprigg William Yates, Robert Douglass, William Webb, Daniel Weisel Robert Smith, Joseph 'Price George Scott, George Nigh, Henry Ankeny James McClain, Thomas Kennedy, William S Compton, George Smith, Jacob Schnebly Martin Kerschner, Philip Mauns, John Langley, John Bowles, and James Prather

1807 — The appointments of 1807 were the same as the preceding year except that the name of Daniel Weisel was dropped and John J Mason added to the list

1808 — The same were reappointed in 1808 except Webb, deceased and the addition to the list of William Gibby and Robert Hughes

1809 — Appointments same as preceding year

1810 — The only changes made in 1810 were occasioned by the death of Gen Sprigg and appointments of Matthew Collins and Henry Lochner, Jr

1811 — Thomas Crampton Adam Ott, Samuel Ringgold, John Hunter Wm Yates, Robert Douglass, Robert Smith, Josiah Price, James McClain, Thomas Kennedy, William S Compton, George Smith, Jacob Schnebly, Martin Kerchner, Philip Mauns, John Langley John Bowles, James Prather, William Gibby, Robert Hughes, Matthew Collins, and Ezra Shfer

1812 — In January, 1812, the same were reappointed, except that Langley was dropped, and John Blackford, William B Williams, John Wolgamott, Charles Heseltine, and William Fitzhugh, Jr, added

1813 — No record

1814 — Adam Ott William Yates, James McClain, George Smith, Jacob Schnebly, John Bowles, James Prather, Robert Hughes, John Blackford, Edward Boteler George Nichols, James D Moore, John Witmer, John Barr, Christopher Burkhart, John Hershey, William Van Lear, William Fitzhugh, Jr, Isaac Hauser, Jr, Alexander Grimm, Edmund H Turner, Jonas Hogmire Joseph Ingram, Matthew Van Lear, Frederick Grosh David Newcomer, Lancelot Jacques, Cornelius Ferree Jeremiah Mason, Ephraim Davis and John Adams

1815 — George Smith, John Blackford, Edward Boteler, George Nichols, Alexander Grimm, Edmund H Turner, Jonas Hogmire, Isaac Hauser Jr, Joseph Ingram, Matthew Van Lear Robert Hughes, John Witmer, John Barr, Christophor Burckhart John Hershey, Wm Fitzhugh, Jr, Frederick Grosh, David Newcomer James McClain, John Bowles, James Prather, James D Moore, Lancelot Jacques, Wm Yates, Cornelius Ferree, Jeremiah Mason, Ephraim Davis, John Adams, Jacob Schnebly, Archibald M Waugh, Joseph C Keller, Seth Lowe, and Robert McCulloh

1816 — The same as 1815, except James Prather deceased, and the additions of Dr Christian Boerstler, John Young Septimus Stephens, and George Brumbaugh

1817 — George Smith, John Blackford, Edward Boteler George Nichols, Alexander Grimm, Edmund H Turner, Isaac Houser, Jr Joseph Ingram, Matthew Van Lear, Robert Hughes, John Witmer, John Barr, Christopher Burckhart, John Hershey William Fitzhugh, Jr, Frederick Grosh, David Newcomer, John Bowles, James D Moore, Lancelot Jacques, William Yates, Cornelius Ferree, Jeremiah Mason, Ephraim Davis John Adams Jacob Schnebly, Arch M Waugh Joseph C Keller, Seth Lane, Robert McCullough, Dr Christian Boerstler, John Young Septimus Stevens, George Brumbaugh, John Davis, Thomas C Brent, and Ezra Shfer

1818 — George Smith John Blackford, Edward Boteler, George Nichols, Alexander Grimm Isaac Houser, Jr, Matthew Van Lear, Robert Hughes, John Witmer, John Barr, Christopher Burckhart, John Hershey, William Fitzhugh Jr, David Newcomer, John Bowles, James D Moore Lancelot Jacques, William Yates, Cornelius Ferree, Jeremiah Mason, Jacob Schnebly Arch M Waugh, Seth Lane, Robert McCulloh Christian Boerstler, John Young George Brumbaugh, John Davis, Thomas C Brent, Ezra Shfer, and The Baker

1819 — The same were appointed in 1819, with Milton H Sackett, James H Bowles, David Stephens, and Edmund H Turner as additional justices

From and including the year 1820 the names of those only are given who qualified according to law, and as shown in the test books on file in the office of the Circuit Court clerk

1814, A M Waugh, 1815, Robert McCulloch, Jacob Schnebly, Seth Lane, 1816, Christian Boerstler, John Jung, John Adams George Brumbaugh 1817, George Nichols Ezra Shfer, M Van Lear, 1818, Thomas C Brent, 1819, Milton H Sackett, 1820, Benjamin Yoe, Thomas Compton, Andrew Kershner, John McClain, Thomas Kennedy, Edward G Williams, William Fitzhugh, Jr, John Rench Dennis Burns, George Shafer, Jacob Miller, Michael Fenninger, William Webb, James Hemphill, John McKee, John Smith, Frederick Dorsey William Gibby, Daniel Reinhard, George Lochner, Stewart Herbert, Philip Mauns, 1821, Charles Heseltine, William S Compton, John D Moore, Henry Schnebly, Benjamin F Hickman, Joseph Gibby, Jacob Zeller, 1822, Ezra Shfer, John Bowles, Ignatius Drury, Nathaniel Summers, Samuel Bayley, John Horine, James H Bowles, Benjamin Poteler, 182[illegible], Thomas B Hall, Daniel Malott, Jonathan Shafer, Daniel Donnelly, Robert Clagett, David Kohler 1824, William Kreps, Jacob Kissinger, John M Rohrer Marmaduke W Boyd 1825, James Leggett, Joseph Gabby, Samuel Ringgold, George H Lambert John [illegible] 1826 David Brookhout, John A Carter William [illegible] William Booth, Henry Tracy, J[illegible] M M H[illegible] [illegible] Hinny, 1827,

Thomas Post, Isaac S Swearingen, 1829, Washington W Hitt, Charles Nouse, Henry Crosby, William Webb, 1830, Henry Lewis, Jacob Kessinger, J M Welch, Henry C Schnebly, Anthony Snyder, Thomas Johns, Van S Brasheur, George Seibert John Hall, William Booth, Samuel Dietrich, Jacob Baker, Henry Wade, 1831, S Herbert, Benjamin Oswald, Jr, Joseph West, John A Wagoner, 1833, Jacob Kausler, John D Kiefer, Richard M Harrison, John Lambert, 1834, John Newcomer, Daniel Grim, 1835, David Hughes, Watkins James, Jr, 1836, Joseph Gabby, John Horine, Jacob Lambert, Lewis Tuttle

Among other justices who qualified in years prior to March, 1839, but the date of whose qualification is not shown on the records, were

Samuel Mitchell, Patrick Byrne, John Herr, Charles Rousse, David Schnebly, Peter Seibert, George Shifer, Solomon Sherfy, Andrew Smith, Samuel Claget, Perry Prather, George M Elliott, John D Ridenour, Joseph Gray, Alex H Laflon, Wm H Handey, John D Dutton, William Downs, Isaac Nesbitt, D H Keedy, Thomas Boteler, John J Keedy, James P Mills, Abel Dunham, George Stubblefield, David Smith, David Showman, Elias Davis, Thomas D Grim, H Dyron, George Shafer, G W Rodgers, William S Morrison, Abraham Witmer, Thomas Patterson, James Maxwell, Jonathan Newcomer, A Mcbride, David Brumbaugh, George Shief James Hurley

Subsequent justices of the peace to date, who have exercised their duties, are as follows

1839.—George W Smith, Jacob Powles, Daniel Giesbart, Samuel S Prather, Daniel Flory, Daniel South Daniel Hauce, Emanuel Knodle, Anthony Snyder, Michael Iseminger, Jacob Reichard, D Osler, George Feidt Jacob Smith, John Witmer, John M Rohrer, Wm McK Keppler, George Spiecher, John Beard, Henry Wade, Daniel Grim, Eli Mobley, John Cool Hugh Logan John Cunning, Jacob Miller, E S Poteler, D Keedy, B Beam, Andrew Smith, William Webb, Benjamin Hartman, David T Wilson, Nathaniel Summers, John D Dutton Solomon Helser, H C Schnebly, David Newcomer, Eli Crampton, George Brown, Ethelbert Tracey, Arthur Blackwell, Joseph Knox, Conrad Wolf, William McAuley

1840.—C F Gelwick Geo W Smith, Samuel Bleche, Henry Mills John Baker, John J Grim, Abel Williams, Daniel Root, Hiram G Reese, John T Grow, Roger E Cook, John Weis, Conrad Wolf, George Geity

1841.—Alexander H Lappon, Jacob A Miller, John B Bechtell, Jonathan Keller, Wm McK Keppler

1842.—John Johnson, I A Grim, Joseph A Skinner, Joseph Unger, John R Curtis, John Binger, H Snyder, James Mongan, William Kreps, Christian Sheppard.

1843.—John K Smith, Jacob R Martin, Jacob Shoop, Elijah Swope, Samuel Blecher, George Colliflower, M W Boyd, H Downie, Philip Mcade, Wm C Webb, William Hunter, Samuel H Smith, Samuel Lyday

1845.—George Hill, Wm H Boyd, Wm H Handey, S L Ditwiler, Henry Ridenour, Stewart Herbert, Jacob Shanebyer, Wm R Hughes Daniel Flory W M Tice, John Herr, W W Bucher, C F Gelwick, Robert Wilson, H H Snyder, Joseph Brewer, John Brown, John A Wagoner, Abraham H Ganer, Jacob Lambert, Jacob Kansler, Peter Springfield, William H Miller, David Reichard, William Eakle, David Newcomer, Henry C Welty, John M Rohrer, Isaac Garver, James Wa[illegible], John D Ridenour, O H Williams, [illegible]baugh, Washington McCoy Nathan M Dunnell, James Brown, George W Grosh Wm McAuley Charles G Lane John L Smith John J Keedy, Samuel Brown Matthew McClannahan, Jesse Hair, Peyton Skinner, Andrew Newcomer, Elias O'Neal, J P Stephey, Thomas Boteler, David Hughes, Jonathan Smith, Daniel Donnelly

1846.—John W Heard Lewis Fletcher, Isaac H Allen, Joshua C Price, Elisha C Wells, Elias J Ohr

1847.—Francis C Shief, Joseph Cunningham, Solomon Florry

1848.—C Sheppard, John Cook, Wm McK Keppler, Joseph A Skinner, Samuel Lyday, Moses Dillon, Jacob Bleacher, Jacob Smith, John Corby, D H Keedy, John Weis, George Long, Samuel Houser, J P Mayhugh, O McClain, Charles W. McMinn, Jeremiah Kuhn Joseph Knox, George W Smith, S S Downin, John R Williams, R E Cook, D E Price, W H Fitzhugh, Hugh Logan, George Knodle, Joseph D Price, Chas W Bigham, Henry Gray, Martin Eakle, John Hershberger, D Haner, John Snyder Eli Crampton, D H Myers Wm C Kirkhart, Thomas Clingan, F A Grim, Jacob Powles Jacob Shoop, Josiah Buck, Jonathan R Humphries, John B Bechtell, J A Miller, Michael Iseminger, Jr, William Firefoot, John Moore, James Cassidy

1849.—Geo I Hawken, Thomas H Crampton, David Fortney

1850.—Daniel Grim, W T Amba, Thos L Schleigh, Horatio N Harne, William Merninger, Jacob Fonk, G W Brown

1851.—James Mongan, Absalom Eakle, John Snyder, John S Wolf

1852.—C Sheppard, J P Mayhugh, John Cook, T E Schleigh, Daniel Grim, George Knodle, John Hershberger, D H Keedy, J R Humphries, Joseph A Skinner, Jacob Blecker, Jeremiah Kuhn George I Hawkens, John Corby, Samuel Houser, George Long, John Wachtell, Martin Eakles, Absalom Eakles, G W Brown, John Snyder, Jacob Shoop, Henry L Teatian, Owen McClain, K Ellsworth Cook, Jonathan Hawer, Michael Iseminger, Jr, D Hauer, Hugh Logan, Joseph D Price, David E Price, Lewis Bell, Daniel H Myers, David Fortney, Alex Neill, Jr, William Monninger

1853.—John Knodle, William Miller, F Humrichouse, James Mongan, Samuel Houser, William M Tice, William H Handey, John Cook, John L Smith, M Iseminger, Jr, Daniel Grim, F C Shief, George I Hawkens, J P Wolfersberger, Elias O'Neal Samuel Boyd, Benjamin Schimel, David Reichard Daniel Flory, J R Humphries, George M Knode, George Hill, Isaac Garver, Thomas Watkins, Joseph Brittain, John Corby, John D Hart, R E Cook, Elias J Ohr, George Wolf, James Mongan

1854.—John Troxell

1855.—Josiah Buck, Otho B Castle, John Troxell, Thomas Watkins, John W Dienner, Jeremiah Kuhn, Samuel Boyd, Josiah Buck Jacob Powles, J R Humphries, M King J Cook, Tacitus V Bailey, David Wilhelm, Joshua Dayhoff, William Kreps, George Pearson, James W Leggett, David M Hoover, Elias O Neal, Daniel H Myers, George Hill, Owen McClain, John L Smith, M Iseminger, Jr, Solomon Davis

1856.—Peter Muterbaugh

1857.—Jeremiah Kuhn, James Mongan David Wilhelm, Samuel Nigh, Thomas Curtis, David Hughes, Owen McClain, J Cook, William Kreps James P Hays Ezra Munson, Elias O Neal, John Savin, John Troxell, D G Potter, Tacitus V Bailey James Pruttzah Elias Sprecher, M King, Isaac Garver, Thomas Boteler Peter Hull, James Hurley J R Humphries

1858.—Otho B Castle, George T Hawkens, [illegible] [illegible] [illegible] [illegible] [illegible] B F Keller,

M King, John McKing, John Stonesifer, Solomon Calklesser, J R Hode, George Caswell, Samuel Boyer William Kreps, R E Cook, Owen McClain, Joseph Green, Joseph Harrison, Robert Shives, David Hughes, George W Bowers, J O Fiery, Isaac Garver, E F M Hurley, Thomas Boteler, David G Potter, Joseph S Grim, Tacitus N Halley

1860 —Jeremiah Kuhn

1861 —William Bershing John Cook, William M Tice, William Phreaner, James Mongan, Thomas Watkins, Cornelius Vatts, Samuel Houser, Frederick Harmon, James P Hays, Adam Devilbiss, John Hershberger, Jacob Good, D G Potter M Iseminger, Jr, John Stonesifer, George Fulton, George Hill, John T Wolverton, Joseph Harrison, Peter Ardinger, Isaiah S Pee Joseph S Grimm, J R Hode

1862 —James Dorrance, Samuel Boyd

1863 —Jacob Craig, Moses Poffenbarger, Jacob Good, J O Firey, Lewis L Mentzer, D G Potter, Jacob C Thompson, Frederick Harmon, Tacitus Halley, J Cook, Samuel Meredith, John Troxell, Samuel Houser, J R Hode, William M Tice, Andrew J McAllister W Bershing James Dorrance, George Fulton, M Iseminger, James R Myers, Peter Ardinger, Thomas Watkins, James Mongan, Adam Devilbiss George Hill, Joseph S Grimm

1864 —James Dorrance, Jacob Good, William M Tice John Cook, Samuel Meredith, Adam Devilbiss, William Beirshing, D G Potter, Samuel Houser, George Fulton, Tacitus V Halley, Frederick Harman, Michael Iseminger, Samuel Boyer, J R Hode, Jacob C Thompson, Peter Ardinger, D J Pittenger, Joseph S Grimm

1865 —Jacob Craig Lewis L Mintzer, George Hill, Thomas Watkins David Pennel James Dorrance, David Pennel, William Beirshing, Josiah Knodle, John Cook, Tacitus V Halley, Thomas Watkins Frederick Harman, George Fulton Samuel Houser William M Tice, Samuel Boyer, Adam Devilbiss M Iseminger, Peter Ardinger, D C Potter John J Thomas, N Mckinley, Jacob C Thompson

1866 —George Hill, J R Hode, James Hurley, James W Leggett David S Reily, John Snyder

1867 —William Beirshing William M Tice, George Long, O McClain, Jacob Blecker John H Lakin, Thomas Taggert, Elijah Swope, M H Clarke, Joseph C Hershberger, Joseph Harrison J A McCool George W Hicks, John J Watson, John Snyder, B F Keller, Samuel B Preston, Josiah Buck, Jacob Craig, James A Skinner David M Hoover, Tacitus V Halley, James W Leggett, Jacob Motz, James P Myers, John G Hine, John G Frnt

1868 —Daniel H Myers, John G Hine, Joseph Harrison, W H Grove, Dennis Cain, John Snyder, O McClain, George H Shafer, Josiah Buck, John H Lakin, Jacob Blecher, Jacob Craig, Elijah Swope, Tacitus V Halloy, Thomas Taggart, Wm M Tice, Wm Beirshing, M H Clarke, Solomon Davis, James A Skinner, John Clark, Andrew R Schnebly

1869 —John Long, J R Hode, John H Read, Samuel Boyer

1870 —H F Perry, John H Lakin, John Murdock, George Long, Jacob Craig James A Skinner, John Snyder, Wm H Grove, Tacitus V Halley, Thomas Taggart, Josiah Buck, William M Tice, Joseph Harrison, Wm Bershing, Owen McClain, Joseph C Hershberger, John G Hine, G W Hicks, Elijah Swope M H Clarke, T E Schleigh, John Long, James W Leggett, Samuel Boyer, Thomas Watkins, James H Harne, Thomas Boteler, Jonathan Lowser

1871 —Hiram R Stickel

1872 —William H Myers G W Smith, Wm H Lowe Thomas Boteler, Wm H H[illegible] Charles Harvey, Wm M Tice Peter Middlekauff, John Murdoch, Joseph A Skinner, Morgan Miller, W H Grove, Jacob Craig, Elijah Swope, Samuel Boyer, W H Lowe, John F Gray, Thomas Watkins, G W Smith, Wm H Myers, John S Hine, Thomas Taggart, George W Hicks, John Long, Joseph Hershberger, Thomas E Schleigh, Josiah Buck Hiram R Stickel, Jacob Losey, James W Leggett, Tacitus V Halley, George Long, John H Lakin A A Cook, I D Claggett H F Perry

1874 —John Buck, W H Grove, J A Skinner, W H Lowe, Aaron F Baker, John Murdock J A Wright W V Harne, Samuel Boyer, John F Gray, Jacob Fiery, Wm H Myers, Morgan Miller, Jacob Craig, Thomas Watkins William M Tice, Thomas Taggart, S Colklesser, Thomas Boteler, John H Lakin, Wm H Hawken, Josiah Buck, R E Cook, James W Leggett, John W Hine, Peter Middlekauff, Elijah Swope, T L Schleigh, H F Perry, H R Stickler, Robert Shives, John Long, Jacob Motz, D S Pittinger, Tacitus V Halley, Joseph C Hershberger J R Cushwa

1875 —J Irvin Bitner, M H Clarke, J Snively, J P Anderson, Albert C Tice

1876 —John Buck, Christian G Brezler, J A Skinner, Thomas Taggart, S Colklesser, J Irvin Bitner, R L Cook, Joseph H Dreamer, J A Wright, John H Lakin, W H Grove, John Murdock H F Perry, Wm H Myers Elijah Swope, Daniel W Blessing, W H Lowe, Josiah Buck, John G Hine, W V Harne, Morgan Miller, Otho Oliver, J Snively, Peter Middlekauff, Robert Shives, Tacitus V Halley Wm H Hawken, Thomas Boteler, J H Wade, John Long Charles Harvey, D S Pittenger, Thomas Watkins, John H Fiery, Joseph C Hershberger, M H Clarke

1877 —John S Wolf, Charles H Dickel, James W Leggett

1878 —T Belt Johnson, Allen A Nesbitt, James R Myers, Joseph Harrison, A D Sagar, J Irvin Bitner, John Buck, James L Elgin, Peter Middlekauff, Allen A Nesbitt, John H Lakin, John H Wade Elijah Swope, George H Weld, R W Grove, C G Brezler, Wm H Myers, T Belt Johnson, J Snively, Otho Oliver, J A Wright, H V Harne, R E Cook Jacob Lakin, John G Hine, C H Dickel, J A Skinner, S Summers, John E Brown, Thomas Taggart, Joseph C Hershberger, Lancelot Jacques, John Long S Corklesser, Wm H Hawken, Josiah Buck, D W Blessing, John Murdock, John S Wolf, Eli Stemm, Jr, John Lambert

1880 —L Colklesser, John Buck, Wm H Myers, R W Grove, T Belt Johnson, J I Bitner, Philip Sprecher, C G Brezler, H H Long, John H Lakin, Morgan Miller, Peter Middlekauff, P Oswald, John Lambert, Elijah Swope, S Summers, David Dick, John Long, Thomas Taggart, John Clarke, Aaron Sagar, Joseph C Hershberger, J Snively, R E Cook, W V Harne, J L Evessole, Lancelot Jacques, Silas Wolfersberger, George H Weld J A Skinner, J L Elgin, Allen A Nesbitt, John Murdock, John S Wolf, Wm H Hawken Josiah Buck, John G Hine, J A Wright, John E Brown, C H Dickel, Joseph Harrison, Garey S Betts, Thomas J Halley, Scott Palmer

The judges of elections in 1823 for the county were

District No 1, Sharpsburg —Jacob Miller, Robert Clagett, John D Grove

District No 2, Williamsport —Isaac S Swearingen, Milton H Sackett, Ignatius Drury

District No 3, Hagerstown —Peter Humrickhouse, John Wolgamott, Henry Shafer

District No 4, Clear Spring —Michael Bovey, David Cushwa, Jac[illegible]

District No 5, Hancock —William Yates, James H Bowles, Anthony Snyder

District No 6, Boonsboro' – John Shafer, Matthias Shaffner, Michael Piper

District No 7, Cavetown —William Gabby, William H Fitzhugh, Peter Seibert

Col Henry Lewis was appointed coroner by the Governor in 1822

CHAPTER XLII

INTERNAL IMPROVEMENTS

Roads — Bridges — Turnpikes — Stage-coaches — Mails — Railroads

WASHINGTON COUNTY is better provided with transportation facilities than any other county in the State Some of its far sighted and enterprising citizens at a very early period inaugurated a system of turnpike roads which not only has given the county most admirable roads where they were most needed, but has also resulted in bringing from their tolls, large revenues into the county treasury The county is also traversed by several railway lines The Chesapeake and Ohio Canal passes through the whole extent of its southern border, giving all necessary transportation to this section of the county and full intercourse with the coal-fields in Allegany County The main stem of the Baltimore and Ohio Railroad passes through the southeastern border, at the foot of Pleasant Valley, while the Washington County Branch of the same road beginning at Weverton, on the Potomac, passes northward through Bartholow's, Brownsville Claggett s, Beeler's, Summit, Rohrersville, Eakle's Mills, Keedysville, and Breathed's Stations to Hagerstown, a distance of twenty-four miles

The Shenandoah Valley Railroad, beginning at Hagerstown, its northern terminus, passes through St James, Grimes, and Sharpsburg Stations, or a distance of about fourteen miles in Washington County The Cumberland Valley Railroad, which extends from Harrisburg, Pa, to Martinsburg, W Va, has as stations in this county State Line, Morgantown, Hagerstown, and Williamsport, while the Western Maryland Railroad in its route from Baltimore passes that picturesque locality known as Pen-Mar, also Edgemont, Smithsburg Cavetown, Chewsville and Hagerstown to Williamsport These roads all converging at Hagerstown, which is centrally located and the county-seat, have contributed greatly to its business activity and wealth, as well as to the prosperity of all parts of the beautiful and rich agricultural region surrounding it In turnpike roads this county is better provided than any other in the State

Rumsey's Steamboat —Washington County may also claim to no inconsiderable share in the construction of the first steamboat ever built in the United States This was the vessel built by James Rumsey, of Shepherdstown, W Va, in 1785 Blasco de Garay in 1543, the Marquis of Worcester in 1655, Denys Papin in 1695, Savery in 1698, and others had prophesied, proposed, or tried steam navigation, and various experiments with rude vessels had been made in Europe from time to time It was not, however, until the experiments of Fulton in 1807, and his trip up the Hudson, that the practicability of propelling vessels by steam was fully and finally demonstrated But Fulton had been anticipated by Rumsey, who as early as 1785 constructed a boat at Shepherdstown, and had it fitted up with machinery partly manufactured at the Catoctin Furnace of the Johnson Brothers near Frederick The boiler, two cylinders, pumps, pipes, etc, were manufactured in Baltimore by Christopher Raborg and Charles Weir Some portions of the works were made at the Antietam Iron-Works March 14, 1786, a public experiment was made on the Potomac River (the first of the kind ever undertaken in this country), and Rumsey succeeded in attaining a speed of four miles an hour against the current The boat was eighty feet long, and propelled by a steam engine working a vertical pump in the middle of the vessel, by which the water was drawn in at the bow and expelled through a horizontal trunk at the stern She achieved the speed above stated when loaded with three tons, in addition to the weight of her machinery,—one-third of a ton The whole of the machinery, including the boiler, occupied a space but little over four feet square A newspaper account of the vessel, under date of April 25, 1793, gives the following description of her, viz

> "The vessel of the late lamented Mr Rumsey to sail against wind and tide has lately been tried, and was found to sail four knots an hour The following is the principle upon which it moves A pump of two feet diameter, wrought by a steam engine, forces a quantity of water up through the keel The valve is then shut by the return of the stroke which at the same time forces the water through a channel or pipe of about six inches square, lying above and parallel to the keel on out at the stern, under the rudder, which has a less dip than usual to permit the exit of the water The impress of the water forced through the square channel against the exterior water acts as an impelling power upon the vessel"

Gen Washington and Governor Thos Johnson, of Maryland, were patrons of Rumsey's experiment, which was made in the interest of the proposed Chesapeake and Ohio Canal The demonstration that

a boat could be propelled up stream against the current was regarded by them as being very satisfactory Thus we find that the first steamboat was propelled on the Potomac, and the first machinery was made in Western Maryland, twenty years before Fulton's experiment on the Hudson Rumsey's claim to priority was disputed by John Fitch, a Philadelphia watch-maker, but the evidence in favor of Rumsey is very clear and convincing Fitch did not make public his plan until 1786 It consisted in "paddling a ship by steam," the device resembling vertical paddles, six on each side working alternately The vessel was launched at Philadelphia in 1788, and proceeded to Burlington, N J, twenty miles distant, where she burst her boiler She was floated back to Philadelphia and repaired, and made several subsequent trips The cylinder was twelve inches in diameter and three-feet stroke Rumsey who was a native of Cecil County had petitioned the Maryland Legislature for the passage of an act vesting in him "the sole and exclusive right, privilege, and benefit of constructing, navigating, and employing boats, constructed upon a model by him newly invented, upon the creeks, rivers, and bays within this State" It was read and referred to Messrs McMechen, O'Neale, and James Scott, who on the same day reported that they had "examined the allegations therein contained and find them true, and are of opinion that the said invention will be of great utility to facilitate the inland navigation of this State and that a law pass agreeably to the prayer of said petition" At the same session the Legislature passed an act to invest Rumsey "with an exclusive privilege and benefit of making and selling new invented boats on a model by him invented" The experiment which preceded this application took place in September, 1784, and had been witnessed by Gen Washington, who was highly gratified, and gave Rumsey the following certificate, viz

'I have seen the model of Mr Rumsey's boats constructed to work against stream, examined the powers upon which it acts, been eye witness to an actual experiment in running water of some rapidity, and give it as my opinion (although I had little faith before) that he has discovered the art of working boats by mechanism and small manual assistance against rapid currents, that the discovery is of vast importance may be of the greatest usefulness in inland navigation, and if it succeeds, of which I do not doubt, that the value of it is greatly enhanced by the simplicity of the works, which when seen and explained may be executed by the most common mechanic'

The boat appears to have been propelled by paddles and setting-poles, the power being communicated by hand But soon afterwards Rumsey turned his attention to the possible application of steam as the motive power He worked hard all that fall and winter, and was fortunate enough to secure the assistance and patronage of Governor Thomas Johnson The latter was part proprietor, with his brothers, of the Catoctin Iron Furnace The boat itself was built at Shepherdstown, and in December, 1785, was brought down to the mouth of the Shenandoah, and at Harper's Ferry a trial was made with successful results, as previously stated In 1786, Benjamin Franklin and Oliver Evans suggested substantially the same method of propulsion, namely, the power of steam upon a column of water received at the bow and ejected at the stern on a line with the keel The plan has been lately revived, and several vessels have been built in England to test it In 1788 the Rumsey Society, of which Franklin was a member, was formed in Philadelphia to aid the Maryland inventor He went to London, where a similar body was formed, a boat and machinery built for him, and patents obtained in Great Britain, France, and Holland A successful experiment was made on the Thames in 1792, and he was preparing another when he died, December 23d of that year In 1839 the Legislature of Kentucky presented a gold medal to his son, "commemorative of his father's services and high agency in giving to the world the benefits of the steamboat" There was an acrimonious controversy between Fitch and Rumsey, growing out of the latter's having charged the former with appropriating his idea of a steamboat from a description of Rumsey's boat given him by a Capt Bedinger Rumsey published a number of affidavits to prove that he was the original inventor of the steamboat, and among the other documents exhibited by him was a letter from Gen Washington to show that he had spoken to him (Washington) of employing steam as a motive-power In January, 1786, after Rumsey's experiment, John Fitch petitioned the Maryland Legislature for assistance in "bringing his theory of the elastic force of steam to experiment," but although the Legislature could not advance any money, owing to the condition of the public funds at the time, it passed a resolution stating that it was "strongly inclined to believe the probability of the success promised by the theory" Rumsey and Fitch were followed by many experimenters, but, as stated, Fulton's steamboat, the "Clermont," achieved in 1807 the first decisive and permanent success

Public Roads—As early as 1666 the Assembly of Maryland began the work of expediting inter communication between the different parts of the colony, and for this purpose passed an act for "marking highways and making the heads of rivers, creeks, branches, and [illegible], p[illegible] horse and foot,"

and in 1704 the width of roads was established at twenty feet, and provision was made for marking their route by notching trees and branding them with marking irons, and in 1774, Isaac Griest, Benjamin Griffith, Jesse Hollingsworth, and others were appointed commissioners to direct the expenditure of nearly eleven thousand dollars to construct the three great roads leading to Baltimore The Frederick, Reisterstown, and York roads were laid out in 1787

The inhabitants about the Monocacy River and to the northward of the Blue Ridge petitioned, May 14, 1739, that a road be cleared through the country to Annapolis, to enable them to bring their grain and other commodities to market The petition was laid over until the next session

On the 1st of September, 1796, a number of the citizens of Elizabeth Town (Hagerstown) met at the court-house to discuss the utility of a turnpike road to the seaboard Thomas Sprigg was appointed chairman of the meeting, and resolutions were unanimously passed to the effect that while agricultural prosperity depends on good markets and the best prices for the produce of the land, the interests of the citizens demand that every possible avenue of communication with the seaport towns, by land or by water, be opened, and that intercourse with them should be as cheap, easy, and convenient as possible The resolutions further declared that it was very much within the power, disposition, and means of those present to provide such a road to Baltimore Town as would enable the farmers to make use of that season of the year in which they were unable to work upon their farms for the transportation of their produce to market After calling attention to the advantages of the road to the State of Maryland, to the counties through which it was proposed to have it pass, and especially to Washington and Allegany Counties, the furthest removed from the seaboard, the resolutions proposed an address to the Washington County delegates in the Assembly, requesting them to use their efforts in obtaining a charter for the constructing of a turnpike road from Baltimore Town to Elizabeth Town and Williamsport, giving to Washington County the right to assume one eighth of the whole expense, and to Allegany County a specified portion, provided this privilege was availed of within two months after the opening of the subscription-books It was also determined that if the law should provide for only one commissioner from each county to lay out the road, that Gen Heister was the choice of the convention, but if more than one was provided for, that the delegates should themselves appoint the other or others. The Williams, William Clagett, Samuel Ringgold, Daniel Hughes, Nathaniel Rochester, and Adam Ott were appointed to form and present the address to the delegates in the Assembly, and Cephas Beall, Robert Hughes, Abraham Woning, Jacob Schnebly, James Kendal, Benjamin Clagett, George Price, Jacob Myers, John Clagett, and Dr Henry Schnebly to open petitions for signature by the citizens of Washington County, to be presented by their delegates to the Assembly of Maryland The committee having in charge the address to the Washington County delegates on December 2d submitted the proceedings and resolutions of the convention as directed, and in addition thereto stated that it was the general sense of those present that it should be left to the Legislature to decide whether or not the road should fork on the upper side of the South Mountain, one fork to extend to Hagerstown and the other to Williamsport, if but one road should be thought necessary, then it was desired that the same should extend to Hagerstown, and thence to Williamsport

An act was passed by the Assembly in March, 1797, to lay out a turnpike road from Baltimore "through Frederick Town in Frederick County to Elizabeth Town and Williamsport in Washington County" Another public meeting was held on the 19th of September of the same year to aid in the work, at which Nathaniel Rochester acted as chairman, and Elie Williams, Daniel Heister, Samuel Ringgold, Charles Carroll, and Nathaniel Rochester were appointed a committee to carry out the object of the meeting

On the 8th of October, 1797, Samuel Newcomer, Christian Newcomer, John Snavely, Christian Martin, Henry Martin, and Jacob Martin gave notice that they intended to petition the next General Assembly to pass an act empowering the justices of the Levy Court of Washington County to make such alterations in the public road leading from Newcomer's mill to the South Mountain, and passing through the petitioners' land, as the justices may deem necessary for the public good In the year 1801 the shares of stock issued for the purpose of building a bridge over the Eastern Branch of the Potomac were subscribed for immediately upon their being offered to the public The company was authorized to call for forty five thousand dollars, if necessary Notice was given, Sept 14, 1801, that certain of the inhabitants of Washington County intended petitioning the General Assembly for a law to remedy the errors in the returns of the commissioners in laying out and straightening the road from Christian Newcomer's mill to the top of South Mountain [illegible] Frederick Town, and to

authorize the taking of the best ground on said road and going up said mountain The Westminster and Hagerstown turnpike road was the first pike projected in Washington County, and formed part of the line of the grand national road It was built in 1812–16, the managers being John Welty, Walter Boyd, Robert Hughes, and William Gabby

John Scott was treasurer of this company in 1814, and it was then proposed to commence work at the foot of South Mountain, on the west side, provided sufficient subscriptions could be obtained in Washington County to build five miles of the road

In 1805 the Baltimore and Frederick Town Turnpike Company was incorporated, and in 1815 it was empowered to extend its road from Boonsboro' as the beginning of the Cumberland turnpike road In 1813 the presidents and directors for the time being of the several incorporated banks in the city of Baltimore, of the Hagerstown Bank, of the Conococheague Bank, and the Cumberland Bank of Allegany were incorporated as the president, managers, and company of the Cumberland turnpike road In 1821 the presidents and directors of the banks in Baltimore, except the City Bank, and the president and directors of the Hagerstown Bank were incorporated as the president, managers, and company of the Boonsboro' Turnpike Company

The Baltimore, Liberty and Hagerstown turnpike road was chartered during the winter of 1815–16 The commissioners of Washington County appointed to receive subscriptions to the stock were Henry Lewis Martin Kershner, Richard Ragan, Wm Heyser, John Witmer, and Daniel Hughes, Jr

From 1816 to 1825 a fever for turnpike companies seems to have raged They were mostly stock companies authorized by special acts of the State

In 1817, John Kennedy Jacob Zeller, Upton Lawrence, O H Williams David Schnebly, Henry Witmer, William Heyser, Alexander Neill, and Henry Lewis were appointed commissioners to receive subscriptions to the stock of the Hagerstown and Conococheague Turnpike Company In the same year John Davis, who had a store at the time at Hancock, contracted to construct the turnpike road from the Big Conococheague to Cumberland

On the 27th of January, 1818, the Hagerstown and Conococheague Turnpike Board entered into a contract with Messrs Kincaid, McKinlay, and Ramsay for turnpiking the whole of their road from the court-house in Hagerstown to the Conococheague Creek to the point near Witmer's where the Cumberland turnpike road, then in course of construction, commenced

The road, according to the contract, was to be completed by the 1st of January, 1820, in a style not inferior to the United States road west of Cumberland

The board also contracted for a first-class stone bridge across the Conococheague two hundred and ten feet long, including abutments and wing-walls This bridge was intended to connect the road with the Great Western turnpike, thus bringing the latter down to Hagerstown, where it intersects with the Westminster and Hagerstown and the Baltimore and Frederick turnpike roads The completion of the Westminster and Hagerstown road to Hagerstown lessened the distance from Baltimore to that town four miles

The turnpike from the west side of Conococheague to Cumberland was located in 1818, and completed a few years later This road, together with the United States road, furnished a turnpike road from Wheeling to Baltimore (with the exception of eleven miles between Hagerstown and Boonsboro'), two hundred and eighty-two miles long, one hundred and twenty-seven of which were free of tolls

About this time the Legislature of Pennsylvania passed an act constituting a company whose purpose it was to open a turnpike road from Gettysburg to the division line between the States, thence to connect with a road to be constructed in Maryland, which, when completed, would furnish a direct turnpike communication between Philadelphia and Wheeling *via* Hagerstown, a distance of three hundred and thirty-three miles

The subscription books of the Gettysburg and Hagerstown Turnpike Company were opened on the 21st of April, 1828, and the following commissioners were appointed to receive subscriptions John Herch, Sr, Bernhart Gilbert, Andrew Marshall, James McKesson, William McMillan, Lewis Ripple, and Alexander Gordon

Messrs Thomas Cresap, Michael Cresap, James Wood, Jonathan Hagar, John Swan, James Caldwell, John Caldwell, and Richard Yeates were in 1773 appointed managers of a lottery to raise thirteen hundred and fifty dollars for repairing the road from Connoltoway to the Winding Ridge There were three thousand tickets at two dollars each, and ten hundred and forty prizes

A proclamation was issued by Governor J H. Stone, Sept 22, 1797, offering a reward of five hundred dollars for the arrest and conviction of any one committing highway robbery

The following notice was issued on the 28th of February, 1[illegible]

"All persons who may for the time to come have occasion to pass flour or other articles at the toll-places of the Potomac Company are required to pay the tolls fixed by law before the same shall be allowed to pass it being understood that at Watts' Branch and the Great Falls tolls will not be exacted when the above mentioned articles are deposited in the Company's stores, until they are taken therefrom"

This notice was signed by James Keith, president, and by John Mason and Isaac McPherson, directors

Thomas Kennedy informs the public, Feb 27 1799, that the tolls leviable at the mouth of the Conococheague will continue to be received by him

Pursuant to public notice a number of the citizens of Hagerstown and Funkstown convened at the Town Hall in Hagerstown on Saturday, the 3d of November, 1827, for the purpose of making arrangements for planting trees along the sides of the turnpike road between the two towns

Frederick Grosh having been called to the chair and William D Bell appointed secretary, the following resolution was offered and unanimously adopted

"*Resolved*, that Dr C Boerstler, Frederick Grosh, H Shafer, J D Keifer Thos Davis, John Kennedy Daniel Heister, John Wagoner, Samuel Steele, and William D Bell, be and they are hereby appointed a committee with full power to make every arrangement necessary to carry into effect the desirable objects of this meeting, and that they be requested to obtain the consent of the landholders and such pecuniary aid as may be requisite from all persons disposed to afford it

"FREDERICK GROSH, *Chairman*
"WILLIAM D BELL, *Secretary*"

The Hagerstown and Sharpsburg turnpike was finished about the year 1860, at a cost of twenty-six thousand dollars, or two thousand dollars a mile Before the building of the pike it cost the county two hundred and forty dollars per annum to repair the mud road, yet the county commissioners were reluctant to subscribe to the stock of the company, fearing that it would not pay Three thousand five hundred dollars were, however, subscribed, and the dividends received by the county from 1860 to 1880 on this amount of stock aggregated four thousand one hundred and forty-seven dollars

In 1822 steps were taken by certain gentlemen to ascertain the proper location for the turnpike road from Hagerstown to Boonsboro' The construction of this road was of importance to those interested in the Cumberland or Bank road, as its completion materially increased the value of the Bank road, in which the banks of Baltimore, the Hagerstown Bank, the Conococheague Bank, and the Cumberland Bank had together invested $486,170 71

The Westminster and Hagerstown turnpike, *via* Herman's Gap, was incorporated by an act of the Legislature, [illegible] 10, 1810, and Charles [illegible] Upton Lawrence, William Heyser, William Downey, and Robert Hughes were named as commissioners to receive subscriptions for the road in Washington County A citizen of the county, writing March 21 1810, said, "Let this road be once completed to Hagerstown and a good common, well graded road be extended thence through Hancock Town to Fort Cumberland to meet the Great Western road, now making by Congress from Cumberland to Wheeling, and through the State of Ohio, and then Hagerstown will become most certainly the thoroughfare for the whole of the Western wagons and travelers, and will without doubt become one of the very first and most flourishing inland towns in Maryland, or perhaps in the United States"

In 1821 the road from Hagerstown to Boonsboro' was the only portion of the distance from Baltimore to Wheeling that was not turnpiked, and in winter the stages were generally from five to seven hours passing over this space of ten miles

Two stone bridges over Antietam Creek, one at John Shafer's mill, and another at or near Frederick Ziegler's ford on the road leading from Hagerstown through Nicholson's Gap to Gettysburg, were built by James Lloyd in 1824, and one over the same creek, on the road leading from Boonsboro' to Sharpsburg, at Mumma's mill, was erected by Mr Silas Harry in the same year A stone bridge was also built by Jabez Kenney over Beaver Creek, on the road leading from Boonsboro' to Williamsport, during the year 1824

In 1881 the officers of the Hagerstown and Conococheague Turnpike Company were James W Troupe, president, Joseph Kausler, secretary and treasurer, Directors, Joseph B Loose, Frederick Fechtig, D C Hammond, P H Wingert, and Joseph Kausler

In 1819 the roads in Washington County were the following

District No 1 —From Henry Keedy's to the top of South Mountain by Thomas Crampton's from the forks of the road near Hogg's old place to Mackey's stone mill on the Potomac River, from the maple swamp until it intersects the main road leading by Mumma's mill to Fox's Gap, and from Harper's Ferry to the Frederick County line Distance, twenty miles Daniel Brown, supervisor

No 2 —From the turnpike at Mumma's mill to the Frederick County line at Fox's Gap, from George Geeding's store to Antietam bridge at Hess mill Distance, nine miles, John Shuey, supervisor

No 3 —From Swearingen's ferry to Sharpsburg Distance, three miles John Blackford, supervisor

No 4 —From Sharpsburg to the cross roads at Stover's, and from the cross roads at Carey's to Smith's bridge on Antietam Creek Distance, eleven miles, Christian Middlekauff, supervisor

[illegible] er's mill on Little

Beaver Creek Distance seven miles, Jacob Knode, Jr supervisor

No 6 —From Newcomer's mill on Little Beaver Creek to Boonsboro' Distance, four miles, Samuel Hager, supervisor

No 7 —From the cross-roads at Stover's by Booth's mill, to where the road from John Shafer's mill intersects the Boonsboro' road Distance, three and a half miles William Booth, supervisor

No 8 —From the lower end of Samuel Ringgold's line on the Williamsport road by John Shafer's mill, until it intersects the aforesaid road and from thence to Boonsboro', from John Shafer's mill to Petry's school-house Distance, seven miles, John Shafer, supervisor

No 9 —From L G Williams' line near Williamsport to the cross-roads at Carey's Distance seven miles Daniel Rench, supervisor

No 10 —From Williamsport to the cross-roads at Stover's Distance five miles, Thomas Kennedy, supervisor

No 11 —From the manor cross-roads to the corner of Christley Rohrer's fence where it intersects the road from Hagerstown to Sharpsburg Distance four miles, John Dusing, supervisor

No 12 —From Williamsport to Hagerstown until it intersects the Sharpsburg road, and from Williamsport to Miller's mill on the Conococheague Distance, eight miles, Jacob Hershey, supervisor

No 13 —From the cross-roads at Stover's to Wise's smith shop at the south end of Potomac Street, in Hagerstown Distance six miles Frisby Tilghman, supervisor

No 14 —All the streets in Williamsport, including the road to the ferry, Joseph Hollman, supervisor

No 15 —From the Frederick County line at Orr's Gap to Funk's mill on Beaver Creek Distance, four miles, Samuel Funk, supervisor

No 16 —From Hagerstown to the Antietam bridge on the Charlton's Gap road Distance two miles, David Middlekauff, supervisor

No 17 —From Cavetown to the Frederick County line Distance, four miles, Conrad Mentzer, supervisor

No 18 —From Hagerstown to Antietam Creek below Lantz mill on the Nicholson Gap road Distance, six miles, Joseph Miller, supervisor

No 19 —From Antietam Creek below Lentz' mill to the Pennsylvania line Distance, six miles, George Shiefs, supervisor

No 20 —From the Pennsylvania line near Peter Baker's until it intersects the Charlton's Gap road near Robert Hughes' Distance, seven miles, John Mentzer, supervisor

No 21 —From Hagerstown, by David Schnebly's, to the Pennsylvania line Distance, six miles, Henry Schnebly, supervisor

No 22 —From the forks of the road near Hagerstown, on the Mercersburg road, until it intersects the Greencastle road Distance five miles, Daniel Reiebard, supervisor

No 23 —From the Greencastle road to the Pennsylvania line, in the direction of Mercersburg Distance, three miles, Josiah Price, supervisor

No 24 —From the forks of the road near Upton Lawrence's plantation, on the broad fording road, to John Long's cross-roads Distance 4 miles Henry Stitzell, supervisor

No 25 —From Miller's mill on the Conococheague, by Kershner's cross-roads near the turnpike, until it intersects the roads at Long's from Miller's mill to Ashford's, and from the forks of the Williamsport road near Wolgamott's, by Huff's mill, until it intersects the road to the Broad Ford Distance, six miles [illegible]

No 26 —From the Broad Ford on Conococheague Creek, by Nicholas King's to the Pennsylvania line Distance, 4 miles, Nicholas King, supervisor

No 27 —From the forks of the road at Henry Ford's to Jacques' furnace Distance, five miles, James D Moore, supervisor

No 28 —From Williamsport until it intersects the road from Hagerstown to Hancock by the Big Spring, from Ash's ford on the Conococheague to Lick Run, thence until it intersects the Williamsport road near Baltzer Moudy's old place Distance, six miles John McClain, supervisor

No 29 —From Jacques' furnace to the turnpike road near Licking Creek Distance, five miles, John O Moore supervisor

No 30 —From the Big Tonoloway, by Henry Davis' mill, to the Pennsylvania line, and from Hancock Town, by Jeremiah Stillwell's, to the Pennsylvania line near Samuel Graves' Distance, nine miles, John Ressley, supervisor

No 31 —From Little Tonoloway to Sideling Hill Creek, near Goulding's Distance, ten miles

No 32 —From near Christian Shepherd's saw-mill, by George Rizer's, to Sideling Hill Creek Distance, three miles

No 33 —From the Pennsylvania line on the Little Cove road, near Lake Williams' saw mill, until it intersects the main road leading from Hagerstown to Cumberland, near Jacques' furnace Distance, eight miles, Henry Bragonier, supervisor

No 34 —From the forks of the road near the Widow Robey's, by Wolgamot's mill, until it intersects the Sharpsburg road, and from thence until it intersects the Williamsport road near Booth's mill Distance, three miles, Andrew Hogmire, supervisor

No 35 —From the east end of Washington Street, in Hagerstown, by Stull's old mill, to Funk's mill on Beaver Creek, from Funkstown till it intersects a road near David Hershey's Distance, five miles, David Hershey, supervisor

No 36 —From Jonathan Street, in Hagerstown, to the Williamsport road Henry Dillman supervisor

No 37 —The streets of Hagerstown Commissioners of Hagerstown, supervisors

No 39 —From the new bridge on the Charlton's Gap road to Cavetown Distance five miles, Levi Housely, supervisor

No 40 —From the north end of Jonathan Street, Hagerstown, to the Pennsylvania line Distance, five miles, David Brumbaugh, supervisor

No 41 —From Henry Snyder's mill to the turnpike road near Summer's house Distance, three miles

No 42 —From the Pennsylvania line, in Jacob Seirs' field, where the new road from Mercersburg to that point ends, to McCoy's ferry on the Potomac River Jonathan Nesbitt, supervisor

No 43 —From near Nicholas Parrott's, by Leopard's, to Tices' Distance, ten miles, Paul Summers, supervisor

No 44 —Streets of Sharpsburg Jacob Miller, supervisor

No 45 —From the west end of Salisbury Street, in Williamsport, to the Potomac River Peter Ardinger, supervisor

No 46 —From Funkstown to David Hershey's Jacob Knode, supervisor

No 47 —From John Long's to the new bridge on the Conococheague near Union Mills, from thence until it intersects the old road near Henry Ridenour's, and from Long's road to the Pennsylvania line Jacob Zeller, supervisor

No 48 —From the old Harman's Gap road near Robert Hughes' to the top of the mountain at the Frederick County line, where it meets a public road leading through Frederick County to Frederick Town Distance one and a half miles, [illegible]

No 49 —From the Opecken road near Nicholas Swingley's, by Clagett's mill, to intersect the road from Funkstown to Boonsboro Distance, four miles David Clagett, supervisor

No 50 —From Sharpsburg to Antietam Forge Distance, three miles, Jacob Miller, supervisor

No 51 —From the Broad Ford until it intersects the road from Hagerstown to Hancock, near Jacques' furnace Distance, six miles, Daniel Gehr Jr, supervisor

Laws Passed by the Legislature for the Laying Out of Roads in Washington County —In 1801-2 a road was authorized to be opened from Hancock town, by Tong's mill, to intersect a road from Cumberland, in Allegany County, to Sideling Hill Creek In 1801 a road from Elizabeth town by Barrett's Ford to the Pennsylvania line In 1801 part of a road from Turner's Gap to Williamsport to be reviewed In 1801 the road by Bainbridge's and Newcomer's mill to Elizabeth town to be reviewed and laid out In 1801 a road to be laid out from Williamsport to the Pennsylvania line In 1801 an act respecting a road from Elizabeth-town (Hagerstown) to the Pennsylvania line, in Nicholson's Gap In 1803 the Levy Court authorized to change the direction of the road from Hagerstown towards Hancock-town In 1803 a road to be opened from Bennett's ferry to intersect the old road from Hancock town to Fort Cumberland In 1804 a company incorporated for making a turnpike road from Baltimore, etc, to Boonsboro' In 1804 the road to be extended to Hagerstown and Williamsport In 1806 the direction of the road from Ashe's ford on Conococheague Creek to the intersection thereof with the main road from Hagerstown, etc, to be altered

In 1806-7 a road to be laid out from the State line (where a road from Greencastle joins the same) to intersect the main road from Hagerstown to Baltimore through Charlton's Gap In 1806 the road from Hancock-town to Cumberland to be laid out and improved In 1809-11 the road from Baltimore through Frederick-town, etc, to Boonsboro' confirmed In 1809 the Levy Court authorized to open a road to intersect a road from Hagerstown to Williamsport In 1809 a road to be laid off from Boonsboro' to intersect the Sharpsburg road, and to Blackford's ferry on the Potomac In 1812-13-16 a company incorporated to make a turnpike road from Westminster to Frederick-town, through Harman's Gap to Hagerstown In 1809 a road to be opened from Little Tonoloway Creek, at the ford near Hancock town, to intersect the road from Bedford towards Hancock town at the Pennsylvania line In 1810 a road to be laid off from the Pennsylvania line on the Little Cave road, etc, to intersect the main road from Hagerstown to Cumberland, near Jacques' old furnace In 1810 the act of 1809, to clear and make public a road in Washington County, repealed In 1810 the road from Hagerstown to Hancock-town to be straightened In 1811-12 a road to be laid out from Snider's mill to intersect the turnpike road between the foot of the mountain and Boonsboro' In 1811 a road to be laid off from a point on the road from Hagerstown to Sharpsburg, as therein directed, to intersect the road to Baltimore, etc In 1811 the road from Boonsboro' to Funkstown to be straightened, etc In 1811 a road to be laid out from the Charlton's Gap road to the divisional line between Frederick and Washington Counties In 1812 a road to be laid out from Shank's mill to intersect the main road from Hagerstown to Hancock town from McSrum's, or Taylor's ferry on the Potomac, or Crampton's Gap on the South Mountain In 1812 the road from Hancock to Cumberland, as located by Williams and Moore, declared to be a public road In 1813 the old road from Hagerstown to Mercersburg, etc, to be straightened and amended

In 1814 a road to be laid out from the Pennsylvania line, where the new road from Mercersburg ends, and thence to the Potomac River In 1814 a company incorporated to make a turnpike road from Boonsboro' to Swearingen's ferry on the Potomac In 1815 a road to be laid out from Jonathan Street, in Hagerstown, towards Greencastle, as far as the Pennsylvania line In 1815 a company incorporated to make a turnpike road from Baltimore through Liberty town to Hagerstown

In 1815 the Washington and Frederick Turnpike Company incorporated In 1815 a road to be laid out from the farm of N Parrott, near Hancock town, to intersect the old public road near W Sedbum's In 1816 a company incorporated to make a turnpike road from Hagerstown to intersect the Cumberland turnpike road on the west bank of the Conococheague In 1817 companies incorporated to make a turnpike road through Montgomery County to Crampton's Gap in South Mountain and thence to Williamsburg In 1817 a company incorporated to make a turnpike road from Boonsboro', through Williamsport, to intersect the road then making from Cumberland to the west bank of the Conococheague In 1818 a company incorporated to make a turnpike road from the west bank of the Conococheague Creek at Williamsport to intersect the Cumberland turnpike road at or near Stone Quarry Ridge In 1818 a company incorporated to make a turnpike road from Hagerstown to intersect the turnpike road leading from Gettysburg through Nicholson's Gap to the Pennsylvania line In 1818 a company incorporated for making a turnpike road from Hagerstown to Boonsborough

In 1821 a company incorporated to make a turnpike from Boonsborough to Hagerstown In 1825 alteration authorized to be made in the location of the road from Sharpsburg to Hagerstown

In 1849 an extension of Adams' Express Company's services from Baltimore through Frederick and the intervening towns to Hagerstown was effected by E M Mealey & Co

Early Stage-Lines —In 1781, Gabriel Peterson Vanhorn ran his "carriage" from Daniel Grant's

THE FOUNTAIN INN, BALTIMORE

Fountain Inn, Market Space Baltimore at eight o'clock, to Capt Phillips', "where the passengers may dine" and thence to Harford Town where they re-

gained overnight, and proceeded next morning to the Susquehanna for breakfast at Capt Twining's, meeting here the stage from Philadelphia and exchanging passengers, returning by same route to Baltimore, fare, four dollars specie, and the like sum for one hundred and fifty weight of baggage" Nathaniel Twining and Gershon Johnson, of Philadelphia, ran the stages connecting with Vanhorn's line, and assured the passenger leaving "Baltimore on Monday morning of completing his journey to Elizabeth Town by Friday at two o'clock" Letters were carried by this line,—for "every letter one eighth of a hard dollar to be paid by the person sending the letter"

A bi weekly line of stage coaches ran in 1783 between Baltimore and Frederick Town, William Davey and Richard Shoebels, proprietors, "stopping for the entertainment of passengers at Mr Hobbs', Mr Simpson's, and Mr Ricketts, where good fare may be had for fifteen shillings"

A weekly passenger stage from Elizabeth Town to Baltimore was announced Aug 1, 1797 Leaving Elizabeth Town on Tuesdays, and passing through Frederick Town and New Market, it arrived in Baltimore on Wednesdays After remaining there one day, it returned to Elizabeth Town by the same route, arriving on Saturdays

John Ragan in 1797 ran a stage three times a week from Baltimore to Hagerstown

An announcement dated Dec 18, 1797, stated that proposals for carrying the public mails would be received at the General Post office on the following routes From Yorktown (now York, Pa), by Hanover, Petersburg, Taneytown, and Frederick Town, to Leesburg, Va , once a week

Leaving Yorktown on Monday morning at eight o'clock, the stage arrived at Frederick Town at five o'clock P M on the following day, and at Leesburg on Wednesday at two o'clock P M Returning, it left Leesburg at noon on Friday, and arrived at Yorktown at six o'clock P M on Sunday

From Yorktown, Pa , by Abbottstown, Gettysburg, Fairfield, Elizabeth Town, Williamsport, Martinsburg, Winchester, Stevensburg and Strasburg, to Woodstock once a week

The stage on this line left Yorktown at noon on Sunday, and arrived at Martinsburg at eleven o'clock A M on Tuesday After an hour's pause the journey to Woodstock was resumed, and was finished on Wednesday at six o'clock P M Returning, the stage left Woodstock at six o'clock A M on Thursday, arriving at Martinsburg on Friday at eleven o'clock A M , and in Yorktown at the same hour on Sunday

From Baltimore to Frederick Town Elizabeth Town, Greencastle, and Chambersburg, to Shippensburg, Pa , once a week

The stage left Baltimore on Friday at eleven o'clock A M , and arrived at Frederick Town at ten o'clock on Saturday morning, at Elizabeth Town in the evening of the same day, and at Shippensburg on Monday at seven o'clock P M Returning, it left Shippensburg on Tuesday morning at nine o'clock, arriving in Elizabeth Town in the evening at eight o'clock, in Frederick Town the next day at noon, and in Baltimore at five o'clock P M on Thursday

From Elizabeth Town, by Hancock and Old Town, to Cumberland once a week

Leaving Cumberland at six o'clock on Saturday morning, the stage arrived at Elizabeth Town on Monday morning at eight o'clock, and arriving in Cumberland on the return trip at six o'clock P M on Tuesday

Basil Brooke & Co announced to the public on the 24th of May, 1798, that they had commenced running a stage for the accommodation of passengers on the road leading from Hagerstown to Baltimore The stage left Hagerstown on Tuesdays, and passing through Middletown, Frederick Town, and Liberty Town, arrived in Baltimore on Wednesdays Remaining there until Friday morning, it then started on the return trip, pursuing the same route, and arriving in Hagerstown on Saturdays

The same parties also announced that hack-stages from Hagerstown to Bath and from Liberty Town to the Sulphur Springs, in Frederick County, could be had during the season

An announcement is made by Henry Winemiller, May 16, 1799, that the Frederick and Georgetown mail stage starts from the house of Mrs Kimball every Thursday morning at three o'clock, and arrives at Georgetown the evening of the same day, stopping at the Union tavern Starting the next morning at three o'clock, it returned to Frederick Town, arriving there in the evening

The stage of Messrs Scott & Barrick also started from Mrs Kimball's house, leaving on Saturday morning at five o'clock and arriving at Lancaster on Sunday evening, where it stopped at Mrs Ferree's tavern The return trip was commenced at five o'clock on Tuesday morning, Frederick being reached on Wednesday morning

The stage of Messrs Peck & Coale started at five o'clock every Tuesday from Mr Peck's, in Hagerstown, arriving at Frederick Town at noon It there stopped at Maj Henry Butler's tavern, leaving which it arrived at Liberty Town the same evening The stopping place in that town was Mr Orndorff's tavern,

whence it started on Wednesday morning at five o'clock, and arrived in Baltimore in the evening of the same day Mr Evans' tavern was the stopping-place in Baltimore, and there the stage remained until Friday morning at five o'clock, when it started to return by the same route, arriving at Frederick Saturday morning, and reaching Hagerstown the same evening The announcement of these lines concludes with statements to the effect that passengers going to Georgetown, York, Lancaster, Philadelphia, Baltimore, or Hagerstown may, by taking the Georgetown stage on any one of these routes, arrive at his destination without longer detention on the road than is necessary to feed and change horses The fares charged were three dollars from Georgetown to Frederick, four dollars and a half from Frederick to Lancaster, fourteen pounds of baggage being allowed to be carried by each passenger free, and one hundred pounds weight being considered equivalent to an additional passenger and charged for accordingly It was further announced that the public houses on these roads were excellent, and the charges as reasonable as any on the continent

H Peck announced on the 25th of July, 1799, that he would run a hack-stage during the ensuing season for the accommodation of passengers going to Bath or elsewhere, furnishing "a good comfortable stage, active horses, and steady, sober, and attentive drivers," all at reasonable prices

On the same day John Home announces that his hack-stage will run as usual to Bath, applications to be made to Mr Henderson at the Fountain Inn, on the corner of the Public Square, near the court-house, in Hagerstown

In 1801, Peter Orndorf ran a line of stages between Frederick and Hagerstown

On June 2, 1802, George Giffinger informs the public that he continues to keep a good stage and horses, which may be had at the shortest notice and on the most reasonable terms by applying to his house or at Mr Stoner's tavern, near the court-house

In an announcement made June 9, 1802, Peter Orndorf informs the public that as many inconveniences have arisen from there being but one stage a week between Baltimore and Hagerstown, he has gone to a very considerable expense and trouble to arrange for running in future two stages a week He announced that stages would leave the Indian Queen Stage office, Baltimore, every Tuesday and Saturday at four o'clock A M and arrive in Frederick at six P M, leaving there the next morning at four o'clock A M, and arriving at H[illegible] at four P M [illegible]turning to Ba[illegible] the stages were to leave Ha[illegible]town on Tuesdays and Saturdays at eight o'clock A M stopping at Frederick during the night, and arriving in Baltimore at six o'clock in the afternoon of the next day

In 1803, Messrs George Cissinger, of Hagerstown, and John Geyer, of Frederick Town established a line of mail stages from Hagerstown to Baltimore, which left Jonathan Hager's tavern, at the "Sign of the Ship," near the court house, Hagerstown, every Tuesday and Saturday at ten o'clock A M, and arrived at Mrs Kimball's, Frederick, the evening of the same day, and at the Columbian Inn, Baltimore, the next afternoon at six o'clock Returning, they left Baltimore on Tuesdays and Saturdays at four o'clock A M, and stopping at Frederick during the night, arrived in Hagerstown the next evening The fare charged on this line was two dollars to Frederick and from Frederick to Baltimore, three dollars and a half

George Cissinger further announces that he will, if necessary, run an additional stage on Thursday, arriving in Frederick in the evening, and returning to Hagerstown next day

On the 29th of March, 1805, George Cissinger and Joseph Boyd informed the public that they had commenced running a line of mail-coaches from Frederick Town, via Middletown, Boonsboro', Hagerstown and Greencastle, to Chambersburg twice every week to and from the above places

Starting from Mrs Kimball's every Tuesday and Saturday at five o'clock P M, they arrived at Hagerstown the same night, stopping at the house of George Beltzhoover (late Ragan's), and leaving the next morning at four o'clock, they arrived at the house of Thomas Hetich, in Chambersburg, by eleven o'clock A M

They left Chambersburg on their return trips on Sundays and Wednesdays at one o'clock P M, and reached Hagerstown at six P M, and leaving Hagerstown on Tuesdays and Thursdays at six A M, they arrived in Frederick Town by one P M This line met at Frederick Town Mr Scott's line from Philadelphia via Lancaster, Columbia, York, Hanover, and Petersburg, and also Mr Winemiller's from Washington City via Georgetown, Montgomery Court house, and Clarksburg, and Mr Orndorff's from Baltimore via New Market At Chambersburg it met the line of Mr Tomlinson & Co from Philadelphia via Lancaster, Elizabeth Town Middletown, Harrisburg, Carlisle, and Shippensburg, also theirs from Pittsburgh via Greensburg, Somerset, Bedford, and McConnellstown The fare charged from Frederick Town to Ha[illegible] [illegible] to Chambersburg, [illegible] with the usual allowance

for baggage A line of stages from Baltimore to Pittsburgh and Wheeling, *via* Frederick Town, Hagerstown, Cumberland, and Brownsville, commenced running Aug 1, 1818, starting from Gadsby's Hotel in Baltimore, every Sunday, Tuesday, and Thursday, it arrived at Hagerstown at eight o'clock P M same day, left Hagerstown Mondays, Wednesdays, and Fridays at three o'clock A M, arriving at Pratt's tavern same evening at six P M, left Pratt's Tuesdays, Thursdays, and Saturdays at two A M, and arrived at Uniontown, Pa, at nine P M, leaving there at four A M, and arriving at Pittsburgh and West Alexandria the same evening, thence at four A M, arriving in Wheeling at seven A M, through in four days

A new line of post coaches from Gettysburg to Hagerstown, for the accommodation of passengers from Philadelphia to Wheeling or Pittsburgh, was started in 1821, Stockton & Stokes being the proprietors

On the 2d of April, 1822, it was announced that the Hagerstown and Gettysburg line of stages had recommenced running three times a week, connecting with the Philadelphia mail line at Gettysburg The journey from Wheeling to Philadelphia, a distance of three hundred and forty six miles, was accomplished in little more than four days, and the fare charged was twelve dollars

The Hagerstown and Boonsboro' Turnpike Company was incorporated by the Legislature during the session of 1822–23

In 1823 a new line was started by A Lindsay between Hagerstown and McConnellsburg, Pittsburgh, Chambersburg, Bedford, and Greensburg Travelers by these routes were conveyed from Pittsburgh to Baltimore or Washington in three days

The following announcement is dated March 28, 1823 "The United States Mail Stage for Wheeling *via* Frederick Town, Hagerstown, Cumberland, etc, leaves the office, adjoining Barnum's Hotel, on Sundays, Tuesdays, and Thursdays, at four o'clock A M, arriving at Wheeling in three and a half days where boats are always in readiness to convey passengers down the river On the 1st of April next an accommodation stage will leave the same place for Frederick Town and Hagerstown on Mondays, Wednesdays, and Fridays at four o'clock A M, dining at Frederick Town, and lodging at Hagerstown, affording a conveyance to the two latter places six days in the week" An announcement dated Feb 7, 1826, said "The extra mail or accommodation line leaves Baltimore on Mondays, Wednesdays, and Fridays at four o'clock in the morning, and reaches Wheeling on the fourth afternoon [illegible] the Friday [illegible] which arrives there on the fifth day after leaving Baltimore The old mail line runs as usual on Sundays, Tuesdays, and Thursdays, going through in three and a quarter days" A line to run only during the day (except at special instance of the passengers) is also announced to commence running on the following 1st of March, making the trip to Wheeling in five and a half days The fares charged were, from Baltimore to Hagerstown, $5 50, from Hagerstown to Cumberland $5 00, from Cumberland to Uniontown, $4 00, from Uniontown to Wheeling, $4 25, making the total charge for the trip from Baltimore to Wheeling, $18 75 To Emmittsburg, *via* Union and Taneytown, a bi-weekly line was run in 1826, and in the same year a line to Chambersburg was running every Thursday and Saturday

A new line of stages commenced running Jan 1, 1827, between Boonsboro', Md, and Winchester, Va, by way of Shepherdstown, Martinsburg, etc, Mr Humrickhouse, of Hagerstown, being part contractor

The Hagerstown and Winchester mail line, *via* Williamsport, Falling Waters, Martinsburg and Bucketstown, was run by Maxwell & Ringer in 1839, leaving Hagerstown on Tuesdays, Thursdays, and Saturdays, and leaving Winchester on Mondays, Wednesdays, and Fridays

The Good Intent and Pilot lines to Pittsburgh and Wheeling and Cincinnati in 1838 ran *daily*, with United States mail

In their "day and generation" these were the fast lines of our fathers, but they have passed away forever, leaving behind them only their advertisements for travelers to show who were the men of energy and enterprise that preceded the "railway kings" of the present time

Mails—The first protection to public and private letters in Maryland was given by an act of Assembly passed at the session of 1707, by which the opening of letters by unauthorized persons was made a penal offense

Letters at that time were generally, in the absence of post-roads and post-offices, deposited in public-houses, to be sent by the first conveyance of which the landlord could avail There was very little correspondence at that time between the towns along the coast, as most of the trade was direct with England from each port Letters on business sometimes containing bills of exchange on Liverpool and London merchants, were left at the public houses, and forwarded by the hands of the captains of vessels sailing from the particular port to England, but were accessible, as well as the answers, to any designing person [illegible] to bills of ex-

change were frequently intercepted, and it became necessary to protect such communications by law. This act was repealed and re-enacted at the session of the Assembly in 1713, the protecting clauses and penalties for breaking open letters by unauthorized persons were re-enacted, and additional clauses enacted making it the duty of the sheriff of each county to convey all public letters to their destination within his county, but if beyond, to the sheriff of the next county on the route. The sheriff of each county was allowed for this service so many pounds of tobacco annually.

The first regular post-office established in the colonies was by an act of the Parliament of England passed in 1710. By its provisions a general post-office was established in North America and the West Indies, and in 1717 a settled post was established from Virginia to Maryland.

It was not until 1753 that the practice of delivering letters by the penny post or letter carrier and of advertising letters on hand commenced. Newspapers were carried by mail free of charge until 1758, when, by reason of their great increase, they were charged with postage at the rate of ninepence each year for fifty miles, and one shilling and sixpence for one hundred miles.

At this time the postal routes were few and far between, and did not afford sufficient facilities for the convenience of the public. Gentlemen of a town or a neighborhood were in the habit of making up a purse to supply a regular mail-rider, generally going to the single post-office of the province, as in Maryland to Annapolis, and depositing all letters they were intrusted with, and on their return bringing letters and papers to remote correspondents and subscribers. Stage-shallops were sometimes used between important places to carry passengers. The stage-shallop resembled a dug-out rigged upon wheels, at that time a very essential combination, as it often became necessary on these routes to cross streams that were not fordable and without a ferry.

The new post-rider between Frederick and Hagerstown made an announcement, Dec. 29, 1786, that he had made Mr. Steel's tavern, the "Sign of Gen. Hand," in Market Street (opposite Mr. William Stenson's), his stopping-place, where letters for and from those places would be received and carefully delivered.

The mails of Western Maryland, in March, 1792, were carried as follows: From Baltimore to Fredericktown, Sharpsburg, and Hagerstown, and thence to Chambersburg, once a week, the mail leaving Baltimore on Saturday at three o'clock in the afternoon, and arriving at Chambersburg the following Monday at seven in the evening, or on Tuesday at seven in the morning. Returning, it left Chambersburg on Wednesday morning at five o'clock, and arrived at Baltimore on Friday at four in the afternoon.

In 1815, William Kreps, postmaster, advertised for a letter-carrier. A daily mail for Washington City, Baltimore, and Wheeling was first made up at Hagerstown in May, 1822.

In June, 1869, the location of the Hagerstown Post-office was changed from the old stand on North Potomac Street to the new building erected by Postmaster Logan on West Franklin Street, north side, a short distance east of Jonathan. The building is one story high, is commodious, airy, light and high-ceiled, and is sufficiently large to accommodate the business of the post-office for some years to come.

The following is a list of the postmasters of Hagerstown from the establishment of the office to the present time:

Oct. 1, 1803, Nathaniel Rochester;[1] October, 1804, Jacob D. Dietrick; April, 1807, William Kreps; March 18, 1822, Daniel Schnebly (predecessor died); Aug. 23, 1826, Thomas Kennedy; July 8, 1827, O. H. W. Stull; Nov. 17, 1829, Howard Kennedy; April 5, 1838, Frederick Humrickhouse; Feb. 23, 1843 (under Mr. Humrickhouse, the office became a Presidential appointment); March 2, 1847, Christopher Hilliard; June 21, 1849, George Updegraff; April 11, 1853, Samuel Rudenour; May 29, 1861, John Schleigh; April 21, 1869, William Logan; Sept. 5, 1878, Margaret Logan, who is the present incumbent.

Cumberland Valley Railroad extends a distance of seventy-four miles, from Hagerstown to Harrisburg, Pa., in one direction, and to Martinsburg, Va., in the other, only a small portion of the road being in Maryland. This road was chartered on the 2d of April, 1831. The work of construction was commenced in January, 1836, and the road was completed from Chambersburg to the Susquehanna River, opposite Harrisburg, in December, 1837, a distance of forty-nine miles. The company obtained leave by an act of the Legislature approved Feb. 2, 1836, to construct a bridge over the Susquehanna, and to extend the road through Harrisburg three miles to the Pennsylvania Canal, and also to connect with the other roads centering in Harrisburg. That portion of the road extending from Chambersburg to Hagerstown was originally the Franklin Railroad, and was constructed under charters obtained from the Legislatures of Pennsylvania and Maryland in the year 1832. The road was built in 1838, and after passing through

[1] Col. Rochester was postmaster for years previous to 1803. He was appointed an associate judge of the Washington County Court in 1793, and his nephew, Robert Rochester, succeeded him. [illegible]

the hands of several owners, was finally transferred, in 1859, to the Cumberland Valley Railroad, by which it is now operated. The road was opened to Martinsburg in 1874. During a flood in the latter part of 1877 the Cumberland Valley Railroad bridge across the Potomac River was destroyed, the superstructure of wood, covered with tin, being entirely washed away. A ferry across the river was improvised, and trains were run as usual, the only interference with travel resulting from the disaster being an addition of thirty minutes to the regular time consumed in travel between Hagerstown and Martinsburg. The Cumberland Valley road is managed by the Pennsylvania Railroad Company.

Western Maryland Railroad.—Of all the railroads that centre at Baltimore, the Western Maryland was the last to be completed. Although projected in 1830, its trains did not enter the city on its own track till 1873. It is difficult for those who pass over the road to understand why its building was delayed so long. Fully fifty years ago the people of Baltimore were most anxious to establish communication by rail with the fertile and populous region which it traverses. The Baltimore and Ohio road would have been located upon this line if the engineers could have found a practicable route across the South Mountain. Railroad building was in its infancy when these explorations were made. After the Baltimore and Susquehanna Company (now the Northern Central) had completed eight miles of its main stem it turned to the west and built nine miles of road through the Green Spring Valley, with the intention of continuing the line to the Blue Ridge. The completed portion of this branch was opened for travel May 26, 1832. When work was resumed on the main stem, the western extension of the Green Spring branch was suspended, and nothing further was done for twenty years.

An act was passed May 27, 1852, incorporating the Baltimore, Carroll and Frederick Railroad Company. The corporators were George Brown, Robert M. Magraw, Zenus Barnum, William F. Johnson, Charles Painter, Richard Green, Richard Worthington, Nicholas Kelly, Edward Remington, Jacob Reese, John Fisher, Jacob Mathias, David Roop, Joshua Smith, J. Henry Hoppe, David H. Shriver, John Smith, Samuel Ecker, Joseph Moore, Reuben Haines, of W., Daniel P. Sayler, John Cover, Peregrine Fitzhugh, Joshua Motter, Robert Annan, David Rinehart, Jervis Spencer, Isaac Motter, and John Baker. This company was authorized to build a railroad to the "head-waters of the Monocacy River," with the option of beginning at Baltimore or at the terminus of the Green Spring branch of the Baltimore and Susquehanna road (Northern Central). In the following year the corporate name was changed to "The Western Maryland Railroad Company," and an act was passed at the same session of the Legislature authorizing the company to issue bonds to the amount of $1,000,000, and to extend the road to Hagerstown. Robert M. Magraw was the first president of the new company. Nothing was done for five or six years except that it was decided to begin building at the terminus of the Green Spring branch, and to use the main stem of the Northern Central Railway from Lake Roland to the city. The road was opened to Owings' Mills Aug. 11, 1859, and to Westminster June 15, 1861. One year afterwards trains began to run to Union Bridge, twelve miles beyond Westminster, and this place remained the terminus of the road until Jan. 9, 1871, when it was opened to Mechanicstown, fifty-nine miles from Baltimore.

The construction of the road on the west side of the Blue Ridge was begun in 1866. In that year the Legislature passed an act authorizing the county commissioners of Washington County to subscribe $150,000 to the capital stock of the Western Maryland Company, the money to be expended in grading the road from the western slope of the mountain to Hagerstown. The commissioners of Washington County subsequently indorsed the bonds of the Western Maryland Company to the amount of $300,000. There was some delay in getting over the mountain, and the eastern and western divisions were not united until June 6, 1872, when trains began to run to Hagerstown. The Williamsport "extension" and the "short line" from Baltimore to Owings' Mills were built simultaneously, and the road was opened to the Potomac River Dec. 17, 1873. After the completion of the direct line from Owings' Mills to Baltimore, the nine miles of track between the Green Spring Junction and Lake Roland reverted to the original owners, and this division is again operated as the Green Spring branch of the Northern Central Railway.

Baltimore City and Washington County furnished the greater portion of the capital used in building the Western Maryland Railroad, and the board of directors and the officers of the company were subject to the mutations of municipal politics. A great deal of money was wasted, and although the route presented no extraordinary difficulties, the cost of construction per mile far exceeded that of any other railroad in Maryland. The funded debt amounts to $1,265,250, or something more than $18,000 for every mile of the main stem. To this must be added the capital paid in by the stockholders. Bonds representing the funded debt of the road [illegible] dorsed by the

city of Baltimore and bonds amounting to $300,000 are indorsed by Washington County.

Early in 1874 Col. J. M. Hood, a practical engineer of large experience, was elected president of the company and general manager. With his administration began a new era in the history of the Western Maryland Railroad. The management was completely divorced from municipal politics, and the president became in fact as well as in theory, the chief executive officer of the company. The net earnings of the road increased from year to year, new sources of revenue were developed, the floating debt was paid, the overdue interest on the mortgage debt was funded, and the liquidation of the principal provided for on terms satisfactory to the bondholders. The old portion of the main stem was rebuilt, additional passenger-trains were put on the eastern division and special inducements were held out to summer excursionists to visit the romantic spots on the line of the road. The increased facilities for getting to and from the city attracted a large number of people to the suburban towns on the line of the road, and the movement of population in this direction is seen in the constantly increasing receipts from passengers on the eastern division. A summer resort was established at Pen-mar on the summit of the Blue Ridge, which was visited by more than one hundred thousand persons last season. In 1874 a contract was concluded with the Baltimore and Potomac Railroad Company, under which the trains of the Western Maryland Company enter Baltimore through the Baltimore and Potomac Railroad tunnel and run direct to Hillen Station. This fine depot was built in 1875 with funds loaned by the city. Early in 1880 the Baltimore and Hanover Railroad was completed to Emory Grove Station, nineteen miles from the city, where it connects with the main stem of the Western Maryland road. Its trains run to Hillen Station on the Western Maryland track, and the business drawn from the section of country traversed by the new road has added considerably to the revenues of the Western Maryland Company.

The projected line of the Western Maryland Railroad ran through Emmittsburg and Waynesboro' in all the old surveys, but in the multitude of counsels which prevailed between 1867 and 1870 the route was changed to its present location. It then became necessary to reach these two important towns, each lying five miles north of the main stem by means of lateral branches.[1] The Emmittsburg branch, which diverges from the Western Maryland road at Rocky Ridge, fifty-four miles from Baltimore and connects the road with Emmittsburg, was completed in 1875. The Waynesboro' branch, which has developed into the Baltimore and Cumberland Valley Railroad, leaves the main stem at Edgemont, on the western slope of the Blue Ridge, and extends to Waynesboro', seven and a half miles, thence to Shippensburg, by way of Chambersburg, twenty six miles, the whole length of the road being thirty three and a half miles. This, in fact, is an extension of the Western Maryland road into the very heart of the Cumberland Valley. The Baltimore and Cumberland Valley road was opened on the 5th of September, 1881, to Chambersburg, and has since been completed and opened to Shippensburg. The Cumberland Valley of Pennsylvania, which is brought into close connection with Baltimore by this road, extends from the Susquehanna River on the north to the Potomac on the south, a distance of eighty one miles, and is an extremely rich and thickly-populated section. The land is well watered by small streams, and the North Mountain on the west, and the Blue Ridge on the east, protect the valley from violent storms in winter. Every product of the soil known to this climate is successfully raised. By this route Chambersburg is ninety-seven and a half miles from Baltimore, while it is one hundred and fifty miles from Philadelphia by way of Harrisburg, and Shippensburg is one hundred and eight and a half miles from Baltimore, and one hundred and forty miles from Philadelphia. It is confidently expected that this difference in distance in favor of Baltimore will have a marked influence upon the course of trade. The Frederick and Pennsylvania Railroad, completed in 1872, connects Frederick City with the Western Maryland Railroad at Bruceville Station, and extends northward into Pennsylvania to Littlestown, where it connects with the Pennsylvania system. The Hanover Junction, Hanover and Gettysburg Branch Road, recently extended, taps the Western Maryland at Glyndon, nineteen and a half miles from Baltimore.

The Western Maryland Railroad is one of the most attractive in the country for the variety and picturesqueness of the scenery along its route. From the deep cut at Fulton Station until the traveler reaches the terminus of the road at Williamsport, on the Potomac River, a constant succession of beautiful

[1] A company [illegible] chartered in 1860 called the Gwynn's Falls Railroad. A [illegible] amount of stock having been subscribed, a company was [illegible] following officers: George Slothower, president, and John Weathered, J. F. Myers, J. Howard McHenry, Mr. Harris, and Theodore Mottu, directors. Notwithstanding an earnest spirit was manifested, nothing more was done under the charter. It [illegible]

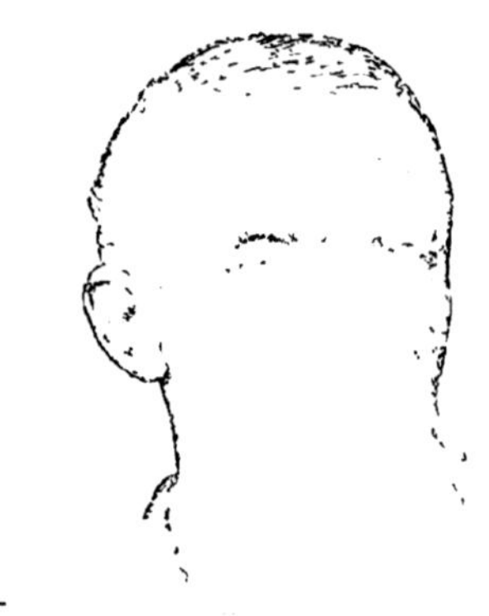

...ures meet the eye. After passing the elegant ...ntry residences along the Liberty and Hookstown ...ls, the first point of interest reached is Greenwood ...rk, a fine grove of shade-trees situated on elevated ...und, which is used as a public resort for excur...ns, picnics, etc. Leaving Greenwood Park, the ...n passes Owings' Mills, Reisterstown, Emory ...ove, Westminster, and Union Bridge, where the ...pany's shops are located. The country from ...ings' Mills to Mechanicstown is beautifully diver...ed and undulating, and embraces one of the richest ...cultural sections of the State. Numerous hand...me farms in the highest state of cultivation, with ...fty-looking homes and huge barns and stables, dot ... landscape in every direction on either side of the ...d. Ascending the Blue Ridge from the east, the ...d makes a complete semicircle around the town of ...illasville, which is familiarly known to excursion...s as the "Horse-shoe Curve." Here a lovely view ... the beautiful Harbaugh's Valley is obtained. ...veral years ago the station "Penmar" (the word ...ing a contraction of Pennsylvania and Maryland) ...s established, where passengers alight for High ...ck, a point one mile distant, and situated near the ...mmit of the mountain, whence a view is had of the ...mberland and Shenandoah Valleys on the north, ...st, and south, covering an area of two thousand ...uare miles of the most charming scenery. High ...ck is about two thousand feet above the sea-level, ... fourteen hundred above the base of the mountain. ...e panorama of the Cumberland Valley is without ...ubt one of the grandest to be seen in any portion ... the country east of the Mississippi. Of course ...re are loftier mountains and bolder effects, but for ...riety, richness, and sublimity combined it is scarcely ...ualed in any other portion of the Union. As far ... the eye can reach the valley is thickly studded with ...wns, villages, hamlets, and farm-houses, and the land...ape consists of undulating plains, silvery streams, ...jecting mountain peaks, and, in the distance, the ...e crests of the loftier ranges. An observatory has ...n erected on the Rock, from which the spires of ...urches in Chambersburg, twenty-four miles away, ... be seen. Monterey Station is a near point, where ... road passes over a corner of Pennsylvania, for ...ich no charter has ever been granted by the State. ...order to obviate the necessity of applying to the ...islature for one, the railroad company purchased ... farm through which the intended route was to ... and built the road without a charter. From ...nterey, where a view of Monterey Springs is ob...ned, to Waynesboro' the grade is on a descending ...le. From Waynesboro' ...tion to H... ... the scenery is charming, and though its character is changed after leaving Hagerstown, it is none the less attractive. When the Potomac is reached the view from Williamsport is one of the handsomest to be found anywhere along the banks of that beautiful stream.

President John Mifflin Hood, through whose exertions and under whose personal direction these important extensions have been made, is one of the youngest of the prominent railroad men of the country. He was born at Bowling Green, the old family residence, near Sykesville, in Howard Co., Md., on the 5th of April, 1843. His father, Dr. Benjamin Hood, was the son of Benjamin and Sarah Hood, and was born at Bowling Green in 1812, and died in 1855, in the forty-third year of his age. His mother, Hannah Mifflin Hood, was the daughter of Alexander Coulter, of Baltimore, where she was born. Young Hood was educated in Howard and Harford Counties, completing his course at Rugby's Institute, Mount Washington, in 1859. He then commenced the study of engineering, and in July of the same year secured employment in the engineer corps engaged in the extension of the Delaware Railroad. The same corps was next employed in the construction of the Eastern Shore Railroad of Maryland, Mr. Hood soon becoming principal assistant engineer, and for part of the time having sole charge of the operations. In August, 1861, he went to Brazil, but finding the field for engineering unpromising, returned to Baltimore in January, 1862, and after studying marine engineering, ran the blockade, and reported to the Confederate authorities at Richmond, Va., for service. He was at once assigned to duty as topographical engineer and draughtsman of the military railroad then building from Danville, Va., to Greensboro', N. C. (since known as the Piedmont Railroad), and upon the completion of his work declined a commission offered in the Engineer Corps, and enlisted as a private in Company C, Second Battalion Maryland Infantry. He served with distinction in the Maryland Infantry until the spring of 1864, when, owing to the scarcity of engineers, he accepted a lieutenant's commission in the Second Regiment of Engineer Troops, in which service he continued until surrendered at Appomattox. Mr. Hood was several times slightly wounded, and at Stanard's Mill, in the Spottsylvania battles, had his left arm badly shattered above the elbow. While still incapacitated for duty he ran the blockade, and, wading the Potomac at night, visited his family, and came to Baltimore, where he had his wound treated by Prof. Nathan R. Smith, returning to his command before Richmond with a large party of re... ... to the C... ... ...ptember, 1865,

he was employed by the Philadelphia, Wilmington and Baltimore Railroad to make surveys for the extension of the Philadelphia and Baltimore Central line between the Susquehanna River and Baltimore, he was next placed in charge of the construction of the Port Deposit branch of the Philadelphia, Wilmington and Baltimore Railroad, and made chief engineer of the Philadelphia and Baltimore Central Railroad, and constructed its line through Cecil County to the Susquehanna River He was soon afterwards elected engineer and superintendent of the same company, and in April, 1870, became general superintendent of the Florida (now Atlantic, Gulf and West India Transit) Railroad His health failing, in November, 1871, he accepted the position of chief engineer of the Oxford and York Narrow-Gauge Railroad, in Pennsylvania, and while holding this position he became also chief engineer of a new line, known as the Baltimore, Philadelphia and New York Railroad, the construction of which was stopped by the panic of 1873 On the 14th of January 1874, Mr Hood was elected vice-president and general superintendent of the Western Maryland Railroad and on the 24th of March following he was made president and general manager of the road, including the office of chief engineer, in which position he continues to the present time On the retirement of Mr Keyser in 1881, Mr Hood was tendered the office of second vice president of the Baltimore and Ohio Railroad, but declined the office Mr Hood married on the 17th of July, 1867, Florence Eloise Haden, of Botetourt County, Va, and has five children The presidents of the Western Maryland Company and the dates on which they were respectively elected are given in the following list

	Elected
Robert M Magraw	Feb 21, 1853
Nathan Haine	1851
William Roberts	June 23, 1858
Augustus Shriver	June 1[illegible], 1860
Nathan Haines	October, 1861
John Smith	Nov 6 1862
Robert Irvin	Jan 6, 1863
John Lee Chapman	Nov 8, 1866
Wendell Bollman	April 2, 1868
George M Bokee	May 17, 1870
Robert F Banks	Oct 18, 1871
James L McLane	Nov 21, 1871
Alexander Rieman	Dec 2, 1873
John M Hood	March 24, 1874

Classification of Tonnage Receipts on Western Maryland Railroad for the Year ending Nov 30 1880, compared with Two Previous Years

	1880 Tons	1879 Tons	1878 Tons
Lumber and bark	11,808	10,151	11,016
Coal	31,125	10,081	9,9[illegible]
Miscellaneous	47,882	39,037	42 225
Live-stock	7,890	3,081	3,[illegible]30
Grain and feed	30,986	27,949	26,[illegible]
Lime and limestone	5,115	1,551	4 111
Wood	[illegible]	1,[illegible]	[illegible]
Ores	12 863	93 692	911
Flour, barrels	61,820	92,562	89,841
Net tonnage	154,795	108,906	

Distances on Western Maryland Railroad

	Stations	Miles		Stations	Miles
	Baltimore	0	2.4	Linwood	[illegible]
	Fulton	3.0	1.8	Union Bridge	4[illegible].3
2.8	Oakland	5.8	2.5	Middleburg	47.8
1.0	Arlington	6.8	1.1	Frederick Junction	49.2
1.4	Mount Hope	8.2	0.1	York Road	49.[illegible]
0.9	Howardsville	9.1	1.7	Double Pipe Creek	51.0
1.6	Pikesville	10.7	3.1	Rocky Ridge	54.1
1.3	Greenwood	12.0	1.6	Loys	55.7
1.7	Junction	13.7	1.7	Graceham	57.4
1.1	Owings' Mills	14.8	2.0	Mechanicstown	59.4
2.9	Timber Grove	17.7	1.3	Deerfield	6[illegible].7
1.8	Glyndon	19.5	2.2	Sabillasville	[illegible].9
0.4	Emory Grove	19.9	3.1	Blue Ridge	69.0
2.8	Glen Falls	22.7	2.4	Pen Mar	[illegible]
3.4	Tank	26.1	3.7	Edgemont	7[illegible].1
2.7	Carrollton	28.8	2.5	Smithsburg	77.6
1.5	Gorsuch Road	30.3	3.4	Chewsville	81.0
3.4	Westminster	33.7	5.0	C V Crossing	86.0
2.9	Avondale	36.6	0.6	Hagerstown	86.6
2.8	Wayside	39.4	6.4	Williamsport	93.0
1.7	New Windsor	41.1			

Distances on Baltimore and Cumberland Valley Branch of the Western Maryland Railroad

	Stations	Miles		Stations	Miles
	Edgemont	0	4.5	Chambersburg	21.8
3.1	Midvale	3.4	4.9	Green Village	26.7
3.9	Waynesboro'	7.3	3.1	Southampton	29.8
3.6	Five Forks	10.9	3.8	Shippensburg	[illegible]3.6
3.1	Altenwald	14.0			
3.3	New Franklin	17.3			

Washington County Branch of the Baltimore and Ohio Railroad —The first action looking to the construction of a railroad connecting Hagerstown with the main stem of the Baltimore and Ohio was taken by the citizens on the 17th of March, 1857, when a convention from the various districts was held at Hagerstown Resolutions were adopted petitioning the State Legislature to pass an act enabling the county to issue two hundred and fifty thousand dollars' worth of bonds for the construction of the road, and a committee, consisting of J Dixon Roman, T G Robertson, Dr Thomas Maddox, William Dodge, and James Wason, was appointed to confer with the authorities of the Baltimore and Ohio Railroad Company Andrew Rench presided at the meeting, and George F Heyser acted as secretary Addresses were made by Judge Weisel, William Motter, Elias Davis, David Reichard, William Price, and Robert Fowler On the 10th of March, 1864, the Legislature passed an act incorporating the Washington County Railroad, and naming Isaac Nesbitt, George S Kennedy, Jacob A Miller, Johns Hopkins, Galloway Cheston, Peter B Small, and Robert Fowler as commissioners and first directors Th[illegible] dollars, with

permission to increase it to a million and a half The shares were to be of the value of twenty dollars each The commissioners of Washington County and the mayor and Council of Baltimore were also empowered to subscribe each two hundred and fifty thousand dollars to the work, to be raised by issuing bonds

In September, 1865, the county commissioners, William Rulett, Elias E Rohrer, and John Reichard, accompanied by their clerk, John L Smith, and by George S Kennedy, Jacob A Miller, Peter B Small, Dr Thomas Maddox, Thomas A Bolt, Dr Biggs, and A Appleman, had a conference with the Baltimore and Ohio authorities at Camden Station, and were informed by Mr Garrett that the company had decided to make a liberal subscription to the work The county commissioners then subscribed $150,000, and the following additional subscriptions were recorded Johns Hopkins, $12,000, Robert Garrett & Sons, $10,000, Robert Fowler, $10,000, A Gregg & Co, $4000, Samuel Wilhelm, $2000 The work of construction was begun soon afterwards, and the first president under the original incorporation was E W Mealey

The second board of directors was composed of Robert Fowler, Galloway Cheston, Johns Hopkins, Jacob A Miller Peter B Small, and Walter S Kennedy, Sr P B Small was the secretary and treasurer

It was not long, however, before it became apparent that the work could not be accomplished under the original management, and the Baltimore and Ohio came to the aid of the president and directors and finished the construction The last rail was laid on Wednesday Nov 21, 1867, and arrangements were at once completed for running regular passenger and freight-trains between Hagerstown and Baltimore, beginning with Monday November 25th Until the opening of this road the large travel from Hagerstown and its vicinity which reached the Baltimore and Ohio Railroad at Martinsburg and Frederick was conveyed in stage coaches The first shipment over the new road was a consignment of wheat, a car-load of which reached Baltimore on the 22d of November, 1867 The grain belonged to Samuel Emmart, and was consigned to A W Goldsborough Mr Mealey was succeeded in the presidency by Robert Fowler, who retained the position until his death, after which the corporation was merged into the Baltimore and Ohio The road extends from Hagerstown to Weverton, on the main stem of the Baltimore and Ohio Railroad, a distance of twenty-three miles, and passes through the districts of Funkstown Tilghmanton, Keedysville, Rohrersville, and [illegible]

LOCAL RAILWAY STATIONS BALTIMORE AND OHIO RAILROAD

Main Stem—Old Line

Stations	Miles	Stations	Miles
Camden Station, Balto	0	Brady's	185
Relay	9	Rawling's	191
Ellicott City	15	Black Oak	194 5
Hollofields	18 7	Keyser	201
Ilysville	20	Piedmont	206
Woodstock	24 5	Bloomington	208 2
Marriottsville	27 2	Frankville	212
Sykesville	31 5	Swanton	217 2
Gaither's	33	Altamont	221
Hood's Mill	34 2	Deer Park	223 7
Watersville	40	Oakland	2[illegible]
Mount Airy	42 5	Hutton s	235
Plane No 4	46	Snowy Creek	2[illegible]
Monrovia	50	Cranberry	240
Hartman s W S	51	Rodemer s	245
Frederick Junction	58	Rowlesburg	251
Adamstown	64	Buck Eye	252 5
Doub s	65	Tray Run	258
Washington Junction	68 7	Tunnelton	258 5
Point of Rocks	69	West End	259 5
Berlin	75 2	Newburg	265
Weverton	78 5	Independence	266 2
Sandy Hook	80	Thornton	272 2
Harper s Ferry	81	Grafton	277 7
Duffield s	87 5	Fetterman	279 5
Hobb's	89 2	Valley Falls	285 7
Kerneysville	92	Texas	292 2
Vanclevesville	95	Fenton's Ferry	295
Opequon	97	Fairmont	299 5
Martinsburg	100	Barnesville	302
North Mountain	107	Barracksville	305
Cherry Run	113	Farmington	310 5
Miller's	115 5	Mannington	317 5
Sleepy Creek	117	Glover s Gap	324 7
Hancock	122 5	Burton	329 2
Sir John s Run	128	Littleton	335 2
Great Cacapon	132	Board Tree	337 5
Orleans Road	138 5	Bellton	342
Doe Gully	140 5	Cogley s	345 7
No 12 W S	148 5	Cameron	349 2
Paw Paw	153 5	Easton s	354
Little Cacapon	156 5	Roseby s Rock	360
French's	161	Moundsville	366 2
Green Spring	163 7	McMechen s	372
Patterson s Creek	170 5	Benwood	373
Cumberland	178	Wheeling	377

Main Stem via Washington to St Louis

Stations.	Miles	Stations	Miles
Baltimore	0	Rowlesburg	267
Relay Station	9	Tunnelton	275
Laurel	22	Newburg	281
Bladensburg	31	Thornton	288
Washington	40	Grafton	291
Metropolitan Junction	41	Bridgeport	311
Rockville	56	Clarksburg	316
Barnesville	73	Salem	330
Washington Junction	83	Long Run	335
Weverton	93	West Union	343
Sandy Hook	94	Central	346
Harper s Ferry	95	Pennsboro'	356
Shenandoah Junction	103	Ellenboro'	361
Kerneysville	106	Cairo	369
Martinsburg	114	Petroleum	376
North Mountain	121	L [illegible] Junction	378
Hancock	137	Kanawha	388
Sir John's Run	142	Parkersburg	398
Paw Paw	168	Athens	435
Green Spring	178	Chillicothe	495
Cumberland	192	Cincinnati	593
Keyser	215	North Vernon	666
Piedmont	220	Louisville	721
Altamont	237	Seymour	780
Deer Park	240	Vincennes	785
Oakland	246	Odin	868
Cranberry	[illegible]	[illegible]	933

Harper's Ferry and Valley Branch

Stations	Miles	Stations	Miles
Harper's Ferry	0	Strasburg Junction	51
Halltown	6	Tom's Brook	55
Charlestown	10	Maurertown	57
Cameron	11	Woodstock	61
Wadesville	23	Edinsburg	66
Stephenson's	27	Mount Jackson	74
Winchester	32	New Market	81
Kernstown	36	Broadway	88
Newtown	39	Lanville	94
Middletown	41	Harrisonburg	100
Cedar Creek	46	Pleasant Valley	10[illegible]
Capon Road	50	Fort Defiance	117
Strasburg	52	Staunton	126

Metropolitan Branch

Stations	Miles	Stations	Miles
Washington	0	Gaithersburg	21.5
Metropolitan Junction	1	Germantown	26.5
Queenstown	3.2	Boyd's	29.5
Terra Cotta	4	Barnesville	3[illegible].2
Silver Spring	7	Dickerson	35.7
Knowles'	11	Tuscarora	39
Rockville	16.2	Sugar-Loaf	41.7
Washington Grove	20.7	Washington Junction	42.7

Washington Branch

Stations	Miles	Stations	Miles
Camden Station	0	Savage	20.2
Camden Junction	4.5	Laurel	22.2
Relay	9	Contee's	24.5
Elk Ridge	9.5	Beltsville	28
Hanover	11.5	Paint Branch	31.7
Dorsey's	14.2	Alexandria Junction	31
Jessup's	16.5	Bladensburg	34.2
Bridewell	16.7	Metropolitan Junction	39
Annapolis Junction	18.6	Washington	40

Baltimore, Columbus and Chicago Line

Stations	Miles	Stations	Miles
Baltimore	0	Mount Vernon	520
Washington	40	Frederick	527
Harper's Ferry	95	Lexington	549
Martinsburg	114	Mansfield	557
Cumberland	192	Shelby Junction	569
Piedmont	220	Plymouth	577
Deer Park	240	Chicago Junction	583
Oakland	246	Monroeville	596
Grafton	291	Sandusky	611
Fairmont	316	Tiffin	607
Mannington	334	Fostoria	620
Cameron	365	Bloomdale	627
Moundsville	382	Deshler	645
Benwood	389	Holgate	657
Bellaire	391	Defiance	671
Wheeling	395	Hicksville	691
Quincy	406	Auburn Junction	708
Belmont	410	Garrett	711
Barnesville	418	Avilla	716
Spencer's	425	Syracuse	744
Cambridge	443	Milford Junction	749
Concord	452	Walkerton Junction	782
Zanesville	469	Wellsboro'	796
Pleasant Valley	478	Alida	804
Newark	495	Michigan Central Junc	820
Columbus	528	Kingston	842
Louisville	504	Chicago	854
Utica	509		

Washington County Branch

Stations	Miles	Stations	Miles
Weaverton	0	Rohrersville	8
Barthelow's	4	Eakle's Mills	11
Brownsville	5	Keedysville	13
Claggett's	6	Breathed's	18
Baker's Summit	7	Hagerstown	[illegible]

Baltimore, Washington and Pittsburgh Line

Station	Miles	Station	Miles
Baltimore	0	Connellsville	284
Washington	40	Broad Ford	287
Washington Junction	83	Dawson	290
Harper's Ferry	95	Oakdale	29[illegible]
Martinsburg	114	Layton	297
Sir John's Run	142	Jacob's Creek	301
Cumberland	192	Smithton	303
Mount Savage Junction	196	Port Royal	305
Cook's Mills	201	Snyder	307
Hyndman	206	West Newton	309
Sand Patch	225	Suter	313
Keystone	227	Shaner	317
Meyersdale	229	Guffey	318
Garrett	2[illegible]4	Ellrod	324
Rockwood	2[illegible]	McKeesport	3[illegible]7
Casselman	245	Port Perry	331
Pinkerton	249	Braddock	332
Ursina	256	Glenwood	3[illegible]7
Confluence	258	Hazlewood	338
Ohio Pyle	268	Pittsburgh	342
Indian Creek	277		

The Shenandoah Valley Railroad was started as a local work, with home capital and home talent to guide it, and was finished by the Shenandoah Construction Company, the headquarters of which were at Philadelphia. Upon taking charge of the road, the company determined to extend it to Hagerstown, Md., and Waynesboro', Va. On the 4th of September, 1880, the first train from the Valley of Virginia entered Hagerstown, and the last spike in the track between the towns named was driven in March, 1881. The Construction Company is no longer in existence, having been succeeded by the Shenandoah Valley Railroad Company. The stations on this road and their distances from Hagerstown are as follows:

Stations	Miles
Hagerstown, Washington Co., Md.	0
St. James, " "	5.9
Grimes', " "	9.0
Sharpsburg, " "	13.6
Shepherdstown, Jefferson Co., W. Va.	16.9
Shenandoah Junc., " "	23.1
Charlestown, " "	28.4
Ripon, " "	33.9
Fairfield, Clark Co., Va.	36.2
Berryville, " "	39.9
Boyceville, " "	46.2
White Post, " "	49.2
Ashby, Warren "	53.2
Cedarville, " "	56.4
Riverton, " "	59.2
Front Royal, " "	62.1
Manor, " "	66.4
Bentonville, " "	72.9
Overall, Page "	75.6
Rileyville, " "	79.8
Kimball, " "	85.1
Luray, " "	88.8
Marksville, " "	95.6
East Liberty, " "	101.9
Grove Hill, " "	104.0
Shenandoah Iron-Works, Page Co., Va.	106.7
Elkton, Rockingham Co., Va.	112.5
Port Republic, " "	127.2
Weyer's Cave, Augusta Co., Va.	129.1
Patterson, " "	1[illegible]2.1
Crimora, " "	136.9
Waynesboro', " "	1[illegible]3.7

CHAPTER XLIII

REPRESENTATIVE MEN AND FAMILIES OF WASHINGTON COUNTY

WASHINGTON COUNTY has been the mother of a long line of distinguished men in every walk of life Although one of the youngest of the counties of Western Maryland, she has enriched the bench, the forum, the pulpit, the medical profession, and the halls of legislation with earnest and able men, whose lives have been conspicuous and honorable far beyond the small confines of their native county and State

Many of those eminent men have contributed to the glory of their country on the field of battle, in literature, and in art, and some of them are a part of the history of the county itself, and probably no county in Western Maryland has been more prolific of men of force and character in private life than Washington Her sons have held high and honorable positions in every section of the State, and some of them have left her bounds to find fortune and found honorable names in other States

The Hughes family Barnabas Hughes, the ancestor of the Hughes family in Maryland, emigrated from the county of Donegal, Ireland, in 1750 and settled at Lancaster, Pa He married Elizabeth Waters, of Elizabethtown, Pa, and after residing some years at Lancaster removed to Baltimore After a short stay in that town he decided to remove to Western Maryland, and finally located himself in a portion of Frederick County which afterwards fell within the boundaries of Washington County Here he engaged in the iron trade, and built Mount Etna and other furnaces near the Black Rocks, above Beaver Creek He died in 1780 His eldest son, Daniel, was born in 1730, and his second son, Samuel, was born in 1741. Both the brothers became conspicuous in the Revolution for their zeal in behalf of the patriot cause, and from the fact that many of the cannon used by the Continental army were cast at their forges Besides Daniel and Samuel, one son and five daughters were born to Mr and Mrs Barnabas Hughes, but all of them died in infancy On the 9th of August, 1759, was born another son, John Hughes, who afterwards became a captain in the Revolutionary army He married Miss Chamberlaine, of the Eastern Shore After John were born Elizabeth, who married Hon Richard Potts, of Frederick, Margaret, who died single, and Barnabas, who married Miss Beltzhoover, of Hagerstown, and died aged twenty-three

Daniel afterwards colonel, married Rebecca Lux, of Baltimore His children by this marriage were Robert, born [illegible] William, born M[illegible] 1769, Nancy, or Ann, born in April, 1771, Samuel, born in July, 1773, and James, born in 1775 The latter died unmarried Both James Hughes and his mother, first wife of Col Daniel, were buried in the Lutheran church at Hagerstown Rebecca Lux, second daughter of Daniel Hughes, died in 1800, aged twenty three In 1780, Col Daniel Hughes married Susannah Schlatter, of Germantown, Pa, whose father, Rev Michael Schlatter, was one of the early missionaries to the German Reformed Church in this country The children of Col Daniel Hughes and Susannah Schlatter were Susannah, who died single, in 1826, and was buried in the Episcopal Cemetery, Hagerstown, Mary Ann (who married Joseph I Merrick, the well-known lawyer, of Hagerstown, and had two children,—Daniel, who died in infancy, Mary, who died in 1824), Esther, born July 4, 1794 (who married Amasa Sprague of Rochester, N Y, and died in January, 1868), Daniel, who died single, in 1824, John Henry, who married Nancy Lyon John Henry Hughes left one son, William Schlatter Hughes, who now resides in San Rafael, Cal William S. Hughes married Mary Ashberry, and has seven sons and one daughter At the age of seventy, Col Daniel Hughes married his third wife, Mrs Ann Elliott, of Carlisle, Pa, mother of Commodore Jesse D Elliott, U S N By this marriage he had one daughter, Rebecca Lux, who married Dr Joseph Martin, of the Eastern Shore, and died leaving no issue Both Mrs Martin and her mother were buried in the Presbyterian graveyard at Hagerstown, but Col Daniel Hughes and the other members of his family were interred in the Episcopal graveyard at the same place

Robert Hughes, eldest son of Col Daniel Hughes, married Susannah Purviance, daughter of Samuel Purviance, of Baltimore Mrs Hughes' brother, John Henry Purviance was in the diplomatic service of this country, and for twenty years was the bearer of dispatches between this country and France He accompanied the commissioners who contracted the treaty of Ghent Another brother, Henry Purviance, studied law with Henry Clay Mrs Hughes' father left Baltimore in 1780, accompanied by Nicholas Raguet, of Philadelphia, and Samuel Ridout, of Annapolis They traveled westward by way of Fort Pitt, now Pittsburgh, their purpose being to take legal possession of one hundred thousand acres of land owned jointly by Samuel and Robert Purviance While descending the Ohio River in a flat boat they were attacked by Indians, near the site of the present city of Cincinnati Purviance and Raguet were [illegible] ained to An-

napolis, where his descendants still reside Mr and Mrs Robert Hughes had six children,—Elizabeth Isabella, Henrietta Frances (who married Dr Horatio Nelson Fenn, of Rochester, N Y), Henry C, Rebecca L Letitia Purviance (who married Dr H H Harvey), and Henry Courtney, who died in 1862 William Hughes, second son of Col Daniel Hughes, married Margaret Coale, of Cecil County, and had the following children William, Joseph Samuel, Barnabas, Emily, Ann, Rebecca Hollingsworth, Augusta, and Helen William and Joseph died early in life Emily married George Clarke, of Baltimore, and lived many years in Louisville, Ky, where her descendants still remain Rebecca H married Nathaniel Ruggles of Boston Augusta married Dr Alvas, of Henderson, Ky, and Helen married a Mr Taylor, and still resides at Paducah, Ky William Hughes removed to Henderson, Ky, after his marriage, and he and his wife died there Samuel Hughes, third son of Col Daniel Hughes, married Miss Holker, and had five sons, his eldest being John Holker, second, James, third, Napoleon, fourth, Henry, fifth, Lewis, and four daughters,—Marie Antoinette, Louisa Adelaide and Catharine Marie A Hughes married Col William Fitzhugh, Louisa married Dr John Claggett Dorsey of Hagerstown, Adelaide married John Savage, of Philadelphia, Catharine married William Coleman Birch, and afterwards Rev Tryon Edwards John Holker Hughes died unmarried, Napoleon B Hughes married Nancy Thompson, sister of Gen Thompson, of Baltimore, Dr. Henry Hughes died unmarried, and Lewis Hughes married Laura Gray, of Baltimore

Ann, or Nancy daughter of Col Daniel Hughes married Col William Fitzhugh, of Prince George's County, and they had seven sons and five daughters The Fitzhugh family removed from their mansion, "The Hive," four miles from Hagerstown, to Genesee, N Y, where Col Fitzhugh assisted in founding the city of Rochester

The eldest son of William Fitzhugh and his wife, Ann Hughes Fitzhugh, was William, who married, March 10 1818, his cousin, Marie Antoinette Hughes, daughter of Samuel Hughes, of Mount Alto

The second son, Daniel Fitzhugh, married Anna Dana a second cousin Her mother was the daughter of Peregrine Fitzhugh, who was a brother of the elder Col Fitzhugh She married Mr Dana, an English gentleman Anna was the only child

John Henry Hughes, who married Nancy Lyon, of Philadelphia, died at Mount Etna Furnace His widow married Thomas Curtis, of Mount Holly, Pa The first furn[illegible] of the Hugh[illegible] brothe[illegible] w[illegible] built at Black Rocks, near South Mountain, in partnership with Mr Buchanan of Baltimore, before the Revolutionary war The second furnace, now known as Mount Etna, was about a mile lower down After these were built, Col Daniel Hughes formed a partnership with Col Wm Fitzhugh and built a forge and nail furnace, now known as the "Old Forge," between Hagerstown and Leitersburg, on the Antietam The fourth and last furnace was built by Col Daniel Hughes and his two sons, Samuel and Daniel Hughes both lawyers of Hagerstown, at Mont Alto, Franklin Co, Pa, now known as Mont Alto Park, a summer resort It was sold by the Hugheses to Col Weistling, of Harrisburg John Horine purchased Mount Etna Furnace The Mount Pleasant Furnace, near Havre de Grace, in Harford County, Md, was built by Samuel Hughes son of the first Barnabas, and brother of Col Daniel Hughes, of Antietam There are cannon now in existence in the Boston Navy-Yard cast at this furnace during the Revolutionary war

Capt John Hughes, the youngest son of the first Barnabas Hughes, was in the Revolutionary war, and was a great friend of André, and attended him during his last confinement, and received letters and his picture with a request that they should be sent to his affianced in England He performed all of André's bequests with scrupulous exactitude, and corresponded with André's intended bride, giving her all the particulars of his confinement and death

Richard Stockton, formerly of Baltimore, married a daughter of Capt John Hughes Another daughter married Mr Stokes, his partner Stockton & Stokes were the great stage-men in the days before railroads were invented Mr Stokes also lived in Baltimore His son is Dr W H Stokes, of Mount Hope Institution, near Baltimore

The Lawrence family Among the leading citizens of Washington County in the early part of the present century, and one of the most conspicuous figures in the social, legal, and political circles of Hagerstown, was Upton Lawrence, a gentleman of exceptional talents and of a high standard of moral and intellectual attainment Mr Lawrence's father was John Lawrence, of Linganore, Frederick Co, who married Martha, a daughter of Sir Stephen West Sir Stephen was the son of John West, of Horton Buckinghamshire, England, and emigrated to this country at an early date He settled in Anne Arundel County and left six children of whom Martha was the fourth Upton Lawrence, son of John Lawrence and Martha West, married Elizabeth, daughter of Col Jonathan Hager, and granddaughter of Jonathan Hager, founder [illegible] Lawrence, like

mother, the gifted Mary Orndorff, was lovely in person and in character, and was one of the belles of Hagerstown About that time the Messrs Buchanan, afterwards learned jurists,—one of them becoming a member of the Court of Appeals and the other a circuit judge,—were regarded as being among the most attractive and entertaining beaux of Washington County which was famous for the culture and refinement of its early society Miss Heister, daughter of Gen Daniel Heister, and niece of Jonathan Hager, in writing of one of them, said briefly but impressively, "I like Mr Buchanan and think him a gentleman" Mr and Mrs Upton Lawrence were married by the Rev George Bower, rector of St John's Episcopal Parish, a genial parson of the old school, who is said to have frequently danced the first cotillion at the gay assemblies in his parish Mrs Lawrence's grandfather, Christopher Orndorff, was of German extraction, and lived in great state on his plantation near Sharpsburg He was a handsome man of commanding presence, and very free and genial in his manners He kept open house and dispensed a generous but by no means ostentatious hospitality He reared twelve children, all of whom were educated with unusual care Mr Orndorff served as an officer in the Revolutionary army, attaining the rank of major, and all the officers of the Continental army passing to and fro from the theatre of war were received and entertained at his house with the utmost cordiality Upon one occasion, when Gen Horatio Gates was a guest of Maj Orndorff's, Mary Madeline, a daughter of his host, passed him in the hall without seeing him, and entered the parlor to view herself in the large mirror there She was very young and had on a new cap of the latest style, and doubtless wished to discover if it was becoming As she passed him Gen Gates turned to her father and exclaimed, "Who is that lovely creature?" Maj Orndorff replied, "That is my youngest daughter" At Gen Gates' request she was placed at the tea table so that he could see her A few days afterwards Gen Gates proposed, through her father, to make her his wife, but as she was of a somewhat *romantic* temperament, she could not reconcile herself to a marriage with a person as old as her father, and promptly rejected him In the same manner, while stopping at Maj Orndorff's house on his way from the scene of military operations Col Jonathan Hager met Mary Orndorff and surrendered at discretion He was, however, more fortunate in his suit than Gen Gates, for he paid his addresses one day and was married the next Their only child was a beautiful girl, Elizabeth Hager, who when [illegible] married Upton Lawrence, who afterwards became a distinguished lawyer, and whose house was frequented by many of the leading people of Maryland Among them was Luther Martin, the famous lawyer, who was at one time engaged to be married to Mrs Lawrence's mother, the beautiful widow of Jonathan Hager The match, however was broken off because Mrs Hager became convinced that Mr Martin was intemperate[1] Mr Martin, however, appears to have been sincere in his expressions of admiration and esteem and always treated her daughter, Mrs Lawrence with the utmost affection, making Mr Lawrence's house his home whenever business called him to Hagerstown Roger B Taney and John Thomson Mason were also frequent guests at Mr Lawrence's mansion Mr and Mrs Lawrence had five children,—two sons, Jonathan and Upton, who are dead, and three daughters one of whom is Mrs Robert J Brent, whose daughter is Mrs William Keyser, wife of one of the former vice-presidents of the Baltimore and Ohio Railroad Company The other two daughters remain unmarried and continue to reside in Hagerstown, occupying the building erected by the late Dr John Reynolds upon land owned by their father It is situated on Prospect Hill, West Washington Street The Misses Lawrence are now the sole representatives in the third generation of the original proprietor of Hagerstown, and preserve with creditable pride many rare and curious relics of the Hager family[2] They reside in

[1] Mrs Hager afterwards married Col Henry Lewis, of Virginia

[2] Following are copies of some of the letters addressed by Mr Martin to Mrs Hager during his courtship

(No 1)

"May 12, 1800

"My dear Madam,—I twice called at Mr Wyant's yesterday to see you, and you were not at home Being obliged to leave town this morning, I take the liberty of expressing to you in writing those sentiments which I should have been happy to have done in person You have a charming little daughter who wants a father I have two who stand in need of a mother By doing me the honor to accept my hand our dear children may have the one and the other, and I promise you most sacredly that in me you shall ever find a tender, indulgent, and affectionate husband, and your present little daughter shall find in me everything she could wish for in a father My fortune, my dear madam, is not inconsiderable I have a large landed estate in Maryland and Virginia, and my practice brings me more than twelve thousand dollars a year Our estates united will enable us to live in a style of happiness equal to our wishes And so far am I my dear madam, from wishing my little girls to be benefited by your estate, that if we should not increase our family, your fortune whatever it may be, shall be your own if you survive me, or if you should not survive me, your daughter's Forgive my dear madam, the liberty I have taken in thus laying before you my wishes and my hopes, and do me the honor to write to me and treat me with the same [illegible] fly to you [illegible]

the old mansion in unostentatious but liberal style, and dispense a generous but charming hospitality. The atmosphere of their household is quaintly antique, and there is everywhere apparent a tender reverence for the traditions and associations of the past. Both ladies enjoy the confidence and respect

first moment in my power, and express my gratitude at the feet of her on whom, from that time, I shall depend for my happiness. With the most perfect esteem and affection, I am, my dear madam, your sincere friend and lover,

"LUTHER MARTIN."

(No. 2.)

"AT MRS. WYANT'S (no post-mark),
"ANNAPOLIS, May 14, 1800.

"MY DEAR MADAM.—Believe me when I assure you that I feel for you the most perfect respect, and it would give me infinite pain should you consider my letter to you as being in any manner wanting therein. It was the apprehension that you would leave Baltimore before I could return from this place that caused me to lay before you in the manner I have done those wishes which I otherwise intended to have declared personally, and which have not been hastily formed, for though I have not had the happiness of much personal acquaintance, I am no stranger to your merit. I wish to obtain for myself a kind and amiable companion for life, and for my two little daughters a worthy mother. You, my dear madam, are the lady who for some time past I had selected from your sex, as far as depends on myself, to supply that place, and I regret that I did not sooner know of your visit to Baltimore. Permit me once more, my very dear madam, to assure you most solemnly that if you can prevail on yourself to accept my hand and consent to my wishes, the unremitted study of my future life shall be to render you happy and to promote the interest of your amiable daughter.

"Permit me also most respectfully to solicit that you will honor me with an answer, and that you will not forbid me to hope that to you I may be indebted for my future happiness.

"With the sincerest esteem and affection, I am your friend and lover, and ardently wish you may honor me so far as also to give me a right hereafter to sign myself your tender and affectionate husband,

"LUTHER MARTIN."

[No. 3.]

"BALTIMORE, July 26, 1800.

"MY VERY DEAR AMIABLE MRS. HAGER,—Unless you have experienced something like it yourself, you cannot imagine the vacancy in my existence which your absence hath occasioned. I feel quite a solitary being, and shall so feel until I am blessed with the animating presence of my other, my better half. With what solicitude do I look forward to that period, and how tedious will be each hour until that time pass away. To you, my dearest, best of women, I have avowed my love and affection. Will you not then bestow on me the dear delight, by way of softening the pains of absence, of an assurance that you can, without a sacrifice of your own wishes, reward my love and affection by reciprocal affection on your part? You know not with what anxiety I shall on my return from New York fly to the post office for a letter. Do not, dearest madam, disappoint me.

"I have been told since you left town that on last Sunday week, in the evening, I was at your lodgings. Of this I had no recollection. I doubt not I made a very foolish figure, but I think it impossible that I should have behaved with rudeness or impropriety. Was that the reason, my very dear Mrs. H., of the coldness and reserve you appeared to me with on the Monday morning when I called on you before I went to Annapolis? If so, I wish [illegible] you [illegible] but [illegible] [illegible] never see me again in a situation that I know not what I do, unless it should proceed from the intoxication of love! In the heat of summer my health requires that I should drink in abundance to supply the amazing waste from perspiration but having found that I was so unexpectedly affected as I was by cool water and brandy, I have determined to mix my water with less dangerous liquors, nay, I am not only confining myself to mead, cider, beer, bock, mixed with soda water but I am accustoming myself to drink water alone. Thus if we live to see each other again, you will find me most completely reformed and one of the soberest of the sober. I hope, my dearest madam, that you arrived at your home in health and that you remain so. The heat was so great that it is impossible you could have traveled with much satisfaction. Be so good as to express my affectionate regard to our amiable daughter, and be assured that the first wish of my heart is that her very amiable mother will give an undisputed right that she should be so called to her sincere and affectionate friend and lover,

"LUTHER MARTIN."

(No. 4.)

"BALTIMORE, Sept. 4, 1800.

"MY DEAR MADAM,—I returned from Richmond, in Virginia, on last Monday. I was one week gone. I returned much fatigued but in good health. But alas, alas what is health to me? To a poor wretch, who, before you hear of him again, will most probably be tucked up, swinging from the limb of some convenient gallows formed tree, something like those figures—a little resemblant of the human shape which some prudent farmers hang up in their corn fields to scare the birds from their corn. Yes, my dearest madam, be not alarmed should you hear that your swain, in a fit of despair, has in the French style given you the slip by sticking his neck into a noose. For alas! my dearest madam, I have been this day informed that some time past at Mr. Peck's tavern, some of the company having introduced our names, for you know impertinent people will take these liberties, some wight of great self-consequence, but whose name I cannot yet learn, most solemnly pledged himself that our union should not take place, and that he would under take to prevent it. Nay, further, that some kind friend who would be eternally miserable should you throw yourself away upon such a miscreant as myself, has sent you a cautionary letter, in which are enumerated all my sins and indignities. Now, my very dear madam, can you wonder should you after this hear that I had hung myself in despair? But to be serious, I have infinitely too good an opinion of your understanding and judgment to believe that you will suffer any person to put you, like a child in leading strings and compel you to move only subservient to their wills, and I have infinitely too good an opinion of the candor and generosity of your heart to believe that you will ever suffer your conduct towards me to be influenced by the cowardly attacks of an assassin in the dark. I have no doubt there are persons who would go half-way to the devil to prevent our union and who can lie and misrepresent almost equal to their old master, but as I feel conscious less that there is nothing in my situation in life, in my fortune, in my character, in my past or present life, which ought to justify to deprive me of that happiness I solicit, or render me unworthy of that blessing, I only ask that I may have an opportunity of explaining or falsifying any suggestions to my prejudice before they shall be supposed to influence your conduct towards me. [illegible] to think you,

the entire community of Hagerstown, which regards them with affectionate pride as the oldest representatives now living in the town, of the original proprietor, Jonathan Hager.

From memoranda in their possession, it is evident that eighty or ninety years ago Hagerstown was the centre of an exceptionally refined and highly cultivated society. In addition to the intelligent German families who had settled in the vicinity or in the town itself, it had received valuable accessions from the wealthiest and most aristocratic of the leading Southern Maryland and Eastern Shore families, such as the Ringgolds, the Tilghmans, the Buchanans, the Spriggs, the Bells, the Fitzhughs, etc. The period was one of fine dress and courtly equipage, of lace and ruffles, of powdered hair and silken hose, of "routs" and other entertainments of the most elaborate and lavish character. A gentleman's full dress at that time consisted of long silk stockings, short-clothes, embroidered vest, cut low in order to display

... dearest madam, for your favor of the 1st instant. You are so ... to receive the trifles I send you and express your thanks ... them. I am equally actuated in sending them, as they may ... pleasure in the enjoyment to yourself and our dear child, ... as they are proofs of my affectionate attention to you,—another proof of which be so good as to accept in the few watermelons and cantaleups which will accompany this. The moment, my dearest madam, I receive from you the promised papers I will address the most immediate measures for your interest, and I will give you my services in the execution of those measures. Why have you not mentioned to me my dear Elizabeth? I hope my sweet girl is well, and that she doth not hate me; present to her my sincerest wishes for her happiness. Promise me, my dearest Mrs. H., a longer letter by the return of the stage or ... Oh, my dearest madam! let me hope that you will throw off that unaccountable reserve which you have so long assumed, and which I am willing to suppose you mean as a trial of your power and of my patience. Indeed, my dearest madam, you have had proof sufficient of both, now be so very good as on your part to bless me with the assurance that you can without a sacrifice of your own wishes promise to receive as an affectionate, indulgent, tender husband him whom you have found a sincere and affectionate friend and lover.

"Yours, L. Martin."

(No. 5.)

"Baltimore, Dec. 17, 1860.

"It was, my dearest Mrs. H., with inexpressible delight that I once more received your handwriting. Indeed, you had been very cruel in so long neglecting me, and I felt it most sensibly. Were you really impressed with the belief that I love you with that tenderness and sincerity which is truly the case, I think you have too much generosity of disposition and goodness of heart intentionally to give me pain. But I will not, my dear madam, trouble you with complaints at present, whatever injustice I may have to charge you with. I will defer the charge until we are so happy to be 'by ourselves' in one of our habitations in Baltimore, where I shall demand personal satisfaction, which, I hope, you will not refuse me. And so my charming widow has really taken a house in Baltimore, and is coming to spend the winter there. Indeed, indeed, my dear, I will try hard to turn you out of possession in a very little time, and you must consent to have me a very constant visitor until that event takes place, for I shall not be able to live out of your company. Why, my ever dear, my tenderly beloved Mrs. H., did not you condescend to assure me that I should not be an unwelcome visitor on the approaching Christmas? With what joy would I have accepted the hint! Why, my best beloved, do you defer your consent to our mutual happiness, a consent which I must hope you intend to bestow on your sincere lover. Why, dearest of women, will you not name the day from which we both may date the happiest period of our lives? Is there anything in my situation of life which you wish to have explained? If so, inform me. I will explain anything you wish to know that concerns me in any respect whatever with truth, with candor, with sincerity; I will make you my judge.

"Let me entreat my dearest Mrs. H. to free me from the suspense she at present keeps me in. Tell me that you will be mine. Name the [illegible] that shall [illegible] all my wishes, and my future life shall speak my joy, my love, my gratitude to you. Though you have been so unkind that you would not ask me to dine with you on Christmas-day, nor permit me to wait you on that day with a license and a ring as I wished to have done, yet, my dearest Mrs. H., permit me to increase your enjoyments at that period. By Joseph I send you a box containing some excellent raisins and currants as ingredients for mince-pies, which is generally a dish at that season, and I also send a jug of as good Madeira wine as this city can furnish. In return sometimes think of me, and think of me as one of those who delights and who always will delight in showing his approbation and affection for you, and on Christmas-day and the day after, exactly at half-past two o'clock, drink a glass of the wine to the health of your lover, exactly at which time I also will drink a glass to the health and happiness of my dearly beloved mistress. Thus we, though absent, shall have the pleasure of knowing that at that moment our thoughts are fixed on each other. Adieu, best, most beloved of women. Do not forget, do not neglect, but bless with another dear letter

"Your Martin."

(No. 6.)

"Annapolis, June 12, 1861.

"My dear Madam,—I have at length received and had deposited in the Chancery office all the exhibits in your case and Kershner's; as soon as I have a moment's leisure I will compare them with the depositions and proceed to do whatever may be necessary in the case. That I will render you and your daughter every service in my power, from *motives of friendship*, you may be assured. I once flattered myself you would have given me an *additional motive* for so doing. I have been for this eighteen days past engaged, without interruption, every day in the trial of causes. You may easily judge I have not had time to attend to anything else, and that my fatigue has been great. My daughters, with their friend Anna Maria Thompson, are at Governor Ogle's. They still love you, and frequently ask me when you and I are to be married. What answer can I give to that question? To my dear Betsey give my sincerest wishes for her happiness, and accept for yourself the same from your friend,

"L. Martin."

[Evidently, Mr. Martin had not yet abandoned hope, but the tone of his letter indicates a fear that his cause was a desperate one, and so it proved, for Mrs. Hager afterwards married Col. Henry Lewis, [illegible]

the elaborate stock with its brooch of brilliants, velvet or satin coat, and pumps with enormous buckles A lady's dress was even more costly and elaborate On one occasion Mrs Jonathan Hager wore plum colored satin trimmed with fine black lace and cord and tassels Her wardrobe also included a bewildering assortment of silk and satin costumes, the colors comprising "old gold," black, bronze, sage, and other hues which the English "renaissance" has made fashionable once more, light blue satin scarfs with trimming of lace and ribbon, capes trimmed with down, a green camel's hair shawl, with green bonnet to match, brocades of light blue and deep pink, embroidered with bunches of flowers, etc All the dresses were "gored," so as to set close to the figure, and all of them had long "trains" Upton Lawrence appears to have been a model entertainer of the old-fashioned type, and was noted for his handsome parties, fine dinners, and well-trained servants He did not, however neglect his profession, but was an eloquent and able lawyer and enjoyed an extensive practice He also managed several farms, and was a gentleman of liberal cultivation and enlarged ideas

The Tilghman family Of the prominent Eastern Shore families represented among the early settlers of Washington County the Tilghmans were among the most conspicuous Col Frisby Tilghman, son of Judge James Tilghman, of Queen Anne's County removed to Washington County prior to 1800 and settled on the estate known as "Rockland" His father, the third son of Susanna and Richard Frisby Tilghman, was a member of the Revolutionary conventions of Maryland of 1774, 1775, and 1776, a member of the Council of Safety throughout the war and afterwards chief judge of the judicial district composed of Cecil, Kent, Queen Anne's, and Talbot He was the first attorney-general of Maryland, and was a judge of the Court of Appeals from 1801 to 1809 On the 29th of June, 1769, he married Susanna, daughter of Dr George Steuart, of Annapolis One of their sons Frisby, was born Aug 4, 1773, and died on the 14th of April, 1847

Col Frisby Tilghman married, on the 24th of March, 1795, Anna Maria Ringgold, daughter of Gen Samuel Ringgold, and had children,—Mary, born on the 8th of February, 1796, George, born on the 11th of May, 1797, Thomas Edward born April 15, 1800, Susan Ann, born March 31, 1801, Frisby, born Oct 23, 1807, and Ann Chester, born Feb 20, 1810 (who married William Hollyday) Mrs Anna Maria Tilghman died on the 21st of February, 1817 Her husband (Col Frisby Tilghman) survived her, and on the [illegible] September, [illegible], married [illegible] daughter of Col William Lamar, of Allegany, and had children, viz Louisa (who married William Hollyday), Margaret Ann (who married Gen Thomas J McKaig), and Sarah Lamar Col William Lamar married Margaret Worthington, daughter of John and Mary Todd Worthington, of Baltimore County Their children were Mary, who married Hon Michael C Sprigg, William L Lamar, who married Maria Briscoe, Richard Lamar who died single, Louisa, who married Col Frisby Tilghman, Ann, who married George Tilghman, and Sarah, who died single Mary, daughter of Col Frisby Tilghman and Anna Maria Ringgold, married Dr William Hammond and had children,—Ann, Richard Pindell, Mary, William, Caroline, George, and Rebecca Hammond

Richard Pindell Hammond entered West Point Military Academy in 1837, and graduated in 1841 After graduating he was assigned as brevet second lieutenant to the Third Artillery On the 10th of September of the same year he was made a full second lieutenant From 1841 to 1842 he served in garrison at Fort McHenry, Baltimore For some years afterwards he served at various military stations in the South, and when the war with Mexico broke out was ordered to the front, and participated in nearly all the important engagements Both at the storming of Churubusco and Chapultepec he distinguished himself by his intrepidity and coolness, and was brevetted major After the war he served on the Coast Survey and in May, 1851, resigned to engage in the practice of the law at Stockton, Cal

George Tilghman (born on the 11th of May 1797, died Aug 25, 1831) was the son of Col Frisby Tilghman, and married twice His first wife was Ann E Lamar, by whom he had children,—Anna Maria and Mary Tilghman, who married Phineas Janney His second wife was Anna B Lynn, daughter of Capt David Lynn, of Allegany Their children were Fanny Lynn, Susan, who married W Bowcue, George, and Frisby L, who married Anna, daughter of Col Bolling, of Petersburg Va

Thomas Edward Tilghman, born on the 15th of April, 1800, was the son of Col Frisby Tilghman, and married Rebecca Hammond His children were Edward Sommerfield, born Jan 21, 1827, William Frisby, born Feb 23, 1828, Thomas Hammond, born Jan 7, 1830 His second wife was Sarah Bugbee by whom he had the following children William Ridgeley, Anna Maria, Sarah, Charles Ringgold, Antoinette, Ida, and Henry

Dr Frisby Tilghman son of Col Frisby and Anna Maria Ringgold Tilghman, studied medicine in P[illegible] [illegible] Hage[illegible]

He married his cousin, Henrietta Maria Hemsley, daughter of Alexander Hemsley and Henrietta Maria Tilghman Alexander Hemsley was the son of William Hemsley, of Queen Anne's County, a member of the Continental Congress from the Eastern Shore, and Henrietta Maria Tilghman was the daughter of Richard Tilghman, son of Matthew, the youngest son of the second Richard Tilghman, of the Hermitage Dr Frisby Tilghman died, leaving no children

Nathaniel Rochester was one of the earliest residents and most influential business men of Hagerstown His father was John Rochester, son of Nicholas, who emigrated from England to Virginia, and settled in Westmoreland County, where he died, leaving two sons,—William and John John married a daughter of William Thrift, of Richmond, Va, and died in 1754, leaving three daughters and two sons,—John and Nathaniel The latter was born on the 21st of February, 1752, in Westmoreland County, Va He was only two years old when his father died Two years afterwards his mother married Thomas Critcher, and in 1763 the family removed to Granville N C Mrs Critcher died the same year, and Thomas Critcher died in 1778 Nathaniel's opportunities for education in early life were of the most limited description, but he possessed a vigorous mind and great energy of character, and whenever and wherever he could obtain it never failed to store his mind with information that might prove useful in later years His youth was spent in mercantile business and at the age of twenty he engaged in business with Col John Hamilton, who afterwards held the consulate of the British government for the Middle States When the Revolutionary war broke out he entered the Continental service, and by his gallantry and good conduct attained the rank of lieutenant-colonel at a very early age After the war he again engaged in mercantile pursuits, first in Philadelphia and afterwards in Hagerstown, where he associated himself with Col Thomas Hart, who in 1793 removed to Lexington, Ky Two of Col Hart's daughters married, respectively, Henry Clay and James Benton, father of the celebrated Thomas Hart Benton

The names of Hart & Rochester of N & R Rochester, of Thomas Hart & Son, and of William Fitzhugh are constantly recurring in the brief "notes" of the early enterprises and business of Hagerstown Thomas Hart, N Rochester, and William Fitzhugh were citizens of Hagerstown at the end of the last and the beginning of the present century The following old advertisement sets forth alike their kind of business and the prices [illegible] at that time

"HART AND ROCHESTER

Have, and will constantly keep, for sale a

LARGE QUANTITY OF

NAILS, BRADS, AND SPRIGS,

of their own manufacturing, in Hager's Town, at the following Prices —Twenty-penny nails and flooring brads, at nine pence per pound, or thirteen shillings and six-pence per thousand, sprigs of different sizes, in proportion (the quality of these nails being far superior to those imported from Europe, they have not a doubt of the preference being given to them at the above-mentioned prices), Twelve penny, or shingle-nails at nine-pence per pound, or eleven shillings three-pence per thousand, ten penny nails at nine pence per pound, or ten shillings per thousand, eight-penny nails at ten pence per pound or eight shillings and four-pence per thousand, six-penny nails at eleven-pence per pound, or seven shillings per thousand, four-penny or case nails, at four shillings and six-pence per thousand

Hager's Town, August 20, 1790"

Nathaniel Rochester, the other member of the firm, was well known to the old inhabitants of Washington County as a distinguished merchant, politician, and agriculturist He was a candidate, and elected, on the electoral ticket in 1808 (in connection with Dr John Tyler, of Frederick Town) in favor of the election of James Madison to the Presidency,—Frederick, Washington, and Allegany Counties constituting the district In 1810 he removed from Washington County, Md, to the Genesee country in Western New York, and settled in what is now known as Monroe County He purchased land on which the city of Rochester (named after him) is now built *at a pound of bacon for an acre of land*

Col Rochester, June 25, 1791, "declined the mercantile business in this place" (Hagerstown), and earnestly requested "all those indebted to him or to the late concern of Nathaniel & Robert Rochester, to make immediate payment, that he may be enabled to continue and enlarge his nail and rope manufactories" In October, 1804, he was elected sheriff, and resigned then the office of postmaster, having been the first postmaster of Hagerstown Nov 20, 1810, Col Rochester advertised for sale his Hagerstown residence,—"a brick dwelling-house sixty-eight by twenty two feet," with rope-house and rope-walk On the 13th November, 1800, Mr William Fitzhugh advertised for sale his residence and seven hundred acres, four miles from Hagerstown, and on November 4th, Col Charles Carroll advertised his estate of one thousand and fifty acres adjoining Hagerstown Whether the sales were then effected is not stated, but the three gentlemen emigrated to the Genesee Valley in New York

Col Rochester married Sophia, daughter of Col William Beatty, of Frederick County, Md, on the 20th [illegible] died on the 14th of May,

1831, in Rochester, N Y, in his eightieth year His widow died in the same place They had twelve children Col Rochester was the first president of the Hagerstown Bank, and his portrait, painted while he held that position, is now in possession of the bank, and is highly prized by the officers of that institution Col William Beatty's wife and Mrs Rochester's mother were the daughters of John Conrad Grosh, a respectable German immigrant, who settled in Frederick County about 1750 Col Rochester removed to the Genesee country early in the present century, in company with Charles Carroll, of Bellevue, and Col William Fitzhugh He left his home in Hagerstown when over sixty years of age, and with his family and household goods journeyed across the State of Pennsylvania, in wagons and carriages, to the site of the city of Rochester At his death he had amassed great wealth

Col Rochester's sons were William, who was lost at sea, Thomas, a judge of the court at Rochester, died a few years since, Nathaniel, a lawyer, Henry E,[1] now living at Livingston Park, near Rochester, Mrs Childs (Sophia), Mrs Dr Montgomery (Mary), Mrs Bishop (Caroline), Mrs Dr Pitkin (Louisa), and Mrs Coleman (Anna)

The Carrolls Charles Carroll, who was one of

[1] The Hagerstown *Mail* of June 10, 1881, gives the following account of a visit of Henry E Rochester, son of Col Rochester, to that place in 1881

"In 1810, Col Nathaniel Rochester, one of the pioneers of the Genesee Valley in Western New York and co-founder of the great city there which bears his name, left his home in Hagerstown at the mature age of sixty-one years, and, with his family, started, in carriages and wagons, across the State of Pennsylvania, taking with him most of his household goods, for his new home in the rich wilderness, now one of the garden-spots of the American continent Of that cortege the youngest member was Henry E Rochester, the youngest son, then four years old, and who on Wednesday last, seventy-one years after he had left the place of his birth, returned to it a father and a grandfather, in the full possession of health and of a mind and heart capable of taking in the full enjoyment of such a return A few weeks before we had taken the liberty of publishing, with his initials, a private letter, in which was shown the deep interest which remained with him in matters pertaining to his old home, and it was with exceptional pleasure that we greeted him on Wednesday morning, and walked with him through the streets so familiar to and so much cherished by both

"One of the first persons encountered in the stroll was Governor Hamilton who was about to get into his buggy, on his way to his farms on the northern borders of Hagerstown, one of which was, when Mr Rochester left here a child, owned by his mother's brother, Elie Beatty, and the other by Maj Charles Carroll, who, with Col Rochester and Col Fitzhugh, were the co-partners in the pioneer enterprise of opening the Genesee country to agriculture, and in locating and founding the city which bears the name of 'Rochester,' and has to-day a population of one hundred thousand souls That this ride with the Governor of the State and present proprietor of those farms was a pleasant one to the visitor we can readily imagine, and in addition have his own assurance That portion of the valley was seventy years ago as it is now noted for its fertility, and many changes, which are improvements, have been made, particularly in r[illegible] which those farms are approached, and in additions to the original mansions, but the old Beatty house was still on 'Old Hill,' as the place was then called, and the old Carroll house still stands on the Bellevue farm, almost unchanged from what it was when Charles Carroll, of Bellevue, left it nearly seventy years ago to join his partners in the Genesee Valley

"Later in the day, and after his return on Wednesday from those old scenes, we accompanied Mr Rochester to [illegible] Franklin Street, to see one of the oldest of the old men of Hagerstown,—Mr William Miller, now in his eighty-ninth year, and with a memory as accurate as it was at twenty-nine,—between whom and Mr Rochester a mutual desire to meet had been expressed Mr Miller had previously, in conversation with us, shown a perfect recollection of the persons, characters, peculiarities, and homes of both Col Rochester and Maj Carroll, and could describe the latter as he rode from his estate into Hagerstown, around the corner at the Catholic church, eighty years ago, with as much precision as if it were but yesterday His courtly manners and genial bearing made an impression upon the boy which survives in the nonogenarian Mr Miller's recollection of Col Rochester was equally vivid, and when he and Mr Henry E Rochester met they at once launched out into reminiscences of the past, which showed how vivid was their recollection, and how deeply they had been impressed as youths Mr Miller spoke of the time when Col Rochester lived in the stone house on North Potomac Street, now owned by Mr William S Williamson, and Mr Rochester asked if that place was not then called 'Potato Hill,' to which Mr Miller replied, 'Yes, and is so called now' At a later hour, as we passed the old stone house, now owned by Governor Hamilton and occupied by Mr Daniel White as a saloon, next the Antietam House, Mr Rochester paused, and pointing out the alteration in the doorways, which now reach to the pavement, and in front of which there was once quite a high porch, said that he well recollected, though but a child, the vendue of his father's effects before leaving for New York which took place in front of the porch, and especially did he recollect the man with a bell, who stood on the porch ringing it to bring the bidders to the sale It is hardly necessary to say that it is in that very same spot every week farms and stocks and bonds are sold by thousands, just as Col Rochester's household effects were seventy years ago

"In a subsequent conversation with our friend Mr Rochester, we had a description of the passage of the emigrant family across the State of Pennsylvania, with the farmers' six horse covered wagons to convey the effects and carriages the family, attracting attention wherever they passed, and this movement being followed by other families from this section, whose descendants are now among the prominent people of Western New York Particularly did he recollect that a Mr Schnebly who afterward kept the 'Globe Hotel,' and was for many years register of wills of our county, then a young man had permission of Col Rochester to go along with the party, he acting as driver of the family carriage, in order that he might see the country, which then attracted such interest But it is hardly necessary to add that this young adventurer returned to his old home and died here at a ripe old age

'Yesterday Mr Rochester had set apart to dine with some friends and to revisit the bank, to see his father's portrait, which is still preserved there, he being the first president of th[illegible]

Rochester's associates in settling the Genesee ...try in New York, was one of the wealthy men of ...hington County about 1800. He owned a tract ...even or twelve hundred acres of the best land in ...county, on the northern border of Hagerstown, ...in part the property of Governor Hamilton and ...t the site of Bellevue Asylum, erected several ...s ago by Washington County. Mr. Carroll's resi... was a large stone mansion, one hundred and ... feet in length. It is still standing, and is now ...pied as a country seat by Hon. William T. Ham... The property has been improved by Mr. Ham... by the construction of a macadamized road from ... turnpike, with a substantial stone fence on either ... and in many other ways. Mr. Carroll left three ...—Charles, a man of great wealth and prominence, ... remained in New York, William, who removed ... Washington, and David. Charles H. Carroll, born ... Washington County, was a representative in Con...s from New York from 1843 to 1847, and a ...ber of the Assembly in 1836, a State Senator in ...37. He was a lawyer by profession, but devoted ... whole time to the management of a large estate in ...nesee County. He died at Groveland, Livingston ... N. Y., in 1865, aged seventy-one.

The Wetzels. The celebrated Indian fighters, ...is and Jacob Wetzel, were natives of Lewistown ...rict, in Frederick County. They were born a ...rter of a mile from Lewistown Village, on a farm ... owned by George Eisenangle, and when young ...ved with their parents to near Wheeling, W. ... where their father and mother were, with their ...thers and sisters, cruelly massacred by the Indians. ... boys Lewis and Jacob swore eternal vengeance ...inst the savages, and roamed the forests killing ...lians whenever and wherever they met them. ...mont County, Ohio, was the scene of two of the ...ing adventures of Lewis Wetzel, the far-famed ...berer, whose exploits alone would fill a volume.

The road along what is now the Cincinnati water...nt, leading from Storrs' to Delhi, crossed what was ... early days the outlet of a water-course, and not...hstanding the changes made by the lapse of years ... the building improvements adjacent, the spot still ...sesses many traces of original beauty. At the ...iod of this adventure, Oct 7, 1790, Jacob Wetzel ... been out hunting, and was returning to town, ...h at that time consisted of a few cabins and huts ...ted in the space fronting the river. He had ... very successful, and was returning to procure a ... to bear a load too heavy for his own shoulders. ... the spot mentioned he sat down on a decaying ... trunk to rest ... While ... thus he heard the rustling of leaves and branches, and silencing the growl of his dog, who sat at his feet and appeared equally conscious of danger, he sprang behind a tree and discovered the dark form of an Indian half hidden by the body of an oak, who had his rifle in his hands ready to fire. At this instant Wetzel's dog spied the Indian and barked, thus informing the Indian of the proximity of an enemy. Discovering Wetzel behind the tree, he took aim and fired, and the crack of the two weapons was almost simultaneous. The Indian's rifle fell from his hands, the ball of the hunter having penetrated and broken his left elbow, while Wetzel escaped unhurt. Before the Indian could reload, Wetzel rushed swiftly upon him with his knife, but not before the Indian had drawn his own. The first thrust was parried by the Indian with the greatest skill, and the hunter's knife was thrown some thirty feet from him. Nothing daunted, he threw himself upon the Indian and seized him around the body, at the same time grasping the right arm in which the Indian held his knife. The savage, however, was very muscular, and the conflict was a doubtful one at first. In the struggle their feet became interlocked, and they both fell to the ground, the Indian uppermost; this extricated the Indian's arm from the iron grasp of the hunter, and he endeavored to stab Wetzel, but the latter forced him ever on his right side, and consequently he could have no use of his right arm. By a desperate effort, however, he succeeded in getting Wetzel underneath him again, and raised his arm for the fatal plunge. Just at this moment the hunter's faithful dog sprang forward and seized the Indian by the throat, and caused the weapon to fall harmless from his hand. Wetzel then made a desperate effort and threw the Indian from him. Before the prostrate savage had time to recover himself the hunter had seized his knife, and rushing upon him, plunged the weapon into his breast, killing him instantly.

As soon as Wetzel had possessed himself of his rifle, together with the Indian's weapons, he started on his way again, but had gone but a short distance when his ears were assailed by the startling war-whoop of a number of Indians. He ran down to the river, and finding a canoe on the beach, near the water, was soon out of reach, and made his way in safety to the town.

Lewis Wetzel roamed through the Ohio Valley, and Belmont County, Ohio, was the scene of two of his daring adventures. While hunting he fell in with a young frontiersman who lived on Dunkard's Creek, and who persuaded him to accompany him to his home. On their arri... ... in ruins and all

the family murdered except a young woman who had been raised with them, and to whom the young man was ardently attached She had been carried off alive, as was found by examining the trail of the enemy, who were three Indians and a white renegade Burning with revenge they followed the trail until opposite the mouth of the Captina, where the enemy had crossed They swam the stream and discovered the Indian camp, around the fires of which lay the enemy in careless repose The young woman was apparently unhurt but was making much lamentation and moaning The young man, hardly able to restrain his rage, was for firing and rushing instantly upon them Wetzel, more cautious, told him to wait until daylight, when there would be a better chance of killing the whole party At dawn the Indians prepared to depart The young man selecting the white renegade and Wetzel an Indian they both fired simultaneously with fatal effect The young man then rushed forward knife in hand to release the girl, while Wetzel reloaded and pursued the two remaining savages, who had taken to the woods Wetzel, as soon as he was discovered, discharged his rifle at random, in order to draw them from their covert The ruse took effect, and taking to his heels, he loaded as he ran, and suddenly wheeling about discharged his rifle through the body of his nearest enemy The remaining Indian, seeing that his enemy's rifle was unloaded, rushed forward in eager pursuit, but Wetzel led him on, dodging from tree to tree until his rifle was again ready, when suddenly turning he fired, and his remaining enemy fell dead at his feet After taking their scalps Wetzel and his friend with their rescued captive returned in safety to the settlement A short time after Crawford's defeat, in 1782, Wetzel accompanied Thomas Mills, a soldier in that action, to obtain his horse, which he had left some distance away They were met by a party of about forty Indians at the Indian Springs, two miles from St Clairsville, on the road to Wheeling Both parties discovered each other at the same moment, when Lewis instantly turned and fired, killing an Indian A shot from the Indians wounded his companion in the heel, and the savages overtook and killed him Four Indians pursued Wetzel, who wheeled on one of them and shot him He then continued his flight and less than a mile farther a second Indian came so close to him that as Wetzel turned to fire he caught the muzzle of his gun After a severe struggle Wetzel succeeded in pointing it at his chest, and firing his opponent fell dead Wetzel still continued on his course pursued by the two Indians, all three were pretty well fatigued, and often stopped and [illegible] than a mile, Wetzel took advantage of a piece of open ground over which the Indians were passing and stopped suddenly to shoot the foremost, who thereupon sprang behind a small sapling Wetzel fired and wounded him mortally The remaining Indian then turned and fled About 1795 Wetzel went farther west, where he could trap the beaver, hunt the buffalo and deer, and occasionally shoot an Indian

The Poes In the present tavern of George H Clem, situated in Lewistown District, Frederick County, were born the two brothers, Adam and Andrew Poe the noted Indian fighters Their father had the old mill on Fishing Creek, the first ever built in the district When these brothers were small their father removed to near Wheeling, W Va, and throughout that section and portions of Pennsylvania the Poe boys became the terror of the savages Adam finally settled in Columbiana County, Ohio, and in that and Portage County of the same State are found many of his descendants The following is a narrative of the celebrated fight of these two brothers with the Indians nearly opposite the mouth of Little Yellow Creek, in Columbiana County, Ohio

In the summer of 1782 a party of seven Wyandots made an incursion into a settlement some distance below Fort Pitt, and several miles from the Ohio River Here, finding an old man alone in a cabin, they killed him, packed up what plunder they could find and retreated Among their party was a celebrated Wyandot chief, who, in addition to his fame as a warrior and counselor, was a giant in size and strength The news of the visit soon spread through the neighborhood, and a party of eight good riflemen was collected in a few hours for the purpose of pursuing the Indians In this party were the brothers Adam and Andrew Poe They were both famous for their courage, size, and activity This little party commenced the pursuit of the Indians, with the determination, if possible, not to let the murderers escape, as they usually did on such occasions, by making a speedy flight to the river, crossing it, and then dividing themselves into small parties to meet at a distant point in a given time The pursuit was continued the greater part of the night In the morning the party found themselves on the trail leading to the river When they arrived within a short distance of the river, Adam Poe, fearing an ambuscade, left the party, who followed directly on the trail, and crept along the river-bank, under cover of the weeds and bushes, to fall on the rear of the Indians should he find them hidden there He had not gone far before he saw Indian rafts at the water's edge Not seeing [illegible] dily down the

bank with his rifle cocked. When about half way down he discovered the Wyandot chief with a small Indian within a few steps of him. They were standing with their guns cocked and looking in the direction of the party who by this time had gone lower down into the bottom. Poe took aim at the large chief, but his rifle missed fire. The Indians hearing the snap of the gunlock instantly turned and discovered Poe, who, being too near them to retreat, dropped his gun and instantly sprung from the bank upon them. Seizing the large Indian by the cloths on his breast and at the same time embracing the neck of the small one, he threw them both down on the ground and fell with them. The small Indian soon extricated himself, and running to the raft procured his tomahawk and attempted to dispatch Poe while the large Indian held him fast in his arms. But Poe watched the motions of the smaller Indian, and when he was in the act of aiming his blow at his head, by a vigorous and well directed kick with one of his feet staggered the savage and knocked the tomahawk out of his hand. This failure on the part of the smaller Indian was rebuked by an exclamation of contempt and disgust from the large one. In a moment the Indian caught up his tomahawk again and approached more cautiously, brandishing and making a number of feints at his intended victim. Poe averted the real blow from his head by throwing up his arm and receiving it on his wrist, in which he was severely wounded, but not so much so as to lose entirely the use of his hand. In this perilous moment Poe, by a violent effort, released himself from the Indian, and snatching up one of the guns shot the smaller Indian through the breast as he ran up the third time to tomahawk him. The large Indian who was now upon his feet, grasped Poe by a shoulder and leg and threw him down on the bank. Poe instantly disengaged himself and got on his feet again. The Indian then seized him again, and a new struggle ensued, which, owing to the slippery state of the bank, ended in the precipitation of both combatants into the water. In this situation it was the object of each to drown the other. Their efforts to effect their purpose were continued for some time, until Poe at length succeeded in grasping the savage's scalplock with which he held his head under the water until he supposed he was drowned. Relaxing his hold too soon, Poe instantly found his gigantic antagonist still living and ready for another combat. While struggling they were carried into the water beyond their depth. In this situation they were compelled to loose their hold on one another and swim for mutual safety. [illegible] Indian [illegible] the [illegible] reached the land first. Poe, seeing this immediately turned back in the water to escape being shot by diving. Fortunately, the Indian caught up the rifle with which Poe had killed the other warrior, and which therefore was unloaded. At this juncture Andrew Poe, who had missed his brother from the party, and supposing from the report of the gunshot that he was either killed or engaged in a conflict with the Indians, hastened to the spot. On seeing him Adam called out to him to kill the big Indian on shore. But Andrew's gun, like the Indian's, was empty. The contest was now between the white man and the Indian as to who should load first and fire. Very fortunately for Poe the Indian in loading drew the ramrod from the stock of the gun with such violence that it slipped out of his hand and fell a little distance from him. He quickly caught it up and rammed down his bullet. This delay gave Poe the advantage. He shot the Indian as he was taking aim at him. He then leaped into the water to assist his wounded brother ashore, but Adam, thinking more of the honor of carrying the big Indian home as a trophy of victory than his own safety, urged Andrew to go back and prevent the struggling savage from rolling himself into the river and escaping. Andrew's solicitude for the life of his brother prevented him from complying with this request. In the mean time the Indian, jealous of the honor of his scalp even in the agonies of death, succeeded in reaching the river and getting into the current, so that his body was never obtained. Just as Andrew arrived at the top of the bank for the relief of his brother, one of the party who had followed close behind him, seeing Adam in the river and mistaking him for a wounded Indian, shot at him and wounded him in the shoulder. He recovered however from the wound. During the contest between Adam Poe and the Indians the party had overtaken the remaining six of them, and a desperate conflict had ensued, in which five of the Indians were killed. The loss of the whites was three men killed and Andrew Poe badly wounded.

The slaughter of the Indians, especially of their chief, caused great excitement among the Wyandots, the chief with his four brothers, all of whom were killed at the same place, being among the most distinguished warriors of their nation. The chief was magnanimous as well as brave, and, more than any other individual, contributed by his example and influence to the good character of the Wyandots for lenity towards their prisoners. He would not suffer them to be killed or mistreated. On learning the re- [illegible] companions

the Wyandots determined on revenge Poe then lived on the west side of the Ohio River, at the mouth of Little Yellow Creek They chose Pohn-yen-ness one of their warriors, as a proper person to murder him and then make his escape He went to Poe's house, and was met with great friendship, Poe not having any suspicion of his design The best food in the house was furnished him, and when the time came to retire for the night Poe made a pallet on the floor for his guest He and his wife went to bed in the same room Pohn-yen-ness afterwards said that they soon fell to sleep, and there being no person about the house but some children he thus had the desired opportunity to execute his purpose But the kindness they had shown him worked on his mind, and he asked himself how he could kill an enemy who had taken him in and treated him like a brother On the other hand, he had been sent by his nation to avenge the death of some of their most valiant warriors, and their ghosts would not be appeased until the blood of Poe was shed He continued undecided until about midnight, when the duty he owed to his nation and the spirits of his friends aroused him He seized his knife and tomahawk, and crept to the bed-side of his sleeping host Again the kindness he had received from Poe recurred to him, and unable to execute his crime he crept back to his pallet and slept until morning His host then repeated the kindness of the previous night, and told him they were once enemies, but he had buried the hatchet and were brothers, and hoped they would always be so Pohn-yen-ness returned to his tribe, and subsequently became a convert to Christianity

Maj Gen Perry Benson, of Washington County, was another of the distinguished soldiers whom Western Maryland gave to the country during the Revolutionary struggle He displayed conspicuous gallantry at the battles of Cowpens and Guilford Court-house, at Hobkirk's Hill, and at Ninety Six, where he led the forlorn hope At Hobkirk's Hill Capt Benson commanded the picket-guard, consisting of about two hundred and twenty men, and checked the advance of the whole British army until the American forces, which were separated and unprepared for an attack, could be concentrated and formed for battle, and did not retire until his command had poured six deadly volleys into the enemy, and he had lost in killed and wounded all but thirty-three of his men In the attack on Ninety Six Capt Benson commanded the forlorn hope, and was shot down within a few yards of the enemy's works, while encouraging his command He did not recover from the effects of this wound for many years and even to the end of his life was occasionally a sufferer from it During the Whisky Insurrection he joined the army with the rank of colonel, and in 1812 in spite of the infirmities of advancing age, he took an active part in the defense of the State as brigadier general of militia, on one occasion handsomely repulsing a British attack on the town of St Michael's with a small body of raw militia Previous to the war of 1812 he had represented his county in the Lower House of Assembly, which was the only civil office he ever held He died on the 2d of October, 1827, in the seventy-second year of his age, and was interred in the family burial-ground

The Williams family There is scarcely any family of Western Maryland that has played a more conspicuous rôle in its early history than did the Williamses Otho Holland and Elie Williams were sons of Joseph Williams and Prudence Holland Their father was of Welsh ancestry of gentle blood In 1750 he removed to what was then Frederick County, near the mouth of Conococheague Creek Otho Holland Williams was appointed at a very early age to a position in the clerk's office of Frederick County, which he held for several years, after which the office was given entirely into his charge He subsequently held the position of Collector of the Port of Baltimore At the breaking out of the Revolutionary war he enlisted in the colonial service, and became a distinguished officer[1] Gen Williams died July 15, 1794

His brother, Col Elie Williams, who died at Georgetown, D C, in 1823, in his seventy-third year, was also conspicuous during the Revolution and in the latter part of his life was an ardent advocate of internal improvements, especially the Chesapeake and Ohio Canal, in which he retained an active interest up to the time of his death

Col Elie Williams left two sons, Col John S and Gen Otho H Williams Col John S Williams, who died at Washington, D C, June 14 1868, served as major in the war of 1812, and published an interesting narrative of the battle of Bladensburg He lived for many years in Washington, and was president of the Association of Oldest Inhabitants of that city

Gen Otho Holland Williams, the younger, was born in 1784, and died Oct 24, 1869 He was appointed clerk of Washington County Court in 1800, and continued to hold this office until February, 1845, period of nearly forty-five years, during which time he discharged his duties to the entire satisfaction of the public He was also at one time a judge of the

[1] For a sketch of Gen Otho H Williams, see the history of Wil[illegible]

Orphans' Court of Washington County Mr Williams was an ardent Whig and the intimate friend and warm personal admirer of Henry Clay

He derived his military title from his appointment by the Governor of Maryland as brigadier-general of militia Mr Williams was a very active politician in his earlier years, and enjoyed great personal popularity throughout his career

Gen Samuel Ringgold was the son of Thomas Ringgold and Mary Galloway, and was born in Kent Co, Md, about 1770 The Ringgolds were among the earliest settlers of that section of Maryland, and the family in subsequent generations maintained a conspicuous position among the landed gentry of the State On the 3d of May, 1792, Samuel Ringgold married Mary, daughter of Gen John Cadwalader Soon afterwards he removed from Kent to Washington County, and located himself at "Fountain Rock," near Hagerstown He owned an immense estate, containing, it is said, some seventeen thousand acres of land in one of the most fertile and attractive sections of the State, and known as "Ringgold's Manor" He was also interested in an extensive tract in Pennsylvania [1]

At Fountain Rock, Gen Ringgold erected a splendid mansion which in later years was converted into St James' College It was decorated with stucco-work and wood-carving executed with great taste and care Many of the doors of the mansion were of solid mahogany, and the outbuildings, appointments, etc, were of the handsomest character The architect was the distinguished Benjamin H Latrobe, who was also one of the architects of the National Capitol at Washington It was Gen Ringgold's practice to drive to Washington in his coach and four with outriders, and to bring his political associates home with him Among his guests were President Monroe and Henry Clay Gen Ringgold lived in great elegance and state, and is said to have squandered a large fortune One local tradition even has it that he was wont to light his cigars with bank-notes He was famous for his hospitality and for his pleasant genial manners Towards the latter part of his life he became financially embarrassed, and died at the residence of his son-in-law, William Schley, in Frederick, on the 18th of October, 1829, aged about sixty years Gen Ringgold, who was very popular with all classes, was one of the most successful and influential politicians of his day He was a member of Congress from 1810 to 1815, and again from 1817 to 1821, and held various local offices from time to time He was also very active in organizing the militia of his section of the State, and was appointed brigadier-general Probably no man ever lived in Western Maryland who exerted a wider influence or enjoyed a more unqualified popularity "Fountain Rock" was sold to liquidate his debts, and went into the possession of the Hollingsworth family [2]

When Rev Dr J B Kerfoot, afterwards Bishop of Pittsburgh, purchased the building for the use of St James' College it was in a very neglected and dilapidated condition In the family graveyard at "Fountain Rock" the following persons are buried

Samuel Ringgold, died Oct 18, 1829, aged sixty

Maria Ringgold, his wife, died Aug 1, 1811, aged thirty-five

[1] The following advertisements afford some idea of the extent of his landed possessions

"ENCOURAGEMENT FOR SETTLERS

"The subscriber wants to engage with a number of persons to settle a large quantity of land situated in the back part of Pennsylvania, about 45 miles above Pittsburgh, on the Allegany River, which is navigable to Pittsburgh, and from thence down to New Orleans The terms are as follows Apply to the subscriber near Williamsport

"SAMUEL RINGGOLD

"WASHINGTON COUNTY, June 16, 1795"

"TO THE CITIZENS OF WASHINGTON COUNTY

"I shall offer at the next election to represent this county in the next General Assembly, and would thank you for your suffrages should you think me a proper character to fill so important an appointment I am, Gentlemen,

"Your obedient servant,

"SAMUEL RINGGOLD

"September 22, 179[illegible]"

In October, 1799, Tench Ringgold advertised that he would sell one thousand acres of land, lying in Washington County, within a mile and a half of Hagerstown Following is a copy of the advertisement, viz

"I will sell one thousand acres of land, lying in Washington County, State of Maryland, within one mile and a half of Hagerstown

"The above land is one of the reserves of Ringgold's Manor, well known for its fertility and advantageous situation, and it being presumed that those willing to purchase will view the premises, it will only be necessary to add that its distance from [illegible] is about 70 miles from George town and the Federal City the same, from the [illegible] mile [illegible] on Antietam Creek, having four merchant mills within one mile

"The land will be shewn and the terms of sale made known by applying to Samuel Ringgold, esquire, at his seat, near the premises, or the subscriber, living in George Town, on the Potomac

"TENCH RINGGOLD

"September 19, 1799"

[2] Sophia Givens, a former slave of Gen Ringgold's, who was sold from the steps of the mansion, died in 1877 It was asserted that she had attained the age of one hundred and six ye

Edward Lloyd Ringgold, son of Samuel Ringgold, died July 28 1822, aged sixteen

Charles Ringgold, son of Samuel Ringgold, died May 28, 1817, aged six

Charles Anthony Ringgold, son of Samuel Ringgold, died Sept 25, 1825, aged fifteen

Benjamin Ringgold, brother of Samuel Ringgold, died in August, 1798, aged twenty five

Thomas Ringgold, brother of Samuel Ringgold, died in March, 1818, aged forty

The children of Gen and Mrs Samuel Ringgold were Anna Maria, born on the 10th of July, 1793, and died on the 4th of March, 1828, John Cadwalader, born 15th November, 1794, died young, Samuel, born 16th October, 1796, Mary Elizabeth, born Dec 18, 1798, died March 9, 1836, Ann Cadwalader, born Jan 10, 1801, and married William Schley, of Frederick, Cadwalader, born Aug 20, 1802, Cornelia, born Jan 27, 1809, and Charles and Frederick, twins, born 22d and 23d of July, 1810 Gen Ringgold married in Washington at the Executive Mansion, a second time, Maria Antoinette Hay, granddaughter of President Madison, and had children, viz George H Ringgold, U.S.A, Fayette Ringgold, at one time United States consul at Peru, Virginia Ringgold, who married John Ross Key, and Rebecca Ringgold who married Dr Hay, of Chicago

Three of Gen Ringgold's sons entered the military service, viz Samuel, Cadwalader, and George H

Maj Samuel Ringgold was born October 16, 1796, and in 1814 entered West Point Military Academy On the 24th of July, 1818, he was appointed second lieutenant of artillery Upon his entrance into the army he received the appointment of aide to Gen Scott, and repaired to Philadelphia, where that officer had his headquarters After three years' service in this capacity he was detailed as an engineer under Maj Bache to make an examination of a part of the Southern coast At a later period he performed the duties of ordnance officer at New York His improvement on the percussion cannon-lock, which was perfected while he was stationed in New York, brought his name prominently before leading military officers and inventors throughout the world The lock at that time in use, not only in our own country but elsewhere, was peculiarly liable to injury from the unyielding manner in which the hammer fell upon the cap at the breech of the gun The recoil was so great as frequently to throw the hammer from its position, and thus disable the piece After much time and labor Maj (then Lieut) Ringgold succeeded in imparting a lateral motion to the hammer by means of a spring which drew it sideways and backward the moment after it gave the blow by which the cap was exploded This invention formed the basis on which all the modern improvements were made The military saddle was also an invention of Maj Ringgold's

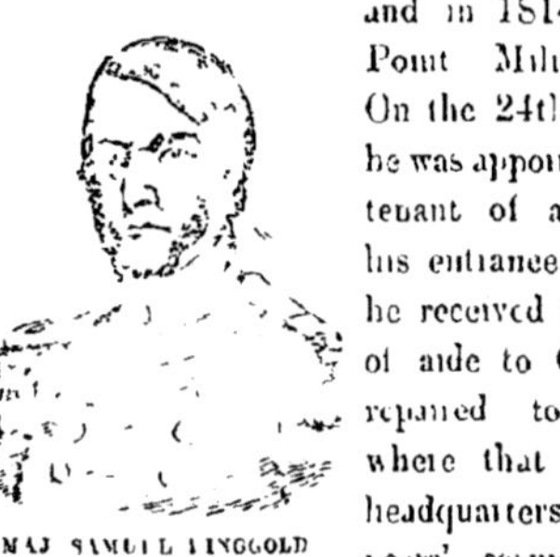
MAJ SAMUEL RINGGOLD

On the 21st of May, 1821, Lieut Ringgold was assigned to the Second Artillery, and on the 21st of August of the same year to the Third Artillery In May, 1822, he was promoted to a first lieutenancy In May, 1832, he was brevetted captain for ten years of faithful service In August, 1836, he was promoted to the captaincy, and on the 15th of February, 1838, was brevetted major "for meritorious conduct in activity and efficiency in war against Florida Indians" He was appointed major in 1843, was mortally wounded in the battle of Palo Alto, in Mexico, and died on the 11th of May, 1846, at Point Isabel, Texas The action of Palo Alto was a very spirited one, and Maj Ringgold behaved with remarkable gallantry Fire was opened by the Mexican batteries, and was responded to by Maj Ringgold's battery Maj Ringgold pointed the guns with his own hands, directing the shot not only to groups and masses of men, but to particular individuals in the line He saw them fall in numbers, and their places occupied by others, who in turn were shot down Maj Ringgold continued his fire for several hours, until he was shot through the thighs by a cannon ball, passing from right to left, and carrying with it a mass of muscle and integuments, and tearing off a portion of the saddle and the withers of the horse which he was riding He fell slowly, and before he reached the ground Lieut Shover came to his assistance and supported him While doing this the lieutenant called for aid to carry him to the rear "Never mind, sir," said Maj Ringgold, "you have work to do, go ahead with your men, all are wanted in front" Finally, however, the lieutenant persuaded him to allow him to carry him from the field His body was taken to Baltimore, and buried there with civic and military honors on the 22d of December, 1846 [1]

[1] The following account of the death of Maj Ringgold is taken from a letter published in the Washington *Union* The letter is as follows

"Camp Isabel, near the Mouth
"of the Rio Bravo Del Norte May 9, 1846

"The numerous friends of Maj Ringgold will doubtless be [illegible] melancholy end,

Soon after notice of Maj Ringgold s death was received at Hagerstown a public meeting was held for the purpose of giving expression to the deep sense of popular regret at the unfortunate end of the gallant officer Gen O H Williams was appointed president, and Col Charles Macgill and Capt W B Clarke, vice-presidents, and John A Wagoner and Andrew Kershner, secretaries On motion of John T Mason, the following resolutions were adopted

"*Resolved*, That while we unite in the general feeling of sorrow that pervades the whole nation at the loss of the noble and gallant officers and men who lately fell in Texas in defense of their country, we feel that in addition to our national bereavement we have sustained in the death of Maj Samuel Ringgold the loss of one who was united to us by the ties of friendship, by the associations of youth, and by the relation of a companion and fellow citizen

"*Resolved*, That though we regret the death of the gallant Ringgold, yet we rejoice in the character and manner of that death, crowned as it was by the heartfelt joy which the patriot feels in the consciousness of dying in support of the dignity, the freedom and happiness of his country

"*Resolved*, That it is a source of pride and congratulation to know that Washington County has not only furnished for the nation's defense the officer whose distinguished services we are called at present to commemorate, but that she has given a number of the flowers of her youth, who now fill the ranks of her country's noble army, and that the names of Sergt John Anderson, Privates David Anderson, Jeremiah Carey, Calvin Bowers, Thomas Philips, and Upton Wilson will always be cherished as faithful citizens and well tried soldiers

"*Resolved*, As the sense of this meeting, that in time of actual war, regularly and constitutionally declared by the United States, it is too late to hesitate and inquire into the causes of hostilities, but that it is the duty of every American citizen on such an occasion to sustain his country, 'right or wrong'

"*Resolved*, That the State of Maryland has nobly sustained on the plains of Texas her character for gallantry and patriotism by the conduct of her sons, Cross Ringgold, May, Walker, Ridgely, and the many others who aided in the achievement of our late victories, and that she has shown that though small in territory, she can vie with the largest of her sisters in spirit, patriotism, and effective service"

On motion of Capt W B Clarke, it was

"*Resolved*, That each citizen here present will lend his aid in encouraging the formation of a volunteer corps of sixty-four men, to attach themselves to the regiment now forming in this State under the organization of the President of the United States"

On motion of Isaac Nesbitt,

"*Resolved*, That this meeting heartily concur in the suggestion and movement of the Hagerstown Horse-Guards, on the 28th instant, respecting the erection of a monument to the memory of the gallant Ringgold, and will co operate with them in carrying out the object set forth in their proceedings in relation thereto

"*Resolved*, That a committee of three be appointed by the chair to unite with the committee of the 'Horse Guards' in maturing the necessary plan and arrangements for the erection of the monument"

The Potomac Dragoons, being represented in the meeting appointed Maj Thomas G Harris, Lieut Hays, and Lieut Grimes a committee to act with the committee appointed by the meeting and the committee on the part of the 'Horse Guards" for the erection of the monument

At a meeting of the Hagerstown Horse Guards, held at Hagerstown on the 28th of June, 1846, Capt William B Clarke after referring to the triumphs [illegible] Rio Grande

and I hasten to give them to you The engagement of the 8th was entirely in the hands of the artillery, and Maj Ringgold took a most active and important part in it About six o'clock he was struck by a six pound shot He was mounted, and the shot struck him at right angles, hitting him in the right thigh, passing through the holsters and upper part of the shoulders of his horse, and then striking the left thigh in the same line in which it struck him On the evening of the 9th he reached the camp, under the charge of Dr Byrne, of the army He was immediately placed in comfortable quarters and his wounds dressed An immense mass of muscles and integuments were carried away from both thighs The arteries were not divided, neither were the bones broken I remained with him all night He had but little pain, and at intervals had some sleep On dressing his wounds in the morning they presented a most unfavorable aspect, and there was but little reaction During the night he gave me many incidents of the battle, and spoke with much pride of the execution of his shot He directed his shot not only to the groups and masses of the enemy, but to particular men in the line, he saw them fall and their places occupied by others, who in their turn were shot down He said he felt as confident of hitting his mark as though he had been using a rifle He had he said, but one thing to regret, and that was the small number of men in his company He said that he had made use of all his exertions to have his company increased to one hundred men, but without success From the small number of his men, as they were disabled at their guns he was without others to take their places During the day he continued to lose strength, but was free from pain and cheerful He spoke constantly of the efficiency of his guns, and of the brave conduct of his officers and men He continued to grow worse, and a medical officer remained constantly by his side Dr Byrne remained with him during the night, using every means which could be devised to save his valuable life, but without effect He continued to grow worse until one o clock last night, when he expired He survived his wounds sixty hours During all this time he had but little pain, and conversed cheerfully, and made all his arrangements for his approaching end with the greatest composure and resignation He will be buried to-day at three o'clock P M, lamented by the whole camp The wounded are generally doing very well

'I am your obedient servant,

"J M FALTZ,

"*Surgeon United States Navy*"

A letter from a young officer of Baltimore gives the following account of the wounding of Maj Ringgold

"About twenty minutes after the commencement of the action [illegible] Maj Ringgold was struck by a six pound shot and mortally wounded (he has since died) I had lent him my pistols on going into the fight The shot struck one holster, cut it and the pistol in two pieces, cut all the flesh off the upper part of the major's thigh, [illegible] the other pistol [illegible]

submitted the following resolutions, expressive of the feelings of the corps in receiving the news of the death of Maj Samuel Ringgold, of the Third Artillery

The resolutions were prefaced by appropriate remarks upon the life and services of this distinguished officer, and were as follows

"*Resolved*, That this corps will cause to be erected in Washington County, the place of his birth, a suitable monument as a mark of respect to his memory, and that the several volunteer corps of the county be requested to co-operate in carrying out this resolution"

The above resolution being unanimously adopted, a committee to consist of the commissioned officers of the corps was selected to report the design for the monument, and to take the necessary steps to insure its erection The monument, however, was never erected

Cadwalader Ringgold, son of Gen Samuel Ringgold was a distinguished officer of the United States navy, and died with the rank of rear-admiral He was born at Fountain Rock in 1802, and was appointed midshipman on the 4th of March, 1819, and was promoted to a lieutenancy May 17, 1828 He was made lieutenant-commander July 16, 1849, captain, April 2, 1856, commodore, July 16, 1862, and rear-admiral in March, 1867 While a lieutenant commander he was for a short time in charge of the surveying and exploring expedition to the North Pacific and China Seas At the breaking out of the civil war he was transferred to the command of the frigate "Sabine" On Friday, Nov 1 1861, the blockading fleet to which the "Sabine" was attached encountered a terrific storm The steamer "Governor," which had on board a battalion of marines, was seen to be in a very dangerous condition, and Capt Ringgold went to their assistance He succeeded in rescuing the marines and the crew, and shortly afterwards the steamer sank

Admiral Ringgold rendered the Federal government valuable service in blockading the Southern ports, and in the operations against Port Royal and other ports on the Atlantic He was made a rear-admiral in 1867, and died in New York City on the 29th of April in that year

George Hay, son of Gen Samuel Ringgold and his second wife, Marie Antoinette Hay was born at Hagerstown in 1814, and was educated at the West Point Military Academy He was appointed brevet second lieutenant of the Sixth Infantry on the 1st of July, 1833, and served on frontier duty at Jefferson Barracks, Mo, Fort Jesup, Fla and Camp Sabine, La On the 15th of August, 1836, he was promoted to a second li[illegible] ing resigned, in order to engage in agriculture and in the manufacture of flour Subsequently, from 1842 to 1846, he served in the United States Ordnance Bureau at Washington On the 4th of August, 1846, he was reappointed in the army with the rank of additional paymaster During the Mexican war he served as paymaster, with the rank of major, and during the civil war as deputy paymaster-general, with the rank of lieutenant-colonel He died on the 4th of April 1864, at San Francisco Col Ringgold was a gifted scholar, an accomplished draughtsman and an amateur poet, and in 1860 published a volume of poetry entitled "Fountain Rock, Amy Weir, and other Metrical Pastimes"

The Fitzhughs Among the early families of Washington County there was scarcely any which had a wider connection or enjoyed greater influence than did the Fitzhughs The founder of the Western Maryland branch of the family was Col William Fitzhugh an officer in the British army, who threw up his commission at the beginning of the Revolutionary war and retired to his estate in Prince George's County Towards the latter part of his life he removed to the residence of his son, Col William Fitzhugh, known as "The Hive," in Washington County, and there spent the remainder of his days His remains are buried in the Episcopal cemetery at Hagerstown

Col Fitzhugh's wife was Anne Frisby, the daughter of Peregrine Frisby, of Cecil County, who was born Sept 5, 1727 Her first husband was John Rousby, and their only daughter married John Plater

On the 7th of January, 1759, Mrs Rousby was united to Mr Fitzhugh, a colonel in the British service Col Fitzhugh had won considerable distinction in his military career in the West India expedition At the commencement of difficulties between the colonies and the mother-country he was living on his half-pay The large estate, highly improved, on which he resided lay at the mouth of the Patuxent River, and he had in operation extensive manufactories of different kinds

When discontent ripened into rebellion, though he was advanced in years, in feeble health, and had almost entirely lost his sight, neither the infirmities of age nor any advantage to be derived from adhesion to the government prevented his taking an open and active part with the patriots On account of his influence in the community he was offered a continuance of his half pay if he would remain neutral, but he at once declined the offer, resigned his commission, and declared in favor of the colonies Unable himself to bear arms he furnished his two sons—Peregrine and W[illegible] them with the

command to be true to the interests of their country They were both officers, and served with distinction under the Continental standard Their father took his seat in the Executive Council of Maryland, giving his vote and influence to the debates till the political opinions of that body were no longer wavering Not only thus did he render service, but he was seen and heard at every public meeting, going from place to place through the county, haranguing the people in stump-speeches, and devoting all his energies to the task of rousing them to fight for their rights This active zeal for American freedom did not fail to render him obnoxious to the British He was often apprised of danger, but no risk could deter him from the performance of duty At one time, when he had disregarded a warning from some unknown hand, Mrs. Fitzhugh was surprised in his absence by news of the near approach of a party of British soldiers She instantly decided to collect the slaves, whom she furnished with such arms as could be found Then, taking a quantity of cartridges in her apron, she led the way out to meet the enemy, resolved that they should have at least a round of shots by way of welcome Finding preparation for resistance where they probably expected none, the British party retired from the grounds without doing any damage At another time, when they received information of a design on the enemy's part to attack the house that night take the colonel prisoner, carry off what plunder could be found, and lay waste the premises, Col Fitzhugh was dissuaded by his family from making any attempt at defense Perhaps thinking that, meeting no opposition, they would be content with plunder, he reluctantly consented to leave the place with his household Next morning nothing remained of the mansion but a heap of smoking ruins The family then removed to Upper Marlboro', where they continued to reside until the close of the war

In the fall, before peace was declared, a detachment of British soldiers having landed on the Patuxent, marched to the house of Col Fitzhugh It was about midnight when he and his wife were roused from sleep by a loud knocking at the door The colonel raised a window and called out to know who was there The reply was, "Friends" He asked, "Friends to whom?" "Friends to King George," was shouted in answer, with a peremptory order to open the door Knowing that remonstrance or resistance would be useless, and that delay would but irritate the intruders, the colonel assured them that his wife—he being blind—would immediately descend and admit them Mrs Fitzhugh did not hesitate Her distress was great when, putting the [illegible] tains for an instant, she saw the court-yard filled with armed men Hastily lighting a candle and putting on her slippers, she went down-stairs, stopping only for a moment to give her sons, who happened to be in the house, their pistols, and warn them that they must lose no time in making their escape They left the house by the back door as their mother with difficulty turned the ponderous key which secured the front door

The British soldiers instantly rushed in, touching her night dress with their bayonets as she turned to leave the door She walked calmly before them into the parlor, and addressing the officer said she hoped they intended to do the inmates of the house no harm He replied that they did not, but he must see Col Fitzhugh at once Then, his attention being suddenly attracted by some articles of military dress, he demanded quickly, "What officer have you in the house, madam?" "There is no one here but our own family," answered Mrs Fitzhugh

The men spoke together in a low voice, and then the question was repeated, to which the same reply was given She noticed a smile on the countenance of the officer as he said, "We must take these," pointing to the cap, holsters, etc Nothing else was touched in the house, although the supper-table, with silver plate upon it, was standing as it had been left at night, and the sideboard contained several other valuable articles Mrs Fitzhugh, in obedience to the order that her husband should come down, went to assist him in dressing, and returned with him, unmindful in her anxiety that she had taken no time to dress herself The officer informed him that he was his prisoner and must go with them to New York, then in possession of the British Col Fitzhugh replied that his age and want of sight made it scarce worth their while to take him, as he could neither do harm nor service, being unable indeed to take care of himself Such arguments, however, availed nothing, and he was hurried off Mrs Fitzhugh had made no preparation for a journey Walking up to her husband, she took his arm, and when the officer endeavored to persuade her to remain, saying she would suffer from exposure, she answered that Col Fitzhugh was not able to take care of himself, and that even if he were she would not be separated from him The officer then took down a cloak and threw it over her shoulders With only this protection from the cold and rain she left the house with the rest Their boat lay about half a mile away, and in going to the shore they had to walk through the mud, the ground being soaked with rain

When t[illegible] however, the officer

consented to permit Col Fitzhugh to remain on his parole, which was hastily written

On their return to their residence, the colonel and Mrs Fitzhugh were much surprised to find all the negroes gone except one little girl who had hid in the garret They had evidently been taken or persuaded to go off in their absence, and there was ground for the suspicion that the enemy's real object had been to obtain possession of the slaves without any resistance that might alarm the neighbors Many of those missing returned to their master of their own accord, the fair promises made to allure them from his service not having been kept Miss Plater, the granddaughter of Mrs Fitzhugh, displayed much courage upon this occasion After her grandparents had left the house in charge of the soldiers, one or two of the men came back to obtain some fire, and in carrying it from the room let some of it fall on the carpet The young girl started forward put her foot upon it, and asked if they meant to fire the house They answered kindly that the house should stand and no harm come to her They then asked for wine, which she ordered to be set before them They would not drink, however, fearing it might be poisoned, till she had tasted each bottle This young lady was afterwards the wife of Col Forrest Capt Peregrine Fitzhugh, one of the sons already mentioned, who was for some time aide to Gen Washington, married Elizabeth Chew, of Maryland, and removed in 1799 to Soders' Bay, on Lake Ontario, where he spent the remainder of his days Col William Fitzhugh married Ann, daughter of Col Daniel Hughes, of Hagerstown, and removed to the vicinity of Genesee, Livingston Co, N Y, in company with Messrs Carroll and Rochester, and assisted in founding the city of Rochester

Col Fitzhugh's family consisted, in part, of seven sons William H, three times sheriff of Washington County, and owner of "The Hive," Dr Daniel, one of the wealthy men of Western New York, Samuel, a judge in New York, James, who moved to Kentucky, Henry, of New York, Richard, killed on the railroad by an accident, and Robert His daughters were the wife of the Rev Dr Backus, a celebrated divine of the Presbyterian Church, the wife of James Birney, once Abolition candidate for the Presidency, the wife of the late Gerritt Smith, philanthropist and abolitionist, of Petersboro', N Y, whose son, Green Smith, was married to the youngest daughter of his uncle, Col William H Fitzhugh, and died at Petersboro', Mrs Tallman, of Rochester, and Mrs Swift, wife of Commodore Swift, of Geneva, N Y

William H Fitzhugh, eldest son of Col William, married M[illegible] and granddaughter of Col Daniel Hughes, his own cousin Dr Daniel Fitzhugh married Ann Dana, his cousin Judge Samuel Fitzhugh married Ann Addison, and had one son, who died unmarried James Fitzhugh married a lady of Kentucky Henry Fitzhugh married a daughter of Charles Carroll, of "Bellevue," Washington County, cousin of Charles Carroll of Carrollton He went with the Fitzhughs, Rochesters, Hogmires, and others to Genesee Robert married Maria Carroll, daughter of Daniel Carroll, son of Daniel Carroll, of Duddington She has a son living, Carroll Fitzhugh, now of New York Richard married a Miss Mary Jones, of Mount Morris, Livingston Co, N Y.

Jesse Duncan Elliott[1] was born at Hagerstown on the 14th of July, 1782 He was descended from an Irish family of Fincastle, County Donegal, and his parents were Pennsylvanians In 1794 his father, Col Robert Elliott, was killed by a party of Indians on the Muskingum, whilst on the way to join Gen Wayne's army[2] The death of Col Elliott rendered the family destitute, but through the efforts of John Thomson Mason, Congress granted a small pension to the widow, and President Jefferson forwarded commissions as midshipmen in the navy to the two brothers, St Clair and Jesse D Elliott The latter had been educated at Carlisle, Pa, and had studied law The warrants were dated April 2, 1804, and were accompanied by orders attaching St Clair to the "President," Commodore Samuel Barron, and Jesse to the "Essex," Commodore James Barron The two vessels proceeded to the Barbary States, and having humbled them, negotiated a treaty with Tripoli, and brought home the crew of the "Philadelphia," who

[1] On the 24th of November, 1813 Messrs J J Merrick, O H Williams, Jervis Spencer, Charles Macgill, John Thomson Mason, and George Schley addressed a note to Commodore Jesse D Elliott, conveying the request of a number of their fellow citizens that he would accept the compliment of a public dinner on the following day The commodore replied that he had come to Hagerstown for the purpose of visiting the graves of his mother and sister, who were buried there, and for that reason, and because he had an appointment at Baltimore, he was constrained to decline The committee, however, prevailed upon him to make an address to his early companions and friends at the court-house, and from the speech delivered on that occasion, and from "A Biographical Notice," by a citizen of New York, the accompanying sketch was compiled

[2] Col Robert Elliott was an army contractor, and while traveling with his servant from Fort Washington to Fort Hamilton, was waylaid and killed, in 1794 Being somewhat advanced in life, the colonel wore a wig The savage who shot him hurried forward to scalp him, but when, having drawn his knife, he seized him by the hair, the scalp, to his astonishment, came off The Indian looked at it and then exclaimed, "Damn lie!" His companions were much amused at his discomfiture, and made a [illegible] wig

[illegible] been confined in the dungeons of that city. Having remained on shore until 1807, Jesse was attached to the ill-fated "Chesapeake," Capt. J. Barron, and on the 22d of June departed for the Mediterranean. She had scarcely cleared the American coast before she was attacked by the British ship of the line "Leopard," of greatly superior force, and such was the defenseless condition of the "Chesapeake," owing chiefly to her ignorance of the intended attack of a vessel belonging to a nation with which the United States were then at peace, that in a short time she was compelled to strike her flag. Commodore Barron was court-martialed on his return to the United States, but Commodore Elliott declared that he did all that a brave and skillful officer could have done under the circumstances. Commodore Elliott was so zealous in defense of Commodore Barron that he was challenged to fight a duel by one of Barron's detractors, and accepted. His antagonist fell, badly wounded, but afterwards recovered, and became a warm friend of the commodore's. Young Elliott was appointed, about this time, acting lieutenant on the "Enterprise," and subsequently was promoted, and commissioned to a lieutenancy on the "John Adams," and bearer of dispatches to the United States minister, William Pinkney, at the Court of St. James.

COM. JESSE D. ELLIOTT.

While in London he was insulted by "a person having the appearance of a gentleman," who took a seat near him in a coffee-house, and to whom he handed his card, expecting that a duel would follow. The man had mistaken him for a British officer, and "lavished all manner of abuse against the Yankees and their country," whereupon Elliott informed him that he was a Yankee, and when he made no sign of apologizing or handing Elliott his card, the future commodore, to quote his own language, "stepped to the person in waiting and observed, 'Sir, you put a scoundrel instead of a gentleman in the box with me; he has grossly insulted me. There's my card; give it to him and tell him I demand his.'" By this time, however, the man had disappeared, and Elliott never heard of him again. Mr. Pinkney, hearing of the affair, advised Elliott not to appear on the street in his uniform, since otherwise he would be subjected to many annoyances and insults. Elliott took his advice, and besides exchanging his uniform for a private dress, [illegible] to be the object of curiosity or suspicion. Returning to the United States, he shortly afterwards married. Immediately succeeding this event, war having been declared against Great Britain, he parted with his wife in order to join his ship at New York, but the vessel had sailed before his arrival in that city. Having learned that the British Admiral Sir John Borles Warren had information of the instructions to Commodore Rodgers to rendezvous in the Chesapeake, he volunteered to bear the news to the American fleet, hoping that he might be able to join the "Argus," of which he was the first lieutenant. For this purpose he hired a small pilot-boat called the "Patriot" (the ill-fated schooner on which Aaron Burr's daughter Theodosia was afterwards lost at sea), put one gun and thirty men on board, and cruised forty days, during which he was chased by two British gun-brigs and narrowly escaped. He then returned home and was ordered to report for service. Commodore Chauncey invited him to join his command, and he accepted. He was ordered to proceed to Genesee Falls, on Lake Ontario, and to Black Rock and Buffalo, on Lake Erie, there to communicate with Gen. P. B. Porter, Mr. Granger, the Indian agent, and Gen. Van Rensselaer upon the subject of obtaining vessels for operations on the lakes. Soon afterwards, Commodore Elliott, assisted by Capt. Nathan Towson, of Baltimore, effected the capture of the British vessels "Detroit" and "Caledonia." In his official report to the Secretary of the Navy he states that on the morning of Oct. 8, 1812, the "Detroit," formerly the United States brig "Adams," and the "Caledonia" came down the lake and anchored off Fort Erie, under the protection of its guns, and that he determined to attempt their capture. Accordingly, with two boats, each containing fifty men, he put off from the mouth of Black Rock (where he was engaged in the construction of an American fleet) at one o'clock on the following morning, and at three was alongside the vessels. In less than ten minutes he had captured both vessels and secured their crews. Being exposed to the fire of Fort Erie he beached the "Caledonia" under the protection of one of the American batteries, and succeeded in getting the "Detroit" out of range of the fort, but the pilot having deserted her, the vessel ran ashore on the American side. She had [illegible] the fort and

GEN. NATHAN TOWSON.

the flying artillery that she was incapable of being floated again The "Caledonia" was loaded with furs worth two hundred thousand dollars The crew of the "Detroit" consisted of fifty-six men, and that of the "Caledonia" of twelve men Commodore Elliott's loss was two men killed and five wounded Elliott encountered the first man on boarding, and opposed three of the enemy with no other weapon than his cutlass He captured nearly one hundred prisoners, and released forty of his own countrymen belonging to the Fourth Artillery who were confined on board Congress voted Elliott a sword, and appropriated twelve thousand dollars as prize-money to the lieutenant and his crew He then joined Commodore Chauncey on Lake Ontario, and assisted in driving the enemy into the harbor of Kingston Subsequently he accompanied Gen Dearborn and Gen Pike in the operations against York, in Canada, and against Fort George, both of which were captured He then joined Capt Oliver H Perry on Lake Erie, and took a conspicuous part in the famous naval engagement known as the Battle of Lake Erie, which was fought on the 10th of September, 1813 Capt Elliott commanded the "Niagara" in that engagement until she was boarded by Perry, and the latter did not hesitate to say that he owed the victory to Elliott's coolness and skill Elliott himself gives a very spirited and interesting account of the action "At this time," he says, 'the 'Lawrence' (Capt Perry's ship) ceased her fire entirely, and no signal being made after the first to form in the order of battle, I concluded that the senior officer was killed The breeze now freshening, I observed that the whole British fleet drew ahead, cheering along their entire line I then set topgallant-sail, fore and aft mainsail and foresail, and passed within twenty yards of the 'Lawrence,' still not seeing Capt Perry Having now exhausted nearly all my twelve-pound round-shot, I ordered Mr. McGrath with a few bracemen to proceed in my boat to the 'Lawrence' and bring me all hers, and immediately steered directly for the head of the British line, firing continually my whole starboard battery on them as I passed When I reached within two hundred and fifty yards of the beam of the 'Detroit,' and ahead of the 'Queen Charlotte,' I luffed on a wind and commenced a most deadly fire, the 'Niagara' then being the only vessel of our fleet in what I call close action The British were just before cheering for victory, but their cheers were now turned into groans, and the blood ran from the scuppers of the 'Detroit and 'Queen Charlotte' like water from the spouts of your houses in a moderate rain " While thus engaged the "[illegible]rs" w[illegible] by Cap[illegible] Perry, who was much agitated Elliott asked him what was the result on board his brig He answered, "Cut all to pieces, the victory's lost, everything's gone! I've been sacrificed by the d—— d gunboats!" To this Elliott replied, 'No sir, victory is yet on our side I have a most judicious position, and my shot are taking great effect You tend my battery, and I will bring up the gunboats " "Do so," said Perry, "for heaven's sake!" Elliott then got into Perry's boat and passed down the line exposed to the enemy's fire, and ordered the gunboats to cease firing at the small vessels and to press up to the head of the line He then took command of the foremost gunboat, the "Somers," and led the squadron into action The "Detroit ' and Queen Charlotte ' fouled at this juncture, and the "Niagara" and the gunboats rushing in upon them, the British were whipped and compelled to surrender As soon as the firing had ceased Elliott went on board the 'Detroit," and so slippery were the decks with blood that he slipped and fell, his clothing becoming completely saturated and covered with gore Capt Barclay, commanding the "Detroit," handed Elliott his sword, but the latter refused it, assuring him that every kindness would be shown him and the other prisoners On meeting Capt Perry that officer said to Elliott, "I owe the victory to your gallantry " The British flag on the "Detroit" was nailed to the mast, and Commodore Elliott, having had the nails extracted, afterwards presented them to the distinguished statesman Henry Clay Mr Clay was a warm friend of Elliott s, and was closely identified with the people of Hagerstown, having married Lucretia Hart, of that place [1]

After the action on Lake Erie Elliott returned to Lake Ontario, designing to act as flag-captain on Commodore Chauncey's ship "Superior " On his arrival, however, he found a vacant brig, the "Sylph," a fast sailer of twenty guns, and by agreement accepted that vessel for the purpose of bringing on an action with the British fleet Late in the summer he met a British brig and attacked her, but the captain ran her ashore and blew her up

In 1818 began an acrimonious controversy between Commodore Oliver H Perry and Commodore Elliott, which ended disastrously for the latter Commodore Elliott appears to have been of a bluff, outspoken temperament, and to have made numerous enemies, partly on

[1] In his memoir Commodore Elliott speaks in high terms of the brave Israel, another Washington County boy, who threw himself on board the "Intrepid ' at Tripoli for the purpose of destroying the Tripolitan fleet, and who when discovered, rather than yield himself a prisoner, with his brave companions [illegible] in one common [illegible]

account and partly owing to his pronounced political views His troubles commenced with the battle of Lake Erie, it being asserted by those unfriendly to him that he had not behaved well in that engagement When this assertion came to his ears he at once wrote to Capt Perry, who replied that he was indignant that such a charge should be brought, and declared that Elliott's conduct had been such as to merit his warmest approbation, and to contribute largely to the victory Notwithstanding this, however, the accusation was persisted in, and subsequently gave the commodore no little annoyance After some service on Lake Ontario he proceeded to Baltimore to take command of the sloop-of-war "Ontario" That vessel sailed for New York, and while she was fitting out at the latter port Commodore Elliott received information that doubts were being circulated as to his conduct at the battle of Lake Erie He thereupon asked for a court of inquiry, which was granted, and he was acquitted with honor His enemies, however, continued to persecute him with defamatory publications, and Fenimore Cooper, the novelist, having given a correct account of the engagement in his "Naval History of New York," was assailed by R S Mackenzie, author of a "Life of Perry," whom he sued for libel Cooper won his suit, and demonstrated the truth of his narrative Sectional prejudice against Elliott was skillfully excited, and the Legislature of Rhode Island gratuitously and by proceedings wholly *ex-parte* considered the circumstances of the battle, and pretended to decide the relative merits of the parties concerned" Mackenzie's "Life of Perry," which was grossly unfair to Elliott, was admitted into the libraries of the public schools of New York Elliott challenged Perry to fight a duel, but Perry did not accept Elliott next proceeded, in command of the "Ontario" as one of Commodore Decatur's squadron to the Mediterranean against Algiers, and contributed to the capture of a large Algerian frigate by pouring a heavy fire into her Three days afterwards a brig of twenty-four guns and three hundred men was taken by the squadron Peace being concluded with Algiers, the fleet proceeded to Tunis, and compelled the Bey to surrender a large amount of property belonging to the United States, captured from the British by American privateers In a negotiation with the Bey, the American consul, M M Noah, went to the palace accompanied by Capts Gordon and Elliott The Bey's son was very insolent, whereupon Capt Elliott observed, "We did not come here to be insulted This interview must be cut short Will you or will you not pay for these vessels?" Answer ... that" ... was furious, but the ... payment During the interview thirty Mamelukes entered the room with drawn cimeters Perceiving that the intention was to intimidate them, Capt Elliott placed his back against the wall and, drawing his sword, declared that he would sell his life dearly This action and his peremptory manner had a salutary effect on the Bey Capt Elliott returned home, and in 1817 was appointed a commissioner, with Gen Bernard, Gen Swift, Capt Warrington, and Cols. Armistead and McCrea, to examine the coast of the United States for selecting sites for permanent dock yards and fortifications, and for lighting the coast of North Carolina In this position he continued until 1824

Whilst discharging its duties he was informed by Mr Crawford, then Secretary of the Treasury, that owing to the supposed danger of locating a light-ship and occupying it during a gale, no person could be found willing to perform such service Capt Elliott at once volunteered to locate one, and successfully accomplished the task in a storm, thus demonstrating the practicability of using the light-ships at dangerous points during a high wind March 27, 1818, he was promoted from the rank of master commandant to that of full captain On the termination of the Coast Survey Commission, in December, 1823, he received a highly complimentary and friendly letter from the chief, Gen Bernard, afterwards French Minister of War In 1825 he was sent in the frigate "Cyane" to the coast of Brazil, where, in the presence of a greatly superior force, he boldly asserted and maintained the right of an American war-vessel to enter a blockaded port Before leaving Brazil he was offered by the emperor the post of admiral, with the highest salary paid to any Brazilian naval officer, but declined the offer On his return from Brazil he was, in 1829, appointed to the command of the naval forces in the West Indies and Gulf of Mexico On arriving at Pensacola he found a letter from Hon J R Poinsett, United States minister to Mexico, stating the difficulties by which he was surrounded, and advising a demonstration of the squadron at Vera Cruz Accordingly the squadron proceeded to the Mexican coast, and having taken Mr Poinsett on board at Tampico, returned to the United States While in Mexico the commodore was entertained by Gen Santa Anna at his hacienda or farm Having returned from the West Indies in 1831, his aid was asked in suppressing an insurrection of slaves in Southampton County, Va Accordingly he ordered a force of one hundred seamen and sixty marines under Capt ... S Newton of the sloop-of-war ... the scene of

disturbance Commodore Elliott, with the fleet-surgeon, accompanied them They arrived in time to succor the terrified inhabitants, who were assembled at Jerusalem in such numbers that they were obliged to sleep in stables and outhouses In this connection Commodore Elliott records an act of remarkable gallantry on the part of a child "The hero," he says, "was a youth of less than thirteen years of age, the son of an aged and diseased gentleman of Southampton, Dr Blount, who could not be removed to a place of safety on account of his extreme illness His little son, the lad spoken of, assured his father that he, with the overseer and his two sons, could defend him, and accordingly when night came he barricaded the doors, opened the windows, gathered all the arms he could find about the house, consisting of a few old pistols, etc, and awaited the attack About two o'clock in the morning the insurgent negroes to the number of two hundred and fifty, well mounted and armed, rode up, and were in the act of dismounting when the little fellow commenced a slow and steady fire upon them, which had the effect to intimidate them and they went off, leaving their dead and wounded on the ground It was the last attack the negroes made" Commodore Elliott procured the boy, S F Blount, an appointment as midshipman, and he afterwards became a distinguished officer During the nullification troubles in South Carolina, Commodore Elliott was in command of the naval forces at Charleston, and afterwards took charge of the navy yard at Boston In 1835 he was deputed to take the Hon Edward Livingston, United States minister to France in the frigate "Constitution" This duty was performed, but on the return voyage the vessel narrowly escaped being wrecked during a heavy storm in the English Channel Capt Elliott's daring and skill in handling the vessel alone prevented her from being dashed on the Scilly Rocks, in which event her destruction was inevitable Subsequently he took command of the Mediterranean squadron, and on returning home from that duty in 1839 found that reports derogatory to his professional character were again being circulated by his enemies The charges were based on the commodore's conduct at Lake Erie and during the nullification troubles and his treatment of certain midshipmen who had been engaged in a duel He was also accused of using the ship's stores, receiving presents, and harsh treatment to sailors He immediately demanded a court of inquiry, which was granted The result was that the commodore was subjected to a court-martial At the trial he claims he was deprived of some of his important witnesses, upon the ground that [illegible] under sailing [illegible] and could not be detached from their vessels A verdict against him was rendered, and he was suspended from the service until the 6th of July, 1844, with loss of pay The latter, however, was remitted by President Van Buren After living in retirement for nearly four years, he succeeded in obtaining a rehearing of his case, with the result of being reinstated in the navy with his former rank of commodore During his suspension, which lasted from the 22d of June, 1840, to the 18th of October, 1843, he resided near Carlisle, Pa, and was engaged chiefly in farming[1] He devoted much time and attention to the breeding of fine sheep and swine which he had imported He was a man of indomitable energy and courage, and though suffering keenly under the ignominy of an unjust sentence, applied himself bravely to the work which lay next his hand At the age of fifty five he learned how to plow, and boasted that he could "plow as good a furrow as any man in Pennsylvania"

While stationed in the Mediterranean, Commodore Elliott, in company with Gen Lewis Cass, minister to France, visited various places in Europe, and along the African and Turkish coasts At Rome he was cordially thanked by the Pope for the protection which he had given to the Sisters of the Ursuline Convent, near Boston, after the burning of the convent by the anti-Catholic mob while he was in command of the Boston navy-yard At Athens the King and Queen of Greece were entertained on board the "Constitution," and afterwards gave a ball in honor of the commodore and his officers[2]

Commodore Elliott was a rigid disciplinarian and an earnest political partisan, and to this fact doubtless he owed much of the persecution to which he was so relentlessly subjected He was a firm friend and admirer of Gen Jackson, and during a period when

[1] His restoration to the service was due to President Tyler, who, having read a statement prepared by the commodore, instructed the Secretary of the Navy to place him on waiting orders The letter restoring him is as follows

"NAVY DEPARTMENT, Oct 19, 18[illegible]

"SIR,—The President of the United States having carefully considered the facts in your case in connection with evidences recently furnished, and considering also the long period of your suspension from the public service, and the gallantry exhibited by you on more than one occasion during the late war with Great Britain, has thought proper to remit the remaining period of your suspension, and to restore you to the public service You will accordingly consider yourself as waiting orders, your restoration dating from the 18th inst

"Your obedient servant,

"DAVID HENSHAW

"COMMODORE J D ELLIOTT, U S NAVY"

[2] Among his officers Elliott mentions Lieut Cadwalader Ringgold, of Washington County, "a fine young officer," whom [illegible]

general was very unpopular in Boston insisted on adopting a statue of the old warrior as the figure-head for the "Constitution," then lying at the Boston navy yard The figure was placed on the ship despite a furious popular outcry, and during the night was sawed off and carried away by some one who obtained admission to the navy yard Commodore Elliott attributes much of his undeserved misfortune to the resentment of Hon J K Paulding, Secretary of the Navy, who, he declares was his bitter enemy while professing to be his friend There seems little reason to doubt that his conviction by court-martial was brought about by unfair means, and that he was absolutely guiltless of the charges preferred Many of these charges were so trivial as to have been unworthy of notice, but they seem to have been considered serious by a court martial which was evidently determined to find the commodore guilty, and to humiliate him as much as possible There does not appear to have been one of them which was not refuted by the most conclusive testimony Commodore Elliott himself compared his conviction to the treatment of Commodore James Barron, and of the unfortunate Admiral Byng, and the comparison would seem to be fully justified by the records

Commodore Elliott was appointed to the command of the Philadelphia navy-yard, and died there Dec. 10, 1845

Commodore Elliott had a brother Wilson who was captain in the Nineteenth Regiment United States Infantry, and one of those who accompanied Col Campbell in the Mississineway expedition, in which there was so much suffering from hunger and cold He was also one of the four captains who successfully charged the left flank of the British batteries when they had invested Fort Meigs He contracted disease at Fort Meigs, which continued to weaken him until it caused his death

The Kennedy family Among the earliest and most successful business men of Hagerstown were the Kennedy brothers, John and Hugh The Kennedys were a Scotch-Irish family, and were rigid "Covenanters" of the Cromwellian type Their home was in the county of Derry, Ireland, where they occupied a respectable position John Kennedy, the first immigrant was born at Ballyavlin, a small farm near the town of Newton Limavaddy, in the county of Londonderry, June 1? 1767 His parents were James Kennedy, Jr, born Nov 23, 1739, and Rachel, whose maiden name was George Their children were John, Hugh Priscilla, James, Joshua, and [illegible] John Kennedy received a good education and being of [illegible] home at the age of nineteen to sail for America He landed at Philadelphia, and thence proceeded to New Castle, Del, where he taught school Subsequently he removed to Hagerstown, where he was befriended by a fellow-countryman, James Ferguson, a merchant, who transacted a large miscellaneous business in Hagerstown Ferguson employed him as clerk, and young Kennedy finding that a knowledge of the German dialect spoken in Pennsylvania and Maryland was indispensable to success in business, set to work to master it and made such progress that he was soon enabled to render valuable service to his employer As soon as he became firmly established in Hagerstown he sent over to Ireland for his brother Hugh, who came to this country and joined him in business Mr Ferguson being desirous of relinquishing the business, offered it to the Kennedys on condition that they would take into partnership with them Richard Ragan, also a clerk in Ferguson's employ This they consented to do, and the firm became Kennedy & Ragan For many years the firm practically divided the business of the county with another thriving house, that of Stonebraker & Co, at Boonsboro' Both the Kennedys succeeded in thoroughly mastering the German dialect, and to this fact much of their success is doubtless to be ascribed John married on Christmas day, 1804, Mary Wagoner Hugh remained a bachelor Mary (Wagoner) Kennedy was the daughter of John Wagoner, who lived on the old "End Strife" farm, now "Ravenswood," nearly equidistant between Hagerstown and Funkstown Mrs Kennedy's mother (wife of John Wagoner) was the daughter of Peter White and Margaret Stull Peter White was the son of John White, an Englishman, who settled in New Jersey Peter White took up large tracts of land on both sides of the Antietam, called "End the Strife," "Whisky," and "Toddy" Eight children were born to Mr and Mrs White They were Sarah, who married John Wagoner, who was sheriff of Washington County for two terms, Margaret, who married Mr Geary, and was the mother of the late Governor Geary, of Pennsylvania, and of Rev Edward Geary, a Presbyterian minister, now living in Portland, Oregon, Isaac Stull White, who was also sheriff of Washington County, and who married a Miss Rench, John, who was afterwards the father of Mrs Judge Carson, of Mercersburg Pa, two sons who died single, and two daughters who also remained unmarried Mrs Peter White (Margaret Stull) was the niece of Judge Stull Mrs White's sister Susan married Col Jack Swearingen of racing fame In May 1818 Mrs John Kennedy died leaving four [illegible] Benjamin Price,

the lawyer of Frederick, and afterwards of Hagerstown, Louisa Margaret, who married Hon James Dixon Roman, John Wagoner, who married Mary Elizabeth McPherson, only daughter of Dr William Smith McPherson, of Prospect Hall, Frederick County, and James Hugh, who married Lydia, second daughter of Col Jacob Hollingsworth, of Hagerstown

On the death of their parents in Ireland, the Kennedys sent for their younger brother, James, who had remained at home to take care of his mother and father He came over to this country with his wife and eight children and settled on a farm near Greencastle, Pa, which his brothers had purchased and stocked for him On this place still resides the eldest son (John) of James Kennedy After continuing for a number of years, the firm of Kennedy & Ragan dissolved, the Kennedys retaining the old stand, at the southeast corner of the public square, in the centre of which stood the court-house Mr Ragan established a new store two doors away John and Hugh Kennedy then took into partnership two young men, James O Carson, of Greencastle Pa, and John McCurdy, of Mercersburg, Pa Mr Carson married Rosanna White, daughter of John White, and a cousin of Mrs Kennedy Mr McCurdy married Rachel McClelland, a niece of John Kennedy The firm continued in business for some twenty years, when Mr McCurdy established a store in Hagerstown, and Mr Carson removed to Mercersburg Hugh Kennedy also retired from business, in favor of his nephew, John Wagoner Kennedy, and the firm became John Kennedy & Son Hugh Kennedy died in 1835, aged sixty six, and John Kennedy died in 1847, aged eighty James Kennedy died in November of the same year, aged seventy-three Of John Kennedy's children, Sarah Anne, widow of Benjamin Price, who died in 1840, still survives with two children,—Louisa Kennedy, who married Francis M Darby, a lawyer of Hagerstown and died about two years ago, and Kennedy, now living in Siskyou County, Cal Mrs James Dixon Roman (Louisa Margaret Kennedy) died on the 1st of August, 1878, having had the affliction to survive the death of her entire family,—her younger daughter Louisa, her husband, her daughter Sallie, wife of C C Baldwin, of New York, and her son, James Dixon Roman John W Kennedy and his wife and two children are still living One of their children, John Wagoner Kennedy, died when seven months old The other children are McPherson Kennedy, of New York, who married Esther Walden Tomlinson, of that city, and has two children—McPherson and Esther Walden, and Antoinette Kennedy, who [illegible] more Mr and Mrs Crichton have six children—William, Nettie Malcolm, McPherson James and Mary Elizabeth

James Hugh Kennedy, youngest son of John Kennedy, was attacked by a mob in Carlisle, Pa, while seeking to recover some runaway slaves, and so badly injured that he died He left a wife and two daughters His widow married Rev Dr William Jackson, at that time rector of St John's Parish, Hagerstown and died in Jacksonville His eldest daughter, Nannie Hollingsworth Kennedy, married Dr Lehman Adams Cooper, of Baltimore, who died recently in New Mexico Mrs Cooper died in Hagerstown in 1872, leaving a son, Lehman Adams Cooper, and a daughter, Marie Louise Cooper, both of whom survive her James H Kennedy's youngest daughter, Lydia Hollingsworth Kennedy, married Tryon Hughes Edwards, a lawyer practicing in Hagerstown Their children are Catharine Hughes, Lydia Hollingsworth, and Tryon Pierpont They have lost one daughter, Nannie Kennedy, about one year old

All three of the Kennedy brothers were strict members of the Presbyterian Church John Kennedy was a ruling elder and for many successive years was a delegate to the General Assembly from the Presbytery of Carlisle He was an uncompromising believer in and advocate of the orthodox Presbyterian doctrine, but at the same time was very tolerant, and enjoyed the friendship and confidence of Fathers Dubois and Dubarrel of Emmittsburg, in whose society he took great pleasure Both the brothers were earnest Whigs, but neither took any active part in politics They restricted their energies to their business and to promoting the interests of their church Both of them amassed considerable property, and both led sober, well balanced lives, whose influence upon all who came in contact with them, and upon the community at large, was of the most wholesome and beneficial character

The Beatty family Col William Beatty, one of the earliest settlers of Washington County, was a man of remarkable energy and force of character He married Mary Dorothy daughter of John Conrad Grosh, one of the pioneer German immigrants of Western Maryland They had twelve sons and four daughters as follows

1 William, born 1758, killed at the battle of Hobkirk Hill, near Camden, S C, April 25, 1781

2 Henry Beatty, born 1760

3 Elizabeth Beatty, born 1762

4 John Conrad Beatty, born 1764

5 Cornelius Beatty, born 1766

6 Sophia Beatty, born 1768, married Col Nathaniel [illegible]

[illegible] Dec 5 1[illegible]5

7 Mary Beatty, born 1769
8 George Beatty, born 1771
9 Otho Beatty, born 1773
10 Eleanor Beatty, born 1774
11 Elie Beatty, born 1776
12 Adam Beatty, born 1777
13 John Michael Beatty, born 1779
14 Daniel Beatty, born 1780
15 William Beatty (2), born 1782
16 Lewis Augustus Beatty, born 1784

Peter Grosh's second daughter, Catharine, married William Kimball His son Michael married Christiana Raymer His daughter Anna B married E. Williams His son Adam was killed at the battle of Germantown

William Beatty, son of Col William Beatty and Mary Dorothy Grosh, was born in Frederick County Md, on the 19th of June, 1758 He was the eldest of twelve sons In stature he was erect and stately, and in person vigorous and athletic, capable of enduring the greatest fatigue and of suffering the utmost privation His attachments were warm and permanent, and his patriotism ardent and almost romantic[1]

The venerable Frederick Hummrichouse, one of the best known citizens of Washington County, died on the 5th of October, 1876, at the age of eighty-five years, two months, and twenty days, and his remains were laid beside those of his ancestors, who were among the earliest citizens of Hagerstown, in the graveyard of the Old Reformed Church Mr Hummrichouse removed to Hagerstown with his father in 1798, when nine years old, and continued to remain in the same spot for the remainder of his life

The father of Frederick Hummrichouse enlisted as a private in the Revolutionary army two months before the Declaration of Independence was signed, and on the 1st of July, 1776, was commissioned as an ensign He participated in the great battles of the war, was at Valley Forge, and did not lay down his sword until the struggle was ended He then lived in Philadelphia until the yellow fever epidemic, when he removed to Hagerstown The maternal grandfather of Frederick Hummrichouse was the Rev Christian Frederick Post, of the Episcopal Church of England, who came to this continent first to Labrador as a missionary, where he remained twenty-two years His second mission was to the then wilderness of which Pittsburgh is now the centre, and his third mission, to the same locality, to quiet the hostile Indians, was upon a commission issued by William Denny, the Governor of the province of Pennsylvania, and bears date Oct 23, 1758

Frederick Hummrichouse represented the county in the General Assembly of Maryland, filled the office of postmaster at Hagerstown, was a director in most of the banking and other companies, and was, up to within a few months of his death, one of the most active and experienced working directors of the Hagerstown Bank and the Washington County Mutual Insurance Company He "died in harness," with a mind as clear and strong as at any previous period of his life,—a useful man and earnest Christian

William Heyser, who died on the 15th of January, 1875, aged eighty-four years and four months, was the son of William Heyser, for many years president of the Hagerstown Bank, and grandson of Capt William Heyser, who was an officer in the Revolutionary army

William Heyser, the great-grandfather of John H Heyser, of Cold Spring, was the original settler of the family in Hagerstown Valley, and was contemporary with Hager and Funk, the first settlers The first Heyser commenced the building of the German Reformed church of Hagerstown, whose "centennial" was celebrated in 1874, and it was with his means mainly that that building was erected The finishing of it was suspended for a few years by the absence of Capt Heyser with the army

The following letter from his son William, aged nine, written to the captain during the Revolutionary struggle, provides a signal illustration of the universality of the patriotic and martial spirit of that period The letter is as follows

"*To Capt William Heyser, at the American Camp, Philadelphia*

"DEAR FATHER

"Through the mercies of almighty God, I my Mammy, my brother and Sisters are well, in hopes these may find you enjoying these Felicities, which tend to happiness in life, and everlasting Happiness in Eternity your long absence and great distance is the only matter of our trouble but our sincere Prayers, is for your Welfare and Prosperity, begging that God may prosper you, and your united Brethren, in your laudable undertaking, and in the end crown you with the laurels of a Compleate Victory, over the Enemies of the inestimable Rights, Liberties, and Privileges of distressed America, and hand them down inviolate to the latest Posterity My Dear father, my greatest Grief is, that I am incapable of the military Service, that I might enjoy the company of so loving a father, and serve my country in so glorious a cause but tho' absent from you yet my constant prayer is for your Safety, in the Hour of danger, your compleate victory, over the Enemies, of the united States of America, and your Safe Restoration to the government of your family I and my brother Jacob Continue at School, and hope [illegible] in our [illegible] Mammy, my

[1] A brief sketch of [illegible] Frederick [illegible]

brother and Sister do join me in their Prayers and well wishes for you

"HAGERS TOWN, October 12th 1776 } I am Dr Father your most dutiful and obedt Son,
WILLIAM HEYSER"

William Heyser, grandson of Capt William, was born in Hagerstown, and resided within a mile of that place He was a man of powerful physique, indomitable energy, and great self control He built a number of houses,—the large stone house and buildings on the Heyser farm, and subsequently the houses for his son John, his grandson, Oscar Bellman, and his daughter, Henrietta Snyder His remains were interred in Rose Hill Cemetery

Mary Wolgamot, wife of Col David Schnebly, attained the remarkable age of one hundred and three years, nine months, and two days

The family Bible in which the record is kept is of the edition of 1807, Philadelphia, Mathew Carey At the head of the list of "births" are recorded those of Col David Schnebly and Mary Wolgamot, husband and wife, as follows

"BIRTHS

"David Schnebly, born May the 8th, 1770

"Mary Wolgamot, born Feb the 10th, 1773

On the opposite page is recorded the marriage of the above

"MARRIAGES

"David Schnebly, married to Mary Wolgamot, May 7th, 1793,"

And on the last page of the family record we find the death of Col Schnebly thus recorded

"DEATHS

"October 1, 1842 This day Col David Schnebly died, aged 72 years, 4 months, and 22 days"

After the death of her husband, whose remains were buried in the Reformed church, Hagerstown, Mrs Schnebly continued to reside at the farm "Garden of Eden," lying near the Cumberland Valley Railroad, five and a half miles north of Hagerstown Here Col David Schnebly was born Mrs Schnebly's birthplace was the farm afterwards owned by Joshua Emmert, and at the time of her birth the property of her father, Col John Wolgamot, about four miles southwest of the "Garden of Eden," near the Conococheague At this place Mrs Schnebly was married, and on the 8th of May following removed to the "Garden of Eden" farm, where she resided for eighty-two years Her father was a soldier in the Revolutionary war, and died when she was a little child Mrs Schnebly was last seen in public at the centennial celebration of the Reformed Church, which took place in Hagerstown in the spring of 1874

From an account published in the Hagerstown *Herald and Torch* in February, 1873, of a visit to Mrs Schnebly, we make the following extracts viz

"The aged and venerable lady, seated erect as in early life in her arm-chair, received the congratulations of every visitor, and expressed in strong, unshaken voice her thanks and her happiness at seeing them all Her portrait, taken in her prime by Eichholtz (whose colors never fade), was suspended near her on the wall, and all could mark the contrast between the youthful beauty and the beauty of serene age

"Mrs Schnebly's vision is impaired, and her hearing somewhat dulled, but her voice is strong, and she converses with wonderful facility for one of such extreme age She told several amusing incidents of her life, and joined heartily in the merriment produced Being in her fourth year when the Declaration of Independence was adopted, she was well grown when Gen Washington visited this county and she saw him and has a vivid recollection of him She was born and reared within four miles of the residence to which she was transferred in her twentieth year by her marriage with the late Col David Schnebly, whom she has survived about twenty eight years And there she has lived during her long life her husband during his life in the peaceful occupation of agriculture, and she the dutiful frugal, industrious, domestic wife, dispensing as oft they did a welcome hospitality The carpet which now adorns her parlor, in colors bright as if new, was laid in 1812 —sixty years ago,—a beautiful Brussels The white, beautiful table linen which covered the festal board on this occasion was made by her own tender hands in 1790,—eighty years ago Since the death of her husband she has been conducting the farm (and that no small one) herself, with the aid of a worthy citizen who attends to the out door employments

"On the anniversary here referred to her board was plentifully supplied with the good things of her household and all partook, she herself being seated at the head of the first table and partaking liberally of the food she had so bountifully spread for her guests After all had dined the entire party reassembled in the parlor for religious services Appropriate passages were read from the Bible by the Rev Dr Kieffer, of Greencastle, Pa The assembly then rising, the Creed was repeated by all Then kneeling, a very touching prayer was offered up by that gentleman, and the benediction pronounced During all these services and entertainment this aged and most interesting lady manifested no fatigue whatever"

Col Jacob Hollingsworth, who died from a pistol wound inflicted accidentally by himself, in March, 1868, was about seventy eight years of age, and was one of the prominent citizens of Washington County About 1835 he purchased "Fountain Rock" the former residence of Gen Samuel Ringgold, and removed from Anne Arundel to Washington County Soon after he established his residence in Hagerstown and invested his means, after selling the Ringgold property in a sugar plantation in Mississippi The war inflicted heavy loss on him, and in his later years he led a very retired life He had an extensive family connection, among them the late Dr Gibson, an eminent surgeon of Philadelphia, Gen Charles Sterett Ridgely and Dr John B Morris The manner of Col Hollingsworth's death was a great shock to his relatives and friends [illegible] living alone in his

room, across the foot of the bed and insensible, the blood oozing out of a small wound a little behind and above the left ear. Under his body was found a Colt's revolver of the smallest size, loaded with the exception of a single charge. The report of the pistol had been heard by one of the colonel's daughters, about eleven o'clock, but it excited no alarm at the time. But the colonel's wife, whose mind has been enfeebled by age, entered the parlor about noon and told her daughter, Mrs. Watts, that something was the matter with her father. Mrs. Watts, on discovering the prostrate form of her father, called to her husband, Maj. Edward Watts, when the facts above related were developed.

The first impression was that the act might have been designed; but later in the day this impression was changed into the belief among those persons who attended the bedside of the wounded man, that it was the result of accident. The Rev. Henry Edwards, former pastor of St. John's Parish, called at the bedside of the dying man, Drs. Regan and Dorsey, Maj. Hughes, Judge French, Maj. Watts, John W. Kennedy, and several ladies, friends of the family, were also present. The impression having rapidly gone abroad that the act might have been one of attempted suicide, Mr. Edwards felt it to be his duty to inquire into the circumstances of the case. Mr. Edwards subsequently stated that Col. Hollingsworth, both on the occasion of this visit and of a subsequent visit three hours later, was entirely conscious; that he answered the questions put to him knowingly and intelligibly; that he pronounced his (Mr. Edwards') name, as well as those of Maj. Hughes and Mr. Kennedy, when pointed out to him, quite distinctly; and that, although suffering severe pain which caused moaning, while Mr. Edwards was reading the church service he remained perfectly still and attentive. Mr. Edwards, again and again, in various forms, propounded the questions, "Had he done it on purpose?" "Was it accidental?" To the first he received the consistent answer "No!" and to the latter "Yes!" Mr. Edwards was satisfied, as fully as it was possible to be under such circumstances, that the act was one of accident, and in this view the other gentlemen present concurred. For a long while Col. Hollingsworth had been in a highly nervous state, mentally as well as physically. He had fancied that he was threatened by robbers, and one of his idiosyncrasies was that he must have a pistol constantly about him for his defense.

Among the thrifty and enterprising Swiss emigrants who crossed the ocean to America in the early part of the eighteenth century were the parents of Wolfgang Newcomer, who [illegible] ylvani[illegible] about 1720, and settled in the city of Philadelphia. They probably belonged to that large class of artisans and mechanics who poured into Pennsylvania in a steady stream at this period from Germany and Switzerland, and proved such valuable acquisitions in a land where skilled labor and steady workmen were difficult to obtain. The son, Wolfgang, was a carpenter by trade. He was twice married. His first wife, a Miss Baer, only lived about a year after their marriage; and about two years after her death he married Elizabeth Miller, by whom he had three sons,—Henry, Christian, and Peter,—and five daughters.

The three brothers removed from Lancaster County, Pa., where their father settled, to Washington County, Md., and became owners of large landed estates in the vicinity of Beaver Creek, near Hagerstown. All three of them soon took prominent positions in their new homes. Christian became a noted minister of the German Reformed Church, and eventually a bishop of that denomination, while Henry and Peter made their influence felt for good in more private walks of life. Among the descendants of Henry was John Newcomer, who was born on the 18th of December, 1797, in Washington County, Md., where he died on the 21st of April, 1861. John Newcomer would seem to have inherited in a special manner all the highest virtues and best qualities of the sturdy, honest stock from which he sprung. Although naturally quiet and retiring, his strong character and no less strong intellect made him a [illegible] of prominence all through his life, and in spite of his own personal tastes and wishes kept him almost constantly before the public, so that, even when permitted to escape the burden of official responsibilities, he still occupied by general consent a semi-official position, and as a sort of business oracle of the community in which he lived, was made by his friends and neighbors the judge and arbiter of their business disputes. His strict integrity and veracity, his frankness, sincerity, and disinterestedness, gave to these decisions the weight of law with the contending parties, and procured for him the genuine and universal respect of the community.

In 1836 he was elected sheriff of the county, and in 1840, after the expiration of his term, was sent to the State Senate, where he served his constituents with credit to himself and satisfaction to them for the period of six years. In 1846 he was elected county commissioner, serving until 1849, and in 1850 was elected a member of the convention which framed the constitution adopted in that year. In 1859 he reluctantly consented to become a candidate for county [illegible] five consti-

dates on the ticket with him who was elected to that office, which he held at the time of his decease While thus holding many political offices of trust and honor, he never sank to the level of the politician, nor lost in public station the virtues which adorned and beautified his private life

His wife Catharine Newcomer, was a lady of the most admirable and excellent character, and to her loving and judicious training her eldest son, Benjamin Franklin Newcomer, who has won such well-merited distinction in the business world, attributes much of his success Born on the 28th of April, 1827, at the old homestead of his great grandfather, Henry Newcomer, which is still in possession of the family Benjamin F Newcomer was educated at the Hagerstown Academy with a view to civil engineering as his future calling, for which he seemed peculiarly adapted by his strong natural talent for mathematics In the year 1842, however, his father formed a connection with Samuel Stonebraker and establishing in Baltimore the house of Newcomer & Stonebraker, wholesale dealers in flour and grain, sent his son, then but sixteen years of age, to represent his interests in the business In a short time the firm stood among the leaders in the flour and grain business of Baltimore, and for many years their sales aggregated one-tenth of all the flour sold in that city Two years after he had entered upon his business career, at the youthful age of eighteen, B F Newcomer purchased his father's entire interest in the establishment, having at that period sole charge of the correspondence and financial department of the house In the mean time however, anxious to complete as far as practicable, the education which had been interrupted by his call to the pursuits of active life, he had become a member of the Mercantile Library Association, and very soon afterwards a director in that institution, spending his evenings in reading, study, and attending lectures, including several courses in philosophy, astronomy, and chemistry In 1862 the firm of Newcomer & Stonebraker was dissolved and the present house of Newcomer & Co established in the same line,—a house which stands second to none in the country for business enterprise, careful management, and financial integrity

While laying the foundations of a great business house and building up an enviable reputation for himself personally, Mr Newcomer was not indifferent to the calls of benevolence, and at the early age of twenty five, in connection with Judge John Glenn, Jacob I Cohen, William George Baker, J Smith Hollins, J N McJilton, and David Laughery, became one of the incorporators of the "Maryland Institution for th[illegible] Newcomer is now the only survivor of the original incorporators, but his interest in the institution has only increased with time, and with its development and progress Since its establishment a quarter of a century ago it has done a noble work in the education of the blind, and it is indebted to Mr Newcomer, who was for many years its treasurer and is now its president, for much of its past success and present prosperity In 1854, Mr Newcomer was elected a director in the Union Bank of Maryland (now the National Union Bank of Baltimore), and during the whole of his connection with it was the youngest member of the board, upon which he continued to serve until 1868 when the increasing pressure of private business compelled his resignation He was also one of the original promoters of the Corn and Flour Exchange, organized in 1853, which has become one of the most important mercantile institutions in Baltimore In 1861 he was elected a director in the Northern Central Railway Company, and was soon afterwards made chairman of the finance committee, holding that position until his resignation in 1875 His services were so highly appreciated that at the annual meeting of the stockholders in February, 1878, he was strongly urged to again become a member of the board Yielding to this imperative solicitation, he was again elected chairman of the finance committee, and was also made a member of every committee of which the board is composed He is also a director in the Philadelphia, Wilmington and Baltimore Railroad In association with William T Walters he served as one of the finance commissioners of the city of Baltimore from 1867 to 1869 and discharged the duties of the position with signal judgment and ability After the close of the war he acquired large interests in various railroads in North and South Carolina, and assisted with capital and energy in the development of the railway system which has opened up a new era of prosperity in the South He is vice-president of the Wilmington and Weldon Railroad, and a director in the various roads constituting the Coast Line, the management of which is in the hands of himself and his associates In 1868, Mr Newcomer was elected president of the Safe Deposit and Trust Company of Baltimore,—a corporation chartered for the safe-keeping of bonds stocks and valuables of every description, and for the purpose of acting as trustee, executor, guardian, etc The Safe Deposit building is the most complete structure of its character in the country, and is unsurpassed by any similar building anywhere either in security or finish It is strictly fire proof, and the great burglar and fire [illegible] and beauty

The company has supplied a real need in Baltimore and its vicinity, and under the able management of Mr. Newcomer it is daily growing in public appreciation. The authority given it in its charter to act in a fiduciary capacity has proved as valuable to the public as to itself and trusts of all characters are administered not only with fidelity, but with more than ordinary intelligence, owing to Mr Newcomer's thorough familiarity with the laws and the business details connected with their management. Mr Newcomer still retains the presidency of the company, is also a director in the Baltimore and Potomac Railroad Company, in the Chamber of Commerce Building Company, and in the Savings-Bank of Baltimore, and was formerly a director in the National Exchange Bank and in the Third National Bank.

While courteous and kindly in his intercourse with all with whom he is brought into contact, Mr Newcomer is firm and independent in his business transactions, ready to receive suggestions, but relying largely, like all men of strong character who have carved out their own way in the world, upon his own judgment and experience,—guides, it may be added, which rarely lead him astray. With all his business capacity and talent, he possesses the rare virtue of modesty, shrinking from notoriety and prominence, and of all the positions he has been called upon to fill not one was ever sought by him. His attachments and affections are strong and ardent, and he has frequently declared that whatever success he has achieved in life can be attributed to a good mother and a good wife, in both of whom he has been peculiarly blessed.

When a little over twenty-one years of age, Mr Newcomer married Amelia, daughter of John H Ehlen, one of the earliest stockholders and for many years a director in the Baltimore and Ohio Railroad Company, as also in the Chesapeake Bank and in the Firemen's Insurance Company, a gentleman noted for his business integrity, genial manners, and kindness of heart. In the spring of 1870, accompanied by his wife, Mr Newcomer joined at Paris their eldest daughter, who had been sent there to complete her education. Together they made the tour of Southern Europe and Great Britain. In 1877, accompanied by his wife and two younger daughters he made another and more extended tour, embracing France, Italy, Germany, part of Austria, Switzerland, Holland, Belgium, England, and Scotland.

Mrs Newcomer, whose death occurred on the 20th of October, 1881, was a lady more than worthy of the love and esteem in which she was held by all who enjoyed the p[illegible] [illegible] relations of her home circle, and in labors for the relief of suffering she was true, devoted, and self-sacrificing. The beauty and nobility of her character were illustrated by the quiet exhibition of those virtues which best adorn womanhood, and she ever blessed and cheered with voice and hand. Her death was no ordinary loss, and the regret which it occasioned was widespread and sincere.

Mr Newcomer has four children,—three daughters and one son. The eldest, Mary L, is the wife of James M Maslin, of the house of Henry, Maslin & Co, wholesale merchants, of Baltimore, the second, Nannie, is the wife of F H Hack, a member of the Baltimore bar, the third, Hattie, and her younger brother, Waldo, reside with their father.

Christian Newcomer, a bishop of the German Methodist Society, was born in Lancaster County, Pa, Feb 1, 1749. His father, Wolfgang Newcomer, emigrated from Switzerland and settled at Philadelphia. His occupation was that of carpenter. He first married a Miss Baer, who lived only one year after marriage, and after being a widower about two years he married Elizabeth Weller, by whom he had three sons and five daughters. Of the sons, Henry Newcomer was the eldest, Christian the second, and Peter the youngest. Both the parents were members of the Mennonite denomination. At a very early age Christian became deeply interested in religion, and was baptized into the Mennonite Society. He learned the trade of carpenter, which he continued to practice until the death of his father, when he took charge of the homestead. On the 31st of March, 1770, he was married to Elizabeth Baer. In the winter following he had a serious illness, but recovered. During this illness and subsequently, he was assailed by many doubts and scruples concerning religion, and fearing to yield to the temptation to become a minister, sold his plantation in Pennsylvania and moved into Washington County, Md. During the Revolution he was considerably embarrassed by the conflict between his patriotism and the rule of his society forbidding any of the members to take up arms. Subsequently, during a visit to his old home at Lancaster, he rose in a meeting, and having related his mental vacillation, earnestly recommended "to them the grace of God in Christ Jesus." Some time before he had made the acquaintance of William Otterbein and George Adam Geeting, two preachers of the German Reformed Church, whose sermons produced a powerful impression upon him and caused him to withdraw from the Mennonites and attach himself to their communi[illegible] [illegible] [illegible]lly upon the [illegible] [illegible] often traveled

a hundred miles and more to fill appointments He preached both in German and English, though unable to speak the latter with fluency His service extended over the whole of Western Maryland, and into portions of West Virginia, Pennsylvania, and Ohio He continued to labor with wonderful activity and diligence, keeping a daily record of his work, until eighty-one years of age In this year he was elected, with Henry Kumler, a bishop of the society His health now began to fail, but he continued nevertheless to discharge the duties of his office with wonderful punctuality and vigor until his death which occurred on the 12th of March, 1830, in his eighty second year The last entry in his journal reads

"March 1st —This day I rode to Boonsborough and lodged with brother Michael Thomas 2d My intention was to ride to Virginia to-day, but finding the weather rather disagreeable this morning I returned home 3d This morning I was very well satisfied that I had returned home, during the past night I was very ill and had but little rest O God! stand by me for Jesus' sake, true I am unworthy of all Thy mercies, but I am so needy, Lord, bless me, and Thine shall be all the glory Amen Some time in the day my son Andrew sent for a physician 4th This forenoon I tried to write in my journal, but, alas! I find that I am not able to perform the task, so I lay down my pen The Lord alone knows whether I shall be able to resume it again The Lord's will be done Amen, Hallelujah!"

Shortly before his death, Bishop Newcomer rose from his pillow without assistance, and, with those present, offered an earnest prayer He then lay down, and, "reclining his head on his pillow, drew breath but a few times and calmly expired" His funeral was attended by a vast concourse Bishop Henry Kumler preached in German, and Dr John Zahn in English

Robert Fowler, State treasurer of Maryland, was a native of Montgomery County, but removed to Washington County in early life, and married there He pursued the various avocations of hotel keeper, merchant, contractor, and politician, and in all these relations enjoyed the respect and confidence of the community in which he lived His first office was that of county commissioner in which position he displayed, although a very young man, the same qualifications for business and the management of public affairs that distinguished him in after life In 1846, when party excitement was unusually high, Mr Fowler was renominated as a Whig for the House of Delegates in opposition to Hon Wm T Hamilton The contest was a very exciting and extremely personal one, and resulted in the election of Mr Fowler After the expiration of his senatorial term he was engaged in projecting and building various turnpike roads He a[illegible] the construction of the Washington County branch of the Baltimore and Ohio Railroad, and the successful prosecution of that enterprise was largely due to his efforts in its behalf He was elected treasurer of Maryland for several consecutive terms and at the time of his death was regarded as one of the most influential politicians in the State The greater portion of his life was spent in Washington County, but for some years previous to his death he resided in Baltimore County The funeral took place from Barnum's Hotel and was very largely attended The Rev C R Haines, rector of St Timothy's Church, at Catonsville, of which Mr Fowler was a member, and the Rev Fleming James, rector of St Mark's Church were the officiating clergymen

After the funeral service had been read the cortege was formed the clergy leading Then came the honorary pall bearers of the Legislature, viz Senators Walsh, Spencer, Tuck, and Steiner, and Representatives Grimes Leonard, Merryman and Annan Then followed the casket, borne by the following gentlemen who acted as pall bearers Hon Wm T Hamilton, Hon Isaac M Denson, Daniel Dorsey, A S Abell, Dr J Hanson Thomas J B Brinkley, F K Zeigler, Wm B McLaughlin, Henry James, John King, Jr, and Joseph Judick After the family and friends had been seated the members of the Legislature and city officials took carriages in the rear and the cortege proceeded to Loudon Park Cemetery Among those present were Hon Reverdy Johnson Senator Whyte, and Mayor Vansant

Luke Tiernan, importing and shipping merchant of Baltimore, was born in the county of Meath Ireland, in 1757, and came to the United States in 1787 and settled in Hagerstown, Md He married, in 1793, Ann Owen, a descendant of Col Cresap Mr Tiernan removed to Baltimore in 1795 and went into the business of importing dry goods, and was also largely interested in ships His house was on Baltimore Street, where the warehouse of Hamilton Easter & Sons is situated In politics he was a Whig and a warm admirer of Henry Clay who frequently stopped at his house, and always spoke of him as the patriarch of the Whig party of Maryland He was a Presidential elector for John Quincy Adams, he was the head of the list of the founders of the Hibernian Society He was one of the committee appointed in 1826–27 to urge upon the Legislature the incorporation of the Baltimore and Ohio Railroad The "Herald," one of his ships, brought the first locomotive for that road from England He was one of the organizers and president of the Screw Dock Company he was one of the trus[illegible] [illegible] of the com

mittee at the inauguration of the Washington Monument. He died Nov. 10, 1839, aged eighty-three, and left eleven children. He was greatly respected and beloved in the community, and strongly attached to the people and government of his adopted country.

Adam J. Glossbrenner was born in Hagerstown, Md., Aug. 31, 1810. His school was the printing-office, to which he was apprenticed, and at seventeen he became foreman of the *Ohio Monitor*, and afterwards of the *Western Telegraph*. In 1829 he returned to Maryland, and afterwards removed to York, Pa., where he published the *York Gazette*. In 1849 he was elected sergeant-at-arms to the House of Representatives for the Thirty-first Congress, and was re-elected for four Congresses. In 1861 he was private secretary to President Buchanan; in 1863 he founded the *Philadelphia Age*, and in 1864 was elected to the Thirty-ninth Congress, and served on the Committee on Public Lands, and on Engrossed Bills. He was re-elected to the Fortieth Congress, serving on the Committees on Expenditures in the Navy Department and Executive Mansion.

Edward Merryman Mealey was born in the New Market District of Frederick County about 1810. His mother was a native of England, and his father a native of Ireland. On attaining his majority he removed to Hagerstown, where he became a clerk for Stockton & Stokes, the stage proprietors. The latter sold out to Dr. Howard Kennedy and James Cowdy, of Hagerstown. Dr. Kennedy afterwards sold his interest to Mr. Cowdy and George Sinn, of Hagerstown. In 1865 the proprietors sold their rights to Pretzman & Appleman, and in 1849, Mr. Adams, who was then endeavoring to organize the express company which now bears his name, visited Hagerstown and gave the elder Mealey a certain portion of the stock in payment for combining the express business with his stage-lines. Mr. Mealey was elected to the House of Delegates on the Whig ticket in 1858, and was president of the Washington County Railroad from commencement to completion, and director in the Hagerstown Bank.

In 1841 he married Elizabeth Frances Windsor, of Kentucky, and had one son, Edward W. Mealey, who was born on the 23d of August, 1846. E. W. Mealey, Jr., was educated at the College of St. James, where he graduated in 1864, and at Harvard College, where he graduated in 1867. He studied law, and on the 1st of June, 1876, married Gertrude Parks, of New York City, whose father was rector of Trinity Church. Mr. Mealey is a director of the Western Maryland Railroad, Hagerstown Steam-Engine and Machine Com[illegible] Washington County Water Company, and is one of the owners of the Baldwin House at Hagerstown.

George C. Washington was born in Westmoreland County, Va., Aug. 20, 1789, and died in Georgetown, D. C., July 17, 1854. At the time of his death he was the eldest and nearest surviving relative of his grand-uncle, Gen. Washington. He represented Western Maryland in the Congress from 1827 to 1833, and from 1835 to 1837. He was also president of the Chesapeake and Ohio Canal and a commissioner for the settlement of Indian claims. He was spoken of for Vice-President on the ticket with Gen. Scott.

Frederick Bodmann, who died on the 29th of July, 1874, was born at Hanau, near Frankfort-on-the-Main, July 16, 1801, and was therefore at the time of his death a little more than seventy-three years of age. His father, Louis Charles Bodmann, was a judge of the Superior Court of a German principality near Frankfort. Ferdinand graduated with honor at Bamberg College in 1817, and subsequently received a liberal commercial education in a large banking-house in Frankfort. In 1822 the father, with three sons, Ferdinand among the rest, arrived in Baltimore, Md., and soon after settled in Hagerstown, where Ferdinand was engaged in commercial business until the death of his father, which occurred about six years after the immigration to this country. In a short time after the father's death Ferdinand disposed of his business and went to Cincinnati and engaged in the tobacco business, which he followed until his death.

Mr. Bodmann had considerable means,—about thirty thousand dollars, it is said,—and on this as a foundation he amassed a great fortune. Immediately on his arrival in Cincinnati he commenced the erection of a tobacco-factory on Main Street, between Sixth and Seventh. Remaining in this place a few years, he removed across the street, to what is now No. 273, and there remained in business until he died.

He was married Dec. 14, 1825, to a daughter of George M. Popline, of Baltimore. Of the six children born three survive, they being Charles, one of the largest tobacco dealers in Cincinnati; a younger son, George, engaged in business in Brussels, Belgium; and Lauretta L., widow of the late Joseph Reakirt, the wholesale druggist.

Mr. Bodmann was for ten years Master of Cincinnati Lodge, No. 133, Free and Accepted Masons, a member of McMillan Chapter, of the Cincinnati Council and Cincinnati Commandery of Knights Templar, and an honorary member of Hanselmann Commandery. Upon his arrival in this country he was made a Mason i[illegible]

At the old business stand, No 273 Main Street, Cincinnati, where he remained for about forty years, Mr Bodmann at one time did a large wholesale and retail business in tobacco, considering the extent to which the trade was carried on in those days

He lived with his family in a very unpretentious manner over the store until he moved to Mount Auburn, about twenty-six years before his death

The vast property which he gathered was not the result of speculation He never entered into a speculation in his life His wealth, consisting of about a million of dollars' worth of real estate and other possessions, swelling his fortune to a million and a half or two millions of dollars, was the slow accumulation of years through industry, economy, and sagacious investment Thus the years made him the oldest, and the product of his toil the wealthiest, German citizen of Cincinnati To his estate belonged the tan yard at the Great Western Stock Yards, the carrying on of which was his principal business for the last few years of his life He owned a large amount of real estate in the vicinity of his store on Main Street At an early day, with John Groesbeck as president, he was a director of the Franklin Bank, in which he owned considerable stock

Mr Bodmann had many strong eccentricities of character, some of which were admirable In his business investments he would not, under any circumstances, purchase a building unless he could own in fee-simple the ground upon which it stood When real estate came into his possession he held on to it permanently The only property of this kind he was ever known to part with was some eighty thousand dollars' worth on Fifth Street, which he sold to the government for room upon which to erect the new custom-house He frequently afterwards regretted the sale He was never known to give a note or a due-bill When he purchased a piece of property upon which there were to be deferred payments, he invariably refused to give his notes for these payments He simply had made on his books an entry of the amounts due, which as he always had the cash ready when pay day came around, was deemed perfectly satisfactory to the other parties He was a man whose word was as good as his bond

He often spoke of his native land, but never went back to see it Indeed, with a residence of nearly half a century in Cincinnati, it is said that during all that time he was never outside of the city except in the immediate vicinity He was fond of hunting game, and occasionally, in early times, went out for sport in the neighboring woods and fields He never trusted hims [illegible]

A friend relates that he was once urged to take the cars for Dayton to attend a Masonic meeting there Though he answered that he had property in that city which he had not seen for thirty years, he could not be induced to make the trip

Mr Bodmann was most remarkably methodical in his habits Though a millionaire, he until the last attended his plain little tobacco store, with unplastered walls, on Main Street He made this his office, where he loaned large sums of money and transacted the business connected with his large estate, but at the same time he did a share in waiting on customers, and with alacrity weighed out small quantities of tobacco, snuff, etc, for them He took pleasure in it, for with him his simple habits appeared a pleasure

Mr Bodmann was quite a bird-fancier, and in nothing else were his eccentricities more strongly marked than in this particular He is said to have intimated that one great inducement for moving on Mount Auburn was the comfort of his pets He had a large number of singing birds in his store, and at his home was a much larger collection, which in point of size and variety was one of the finest in the country In this were about six hundred pairs of pigeons of all varieties and colors The master fed the birds and animals from his own hand, and they became much attached to him Only the morning before he died, against the advice of friends, who regarded his health too precarious, he went out early to feed and fondle his pets

The Neill family William Neill, the great grandfather of Alexander Neill, was born in 1751 in County Antrim, Ireland, and emigrated to America, in company with his two brothers, about 1770 He landed in Baltimore, and engaged in business there, becoming one of the leading merchants of that town His son Alexander was born in Baltimore, Dec 22, 1778, and married Sarah Owen about 1803 He removed to Hagerstown the same year and entered into business He was elected sheriff in 1826, and subsequently retired from business He was for a long series of years president of the Hagerstown Bank He had ten children, four girls—Sarah, Rebecca, Mary Chandler, and Isabella Callender—and six boys,—William Kennedy, Robert Callender, William, Alexander, Kennedy, and Luke Tiernan

Alexander, father of Alexander Neill, now a prominent member of the Hagerstown bar, was born in Hagerstown, Dec 5, 1808 He married Mary Sim Nelson, of Frederick, daughter of John Nelson, who was attorney general under President Tyler

Mary Sim Nelson was born March 22, 1819 She [illegible] commander

of the United States sloop-of-war "Enterprise," to whom Congress awarded a gold medal for gallant conduct in destroying the British brig "Boxer" during the war of 1812.

The fruits of this marriage were eight children: Alexander, John Nelson, William, Sally, Harriet Barrows, Mary Chandler, Isabella, and Rose Nelson.

Alexander Neill, Jr., was born Aug. 5, 1844. He was educated at St. James' College, graduating in 1863, and commenced studying law with his father. After the death of his father he pursued his studies in the office of Judge William Motter. He was a member of the Legislature in 1870 and also a school commissioner, and was auditor of Washington County Court in 1876. Besides his public services, he has held numerous positions of trust in connection with private corporations, among them the treasurership of the Washington County Savings Institution in 1871, and a directorship in the Mutual Insurance Company of Washington County, for which company he was also attorney.

He married, April 27, 1871, Ellen, daughter of William Loubridge, of Baltimore, and has four children.

William Neill married Grace Kennedy, sister of Dr. Howard Kennedy.

Jonathan Hager's brother, George Hager, was born at Hagerstown, July 21, 1787, and settled in Terre Haute, Ind., in 1835. He was an active, enterprising business man, and contributed much to the growth and prosperity of Terre Haute. His character was a kindly, benevolent one, and he was extremely popular among his fellow-citizens. He died in April, 1870, in his eighty-third year.

J. Philip Roman was a native of Cecil County, of Quaker descent, and removed in early life to Washington County, where he studied law with his elder brother, Hon. J. Dixon Roman. Mr. Roman took a conspicuous part in the politics of Western Maryland, although, with the exception of representing Allegany County (in part) in the Constitutional Convention of 1867, he never held public office. In 1852 he was the Whig candidate for Congress, but was defeated by Hon. William T. Hamilton. In 1868 his name was before the convention which nominated Hon. Patrick Hamill for Congress, but after two days of fruitless balloting it was withdrawn. Mr. Roman was a man of unusual energy and decision of character, and was extremely popular with the masses. In the course of a long and active business life he amassed a handsome fortune. He owned several large tracts of valuable coal-lands, a shipping wharf to Locust Point [illegible] and [illegible] property. Mr. Roman was so engrossed in his business enterprises that he was not able to give much attention to his profession, the law. Soon after being admitted to the bar (1843) he removed to Cumberland, where he resided until his death. Mr. Roman married Miss Louisa Lowndes, daughter of Lloyd Lowndes, of Cumberland, who survived him.

Lieut. Louis M. Hughes, of the United States army, was killed on Feb. 14, 1870, by falling into a shaft at "Miners' Delight," a small town in the Sweetwater mining district of Wyoming Territory. He was a native of Hagerstown, and was appointed a second lieutenant from Maryland in the Thirty-sixth Infantry, July 28, 1866. On Feb. 22, 1869, he was promoted to a first lieutenancy, but as the consolidation of regiments about that time left him unassigned, he was at his own request continued in active service, and was attached to the Second Cavalry, then about to march to Montana. Subsequently he was assigned temporarily to the Seventh Infantry, and was ordered on duty in the locality where he was killed. Hearing that a notorious character who had stolen a number of government animals was concealed in a neighboring cabin, he obtained permission to try and capture him. With a detachment of soldiers he visited the place where the outlaw was supposed to be secreted. This proved to be the covering of a mining-shaft, through which Lieut. Hughes accidentally fell and received fatal injuries. His remains were brought to Hagerstown, where his mother resides, and were there interred.

Among the officers of the Army of Northern Virginia none were more celebrated for courageous daring, military gallantry, or affective aid to the "lost cause" than Maj. James Breathed, of Stuart's celebrated horse artillery, and in the civil war he won a reputation that will live for generations to come with those whose ancestors were sympathizers with the South in that sectional struggle. Maj. James Breathed was the eldest son and child of John W. Breathed, the founder of Breathedsville, Washington Co., and was born Dec. 15, 1838, in Morgan County, Va. In his infancy his father removed to Washington County, and James was educated at St. James' College. Upon concluding his studies he graduated as a medical doctor in Baltimore City and went to Missouri, where he settled near the city of St. Joseph. In his new home he soon became distinguished in his profession, which he abandoned at the breaking out of the war, and came East to cast his fortunes with those of his native State. On the journey he had for a traveling companion Gen. Stuart, who was afterwards his commanding [illegible] Virginia, and whose

errand was identical with that of young Breathed, but neither knew at that time of the mission of the other. Young Breathed first proceeded to the home of his parents to await the result of the action of the Maryland Legislature, which was about to convene in extra session. About this time, while in Chambersburg, Pennsylvania, he was suspected by the Federal authorities, who seized and searched his baggage, but released him after a short delay. Finding that the Legislature hesitated about the future course of the State, young Breathed, against the wishes of his parents, who counseled further deliberation, departed for Virginia and joined a company of cavalry commanded by J. Blair Hoge, of Martinsburg, afterwards known as Company B, First Virginia Cavalry. It was, together with other companies, placed under the command of Gen. J. E. B. Stuart, who was charged with the duty of retarding Gen. Patterson's advance upon Martinsburg. Recognizing in young Breathed his traveling companion of a few weeks previous, Gen. Stuart assigned him to scouting duty and other detached service, in the fulfillment of which he more than met the expectations of his commander. It was at this time that young Breathed displayed the elements of courage and daring which afterwards led to his rapid promotion.

Early in 1862, when Gen. Stuart organized a battalion of horse artillery, young Breathed was selected as first lieutenant of the first battery, of which John, afterwards Maj., Pelham was made captain. With this battery Maj. Breathed passed through the Peninsula campaign, Fair Oaks, the seven days' fighting around Richmond, Antietam, Gettysburg, and other celebrated engagements, in all of which he was more or less conspicuous. At the battle of Antietam the guns of this battery, commanded by him, opened the engagement. His guns were also the last to cross the Potomac at Shepherdstown on the occasion of Lee's retreat, and were constantly employed at the front of the Federal army as it moved on to Richmond. Just before the battle of Fredericksburg Lieut. Breathed was promoted to a captaincy. At the battle of Chancellorsville Capt. Breathed especially distinguished himself and won encomiums of praise from his commanding general, and at Gettysburg his company was in the fiercest of the fight and lost heavily.

Passing near his father's house on the return from Gettysburg, Capt. Breathed made it a visit, and while there was surprised by a company of Union cavalry and narrowly escaped capture.

On Sept. 25, 1863, Capt. Breathed, while in camp near Orange Court-House, tendered his resignation to Hon. James [illegible], [illegible] tired of my arm of service, and know that I can do better service in another arm of service."

Brig. Gen. Wickham, in forwarding it, said, "Strongly disapproved." "Capt. Breathed is the best man for the management of a battery of horse artillery that I ever saw."

Brig.-Gen. Fitzhugh Lee indorsed it, "Disapproved." "Capt. Breathed is an excellent officer. He can do no better service in another arm of the service."

Maj. Gen. J. E. B. Stuart, in his indorsement, said, "Respectfully forwarded disapproved." "I will never consent for Capt. Breathed to quit the horse artillery, with which he has rendered such distinguished service, except for certain promotion, which he has well earned."

The resignation of Capt. Breathed was also "disapproved" by Gen. Lee and the Secretary of War, and on April 22, 1864, he was promoted to major of artillery, to rank as such from Feb. 27, 1864. On the 26th of April following he was assigned by Gen. Lee to duty with the battalion of horse artillery serving with the cavalry corps of the Army of Northern Virginia.

Maj. Breathed's commission as lieutenant of artillery was dated April 1, 1862, and signed by Governor Fletcher, to rank from March 23, 1862, in the provisional army of the State of Virginia. His commission as captain in the provisional army of the State of Virginia, to rank from Aug. 9, 1862, was dated Sept. 22, 1862, and his commission as major was for "the provisional army in the service of the Confederate States."

After his last promotion Maj. Breathed went into winter quarters near Charlottesville. During this encampment he was surprised by a portion of Custer's brigade, then on a secret raid on Charlottesville. He drew two pieces on a neighboring hill, and as the first companies of the enemy charged through his camp fired upon them, and then with a small band of artillerists, under cover of the confusion created by the guns, charged them and drove them back, and chased and harassed them for many miles. For this daring act he received the thanks of the residents of Charlottesville, and the ladies of the town presented him with a stand of colors. In the campaign of '64, during Grant's march on Richmond, Maj. Breathed's battalion occupied the Confederate flank, and was fighting almost incessantly, sometimes as cavalrymen, again as artillery, and always with the dash and courage for which he was noted. Early in May of that year Fitzhugh Lee was endeavoring to hold the Federal [illegible] Court House,

and received information that Longstreet's first division was hurrying to his relief. He was urged by Gen. Stuart to hold out at any sacrifice. At a moment of great importance, when the advance had been held at terrible cost, Fitzhugh Lee called on Maj. Breathed to check the advance of a fresh column of the enemy. The result Gen. Lee told afterwards, as follows:

"Maj. James Breathed, by my order, placed a single gun on a little knoll, and as we were falling back, disputing the enemy's advance towards Spottsylvania Court-House, we knew the enemy's infantry were marching in column through a piece of woods, and the object was to fire upon the head of the column as it debouched, to give the idea that their further advance would be contested and to compel them to develop a line of battle, with skirmishers thrown out, etc. Under Maj. Breathed's personal superintendence shells were thrown, and burst exactly at the head of the column as it debouched; the head of the enemy's advance was scattered, and it was only with some difficulty a line of battle with skirmishers in front was formed. I was sitting on my horse near Breathed and directed him to withdraw his gun, but he begged to be allowed to give the enemy some more rounds. He fired until their line got so close that you could hear them calling on him to surrender the gun. Breathed's own horse had just been shot. The cannoneers jumped on their horses, expecting, of course, the gun to be captured, and retreated rapidly down the hill. Breathed was left alone. He limbered the gun up and jumped on the lead-horse. It was shot from under him. Quick as lightning he drew his knife, cut the leaders out of the harness, and sprang on a swing-horse. It was also shot from under him just as he was turning to get into the road. He then severed the harness of the swing-horse, jumped upon one of the wheel-horses, and again made a desperate trial for life. The ground was open between the piece and the woods; the enemy had a full view of the exploit; and Breathed at last dashed off unharmed, almost miraculously escaping through a shower of bullets."

Many such exploits are told of the young officer, but one especially at "High Bridge," on the Appomattox, illustrated his reckless indifference to danger and dauntless courage. Breathed was sent with Gen. Rosser to prevent the Federals from obtaining possession of it, and finding them already there he gave battle. The fighting was so intense and close-handed that Gen. Reid, of Philadelphia, in command of the Federals, was killed by Brig.-Gen. Deering, a young Confederate [illegible] and Maj. Thompson had fallen on the Confederate side. When the fight was at its height and the result was doubtful, Maj. Breathed was commanded to lead a dismounted charging column. He went to the front and ordered the advance, but the men faltered and refused to move. Breathed galloped about forty paces and called upon his men again. At this moment two captains left the ranks of the enemy and came galloping upon him. Breathed received them with extended sabre, killed the first, and in the effort to avoid the stroke of the second was dismounted. This would have been fatal had not a soldier reached the spot and shot his antagonist. Maj. Breathed was dangerously wounded early in July, 1864, and Gen. Robt. E. Lee, commander-in-chief of the Confederate forces, on hearing of this, dispatched to him the following:

"MAJOR,—I heard with great regret that you were wounded and incapacitated for active duty. I beg to tender you my sympathy, and to express the hope that the army will not long be deprived of your valuable services. The reports I have received from your superior officers of your gallantry and good conduct in action on several occasions have given me great satisfaction, and while they increase my concern for your personal suffering, render me more desirous that your health will soon permit you to resume a command that you have exercised with so much credit to yourself and advantage to the service."

Gen. J. E. B. Stuart, commander of the cavalry of the Army of Northern Virginia, in a letter to Maj. Breathed, dated March 21, 1864, said,—

"I am sensible of the distinguished gallantry which you have always displayed when brought in contact with the enemy, and can also assure you of its appreciation by the commanding general. I feel confident that you will soon be promoted. Labor to get your battery in fighting and flying trim as soon as possible. Your conduct in the late attempt of the enemy at Rio Mills to seize your guns was in keeping with the heroism which has distinguished your career as a soldier, and I regret that necessary absence from my headquarters prevented me from seeing you on your recent visit, and expressing to you in person, as I wished, my congratulations upon your achievement, as well as my high appreciation of your gallantry."

Many were the similar tributes received by Maj. Breathed for his merit, valor, and personal attributes, and the regard in which he was held in the army was continued in private life when, after the declaration of peace, he settled down again in the pursuit of his professional calling. Maj. Breathed died Feb. 16, 1870, in his thirty-second year, and was interred in St. Thomas' Graveyard, at Hancock, Md.

Necrology.—Following is a list of persons either born in or at some time resident in Washington County who have died since 1791. Owing to the impossibility of collecting sufficient material, it is necessarily imperfect, but it contains a large number of the representative people of the county:

At West Conococheague February, 1799, Capt John Ankeny

May 28, 187- Capt David Artz, aged 78 Capt Artz was among the most active and enterprising of the business men of Hagerstown for fully half a century and was also an earnest member of Trinity Lutheran Church He received his title of captain from commanding a local company of militia, but he had also seen real service under Capt George Shryock in the war of 1812 His remains were interred in Rose Hill Cemetery, having previously been taken to Trinity church, where the usual exercises were held by the Revs Lepley, Eyester, Hill, and Luckenbach, the latter, as pastor of the church, delivering an appropriate discourse

May, 1804 Christopher Alter

Jan 1, 181-, Frederick Alter, overseer of the almshouse, aged 73

In June 181 , William Adams, who lived six miles from Hagerstown, aged 87

May, 1810 at West Conecocheague, Henry Ankeny

Feb 14, 18-0, Capt John Ashbury, near Ringgold's Manor

Mrs Bowman, at Brownsville, Pa, Dec 19, 1822, in the 79th year of her age She was one of the earliest settlers of Washington County, and had resided at Hagerstown from its founding to 1816

At the Globe Tavern in Hagerstown, Dec 3, 1823, Thomas Belt, aged 83 An obituary notice said of him, "He was almost one of the last of the good old fathers of Washington County who have rendered it ever memorable for its ancient hospitality

Sept 9, 18-1, at Shepherdstown Va, in the 20th year of his age, Samuel Bell youngest brother of the editor of the Hagerstown *Mail*

Dec 12, 18-, at the residence of Alex Kennedy, near Boonsboro', Bartholomew Booth son of John Booth

March 30, 1879, Lily, wife of Frank O Brush, of Cumberland, and daughter of Hon A K Syester, of Hagerstown

November, 1870 at Mobile, Col Daniel Beltzhoover, son of the Mr Beltzhoover who kept the Globe Tavern at Hagerstown The deceased graduated at West Point in 1845, served through the Mexican war with gallantry and resigned his commission in 1856, when he was appointed professor of geometry and the higher branches of mathematics at Mount St Mary's College, Emmittsburg Md When the war between the States broke out, though not a native of the South he offered his services to the Confederacy, and was appointed on Gen Twiggs's staff at New Orleans, and was afterwards made captain of the famous Watson's battery, and for gallant conduct under Sidney Johnston was breveted major, afterward lieutenant colonel was chief of artillery at Vicksburg, and whilst in command there received his commission as colonel of artillery During the siege of Fort Powell, in Mobile Bay he rendered further important services After the war he devoted himself to the instruction of youth He was a proficient in music, and the composer of many pieces of much instrumental merit

Feb 16, 1870, Maj James Breathed, at Hancock Maj Breathed was a distinguished officer in the Confederate service, but after the war engaged in the practice of medicine at Hancock

In May, 187- John Boswell, an old resident of Hagerstown

May 10, 18- , near Bakersville, Otho Baker, in his 68th year

July (Monday prior to July 25), 1873, Dr John Beckenbaugh, son of John Beckenbaugh aged 29 He had acquired an extensive practice at and near Sharpsburg, but his health failed, and he was forced to retire His wife was the daughter of the Rev Robert Douglas Mr Beckenbaugh was a brother-in-law of Hon [illegible]

April 10 1873, Mrs Sallie Roman Baldwin daughter of the Hon J Dixon Roman of Hagerstown, and wife of Columbus C Baldwin, of New York She was a very estimable lady

Dec 6 1878 David Brumbaugh, aged 76 years, 6 months, and 11 days Mr Brumbaugh was a thorough business man, as also an ardent politician and a devoted member of the Presbyterian Church He also took a deep interest in agriculture, and for many years was president of the County Agricultural Society

April, 1879, Rachel, widow of the late Henry Biershing, in the 80th year of her age She was a Miss Steele, born in Hagerstown, of a family which was among the original settlers Her husband, Henry Biershing was a prominent and influential citizen of Hagerstown of vigorous intellect, strongly marked character and in his political convictions an original and decided Democrat He was one of the leading citizens of the town, and as a watchmaker and silversmith acquired a very handsome independence for those days He died in April, 1843

July 29, 1874 in Cincinnati, Ohio, Ferdinand Bolmann, a former resident of Hagerstown Mr Bolmann had amassed a large fortune, and was a very influential citizen

September, 1876, John Bowman, of Beaver Creek, in his 87th year

May 1881, David Brewer, of Clear Spring District, aged 83

January, 1879, David Brumbaugh, vice president Washington County Agricultural Society

Oct 19, 1804, in Leitersburg District, John Barr, in the 78th year of his age

March 22, 1893, Henry Brumbaugh, aged 77

In 1806, Samuel Bowles, an old resident of Hagerstown

In February, 1808, Sebastian Baker, for many years crier of the Washington County Court

June, 1812, near Williamsport, Nicholas Baker, a native of Germany

Jacob Bresnis, for many years a resident of Hancock, Dec 6, 1822, in the 78th year of his age

At the Globe Tavern Hagerstown, on Wednesday Aug , 1823, Thomas Belt, in the 8- year of his age

At his residence, in Washington County, Nov 2 1852, John Breathed, aged 73 Mr Breathed, who was a man of considerable means, was noted for his liberality in aiding deserving relatives and friends

In 1844, Judge John Buchanan

Near Hagerstown, suddenly of apoplexy, Sept 27, 1847, Judge Thomas Buchanan

At Wheatland, Oct 2 1827, Maj-Gen Perry Benson in the 72d year of his age

Near Hagerstown, on the 2 d of August, 1800, Mrs Eleanor Baird

On the 27th of August, 1800, Mrs Margaret Baird, relict of the late Maj William Baird

On his plantation in Washington County, in the latter part of June, 1800, Col John Barnes

Near Hagerstown, Feb 27, 1799, Martin Barr

Nov 20, 1801, Harriet R Beatty, wife of Col Cornelius Beatty, of Hagerstown

At Williamsport, May 2 1801, Rudolph Bell, merchant

May , 1859, The Beatty, aged 8-

April 2- 1859, Rev James Brown, aged 84 a colored preacher He had been a slave of Benjamin Galloway, and at the time of his death was one of the oldest colored preachers in the county

June 7 18-1, Henry J Bentz, aged 52

Oct 7, 1811, William D Bell, aged 1- the founder and pro

May 11, 1791, Maj. Wm. Baird, of Hagerstown, at an advanced age. He was an officer at Braddock's defeat, magistrate [illegible] many years, and coroner for Washington County from the [illegible] it was separated from Frederick.

[illegible] 28, 1873, George Beard, a descendant of one of the [illegible] settlers of Hagerstown Valley.

At New Orleans, Nov. 21, 1817, Maj. Charles Boerstler, late [illegible] U. S. army, and son of Dr. Christian Boerstler, of Funks-[illegible].

March 14, 1828, in Blair's Valley, James Blair, in his 93d [illegible]. Mr. Blair was one of the earliest settlers of this portion [illegible] Washington County, and was engaged in many skirmishes [illegible] the Indians.

[illegible] Frederick Town, May 8, 1819, Richard Brooke, formerly [illegible] Hagerstown, in his 44th year. Mr. Brooke was a distin-[illegible] member of the Maryland bar, and a consistent mem-[illegible] the Catholic Church. At a meeting of the bar of Fred-[illegible], Hon. Abraham Shriver presiding, and Frederick A. [illegible] acting as secretary, it was resolved that those present [illegible] crape on the arm for one month as a mark of respect for [illegible] deceased.

Feb. 12, 1870, J. F. Broderick, merchant, of Hancock.

February, 1872, Robert J. Brent, the distinguished lawyer, [illegible], at Baltimore.

September, 1791, Robert Elliott, surveyor, killed by Indians [illegible] the West. He was the father of Com. Elliott, U.S.N.

June 12, 1851, at the residence of his son-in-law, John R. [illegible], in Hagerstown, William Eakle, in his 6[illegible]th year. Mr. Eakle had long been a useful and highly-respected citizen of [illegible]-town.

In October, 187[illegible], at Williamsport, Charles Embrey, in his [illegible] year, formerly judge of the Orphans' Court of Washington County.

May 7, 1878, Martin Eakle, aged 6[illegible]. Mr. Eakle in 18[illegible] was [illegible] county commissioner, and served as the president of the [illegible] for two years, and in 185[illegible] was elected to the House of Delegates, of which body he was a useful member. He also was extensively known as a business man. Up to the time of his [illegible] he conducted the flouring-mill at Eakle's Mill, and was [illegible] agent of the Baltimore and Ohio Railroad at that place, [illegible] the senior member of the mercantile firm of Eakle & Son, [illegible] at one time was the active member of a firm which con-[illegible] the Antietam Iron-Works.

February, 1854, at Frederick, Md., at an advanced age, George M. Eichelberger. Maj. Eichelberger served in the war [illegible] 1812, and contributed much to the result by his patriotic and [illegible] example.

April 27, 1822, John Eichelberger, in the 60th year of his age.

At Hagerstown, on the 31st of August, 182[illegible], aged 65, Mrs. Ann Hughes, widow of Robert Elliott, and mother of Com. Elliott, of the U. S. navy.

April 11, 1856, Daniel Creager, a soldier of 1812, aged 65 years, 6 months, and 2 days.

At his residence in Libertytown on the 14th of November, 182[illegible], Maj.-Gen. Robert Cumming, commander of the Second Division of Maryland Militia, in the 72d year of his age.

At Hagerstown, on the 25th of March, 1818, after a lingering illness, William Clagett, an associate judge of the Fifth Judicial District of Maryland.

May 12, 1802, James Coombs, son of Coleman Coombs.

July 21, 1801, Jeremiah Callahan, an overseer for Charles [illegible], fell from a stairway outside a still-house, and was [illegible] instantly killed.

March, 1849, in Funkstown, David Claggett, aged 79. He had [illegible] engaged in farming and milling for more than half a century.

Near Clear Spring, Sept. 9, 1857, George Cushwa, at one time a member of the House of Delegates. He was in his 54th year.

At Sharpsburg, Dec. 25, 182[illegible], John Clarke, aged 61.

March 6, 1819, at his residence in Washington County, Col. John Carr, an officer of the Revolution.

At his residence in Pleasant Valley, May 20, 1819, Thomas Crampton, in his 84th year.

Dec. 6, 1875, Mrs. Mary Claggett, widow of Dr. Horatio Claggett. Dr. Claggett, who died in 18[illegible]0, was among the most eminent men in the State.

May, 18[illegible]1, Dr. Charles Magill, at the residence of his son-in-law, Dr. S. D. Drewry, of Chesterfield County, Va., in the 75th year of his age.

March 2[illegible], 18[illegible], at Chicago, Joseph P. Clarkson, formerly professor at St. James' College, and afterwards a member of the Hagerstown bar. Mr. Clarkson, who was a brother of Bishop Clarkson, of Nebraska, was killed by the accidental discharge of a pistol.

Dec. 5, 1878, Daniel Coarfee, an active citizen, and a member of the Maryland House of Delegates during the civil war.

At Williamsport, in May, 18[illegible], Daniel W. Cyster.

February, 18[illegible], Thomas Curtis, aged about [illegible] years. Mr. Curtis was a teacher at the Hagerstown Academy for a number of years, and after he gave up teaching he held a number of local offices, embracing those of magistrate, collector of town taxes, registrar of voters, etc., the duties of all of which he discharged with care and fidelity.

February, 1876, Capt. Wm. Colkleser, in his [illegible]th year. He resided in Hagerstown when the war commenced, and when Company A of the Seventh Maryland Regiment (Mobley's) was formed Capt. Colkleser was elected first lieutenant, and subsequently, when Capt. Mobley was promoted, he took charge of the company, and remained in the service to the close of the war.

March, 179[illegible], Denton Jacques, of this county; and Robert Clarke, of Allegany, formerly of Hagerstown.

April 1[illegible], 18[illegible], Wm. B. Clarke, aged 5[illegible]. Mr. Clarke represented Washington, and afterwards Baltimore County, in the State Senate, and was a highly esteemed and distinguished citizen of Washington County.

January, 1827, Joseph Cresap, at an advanced age, at the residence of his daughter, Mrs. James Scott, in Cumberland.

At Williamsport, in December, 1824, William S. Compton, in his 67th year.

January, 182[illegible], Dr. Zachariah Clagett, of Pleasant Valley, in his 65th year.

June 12, 18[illegible]4, David Cooke, founder of Marietta, Pa., aged 74.

Jan. 12, 180[illegible], in Baltimore, Frances, wife of Hezekiah Claggett.

Dec. 23, 180[illegible], Richard Cromwell, a member of the House of Delegates.

Dec. 28, 18[illegible], George Crumbaugh, in his 67th year.

At Vincennes, Ind., Dec. 11, 1802, William Clarke, first judge of the Territory of Indiana, and formerly a member of the Hagerstown bar. In 179[illegible], Mr. Clarke was appointed United States attorney for the District of Kentucky, which position he retained until the organization of the Territory of Indiana.

At the residence of her son-in-law, Thomas Martin, on Beaver Creek, June 8, 1805, Mrs. Margaret Carnes, aged 90. She was a sister of George Doyle, who died aged 8[illegible], and her father was one of the original settlers of Hagerstown Valley.

Dec. 7, 1840, near Clear Spring, Mark Coyle, aged 86. Deceased was a soldier in the Revolutionary war, and participated in the battles of Monmouth and Princeton and in other [illegible]

June 1', 1821, Alexander Clagett aged 77 Mr Clagett was a zealous and earnest patriot during the Revolution, and for three years was sheriff of Washington County He removed from Hagerstown to Baltimore in 1818

September, 1808, John Clagett

March 25, 1810, William Clagett, associate judge of Washington County

May, 1819, at his residence in Pleasant Valley, Thomas Crampton, aged 84

Feb 23, 1822, Mrs Catharine Carli aged 109 She was a native of Germany and had been a resident of Hagerstown since 1761

At Williamsburg Livingston Co, N Y Oct 28 1829, Maj Charles Carroll, who prior to 181 resided near Hagerstown

Aug 31, 1801 Capt Joseph Chaplin in the 75th year of his age Capt Chaplin was a soldier of the Revolution

March 17, 1809 Rezin Davis, aged 53 Col Davis served in the Revolutionary war and also filled the offices of sheriff and coroner for a number of years

Oct 9, 1824, Rev Patrick Davidson, minister of the Presbyterian Church at Hagerstown

Nov 1, 1813 Dr Wm Downey, in his 33d year He was highly respected, and had filled a number of important trusts

December, 1806, John Dagy and wife living at the foot of South Mountain were murdered

Feb 7 1856, Rev Robert W Dunlap in his 41st year, pastor of the Presbyterian Church of Hagerstown

May 30, 1829, Dr James Dixon, aged 32

Oct 26, 1808, Dr Frederick Dorsey, Sr, in his 83d year Dr Dorsey was one of the oldest practitioners in the country, and was widely known and highly respected for his professional skill and attainments

Aug 10, 182 William Dillehunt, in his 58th year

At Hancock Dec 24 1879, James L Ditto Sr, one of the oldest and most respectable citizens of the place

Near Fort Smith, Ark July 12, 1851, Col William Duvall, aged 67

Aug 2, 187-, near Keedysville, Samuel Doub, a leading farmer He was a man of considerable means, and had served as county commissioner

February, 1801 Joseph Downey, innkeeper at Hagerstown

July 26 1801, Capt Richard Davis aged 53

At his residence in the Williamsport District, early in March, 1859, Jacob Dellinger at an advanced age

Sept 25 1808, Col Daniel Donnelly, for many years commander of the Fifty fourth Regiment Maryland Militia He was buried at Williamsport with military honors

Near the College of St James, Jan 28, 1859, Daniel Reichard, Sr, aged 78 Mr Reichard had been a bishop of the Tunker denomination for a number of years

Jan 10, 1808, at New Market, Frederick Co, Rhuderick Dorsey, brother of Dr Frederick Dorsey, aged 73

Feb 6, 1818, at Mount St Mary's College, Rev Charles Duhamel, formerly of Hagerstown

Dec 27, 1875 Dr Thomas Buchanan Duckett, aged 7 Dr Duckett was nephew of the Judges Buchanan, and was married to a daughter of Joseph Gabby, in the olden time a leading man, and once a member of the Executive Council of the State before the formation of the first popular constitution The deceased had two sons one of whom, Joseph Gabby Duckett, was shot in the early days of the war while crossing the Potomac River to join the Southern cause

Aug 2, 17 Maj David Funk

Feb 16 1791 Helena wife of Michael Fackler

May 2, 18 at Hagerstown Wm Fitzhugh Jr in his 13 year He was

April 12, 1870, William Freaner aged 79 Mr Freaner served in the war of 1812, and was one of the most valuable citizens of Hagerstown

Nov 10, 1878, Maj George Freaner, aged 47

March —, 1875, Ann Carroll Fitzhugh, daughter of Wm Fitzhugh, of Hagerstown She was born on the 11th of January, 1805, and was consequently in her 71st year at the time of her death In 1822 she was married to Gerrit Smith, of New York, the famous abolitionist One of her sisters was the wife of James G Birney, the Liberty party candidate for President in 1840 and 1844

In the spring of 1881, Dr Daniel H Fitzhugh, of Rochester, N Y, aged 87 Dr Fitzhugh was the son of Col Wm Fitzhugh, who emigrated to New York in the early part of the century, and assisted in founding the city of Rochester

Dec 19, 1813, Henry Fiery, aged 18, at his residence, nine miles from Hagerstown

March 24, 1813, at Big Springs, Dr Emanuel Fritner, aged 64

In September, 1823, at Washington, D C, Rev Louis R Fechtig, son of Christian, a native of Hagerstown, aged 36 At the time of his death he was presiding elder of the Baltimore District, Methodist Episcopal Church

On Christmas day, 1869, John Fiery, aged 64, a wealthy and highly respected citizen of Washington County Mr Fiery was drowned accidentally in the Conococheague Creek

June, 1872, Mrs Fox, widow of George B Fox aged 102 years and 6 months She was born in Frederick County, where she was married, and shortly afterwards removed to Hagerstown, where she resided up to the time of her death, through a period of probably seventy five or eighty years She had fourteen children, fifty six grandchildren, and sixty-seven great-grandchildren When she first lived in the village it had just begun to assume its new name of Hagerstown, it having been known as Elizabethtown up to that time, and nearly the whole of that portion of it now covered by the block bounded by Washington, Potomac, Franklin, and Jonathan Streets was a marsh filled with stagnant water and weeds, the centre of which was the present Oak Spring, and the stream flowing therefrom, that now passes under the Wingert buildings on Potomac Street, then flowed through what is now the Public Square

Jan 10, 1870, Abram Freaner, youngest brother of William Freaner, of Hagerstown Mr Freaner was born in Hagerstown, and at an early age located in Pennsylvania After passing a number of years at Lebanon, Annville, Hummelstown, and Spring Creek, he removed to Harrisburg, where he resided for many years In 1848, Mr Freaner was elected recorder of deeds and clerk of the Orphans' Court of Dauphin County Pa, which position he filled with so much credit that he was honored with a re election, serving six years in all At the time of his demise he was tax collector of the First and Second Wards of Harrisburg, and had reached nearly seventy years of age

September, 1878, Jeremiah Funk, aged 37, son of Jacob Funk, and brother of Henry Funk, late president board of commissioners of Washington County

August, 1878, George French, ex judge Circuit Court

April 28, 1881, Sophia Van Lear Findlay Mrs Findlay was the daughter of Matthew Van Lear one of the leading men of Western Maryland in days of yore, of most pronounced character, and a decided Federalist of the old school He contested the western district of the State for Congress with Gen Samuel Ringgold, a decided Democrat, by whom he was defeated and who generally sold a farm in the Manor which April ures in

[illegible]gress each term. The father of the deceased had a large family, the oldest of the sons being John Van Lear, for many years at the head of the Washington County Bank, and a man of as marked character as any in Western Maryland in his day. Matthew and Joseph were also brothers, and conspicuous among the sisters of Mrs. Findlay were Mrs. Ramsay, whose daughters were pre-eminently beautiful, and Mrs. Irwin, connected with the family of Gen. Harrison, over whose household, while President of the United States, members of this family presided. The husband of the deceased was Mr. Archibald Findlay, of the Chambersburg bar, son of William Findlay, Governor of Pennsylvania, and during one term United States senator from that State, whilst at the same time two of his brothers—Col. John, of Pennsylvania, and Gen. James, of Ohio—were members of the House of Representatives. At this period of her life Mrs. Sophia Van Lear Findlay spent much of her time at the national capital, and was an active participant in the social engagements of those times, when Henry Clay, whose personal relations with the Findlays were the most intimate, was particularly conspicuous in the Senate and in society. Mrs. Findlay was a woman of remarkable decision of character, conspicuously in advocacy of what she believed right and in adhesion to principle. In the late struggle between the North and the South she entered with her whole soul into the cause of the former. She was a sturdy Unionist, and supported the government during the war neither as a Republican or a Democrat, but as a patriot, concerned not so much about this or that principle of constitutional construction as the maintenance of the Union in all its territorial integrity. Guided and governed by this sentiment, she was active in promoting the Union cause in every way she could, and there were few Union officers stationed at Williamsport and vicinity who were not at one time or another partakers of her generous hospitality.

Jan. 15, 1846, Peter Feigley, aged 97, a soldier of the Revolution. Mr. Feigley participated in a number of important battles, and was present at the surrender of Lord Cornwallis at Yorktown. The remains were buried with military honors, being escorted to the grave by the Hagerstown Cadets, commanded by Capt. Schley, and the Union Riflemen, Lieut. Helfelstein, accompanied by the Hagerstown Mechanics' band.

At Beaver Creek, Aug. 16, 1840, Samuel Funk, aged 65.

August, 1851, Jacob Fechtig, in his 52d year.

In Hagerstown, on Aug. 18, 1831, in the 79th year of his age, Benjamin Galloway, a native of Anne Arundel County, and for more than thirty-five years a resident of Washington County. He was appointed soon after the adoption of the constitution of Maryland the first attorney-general of the State.

Aug. 6, 1826, at the residence of Andrew Ramsey, Washington, D. C., Hon. John Graham, formerly minister to Brazil.

April, 1799, William Gordon, a highly-respected citizen of Hagerstown, at an advanced age.

Near Leitersburg, on the 4th of September, 1841, William Gabby, aged 78. Mr. Gabby had frequently been a member of the State Legislature, and was a judge of the Orphans' Court. For more than half a century he had been a communicant of the Presbyterian Church, and for forty years an elder of that denomination.

Dec. 29, 1851, John Gruber, founder of the well-known Hagerstown Almanac, aged [illegible] years.

About Dec. 1, 1877, Sophia [illegible], a colored woman, said to be 105 years old, who claimed to have been born in the family of Mrs. Arthur Nelson, mother of Gen. Roger Nelson, of Revolutionary fame. She also asserted that she was present at the funeral of Gen. Washington at Mount Vernon. She was sold as a slave to Gen. Samuel Ringgold, of Fountain Rock, and when the estate became involved [illegible] on the emancipation of the slaves. Subsequently she lived in Hagerstown, being cared for by the descendants of the Nelson family and others.

At Atchison, Kan., Feb. 17, 1877, Dr. William H. Grimes, formerly of Hagerstown, aged 74.

January, 1874, Jacob H. Grove, of Sharpsburg District, aged 75. Mr. Grove was a county commissioner about 1831, and served in the Maryland Legislature with the Hon. John Thomson Mason and William T. Hamilton.

July 7, 1881, George W. Grove, ex-sheriff of Washington County, aged 72. For many years he had been one of the directors of the County Agricultural and Mechanical Society, and always took an active part in its development. He was also connected with other institutions, and was one of the first selected as a director of the Washington County Water Company.

Nov. 15, 1824, Mrs. Christian Grober, in her 58th year.

Oct. 10, 1812, Henry Gaither, a prominent citizen.

November, 1823, Henry Gooding, innkeeper at Hancock.

November, 1856, Joseph Gabby, at his residence near Leitersburg, aged about 78 years. Mr. Gabby for many years in succession represented Washington County in the Legislature of Maryland; was a member of the Governor's Council, and a very prominent and useful citizen.

April 22, 1866, in Hagerstown, Henry H. Gaither, in the [illegible] year of his age. Mr. Gaither was a prominent citizen, and for many years an active and successful member of the bar.

December 21st, at Hagerstown, John M. Hauck, aged 52. In 1869, Mr. Hauck was elected sheriff of Washington County, and served his full term. In May, 1879, he was appointed weigher of hay at Baltimore, and occupied that position at the time of his death.

At Mount Alto, Franklin Co., Pa., in the latter part of March, 1877, Col. Napoleon B. Hughes, son of Samuel Hughes, and brother of Col. Holker Hughes, aged 71.

Friday, July (next to 20th), 1843, Mrs. Hager, relict of the late Jonathan Hager, at the residence of S. D. Straub, her son-in-law, on South Potomac Street, Hagerstown, in the 78th year of her age. Mrs. Hager was a daughter of Jonas Hogmire, Esq., one of the first surveyors of the county, and a very prominent, wealthy, and influential citizen in its early days, and was his last surviving child.

April (Friday preceding) 11, 1873, Isabella Hughes, daughter of Robert Hughes, one of three brothers (Robert, Samuel, and Daniel) who took up vast tracts of land, one of which covered almost the entire western face of the South Mountain, from a point near the Black Rock to a point far within the limits of Pennsylvania, above Mount Alto. Three other brothers located farther west, in Kentucky and elsewhere. Isabella, daughter of Robert, was born at the old homestead at the foot of the mountain, a mile east of Smithsburg, known as Oswald's tannery. The Hughes tract of land, which originally covered not only the mountain side, but extended as far down into the valley at least as the Antietam, was a princely estate, and upon it were located by the members of that family the old furnace of Mount Ætna (now in ruins), Mount Alto (still in full blast), "The Forge," near the Antietam, and the tannery, which was sold a short time since to David Winter. These establishments were run by the two brothers Samuel and Daniel, Samuel having been at the same time a leading member of the Hagerstown bar, whilst the tannery and farm were [illegible] the elder brother, Robert.

March 22, 1843, David Harry, aged [illegible], a soldier of the Revolutionary war.

At the residence of her son, Jacob Hewitt, near Cavetown, [illegible]

Jan 13, 1873 Overton C Harne, aged 92 years, 3 months, and 28 days, said to be at that time the oldest printer in Maryland

March 20, 1868, Col Jacob Hollingsworth, aged 78, from a pistol-wound supposed to have been accidentally inflicted by himself

Oct 5, 1876, Frederick Humrichouse, aged 85 years, 2 months, and 25 days

Jan 1[illegible], 1875, William Heyser, aged 81 years and 4 months

July 1871, Capt George F Heyser, in his 56th year Death resulted from an accidental fall on the railroad track

April 21, 1880, Hannah Humrichouse, daughter of Jacob Harry and wife of Frederick Humrichouse Mrs Humrichouse was 83 years old

April 2[illegible], 1880, Rebecca, widow of Stewart Herbert, and daughter of George Doyle, members of two of the original families of the county, aged 80

In March 1870, at Terre Haute, Ind, George Hager, in his 83d year Mr Hager was a brother of Jonathan Hager, Jr, and one of the descendants of the founder of Hagerstown He was born in that town July 21, 1787, and was most active and energetic in promoting the interests of Terre Haute

Nov 6, 1878 Solomon Helser, aged 76 Mr Helser had served as county commissioner and also as a member of the House of Delegates in the Maryland Legislature He left two sons, John and Henry Helser

May, 1870 John Harrington, aged 88, a soldier of the war of 1812

June, 1879, Jonathan Hurbaugh, of Ringgold's, aged 75

June, 1793 Mrs Hughes mother of Col Daniel Hughes

Oct 3, 1795, James Hughes, son of Col Daniel Hughes, in his 19th year

Sept 13, 1826, at Williamsport John Hogg, aged 70

March 2, 1825, Daniel Hughes, of Hagerstown

At his farm near Reading, Pa, Sept 3, 1826, Gabriel Heister, in his 76th year

Aug 6, 1824, Anna widow of the late Jonathan Hager, in her 68th year

Sept 27, 1823, Job Hunt

November, 1862, Mr Hanne, aged 106, his wife, who died six months before him had reached the age of 102 years

August, 1803, very suddenly, Michael Helfley

November, 1853, Nathaniel Harmison, run over by cars at Cumberland He imagined himself a successful politician and candidate for Congress, his head being turned by the fact that many years previously he had really been a candidate

In Hagerstown, June 30, 1828, Susan Hughes, daughter of Col Daniel Hughes

June 4, 1881, W W Hoffman, founder of the banking-house of Hoffman, Eavey & Co, Hagerstown, aged 46

In Washington, D C, March 14, 1804, Gen Daniel Heister, representative in Congress from Maryland He resided in Hagerstown, whither his remains were carried

In May 1802, Mrs Hinon, aged 102 Her husband, with whom she had lived for eighty years, died in the following November at the age of 105 years

In June, 1854, Capt John D Hart, of Hancock

March 15, 1853, Esther widow of Christian Hoover, aged 74 years 4 months, and 22 days

March 1818, Dr Arnold Havenkauft

Aug 1 1808 Thomas Helm, innkeeper of Williamsport

July 11, 1806, Jacob Harry, aged 50, a merchant of Hagerstown

Dec 5 1818, Col Daniel Hughes, in his 74th year

In January 1819 Jacob Hose, a Revolutionary soldier, aged 79

Jan 16, 1819 at Sharpsburg, Dr John Hartman [illegible] year

In July, 1823, near Sharpsburg, Dr John J Hays

Sept 8, 1821, at Williamsport, in the 32d year of her age Catharine, wife of John Herr, Jr

Aug 20, 1836, at the residence of Mrs Susan Harry Hagerstown, the Rev William Lane, pastor of the Presbyterian Church at Sykesville, Md He was born in the town Roumalton, in the north of Ireland, on the 29th of October 1818 and was educated and graduated at the college in Belfast Ireland He emigrated to this country in 18[illegible], and entered the theological seminary at Princeton, N J His first service as a pastor was in the Presbyterian Church of Hagerstown

March, 1829, Robert Hughes

April 6, 1816, Susan, wife of Robert Hughes

—— ——, Henry Courtenay Hughes, son of Robert and Susan Hughes

April 4, 1873, Elizabeth Isabella Hughes

Feb 24, 1880, Letitia Purviance Hughes, wife of Dr H H Harvey

March 21, 1879, Henrietta Frances Hughes, wife of Dr Horatio N Fenn

Aug 29, 1825 at her residence in Hagerstown, Mrs Ann Hughes, widow of Col Daniel Hughes

On the 17th of October, 1825, the Rev Daniel Hitt in the 58th year of his age, and the 38th of his itinerant ministry in the Methodist Episcopal Church For many years he filled the station of presiding elder, and for eight years the position of book agent for the Methodist Church

On the 3d of May, 1818, at his residence at Mont Alto Furnace, Samuel Hughes, in the 71st year of his age Mr Hughes was formerly a resident of Hagerstown, and was long known as one of the most distinguished lawyers of the State

Jan 31, 1873, at Memphis, Tenn, Julia P M Hahn, daughter of Prof and Mrs R Hahn, of Hagerstown Miss Hahn was born near Vienna, Austria Both her parents were accomplished musicians, and their daughter was thoroughly educated as a pianist At ten years of age she was placed by her father under the instruction of competent teachers in Paris, where she remained five years, in which period she acquired a thorough mastery of the instrument She gave concerts in New York and Baltimore, which were very successful Subsequently she returned to Paris, and was admitted as one of five members to the famous Conservatory of Music, being chosen after a competitive examination of one hundred applicants She was in Paris during the Prussian war, and performed at several concerts there with great success At the close of the war she returned to Hagerstown and performed with Strakosch and in Nilsson in Baltimore Strakosch engaged her to play at his concerts if she were strong enough, but her health, which had been precarious now grew worse, and she was forced to go South for its benefit She seemed to improve but in January, 1873, grew suddenly worse and died Miss Hahn had many friends in Hagerstown, to whom she had endeared herself by an amiability and sweetness of disposition which greatly enhanced the effect of her wonderful proficiency as a musician

In Hagerstown April 8, 18[illegible] Stewart Herbert, aged [illegible] Mr Herbert was the son of the founder of the Hagerstown *Spy and Herald* and worked in that office as a compositor

In December 1798, Jonathan Hager, proprietor of Hagerstown and son of the founder

April 9, 17[illegible] William Hu[illegible] county [illegible]

In Smithsburg, Dec 24, 18[illegible], M[illegible] Thomas Hollingsworth, in his 42d year

June 11 1791 Mrs Catharine Hughes, widow of Bernard H[illegible]

Sept. 11, 1822, in Washington, D. C., Leonard Harbaugh, aged 74. Mr. Harbaugh was a large contractor for works of internal improvement, including those on the Potomac and the Shenandoah.

Jan. 16, 1843, at Sharpsburg, Andrew Hines, aged about 50.

Jan. 15, 1818, Rev. Thomas Pitt Irving, aged 48, principal of the Hagerstown Academy. A funeral sermon was preached in the Lutheran church by the Rev. Mr. Hatch, of Frederick, from the 4th and 12th verses of the 102d Psalm,—"My days are like a shadow that declineth," etc.

Near Big Spring, April 15, 1818, Denton Jacques, in the [illegible] year of his age.

Jan. 21, 1820, John Julius, an old and respected citizen of Hagerstown.

Nov. 10, 1881, Watkins James, in his 71st year. Mr. James was thrice married, first to Miss Louisa Baker, daughter of the late Maj. Baker, from whom Bakersville derived its name; second, to Miss Maria Davis, sister of Wm. Davis, now residing in Fairplay; and third to Miss Maria Reynolds, sister of the late Wm. and John Reynolds. The deceased was a man of more than ordinary activity and was engaged in various pursuits. For a number of years he was chief clerk and manager of John McPherson Brien's iron-works, three miles from Sharpsburg. He was also employed at the Catoctin Iron Works for a time. He moved from Washington County to Woodstock, Va., and resided there some nine years. After the war he was United States internal revenue assessor in that district, after which he returned to Washington County.

At Hancock, in the latter part of July, 1824, Hon. John Johnson, chancellor of Maryland.

Aug. 1, 1845, Arthur Jacques, aged 62.

April 1, 1859, Thomas Keller, aged 73.

At his residence, near Hagerstown, Oct. 6, 1857, Andrew Kershner, aged [illegible] years, 5 months, and 22 days. On the 8th he was buried in the German Reformed church at Hagerstown, his remains being followed to the grave by a large number of persons. He had represented the county in the Maryland Legislature seven times, and was a man of wide-spread influence and popularity.

Nov. 19, 1817, at his residence, near Hagerstown, Maj. Martin Kershner, aged 74. Maj. Kershner had several times represented the county in the State Legislature, and had also served acceptably as justice of the peace.

At Boonsboro', Aug. 18, 1876, Daniel Keedy, father of H. H. Keedy, of the Hagerstown bar, and Rev. C. L. Keedy, principal of the Hagerstown Female Seminary, aged 76. Deceased was a farmer of considerable means, and resided for a number of years on his estate in Rohrersville District, at the head of Pleasant Valley.

July 26, 1881, Howard Kennedy, eldest son of Dr. Howard Kennedy, aged 35. He was employed on the United States Coast Survey, and afterwards settled in Southern California for his health.

In April, 1875, Jacob Kaylor, at his residence on Beaver Creek, in the 81st year of his age. Mr. Kaylor was a soldier in the war of 1812.

Jan. 20, 1874, Mrs. Catharine Kausler, aged 84, daughter of Capt. George Shawl, and widow of Jacob Kausler. The deceased was the mother of eleven children, forty-eight grandchildren, and twelve great-grandchildren.

April 17, 18[illegible], Catharine, widow of Englehard Kuthe, aged [illegible]. She was a native of Germany, and had resided in Hagerstown over forty years.

Feb. —, 1825, William Kreps, postmaster at Hagerstown, in the 51st year of his age.

September, 18[illegible] [illegible] Mr. K[illegible] [illegible] was an enthusiastic farmer, although during part of his life he was a member of the firm of Huyett, Kendall & Co., bone-mill, Hagerstown. He was also for fifty years an earnest member of St. John's Lutheran Church.

July, 1881, Rev. John Barrett Kerfoot, D.D., bishop of the Protestant Episcopal diocese of Pittsburgh, and professor in and rector of the College of St. James from 1842 to 1863.

October, 1880, Rev. Levi Keller, from an amputation rendered necessary by a fall. Mr. Keller, who belonged to the Lutheran denomination, entered the ministry in 1849, at Strasburg, Va.

July 26, 1821, Daniel Keedy, farmer and miller, in his 59th year.

Aug. 15, 1823, Joseph Kershner.

September, 1831, Michael Kapp, for many years an inn-keeper at Hagerstown.

Feb. 17, 1867, in Boonsboro', David H. Keedy, aged 71 years, 5 months, and 2 days.

June 12, 1855, Dr. Howard Kennedy, in his 47th year. Deceased, who was a son of Hon. Thomas Kennedy, was at one time postmaster at Hagerstown, and afterwards for a number of years special agent of the Post-office Department. He was also an extensive stage contractor, a member of the express firm of Adams & Co., and a State director of the Baltimore and Ohio Railroad Company.

June 25, 1847, James Hugh Kennedy, from injuries received at the hands of a mob in Carlisle, Pa., while attempting, in company with G. Howard Hollingsworth, to rescue some slaves that had absconded. Mr. Kennedy was very popular in Hagerstown. He was buried from the residence of his father-in-law, Col. Hollingsworth, and his remains were followed to the grave by the Hagerstown Home Guards, the Antietam Fire Company, and an immense concourse of citizens.

Dec. 28, 1827, at the mill of John Kennedy, near Hagerstown, Lewis, the "old Antietam fisherman."

In October, 1816, a colored woman known as "Mammy Lucy," and said to be 130 years old. Her son is said to have been a servant of Col. Thomas Cresap.

March 2, 1818, Abraham Leiter, aged 78.

May 21, 1826, Capt. William Lewis, of the Revolutionary army, in the 124 year of his age. Deceased was in the battles of Trenton, Princeton, Brandywine, Germantown, and Monmouth, and engaged in several skirmishes. He also served under Gen. Wayne in the Indian campaigns, and was at the battle of Miami in 1793.

At Boonsboro', May 19, 1880, Abraham Lemaster, aged 78.

September, 1874, Mary, aged 84, widow of John Lushbaugh, a soldier of the war of 1812.

May 16, 1875, William P. Lavely, in his 67th year.

August, 1878, William Logan, postmaster at Hagerstown, aged 58. Mr. Logan devoted his earliest years to business, and was recognized in that capacity, as he was afterwards in others, as a man of remarkable popularity. This led, in 1849, to his appointment as collector of State and county taxes, when he removed from Leitersburg to Hagerstown. In 1853 he was elected sheriff of the county by a large majority, and in 1857 register of wills, at the head of his ticket. He was re-elected to this office in 1863, and held it until 1869, when a change of parties took place under the new constitution, and M. S. Barber was his successful competitor. In 1869 he was appointed postmaster at Hagerstown; was reappointed in 1873, and filling both of those full terms, was reappointed for a third term in 1877, and died in harness.

Sept. 20, 18[illegible], Rev. John Lind, pastor of the Presbyterian congregations at Hagerstown and Greencastle, Pa.

April [illegible], 18[illegible], Upton Lawrence, aged [illegible], a distinguished lawyer [illegible] of the county.

In July, 1823, at Conococheague, John Long

At Hagerstown, on Thursday, Dec 31, 1840, Joseph Little, Sr, in the 81st year of his age

July 21 1873, Rev Henry Myers, pastor of St Vincent's Roman Catholic Church, aged 67

May 1871, Maj Edward M Mealey aged 60 Mr Mealey was for many years a prominent citizen of Hagerstown, taking an active part in local State, and national affairs, and always maintaining intimate connections with the leading men of other portions of the State, by whom he was much respected for his sound judgment and sterling integrity He was for two sessions a member of the Legislature, for several years president of the Washington County Railroad, and also a director of the Baltimore and Ohio Railroad Company

February, 1874, John Mentzer, of Ringgold District, aged 79

Nov 6, 1797, Maj Alexander Monroe, at an advanced age, a native of North Britain and formerly an officer in the English service

Near Smithsburg, November 2'd, James McKissick, in his 65th year

In 180" William McIntosh, leaving a widow and five children

Oct 26, 18[illegible], Thomas McCardell, aged 67

Oct 25, 185[illegible] Susan, widow of John Gettillag, aged 77

In November, 18[illegible], at the residence of his son-in-law, Joshua P Crist, Dr Frederick Miller in his 82d year Dr Miller, who settled in Hagerstown in 1797, established the first drug store in that place

March 13 1848, at Camp Mier Lieut Edward McPherson, of Washington County Lieut McPherson was an officer in Capt Merrick's company of dragoons, U S A, and fought a duel with Lieut Maddox, of St Mary's County Two rounds were fired with dueling pistols, after which McPherson called for his horse pistols At the first fire he fell mortally wounded, the ball passing through the hip and loins He died in about an hour Upon falling he called for Lieut Maddox, took him by the hand and said that he (Maddox) was a brave man

In January 18[illegible], Daniel Middlekauff, a leading farmer of Washington County

June 19, 18[illegible], Joseph I Merrick an old citizen of Washington County, aged about 6[illegible] Mr Merrick, who was a prominent lawyer, resided in Washington D C, for some years before his death

In June, 1854, Thomas Mills, a substantial farmer of Clear Spring District, and a veteran of the war of 1812 Mr Mills was chosen several times a member of the Maryland House of Delegates, and also held other offices of trust and honor

April 1817, Capt Charles McCully, aged 64

Aug 28, 1822, Rev Colin Macfarquhar, a native of the Highlands, Scotland, in his 91st year, at the residence of his son-in law, David Cook, Hagerstown He came to America in 1774, and before coming to Hagerstown lived over thirty years in Lancaster County, Pa

Oct 20, 1822, Jacob Myers, in the 64th year of his age

March 5, 1804, Walter Machall, at his seat in Washington County His remains were taken to Calvert County to be buried in the family burial ground there

June 3, 1856, at Washington, D C in the 35th year of his age, Horatio McPherson cashier of the Washington County Bank

Feb 3, 180[illegible] Rev Thomas McPherrin

Nov 6, 1841 James Maxwell, aged 44 Mr Maxwell was the original editor and proprietor of the Hagerstown *Mail*

At Clear Spring, Sept 28, 1849, Rev Jeremiah Mason, in the 64th year of his age

At Elkton Maryland, March 28 187[illegible], Hon John Thomson Mason a native of Washington County and a prominent jurist of Maryland

At the residence of Col Daniel Malott, Nov 16 1827, [illegible] McQuinney, aged 8[illegible], a soldier in the Revolutionary war He was a native of Ireland, and enlisted at Elkton, Md, in the 5th Maryland Regiment, serving under Maj Lansdale Capt Muse and Capt Lynn, of Allegany, Monday before

Dec 7, 1877, Isaac Motter, of Williamsport, aged 7[illegible] Mr Motter was one of the best known farmers of that section and was always prominent in movements for the development of the natural wealth of the county He was a director in the Western Maryland Railroad, the Washington County Bank, and the two turnpike companies leading from Hagerstown to Williamsport and to Greencastle, Pa In 1844 he was a delegate to the State Legislature

Aug 20, 1877, Joseph M Mish [illegible]

September, 1872, Mrs Martin, widow of Nathaniel Martin, aged 97

In May, 1872, Joseph P Mong, aged 62 Mr Mong was widely known both in business and in local politics His remains were interred in the Dunkard burial-ground at Beaver Creek Rev Leonard Lemert delivering the funeral discourse

June 24, 1843, Sarah wife of Alexander Neill, president of the Hagerstown Bank, in the 62d year of her age

July 20, 1807, Nathaniel Nesbitt aged 82

Jan 4, 1826, at his residence on Beaver Creek, Rev Peter Newcomer, aged about 7[illegible]

Jan 22 1826, Mrs Isabella Neill, mother of Alexander Neill, in her 69th year

In Hagerstown, June 17, 1856, Isabella Neill, aged about 75 years

At his residence, near Clear Spring, on the 3d of April, 1856, Jonathan Nesbitt, Sr, aged 86

On the 19th of June, 1856, at his residence, near Kenton Hardin Co, Ohio, Jacob Nesbitt, aged 81 years and 10 days The deceased was born in Washington County, Md and in 1813 moved to the State of Ohio, and settled on Beaver Creek in 1814

March 12, 1830 Rev Christian Newcomer, bishop of the German Methodist Society in his 82d year

Aug 2, 1858, Alexander Neill Sr, aged 82

Aug 28, 1877, Jonathan Nesbitt, in the 73d year of his age He was a farmer by profession, but took an active part as a writer and a politician in national and State affairs He was at one time a member of the Maryland Legislature He left two sons, C J Nesbitt and Jonathan Nesbitt, who emigrated to the West

Aug 29, 1879 at his home near Boonsboro', John Nicodemus, in his 79th year Mr Nicodemus was a leading farmer and miller, and amassed a handsome competence, which he did not hesitate to employ freely in acts of benevolence

April 2, 1881 Michael Newcomer, aged 81, at his residence on Beaver Creek He was born within half a mile of where he died, and passed his whole life in that district His family was, and is perhaps, the largest connection, by blood and intermarriage, in Washington County, and has always been prominent in political and industrial affairs the deceased taking a leading part at all times He was a Democrat, and in 1836 was elected to the Legislature, serving one term In 1839 he was re-elected to the House of Delegates He was elected to the Constitutional Convention of 1851 and served in that body During the war he was elected to the board of county commissioners, in which capacity he served a term At all times he took an active part in local politics He was a farmer and miller during the greater part of his life his father being a miller John Newcomer former sheriff of the county, who was his colleague in the Legislature on the opposite side of politics, was an elder

Aug. 6, 1880, Mary Sim Neill, widow of Alexander Neill, and daughter of Hon John Nelson

August, 1878, Lewis B Wyman, ex-clerk Circuit Court and corresponding clerk Baltimore custom-house

June 8 1803, Abraham Neff, an old and respected citizen of Hagerstown

Aug 10, 1827, Col Adam Ott, a Revolutionary soldier, in his 74th year He was commissioned an officer of the Pennsylvania Line in January 1776, and served with credit in the war Afterwards he became sheriff of Washington County, in addition to which he occupied other civil positions of honor and trust

Oct 3, 1824, Capt Christian Orndorff, in his 67th year Capt Orndorff served in the Revolutionary army, and was present at the surrender of Fort Washington

Sept 11, 1823, in Logan Co Ky Christopher Orndorff, formerly of Hagerstown, in his 72d year

In February, 1812, near Hughes' furnace, John Oswald

Aug 17, 1827 near Cadiz Ohio, Neale Peacock, formerly of Washington County, and for many years a soldier in the Revolutionary Maryland Line

In Hagerstown, on the 7th of May, 1877 Charles Poffenberger, in his 32d year Mr Poffenberger was a Federal soldier during the war, and was buried with honors by Reno Post, No 4, of the Grand Army of the Republic

Feb 13, 1879, Dr William S Pittinger, of Fairview, Conococheague District, in his 60th year

Aug 4, 1794, Mrs Eliza Pindell, wife of Dr Richard Pindell, and daughter of Col Thomas Hart, of Hagerstown

Aug 23, 1804, near Hancock, Rev Joseph Powell

Dec 18, 1825, Col Josiah Price, at an advanced age

In Baltimore, Nov 2?, 1868, William Price aged 7?, a native of Washington County, and a prominent member of the Maryland bar

November, 1840, Benjamin Price, a distinguished lawyer

At Annapolis Nov 8, 1803, Allen Quynn in his 77th year, long a resident of that city, and for twenty-five years a member of the House of Delegates

July 25, 1826 at Tammany Mount, the residence of Mrs Van Lear, Matthew Van Lear Ramsay, aged 21, son of Col John Ramsay, of Pittsburgh

About Aug 31, 1798, Benjamin Ringgold

At St Joseph, Mo, on the 1st of February, 1860, David Reichard, aged 52 Mr Reichard was a member of the Maryland Legislature from Washington County in 1856

May 4, 1816, at his residence in Hagerstown, in his 86th year, Col John Ragan He was appointed a captain in the United States army in 1808, and served in that capacity at New Orleans and Camp Terre au Bœuf about eighteen months In 1810 he returned to his native place, and upon his marriage resigned his commission He was afterwards appointed by the Governor of Maryland lieutenant colonel of the Twenty-fourth Maryland Militia

Aug 8, 1811, Maria, wife of Gen Samuel Ringgold, and daughter of Gen Cadwalader, of Philadelphia

April 3, 1807, Capt John Ritchie, for many years manager of the Antietam Iron Works

September, 1823, at his residence, five miles from Hagerstown, John Rice, an old inhabitant of the county

Jan 28, 1826, at Newcomer's Hotel Hagerstown, John Rohrer, Sr, of Pleasant Valley, aged 65

At Fountain Rock, July 28, 1822 in the 16th year of his age Edward Lloyd Ringgold son of Gen Samuel Ringgold

On the 5th of April, 18?2, in Hagerstown, Jacob Rohrer, in the 70th year of his age

At Frederick [illegible]

Redmond, aged 47 years pastor of the Catholic congregations of Washington and Allegany Counties

At Hagerstown, Tuesday Aug 26 1856, John D Ridenour, aged 53 years Mr Ridenour was a merchant and a deputy in the sheriff's office, and subsequently clerk in the Hagerstown Bank

At Centreville, Md, Feb 6, 1801 Rev Elisha Rigg formerly rector of the Episcopal Church, Lancaster, Pa, and well and favorably known in Western Maryland

Sept 29, 1801, David Ridenour in the 5?th year of his age

Oct 13, 1804 Jacob Rohrer in the 6?d year of his age

July 27, 185? Maj Jacob Rohrbach a soldier of 1812

Dec 2?, 1840, Dr John Reynolds, in his 59th year

Oct 18, 1829, at the residence of his son-in-law William Schley, in Frederick Town, Gen Samuel Ringgold, in the ??th year of his age

October, 1801 Jacob Rohrer, an old resident, near Hagerstown

At Greensburg, Pa, Sept 21, 1823, Frederick Rohrer, aged 81

Oct 7, 1823, at his residence near Mount Etna Furnace William Reynolds, son of a wealthy farmer of Washington County, who was one of the first persons to purchase lands in Kentucky The elder Reynolds was killed by the Indians while descending the Ohio His family were captured and carried to Canada, but subsequently were permitted to return to Washington County, where his son, William M, settled and acquired considerable property, which he lost shortly before his death through his own generosity

Sept 23, 1817 Rev Jonathan Rahauser, pastor of the German Reformed Church in Hagerstown in his 53d year

In February, 1826, while visiting friends in Frederick, Maria, eldest daughter of Gen Samuel Ringgold

Near Cavetown, Sept 21, 1827, Jacob Ridenour, a soldier of the Revolution

In June, 187?, aged 21, J Dixon Roman son of the Hon J Dixon Roman, and grandson of John Kennedy The deceased had attained his majority only a few days before, and was about to graduate from Harvard University His remains were interred in the old Presbyterian churchyard, and were followed to the grave by a large concourse of citizens among whom he was extremely popular

March 1881, at Smithsburg, Dr Riddlemoser

At Cumberland, in April, 1878, John Kabold, a veteran bricklayer and builder, formerly of Hagerstown He had the reputation of being the best workman in his section of country, and was the builder of most of the brick houses on Prospect Hill, Hagerstown from 1832 to 1806 which stand as monuments of admirable workmanship He it was who built Dr Reynolds' house, now owned by the Misses Lawrence, that of Gen Williams, now owned by Dr Fahrney, and that of Maj Yost, now the property of the Hon W T Hamilton

In September, 1879, Joseph Rench, at one time a judge of the Orphans' Court, and the senior of the Presbyterian Church at Hagerstown, aged 72 There was an immense attendance at the funeral and an appropriate discourse was delivered by the Rev Mr Loudthaler

March 16, 187?, Magdalena Rohrer, mother of Solomon Rohrer, in the 8?th year of her age She was the only surviving child of Martin Rohrer, who moved into Washington County then a portion of Frederick County, about 1740, and who located near Hagerstown, on what is now known as the Brien farm, lying on the Antietam Creek, and near the Cavetown turnpike Martin Rohrer had seven daughters all of whom married and gave rise to a large connection, extending [illegible] Mrs

Rohrer was a member of the Reformed Church, and was known in the neighborhood in which she lived as a most kind and charitable woman

February, 1874, Martin Rickenbaugh, aged 81

Feb 1, 1870, Rev John Rebaugh, in his 69th year In 1831 he became pastor of the Boonsboro' charge, Washington County, Md, which then consisted of four congregations, namely, Boonsboro, Sharpsburg, Cross-Roads, and Pleasant Valley In this field he labored until 1837, when he removed to Greencastle Franklin Co, Pa, and took charge of the Reformed Church in that place, and of several other congregations in the vicinity In 1851 he resigned the pastorate of the Greencastle congregation, which was then constituted a separate charge He continued to serve the congregation at Middleburg, five miles south from Greencastle, in connection with other congregations until he became disqualified through disease for the further prosecution of the work of the ministry in 1863 During the greater part of this latter period he preached regularly to the congregations at Clear Spring and St Paul's Church, Washington County, Md

November, 1794, John Leneh and Martin Ridenour

At Fredericktown, Sept 22, 1824, Robert Ritchie, editor of the *Political Intelligencer and Republican Gazette*

May 8, 1846 in the battle of Palo Alto, Mexico, Maj Samuel Ringgold, of Washington County

May 8, 18 Dr Andrew P Ringer, in his 45th year Deceased was a native of Hagerstown, but emigrated to Iowa, in which State he died For some years he was a minister of the Christian or Campbellite Church but later in life was actively engaged in the practice of medicine

July 21 1881, Christiana Rohrer, aged 83, wife of Jacob Rohrer

March 22, 1882, David Rohrer, aged 63, an influential and worthy citizen

In Baltimore City on the 16th of June, 1850, Rev James Reid, a former resident of Hagerstown Mr Reid was a minister of the Methodist Episcopal Church, and was in his 71st year at the time of his death

Nov 24 1857, in the Clear Spring District, Martin Reckert, aged 106 years, 11 months He was a native of Germany, and came to this country in company with the Rev George Schmucker, father of the Rev S S Schmucker, D D He settled in Lancaster County, Pa, but removed to Washington County toward the close of the last century He voted for George Washington and for every succeeding President down to and including the election preceding his death

At his residence Green Spring Furnace, on the 2d of January, 1863, B Franklin Roman, brother of the Hon J Dixon Roman Mr Roman was a partner in the firm and manager of the furnace

Oct 18, 1791, Susan, wife of Col Moses Rawlings, of Washington County in her 46th year She left no issue

Jan 19, 1867, Hon J Dixon Roman, a distinguished lawyer and ex-member of Congress

November, 1878, Louisa, wife of the Hon James Dixon Roman Mrs Roman was the daughter of John Kennedy, one of the early settlers of Western Maryland, and a leading business man in Hagerstown Her life was clouded by the death of her husband, daughter, and son, the latter just arrived at manhood, and with a very promise of a highly honorable and successful career before him Mrs Roman resided during the winter months with her son-in-law, Columbus C Baldwin, in New York

Near Hagerstown, in the latter part of May, 18, John Shafer, president of the board of county commissioners, aged 53

Sept 6, 1801, Elizabeth Schnebly, wife of Leonard Schnebly

Nov 28, 1801, Mrs Magdalena Steidinger, mother in law of Col A Ott, aged about 80

September, 1793, at an advanced age, Elizabeth Schnebly, wife of Dr Henry Schnebly

Dec 7, 1848, John W Summors, a former member of the State Legislature, drowned by accidentally falling into a canal-lock near Hancock

At Augusta, Ga, Nov 20, 1858, William Schley Mr Schley was at one time Governor of Georgia, and was a brother of Frederick A Schley, of Frederick

March 16, 1843, Nicholas Swingley, aged 91 He had been a citizen of Washington County ever since its formation, and is presumed to have been at that time the oldest person within its boundaries

Dec 20, 1807, John Shepherd, Sr, of Hancock District, aged 77 years and 6 months

1791, Dec 25, Frederick Steidinger, one of the oldest inhabitants, in the 61th year of his age

April 9, 1791, Col John Stull, president of the County Court, and formerly representative of the county in the General Assembly Rev George Lower preached his funeral discourse

July 26, 1818, Col Charles Swearingen, in his 83d year Col Swearingen was one of the most influential and respectable men in the county

July 15 1819, John M Smith, principal of the Hagerstown Academy, aged 25

Oct 14, 1818, at his residence, near Sharpsburg, Robert Smith, aged 81 years Mr Smith served several terms in the State Legislature, and was a popular and influential citizen

April 15, 1876, Col A K Stake, aged 57 His father was a captain in the Revolutionary war Col Stake, the youngest of a large family, learned the trade of a joiner or carpenter, and before he was 21 went to the Western States and spent several years there In 1840 he returned to Washington County, and was appointed to a responsible position on the Chesapeake and Ohio Canal Up to the time of his death he was employed in various capacities on that work In 1854-56 he was general superintendent of the entire line from Georgetown to Cumberland, and his administration was remarkably efficient and prosperous He served in the State Legislature during the sessions of 1850, 1860, and 1874

November, 1809, at the residence of her son, A K Stake, in Hagerstown, Mrs Rosanna Stake, aged 102 years and 3 months At the time of her death her descendants numbered over one hundred persons

May 19, 1814, at his residence, in Shenandoah County, Va, Col Henry Shryock, aged 78 He was a soldier for many years in the wars preceding the Revolution, and also during that period In politics he was a follower of Washington After the Revolution he settled at Hagerstown, Md, and filled various offices, being several times high sheriff of Washington County Though at one time rich, he died poor

In 1858, Daniel H Schnebly, an old and respected citizen of Washington County

April 9, 1791, at Hagerstown, Col John Stull,

Oct 24, 1879, John R Sneary, in his 61st year

Nov 17, 1870, Mary Wolgamot, widow of Col David Schnebly Mrs Schnebly was born Feb 15, 1777, and was therefore 103 years, 9 months, and 2 days old

In April, 1880, Peter Stoufter, of Funkstown District, in the 80th year of his age

March 6, 1879, at St Charles, Mo where he had settled after removing from Funkstown, Oliver Stonebraker aged 61

In September, 1877, near Williamsport, George Snifer, aged 70 [illegible] ing various im-

[illegible] business operations at the extensive mills of the family in [illegible]town, which many years ago were destroyed by fire and [illegible] by this circumstance still more generally advertised through a lottery granted by the State to replace them but [illegible] drawn. Of late years Mr. Shafer had lived a wholly re[illegible] life, and left behind him descendants highly esteemed and respected.

In April, 1877, John W. Stouffer, in his 7[illegible]th year. Mr. Stouffer was a substantial farmer, an active politician, and a man of general influence and popularity.

In November, 1879, Richard Scheckles, a popular auctioneer of Hagerstown. The deceased had a host of devoted friends, and was exceptionally conspicuous as a leader and founder of beneficial and other associations in Hagerstown. He was one of the original members and highest officer in both the Masonic and Odd-Fellows' lodges, and was particularly conspicuous in the latter order.

At Funkstown, in April, 1873, Thomas Smith, aged 91, a veteran of the war of 1812.

May, 1874, Conrad Semler, of Hagerstown.

May, 1874, Daniel Shank, Sr., of Leitersburg, aged 81.

May 31, 1869, Jacob Snyder, Sr., in the 93d year of his age.

Sept. 11, 1879, between Des Moines and Grand Junction, Iowa, Daniel Strite was shot and killed in some manner unknown. Mr. Strite was born near Leitersburg, and was a brother of Samuel Strite, associate judge of the Orphans' Court. He was 59 years of age, a man of liberal education and fine business qualities, and before removing to Iowa had filled the important posts of teller in the Washington County Bank, book-keeper of the Hagerstown Bank, clerk in the office of register of wills, and collector of internal revenue under President Johnson.

June, 1870, D. Sprigg, cashier Merchants' Bank of Baltimore, aged 81. Previous to 1830, Mr. Sprigg had been for several years the cashier of the Hagerstown Bank. In 1830 he became cashier of the Branch Bank of the United States at Buffalo, N. Y., and subsequently cashier of the Merchants' Bank.

Aug. 2, 1871, Eliza Schnebly, aged 81. She was the daughter of Dr. Jacob Schnebly, and grand-daughter of Dr. Henry Schnebly, who in the year 1762 built the house in which she died, which is yet in a perfect state of preservation, and one of the most desirable pieces of property in Hagerstown. The elder Schnebly was one of the early settlers of Washington County, then a part of Frederick County, and was one of the framers of the first constitution of the State of Maryland. At various times members of this family have filled the most important offices of the county. One of the first, if not the first, departures from the old Ramage printing-press, and an invention which preceded the present power-press, was the invention of Thomas Schnebly, a brother of Miss Eliza.

At the residence of his son-in-law, James M. Schley, in Cumberland, on the 23d of July, 1867, O. H. W. Stull, in the 84th year of his age. This venerable gentleman was a native of Washington County, and the son of John Stull, of Revolutionary memory. He was in 1814 associated with the late William D. Bell in the editorship of the *Torch-Light*, and during Gen. Harrison's administration was secretary of the Territory of Iowa.

Dec. 22, 1873, Geo. W. Smith, aged 65. In 18[illegible] he was appointed a justice of the peace, and for many years served in that capacity. Subsequently he was appointed a judge of the Orphans' Court, and for a number of years filled that position with exceptional ability. About this period he became editor of the *Washington County Democrat*, a Democratic newspaper, printed for several years in Hagerstown. In 1[illegible] he was a candidate for the Legislature on the Democratic ticket and was defeated, but in 1[illegible] he w[illegible] [illegible] majority, and served one term in the House of Delegates. In 1850, Mr. Smith was admitted to the bar of Washington County Court, at which he continued to practice, particularly as advising counsel, up to a few months previous to his death. He was one of the founders of the Franklin Debating Society, and also a director of the Washington County Bank.

February, 1881, Peter B. Small, cashier First National Bank of Hagerstown. Mr. Small was also a director of the Washington County Railroad, and of the Agricultural and Mechanical Association of the county. He also served a term as judge of the Orphans' Court.

Aug. 5, 1791, Peter Shugert, of Hagerstown, at an advanced age. At one time he was sheriff of York County, Pa., and held several other offices of trust.

Jan. 21, 1794, Mrs. Mary Shugert, wife of Peter, in her 6[illegible]th year. She left nine children and thirty-nine grandchildren.

In the latter part of January, 18[illegible], Nicholas Smith, in the 71st year of his age.

Aug. 30, 18[illegible], Mrs. Schnebly, wife of Dr. Henry Schnebly.

In April, 18[illegible], J. Henry Shafer, of Funkstown. Mr. Shafer was born in Pennsylvania, Jan. 11, 17[illegible], but removed to Washington County at an early age, and settled at Funkstown, then called Jerusalem, in 1798. He resided there up to the time of his death. He was received into the German Reformed Church by the Rev. Jacob Weimer, at Hagerstown, about 1797. He afterwards united with the church at Funkstown, and was a member of the church council for half a century.

On the 2d of January, 1814, in Montgomery County, Ohio, Henry Schlenker, aged 68, a former resident of Washington County.

January, 1854, Henry Shriver, aged 73.

Aug. 16, 1858, Thomas Shaw, aged 66.

Dec. 13, 18[illegible], Gen. Thomas Sprigg, aged 62. Gen. Sprigg resided in Washington County, and was conspicuous both in the Revolutionary war and as a member of Congress.

On Conococheague Manor, Oct. 27, 1820, Susanna, widow of Col. Charles Swearingen, in her 82d year. Col. and Mrs. Swearingen lived together harmoniously for upwards of fifty-nine years, and left numerous descendants in various parts of Maryland, Virginia, Kentucky, and Illinois.

Gerard Stonebraker, at Funkstown, in June, 1815, at the age of 70.

Rev. Solomon Schaeffer, pastor of the Hagerstown Lutheran Church, March 30, 1815, aged 25.

Robert Smith, aged 51, at his residence, near Sharpsburg, Oct. 14, 1818. He had served several terms in the State Legislature, and for a number of years was a member of the county Levy Court.

Oct. 5, 18[illegible], at his residence, near Chambersburg, John Shryock, in the 8[illegible]th year of his age. Mr. Shryock was born at Hagerstown, on the 17th of October, 1771. His paternal ancestors immigrated to this country from Prussia between the years 1715 and 1730, and settled in what is now York, but which was at that time included in Lancaster County, Pa. His maternal grandfather was a Lutheran minister from Hanover, who came to America in company with Dr. Muhlenberg, and preached throughout Pennsylvania previous to the year 1755.

July 16, 18[illegible], Jacob Shever, farmer.

Sept. 2, 18[illegible], George Scott, of Boonsboro', formerly an associate judge and a justice of the peace.

Feb. 1[illegible], 1810, Jacob Seibert, at his residence, West Conococheague.

July 24, 18[illegible], Dr. Henry Schnebly, aged 77. Dr. Schnebly was prominent during the Revolution, and was one of the most highly [illegible].

At Kaskaskia, Ill, Dec 5, 1821, Joseph Sprigg, aged 62, who removed to Illinois in 1816

At Williamsport, May 23, 1822, Capt Peter Stake, aged 57

At Hagerstown Aug 12, 1823, Dr Samuel Sherman

Dec 1, 1825, Lucy, widow of Thomas Sprigg, in the 74th year of her age

Oct 28, 1822, near the Maryland Tract, Frederick County, John Shafer, Sr aged 79 years, 5 months, 3 days

On the 9th of September, 1821, Nicholas Smith, farmer, near Williamsport

Jan 19, 1823, James W Steele, formerly of Hagerstown, near Lake Champlain, New York

In Hagerstown, October, 1802, John Byers Taylor

Feb 6, 1830, Rebecca Tilghman, wife of Thomas Tilghman

Jan 14, 1820, John Teisher, aged 73

Dec 6, 1818, Jonathan Turner, aged 28

July 19, 1819, Jonathan Tutweiler, a Revolutionary soldier

Aug 4, 1872, Hugh Taggart, aged 87

November, 1871 Rev Septimus Tustin D D, for several years pastor of the Presbyterian congregation in Hagerstown Dr Tustin, although for a considerable period in the latter portion of his life engaged in a secular pursuit as clerk in some of the departments at Washington had occupied many prominent positions in his church, the most conspicuous of which, probably, was that of chaplain to the Senate of the United States Dr Tustin was a brother-in-law of Maj-Gen Macomb, those gentlemen having married daughters of the late Rev B Balch, D D, of the District of Columbia He was also chaplain of the University of Virginia in 1836, chaplain to the House of Representatives of the United States in 1840, chairman of the Committee of Foreign Correspondence of the General Assembly, and was the first clergyman to initiate the measures for reunion, and president of the board of trustees of Lafayette College, Easton, Pa, as well as pastor of several churches in Pennsylvania and Maryland

March, 1824, Ann Eliza, wife of George Tilghman, and daughter of Col Lamar, of Allegany

Sept 30, 1840, Thomas Trice, editor Williamsport *Banner*, in the 31st year of his age

Oct 5, 1853, Dr Frisby Tilghman

In September, 1807, Ignatius Taylor, judge of the Orphans' Court and a man of exceptionally high character

In Hancock, on the 16th of March, 1856, George Thomas, in the 59th year of his age

In December a colored woman known as "Aunt Tabby," said to be 104 years old, was burned to death at the home of her son-in-law Hilary Wilson, in Sharpsburg

Aug 10, 1869 George Updegraff, aged 70 years 11 months, and 29 days

July 20, 1801, John Van Lear, aged 77

July 5, 1822, Matthew Van Lear, a prominent citizen of the county

At his residence in Williamsport, on Friday evening, April 24, 1859, in the 71st year of his age, John Van Lear, Jr, cashier of the Washington County Bank Mr Van Lear was connected with the bank from its organization, first as its president for four years, and afterwards as its cashier, which position he held from the year 1836 He was also a strong friend of African colonization, and in support of this, as well as other schemes of Christian benevolence, he gave liberally in money, and furnished constant encouragement and example

Feb 11, 1815, Col William Van Lear, in his 58th year Col Van Lear served as brigade-major under Gen Wayne, and inspector of the Marquis de Lafayette's division shortly before the surrender [illegible] Green Springs, but afterwards returned to active service At the close of the war he settled in Washington County

Died at the farm of Matthew Van Lear, near Williamsport, Sept 1, 1816, Dr Matthew Simms Van Lear, in the 28th year of his age

July 15, 1794, Gen Otho Holland Williams

At Georgetown, D C, in 1823, Col Elie Williams, in the 73d year of his age Col Williams was an ardent patriot during the Revolution, and in the latter portion of his life was deeply interested in the Chesapeake and Ohio Canal, being elected to the Legislature from Washington County with the special object of promoting the interests of that great enterprise

June 13, 1819, Daniel Witmer, Jr, inn-keeper at Hagerstown, aged 60 years

May 11, 1852 Gen O H Williams, for many years clerk of the Washington County Court, in his 78th year

July, 1854, Col George C Washington, formerly a representative in Congress from Maryland, and at one time president of the Chesapeake and Ohio Canal in the 69th year of his age The deceased was a relative of the great Washington, and a man highly esteemed for his elevated character, public spirit, and social and generous qualities

At Washington, D C, June 14, 1868, Col John S Williams, aged 84 Col Williams was a brother of Otho H Williams, so long a clerk of Washington County Court, and a nephew of Gen O H Williams, of Revolutionary fame Col Williams was born in Maryland in 1785 and when a young man resided for several years in Georgetown, but again removed to Maryland and after a residence of several years again removed to Washington where he resided for many years He was a major in the war of 1812 At the battle of Bladensburg he was an adjutant, and published an interesting history of that battle He was vice president of the Association of the Oldest Inhabitants of Washington and the presiding officer of the soldiers of the war of 1812

In March, 1879, Benjamin Witmer, of Beaver Creek, in the 71st year of his age Mr Witmer was elected a member of the State Legislature in 1855, and was an active and influential citizen

May 5 (?), 1880, John Weltz, aged 67

Oct 24, 1869, Otho Holland Williams, in his 86th year

At Williamsport, Sept 25, 1880, Judge Daniel Weisel, aged 77

July, 1804, John George Weiss, aged 83, who had been a teacher in Hagerstown upwards of thirty years His death was followed by that of his widow within a week

Oct 20, 1811, at his residence, near Hughes' furnace, Col James Walling

Aug 3, 1806, Dr T Walmsley Dr Walmsley removed to Hagerstown from Philadelphia in 1805, and was extremely popular

In January, 1807, William Webb, for many years magistrate at Hughes' forge

Archibald M Waugh, died May 23, 1823, aged 47 He was a man of great integrity of character, and respected by all who knew him

July 1823, at Cavetown, Samuel Webb

May 6, 1880, John Welty (nephew of John Welty), farmer and distiller His farm was one of the richest and most carefully improved in Cumberland Valley On it was a trout pond which had quite a local celebrity Mr Welty was at one time a member of the State Legislature, and also a county commissioner, director of the Western Maryland Railroad, etc

April 19 1856, Robert Wason, at the residence of his nephew, [illegible] year of his [illegible]

Mr. Mason served in both branches of the Legislature of Maryland, and was an influential politician as well as successful business man.

At Charleston, Va., April 5, 1852, Richard Williams, a former resident of Hagerstown, and editor of the *Farmers' Repository* from 1802 to 1807. He was the first apprentice in the Hagerstown *Herald* office, having commenced work in that establishment in 1790.

At his residence in Hagerstown, April 5, 1842, Rev. Richard Kynthoop, pastor of the Associate Reformed congregation.

March 16, 1843, Joseph Weast, aged 53. Mr. Weast was a member of the first board of county commissioners, and a man of considerable local influence and standing. He had served three times in the State Legislature, and was county collector at the time of his death.

March 16, 1843, Samuel Wolfersberger, aged 24.

At Charleston, S. C., March 16, 1818, Otho H. Williams, of Baltimore, youngest son of the late Gen. Otho H. Williams, in his 23d year of his age.

January, 1872, Dr. Samuel Weisel, in his 63d year.

At New Orleans, on the 8th of May, 1875, Dr. John O. Wharton, at the residence of his son, Col. Jack Wharton, aged 7-.

Feb. 2, 1876, Matilda, wife of Judge Daniel Weisel.

March 26, 1791, Jacob Young, in his 59th year.

April 26, 1793, Rev. George Young, aged 51 years, who for about nineteen years officiated as minister of the gospel in the German Lutheran Congregation of Hagerstown. He was a man of great piety and learning. He left a young wife and a number of children. After the funeral was over an appropriate sermon was preached by the Rev. Yonck from 2d Epistle of Paul to the Corinthians, 8th and 9th verses.

At Sharpsburg, Feb. 6, 1829, Henry Young, a Revolutionary soldier, in his 97th year. After the war he was a teacher of English and German, and resided in Sharpsburg for upwards of thirty years.

July, 1878, Barnett Young, aged 89 years.

Feb. 23, 1803, Rev. John Young, in his 40th year. Member of the Associated Reformed Synod, and pastor of the united congregations of Greencastle, West Conococheague, and Great Cove.

June 8, 1863, Dr. John R. Young, at a comparatively early age.

March 3, 1863, Lewis Zeigler, a former member of the Maryland Legislature.

In the latter part of November, 1875, Rev. W. R. Zimmerman, in his 56th year. Mr. Zimmerman studied for the ministry under the late Rev. Dr. Zacharias, and upon the completion of his studies went to Clear Spring, in Washington County, where he preached for several years, but owing to physical disabilities he retired to his farm in this county, where he resided until his death.

At Frederick, March 31, 1875, Rev. Daniel Zacharias, D.D. "Dr. Zacharias was a native of Washington County, having been born near Clear Spring. His classical education was received at the Hagerstown Academy and Jefferson College (Canonsburg, Pa.). His theological studies were prosecuted at the Theological Seminary of the Reformed Church (then located at Carlisle, Pa.), under Rev. Dr. Lewis Mayer. During this time he attended some of the lectures in Dickinson College, which was then in charge of Dr. Nesbitt. Shortly after the completion of his theological studies he was chosen as pastor of the Reformed Church of Harrisburg, from which place he was called to Frederick in 1835. He was one of the most prominent ministers in his denomination, and was frequently selected by the preference of [illegible] to preside over their ecclesiastical assemblies. In 1835 he was associated with Rev. Dr. Wolff in the preparation of the appendix to the church hymn-book. At a later date the German hymn-book was chiefly compiled by the Rev. Dr. Schneck and himself. In the preparation of the 'Liturgy of the Church,' and its revision, known as 'An Order of Worship for the Reformed Church,' he was a prominent member of the committees appointed by the Synod, and he likewise took a part in the preparation of the edition of the Heidelberg Catechism in German, Latin, and Greek, which was published by the church in 1863."

Sept. 27, 1826, Mrs. Elizabeth Zeller, aged 57.

At his residence near Leitersburg, on May 31, 1867, Frederick Zeigler, Sr., aged 79 years. Mr. Zeigler was one of the wealthiest and most respectable citizens of Washington County.

CHAPTER XLIV.

HAGERSTOWN.

The First Settler—Jonathan Hager—Cresap's Fort—Incorporation of the Town—The First Officers—Reminiscences—Prominent Events.

HAGERSTOWN, the county-seat of Washington County, is beautifully situated near Antietam Creek, eighty-seven miles from Baltimore, and lies five hundred and sixty-six feet above tide. It is located in the midst of the charming Hagerstown Valley, and is one of the most attractive and thrifty towns in the country. The streets are regular and in good condition, and the buildings substantial, and in many instances unusually handsome. Stores and shops of various kinds are numerous. The railway lines which centre here are the Washington County Branch of the Baltimore and Ohio, the Western Maryland, the Cumberland Valley, and the Shenandoah Valley. These roads drain a magnificent section of country, decidedly the richest in Maryland, and embracing also some of the fairest portions of Pennsylvania, Virginia, and West Virginia. From an elevated position in the town may be seen for miles the fertile fields of the Hagerstown Valley, while on the south lies the bleak battle-field of Antietam, and on the eastward that of South Mountain. From a point northwest of Hagerstown the line of intrenchments thrown up by Lee's army in his last invasion of Maryland extended in a southerly direction to the Potomac. At some points the intrenchments were not more than three-quarters of a mile or a mile and a half from the town, which was completely covered by the Confederate guns. The Union fortifications were also very extensive. In fact, Hagerstown was the theatre of some of the most important events of the war, and the [illegible] of the havoc wrought

by both armies are by no means effaced even yet In addition to its railroad facilities, the town enjoys the advantage of being the point of convergence for a number of admirable turnpike roads, which have largely contributed to building up its flourishing trade It is abundantly supplied with water-power which, with the richness and productiveness of the surrounding country, has contributed to give it not only the appearance but the reality of remarkable prosperity and enterprise

Looking eastward, towards the South Mountain ridge, the scenery is of the most imposing character Splendid farms, teeming with richness of soil and all under perfect cultivation, are within visual range in every direction, whilst blue mountains rise up in the distance, making altogether a panorama that has few equals anywhere Beautiful springs gush forth from limestone rocks at frequent intervals, and sparkling streams are seen winding through the rich fields like threads of glittering silver To all this rural beauty is added a pure, salubrious atmosphere One of the most attractive features of the town itself is the number of beautiful gardens and green inclosures attached to private residences

The town is divided into five wards The principal streets are Washington and Potomac Washington runs nearly east and west, and Potomac north and south Each is divided by the other into two sections thus making East and West Washington and North and South Potomac Streets The streets running parallel with Washington Street, beginning on the north, are North, Bethel, Church, Franklin, Antietam, and Baltimore Those running parallel with Potomac Street, beginning on the east, are Mulberry, Locust, Jonathan, Walnut, Prospect, and High Green Lane is an extension of West Washington Street, and Pennsylvania Avenue is a continuation of Jonathan Street The Washington Branch of the Baltimore and Ohio Railroad enters the town from the south, passing between Potomac and Jonathan Streets The depot is situated at the intersection of South Jonathan and West Antietam Streets, a short distance northwest of St John's Lutheran church, which fronts on Potomac Street near the intersection of Antietam Street The Cumberland Valley Railroad passes through the western portion of the town, along Walnut Street The depot is situated at the intersection of South Walnut and West Washington Streets For some distance the course of the Western Maryland Railroad is parallel with and westward of that of the Cumberland Valley, which, however curves suddenly to the northward and intersec s the W t n Mar l a l n th n th [illegible] western section of the town The depot is situated on West Washington Street

The principal buildings in Hagerstown are the court house, on West Washington Street, at the corner of Jonathan, near which stands the banking-house of Hoffman, Eavey & Co , the Baldwin House, a handsome new hotel located on Washington Street, diagonally opposite from the court-house, to the eastward , the market-house, on the east side of Potomac Street, at the corner of Franklin , county jail, on Jonathan Street, at the corner of West Church , Hagerstown Female Seminary, located in the extreme southeastern portion of the town and the Hagerstown Academy, which is situated in the southwestern portion, near Walnut Street The town hall is situated at the corner of Franklin and Potomac Streets, with market house under it

The churches are located as follows Catholic, Washington and Walnut Streets , St John's Episcopal, Antietam and Prospect Streets, St John's Lutheran, Potomac Street near Antietam , Presbyterian, corner of Washington and Prospect Streets and another on South Potomac near Baltimore Street, Methodist, Jonathan Street near Franklin, Trinity Lutheran and the Reformed churches, on Franklin Street between Jonathan and Potomac Bethel Methodist Episcopal church, on Bethel Street near Potomac, Colored Methodist church, on Jonathan near Church , United Brethren, at the corner of Locust and Franklin Streets , and St Matthew's German Lutheran church, on the corner of Antietam and Locust Streets Besides these there is another Reformed church on Potomac Street near Church The handsomest and most conspicuous church in Hagerstown is St John's Protestant Episcopal, a beautiful structure of graystone, with an imposing tower The court house is a spacious building of brick , with tower, and is one of the finest structures of the kind in the State The Baldwin House is the principal hotel, and is a new, roomy and well appointed structure The other hotels are the Franklin House, on Potomac Street, Antietam House, on West Washington Street, Hoover House, corner Franklin and Potomac Streets, and the Mansion House, near the depot of the Cumberland Valley Railroad The Hagerstown Bank, one of the oldest institutions of the kind in Western Maryland, is situated on Washington Street opposite the Baldwin House, and the First National Bank is now erecting a new building on Washington Street, opposite the court-house

The sidewalks are paved with brick, and the streets are substantial turnpike roads The site of the old [illegible] tion of Poto-

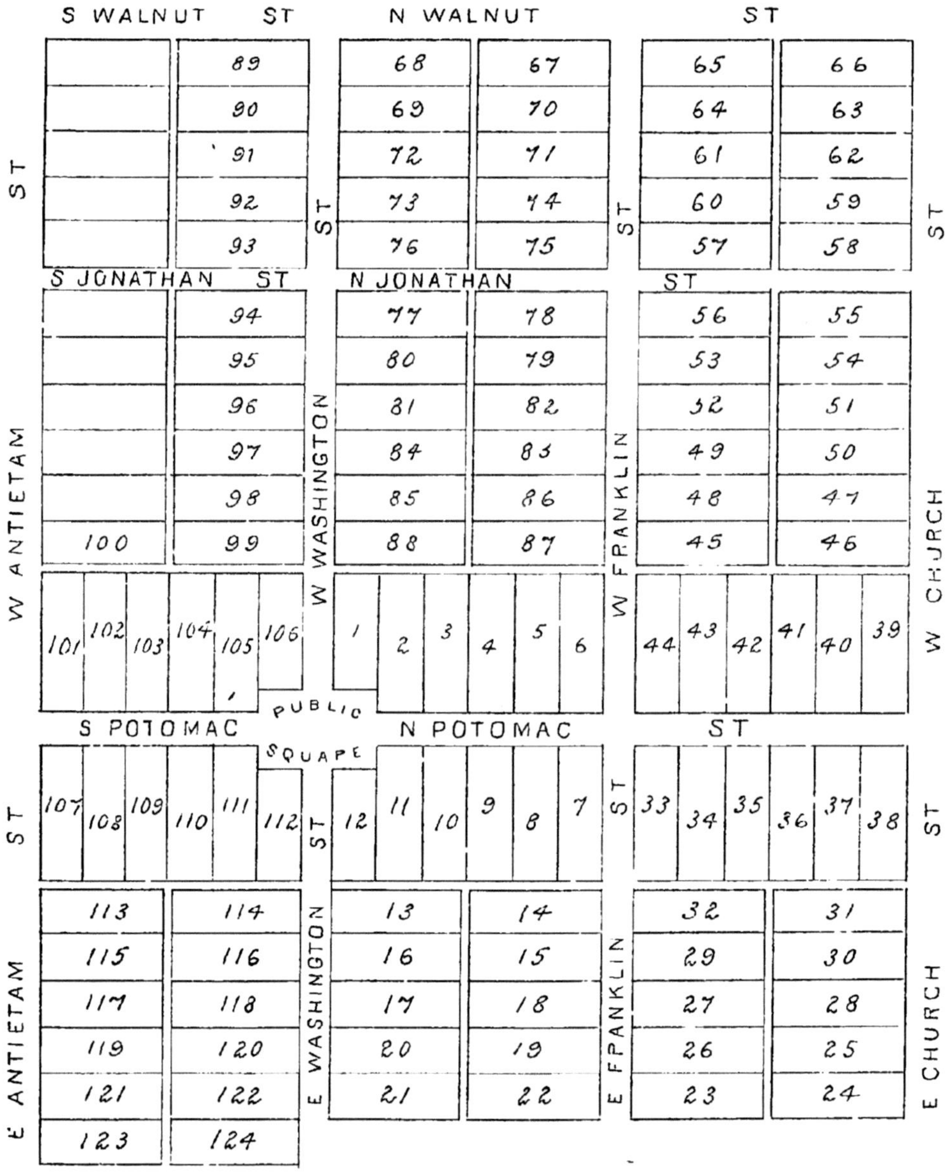

S WALNUT ST — N WALNUT ST

89 90 91 92 93

68 67 69 70 72 71 73 74 76 75

65 66 64 63 61 62 60 59 57 58

S JONATHAN ST — N JONATHAN ST

94 95 96 97 98 100 99

77 78 80 79 81 82 84 83 85 86 88 87

56 55 53 54 52 51 49 50 48 47 45 46

W ANTIETAM ST — W WASHINGTON ST — W FRANKLIN ST — W CHURCH ST

101 102 103 104 105 106

1 2 3 4 5 6

44 43 42 41 40 39

PUBLIC SQUARE

S POTOMAC ST — N POTOMAC ST

107 108 109 110 111 112

12 11 10 9 8 7

33 34 35 36 37 38

113 114 115 116 117 118 119 120 121 122 123 124

13 14 16 15 17 18 20 19 21 22

32 31 29 30 27 28 26 25 23 24

E ANTIETAM ST — E WASHINGTON ST — E FRANKLIN ST — E CHURCH ST

ORIGINAL PLAT OF HAGERSTOWN.

mac and Washington Streets, is now used as a public square. It is a great rendezvous for market people. The finest private residences are situated on Prospect, and at the head of West Washington and North Potomac Streets, but there are also a number of others scattered about in different localities. The houses are mostly of brick, but some graystone is also used with handsome effect.

Hagerstown was laid out as a town in 1762 by Capt. Jonathan Hager, and its site is said to have been in the main a dreary, uneven swamp. Capt. Hager came from Germany about 1730 and settled in what is now Washington County, about two miles west of the present site of Hagerstown, on a tract of land which was known as "Hager's Delight," and which was owned recently by the late Samuel Zeller. The earliest information of Jonathan Hager, Sr., is found in the statement that he received a patent of certain land on which a portion of the city of Philadelphia now stands. He was a man of much independence and force of character, and pushed on to Maryland. Having obtained patents for extensive tracts of land in Washington County, he settled, as stated above, in the vicinity of Antietam Creek. On this farm was built the first two-story log house, with an arched stone cellar so constructed that if the family were attacked by the Indians they could take refuge there. Capt. Hager was frequently assailed by the savages, and his family found the cellar a most useful asylum. It was often necessary to protect the dairy-maids with armed men while engaged in milking the cows. As a rule, however, Capt. Hager generally managed to keep on pretty friendly terms with the Indians of the vicinity.

Jonathan Hager was not, however, the first settler in the neighborhood of Hagerstown. He was no doubt preceded several years by Capt. Thomas Cresap, the famous Indian-fighter, and other fearless settlers. Capt. Cresap at a very early period built an Indian fort of stone and logs over a spring at "Long Meadows," on the farm now owned by George W. Harris, about three miles from Hagerstown, which was known for many years as "Old Castle Cresap." During the Indian wars Cresap's fort was an important point, as it afforded protection to those who fled to it for safety. It was also a general rendezvous for the rangers established in the county for the protection of the back settlements. When the inhabitants increased and the Indians were driven farther into the interior, Cresap abandoned his castle near Hagerstown and erected a more formidable one at his new home at Skipton, or Old Town, in Allegany County. Some of the ruins of his old fort are yet visible; indeed, the old stone barn, on the [illegible] Mr. R[illegible] which was [illegible] chased by him in 1868 from the executors of the late Richard Ragan, was built out of the stone of Castle Cresap, which stood on that farm. "Long Meadows" was the favorite abode of the early settlers of Washington County, and within the memory of many living the farms in that locality were owned by the Harts, Spriggs, Thomas B. Hall, and other names once familiar, but now extinct.

Jonathan Hager was attracted to Washington County by the fertility of its soil and the great abundance of pure and wholesome water, and was not disappointed in the hope of speedily accumulating a comfortable maintenance.

About 1740 he married Elizabeth Kershner, who lived in the same neighborhood. They had two children, Rosanna and Jonathan. Rosanna married Gen. Daniel Heister, and Jonathan married Mary Madeline, daughter of Maj. Christian Orndorff, who lived near Sharpsburg. Maj. Orndorff's house was the headquarters of the Revolutionary officers who passed that way to or from the scene of military operations in the North or South. Mrs. Jonathan Hager, Jr. (Mary Orndorff), was a great belle and beauty in her day, one of her suitors being the famous Gen. Horatio Gates. She rejected him, however, and when fifteen years of age accepted Jonathan Hager, Jr., and was married to him. They had one daughter, Elizabeth, who married Upton Lawrence. Nine children were born to Mr. and Mrs. Lawrence, and their descendants are very numerous. Among them are the two Misses Lawrence, who reside in the Lawrence mansion, and who have many interesting relics of the Hagers in their possession. Among them is the original plat of the town, as shown in the cut. They also have Jonathan Hager, Sr.'s, old-fashioned silver watch of the "turnip" pattern, the massively engraved silver shoe-buckles worn by Jonathan Hager, Jr., and the latter's suspender-buckles of silver, with his initials engraved on them. Among the other articles in their collection is a handsome silver stock-buckle set with brilliants and attached to a stock of black lace and blue satin, a brooch of brilliants for the shirt, a gold ring set with a ruby and diamonds, and a full-dress suit with lace and ruffles. This costume consists of two vests,—one of them of white satin embroidered with spangles and colored silks, and the other of apple-green silk embroidered with spangles, gold thread, and colored silks. The spangles and embroidery are still as bright, probably, as when they were first put on. They also have Mr. Hager, Jr.'s, silver shoe-buckles, magnificently set with brilliants, and retain possession of all the old silver and plate.

Th[illegible] the new village

Elizabeth Town in honor of his wife, Elizabeth, but in after years it came to be written Elizabeth (Hager's) Town, and gradually the Elizabeth was discarded and it was denominated solely Hagerstown Capt Hager laid off the town in about 520 lots of 82 feet front and 240 feet deep, making half an acre each, which were leased for £5 consideration money, $1, or 7 shillings and 6 pence, per annum as a perpetual ground rent He reserved all the lots outside the town which were not numbered in the original, but these were afterwards sold by his heirs There are still in the possession of his descendants about 300 ground rents of the original town lots A large square was laid out, and a market-house was erected in the centre, at the intersection of what is now Washington and Potomac Streets Afterwards a court-house and market-house combined was built, the market house being below and the court-house above When Washington County was created out of Frederick in 1776, Mr Hager, we are told, "rode down to Annapolis and had his town made the county town" This must have been Jonathan Hager, Jr, as the date of his father's death is given as being 1775[1] In the previous year (1773) Jonathan Hager, Sr, had been returned as a delegate to the General Assembly of Maryland from Frederick County, but not being a native subject of the English crown nor descended from one, but naturalized in 1747, was declared ineligible by the House The act created a considerable stir and the Governor and Council declared it unprecedented He was also a member of the House of Delegates in 1771 The course of the Assembly in 1773 was predicated on a petition from Samuel Beall setting forth that a number of voters in Frederick County had not produced certificates of their naturalization, and on account of their religious tenets had refused to take the oaths required by law The old Hager residence, a massive stone building on the eastern side of the public square and fronting on Washington Street, was torn down a few years ago in order to make room for a store In this ancient structure the Hagers resided for a number of years, and after them Col Henry Lewis, who married Mrs Mary Hager, widow of Col Jonathan Hager, Jr Mrs Mary Hager was still a very beautiful woman, and still young when Col Hager died At one time Luther Martin, the great lawyer, was an ardent suitor for her hand, but she rejected him and married Col Lewis Both the Jonathan Hagers, father and son, were very popular with the citizens of Hagerstown, and enjoyed almost unbounded influence The elder Hager was accidentally killed on Nov 6, 1775, in his sixty first year, at a saw-mill near the site of Hager's mill, by a large piece of timber rolling upon and crushing him The timber was being sawed for the German Reformed church, which Mr Hager was very active in building Jonathan Hager, Jr, entered the Revolutionary army, and served through the war After his marriage he resided in Hagerstown, and died in December, 1798 In its issue of the 20th of that month the Hagerstown *Herald* paid him a warm tribute as a worthy citizen and an affectionate husband and father His daughter, Elizabeth, married Upton Lawrence, a distinguished lawyer of Hagerstown

In 1791, Henry Shryock, Matthias Need, and Martin Harry were appointed commissioners, with power and authority to lay out a portion of ground in Elizabeth Town for the purpose of building a market-house thereon not less than fifty feet in length and thirty in breadth By the act of 1793 all the powers to these commissioners were transferred to the commissioners of the town By an act passed by the General Assembly in 1791 "to improve the streets," etc, Elizabeth Town was incorporated By this act Thomas Hart, Ludwick Young, William Lee, John Shryock, John Geiger, Peter Heighley, and Baltzer Gole were appointed the first commissioners

The preamble of the act sets forth that the citizens of the town petitioned for the act of incorporation, stating in their petition that the streets of the town were frequently rendered almost impassable by means of many of the inhabitants raising the ground before their own houses, and turning the water with a view to their private convenience only, and that disputes often arose respecting boundaries of lots by filling up the [illegible] commissioners were

[1] Extract from the family Bible of Jonathan Hager, translated from the German

"I entered into marriage with my wife, Elizabeth Grischner, in the year 1740 On the 21st of April, 1752, in the sign of the Lion, there was born to us a daughter, who was named Rosina

"On the 13th of December, 1755, there was born to us a son, who was named Jonathan

"We lived together until the 16th of April, 1765 Then it pleased the Lord to call her, after severe suffering, out of this world 'What God does is well done' Her funeral text is recorded in 2 Tim i 12 The hymn was sung, 'Lord Jesus Christ, true man and God' also the hymn, 'Think ye, children of men, on the last day of life' O, my child, lay rightly to heart the words of this hymn and do right and fear God and keep His commandments And if you have anything, do not forget the poor, and do not exalt yourself in pride and haughtiness above your fellow-men For you are not better than the humblest before God's eyes, and perhaps not as good And so, if you have no fear of God within you, all is in vain My child keep this in remembrance of your father, and live according to it, [illegible] will with you [illegible] while you live and there [illegible]

empowered to levy a tax not exceeding three shillings on one hundred pounds, to dig wells, purchase a fire-engine, etc

The commissioners were also made a body corporate by the name of the Commissioners of Elizabeth Town, and to have a common seal and perpetual succession Additional powers were conferred on the commissioners by the act of 1792 At this time the lower part of the town was built on very low and swampy land, the streets have been raised many feet above the original level, and were often in a very bad condition The marsh at the southern edge of the town accounts for the bend in South Potomac Street, as it was bent east of the straight line to avoid it In the year 1802 the General Assembly authorized a lottery for the purpose of raising money to repair the streets About 1810, Samuel Rohrer made an addition to the original town

The first census of Hagerstown of which any record remains was taken in 1810 At that time the population numbered 2342, of which 1951 were whites, 297 slaves, and 94 free negroes

In 1820 the population was as follows Whites, males, 1161, whites, females, 1137, total whites, 2298, slaves, males 147, slaves, females, 133, total slaves, 280, free colored persons, males, 55, females, 57, total, 112, total population, 2690

For the censuses of 1850, 1860, 1870, and 1880, the only years we have been able to obtain the official figures, the returns were as follows

	Total	Native	Foreign	White	Colored
1850	3879			3261	618
1860	4132			3623	509
1870	5779	5142	637	4910	860
1880	6627				

A writer describing Hagerstown in 1822 says

There are perhaps few towns in this county which have risen more rapidly in importance within the last few years than this town Nor are its advantages in other respects less important The arrivals and departures of stages in one week amount to forty-two,—seven arrive from Wheeling, seven from Washington, Georgetown, and Baltimore *via* Frederick, three from Baltimore *via* Westminster, Taney Town, and Emmittsburg which line is intersected twenty miles from this place by a direct line from Philadelphia *via* Gettysburg, three from the respective sections of Pennsylvania *via* Chambersburg, and one from Virginia *via* Winchester, Martinsburg, and Williamsport, making twenty-one arrivals from, and the same number of departures for, the respective places above named An idea of the progress of improvement may be gathered from the fact that a court-house equal, perhaps, in elegance and taste to any in the country has just been completed, and that there are now in progress a market house, connected with a town hall and Masonic Hall, independent of a large Episcopal church and several private dwellings The number of well conducted public houses is not, perhaps, surpassed by those of any inland town in the country, the enterprise and activity of our mercantile men are proverbial, and the industry and perseverance of our mechanical po[illegible] various branches of active [illegible]

In connection with the town hall and market alluded to an animated discussion arose It seems that the steeple of the old market-house was surmounted by a little old man of tin, with a rotund abdomen, who was popularly known as "Old Heiskel," doubtless from his resemblance, real or fancied, to some well-known resident of the town The citizens generally wanted to have "Old Heiskel" placed on the steeple of the new building, but the Freemasons desired a compass and square to indicate the character of the edifice Neither party would give way at first, and a violent controversy in and out of the newspapers was the result The Masons finally triumphed, however, and the compass and square were placed on the vane

Early Residents — Among the residents of Hagerstown and its immediate vicinity from 1800 to 1805, inclusive, were the following

Arnold, Henry, weaver
Alter, Frederick, overseer of almshouse
Adams, Nathan, farmer
Artz, Christian
Beatty, Elie, the first cashier of Hagerstown Bank
Bower, Rev George
Beltzhoover, Melchor, tavern keeper
Brazier, William, bridle, bit and stirrup maker
Bower, Abraham
Bowers, Mrs, owner of brick-yard
Belt, Thomas, register of deeds
Blaire, L, classical teacher
Byers, John, tailor and habit-maker
Burke, John, stocking-weaver
Bender, George, wheelwright
Bender,[1] John, laborer
Baker, Sebastian, crier of Washington County Court
Boreoff, Adam, blacksmith
Coffroth, Conrad, merchant
Crissinger, George, proprietor hackney stage
Clagett, Alex, merchant
Clapsaddle, Daniel, farmer
Compton, Thomas, justice of the peace
Clagett, William, associate judge
Crumbach, John, potter
Cake, Henry
Conrad, John
Crumbach, Conrad, potter, also brewer
Clagett & Miller, merchants
Clagett, Benjamin
Carroll, Charles, farmer
Coburn, A, teacher of music
Cook John, tavern-keeper at stone house, "Sign of Gen Washington"
Carlos, Francis, barber
Douglass, Robert, weaver
Doyle, Dorris
Dunn, William, tailor and habit maker
Devine, John, tailor and habit maker
Dietrich, Jacob D, merchant, also bookbinder
Diffendorfer, Mrs, milliner

[1] [illegible], 1803

Devine, Mrs John, milliner and mantua maker
Dorsey, Frederick, physician
Dunnington, James merchant
Donaldson, John, whitesmith
Dietz, J, bookbinder
Davis, Samuel B, teacher and bookbinder
Davis, Col Rezin, a veteran of '76
Eichelberger Devalt
Fechtig,[1] Christian, potter
Ferguson, James, & Co, merchants
Forman & Keller, merchants
Foutz & Stucky, hatters
Gibbs & Westover, who had carding-machines on the Antietam
Galloway Benj, politician
Greiner, John, brass-founder
Geiger, John, tanner
Grieves, Thomas, publisher and bookseller
Geiger & Harry, merchants
Green, Wm, proprietor of grist-mill situated near the town
Garrett, Thomas, weaver
Gruber, John, printer and publisher
Gilberts, Wendel, farmer
Grubb George, cooper
Hughes Daniel, Jr
Harry, Jacob merchant
Harry, David, wagon maker
Hawken, Capt Christian, gunsmith
Hawken, George, gunsmith
Hogmire, Conrad, dealer in flour, corn-meal, etc
Haynes, Richard
Hughes, Samuel
Heyser, Wm, coppersmith and fire department chief
Henderson George, miller
Heddinger, ——, auctioneer and market clerk
Hager, Jonathan, proprietor tavern, "Sign of the Ship"
Hefleich, Peter
Hose, Jacob Revolutionary veteran
Heister, Gen Daniel, member of Congress
Hawkin, William, gunsmith
Hess, William
Herndige, Philip, candle maker
Herr, John P, tailor and lumber-dealer
Hieshen, J, teacher of private school
Hartshorn, D, teacher of dancing
Heffley, Michael, farmer
Hilliard, James, farrier
Heddington, James
Herbert, Stewart, printer
Hershey, John, tanner
Hart, Thomas, merchant
Johnson, Arthur, clock and watchmaker
Kershner, Martin
Kennedy, John, merchant
Kreps, William, merchant
Kreps, George, gunsmith
Kreps, Martin, carpenter
Kemmelmeyer, F, limner and portrait-painter
Kealnofer, Jacob, boot and shoemaker
Kelly, John V, fuller and dyer at Bechtel's mill
Kendall James attorney at-law and deputy county clerk
Kupp, Michael, tavern-keeper
Keller, Christian

Keller, Philip, blacksmith
Light, Benjamin, tavern keeper
Light, John
Lewis, Henry farmer
Little, P W, firm of Little & Miller
Little & Miller, merchants
Lawrence Upton, attorney-at-law
Lane, Seth, cabinet maker
Middlekauff, Henry
Monahan, Timothy, plasterer, and captain of militia
Miller, Frederick, firm of Little & Miller
Miller, James, weaver
Miller, John, weaver
Miller, Peter, tavern keeper
Miller, Jacob, tavern keeper, house, "Sign of the Indian Queen"
McNamee, George and Job dealers in plaster, etc
McCloskey, Stephen, who charged $1 per year for water taken from his well
Mahony, Mr, scrivener
Mahony, Mrs, teacher of private school
Middlekauff, David, tavern keeper, house, "Sign of the Swan"
McCoy, John, merchant
Miller, Peter, merchant
McCardell, James
McIntosh, William, scrivener
McDonald, Richard
McKinley, Josiah, painter and glazier
McIlhenny, John, merchant
McIlhenny, Joseph merchant
McCardell, Thomas
Neill, Alexander, merchant
Neid, Capt Daniel, tanner
Nigh, George, justice of the peace
Nichol & George gunsmiths
Oldwine, Parney, Revolutionary veteran
Ott, Col Adam, justice of the peace
Oldwine, Charles, plasterer and bricklayer
O Neill John
Orndorf, Peter, stage proprietor
Pindell,[2] Richard, physician
Parsons, Daniel, tailor and habit-maker
Pinkley, George, & Co, merchants
Pinkley & Middlekauff, merchants
Pinkley, George, blue dyer
Pinkley, Jacob, blue dyer
Price, George, collector of revenue
Quantrill, Thomas blacksmith
Quantrill, Thomas, Jr blacksmith
Rochester & Beatty, merchants
Rochester, John C
Rochester, William B
Ralph, John
Ragan, Richard, merchant
Reed & Byers, tailors and habit-makers
Ragan, John, tavern keeper, house,[3] "Sign of the Indian King" also stage proprietor
Ragan, John, Jr, an officer of the war of 1812
Ridenour, David, tavern keeper
Ridenour, Samuel, tanner

[1] The pottery business then carried on by Christian Fechtig and George V[illegible] [illegible] controlled by [illegible]

[2] Dr Pindell served as surgeon in the Continental army He removed to Kentucky in 1814

[3] On the 20th of July 180[illegible] Hon John Randolph, M C from V[illegible] [illegible] the citizens of H[illegible]

P[illegible]her Samuel
Rahauser, Rev Jonathan, pastor German Reformed Church
Reynolds, Capt John, clock and watchmaker
Reynolds, William, spinning wheel and chair-maker
R[illegible]bardet, James (of Baltimore), teacher of dancing
R[illegible]our & Binkley, merchants
Rochester, Col Nathaniel, postmaster
Rohrer, Frederick, farmer
Schmucker, Rev George, Lutheran pastor
S[illegible]h, Peter, shoemaker
S[illegible]th, Geo shoemaker
Steele, Benjamin, stocking weaver
Schnebly, Dr Jacob, sheriff 1802 to 1804
Stoner, Michael, tavern-keeper
Stonebreaker, George, shoemaker
Shure, Peter, farmer
Shall, George
Simpson Alexander, jeweler, watch and clock-maker
S[illegible], George C, scrivener
Sharkey, George, carpenter
Smith, George, painter and glazier
Shene, Henry, tavern-keeper
S[illegible]k, George
S[illegible] Thomas, tinman and tavern keeper, house, "Sign of the Golden Swan"
Sleigh, Samuel, plasterer
Sleigh, John, blacksmith
Shrine, Samuel, school teacher
Stull, Capt Daniel, mill owner
Sample, Christian, blacksmith
S[illegible]mus, Henry dealer in mill supplies
Shryock, Samuel, saddle, cap, and harness maker
Stull, John I
Stull, Otho H W
Stull, William B
Townshend Henry, tailor and habit-maker
Tibbs, Capt Moses
Vogelsang, George, potter
Williams, Otho H, clerk of Circuit Court
Watt, John
W[illegible]land Charles, saddler
Woltz, Dr Peter
Waugh, Archibald M, scrivener
Woltz, Samuel, clock and watchmaker
Woltz, William, cabinet maker
W[illegible]sey, T, physician
Young, Samuel, physician
Young,[1] John R, physician
Young, P C, teacher
Young, John, teacher
Yerger Michael, saddle and harness maker
Yakle, Jacob, tin-plate worker

Besides the inhabitants just named, who represented a population of at least three hundred and fifty white inhabitants, and there were probably nearly as many more whose names cannot now be gathered, Hagerstown of that day boasted of four church edifices, viz Protestant Episcopal, German Reformed, Lutheran, and Roman Catholic,[2] the newspaper offices of the *Maryland Herald* and *Elizabethtown Advertiser*, *Elizabethtown Gazette*, and the *German Western Correspondent*, the court house, jail and market buildings, Dietrick's Circulating Library, Mount Moriah Lodge of F and A M, a military company termed the Washington Blues, and a well equipped fire company (The United)

Referring to the files of the *Maryland Herald* and *Hagerstown Advertiser*, we find that the following were residents of Hagerstown during the years from 1805 to 1815, inclusive

Anderson, Franklin, attorney at law
Ashcum, Mr, teacher
Artz & Emmert, merchants
Adams, Henry earthenware manufacturer
Armor, William, tailor
Amba, William, manufacturer of blacking
Albert, John, butcher
Brent, William L, attorney-at law
Bayly Samuel, conveyancer, afterwards an inn keeper
Brumbaugh, George, tavern keeper and brewer
Beall, John L, classical teacher
Brown, William, editor of the *Hagerstown Gazette*
Bowart, George, brick maker
Brendle, George, master cordwainer
Barr, David, tinner
Binkley, George, merchant
Beecher, William, grocer
Barnes, Samuel W, house painter
Brown, Jesse, inn keeper
Bovey, Jacob
Bell, William D, editor of the *Torch Light*
Beeler, Samuel
Buchanan, Judge John
Bean, George, tavern keeper, house "Sign of the Rising Sun"
Beltzhoover, George, tavern keeper
Beecher & Neid, merchants
Beigler, George, baker
Bradshaw, John, wheelwright and chair maker
Bell, Peter, earthenware manufacturer
Creager, Henry, saddler
Creager, John saddler
Cake, John, brewer
Cezerone, Mr, dancing teacher, also painted portraits at ten dollars each
Cramer, Peter, farmer
Crissinger, John proprietor of hack
Cromwell (Nathan) & Martin (A B), merchants
Downey, William, physician
Doyle, George, saddler
Dixon, William, farmer
Dickey, W, agent Antietam Woolen Manufacturing Company
Dillman, Henry, market clerk
Edwards, P, teacher
Ebert, John comb maker
Embich, Philip, blue dyer
Eichelberner, Theobald carpenter
Eichelberner, Mrs F milliner and mantua-maker
Emmert, George, merchant
Edwards, Thomas tavern-keeper
Fo[illegible]e, Abraham, hatter
Freaner John master cordwainer
[illegible]

[1] Son of Dr Samuel Young He died June 8, 1804, at the age of twenty four years

[2] A sect known as the [illegible] Imperialists also had a meeting house in 1806

Fechtig Christian, tavern keeper, the "Coffee House," "Sign of Columbus"
Fechtig, L
Feague, Mr, tavern keeper
Funk, Henry B, merchant
Gelwick, Charles, brewer
Gear, John, proprietor of livery stable
Glossbrenner, Peter, tavern-keeper, house,[1] "Sign of the Billiard table"
Greiner, William, gunsmith
Generes William, Jr, dancing-teacher
Geisendorfer, Mrs, milliner
Groff & Kausler, cordwainers
Glassbrenner, Adam, carpenter
Hilliard, Christopher, merchant
Humrickhouse, Peter blacksmith
Hall, Thomas B, attorney-at-law
Hanenkampft, Arnold, physician
Howard, John, tailor
Harry, John and George, merchants
Hoffman John, master cordwainer
Hammond, William physician
Harry, David, Jr, wagon-maker
Harman John, cordwainer
Harbaugh, Thomas, agent Antietam Woolen Manufacturing Company
Hughes, John H, & Co, merchants
Hawken, Jacob
Hunt, Job, coppersmith
Herr, Samuel carpenter
Henneberger, John and Christian, cabinet-makers
Hatfeld, A, & Co, shoe manufacturers
Hager, George and Jonathan merchants
Humrickhouse, Frederick, silver-plater
Humrickhouse, John
Hager, Samuel, saddler, also tavern-keeper
Harry, John & Co, tanners
Heffleich & Nead, merchants
Irving, Rev Thomas P, pastor Episcopal Church
Irwin, G H tavern keeper, "White Swan Inn"
Irwin, Joseph, barber and umbrella-maker
Justus, Peter, teacher
Kissinger (J) & Artz (P), merchants
King, Abraham, blacksmith
King, John, wagon-maker
Kausler & Graff, merchants
Kissinger & Emmert, merchants
Kennedy, Hugh and John, merchants
Kay, James, teacher
Keen, Knighn & Ragan, hatters
Kreps, George, cabinet maker
Kitchen, Uriah, teacher of penmanship
Kinsell, Frederick, barber
Kuhn Leonard
Kealhofer, John and Henry, saddlers, etc
Klink, George
Keller & Rohrer, merchants
Kurtz, Rev Benjamin
Lighter Abraham
Little David, tailor
Little, Joseph, plow and wagon-maker
Lantz, Christian, tavern-keeper
Lee, William
Linton, Joshua
Lynes (James) & Fuel (Thomas I), coach makers
Lantz, Christian, & Co, merchants
Leopard Adam, tailor
Lewis, Capt William, a veteran of '76
Langnecker Christian
Lawrence, Otho attorney-at law
McComas, Zaccheus
Miller (Geo) & Gibbs (Edward A), cotton spinners
McCall, J, teacher
McLaughlin, P, teacher
McCleery, John, teacher
Martin, Samuel, [illegible]
Martiney, George
Mayer, Michael I
Mayer & Irwin, merchants
Martin, Anthony B, & Co, druggists, etc
May, Daniel, son in-law of John Gruber
Middlekauff & Julius, merchants
McCardell, William
Mason, William T T
Martiney, John, spinning-wheel and chair-maker
Mendenhall, L B, teacher
Nead, Matthias, grocer
Post, Thomas
Post, Rev Frederick
Posey, Nathaniel, hatter
Price, L, tavern keeper
Perrin & Sweitzer
Pettit, Samuel, tavern-keeper, "Sign of Wheat sheaf"
Price (Samuel D) & Hussey (George), merchants
Ringgold & Boerstler, merchants[2]
Rawlins, Mrs Ann, teacher
Richard Daniel, earthenware-manufacturer
Rohrer & Barr, tanners
Roushkulp, Samuel, hatter
Robertson, William, instructor of military school
Ragan, John, Jr, lumber dealer
Rea, Aaron P teacher of penmanship
Rohrer & Motter, tanners
Strause, Henry, inn-keeper "Sign of the U S Arms"
Seitz, John inn-keeper, "Sign of the Buck"
Shaffner, Charles and Matthias, tanners
Smith, George, inn-keeper
Sholl, Jacob, rope-maker
Scoggins, John, harness maker
Stallsmith, John cordwainer
Smith, George, merchant
Schaeffer, Rev Solomon
Smith, Peter, auctioneer
Snyder, Anthony, bridle, bit, and stirrup maker
Savler, Jacob, inn keeper
Snavely, John, earthenware manufacturer
Sweitzer, Benjamin
Sholl & Butler, rope manufacturers
Shank, George, Jr, harness maker
Schiller, Christopher, painter and glazier
Shryock, Col Henry
Shryock, Capt George, pump maker
Sprigg D
Trovell, Peter, weaver
Totwiller, Jonathan, auctioneer
Watterson, George, attorney at-law

[1] [illegible]

[2] They removed their [illegible] goods to Col Samuel Ringgold's [illegible] where they continued the busi[illegible]

[illegible], Maxwell, teacher.
[illegible], George, cabinet-maker.
[illegible]ld, Philip.
[illegible], Arch. M., tobacco-manufacturer.
[illegible]ney, A., auctioneer.
[illegible] (O. H.) & Ragan (John, Jr.), rope-manufacturers.
[illegible], William, cordwainer.
[illegible], John, druggist.
[illegible]man, Perry, harness-maker.
[illegible], John, blacksmith.
[illegible] & Crawford, cordwainers.
[illegible] (L. C.) & Fechtig (F., Jr.), ladies' shoemakers.
[illegible]el, John.
[illegible]y, John, sickle-maker.
[illegible]ster, Frederick, butcher.
[illegible], Benjamin, tailor.
[illegible] & Van Lear, physicians, druggists, etc.
[illegible]merman, Gotlieb, pump-maker.

On Jan. 26, 1814, the Legislature passed an act "to alter and change the name of Elizabeth Town, in Washington County, to Hager's Town, and to incorporate the same." By this act Elizabeth Town was changed to Hagers Town and made an incorporated town. The body corporate consisted of a moderator and four other commissioners, who were elected annually from among the "free white male citizens of the town." They were to be not less than twenty-five years of age and have a freehold estate in the town. They were empowered to elect a clerk and assign him his duties, and to allow him a salary not exceeding sixty dollars per annum. The commissioners were entitled to receive two dollars per day for every day that they met to transact the business of the town. They were to meet upon the business of the town at least four times in every year,—on the third Monday in April, in June, in September, in December,—and oftener if they deemed it necessary. The commissioners were also authorized to appoint a treasurer of the corporation and to affix his salary. The ordinances were orderd to be published at least once in some German and English newspaper printed in the town. The commissioners had power to regulate by ordinance all the public affairs of the town, and to levy on all taxable property in the town and its additions a sum annually not exceeding twenty-five cents on every hundred dollars' worth of taxable property in any one year, and apply the taxes so collected to the expenses of the corporation. The act of 1814 was amended by an act passed Jan. 18, 1815, Feb. 1, 1817, and Jan. 23, 1818, which gave additional powers to the commissioners.

The following have been the corporate officers of Hagerstown since 1814:

Moderators.—1814–15, Henry Lewis; 1816, Archibald M. Waugh; 1817, George Shryock; 1818, Seth Lane; 1819, John Hershey; 1820, Thomas Quantrill; 1821–22, Daniel Schnebly; [illegible].

Clerks.—1814–18, George Bower; 1819–23, George Brumbaugh; 1824, Joseph Graff.

Commissioners.—1814, Henry Lewis, Richard Ragan, George Brumbaugh, Charles Shaffner, and John McIlhenny; 1815, Henry Kraffhoffer, Henry Lewis, David Harry, G. H. Irwin, and George Emmert; 1816, David Harry, Archibald M. Waugh, Charles Shaffner, John Kennedy, and Peter Humrickhouse; 1817, George Shryock, Charles Shaffner, John Hershey, Archibald M. Waugh, and John Schleigh; 1818, John Kennedy, John Hershey, Peter Humrickhouse, Thomas Shuman, and Seth Lane; 1819, George Brumbaugh, John Kennedy, William Kreps, John Hershey, and Theobald Eichelberger; 1820, John Reynolds, George Brumbaugh, John Schleigh, Thomas Quantrill, and George Martiney; 1821, William Heyser, Daniel Schnebly, Theobald Eichelberger, Charles Shaffner, and George Brumbaugh; 1822, Thomas Post (First Ward), Daniel Schnebly (Second Ward), Charles Shaffner (Third Ward), George Brumbaugh (Fourth Ward), John Reynolds (Fifth Ward); 1823, John Albert (First Ward), George Bean (Second Ward), John Hershey (Third Ward), George Brumbaugh (Fourth Ward), George Martiney (Fifth Ward); 1824, John Albert (First Ward) George Bean (Second Ward), John Hershey (Third Ward), George Brumbaugh (Fourth Ward), John Freaner (Fifth Ward).

On the 22d of March, 1848, the Legislature passed an act which changed the corporate body of the town to a mayor and five councilmen, "to be styled the Mayor and Council of Hagerstown," with all the powers heretofore granted to the moderator and commissioners. The mayor was to be elected for two years, and the councilmen (one from each ward) for one year. The compensation was to be the same as formerly allowed to the moderator and commissioners. By the act passed Feb. 4, 1850, Hagerstown is mentioned for the first time as "Hager's City." The mayors of Hager's City since 1859 have been as follows:

1859, D. G. Mumma; 1860, J. Cook; 1862, William Ratcliff; 1863, William Beirshing; 1864–65, John Cook; 1866, William Beirshing; 1868–70, William M. Tice; 1872, E. W. Funk; 1874, C. E. S. McKee; 1876–78, William S. Swartz; 1880, John D. Swartz.

Members of Common Council.—1865, Thomas A. Boult, William Hall, Wm. H. Protzman, M. S. Barber, R. Sliker; 1866, M. S. Barber, Thomas A. Boult, William Hall, R. Sliker, Wm. H. Protzman; 1868, George S. Miller, Thos. A. Boult, M. J. Kinyon, Daniel White, Robert Warner; 1869, M. A. Berry, Upton Rouskulp, M. J. McKinnon, John D. Swartz, Jonathan Middlekauff; 1870, George Fechtig, George Lias, Upton Rouskulp, John D. Swartz, M. L. Bowman; 1871, George Fechtig, Joseph E. Loose, Upton Rouskulp, John D. Swartz, M. L. Bowman; 1872, M. A. Berry, Lewis Schindle, Lewis Delamater; 1878, Joseph H. Firey, J. W. Mousch, D. F. Hell, John D. Swartz, John W. Boward; 1879, Joseph H. Firey, D. F. Hall, Lewis Delamater; 1880, Charles M. Futterer, Henry Deanberger; 1881, J. C. Roulette, Joseph H. Firey, D. F. Hall.

Early Notes and Reminiscences.—In 1805 there were about two hundred and fifty houses on Washington, Potomac, [illegible], and Franklin

Streets They were nearly all built of logs, very substantial and roomy, and a very few were of brick Upton Lawrence, Samuel Hughes Mr Brent, and John Thomson Mason, the elder, were the principal lawyers Brent and Otho Stull, who succeeded Mr Beltzhoover as the proprietor of the Washington Hotel, fought a duel in 1805, in Virginia, and Brent was shot in the knee Old Dr Frederick Dorsey attended them as their surgeon Joseph I Merrick removed to Hagerstown soon after, and was a very brilliant lawyer

Two of the oldest houses in Hagerstown are Kirschtenfeter's, on Potomac Street, built by the elder Knapp in 1778, and the stone house now occupied as the office of the Hagerstown Agricultural Works, on South Washington Street, which was built in 1781

From time immemorial Tuesday has been observed as "public day" in Hagerstown The same custom prevails in most of the other county towns of Maryland, but in Hagerstown it has always been marked with peculiar observances Even at the present day the people from the surrounding country assemble from miles around in order to transact their business and discuss the political situation On these occasions peripatetic "fakirs" ply a thriving trade in "thimble-rigging" and other games shrewdly calculated to deceive the unwary and ease them of their cash, and the whole town is full of bustle and excitement

Harry Cookus was one of the oddities of Hagerstown about seventy years ago He was a large, corpulent man, weighing considerably over two hundred pounds, and was always strolling about, apparently waiting for something to turn up He had been a recruiting sergeant and a soldier in the war of 1812 His favorite occupation like many other prominent citizens in the town, was cock fighting, and his elation or depression as his favorite chicken conquered or was vanquished is described as having been manifested by the most ludicrous writhings and contortions Jacob Yeakle, who carried on the business of tinsmith in a log house on West Washington Street, was also a most peculiar character He kept several fine horses, and rode with the practiced ease and skill of an Arab

When the post-office became vacant by the death of William Krebs, who had been postmaster for many years, there was quite an exciting contest among a number of applicants for the vacancy As there was then no direct travel between Hagerstown and Washington City, except on horseback, each of the candidates started themselves or dispatched couriers to the capital to procure the possession of the desired vacancy Yeakle was employed by Daniel H Schnebly to carry his application to the seat of government Some of them got the start of Yeakle, but he overtook them on the banks of the Monocacy beyond Frederick Town, and while they were waiting to be ferried over he plunged his horse in, swam the river, arrived in Washington first, and procured the appointment for his employer, and came back triumphant ahead of them all Charles Ohlwein also achieved a local reputation by his bluntness in discharging the rather delicate duties of a constable On one occasion he had a bill against a certain "very respectable" gentleman to collect, and instead of approaching him privately, blurted out one day in the street, Say, Mr ——, I've got a warrant for you" The "very respectable" gentleman was, of course, highly indignant, and the constable, concluding that he was the wrong man for the place, gave up his position and returned to his trade, that of a stonemason Maj Benjamin Galloway, who lived on the southwest corner of Washington and Jonathan Streets, in the house now occupied by E W Mealey, was another man of peculiar characteristics He was a graduate of Eton College, England, and often prided himself upon that fact He was quite a politician, and was always in his element when there was any political excitement He was somewhat erratic, but always honest He was frequently desirous of a seat in the Legislature but having but few of the elements of popularity about him, he was often defeated or ruled out On one occasion, however, after the death or resignation of a member of the Legislature, he was returned to fill the unexpired term He was a man of strong prejudices, and vented his feeling against his opponents in placards and in doggerel verse, which he read aloud in the streets whenever he could obtain an audience to listen

Considerable excitement was created one day in Hagerstown, about 1805, by the announcement that the old Episcopal church was haunted The report arose from the fact that a large black dog got into the building on Sunday and went to sleep without being observed When he awoke the door was locked, and his howls and frantic efforts to get out alarmed the neighborhood It is a curious evidence of the prevalence of superstition at the time that the people generally jumped to the conclusion that the church was inhabited by ghosts It was also gravely asserted that when the door was opened the dog sprang over the heads of twenty men

An even more significant illustration of the superstition then prevailing is found in the conduct of the people immediately after the execution of the three Cott[illegible] Some of th

spectators, we are told, struggled fiercely for fragments of the ropes with which the men were hanged. Their object in striving to get possession of them was to treat them as "charms" against disease or misfortune. It is asserted that the bodies of the executed men were stolen from their graves by resurrectionists and dissected by local physicians. Upton Lawrence, the principal lawyer for the defense of the criminals, is described by Dr. W. H. Grimes as having been a genial, whole-souled man, of medium size, with dark complexion, piercing black eyes, black hair, and very pleasing address.

Old "Oak Spring" has been a famous local resort in Hagerstown for a great many years. It is situated on West Franklin Street, and the water flows from beneath the roots of an ancient oak, which is the only one remaining of the original forest. It is related that an aged Indian, who passed through Hagerstown about 1816, recognized the spring as the one at which he had often slaked his thirst in his boyhood. The water is famous for its sweetness and purity. In 1856 the town authorities inclosed the lot in which it stands with a substantial brick wall. The bowl of the spring was deepened and enlarged and a stone wall was thrown up around it.

One of the local features of Hagerstown was the general muster of the county militia, which was held in October of every year. There were sometimes over two thousand men in line.

A peculiar custom, by no means indigenous to Hagerstown, however, was the suspension, on the eve of St. Patrick's day, in some conspicuous place, of a dummy figure, popularly denominated a "Paddy," with the view of annoying the Irish residents of the town and vicinity. On several occasions this foolish practice provoked serious disturbances, which, however, ended without bloodshed.

In 1805, George Strouse built about the first of the large brick houses. It was located at the corner of Locust and Washington Streets. About this time there was a race-track out Locust Street on the Funkstown road, and races were run in four-mile heats. Among those most active in getting them up were Alfred Kline, Jonathan Hager, John Ragan, Maj. Bailey, Thomas McCardell, and William Fegley. Purses of five hundred dollars were contested for, and the meetings were held every fall. Horses from distant points, such as New York, Virginia, and Kentucky, as well as horses nearer home, from many different localities, took part in them. Betting was very heavy. Lafayette and White Stocking were famous winners. White Stocking slipped, while running one day in a light rain, and broke his leg. Gen. Samuel Ringgold had fine horses, but he was unlucky, and never won more than two races. Gen. Williams had a course at Springfield, and used to train his horses there. Gen. Williams was very fortunate in his races.

Stone's tavern, on Potomac Street, was a notorious gambling resort about 1805. George Stone is described as having been very gentlemanly and pleasing in his manners, but was always determined to win his intended victim's money, whether by fair means or foul. It is related that on one occasion a woman entered the tavern and "collaring" her husband, picked up his hat and forced him to leave with her. The tavern was the scene of many fierce brawls and violent deeds.

The old jail stood in an alley between Washington and Franklin Streets, and was an old log house, looking very much like a stable. There were little peep-holes for windows, and the door was thickly studded with huge spikes. Elbert, the jailer, was shot previous to 1805, by a prisoner named Orndorf, while the latter was endeavoring to escape.

About 1805 both town and country people were very sociable, and balls were frequently given at the Globe Tavern. No man was asked to an apple-butter boiling, which was one of the favorite amusements, unless he would consent to dance.

"Fourth of July" was always celebrated at Hagerstown in early days with a good deal of enthusiasm. In 1810, for instance, it was observed with a parade, volleys of artillery, and a dinner at the Cold Spring, south of the town. The cannon used was a large one, which lay unmounted on the hill just east of the town. It subsequently burst, killing one man, George Bower, and so seriously wounding another, George Gelwig, that his leg had to be amputated.

In olden times there was a singular custom prevalent among the people of designating a person by the trade or occupation followed, or from some particular habit or act done or committed. For instance, an old man who drove a two-horse team and did most of the local transportation about town was known everywhere by the pseudonym of "Bopple Miller," from a habit he had of talking a great deal in a loud and rapid manner. He had small bells attached to his horses' necks, so that any one having hauling to do knew by the tinkling of his little bells that "Bopple Miller" was about. A man residing in West Washington Street, who supplied his customers with bread and cakes, was always known as "Berker Hanns." So a man who had appropriated some bacon not legitimately his own was ever afterwards known as "Speck Martin."

"Cold Spring," situated about half a mile from

Hagerstown near the Williamsport road was a very popular resort in early times The water gushes forth from the rock in a pure and limped stream, and the surroundings are of a charming character The spring is situated in a sequestered dale, and was the favorite resort for picnics, etc

Negro "runaways" appear to have been very numerous about 1817, as we find in a single number of the Hagerstown *Herald* under date of Sept 17, 1817, four advertisements of rewards for slaves who had disappeared The rewards offered were ten, twenty, and fifty dollars

In the Hagerstown *Herald* of Feb 7, 1799, Samuel Hughes, Jr, advertised for sale "the house wherein I now keep my office, with a valuable lot belonging thereto"

Fishing in the Antietam was a favorite sport in the latter portion of the last century, so much so that, in 1798 John Booth, Elijah Cheney George Powell, John Shafer, Jeremiah Cheney, Nicholas Broadstone, Matthias Springer, Nicholas Frankhauser, John Smith, Joseph Cheney, Stephen Foller, Edward Breathed Elizabeth South, Christian Binckley, Jacob Sharer, and John Claggett advertised that as very great inconvenience had arisen from sundry persons fishing in the creek, they would not thereafter allow any persons to fish in the creek unless they first obtained permission

On Wednesday afternoon, at two o'clock, Oct 20, 1790, the approach of President Washington was announced in Hagerstown Capt Rezin Davis, of the light horse, with a number of the prominent citizens of the place, met the distinguished visitor about three miles from town and escorted him to its environs, where they were met by a company of infantry commanded by Capt Ott The Presidential escort was then conducted through Washington Street amid the welcoming shouts of the inhabitants who lined the sidewalks and filled the windows, doors, etc, along the route of the procession The bells of the city were also rung during the march President Washington was conducted to Beltzhoover's tavern, where "an elegant supper was prepared by direction, of which the President and principal inhabitants partook" In the evening the town was illuminated, bonfires appeared in all quarters and every demonstration of joy and enthusiasm was indulged in At the close of the banquet the following toasts were drunk, accompanied with a discharge of artillery and volley of musketry to each

1 "The President of the United States"

To this toast Gen Washington responded in a few fitting remarks, and proposed the toast, "Prosperity to the inhabitants of Elizabeth Town"

2 "The Legislature of the United States"

3 "The land we live in"

4 "The river Potomac"

5 "May the residence law be perpetuated, and Potomac view the Federal City"

6 "An increase of American manufactories"

7 "May commerce and agriculture flourish"

8 "The National Assembly of France"

9 "The Marquis de Lafayette"

10 "May the spirit of liberty liberate the world"

11 "The memory of those who fell in defense of American liberty"

12 "The memory of Dr Franklin"

13 "May America never want virtuous citizens to defend her liberty"

The feast terminated before ten o'clock, and on the following morning, at seven o'clock, Gen Washington resumed his journey to Williamsport, where, after a short stay, he took his passage down the river to his home at Mount Vernon During his visit at Hagerstown the following address was presented to him by the citizens

"To the President of the United States

"Sir,—We, the inhabitants of Elizabeth Town and its vicinity, being deeply impressed with your illustrious character, and sensibly aware to your resplendent and innumerable virtues, hail you a hearty welcome!

"We are happy to find that notwithstanding your perils, toils, and guardianship, you are still able to grant us this first, this greatest of all favors,—*your presence*

"We felicitate ourselves on your exploring our country and as you already reign in our hearts, so we should think ourselves doubly blessed could we have the honor to be included within your more especial command and jurisdiction,—within the grand centre of virtues

"Our beloved Chief! Be pleased to accept our most grateful thanks for this honor conferred on us And may the disposer of all things lengthen out your days, so that you may behold with satisfaction the virtue and prosperity of the people whom you have made free! And when you come to close the last volume of your illustrious actions, may you be crowned with a crown not made with hands!

"Thomas Sprigg,
"Henry Shryock,
"William Lee,
"In behalf of the whole"

The President returned the following reply

"Gentlemen,—The cordial welcome which you give me to Elizabeth Town, and the very flattering expressions of regard contained in your address, claim and receive my grateful and sincere acknowledgments

"Estimating as I do the affection and esteem of my fellow citizens, and conscious that my best pretension to their approbation is founded in an earnest endeavor faithfully to discharge the duties which have been assigned me I cannot better repay their confidence than by assuring them that the same impartiality which has heretofore directed, will continue to govern my conduct in the execution of public trusts

"I offer sincere wishes for your temporal happiness and future felicity

"G Washington"

Washington Street, Hagerstown, was so named because Gen. Washington and his escort passed down that thoroughfare in proceeding through the town.

June 8, 1791, the editor of the Washington *Spy*, Hagerstown, announced that he had been disappointed in receiving any papers from Baltimore by the last post. "The reason assigned by the person who carries post was that owing to a horse-race at Baltimore the post-office was shut."

On the 28th of December, 1792, the commissioners of Hagerstown prohibited the firing of guns and pistols in the town.

In March, 1792, by direction of the town commissioners, the Hagerstown market was ordered to be opened at sunrise on each market-day, of which notice was to be given by ringing the court-house bell.

On the 4th of May, 1801, Albert Gallatin, then recently appointed Secretary of the United States Treasury, stopped at Hagerstown with his family, on his way to Washington to assume the duties of his office.

In 1794 the following advertisement appeared in the Washington *Spy*:

"100 DOLLARS REWARD.

"Whereas, some evil-disposed person or persons set up at the Market-House in this Town, last night, an advertisement in the German Language, charging us with having cut down the pole lately erected in this town, termed by the deluded authors of its erection a liberty-pole, and commanding us in menacing terms to erect another in its stead, or that we shall surely be put to death by the sword. And as the authors of said dangerous threats ought to be brought to condign punishment, We hereby offer a reward of One hundred Dollars to any person or persons who will give such information of the author or authors of the said advertisement, or of the person or persons who set up the same, that he or they may be brought to justice; to be paid on conviction.

"HENRY SHRYOCK,
"REZIN DAVIS,
"ALEXANDER CLAGETT,
"ADAM OTT,
"JOHN GEIGER,
"JACOB SHRYOCK,
"WILLIAM WILLIAMS."

This pole had been erected by the whisky insurrectionists, but was cut down at night, and, as shown above, a placard was posted ordering some of the principal inhabitants, mentioning them by name, to put up another pole, but the threat was not regarded except by the publication of the above reward.

One of the earliest celebrations of the Fourth of July was that which took place in 1796. The Washington Blues, commanded by Capt. Jacob Schnebly, the mechanics of the town, and other citizens took part in the parade. A public dinner was given, and toasts were drunk, accompanied by discharges of artillery. Thomas Sprigg was chairman of the meeting, and Daniel Heister was vice-president. In the following year, on the same anniversary,

"a number of citizens, and the Washington Blues, Capt. J. Schnebly, met at Mr. Hager's, at Fountain Inn. After the usual evolutions they proceeded to Mr. Smith's tavern to dinner, where a number of toasts were drunk."

On the 15th of June, 1798, the companies of light infantry commanded by Capts. Rutledge and Davis held a meeting at Hagerstown, and adopted an address to the President concerning the threatened troubles with France. The correspondence which resulted was as follows:

"TO THE PRESIDENT OF THE UNITED STATES:

"Permit us, sir, the companies of infantry commanded by Capts. Rutledge and Davis, of Washington County, and the State of Maryland, to join the general voices of our countrymen in addressing you upon the present important and critical situation of our national affairs; to express our sincere affection for the government of our choice, and our firm determination at every hazard to support it. While we contemplate with the liveliest emotions of sorrow the unhappy issue which your late attempts to accommodate our differences with France are likely to experience, we cannot but derive peculiar consolation from the belief that nothing has been left undone on your part to have insured them a very different fate, and we are persuaded, sir, if the friendly disposition manifested by your instructions to our envoys at Paris had been met with a similar disposition on the part of the present rulers of that nation, the two republics would ere now have been reunited in the closest bonds of amity and friendship. Under this impression, and with full confidence in the wisdom, patriotism, moderation, and energy of our united councils, we deem it our duty to declare that we will support with promptitude and firmness such measures as they may find themselves indispensably called upon to adopt for our mutual defence and security. We hope, sir, that this address will not be less acceptable because a majority exercising the rights of freemen have not only indulged, but freely expressed their opinions, in opposition to certain measures of government. It ought, we conceive, rather to enhance its value, inasmuch as it offers to the world an animating proof that the American people, however they may differ in their sentiments as to their interior arrangements and regulations, will always be found ready to unite and defend with their lives and fortunes, the honor, dignity, and independence of their country, whenever they shall be assailed by any foreign power on earth.

"Signed by desire and in behalf of said companies.

"ABRAHAM RUTLEDGE,
"DENNIS DAVIS,
"*Captains.*

"*June 15, 1798.*"

The following was President Adams' reply:

"TO THE COMPANIES OF INFANTRY COMMANDED BY CAPTS. RUTLEDGE AND DAVIS, OF WASHINGTON COUNTY, IN THE STATE OF MARYLAND.

"GENTLEMEN,—I thank you for this address, presented to me by your representative in Congress, Mr. Baer.

"The sincere affection you express for the government of your choice, and determination at every hazard to support it, are the more acceptable, because a majority of you, exercising the rights of freemen, have not only indulged, but freely expressed their opinions in opposition to certain measures of govern-

ment I cannot, however, upon this occasion, forbear to lament the gross misrepresentations which have misled so many citizens in their opinions of many measures

"JOHN ADAMS

"PHILADELPHIA, June 25, 1798"

In the Hagerstown *Herald* of Feb 14, 1799, the following advertisement appeared

"To be rented, for one or two years, and possession to be given the 1st of April next, the house and lot where George Diffenderfer now lives, three doors above Mr Shill's tavern

"This stand is well calculated for a tradesman, as there is a convenient brick building adjoining the house very suitable for a store For terms apply to

"HENRY HOOVER

"HAGERSTOWN, Feb 14, 1799"

In the same paper of July 7, 1802, appeared the following

"All persons are hereby forewarned from taking assignments on certain bonds given by me to Capt Peregrine Fitzhugh, late of Washington County, in consideration of a tract of land called Chew's Farm, which I purchased from him, he not having complied with his agreement concerning the same I am, therefore, determined not to pay said bonds, or any part thereof until he shall have complied with his contract, unless compelled by law

"HENRY LOCHAR

"WASHINGTON COUNTY, July 5, 1802"

On the Fourth of July, 1799, Capt Schnebly's troop of Washington Blues, after parading and going through various evolutions, repaired to Peck's Garden, in Hagerstown, where they had dinner and drank a number of toasts The garden was handsomely illuminated, and was visited by a number of citizens On the same day "a respectable number of the citizens," together with a company of the Twenty-fourth Regiment of militia, assembled "at the usual place of parade," before Maj Ott's, "to celebrate the national anniversary" Maj Ott presided, and Capt Douglass acted as vice-president After appropriate addresses, etc, they marched to "Mr Rohrer's Spring, near town, where a handsome entertainment was prepared for them" Having refreshed themselves, "they withdrew to an adjoining eminence and drank a number of toasts, accompanied with cheers and discharges of cannon and small-arms"

Gen Washington's death was announced by the Hagerstown *Herald* in the following extract from the *Rights of Man*, published at Frederick

"FREDERICKTOWN, Tuesday evening,
"9 o'clock, Dec 16, 1799

"Disagreeable as the talk is to me, I think it is my duty to announce to the public the dissolution of his excellency George Washington, who died at Mount Vernon (of a few hours' illness) on Sunday morning last about 5 o'clock

"This intelligence was received by two honest countrymen, who left Georgetown yesterday at 12 o'clock, and stopped at Maj Miller's [illegible] for this evening A [illegible] arrived from Alexandria near the same hour, who corroborates the melancholy circumstance, and leaves us to lament it is but too true

"PRINTER OF THE RIGHTS OF MAN"

As soon as the news reached Hagerstown a meeting was held, at which it was resolved to have a funeral procession in Washington's honor on Friday of the following week Elie Williams occupied the chair, and Nathaniel Rochester acted as secretary The following resolutions were adopted

"*Resolved*, That Messrs Elie Williams, Adam Ott, N Rochester, Jacob Schnebly, George Walts William Fitzhugh, Samuel Ringgold, David Harry, Josiah Price, Thomas Sprigg, and Daniel Heister be appointed a committee to make the necessary arrangements for, and to superintend, the said Procession, and that they or a majority of them meet at the Court-house, on Saturday next, to make the arrangements

"*Resolved*, That the Committee consult the Rev Mr Smucker, Rev Mr Rauhauser, and Rev Mr Bower on the oration to be delivered on the occasion

"*Resolved*, That the Military and other citizens of Washington County be, and that they are hereby invited to attend and join the said Procession

"*Resolved*, That the secretary have these proceedings published in the papers of this town to-morrow

"By order
"N ROCHESTER, *Secretary*"

In May, 1800, while the Tenth Regiment United States troops, commanded by Col Moore, were stopping at Hagerstown on their way from Carlisle to Harper's Ferry, a duel was fought between Capt Gibbs and Lieut Franklin, in which the former was wounded in the side, but not seriously

In January, 1807, a duel was fought in Shepherdstown, Va, between Wm L Brent and Otho H W Stull, both of Washington County Mr Brent was wounded in the leg

Early in July, 1801, ten prisoners broke out of the jail They were Wm Dunn, John Johnson, James McDeid, Michael Ward, J McCreery, Andrew Dowd, John Johnson, Wm Harvey, John Lynch, and William Jolly

Five Indian chiefs of the Pottawotamie tribe passed through Hagerstown in December, 1801, on their return from Washington City, accompanied by a Capt Wells, who acted as their interpreter Among them were the powerful chiefs "Little Turtle" and "The Toad" In January of the following year the "kings" of the Delaware and Shawnee tribes, nine chiefs and two attendants, passed through Hagerstown In March of the same year fifteen Indians of the Seneca tribe passed through Hagerstown Among them was the well-known chief Cornplanter Doubtless many similar delegations passed through Hagerstown from time to time

[illegible] Randolph [illegible] Hagerstown

July, 1803, and was tendered and accepted a dinner at John Ragan's tavern.

In 1804 the Fourth of July was celebrated with the usual artillery salute and the parade of the Washington Blues, under the command of Capt. Otho H. Williams. A public dinner was also served at Ragan's tavern. Gen. Thomas Spring was president of the day, and Capt. Otho H. Williams vice-president. The Declaration of Independence was read by Benjamin Galloway, after which a number of toasts were drunk. On this occasion Sebastian Fink was severely wounded in the thigh by the bursting of a swivel.

George Clinton, Vice-President of the United States, visited the town in June, 1809, while on his way to New York.

In 1821 it was proposed to erect a statue to Gen. Washington in the public square, but no further action appears to have been taken in the matter. The monument was to have been of Washington County marble, and was to have included a fountain, etc. At the November election of that year the sum of one hundred and six dollars was contributed by the voters in the different districts towards the completion of the Washington monument at Washington City, D. C.

During Lafayette's visit to this country in 1824 it was proposed that he should visit Hagerstown among other places in Maryland. In September of that year a public meeting was held at the court-house in Hagerstown, at which William Gabby presided, and J. Schnebly acted as secretary. The following resolutions were adopted:

"The citizens of Hagerstown and Washington County, participating in the general joy of the American people on the appearance among them of the distinguished and gallant Gen. Lafayette; deeply impressed with the importance and value of his services in their eventful and glorious struggle for independence; and being desirous of manifesting in a suitable manner their veneration for his person and character, have therefore

"*Resolved*, That Col. O. H. Williams, Col. F. Tilghman, the Hon. John Buchanan, William Price, and V. W. Randall, Esqs., be appointed a committee on behalf of this meeting to wait on Gen. Lafayette on his arrival in the city of Baltimore, tendering him their hearty congratulations, and inviting him to visit their county.

"*Resolved*, That the proceedings of this meeting be published.

"WILLIAM GABBY, *Chairman*.

"JACOB SCHNEBLY, *Secretary*."

At a subsequent meeting the committee reported their proceedings, as follows:

"That they repaired to Baltimore upon the arrival of the general at that place, and on Friday, the 8th inst., were introduced to him, at his quarters in Light Street, by the city authorities.

"Col. Williams, as chairman of the committee, then addressed him as follows: 'General, the [illegible] grateful enthusiasm which has been elicited by your recent return to the United States is without parallel in the history of any modern people; it is not confined to our populous cities, but has diffused itself to the remotest borders of our country.

"'The citizens of Washington County, Md., largely participating in this general feeling, have deputed us to wait on you, and directed us to tender to you their warm and heart-felt congratulations on your return to a country whose rights you defended and whose liberties you greatly assisted to achieve. They have also directed us to present to you an invitation to visit them so soon as it may suit your convenience. Although we cannot compete with our brethren of the great commercial cities on the sea-board in the reception we shall give you, yet so far as the pure incense of grateful hearts, and the frank and cordial hospitality of republican manners can supply the deficiency of pomp and splendor, we can affirm there shall be nothing wanting.

"'We feel proud, general, of the distinction conferred on us, in being made the organ of a community of freemen, through which this slight tribute of respect is presented to the champion of liberty in both hemispheres, the early and strong advocate of America, and the bosom friend of the illustrious father of our country. Be pleased to accept the assurance of our great personal esteem and affection.'"

To this address the general replied that he felt highly gratified by an invitation from the citizens of Washington County, and that he would, with great pleasure, pay them a visit at the earliest opportunity.

At a meeting of the citizens of Washington County at the court-house in Hagerstown, on Wednesday, the 27th of October, 1824, Col. David Schnebly was called to the chair, and R. M. Tidball was appointed secretary. The following resolutions were proposed and adopted:

"*Resolved*, That the following citizens be appointed a committee to make such arrangements and adopt such measures as they may deem necessary for the reception and entertainment of Gen. Lafayette in Hagerstown, viz.: John Hershey, Dr. F. Dorsey, Richard Ragan, Frisby Tilghman, William Heyser, P. Humrickhouse, Col. William D. Bell, Joseph Graff, Stewart Herbert, George I. Harry, George Brumbaugh, Alexander Neill, Jacob Schnebly, John Robertson, John Harry, Charles Shaffner, John Albert, F. Anderson, John Carry, A. Johnston, Samuel Hughes, Henry Kealhofer, Eli Beatty, Dr. J. Reynolds, T. Eichelberger, John Ragan, George Shryock, Jacob Motter, Daniel Schnebly, Maj. J. Reynolds, John Gruber, J. V. Swearingen, David Artz, Dr. W. D. Macgill, M. Rickenbaugh, Henry Dillman, Frederick Stover, David Clagett, William Gabby, George Shiess, John Witmer, Peter Seibert, William Webb, Col. D. Schnebly, Thomas Keller, Andrew Kershner, John Bowles, Henry Ankeny, John Barnett, Arthur Jacques, B. Kershner, Thomas C. Brent, James H. Bowles, Robert Mason, Benjamin Bean, Anthony Snyder, Dr. M. A. Finley, Daniel Weisel, Dr. W. Van Lear, William Dickey, Col. J. Blackford, Dr. Joseph C. Hays, Jacob Miller, Dr. T. Hammond, George Bedrick, William P. Stewart, Dr. Ezra Slifer, Jonathan Shafer, M. Stonebraker, Alexander Mitchell, Dr. C. Boerstler, Henry Shafer, W. Fitzhugh, Jr., Elias Davis, Jacob I. Ohr.

"*Resolved*, That the members composing the Committee of Arrangements be notified by the chairman and secretary of their appointment, and be requested to meet at the town-hall on Saturday, the 6th of November, at four o'clock A.M., for the purpose [illegible] appointment.

"*Resolved*, That the Military Committee be respectfully requested to communicate with the Civil Committee of Arrangements on the object in contemplation"

On motion of D G Yost, it was

"*Resolved*, unanimously, that a committee be appointed to address the representative in Congress from this District in behalf of this meeting, and to request him to use his influence in procuring a suitable appropriation from our government for Gen Lafayette for his meritorious services in our Revolutionary struggle David G Yost, William Price, and Frisby Tilghman, Esqs, were appointed the committee

"*Resolved*, That the above proceedings be published in the several newspapers of the place for the information of the citizens generally

"DAVID SCHNEBLY, *Chairman*
"R M TIDBALL, *Secretary*"

At a meeting of the officers attached to the Second Brigade, Maryland Militia, convened at the town hall in Hagerstown on Saturday, the 30th inst, Gen Samuel Ringgold was appointed chairman, and Capt V W Randall secretary The following preamble and resolutions were adopted

"*Whereas*, The acceptance by Gen Lafayette of the invitation given him by the citizens of Washington County will soon afford them an opportunity of testifying their respect and affection for our illustrious guest, it becomes necessary that arrangements should be made forthwith for receiving and welcoming him in such a manner as will evince an attachment to the benefactor and friend of our country Therefore

"*Resolved*, That the following officers be a Committee of Ways and Means Col Weller, Col Toule, Lieut Col Wolf, Majs Rohrback, Hall and Sprecker, Capts Barr, Swearingen, Beall, Funk, Kessinger, Grosh, Brookhartt, Donnelly, Fletcher, Baker, Barnett, Lieuts Hallman, H Shafer, and J Zwisler

"*Resolved*, That the Committee of Arrangements and the Committee of Ways and Means assemble at the town hall on Saturday next at 10 o'clock A M, to confer with the committee appointed on Wednesday last by the citizens, and to co operate with them in making the necessary arrangements for the reception of Gen Lafayette"

At the reception in Frederick a company of riflemen from Hagerstown, commanded by Capt V W. Randall, was present, and elicited the warmest commendation for its drill and evolutions

Gen Lafayette was unable to visit Hagerstown, but we give the foregoing account as a curious picture of the times and of the spirit then pervading the counties of Maryland

On the 15th of July, 1826, it was resolved "that the citizens of Washington County be requested to meet at the court-house at Hagerstown on Saturday, July 22d to arrange for a public tribute of respect to the memory of John Adams and Thomas Jefferson" In accordance with this resolution "a large and respectable meeting" was held at the court house in Hagerstown on the 22d of July, 1826 David Schnebly was elected chairman, and Thomas Kellar secretary T[illegible]

"Having heard with the deepest sorrow and most unfeigned regret of the deaths of Thomas Jefferson and John Adams, and desirous to evince to the world in common with our fellow citizens of these United States the great veneration and respect we entertain for the characters of those illustrious patriots of the Revolution, for their pure and exalted worth, pre-eminent talents, and long and faithful public services, we therefore resolve as follows, viz

"1st *Resolved*, That there be a public procession in Hagerstown on Tuesday, the first day of August next

"2d *Resolved* That the citizens of this county be requested to wear crape on their left arm for sixty days, and the ladies be solicited to wear badges of mourning for the same period

"3d *Resolved*, That the clergymen of the different congregations of this county be requested to preach an appropriate sermon in their respective churches at such times as may be convenient

"4th *Resolved*, That in order to impress the minds of the rising generation with the virtues and characters of those illustrious dead, the teachers of the public schools in this county be requested to read at least once a week for two months obituary notices of those benefactors of mankind

"5th *Resolved*, That the committee of arrangements request their fellow citizens to deliver an eulogium on the above solemn occasion, also request two clergymen to address the Throne of Grace

"6th *Resolved*, That the citizens of Hagerstown be requested to abstain from all business during the procession

"7th *Resolved*, That the chairman of this meeting, together with such other persons to be named by him, constitute the committee of arrangements, who shall have power to carry the foregoing resolutions into full effect, and make all other arrangements which the occasion may require

"8th *Resolved*, That the bells in the different churches in this county be tolled for one hour on the morning and evening of the day of the procession"

The following persons composed the committee of arrangements "David Schnebly, chairman Samuel Ringgold, William Gabby, Frederick Dorsey, Thomas Kennedy, George W Boerstler, Otho H Williams

The committee held a meeting soon afterwards and agreed on the following order of procession

Chief Marshal
Revolutionary officers and soldiers in carriages
Committee of arrangements
Choristers
Orator and officiating clergy
Clergy of the county
Moderator and commissioners
Judges and officers of the court
Judges of Orphans' Court
Judges of Levy Court
Members of the bar
Physicians
Students of divinity, physic, and law
Teachers, with their pupils
Representatives in Congress
Delegates of the General Assembly
Officers of the United States army and navy
Militia officers
Band
Masonic brethren

The procession rested with its right near the court-house, at the intersection of Washington and Jonathan Streets, and moved up Jonathan to Franklin Street, down Franklin to Potomac, up Potomac to the "stone" church, then countermarched down Potomac Street to the Lutheran church, which it entered in the same order. The officers of the army, navy, and militia appeared in uniform with crape on the left arm, and the usual badges of mourning on their side-arms. The ladies of the choir and the young girls attached to the different schools were dressed in white with a black ribband around the waist. One gun was fired at dawn, another at twelve o'clock, and a third at sundown, and the bells of the different churches tolled during the procession, which was under the direction of a chief marshal on horseback, with his assistants on foot, all of whom were designated by white sashes and wands.

A public meeting was held at the court-house, in Hagerstown, on the 24th of July, 1827, at which a committee was appointed to meet the engineers employed in surveying the proposed route of the Baltimore and Ohio Railroad and give them all the information in their power. William Gabby was selected as chairman, and William D. Bell was chosen secretary. After remarks by Dr. John Reynolds and Col. Otho H. Williams, the committee was appointed, as follows:

District No. 1, Col. John Miller, Robert Clagett; No. 2, Joseph Hollman, Col. Daniel Malott; No. 3, Gen. Samuel Ringgold, Col. Henry Fouke; No. 4, Lancelot Jacques, Henry Fiery; No. 5, John Johnson, Anthony Snider; No. 6, David Brookhartt, Elie Crampton; No. 7, M. W. Boyd, John Welty.

In December, 1827, the Hagerstown *Torch Light* announced that Lieut. Dillahunt and a party of engineers had examined the route through Harman's Gap to the Antietam, thence down the stream to a point below Funkstown, and thence to Williamsport.

On the 4th of July, 1828, a number of gentlemen from Hagerstown repaired to the Black Rocks on South Mountain and celebrated the day in festive fashion with a good dinner, toasts, etc., and encamped there all night.

In the Hagerstown papers of April 7, 1841, there appeared an advertisement of Wise's twenty-sixth balloon ascension, announced to take place on the afternoon of the 24th day of that month from the prison-yard in Hagerstown.

During the performance of the circus company of J. M. June & Co., in Hagerstown, one evening early in October, 1850, some persons outside pulled down part of the [illegible] circus people and the aggressors. The combatants fought for some time with dirks and clubs, and a number of persons were injured more or less severely.

On the 22d of May, 1872, Alexander Smith, Wesley Finnegan, and Frederick Fridinger were crushed to death by the falling of a wall of the court-house, which they were engaged in taking down. Smith was forty years of age, and lived on the Cavetown turnpike near Hagerstown. He served through the civil war, and was at the battle of Gettysburg. Finnegan was thirty-six years old, and had also been a Federal soldier. Fridinger was about seventeen years of age, and his father lost his life when the court-house was burned during the previous fall. On the Sunday following the catastrophe the three funerals took place, and the bodies were borne to the grave in a procession of Odd-Fellows, the Fire Department, and many citizens.

Hagerstown, like many other communities throughout the country, was invaded by the centennial epidemic, and a Martha Washington tea-party was the result. The entertainment was given on the evenings of the 18th and 19th of March, 1875, at Lyceum Hall. The following ladies were appointed on the various committees which managed the affair:

President, Mrs. Louis F. McComas; Vice-President, Albert Small; Treasurer, Miss Agnes McAtee; Secretary, Miss Nellie Gibson. Members of Committees: Mrs. J. E. McComas, Mrs. P. A. Brugh, Mrs. J. H. Seymour, Miss Lizzie Hagerman, Miss J. E. McComas, Mrs. Kate Fechtig, Mrs. Charles Bechtel, Miss Laura Kepler, Mrs. P. A. Brugh, Mrs. E. C. Bushnell, Mrs. P. B. Small, Mrs. N. B. Scott, Mrs. George Freaner, Mrs. S. D. Straub, Miss M. Robertson, Miss Lily Syester, Miss Ada McComas, Mrs. J. H. Van Lear, Mrs. David Zeller, Miss S. Thompson, Mrs. F. M. Darby, Miss Minnie Moon, Miss Cephie Herbert, Miss Nannie Cushwa.

In addition to these ladies the following gentlemen took part: Messrs. W. S. Herbert, C. A. Small, Albert Small, W. Harry, and Samuel Ogilby.

The executive committee consisted of Messrs. Straub, Small, Brugh, Kendall, and Rev. J. C. Thompson. Mrs. P. A. Brugh, Mrs. John H. Seymour, and Miss Nannie F. Little had charge of the fancy table. Among the interesting articles exhibited were the following: An oil-painting of Gen. Washington when forty-five years old, painted by Charles W. Peale, by order of Congress while the army was encamped at Valley Forge in 1777, which now belongs to Gen. T. J. McKaig; also a head of Washington woven in silk at Paris on a Jacquard loom (which was [illegible] fine-tuned as a steel-

engraving, also an engraving of Gen Otho Holland Williams, the founder of Williamsport, a portrait of Commodore Jesse Duncan Elliott, born in Hagerstown in 1780, a portrait of John Henry Purviance, secretary to President Monroe, with an autograph letter from Samuel Purviance, also Robert Parker's certificate of membership in The Society of the Cincinnati, dated 1785, signed by George Washington On the right of the stage was an oil-painting of Mrs Gen Heister, the only daughter of Jonathan Hager, painted in 1780

On the east side of the stage was an Indian wigwam, in front of which was a table containing a number of articles of Indian workmanship On the left of the stage there hung an engraving of President Monroe, taken from an original painting by I Van der Lyn On the stage was a chair one hundred and seventy five years old, which belonged to Mrs Dr Bates, and a pair of arm chairs, imported by Col Daniel Hughes, of Antietam, in 1770, and another which belonged to Mrs Murdock, of Frederick, one hundred and fifty years old, also a memorial picture worked in silk by Rev Mrs Thompson's grandmother, Mrs Hannah Upham, in 1797, a fac-simile of Washington's headquarters at Valley Forge, an autograph receipt from Gen Washington to Mr William McAnulty, dated Jan 25, 1774, two autograph notes to Capt Van Lear inviting him to dinner, a copy of "John Drane's Poems," published in 1560, and a number of other ancient volumes In addition to these were the watch of Jonathan Hager (founder of Hagerstown) and the watch of Mrs Gen Heister, his daughter, together with articles worn by Capt Jonathan Hager, of the Revolutionary army, including two embroidered vests, shoe buckles, knee buckles, suspender-buckles, stock-buckle, brooch, saddle ornaments, and Mrs Hager's shoe buckles Besides these the exhibits comprised a copper kettle used by Lafayette while in the Revolutionary army, presented by him to Col John Holker of his staff, a medallion on satin of Louis XVI and Marie Antoinette, presented to the Marquis de Lafayette, and given by him to Col John Holker, agent of the French government during the Revolution, a pair of brass candlesticks, one hundred years old, a pair of solid silver goblets, one hundred and fifty years old, which belonged to Col Hughes, a set of teaspoons and sugar-tongs, which were brought from Switzerland one hundred and twenty years before, an amber bead bracelet, which had been worn by six generations in succession, a set of tablespoons made in Hagerstown from Spanish half dollars in 1785

Among the china was a water-pitcher with the coat of arms of the thirteen original States painted in 1778 [illegible] a butter dish and cup and saucer which were used in the family of President Monroe, a small box made out of the table on which the Declaration of Independence was written, a pitcher made the year after Washington died to commemorate his death, which has on it a quaint picture, three dishes which were used in the Mitchell family when Maryland was a colony, an old set of china, used in the Price family over a hundred years, a set of spoons sent during the reign of George III to Mrs Keallhofer's great grandfather, then a missionary on the island of Jamaica [illegible]

The various supper-tables were ranged around the sides of the room, each table having the name and motto of the State it represented on the wall above it The ladies in charge of the tables were

Virginia, Misses Lily Cushwa and Lily Syester, New York, Misses Rene Boullt and Ada McComas, Connecticut, Misses Lily Seymour and Lottie Croynin, South Carolina, Misses Eva Foulke and Maggie Keller, Rhode Island, Misses Lily Scott and Nannie Ogilby, Massachusetts, Misses Kate Marshall and Sue Love, North Carolina, Mrs Allan Yingling and Mrs W H A Hamilton, Delaware, Mrs S D Straub and Miss Sue Herbert, Pennsylvania Misses Bettie Zeller and Cephie Herbert, Maryland, Misses Emma Herbert and Mary McComas, New Jersey, Misses Nannie Cushwa and Lily Ogilby, New Hampshire, Mrs E C Bushnel, Mrs P B Small, and Misses Nellie Gibson, Eliza Keller, Annie Campbell, V Dunn, and Mary Small, Georgia, Mrs Kate Fechtig, Mrs A K Syester, Mrs C Bechtel, Mrs Joseph B Loose, and Misses Louisa Johnson and Laura Keppler

On the 6th of June 1872, the first passenger-train over the Western Maryland Railroad from Baltimore arrived in Hagerstown The run was made from Baltimore, 86 miles, in three hours and twenty minutes with seven stoppages The train comprised the locomotive, which was tastefully decorated with flowers and flags the baggage-car, and a new passenger-car The latter contained a number of officials and invited guests, among whom were the president of the company, James L McLane, and his predecessor in that office, George F Bokee, Robert Hooper, secretary and treasurer, J T Rigney, general superintendent, B H Griswold, agent at Hagerstown, Mr Hutton, chief engineer, Col Longwell, of Carroll County ex-Senator Biggs, of Frederick, John Welty, one of the Washington County directors, Col Fred Raine, of the *German Correspondent*, of Baltimore, and others The conductors in charge of the train were Messrs Besler and R Stoner The train was met by the mayor of Hagerstown and other [illegible] assemblage of

After being entertained at the residence of ... Harris, one of the directors, near the town, the ... inspected the site of the depot, not then ...ted and the officers of the company concluded the ...ations for its purchase with its owner, Richard ... In the afternoon they took dinner at the ...ington House with the mayor and a number of ... citizens of Hagerstown, after which they re...ed to Baltimore

The Fourth of July, 1876, was observed in Hagers... with elaborate and appropriate ceremonies Two ...rms were erected,—one in the southwest angle of ... public square and the other in front of the court-...se The former was erected for the school of ...ph Updegraff, and the latter by the citizens of ...own—a spacious structure, which nearly covered half of the pavement in breadth, and was nearly ... full length of the building

Bunting was extensively displayed all over the town, ...d banners of all nations were flung to the breeze ... eve of the Fourth was celebrated by the school of J...ph Updegraff on their platform on the square, ...ich was brilliantly festooned, and illuminated with ...inese lanterns interspersed among American flags ... exercises consisted of music led by Prof Mentzer, ...clamations, recitations, and songs by members of the ...ool, which continued until after ten o'clock, and were attended by a very large concourse of citizens

At midnight the bells sounded a simultaneous peal, ...ich was accompanied by the steam-whistles of the A...ricultural Works on Washington Street Next ...rning the procession formed as follows

Chief Marshal, R C Thornburg

Aids, M M Gruber, H A McComas, Oliver Ridenour, Dr J ... P Scott, and L Delamarter

The line moved up West Washington Street in the following ...der

Hyser's Silver Cornet Band

Omnibus containing thirteen of the oldest citizens, repre...ting the thirteen original States of the Union as follows ...ederick Humrickhouse, Samuel Newman, Samuel Ridenour, ... Eichelberger, D Zeller, W V Hemil, Frederick Feehtig, Geo ... Kissinger, Michael Frieso, Wm Miller, George Hayes, Charles Martin, Eli Mobley

Choir of young ladies,

...presenting the thirty-eight States, dressed in white, red, and blue and seated on platform drawn by six horses

Judges of Circuit Courts

... R H Alvey Hon D Weisel, Hon William Motter, Hon George French, in carriage

Orator and reader of the Declaration, in carriage

..., of the Orphans' Court, president and members of the board of county commissioners, and mayor and council men, in carriages

Army of the Republic—Reno Post—on foot

Parrott gun, mounted and officered and manned by Lieut S ... Dr Crowther ... ... William ...

Three fired ... ... at sunrise, thirty eight at noon, and balance at sundown, at the rate of four rounds to the minute, from Cannon Hill, east of the town

Boys and Girls Reading Association

Winter's Band

Boys in red, white, and blue

Western Enterprise Fire Company,

in full force, dressed in uniform, red shirts, engine caparisoned and decorated, drawn by four grays, and truck decorated with a picture of Washington

Field piece on wheels, cast at Mount Ætna Furnace in 1774, under command of Capt Wm Sands

Junior Engine,

trimmed with flags, and drawn by four grays

First Hagerstown Hose Company,

upon whose engine was created a temple of liberty, with appropriate canopy, under which was seated the goddess (Miss Sophie Updegraff), with the four corners guarded by Continental officer (Master Leith Cooper), Continental soldier (Master Fred Weiss), naval officer (Master Max Weiss), and sailor (Master Walter Mobley) in the uniform of the Revolution

First Hagerstown Hook and-Ladder Company, with truck and equipments

Gumbert & Mobley carriage in wagon, and attended by work men

"Centennial Band"

Willbide's cigar-works on wheels, and in full operation

Hopple's pottery-works on wheels, and in full operation, turning out pots, and distributing them to the crowd in passing

McComas' coal wagon with load of coal

Hagerstown foundry, represented by a pyramid of castings, drawn by two horses

Singer's sewing-machine on wheels

Bone meal in bags

From the manufactory of Ames, Manning & Ames, at the old Hager mill, the bags packed in large hay wagon and drawn by a full team

Hagerstown Agricultural Implement Manufacturing Company,

led by the president, vice-president, treasurer, and secretary, in carriage drawn by two bays Following this, drawn by distinct teams, were 1 Cutting machine, 2 Cutting-machine, 3 Cutting-machine, 4 Reaper, 5 Drill, 6 Drill, 7 Clover-huller in motion, 8 Workmen with their implements of labor appropriately festooned, and numbering in all forty men

Schindle & Co's leather-works

fitted up in three large wagons, with all of the hands performing their respective labors 1 Working out the leather and shaving it down, 2 Pegging shoes, 3 Sewing leather by machinery

Hagerstown Steam Boiler Company,

with a separator decorated and in working order

McKee & Bro.'s

wagon decorated with hardware

Wm Schlotterbeck,

wagon with emblems of his trade in stoves, etc

Citizens in wagons with appropriate banners

The procession having marched through the streets of the town according to programme, drew up in front of the court house, when the officers of the day the choir, and leading participants in the procession took their seats upon the platform, the Hon Daniel Weisel having been called upon to preside The young ladies ... ... occupied

the eastern division of the platform, the judges of the courts and other officials the western side, and in the centre were the aged men who represented the original States The music was rendered with effect, the Declaration of Independence was read by W H A Hamilton, of the Hagerstown bar, prayer was offered by the Rev S W Owen, of St John's Lutheran Church, and the oration was delivered by Hon A K Syester.

In the afternoon there was a procession of the different Sabbath schools, which concluded the day's proceedings The heat of the day had gradually intensified until five o'clock, the hour fixed for this parade, when rain fell for half an hour, delaying and interrupting the proceedings The ceremonies advertised had to be dispensed with on account of the rain, with the exception of the procession, which was formed in the following order by William H Seidenstricker, chief marshal, with his aides, consisting of the superintendent of each Sunday-school in line, as follows

First Reformed School—William Gassman, superintendent, 200 in line Left resting on Householder's corner

Presbyterian School—W H Herbert, superintendent, 75 in line South side Washington Street

St John's Lutheran School—John Bikle, superintendent, [illegible] in line East side South Potomac Street

United Brethren School—Mr Worst, superintendent, 75 in line Right resting on Beachley's corner

Methodist Episcopal School—J S McCartney, superintendent, 100 in line Right resting on Byers' corner, north side West Washington Street

German Lutheran School—Mr Brey, superintendent, 75 in line East Washington Street, right resting on Martin & Stover's corner

Second Reformed School—John Gassman, superintendent, 65 in line North Potomac Street, right resting on Gassman's corner

Trinity Lutheran School—Jacob Roessner, superintendent, 250 in line North Potomac Street, right resting on J D Swartz' corner

Updegraff's Practical School—Preceded by a drum corps, and each scholar wearing upon his breast a shield emblazoned with the "Stars and Stripes"

In all the procession numbered about twelve hundred and fifty scholars and teachers The line of procession shone brightly with numerous banners and flags, and various expressive devices and mottoes One of these was a large bell, a representation of Independence Bell, made entirely of natural flowers, which was borne by children of the German school

The line of march was from the public square to Antietam, Locust, Franklin, Walnut, Washington Streets to Square, headed by the drum corps and the Heyser Band, and thence by countermarch to the court-house

The display of fire-works was the finest, probably, ever witnessed in the town The illumination and decoration of houses was also very effective, though not so general as might have been desired

On the 31st of December, 1880, an entertainment was given at the Baldwin House by the gentlemen connected with the Shenandoah Valley Railroad, who had previously been entertained by the citizens at a banquet The men from the company's shops at Shepherdstown were brought over to decorate the large dining room of the hotel, and succeeded in making the apartment look very handsome and attractive The colors used were chosen with a view to represent the signals employed in the running of the trains, and the head light of a locomotive was also introduced in the decoration with striking effect Over the entrance were the words "Welcome, 1881," and bunting and evergreens were tastefully draped from the walls, ceiling, and chandeliers A locomotive was stationed so as to appear to be in the act of approaching, and on its head-light was the monogram "S V. R R" On the front of the engine the figures 1880 were so arranged that on the expiration of the old year the figures 1881 would instantly appear At midnight the engine-bell struck and the whistle sounded, announcing the arrival of the new year, and from the smoke stack a banner representing smoke, and bearing the inscription "1880," floated out and then disappeared, only to be followed by another bearing the inscription "A Happy New Year" About two hundred persons were present, and between ten and eleven o'clock dancing commenced A handsome supper was provided, including roast venison, olio, oysters, sweet breads, turkey, and desserts Music was furnished by John Ziegler's band from Baltimore, and the dancing continued until a late hour

---

CHAPTER XLV

RELIGIOUS DENOMINATIONS

As in Frederick County, the honor of having first introduced the Christian religion into the then wilds of Washington County cannot be definitively accorded to any one denomination, but the probabilities are that the Episcopalians were first on the field as an organized body, for it seems to be very clear that the English settlers from Southern Maryland anticipated the Germans and the Scotch-Irish by some years, and most of the Southern Marylanders belonged to the Establishment [illegible] were Catholic

[illegible], the Episcopal Church was established by law, and started out with everything to facilitate its proper organization. Churches of other denominations were founded irregularly and in various localities as circumstances dictated, but the growth of the Episcopal Church was in a logical order of development, and its history may be termed almost identical with that of the county itself. The Lutherans and the German Reformed and Presbyterian denominations also established permanent congregations in many localities at a very early period, while the Methodists, though considerably later on the field, developed rapidly into strong and flourishing communities.

Originally Washington County was part of All Saints' Protestant Episcopal, or, as it was then, Anglican, Parish, which was an offshoot of St John's, or Piscataway Parish. The latter began at the mouth of the Mattawoman Creek, on the Potomac, and ran up the said creek and the branch thereof to the utmost limits of Charles County, and thence ran with the county line to the line of the province, separating it from Pennsylvania, thence westward with that line to the boundary line separating Maryland and Virginia, and southward with that line to the Potomac River, down that river to the mouth of the Mattawoman, its beginning. In 1695 Prince George's County was created, embracing all the territory north of the Mattawoman Creek and the main branch of Swanston's Creek, or, in other words, all between the Potomac and the Patuxent Rivers. St John's accordingly fell into Prince George's County. In 1696 the Rev George Tubman was rector. He was presented in 1698 for bigamy and "sotting," and was suspended. Abraham Ford was made lay reader in his place, but in 1700, Mr Tubman was reinstated in the ministry, and in 1702 again became rector of the parish, and died soon afterwards. He was succeeded by the Rev Robert Owen, who did not continue long in charge. In 1704, Hickford Leman was employed as lay reader. Mr Owen, however, officiated in the church every other Saturday during part of the year. These services were continued some four years, if not longer. In October, 1708, it was ordered that a new church be built. On the 23d of June, 1710, the Rev John Fraser presented his appointment as rector. In 1726 a new parish, Prince George's, was erected out of St John's Parish. It was eighty miles in length and twenty in breadth. Mr Fraser died in November, 1742. Prince George's Parish embraced all the territory included in the then Prince George's County west of the Eastern Branch and East Fork of the Eastern Branch [illegible] Washington City, Georgetown, and [illegible] Montgomery County, part of Carroll, and all of Frederick, Washington, and Allegany Counties. It was a frontier parish, and at the time of its formation had not more than two thousand four hundred inhabitants. The first rector (1726) was the Rev George Murdoch, afterwards rector of All Saints', Frederick, which was created in 1742. The latter parish embraced all the territory north of Great Seneca Run River, and west of a line drawn from its head in the same direction to the head of one of the draughts of the Patuxent, comprising part of Carroll and Montgomery and all of Frederick, Washington, and Allegany Counties. At this time Washington County constituted part of All Saints' Parish, and was known as Antietam Hundred, or District of Frederick County. A chapel of ease was built in this district soon after that date, but in 1761 it was represented in a petition to the General Assembly that it was decayed, and built on so narrow and contracted a plan as not to be capable of holding one-third of the congregation willing and desirous to attend divine service there, and could not be enlarged with profit or convenience, so that it was absolutely necessary to rebuild it upon a better plan and with more durable materials. It is supposed that this was done, though without any legislative aid so far as can be ascertained. This was a frame building, situated about five and a half miles west of Hagerstown, and about a mile from the present site of St James' College. A graveyard still remains there. At a comparatively recent period the structure was transformed into a dwelling, and the late Rev Ethan Allen narrates that the "elder Dr Dorsey" (probably Dr Frederick Dorsey, Sr) told him that he remembered the old chapel well.

In 1770, by an act of Assembly of that year, the Antietam District of Frederick County was created a separate parish, to become such on the removal of the then rector, Rev Bennett Allen. The latter resided in Hagerstown, opposite the old chapel, and a curate officiated for him in the parish church at Frederick Town. Another curate had charge of St Peters' Church, in the Monocacy District. In the fall of 1776 the new county of Washington was created by act of the Provincial Convention, and the legal provision for the maintenance of the clergy was abolished. Thereupon Mr Allen relinquished the rectorship and returned to England. In accordance with the law of 1770, Antietam District now became Frederick Parish, and in 1806 the Diocesan Convention changed the name to St John's Parish embracing the whole of Washington County except the portion comprised in St Mark's Parish. In 1819 [illegible] Episcopa[illegible] [illegible] the Diocesan

Convention for leave to establish a separate congregation at that place This leave was granted and the new parish created Similar petitions were presented from St Thomas' Church, Hancock, in 1835, and from St Andrew's, Clear Spring, in 1839, and in both instances parishes were allowed to be formed Two years later the Episcopal College of St James was founded, the site being the old mansion of Gen Samuel Ringgold Congregations were also formed at Williamsport, Funkstown, Lappon's Cross-roads, and other thriving points

According to the journal of the Diocesan Convention for 1881 the register of the Episcopal Churches in Washington County at present is as follows St John's Parish St John's Church, Hagerstown, St Ann's Chapel, Smithsburg, Rev Walter A Mitchell, rector

College of St James St James' Chapel, Rev Henry Edwards, chaplain

St Andrew's Church, Clear Spring, Rev Coupland R Page, rector

St Mark's Church, Lappon's Cross-roads, Rev. Henry Edwards, rector

St Paul's Church, Sharpsburg, Rev Henry Edwards, missionary

St Thomas' Church, Hancock, Rev Henry Wall S T D, rector

Hagerstown is a city of churches, and no community of its size in Maryland can boast of as many handsome church edifices In point of architectural excellence, it is doubtful if its churches would not bear off the palm in competition with any of the rural cities in the whole country Especially beautiful and even imposing is St John's Episcopal church, belonging to the strongest religious congregation in the city, but several of the other churches are striking enough in their appearance to render any very marked distinction impossible The Lutherans, the Presbyterians, the Catholics, and the Methodists all have fine church buildings, which are really models of style, and finished in a uniformly handsome manner

The records of "The Vestry of Washington County" were begun on April 21, 1787, when "a number of the inhabitants of Washington County professing the Protestant religion of the Episcopal Church" met at the court house in Elizabeth Town (Hagerstown) and elected as vestrymen John Stull, Daniel Hughes, Alexander Claggett, Thomas Sprigg, Richard Pindell, Nathaniel Rochester, and Elie Williams On May 19th the vestry contracted with Henry Bowart for twenty-six thousand bricks for the church, and on June 2d they awarded to John Willar, at forty-five pound the contract for the [illegible] stood near what is now the southern end of Locust Street, and was a substantial brick edifice On June 21 1788 the following accounts for materials furnished for the edifice were submitted to the consideration of the vestry and were settled

	£	s	d
William and John Lee, 600 shingles and 25 pounds white lead	2	5	0
Hart & Rochester, scaffold, poles, hauling, etc	2	11	0
Rezin Davis, for nails and white lead	4	10	9
Alexander and Hugh Claggett for hauling	15	12	3
Alexander Claggett, for hauling	10	[illegible]	3
John Willar, for joiners' work	60	0	0
Frederick Alter, for mason work	43	10	0
Total	138	19	3

On June 25th the vestry examined and passed the following accounts against the church

	£	s	d
Dr Richard Pindell, for part of his account	2	8	3
Elie Williams	9	6	10
Alexander and Hugh Claggett, for 3500 bricks of Charles Hefiley	4	15	0
Henry Bowart, for bricks	37	10	0
John Scott, per account		7	6
Total	193	6	10

On April 13 1789, "a number of inhabitants of Washington County" again met at the court house, and elected as vestry Rev George Bower, Alexander Claggett, Thomas Sprigg, Daniel Hughes, Elie Williams Richard Pindell, and Hezekiah Claggett The church wardens appointed were Rezin Davis and Wm Gordon Col John Stull was allowed £24 16s 3d for "lyme, scantling, and hauling," Alexander Claggett £1 16s 3d for sundries for the use of the church, Alexander and Hugh Claggett, for sundries advanced for the use of the church, £6 8s 4d, and Frederick Alter ten shillings for altering a window in the church At the meeting of the vestry on May 11th of same year the collectors of subscriptions were directed to proceed by legal process against the subscribers who had not paid the amounts for which they had set down their names To collect actual money seems to have been rather difficult at that time and when, on May 18th, the vestry contracted with John Willar to erect a pulpit and lay floors for the sum of £25, in case the parish did not pay him, Alexander Claggett, Daniel Hughes, Hezekiah Claggett, Elie Williams, Thomas Sprigg, and Richard Pindell made themselves responsible for the money Hezekiah Claggett was appointed "to represent this parish as a lay deputy in convention to be held in Baltimore Town on the first Tuesday in June next" On Oct 5, 1789, the vestry meeting drew up a subscription paper "for the purpose of employing Rev George Bower to officiate for the term of one year" from Dec 1, 1789 [illegible] 5, 1790 the [illegible] meeting at the [illegible] vestry were re-

[illegible]ected except that Mr Bower was dropped and John [illegible]gram was elected Nathaniel Rochester was elected [illegible]ster of the vestry, and Daniel Hughes the lay delegate to the Diocesan Convention Capt Rezin Davis was appointed "to confer with a person to execute the duty of sexton, also to direct the grave-digger in what manner the graves are to be dugg (*sic*) in future" At the next meeting, June 7th, Rezin Davis informed the vestry that he had not been able to collect "any of the monies subscribed for furnishing the church," and Samuel Finley was appointed collector, and Rev Mr Bower was requested "to make use of every endeavor to induce those in arrears to discharge the sum due by them, and that he inform such as use further delay that necessity will prevent the vestry from granting further indulgence" On August 2d, Capt Rezin Davis reported that Titus Rynhart had agreed to act as sexton in return for the privilege of digging the graves in the churchyard Benjamin Claggett was appointed to collect moneys due the church and one-half the salary of Rev Mr Bower, which had been for some time in arrears, but at the vestry meeting on November 1st it was still unpaid, and Rezin Davis was appointed to assist Mr Claggett in raising subscriptions both for the pastor and the clerk, the salary of the former being now fixed at one hundred pounds per annum Charles O'Neal accepted the position of clerk, and the vestry agreed to pay him twenty dollars for his services for eight months, from April 1st to November 30th On Feb 7, 1791, Henry Grunwell was appointed to collect the pastor's salary and the balance due on the old subscription papers, for which he was to receive five pounds

The fourth vestry was elected by public meeting May 2, 1791, as follows Daniel Hughes, Alexander Claggett, Elie Williams, Richard Pindell, Hezekiah Claggett, William Gordon, and William Reynolds, who chose Rezin Davis and William Prather to be church wardens On September 19th, John Willar submitted to the vestry his account of forty-five pounds for erecting pews, additional gallery, glass rack, platform with steps, etc He was debited with £19 4*s* 8*d* already paid him, leaving the balance due £25 5*s* 4*d* Willar's family was in distress for the necessaries of life, but up to November 8th the vestry could pay him but £3 5*s* of the money due him, and William Reynolds was commissioned to collect the arrearages of subscriptions Solomon Rawlings was made sexton, and was allowed £3 yearly, in addition to the usual compensation for digging graves Of the latter he was to have a [illegible] the [illegible] of the vestry declaring [illegible] th[illegible]

may be necessary in the English Protestant Episcopal churchyard" Hezekiah Claggett and William Reynolds were directed to procure bags in which a collection shall be taken up by the church-wardens each church Sunday At the meeting on November 28th, Rev Mr Bower consented to remain as rector another year at the same salary, and it was decided to pay £7 10*s* to the clerk, and £5 to a collector of subscriptions On Feb 6, 1792, the vestry settled up Mr Bower's salary for 1790 and 1791, it appearing that they owed him £112 18*s* On Easter Monday, April 1, 1793, the meeting for the annual election of vestry, previously held at the court house, was convened in the church, and Elie Williams, Richard Pindell, Hezekiah Claggett, William Gordon William Reynolds, Samuel Finley, and Rezin Davis were chosen, who elected as church-wardens Alexander Claggett and Cephas Beale Rezin Davis was continued as treasurer, and Nathaniel Rochester as register Solomon Rawlings was voted £3 yearly for taking care of and cleaning the church, and Titus Rynhart was continued as grave digger The treasurer was ordered to pay Mr Bower £20 as soon as it could be collected, to enable him to finish his house On October 14th, Turner Gor was appointed clerk, and it was ordered that "no person attempt to assist him in the clerk's desk but such as he shall invite for that purpose" As the register was directed to serve a copy of the order upon a certain Mr Jones, it is probable that that gentleman had been intruding himself into the position There is no record of the election of vestry in 1794 On June 14, 1795, *The Spy* contained an advertisement of "a lottery to be held at Elizabeth (Hager's) Town, Washington Co to erect a church for the Episcopal congregation There were two thousand tickets at two dollars" the prizes amounted to three thousand dollars, and eight hundred dollars was raised The managers were Daniel Hughes, Thomas Hart, Elie Williams Henry Schnyock, Frederick Rohrer, Alexander Claggett, and Michael Fackler

July 6, 1795, the regular meeting of parishioners elected Elie Williams, Richard Pindell, Rezin Davis, John Claggett, Cephas Beale, Charles Ogle, and William Gordon[1] The record here speaks of All Saints' Parish for the first time On July 21st, Alexander Claggett and Cephas Beale were appointed trustees to superintend the building of an addition to the church In June, 1796, a corpse was stolen from the churchyard, and the vestry offered a reward of thirty dollars

[1] [illegible] pended list a[illegible]

for information leading to the arrest and conviction of the offender On Aug 13, 1797, the church and graveyard were consecrated by Bishop Claggett, who also on the same date confirmed the following persons Mary Stull, Sophia Rochester, Ann Miller, Lucinda Bower, Catherine Swearingen, Matilda Stull, Elizabeth Rawlings, Rebecca Hughes, Susanna Hughes, Elizabeth Hall, Margaret Taylor, Otho Williams, Joseph Williams, Holland Stull, Prudence Williams, Allen Dowlas, Phœbe Grieves, Sarah Owen, and Sarah Dowlas On November 6th the pews were sold to the highest bidders, as follows

			Price	Annual Rent
No	1	Daniel Hughes	$58	$30
"	2	Ignatius Taylor, Thomas Belt, and Charles Carroll	52	"
"	3	John Claggett	45	"
"	4	Samuel Ringgold	60	"
"	5	Elie Williams	58	"
"	14	Richard Pindell	26	15
"	15	Benjamin Claggett	30	"
"	16	William Elliott	26	"
"	17	Rezin Davis and Kennedy Owen	21	"
"	18	Nathaniel Rochester and Daniel Stull	15	"
"	20	John Ragan	20	"
"	21	Thomas Sprigg	25	"
"	22	Alexander Claggett	30	"
"	23	William Fitzhugh	30	"
"	9	George Bean	4	10
"	10	William Gordon	10	"
"	11	William S Compton	12	"
"	12	Edmund Rutter	12	"
"	13	Maurice Baker	14	"
"	24	William Fitzhugh	20	"
"	25	Peter Miller	12	"
"	26	Perry McCoy	11	"
"	27	John Dowlas	11	"
"	19	James and Griffith Henderson		"

Accounts of John Hooper for £101 3s, for joiners' work, and of Cephas Beale for £11 3s 6*d*, for the addition to the church, were passed In 1798, Mr Bower's salary as rector was increased to £150

The act of Assembly for the establishment of vestries in the parishes required that members of the Protestant Episcopal Church should be enrolled on the parish books a month before they could become eligible as vestrymen or electors of vestrymen The earliest enrollments made were on April 8, 1799, as follows Alexander Claggett, William Fitzhugh, Rezin Davis, Thomas Belt, John Carr, Griffith Henderson, Charles McCauley, Nathaniel Rochester, Otho Holland Williams, Eli Beatty, and Thomas Hallam Daniel Hughes, Sr, Robert Hughes, and John Claggett were enrolled on April 19th From November 6th, Mr Bower's salary was cut down from one hundred and fifty pounds to four hundred dollars per annum On Sept 21, 1801, the vestry gave notice that they would prosecute delinquent pewholders who did not promptly settle up their arrearages Still there was a deficiency in the finances

In 1803, [illegible] fact, a lottery scheme was successfully carried out for the benefit of St John's congregation, which was superintended by the following commissioners, who had been authorized by the Legislature to conduct the drawings Col N Rochester R Pindell, J Taylor, R Hughes, and O H Williams The amount of money to be raised was five hundred dollars, "to finish the church edifice of the Episcopal All Saints' Parish in Hagerstown"

On Feb 28, 1805, it was resolved to abandon the system of pew-rents and to resort to the old plan of soliciting subscriptions to meet the expenses of the parish Rev Thomas P Irving was appointed rector Sept 22, 1813, at a yearly salary of four hundred dollars, of St John's Church, All Saints' Parish, as the title then appeared in the records, and on Nov 13, 1814, he was authorized to charge five dollars for officiating at funerals, and four dollars for each christening From this year onward the name appears as St John's Parish Mr Irving resigned the pastorate in February, 1816, because of ill health, and on August 27th, Rev. Joseph Jackson was appointed his successor, but on July 26, 1817, the vestry rejected a resolution to reappoint him, and on October 1st refused him the use of the church to preach a charity sermon for the benefit of the Female Society for Instructing Poor Children In a letter to Levin Mills, church-warden, in reference to Mr Jackson's request, the vestry say that they "have determined, on account of the conduct of that gentleman on Sunday last, to hold no communication directly or indirectly with him" On Oct 25, 1817, Rev John Curtis Clay was chosen rector, his incumbency to date from Jan 1, 1818 At the vestry meeting Aug 31, 1818, it was resolved to raise by subscription a fund for the building of a new church, the subscribers to have the choice of pews according to the amount of their subscriptions On May 10, 1819, the pastor's salary was increased to one thousand dollars per annum On May 12, 1821, one-fourth of the subscriptions for the new church edifice were called in, and Otho H W Stull was appointed to solicit aid in Baltimore On July 2d Eli Beatty, George Bean, Otho H Williams, and Franklin Anderson were appointed the building committee, and a lot on Jonathan Street was bought for six hundred dollars from Christian Fechtig for the site of the new church The committee were authorized to contract with Daniel Sprigg for one hundred thousand bricks with George Bean for stone for the foundation, with Mr Stout for the stone and brick-work and to purchase all the requisite materials Rev Mr Clay resigned the pastorate [illegible] mber 16th, [illegible]

... notified him that they would regret to lose his ...s, and would make any possible exertions to ... them. Mr. Clay removed to Pennsylvania, and Mr. Shaw filled the pulpit for a few months, ... the election of Rev. George Lemmon on Oct. 1822. The salary was fixed at eight hundred ..., and on June 17, 1823, the pews in the new ... were sold, as follows:

		Price.	Annual Rent.
	Frisby Tilghman	$545	$50
	Benjamin Galloway	450	45
	Frederick Dorsey	302	40
	Otho H. Williams	300	50
	Thomas Belt	300	45
	Richard Ragan	212	30
	Eli Beatty	211	30
	John Reynolds	200	"
	Samuel Ringgold	"	"
	Thomas Buchanan and John R. Dall	"	"
	Upton Lawrence	"	"
	Samuel Hughes, Jr	"	"
	Daniel Sprigg	150	"
	David G. Yost	151	"
	John B. Claggett	152	"
	Thomas Grieves	150	"
22.	Franklin Anderson and John Ridout	"	25
27.	George Bear	"	30
	John T. Mason	125	20
	Henry C. Schnebly	"	"
	John Booth	105	18
46.	John Buchanan	"	"
15.	Susan and Esther Hughes and J. I. Merrick	80	12
	Levin Mills and William Fitzhugh, Jr	156	25
	Henry Barnett	76	12
	George C. Smoot	125	20
	William Price and Otho Lawrence	100	16
21.	Otho H. W. Stall	100	16
	William O. Sprigg	125	25

The new church was consecrated June 18, 1825, ... Bishop James Kemp, assisted by Rev. William Armstrong. On Dec. 4, 1827, Rev. Mr. Lemmon ...ered his resignation, and on the following June ...h, Rev. Robert B. Drane was called to the pastor... and in 1834 he opened a school to increase his ...me. He was permitted to officiate every other ...day in the church at Williamsport, and on April ..., 1835, the vestry ordered that a parsonage be ...ilt. He resigned April 26, 1836, and in reply to ... question from the vestry, he wrote that it would be ...possible for him to remain because "of the mali...ous and vindictive conduct of some who had set themselves to destroy my reputation and influence as ... minister of the gospel"; and that such a course on ... part "would involve a sacrifice of the happiness ... me too near and dear to me to be thus destroyed." ... July 29th the vestry extended a call to Rev. Mr. ...man, of Cecil County, Md., but he declined it, ... Rev. John Wiley became Mr. Drane's successor. ... March, 1838, Mrs. Henrietta Johns was engaged ... "play upon the organ" for fifty dollars per annum. On March 24, 1840, the vestry passed a resolution ...olving their ... ...

April 1st, but permitting him to occupy the rectory, and receive a salary at the rate of seven hundred dollars annually for six months from that date, and in case he claimed possession of the church after April 1st, they would not hold themselves liable to him for his emoluments, and would proceed to expel him by law. Joseph I. Merrick, as counsel for Mr. Wiley, addressed a letter to the vestry denying their legal right to terminate the contract, or reduce the salary without the rector's consent, and Mr. Wiley himself refused to accept the terms offered him, declaring that he would do nothing which might be construed into an acknowledgment of their right "thus summarily to cast a minister of the gospel with his family upon the world." The vestry, however, proceeded to elect Mr. Wiley for six months from April 1st, thus reaffirming their theory that they had no authority to install a pastor for an unlimited time. Eli Beatty, Otho H. Williams, David G. Yost, William H. Fitzhugh, Richard Ragan, and Thomas Schnebly voted for the resolutions, and Dr. Frederick Dorsey against them. At the election for vestry on Easter Monday, April 20, 1840, the pastor's party were victorious, choosing Dr. Frederick Dorsey, John S. Hamilton, Peregrine Fitzhugh, Joseph I. Merrick, and Col. Frisby Tilghman, and the controversy was terminated by the passage of a resolution declaring Mr. Wiley to be the lawful rector of the church; but he stated that as he had vindicated the right of the position which he had taken he offered his resignation, to take effect in September. The contention had done much harm to the church, and the vestry requested Rev. Dr. Whittingham, then recently elected Bishop of Maryland, to make his residence in Hagerstown, and act as rector of St. John's until it could be restored to peace and prosperity. The bishop declined the proposition, and recommended for the vacancy Rev. Theodore B. Lyman, who was elected on Oct. 12, 1840, but the vestry stipulated that the contract should only run from year to year, and might be terminated by either of the parties at six months' notice. Mr. Lyman accepted the conditions, although the bishop regretted that they had been imposed. By vigorous effort the church was relieved of the worst of its embarrassments, and on Nov. 14, 1842, Rev. Russell Trevett was made assistant rector. In 1843 a fund of over seven hundred dollars was raised and repairs made on the edifice, which was dedicated anew by Bishop Whittingham on October 26th. In December, Col. Tilghman and Charles Macgill resigned because of their inability to agree with the other vestrymen concerning the position of the furniture in the chancel, ... E. A. ...ms, Richard

Ragan, Jervis Spencer, Alexander Neill, Jr, M W Boyd, Eli Beatty, and William B Nelson, withdrew from the church On April 5, 1845, Mr Trevett resigned as assistant rector, and Dwight E Lyman was chosen in his place The gentlemen above named as having separated themselves from St John's founded Christ Church, and on Oct 29, 1845, the rector of St John's wrote to their vestry suggesting a union of the churches, and avowing a willingness to arrange the chancel furniture as they desired, although he assured them that they were wrong in supposing that doctrinal innovations were concealed in the plan which he had adopted, and which had given offense to them They, however, refused to entertain the proposition

On July 18, 1848, Rev R G H Clarkson was elected assistant rector, to succeed Rev Dwight E Lyman, who had resigned, and in 1849, Mr Clarkson was followed by Rev Joseph C Passmore In the latter year Christ Church ceased to exist, and most of the Separatists returned to St John s, in what was called by Eli Beatty "a nominal membership" On April 1 1850, Rev Theodore B Lyman resigned to go to Trinity Church, Pittsburgh, and at the same time Mr Passmore gave up the assistant rectorship Rev Mr Wheat filled the pulpit temporarily, until the election of Rev William G Jackson, on April 22d, who did not take charge until September, having spent the summer in Europe, and in January, 1851, he was again compelled to accept an indefinite leave of absence on account of his health He resigned in December, 1852, and Rev George C Stokes declining the call that was extended to him, Rev Walter N Ayrault was elected on March 23, 1853, who continued until Sept 1, 1856 Rev William W Lord was offered the position, but could not accept it, and in December Rev Henry Edwards was chosen Gas was introduced into the church in May, 1857, and in April, 1859, Mr Edwards was able to announce that the church had been freed from debt On May 21, 1866, the building was damaged by fire, and was repaired at a cost of eleven hundred and fifty dollars Mr Edwards resigned Jan 18, 1867, and on February 23d, Rev Claudius B Haines was elected On Nov 17, 1869, a portion of the church property, at the corner of Jonathan and Antietam Streets, was sold to Thomas H Grove for two thousand five hundred dollars A protest against the legality of the election of A S Mason, Frederick Dorsey, Henry Bell, and Frank Kennedy as vestrymen in April, 1870, having been made, they resigned, and a new election took place in June Mr Haines tendered his resignation Dec 26, 1871 The church was burned to the ground on the night of December 6th, and Benjamin Reigle, George W Harris, George A Gambrill, Buchanan Schley, and Dr William Ragan were appointed a building committee for the erection of a new edifice, and they recommended that it should occupy the site of the destroyed church Rev Walter A Mitchell entered upon the rectorship in February, 1872, and the congregation worshiped in the chapel of the Reformed Church In May it was decided to sell the old church property for not less than seven thousand five hundred dollars and buy a new site on Prospect Street for two thousand three hundred dollars

Since the formation of Frederick Parish in 1777 the rectors have been

1777-85, Rev Bartholomew Booth, Dec 1, 1786, to 1812, Rev George Bower, Sept 22, 1813, to 1815, Rev Thomas P Irving, Aug 27, 1816, to Aug 1, 1817, Rev Joseph Jackson, Oct. 25, 1817, to December, 1821, Rev John Curtis Clay, D D, Feb 27, 1822, to July, 1822, Rev Samuel B Shaw, D D, Oct 12, 1822, to April, 1828, Rev George Lemmon June 28, 1828, to June, 1836, Rev Robert Brent Drane, D D, April 2, 1837, to 1840, Rev John Wiley, 1840-49, Rev Theodore Benedict Lyman, D D, September, 1850, to 1852, Rev William Gooden Jackson D D, June, 1853, to 1856, Rev Walter Ayrault, D D, January, 1857, to Jan 18 1867, Rev Henry Edwards, April 27, 1867, to 1871, Rev Claudius B Haines, Jan 1, 1872, Rev Walter A Mitchell

The vestries of St John s Church have been

1787 —John Stull, Daniel Hughes, Alexander Claggett, Thomas Sprigg, Richard Pindell, Nathaniel Rochester, and Eli Williams

1789 —Alexander Claggett, Thomas Sprigg Daniel Hughes, Eli Williams, Richard Pindell, and Hezekiah Claggett

1790 —Alexander Claggett, Thomas Sprigg, Daniel Hughes, Richard Pindell, Hezekiah Claggett, Eli Williams, and John Ingram

1791 —Daniel Hughes, Alexander Claggett, Eli Williams, Richard Pindell, Hezekiah Claggett, William Gordon, and William Reynolds

1793 —Eli Williams, Richard Pindell, Hezekiah Claggett, William Gordon, William Reynolds, Samuel Finley, and Rezin Davis

1797 —Eli Williams, Richard Pindell, Rezin Davis John Claggett, Cephas Beall, Charles Ogle and William Gordon

1798 —Alexander Claggett Eli Williams, John Claggett, Rezin Davis, William Fitzhugh, Ignatius Taylor, and Thomas Belt

1799 —Alexander Claggett, Thomas Belt, Rezin Davis, Eli Williams, William Fitzhugh, Griffith Henderson, James Kendall, and Benjamin Claggett

1802 —Nathaniel Rochester, Alexander Claggett Ignatius Taylor, Robert Hughes, Samuel Ringgold, Frisby Tilghman, Benjamin Claggett, and Otho H Williams

1805 —Rezin Davis, Otho H Williams, Robert Hughes, Frisby Til[illegible]n, Benjamin Galloway, John Ragan, Sr, and Nath[illegible] Rochester

1807 —[illegible] Hughes, Thomas Belt, Rezin Davis, William F[illegible], Nathaniel Rochester, Eli Williams, Otho H W[illegible], and Thomas Grieves

1809 —[illegible] Thomas B Hall, Na

thaniel Rochester, William Fitzhugh, Jr, Otho H W Stull, Otho H Williams, and Daniel Hughes Jr

—William Fitzhugh Thomas Belt, Thomas B Hall, Upton Lawrence, Thomas Grieves, William Fitzhugh, Jr, Otho H W Stull, Otho H Williams, and Daniel Hughes, Jr

[illegible] —Daniel Hughes, Sr, William O Sprigg, Otho H Williams, Frisby Tilghman, John Ragan, Jr, Thomas B Hall, Henry Lewis George C Smoot, and William Fitzhugh

[illegible] —Otho H Williams, Frisby Tilghman, Thomas B Hall, William Fitzhugh, Daniel Hughes, Henry Lewis, Eli Beatty, and George C Smoot

1815 —Benjamin Galloway, Thomas Belt, Otho H Williams, William Fitzhugh George C Smoot, Eli Beatty, Thomas B Hall, and Frisby Tilghman

1816 —Benjamin Galloway Eli Beatty, Thomas Grieves, Daniel Sprigg Anthony B Martin Levin Mills, Thomas Compton, and Franklin Anderson

1817 —Same vestry, except that Rev Thomas P Irving and Otho H W Stull took the places of Levin Mills and Franklin Anderson Mr Irving resigned, and his place in the vestry was filled by Frisby Tilghman

1818 —Eli Beatty, Daniel Sprigg Thomas Grieves, Richard Ragan, Franklin Anderson Otho H W Stull, Frisby Tilghman, and A B Martin

1819 —Frisby Tilghman, Eli Beatty, Thomas Grieves, Otho H W Stull, Daniel Sprigg, Otho Lawrence George Bear, and Franklin Anderson

1820 —Frisby Tilghman, George Bear, Richard Ragan, Levin Mills, Thomas Belt, Daniel Sprigg, Edward Gaither, and Franklin Anderson

1821 —Daniel Sprigg, Thomas Grieves, Otho H W Stull, Eli Beatty Frisby Tilghman, George Bear, Richard Ragan, and Franklin Anderson

1822 —Same vestry, except that Levin Mills took the place of Mr Stull

1823 —Eli Beatty, Daniel Sprigg, Thomas Grieves, John B Claggett, Frisby Tilghman, George Bear, Richard Ragan, and Franklin Anderson

1824 —Same vestry, except Otho Lawrence in place of Frisby Tilghman

1825 —Same vestry, except Henry Barnett in place of Otho Lawrence

1826 —Otho Lawrence, Eli Beatty, Daniel Sprigg, John B Claggett, George Bear, Thomas Grieves, Joseph Martin, and Franklin Anderson

1827 —Same vestry, except Richard Ragan in place of Thomas Grieves

1828 —Vestry of 1827 re-elected

1829 —Re-elected as above

1830 —Re-elected as above

1831 —Same vestry, except that Frisby Tilghman took the place of George Bear

1833 —Richard Ragan, Otho Lawrence, J B Claggett, Marmaduke Boyd, Joseph Martin, Frisby Tilghman, J P Dall, and Eli Beatty

1834 —Eli Beatty, Frisby Tilghman Joseph Martin, Jr, Richard Martin, Horatio McPherson Richard Ragan, and Otho Lawrence

1835 —Frisby Tilghman, J R Dall H McPherson, Otho Lawrence, Richard Ragan Eli Beatty, F Tilghman, Jr, and Barton Bean

1836 —F Tilghman, Sr, F Tilghman, Jr Otho Lawrence, O H W Stull, Horatio McPherson, John R Dall, Richard Ragan, and John B Claggett

1837 —Richard [illegible] William H Fitzhugh O H W Stull, Otho Lawrence, Thomas Schnebly, John B Claggett, Frederick Dorsey, and William R Abbott

1838 —Otho H Williams, Eli Beatty, Fred Dorsey, Jacob Hollingsworth, John B Claggett, Thomas Schnebly, John R Dall, and William R Abbott

1839 —Eli Beatty, John B Claggett, William Fitzhugh, Thomas Schnebly, William R Abbott Fred Dorsey, Otho H Williams and Jacob Hollingsworth

1840 —Frisby Tilghman, Joseph I Merrick, John S Hamilton, Peregrine Fitzhugh, Fred Dorsey William H Fitzhugh, Thomas Schnebly, and Jacob Hollingsworth Two members resigned, and their places were filled by John Thomson Mason and Charles F Keerl

1841 —Same vestry, except Jervis Spencer and James R Jones, in place of P Fitzhugh and Fred Dorsey

1842 —Same, except John R Dall in place of Joseph I Merrick

1843 —Jervis Spencer, John Thomson Mason, James R Jones, Fred Dorsey, Charles Macgill, W H Fitzhugh, Frisby Tilghman, and John R Dall

1844 —William H Fitzhugh, James R Jones Jacob Hollingsworth, Thomas Schnebly, J T Mason, Edward Gaither, and Fred Dorsey

1845 —Same, except John R Dall in place of James R Jones, and a vacancy filled by John Ingram

1846 —Same except William Motter, vice John Ingram

1847 —No change

1848 —Same, except Charles Macgill in place of John R Dall

1849 —Jacob Hollingsworth William Motter, J R Jones Fred Dorsey, William H Fitzhugh, J T Mason, and Charles Macgill

1850 —Same, except John D Reamure in place of J R Jones

1851 —Jacob Hollingsworth, John D Reamure, Wm Motter, Fred Dorsey, Charles Macgill, Joshua P Crist, Edward Gaither, and Richard Ragan, Jr

1852 —Same, except Benjamin Pendleton in place of Richard Ragan

1853 —Wm Motter, Jacob Hollingsworth, Edward Gaither, Fred Dorsey Chas Macgill, John D Reamure, J P Crist and Robert Fowler

1854 —Same, except Z L Claggett in place of Robert Fowler

1855 —Same, except W S Berry in place of Z L Claggett

1856 —No change, except Z L Claggett in place of Edward Gaither

1857 —Jacob Hollingsworth Fred Dorsey, Charles Macgill, Wm Motter, John D Reamure, Joshua P Crist, Washington Berry, and Eli Beatty

1858 —Same, except Charles F Keerl and Dr Wm Ragan in place of Washington Berry and Charles Macgill

1859 —No change

1860 —Jacob Hollingsworth, W Berry, James H Grove, Charles F Keerl, Charles Macgill, Joshua P Crist, John D Reamure, and Wm Motter

1861 —No change

1862 —No change

1863 —No change

1864 —Frederick Dorsey John D Reamure, Jacob Hollingsworth, Edward Watts, James H Grove, W Berry, Wm Motter, and Chas F Keerl

1865 —No change.

1866 —Jacob Hollingsworth, Chas F Keerl, James H Grove, W Berry, D G Huyett, Wm Motter, T W Simmons, and Wm Ragan

1867 —No change, except Richard Ragan in place of W Berry

1868 —Same, except Frederick Dorsey in place of Jacob Hollingsworth

1869 —W Ragan, Richard Ragan, T W Simmons, Charles F Keerl, D G Huyett, George W Pole, James H Grove, and Wm Motter

1870 —Henry Bell, George W Pole, D G Huyett, B Riegle, Wm Motter, Frederick Dorsey, T W Simmons, and Charles F Keerl

1871 —No change

1872 —P Riegle, Geo W Pole, Wm Ragan, Wm Motter, D G. Huyett, Geo W Harris, Alonzo Berry, and B H Griswold

1873 —Wm Motter, Geo W Harris, Alonzo Berry, B H Griswold, Wm Ragan, I P Crist, D G Huyett, Buchanan Schley

Following are brief sketches of the rectors of St John's The Rev Bartholomew Booth, who is put down as the rector of St John's from 1777 to 1785, was born and ordained in England, and came over to this country about 1776 He was famous as an instructor, and a sketch of him is given in another place There is no record of his officiating in the church, but as there is no mention of any other minister being there from the time of Mr Allen's departure in 1777 to that of Mr Bower's arrival in 1786, it is to be presumed that Mr Booth performed all the functions of a minister

The first record of the Rev George Bower is that of his arrival, Dec 1, 1786, and his employment at a salary of one hundred pounds, equal to two hundred and sixty-six dollars per annum During this year a subscription was raised for building a church in Hagerstown, then called Elizabeth Town The first records now known date from April, 1787, when the first vestry were elected Mr Bower still continued rector In 1788, however, he left and became rector of Queen Caroline Parish, Anne Arundel County, now in Howard, where he continued a year, at the expiration of which he returned to Hagerstown The Diocesan Convention met on the 2d of June, 1789, in Baltimore Mr Bower was present, and Mr H Claggett represented the parish as lay delegate The first convention met June 22, 1784, but that of 1789 was the first in which St John's Parish was represented In the certificate of appointment of the lay delegate it is stated "that the upper part of the parish [of All Saints', which this had been] has for some time been considered a separate and distinct parish," and so the act of 1770 had made it This the convention recognized, and accordingly Mr Bower and Mr Claggett were admitted to seats from Frederick, now St John's, Parish Mr Bower acceded to this, and ratified the constitution and canons for himself and Mr Claggett in behalf of the parish

Town com[illegible] appointed in 1791, and in the same year Mr Bower appears to have officiated part of his time in Frederick Town It is possible that he had officiated there before In 1795 an addition was made to the church The following letter from Mr Bower to Bishop Claggett gives an interesting picture of the condition of the parish at that time

"Hagerstown, July 11, 1797

"Rev and dear Sir,—It was out of my power to attend the convention this year, as it has been for some years past, owing to the delicate state of Mrs Power's health

"Our congregation in Hagerstown has become very respectable The addition we have made to our church is not yet completed I attend here every other Sunday, at Fredericktown every fourth Sunday, and at Taneytown every fourth Sunday Next Sunday, which is the fifth Sunday after Trinity and the 16th day of the month, I am to officiate here The Sunday after, which is the 23d of the month, I am to officiate at Taneytown The Sunday after that, which is the 30th, I stay here, and the Sunday after that, which is the 6th of August, I go to Fredericktown And so on regularly through the whole year

"Should we be favored with the pleasure of your company this fall, you will be so good, sir, to keep this letter, and you will know where to meet me I have kept a constant register of the marriages, births, funerals, and communicants But the adults I have found it impossible to make out They are so scattered about in this extensive parish, which contains three counties, and is, I believe, near one hundred and fifty miles in length, reaching from Baltimore County to the end of the State

"You would oblige me greatly to write a few lines by the post, to acquaint me with the time you think you can come up

"I am, reverend and dear sir, with great respect,

"Your very humble servant,

"George Bower"

In the following August the bishop visited this parish, and on the 13th of that month consecrated the church In 1799, Mr Bower's salary was four hundred dollars, in 1805, two hundred, in 1806, four hundred, in 1807, five hundred and fifty for half his services

In 1806 a petition was presented to the convention from sundry inhabitants of All Saints' Parish, in Washington County, praying to be allowed to constitute a separate cure by the name of St John's Parish, Washington County An act was passed making the whole of the county St John's Parish except that part of said county which forms a part of St Mark's Parish It would have been proper, doubtless, if desirable, to have granted a change of name and defined its bounds, but it had been made a separate parish before

Very soon after May, 1813, Mr Bower died, after a ministry of twenty-seven years He had been placed on the standing committee five times, and in 1801 preached the convention sermon

The only time when the number of communicants w[illegible] in 180[illegible] The number then was

[illegible] At more than half of the conventions he was absent. He left a widow, three sons, and a daughter. One of the sons died in Frederick. The others of the family went West, but in July, 1815, Mrs. Bower was living in Hagerstown.

Rev. Thomas P. Irving became rector Sept. 22, 1813, at a salary of four hundred dollars. He also taught a school. Mr. Irving was a native of Somerset County, but came into the diocese from the South, having been ordained by Bishop White in North Carolina, where he was principal of an academy at Newbern. In November, 1814, the vestry ordered five dollars to be paid for burial, and four dollars for a christening. In July, 1815, Mr. Irving had formed a Bible Society. Under date of May, 1816, Mr. Irving writes Bishop Kemp that he had been compelled on account of his health to resign his church, though not his academy. He is said to have died in 1817, at the age of forty-one years.

Rev. Joseph Jackson was elected rector Aug. 27, 1816. By birth Mr. Jackson was an Englishman. He was ordained deacon by Bishop Claggett in 1794, and in 1796 was rector of St. Peter's, Talbot, and for fifteen years of William and Mary, St. Mary's. He moved to Hagerstown in 1811, but remained only a year. In 1820 he went as a missionary to Kentucky, where he died that year. He had been twice on the standing committee, twice the convention preacher, and once deputy to the General Convention. His savings formed the nucleus of St. James' College.

Rev. John Curtis Clay was elected rector Oct. 25, 1817, to commence Jan. 1, 1818. He was the son of the Rev. Slater Clay, of Pennsylvania. In giving notice of his becoming a candidate for holy orders, Jan. 16, 1812, he says he had lived with the Rev. George Dashiell since 1809, except a few months spent in the University of Pennsylvania, "under whose direction I have pursued and am still pursuing the studies preparatory to ordination." He was ordained deacon by Bishop White, June 13, 1813, being just twenty-one years of age, and went to North Carolina, whence he removed to Hagerstown. He continued there four years, and resigned Dec. 18, 1821. He returned to Pennsylvania in 1822. In 1831 he became the rector of Gloria Dei Church, Philadelphia, where he died Oct. 20, 1863, in his seventy-second year.

Rev. Samuel B. Shaw was elected rector Feb. 27, 1822. He came from Massachusetts, his native State, having been ordained deacon by Bishop Griswold in 1821. He re[illegible] at H[illegible]town but [illegible] month[illegible], and then return[illegible] Ma[illegible].

Rev. George Lemmon was elected rector Oct. 12, 1822, with a salary of eight hundred dollars. He was a native of Baltimore, and was ordained deacon by Bishop Claggett in 1813. He became the minister of Queen Caroline Parish, in Anne Arundel County, but in 1816 removed to Virginia, where he married. From thence he removed to Hagerstown. In 1823 the new church recently built was consecrated by Bishop Kemp.

Hitherto the parochial reports on the convention journal had been merely statistical; but in 1825 Mr. Lemmon reports that two Sunday-schools had been put into operation, one white and the other for colored children. The congregation had much increased, and some had become the subjects of "spiritual change of heart." In 1826 he speaks of a lecture delivered on every Thursday evening. On the 1st of April, 1828, Mr. Lemmon resigned, after a six years' pastorate, and returned to Virginia, where he died, aged sixty. When Mr. Lemmon resigned Rev. Ethan Allen was invited to the charge, but declined.

Rev. Robert Brent Drane was elected June 26, 1828, but took charge on the 31st of August. He was a native of Rock Creek Parish, a graduate of Harvard College, and was ordained deacon by Bishop Griswold, of Massachusetts, May 3, 1827. Returning to the Diocese of Maryland, he became the rector of Addison Chapel Parish, Prince George's County, and thence removed to Hagerstown. In his report Mr. Drane mentions (1830) the reorganization of the Sunday-school and the formation of an Auxiliary Missionary Society. In 1832 he reports a weekly meeting for prayer and the exposition of Scripture. About this time he officiated once a month at Williamsport, and occasionally at a place seven miles east of Hagerstown. In 1833 he reports that he was continuing to officiate regularly at Williamsport, and also to a congregation then recently formed in Funkstown. In 1834 he reports having officiated every other Sunday at Williamsport from May 10th. During the year 1835 a parsonage was built for St. John's Church, and Mr. Drane had a school. In 1836 he preached the convention sermon. In June, 1836, after a ministry of six years, he resigned, and removed to North Carolina, to the rectorship of St. James', Wilmington. In 1843 he became the president of Shelbyville College, Kentucky, and received the degree of D.D., but at the end of the year he returned to Wilmington, where he continued till his death, in October, 1862. He died of the yellow fever, after a ministry of thirty-five years, and left a wife and children. On Aug. 1, 1836, Rev. J[illegible] W[illegible] was [illegible], but declined.

Rev. John W[illegible] April 2, 1837.

He was a native of Delaware, and a graduate of the General Theological Seminary, and was ordained deacon July 5, 1829, by Bishop Hobart of New York, and coming to Maryland, became the minister of St James' Parish, Baltimore County In 1833 he became rector of All Hallows and Worcester Parishes, Worcester County, and in 1836 of St Peter's, Talbot, whence he removed to Hagerstown Mr Wiley's convention reports are all merely statistical In 1840 he was the convention preacher In 1841 he resigned this parish and went to North Sassafras Parish, Cecil County In 1853 he removed to Trinity, Charles County, in 1866 to Labyrinth, Montgomery County, in 1872 to Sherwood Parish, Baltimore County He has been a deputy to the General Convention twice

Rev Theodore B Lyman became the rector of this parish in 1840, having been ordained deacon by Bishop Whittingham, Sept 25, 1840 He was a native of Connecticut, and graduate of the General Theological Seminary In 1841 St James' College was founded under his auspices In his convention report of 1842 Mr Lyman mentions that since October he had been assisted by the Rev Russell Trevett, deacon, that the church had been open on all holy days and Wednesday and Friday mornings, and that he had a Bible-class, a Sunday-school, a weekly service for the colored people, and weekly offerings. In 1844 the church had been enlarged and repaired, giving it a Sunday-school room and a vestry room In 1848 two silver chalices and two large silver alms-dishes had been presented About 1849, Mr Lyman removed from St John's Parish to Columbia, Pa In 1857 he was in Pittsburgh, in 1857 he received the degree of D D, in 1863 was residing in Paris, France, in 1865 in Rome, Italy, in 1871 in San Francisco, and in 1874 became assistant bishop in North Carolina

Rev William G Jackson took charge of the parish in September, 1850 Mr Jackson was a native of England, the son of Rev Thomas Jackson, rector of All Saints', Frederick, from 1830 to 1836 He graduated at the Virginia Theological Seminary, and was ordained deacon by Bishop Moore, of Virginia, in 1833 He became rector in 1850, and was married in 1852 to Lydia E Kennedy, daughter of Col Jacob Hollingsworth In January, 1851, on account of ill health, he was absent a while, and his place was supplied by the Rev W W Lord Before the convention of 1853, Mr Jackson had removed to South Carolina In 1855 he had returned, and had become rector of Grace Church, Howard County In 1870 he received the degree of D D, and afterwards became dean of the Convocation Rev Walter N Ayrault entered on his charge in June, 1 [illegible] He was a native of New York, and was ordained deacon in 1846 by Bishop De Lancey, and removed from Western New York In 1856 he returned to Western New York In 1868 he received the degree of D D

Rev Henry Edwards became rector in January, 1857 He was born in Connecticut, and was ordained by Bishop Brownell in 1853, but came to Maryland from New York, and became assistant in Emmanuel Parish, Allegany, whence he removed to St John's In 1858 he reported that the daily service had been continued with increasing congregations, and that services had been held in two villages a few miles distant In 1859 the old church debt had been entirely paid off In 1860 were reported a parochial school and a ladies' sewing society of ten years' standing and a new organ During the civil war Washington County was often the scene of extensive military operations, and the parishes suffered greatly Mr Edwards resigned his charge in January, 1867, and became the rector of St Mark's He also assumed missionary charge of St Andrew's, St Luke's, Pleasant Valley, St Mark's, and St Paul's, in Frederick County

The Rev Claudius R Haines commenced his rectorship April 29, 1867 In that year he reported that the church, which had been very much injured by a fire more than a year before, had been repaired at the cost of over three thousand dollars, and that two beautiful stained-glass windows had been presented for the chancel In October, 1861 he became the minister of Christ Church, Anne Arundel County, but received his letters of transfer from Virginia in 1866, and from thence removed to Washington County On the 1st of October, 1869, the vestry declared the church free Its revenue increased, and in 1871 it had proved a great success In that year he became the rector of St Timothy's, Catonsville, Baltimore Co

Rev Walter A Mitchell became rector January, 1872 He is the son of the late Rev Richard H B Mitchell, so many years in St Mary's County He was ordained deacon by Bishop Drane, of New Jersey, in 1856, and in 1857 became rector of St Paul's, Calvert County In 1860 he was a missionary in Baltimore, and in 1866 became rector of St John's, Howard County, whence he removed to Hagerstown

Upon Mr Mitchell's arrival, in the spring of 1872, he at once turned his attention to rebuilding the church It was determined as soon as the matter had been sufficiently discussed, that the wisest plan would be to sell the old site and erect the new church in another [illegible] was accordingly [illegible] et Street, near

the Dry Bridge" The lot is ninety two by two hundred and forty feet, and the position one of the most commanding in the town

The foundations of the church were laid in August of 1872, and it was ready for occupancy on Nov 3, 1875, although not absolutely complete until August 18 1881, when the capstone of the spire was laid, and the cross which surmounts the whole was set up in its place by Geo W Stover, superintendent of the contractors, M Gault & Son As completed, the edifice is one of the most beautiful and convenient in the country It is Gothic in style, and is built of limestone, broken range rock-work, laid in strong lime mortar. It presents a front of seventy-three feet, and is one hundred and nine feet deep The tower is fifteen feet square, and the top of the steeple one hundred and ten feet from the ground, surmounted by a gilt cross four feet five and a half inches high, the whole steeple structure being of hewn stone, and is graceful and imposing in appearance The native limestone is generously relieved by trimmings of brownstone and massive granite over the doorways of the tower The tower and steeple were contributed by C C Baldwin as a memorial to his wife, and he has since ordered to be cast a magnificent peal of bells, which will soon be in place The church building proper was erected under the superintendence of W H Hurley The corner stone was laid on September 4th by the rector, Rev W A Mitchell assisted by the following clergymen Rev Dr Grammer, Rev A J Rich, M D, Rev Wm T Johnson, Rev Henry Edwards, Rev Julian Ingle, and Rev James B Averitt Rev John D Easter, Ph D delivered the address The wardens, vestry, and building committee were prominently engaged in the ceremonies They were as follows Wardens, William Kealhofer and Buchanan Schley, Vestry, Hon Wm Motter, George W Pole, Dr William Ragan, Daniel G Huyett, Geo W Harris, Alonzo Berry, and R Howell Griswold, Building Committee, Geo W Harris, Dr Wm Ragan, Geo Gambrill, and Buchanan Schley Ember C Little, of New York, the architect, was also present At the time of its completion, in 1875, the building committee was as follows Rev W A Mitchell, Dr Fred Dorsey, Geo W Harris, and Geo W Pole, Esqs The main auditorium will comfortably seat four hundred and fifty people, and its plan and decorations are very handsome The walls are of a neutral drab, wainscoted four feet from the floor with alternate beaded walnut and chestnut planks oiled The church is fin[illegible] walnut [illegible] the furn[illegible] of th same w[illegible]

A magnificent organ furnishes the music for the congregation The windows are exceedingly handsome and rich in their coloring The central light of the chancel window is a figure of St John, the two side lights figured stained glass, the three upper circular windows are figures of adoring angels with trumpet, lute, and harp There are three handsome windows in the south transept, one the subject of which is the Annunciation and Nativity, contributed by the Sunday-school of the church, costing about one hundred and sixty dollars, another, representing the presentation in the Temple and our Lord among the doctors, is a memorial of the late Maj Holker Hughes, and a third, in memory of Miss Anna Fitzhugh, is triangular, and represents the adoration of the wise men In the north transept is a large circular window representing the Ascension The other windows are of diamond-shaped buff and white stained glass

The opening services of the church were held on Oct 11, 1875 The following clergymen were present The Right Rev Theodore Lyman, Assistant Bishop of North Carolina, a former rector of the parish, Rev C W Rankin, of St Luke's Church, Baltimore, Rev Fred Gibson, assistant rector St Luke's Church, Baltimore, Rev Dr J Stephenson, of Frederick County, Rev Dr S C Thrall, of Cumberland, Rev Jas Mitchell, Centreville, Queen Anne's Co, Rev Henry Edwards and Rev Jos B Trevett, of Washington County, and the rector, the Rev Walter A Mitchell The procession was headed by thirty choristers of St Luke's Church, Baltimore While marching up the aisle the hymn "Holy, Holy, Holy," was sung The sermon was preached by Bishop Lyman

The graveyard of St John's Church contains the remains of the following old residents

Col Isaac Nesbitt, born Nov 30, 1801, died June 1, 1865, and his wife, Ann Jane, died June 17, 1861, aged 50 years

Capt Alexander H Nesbitt of the Union army, died March 9, 1863, aged 29 years

Alexander Neill, born Dec 5, 1808, died July 18, 1865, and his wife, Mary S, born March 22, 1819, died Aug 23, 1880

Isabella Neill, born March 8 178[illegible], died June 16, 1856

Mary Chandler, wife of Dr Wm Chandler, of Philadelphia, died May 28, 1862, aged 86 years

Mary Magill, daughter of Rev James Magill, first rector of Queen Caroline Parish, Anne Arundel Co, Md, born March 25, 1749, died Aug 18 1824

Dr Wm D Magill, born Jan 6, 1801 died March 22, 1833

Dr N Carroll Magill, born May 13, 1801, died Sept 11, 1839

Henry Howard Gaither, born March 11 1793, died April 22, 1856 and his wife, Catherine K, born Jan 17, 1793, died March 8, 1857

[illegible] Gaither died June [illegible] 184[illegible] her 82d year

[illegible] 7, 1844, aged

Rezin D--, born April 29, 1753, died March 17, 1800, and his wife E-, born April 5, 1737, died March 28, 1815

Eliza - Prebly, born July 16, 1791, died Aug 2, 1871

Mary M-Cardell, died Sept 14, 1841, in her 72d year

Mrs M- Pottinger, died March 7, 1854, in her 88th year

John W-, born in Radnorshire, South Wales, Feb 2, 17-, died March 4, 1843

Martha Stewart, wife of William Stewart, and daughter of Isaac Foun-, of Londonderry, Ireland, died April 8, 1815, aged 7- years

Gottlieb Basler, a native of Germany, died Dec 13, 1831, in his 70th year and his wife Mary, died Feb 28, 1850, in her 8-th year

John N-r, a native of Germany, born May 1, 1750, died Jan 20, 1825

Alexander Neill, Sr, died Aug 2, 1858, aged 80 years, and his wife, -, died June 21, 1843, aged 62 years, 11 months

Mrs I- -ell Neill, died Jan 22, 1826, aged 69 years, 8 months

Parton I- born March 24, 1780, died Aug 24, 1835

Benjamin Galloway, died Aug 19, 1831, aged 77 years, 7 months

Henrietta Galloway, died April 21, 1847, aged 89 years

Wm Fitzhugh, died May 14, 1829, aged 45 years, 8 months

Dr Samuel Young, born in County Down, Ireland, May, 1739, died July 23, 1838, aged 99 years, 2 months

John McLaughlin, died Sept 13, 1804, in his 65th year, and his wife, Susan, died Dec 21, 1831, in her 92d year

Jacob H-ward, died Feb 18, 1867, aged 7- years, 1 month

Stewart Herbert, died March 13, 1795, aged 40 years, 11 months

David Newcomer, born in 1802, died in 1852, and his wife, Eleanor -, in 1806, died in 1833

Mary, wife of James Inglis, Sr, of Baltimore, died Aug 9, 1829 in her 5-th year

Otho Holland Williams Stull, born March 7, 1784, died July 23, 1867, and his wife, -, died Oct 2, 1862, in her 7-th year

Otho Holland Williams, born Sept 27, 1776, died July 11, 1852, and his wife, Elizabeth Bowie, died Nov 14, 1816, aged 74 years - months

Thomas Belt, died Dec 3, 1823, aged 82 years, 1 month, and his wife, Elizabeth Lawson, died July 30, 1816, aged 62 years

Margaret Capito, born in 1789, died Jan 23, 1878

William Beverley Clarke, born Sept 4, 1817, died April 14, 1855

Sally, wife of William Price, born June 2, 1797, died Oct 26, 1837

Thomas Sprigg died Dec 15, 1809, and his wife, Elizabeth, died July 28, 1808

John Reynolds, died Dec 3, 1845, aged 59 years, and his wife Maria Eliza Sprigg, died March 9, 1851, aged 60 years

William O Sprigg, son of Thomas and Elizabeth, died July 29, 1836, aged 63 years

Thomas Curtis, born in 1783, died Feb 15, 1874, and his wife, Ann born Aug 3, 1791 died March 19, 1851

Eli Beatty, died May 0, 1850 in his 84th year

John P Kennedy, died March 1-, 1866, aged 19 years, 7 months

Samuel Hughes, born July 6, 1773, died May 2, 1845, and his wife, Catherine, born March 29, 1781, died Oct 29, 1857

John Holker Hughes, born Sept 19, 1798, died Jan 1-, 1871

Napoleon Hughes, born Dec 23, 1806, died March 29, 1877

Ann Hughes - died March -, 18-

W- [illegible]

William H Fitzhugh died March 13, 1851, aged 57 years

Marie Antoinette Fitzhugh, died April 26, 1861 aged 63 years

William H Handy, died April 7, 1863, aged 77 years, and his wife, Catherine, died July 2, 1866, aged 68 years

Judge Thomas Buchanan, born Sept 25, 1768, died Sept 25, 1847, aged 79 years, and Rebecca Maria, his wife, died Feb 9, 1840, in her 70th year

Harriet Rebecca Anderson Buchanan, born Oct 13, 1803, died Feb 11, 1872

John Robert Dall, born Nov 1, 1798, died May 5, 1851, and his wife, Melvina, daughter of Judge Thomas Buchanan, born Dec 24, 1800 died April 9, 1879

Jacob Hollingsworth, born Aug 6, 1790 died March 19, 1868 and his wife, Nancy, born Sept 10, 1793, died Aug 21, 1872

Hezekiah Claggett, died April 3, 1866, aged 79 years, 7 months, and his wife, Ann, died March 25, 1867, aged 66 years, 4 months

St. John's Lutheran Church, Hagerstown, was organized in 1770, its constitution being signed by sixty members Its first pastor was the Rev Mr Wildbahn, and within one year after its organization it had one hundred and sixty communicants, and a year later two hundred and seventy one From 1772 to 1779 the pastor was the Rev Mr Young, and it is believed that the first church edifice was built during his pastorate In 1782 a collection amounting to £127 19s 6d, was taken to purchase an organ There are no records in existence of the proceedings for the ensuing eleven years except that in December, 1791, the congregation held a lottery for raising nine hundred and sixty five dollars There were two thousand two hundred tickets at two dollars, with seven hundred and forty-one prizes and fourteen hundred and fifty nine blanks The trustees and managers were Trustees, Peter Hoeflich, Henry Shryock, Peter Woltz, Baltzer Goll, David Harry and Jacob Harry Managers, William and John Lee Rezin Davis, Alexander Claggett, Nathaniel Rochester, Henry Schnebly William Reynolds, Melcher Beltzhoover John Geiger, John Protzman, Adam Ott, Michael Kapp, George Woltz, John Ragan Abraham Leider, Robert Hughes, Henry Shroder, Henry Eckhart, William Van Lear, Jacob Miller, F T, Frederick Stemple, Peter Whitesides, Andrew Kleinsmith, Philip Entler, John Ney In 1793 the Rev J G Schmucker, D D, became pastor Dr Schmucker was educated at Halle, Germany and was twenty-two years of age when he came to Hagerstown Previous to his acceptance of the charge of St John's he had been engaged in religious work in York County, Pa, among his charges being "Quickel's" An old sermon contains a graphic picture of the condition of religious society at the time of his [illegible] The Presby[illegible] g God's time,

... the Episcopal minister was "much more at home in the ball room and on the turf than in the pulpit," and the Methodists only were fighting the devil with vigor The new pastor of St John's entered [illegible]nously into the work which was before him, and made a great impression and was very successful In 1795 another building was erected The congregation numbered one hundred and eight members at this time and ten years afterwards it had increased to two hundred and eleven A new constitution was adopted in 1806 D. Schmucker resigned in 1810, and was succeeded by the Rev Solomon Schaeffer, who died young and was buried beneath the church A marble tablet in the aisle near the chancel marks his resting-place In 1815, Rev Benjamin Kurtz, D D, became pastor He also supplied the congregations at Funkstown, Williamsport, Beard's, and Smithsburg In 1816 there were one hundred and seventy-nine communicants, in 1800, three hundred, and in 1822, four hundred and two In 1825 a second bell was purchased, the congregation having paid off an indebtedness of thirteen hundred dollars in the previous year During Dr Kurtz's pastorate, which lasted sixteen years, preaching in English and protracted prayer-meetings were introduced During Dr Kurtz's absence in Europe in 1825, for the purpose of securing assistance for Gettysburg Theological Seminary, the pulpit was supplied by the Rev F Ruthrauff and the Rev J Medtard

In 1827, Mr Kurtz returned from Europe and resumed his pastoral relations with the church, Rev F Ruthrauff removing to Pennsylvania while Rev J Medtard took charge of the church at Martinsburg, Rev Winter being called to Williamsport—an associate charge of St John's—upon Mr Medtard's removal therefrom to go to Martinsburg

Dr Kurtz was succeeded at St John's by Rev Samuel K Hoshour in 1831, who was followed in 1834 by Rev C F Schaeffer, D D The latter resigned in 1840 At the last communion of the latter three hundred and eight names were recorded Rev Ezra Keller, D D, succeeded Dr Schaeffer, and during his pastorate, lasting four years, the number of communicants increased to four hundred and sixty Rev F W Conrad became pastor in May, 1844, and resigned in October, 1850 During his pastorate two hundred and nineteen persons were admitted one hundred and ninety-two buried, two hundred and fifty baptized, and the sum of seven thousand seven hundred and fifty dollars was raised for various objects Four Sabbath-schools were organized in the county, which with that in Hagerstown numbered more than five hundred scholars In the fall of 1850 Rev F R. Anspach, D D, became pastor, and was succeeded by Rev R Hill in 1857, who was followed by Rev J Evans in December, 1860 Mr Evans remained until 1866, and was succeeded in 1867 by Rev T T Titus, who resigned in October, 1869, in order to become pastor of Trinity Lutheran Church, an offshoot of St John's During several intervals the pulpit was supplied by Rev W F Eyster and Rev C Martin, while acting as principals of the female seminary In November, 1869, the Rev S W Owen (the present pastor) took charge He preached his last sermon in the church in its old form on the last Sunday in May, 1870, and the first one in its remodeled form on the third Sunday of April, 1871 During the century and more of its existence this congregation has had fourteen regular pastors and four temporary supplies Of the regular pastors six are still living, viz Revs S K Hoshour, C F Schaeffer, F W Conrad, Reuben Hill, T T Titus, and S W Owen, and eight have died, viz Revs Wildbahn, Young, J G Schmucker, Solomon Schaeffer, Benjamin Kurtz, Ezra Keller, F R Anspach, and J Evans Of the temporary supplies Revs C Martin and W. F Eyster are still living, while Revs F Ruthrauff and J Medtard are dead The original field covered by the pastors of St John's has been divided into half a dozen charges, supplied by as many ministers The older pastors took a prominent part in the organization of the General Synod, and in St John's Church the delegates from the Pennsylvania, Maryland, and North Carolina Synods met on the 20th of October, 1820, to adopt its constitution Here also the committee met to determine the location of the General Theological Seminary and the congregation of St John's subscribed the largest *bona fide* sum, two thousand five hundred dollars, to secure it Three of its pastors became editors of the *Lutheran Observer*, while others have been prominent in educational works It has furnished a number of ministers, among them Dr W M Reynolds, Prof F Springer, and Rev Messrs C Startzman, J H A Kitzmiller, H J Watkins, and J Forthman Its Ladies' Benevolent Association has aided a number of clergymen in obtaining their education The congregation numbers three hundred and twenty-five members, and recently expended seventeen thousand dollars in remodeling its church edifice The old church, built in 1795 and 1796, stood on South Potomac Street Its pulpit was shaped like a wine-glass, and had six sides It was twenty feet high, and entered by a door from a circular stairway, which led down into a latticed room which was used by the [illegible] ing-board, on

which was emblazoned a large eye There was no carpet on the floor, and the church was unheated, it being considered improper that the congregation should enjoy the comfort of a fire while listening to the minister and performing their devotions The collection-bags were attached to rods about ten feet in length, and had a silken tassel and a bell, which was used to attract the notice of inattentive or sleepy members At this period the attendance was not as large or as regular as might have been desired, cock-fighting at Big Spring or Yellow (now Ladle) Spring, horse-racing, bull baiting, and similar sports proving attractions too strong to be resisted by some of the members

In March, 1870, the old church was remodeled, so that the internal dimensions became seventy-five by sixty feet, and commodious access was afforded by means of two spacious stairways to the chief hall of worship on the upper floor The lower floor was fitted up with new seats, and was used by the Sunday school, then containing five hundred scholars and teachers The auditorium on the upper floor was fitted up with the newest style of seats, very handsomely upholstered in crimson damask and soft cushions The old organ gave way to a new one of later pattern and better tone, which cost sixteen hundred dollars The old pulpit and chancel were taken out and replaced, the new ones being of solid curled walnut Previous to this, in January 1870 the two old bells had been taken down, both being cracked so badly as to render them useless One of these bells had been cast in London in 1788, and the other in Boston in 1824 The inscription upon the older bell, although in English had the German spelling

Previous to 1834 the charge of St John's embraced Williamsport, St Paul, Clear Spring, and Martinsburg At these places the church buildings were inconsiderable, there being only a log building even at Williamsport, which was the most considerable of them all When Rev Benj Kurtz returned from Europe in 1827, Rev Mr Winter took charge of the church at Williamsport, and during his pastorate, in 1829, the present brick church was built

In September, 1834, Rev S W Harkey took charge of Williamsport, St Paul, Clear Springs being served by Rev. Winter After serving the charge one year and a vacancy of eleven months Rev Daniel Miller became pastor, and continued to sustain this relation for one year when, after a vacancy of one year and four months, Rev Christian Stutzman became pastor, and remained eleven years During this period Clear Spring was reunited to the charge, but when Rev Henry Bish[illegible] to be pastor in 1[illegible]50, Clear Spring withdrew a second time from the charge In 1855, owing to the removal of Rev Mr Bishop, Rev Wm F Greaver was chosen as his successor He is represented as having been "very much esteemed and beloved by the whole congregation, and under his ministry the church was prospering, but he died Oct 16, 1857

His successor was Rev Jos Barclay, late of Baltimore, during whose ministry the church edifice was enlarged and beautifully frescoed In August or September, 1859 he resigned, and was followed on the 20th of October of the same year by Rev Christian Lepley, who remained until October, 1864 After a vacancy of about a year Rev S Jesse Berlin was called to assume the pastoral care on Nov 1, 1865, but owing to failing health he removed Feb 1, 1867, when he was succeeded by Rev M L Culler, who remained until 1869 when he removed to Martinsburg, W Va In 1870 another division took place in the pastorate by the union of St Paul's with the Clear Spring charge In 1871, Rev W D Strobel became pastor, and after a ministry of about three years he resigned The congregation was now supplied with preaching by Rev J McCrow, of the Hagerstown Female Seminary, and in April, 1874, Rev J B Keller was called to become the pastor During this period the membership has been considerably increased, numbering now about one hundred and forty The church has for the second time been freed from debt, the contributions have been largely increased, a "Dime Society," averaging ninety members, who pay ten cents monthly, has been kept in successful operation for three or four years, the Sunday-school numbers on its roll one hundred and thirty-five pupils and twenty two teachers, and the church has been lately repaired at a cost of about three hundred dollars

One of the leading members of St John's and a pillar of the church for many years was Capt George Shryock George, son of John and Mary (born Teagarden) Shryock, was born in 1783 on the manor in Washington County In 1787 the family removed to Hagerstown, and resided on Franklin Street opposite the Oak Spring In 1796 he accompanied his father and brother John to Westmoreland County, Pa, where they built a log house in the woods The rest of the family followed them in the same year, the wagon conveying their goods being the first ever seen in that portion of the country Heavy wooden sledges were used for hauling and pack-horse trains for transportation between more distant points In 1803, George Shryock returned to Hagerstown [illegible] commenced the [illegible] leading member

of St John's Lutheran congregation, which his father had furnished with a portion of the building materials for the church edifice, erected in 1796. In 1809 he married Elizabeth Lewis, daughter of Capt James Lewis, and in the same year both himself and his wife became communicants of St John's Church. In 1820 he was a lay delegate to the first General Synod of the Lutheran Church in America which met in Hagerstown, and was the last survivor of that body. In 1813 he served as captain in Ragan's regiment, Stansbury's brigade. David Artz was first lieutenant of his company, —— Posey was second lieutenant, and Christian Fechtig was ensign. After the repulse at Bladensburg the company was detailed to support Commodore John Rogers' battery at Fort McHenry, Baltimore, and was present at the famous bombardment on the night the "Star-Spangled Banner" was written. Capt Shryock was one of a family of eleven children, of whom seven reached the age of eighty years and over, one that of seventy, and two that of sixty years and over.

COMMODORE JOHN ROGERS

Among those buried in the old St John's Lutheran graveyard are the following residents of Hagerstown and vicinity:

Samuel Eichelberger, died July 22, 1863, aged 73.

Philip Householder, died Jan 26, 1860, aged 78 years, 5 months, and his wife, Barbara, died April 8, 1863, aged 77 years, 3 months.

George McNamee, born March 27, 1775, died April 17, 1838.

David Startzman, died March 8, 1854, aged 70 years, 1 month.

Thomas Thirston, died Dec 6, 1843, in his 51st year, and his wife, Sarah, died Dec 9, 1876, aged 82.

Susan, wife of William H Hager, born Oct 6, 1820, died Dec 16, 1875.

Henry Kealhapper, born Jan 28, 1776, died Oct 31, 1851, and his wife, Elizabeth, born Sept 6, 1782, died Jan 31, 1852.

George Gittinger, died Nov 9, 1814, aged 80 years, 6 months.

Barbara, wife of John Eckstein, died Sept 2, 1850, aged 73.

George Bowman, born Jan 12, 1793, died April 28, 1870, and his wife, Mary, born Jan 1, 1801, died Jan 27, 1870.

Mary Hinkle, born May 15, 1817, died Jan 5, 1871, aged 53.

Peter Jacob Creek, died April 3, 1838, aged 72 years, 6 months, and his wife, Margaret, died April 8, 1857, aged 78.

Valentine Gliss, died Oct 29, 1857, aged 83, and his wife, Mary Barbara, born April 1, 1781, died Aug 25, 1843, aged 62.

Elizabeth Gelwicks, born March 15, 1775, died Feb 26, 1841.

Thomas Wright, died March 22, 1841, in his 50th year.

Henry Preamer, died July 7, 1863, in his 66th year, and his wife, Sarah, died Jan 17, 1847, in her 43d year.

Susannah Stewart, born Feb 14, 1767, died March 31, 1812.

Joseph Irovinger, born Dec 11, 1790, died May 11, 1851.

John Albert, died April 25, 1860, aged 8 years, 2 months.

Jacob Semler, Sr, died Oct 29, 1853, aged 61 years, 1 month.

John Keilhoffer, died Oct 17, 1856, aged 72, and his wife, Mary, died March 22, 1863, aged 73.

Sophia Smith, died July 28, 1868, aged 72 years, 1 month.

Samuel Rouskulp, died July 31, 1865, aged 81 years, 2 months, and his wife, Sarah, died Aug 12, 1849, aged 57 years, 8 months.

Catharine Smith, daughter of Peter and Ann Maria Heifleib, born Oct 22, 1771, died April 22, 1847.

Jacob Bragunier, died June 14, 1851, in his 57th year, and his wife, Mary, died March 17, 1850, aged 63 years, 7 months.

Jacob Zimmerman, born in Lebanon County, Pa, Oct 19, 1770, died Dec 11, 1868, and his wife, Elizabeth, born in Dauphin County, Pa, April 8, 1803, died April 11, 1871.

George C Gelwicks, born March 16, 1781, died March 31, 1853, and his wife, Mary, born Feb 15, 1788, died March 10, 1868.

James Hawthorn, died Feb 17, 1853, aged 84.

Samuel B and Ann Harris. The former died March 19, 1844, in his 79th year, the latter, June 15, 1844, in her 70th year. Their tombstone records that "they were wedded more than fifty years."

Eliza Woltz, born Sept 23, 1797, died May 2, 1867.

Daniel Gearhart, born Feb 11, 1791, died June 3, 1812.

Nancy Litter, died July 5, 1865, aged 79 years, 7 months.

Peter Kuntz, born March 2, 1779, died Nov 4, 1844, and his wife, Maria, born Nov 14, 1786, died Nov 11, 1853.

Susannah Brown, died June 22, 1862, aged 82 years, 6 months.

Thomas Phillips, born March 22, 1788, died Feb 19, 1844.

Jacob Huyett of Henry, born April 25, 1784, died Feb 2, 1812, and his wife, Mary, died Jan 25, 1851, aged 60 years, 9 months.

Jacob Firey, born Nov 25, 1767, died May 10, 1821.

Susan Firey, died Sept 15, 1872, aged 90 years, 5 months.

John N Zimmer, born Aug 29, 1781, died March 8, 1856.

Sergt David L Smith, Co A, 7th Maryland Regiment, died June 21, 1865, aged 30 years, 1 month.

Daniel Willard, born Oct 5, 1781, died Nov 14, 1846.

George P Baumbaugh, born Sept 9, 1785, died May 22, 1837, aged 53, and Mary L, his wife, born Aug 11, 1778, and died March 29, 1840, aged 61.

Joseph Newman, died May 7, 1862, aged 43.

Joseph A File, died July 9, 1845, aged 48.

John G Lussey, died Nov 7, 1819, aged 57.

Rebecca A Newcomer, wife of Jacob, born Aug 15, 1813, died Nov 1, 1850, aged 37.

Richard Rowe, born May 5, 1805, died Dec 5, 1858, aged 53, and Ann Maria, his wife, born Sept 23, 1805, died May 5, 1839, aged 33.

Thomas Lowery, died Feb 25, 1844, aged 42.

Abraham Cushwa, died Aug 25, 1859, aged 43.

Eliza, wife of Jacob Mummert, died Feb 12, 1851, aged 52.

Jacob Semler, Sr, died Oct 29, 1853, aged 61.

John Moyer, died March 27, 1871, aged 68.

Gottlieb B Lauger, born April 22, 1806, died July 9, 1853, aged 49.

William Baker, born May 6, 1800, died Feb 22, 1853, aged 52.

Catharine Smith, daughter of Peter A and Ann Maria Heifleib, born Oct 22, 1771, died April 22, 1847, aged 75.

Magdalena, wife of John D Middlekauff, died May 29, 1858, aged 45.

Ann Maria Smith, daughter of Nicholas and Catharine Smith, born May 18, 1792, died April 20, 1844, in her 53d year.

Daniel Bragunier, died in September, 1855, in his 55th year.

Rosanna Bragunier, died Sept 16, 1860, in her 55th year.

Elizabeth Startzman, born Aug 15, 1803, and died May 15, 1856

Jacob Zimmerman, born in Lebanon County, Pa, Oct 19, 1790, died Dec 11, 1868, aged 78, and Elizabeth, his wife, born April 8, 1803, died April 14, 1871, aged 68

Christiana, wife of Jonathan Late, born Dec 11, 1811, died July 6, 18[illegible], aged 52

Michael Rudisill, died June 28, 1868, aged 53

Francis C Reed died Feb 26, 1872, aged 64, and his wife, died Aug 7, 1863, aged 52

Susan Coil, died May 27, 18[illegible]2, in her 47th year

John Bentz, died June 9 1847, aged 58

Peter Wright, born May 16, 1806, died May 1 1868 aged 61, and his wife, Susan, died Feb 6, 18[illegible], aged 41

Mrs Elizabeth Hostetler, born Jan 27, 1808, died Jan 25, 1841, aged [illegible]

Thomas Phillips, born March 22, 1788, died Feb 19, 1844, aged 55

Dr Thomas P Phillips, born Sept 25, 1813, died Nov 29, 1841, aged 28

Susan, wife of James Kridler, died Aug 18 1856, aged 19

Daniel Willard, born Oct 5, 1784, died Nov 14, 1816, aged 62

Jacob Newcomer, died April 8, 1859, in his 58th year

Henry Weise, born June 30, 1809, died Sept 11, 1864, aged 55, and Elizabeth, his wife died Aug 4, 1840, aged 27

Trinity Evangelical Lutheran Church—The project of forming a new Lutheran society and erecting a new church edifice in Hagerstown took definite shape in the spring of 1868, the first meeting of those favorable to the enterprise being held in May of that year The circumstance which led to the new church project was the refusal of a majority of the members of St John's to remodel their old edifice After numerous efforts on the part of some of the most enterprising of St John's members to remodel the edifice had failed, about sixty or seventy withdrew from the mother church and proceeded to organize another congregation Before their withdrawal an equitable division of the common church property was proposed, and a committee was appointed to value the property, which they did, and reported the value to be sixteen thousand dollars No division, however, was ever made

On May 13th the friends of the new enterprise held a meeting, and a committee of arrangements was appointed, and other preliminary steps taken At subsequent meetings the following committees were appointed On subscriptions, Martin Startzman, Jonathan Schindel, and John E Herbst, M D and to this number Philip Wingert Jacob Roesner, and A J Weise were subsequently added, for procuring a lot and selecting a site, David Artz, Sr, Otho Swingley and William H Protzman, on constitution and by-laws, A J Weise, William H Protzman, Otho Swingley, Wilson L Hays, and John Byers, in procuring designs Dr J E Herbst and William Hous-holder Subsequently the following members of the building committee were chosen by ballot Dr J E Herbst, Otho Swingley, George W Stover, Lewis L Mentzer, and Jonathan Schindel The following were named trustees of the new congregation M Startzman, W L Hays, and F J Posey

The lot on which the church now stands, on West Franklin Street, was purchased for three thousand five hundred dollars from E M Reche The architect of the present "Trinity Lutheran Church" was C S Witzel, of Danville, Pa Ground was broken for the foundation on Oct 1, 1868, and the ceremony of laying the corner stone occurred in the presence of a large concourse of people on Nov 7, 1868, Rev Joel Swartz officiating The church cost thirty thousand dollars, not including the furniture, which was put in at a cost of two thousand dollars, and when completed ten thousand dollars of debt remained against it The congregation was formally organized on the 29th of August, 1869, with about one hundred and twenty members, the building committee, under whose superintendence the church edifice was erected were as follows Dr J E Herbst, chairman, L L Mentzer secretary, F J Posey, treasurer, and Messrs Jonathan Schindel, Otho Swingley, and Geo W Stover

The church was dedicated on the 3d of October, 1869, on which occasion Rev F W Conrad, D D, preached the dedicatory sermon The congregation at once elected Rev T T Titus, of St John's, pastor of their new church, a call which he at once accepted, and began his ministry In 1870 a chime of bells was placed in the steeple at a cost of fifteen hundred dollars, and a splendid organ placed in the church The total cost of the church has been thirty six thousand dollars, and although a parsonage has been recently purchased at a cost of three thousand dollars, the congregation only owes five thousand dollars On the 3d of April, 1870, Rev T T Titus, in consequence of the impaired condition of his health, was compelled to resign as pastor, and the church was without a pastor until Feb 25, 1872, when Rev W H Luchenbach was elected and served until August, 1874 On the 13th of June, 1875, Rev John R Williams, the present pastor, was elected

Rev T T Titus, first pastor of Trinity Lutheran Church, was born in Loudon County, Va, on the 4th of March, 1829 He was the son of poor parents, and the youngest of ten children He manifested an eager desire for learning when quite young, and was carefully instructed by his mother in the principles of religion At sixteen years of age he became a teacher, to which occupation he devoted some years of his life B[illegible] obliged to

labor with slaves in the field He was converted at a protracted meeting led by the Rev P Willard in 1847, and not long after united with the Lutheran Church In 1848 he went to Gettysburg, and commenced his studies for the ministry in the preparatory department of the General Theological Seminary His extreme poverty made it necessary for him to leave college several times in order that by teaching or selling books he might obtain the money needed to continue his education In 1853 he was rewarded by graduating as valedictorian of his class In the following year he took a class in the preparatory department and at the same time continued his studies for the ministry The double labor, however, was too much for his strength, and he was compelled to go abroad for the benefit of his health He was then ordained, and served in the ministry for eighteen years In 1867 he succeeded the Rev J Evans as pastor of St. John's Church, Hagerstown, and in October 1869, became the pastor of Trinity Church He labored with the greatest zeal, until at last his voice grew so weak that he could no longer be heard from the pulpit As a writer he was vigorous and pointed, and was a valued contributor to the *Lutheran Observer* He was also the author of a useful "Explanatory Question Book for Sunday schools" Mr Titus was very active in temperance work, and was twice elected to the office of G W C T in the order of Good Templars in Ohio A memorial service was held at Trinity Church conducted by Rev Dr McCron and Rev W H Luckenbach, who preached the sermon

The St Matthew's German Lutheran Church, which stands on Antietam Street was founded in 1871, and the congregation was organized on June 12th of that year Work was commenced on the church during the next fall, and the edifice was completed in the spring, the dedication of the church occurring on May 26, 1872 The first church council was as follows Lewis Heist, Y Marsack, William Schlotterbeck, Christian Thomas, Jacob Schneider, Wolfgang Brey, Henry Darnberger, Peter Rauth, G Grebner, John Brey The first pastor was Rev J J Dietrich, who was succeeded by Rev C Steinhauer After him came Rev J G Reitz who immediately preceded the present pastor, Rev G H Brandon The present church council is constituted as follows Christian Krohberger, George Rauth, Jacob Rettberg, Gottlob Schmidt, Frederick Baumbach, Jacob Wunsch, Justus Heinel, Christian Bretzler, Jacob Schlotterbeck

The Reformed Church.—Although the Reformed Church was [illegible] authentic records of the church previous to that year, when the first regular church organization was effected Its first regular pastor was Rev Jacob Weymer, who was first put in charge of the congregation in 1770, and who continued to serve it until his death, which occurred in 1790 During his pastorate the oldest church edifice now standing in Hagerstown was erected, in the year 1774 more than a century ago The congregation elected William Heyser, a member and deacon of the congregation, building-master, who was assisted in the construction of the church by his colleagues, Philip Osten, Peter Wagner, and Jacob Hauser, who carried the work on to the laying of the corner stone

On this occasion Rev Frederick Ludwig Henop, Reformed pastor at Frederick Town, who had been invited to be present, preached on the words contained in Colossians iii 17, "And whatever ye do in word or deed, do all in the name of the Lord Jesus, giving thanks to God and the Father by Him" At this service, which was held on the ground on which the church was to be built, there was likewise present Jacob Weimer Reformed pastor in Elizabethtown, Rev George Young, Lutheran pastor, and Rev ——, also Lutheran pastor of Fredericktown, William Heyser, builder, and Philip Oster, Peter Wagner, Jacob Hauser, deacons The following were the members of the first congregation William Baker, Ernst Baker, Yost Wegand Isin Gnadig, Johannes Karr, Frantz Greilich, Herman Greilich, Andreas Link Eustagnues Jung, Wilhelm Conrath, Henrich Doutweiler, Jacob Fischer, Johannes Steinseyfer, Frantz Wagner Ernst Ditz, Rutholph Bley, Johannes Oster, Michael Eberhart, Matthias Saylor, George Herdn, George Clampett, Johannes Nicholas Schuster, George ——, Hanadam ——, Valentin ——, Jacob Hauser, Peter Diller, George Frey, Johannes Frey, Conrad Eichelberger, Philip Klein, Ernst Kremer The corner stone of this venerable structure was laid on the 10th of August, 1774 The ground occupied by the church was given by Jonathan Hager, founder of the town, and a member of the congregation who was killed by a rolling log while engaged in cutting timber for the church edifice

No record has been preserved of the date of consecration It is known that after the building had been placed under roof the congregation, for want of means to complete it, worshiped in it for four years with the interior unfinished The dedication probably took place about 1778 The succession of pastors is as follows Rev Jacob Weymer, 1770, who continued to serve the congregation and to preach at St Paul's [illegible] rd's Church

near Cavetown, at Besore's, near Waynesboro', and at Apple's, in Frederick County, until the 12th day of May, 1790, when he died, at the age of sixty-six years, and was buried in the graveyard attached to the church, no stone, at his own request, marking his last resting-place Two years afterwards the Rev Jonathan Rahauser succeeded him in the charge of these congregations, and served them for a period of twenty five years, performing an immense amount of labor, and proving an effective preacher and a popular pastor He died Sept 25, 1817, in the fifty third year of his age, and was also buried in the graveyard attached to the church Rev James R Reily was the third pastor, who entered upon the discharge of his duties on the 1st of January, 1819, having on that day preached his introductory sermon He seems to have been a very popular preacher, as well as pastor, and drew immense congregations He resigned on the 25th of April, 1825 Although there was an occasional English sermon preached during Mr Reily's ministry, it was so rare that it might almost be said that the German was the only language used in the services of the church for fifty-five years of its existence With his successor the transition from German to English fairly commenced Mr Reily's successors were Rev Mr Brunner, 1827-32, Rev W A Good, 1833-36, Rev Albert Helfenstein, 1837-43, Rev M Kieffer, 1844-49, Rev D Gans, 1850-55, Rev S H Giesy, 1855-60, and Rev J H Wagner, 1861-64 Rev J S Kieffer became pastor of the congregation in 1868, and still continues to serve in that capacity, being the eleventh in a succession of pastors covering one hundred and eleven years

Improvements in the church building were made from time to time, and the entire structure was remodeled and placed in its present condition in 1867-68 About the same time a chapel was erected beside the church, on the site of the old lecture-room Two or three years afterwards the tower of the church, which had been left unchanged when the remodeling took place, was replaced by a new one The new spire, however, was blown down by a violent tornado in June, 1878,—a heavy loss to the congregation, which it has not as yet been able to repair The Sunday-school connected with the church numbers thirty odd teachers and over two hundred scholars

The Consistory of the congregation consists, in addition to the pastor, of six elders and four deacons These are at present the following

Elders—D C Hammond, H K Tice, M A Berry, A D Bennett, Wm Gassman, E M Recher

Deacons—W H McCardell, J T Seiss, W D Troxell George Shaver

In the cemetery of the Reformed Church are buried the following

Philip Wingert, born Jan 11, 1784, died Aug 30, 1861, aged 77, and Martha Wingert died Jan 20, 1833 aged 40

Gen Daniel Heister, "the patriot, the soldier, and the statesman," died March 7, 1804, in his 57th year, and his wife, Rosanna, daughter of Jonathan Hager, died Jan 11, 1810, in her 58th year

John Henneberger, died Sept 11 1859, aged 74, and his wife, Catharine, died Aug 11, 1869 aged 80

John McNamee, died Aug 11, 1858, aged 51, and his wife, Margaret, died Dec 26, 1873

John Braguner, died Feb 11, 1870, aged 70, and his wife, Susan, died April 24, 1871, aged 73

Sarah, wife of George Thornburg, born Dec 17 1796, died Dec 9, 1830

Daniel Burgesser, died March 14, 1865, aged 80

Philip Keller, died Sept 19, 1846, aged 73 years, and his wife, Ann, died Jan 7, 1841, aged 64

Samuel Braguner, born May 30, 1788, died Jan 16, 1838, and Elizabeth, his wife, died Nov 22 1875, aged 82

Samuel Beecher, died Oct 8, 1821 aged 53

Jacob Knode, born Sept 26, 1751, died Feb 2, 1828, aged 76, and his wife, Margaret, born April 10, 1750, died July 15 1824, aged 74

Peter Humrichouse, died Feb 13, 1807, aged 84 years, and his wife, Mary Ott died Oct 7, 1839

Elizabeth Hager Lawrence, only grandchild of Jonathan Hager, founder of Hagerstown, and the wife of Upton Lawrence, born Aug 1 1785, died Aug 5, 1867

Alexander Armstrong born Sept 8, 1798 and died Oct 29, 1870

Ann, wife of William Williamson, died Aug 16, 1857, aged 75

Frederick Bryan, died July 20, 1871

Martin Rickenbaugh, born April 3, 1794, died Feb 16, 1874

Jacob Stahl, born Feb 2, 1762, and died Sept 6, 1831, aged 69

John Tice, Sr born Nov 26, 1770, died July 27, 1833

John S Barr died July 6, 1856, aged 63

Daniel Middlekauff, born Aug 6, 1794, died Oct 23, 1855

Benjamin Leight, died Oct 11, 1848, aged 74

Jacob Gruber, died Sept 16, 1875, aged 86

Michael Hammond, died Nov 13, 1857, aged 81

Jonas Cramer, born Oct 14, 1755, died Aug 14, 1835

William Heyser, died Sept 10, 1830, aged 67

John C Ulrich, died March 4, 1848 aged 69

Johannes Weller, died Jan 1, 1800, aged 25

John Gruber, died Dec 29, 1857, aged 89, and Catharine, his wife, died Sept 15, 1859, aged 82

Jonathan Rahauser, pastor of the church, born Dec 14, 1761 died Sept 23, 1817

John S Rahauser, born Feb 23, 1794, died June 29, 1815

Daniel Rench, died Dec 2, 1831, aged 61

Andrew Kershner, born April 12, 1787, died Oct 6, 1857 and his wife, Elizabeth, born Oct 31, 1791, died Sept 10, 1860

Frederick Wolfersperger, born May 8, 1780, died Dec 6, 1821

Frederick Humrichouse, born July 6 1791, died Oct 5, 1876 and his wife, Hannah, born Jan 29, 1791, died April 25, 1880

William Freaner, died April 12 1870, aged 80

Andrew Wagoner died Aug 22, 1872, aged 78

John Gottlieb Mittag, born March 7, 1776, died Nov 4, 1828 aged 52, and his wife, Susan, died Oct 18 18[illegible], aged 76

Alexander McCammon died April 6 1869 aged 75

Margaret, wife of Rev Christian F Post died March 7, 1810,

Ludwig Carl Bodman, born Nov 29, 1752, died April 1, 1828
John Seitz, died March 30, 1851, aged 63
Elizabeth, wife of Peter Wingert, and daughter of David [illegible], died Dec 17, 1806, aged 57
George Ross Beall, born April 10, 1796, died May 14, 1843, [illegible] wife, Ellen, born July 8, 1809, died Jan 18, 1840
Isaac S White, Sr, died in 1844, in his 73d year
Henry Middlekauff, born Oct 18, 1766, died March 13, 1837
[illegible] David Schnebly, youngest son of Dr Henry Schnebly, born May 8, 1770, died Oct 4, 1842, and Mary, born Feb 15, [illegible] died Nov 17, 1876, aged 103 years
John F Hoffman, born Oct 23, 1789, died March 6, 1870, [illegible] his wife, Catharine B Hoffman, born Aug 28, 1793, died [illegible] 12, 1877
Wm Kreps, died Feb 28, 1822, aged 50

Christ Reformed Church.—During 1852 religious meetings were held in the lecture room of the First Reformed Church, in Hagerstown for the benefit of those who desired services exclusively in the German language and were attended by Germans, members of the German Reformed and Lutheran Churches, and others not members of any church. Rev Carl Kast, a minister of the German Reformed Church, ministered to the special wants of the new congregation for several years. No organization was, however, effected at this time, although measures were taken to build a Reformed church in which those who desired German services exclusively might worship. A location was ultimately selected on Franklin Street, and the work of building went forward. In March, 1855, the Germans assembled in the First Reformed church and organized a Reformed congregation, after which they proceeded in a body to the new church, where the corner-stone was laid, and the church received the name of "Christ Church," and was popularly known as the Second Reformed Church. The church was completed in 1856, and was dedicated in the spring of the same year. Among the ministers present were Rev Samuel H Giesy, D D, pastor of the First Reformed Church, Rev Philip Schaff, D D, and Rev Dr George Wolff. The following were the officers of the congregation: Henry Winter, Leonard Maisack, Mark Benner, Jacob Gruber, Theobald Kiefer, William Beslard, and George Steinmetz. Rev Mr Kast continued to serve the congregation for a number of years and was succeeded by Rev John B Poerner. Rev Dr George Seifert followed Mr Poerner. In 1868, Rev Henry Louis G Menard became pastor, and served for one year. He was succeeded by Rev [illegible] Scheel, who was in turn succeeded by Rev Theobald Herschman, who was a member of the Lutheran Church, and the only Lutheran minister that ever served its congregation. It appears that he was [illegible] called as pastor of the congregation. During his brief term [illegible] difficulties [illegible], and the Reformed Classis of Maryland, which held jurisdiction over Christ Reformed Church, at its next meeting took into consideration the difficulties and complaints made by the Reformed portion of the congregation, and by resolutions declared its unwillingness to have under its jurisdiction a congregation served in so irregular and unsatisfactory a manner. As a result of this action the German Lutheran portion of the congregation left the church and proceeded to build a German Lutheran church. Rev William F Colliflower succeeded Rev Herschman in 1872.

During his pastorate there was practically a reorganization of the congregation. Quite a number united with the church by confirmation and certificate who were not familiar with the German language, and in consequence there were only occasional German services, and in a short time German services were discontinued. This change from German to English services rendered necessary a change in its constitution, and on Sept 18, 1877, such changes and alterations as were necessary were made. Rev Mr Colliflower continued pastor of the congregation for about three years and three months, and his successor, Rev C H. Coon, was installed in the fall of 1876, and was succeeded on Oct 1, 1878, by Rev Leighton G Kremer, the present pastor. The officers of the congregation are: Elders, George Fridinger, Charles Fridinger, C G Boyer, Henry Haltzapple; Deacons, George G Solliday, John Gassman, Solomon Baker, Theodore Weagley. The present number of communicants is ninety-seven, and Sabbath-school scholars one hundred and sixteen. Extensive improvements were made in the audience-room of the church in the fall of 1878, and the congregation possesses a neat and comfortable place of worship. The basement of the church has lately been fitted up for a Sabbath-school and lecture-room.

The Presbyterian Church.—Traces of the Presbyterian Church are found as far back as 1774, when Rev Thomas McPherrin was called by the united congregations of Conococheague and Jerusalem, the latter being known as "Hagerstown charge," to the pastorate of the Presbyterian congregations west of the South Mountain. In 1788 it is mentioned that, in compliance with a "supplication" from Falling Waters, Hagerstown and Williamsport, Rev Mr Caldwell was appointed by the Presbytery "as a constant supply for those places for one year." There are, however, no known records of the church earlier than 1817, when the society was organized.

Previous to this, from about 1809, John Lind divided his time between Greencastle and Hagerstown. [illegible] Land, and

came from Ireland in 1771, and shortly afterwards organized the Associated Reformed Church his church being erected in Greencastle Under the pastorate of the younger Lind the first church on South Potomac Street was erected Before this, service was held in the German Reformed church

On Nov 15, 1817, Robert Douglas, John Kennedy, Joseph Gabby, and John Robertson were ordained to the office of ruling elder, and the church was known as the Associated Reformed Church On the following day the sacrament of the Lord's Supper was administered for the first time by an English Presbyterian minister The society thus formed comprised thirty seven members The church had just been completed at a cost of $9149 17 This included also the price of the lot

The lot upon which the church was erected was purchased for fifteen hundred dollars from Gotleib Zimmerman Of the one hundred and sixty-seven contributors to the church fund, only one, Frederick Hummickhouse, was alive in 1875 It is mentioned that two of the subscriptions to this first Presbyterian Church amounted to six thousand dollars From the organization of the church until the end of 1824 there were added to its membership fifty seven persons In 1824 Rev Mr Lind died, and was succeeded by Rev Matthew L Fullerton The church, together with that of Greencastle, united in the spring of 1825 with the Presbytery of Carlisle Mr Fullerton was installed as pastor Sept 28, 1825, and ministered to the congregations of Hagerstown and Greencastle upon alternate Sundays He died Sept 17, 1833, and was succeeded by Rev Richard Wynkoop who was installed June 25, 1834, when the severance from the Greencastle Church became final In January, 1836, the Session having determined upon the election of three additional elders on the 26th of that month Messrs Joseph Rench, Samuel Steele, and John McCurdy were elected In the opposition to the ordination of Mr McCurdy was begun a difference which ultimately resulted in a division of the church The pastorate of Rev Mr Wynkoop continued until his death, April 6, 1842 He was succeeded by Rev Herman Douglas, and he by Rev John F McLaren, whose pastorate continued until it became evident that a reunion could be accomplished, when he and Rev Mr Love the pastor of the other church, resigned in order to further it The pastors of the seceding portion of the congregation were Rev Mr Davies and Rev William Love Under the corporate name of the First Presbyterian Church of Hagerstown they perfected and maintained an organization, worshiping in the court [illegible] the Session consisting of Elder William Stewart, Nathan McDowell, and William M Marshall This congregation was admitted to connection with the Synod of the Associate Reformed Church Jan 26, 1838, notwithstanding the Presbytery of Carlisle did not release it nor recognize its withdrawal The reunion of the congregations was effected April 10, 1846, and September 14th, Rev Septimus Tustin, D D, was called, and came in response to the call, but was not installed until the following year John Kennedy, the founder of the church died April 27, 1847 Dr Tustin having resigned, Rev R W Dunlap was next called, and began his ministry in the latter part of 1851 or early in 1852 He died Feb 17, 1856, and was succeeded by Rev Robert A Brown, who was called early in the year 1858 During the summer of 1861, Victor Thomson, who had long been an attendant of the church, died and devised to it the sum of five thousand dollars, which was applied, in accordance with his will, first in placing a substantial iron fence in front of the church, the balance being invested with its annual increment, made it possible to indulge the idea of remodeling the church building, but the war occurring dissipated the project, the ultimate result being the erection of the new structure

In the spring of 1862, Rev Mr Brown resigned, and the pulpit was afterwards filled and until Sept 24, 1866, by Rev W C Stitt, first as stated supply and then as pastor Feb 18, 1867, Rev Tryon Edwards D D, was called and entered upon the ministry He resigned Oct 29, 1872 In April following the congregation, at the annual meeting, directed the building of the new church July 24, 1873 Rev J C Thompson was called, and he was installed November 18th of that year

Mr Thompson resigned in 1879, and was succeeded by Rev J A Roundthaler, the present pastor The old church on South Potomac Street was sold to the Christian Church in 1878, but the last service held in it by the Presbyterians was on Sunday, Dec 18, 1875 The sacrament having been a part of the opening services of the church fully eight years before, it was deemed proper that the final services should be also completed with the sacrament There was not, however, a single person who was present on both occasions The new church was dedicated on Sunday, Dec 25, 1875, the sermon being preached by Rev J T Smith, of Baltimore Rev George P Hayes, D D, president of Washington College, preached in the evening, and raised four thousand dollars with which to help pay off the debt of ten thousand dollars The edifice, which was designed [illegible] of graystone,

[illegible] is simple but imposing in style. The main audi[illegible]m is forty-three by seventy-five feet, and is en[illegible] from a vestibule nine by forty-five feet, which [illegible] on Washington Street. A tower occupies the [illegible]thwest corner, and faces both Washington and [illegible]pect Streets. When completed this tower will [illegible] one hundred and twenty-five feet high. The finish [illegible] the audience-room is of black walnut oiled, the [illegible]s being cushioned in crimson terry, the floor car[illegible]d in crimson and drab. The triple window in the [illegible]nt is a memorial in stained glass to Victor Thom[illegible], whose bequest formed a valuable part of the [illegible]ilding fund. The windows upon the sides are [illegible] of stained glass in simple style. The ceiling is [illegible]oken by heavy white mouldings running across, and [illegible] of a lavender tint. It is lighted artificially by four [illegible]rge reflectors, circular in pattern, and neat and or[illegible]mental in design.

In the Presbyterian graveyard on Potomac Street the following are buried:

John McIlhenny, died Oct. 15, 1832, aged 51.

Susan, wife of W. D. Bell, born Dec. 3, 1799, died Feb. 22, 1876.

Mary Bell, died July 19, 187[illegible], aged 67.

Thomas Sturr, died April 10, [illegible]58, aged 72.

Thomas Kennedy, born Nov. 29, 1776, died Oct. 18, 1832; and Rosamond Kennedy, born May 19, 1774, died March 30, 1857.

James Ferguson, died March 24, 1839, aged 79.

John Wagoner, died Nov. 21, 1831, aged 76; and Sarah Wagoner, died July 13, 1832, aged 81.

Edith Kellar, died March 14, 1843, aged 60.

In the Roman family lot, which is marked by a simple pedestal and shaft of white marble, are buried the following: James Dixon Roman, born Aug. 11, 1809, died Jan. 19, 1867; Louisa Margaret, widow of James Dixon Roman, born May 7, 1809, died Aug. 1, 1879; Sallie Roman, wife of C. C. Baldwin, born Nov. 4, 1843, died April 3, 1873; James Dixon Roman, born June 8, 1854, died July 1, 1875.

Elizabeth, wife of Joseph McIlhenny, died Nov. 3, 1857, aged 7[illegible].

William D. Bell, born Sept. 20, 1763, died Oct. 7, 1841.

William Gabby, born April 25, 1762, died Sept. 5, 1841; and Emily Gabby, died July 9, 1[illegible], aged 59.

Hannah Kellar, born Dec. 20, 1779, and died Sept. 13, 1857.

John Kennedy, born in Ireland June 13, 1767, died April 27, 1847; and Margaret Kennedy, died May 30, 1813, aged 35 years.

Hugh Kennedy, died March 11, 1835, aged 66.

Joseph Rench, died Sept. 6, 1879, aged 73.

Mrs. Rebecca L. Martin, daughter of Col. Daniel and Ann Hughes, died March 20, 18[illegible], aged 25.

A monument marking the grave of the Rev. Mr. Fullerton bears the inscription: "A memorial of their late beloved pastor, Rev. Matthew Lind Fullerton, erected by his congregation. He was born Oct. 22, 1801, ordained and installed pastor of the Presbyterian Church in Hagerstown, Sept. 25, 1823, and departed this life Sept. 17, 18[illegible]."

Another memorial reads: "Dedicated to the memory of the Rev. Richard W[illegible] the [illegible] after a short illness of [illegible]

Rev. Colin MacFarquhar, a native of Scotland, and for thirty years pastor of the Presbyterian Church of Donegal, Lancaster Co., Pa., died Aug. 22, 1822, aged 93.

Mrs. Daniel Hughes, died Aug. 29, 1823.

Methodist Church.—The section of country surrounding Hagerstown was visited by Strawbridge, Owen, King, Asbury, and other pioneer preachers. In 1776, Asbury wrote, "It seemed as if Satan were the chief ruler there; the people were very busy in drinking, swearing, etc." In 1812 he revisited the place, and says that he "preached in the neat, new Methodist chapel to about one thousand hearers." It was for a number of years included in the Chambersburg Circuit, but in 1822 appears as a separate circuit, with John Emory, subsequently bishop, as pastor. As early as 1793 the Methodists had a congregation in Hagerstown, for they are mentioned in connection with Dr. Schmucker's first appearance, which was in that year. They held camp-meetings at Enoch Jones', five miles from Hagerstown, about 1807, of which Rev. Hambleton Jefferson had charge. They had built a church in the town early in the present century, and Rev. William Rylan preached there as early as 1810. A new church was dedicated in 1867, and on Sunday, Dec. 14, 1879, the present Asbury Methodist Episcopal church was dedicated. It is situated on North Jonathan Street, and was completed during the pastorate of Rev. J. W. Waters. The structure is of brick, and is built upon the site of the old building, in which the Rev. James Brown led in worship for so many years. Its gable front abuts upon the street. The main auditorium is on the second floor, and is quite plain in its appearance, a single motto in an arch upon the wall back of the pulpit being its only ornamentation.

The church lecture-room is upon the ground-floor. Thurston & Beck, contractors, commenced work on the edifice in July, 1879, and it was dedicated on Sunday, December 14th. Rev. N. M. Carroll, of Baltimore, preached the dedicatory sermon, and the services were conducted by Presiding Elder H. A. Carroll. Sermons were also delivered during the day by Rev. James Thomas, of Baltimore, and Rev. Robert Steel, of Baltimore. On the Sunday of the dedication Presiding Elder J. H. A. Johnson, of the African Methodist Episcopal Church, and Rev. Mr. Wayman, bishop of the African Methodist Episcopal Church, participated in the ceremonies. The following members of the congregation conducted the collection, which amounted to a considerable sum: John Harden, H. W. Dorsey, Benjamin Myers, H. D[illegible] C. Do[illegible] P. N[illegible] G. Miller, and J. T. W[illegible].

The colored people of Hagerstown had maintained a Methodist Church organization for many years previous to the building of their church, in July, 1879 Their church edifice was completed in the fall following, and is a commodious and convenient place of worship

Catholic Church—The Catholics, although they had a congregation in Hagerstown previous to that time, built their first church in the spring of 1794 Proposals for this church, or "stone chapel," were received at the house of John Worland on the 29th of January The walls of this chapel were fifty feet long, thirty-five feet wide, and nineteen feet high The advertisement soliciting proposals for the building of this church was signed by William Clark, who stated that he would show the plan for the chapel upon application, and proceeded to say that the person undertaking to build the walls must find stone, lime, clay, sand, and all other materials, laborers, etc, "so that the whole work may be done within himself, and the walls delivered by him ready built His proposals must mention what he will do it for by the perch of the wall,—that is, sixteen feet and one-half of a foot in length and one foot in height of the whole thickness of the wall Stone can be had on the lot where the house is to be built, and the quarry is already opened, which will save a great deal of expense in hauling"

In 1804, Rev Charles Duhamel was pastor, and Patrick Edwards was parish teacher of the congregation In 1828 a new church was built, and dedicated on October 5th of that year On June 9, 1837, Rev T Ryan, who had been for many years pastor of the church, died After this, for twelve years, Rev Henry Myers was pastor of the Hagerstown Church, it being embraced in his parish, comprising all of Washington County Father Myers was one of the most highly esteemed pastors of the church He was born in Conewago, Adams Co, Pa, in 1806, and studied at St Mary's Seminary, Baltimore He was ordained in 1830, and prior to his pastorate at Hagerstown was stationed at St Patrick's, Washington, D C, and afterwards at Cumberland, Md, where he built a church He went to Pikesville, Baltimore Co, after twelve years of labor at Hagerstown, and in 1860 succeeded Rev Leonard Obermyer as pastor of St Vincent de Paul's on Front Street, Baltimore City, where he remained until the time of his death, in July, 1873

The old Catholic church in Hagerstown was repaired in the fall of 1870 and was re dedicated on January 29th of that year The improvement to the church, which [illegible] large, consisted in the erection of a tow [illegible] of a beautiful spire, the height of which from the ground to the summit of the cross is one hundred and twenty feet The length of the church is one hundred and nine feet, and it is forty-eight feet wide These improvements were made from designs furnished by George A Fredericks, of Baltimore, under the direction of Mr Hurley, Mr Wright, and Mr Cushwa The total cost was seven thousand dollars, of which all but fifteen hundred had been paid on the day of dedication The dedication services were conducted by Rev Henry Myers, who was then pastor of St Vincent de Paul's, Baltimore The Very Rev Dwight Lyman, of Baltimore, delivered the dedicatory sermon

The Catholic cemetery at Hagerstown embraces four acres of land on West Bethel Street Among the interments are the following

Susan McLaughlin, died Dec 1 1846, aged 70 years

Elizabeth Brooks, died ———, in her 8?th year

William Couden, born in Queen's County, Ireland, died March 14, 1822, in his 52d year

Francis McBride, died Feb 25, 1874, in his 60th year

Bridget, wife of Francis McMullin, died Nov 20, 1863, in her 75th year

Thomas McCardell, died Oct 26, 1843 aged 66 years, 8 months, and his wife, Ann, died March 21, 1861, aged 84 years, 3 months

Joseph Reel, died Jan 17, 1831, aged 76 years, 30 days

Elizabeth Reel, died Feb 16, 1822, aged 51 years, 4 months

Hugh McKuskerd, died Dec 14, 1867, aged 64 years, 9 months, and his wife, Margaret, died March 13, 1879, aged 71 years, 1 month

James Adams, died in 1836, aged 56 years, and his wife, Elizabeth, died Feb 5, 1836, aged 52 years

Patrick Mooney, died Nov 24, 1838, aged 65 years

Margaret Adams, died Aug. 21, 1846, aged 63 years, 3 days

Patrick Donnelly, died May 27, 1837, in his 54th year, and his wife, Margaret, died March 29, 1852, in her 59th year

Richard Welsh, died Nov 9, 1828, in his 61st year

James McGonigle native of Londonderry, Ireland, died Oct 13, 1838, aged 70 years

Jeremiah Lyons, died May 16, 1876, in his 75th year

Mary Roach, native of Limerick, Ireland, died Sept 6, 1876, aged 80 years

Philip Bradley, native of Londonderry, Ireland, died March 1, 1875, aged 63 years

Hugh Murphy, born in County Carlow, Ireland, died March 9, 1878, in his 71st year

George Moore, died March 8, 1865, aged 77 years, 7 months

William E Doyle, died June 28, 1865, in his 61th year, and his wife, Margaret, died Dec 15, 1860, in her 57th year

Thomas Shirvan, died Oct 17, 1868, in his 84th year, and his wife, Isabella, died July 29, 1867, aged 67

Casper Schwab, died Feb 22 1855, aged 77 years

Rev Joseph J Maguire, died Sept 15, 1852, in the 36th year of his age

Susan McLaughlin, died Dec 1, 1846, aged 70

Christopher Murphy, born in Armagh, Ireland, aged 61

Adam Crist died Aug 13, 1852, aged 50

Margaret, wife of Richard Barry, of County Limerick, Ireland, died Feb 11 1858, aged 68

[illegible] [illegible] aty, Ireland, died [illegible]

[illegible], wife of Isaac Rowland, born Dec. 17, 1808, died [illegible] 1869, aged 60.

[illegible], wife of Robert Lewis, died Dec. 20, 1856, in her 47th [illegible].

[illegible] Shilling, died March 8, 1859, in his 52d year; and [illegible], Francesca, died Feb. 11, 1852, aged 42.

[illegible] Butts, died May 16, 1861, aged 54.

The Church of the Disciples was dedicated on [illegible] 1, 1859, by Bishop Glassbrenner, the Rev. Mr. [illegible]y, and the Rev. Mr. Lowber. The only debt [illegible] church at that time was four hundred and [illegible]y-four dollars, which amount was contributed [illegible] the day of dedication. Among those buried in [illegible] church of the Disciples are the following:

[illegible]ville E. Smith, adjutant 6th Maryland Volunteers, U.S.A., [illegible] at Cedar Creek, Va., Oct. 19, 1864, died Nov. 17, 1864, [illegible] 19 years, 11 months.

Nathan McDowell, born Aug. 5, 1803, died Oct. 30, 1860.

Capt. Lodovick Leeds, born in Groton, Conn., Sept. 14, 1776, [illegible] Sept. 7, 1863; and his wife, E. M., died July 10, 1848, in [illegible] [illegible]th year.

[illegible]n, wife of Andrew Thomson, of Belfast, Ireland, died April [illegible], 1844, aged 71.

Francis C. Thomson, born in Belfast, Ireland, July 24, 1800, [illegible] Nov. 20, 1876.

Victor Thomson, born in Belfast, Ireland, March 18, 1810, [illegible] July 17, 1860; and his wife, Margaret, died Jan. 9, 1842, [illegible] 33d year.

Nathaniel Martin, died Oct. 7, 1863, aged 93; and his wife, [illegible]zabeth, died Sept. 7, 1872, aged 97.

Jacob Keller, died April 4, 1859, aged 72.

Capt. James Biays, born in Baltimore, died Sept. 29, 1865, aged 74 years, 4 months; and his wife, Margaret, born in Philadelphia, Feb. 8, 1797, died near Hagerstown, March 21, 1871, aged 74.

George L. Harry, died March 19, 1847, aged 64; and his wife, [illegible], died Jan. 13, 1873, aged 74.

John McKee, born Feb. 21, 1787, died January, 1871; and his wife, Isabella, died Dec. 17, 1851, aged 62 years, 7 months.

Sally McKee, died May 2, 1871, aged 81 years, 8 months.

Ann, wife of Gabriel Nourse, died Aug. 16, 1853, aged 80.

Charity Hagerman, died Dec. 3, 1852, aged 81.

Wm. Pott, died Dec. 4, 1848, in his 80th year; and Sarah, his wife, died Feb. 10, 1852, aged 59.

Dr. Thomas Buchanan Duckett, died Dec. 27, 1875, in his 16th year.

Joseph Taylor, born in Charlton, Saratoga Co., N. Y., Aug. 26, 1775, died in Hagerstown, June 3, 1829, while on a journey for his health. He held several prominent offices in his native State, and at the time of his death held one in the General Post-office Department at Washington.

Dr. Howard Kennedy, born Sept. 15, 1808, died June 12, 1855.

Jane Carroll, died Jan. 9, 1851, aged 75 years, 11 months.

Joseph Gabby, born April 25, 1779, died Nov. 30, 1856; and his wife, Ann, born April 25, 1777, died Jan. 6, 18[illegible]2.

[illegible], mother of Rev. Septimus Tustin, died Aug. 22, [illegible], aged 7[illegible].

[illegible] McKee, died April 5, 1854.

[illegible] Robertson, died June 8, 1847, aged 55.

[illegible], wife of Dr. James Johnson, born Sept. 28, 1807, and [illegible] in 18[illegible].

Sarah Johnst[illegible], [illegible] [illegible]ston, died March 12, 1821, aged 47.

The Christian Church.—The youngest religious organization in Hagerstown is the congregation of the Christian Church, which began in 1876, with eighty members. The original officers were John D. Newcomer, J. H. Wagoner, elders, and Abraham Corbett and Alfred Stouffer, deacons. At first worship was conducted in Hoffman Hall, but in a short time the old Presbyterian church on South Potomac Street was purchased. In March, 1877, Elder Louis H. Stein, of Kentucky, was called to the pastorate of the church, being its first regular minister. He remained but a little more than a year, during which time Elder John H. Wagoner resigned his eldership, and Henry S. Eavey was elected in his place. In September, 1878, Elder S. B. Moore, of Iowa, became the second pastor of the church. In the summer and fall of 1879 the old Presbyterian church building, recently purchased, was remodeled and repaired, making it one of the neatest and most comfortable church edifices in the city. The congregation has had an uninterrupted and steady growth, until it now numbers one hundred and sixty-eight communicants, and owns a church property valued at nine thousand dollars, free of debt. The present officers are: Elders, John D. Newcomer, Henry S. Eavey, A. M. Wolfinger; Deacons, Abraham Corbett, Alfred Stouffer, John W. Newcomer, George D. Keller. The pastor is S. B. Moore, and the treasurer Levi Middlekauff. The Sunday-school numbers one hundred, including officers and teachers. Superintendent, J. Irvin Bitner; Assistant Superintendent, Levi Middlekauff. In connection with the church is a "Ladies' Aid Society," the object of which is to raise money by weekly contributions for the aid of the poor in the congregation, and for other purposes.

Rose Hill Cemetery was incorporated March 16, 1866, Governor William T. Hamilton being one of the original incorporators. The others were B. H. Garlinger, W. M. Marshall, David Zeller, Chas. T. Nesbitt, Geo. F. Heyser, William Updegraff, W. H. Protzman, Samuel T. Zeigler, William McKeppler, N. I. Magruder, Chas. Knodle, and Geo. B. Oswald. Governor Hamilton was made president. The cemetery grounds were purchased from the wife of T. H. Norman, and consist of twenty-six acres, beautifully situated on the southern borders of the town, facing the Sharpsburg turnpike and the Washington County Railroad. The cemetery is one of the ornaments of the town. The grounds were laid out by Jno. Wilkenson, of Baltimore, and were dedicated in September, 1867, the Rev. T. T. Titus, of the Lutheran Church, deliv[illegible] the address. The present officers of the [illegible] [illegible] Governor W. T.

Hamilton, Secretary and Treasurer, W Updegraff, Directors, D B Sath, L D Herbert, D W Ragan, James I Hurly, M E Barber, B A Garlinger, C W Humrickhouse, William Updegraff, E M Mealey

The following are among those interred in Rose Hill Cemetery

Rev Robert W Dunlap, pastor of the Presbyterian Church, born in Lancaster District, South Carolina, in September, 1815, and died in Hagerstown Feb 17, 1856 He was a graduate of the theological seminary at Princeton, N J, was ordained in April, 18[illegible], and was called to the congregation at Hagerstown in 18[illegible] A marble monument with a brownstone base was erected to his memory by the people of his charge

Benjamin Price, born Jan [illegible], 1793, died Nov 16, 1840

Mary McCardell died Sept 14, 18[illegible] aged 72

William McCardell, died Aug 21, 1870

Christian Fechtig born Feb 6 1794, died Sept 7, 1835

Isabella Fechtig, born Feb 26, 1800, died Aug 1, 1866

Christian Fechtig born Feb 18 1759, died Jan 14, 1834

Susan Fechtig born July 12, 176[illegible] died April 9, 1810

John Fechtig born March 14, 1799 died April 10 1869

Jonathan Hager, died April 16 1864 aged 72, and his wife, died July 18 1873, aged 78

John I Heyser, died July 11, 1871 aged 55

Joseph Lummert, born April 1 1799, died Sept 2[illegible], 1[illegible] and Elizabeth, his wife, born July 2[illegible] 1799, died Sept 17, 1866

Catharine Wagner, wife of William, died Sept 10, 1877, aged 30 Her grave is marked by a handsome monument, surmounted by an urn

Zaccheus McComas, born March 31, 1792, died May 15, 1867

Susan I McComas, born Jan 7, 1796, died Sept 7 1859

T G Robertson, born April 17, 1823, died June 28 1869

Both these graves are marked by tasteful monuments

Francis Dieterich, died Feb [illegible], 1878, aged 86

Margaret Kreigh, wife of William, died Nov 28, 1864, aged 66

Timothy Monahan, died Oct 15, 1806, aged 11

Francis McKiernan, died June 18, 1859, aged 86

Eliza T Monohan, born Feb 12, 1803, died Nov 15, 1874

Martin Speck, Sr, born Nov 15, 1789, died March 24, 1852, aged 62, and his wife, Ann, born July 21, 1790, died Oct 21, 1858, aged 68

Martin Speck, Jr, born Jan 3, 1817, died April 11, 1877, and his wife, Isabel, born Oct 28, 1824, died Jan 3, 1875

George G Middlekauff died Aug 6, 1877, aged 43

J E Rowland has a very handsome lot, with a monument of marble Two children are interred in it

Dr Frederick Dorsey, died Oct 26, 1858, aged 82, and Sarah, his wife, died Oct 5, 1860, aged 75

Catharine Kuntz aged 63

Christiana, wife of Michael Miller, died Aug 3, 1860, aged 54

Philip Schindel, died Aug 15, 1854, aged 72, and Mary A C, his wife, died April 28, 1869, aged 82

Elizabeth, wife of Daniel Dunn, died April 8, 1861, aged 19

William M Tice, born Sept 23 181[illegible], died June 2[illegible], 1875, Ann C his wife born March 22, 1818, died June 9, 18[illegible]

Catharine, wife of James Hockley, born Oct 18, 1801, and died Dec 11, [illegible], aged 62

Jane S P Kench, wife of Andrew, born May 15, 1802, died March 15, 1861

David Johnston died Oct 12, 1855, aged 57

John Gamble born Sept 5, 1815, died June 21, 1862, aged 46, and his wif[illegible] na, [illegible] May 24, 1861 [illegible]

Solomon [illegible]

D Artz, died May 28, 1872 aged 78, and his wife, Catharine, died May 20, 1832, aged 41

Lewis Horst, died Jan 18, 1877, aged 69

Archibald McCoy, died Sept 10, 1868, aged 6[illegible]

Charles Ulrich, Sr died Jan 12 1879, aged 64

Isaac Motter, born Oct 28, 1805, died Dec 3 1877 A fine monument of marble with granite base, and with a cross carved on it, marks Mr Motter's grave

Henry Stonebraker, born July 21, 1815, died Feb 21, 1877

John Zeller, died Feb 16, 1873, aged 60

Philip Seibert, died Nov 2[illegible], 1859, aged 66, and his wife, Elizabeth, died Feb 23, 1880 aged 73

George Buch, died July 8, 1878, aged 71, and his wife, Anna Eve, died Oct 17, 1870, aged 58

Marinda Etta, wife of Elias Brumbaugh, died Aug 26, 1878, aged 61

Samuel Schindel, born Dec 23, 1791, died Aug 11, 1863, aged 72, and his wife, Julia Anna, died Oct 19, 1858, aged 61

B Franklin Roman, born Dec 29, 1819, died Jan 3, 1863 aged 43

Lewis K Fouke, died Nov 17, 1872, aged 82

Edward B Murray died July 16, 1860

Elizabeth, wife of Blakiston Lynch, died July 23, 1872, aged [illegible]

George W Smith, born Jan 12, 1810, died Dec 22, 1873

Melissa wife of H G Wiles, born April 17, 1828, died Feb 13, 18[illegible]8

Capt Henry Clopper, died March 1, 1879, aged 77

Sarah Ann, wife of George W Martin, aged 64

Jacob S Huyett, died April 23, 1877, aged 56

Jacob Yeakle, born in Hagerstown, Sept 26, 1779, and died Jan [illegible], 1841, and his wife, Elizabeth, aged 95

Amelia, wife of Jacob K Harry, died Sept 27, 1874, in her 62d year

Adam Andreas, born in Hesse Cassel, Nov 17, 1801, died Sept 29, 1873

William Cramer, born Oct 4, 1806 died March 2 1871, aged 6[illegible]

Frances, wife of Jonathan Schindel, died Aug 13, 1871, aged 50

Daniel Startzman, died March 17, 1863, aged 62, and his wife, Anna, died Dec 19 1872, aged 7[illegible]

John Booth, Sr, died Jan 18, 1872, aged 51

John Booth, Jr, died April 13, 1865, from wounds received in the civil war, aged 20

Overton C Hume born Sept 15, 1780, died Jan 15, 1873, aged 92, and Susannah, his wife, born July 6, 1784, died July 29, 1873, aged 89

Alexander Mitchell, Sr, died Nov 29, 1860, in his 61st year

Eliza Carr, died Sept 30, 1852, in her 52d year

Benjamin Riegle, born May 31, 1798, died Jan 11, 1876

Joseph G Protzman, born March 24, 1803, died June 11, 1862, aged 59

Simon G Knode, died May 3, 1868, aged 57

Mary wife of Rev S W Hartsock, died March 5, 1867, aged 24

John Noel, died July 19, 1866, aged 71, and his wife, Catharine, died Sept 1, 1868, in her 71st year

Benjamin Harris, born Oct 27, 1813, died Dec 30, 1870 aged 57

Thomas Hagerman, died Oct 5 1865 aged 68 and his wife, Hannah died June 27 1879, aged 74

Esther, wife of William A Hagerman, died March 17, 1872, aged 49

Upton H Braguner died Dec 22, 1879, aged 57

Christian Winter, born April 22, 1807, died Feb 15, 1858

Sop[illegible] d Jan 21, 18[illegible],

[illegible], wife of Jacob Griffe, died Sept. 5, 1870, aged 75.

[illegible] Crum, died Sept. 1, 1856, aged 60; and his wife, [illegible], born Sept. 1, 1799, and died Aug. 10, 1875, aged 75.

[illegible] W. Boswell, died May 10, 1877, aged 68.

[illegible] S. Middlekauff, died Feb. 20, 1873, aged 78.

[illegible] Beck, died May 3, 1878, aged 83; and his wife, Ann, [illegible] June 4, 1873, aged 73.

[illegible] Bean, died Nov. 30, 1863, aged 73.

Mary E. Helmar, died April 28, 1876, aged 51.

[illegible], wife of Geo. H. L. Chrisinger, died Feb. 10, 1873, [illegible].

Frederick Peters, died July 9, 1875, in his 70th year; and his [illegible] Mary, died Aug. 28, 1871, in her 54th year.

[illegible] Figeley, died June 8, 1862, aged 82.

Margaret Figeley, died April 13, 1850, aged 65.

[illegible] Brengler, died Feb. 18, 1879, aged 71; and his wife, Margaret, died Nov. 7, 1853, aged 42.

John C. Most, died Jan. 11, 1865, aged 65.

Anna Margaret Most, died Sept. 28, 1878, aged 72.

Zacharias Hamrich, died Dec. 21, 1871, aged 43.

Sarah A., wife of Philip D. Blair, born April 25, 1825, died [illegible] 6, 1874, aged 49.

Henry Schubert, born March 16, 1824, died Sept. 10, 1880, aged 56.

John Smith, born Feb. 15, 1827, died June 6, 1878, aged 51.

John Smith, born March 1, 1800, died Jan. 4, 1875, aged 74; and his wife, Catharine B., born Feb. 12, 1798, died July 6, 1871, aged 73.

Barbara, wife of John Mead, born Feb. 18, 1801, died July 16, 1870, aged 69.

Elizabeth, wife of Christian Krabberger, died Aug. 23, 1879, aged 59.

Mrs. George Sommar, died Sept. 23, 1880, aged 70.

Jacob Giesnour, born Feb. 9, 1791, died Dec. 31, 1876, aged 85.

Thomas Boyd, Sr., died Nov. 8, 1869, aged 55.

Stewart Herbert, died April 8, 1853, aged 61 years, 11 months, and 1 day; and his wife, Rebecca, died April 26, 1880, aged 86 years, 5 months, and 5 days.

Frederick Stover, died Oct. 24, 1861, aged 80; and Magdalene Stover, died April 30, 1872, aged 80.

George French, born Dec. 8, 1818, died Aug. 1, 1878.

Bernard B. Smith, died Feb. 16, 1841, aged 36; and Elizabeth B., died March 19, 1875, aged 67.

George Brundel, died Aug. 6, 1855, aged 81; and Maria Brundel, died Jan. 13, 1868, aged 66.

David Barr, born Oct. 17, 1788, died April 14, 1846.

Matilda S., wife of Daniel Weisel, died Feb. 1, 1876.

John S. Hamilton, born Oct. 20, 1801, died March 25, 1869.

Henry Schriver, died March 4, 1872, aged 65; and his wife, Barbara, Aug. 18, 1854, aged 46.

Samuel Yeakle, born Oct. 15, 1806, died Nov. 22, 1876.

Johanna Kutzherbst, died Oct. 17, 1878, aged 84.

G. Henry Hargis, died Dec. 31, 1874, aged 78; and his wife, Sabilla, died Feb. 10, 1852, aged 50.

John Tice, died Nov. 16, 1868, aged 73.

Henry Winter, born Aug. 31, 1815, died March 18, 1874.

Corp. Henry A. Gyer, killed in battle in front of Petersburg, Aug. 21, 1864, aged 26.

David Beeler, died Sept. 14, 1874, aged 76.

William Brazier, died Sept. 27, 1861, aged 78; and Mary Brazier, died May 9, 1872, aged 83.

John Appleman, born June 29, 1793, died Dec. 25, 1862.

Mary Swingley, died Sept. 8, 1867, aged 75.

George Boyd, born Jan. 2, 1812, and died June 16, 1871.

John Hagerman, [illegible] 187[illegible], aged [illegible].

Sarah Hagerman, died Sept. 30, 1870, aged 58.

Daniel Carver, born July 28, 1796, died Feb. 9, 1872.

John Cook, died Feb. 5, 1874, aged 68; and Eleanora Cook, died Nov. 28, 1872, aged 57.

Rev. H. C. Fouke, died July 15, 1879, aged 45.

Barbara, wife of Christian Negley, died Sept. 17, 1869, aged 75.

Richard Ragan, Sr., died Nov. 13, 1850, aged 75; and Elizabeth Ragan, died July 20, 1835, aged 52.

Barbara Sellner, died Aug. 3, 1873, aged 67.

Michael Graybill, died April 26, 1875, aged 93; and Esther Graybill, born Aug. 24, 1785, died June 17, 1846.

Christian Thomas, died Dec. 15, 1880, aged 77.

Magdalene Nef, died Nov. 28, 1808, aged 77.

J. Conrad Simler, died April 28, 1874, aged 76.

William Kitzmiller, died Dec. 23, 1866, aged 55; and Catharine Kitzmiller, died Feb. 13, 1869, aged 55.

Charles E. Gelwicks, died May 14, 1875, aged 65.

George Shryock, died May 21, 1872, aged 85; and Elizabeth Shryock, died Feb. 7, 1865, aged 81.

Anthony W. Lewis, born Nov. 20, 1801, died March 27, 1876.

William Bester, died Sept. 28, 1859, aged 57.

Susan Beck, born May 30, 1793, died Aug. 11, 1855.

William Knodle, died Nov. 16, 1851, aged 65; and Rebecca Knodle, died March 6, 1828, aged 43.

Jacob Winter, died March 6, 1877, aged 72.

Charles G. Lane, born March 17, 1804, died Jan. 4, 1873; and Maria Lane, born July 4, 1806, died April 13, 1869.

Seth Lane, born Feb. 1, 1774, and died Dec. 7, 1821; and Catharine Lane, born June 17, 1777, and died April 26, 1825.

Margaret A. Black, died July 4, 1879, aged 83.

Catharine, wife of J. Q. Smith, died May 14, 1873.

Joseph Fiery, born Jan. 15, 1807, died Nov. 27, 1866.

John R. Sneary, died Oct. 24, 1879, aged 60.

Barbara Rowland, died Aug. 2, 1861, aged 71.

M. C. Hammelhouse, born Aug. 7, 1804, died Feb. 3, 1878.

Joseph Ignatius Merrick, born Sept. 20, 1790, died June 19, 1854; and Sophia Buchanan Merrick, born Aug. 11, 1790, died June 11, 1873.

Rebecca Snider, died March 22, 1854, aged 70 years.

Elizabeth Perry, died June 27, 1878, aged 79.

Elizabeth, wife of Allen Glassbrenner, born Feb. 18, 1790, died March 18, 1856.

Daniel C. Miller, born July 19, 1791, died March 22, 1860; and Rachel, died Sept. 16, 1874, aged 76.

John Ringer, died March 29, 1864, aged 77; and Magdalene S. Ringer, died Nov. 15, 1868, aged 64.

Susan Miller, died Nov. 11, 1880, aged 83.

Mary McDaniel, died Sept. 6, 1845, aged 65.

Andrew Swartz, died Jan. 15, 1867, aged 63 years.

Eleanora, wife of Leonard Maisack, born July 6, 1797, died April 26, 1869.

Andrew Schwinger, born Feb. 3, 1802, died Feb. 28, 1869.

H. H. Harvey, died Nov. 22, 1875; and his wife, Letitia Purviance Harvey, died Feb. 2, 1880.

Henry Courtenay Hughes, died Feb. 23, 1862.

Isabella Hughes, died April 4, 1873.

Among the conspicuous lots in the cemetery are the following:

The Hughes lot, containing the bodies of Robert Hughes, who died March 26, 1839, and his wife, Susan Purviance, who died April 6, 1846. In the lot of D. H. Wiles is a monument in marble to his only child, Frederick M. Wiles. The lot of the Mealey family is marked by a monument of granite with a [illegible] lot of the Dillon

family is elaborately carved and surmounted by a cross The Russell family monument is a tall granite shaft, on the panels at the base are the names of the family A handsome monument of granite polished and carved and surmounted by a draped urn marks the grave of Elizabeth, wife of Samuel Goheen, who died Nov 27, 1857, aged 73, having been a member of the Methodist Episcopal Church for fifty four years The grave of F Dorsey Herbert is also marked by a fine marble monument A monument erected by Potomac Lodge, No 31, I O O F, bears the inscription, "To Our Dead," and is decorated with emblems of the order on the panels Another monument is dedicated to the memory of Charles E, son of John Gale, who was murdered by a mob "while in the fearless discharge of his duty as a member of the Hagerstown police force, Oct 20, 1866, aged 24 years"

Washington Cemetery —In 1870 the Legislature appropriated five thousand dollars to pay the expense of removing the bodies of the Confederate dead from

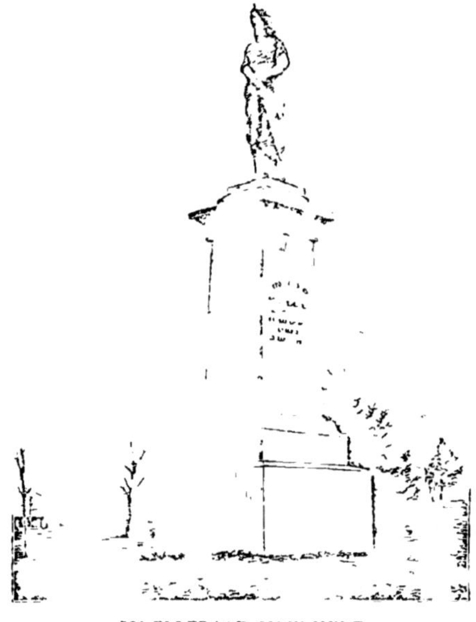

CONFEDERATE MONUMENT

the battle-fields in this section, and the commission appointed selected a portion of Rose Hill as the most suitable place The removals began in September, 1872 On Feb 28, 1877, a beautiful monument was erected by the managers of the cemetery and dedicated to the Confederate dead The body of the monument is of Scotch granite of Aberdeen, of a beautiful brown dappled with varied hues, the base is a solid, heavy stone of American granite from Richmond, upon the top is a marble figure more than five feet in height, representing Hope leaning upon her anchor, with flowing robes, and upon her brow is set a star (perhaps the "single star of the Confederacy") [illegible] the front of the [illegible] the cemetery is the inscription, "The STATE OF MARYLAND has provided this cemetery and erected this monument to perpetuate the memory of the Confederate dead who fell in the battles of Antietam and South Mountain" On the right side we read, "The State of Virginia has contributed toward the burial of her dead within this cemetery," and on the left the same of West Virginia

On Tuesday, the 15th of June, 1877, the Washington Confederate Cemetery, near Hagerstown, was dedicated and decorated for the first time The weather was very fine, and there was an immense concourse of people within the grounds The arrangements were under the direction of Col H Kyd Douglas, president of the board of trustees of the cemetery, seconded by Mr P A Witmer The first arrival occurred about eight o'clock in the morning, when a train from Martinsburg, *via* the Cumberland Valley road, reached Hagerstown with over six hundred excursionists Among these was Capt Charles J Faulkner's company of the Berkeley Light Infantry, numbering eighty men About the same time the two regular trains of the Baltimore and Ohio Railroad came in, bringing about two hundred people from the lower districts of the county At half past eight o'clock a delegation from Shepherdstown, headed by Col W A Morgan, trustee of the cemetery on behalf of West Virginia, and accompanied by the Shepherdstown Cornet Band, arrived on the scene, and shortly before noon a special car of the Baltimore and Ohio Railroad bearing Gen Fitzhugh Lee reached Hagerstown, and was met by Maj George Freaner, Col H Kyd Douglas, and Dr A S Mason, who conducted Gen Lee to Maj Freaner's residence, where he was entertained Maj Freaner had been a member of Gen Lee's staff during the war At noon a train arrived from Baltimore, *via* the Western Maryland Railroad, and soon after two trains of the Baltimore and Ohio Railroad came in, one of them from Washington, and the other from Baltimore The excursionists from Frederick returned home on learning of a railroad accident which had occurred at Point of Rocks Among them was James Gambrill, one of the trustees of the cemetery In Hagerstown the day was universally given up to the celebration Many of the citizens kept open house and invited persons to lunch or dine with them Although it was Tuesday the county "public day" very little business was transacted It is thought that at least six thousand people visited the cemetery during the day, and that there were five thousand present at one time

[illegible] formed in the

public square at Hagerstown, with Col. R. E. Cook, chief marshal, assisted by Marshals A. J. Schindle, A. K. Syester, Jr., Edwin Schindle, George M. Stonebraker, Frank Emmert, and Upton Brumbaugh. In half an hour the different organizations had taken their proper places and the march to the cemetery was commenced. At the head of the column, preceded by the Martinsburg Band and Drum Corps, were the Berkeley Light Infantry, Capt. Charles J. Faulkner, who were followed by the mayor and City Council of Hagerstown, Gen. Fitzhugh Lee, Hon. D. B. Lucas, Gen. I. R. Trimble, and others in carriages. After these came the delegation from the Society of the Army and Navy of the Confederate States and other citizens of Baltimore, accompanied by the Fifth Regiment Band, and commanded by Capt. McHenry Howard, president of the society. Next in order came the Fire Department of Hagerstown, their engines handsomely decorated with flowers, and accompanied by the Keedysville Band. These companies were followed by the delegation from Shepherdstown, W. Va., commanded by Col. W. A. Morgan, assisted by Capts. J. S. Melvin and Lee H. Moler, and led by Criswell's Cornet Band. After the Shepherdstown delegation came various other delegations from Washington County and elsewhere. Those from Williamsport, Funkstown, and Sharpsburg were noticeably large, and carried masses of beautiful flowers. On the route from Hagerstown to the cemetery the different bands played lively and spirited airs, but when the inclosure was reached they were succeeded by solemn marches and dirges.

At the cemetery the light infantry were drawn up in line facing the graves and near the speaker's stand. The bands were stationed at various points. The mayor and Council, the speakers, and the guests were then conducted to the stand by the trustees of the cemetery. A choir of sixty persons, with an organ, were placed in front of the stand, and the engines of the Fire Department were stationed along the main drives, upon a conspicuous eminence.

The exercises began with prayer, which was offered by the Rev. Levi Keller, of Funkstown. He thanked Almighty God for the restoration of love and unity between the late contending armies, and offered an earnest supplication for the President and other civil functionaries of the United States. After music by the Fifth Regiment Band, Maj. George Freaner, secretary and treasurer of the cemetery association, delivered a historical sketch of the cemetery. The burial of the Confederate dead who fell in the battles of Antietam and South Mountain in an appropriate place was, he said, the result of a series of efforts made by the State of Maryland. Less than eighteen months after the battles were fought the Legislature passed an act organizing the Antietam National Cemetery. This act, which was amended and re-enacted at the succeeding session of 1865, provided for the purchase of ten acres of land, "a part of the battlefield of Antietam," as a burial-place for the soldiers who fell in that battle. These acts made it the duty of the trustees of all States joining the corporation to remove the remains of all the soldiers who fell in the battles of Antietam and have them interred in this national cemetery, the remains of the soldiers of the Confederate army to be buried in a portion of the ground separate from that in which the bodies of the soldiers of the Union army were interred. To carry out this scheme the sum of fifteen thousand dollars was appropriated and expended in the purchase of the grounds, etc., near Sharpsburg, now the National Cemetery. Many thousands of dollars were contributed by fourteen other States, but, in violation of the law, the remains of the Confederate soldiers were not reinterred, but were permitted to remain where they had been hastily buried. In many instances the trenches were so washed by the rain that their bones were laid bare and were turned over by the plow.

In a letter dated Dec. 3, 1867, Governor Fenton, of New York, called the attention of the trustees of the Antietam National Cemetery to the sad condition of these Confederate dead, and to the requirement of the Maryland acts of Assembly, which they had disregarded, viz., that the remains of Confederate as well as Federal soldiers should be removed to their cemetery. In this connection, Governor Fenton said, "The hostility of the generous and heroic ends with death, and brief as our history is, it has furnished an early example. The British and Americans who fell at Plattsburgh sleep side by side, and a common monument on the Plains of Abraham attests the heroism of Wolfe and Montcalm." Influenced probably by this appeal and the earnest entreaties of Thomas A. Boullt, secretary and treasurer of the board, the trustees passed a resolution designating and setting apart for the burial of the Confederate dead who fell in the battle of Antietam, in the first invasion of Lee, the southern portion of the grounds, not occupied, and separate from the ground devoted to the burial of the Union dead. At the next session of the Maryland Legislature five thousand dollars was appropriated to the cemetery, presumably for the reinterment of the Confederate dead. But the trustees in 1868 finally postponed any further action towards the removal of these remains. The five thousand dollars appropriated by Maryland [illegible] State treasury,

and at the January session of the Legislature of 1870 an act was passed organizing the Washington Cemetery and appropriating the five thousand dollars to its use. The charter provides for the burial of the dead of both armies remaining unburied at the date of that instrument, and for the appointment of three trustees from Maryland and one from any State which may join the corporation. It gives the trustees full power to accomplish the work intrusted to them, and enables them to receive and hold all contributions by way of gift, devise, bequest, etc.

During the summer of 1870, Governor Bowie appointed as trustees on behalf of the State of Maryland Col. H. K. Douglas and Maj. George Freaner, of Washington County, and James T. Gambrill, of Frederick County. The first meeting of the trustees was held in the fall of 1870, and Col. Douglas was elected president. The summer of 1871 was consumed in seeking sites for the cemetery. The charter required that it should be located within one mile of Hagerstown, and the trustees finally purchased two and a half acres and ten perches of land from the Rose Hill Cemetery Company for two thousand four hundred dollars. The Rose Hill Cemetery Company agreed, in making the sale, to keep the grounds in the same condition as their own. After securing the ground, the trustees commenced the removal of the dead, first from the fields of Antietam about twelve miles south of Hagerstown. With the aid of H. C. Mumma, of Sharpsburg, the trustees disinterred and removed from the battle-fields of Antietam seventeen hundred and twenty-one bodies. The remains when known were placed in single boxes, and when unknown were deposited two in a box. They were removed to Washington Cemetery and buried at an average cost of one dollar and a half per head. This closed the work for 1872 and nearly exhausted the money appropriated, leaving the dead of South Mountain and in isolated parts of the county unburied.

A further appropriation of five thousand dollars, however, was made by the Legislature of Maryland at its January session in 1874, and the Legislatures of Virginia and West Virginia each appropriated five hundred dollars. On receiving these appropriations, the trustees elected Col. W. A. Morgan, of West Virginia, and Maj. R. W. Hunter, of Virginia, to represent their respective States in the board of trustees. In 1874 the trustees resumed work, and buried two thousand four hundred and forty-seven dead, of whom two hundred and eighty-one were identified. The graves were sodded and the grounds decorated as far as the funds of the trustees permitted after they had set apart [illegible] dollars, which invested, would yield an income sufficient to keep the cemetery in good repair. A monument was also erected, the work of A. Steinmetz, of Philadelphia, at a cost of fourteen hundred and forty dollars. At the close of his remarks Maj. Freaner said, "It is our intention to make this cemetery a beautiful spot, worthy of an annual pilgrimage from those whose friends and kindred lie here buried, as well as all those who may wish to render homage to a race of men who were willing to die rather than submit to humiliation."

The dedication dirge (words by Col. H. Kyd Douglas, music by F. J. Halm) was then sung by the choir, led by Prof. Halm, with organ accompaniment by Mrs. John Cretin. During the singing Capt. Faulkner's company stood at "present arms." The dirge and music were dedicated to Gen. Fitzhugh Lee. Gen. Lee, the orator of the day, was then introduced, and delivered an eloquent address, in which, after giving rapid sketches of the conspicuous Southern generals he said that the people of the two sections now had a common country, and that it behooved his hearers to love and cherish it, and to banish discord and strife. After Gen. Lee's address there was music by the Martinsburg Band, which was followed by a poem delivered by its author, Hon. Daniel B. Lucas, then music by the Keedysville Band, after which a letter was read from Brevet Maj. Gen. J. W. Crawford, of the Federal army, then living at Chambersburg, Pa., in which he said that he would most willingly add his testimony to the bravery and devotion of the gallant men who rest at Washington Cemetery. "In their devotion to principle," said he, "and in those high qualities which enabled them to die for it they have the respect of every true American." After the reading of this letter the graves were strewn with flowers, the monument was decorated with roses and evergreens, and a handsome magnolia was placed at the base. On the mound whereon the monument stands and in front of the monument stood a shield, with the ground in white roses and a St. Andrew's cross in red roses, and on the three remaining sides the words, in large letters, Gettysburg, Antietam, South Mountain, in red, white, and pink roses respectively. Besides these there was a great profusion of flowers and of floral decorations placed on the green turf near the monument. During the ceremony of strewing the graves with flowers the different bands played funeral marches and requiems. When the decoration was finished Harry Greenwood, of Shepherdstown, aged five years, performed a "solo" on the drum, accompanied by his father with the fife. The choir then sang "[illegible] th[illegible] [illegible] arranged by A. D.

[illegible]ok, and the long metre doxology, with accompa[illegible] by the Hagerstown Band, after which the Rev. [illegible] A Mitchell, rector of St. John's Protestant [illegible] Church, pronounced the benediction. The [illegible] Light Infantry then discharged three volleys [illegible] the graves of the dead soldiers, after which the [illegible]sion formed again and marched back to Hagers[illegible], and the visiting delegations took the trains for [illegible] respective homes.

The following committees made the necessary ar[illegible]ements for the occasion:

[illegible] of Arrangements.—P. A. Witmer, Alexander Arm[illegible], William Weller, Buchanan Schley, Christ. F. Bikle, A. [illegible], J. C. Lane, George Lias, George W. Grove.

[illegible] of Reception.—Col. Geo. Schley, Dr. A. T. Mason, [illegible] W. Hamrickhouse, Lewis C. Smith, Alexander Neill, T. [illegible] Williams, Dr. C. B. Boyle, William Kealhofer, W. McK. Keppler, W. H. Armstrong.

Committee on Music.—John H. Heyser, F. J. Halm, A. D. Merrick, Dr. M. W. Allison, Thomas E. Hilliard, Henry Winter, Mrs. John Cretin, Miss Mollie Schley, Miss Cora Heffinger, Mrs. H. C. Koehler.

Committee on Decoration of Monument.—Edward W. Mealey, Mrs. W. T. Hamilton, Mrs. H. H. Keedy, Mrs. Alonzo Berry, Miss Minnie Moore, Claggett D. Spangler, Frank Kennedy, Mrs. C. E. Ways, Miss Ida Hammond, Miss Eliza Stanhope, Miss Lizzie Ragan, Mrs. Nannie Beckenbaugh, Mrs. William Martiney.

Committee on Flowers.—Dr. William Ragan, Mrs. A. K. Syester, Miss Mamie Motter, Mrs. George Phreaner, Miss Allee Boyd, Mrs. George D. Keller, Mrs. E. Y. Fechtig, Miss Adelaide Berry, Miss Blanche Shindle, Miss Bessie Rowan, Miss Ella Taggart, Miss Ella Smith, Mrs. J. C. Cookerly, Miss Susie Fiery, Miss Leila Cushwa, Miss Sophia Herbert, Miss Bettie Barber, Mrs. W. T. Williamson, William Bester, D. A. Peters.

DISTRICT COMMITTEES.

1. *Sharpsburg.*—George M. Stonebraker, Jacob Marker, Henry C. Mumma, Reuteh Miller, W. F. Blackford, Mrs. Dr. Russell, Mrs. Jacob McGraw, Miss Julia Grove, Miss Savilla Miller, Miss Lottie Grove.

2. *Williamsport.*—J. L. McAtee, J. M. Sword, I. L. Motter, William E. Taylor, D. O. Witmer, Dr. Booth, Miss Mary Clark, Miss Naonie Motter, Miss Maria Hollman, Miss Mary Gruber, Miss Annie Miller.

4. *Clear Spring.*—David Seibert, Lewis Brewer, J. H. Wilson, William Smith, J. T. Cushwa, Mrs. Samuel Reitzell, Miss Seibert, Miss Creigh, Miss Cushwa.

5. *Hancock.*—Joseph Murray, Dr. Delaplane, Robert Bridges, Samuel Rinehart, Miss Mary Broderick, Mrs. Henderson, Miss Bridges.

6. *Boonsboro'.*—O. B. Smith, John L. Nicodemus, J. S. Henry, Henry Wade, Kennedy Wilson, William Welck, Mrs. A. W. Lakin, Mrs. George W. Hoffman, Mrs. Dr. Gaines, Misses Brining, Miss Annie Binger, Miss Rachel Smith.

7. *Cavetown.*—Dr. Riddlemoser, Joseph B. Wishard, T. Harry Davis, David Winters, Mrs. Joseph Winters, Miss Emily Bishop, Mrs Ida Riddlemoser, Miss Santee, Miss Nettie Little, Miss Emma Fiery.

8. *Rohrersville.*—Augustus Young, George W. Brown, John S. Miller, Josiah Buck, Mrs. John Shifler, Mrs. Joshua C. Miller, Mrs. Ezra D. Miller, Miss Jane Gouff.

9. *Leitersburg.*—Dr. Charles Harper, Daniel Beck, Henry Schriver, Jr., Mi[illegible] Mi[illegible], M[illegible].

10. *Funkstown.*—Charles South, William H. Myers, Nathaniel Fiery, Joseph Williams, Henry Eyler, Charles Keller, Miss Libbie Keller, Miss Laura Shafer, Miss Ella Keller, Miss Sallie Knode, Miss Carrie Brewer, Miss Sallie Gower.

11. *Beaverton.*—B. Clay Elgin, Edward Garrett, George H. Stonebraker, Marlow Thrasher, Mrs. Warren Garrett, Mrs. Samuel B. Preston, Mrs. J. H. Elgin, Miss Moore.

12. *Tilghmanton.*—Thos. J. Warfield, J. H. Beeler, B. A. Poffenberger, George Eakle, J. W. C. Beeler, Mrs. Dr. Grimes, Miss Sue Booth, Mrs. John Henry Reynolds, Mrs. Dr. Duckett, Miss Nannie Maddox.

13. *Conococheague.*—E. I. Spickler, George W. Beckenbaugh, David C. Byers, Philip Neibert.

14. *Ringgold.*—Dr. F. Barkdoll, Jacob C. Reecher, Lewis Barkdoll, A. H. Schockey, Miss Sue Shockey, Miss Barkdoll.

15. *Indian Spring.*—Alexander Flora, E. G. Kinsell, John D. Ties, Tom Moore.

16. *Beaver Creek.*—A. B. Martin, J. J. Bitner, John M. Newcomer, Elias Rowland, Miss Ella Newcomer, Mrs. James Kridler, Mrs. Elias Martz.

18. *Chewsville.*—John B. Baechtel, John H. Hartle, Jacob Huyett, Mrs. Emma Huyett, Mrs. Jacob Wolf, Mrs. Abner Betz, Miss Martha Hoover, Miss Ida Baechtel.

19. *Keedysville.*—Dr. Keedy, Daniel Neikirk, Frisby Deah, George W. Miller, George Snively, Miss Minnie Eakle, Miss Susan Hoffman, Miss Fannie Deaner, Mrs. Otho Miller, Miss Kate Hammond, Miss Barbara Neikirk, Miss Susie Snively.

The managers of the cemetery are H. Kyd Douglas, George Freaner, and James H. Gambrill.

CHAPTER XLVI.

THE BENCH AND BAR OF WASHINGTON COUNTY.

The Court-house—Early Trials and Executions—Jail—Early Court Notes—Distinguished Judges and Lawyers.

WASHINGTON COUNTY has erected three court-houses since the formation of the county in 1776. The first building was a quaint-looking brick structure, standing in the centre of the public square, and was erected soon after the establishment of the county.

The court-room was on the second floor, and was reached by a flight of steps on the outside. For a time all elections were held in this room, the voting being *viva voce*. The elections lasted several days, and were conducted in a very primitive manner. All the candidates sat in a row behind the sheriff, who took the votes. As each elector approached the candidates would take off their hats, bow politely, and solicit his vote. When the contest was very spirited there were, of course, some animated scenes, and not infrequently disturbances took place. The windows on one side of the court-house were protected with wire from random balls, there being a public alley for ball-playing on that side of the building. The lower story [illegible] market-house.

At a regular session of the General Assembly of the State of Maryland, held in Annapolis during the winter of 1815–16, an act was passed and approved authorizing the inhabitants of Washington County to levy a tax and erect a new court-house This was done in accordance with the wishes of a majority of the tax-paying citizens, who in their petition represented

"that the existing court-house of said county is in a state of ruinous decay, and the Public Records deposited therein are considerably endangered, that it is too contracted in its plan to accommodate the court and its officers, and that, standing in the Public Square, directly on the intersection of the two principal streets, it greatly injures the appearance of Hagerstown"

The chief provisions of the act were these

"Sec 2 *Therefore be it enacted by the General Assembly of Maryland*, That John Blackford, Samuel Ringgold, William Gabby, John Bowles, and Thomas C Brant be and they are hereby appointed commissioners to select and purchase such lot or lots of ground within the limits of Hagerstown, or the additions to said town, as in their judgment they or a majority of them shall consider the most eligible and proper site for a new court house for the county aforesaid

"Sec 3 *And be it enacted*, That the commissioners hereinbefore named, or a majority of them, be and they are hereby authorized and empowered to contract for and superintend the building of a new court house, with suitable apartments for the court and juries, clerks, sheriff's, and register's offices, and fire-proof places of deposit for the public records, on the site as above by them to be selected and purchased, upon such terms and in such manner as to them shall seem most advantageous to the community

"Sec 4 *And be it enacted*, That the commissioners hereinbefore named, or a majority of them, shall have power to appoint some capable person to superintend and direct the erection of the building aforesaid, under the order of the commissioners aforesaid and that they be and they are hereby empowered to allow such person so employed such compensation as they or a majority of them may deem adequate to his services

"Sec 5 *And be it enacted*, That the Levy Court of Washington County be and they are hereby authorized and required to assess and levy upon the assessable property of said county, in five successive, equal annual installments, a sum not exceeding thirty thousand dollars, the first installment to be assessed by the said court at the second annual session which, after the passage of this act, they shall hold for the purpose of laying the county levy, and to be collected by the sheriff of said county

* * * * * * * *

"Sec 9 *And be it enacted*, That when the said court-house shall be completed and finished, the said commissioners or a majority of them may pull down the old court-house and sell the materials of the same, the proceeds of which may be applied to discharge any debt contracted for the building of the new court-house over and beyond the sum hereinbefore mentioned

* * * * * * * *

"Sec 11 *And be it enacted*, That the public ground on which the court-house now stands shall be condemned as a public street of Hagerstown, not to be built upon or used but as one of the streets of the said town

"Sec 12 *A*[illegible] That the [illegible] said shall meet [illegible] in Hagerstown on the first Monday in April next (1816), and may proceed to the discharge of the several duties provided by this act, and may adjourn from time to time, as may be convenient and necessary and each commissioner shall be entitled to receive two dollars for each day in which he may be engaged in the discharge of the duty imposed by this act"

Thomas Harbaugh was employed as architect and contractor, and work was commenced soon afterwards to erect a new court house at the corner of Washington and Jonathan Streets, on the site of the present edifice, the greatest care being taken in building the walls The court-room was originally on the ground-floor, and extended up to the dome, and was hung around with red tapestry The effect of this was very handsome, but it was impossible for a speaker to make himself heard in it Subsequently an upper floor was built, and the court removed up-stairs, but being still under the dome, its acoustic properties were as bad as before The floor was removed and the hall brought back to its original position, and the next improvement attempted was a floor made directly beneath the dome, in which position it remained until a back building was constructed by R C Thornsburg, the contractor, in 1859 The floor in the old building was then restored, and the space above was fitted up for offices The court hall was then removed to the back building, and no further change was made until the whole building was burned on the night of the 6th of December, 1871

In 1821, soon after the completion of the second court-house, the subject of erecting a statue to George Washington upon the site of the old building in the public square was agitated, but the movement never reached a satisfactory result Washington's name is honored in the town, however by being given to the most prominent street and the public square After the fire in 1871 steps were taken for the erection of a new court house, and a committee was appointed by the court to select temporary accommodations until the completion of the new building The committee consisted of Hon George French, George W Smith, Jr, H H Keedy, Edward Stake, L C Smith, L E McComas, and J C Zeller After examining a number of proposed locations, it was concluded to select the basement story or lecture room of the Methodist church, which is but half a block distant from the record office, on North Jonathan Street The term for which this room was rented began March 1 1872, and ended March 1, 1873, with privilege of renewal at the rate of four hundred dollars a year In the mean time preparations were made for the erection of the new building The county commissioners intrusted the selection of the plan to a committee of lawyers, con- [illegible], Col George

Schley, John C. Zeller, F. M. Darby, Albert Small, Henry K. Douglas, and George W. Smith, Jr. The corner-stone was laid in October, 1872, by the Masonic order at the invitation of the county commissioners, the ceremonies being conducted by Friendship Lodge, No. 84, of Hagerstown, assisted by representatives of lodges from Westminster and other points in the surrounding country. The building was dedicated in the spring of 1874, and the charge of Chief Judge Alvey was listened to by an audience that filled the spacious hall. The new building has given satisfaction in all particulars, the acoustic properties being excellent. The building occupies the site of the old court-house, at the corner of Washington and Jonathan Streets, fronting ninety-one feet on the former and running back about one hundred and twenty feet. This includes a back building, which is sixty-two and a half feet long by fifty-nine and a half wide. The material is brick, unpainted, and pointed with black mortar, and the building is surmounted by a mansard-roof. Over the main entrance is a large iron plate bearing the coat of arms of the State, and at the angle on Jonathan Street, where the main and back buildings join, is a small belfry, which is about the same height as the highest point in the roof of the main building.

In this tower, facing on Jonathan Street, is a brown-stone tablet bearing the names of the county commissioners by whom the building was erected, the architects, and the contractor.

The sides of the building are relieved by pilasters surmounted by urns. A great deal of brownstone has been used in the structure, and the cornice, which is of galvanized iron, is painted and sanded in imitation of stone. The entrance-doors are of paneled oak, varnished, and are quite handsome. On the right of the main entrance, going in, is the register's office, and on the left the clerk's office, and in the rear of each is a commodious fire-proof vault in which to keep the records of the respective offices. Going down the passage, on the right-hand side, is the county commissioners' room and the main stairway, which is of solid oak. On the left-hand side of the passage are the rooms of the school commissioners, the sheriff, and collector, and a private stairway for the use of the court and members of the bar, leading to a door which opens inside the bar of the court-hall.

The court-hall occupies the whole of the second floor, with the exception of a library and a witness-room at the eastern end, and is lighted by large and well-proportioned windows. About one-half of the hall is taken up for the court and the bar. The petit jury box is o[illegible] the bench and the grand jury box faces the petit jury. The hall is seventy-two feet long by fifty wide. The ceiling is coated with plaster of Paris, as are those of the other rooms, and ornamented with stucco; all the walls throughout the building are left unpainted and unwashed. Near the centre of the ceiling is a large circular opening, which is designed by the architect to secure ventilation; it has two semicircular lids, which can be raised or lowered at pleasure. When both of these lids are raised, the heated air will ascend on one side of them and the cool air descend on the other. The rooms on the second floor of the back building are occupied by the State's attorney and the grand and petit juries. All of the rooms in the building have the purpose for which they are designed painted on the doors. The vaults are furnished with iron window-shutters and double iron doors with patent combination locks. Outside of the private entrance to the court-hall is a stairway leading to the roof, from which point there is a grand view of the town and the surrounding country.

Jail.—The first jail was a small rough building of round logs, and occupied the lot where the tannery of the Washington County Leather Company stood. It was used for a number of years, and then the building afterwards occupied by Richard Sheckles was erected for that purpose. Thence it was removed to the jail building, which was destroyed by fire in 1857. The building of this jail became necessary, and was authorized by the Legislature in 1818. The commissioners having in charge the erection of the structure were S. Ringgold, William Gabby, O. H. Williams, William Heyser, and Henry Lewis, the same who erected the second county court-house. This jail was built of limestone, rough-casted outside, and was inclosed by a wall on the north, west, and south. The approach to the entrance was through a neat plastered house, which was generally occupied as a residence by the sheriff and his family.

In passing through the hall of the sheriff's house, the visitor approached the outer door of the prison. This door was large and massive, being constructed of oak, and traversed in all directions by spikes and screws, and lined between the bars of wood with substantial sheet-iron.

This building was destroyed by fire in April, 1857, the entire wood-work of the jail proper being consumed. The sheriff's house, separated by a few feet from the prison, escaped destruction. The old jail was erected in 1826, at a cost of twelve or fifteen thousand dollars.

Steps were immediately taken to provide a new prison for the [illegible] county. [illegible] work on the

building was commenced under the direction of John B Thurston The structure is seventy three by forty-seven feet and is one story high It is roofed with tin, covered with Childs' elastic cement roofing, and is heated by a furnace placed in the cellar It is fire-proof throughout The cost of the building was about seven thousand dollars The transfer of prisoners, some eight or nine in number, to this jail was made by Sheriff Hauck in May, 1858, each of them being placed in a separate cell

Notable Early Trials and Executions—In early days in Maryland the penalty even for misdemeanors was excessively and cruelly severe, our ancestors acting upon the idea that the greater the punishment the more effective the check to crime Even imprisonment for debt was used as a means of private malice An instance of this is afforded by the case of a colored barber, who had a tipsy customer imprisoned for a debt of six and a quarter cents, and paid three pounds in fees before his malice was satisfied Persons offending against the somewhat puritanical laws of the province were imprisoned during the pleasure of the court, not exceeding one year Among other punishments were banishment, boring through the tongue with a red-hot iron, slitting the nose, cutting off one or both ears, whipping, branding with a red hot iron, in the hand or on the forehead, with the initial letter of the offense for which the sufferer was punished,—"S L" for seditious libeler, on either cheek, "M" for manslaughter, or "T" for thief, on the left hand, "R" for rogue, on the shoulder, and "P" for perjury, on the forehead,—"flogging at the cart's tail," when the criminal was tied to the end of a cart and flogged on his naked back while the cart was driven slowly through the town At the Baltimore County Assizes in 1748 an old, gray-haired man was convicted of blasphemy, and his tongue was bored through, and he was sentenced to remain in jail until he paid a fine of twenty pounds The pillory and whipping post were also used as a sort of preliminary punishment to the more severe penalties to follow In 1819 the pillory was used for the last time in Maryland for a revolting crime The last man whipped in the State was a postmaster, for tampering with the mails in Annapolis He was tied to one of the pillars of the portico of the State-house and whipped, while Judge Chase was holding court in the Senate chamber

On the morning of April 12, 1799, two negroes, known as Emanuel and Jack, sentenced to death for the murder of their overseer, Mr. Todd, were taken from the jail at Hagerstown, about nine o'clock, to the place where they h[illegible] committed th[illegible] murd[illegible] and at twelve o'clock were hanged in the presence of a great multitude of spectators

On the 3d of December, 1799, John Jacob Werner, an old man living with his family in the vicinity of Hagerstown, entered the room where his four children were sleeping, and with a tomahawk proceeded to butcher them, fracturing their skulls by repeated blows upon the backs of their heads When he had completed the work of destruction he left the room to search for his wife, whom he found gathering wood in the yard Telling her that he had something very extraordinary to say to her, he called her into the house and, as she was entering the door, assaulted her with the tomahawk, and fractured her skull in several places Leaving her for dead, he returned to the room where his first victims lay, locked the door, and, seizing a razor, cut his own throat from ear to ear, and fell down and expired Two of the children died instantly The wounds of the mother and of the two other children were of a desperate nature, but they survived

The cause of the deed was supposed to have been despair, engendered in the mind of the perpetrator by apprehensions that a law suit in which he was engaged, and which was then pending in the County Court, would be decided against him His wife stated that for eight or ten weeks previous to the catastrophe he had been subject to fits of insanity

On the 15th of April, 1803, John McDaniel was executed, in pursuance of his sentence, for breaking open and robbing the house of Jonas Stevenson The execution took place back of the new jail at Hagerstown The condemned man acknowledged having committed many crimes, but utterly denied the crime for which he was to be hung, as well as three others, for which he was tried and sentenced to hard labor

On the 24th of August, 1803, Peter Light was arraigned at the bar of Washington County Court, charged with making counterfeit dollars He was tried and found guilty, and was sentenced to be whipped, pilloried, and cropped, which sentence was duly executed by the sheriff

Thomas Burk (colored), who had been sentenced to death by Judge J Buchanan for rape, committed in 1808, on Maria Branner, under twelve years of age, escaped from the Washington County jail July 4, 1809

In 1811, Elizabeth Cope was tried and convicted of having cut off the ears of a boy about six years of age, for which she was sentenced to the Maryland Penitentiary for nine years, and to be kept in a cell on low diet for eighteen months of that time

[illegible] that ever took

[illegible] in Washington County was that of the Cotterills, [illegible] and two sons, for the murder of James Adams, [illegible] Allegany County, on the 9th of May, 1819.

The circumstances attending the murder were as follows: William Cotterill, Sr., and his two sons, William and John, in company with their victim, sailed from Liverpool for Baltimore about the 1st of February in the ship "Ceres," Adams having in his possession a considerable sum of money and a check on a mercantile house in Baltimore for a further amount. Arriving in Baltimore in the latter part of April, the four took lodgings together, and remained in the city a few days, when, not finding employment, they determined to seek their fortunes in the West. Reaching Allegany County, they contracted on Thursday, the 6th of May, with Messrs. Wood & West for employment as laborers on the turnpike road. They continued to work for them until the following Saturday evening. On Sunday morning Adams, believing that he had lost the check which he had brought with him from England, determined to return to Baltimore in search of it, and if unsuccessful in this, to stop payment upon it and return to England. He started down the road in pursuance of this determination, accompanied by the two younger Cotterills, the father remaining at the house of Messrs. Wood & West. Two or three hours later the Cotterill brothers returned, not by the road, but through the woods, having their pantaloons wet up to the knees. Their father, who had manifested much uneasiness and agitation during their absence, met them as they approached the house, and a short conversation ensued, during which one of the sons was heard to say, "Father, we have done it."

They immediately applied for the wages due them, announcing their intention to return to England, and in about three-quarters of an hour after the return of the two sons the three left the house, going through the woods in the same direction in which they had come. One week afterwards the dead body of Adams was found in Fifteen Mile Creek, a short distance below the road. The head and breast were terribly mangled, the clothing torn, and the pockets rifled of their contents.

The place was a secluded spot, situated between two mountains, and the surroundings were dreary and wild. Men seldom ventured to intrude upon its solitude, and only accident revealed the dark deed that had been perpetrated there. The murdered man was known in Baltimore, and was said to have been a respectable farmer from Cadworth, England. Circumstances strongly indicated that the three Cotterills were the authors of the murder, and they were [illegible] to Baltimore, where they were found on the point of embarking for England in the ship "Franklin." Their trunk was searched, and in it were found a watch, clothing, and other articles known to have belonged to Adams, and also some money believed to have been a part of that which Adams was known to have possessed. Upon this evidence they were committed to the Baltimore City jail, where they remained until the session of the Allegany County Court was convened. At the request of the prisoners the trial was removed to Washington County. The prosecution was conducted by Roger Perry, and the two younger prisoners were defended by Beal Howard, Samuel Hughes being associated with him in the defense of the elder. The trial was conducted with great ability and ingenuity by the counsel engaged in the case, and after a patient hearing the three prisoners were found guilty of murder in the first degree. The case of each of the three murderers was tried before a different jury. The one which convicted William Cotterill, Jr., was constituted as follows: Jacob Zeller (foreman), John Barr, John McLain, Theodore Mills, Michael Smith, Ignatius Drury, William Gabby, Jeremiah Mason, Archibald Ritchie, Alexander Grim, William Dillehunt, and Frederick Fishaugh.

John Cotterill's jury was composed of the following: John Johnson (foreman), John Neff, Michael Smith, John Hedrick, Daniel Reuch, John Ragan, Isaac S. White, William H. Fitzhugh, John Schnebly, Adam Myers, John Hall, and Thomas Brent.

The following were the jury which tried William Cotterill, Sr., viz.: Daniel Schnebly (foreman), Jacob Zeller, William Gabby, Isaac S. White, Theodore Mills, John Hedrick, Archibald Ritchie, Daniel Reuch, William Fitzhugh, Jr., Frederick Fithzugh, John Neff, and William H. Fitzhugh.

Friday, February 25th, the day appointed for the execution, was wet and cheerless, yet thousands were gathered in the streets of the town, and along the roads leading into it from the surrounding country. Various estimates have been made of the number present at the execution, ranging from ten thousand to forty thousand. At half-past ten o'clock a wagon left the jail door, bearing the three criminals and their spiritual advisers, guarded by the troops of horse of Capts. Barr and Swearingen, and the foot companies of Capts. Dewey and Bell. Preceded by the coffins of the doomed men, the procession passed on to the place of execution. On reaching the scaffold, the Rev. Messrs. Allen and Kurtz ascended the platform and conducted religious services. The criminals then ascended, accompanied by the Rev. Mr. Clay, who offered prayer, the prisoners kn[illegible] and j[illegible] apparent earn-

estness in the devotions Several hymns were then sung, after which the youngest son, John, addressed the vast crowd present He confessed that he and his brother had murdered Adams, and that they suffered justly the penalty of death, but he strongly denied that his father had participated in the crime William, the elder son, also declared the innocence of his father, and the father himself asserted to the last that he was not guilty The condemned men continued to pray until the drop fell

The trial of George Swearingen for the murder of his wife which was another celebrated case, commenced Aug 11, 1829, and lasted eight days The accused was one of the most popular young men in Washington County, and had been elected sheriff in 1827 He married in Allegany County, and in that county was committed the crime for which he suffered death The testimony during the trial tended to show that Swearingen had married his wife from mercenary motives, and his conversations not only indicated that this was true, but also that his affections were engaged and were reciprocated in another quarter Evidence of his indifference towards his wife was produced, and it was also stated during the trial that in June or July, 1827 he had upset her in a gig on Martin's Mountain, injuring her severely It was proven that in August or September, 1827, just previous to his election, he formed an intimacy with a lewd woman, Rachel Cunningham, whom he took to a camp meeting in Washington County in a barouche, and for whom he built a house in Hagerstown which is still standing His connection with the woman becoming notorious, he was threatened by a mob, who intended to demolish the house, but, arming himself, he declared that he would kill the first man who approached him, and thus deterred the rioters After this he sent the woman Cunningham to Virginia, and finally removed her to a farm which he held in his wife's name in Allegany County

His wife left him, but subsequently consented to live with him again on condition that he gave up his intimacy with Rachel Cunningham After this his conduct towards her underwent a change He treated her with more attention, and promised to reform his habits One Sunday he left Cumberland with his wife, traveling as far as Mrs Peggy Cresap's, where they spent the night Next morning they started for the house of another Mrs Cresap's Upon arriving at a point opposite his farm, Swearingen and his wife left the road just as a drove of cattle came up, at the head of which was a young man named Hillary This man swore that he saw the accused leave the road, he leading the way and carrying the baby while his wife followed a short distance in the rear Traveling about two hundred yards in this direction, they reached the foot of a steep hill, where he dismounted, put down the child, and fastened his horse He then took his wife's horse by the bridle and led him up the hill, where Hillary lost sight of them The drover had gone about three-quarters of a mile when Swearingen, riding at a moderate gait and carrying the child in his arms overtook him inquired his name, where he was from, etc, and then informed him that his wife had been thrown from her horse, and that he feared she was dead He requested him to take his horse and ride to Cresap Town and send Robert Kile to him immediately This Hillary did Kile received the message and started for the scene of the catastrophe While passing along the road leading to Swearingen's farm he heard a whistle, and looking in the direction from which it came, discovered Swearingen sitting by the dead body of his wife This spot was about a mile from the main road, and about a quarter of a mile from the place where Swearingen said the horse had fallen with her The coroner's inquest, held the next day, rendered a verdict that the deceased came to her death by an act of Providence Two days after the death of Mrs Swearingen the ground was carefully examined from the point where Hillary lost sight of the party to the place where Kile found Swearingen by the side of the body

The track of a horse was traced by some persons through a laurel thicket, over the hill, from the former of these points to a point in the road about fifty yards above where the corpse was first seen, and a place was discovered where a hollow had been formed by the leaves having been pressed down Beside this depression was a log, and upon the log a stone Not far off was a place where a horse had evidently been hitched, and a club was found, which had apparently been cut in a hurry

Some of the witnesses testified that the leaves were spotted, as they thought, with blood, although others considered this as not being certain There were also some who did not think that the tracks discovered were those of a horse, and one witness stated that there were, in his opinion, no tracks at all The statements of the accused were very contradictory He asserted on one occasion that his wife's fall from the horse had killed her at once, on another, that he had placed her again on the horse after her fall to take her to a place of safety, and that she had again fallen, being killed by the second fall To some he stated that the drove of cattle came in view when she fell [illegible] occurred just as the [illegible]

Another inquest was held, and several physicians were called upon to examine the body Its advanced state of decomposition rendered it apparently impossible to obtain any evidence from the examination, and the physicians so stated in writing They afterwards, however came to the conclusion that the deceased had suffered death from suffocation This later conclusion was based upon the swollen state of the neck but some of the physicians contended that this was not sufficient evidence upon which to establish death by suffocation and that an examination of the lungs and brain should have been made to render the judgment conclusive No such examination was undertaken After this second inquest Swearingen fled, and a summons was issued for him by the coroner The knees of the horse ridden by the deceased were examined and several witnesses swore positively that the injuries had been inflicted by some sharp instrument, and could not have been produced by a fall While Mr Price was making the closing argument a letter from the accused to Rachel Cunningham, written by him in the jail, was produced and read by the prosecuting attorney Within ten minutes after the case had been given to the jury a verdict of murder in the first degree was rendered The case was tried before Judges John Buchanan, Abraham Shriver, and Thomas Buchanan Mr Dixon appeared for the State, and the defense was conducted by Messrs William Price, J V L McMahon, and Bushkirk The report states that Mr Price argued five hours before the jury, and Mr McMahon seven hours and a half

On Monday Judge John Buchanan sentenced him to be hanged, and October 2d was fixed for the execution The place selected was on the west bank of Will's Creek, in the vicinity of Cumberland The condemned man was taken from the jail precisely at ten o'clock and proceeded to the scaffold on foot, escorted by five companies of infantry from Somerset and Bedford Counties, Pa, and by a troop of horse from the former of these counties, under command of Capt Forward Swearingen was attended to the scaffold by the sheriff and by Revs Messrs John Miller, C B Young, N B Little, L H Johns, and H Haverstick, who conducted religious services The rope was then adjusted and the cap drawn by the sheriff A few moments before the platform fell Swearingen assured the sheriff and the Rev Mr Little "in the presence of the Judge of all the earth," that certain particulars previously communicated to them were true A full confession was made by the prisoner to the Rev Mr Little and the particulars mentioned also [illegible] nected with the crime for which he died About twenty minutes before twelve o'clock the sheriff told the doomed man that his last moments had arrived, and let the platform fall from under him His death was comparatively easy

Rachel Cunningham, his mistress, died a pauper in Bayview Asylum, Baltimore, several years ago

On Friday, April 10, 1863, Frederick Smith was hung at Hagerstown for the murder of Agnes Tracy It is estimated that from six to eight thousand persons were present at the execution

Early Court Notes—In December, 1793, Nathaniel Rochester was appointed one of the associate judges of Washington County In April, 1800, the justices of the Washington County Court appointed Otho H Williams clerk of the court in place of Elie Williams, resigned In 1802, William Clagett was appointed chief justice of the Washington, Frederick, Montgomery, and Allegany Courts The justices of the Levy Court were Thomas Sprigg, Samuel Ringgold, Adam Ott, Richard Cromwell, John Good, Charles Carroll, and William Yates In the same year Ignatius Taylor, Elie Williams, and Jacob Harry were appointed judges of the Orphans' Court, and Thomas Crampton, Adam Ott, Richard Cromwell, Lancelot Jacques, John Downey, Samuel Ringgold, Thomas Brunt, William Van Lear, John Good, John Hunter, Isaac Baechtel, George Kennedy, Thomas Sprigg, William Yates, Charles Carroll, Robert Douglass, William Webb, Benjamin Clagett, Henry Shroeder, Daniel Weisel, and Jacob Harry were appointed justices of the peace for Washington County In an advertisement dated Feb 23, 1802, Nathaniel Rochester announced that, having observed in the newspapers a notice calling the attention of the voters to the next election for sheriff, in which it was stated that a poll would probably be opened in his favor, he felt called upon to make known his intentions He therefore informed the voters of the county that he was a candidate, and would thank them for their votes

In 1804 the Governor and Council appointed Martin Kershner to be associate justice of the Washington County Court in place of Benjamin Galloway, resigned

Distinguished Jurists and Lawyers of Washington County.—The bench and bar of Washington County has always sustained the lofty character that has been accorded to the Maryland bar in two hemispheres Its high professional honor has never been questioned, and to-day among leading jurists and counselors it ranks with any county in the State Among these citizens of Washington County who [illegible] in the pleadings

and practice of the law we have selected a few of the most prominent

One of the most brilliant intellects that the bar of Western Maryland has ever boasted was that of Frederick A Schley Mr Schley was the fourth son of John Jacob Schley and was born at Frederick Md, on the 14th of May, 1789, and died there on the 5th of February, 1858 His grandfather, Thomas Schley, the progenitor of the Schleys of Western Maryland and Georgia, was born in the Palatinate, in Germany, in 1712, came to America in 1745, and selected the site of Frederick City as his permanent home He there erected, in 1746, the first house of the future town, and died there in 1790, aged seventy-eight years He had the reputation of being a gentleman of polished and refined manners, of extensive and varied learning, and the possessor of ample means One of Thomas Schley's sons, John Jacob Schley, married Ann Maria Shelman, and there were born to them while they lived in Frederick Michael, John Ann Maria, William, Frederick Augustus, and George About 1793, John Jacob Schley removed from Frederick to Louisville, Ga, where were born Philip Thomas and Catharine Schley Michael died early in life John was a lawyer, and for years prior to his death was a judge William was a lawyer, a member of Congress, judge, and afterwards Governor of Georgia One of the counties of the State was named after him George was an insurance lawyer Philip Thomas was also a lawyer, amassed a fortune, and retired from the bar The above all died in Georgia leaving numerous descendants, of whom five have been lawyers One of them, ex-Judge William Schley, resides in New York Another member of the family is a judge, and several of them have been physicians

Frederick Augustus Schley, the special subject of this sketch (born as stated, May 14, 1789, and died Feb 5 1858), removed to Georgia with his father, John Jacob Schley, but the climate not agreeing with him, he left the University of Georgia when seventeen years of age and returned to Frederick, his birthplace, in the hope that the change would benefit him Finding that his health improved he remained in Frederick, and completed his education at the Frederick Academy While a student at the academy his tall figure, genial manner, and bright intellect attracted the attention of Roger B Taney, future chief justice of the United States, who was then a leading member of the Frederick bar On completing his studies, at the invitation of Mr Taney he entered the latter's office to prepare himself for the bar In 1809 or 1810 he was [illegible] considerations of health to remain in Frederick instead of returning to Georgia He soon achieved success, and gradually built up an extensive and lucrative practice Mr Schley was a gentleman of commanding

FREDERICK A SCHLEY

stature, being over six feet in height, refined and polished in manner, profoundly versed in his profession, a close and accurate reasoner, and possessed of great oratorical powers The latter talent was enhanced by reference to a treasury of poetry and literature which was ever at his command, and which was used with rare and striking effect in his addresses to the jury He possessed in a pre-eminent degree the "*fortiter in re et suaviter in modo*" His knowledge of law was full and precise, and in the argument of difficult and abstruse points his clearness of statement and aptness of illustration always elicited admiration, while his reasoning seldom failed to convince The late John Nelson, at one time Attorney-General of the United States, and William Schley, of Baltimore, his relative and former student in his office, were often his opponents at the Frederick bar, where both those gentlemen practiced law for many years

Like all lawyers of a past generation, Mr Schley is now known only by his arguments in the Court of Appeals, reported in the Maryland Reports Whoever will examine them will find there some record of his learning and research, the imprint of a vigorous and thoroughly disciplined legal mind, and the evidence of a comprehensive knowledge of law, and rare [illegible] se, the person-

ty of the orator the pleasant and graceful manner, eye beaming with intelligence, and the charm of cation, which formed such important factors of his success at the bar, are not to be found on the formal records of his achievements, nor can they be perpetuated in words. Mr Schley's reputation was not confined to Western Maryland, but extended throughout the State. He was often urged to remove to Baltimore, where he would have had a wider and more promising field for his talents, but he preferred to remain in Frederick. Mr Schley left four sons, of whom three are distinguished lawyers, George and Buchanan Schley, residing in Washington County, and James M Schley residing in Allegany County.

John Thomson Mason, father of the late Judge Mason, was for a long time a prominent lawyer and country gentleman of Western Maryland. He moved there in early life from Georgetown, D C, while in active practice owing to his impaired health, and a large and influential family grew up around him. He was a son of the well known Thomas Mason, of Virginia, and nephew of George Mason, of Virginia, whose statue in Richmond perpetuates his great memory and deeds as one of the country's distinguished men and a signer of the Declaration of Independence.

The subject of this sketch lived at "Montpelier," which place originally belonged to John and Richard Barnes, and here were received many prominent guests from all parts of the country,—Thomas Jefferson used to drive there in his coach to visit Mr Mason.

As a brilliant lawyer and orator he was accorded a high place but his singular modesty and impaired health prevented him from seeking or accepting any political office, though any were at his disposal. In this respect he was much like the late John V L McMahon. He was tendered the office of attorney-general under President Jefferson, but declined it.

The early Maryland Reports and legislation bear the impress of Mr Mason's legal and literary ability and statesmanlike mind.

The following letter from William Price, the distinguished lawyer, to Judge Mason supplies some interesting reminiscences of John Thomson Mason, viz.

"Baltimore, Aug 26 1865

"My dear sir —My recollections of your father are all of the most agreeable kind. He was the object of my youthful admiration and I sought his society constantly and eagerly.

"I was married at the age of twenty three, and a week or two afterwards Mr Mason came to my house, sent for my wife and self, and gave us a lecture upon the conduct of life business etc, the substance of which was that I was to study hard, my wife to be [illegible] and live as much at home as possible. We had occasion long to remember his good advice and the kind feeling which prompted it.

"His last case at the bar was my first. It was a prosecution against a man named Duncan for purchasing wheat from his negroes. I have no doubt the fellow was guilty, but the proof was very scant, and I got him off.

"He was in the habit of settling the disputes which arose among his neighbors. If one party came to him he would send for the other, then hear patiently all they had to say, examine their papers if they had any, and finally give his decision, which was generally final. On one occasion Henry Fiery and a person with whom he had a dispute came to Mr Mason. They made their statements, and during the investigation Fiery produced a receipt which the other party snatched up and put into his pocket. Your father deliberately arose from his chair, caught up the poker, and advancing to the person, said to him, 'Lay down that receipt, you d—d rascal, or I will break your head.' The receipt was at once produced, and the settlement proceeded.

"Col John Barnes, your father's uncle, occupied the Montpelier estate to the time of his death, shortly after which event Richard Barnes of St Mary's, died, leaving the estate to your father. It was a magnificent property, which my father estimated at three hundred thousand dollars. Your father had been laboriously engaged in his profession, until one bright morning, finding this on his table, he determined to remove upon the estate and never entered a court house afterwards, except to prosecute Duncan. It was perhaps unfortunate that he ever acceded to this immense estate, as he gradually thereafter lost his knowledge of the law and perhaps the vigor of his intellect.

"He was an admirable lawyer. Many a time have I, a mere child, played truant to hear him speak. His explanations and reasonings were so plain that I, even at that early age, could understand everything he said. I once heard Luther Martin say that he had practiced law with him for forty years and never knew him once to be taken by surprise.

"He once remarked to me that Blackstone was a great misfortune to the profession,—that it made the law too easy. He thought that knowledge acquired without labor did not stick by one, nor was it so well understood as that which was dug out by incessant toil and then arranged for yourself.

"I was once dining at Montpelier, and your father seeing my glass remaining untouched, though nearly full of wine, called out to me, 'Will, drink your wine, come, sir. You poured it out. If I had helped you, you would not be bound to drink more of it than you pleased, but it is not so when you have helped yourself.' Of course I turned off the whole whether I liked it or not.

"I take it for granted you have heard of what occurred between your father and Judge Stull in relation to the trial of a man who was indicted for stealing a horse. The proof was very strong, and the theft clearly proven, but in the course of the evidence the fact was disclosed that the horse was stolen in Pennsylvania and never was in possession of the thief on this Maryland side of the line. Your father, therefore, made the point that the court had no jurisdiction of the case,—that the stealing of a horse in Pennsylvania was no violation of the laws of Maryland. The judge, however, seemed to be incredulous, and said, in his broken English, 'I don't know pout dat Mishter Mason.' 'But,' rejoined your father, 'you have no authority to try him. If you convict him, and punish him, he may still be punished for the same offence in Pennsylvania.' 'Vell, Mishter Mason, ve'll see about dat [illegible] his office for the

books, to show that he was right The court-house was above the market house, and the whipping post was in the centre of the latter And as your father was ascending the steps with an armful of books he heard an outcry in the market-house, and looking under the arch, saw that his client was lashed to the whipping-post and the sheriff was diligently engaged in giving him the benefit of the law of Moses on his bare back. Your father went into the court house in a towering passion and commenced a fracas with the court He found the judge, however perfectly satisfied with what he had done, who remarked in a very business style, 'Dat de man had stole de horse, and was whipped for it, and te ting was now over'

"It was said that while the altercation between your father and the judge was in progress the man, who had come into court, asked what his lawyer was doing with the court, and was answered that he was applying for a new trial 'Oh, for God sake!' said he, 'I don't want any more trials I've had one trial too many already'

"But this last was the improvement of some one who was fond of adding to history his own embellishments The story, I think, properly closes with the scene at the whipping post and the remonstrance of your father in court

"Your father honored me with his confidence, and spoke to me always with the freedom which might characterize the intercourse of persons more nearly approaching the same age On one occasion at Montpelier he said to me, 'Will, avoid the horrible vice of gaming I should have been ruined by it but for a vow I made never to play after I had lost all my cash Frederick,' he continued, 'was the worst place for excessive play I ever saw I have lost as much as five thousand dollars at a sitting, but when my money was gone I have said, "Well, gentlemen, you have now got all I had to lose, and I suppose my company is no longer agreeable to you" And he quit the table

"Judge Stull was a remarkable man He had certainly no pretentions to legal knowledge, yet his services as president of the Committee of Observation for Elizabeth (now Hagerstown) District during the years 1775-77, which committee assumed and exercised all powers of government, legislative, judicial, and executive, during a period of great difficulty and disorder,—and his will, owing to his excellent judgment and extraordinary force of character, was received as law,—were regarded as sufficient to insure him a place of especial dignity and trust in the community which he had served so faithfully He was on the bench, therefore, from the habit of the people to look up to him for advice, and he was not the man to suffer the forms of law to stand in the way of what he considered the justice of the case

"Many amusing stories were told of him, one of which, on account of your father being connected with it, I will mention Judge Claggett was the chief justice of the court, and was a man of ability On one occasion the term of court commenced, and in the absence of the chief justice, who had not arrived, Judge Stull was forced, much against his will, to address the grand jury. It was his duty, however, and he was not the man to shirk from it Addressing them as 'Shentlemens of te Grand Inquesht for te pody of Washington County,' he went through the whole list of crimes, which by the aid of your father he defined as he proceeded Some of the definitions were a little extraordinary, but were, nevertheless, propounded with a very grave face At last they came to 'burglary' 'Wat te tevil is dat pooglary, Mason?' 'Oh,' said your father, 'that is selling liquor by the small' And the judge gave that explanation of 'pooglary' to the jury

"Your father acquired great distinction by the ability displayed by him in [illegible] of Harper [illegible] It was [illegible] before my time [illegible] Court in the year 1803, but I have frequently heard the old people talk about it Robert Goodloe Harper was the plaintiff, and Gen Wade Hampton, of either Georgia or South Carolina, the defendant Your father, William Pinkney and John Johnson, the father of Reverdy Johnson, an admirable *nisi prius* lawyer, were for the defendant and Luther Martin, Philip Barton Key, and Alexander C Magruder for the plaintiff The prominence of the parties the great distinction of the counsel, and the large amount involved in the controversy gave to the trial an uncommon degree of interest Mr Harper took part in his own case, and, although not so well trained as lawyers of his standing at the Maryland bar, was notwithstanding a very formidable man to encounter Your father and he came in contact [illegible] in the trial, [illegible] which made it extremely difficult to avoid personalities of the most pointed character And it was said that your father, who was very competent to hold his own in such a quarrel made the trial an extremely unpleasant one to Mr Harper There were some letters of Mr Harper which were given in evidence, and which offered free scope for sarcasm and invective, and your father did not feel himself particularly called upon to spare either

"After I had been reading law for a year or more I went home for about six months, and had the use of your father's books I was of course frequently at Montpelier, and had very frequent conversations with him about the course of study and the practice of the law. He has frequently said to me that I had better be a respectable mechanic than a second-rate lawyer, and admonitions of this character coming from him stimulated me to greater exertions, than without them I should not have used He was a very good talker possessed an even flow of spirits which I never saw ruffled It was said that at the bar he was remarkable for calmness and equanimity that nothing was ever permitted to put him out of temper, and although his adversary might be furious, he was perfectly cool, and would say the most cutting things with a smile on his countenance

"My engagements are such that I cannot continue these reminiscences I began intending to write a short letter, but the matter has grown under my hand, and I must here stop for want of leisure

"Very truly yours,

"William Price

"Hon John Thomson Mason"

Judge John Thomson Mason, son of John Thomson Mason, was born at the family-seat "Montpelier," Washington County, May 15, 1815 He was one of a large family, whose home was a resort of many prominent persons of this and other States

After a preliminary course at Mount St Mary's College, Emmittsburg, Judge Mason entered Princeton College, where he graduated in 1836 with high honors and the valedictory Returning to Hagerstown, the county seat, and about ten miles from the Mason family home, he entered the law-office of the late William Price, one of Maryland's most prominent lawyers After passing the bar he at once began a successful and active life, both professionally and soon politically In this latter field it was his happy portion, and for which he received the just tribute and love of both personal and political friends and those opposed, to [illegible] kept himself [illegible] es, and defeats

retaining to the day of his death an ardent love for agricultural pursuits, his attention was frequently directed to his farms lying near Hagerstown.

In 1845 he was sent to Congress from the district to which Hagerstown then belonged, and after one term returned to his profession. In 1851 he was elected one of the judges of the Court of Appeals of Maryland, under the old constitution, which then provided for only four judges for that tribunal. He then removed to Annapolis permanently. His associates were Judges Tuck, Legrand, and Eccleston. After six years' service, during which time his decisions were marked and his labors conspicuous (the case of Ware vs. Richardson, 7 Maryland, demonstrating the applicability of the rule in Shelley's case in Maryland, being one of his important opinions), he resigned, upon the accession of Mr. Buchanan to the Presidency, to accept the position of collector of the port of Baltimore under that Executive. Upon the breaking out of the war Judge Mason, whose sympathies were warmly with the South, retired to private life, and during the exciting scenes of our civil war he quietly yet firmly gave his time and counsels as he thought best to those of his friends and such measures as demanded his attention. He was imprisoned twice, once in Western Maryland while upon his farm, and also in Fort McHenry with many other prominent gentlemen.

At the close of the war Judge Mason, whose residence was still in Annapolis, resumed the practice of law in Baltimore, associating himself with the late Maj. Thomas Rowland. When Hon. William Pinkney Whyte was elected Governor, he appointed Judge Mason his Secretary of State, which position he held to the day of his death, which occurred very suddenly on March 28, 1873, at Elkton, Md. His busy professional life would not admit of his sparing himself, even with the duties above mentioned, and he may be said to have literally "died in harness." At the close of a long and important case in Elkton (Mow *vs.* McHenry), and just as he sat down to his dinner and was receiving the congratulations of his friends and brother attorneys upon his able speech in the case, and before hearing the verdict in his favor, a few minutes previously announced, his head fell back, and he died peacefully, in a moment, a victim to apoplexy. He was buried in the county and near the mountains he loved so well. He was a man of large and liberal views, of great experience and learning both as judge, lawyer, and politician; and, withal, possessing a large, warm heart, simplicity of manner, and a zealous and devout religious nature, he was equally loved and [illegible] in public and private life, and the humblest citizen seemed to know and feel his loss, as did his companions everywhere throughout the State.

At the close of the war Judge Mason espoused the Catholic religion, and soon, with his hearty, zealous nature, became an important and prominent member. He delivered the address at the Cathedral upon the occasion of the twenty-fifth celebration of the pontificate of Pope Pius IX., and in many ways gave prominence to the lay representation of the church.

He died in the fifty-eighth year of his age, in the full vigor of manhood and intellectual brightness, and his loss was one that the "new school" cannot perhaps supply. He leaves a widow, two married daughters, and one son, the latter bearing his name (the third in succession), and now a member of the bar of Baltimore.

Judge John Buchanan, a brother of Judge Thomas Buchanan, was the second son of Thomas and Anne Buchanan, and was born in Prince George's County in 1772. Losing his parents quite early in life, he was sent to Charlotte Hall Academy, Charles County, where he received the usual education of that day, and when still but a youth was sent to Winchester, Va., to read law with Judge White, a learned jurist of that place, but soon afterwards was transferred to Washington County, where he continued his studies with John Thomson Mason, the elder, at that time one of the most distinguished lawyers in the State. After a successful practice of a few years, he married the daughter of Col. Elie Williams (niece of Gen. Otho H. Williams), and shortly afterwards was placed on the Supreme Bench of Maryland. He continued to occupy and adorn this conspicuous office for a period of forty years and up to his death, winning, as a jurist of remarkable profundity, the admiration and respect of such legal minds as those of Luther Martin, Pinkney, Roger B. Taney, Reverdy Johnson, and many others. In personal appearance and manners he was regarded as being one of the most elegant men of his age, and his public worth may be measured by the many valuable decisions which he rendered from time to time throughout the long period of his official career. Judge Buchanan died in November, 1844.

The family is descended from the Buchanans of Loch Lomond, Scotland, one of whom, George Buchanan, was tutor to the royal Earl of Murray, and another, Alexander Buchanan, distinguished himself at the battle of the Boyne.

Judge Buchanan's death was announced to the court of Baltimore County by I. Nevett Steele, deputy attorney-general, in the following words:

"May it please the court: I rise to discharge the melancholy duty of announcing to the court the death of the Hon. John Buchanan, chief judge of the Court of Appeals. For nearly forty years he has adorned the judiciary of our State, and in his death he has left behind him, in the reported decisions of our highest legal tribunal, the most enduring evidences of his profound learning and great judicial ability. Without attempting here any eulogy upon his private character, Mr. Schley has most truly observed that the announcement of Judge Buchanan's death would be the occasion of the deepest regret to the court. He has filled for thirty-eight years the station of chief judge of the district in which he resided, and has presided for upwards of twenty years as the chief justice of this State. The reports of the decisions of our court evince his learning and will pass his name to succeeding generations, as long as our free institutions and the principles of the common law are respected. Few men, in any age or country, have lived who possessed more generous feelings, a kinder heart, or a wiser head. It has been my good fortune to have lived in intimate friendship with him, and to have acted with him for more than one-half of his judicial career, and I can say, with truth and sincerity, that in all my intercourse with the world I have met with no man of a more scrupulous sense of honor, of a better regulated judgment, or of more urbane manners. He had lived beyond the age allotted to our race, but he quit our earthly and temporary habitation for his eternal abiding-place with an intellect unimpaired by age, leaving behind him a character distinguished for virtue and for every quality which could adorn our nature."

In announcing the death of Judge Buchanan the Hagerstown *Torchlight* said,—

"It is with feelings of the most profound sorrow that we announce the death of his Honor John Buchanan, chief justice of the State of Maryland, in the seventy-first year of his age. He expired at Woodland, his late residence, on Wednesday last, at eleven o'clock. Judge Buchanan was appointed associate justice of this judicial district in 1806, and in 1824 took his seat as chief judge of the Court of Appeals, from which time to the present he has presided in such a manner as to have conferred upon himself the reputation of one of the ablest jurists in the country. During this period, notwithstanding his precarious health, he has labored with indefatigable perseverance in his vocation, and has bequeathed to his State a series of decisions which will always be looked upon as one of the proudest monuments, and from which her sons, so long as she exists, will continue to reap the wholesome and vivifying fruits. Deeply do we deplore his decease, and most deeply do we sympathize with his bereaved family in the loss which not only they, but the public, have sustained."

Judge Thomas Buchanan was the eldest son of Thomas Buchanan and Anne Cooke, of Chester, England, and was born Sept. 25, 1768, on his father's plantation near Port Tobacco, Md. He graduated in the law quite early in life, and practiced in the courts of Anne Arundel and St. Mary's Counties until his marriage with Miss Anderson, granddaughter of Samuel Ogle, Governor of Maryland, in April, 1797, when he removed to Baltimore, and afterwards to Washington County, where he had large landed estates. He succeeded the Hon. Roger Nelson as judge of the Circuit Court, May 5, 1815, and died Sept. 27, 1847, of apoplexy, with which he was seized while returning home from court at Hagerstown. During his long career at the bar and on the bench Judge Buchanan was noted for his learning, integrity, and lofty sense of professional honor.

In announcing his death a Hagerstown paper said:

"We have the melancholy duty to perform this week of announcing the sudden death of this very distinguished citizen of our county. Never before have we felt ourselves so utterly incompetent to the right performance of any duty as that which devolves upon us in briefly portraying in suitable and becoming language the merits of this able and profound jurist. The circumstances immediately surrounding his last moments are sad and deeply affecting. He had come to town in the forenoon of Tuesday last, and opened a court for the purpose of hearing an argument in chancery of considerable importance, and the near approach of the election brought to town some fourteen or fifteen persons, to avail themselves of his presence to become naturalized. This duty he performed with more than usual strictness, as we are told, and then listened with his usual patience to the arguments of the case just alluded to for about three hours, during all of which time he exhibited no symptoms of indisposition, nor did he at all complain. After a session of some five hours he rose from his seat, and having appointed Monday following for the meeting of the court again, in order to despatch some other pressing business before he should leave for the court in Allegany, he took leave of those who were present with his usual kind manner, and in company with his amiable daughter and an old valued servant, he started for his residence, some ten miles distant. On the way, as we learn, he seemed very well, and conversed with cheerfulness, until within about two miles of his home, when he was suddenly seized in his carriage with apoplexy, and died instantly, without a groan or struggle. Thus passed from earth to heaven the late venerable and venerated senior associate judge of this judicial district, the Hon. Thomas Buchanan. But few are the men, indeed, if any, who have ever descended to the tomb in Western Maryland whose death was more deeply mourned, or whose loss was more severely felt.

"He was the very model of a judge, and has left behind him an ermine of spotless purity, which but few could wear and not soil. For upwards of *thirty-two* years—having been commissioned on the 5th of May, 1815—he sat upon the bench, dispensing justice alike to the rich and to the poor, administering the laws of the land with an impartiality that knew no friend, with a judgment that seldom erred, and with a dignity, yet easy grace, entirely free from ostentation, that would at once have made insolence stand rebuked in his presence. And although in him was found the stern and upright judge, yet for the misfortune of a fallen fellow-creature no one possessed a more kindly heart, as all who knew him can bear witness. As a citizen he was equally exemplary, discharging the duties of neighbor, and the nearer relation of family, in a way that secured the love and esteem of all, and in these varied relations, whether as a public minister of the law or as a private citizen, he has left a vacuum that we fear will not be easily filled. His remains were, on Thursday following his demise, brought to this place and interred in the Episcopal burying-ground, amidst the tears and regrets of a vast assemblage of his neighbors, friends, and acquaintances."

At a meeting of the bar of Washington County Court convened at the clerk's office, in Hagerstown, on the 29th day of September, 1847, R. M. Tidball was called to the [illegible] Spencer appointed

William T Hamilton

secretary The following preamble and resolutions, submitted by Daniel Weisel and prefaced by him with some remarks, were unanimously adopted

"*Whereas*, This meeting has learned with equal surprise and sorrow the sudden death of Hon Thomas Buchanan, late the senior and associate judge of the Fifth Judicial District of Maryland, which occurred yesterday evening in his carriage on his way home from this place, where he had on that day mingled with us, in health, in the discharge of official business

"*And whereas*, The pure and elevated character, private and judicial, of the deceased, the relation which he bore to us and his long, able, and faithful service to the public, demand from us a suitable expression of the sentiments with which we have received the intelligence of this mournful dispensation of Providence Therefore

"*Resolved*, That this event, so sudden and affecting and depriving us and the community of one so endeared and distinguished as was the late Judge Buchanan, has impressed us all with the most profound sorrow

"*Resolved*, That we recognize in the deceased the true gentleman, the valued and valuable citizen, the pure, learned, and upright judge, and a public benefactor, whom any community might have been proud of and blessed to call its own, and whose loss cannot but be most sensibly felt and deplored

"*Resolved*, That the members of the bar have by this event been deprived of a valuable friend, society of a highly respected and venerated member, the bench of an ornament, and the cause of public justice of a firm and noble pillar"

William T Hamilton, the present Governor of Maryland, was born at Hagerstown on the 8th of September, 1820 His father was Henry Hamilton, who resided at Boonsboro', where his son, William T, received the rudiments of his education from James Brown, at one time surveyor for Washington County His (William T's) mother died when he was about six years old and his father about two years later Left thus unprotected, he was received into the family of one of his uncles on the maternal side, who was noted for his devotion to the principles of the old Jefferson school and for his strict attention to business The future Governor and senator was placed at the Hagerstown Academy, where he remained for some time, making for himself an honorable record as a close and diligent student He then entered Jefferson College, at Canonsburg, Pa, and after completing his studies returned to Hagerstown, and entered the law-office of Hon John Thomson Mason as a student of law In 1843 he was admitted to the bar, and in 1846 was nominated upon the Democratic ticket and elected to the House of Delegates, the ticket, after a hard fought contest, being divided, with William Beverly Clarke, a Whig, elected to the Senate One of the most prominent topics before the Legislature was the question as to whether the interest upon the State debt should be paid or not Mr Hamilton advocated its payment with great earnestness a[illegible] In 1847, Mr Hamilton was renominated, but, although he led his ticket by a large majority, he was defeated by his Whig opponent

In 1848 he was placed upon the Cass electoral ticket, and in 1849 was nominated by the Democratic party for Congress After a close and exciting contest he was elected, although in the previous year the county had given a large majority for Gen Taylor, the Whig candidate for President The absorbing issue of the day was the tariff question, and Mr Hamilton did not hesitate to affirm and demonstrate in the most forcible manner the theories of the Democratic party looking to a tariff for revenue only, although many of his constituents were strongly tinctured with Protectionist ideas His opponent was Thomas J McKaig, who received 7191 votes against 7307 for Hamilton During his first term in Congress Mr Hamilton distinguished himself by the ability and eloquence with which he supported and advocated the Clay Compromise Bill In 1851 he was again elected to Congress, receiving 6863 votes against 6626 cast for Mr Roman, the Whig candidate At the expiration of his second term Mr Hamilton determined to retire from politics, but being urgently pressed by his friends, consented to be placed in nomination in 1853 His opponent, Hon Francis Thomas, was an independent candidate, and in the contest which ensued the two candidates were pitted against each other in joint discussions The result was a larger majority for Hamilton than at either of the two preceding elections, the vote being, Hamilton, 7545, Thomas, 6429 During his third term in Congress, Mr Hamilton gave an energetic and loyal support to the administration of President Pierce As chairman of the Committee on the District of Columbia, he took a leading part in the prosecution of the vast work by which the city of Washington is now supplied with water from the Great Falls of the Potomac At the expiration of his term Mr Hamilton again announced his desire and intention to retire to private life, but his constituency demanded that he should continue in the field, and he was obliged to yield to their wishes In 1855, therefore, he was for the fourth time a candidate for Congress, but the Know-Nothing, or "Great American," party having suddenly gained phenomenal, though temporary strength, he was defeated Thenceforward Mr Hamilton devoted himself assiduously to the practice of his profession, in which he achieved the most gratifying success, demonstrating in a variety of cases remarkable argumentative powers and a thorough and comprehensive knowledge of the law During his career as Congressman Mr Hamilton was assisted in his l[illegible] eminent judge

of the Court of Appeals In 1861 he was strongly urged to accept the Democratic nomination for Governor but declined the honor In 1868 he consented to stand as a candidate for the United States Senate, and was elected for six years from the 4th of March, 1869 His predecessor, Governor Whyte, had been appointed to fill the unexpired term of Reverdy Johnson, who had been sent by President Johnson as United States minister to England The vote stood Hamilton, 56 (exactly the number necessary for a choice), Swann, 16, and Merrick, 7 In the Senate Mr Hamilton proved himself to be a fluent and forcible debater, and made a marked impression upon that body at a period when it was exceedingly difficult for a senator of his political persuasion to obtain even a respectful hearing His term expired in 1875, in which year the Democratic convention met to nominate a candidate for Governor of Maryland In an eloquent and forcible speech Hon John Ritchie, of Frederick, presented the name of ex-Senator Hamilton, but Mr Hamilton failed to receive the nomination, and Hon John Lee Carroll was chosen by the convention and elected by the people On the 7th of August, 1879, however, Mr Hamilton was unanimously nominated by the Democratic State Convention to succeed Gov Carroll, and in the following autumn was elected, his majority over his Republican opponent, James A Gary, being 22,208 His inauguration was the occasion of an enthusiastic popular demonstration, and the ceremonies at the State-house were of an exceptionally interesting and impressive character Governor Hamilton devotes much time and attention to the management of his farms, which are considered to be among the most intelligently and carefully tilled and among the most productive in Washington County He has a handsome residence in Hagerstown, besides his country seat about two miles distant, and alternates between these two points and Annapolis He has six children,—four daughters and two sons,—the latter being Richard and William T Hamilton, Jr Governor Hamilton is a man of remarkable force of character, strict integrity, and a lofty appreciation of the duties incumbent upon a public official As an executive, he has shown invariably an earnest disposition to prevent and reform abuses, and to reduce the burden of taxation to the lowest possible point As a lawyer, he ranks among the foremost members of the bar of Western Maryland, and in all matters of business or of agriculture he is quoted by his neighbors and friends as an authority from which there should be no appeal

William Price, one of the most distinguished lawyers that Maryland has produced, was a native of Washington County, his father being an officer of the Revolution, and died Nov 25, 1868 He was educated at Dickinson College, and studied law with Judge Cooper, of Carlisle, Upton Lawrence, of Hagerstown, Judge Nicholas Brice, of Baltimore, and John Thomson Mason, the elder While a resident of Washington County he was elected a member of the State Senate by the electoral college about 1825 He was afterwards a candidate for Congress He moved to Cumberland, Allegany Co, and after a few years removed to Baltimore He was elected a member of the State Legislature from Baltimore in 1862, and was afterwards appointed United States District Attorney by President Lincoln, which office he held for one term Mr Price was one of the commissioners appointed by the Legislature to simplify the forms of pleading and practice in Maryland He was a prominent member of his profession, by whom his social qualities and personal character were held in high regard The courts of Baltimore, in which tributes of respect were paid to his memory, all adjourned to attend his funeral

In the Superior Court George M Gill announced the death of Mr Price He spoke of the deceased in becoming terms, and moved that the court adjourn in respect to his memory

Hon J Thomson Mason rose to second the motion He gave a sketch of the life of the deceased, and said his abilities as a lawyer were generally recognized, and his high personal character was as well known as his professional abilities

In response to the remarks of the members of the bar Judge Dobbin said,—

"The whole bar of Maryland will unite with us in mournful regret at the death of our brother Price Enjoying in his younger life a large practice in the western counties of the State, Mr Price followed his cases to the Court of Appeals, where all remember how his majestic presence, his genial urbanity, and his rich colloquial gifts adorned the professional circle which assembled at Annapolis Mr Price possessed also an extensive and varied scholarship, which he so gracefully blended with the severer labors of his vocation that he was always an engaging and instructive orator The liberal view which he took of the science to which he was devoted carried him ahead of most of his contemporaries in those simplifications of the law now so apparent upon our system of conveyancing and pleading, and he was the first, under legislative appointment, to get rid of many of the technical embarrassments of the older law After his removal to Baltimore, and in the late troubles of the country, William Price became the law officer of the general government in this district, and while he faithfully discharged his duty to the public, he made what was often a painful exercise of office as little offensive as possible to those of his fellow-citizens who differed from him in opinion He belonged to a generation of lawyers fast passing away and when our younger professional brethren shall look back in the forensic circle of the State to find a type of the old Maryland

[illegible] man and lawyer, none will be more likely to furnish the [illegible] than the late Mr. Price.

[illegible] of respect for his memory, and in order that we may at [illegible] his remains to the grave, I shall now order the court to [illegible] adjourned."

Mr. Price once appeared as a writer of romance, and produced the novel entitled "Clem. Falconer, or the Memoirs of a Young Whig." It was not a success, and was his only attempt. He also at one time contemplated the publication of work on chancery practice, which no doubt would have met a different fate from the novel, for the inclination of Mr. Price was law, in which he was profoundly versed. He also frequently essayed politics, but without a success commensurate with his natural ability; and was also once connected with an edge-tool manufacturing company, which proved a failure. His sphere was emphatically the law, and nothing else appeared to suit him. He was an enthusiastic Union man at the commencement of the war, and while in the Legislature introduced the "Treason Bill," with which his name became familiarly associated, and which, owing to peculiar circumstances, subjected him to severe animadversion. Towards the conclusion of the struggle he became pre-eminently conservative, and before his death those estrangements which sprang from his zeal at a more early stage of the war, were entirely removed.

In a letter to the Hagerstown *Mail*, correcting certain misstatements, the late Judge Mason gives the following interesting reminiscences of Mr. Price:

"It would be unnecessary to refer to the prominent incidents in the life of Mr. Price, as the recollection of them is still fresh in the minds of most of your readers. His urbane manners, his commanding personal appearance, his fascinating powers of conversation, his earnest, distinguished, and apostolic style of public speaking are all well remembered by his former friends and neighbors. Of his father, who was no less remarkable in his way, little is now known. Col. Price lived and died on the banks of the Conococheague, and was distinguished no less for the vigor of his intellect and personal integrity than for his great eccentricities. His history and peculiarities, of which I heard so much when a child, have passed, amid the changes and vicissitudes of Washington County, almost entirely out of the memory of the people. In many respects he was a wise man. He showed this in the course he pursued towards his four sons. Having but a moderate estate, he summoned his sons before him, and after a thorough explanation of his purpose, their consequences, etc., to the effect that his means would not enable him to give to them all a complete and polished education and leave them property besides, he proposed to those of his sons who preferred that they should receive such an education, but at his death should get no part of his estate, while the others, who might be content with the common education which the neighborhood could furnish, should have his property. William and Benjamin selected the education, and the other two the property; but by a strange decree of Providence the two last referred to died while young, and their surviving brothers thereby succeeded to the property as well as to the education. In regard to this compact Col. Price carried it out in perfect good faith, for he spared no pains in affording his two sons, William and Benjamin, every advantage of education which his judgment could suggest and his means furnish, and they in turn no less appreciated these advantages, as was abundantly shown in the highly cultivated state of their minds, evinced as well in legal attainments as in general literary tastes and acquirements. But they commenced life without a dollar.

"I have heard one anecdote of Col. Price, which is so well vouched for and so creditable to his good nature and neighborly feelings, if it even does not reflect much honor upon his loyalty (as now understood), that I think it worthy of public notice.

"During the famous 'Whisky Insurrection,' in Washington's administration, Col. Price held a military position under the government. The spirit of rebellion was not confined to Western Pennsylvania, but it extended to other parts of the country, and even in the secluded region where Col. Price lived it had taken strong hold. A public meeting of Republicans, as they were then called, which was composed of many of the most substantial and respectable of Col. Price's neighbors, had been held at Rockdale to express sympathy with the Pittsburgh insurgents. The movement had assumed such proportions that the government determined it should be thwarted. Accordingly a body of soldiers was ordered to report to Col. Price, with instructions that some fifteen or twenty, whose names were furnished, of those who had participated in the meeting should be arrested. The soldiers reached his house early in the afternoon and delivered their instructions. He received them with his usual hospitality, but instead of proceeding at once to the execution of the orders, he insisted they should remain with him till morning, when he would see that their mission was fulfilled. They accordingly did so, and early the next day, accompanied by a guide, they started on their assigned duty. Late in the evening they returned with but one prisoner, and that was Philip Kriegh, a man well known in his day for respectability, probity, and frankness, in all of which qualities he is well represented by his son William, still living in Washington County. Col. Price met him at the gate in the most cordial manner, and inquired 'where the rest of his neighbors were?' Mr. Kriegh seemed a little surprised at this question, and with more frankness than prudence presently responded, 'Didn't you send your son all through the neighborhood last night to tell us to run away, that the soldiers were after us?' And he then explained that the reason he did not run with the others was that, being sick, he had not been able to attend the Rockdale meeting. At first the colonel was a little confused and discomfited at this unexpected public disclosure of disloyalty, but he soon recovered his presence of mind, and turning to the commanding officer, said, 'What can my good, harmless neighbors do to injure this great government? Come in! come in! and let us drink the health of Gen. Washington.' Greatly given to conviviality, as well as hospitality, it may be well imagined that Col. Price and his friends had a merry night. It was sufficient at all events to forever obliterate from the mind of the government all memory and resentment for the Rockdale treason."

In August, 1840, Mr. Price fought a duel with the Hon. Francis Thomas, which caused no little excitement throughout the State. The Baltimore *Sun* in its issue of Aug. 6, 1840, said,—

"Our city was thrown into considerable excitement yesterday by a painful report, said to be brought by passengers in the railroad cars, that a hostile meeting had taken place somewhere on the Virginia shore of the Potomac between the Hon. Francis Thomas, member of Congress from this State, and president of

the Chesapeake and Ohio Canal Company, and William Price, Esq, an eminent member of the Hagerstown Bar"

On the following day the same paper added,—

"In a part of our edition yesterday morning we added a postscript containing authentic intelligence of the result of a duel between Mr Thomas and Mr Price, and we must now repeat it for the benefit of those who did not see it The parties met on Wednesday morning in Morgan County, Va, between Bath and Hancock, Md, one shot was exchanged without effect, and the difficulty was then compromised on the interference of friends We rejoice exceedingly at the result Mr Thomas is a gentleman well known in this State, and as a politician throughout the country, and few men have had greater share of the confidence of their immediate constituents than he He now, besides his place in Congress, holds a responsible situation in the Chesapeake and Ohio Canal Company, that of president From this his position in society may be inferred In Congress he was looked upon by his party as a man of more than ordinary discrimination and talent having been placed at the head of the Judiciary Committee, one of the most important committees in the House The distance at which the gentlemen fought was twelve paces"

The particulars of the affair, as given in the Hagerstown *Mail*, were these

"The difficulty originated in a speech delivered by Mr Price at Cumberland some time since There are various rumors afloat about the rise, progress, and settlement of the affair, but we have not been able to obtain a statement that could be relied upon, because, as we understand, it was agreed among the friends of the parties that no publication should be made except the following

"'A CARD —Understanding that the public are aware that a misunderstanding between William Price Esq, of Washington County, and Francis Thomas, Esq, of Frederick County, in this State, has resulted in a hostile meeting the undersigned, who acted as the respective friends of the parties upon the ground, take pleasure in stating, with a view to correct all error upon the subject, that after an exchange of shots, at our instance the difficulty was adjusted to the entire honor of both gentlemen

"'WM H NORRIS,
"'JOHN MCPHERSON
"'J HOLLINGSWORTH

"'HANCOCK, Aug 5, 1840'"

Robert J Brent, one of Maryland's most gifted lawyers, was born in Louisiana, and died in Baltimore City in February, 1872 Mr Brent married a daughter of Upton Lawrence, of Hagerstown, and was otherwise identified with the people of Washington County His grandfather, Mr Fenwick, was for many years a member of the Maryland State Senate from Charles County, and his father practiced law in Louisiana and in Washington, D C Robert J Brent studied law in the office of his father, and in that of Gen Walter Jones, of Washington and was admitted to the bar in 1831 After practicing a short time in the courts of Washington he removed to Frederick City, and thence to Hagerstown, where he married A few years later he removed to Baltimore, where he [illegible] acquired a large practice He also frequently appeared before the Court of Appeals, and in the courts at Washington His associate and intimate friend was the Hon Henry May

Mr Brent was originally of the old Whig school of politics, but becoming dissatisfied with the party during the administration of Gen Harrison, allied himself with the Democrats, and afterwards remained an active and influential member of that party Although he was never a seeker for office, he was on several occasions chosen delegate to the Presidential Nominating Conventions, served several terms in the State Legislature and was a member of the Constitutional Convention in 1850 and 1851 While in the latter body he was appointed State's attorney for Baltimore City on the death of George R Richardson, by Governor Lowe Mr Brent was engaged in a number of the most important cases, not only in Baltimore, but in the various counties in the State, in the Court of Appeals and in the Superior Court As an advocate he was fearless and faithful, so devoted to the interests of his client that he sometimes failed to see the imperfections of the cause in which he was engaged To his associates he was always polite and courteous and to the younger members of the profession he was kind and considerate In social life he was genial and entertaining never, however, carrying any pleasure or sport to excess During his leisure hours in summer he indulged his love of aquatic sports, and his yacht "Minnie" was well known in the Patapsco The last time Mr Brent appeared as counsel was for the defendant in a civil suit in the Superior Court and during the trial complained of a pain in the heel which finally became so acute as to cause him to retire to his home The disease was finally pronounced acute rheumatism which, extending to vital parts, terminated his life Mr Brent left a widow several daughters, and one son, who was associated with his father in the practice of law

Hon Richard H Alvey, chief judge of the Fourth Judicial Circuit and judge of the Court of Appeals, was the eldest child of George and Harriet (*née* Wicklin) Alvey, and born on the 6th of March, 1826, in St Mary's County Md Both of his parents were of English descent, and belonged to families which were among the oldest and most distinguished in Southern Maryland Straitened family circumstances, however, did not permit them to give their eldest son a liberal education, and his early intellectual training was confined within the unpretentious limits offered by the curriculum of a county school taught by his father In 1844, when only eighteen years of age, he entered the clerk's office of Charles County, where h[illegible] clerk for several

… and while thus employed began the study of … which he prosecuted principally at night, after daily routine of regular duties had been brought … a close In 1819 he was admitted to the bar in

Charles County, and in the early part of 1850 removed to Western Maryland and settled in Washington County, where he has ever since resided He commenced his professional career in partnership with the late Judge John Thomson Mason, and was subsequently associated for a time with the present Governor of Maryland, Hon William T Hamilton

He had been at the bar but a short time when he discovered (as the great majority of young lawyers soon discover), that it was necessary to supplement his previous preparation by thorough reading and a systematic course of study He did, however, what so few young lawyers do on discovering their deficiencies, —set at once and energetically to work to supply them Law schools and learned professors to make smooth the road of professional knowledge were not so abundant as at the present day, and aspirants for legal honors were forced to rely to a large extent upon their own judgment as to the best method of mastering the unarranged material which was to be digested and assimilated The subject of this notice had the good sense to appreciate the necessity for systematic and intelligent … and … comprehensive plan, pursued a regular course from the foundation up, beginning with Littleton and Coke This course, in connection with his practice, which was meantime steadily increasing, occupied him for several years, and when completed gave him a professional soundness and thoroughness of which few young lawyers can boast His natural aptitude for the law, his conscientious and thorough preparation of his cases, his fidelity to the interests of his clients, his marked ability, and his spotless integrity rendered anything but success impossible, and he soon stood in the front rank of his profession in Western Maryland

Although Judge Alvey came of a strong Whig family, he became an earnest disciple of the political principles of Mr Jefferson at the very outset of his career His political opinions were formed in rather an accidental way Just before he arrived at manhood he happened to become the owner of a copy of Prof Tucker's "Life of Jefferson," and as he was not then the owner of many books, he read and reread this with great care He thus became thoroughly acquainted with Jefferson's doctrines with respect to questions of civil government, national policy, and constitutional law, and the opinions then formed have been only strengthened and confirmed by the experience of succeeding years In addition to the influence exercised in the formation of his political views by the work already mentioned, one of the earliest law-books which fell into his hands was an old copy of that now much neglected but still valuable treasury of political and constitutional law, Tucker's "Blackstone" He not only read carefully the text of Blackstone, but Judge Tucker's admirable appendix, wherein are discussed most clearly the questions of the sources of sovereignty and the power of legislation, the forms of government, the various provisions of the Constitution of the United States, and the sources of the unwritten or common law as it has been introduced and practiced in this country The theory that pervades Mr. Tucker's discussion of these subjects is that of Mr Jefferson, and it made a very deep and lasting impression upon the mind of the youthful reader

Thus Judge Alvey commenced life with views upon political and constitutional questions which were the result of independent investigation, not of training or prejudice, and brought to the discharge of his duties as a citizen an amount of information on these subjects that is rarely possessed by much older men His familiarity with the political history of the country, and his thorough and clear comprehension of the great principles of constitutional government enunciated by Mr J… … ce, and the

year after his removal to Washington County he was induced to become the Democratic candidate for the State Senate, the opposition candidate being the late Judge French The county was then strongly Whig, and the Democratic candidate was a comparative stranger, but, nothing daunted by the discouraging prospect he canvassed the county in company with his Whig opponent, and the result, to their mutual surprise, was a tie vote The Whigs, however, grew alarmed, and, redoubling their efforts, succeeded in defeating Judge Alvey in the second election by a few votes only Probably this defeat was the most fortunate circumstance for the State that could have occurred as it doubtless prevented his being tempted from the severer duties of his profession to the more seductive sphere of political life —a result which would have given the country a profound constitutional lawyer and a great statesman, but would have lost to Maryland one of the brightest ornaments of her bench In 1852 Judge Alvey was nominated as one of the Pierce electors, and with several of his associates canvassed the greater portion of the State, which they carried triumphantly for the Democratic candidate

While Judge Alvey, in common with a very large majority of the people of Maryland at the beginning of the sectional troubles in 1860, felt that many of the grievances of the South were well founded, and that there was no constitutional authority for a war of coercion he never believed in the doctrine of secession and never advocated the extreme and unwise measures adopted by the Southern States The idea of hostile invasion of one section of the country by another seemed to the great majority of the people of Maryland at that time as nothing less than the total subversion of the fundamental principles of the union of States Judge Alvey did not hesitate to proclaim his opinions, which in his view were entirely consistent with his obligations to the general government, and his known opposition to the war soon made him a marked man On the 2d of June, 1861, immediately after the arrival of the Union army at Hagerstown, he was arrested in his office at night by a military squad upon the charge (which was totally unfounded) that he was holding communication with the enemy, and taken to the headquarters of the army, where he was treated with great rudeness and indignity After being closely confined in Hagerstown for several days he was sent to Fort McHenry, at Baltimore from there to Fort Lafayette, New York, and thence to Fort Warren, in Boston Harbor, where he was detained, with the other Maryland State prisoners, until the full [illegible] February when he was allowed to return home [illegible]

The close of the war found a large portion of the people of the State disfranchised and otherwise deprived of their rights as citizens, and Judge Alvey was among the first in Western Maryland to move for the restoration of their liberties A large number of the best citizens had been excluded from the juries, and one of the first measures deemed essential to rectify this evil was the adoption of a new jury system Judge Alvey, accordingly, drafted the present jury law in force in the counties, with the exception of some slight changes recently made, and attended the Legislature at the session of 1867 to procure its passage The bill was passed as he prepared it first, as a local law applicable only to Washington, Frederick, and Carroll Counties, but before the session closed it was converted into a general law, and passed for all the counties in the State

The same Legislature which passed the jury law passed the act calling the Constitutional Convention of 1867, which framed the present constitution of the State Judge Alvey was sent to that convention as a delegate from Washington County, and was made chairman of one of the principal committees of that body —that on representation He took an active and influential part in all the proceedings of the convention, and contributed greatly to the satisfactory completion of its labors by his large experience, broad views, and profound knowledge of political and constitutional questions Under the new constitution he became a candidate for chief judge of the Fourth Judicial Circuit, embracing the counties of Allegany, Washington, and Garrett and judge of the Court of Appeals of Maryland and was elected in the fall of 1867 He has held these positions ever since, participating in the decision of many important cases, some of them affecting most deeply the welfare of the entire State, and has discharged the duties of his high office with honor to himself and to the universal satisfaction of the people of Maryland Few men have ever been upon the bench in Maryland who have graced it more, who have better sustained the dignity and strict impartiality of the judicial office, or have brought to the discharge of its important duties a richer store of legal knowledge, a more discriminating judgment, or a clearer and more vigorous intellect

Judge Alvey was first married in 1856, to Mary Wharton eldest daughter of the late Dr John O Wharton and niece of Judge Mason She died in 1860, leaving one child surviving her In the fall of 1862 Judge Alvey married Julia I Hays, only daughter of the late Dr Joseph C Hays, of Washington C[illegible] large family of chil[illegible]

George Freaner was born on the 20th of January, 1831, and was a member of one of the oldest and best-known families of Washington County. His death, which occurred on the 10th of November, 1878, was rather sudden, and was a sad shock to his large circle of friends and acquaintances. Mr. Freaner was educated at Dickinson College, read law in the office of Alex. Neill, Sr., and was admitted to the bar in 1853. Later in the year he emigrated to the Pacific coast, and it was there that one of the most adventurous portions of his life was passed. Among the first and most prominent of the daring spirits who laid the foundation of American empire on that coast were two of his cousins, natives also of Hagerstown,—James L. and John A. Freaner. The former had become world-famous as "Mustang," of the New Orleans *Delta*, during the Mexican war, having in an extraordinary ride from the City of Mexico to Washington brought on the treaty which attached California to the United States. James L. Freaner directed his energies and his influence to the opening of a line of communication through the unexplored wilds of Northern California infested by the most savage of Indian tribes, then known as the "Pitt River Indians," and still later as the "Modocs." The California Legislature granted to James L. Freaner and his associates the charter of a wagon-road through the northern portion of California to the Oregon line, with extraordinary privileges. It was in exploring this route, accompanied by a single companion, that James L. Freaner was lost. Years after captured Indians told how desperate was the struggle of a single white man at the crossing of Pitt River, when, in the middle of the stream, he was beset by foes on all sides and literally crushed by numbers, many of whom fell before he perished. The gold filling in his teeth, which were preserved by the Indians, established his identity as James L. Freaner.

Upon his arrival in California in 1853 the first impulse of George Freaner was to commence the practice of the law in San Francisco. As that bar was then crowded, he was compelled to locate instead at Oakland, which sustains pretty much the same relation to San Francisco as Brooklyn does to New York. After practicing his profession for some time with indifferent success, he accepted a position as associate editor of the Oakland *Times and Transcript*. Subsequently he was tendered and accepted the editorship of the leading Democratic organ at Yreka. In this capacity he at once took a commanding position, particularly in his advocacy of the principles of law and order as opposed to the p[illegible] of the vigilance committees. Mr. Freaner was [illegible] delegate to the Democratic Convention of 1856, and was selected as one of the candidates for Presidential electors. The ticket was successful, and Mr. Freaner was delegated to be the bearer of the Electoral College vote to Washington. After being in that city some time he concluded a partnership in the practice of the law with James Wason and George W. Smith, Jr. In 1859 he was elected a member of the House of Delegates from Washington County, and at once took a commanding position in that body.

He was made chairman of the special committee appointed to investigate the alleged frauds in the Baltimore election, that city having fallen under "Plug-Ugly" domination, and so searching was the investigation under his direction, accompanied by a report that was conclusive of the controversy, that the entire delegation were expelled from their seats. Following immediately upon this triumph was the discovery that Mr. Freaner himself was not, under a strict construction of the constitution of the State, eligible. The constitution required a continuous resid[illegible] of three years in the State, and Mr. Freaner's sojourn in California had broken this, and, as was believed, rendered him ineligible. Mr. Freaner, upon having his attention called to the matter by a friend, arose in his seat, and upon the impulse of the moment tendered his resignation. His resignation was accepted with regret.

Returning to Hagerstown, Mr. Freaner pursued his profession in connection with Messrs. Wason and Smith until the breaking out of the war, when he cast his lot with the South. During the whole war, from the fall of 1861 to the capitulation at Appomattox, Maj. Freaner was in the saddle and field, participating in nearly all the great battles of the Army of Northern Virginia. Gen. J. E. B. Stuart very soon discovered his high qualities as a soldier, and he was solicited to become one of the aides upon the staff of that distinguished cavalry officer, which position he filled up to the time of the death of Stuart. Maj. Freaner was then attached to the staff of Gen. Fitzhugh Lee. At earlier periods of his military career he filled the positions of adjutant of the First Virginia Cavalry, commanded by Col. L. Tiernan Brien, and that of assistant adjutant-general of the brigade to which that regiment belonged. He also for a time served on the staff of Gen. Wade Hampton, in command of the Confederate cavalry, and was by the side of that distinguished officer, who then commanded a division, when one of his sons was killed and another wounded in one of the fiercest battles of the war, and p[illegible] removal from the field.

Upon the re-establishment of peace, Mr Freaner returned to Hagerstown His former law-firm had been dissolved, and he entered in 1866 into permanent connection with A K Syester, then one of the leading members of the bar of Washington County, and afterwards attorney-general of Maryland From that day to the day of his death the law-firm of Syester & Freaner held a commanding position in Western Maryland

In 1867 he was appointed auditor of the Circuit Court for Washington County In 1874 he was again elected on the Democratic ticket to the House of Delegates, where he at once assumed a leading position both in debate and on committees

Mr Freaner was noted for his lofty purity of character, as well as for acuteness and force of intellect Mr Freaner left a widow, daughter of the late George Fechtig, of Hagerstown, and two daughters His remains were attended to the grave by an unusually large concourse The funeral services were conducted by the Rev Mr Thompson, of the Presbyterian Church, assisted by the Rev Mr Hank, of the Methodist Episcopal Church An escort of honor, consisting of eight ex-Confederate soldiers, walked on either side of the hearse to the grave, and the pall-bearers were the following members of the bar H H Keedy, H Kyd Douglas, F M Darby, Alex Neill, Edward Stake, and G W Smith Jr

At a meeting of the members of the bar and officers of the Circuit Court for Washington County, held at the court-house, Nov 11, 1878, on motion of Hon Wm T Hamilton, the Hon Daniel Weisel was called to the chair, and Geo B Oswald was appointed secretary

The chair stated that the object of the meeting was for the purpose of taking suitable action upon the death of the Hon George Freaner, a member of this bar and auditor in chancery

On motion of Hon A K Syester, a committee of three was appointed to draft suitable resolutions, when the chair appointed Hon A K Syester, H H Keedy, and Louis E McComas, Esqs, as the committee

The committee then prepared and presented the following preamble and resolutions, which were upon motion unanimously adopted

"*Whereas* The sudden death of Maj George Freaner, a member of this bar, and for eleven years auditor of this court, cut down in the strength of his days and the maturity of his intellect, has affected his brothers of the bar with a sad and painful bereavement, therefore,

"*Resolved*, That we have heard with feelings of deepest grief of the sudden and untimely death of our friend and brother, Maj G[illegible] F[illegible]ner, cut off in the prime of a u[illegible]ful and distinguished life, which gave abundant promise of still greater usefulness and honor in the future

"*Resolved*, That in the death of our brother the whole community have lost one of its most honorable, active, and useful citizens, the bar of Washington County one of its brightest ornaments and ablest advocates, his more intimate friends and associates a warm hearted, generous, and devoted friend, his afflicted family a tender and considerate husband and father, and the State itself one of her most promising and honored sons

"*Resolved*, That whether in the walks of public or private life, or the practice of the arduous and responsible duties of his profession, the community generally has sustained no ordinary loss in the sudden and unlooked for death of one who was at all times and under all circumstances an attractive and instructive companion, an eminent, honorable, and upright lawyer, and in all the varied pursuits of life a dignified, polished, and courteous gentleman, without fear and without reproach

"*Resolved*, Whether as a gallant soldier in the field, an eloquent orator on the hustings, or a faithful advocate in the forum, or above all as a citizen of spotless integrity, his name will not soon be forgotten, and his memory will long be especially cherished by this bar for his many manly, generous, and winning social traits, and for his lofty standard of professional conduct

"*Resolved*, That we tender to his afflicted family, to whom most especially the loss is indeed an irreparable one our most heartfelt and deepest sympathy in this dark hour of their distress

"*Resolved*, That a copy of these resolutions be sent to his family, and that the chairman of the committee be instructed to present the same to the Circuit Court at its next session, with a request that they be entered on the minutes of the court

"*Resolved*, That as a further mark of respect we attend the funeral in a body and wear the usual badge of mourning for thirty days

"D WEISEL, *Chairman*

"GEORGE B OSWALD, *Secretary*"

At this meeting eloquent tributes of respect to the memory of Maj Freaner were paid by ex-Attorney General Syester, ex Senator Hamilton, and Judges Weisel, Motter, and Pearre

Andrew K Syester, ex-attorney-general of Maryland, and one of the leading lawyers of the State, was born on the 11th of March, 1827, in Berkeley County, Va His father, Daniel Syester, was a native of Berkeley County, and his mother, Sarah Moudy, was born in Washington County, Md A K Syester was educated at Franklin-Marshall College, Mercersburg, Pa, where he graduated in 1849 He removed to Hagerstown in 1850, and during the following winter was a committee clerk in the House of Delegates of Maryland In January, 1852, he was admitted to the bar, and in the autumn of the following year, 1853, was elected to the House of Delegates In 1854 he was elected State's attorney, which office he held for four years from the 1st of January, 1855 In 1859 he was nominated by the Whig party for judge of the Court of Appeals in opposition to Jas L Bartol, Democ[illegible] tes, after a very

... and exciting contest At that time the judicial ... comprised Allegany, Washington, Frederick, ...ll and Harford Counties In 1861, Mr Syester was a candidate for Congress against Hon Philip ... Thomas, and was defeated in common with other Democrats at that period In the spring ... 1867 however, he was elected a member of the ...stitutional Convention, and in the following au... to the House of Delegates In 1872 he was ...minated by the Democratic party and elected at... general of Maryland During his tenure of ... office Mr Syester was called on to assist James ... Revell, of Annapolis, State's attorney for Anne ...undel County, to which the case was removed from Baltimore, in the prosecution of Mrs Mary E Whar...on for the murder of Gen Ketchum, of the United States army, by poisoning, and for attempting to ...ison Eugene Van Ness Mrs Wharton was acquitted on the charge of murder, but on the charge of attempting to poison Mr Van Ness the jury failed to agree During this trial Mr Syester, who was pitted against I Nevett Steele John Thomas, and Herman ...amp, exhibited a legal acumen and shrewdness in cross examination, as well as oratorical power, which placed him in the foremost rank of Maryland's trial lawyers Among the witnesses in this celebrated case was Gen W S Hancock, Democratic candidate for President of the United States in 1880 Another famous trial in which Mr Syester was engaged as counsel for the prosecution was that of Rousby Plater, who was tried at Cambridge for the murder of his wife Plater was a man of good family, and the circumstances of his wife's death were of a most pecu...ar and extraordinary character Plater was found guilty of manslaughter, and was sentenced to a term of years in the penitentiary Mr Syester also conducted the prosecution of Joseph Davis for the murder of Lynn, in Carroll County Davis was convicted Probably the most interesting and difficult case in which Mr Syester has ever been engaged was that of Harry Crawford Black, charged with the murder of William McKaig Black shot McKaig in Cumberland, but the case was removed to Frederick County, and tried there in May, 1872 The result of the trial depended on Mr Syester's introduction of testimony showing that Black's sister had been betrayed by McKaig At first it seemed very doubtful whether he would be allowed to introduce this testimony, but he finally succeeded in getting it before the jury and secured the acquittal of young Black The progress of the case was watched with the keenest interest throughout the State and Mr Syester's eloquent and able defense of th... ... ...sted ...tly in obtaining him the nomination for the attorney generalship In 1880, Mr Syester defended Mrs Mary E Rowland, charged with the murder of her husband This was a most remarkable case In Washington County the tide of public opinion ran so strongly against Mrs Rowland that two hundred and ninety-three jurors disqualified themselves The case was removed to another county, and Mrs Rowland was acquitted after a very brief deliberation on the part of the jury In the course of his professional career Mr Syester has been engaged in thirty two cases of homicide In one case he secured the acquittal of a lad accused of the murder of a canal boat captain who had brutally maltreated him, although the evidence as to the homicide was perfectly clear and positive Some years ago Mr Syester received a deed for one hundred and sixty two acres of valuable land from the accused, who, having settled in the West, had succeeded in business and had secured the confidence and respect of his neighbors From his earliest experience as a lawyer Mr Syester has always had a large trial practice, and is generally regarded as being one of the ablest criminal lawyers in the State His civil practice has also been very large, and is now heavier than ever before Mr Syester has always been an industrious, busy lawyer, and is in the full bloom of intellectual vigor Reared in a Whig family and surrounded by Whig influences, he nevertheless cast his fortunes wholly and unequivocally with the Democratic party, and during the war was an earnest sympathizer with the South Mr Syester was raised in the family of Andrew Kershner, whose wife was his aunt Mr Kershner was a leading Whig in Washington County for many years, representing it in the House of Delegates continuously from 1818 to 1832, but notwithstanding the training which he received in Mr Kershner's household, Mr Syester adhered to the Democratic party at an early age, and continues to be one of its most earnest, consistent, and eloquent exponents Mr Syester resides in Hagerstown, where he is engaged in the practice of the law, and is regarded as being one of the most influential and popular citizens of Washington County

Daniel Weisel was born at Williamsport on the 25th of September, 1803, and died on the 25th of September, 1880, aged seventy-seven He was educated at Princeton, graduating in 1824, and having read law and been admitted to the bar (in 1826), began the practice of his profession in Hagerstown and Williamsport On the 2d of January, 1830, in connection with Mr Tice, he established at Williamsport the *Republican Banner*, a Whig organ, which they conducted for several years at Williamsport ... ... a niece of

Gen O H Williams In 1838 he removed to Hagerstown, where he obtained a lucrative practice In 1847, Judge Weisel was appointed by Governor Pratt associate justice of the judicial district then composed of Frederick, Washington, and Allegany Counties, to fill the vacancy occasioned by the death of Thomas Buchanan This position he retained until the constitution of 1852 vacated it by establishing the single judge system In 1861 he was elected judge of the Fourth Judicial Circuit, then composed of Washington and Allegany Counties, and in 1864 was elected a judge of the Court of Appeals, but went out of office with the change of the judicial system under the new constitution of 1867

Judge Weisel assisted in founding and promoting the Hagerstown Lyceum and the Hagerstown Female Seminary He was founder of the Williamsport Bank, and its president for many years In 1868 he was the Republican candidate for Congress in the Sixth District, and reduced the Democratic majority from 2800 to 480 In 1872 he was delegate at large from Maryland to the National Republican Convention which nominated Grant and Wilson During the closing years of his life he was weighed down by physical infirmities and financial embarrassments He was a man of sturdy independence of character, sincere convictions, and great earnestness of purpose

For a long period Judge Weisel was a member of the board of visitors at the Deaf and Dumb Asylum at Frederick, and always manifested a keen interest in the working of that institution At a meeting of the bar of Washington County, immediately after his death, Judges Alvey and Motter presiding, and George B Oswald acting as secretary, a committee, consisting of Z S Claggett, A K Syester, F M Darby, George Schley, L E McComas, H Kyd Douglas, and D H Wilds, was appointed to draft resolutions, and after retiring presented the following, which were unanimously adopted

"The bench and bar of Washington County having met together to give formal expression of their regret at the death and their respect for the memory, and of their sense of the worth of Hon Daniel Weisel, LL D, their senior brother, who for more than fifty years was a member of this bar, a judge of this court for two terms,—from 1847 to 1851, and from 1861 to 1864,—and a judge of the Court of Appeals of this State from 1864 to 1867, do present the following

"1 In the death of the Hon Daniel Weisel the bar of Maryland has lost one of its oldest and wisest members, one who, in a long professional life, was always the personification of gentlemanly bearing and professional courtesy, qualities which, both in his official administration upon the bench and as a practitioner at the bar, endeared him in a peculiar manner to the profession

"2 To dili[illegible] there was added practical legal learning, gain[illegible] which [illegible] elucidate difficult legal subjects with that force and precision which attested a well disciplined mind stored with the varied and exceptional learning of his profession

"3 In the discharge of his professional duties he was ever characterized by amenity of manner and profound respect to the court and jury, and for his uniform courtesy to his brothers of the bar, especially to the younger and more inexperienced, whether as associates or opponents, he will be held in tender remembrance by us all

"4 The elements which made up his professional character and achieved his success were simplicity of style, directness of thought, patience, industry, and perseverance, both in his office and at the trial table

"5 His life was not lighted up by occasional brilliant displays of ability, but he used his powers steadily and earnestly, adding something by each year's study and experience until he was fitted to fill with honor to himself and the State every professional and public position in which he was tried

"6 As a citizen, he was for more than half a century the first and foremost in all the undertakings in our midst which encouraged and fostered the culture and education of the people He was prominent and foremost in all the enterprises which in later days have so wonderfully enlarged the business and industrial activities, and developed the natural resources of our town and county, and his name will continue to be associated with all the various public improvements in our midst which his early and indefatigable exertions so largely contributed to establish

"7 A life devoted to belles lettres and congenial studies, apart from the labors of the law, endowed him with an excellent style as a writer, made him a favorite lecturer before literary and other societies, and decorated his general learning

"8 Ordered, that a copy of these resolutions be sent to the kinsfolk among whom Judge Weisel died, and that the chairman of this committee present them to the Circuit Court at its next session, with a request that they be entered upon the minutes of the court, also that the proceedings of the meeting be published in the county papers, and that the members of the bar attend the funeral of the deceased in a body, and wear the usual badge of mourning for thirty days"

Among other eulogistic addresses was that of Mr Z S Claggett, who, in the course of his remarks, said,—

"His reputation as a *nisi prius* judge was of the highest order of excellence His acknowledged legal learning and ability and his large experience in the discharge of circuit duties designated him for a position of more extended usefulness, and in the year 1861 he was elected to the bench of the Court of Appeals The opinions of the court delivered by him furnish abundant evidence that he possessed judicial talents and capacity of a high order They show great care and labor in their preparation, and are characterized by purity and perspicuity of style, elaborate research, lucid arrangement, vigorous argument, and ardent love of justice They are an enduring record of his learning, and have secured to him the reputation of a faithful, able, upright, and impartial judge

Personally, Judge Weisel was one of the warmest hearted and most benevolent of men He was extremely hospitable and fond of social recreation, and enjoyed an extensive popularity

At th[illegible] Judges Alvey Motter [illegible] unt, and Find

of the Orphans' Court, George B Oswald, clerk of the Circuit Court, and Messrs William Updegraff, Nathan Late, and Jacob Roessner The funeral services were held in Trinity Lutheran church, and were conducted by Rev J R Williams, pastor, and Rev Maybeiry Goheen, of the Methodist, and Rev J A Rondthaler, of the Presbyterian, Church

George French was a native of Washington County, and was born in 1818, and died on the 4th of August, 1875 He was reared as a farmer, but while serving a term in the House of Delegates his mind was powerfully attracted to the law, and having sold his farm, he entered the office of Judge Weisel as a student

After Judge Weisel's first judicial term had ended he formed a partnership with Mr French, with whom he continued for ten years During this period Mr French was a close student, especially of the decisions of the Maryland courts When Judge Weisel was elected a member of the Court of Appeals a vacancy was created in the Circuit Court, which was filled by the appointment by the late Governor Bradford of Mr French as associate judge Judge Weisel once said that, so far as he knew, not one of Judge French's decisions was ever reversed by the Court of Appeals

In 1867 he retired to private life It was one of Judge French's prominent traits of character that he never took part in a trial before a jury if he could help it, his modesty and timidity causing him to shrink from public exhibition of any kind In an address at a meeting of the bar called to take action on Judge French's death, Hon William T Hamilton said —

He was a schoolmate in our early boyhood days, and we were in the same class In our early manhood we were competing candidates for the Legislature, and were both elected In that body he was respected for the faithful and intelligent discharge of his public duties Upon the leading measure of [illegible] policy at that session, although differing in political opinion we were in full accord His career in the Senate and House of Delegates was marked by a conscientious desire to perform his duty

"He was engaged in farming for many years, but having a liberal education he after some time directed his attention to the study of the law, and became a member of this bar His sensitive nature and diffident disposition repelled him from entering into the strifes of the law, but his daily attendance upon the sessions of the court and his diligent and extensive reading gave him many of the requirements of a lawyer

He became the judge of this court during our late civil [illegible] Some feared that here he would fail They were [illegible] mistaken Our venerable friend Judge Weisel being [illegible] to a higher sphere, the Court of Appeals, says that he [illegible] particularly speak from personal observation and ex[illegible] of Judge French's course upon the bench I can Dur[ing] that gloomy period when turbulence and violence afflicted [illegible] apprehensive nature he never failed in giving to all the impartial benefit of the law just as it was He was a just judge

"He possessed all the amenities of life He was distinguished for integrity and Christian deportment, and he left the world with an unblemished name behind him"

William B Clarke was born in Washington County in 1817, and died at the Eutaw House, Baltimore, on the 14th of April, 1855, in his thirty eighth year. Mr Clarke was a native of Washington County, and one of the most distinguished men in Western Maryland He was elected to the State Senate from Washington County, and was the Whig candidate for Governor in opposition to the Hon Enoch Lewis Lowe, but was defeated During the four years preceding his death he resided in Baltimore His remains were taken to Hagerstown for interment, but the funeral service of the Protestant Episcopal Church was read before the departure from Baltimore by the Rev H V D Johns Mr Clarke made a will in which he bequeathed two thousand dollars, to be invested in some safe and judicious manner, and the interest thereof to be annually appropriated to the poor of Hagerstown, one thousand dollars for the improvement of the Episcopal graveyard in that town, one thousand dollars for the use of his negro boy Cato, and five thousand dollars for the support of an aged and infirm aunt Mr Clarke having subsequently disposed of a large portion of his real estate, or exchanged it for other property, it became necessary to revoke his will, and before he had time to make another, in which all the above bequests would have been continued he was overtaken by death

Mr Clarke removed to Washington County in 1836, and entered the law office of William Price, whose daughter he afterwards married He had scarcely attained his majority before he became locally prominent and influential In the campaign of 1840 he was one of the most conspicuous of the Whig debaters, and in 1841 he was nominated for the House of Delegates In 1846 he was elected to the State Senate, and retained his seat until the adoption of a new constitution changing the mode of electing the officers In 1850 he was nominated by the Whigs for Governor, but was defeated Mr Clarke was not only a successful lawyer, business man, and politician, but he was also in private life a most attractive and amiable gentleman His remains were interred in the Episcopal graveyard at Hagerstown

Among the many distinguished families of Western Maryland none have been more prominently or honorably identified with its history than the Schleys They were among the early settlers in Frederick County [illegible] in the

development and adornment of the western section of the State One of the earliest representatives of the family in Western Maryland was John Thomas Schley, who built the first house in Frederick Town, now Frederick City, in 1746

Among other early representatives of the family was John Jacob Schley, who married Ann Maria Shelman They were both natives of Frederick, but removed to Georgia, where they spent the remainder of their lives Frederick Augustus, the son of John Jacob Schley, was one of the most distinguished lawyers that have adorned the Maryland bar He was born in Frederick, May 14, 1789, and studied law in the office of Chief Justice Taney, whose friendship he enjoyed throughout his entire life He soon acquired a very large and lucrative practice in Frederick, Washington, and Allegany Counties, and a reputation which extended far beyond the limits of his native State Severely logical in legal argument, easy, graceful, and forcible before a jury, gifted with a wonderful memory, and possessing a richly-stored intellect, he illustrated in a striking manner the "*suaviter in modo, fortiter in re*" He was a man of fine presence and commanding stature, being six feet two inches in height, and though, unfortunately, many of his addresses and orations have been lost to us, the earlier volumes of the Maryland Reports contain evidences of his professional ability which fully entitle him to be classed with the great legal minds with which he was contemporary His wife, Eliza Asbury, daughter of James McCannon, of Baltimore, was born Sept 10, 1794, and died suddenly in 1816, leaving two sons to the care of their father

George, the elder, was prepared for college at the Frederick Academy and at a private school near Frederick, kept by the late Rev Jonathan Woodbridge, of Massachusetts In 1829 he entered the sophomore class of Yale College His father accompanied him and the late John J Steiner to the college, and was present at their examination for admission by Profs Kingsley and Silliman Both of the young men, being very ambitious and to a certain extent rivals, were at first a little nervous, but were relieved by Prof Kingsley's interrupting the examination, on the reading of the words in the first book of the Æneid—"*et mens sibi conscia recti*,"—to tell the story of two rival shoemakers, one of whom had hung up a new sign with these words upon it, given to him by a friendly scholar, whereupon his competitor, not meaning to be outdone, got up his new sign also, with the words "*mens and women's conscia recti*" upon it

This plea[illegible] the equilibrium of the young men, and the examination proceeded to the satisfaction of all concerned After remaining at Yale a year young Schley spent two years and a half at the University of Virginia, where, in 1833, he graduated in the schools of ancient and modern languages Thereupon, simply in pursuit of science, he

studied and practiced chemistry at Baer's chemical-works, in Carroll County, Md, for six or seven months He then read law in his father's office in Frederick, was admitted to the bar in 1836, and commenced the practice of law in Frederick Within a very few months after he opened his office he was much astonished by the announcement to him that he had been nominated for the Legislature His astonishment may be imagined when it is stated that he did not even know that a political convention was being held, or that his name had even been mentioned in that connection That year, however, the party (Whig) was defeated, the next year he was renominated and elected After the adjournment of the Legislature, in May, 1839, he removed to Hagerstown, Washington Co, where he has since resided In 1850 he was elected a member of the Constitutional Convention of Maryland, and took an active part in its proceedings In 1852 he was elected to the State Senate, serving during the sessions of 1854 and 1856 He was chairman of the most important committees of that body, and chair[illegible] of the [illegible] houses upon

reform of conveyancing, civil proceedings, and pleadings. In 1862 he was nominated for Congress, but declined the nomination. Since that time he has confined himself to the practice of his profession. In 1872 he was nominated for judge of his circuit, but failed of election owing to pride of county feeling in one of the counties composing the district. In 1873 he was elected president of the First National Bank of Hagerstown, a position which he still holds.

As a lawyer Mr Schley has won a deservedly high reputation throughout the State. He possesses many of the intellectual characteristics of his father, is a powerful and forcible advocate, a clear and logical reasoner, and an impressive and eloquent public speaker. His legal attainments are varied and profound, and are supplemented and strengthened by a rich culture and a wide reading which raise even the highest of professional efforts far above the ordinary level of legal argument. He has been connected with some of the most interesting and important cases that have come before the Court of Appeals during his professional career, and has frequently been associated with the best legal talent of Maryland. He is now the senior member of the Hagerstown bar. Mr Schley is extremely popular, and by his kindly nature and generous qualities of heart and character has won the strong esteem and affection of all who know him.

In June, 1839, he married Mary Sophia Hall, daughter of Thomas B. Hall, and grandniece of Chief Justice John Buchanan and Associate Judge Thomas Buchanan, her grandmother being Mrs Mary Pottenger, widow of Dr Pottenger, of Prince George's County, Md. Mrs Schley died suddenly in Boston, January, 1880, while on a visit to a daughter, Mrs Eliza M. Stellman. Mr Schley's only son, Frederick, graduated in medicine at the University of Maryland in 1866, and immediately thereafter was elected clinical assistant by the faculty. In the discharge of his duties he contracted malignant typhus fever, and died after five days' sickness. His eldest daughter is married to Washington Bowie, and his youngest to Joseph F. Stellman, who resides in Brookline, Mass, but is engaged in business in Boston. His second daughter is unmarried and resides with her father.

William Motter, associate judge of the Fourth Judicial Circuit of Maryland, was born at Emmittsburg, Frederick Co., on the 29th of March, 1817. After one year's attendance at Pennsylvania College, Gettysburg, he entered Princeton College and after graduating in 1836 studied law with William Schley and afterwards with Edward A. Lynch, at Frederick City. After [illegible] legal studies he was admitted to the bar at Hagerstown. For six months he practiced law in Cumberland in partnership with Judge Pearre, who had been his fellow-student. He then retired from practice and went to Wheeling, W. Va., from which place he removed in 1845 to Hagerstown, where he has since remained. In 1857 he was a candidate for the State Senate, but was defeated. In 1859 he was elected State's attorney. In 1867 he was a member of the State Legislature, being a member of the committee on judiciary and printing, and was regarded as being one of the most active and useful members of the Convention. At the first election for judges under the new constitution in 1867, he was elected associate judge of the Fourth Judicial Circuit of Maryland. Judge Motter is universally recognized as a jurist of unusual learning and strict impartiality, and enjoys the confidence and esteem not only of the community in which he resides, but of the people of his entire district.

Henry Kyd Douglas, born Sept 29, 1840, at Shepherdstown, W. Va., is the son of the Rev. Robert Douglas and Mary, daughter of Col. John Robertson. He was educated at the Franklin-Marshall College, Pennsylvania, and graduated in 1859, after which he studied at the law-school of Judge Brockenborough, at Lexington, Va., graduating in 1860. He continued his studies under the instruction of Judge Weisel, and was admitted to the bar at Charlestown, W. Va. Before he entered fairly upon the practice of the law, however, the civil war broke out, and he entered the Confederate army as a private, enlisting at Harper's Ferry in the Shepherdstown company of the Second Virginia Infantry, "Stonewall" Brigade. He rose rapidly through the grades of non-commissioned officer, lieutenant, and captain of the same company. Subsequently he was promoted to the position of adjutant and inspector-general of the "Stonewall" Brigade, from which he was transferred to a post as aide-de-camp on Gen. Jackson's staff. He was afterwards made assistant inspector-general of Gen. Jackson's corps, and occasionally acted in the capacity of adjutant-general. After Jackson's death he served as adjutant-general to Maj. Gens. Edward Johnson, John B. Gordon, Jubal A. Early, and others, commanding the "Stonewall" division and Jackson's corps. He was made colonel of the Thirteenth and Forty-ninth Virginia Regiments consolidated, and was assigned to the command of the light brigade formerly commanded by Gen. Early and Gen. A. P. Hill. While in command of this brigade he assisted in the assault on the [illegible] burg. On

the retreat of Gen. Lee from Petersburg and Richmond he was placed in command of the rear-guard, and was engaged with the enemy several times during the retreat, especially at High Bridge, where he lost forty-five per cent. of his command in two hours and was shot twice, his wounds being severe but not dangerous. After Gen. Lee surrendered he was engaged for half an hour on the extreme right of the line, not knowing that Lee had been defeated. During the war Col. Douglas was wounded six times, once very seriously at Gettysburg. After the war he went to Winchester, Va., where he practiced law for two years. In 1868 he removed to Hagerstown, and has been practicing there ever since. Col. Douglas was a member of Governor Carroll's staff, and during the railroad strike of 1877 was placed in command of the department of Western Maryland, with his headquarters at Cumberland. Here he superintended the movements of the troops who opened the Baltimore and Ohio Railroad, and afterwards moved his headquarters to Sir John's Run and opened the Chesapeake and Ohio Canal. While thus engaged Col. Douglas arrested fifteen of the rioters and handed them over to the civil authorities. Upon the organization of the Hagerstown Light Infantry in the fall of 1880 he was unanimously elected captain, and subsequently, in 1881, was appointed, with the rank of lieutenant-colonel, to the command of the First Maryland Infantry, composed of the militia of Washington and Frederick Counties, with assigned companies from Baltimore County. In October, 1881, Col. Douglas was present at the celebration of the Yorktown Centennial, in command of the First Regiment, and was one of the three field-officers of the day for the encampment appointed by Gen. Hancock. Col. Douglas represented the Southern troops, Gen. De Russey the regular army, and Gen. E. Burd Grubb the Northern volunteers. Col. Douglas has devoted himself since the war to the practice of the law, but has also contributed a number of articles, chiefly military sketches and reviews, to the press. He has also delivered a number of lectures and addresses, and has taken the "stump" in every campaign for President and Governor since he has been in Hagerstown. In 1875 he was a candidate for the State Senate on the ticket with Governor Carroll, and was defeated, but ran ahead of the ticket in Washington County by nine hundred votes.

Francis Moore Darby, one of the leading members of the Hagerstown bar, was born near Monrovia, Frederick Co., Md., on the 11th of March, 1838. He is the son of Charles A. and Martha (Chandler) Darby, and was educated principally at Rockville Academy. His grandparents were of English descent, and were among the earliest settlers of Montgomery County. After completing his education he at once began the study of law in the office of the Hon. James Dixon Roman, and in November, 1858, was admitted to the bar. Since then he has been actively and profitably engaged in the practice of the law in Hagerstown. In 1859 he was married to Louisa Kennedy, daughter of Benjamin Price, and granddaughter of John Kennedy. Mrs. Darby died on the 5th of July, 1879. In 1863, Mr. Darby was elected State's attorney for Washington County on the Republican ticket. He was a Union man throughout the war and has been a Republican ever since. Mr. Darby's personal popularity is such that he has been appealed to by the party on a number of occasions to accept nominations when defeat seemed inevitable. In 1859 he ran for State's attorney, but was not elected. In 1869 he was a candidate for the State Legislature, but the Democratic majority was so large that in common with his ticket, he was defeated. In 1871 he ran for the State Senate under similar circumstances and with a similar result. In 1879 he was the Republican candidate for attorney general of the State, and led the ticket. Mr. Darby has been a director in the Hagerstown Bank since 1859, and is president of the Washington County Mutual Insurance Company. He has been elected several times as a member of the Republican State Central Committee, and has taken an active part in all the national and State campaigns since his first appearance in the political arena. Mr. Darby is a fluent and graceful speaker, and is one of the leading members of his party. On the 25th of October, 1881, he was married to Ella V., daughter of John S. Leib, treasurer of the Northern Central Railway.

John F. A. Remley was born in Greencastle, Pa., Nov. 12, 1843. His earlier education was obtained in the public schools, after which he attended the Allegany Seminary, in Bedford County, Pa., the high school in McConnellsburg, Fulton Co., Pa., and the Iron City Commercial College, in Pittsburgh. In 1859 he began teaching. He removed to Washington County in 1862, and was principal of Antietam Grammar School for six years. He was also for two years principal of the Hagerstown Academy. He commenced reading law with Judge Weisel and Louis E. McComas in 1873 and was admitted to the bar in 1876. He was elected State's attorney in 1879, and now holds that office.

Jervis Spencer, who was elected State's attorney of Baltimore County in the reform movement of 1875, is a native of Washington County, and a son of Jervis Spen[illegible] died at C[illegible]tons-

[illegible] in 1875. Mr. Spencer is about thirty-six years [illegible]ge. He was in the Confederate army, and served through the war in Company C, First Maryland [illegible]talion of Infantry. He was captured when Brad[illegible] T. Johnson was surprised at Moorefield, remained [illegible]isoner some time, was exchanged, and rejoined the [illegible]talion before the Appomattox surrender. After [illegible] event he went with the battalion to join Joseph [illegible] Johnston in North Carolina, and, when that com[illegible]nd surrendered, returned to Baltimore and com[illegible]nced the study of law. He afterwards removed to [illegible]ltimore County, and in the beginning of the cam[illegible]gn of 1875 he came before the people before the [illegible]orm ticket was decided upon as an independent [illegible]ndidate, and, being endorsed by the reformers, was [illegible]cted. Mr. Spencer was married to Miss Elder, of Baltimore County, in 1875.

The following is a list of attorneys who have quali[illegible]d in Washington County from an early period:

[illegible]r to 180[illegible], William Clagett, Daniel Hughes, Jr., Samuel Hughes, James Kendall, Upton Lawrence; prior to 1815, Franklin Anderson, William L. Brent, Thomas T. Hall, Otho Lawrence, George Watterson; established in 1816, Joseph I. Merrick, William Price; established in 1822, Henry H. Gaither, Thomas Kennedy (the poet), R. M. Tidball, W. V. Randall; dates not given, John A. G. Kilgour, Colin Cook, Dennis Hagan, George Chambers, John Nelson, Wm. Price, William Ross, Joseph M. Palmer, Thomas C. Worthington, Roger Perry, David G. Yost, Isaac Howard, Zadok Magruder, Robert Mackey Tidball, Almon Fortwell, Frederick A. Schley, Henry H. Gaither, Benjamin Price, J. Dixon, J. Reynolds, William Wirt, W. Jones, V. W. Randall, Geo. Swearingen, Singleton Duval, Robert P. Henger, John A. McKesson, John T. Brooke, James Raymond, Thomas Anderson, William Schley, Calvin Mason, Thomas Van Swearingen, John R. Key, Samuel M. Semmes, Jonathan H. Lawrence, Edward W. Beatty, Edmond J. Lee, Jr., Richard J. Bowie, R. V. Hollyday, J. Dixon Roman, Mountjoy B. Luckett, Wm. Henry Daingerfield, David H. Schnebly, C. Schnebly, George C. Patterson, William Pitts, William I. Ross, William B. Clarke, George Schley, William Motter, A. H. Pitts, Thomas J. McKaig, John Thomson Mason.

	Qualified.
John V. L. McMahon	1824.
Francis Thomas	1825.
Benjamin F. Yoe	1826.
D. Weisel	1826.
Calvin Mason	1827.
John H. McElfresh	1827.
John D. T. Custer	1827.
Richard M. Harrison	1827.
Clement Cox	1828.
John Davis	1829.
C. Ringgold	1829.
Richard Henry Lee	1831.
Robert James Brent	1833.
John Thomson Mason	1834.
J. R. Hall	November, 1839.
M. Swartzwelder	" "
Joseph S. Dellinger	" "
Richard H. Marshall	March, 1841.
Robert I. Taylor	" "
George H. Hollingsworth	April, 1842.
Edwin Bell	" "
Thomas Perry	November, 1842.
Wm. Meade Addison	" "
James Wason	" "
Joseph Rowland	" "
W. B. Nelson	March, 1843.
James McSherry	" "
John Miller	April, "
Zachariah S. Clagett	November, 1843.
J. Philip Roman	" "
William T. Hamilton	December, "
Luther Martin	March, 1844.
James M. Spencer	November, 1844.
Samuel Martin, Jr.	" "
Joseph Hollman, Jr.	March, 1846.
Rufus H. Irwin	" "
S. Addison Irvin	" "
Joseph Chambers	April, "
Thomas Harbine	" "
William F. Brannon	" "
Daniel O'Leary	October, 1846.
J. Manhold	March, 1847.
A. H. Mclown	November, 1847.
W. G. Van Lear	" "
Daniel Negley	" "
J. W. Heard	" "
C. P. Thurston	" "
M. Topham Evans	December, 1848.
George A. Pearre	" "
George French	" "
Peter Negley	April, 1849.
R. H. Allen	May, "
John F. Tolan	November, 1849.
R. H. Lawrence	" "
Wm. M. Merrick	" "
Bradley T. Johnson	April, 1851.
Joseph P. Clarkson	July, "
Andrew K. Syester	November, 1851.
T. E. Buchanan	" "
J. M. Schley	" "
J. J. Merrick	February, 1852.
J. Spencer	" "
R. H. Allen	" "
Thomas Harbine	" "
J. Dixon Roman	" "
H. H. Gaither	" "
George Schley	" "
Peter Negley	" "
Z. L. Claggett	" "
R. M. Tidball	" "
D. Weisel	" "
G. H. Hollingsworth	" "
Wm. F. Brannan	March, "
A. H. Mclown	" "
Wm. F. Morgan	" "
John M. Smith	" "
G. W. Smith	April, "
Alex. Neill, Jr.	" "
Edward E. Cheney	July, "
Richard R. Magill	" "
Alfred D. Merrick	November, "
Marshall McIlhenny	December, "
George French	" "
Grayson Eichelberger	" "
William J. Rose	March, 1853.
George Freaner	" "
Henry May	September, 1853.
J. Willie Price	March, 1854.
G. A. Hanson	" "
James W. Shank	" "
J. T. M. Wharton	July, "
David H. Wiles	August, "
Jerome D. Brumbaugh	December, 1854.
James H. Groove	August, 1855.
A. N. Rankin	November, 1855.
George W. Smith, Jr.	August, 1856.
William P. Maulsby	December, 1857.
Kennedy Price	April, 1858.
Francis M. Darby	November, 1858.
F. S. Stumbaugh	March, 1859.
Snively Strickler	" "
Eli Day	November, 1859.
Charles J. Nesbitt	December, "
James D. [illegible]	" "

	Qualified
John A Lynch	December, 1859
George K Shollman	“ “
Samuel M Furey	March, 1860.
E L Lowe	“ “
George W Brown	August, “
J H Gordon	December, 1860
Thomas Devecmon	“ “
Joseph A Skinner	January, 1861.
J Mortimer Kilgour	March, 1861
John V L Findlay	“ “
William Walsh	March, 1863
C B Thurston	“ “
J E Longbridge	“ “
Albert Small	November, 1863
James Murdock	December, “
Fred J Nelson	“ “
Y I Lodder	“ “
William McK Keppler	March, 1864
J Addison McCool	“ “
P Wilson Jr	September, 1864
George A Thruston	December, “
James P Mathews	March, 1865
William Keilhofer	“ “
Albert Small	June, “
James H Grove	“ “
Alexander Neill	“ “
George W Smith, Jr	“ “
William Keilhofer	“ “
A K Syester	“ “
D H Wiles	“ “
F M Darby	“ “
William T Hamilton	“ “
K H Alvey	“ “
George Schley	“ “
W Motter	“ “
James P Mathews	“ “
William McK Keppler	“ “
Z S Claggett	“ “
Peter Negley	“ “
G W Smith	“ “
F F Anderson	July, “
W L Powney	“ “
H B Keedy	“ “
Albert L Levy	November, 1865
J Addison McCool	December, “
Alexander Neill	“ “
Edward Y Goldsborough	March, 1866
B I M Hurley	July, “
J C Zeller	“ “
Thomas W Berry	November, 1866
I Cook Hughey	April, 1867
John Williams	July, “
Alfred D Merrick	“ “
R H Jackson	“ “
George Freaner	“ “
A K Syester	November, 1867
William T Hamilton	“ “
D H Wiles	“ “
George French	“ “
Alfred D Merrick	“ “
James P Mathews	“ “
George W Smith, Jr	“ “
H Kyd Douglas	“ “
James H Grove	“ “
F M Darby	“ “
H H Keedy	“ “
Albert Small	“ “
Z S Claggett	“ “
George Freaner	“ “
Wm Keilholer	“ “
G W Smith	“ “
J C Zeller	“ “
H C Kizer	“ “
John Thomson Mason	“ “
Edward Stake	“ “
George Schley	“ “
Alex Neill	“ “
Thomas W Berry	“ “
D Weisel	December, “
Thomas H Grove	March, 1868
Peter A Witmer	April, “
Louis E McComas	August, “
James A Skinner	“ “

	Qualified
Lewis M Blackford	November, 1868
R P H Staub	December, “
Lewis C Smith	“ “
W D P Motter	March, “
Edw W Mealey	“ “
J H McCauley	“ 1869
Richard T Semmes	“ “
S A Cox	November, 1869
C P Hikes	March, “
E J Lee	April, “
Albert Ritchie	March “
F Watts	“ “
A B Martin	August, 1870
James M Sherry	December, 1870
John S Grove	March, 1871
J Thomas Jones	July, “
C V S Levy	“ “
Alexander Armstrong	November, 1871
Buchanan Schley	“ “
T I C Williams	March, 1872
Tryon Hughes Edwards	“ “
C S Devilbiss	“ “
Wm J Read	“ “
John L Smith	September 1872
J A C Bond	“ “
N B Norment	“ “
S L Heflenger	November, “
Stephen H Bradley	“ “
Wm P Maulsby	“ “
Thos Donaldson	December, “
Wm A Fisher	“ “
T C Kennedy	August, 1873
John K Cowen	“ “
Wm McK Keppler	“ “
J W G Beeler	“ “
Fred F McComas	March, 1874
Reinhold J Halm	“ “
William H A Hamilton	July, “
J Clarence Lane	“ “
W P Lane	November, 1874
W M McDonell	March, 1875
J M Mason	May, “
Charles Davis	“ “
W M Price	“ “
R Chew Jones	“ “
B F Winger	August
V R Martin	November, 1875
Frederick J Halm	February 1876
N S Cook	“ “
A I Munsell	March, “
Isaac Motter	May, “
Charles Negley	“ “
S B Loose	“ “
Charles G Biggs	November “
John F A Remley	December, “
George W Graham	February, 1877
A Hunter Boyd	May, “
H W Hoffman	June, “
William Bruce	“ “
Benjamin A Richmond	“ “
Ferdinand Williams	“ “
James D Butt	“ “
John C Motter	May, 1878
John L McAtee	June, “
John D McPherson	“
William Shepard Bryan	“ “
George A Davis	December, 1878
John Ritchie	“ “
Clayton O Keedy	“ 1879
James E Ellegood	November, 1880

CHAPTER XLVII

MEDICINE AND PHYSICIANS

As early as Nov 21, 1785, attention was called, through the columns of the *Maryland Gazette*, to the necessity of [illegible] in Washington County a “med

society for the suppression of quackery," and proposing a State board of medical examiners appointed and paid by the State, which might be the nucleus of a future medical school "Physic, Thoughts on a Reform in the Practice of," is the title of a paper in the *Maryland Gazette* of Dec 13, 1785, suggesting a plan for the better regulation of the profession

A public meeting of the inhabitants of Hagerstown, held Oct 13, 1793, with Col Henry Shryock in the chair, established quarantine against "Philadelphia and other places supposed to be infected with that contagious fever now raging in Philadelphia" By the meeting a board of health was established, composed of Drs Samuel Young, Peter Woltz, and Jacob Schnebly, and Thomas Hart, William Lee, George Schall, Rezin Davis, John Geiger, George Woltz, Andrew Levy, Jacob Harry, David Harry, and Wm Reynolds, who were empowered to take such measures to secure the town from infected persons as their judgment might suggest The magistrates of the county were earnestly requested to vigilantly execute the powers given to them by the Governor's proclamation of the 12th of September, 1793, and it was also

"*Resolved*, That the clothing from Philadelphia sent forward to the troops now in this place shall not be received in this town, or suffered to come within seven miles thereof"

"Quackery" was not by any means suppressed, for Dr Robinson, practitioner of animal electricity and magnetism, was in Hagerstown Jan 17, 1794, and William Kerr continued every day to instruct ladies and gentlemen in the curious and definite arts of animal electricity and magnetism for three pounds each, with a written promise not to teach or cause to be taught any other person whatsoever for the next twelve months

Dr Richard Pindell removed from Hagerstown to Lexington, Ky, with Thomas Hart, in 1793, and was Mr Clay's family physician for twenty-five years Dr James Scott in 1793, Dr Henry Schnebly in 1794, Dr Samuel Young in 1797, Dr J Schnebly in 1798 were practicing medicine in Hagerstown Dr B Fendall, surgeon dentist (the same who advertised in 1779 that "those who have had the misfortune of losing their teeth may have natural teeth transplanted from one person to another, which will remain as firm in the jaw as if they originally grew there," and who also "grafted natural teeth on old stumps") was in Hagerstown in 1797, Dr Runkel in 1799, Mr Hayden, dentist, from Baltimore, in 1801, Drs Pindell and Dorsey in 1803, J Wansley, John R Young, Wm Downey, Arnold Hennenkemph, Wm Hammond, Young & Van Lear, from 1800 to 1818, Samuel Showman, J Reynolds —— Ridout, from 1818 to 1821, J Fitzhugh, A F Belzer, Joseph Martin, Charles H Goldsborough, Wm Macgill, and T B. Duckett to 1824 Dr Wm Macgill in 1825 performed the first operation for lithotomy "ever performed in the county"

From the constitution and by-laws of the Washington County Medical Society, we find that the following were members of the society in 1866 District No 1, Augustin A Biggs, Benjamin D De Kalb, District No 2, J Johnson, S Weisel, H Zeller, J A Croft, Hagerstown, J B McKee, N B Scott, M J McKinnon, T W Simmons, John E Miller, Frederick Dorsey, Joshua Jones, R H Kealhofer, William Ragan, District No 4, H F Perry, Fred C Doyle, W W Shapely, District No 5, J B Delaplane, Jas Breathed, Edward Borck, District No 6, H B Wilson, Otho J Smith, J F Smith, J. D Keedy, and N D Tobey, District No 7, E Bishop, E Tracey Bishop, W A Riddlemoser, District No 8, James H Claggett, District No 9, Samuel M Good, O M Muncaster, District No 10, Wm Booth, R H E Boteler, District No 12, Thomas Maddox, Wm Grimes, R J Duckett

The County Medical Association was formed July, 1881, with the following officers President, Dr William H Perkins, Vice-Presidents, Drs William Ragan and E Tracy Bishop, Secretary, Dr J W Humrickhouse, and Treasurer, Dr T W Simmons

Drs A S Mason, E T Bishop, William Ragan, J McP Scott, and H B Wilson were appointed a committee to prepare rules and regulations

The County Board of Health was organized March 10, 1881, and is composed as follows

No 1 Hagerstown, Funkstown, and Conococheague Districts —Mayor John D Swartz, State's Attorney F A Remly, Dr A S Mason, Dr T W Simmons, Dr J McP Scott, Dr O H W Ragan, Dr J W Humrickhouse, Dr Victor D Miller, and Dr H B Gross

No 2 Sharpsburg Keedysville, and Tilghmanton —Dr C W Russell, Dr Thomas Maddox, Dr William Grimes, Dr R Duckett, and Messrs Thomas Smith and Albert G Lovell

No 3 Sandy Hook and Rohrersville —Dr J E Holmes, Dr Boteler, Dr Yourtee, and Messrs George H Weld and Augustus Young

No 4 Boonsboro' and Beaver Creek —Dr John M Gaines, Dr H B Wilson Dr S S Davis, and Messrs Albert B Martin and A Will Lakin

No 5 Chewsville and Cavetown —Dr E T Bishop, Dr John Ames, Dr Baldwin, and Messrs John H Harp and L D Betts

No 6 Leitersburg and Ringgold —Dr F Barkdoll, Dr C W Harper, and Messrs Josephus Ground, Abraham Frick, and Samuel Strite

No 7 Hancock, Indian Spring, and Clear Spring —Dr Gale, Dr W H [illegible] Dr [illegible] Dr [illegible]erick, and Moses Whit[illegible]

No. 8. Downsville and Williamsport.—Dr. H. Y. Zeller, Dr. Lesher, and Messrs. Victor Cushwa, Henry Onderdonk, and August Shorb.

Dr. Frederick Dorsey, one of the earliest physicians of Washington County, and one of the most distinguished, was born in Anne Arundel County, Md., on the 4th of May, 1776, and was the son of Nicholas and Mary B. Dorsey. He was well educated, and in 1795, before he was of age, removed to Washington County, where he spent the rest of his life in the active pursuit of his profession, that of physician, and

died Oct. 26, 1858, in the house in which he had lived since his marriage, aged eighty-two. He continued in active practice up to the last hour of his illness, a period of nearly seventy years, and was associated in practice at the time of his death with his son and grandson. He left behind him also great-grandchildren. Dr. Dorsey lived through the American Revolution, was a witness from afar of the bloody Revolution in France, and watched with more intelligent eyes the brilliant and afterwards disastrous career of Napoleon from beginning to end. He had shaken hands with Washington, and was a personal admirer of Thomas Jefferson. Dr. Rush was his instructor and friend, while among his early associates are to be found the familiar names of Henry Clay, Col. Nathaniel Rochester, the Fitzhughs, the Barneses, the Ringgolds, the Tilghmans, the Masons, the Lawrences, the Hugheses, the Spriggs, the Carrolls, the Buchanses, and the Kershners,—men who like himself made an indelible impression upon the history not only of their county, but the whole of Western Maryland. When he first arrived at Hagerstown (then Elizabethtown) Dr. Dorsey considered himself to have reached almost the farthest point of Western civilization; but before the close of his long and eventful life he witnessed the settlement of all those vast tracts of fertile land between the Alleganies and the Pacific coast which are now known as "the West." Probably no man ever lived who was more thoroughly identified with a community than was Dr. Dorsey. He was well known to every man, woman, and child, his peculiarities making him a most conspicuous personage, while his benevolence and generosity gave him an enviable prominence. In his profession he could scarcely have been surpassed. Prof. Nathaniel

Potter, an eminent authority, pronounced him as good if not the best judge of the pulse he ever knew "A single touch of that mysterious fibre was for him sufficient to know whether it beat the cheerful notes of life or the sad, muffled toll of death His predictions of life and death were almost superhuman He could fix with miraculous precision the last moment of a sinking patient, and in his own case he foretold with as much calmness and precision as Wolsey had done of himself the very moment when his spirit would take its flight"[1]

In the department of midwifery he was admitted to stand in the front rank of his profession He entered upon this branch of medical science at the age of seventeen, and before he died officiated in upwards of eleven thousand occurrences The great secret of Dr Dorsey's success, as revealed by himself, was to secure the confidence of the patient first, and in order to accomplish this he would seem to humor any and all of their whims, but if questioned he would generally reveal intimately his theory and treatment of the case Dr Dorsey was also a skillful surgeon, and performed a number of extremely difficult operations with rare success Although indifferent to popular approval, and scorning to make the slightest effort to secure it, Dr Dorsey was one of the best-known and, in the popular judgment, most eminent physicians in the country, his death being mentioned with terms of compliment "in almost all the papers from Maine to Texas"

Dr Dorsey had been a student of the famous Dr Rush, and continued throughout his career an ardent disciple and admirer of that great man He was among the first American physicians to adopt etherization in surgical operations, but he held steadfast to the Rush doctrine of calomel and blood-letting for certain forms of disease, although extremely careful to use these remedies only in cases of absolute necessity His skill in the treatment of children's diseases was very remarkable, as was also his intuitive perception of the real character of a disease Thus, for instance, on one occasion, when a gentleman who had been treated by other physicians for consumption came to him, he bluntly told him that "a pound of calomel" would cure him, as his liver, and not his lungs, was diseased Calomel did cure him His ingenuity was no less remarkable than his professional skill Upon one occasion he was called in to prescribe for a hypochondriac who imagined that he had swallowed a spider Knowing that argument would be useless, Dr Dorsey procured a blue-bottle fly, and having had the room darkened and the patient's eyes bandaged, bade him open his mouth, and passed the fly several times before his face, at the same time exclaiming, "I see him!" "He's coming!" etc The fly was finally exhibited to the man, who believed firmly that it was the insect which had tormented him

Dr Dorsey was not a regular graduate of any medical college, though he attended one or two courses of lectures In 1824, however, the honorary degree of Doctor of Medicine was conferred on him by the University of Maryland Twenty years previously (1804) he had received a diploma of honorary membership in the Philadelphia Medical Society, of which he was at the time of his death the oldest honorary member Dr Dorsey's practice was probably as extensive as any ever obtained by a physician, either in this country or in Europe It is said that he often made a circuit of eighty miles in twenty-four hours On a single day he visited and prescribed for one hundred and eighty-six patients On his last birthday he rode on horseback upwards of twenty five miles For some forty days preceding his mother's death he saw her every day, although she lived thirty two miles from Hagerstown, besides attending to his other practice During this period, too, he had a patient at Chambersburg, twenty miles distant, whom he occasionally saw

In his private character Dr Dorsey was an earnest hater of hypocrisy and sham, so much so that he often strove to make himself appear worse for fear he might seem better than he was[2]

He was, however, a profound respecter of religion and a prominent member of the Protestant Episcopal Church And yet he could not resist a fondness for such sports as fox-hunting, horse-racing, and chicken-fighting, and though never a gambler, his love for these out-door sports continued to be an absorbing passion with him, and after he was sixty years of age he went all the way to New York to attend a main of famous cocks

"He would often," says Judge Mason, "economize his time so that he could make the same visit from home subserve both

[1] Address upon the life and character of Dr Frederick Dorsey, by John Thom[illegible] M[illegible]

[2] To listen to some of the sentiments he would utter you would suppose him a monster, while to witness his unobtrusive acts of benevolence and virtue you would esteem him a model of goodness I have known him in apparent seriousness to advocate the burning of all Christian churches, and the hanging of all Christian ministers Yet who contributed more liberally and cheerfully to the support of both? He would denounce certain persons at one moment, and yet in the next quietly heap upon them the most substantial benefits You would hear him recommend the most cruel punishment to slaves, [illegible] of masters" —[illegible]

an Episcopal convention and a chicken fight." His peculiarity in this respect was the result not of any moral obliquity, but of an uncontrollable vivacity and zest for lively amusements. He had, we are told, the spirits of a boy to the end of his days, and "his long life was one unbroken season of youthful enjoyment and sunshine." His generosity was so great to it, it is asserted, he perhaps lost more money by securityship and long indulgence than any man who ever lived in Washington County. He was the main support of his church in Hagerstown, and was a member of its vestry for half a century. At times he was "president, secretary, treasurer, collector, and everything else," and even made the fires and rang the bell. Dr. Dorsey was the leader of the High Church party in his vicinity, and by his vigorous and aggressive course succeeded in carrying the day at the church elections. He was also a warm and steadfast friend of St. James College, and was one of its trustees from the first organization, and among the earliest and most liberal contributors. In all business transactions his integrity was unquestioned. In his personal habits and dress he was scrupulously simple and unaffected, and often boasted of having worn certain articles of clothing for a number of years.

"His hospitality was proverbial, and his conversation extremely interesting. He was a famous talker, and somebody once said of him that he had an assortment of stories for his journeys, which varied from one to twenty miles in length. When he had no one to narrate them to he would talk to his horse. "On one occasion," we are told, "for *nine* days and nights, so pressing were his professional engagements, he never went to bed. On the *tenth* he presided as chief judge at the great race between the famous horses Industry and Bachelor, and was the merriest man on the ground."

In an obituary notice the *Herald and Torch*, of Hagerstown, in its issue of Wednesday, Nov. 3, 1858, said of him,—

"Dr. Dorsey was personally known to almost every citizen of the county. Far and near his fame had spread, and it will be long before the recollection of his great usefulness, his remarkable activity and endurance, his wonderful and untiring energy, and above all his great benevolence and his generous sacrifices, shall fade away from the memory of those among whom he lived and died. As a citizen he was distinguished for his love of justice and reverence for law. Possessed of a sound and enlightened judgment, enlarged and comprehensive views, enterprising, and eminently useful, his large influence and honored position suffered no abatement with his declining age. He filled as large a space in the community under the weight of many years and the infirmities of age as he did in the full strength and vigor of ripened manhood. No man was ever more honored in the confidences and affections of a people, none more venerated and beloved, and few so richly deserving it all. He lived to an unusual age, and the flower of his youth, the strength and vigor of his manhood, and the unequaled and matured experiences of his old age were given to his profession with a constancy and devotion seldom if ever equaled.

"He loved his profession for its own sake, and the blessings which its proper practice would confer on others he devoted all the energies of his remarkable life to its practice, not with a view to the accumulation of wealth, but with the high and noble purpose of mastering its complex and delicate principles, and faithfully discharging its momentous and solemn responsibilities. He was eminently successful. Faithfully, completely, amply, to the full extent of human ability and the furthest stretch of human endurance, did he discharge the heavy responsibilities and delicate duties of his laborious calling. No call was ever unanswered. Heat and cold, darkness and light, cloud and sunshine, the dashing fury of the storm, the blackness of the midnight hour found him, up to the moment when he was prostrated on his bed of extreme suffering, exposed to their perils and inclemencies. He never stopped to inquire, in the midst of his heaviest practice, concerning the pecuniary ability of his patient. He gave his services alike to the rich and the poor. He never pressed the needy or unfortunate. To them his acquirements, his skill, experience, and labor were ever a gratuity. Even in extreme old age, endowed as it was with an unparalleled power of endurance, when others claim that immunity and repose from service and labor so much needed, and so cheerfully given, in the face of the fiercest and bitterest storms that howl around us, and under the darkness of the blackest midnight sky, he was on his errands of benevolence, his aged and welcome form bent over the bedside of the dying and unfortunate, or carried hope and health to the wasted frame of the poor and neglected. The gratification of having relieved the afflicted, of having restored strength and health to the homes of want and suffering, was the only reward he ever asked, and to him that reward was a treasure which money could not buy. In the cherished affections and lasting remembrances of thousands of our people this rare and noble characteristic of his nature will live enshrined. It will embalm his name in the purest impulses of our hearts, and passing down from parent to child will perpetuate his memory, and long survive that ephemeral fame which waits on the unsubstantial gratification of wealth or the uneasy and unstable honors of a public life.

"In the course of his long and active life he was never known to occasion distress or embarrassment to any one, though he was schooled in misfortune himself, and was called on frequently to endure anxieties and make heavy sacrifices for others, owing to the confiding generosity of his nature. He chose to suffer himself rather than cause others distress. In the midst of cruel perplexities and severe embarrassments he was always cheerful, self-possessed, and just, and difficulties which would have bent others to the earth, or have dashed their temper with a shade of sullen and morose bitterness, seemed only to nerve him with increased energy and a firmer resolution, or develop in bolder relief the innate strength and manliness of his character, and illustrate the great superiority of his nature."

On the morning after his death all the church-bells of the town were tolled in honor of the deceased. Friday morning at ten o'clock was the hour fixed for the funeral, but at that time it was raining in torrents, as it had been from an early hour. A postponement until two o'clock in the afternoon was then announced, at which hour, though still raining, the body was borne to the Episcopal church, followed by an immense concourse of people. Arrived in the church an anthem was chanted and the service read, after which an appropriate discourse was pronounced by the Rev. Dr. Kerfoot, rector of the College of St. James. The remains were then taken and deposited in their last resting-place.

On the 17th of March, 1859, an address upon Dr. Dorsey's life and character was delivered by the late Judge John Thomson Mason in the Lutheran church at Hagerstown.

At a meeting of the vestry of St John's Parish, Washington County, held at the parsonage, on Wednesday, Oct 28, 1858, the following preamble and resolutions were unanimously adopted

"WHEREAS, It has pleased Almighty God, in His wise providence, to remove from this world Dr Frederick Dorsey, Sr one of the oldest and most useful citizens of our county, and one who has, for many years, been a member of this vestry, and has also filled the offices of warden, treasurer, and register in this parish therein,

"*Resolved*, That while we desire to bow in submission to the will of Him who doeth all things well, we feel that in the removal hence of our associate, we have lost one in whose wisdom and experience we have learned to confide, and one who was always ready to the extent of his ability to aid in everything which he supposed would promote the material prosperity of the parish, and, therefore, we know that we express the feelings of the parishioners in general when we say that in his death the parish has to mourn the loss of one of its truest friends, and the Church of God a faithful servant

"*Resolved*, That in our estimation a great and a good man has been taken away a great man, because in his prominence and success in his profession we recognize talents and abilities which would have fitted him for any station in life to which, in the providence of God, he might have been called, a good man, because in all the relations of life, whether as a citizen of the State, a member of the social circle, or in the practice of his profession we have always found him faithful in the discharge of his duties But we desire to record our sense of his worth particularly in reference to the special business of his calling —the practice of the medical profession In skill he was proficient, and in the bestowal of his services he was altogether disinterested, for the relief of suffering humanity seemed to be the aim of his life, and the lowly and the poor were as sure of his assiduous attentions, when called for, as those who from their circumstances and position in life were able to command them

"*Resolved*, That we sympathize most deeply with the family of Dr Dorsey in their bereavement, but more especially with her who has been so long associated with him in affairs of love

"*Resolved*, That we will wear the usual badge of mourning for thirty days, in token of our respect for the memory of the deceased

"*Resolved*, That these resolutions be entered upon the records of the parish, and that a copy of them be sent to the family of Dr Dorsey, and also that they be published in the newspapers of the town

"HENRY EDWARDS, *Rector*

"WM MOTTER, *Register*"

The board of trustees of the College of St James having been specially convened to take some action in regard to the decease of Dr Dorsey, it was unanimously

"*Resolved*, That this board, in common with the public in general, has sustained an irreparable loss in the death of that venerable physician who for more than sixty years has been actively engaged in the practice of his profession, whose eminent skill has always been freely given to the destitute, and whose great goodness of heart has secured him a multitude of friends in all ranks of the community

"*Resolved*, That as a trustee of the College of St James from its beginning the deceased has always been one of the most useful and un[illegible] friends [illegible], the board therefore desires to acknowledge that, for the space of sixteen years, his labors, his counsel, and his friendship have been to the college of inestimable value

"*Resolved*, That the surviving members of this board will ever cherish an affectionate remembrance of their venerable associate and beloved friend, as one who, having been in his generation a prominent benefactor to his fellow men, has in a good old age been 'gathered to his fathers, in the communion of the Catholic Church, in the confidence of a certain faith, in the comfort of a reasonable, religious, and holy hope, in favor with his God, and in perfect charity with all the world'

"*Resolved*, That a copy of these resolutions be sent to the family of the deceased, to the diocesan church paper, and to the county newspapers

"A true copy from the minutes

"J C PASSMORE, *Secretary of the Board*"

At a meeting of the medical faculty of Washington County, Oct 29, 1858, Dr Thomas B Duckett in the chair the following resolutions, reported by Dr Charles Macgill and Dr Thomas Maddox, were unanimously adopted

"*Resolved*, That we have heard with deep regret of the death of the venerable Dr Frederick Dorsey, Sr, a distinguished member of the medical profession for more than half a century, and that we sympathize with his family and friends in the loss they have sustained

"*Resolved*, That in testimony of our respect to the memory of the deceased, the usual badge of mourning shall be worn by the faculty for thirty days

"T B DUCKETT *President*

Dr Dorsey married Miss Sally Claggett, of Hagerstown, daughter of John and Ann Claggett, by whom he had three sons and one daughter, viz Richard Pindell Fitzhugh, Freeland, John Claggett, and Lucy Richard P Fitzhugh and Freeland died young, and Lucy in infancy John Claggett Dorsey married Louisa Hughes, daughter of Samuel Hughes, in 1828 Dr J C Dorsey was born Oct 6 1805, and educated at Washington College, Pennsylvania, where he graduated He then studied medicine with his father, and entered the University of Maryland at Baltimore, where he also graduated He then practiced medicine with his father, and entered into partnership with him, continuing in this relation until 1856 His son, Dr Frederick Dorsey, Jr, entered into partnership with him in that year continuing until his father's death, July 30, 1863 Dr Dorsey, the elder, acted as consulting physician to his son and grandson until his death, Oct 26, 1858 Thus representatives of three generations of the same family practiced medicine together At one time Dr John Claggett Dorsey was a member of the board of county commissioners A peculiarity of the Dorseys was that they never put out a sign and never had an office The people knew them so well that there was no necessity for resorting to such advertisement The patients were always received in th[illegible] [illegible] families of

Hagerstown never had any physician except a Dorsey for three generations

Dr Lancelot Jacques, of Washington County, was a native of England, and emigrated to this country in early life He was educated at Newark School, served a short time as surgeon in the American army during the Revolution, was three times elected to the General Assembly, and filled several other official positions with honor and credit to himself and general satisfaction to the public He died at his residence near Hancock on the 29th of October 1827, in the seventy-second year of his age

Dr James Dixon was the son of English emigrants, and was born in St Mary's County, Md , on the 7th of January, 1797 After receiving a suitable education he studied medicine under the direction of Dr Dorsey, of Hagerstown, and, after attending the customary lectures in Philadelphia, he commenced the practice of medicine in 1818 in Hagerstown For ten years he continued to advance in practice, and at the time of his death was regarded as being one of the best physicians in the county In 1824 he married a daughter of Judge King, by whom he had a son and daughter

Dr Charles Macgill, who died at the residence of his son-in-law, Dr S D Drewey, near Richmond, Va , May 5, 1881, was a lineal descendant of Thomas Jennings who filled the position of king's attorney under the colonial government of Maryland, and of Rev James Macgill, of Scotland, who settled in Maryland in 1728 He was educated at the old Baltimore College, completing his studies in 1823 He became a student of medicine under Dr Charles G Worthington, of Elkridge, Md , and subsequently at the Baltimore Hospital, and graduated from the Maryland University in 1828, and entered upon the practice of medicine at Hagerstown, Md , in 1829 He married a daughter of Richard Ragan, of that place In 1840 deceased was Presidential elector on the Van Buren ticket He assisted in establishing the Hagerstown *Mail* in 1828, and subsequently the Martinsburg *Republican* He was appointed by Governor Francis Thomas lieutenant-colonel of the Twenty-fourth Regiment Maryland Militia, subsequently commissioned colonel, and later promoted to the rank of major-general, Fourth Division Maryland Militia In 1861, Dr Macgill was arrested by order of the government on account of his Southern sympathies He was sent to Fort McHenry, thence to Fort Lafayette, and afterwards transferred to Fort Warren, Boston harbor The doctor was several times offered his release during his imprisonment if he would take the oath, which he declined In 1862 he was released and returned to his home, where he resumed practice In 1863, when Lee invaded Maryland, he established a hospital at Hagerstown When the Confederate army fell back Dr Macgill went to Virginia with it, and was appointed a full surgeon by President Davis, which position he held till the close of the war After that time he settled in Richmond and practiced his profession

In its issue of May 7, 1881, the Baltimore *American* gave the following sketch of his life

"The death of Dr Charles Macgill, in Richmond, Va , Thursday, which was announced in yesterday's *American*, caused general regret in this city and State, where he lived for many years, and was widely known and respected Messrs L G and P H Macgill, of the firm of C A Gambrill & Co , and Mr Oliver P Macgill, of Baltimore County, are nephews of the deceased, and he also leaves a niece, Mrs James Gittings From inquiries among his friends in this city further details as to the career of the deceased were learned yesterday, and will doubtless prove a source of regretful interest to all who knew him personally, as well as the many who can recall his political and professional standing in this State when the present generation was in its infancy

"Dr Macgill was educated at the old Baltimore College, and completing his collegiate studies in 1823, entered the office of Dr Charles G Worthington, of Elkridge Landing, Howard Co , Md , where he remained two years Subsequently he became a student of the Baltimore Hospital He graduated with high honors in the University of Maryland in 1828, and entered upon the practice of his profession in Hagerstown, Md , in connection with his brother, Dr William D Macgill This partnership continued up to the fall of 1828, when he removed to Martinsburg, Va In 1829 he married the daughter of Richard Ragan, Esq of Hagerstown, Md , and returned to Hagerstown in 1833, where he was active in many public undertakings He assisted in establishing the Hagerstown *Mail* in 1828, and subsequently the Martinsburg *Republican*

"His decease recalls to mind an era in the political history of the State in which he was a leading actor The State Senate in 1836 was not then, as now, elected by the people, but by electors, each county and the city of Baltimore being entitled to two electors, who convened at the capital and selected the Senate In the year named after an exciting contest, twenty one Whigs and nineteen Democratic electors were chosen

"Upon attempting to organize the latter insisted that their party should be recognized as the dominant one, inasmuch as it had received a popular majority To this the Whigs refused to consent, upon which the Democrats, or 'the glorious nineteen,' as they called themselves,—two of whom, Hon Joshua Vansant and Maj Sprigg Harwood, still survive,—seceded from the convention, came on to Baltimore, and organized by electing Dr Macgill president The excitement throughout the State was intense, and a riot was only averted by Governor Veazey threatening to call out the militia Shortly after several members of the 'glorious nineteen' returned to the main body, thus forming a quorum, which elected the Senate Dr Macgill, however, held aloof, and would never recognize their authority In 1838 he was appointed a visitor to West Point by President Van Buren, and was in 1840 a State elector on the ticket of Martin Van Buren in the Presidential contest of that year He was appointed by Governor Philip Francis Thomas lieutenant-colonel of the [illegible] and was sub [illegible] He [illegible] was afterwards

raised by the Governor to that of major-general of the Maryland Militia, Fourth Division.

"In September, 1861, while Dr. Charles Macgill was at home with his family at Hagerstown, the rattling of sabres and the tramp of soldiers were heard. In a moment a squad of soldiers entered his house. The leader said, 'Dr. Macgill, you are my prisoner.' 'By whose order?' inquired the doctor. The reply was, 'By order of Col. Kenly, who has instructions from the Secretary of State.' Dr. Macgill asked permission to visit his wife, who was ill, upstairs, and started on his way, when the command was given to stop him. A number of privates advanced to seize the prisoner, when he turned upon them and dashed two of them down the stairway. This provoked a desperate struggle.

"Dr. Charles Macgill, Jr., went to the assistance of his father, and Miss Macgill, a daughter, who had returned from riding, and was equipped in a riding habit, and carried in her hand an ivory-headed riding-whip, bravely defended her brother, who had received a sabre cut in the neck.

"At this juncture the soldiers drew their sabres and pistols on Miss Macgill, and but for the timely interference of their captain the consequences might have been serious. The father and son were both arrested, and were carried to Camp Banks, near Williamsport. The colonel commanding ordered the release of the son, and Dr. Macgill was sent to Fort McHenry. From Fort McHenry he was transferred to Fort Lafayette, and afterwards was removed to Fort Warren, in Boston harbor.

"The doctor was offered his release several times during his imprisonment upon the condition of his taking the oath, which he emphatically refused. In 1862 he was released, and returning to his home, quietly resumed the practice of his profession.

"In 1863, when Gen. Lee invaded Maryland, Dr. Macgill established at Hagerstown a hospital for the sick and wounded Confederates, which he superintended in person. When Gen. Lee was compelled to fall back, Dr. Macgill went to Virginia with him, and was appointed by President Davis a surgeon in the army of Northern Virginia, a position which he held until the surrender, after which event he settled in Richmond, and built up a lucrative practice.

"The following document, now on the records of the parish of 'Queen Caroline,' at Elkridge Landing, will be read with interest:

"'*By the honorable Benedict Calvert, Captain General and Commander-in-Chief, &c. To the vestry of the vestry of Queen Caroline Parish, in Anne Arundel county greeting:* Whereas, the Rev. Mr. James McGill, clark, has been sent and recommended by the Right Rev. Father in God Edmund, Lord Bishop of London, &c., diocesan of this province, to officiate as minister of the Church of England, I do hereby appoint said James McGill minister of your parish, wishing and requiring you to receive him as such; and I do strictly command you to be aiding and assisting unto him, to the intent that he have the full benefit of the forty pounds of tobacco per poll raised for the support of the minister of your parish, and other rights, dues, and perquisites to his said office belonging.

"'Given at Annapolis this 13th day of May, in the 3d year of the reign of our sovereign Lord, King George the Second, and the sixteenth of his Lordship's dominion, anno Domini 1730. 'BENEDICT LEONARD CALVERT.'

"The Rev. James McGill referred to was the ancestor of Dr. Charles Macgill, and consequently of the present well-known Maryland family of that name."

Dr. John A. Wharton, who died at the residence of his son, Col. Jesse Wharton, in New Orleans, on the 8th of May, 1875, was son of the Hon. Jesse Wharton, formerly United States senator from Tennessee, and was born about the year 1805, near Nashville, in that State. At about the age of twenty-five, having studied medicine there, he left his home with a view to complete his education at Edinburgh, Scotland. On arriving in Baltimore *en route* for Europe, he ascertained that the lectures at the Edinburgh University had commenced, and that he would lose no time by remaining in Baltimore for the season, which he did, and there resumed his studies under Dr. Potter of that city. Whilst living in Baltimore he had made the acquaintance of Miss Mason, daughter of John Thomson Mason, of Montpelier, who subsequently became his wife. The Edinburgh trip was abandoned, and his medical studies were completed at Baltimore, where he graduated after a residence of two years. Dr. Wharton then returned to Nashville, where he commenced the practice of medicine, and after establishing himself there returned to Maryland for his bride, was married at Montpelier about the year 1828 or '29, and returned to Tennessee to live. After the residence of a year in her new home it was found the climate did not agree with Mrs. Wharton, and the doctor and his wife returned to Maryland and took up their abode on one of the farms of the Montpelier estate, "Avondale," where the former abandoned his profession and devoted himself to agriculture, and where he continued to reside for a number of years.

But farming, though entirely congenial to his tastes, was not the natural bent of his mind, and in a short time Dr. Wharton became deeply immersed in politics, and for the balance of his life he made the politics of his county a study, almost as long as he continued to be a citizen of Maryland, and up to a late period of his life. His first appearance as a candidate was in 1833, when he was elected to the Legislature, with Messrs. Man, Grove, and Humrickhouse, on the regular Democratic ticket, he having received a majority of fourteen hundred and fifty-four votes over Zwisler, the highest on the opposition ticket. This was the year in which Dixon beat Thomas in Washington County. In 1834 he was again elected to the Legislature, the only one on his ticket, with Messrs. Andrew Kershner, John Welty, and Joseph Weast, and was one of the most active members of that memorable session. That year his colleagues on the Jackson ticket, who were defeated, were Robert Wason, Joseph Hollman, and Dr. J. C. Hays. Dr. Wharton beat Joseph I. Merrick, the lowest man on the anti-Jackson ticket, twenty-nine votes. Again, in the fall of 1835, he was a third time a candidate on the Jack-

son Republican ticket for the Legislature, and was elected at the head of his ticket, his colleagues being Michael Newcomer, David Brookhart and Jacob Fiery The opposition ticket consisted of Isaac Nesbitt, Joseph Weast, John Horine, and E Baker

Some years later Dr Wharton was the Democratic candidate for the State Senate, and was defeated by the Hon William B Clarke by a few votes This completed his legislative career, but for the rest of his life he continued to take a keen and active interest in politics

Whilst a member of the House of Delegates the great "Indemnity" question, growing out of the demolition of the residence of John Glenn and Reverdy Johnson, in Baltimore, by a mob was brought before that body The House was Whig by a majority of one, and the payment of an indemnity was chiefly urged by the Whig party of that day, and opposed by the Democratic party in the Legislature The Republican newspaper of Baltimore, the then recognized organ of the Democratic party of the State, edited by Gen Richardson, desperately resisted the passage of the appropriation, and as the final day for the vote drew near it was ascertained that a majority of one in favor of the indemnity existed in the House There were three Whigs who were opposed to the bill and three Democrats in favor of it Among the latter was Dr Wharton, whose position was boldly defined, and who in consequence thereof brought down upon himself personally the censure of the leading organ of his party, as well as of many of the leading men of his party

In 1847, Dr Wharton was in the Democratic State Convention which nominated the Hon Philip Francis Thomas for Governor, and it was in a great measure through his personal exertions that that gentleman was nominated By Governor Thomas he was appointed lottery commissioner at Baltimore, one of the most lucrative offices in the State Upon the election of Gen Pierce, Dr Wharton received at his hands the appointment of surveyor of the port of Baltimore, which he held until the installation of the Buchanan administration. He then originated the Agricultural College, near Washington City, which was established and endowed by the State Legislature, and of which Dr Wharton was register of the board of trustees This position he held until the close of the war, making the college his place of residence After peace was established and order restored at the South, he was induced by his son, Col Jack Wharton, to remove to Mississippi and become a planter He accordingly located himself near two of his brothers, in the vicinity of Jackson, and there he was living with his only surviving daughter three weeks before his death, when he was induced by his son, the colonel, to pay him a visit at New Orleans In that city he was attacked with a gastric fever, subsequently ascertained to have been accompanied by organic disease of the heart and there he died, attended by his daughter Elizabeth and his son, the colonel Besides these, his only other child is William F Wharton, a member of the Towson bar, Baltimore County, Md

Dr Wharton's remains were transported to Hagerstown and interred at the Episcopal burying-ground at that place The pall bearers were Hon W T Hamilton, Col George Schley, Hon William Motter, Hon Z S Claggett, Dr J F Smith, Frederick Humrickhouse J P Crist, and J I Hurley The funeral cortege was preceded by Rev Walter A Mitchell, rector of St John's Church who officiated

Dr Samuel Weisel was born in Williamsport on the 16th of May, 1810, and died on the 26th of January, 1872 His father having died when he was still a mere lad, his training devolved upon his brother, Judge Daniel Weisel, and after a course at the Hagerstown Academy he began the study of medicine under the direction of Dr Michael A Finley, of Williamsport In April, 1832, he graduated as a doctor of medicine at the University of Maryland, and at once commenced the practice of his profession in his native town, and there remained for the rest of his life, a period of forty years Dr Weisel maintained throughout his career a lofty character as a Christian gentleman and careful, laborious physician His funeral was very largely attended, and the services were conducted by Rev Mr Smith, Presbyterian, and Rev Mr Strobel, Lutheran

Joseph Edward Claggett, M D, was born in Pleasant Valley, Washington Co, Md, Sept 5, 1830 He attended the course of medical lectures at the Winchester Medical College of Virginia, and subsequently in Baltimore, Philadelphia, New York, Richmond, and Charleston After his health failed he visited the Southern States, and having recruited his health returned and settled in the drug business at Harper's Ferry, where he remained from 1855 to 1861 He was at Harper's Ferry during the John Brown raid and knew John Brown very well In 1861, when the Confederate army retired from Harper's Ferry, he abandoned his home and business and went to Richmond, and was appointed a full surgeon, and remained with the army of Gen Lee until the surrender at Appomattox He was chief surgeon of the receiving and forwarding hospital of the Army of Northern Virginia [illegible] ssor of materia

medica and therapeutics of the medical department of the Washington University, Baltimore He is a member of the Medico Chirurgical Faculty of Maryland He married, in 1850, Sidney C Lindsay, daughter of Lewis Lindsay, of Winchester, Va

Dr James Thomas Notely Maddox was born at Chaptico, St Mary's Co, Md, April 3, 1810 He is the son of Samuel and Sarah Fowler Maddox, and a descendant of Thomas Notley, Proprietary Governor of Maryland Dr Maddox was born on the farm "Green Spring," which has been in the Maddox family since a few years after the settlement of the State In 1832 he graduated at the University of Maryland, school of medicine, and a few years later removed to Louisville, Ky, then a small town, and there engaged in the practice of medicine He was in that town during the prevalence of the Asiatic cholera In 1840 he returned to St Mary's on a visit, and in consequence of his father's ill health remained In 1846 he married Mary Claggett, of Frederick County a granddaughter of the Right Rev Thomas John Claggett, Bishop of the Protestant Episcopal Diocese of Maryland Two years later he removed to Washington County and purchased a portion of the Tilghman estate, upon which he now resides At that time it was a rough and unpromising tract, but skillful farming has converted it into one of the most productive properties in the State Dr Maddox gradually became so absorbed in farming that he abandoned the practice of medicine and devoted himself to agriculture exclusively, carrying into that occupation a zeal, sound judgment, and intelligence which not only accomplished important results in the improvement of his own farm, but communicated to his neighbors a spirit of emulation in the improvement of their lands and stock, which has borne most valuable fruit He was probably the first farmer in the county who made any practical application of agricultural chemistry, and although his use of chemical fertilizers was the subject of much good-natured banter upon the part of his neighbors, they were not slow to follow his example when they saw the results of his methods It is believed also that Dr Maddox was the first farmer of his section to use a drill in sowing his wheat It may here be stated that Mrs Maddox's grandfather, Bishop Claggett, conferred a great boon upon the farmers by the introduction of clover, the seed of which he brought from England Dr Maddox steadily refused to be a candidate for office, and the only public position he has ever held was that of school commissioner In politics he was originally a Whig, and during the war was a "Union" man, but since then he has been a Democrat He is a zealous member of the Episcopal Church, and has been a vestryman for forty years He has raised five children,—two sons and three daughters One of his sons is a member of the Washington (D C) bar, and the other is a surgeon in the United States army

---

CHAPTER XLVIII

THE PRESS OF HAGERSTOWN

UNTIL 1790 the inhabitants of Washington County, but more particularly Hagerstown, were entirely dependent on Annapolis, Baltimore, and Frederick Town for the current news of the day and a medium for advertising their merchandise or wants On the 1st of January, 1790, the first number of the *Washington Spy*, the first newspaper published in Hagerstown, was issued and distributed throughout the town It was handsomely printed on stout paper, fifteen and one half inches by ten, in good clear type, and contained four pages, with three columns to the page, without rules The last line in the first column of the fourth page contained the publisher's notice, as follows "Elizabeth (Hagers) Town, Printed by Stewart Herbert" The *Spy* was published weekly by Mr Herbert, and at his death was continued by his widow

Newspapers were not edited at this time but only printed, and all comments upon affairs came from the outside, in the shape of communications, or, as they were styled, "letters," to the printer, signed by "Manlius," "Home," "Junius," and the like Herbert made a success of his new enterprise at the start He was full of work, and at once established posts to all principal points The *Spy* was furnished to subscribers at fifteen shillings per annum Mr Herbert died in April, 1795, but the paper was continued by his wife, Phebe Herbert, and John D Cary This partnership was dissolved in March of the following year, and Mrs Herbert assumed the management, which she continued until she married Thomas Grieves, when he published the paper

The *Spy* was not the only newspaper enterprise in Hagerstown at this time John Gruber, whose name has since been inseparably connected with the famous almanac which he founded, and which has become a household word in Western Maryland and Southwestern Pennsylvania, came over from Philadelphia in 1795, where he had been engaged in the printing business, and, at the solicitation of Gen Ringgold, started a paper, which was printed in the German langu[illegible] and [illegible] *Washington*

Correspondent This German paper was continued for a number of years, but it was not a permanent success While Mr Gruber was printing his German sheet Gen Ringgold suggested that he should establish an English paper, and, for the purpose of encouraging and supporting the venture, a supper was given by Gen Ringgold and his political friends The paper was to sustain the policy of the Republican (anti-Federal) party, and was published under the title of *The Sentinel of Liberty* It was not at all successful, and in a very short time was discontinued Mr Gruber continued his German paper for some years afterwards, and it was at one time published under the management of his son-in-law, Samuel May The paper was finally discontinued With this enterprise off his hands Mr Gruber planned and projected his famous almanac, which has made his name locally famous with all generations since, and which has been widely known throughout the country

The almanac was first published in the German language in quarto form, and was called "The German Almanac" The material and press used in printing the almanac were made and purchased in Philadelphia, and were used and in good condition up to 1857 The workmanship upon the almanac was Mr Gruber's up to the last three years of his life It finally became "The Hagerstown Town and County Almanac," by which title it has appeared every year since It was first published in English and German in 1812 It had at once a wide circulation There were then as now cuts on the title page, with borders around them, representing pictures of farm labors from January to December Selections for fireside reading, wise sayings of sages and philosophers, homely common-sense quotations from Franklin, and kindred matter filled up the pages not taken up with the almanac proper Many elaborate almanacs have been printed since, but none of them have been able to supplant Mr Gruber's publication, of such homely associations and practical value among a large circle of readers After Mr Gruber's death the almanac passed into the hands of his heirs, and its publication was continued by them until it was transferred to its present publishers, M A Berry & Co

John Gruber, the founder of "The Hagerstown Town and County Almanac," was born in Strasburg, Lancaster Co, Pa, on Oct 31, 1768, and lived to be eighty-nine years of age Mr Gruber was of German descent, his family record dating back as far as 1555, and locating his ancestors at Marburg, in Hesse His paternal ancestors were highly respectable and honorable, several of them being learned divines and pastors, one of whom [illegible] Gruber[illegible] was in one parish for forty-eight years, and had lived fifty-two years, as the record says, "in connubial felicity" On the maternal side his lineage is traced from noble blood His grandfather, John Adam Gruber, emigrated to Philadelphia in 1726, and settled in Germantown, Pa, where several of his children were born, and among them the father of John Gruber, in 1736, whose name was John Everhard Gruber His great-grandmother died at the age of seventy-six, his grandfather (J Adam Gruber) at the age of seventy His father John Everhard Gruber (a physician by profession), was married to Christiana Pain, of Philadelphia, in 1763, and he and his wife both spent the concluding years of their lives with their son in Hagerstown, the former dying in 1811, aged seventy-eight, and the latter in 1824, aged eighty-six

John Gruber, the subject of this sketch, was apprenticed to the printing business in the city of Philadelphia, and served six years in learning his trade Being in feeble health he visited the island of San Domingo, and while there was engaged as a compositor upon a French paper The insurrection broke out during his stay upon that island, but he escaped its horrors He came to Hagerstown in 1795, at the suggestion of Gen Ringgold, then a young and active citizen and influential politician of the county His connection with the publication of several newspapers late in the eighteenth and early in the nineteenth centuries has already been shown The most important of these enterprises, of course, was the founding of "The Gruber Almanac," which still has the imprint of John Gruber

Besides the regular publications which have been spoken of, Mr Gruber was from time to time engaged in other literary works He published the first edition of the psalms and hymns of the German Reformed Church, under the supervision of the Synod of that church, in 1831 Under his care and instructions many young men were trained at the printing business, who afterwards had honorable and successful careers in life The sergeant at arms of the House of Representatives of the United States in 1857, Adam Glossbrenner, served an apprenticeship to him Mr Gruber was never a violent politician He calmly formed his opinions and consistently adhered to them, without the prospect or desire of political preferment He voted at every Presidential election, beginning with that of Washington, and was a disciple of the Jefferson school of Republicanism In later times he joined the Democratic party, and held office once (that of notary public), forced upon him by his friends and [illegible] until the incum[illegible] accepting it

Through a long life Mr. Gruber was distinguished by marked and uniform quietude and equanimity of temper. Strictly industrious and attentive to his business and concerns, he was never known to speak ill of any human being. He had a heart and a hand for every one in affliction and distress that came within the range of his charity, but so quiet and unostentatious were his deeds of benevolence that generally none but those whom he relieved knew of them. He died on Dec. 30, 1857, and his remains were interred in the burying-ground of the German Reformed church in Hagerstown, on the morning of the last day of that year, in the presence of a very large number of friends, the religious services being performed by the Rev. Mr. Giesy, pastor of that church.

The *Spy* was published until the early part of 1797, and was succeeded in March of that year by the *Maryland Herald*, under the direction and control of Mr. Grieves, the first issue bearing date of March 2, 1797. On the beginning of the year 1804 the publisher of the *Herald* discontinued the use of the old-fashioned letter s, and two months later changed the title of his paper to that of the *Maryland Herald and Hagerstown Weekly Advertiser*. The price of the *Herald and Advertiser* in 1806 was $2.25, which was payable "half yearly, in advance," as the publisher's notice announced, and its advertisement rates were one square three times for one dollar, and one-fifth of a dollar for every subsequent insertion.

Files of the old *Herald and Advertiser* from March, 1802, to January, 1826, are preserved. The earliest number is Vol. VI., and is dated "Elizabeth (Hager's) Town (Maryland), Wednesday, March 31st, 1802." The same heading also informs the reader that it was "Printed by Thomas Grieves, near the Court-House." Beneath the heading "Elizabeth-Town Weekly Advertiser" appeared the motto, "Open to All Parties—Influenced by None." There is nothing to show, however, upon what terms it was delivered to subscribers, or what were the publisher's rates for advertising.

The size of the *Herald and Advertiser* was that of a four-column folio, each page of printed matter occupying a space of nine and one-half by sixteen and one-half inches. The absence of local news and editorials was characteristic of all the newspapers of that period, and indeed, for some thirty years later, but they usually contained considerable home and foreign news of a general character. Thus the issue in question contained the proceedings of the United States Congress during the last days of March, 1802, "Both Sides of the Matter," or two political articles copied from the *Monitor* and *Aurora*, which respectively controverted and coincided with the positions assumed by President Jefferson, letters from Gen. Samuel Ringgold and Matthew Van Lear, then engaged in a bitter newspaper war regarding some business transactions, and news of the troubles between the French and negroes in San Domingo.

In 1809 a newspaper was started in Hagerstown, which was called the *Gazette*. Its first issue was dated May 23d. It was published until June, 1813, when its brief life closed. At the time of its collapse the paper was the property of William McPherrin, who in December, 1811, made an assignment to Henry Switzer for the benefit of his creditors, under which the paper, press, type, etc., were sold.

It is somewhat curious to observe the amenities of journalism in Hagerstown in the early part of the present century. In September, 1809, for instance, in an editorial paragraph, the *Herald* speaks thus of the editor of its only English contemporary, the *Gazette*: "Billy Brown is certainly a poor thing. He neither knows how to write, spell, print, or talk. Although a friend of order, good government, and religion, it appears from his last paper that he does not look at his catechism even on the Sabbath." It would seem that soon after this Mr. Brown was the victim of some violent person who had been offended by his paper, and the *Herald* of Sept. 20, 1809, thus exclaims, "Halloo, Billy! how do you feel after the caning you got last evening!!!"

In February, 1813, upon the beginning of the thirteenth volume of the *Herald*, Mr. Grieves associated with himself in its management his step-son, Stewart Herbert, the son of the founder of the *Spy*. Mr. Grieves was a strong Democrat of the old school, who, had he supposed that there was a drop of Federal blood in his veins, would have had it drawn out. His step-son and partner was very popular, and was a gentleman of warm heart and generous impulses. Between the two the old *Herald* became a power in its day. Until 1813 the *Herald* was the only newspaper in the English language published in Hagerstown. It was not, however, to remain without a rival, and in that year O. H. W. Stull and a few other prominent gentlemen put their capital together and started the *Torch-Light*, its first editor being William D. Bell, whose industry and ability made the paper a complete success. It was a weekly issue, of course, a daily paper being something unknown in Hagerstown at that early day. The *Torch-Light* flourished and was prosperous. It met with a misfortune some little time after its birth, when the office—a part of Major William Lewis' house on the [illegible] corner of the public square—

was burned, and a removal was made to the brick house, which it occupied for a number of years, near the Hagerstown Bank

The *Torch-Light* in a few years got possession of the old *Herald* through Dr John Reynolds, who had purchased it of Mr Grieves and transferred it to W D Bell The *Torch* thus came in the regular line of succession, and could claim to be the continuation of the oldest paper in Washington County The old *Spy* was first presented to the public in January, 1790 For some time afterwards the *Spy* stood in the front rank of American newspapers, and was very far in advance of any of its contemporaries in Maryland It is a curious fact worthy of mention that as late as 1854 the *Torch* had in its office and successively used some of the very type used in the printing of the first issue of the *Spy*

After selling the *Herald* Mr Grieves, who had been for so long a time its publisher, moved away from Hagerstown He had been for thirty years connected as proprietor and editor with the paper His parents were natives of Scotland, and he was himself born in that country He died at Cumberland in 1840 His old partner and step-son, and the son of the founder of the *Spy*, Stewart Herbert, died on April 13, 1853 Mr Herbert remained in Hagerstown after the *Herald* had been purchased by the *Torch*, and occupied a number of local public offices He was for years justice of the peace, and was elected to the State Legislature He was a man of great equanimity of temper and composure of mind, and his manner was very dignified and impressive He was one of the most prominent and influential men in Washington County up to the time of his death

Mr Herbert's father was not only the first editor but the first printer in Hagerstown On the 5th of April 1852 Richard Williams, who was Mr Herbert's first apprentice, died at Charlestown, Va Mr Williams, after leaving the business in the office of the *Spy*, became the editor of the *Farmer's Repository* in 1802, and remained in that position until 1827 He was a lieutenant in the war of 1812

In 1816 the *Herald* felt justified in putting on a little more style as well as four more columns of space On the 14th of August of that year the following announcement was made by the publishers

"We have this week the pleasure of presenting our readers with the *Maryland Herald and Hagerstown Advertiser* on a super royal sheet and on new type By this arrangement we shall in future be able to enrich our columns with a greater variety of news, both foreign and domestic, and at the same time accommodate our advertising friends, whose liberality we cannot enlarge on [illegible] The [illegible] will observe, are the [illegible]"

The enlargement consisted of a change from a four-column to a five column folio

The *Torch-Light* continued to be controlled by W. D Bell, its first editor, until the time of his death, in 1841, twenty-seven years after he had founded the paper Mr Bell was a Whig, and was an able advocate of his political faith At the time of his death the *Torch Light* was a widely-circulated and widely read journal He left a widow and a number of children

For nearly a decade after the death of his father, Edwin Bell, a son of the founder of the *Torch-Light*, and now one of the editors and proprietors of the Hagerstown *Mail*, continued to edit the paper with ability and success His health, however, was not good, and in the spring of 1850 he permanently settled in California, and Mrs Susan Bell, his mother, announced that she had formed an association with Otis W Marsh, formerly of the office of the Washington *National Intelligencer*, and that he would edit the paper Mr Motter, who for a year had been filling the editorial chair for his friend Mr Bell, took graceful leave of the readers of the *Torch* Marsh did not for some reason remain long at the helm On Jan 4, 1851, a second change was announced, when Mrs Bell the proprietress, stated that she had made such an arrangement for the conduct of the journal as she trusted would make it [illegible] hardly less welcome to its readers than it had been for the thirty-eight years of its existence" Mrs Bell discovered in the end that she could not manage her property so satisfactorily as she anticipated, and the result was that in the August following the paper was sold to Messrs Mittag & Sneary, who had successfully re established the *Herald of Freedom* The consolidation of these two papers by Messrs Mittag & Sneary has transmitted to the present generation the Hagerstown *Torch-Light* Mittag & Sneary had taken possession of the *Herald of Freedom* in 1839, soon after James Maxwell, after a brief and not successful experience, had given it up in despair The *Herald of Freedom* had been established by Mr Maxwell early in 1839 for the purpose of making it the organ of that faction of the Democratic party in Western Maryland which had fallen out with President Van Buren, and which was known as the Conservative party The failure of "the Conservative Democrats" of that period is historic, it soon fell to pieces, and with it fell the hopes of Mr Maxwell and others On the 10th of December, 1839, the firm of Mittag & Sneary was formed, and the moribund organ was put on its feet as a "[illegible]" [illegible]

The [illegible] published by

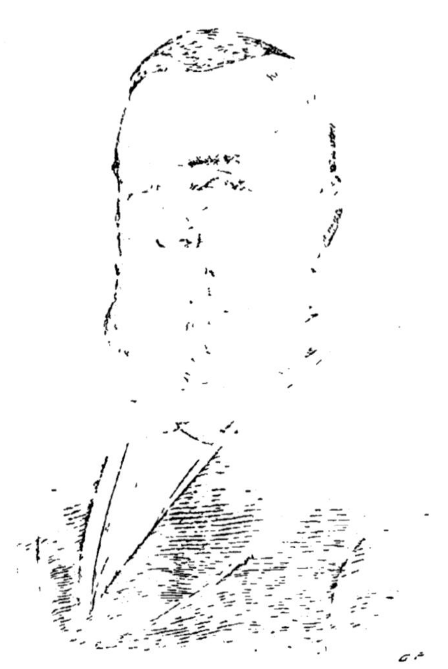

PETER NEGLEY

Mittag & Sneary until it was sold to Carridan & McCurdy, who did not, however, continue its publication for a very long time. Subsequently the old partnership was revived, and the paper was published by them until August, 1879, when Mr. Sneary sold his interest to Charles Negley, and retired finally from the editorial desk. He was the first of the old firm to succumb to old age and disease. He died of dropsy of the heart on the 24th of October, 1879. His career was almost entirely confined to the printing-office. He began life in the composing-room of the *Torch-Light and Advertiser* when seventeen years of age, and before he had reached his majority, in 1839, entered into the partnership, which existed for over forty years. He was a member of the State Constitutional Convention in 1867, and was a director in the First National Bank of Hagerstown, which was the only official position he ever held.

In 1880, Mr. Mittag, on account of failing health, also retired from his long connection with the *Torch-Light*, and sold his interest to Peter Negley, who, with his son, Charles Negley, has since conducted the paper.

Peter Negley, although by birth a Pennsylvanian, has resided nearly all his life in Washington County. He was born Aug. 29, 1818, on Welsh Run, in Franklin County, Pa., to which place his father, Christian (a native of Cumberland County, Pa., where he was born Oct. 19, 1791), removed when a lad with his father, Eliab, in 1800. Eliab Negley was a native of Lancaster County, Pa. His father was one of the pioneers in that county, and one of the founders of the first Seventh-day Baptist Society, organized at what is now known as Ephrata Springs.

Christian Negley, the youngest of four sons, inherited from his father a farm on Welsh Run, and in 1832 exchanged it for a place near Hagerstown, where he passed the rest of his life in the pursuits of agriculture, dying there May 18, 1880, in his eighty-ninth year. In 1814 he was married in Washington County to Barbara, daughter of Peter Newcomer, who with his three brothers moved to Beaver Creek from Lancaster County, Pa. The ancestors of the Newcomers were immigrants from Switzerland. Peter Newcomer died about 1825. From the four brothers sprang the numerous family of Newcomers of Washington County, a name that represents much wealth, intelligence, and influence. Mrs. Christian Negley, who was born in Washington County in 1793, died Sept. 17, 1869. Three daughters and one son (Peter) were born to Mr. and Mrs. Christian Negley. The only surviving daughter is Mrs. George I. Foulke, of Washington County.

Peter Negley remained upon his father's farm until he reached his seventeenth year, attending school meanwhile at the Salem school-house. He then entered a store at Greencastle, Pa., and continued to serve as a clerk about two years and a half, at the expiration of which he was placed in the preparatory department of Dickinson College, Carlisle, of which Rev. Dr. Durbin was then president. Rev. Stephen Asbury Roszell was principal of the preparatory department. In the spring of 1839 young Negley was transferred to the preparatory department of Marshall College, at Mercersburg, Pa., Rev. Dr. Rauch being then president, and in the fall of 1839 he entered the freshman class. Ill health compelled a cessation of his studies for a year, at the end of which he returned, and graduated in 1844. In that year he commenced the study of the law with James Dixon Roman, of Hagerstown, and in 1848 was admitted to the bar. He located himself in Hagerstown, and at once began the active practice of his profession. In 1851 he was brought forward as the Whig candidate for prosecuting attorney against Thomas Harbine (Democrat), by whom he was defeated by one hundred and thirty-seven votes. In 1852 continued ill health led him to abandon his law practice for an appointment as treasurer of the Hagerstown Savings Institution, and when, in 1851, that institution was chartered as a State bank, he was chosen its cashier. In 1864 he was elected a Republican member of the State Constitutional Convention.

Mr. Negley and H. W. Dellinger, of Clear Spring, are the survivors of the six Republican delegates on the Union ticket. In 1866, Mr. Negley purchased a half-interest in the *Herald and Torch-Light* newspaper, and became one of its editors. He is still the editor of that journal, and with his son Charles owns the establishment. He maintained his connection as cashier with the Hagerstown Savings-Bank until it was re-chartered as the First National Bank in 1865, and until 1870 was the cashier of the latter institution. In June, 1870, when the United States depository at Baltimore was made a sub-treasury, Mr. Negley was appointed by President Grant assistant treasurer in charge, and he thereupon resigned his place as cashier to take possession of his new office, which he first occupied Aug. 1, 1870. In 1874 he was reappointed by President Grant, and in 1878 by President Hayes, and still holds the position under the last appointment. His residence is and has been since 1844 at Frederick. During 1878 and 1880 he was president of the Hagerstown Agricultural Implement Manufacturing Company, and later was chosen its treasurer. On the 8th of May, [illegible], Mr. Negley married [illegible], daugh-

ter of Martin Rickenbaugh of Washington County, by whom he had three sons and one daughter, all of whom survive Of the sons, Walter and Charles graduated at Amherst, and William was educated at Cornell Walter and William are now extensively and prosperously engaged in sheep-raising in Texas Charles is associated with his father in the proprietorship of the *Herald and Torch Light* Mr Negley's first wife died Feb 12, 1859 In October, 1861, he married, at Cambridge, Mass, Mrs Brooks, a native of Massachusetts

The *Torch Light* maintains under its present management the high reputation which it has so long enjoyed as a carefully-conducted, vigorous, and intelligent journal Its editorials are ably written and always pertinent to the leading issues of the day, while its news columns every week are filled with interesting local intelligence and news presented in a condensed and attractive form from all quarters of the globe Its miscellany is notably fresh, interesting, and varied, and in fact the *Torch-Light* may be said to be a model county newspaper

Its former editor, Mr Mittag, is living in Hagerstown, in the enjoyment of vigorous health, and is one of the best known and most popular members of the fraternity in Maryland The author is greatly indebted to Mr Mittag for much valuable assistance and many important suggestions in collecting historical material, but more especially for a nearly complete file of the *Torch-Light* which he kindly loaned for the preparation of this work

Numerous journalistic enterprises have been started in Hagerstown In June, 1828, a weekly paper called *Our Country* was published, and continued to be printed until the Presidential election in the fall It was run in the interest of Mr Adams, and was discontinued as soon as the election was over The *Maryland Free Press* was a venture made by Andrew G Boyd, who had been the editor of the *Weekly News* The *Free Press* was first issued in November, 1862, it was not a permanent success The *Bloomer* came out in August, 1851, and its name tempted the Baltimore *Sun* to express the hope that the paper would make its way in the world faster than did the costume of its name The *Bloomer* was published by Blair & Ryan, but the hope of its Baltimore contemporary was not realized The Hagerstown *Times and Farmers' Advertiser* was published as far back as 1827, at two dollars a year, by Reynolds & May, and was another failure In 1850–57 and afterwards the *Chronicle* was published by Mr Marshall, and then by M Prittingham, it did not long survive The *Weekly* [illegible] in November, 1[illegible], but the *Torch-Light* was too much for it, and the *Times* did not get along and was finally suspended In 1852, John C Wise purchased the Clear Spring *Whig* and removed it to Hagerstown, where he published it for a little while, but it did not pay, and was also discontinued

In April, 1842, John A Freaner and John W Boyd launched the weekly and semi-weekly *News* The paper was continued by Boyd after 1846, when his partner sold out and became one of the publishers of the *Mail* The *News* was subsequently sold to A G Boyd, who published it until 1851, when he disposed of the office to S M E Cook, who kept it afloat until 1854, when it finally suspended

The *Odd-Fellow* was first issued in Boonsboro', on Dec 17, 1841, its first publisher and editor being Josiah Knode, a self-made printer, never having served an hour's apprenticeship in any office He was something of an inventor, and his first press was of his own construction In a short time the success of the enterprise warranted the purchase of a "Ramage press" from the *Torch-Light*, of Hagerstown Mr Knode continued in control of the *Odd-Fellow* until November, 1855, when he sold out to Isaiah Wolfersberger and retired from business on account of failing health Mr Wolfensberger only published the paper for two years, and in April, 1860, F H Irwin took possession, and after a short time associated with himself in the management of the enterprise Rev L A Brunner, of the Reformed Church at Boonsboro', who in July, 1860, became sole proprietor, but retired after a brief experience Mr Irwin, in February, 1861, resumed entire control He was a strong Union man, and during the civil war his office was raided and his type destroyed by Confederate soldiers, on account of the strong Northern sentiments expressed in the paper The *Odd Fellow*, however, survived all the vicissitudes of the war, and Mr Irwin in 1866 sold out to Capt John M Mentzer, of Franklin County, Pa, who made the tone of the paper intensely Republican So bitter was the feeling which his editorials created in the community that his office was several times assailed with stones, etc He, however, was not intimidated, and continued to advocate the views which he had professed at first In July, 1880, the *Odd Fellow* was removed from Boonsboro' to Hagerstown, and published on South Jonathan Street, in the "Bentley Building" So favorably was the paper received in its new home that an enlargement was necessary, which was made in October, 1881, and on the 6th of that month the first issue of *The Hagerstown Odd Fellow* was published [illegible] handsome thirty

two column paper, twenty seven by forty inches Capt Mentzer continues to be its editor and publisher He was born in Franklin County, Pa, near Fayetteville The paper is ably managed, and its editorial page commands general attention and respect

The *Hagerstown Mail* is the oldest paper published under the same title in Western Maryland For some years prior to the election of Gen Jackson the Democratic party had no mouth piece in Washington or the adjoining counties Party spirit ran high Jackson was pressed for the Presidency and was bitterly opposed by the Whigs It was in this exciting campaign that a number of citizens of Washington County got together and made up a sum of money to start a Jackson paper It was accordingly established, with James Maxwell, of Martinsburg, Va, as editor, and the first number was issued on the 4th of July, 1828 The following is an extract from the prospectus of the paper

"PROPOSALS *for publishing in Hagerstown, Washington Co, Md, a weekly newspaper, under the title of* THE HAGERSTOWN MAIL

"The *Mail* will convey 'news from all nations,' particularly those most interesting to our own country, and will be conducted so as to give early and correct information of affairs generally, of political occurrences in the different States, of the rise and fall of American produce in our principal cities, and the prices in foreign markets

"The political principles of this paper will be as purely Republican as those contained in the Declaration of Independence, and the rights of the people shall be at all times zealously, firmly, and fearlessly supported, whoever may be in power The establishment is intended to be a permanent one, and as such every endeavor will be used to render it a first-rate country paper deserving of public patronage

"With regard to the Presidential question which now agitates the whole Union, the *Mail* will decidedly and openly advocate the election of ANDREW JACKSON And when it is considered that there is only one press in Baltimore, and only one between Baltimore and Cumberland that espouses his cause, it will readily be allowed that in so large an extent of country there is room for at least another, more particularly as all the other presses in this rich and populous county, where he has so many disinterested friends, are against him The times, too, emphatically demand the establishment of such a press, for at no period of our political history has such *unfair* and *unjustifiable* means been resorted to in order to destroy the character of a public man as have been, within the last year, to injure the well-earned fame of the hero of New Orleans, and merely because he is a candidate before the people for a high and important office, although he was brought out by the people themselves, but the *Mail* will never leave him until he safely arrives at Washington, and receives from the hand of the people the honors justly due to one whose whole life, in peace and in war, has been devoted to his country's liberty, welfare, and happiness

"*Terms of Subscription* —For a single paper, three dollars per annum, but this may be discharged by two dollars in *advance*, or two dollars and fifty cents in six months Persons obtaining ten subscribers, and becoming responsible for the money, shall have a paper *gratis*

"HAGERSTOWN MAIL, *printed and published by James Maxwell, between the bank and court-house, West Washington Street*

"The *Hagerstown Mail* will be published every Saturday morning, at three dollars per annum, but this may be discharged by two dollars paid in *advance*, or two dollars and fifty cents in six months No subscription will be received for less than six months, and no paper discontinued until all arrearages are paid up

"Advertisements not exceeding one square inserted three weeks for one dollar, longer ones in the same proportion, and twenty five cents for every subsequent insertion"

The following is an extract from its salutatory editorial

"And on this day, and in this State, the only surviving signer of that memorable state paper, Charles Carroll of Carrollton, instead of the pen with which he inscribed his name, pledging his life and fortune and sacred honor to the cause of his country's independence, will be seen with spade in hand breaking ground in a great work,—the Baltimore and Ohio Railroad a work which, from his letter to a citizen of this county, published in this day's paper, he considers as only second in importance, to Maryland, to the Declaration of Independence

"And on this day another, and, in our estimation, a still greater, a still nobler national work will be commenced,—we mean the Chesapeake and Ohio Canal,—a work which is destined to bind the East and the West in indissoluble ties a work first patronized by our beloved Washington, a work which through life and until death was with him a favorite public work, and which has at last been rendered certain of completion It, too, commences this day, and an attempt to revoke and annul the Declaration of Independence would now be as likely to succeed as any efforts to impede the progress of the Chesapeake and Ohio Canal It will go on"

The paper as first published had six columns to the page, and was well printed on good paper The news it contained was mainly European, and its columns were well filled with communications upon national politics The paper immediately secured a wide circulation and a valuable patronage It was first published in a room of the Indian Queen Tavern, on West Washington Street, a few doors east of the court-house In 1831, Mr Maxwell published a number of articles which were distasteful to the proprietors of the paper His future services were therefore dispensed with, and on the 1st of April in that year Mr Thomas Kennedy, postmaster of the town, was appointed editor The printing-office was then removed a few doors farther west on the same street, and from there to South Potomac Street, next door to the post-office Mr Kennedy was nominally editor of the paper until Jan 9, 1835, but the paper was conducted by his son, Dr Howard Kennedy In the issue of Nov 11, 1831, John D Ott's name appears at the head of the paper as "Printer" On the 9th of January, 1835, John D Ott and William Weber took control of the paper, and published it under the firm-name of [illegible] the mean

time, when James Maxwell left the *Mail*, he bought up a little literary or neutral paper called the *Courier and Enquirer*, which was published in a building which stood where the *Mail* office now is He changed its name, and endeavored to keep up an opposition Democratic paper, but it failed in a short time The next change in the firm was that occasioned by the sale of William Weber's interest to John A Freaner The firm then continued for some years to be Ott & Freaner Mr Weber is now living in Cumberland, Md, and Mr Freaner in Oakland, Cal, of which he is a prominent citizen About the year 1847 or 1848, Mr Ott sold his interest in the paper to William F Brannon, and for a time the publishers were Freaner & Brannon Mr Brannon left after a short editorship, and became one of the public school teachers of this county In 1851 he was appointed by Judge Perry auditor of the Circuit Court After Brannon left the paper it was published by Mr Freaner alone until 1849, in which year he sold out to John Robinson, who was a brother-in-law of Col Kunkel, of Frederick In 1855, Daniel Dechert bought a half interest in the paper, and some time afterwards bought the other half from Mr Robinson, or rather from Mr Kunkel, into whose hands it had passed as Mr Robinson's trustee In 1856 the first cylinder press, a Hoe, was put into the office In the night of May 24, 1862, the *Mail* office then situated at the northwest corner of the square, above J D Swartz's present store, was destroyed by a mob The presses were broken and the type and other materials were destroyed or scattered broadcast in the square The files of the paper from 1828 were all burned The mob consisted of a number of men and boys variously estimated from fifty to three hundred, who had been wrought up to a high state of excitement by a report that the First Maryland Regiment of the Federal army had been massacred at the battle of Front Royal, and Col Kenly had his throat cut In consequence of this destruction the publication of the *Mail* was suspended for the only time in its career Publication as a smaller paper was resumed in the fall of 1863, having been stopped about eighteen months

In December, 1868, the trial of a suit for damages, entered by Daniel Dechert, representing the *Mail*, against the mayor and City Council of Hagerstown, was commenced, and afterwards decided in favor of the plaintiff, the damages being assessed at seven thousand five hundred dollars The original counsel in the case for plaintiff were Judges Alvey and Motter and Hon Wm T Hamilton These gentlemen becoming disqualified, they were succeeded as counsel by Hon Wm M Merrick, Z S Claggett, H K Douglas, and Geo W Smith The defendants were represented by Hon A K Syester and Judge John Thomson Mason The facts of the riot as testified to by Daniel Dechert, proprietor of the *Mail*, were as follows

"Daniel Dechert testified that he was the editor and proprietor of the Hagerstown *Mail* in the year 1862, that his printing office was located on the northwest corner of the public square, in Hagerstown, that on the night of the 24th day of May, 1862, his establishment was destroyed by a mob and all the printing materials, presses, type, etc, were scattered about and thrown out of the windows, also a large lot of stationery, cards, and paper was destroyed and carried off his ledger and subscription book were burnt, all his furniture, consisting of two desks, a table, sideboard lounge, chairs, etc, with a lot of miscellaneous books, were destroyed That he was paying one hundred and thirty dollars a year rent for the rooms he then occupied for his printing-office, that his printing office, with all the materials, was worth, in the aggregate ten thousand dollars, and by the destruction of his books of accounts he sustained a further loss of four thousand dollars, not being able to collect the accounts therein from memory collected a very small proportion from persons who came and told him that they owed him On the evening his property was destroyed he was working in his garden when he was told that there was considerable excitement down street, and that he had better see about his office that he immediately went down street and found his office-door closed, and thought there was considerable evidence of coming trouble, that he went to see the mayor, Mr B[illegible], whom he met on the street between five and six o clock, on said evening, and there told him, the mayor that there was great apprehension that there would be a riot and destruction of property, and that the property of plaintiff was in danger, and asked that the same should be protected by the authorities of the town, the mayor in reply said that the plaintiff was entitled to no protection whatever, and that he should look to his disloyal articles for protection, that on returning home he called to see Mr Biershing, and asked him to go and see the mayor and use his influence to have his property protected

"On cross examination, he testified that there was considerable excitement in town on the evening before the mob growing out of a report that a Maryland regiment had been slaughtered in the valley, and that Col Kenly had his throat cut There had been threats made frequently before to destroy the office, and had been some demonstrations, and he therefore asked the mayor, in his official capacity, to protect his property on this occasion That he came to the county in the year 18[illegible], and bought one half of the Hagerstown *Mail* printing office for fifteen hundred dollars, and afterwards bought the other half from Mr Kunkel, at the rate of six thousand dollars for the whole, that he purchased the Hoe power-press in 1856, and afterwards made additions of material to the office from time to time That the presses in the office at the time of the mob were a power-press worth eighteen hundred dollars, hand press worth four hundred dollars, and others, that he paid eleven hundred dollars on the power-press, and the balance, seven hundred dollars, was owned by citizens of the county, who held stock in it The next morning after the mob he went down and undertook to gather some of the material together and save what he could, but was run and chased off by a part of the mob still there That he thinks it cost three hundred or four hundred dollars to repair the power-press so that he could use it, that he had two other presses, one worth about five hundred dollars, and [illegible] That he left town

on Tuesday after the mob, and did not return till June 17th following and was then warned to leave for his personal safety, and did leave on the 15th In his absence Mr Boyd took the office and printed the *Free Press*

No effective measures appear to have been taken by the town authorities for the suppression of the mob, which is said to have been maddened by intoxicating drink A short time after the mob of 1862, Charles J Nesbitt, now of Missouri, purchased a half interest, and for a while the proprietors were Dechert & Nesbitt Mr Dechert again became sole proprietor

On the 27th of January, 1867, the old Eagle Tavern, which stood on the square and partly occupied the ground now covered by the *Mail* building, took fire and was consumed, together with the *Mail* office Scarcely anything was saved and the files from the date of the mob were destroyed with the rest Owing to the courtesy of the proprietors of the *Herald*, not a single issue was missed by reason of the fire For four weeks the *Mail*, in rather a diminutive form, was issued from the office of the *Herald* At the expiration of that time a new office was fitted up in the old Hagerstown Hotel building, nearly opposite the old office, and a new outfit and presses procured In October, 1866 James Wason purchased a half-interest in the paper He died on the 11th of August, 1867 On the 9th of August, 1867, a steam engine was first erected in the *Mail* office On Oct 4 1867, Edwin Bell and Robert Wason (a son of James Wason) each purchased a third-interest in the paper Several changes followed in quick succession C P Hickes a member of the bar, was for some years a partner in the firm In August, 1874, F J C Williams, a member of the bar, who had lately come to Hagerstown from Calvert County, Md, purchased an interest in the business, and since that time Messrs Bell & Williams have been the proprietors and publishers of the paper

In March, 1880, the *Mail* office was provided with entire new type and new machinery, and made a new departure in the publication of country papers, in that it condensed its matter into the smallest possible space, and while increasing the matter published, decreased the size of the paper This involved the throwing out of all large type and "display" advertisements This plan proved successful and popular, and has since been adhered to, and fine book paper has been used

The *Mail* is generally regarded as being one of the ablest country papers in the State Its editorials are well written, outspoken, and aggressive, and its columns are abundantly stocked with the freshest news and carefully selected miscellany [1]

Edwin Bell, the senior editor of the *Mail*, is the eldest son of William D Bell, founder of the Hagerstown *Torch Light*, now the *Herald and Torch* W D Bell established the old paper at the close of the war of 1812, and Edwin Bell entered his father's office at the age of sixteen years He studied law in Hagerstown, under the instruction of William Price, and was associated with his father as editor of the *Torch Light* in 1841, and conducted the paper as sole editor until 1849, when he went to California, and the paper was conducted by his brother-in-law, Judge William Motter, until it was sold to the proprietors of the *Herald of Freedom* In California Edwin Bell was connected with the San Francisco *Daily Herald*, published by John Nugent, first as reporter of legislative proceedings, and then as city editor for nearly two years He resigned this position to become joint editor and proprietor of the San Francisco *Daily Placer, Times, and Transcript*, with B F Washington and Joseph E Lawrence, with whom he continued for nearly two years, after which, until his retirement from the Pacific coast he was on the staff of the Sacramento *Daily Union* as general editor In 1858 he organized, and conducted until the war broke out in 1861, the correspondence by "pony express" and telegraph of the San Francisco *Alta California* and Sacramento *Union*, which thus had a monopoly of Eastern news In 1867 he purchased a third-interest in the Hagerstown *Mail*, which experienced several changes of proprietors, with the exception of Mr Bell, who remained in the different firms, and who is now associated with T J C Williams in its publication

Mr Bell is a fluent and vigorous writer, and has succeeded in placing the *Mail* in the front rank of Maryland journalism His influence in the community has always been of a healthy and beneficial character, and he is entitled to great credit for having steadily maintained a high standard of excellence in the matter admitted for publication into the columns of the *Mail* In politics he has strenuously advocated retrenchment and reform, and has never hesitated to point out party abuses wherever they existed, although at the same time he has been a steady and consistent member of the Democratic organization In all public enterprises for the promotion of the interests of Hagerstown and of Washington County generally he has always been

[1] Through the courtesy of the proprietors, Messrs Bell & Williams, the author [illegible] obtain [illegible] of invaluable historical material from the columns of the *Mail*, which had published from time to time many important contributions to the history of Washington County in general and of Hagerstown in particular For their kindly efforts to aid him in his work, as well as for the material furnished, the author desires to return his grateful [illegible]

among the first to lend a helping hand, and the columns of his paper show that he is keenly alive to all opportunities for development and growth as they present themselves from time to time He is now in the full vigor of his intellectual faculties, and is one of the most active and energetic citizens of Hagerstown Mr Bell's brother, Gen George Bell, graduated at West Point Military Academy in 1853, and after serving in the West and in Florida was assigned to garrison duty and on the coast survey During the civil war he served in the Manassas campaign, and was afterwards appointed to a position in the commissary department In March, 1865, he was made brevet lieutenant-colonel for meritorious service, and subsequently brevet brigadier general He now has the rank of major in the regular army and is chief commissary of the Department of the Missouri, with headquarters at Fort Leavenworth

Thomas John Chew Williams, junior editor and proprietor of the Hagerstown *Mail*, was born in Calvert County Md, Aug 6, 1851 His father, the Rev Henry Williams was a native of Hagerstown, of a family which came to that town from South Carolina He was a clergyman of the Episcopal Church He left Hagerstown when quite young, and after having parishes in two other counties took charge of All Saints' Parish, Calvert County, of which he was rector for fifteen years, up to his death in 1852 Soon after going to Calvert he married Priscilla Elizabeth Chew, daughter of Col John H Chew, who became the mother of T J C Williams and four other sons Her family, the Chews, have long been prominent in the State, and their lineage is traced back in England for many generations Chief Justice Benjamin Chew, of Pennsylvania, came from a younger branch of the same family,—the branch which owned the celebrated Chew house, which was stormed at the battle of Germantown Mrs Williams was a granddaughter upon her mother's side of the Right Rev Thomas John Claggett, the first Bishop of Maryland, Delaware, and Kentucky, and the first Episcopal bishop ever consecrated in America He also came of an English family of great prominence

Thomas J C Williams attended the public schools of Calvert, and for a while Columbian College, Washington, D C He left there before his sixteenth year, and at that early age became a teacher in the public schools While engaged in this occupation he studied law under the direction of his oldest brother, Henry Williams, now agent of the Weems line of steamers in Baltimore, but then practicing law at Prince Frederick Md At the age of nineteen he entered the b[illegible] before the late Judge Brent, of the Court of Appeals, and Judge D R Magruder In January, 1872, he removed to Hagerstown, his father's native town, and established himself in the practice of law In less than a year he had obtained a fair practice, and placed himself in friendly relations with a large number of the leading citizens of the county In June, 1874, he was married to Cora Martin Maddox, daughter of Dr Thomas Maddox, one of the best known and most highly-respected citizens of the county Miss Maddox was distantly related to Mr Williams, being, like him, a descendant of Bishop Claggett A little previous to this Mr Williams had commenced contributing articles to the Hagerstown *Mail*, and in October, 1874, he purchased a one-third interest in the establishment For some time he still devoted himself entirely to the law, but in a year or two purchased an additional interest, becoming joint proprietor with his present partner, Edwin Bell From this time he devoted his whole attention to the paper, managing the business part of the concern with vigor and success which with Mr Bell's rare accomplishments and many years' experience as an editor, placed the paper upon a substantial basis Mr Williams is a member of the Episcopal Church, and has been a vestryman for seven or eight years

The first attempt to start a daily paper in Hagerstown was made in 1873, the projector of the enterprise being M E Feetig, a native of the town, who made an arrangement with A G Boyd, then editor of the *Free Press* to use his press and material for the purpose The paper appeared on the 1st of February 1873, its adventurous proprietor spending his last nickel to buy candles to assist his first night's work The *News* was published under many disadvantages by Mr Feetig for about a month, when, owing to some disagreement with Mr Boyd, of the *Free Press*, he was compelled to suspend for want of a press and material Mr Boyd issued the Hagerstown *Daily* in place of the *News*, Mr Updegraff being the ostensible editor and proprietor Mr Feetig, however, soon made arrangements to continue his paper, and Mr George H Nock was taken in as a partner, and a hand-press with barely sufficient type to print the paper was put in the Hoffman building on the public square A large box was used as an editorial desk, and with two chairs comprised the entire furniture of the room The paper came out again on February 25th, under the firm name of Feetig & Nock It was a twenty column paper and has never failed to make its appearance since that time Its early days were full of trouble, and often the little venture was in d[illegible] but it survived

all adverse circumstances, and is now firmly established as one of the institutions of the town. In May of the first year of its publication a new press and additional material were purchased from Jacob Bomberger, of Cumberland County, Pa., and the paper was at last placed on its feet. On June 10, 1873, Mr. Feetig retired from the paper, and Mr. Nock became sole editor and proprietor, but in a few days John M. Adams was taken into partnership by Mr. Nock, and the *News* was continued by the firm of Nock & Adams. Upon completing its first volume the *News* was enlarged to a twenty-four-column paper, and the columns were considerably enlarged.

The great panic of 1873 and 1874 was cleverly weathered by the enterprise and sagacity of the management of the *News*, and, although a little crippled, it came out with fair prospects for future success, which have been fully realized. On July 19, 1875, Mr. Nock retired from the *News*, disposing of his interest to W. S. Herbert, a native of Hagerstown, and a descendant of the founder of the *Spy*, and the paper was published by Adams & Herbert. In October, 1880, the *News* was enlarged to a twenty-eight-column paper, its present size. On Sept. 1, 1881, Mr. Herbert retired from the paper, disposing of his interest to Peter A. Witmer, and the present proprietors of the paper publish it under the firm-name of P. A. Witmer & Co. It is the only morning daily in the town, and commands a generous patronage. The *News* is edited with tact and discretion, and is a remarkably bright and enterprising journal, representing most creditably the community for which it is printed. Its contents are fresh and varied, and its editorials always thoughtful and well considered.

Peter Augustus Witmer, its chief editor and proprietor, was born March 28, 1834, in the Clear Spring District of Washington County, Md. His paternal ancestor, Benjamin Witmer, emigrated from the canton of Berne, in Switzerland, in 1716, and settled in the Conestoga Valley, Lancaster County, Pa. In 1805 his great-grandfather, Henry Witmer, moved from Lancaster County, Pa., to Washington County, and bought property on the Beaver and Conococheague Creeks. In 1820 his father, John Witmer, married Rosanna Brewer (formerly written Brua), of a family of Huguenot extraction, which was one of the largest and most influential in the western portion of Washington County. His father died in 1847, at the age of forty-eight, leaving a widow and six children,—four sons and two daughters,—Peter A. being the second son.

On the death of his father he was placed in a country store, where he remained two years, and then attended the Clear Spring Academy for one year. During the following year he taught school in the neighborhood of his home, after which he again attended school at Williamsport for nearly two years. On leaving school he returned to his former occupation of teaching. In 1856 he accepted a position as

tutor in a private family in Prince George's County, Md. While thus occupied he read law with the late Judge Samuel H. Berry, of that county, but before being admitted to the bar he returned to Washington County in 1859, and engaged in farming and teaching. In 1862 he was nominated by the Democratic party as a candidate for the Legislature, but was defeated. In 1866 he removed to Hagerstown, and entered the law-office of Hon. William T. Hamilton. In 1867 he married Mary Kate, second daughter of John A. K. Brewer, and was admitted to the Hagerstown bar at the March term of court, 1868. In May, 1868, he was appointed secretary and treasurer of the board of public school commissioners and examiner of public schools for Washington County, which office he still holds, having been reappointed for seven successive terms. In 1872 he was appointed a member of the State board of education by Governor Whyte. He has been reappointed by successive Governors, and still holds the office. On the 1st of September, 1881, he became joint proprietor and editor with J. W. Adams, of the H[illegible]town N[illegible] daily, and weekly

paper Mr Witmer has two sons, aged respectively thirteen and four, and a daughter aged eleven He is a member of the Lutheran Church, and his family are connected with the same denomination His public life is best known in connection with, and has been most closely identified with, State and county educational work He has been secretary of the Agricultural and Mechanical Association of Washington County since 1870 He is a member and Grand Vice-Dictator of the Grand Lodge, Knights of Honor, of Maryland, and a member of the Grand Council, Royal Arcanum of Maryland

Mr Witmer ranks among the foremost educators in Maryland and is a thoroughly progressive and enterprising man He is a sound scholar, and having had considerable experience in teaching, knows exactly what should be done in order to accomplish the most desirable educational results He enjoys the additional advantage of being a forcible and interesting speaker, and is thus enabled to emphasize his opinions, and to draw to himself that outside help and co-operation which are indispensable to the successful prosecution of his work Mr Witmer is possessed of fine business capacity and great executive ability When Mr Witmer was first appointed the task before him was an exceedingly difficult one Party spirit ran high, and there was doubt and discontent on every hand He was, however, the man for the emergency He examined all the teachers, visited all the schools, talked with the leading men in all their districts and enlisted their aid, restored the finances to a proper condition, and finally succeeded in putting the school system of the county upon a permanent and prosperous basis New school-houses sprang up in every election district, competent teachers took the place of those who had failed to give satisfaction, the country schools were systematized according to a schedule of graded work, and the old Hagerstown Academy, which for years had been dragging out a feeble and uncertain existence, was remodeled as a county high school Although he was obliged to combat old prejudices and to advocate new theories, he soon acquired the sympathy and respect of the teachers, the approval of the school commissioners, and the confidence of the public So great has been Mr Witmer's success that there are now very few private schools of a primary grade in Washington County, the public schools being of such a character as to render private schools superfluous As a member of the State board of education his influence has been as marked and as potent for good as it has been in the county school board, and his intimate practical knowledge of the working of the system [illegible] that assistance to the State board in the important and difficult task of enacting by-laws for the uniform administration of the school law His thorough knowledge of law and clear judgment have found full scope and exercise in the decision of many important and intricate cases which were brought before the board for adjustment No decision of the board has as yet been reversed by a court of law Few men as young as Mr Witmer, and in his line of work, have made so good a record, or can look forward to a future so full of promise

The *Globe* job printing office was established by Ira W Hays in November, 1876, and continued to be a job office merely, with frequent increases in the facilities of the office, until February, 1879, when a daily evening paper was attempted At first the paper was printed upon a treadle press, but the encouragement proving so liberal, steam was at once supplied In May 1879, the *Weekly Globe* was started under the same proprietorship and in connection with the *Daily Evening Globe* In May, 1880, the daily was enlarged to a twenty by thirty folio, which it still retains Both publications are independent in all things except politics, and in that they are neutral

The *Globe* is a bright, spicy paper, and has contributed largely to the advancement of the material interests of Hagerstown and of Washington County generally It is very enterprising in gathering news, which it presents in attractive shape, and its columns are always filled with interesting matter

One of the best-known printers and journalists of Western Maryland was Overton C Harne, who died on Jan 13, 1873, at his home on the Williamsport pike, at the ripe age of ninety-two years and three months Mr Harne was born near Elk Ridge Landing His family was of old Revolutionary stock, his father having fought as an officer in the Continental army When an infant he was left to the care of Robert Johnson tobacco inspector at Elk Ridge Landing, who sent him at an early age to the printing office of the Baltimore *American* After serving his apprenticeship on the *American* he went to Winchester, Va He did not remain there long, and after his return to Maryland lived with John Thomas, the father of ex-Governor Francis Thomas He married a daughter of Rev Jonathan Forrest and removed to Frederick City, where he published for a year the *Republican Citizen*, in connection with Matthias Bartyn In 1812 he was connected with the *Federal Gazette* and the *Republican Gazette* He afterwards removed to Pipe Creek, taught school, and as deputy sheriff, took the census, being engaged in all these occupations at one time

He [illegible] the negro who

murdered Mrs Baker, a crime which excited the whole of Western Maryland for a long time As a lieutenant he was engaged in the defense of Baltimore, being the only man of his company, formed at New Union, who went to the defense of the city He was honorably discharged on Chinquapin Hill and returned to Hauver District, and became a junior judge of the District Court, justice of the peace, etc He raised seven sons and one daughter All of his children, except one son, live in Washington County

---

CHAPTER XLIX

SCHOOLS AND LIBRARIES

THE first school-teacher engaged in active educational efforts in Washington County was the Rev Bartholomew Booth, who taught school in the county as early as 1776-77 In 1779 he was especially authorized by the Legislature to teach and preach the gospel, and to teach and educate youth in any public or private school At that time he resided on the banks of the Antietam at his home, which was known as Delamere or 'Booth's Mills," and was about a half-mile from what is now Breathedsville, on the Washington County Branch of the Baltimore and Ohio Railroad This property is still in possession of the descendants of this illustrious man Mr Booth had come over to this country from England as early as 1770 In 1754 he was a member of the University of Oxford He was ordained deacon by Edmund Keene, Bishop of Chester, in 1755, and was ordained a minister in July, 1758, and on the same day licensed curate in charge of the chapel of Marple, and the next day an adjunct curate in the chapel of Derby He removed to Washington County, then a part of Frederick County, in the early part of 1776, and settled at Delamere, at which place he remained up to the time of his death, which occurred Sept 13, 1785 His county-seat, where also was his school, contained nearly eleven hundred and fifty acres Previous to his removal to Washington County he had been residing in Annapolis, and it is supposed for a short time in Georgetown, D C, and in Virginia His fame as a teacher appears to have been very great, and his school was patronized by some of the most prominent men of the historic days in which he lived, and he was in frequent communication with them [1]

No record appears to have been kept of the early history of education in Hagerstown, and until the publication of the first paper—the *Spy*, in 1790—

[1] Among the letters which have been preserved which he received during his first years at Delamere were the following, the first one from [illegible], the [illegible] of the Treasury

"YORK IN PENNSYLVANIA, Nov 25, 1777

'SIR,—The high reputation you have acquired by your institution for the education of youth must naturally create a desire in many parents to have their sons admitted into so promising a seminary, and I am amongst the number of those who admire your character and wish my son to partake the advantage of instruction from so accomplished a gentleman

"I expect none but the customary terms, and without inquiring what those are I shall readily comply with them My child reads and writes English tolerably for a boy not yet eight years old, he is just entering on Latin with a master in this place, but we are at a loss for school books, as none are now in the shops for sale I shall write to Europe for some, as soon as possible Understanding that you limit the number of scholars, I address you now to know if my son can be admitted, and if he can, I will bring or send him as soon as convenient With respect and esteem, I remain, sir, your obedt humble servant,

"ROBT MORRIS

'To BOOTH, Esq Near Frederick Town, Md'

The following is from a medical man holding a high position in the Revolutionary army, and a relative—either father or brother—of the wife of Benedict Arnold, who was a Miss Shippen

"PHILADELPHIA, May 29, 1779

"SIR,—From the character you bear, and the very favorable account I have had from some of my friends of your plan of education, I have been very anxious to have my son admitted to a share of your instruction, but till lately have had no expectation of it, from a belief that your number of pupils was complete However, on consulting with Mr Robert Morris and Mr Purviance, I have reason to expect there is still a vacancy, and they both encourage and advise me to send my son by this opportunity Relying, therefore, on their recommendation and opinion that he will not be rejected, I take the liberty of sending him in company with Gen Arnold's son and a son of Col Plater, and at the same time have inclosed in a bundle in my son's trunk the like sum of money which other gentlemen have agreed to pay you I hope, sir, you will have no difficulty in taking him His age is about thirteen, and considering the unfavorable state of the times he has made some progess in his learning If I am not partial you will find him a boy of good dispositions and easily controlled I am told you have sent a bond to the other gentlemen I am, sir, with much respect, your most obedt humble servant, EDW SHIPPEN"

Another of later date was from the traitor Arnold The handwriting is very distinct, although now darkened by age, and its execution is remarkably precise It reads as follows

"PHILADA, May 25th 1779

"DEAR SIR

"Being in daily expectation of sending my Sons to you, has prevented my answering your favor of the 2d April before I am extremely happy in Committing the Care of their Education to a gentleman so universally Esteemed, and admired, not in the least doubting your Care and attention to them in every particular Let me beg of you my Dear Sir to treat them in the same manner as you would your own when they deserve Correction, I wish not to have them spared They have been for sometime in this City which is a bad school, and my Situation has prevented [illegible] I otherwise [illegible] any bad Habits

no traces of the methods or means of mental and mechanical instruction in the town can be found In 1791, Miss Ann Rawlings had a school in which she taught children "reading, sewing, flowering, marking, and open work," and Mr Spicer taught "the rules and practice of vocal music" in the court house on Thursdays and Fridays in the afternoon There were other schools in Hagerstown, and probably a free school of some sort, but of them there has been left no record, and these are the first two teachers of the town mentioned Two years later, in 1793, Mr and Mrs Jones came from Annapolis and opened a boarding-school for young ladies, in which were taught

"Reading, writing, and arithmetic Tambour and Dresden, English, and French embroidery, drawing and painting in water colors, geography, filigree and riband work, plain and colored needle work of all kinds, instrumental music, seed, shell, and paper-work" Mr Jones taught in a separate house a few "gentlemen, English grammar, reading, writing, arithmetic, and book keeping"

In September, 1795, an academy for the education of young men was opened, in which the various branches of science and literature were taught by the president, Mr McDonald, and his assistants The

they are not of a long standing, and I make no doubt under your Care they will soon forget them I wish their Education To be useful rather and learned Life is too Short and uncertain to throw away in speculation on subjects that perhaps only one Man in Ten thousand has a genius to make a figure in,—you will pardon my dictating to you, Sir, but as the Fortunes of every Man in this Country are uncertain I wish my Sons to be Educated in such a Manner that with prudence and Industry they may acquire a Fortune (in Case they are deprived of their Patrimony) as well as to become useful Members of Society

"My Taylor has disappointed me and sent home their cloths unfinished I am therefore under the necessity of sending them undone or detaining the Waggon, I cannot think of doing the latter and must beg the favor of you to procure their cloths finished and some new ones made out of my old ones I must beg you to purchase any little matters necessary for them I have Inclosed three hundred Dollars for their use out of which you will please to give as much to spend as you think Proper, with this Condition that they render to you a Regular account as often as you think necessary of their Expenses, a Copy of which I shall expect they will transmit to me, this will teach them Economy, and Methord so necessary in allmost every thing in Life

"If there is any Books wanting I beg you to purchase them, and whenever you are in want of money to Draw on me

"I shall expect they will write me frequently—of this they will doubtless want reminding

"I have the honor to be with great Respect and Esteem

"Dear Sir

"Your most obedient

"Humble Serv't

"B Arnold

"Rev'd Mr Booth"

Other letter [illegible] written to him by Gen Chas Lee and Mrs [illegible]

thirst for knowledge in Hagerstown seems to have grown wonderfully after this for it justified Mr Barrett in establishing, in October of the same year, a school for the special instruction in "that agreeable and necessary branch of learning,—French" O H Williams was his assistant, and in a public announcement he refers his students to the firm of Ogle & Hael for such books as they would need "The Academy" appears to have been very successful, and to have commanded the respect and admiration of the Spy, for on December 24th, in giving an account of the public examination held by President McDonald, that paper used the following complimentary language

"The young gentlemen were eminently distinguished for the proficiency and knowledge they discovered in the different branches of their education since the commencement of their instructions The general satisfaction they have given the visitors, as well as examinators, in the pertinency and propriety of their answers to the various questions of their examination, sufficiently indicates the justness of their claim to merit, and gives an early presage of their future success in those studies which are either necessary or ornamental"

An announcement was soon afterwards made that Thomas Grieves would open an evening school at "The Academy," for the instruction of such young gentlemen as could not conveniently attend day lectures, in writing arithmetic, and merchants' accounts The hours of instruction were from seven to nine o'clock, and this, the first night-school of Hagerstown, was opened on Jan 18, 1796 There was also an English teacher—Thomas Kirby—at that time in Hagerstown who apparently was successful, for he advertises for an assistant to teach the rudiments of English

On the 1st of January, 1796, Mrs Levy announced that she had opened a boarding school for the reception and instruction of young ladies in every branch of useful and ornamental "needle-work, tambouring, with the art and elegancy of shading and taste in the arrangement of patterns" She designed the work and executed the drawings herself without additional expense Mrs Levy did not, however, confine herself to teaching needle-work alone, but gave instruction in reading and writing

Mr Grieves' night school must have given him a firm hold upon the confidence of the people, for, in September, 1796, he opened a day school, and declined to take more than twenty pupils to whom he gave lessons in French, English, the classics and writing It is probable that Mr Kirby did not remain long at the English school which he established, for on October 5th an advertisement appeared in the Spy [illegible] was wanted im-

mediately, and that any one willing to engage would meet with liberal encouragement. The president of the school board, George Smucker, and the trustees, Jacob Harry, Frederick Abler, and John and Jas. Geiger, stated that the candidate for the place must furnish testimonials of good moral character, but that they will be the judges of his ability.

The advertisement was signed by Jacob Shryock. In November, Mr. Grieves, in connection with his day-school, again opened a night-school, in announcing which he said he

"hopes none may apply but such as will conduct themselves with propriety and decent deportment. Impressed with gratitude for the favors he has already received, he trusts it will ever remain a first object of his ambition, by advancing the literary and moral improvement of his pupils, to deserve the public confidence."

There is a gap in the history of the schools after 1795, and P. Edwards' English school, established in May, 1798, is the first mentioned after the former year. Mrs. Levy seems to have been quite successful with her mental and industrial school, for she continued it after 1794, and is mentioned by the paper and in several private records in very flattering language. A new French teacher, Boileau, had taken the place of Mr. Barrett in 1798. In April of that year Mr. Edwards removed his school to the house formerly occupied by Mr. Hoover, on Main Street. In September, 1799, Mrs. Ragan announced that she would open a school for the instruction of young ladies in needle-work at the two-story brick house belonging to Mrs. Heyser, on Main Street. She was particular to mention that if any young ladies applied she would find suitable accommodations at her house for board.

In the early part of 1800 the first attempt was made to found a seminary for higher education, and a subscription-paper was circulated for the purpose of raising the necessary funds. The *Maryland Herald*, which had succeeded the old *Spy*, strongly indorsed and advocated the movement, Mr. Grieves, the editor of the paper, having been, as we have seen, a teacher in the town himself.

It was maintained that such an institution was a positive necessity; that it would attract a large number of students from abroad, who would give tone and standing to the town and enlarge its fame and fortune; that it would enable the young men of Hagerstown to obtain a full education without being subjected to the temptations and dangers of school life far away from home, and that the establishment of such a school would be an inducement to wealthy people, who had children to educate, to [illegible] in the neighborhood and settle in and about the town. The effort was, however, unsuccessful, and the Hagerstown youths for ten years more obtained all their home instruction through the medium of private schools and the Hagerstown Grammar School, which was under the direction of William L. Kelley, and the trusteeship of Col. Nathaniel Rochester,—the postmaster of the town,—P. Miller, and D. Heister. P. Edwards was still one of the instructors of the town at this time, carrying on both a day and night-school. There was also a school maintained by the Lutheran Church. It does not appear that there were any other schools in the town except these. In March, 1802, J. Hisshen announced that he had opened a school, in which he would teach the English branches, mathematics, etc., and would charge for readers, three dollars per quarter; for writers, three dollars and a half; and for arithmeticians, four dollars. In April following L. Blaire, who was acting under the advice of "prominent gentlemen," published a prospectus of his "institution of learning," which he had established at the house of Col. Rochester, about a quarter of a mile from Hagerstown. This was the first attempt to establish a classical school in Hagerstown, and Mr. Blaire's announcement was that he would teach Greek, Latin, English, and French. It was stated that the number of scholars would be limited unless such a number were obtained as to enable him to employ an usher. Mr. Blaire also offered to take as boarders a few boys, the conditions of boarding to be ascertained "by sending him a letter free of postage." He had taught two years at the academy of Lower Marlborough, Calvert County.

While these efforts were being made to train the minds of the young people of Hagerstown, their deportment was not neglected. A Frenchman named Gabaude was the first dancing-master of Washington County, and modestly announced in the *Maryland Herald* of May 5, 1802, the opening of his dancing-school at Col. Daniel Hughes' country-seat at Antietam Forge. In July, 1803, D. Hartshorne announced to the ladies and gentlemen of Hagerstown, through the advertising columns of the *Herald*, that he would open a school at Mrs. Jonathan Hager's long room, for the purpose of instructing them in the rules of dancing and other graceful deportments which are ornamental to society. He also proposed to devote three hours on the days of his tuition in teaching vocal music. This was some weeks after James Fabardet had made a similar announcement.

From 1803 until 1806 the names of the following teachers appear as giving mental instruction to the [illegible] L. Blaire, J.

Hisshen, Mrs Mahony, P C Young, John A Coburn In 1807 the Hagerstown Library Company was formed, being a subscription stock company

The names of the following teachers appear as having been engaged in educational efforts in Hagerstown from 1815 to 1820 Mrs Ashcum, John L Beall, P Edwards, James Kay, Uriah Kitchen, J McCall, E McLaughlin, John McClurg, E B Mendenhall, Mrs Ann Rawlins, Aaron P Rea, Maxwell Welch, Patrick Devine, Edward Bennett, D C Roscoe

In the spring of 1822, Dr Horwitz, who had made a great reputation in teaching Hebrew, paid a visit to Hagerstown and gave some lessons It was claimed that he gave his pupils a critical and grammatical knowledge of Hebrew in thirty lessons of one hour each, which a writer in the *Maryland Herald* said he would be inclined to doubt if it were not for the many certificates which he brought with him

Hagerstown Academy—In 1810 the attempt to establish an academy for higher education was revived On May 15th a meeting was held, at which Dr Richard Pindell was chairman, and Elie Williams secretary The meeting was addressed by Samuel Hughes who detailed the advantages to be derived from an institution of this character After which the following gentlemen were appointed by the chairman to carry the object of the meeting into effect John T Mason, John Bowles, William Yates, Thomas Brent, John Regan, Sen, Matthias Shaffner, Upton Lawrence, John Kennedy, Otho H Williams, Alexander Neill, Dr P Dorsey, Robert Hughes, Dr Frisby Tilghman, Samuel Ringgold, Jacob Towson, John Ashbury, Benjamin Tyson, John Brien, Dr Claggett, and Henry Locher The committee had obtained up to September 8th three thousand seven hundred dollars, at which time Samuel Ringgold, O H Williams, Frederick Dorsey, Upton Lawrence, and John Ragan were appointed a special committee to inquire as to the best site, and to prepare plans, etc, for the building In December the Legislature passed an act incorporating the academy, and the following incorporators were by the act made the trustees of the institution Richard Pindell, John T Mason, Samuel Ringgold, Samuel Hughes, Jr, Charles Carroll, Upton Lawrence, Frisby Tilghman, Otho H Williams, Moses Tipps, William Heyser, John Kennedy, John Harry, Jacob Zeller, Christian Hager, John J Stull, Jacob Schnebly, Thomas B Hall, John Ragan, Sr, Matthias Shaffner, Alexander Neill, and Frederick Dorsey The capital stock was placed at six thousand dollars, divided into twelve hundred equal shares On Jan 29, 1811 the trustee[illegible]

Williams, president, William Hughes, secretary, Thomas B Hall, treasurer Subscription books were opened at George Beltzhoover's early in March, 1811 A sufficient amount of stock had been subscribed to go on with the enterprise, the subscriptions being made payable in four equal installments of twenty per cent each, the first twenty per cent being paid in cash A site was selected on a pleasant eminence near the town, and on the spot where the present academy now stands The erection of the building was not rapid The last installment of the capital stock was not called in until May 10, 1812, and the academy was not finished until a year afterwards, when Thomas B Hall, the secretary, made the announcement in the public print that the institution was completed in a capacious and handsome manner, calculated for the reception of at least one hundred and fifty scholars, and that the patronage rendered the institution "will enable the trustees to grant liberal salaries to professors in the different branches of education, which it is deemed best by them at this time to have adopted and taught" They solicited applications for the situation of a president, a teacher of the Latin and Greek languages, and a teacher of the English language, mathematics, and geography, "the known healthiness of this country," continues the secretary, "the local situation of the academy, and the reasonable price of board, etc, must offer great inducements to professors, as well as to parents and guardians, to select this place as one highly eligible for the purposes of education Applications to fill the above stations in the academy may be made by letter to me in Hagerstown"

After the academy had been put in operation the following legislation was passed in regard to it In 1811 the Legislature directed the treasurer of the Western Shore to pay $800 annually to the Hagerstown Academy Two years later permission was granted this academy to hold a lottery to raise a sum not exceeding $10,000 In 1816 the Legislature passed a bill directing the treasurer to pay the Levy Courts of Frederick, Washington, and Allegany Counties their proportion of the school fund This fund was created by act of Assembly in 1812 A supplement to the act of 1810 was passed in 1818 providing for the sale of part of the real estate of the Hagerstown Academy, and in 1819 an act to enable the trustees to acknowledge conveyances of any real estate In 1825 Hagerstown Academy was included among those schools declared by the Legislature to have forfeited their donations, but in 1826 a bill was passed for the relief of the academy

The first academic year commenced on June 7, [illegible] military school,

in which William Robertson instructed the pupils in the use of the sword and the manual of arms, and James Robaudet taught fencing with the short sword and cutlass The corporation continued to be kept alive by annual meetings of the stockholders in March and the election of a board of trustees, of which for a number of years O H Williams was president A lottery scheme was organized, and successfully carried out in 1814, to help the institution out of financial difficulty, and the following gentlemen were engaged in the enterprise O H Williams, William Fitzhugh, Sr, Frisby Tilghman, John Buchanan, Jacob Schnebly, Thomas Buchanan, Thomas B Hall, and Upton Lawrence Among the professors during the first years of its existence was Daniel McCurtin, of Baltimore, who taught belles lettres after June, 1814 It is a matter of record that Mrs Philbein was engaged by O H Williams, who was the first president of the academy, to superintend the household department, that John N Smith succeeded Mr Irving as principal, and Cyrus Blood was engaged to take charge of the English department in the early part of 1819, but Mr Smith died in July, 1819, and Andrew Craig, of Long Island, was chosen to take his place

In 1820, Daniel Wilson succeeded Mr Craig, and under his management the tuition per quarter was six dollars, boarding and washing per quarter, thirty one dollars and fifty cents The State some time after this made appropriations to the institution to the amount of eight hundred dollars per year, and thus assumed a *quasi* control In 1828, when W A Abbot was at the head of the classical department, there were about thirty classical students It became an institution of considerable fame, and could boast with truth that it had graduated some of the most distinguished men in Western Maryland After about 1855, however, it began to decay, and in 1867 the building was discarded as being little more than an unsightly mass of bricks and other useful building material It was situated west of what is now Walnut Street, and south of the present depot The old building remained standing until 1877 Efforts had been made to establish and sustain a private academy for years under the management of the trustees, but the academical fund having been transferred, by act of the Legislature in 1861, to the board of school commissioners, the school languished, became involved in debt, was finally sold on May 1, 1877, and purchased by the school commissioners for six thousand dollars The old academy building was at once torn down, and the present handsome Washington County High School was erected in its place, and on Sept 1, 1877 the institution was op[illegible] the [illegible] the board of school commissioners Prof R S Henry was chosen principal, and under his direction in spite of opposition, the school soon won the favor of the people of the county For four years Prof Henry devoted his energies to the building up of the school, and before he retired had the satisfaction of seeing all his opponents forced to acknowledge the school a complete success Prof Henry resigned the position of principal at the close of the school year of 1880–81, and George A Harter, A M, a native of Washington County, was chosen his successor The prospects of the school are excellent The number in attendance at the High School is now larger than ever before, there being fifty four pupils enrolled as high-school pupils

Hagerstown Charity School—In 1815, Miss Isabella Neill, of Hagerstown, while in Philadelphia became deeply interested in the "Ragged Schools" which had been established there, and which were doing so much for the education of the destitute. Free schools were then unknown, and she determined to attempt the establishment of a charity-school at Hagerstown Three other ladies, Misses Susan Hughes, Jane Milligan, and Betsy Harry, joined her in her benevolent undertaking, and "a school for the education of poor children" was soon in active operation The first officers were elected on the 14th of January, 1815, as follows President, Susan Hughes, Treasurer, Isabella Neill, Secretary, Rebecca Fitzhugh, Managers, Betsy Harry, M Hummelhouse, Maria Sprigg, Jane Milligan, Eliza Schnebly and Jane Herbert

The first trustees were Rev J C Clay, John Kennedy, and Alexander Neill The school was opened with twenty five pupils The report of the managers for the first year showed that the receipts had been, from ladies, $395, from gentlemen, $278, from the Masonic lodge, $50 Total, $723 The expenses were for teachers, $300, for clothing, $199 90, stationery, $16 50, rent, $20 sundries, $8 Total $557 During the year thirty children had been thus instructed and taken care of At first the ladies taught the children themselves, but as their work began to be appreciated by the public contributions flowed in, and they were enabled to hire a room in the back building of a house still standing on North Potomac Street, and employ a teacher A sermon on behalf of the charity was preached in some one of the churches every year, and a subscription was taken up for its benefit Singing societies also gave concerts in its behalf, and efforts of various kinds were made to increase its funds In 1827 a statement was made [illegible] educated for the

thirteen years of its existence between thirty and fifty pupils each year

The managers then, as now, were two from each church For many years two of the ladies met the children at the school room on Sunday morning and proceeded with them to church The children were neatly attired, and wore blue bonnets and capes In 1818 the school was incorporated, thus being enabled to receive legacies and funds from its friends In 1832, Miss Susan Hughes left it a legacy of three hundred dollars Since then it has received the following bequests, viz 1833, by Mrs Dr Martin $50, 1835, Hugh Kennedy, $100, 1838, Dr Young, $100, 1842, Martin Hammond, $1700, which was applied to the erection of a school building, 1850, Mrs Pott, $200, 1852, Mrs Tutwiler, $50, 1856, Mrs Dr Reynolds, $100, 1861, Victor Thompson, $1000 The last legacy was bequeathed by Samuel Eichelberger, and amounts to $74 These legacies have been invested, and the school is supported by the income derived from them From the books it appears that over two thousand children have been educated by this noble charity The present teacher, Miss Eliza Keller, has had charge of the school for a number of years The children are taught spelling, reading, writing, arithmetic, geography, and plain sewing Two of the ladies visit the school once a week to instruct the children in needle work, and the garments made by them are given to the needy ones

Washington County Public Schools—There is no history of the public schools of Washington County previous to the organization of the free public schools under the act of the General Assembly of 1865, known as the Van Bokkelen system Under this act the free public school system of Washington County was organized July 11, 1865, with Thomas A Boullt as president, Albert Small, secretary and treasurer, and the following board of commissioners Samuel I Piper, John J Hershey, John A Miller, John S Hedding, Peter S Newcomer, Joseph Garver, and Jacob Funk The number of teachers for the fiscal year ending June 30, 1866, was 118,—schools open seven and a half months, number of different pupils for the year, 6689 There was no county levy, the revenue derived from the State being $25,203 04 The school law was changed by the Legislature of 1868, and under it a new board of school commissioners was appointed by the county commissioners, consisting of one member from each election district, as follows Moses Poffenberger, Dr Jerry Johnson, George W Smith, Sr, John D Houck, Warford Mann, Dr A Will Lakin, Ed and Ingraham, George W Brown, Edward Smith, Jacob Fiery, Warren Garrott, Mr Jones, F T Spickler, Charles Hutechen, James Cullen, and Henry Eakle

This board met and organized on the 5th of May 1868 George W Smith, Sr, was elected president, and Peter A Whitmer, secretary, treasurer, and examiner For that year the receipts were, from the county levy $26,500, and from other sources $62,832, total receipts, $88,332 The expenditures were $85,832, of which amount $26,505 was for the erection of new houses There were employed 138 teachers, and the number of different pupils was 8352

The board, composed of members elected by the people, was reorganized under this law on the 1st of January, 1870, with Jacob Fiery as president, and Peter A Witmer as secretary, treasurer, and examiner

The law was again changed by the Legislature of 1870, which authorized the Circuit Court to appoint the members of the several boards in the counties of their respective circuits Under this law the court appointed as commissioners for Washington County Dr William Ragan, Thomas H Crampton, Henry S Eavey, B A Garlinger, and William B McLain, who met and organized on Jan 2, 1872, by electing Dr William Ragan president, and P A Witmer, secretary, treasurer, and examiner This organization is still maintained, with the exception of Thomas H Crampton, who retired in January, 1880 and was succeeded by Dr William S Stonebraker The following are the statistics for 1880 Receipts from State, $22,731, from county, $36,487, total from all sources, $60,656, number of school-houses, 129, number of teachers, 179, number of different pupils, 8822, average attendance, 5396,—schools open seven and a half months, value of school property, $140,000 In 1877 the board purchased, at a cost of six thousand dollars, the building erected by the Hagerstown Academy trustees, with ten acres of ground attached and converted it into a county high school The building is eligibly located on a commanding position in the western section of the town, between the Western Maryland, Cumberland Valley, and Shenandoah Valley Railroads Since the organization of the high school it has been under the charge of Professor R S Henry During the past year there has been at the institution an average attendance of thirty five pupils, eight of whom graduated in June last In the county there are eighteen graded schools, having from two to ten teachers each The average cost per pupil in average attendance at the public schools in the county for the year 1880 was three dollars and thirty three cents per term, or ten dollars per year, which statistics show [illegible]

HAGERSTOWN SEMINARY,

Hagerstown Female Seminary.—This institution was projected and built by the Maryland Synod of the Evangelical Lutheran Church. Trustees were chosen and a charter was obtained from the Legislature of Maryland, and the first scholastic session was commenced in September, 1853. The first class was graduated in June 1857. Rev. Mr. Baughman was the first principal and had charge of the school for nearly seven years. He was succeeded by Rev. W. Eyster, who remained in charge for two terms of three years each. Between the two terms Rev. Ch. Martin, A.M., was principal for three years. After Mr. Eyster's second term, Rev. J. McCron, D.D., became principal for three years. In June, 1875, Rev. C. L. Keedy, A.M., M.D., the present able principal, took control. In consequence of heavy liabilities incurred in the building and management of the institution, Messrs. C. W. Humrickhouse and J. C. Bridges purchased the property and paid off its indebtedness in 1865. A few years after this Mr. Humrickhouse became sole owner and proprietor, until April 1, 1878, when the present principal purchased it, and has continued to improve it until it has become one of the most beautiful and attractive places in any of the Middle States. The seminary stands upon a commanding eminence just east of Hagerstown, from which may be had a magnificent view of hill and dale and of the town outstretched below. The main edifice is an imposing brick structure, four stories in height, and built in the Romanesque style. There are three wings of equal height with the main building. The grounds, comprising an area of eleven acres, are thickly set with upwards of one hundred handsome evergreens, and about five hundred trees of other varieties. Choice shrubbery marks in graceful lines numerous picturesque divisions of the inclosure, and over the entire surface is spread a bright carpet of rich green-sward. Near the seminary stands the residence of the president, a handsome brick edifice. Under the administration of President Keedy the seminary has continued to be a widely-known and flourishing school. Since its foundation it has received upwards of two thousand pupils and graduated one hundred and fifty. In 1881 the whole number of pupils was one hundred and ten, the graduates, thirteen, and the boarders, sixty. The curriculum of the institution is practical and thorough rather than showy and superficial, provided parents allow their daughters to remain sufficiently long to be graduated. The study of one ancient and one modern language, a complete knowledge of all the English branches, together with some degree of musical culture, are required before a diploma is gi[illegible] and athenæum are valuable and highly appreciated adjuncts to the seminary. The Hagerstown *Seminary Monthly*, founded in 1876, and conducted solely by the pupils, under the supervision of the president, is a prosperous and profitable element in the course of practical experience sought to be developed by the school. The library and apparatus are complete, and the furniture of the buildings is modern and neat in appearance. The school deservedly enjoys a high reputation, and is in a very flourishing condition.

Linden Seminary is comparatively a young institution, having been established in 1878, and was at first known as "Hagerstown Select School," but the name was changed in 1880, since when it has been known as Linden Seminary. It is a strictly private institution, governed and controlled by D. M. Long, the principal. Its beginning was not a favorable one, and the first year it had only nine scholars. The president now congratulates himself on the fact that its roll contains the names of seventy-four students. It is pleasantly situated on South Potomac Street. The institution is intended to be a preparatory school for students who intend completing a collegiate course, but a great many of the pupils are engaged in such studies as they select themselves, without regard to a collegiate course.

The Hagerstown Lyceum, a joint-stock company, was chartered by the Legislature of Maryland on the 5th of February, 1848, and was organized on the 25th of the same month by the election of Wm. M. Marshall as president, and James R. Jones, Jas. I. Hurley, John Robertson, William Stewart, and H. P. Aughenbaugh as managers, who subsequently appointed Edwin Bell secretary and treasurer. The object of the incorporators was to purchase a lot and erect a building mainly for literary and scientific purposes, the whole not to cost over ten thousand dollars. A building committee was appointed, who commenced preparations for the erection of the building on the south side of West Washington Street, Hagerstown. The corner-stone of the building was laid on Tuesday, Sept. 12, 1848, with Masonic ceremonies. A procession was formed, preceded by the Mechanics' Band, consisting of the members of the Masonic and Odd-Fellow lodges of Hagerstown, together with a number of their brethren from other lodges in the county. The Independent, Junior, and the First Hagerstown Hose Companies, the scholars attached to the Hagerstown Academy, the workmen and builders of the lyceum, the officers of the association, ministers of the gospel, etc., the whole under the direction of Col. George Schley and his aides, Mathew S. Barber and [illegible] through the

principal streets of Hagerstown the procession halted in front of the lyceum, and the ceremony of laying the corner-stone was performed by the Masons. The exercises were followed with prayer by the Rev. Mr. Conrad. The procession then moved to the court-house, where an oration was delivered by the Hon. Daniel Weisel. The structure was put under roof and the lower story finished by the 1st of April, 1849. The upper story or hall was finished during the ensuing summer. Hon. Daniel Weisel presided at the preliminary meetings of the stockholders, of whom he was one of those who were most active and energetic, and accepted an invitation to act with the board of managers. The amount of stock subscribed fell considerably short of the expense incurred for the erection of the building and for furnishing the hall. The net annual revenue, therefore, from 1849 to 1855 was applied to the liquidation of the remaining indebtedness. In 1856 a dividend of seven per cent. was paid the stockholders. Since that time regular annual dividends have been paid of from eight to ten per cent., and on several occasions as much as twelve and a half per cent., on a basis of eight thousand dollars, which is about the first cost of the building and furniture.

William M. Marshall was elected the first president, and was re-elected until 1852, when Thomas Harbine was elected, and re-elected in 1853. Mr. Marshall was again elected president in 1854, and re-elected annually thereafter until 1868, when James I. Hurley was elected, and re-elected for 1869 and 1870. In 1871, F. D. Herbert was chosen president, and has been re-elected annually, and is now president. James Wason was elected secretary and treasurer in 1850, and retained annually until 1862, when H. K. Tice was appointed, who served until 1865. F. J. Posey was appointed in 1865, and served until 1876, when H. K. Tice was re-elected, and holds the office at present.

The father of Henry K. Tice was John Tice, who was born in 1770 in Lebanon County, Pa., and married Elizabeth Kerscher, who was born near Hagerstown in 1778. Their ancestors emigrated to this country from Switzerland at a very early date. Henry K. Tice was born near Hagerstown, Oct. 17, 1810, and married in 1838 Mary McCardell, daughter of William McCardell, of Hagerstown, whose wife was Margaret Powles, of the same place. Mr. Tice has had eight children, six of whom are living,—four daughters and two sons. He was educated at the county schools, receiving the rudiments of an English education. He is a member of the Reformed Church, and [illegible] a Henry Clay Whig, but is now a Democrat. The industries which Mr. Tice has aided and promoted are many and various. He was one of the founders of the Washington County Agricultural Society as early as 1852, trustee and secretary of the Hagerstown Female Seminary when it was built, and its chief promoter, and the first to subscribe to the stock of the Hagerstown Gas Company. He was the principal originator of that enterprise, of which he was for many years a director. The Mutual Insurance Company of Washington County owes to Mr. Tice much of its success. For over a quarter of a century he was the treasurer of the company, and indeed nearly every enterprise of Hagerstown for the last twenty-five years has been aided with his means and promoted by his intelligence and energy. The Antietam Paper Company was at one time the property of Mr. Tice and John W. Stonebraker. In 1836 he was in the hardware business in Hagerstown, in which he continued until 1851 in partnership with David C. Hammond. Thus his life has been one of usefulness, energy, and enterprise.

The Thursday Club, composed of ladies of Hagerstown, having, through its dramatic, literary, and other entertainments, accumulated a sum of money, applied it to the formation of a library for general circulation and use in the community, and, as preliminary and auxiliary, determined, if possible, to secure as a nucleus the library of the Belles Lettres Society of the College of St. James, which had not been in use for several years. This object was accomplished in 1878, and the club received from the trustees of the college the library. It consisted of about two thousand five hundred volumes of standard and popular works, selected with great care through a period of eighteen or twenty years by members of the society. These works comprise all standard histories, novels, reviews, all the English poets, and works of general interest.

In order to hold the library thus loaned, and make it a permanent institution, in the advantages of which the citizens might participate, it became necessary to incorporate the club, which was done, with the following ladies as incorporators: Mrs. W. T. Hamilton, Mrs. E. W. Mealey, Mrs. Peter Negley, Mrs. Albert Small, Mrs. Mary Hays, Mrs. H. H. Keedy, Mrs. Alex. Neill, and Miss Anna H. Kennedy. The next step was to secure a proper and permanent place for the accommodation of the library, and accordingly the two large rooms on the second story of Mr. C[illegible] building, West Washington Street, formerly used as the clerk's office, were rented and devoted to this purpose. The annual subscription is three dollars, and th[illegible] thousand

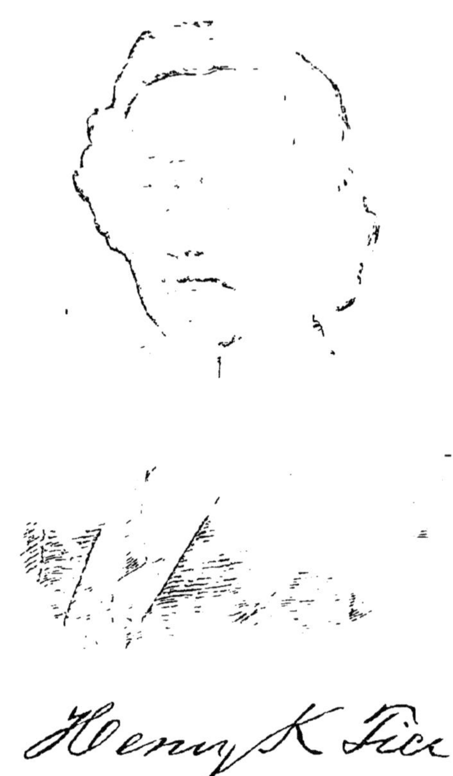
Henry K Fick

CHAPTER L

PUBLIC INSTITUTIONS OF HAGERSTOWN

Market-house—Almshouse—Water-works—Telegraph—Street Lighting—Street Paving

Market-Houses—A market was established by an act of the Assembly as early as June, 1783 It appears from the language of the act that the public labored under many great inconveniences for want of a market-house in Elizabethtown, that a large and commodious space of ground was laid out for that purpose in the centre of said town, and that the petitioners proposed to build thereon at their own expense Permission was therefore granted to Henry Shryock, Matthias Need, and Martin Hairy, as commissioners, to contract for the building of a house not less than fifty feet by thirty feet, to be used for a market house Wednesdays and Saturdays were the market-days, and all victuals and provisions brought to town for sale "except beef by the quarter or large quantity and pork by the hog or hogs," had to be sold in the market-house The following is the eleventh section of the act

"*And whereas* It has been practiced by people coming in from the country to tie their horses in said market house, which is very indecent and offensive to the inhabitants of said town, *Be it enacted* That any person or persons who shall put their own or any other person's horse, mare, or gelding into or under the said market house, on any pretense whatsoever, he shall pay or forfeit *two shillings and* sixpence current money, etc "

In the old market-house, as almost every family had its own vegetable-garden and poultry-yard, there was little else to be seen save the different kinds of meat, butter, and eggs The rules of the market required the butter to be printed in one-pound lumps exactly If a lump lacked even one-half ounce of full weight it was confiscated and taken by the market-master An act of the Legislature, passed at the session of 1818–19, authorized the erection of a new market-house Peter Seibert, Joseph Gabby, and Henry Shafer were named in the act as commissioners, and it was further provided that when the new court-house should be completed the moderator and commissioners of the town should cause the old one to be pulled down and the materials applied to the building of the market house

On the 5th of September 1820 Frisby Tilghman, William O Sprigg, and William H Fitzhugh were appointed by the Levy Court commissioners to select and purchase a site for the market-house These commissioners purchased in October Stump's lot, known as Lot No 7 It had a front of eighty-two feet on North Potomac Street and two hundred and forty feet on East Franklin Street The price paid for this site was one thousand dollars In the following year the first installment of the market-house tax was levied, and the building was opened to public use in December, 1822 Daniel Schnebly was then moderator, and George Brumbaugh was clerk By an amendment to the original act, the commissioners were authorized to erect a town hall over the market-house, and Mount Moriah Masonic Lodge, No 33, were to have the privilege of providing quarters for their use in the building at their own expense This last provision gave rise to a controversy which was conducted with singular bitterness and venom, although the subject at issue was of a very trivial nature The Masonic fraternity, as heretofore stated, had been permitted to erect a portion of the building for their own use, and at their own expense, but the lower story of the building, the portion used as a market house, was built and paid for by the town corporation A cupola was also added at the expense of the town, and the dispute arose concerning the character of the vane to be placed thereon[1]

[1] The nature of the dispute and the manner in which it was conducted can be best illustrated by the insertion here of one of the numerous anonymous communications published in the Hagerstown newspapers during the progress of the affair

"To the Public

"The excessively ridiculous clamor which has been raised by some persons against the moderator and three of our town commissioners [the commissioners at that time were John Albert, George Beam, John Hershey, George Brumbaugh, and George Martiney] makes it necessary to acquaint the public with some facts in relation to the affair It is generally known that an agreement was entered into between the town and Mount Moriah Lodge, by which the latter secured the privilege of building a hall over the market house The contract between the parties guarantees to the lodge the right of constructing their part of the edifice according to their plan, and of carrying it up to the base of the cupola, and no further The cupola, then, is to be considered as not under the control of the lodge, nor can it be presumed for a moment that the agreement gives them any power to construct or ornament it It is not our intention to enter into the details of the compact between the parties, and we refer all those who wish for precise information to the instrument itself The fraternity contains in its body several members of the law, and we take it for granted that however ignorant they may be in the black letter, they know how to interpret plain English

"As well might it be contended that the lodge had a right to plan the market-house beneath this hall as to interfere with the cupola above, but, in fact, the commissioners were indifferent what vane was placed on the cupola, and they were willing that the lodge should construct the whole of it if they bore the expense, but this was refused It can also be stated, and proved, if necessary, that the commissioners did not take the vane down

"Whence, then, comes this disgusting and silly clamor which [illegible] missioners never

Bellevue Almshouse.—The relief of the poor was the subject of early consideration in Hagerstown. On the 28th of March, 1799, the trustees of the poor for Washington County advertised for proposals to erect a brick building in Elizabethtown (Hagerstown) for the poor of the county, thirty-six by sixty feet, two stories high. The advertisement further stated that the plan could be seen in the hands of William Heyser, who would receive proposals for the mason, bricks, and carpenters' and joiners' work upon the building. The trustees signing this notice were Henry Schnebly, William Heyser, and George Ney. The building was completed and was occupied by the poor in 1800.

In March, 1827, a meeting was held at the Charity School-room, on East Antietam Street, to give practical shape to the ideas of those who favored the establishment of a society in the town for the relief of the sick poor, and an organization was soon after effected, the fruits of which were extremely beneficial.

The old county almshouse was situated in the suburbs of Hagerstown, and consisted of two brick buildings, respectively two and three stories high. These buildings for years supplied shelter to the indigent of the county, but in later years their proximity to the town and their situation on one of the principal routes of travel were felt to be serious evils, as the effect of town influence upon the institution was generally acknowledged to be bad, and the public location rendered it a convenient lodging-place for tramps and other idlers. The reports of the grand juries year after year called attention to these facts, and recommended the selection of a more remote site, and the erection of a building better adapted to the purposes of an almshouse. The recommendation was at length submitted to a vote of the people, but on account of the financial condition of the county at the time it was rejected. The subject continued to be agitated, and at a meeting of the Farmers' Club, in 1873, Dr. Maddox read an essay upon the condition of the almshouse, in which he strongly urged that the buildings then in use be sold, and that a farm, remote from the influences and associations of the county-seat, be procured as a site for the institution. These suggestions met with the unanimous approval of the large body of influential tax-payers present, and a committee, consisting of Dr. Maddox and A. K. Stake, secretary of the club, was appointed to draw up a paper for presentation to the county commissioners, in which the opinions of the meeting should be urgently expressed. After a full consideration of the matter the passage of an enabling act was secured from the State Legislature, and the erection of a new building upon a new site was determined upon. In 1878 the generosity of John Nicodemus, of Boonsboro', placed at the disposal of the county a valuable farm, situated north of Hagerstown, on the Hagerstown and Middleburg turnpike. This farm, embracing one hundred and twelve acres, was purchased by Mr. Nicod[illegible] cost of twelve

originated it, nor have they done any precedent act to give rise to it, they have, nevertheless, been industriously attacked, lampooned, and bespattered by a host of petty scavengers, all anxious who should throw the most mud and slime, and this course they pursue, forsooth, by way of ridicule they term it. Really, the Masonic brethren must be miserably deficient in the knowledge of mankind if they do not perceive the effect of the silly plan they have adopted. If they were anxious to cover their craft with dishonor and bring it into disrepute, they could not have adopted a better expedient than the outrage they have committed. Do they think the feelings of good citizens can be sported with with impunity?

"The scorpion lash of ridicule which they pretend to wield with so much effect will surely recoil upon themselves, and devour the hand that brandishes it. Put the moderator and commissioners in one scale and as many of the Royal Arch fraternity in the other, and which will kick the beam? Reader, you know both parties, look at them and then decide, give them in the bargain all their reputation for charity which the trumpet tongue of fame has proclaimed from the house-top. The commissioners are not afraid of the opinion of their townsmen, and they invite an investigation of their acts in a judicial manner, conscious that they have done nothing affecting the privileges of any one in the smallest iota. They defy the brotherhood from A to Z, with their compass, square, trowel, and every implement, jewel, or signet of their mystic art. Let them go on with their childish and harmless mummery, and do all the good they can, but let them respect the rights and persons of others.

"We wish not to be personal, or to retaliate in their own style, but certain it is that if they go on with their unprovoked and silly warfare they may have occasion to wish that their slang had been permitted to slumber in its parent brain. Everybody knows who the commissioners are, they affect no mystery, and they act under the responsibility of their names. The press is free and, although they may not gain admittance into the *Torch-Light*, which appears to be the willing vehicle of all the ribaldry engendered against them, they know that truth and plain facts will not be excluded from the *Herald*.

"We cannot conclude these observations without a word to Mr. Mechanic, the last writer in the *Torch-Light*, and, we presume, the champion of the confederacy. Judging from his style and invective, his elegant punctilio and pertinacities, we presume he intends to flourish his *goose-quill* against the moderator and commissioners in the potent manner that he intends shortly to flourish his glittering steel in the air. He is read in Roman history, too, we perceive, and he concludes his philippic with the threatening prophecy of a ghost who made a considerable figure in the olden times.

"We also have to inform this phantom that we heed not his bravado. We will meet his nothingness when and where he pleases. We have come reluctantly before the public, but if it be rendered necessary by the temper of our assailants, we shall be constrained to sift the affair to the bottom and expose everything to the eyes of our fellow-citizens. We want neither truce nor quarter.

"MANY CITIZENS.

"HAGERSTOWN, [illegible]"

thousand five hundred dollars, and was presented to the county commissioners to be used "for the accommodation of the poor and indigent of the county, and for an almshouse and the general uses of like character which the interests of the county and its people may require" The gift was made free from any embarrassing conditions, the commissioners being empowered, if at any time another location might seem to them more desirable, to sell the land and purchase a farm elsewhere with the proceeds of the sale The public-spirited generosity which inspired the gift was the subject of universal commendation, but some fears were expressed lest the location of the farm might prove to be too close to the town to do away with the evils connected with the location of the old almshouse The county commissioners determined to rent out the farm for one year, and to submit the question of removal to the people at the congressional election in the November following In the mean time the clerk was directed to advertise for proposals to furnish the county with one hundred cords of wood to be used in burning bricks for the new building Dr C W Chancellor, secretary of the State Board of Health, submitted plans for the institution, and was invited by the commissioners to visit and inspect the new location, which invitation he accepted, and pronounced the situation healthy and possessed of many other advantages The final determination was that the site presented by Mr Nicodemus should be used for the new building, and work was commenced in 1879 The farm is a compact body of good limestone land, easily drained, and sloping gently towards the east

Near the northern boundary, and running through the entire length of the farm, is a stream of water, along which are rich bottom-lands, well adapted to the raising of the vegetables necessary for the use of the inmates of the asylum A good barn and a comfortable dwelling-house were on the farm at the time of its purchase The land adjoins the estates of Hon William T Hamilton and Andrew J and Jacob Schindle The new building is situated about three hundred and fifty yards from the pike, on which it fronts It is a plain brick structure, two stories high, and of irregular shape The only attempt at ornamentation in the design is on the front or gable end of the portion in which the main entrance is situated This has a heavy ornamental cornice and a handsome porch, which is approached by a wide flight of steps In this front are placed three tablets, upon the one in the centre is inscribed the name of the asylum, "Bellevue" and the date of its erection, on another are the words "John Nicodemus gave this farm to be a home for the [illegible] the [illegible] are the names of the board of county commissioners, then clerk, J C Dayhoff, and the architect, Frank E Davis

The whole length of the building from the end of one wing to that of the other is one hundred and fifty two feet, and the extension back is one hundred

BELLEVUE ASYLUM

and thirty three feet It contains seven hundred thousand bricks, which were burned on the spot, out of clay dug from the foundation The basement is high, built of stone quarried within a short distance There are in the building seventy-four apartments, which will comfortably accommodate one hundred and fifty inmates The apartments are divided as follows in the keepers' department fourteen, insane department twenty-seven, in each wing nine, and in the centre building fifteen

The keepers' department is in the main front of the building It faces the turnpike, and is forty-one feet in width The main entrance is in this wing and opens into a large hall, upon either side of which is a fine apartment, the one on the right being the parlor and that on the left the office The dining-room is a spacious and lofty room, well lighted and neat in all its appointments A tower surmounts the front wing and commands a fine view of the surrounding country There are separate rooms for the sick and for the harmless insane, who are thus cut off from contact with the violent The latter occupy a wing which has only one means of communication with the rest of the building by means of a single door in the basement Surrounding this wing is a tower, which ext[illegible] a mansard-

roof This is the highest point of the building, and in its roof is placed a boiler iron tank with a capacity for five thousand gallons Water is supplied to this tank from the stream near the building by means of a water ram worked by the stream itself This tank supplies the bath rooms etc in various parts of the building, and also the hose connections for use in case of fire The arrangements for securing good ventilation are very complete Over each wing of the building is an iron ventilator, and each room is provided with a register near the ceiling In addition to this there is a shaft built through the centre of the building, and large ducts lead from this to air chambers formed by making the floors of the rooms double These air-chambers communicate with the rooms by means of openings in the chair boards, by which arrangement floor ventilation is secured The roof of the building is of slate, the brick work is unpainted and unornamented, and the sills are of wood, except those of the basement story The windows are large and numerous, and are all hung with weights so that the upper sashes can be lowered The situation of the building is on the side of a gentle hill, which affords excellent drainage A number of tile pipes are used for carrying off waste water, etc

The height of the ceilings on the first floor is thirteen and a half feet, and of those on the second floor thirteen feet The removal of the last of the inmates from the old almshouse to the Bellevue Asylum took place during July, 1880, Dr Chancellor being present to assist in the classification of the cases The total cost of the building, as stated in the official estimate of the county commissioners, was twenty-six thousand dollars, a portion of which was provided for from the sale of the old almshouse property

In December, 1877, a meeting was held at the court-house, at which Hon A K Syester presided, and J F A Remley acted as secretary The object of the meeting was to provide some means for the relief of the poor of Hagerstown A committee, consisting of A K Syester, chairman, A R Appleman, William Updegraff, M M Gruber, George Lias, F A Heard, E. M Mobley, H H Keedy, P J Adams, J F A Remley, Edward Stake, Michael McDonald, and H A McComas, was appointed to carry into practical effect the benevolent purpose of the meeting The committee held a meeting shortly afterwards and passed the following resolutions

"*Resolved*, That for the purpose of fairly and impartially distributing relief to the actual distress and needs of the unfortunate the following rules and regulations will be observed

"1st All app[illegible] for relief must be presented to this committee in writing signed by the applicant, and giving references

"2d Applications will be considered by the committee, and if upon investigation the object is worthy, the committee will furnish such relief as the exigencies of the case may require

"3d Cases of distress arising from sickness or disability to earn a living shall have precedence

"4th Contributions in money will be given only in the most extreme and exceptional cases

"5th No relief will be granted except to *bona fide* residents of the town and vicinity"

Mr William Updegraff was appointed treasurer of the fund to be raised, and store keeper of the articles which may be contributed, and the following gentlemen were appointed as a committee in each ward to solicit contributions of goods, provisions, money, and fuel

Ward No 1 --Andrew J Schindel William S Swartz, Dr J F Smith, David Zeller, and Rev John M Jones

Ward No 2 —H H Keedy, F A Heard, Joseph S McCartney H S Fiery, and Rev S W Owen

Ward No 3 —J Roessner, Albert Heil, M L Byers, George B Oswald and Rev J C Thompson

Ward No 4 --Lewis Schindel, William S Williamson, John L Bikle, Henry Collflower, and Rev J S Kieffer

Ward No 5 —D S Boyer, Samuel E King, M M Gruber, William S Herbert, and Rev John K Williams

Water-works —For a long time previous to the establishment of the water works the subject of introducing this improvement into Hagerstown was agitated among the citizens Early in 1872 a public meeting relative to the subject was held in Junior Hall, at which it was elicited that the tax-payers of the town were practically a unit as to the necessity of constructing them A committee, consisting of William McK Keppler, George W Harris, F M Darby, B Schley, and Henry Bell, was appointed "to procure counsel to prepare a law to be submitted to the Legislature, the said law to authorize the mayor and Council of Hagerstown to make the necessary appropriations for the introduction of water into the town" Another committee was appointed to form an estimate of the cost of sinking an artesian well, the construction of a reservoir, the laying of pipes, and the other expenses of supplying the town with water This committee consisted of the following H H Keedy, Alexander Neill, William Updegraff, D C Aughinbaugh, David Zeller, and W. M McDowell On the 22d of November, 1880, the Washington County Water-works were incorporated for thirty-nine years, the incorporators being William T Hamilton, William Updegraff, Alexander Armstrong, Edward Stake, Henry H Keedy, George R Bowman, Jacob Roessner, David C Aughinbaugh, George W Smith, John B Thurston, P A Brugh, and Joseph Kausler The capital [illegible] divided into 6600

shares of $10 each The number of directors was eleven, the first board, to serve for one year, being named in the articles of incorporation, as follows William T Hamilton, William Updegraff, Charles W Humrichouse, George R. Bowman, Edward W Mealey, Edward Stake, Henry H. Keedy David S Boyer, William Gassman, George W Harris, and George W Grove At the first meeting of the board of directors, held one week later, Edward Stake, William Updegraff, and H H Keedy were appointed a committee to draft by-laws and propose a plan of operations The source of supply selected was the South Mountain water-shed, and it was deemed advisable at this time to provide for all contingencies by increasing the capital stock from $60,000 to $80,000

To increase the stock a new charter was filed, and the old one, not yet consummated, was withdrawn, and the name of the company was changed by the omission of the word "Works" to that of "The Washington County Water Company" By this company a tract of fourteen acres of land, the property of William Wagley, at the base of the South Mountain, between Cavetown and Smithsburg, and seven and a half miles from Hagerstown, on the line of the Western Maryland Railroad, upon which is a saw-mill, with capacious dam and dwelling houses, has been secured in fee-simple The dam is upwards of two hundred feet above the highest point in Hagerstown It covers a natural basin, and on the tract immediately above the dam nature has carved out a natural reservoir, which may at will be converted into a storage dam capable of retaining a supply for six months' demand by the present population of Hagerstown, without receipts from any auxiliary source But in the mountain and above this natural reservoir is a cluster of from seven to ten other distinct springs, most of which have never been known to fail, which in an emergency or extraordinary growth of the demand for water in the future could in turn be utilized, indefinitely increasing the supply.

It is believed that by care in the collection and utilization of the Wagley stream, and by the cleaning out and opening of fountains now filled up, and the preservation of the water thus lost by diffusion over a large surface, all those persons below the Wagley property through whose farms the stream passes will in no manner be interfered with in the matter of water-supply So copious is the Wagley stream that within half a mile above the Wagley mill two other mills are turned by it The water is as pure as crystal, and bursts from the rocks in the gulch in which the mill stands The spr[illegible] property bought by the company from Wagley is believed to be alone sufficient to supply the town, and the stream from above passes about one hundred yards from the Wagley dam which is used as the reservoir of the company, so that in case of freshets all the surface water will be carried around the dam and none of it will enter into the supply of the town At all times this supply will be pure spring-water, without mud or sediment, equal to the best and purest water on the continent Should the requirements of the future call for an increase of the volume, two plans are open first, a storage reservoir can be constructed on the company's property, or, second, the supply can be indefinitely increased by tapping other fountains and running as many additional springs as may be needed into the dam on the company's property, which is judiciously located on a level below them all The right of way for the water company was procured from the directors of the Western Maryland Railroad Company which authorized them to use the track for the laying of pipes from their property at the mountain to Hagerstown

The reservoir is in charge of the company's tenant, who attends to turning off the surface water and keeping things there in order From the dam to Hagerstown, seven and a half miles, a ten-inch pipe conveys the water, under ground, along the railroad track to the distributing pipes and hydrants within the town There is no reservoir at Hagerstown, the distribution being direct from the mountain dam A clear fall of more than two hundred feet to the highest point in town carries the water by its own pressure to every point, for fire or other purposes, that may be needed A greater altitude and pressure could have been reached, but it was not desired, as a corresponding increase of strength and cost of pipe would have been needed, and the pressure now secured is all that could be desired

A ten-inch pipe will supply 1,131,000 gallons in twenty four hours, or 47,555 gallons per hour The largest quantity consumed in large cities, where every one uses hydrant water, is fifty gallons to each individual, and in those which have a population of twenty thousand or less the quantity required for each person is thirty gallons per day Upon this basis over seven thousand population would require a supply of two hundred and ten thousand gallons daily. The ten-inch pipe in five hours will supply 236,275 gallons, or in a little more than the fifth part of a day will furnish all the water needed by Hagerstown for a whole day The money to construct the water-works was subscribed promptly by the people of the town, and a contract was entered into with William H A[illegible] iron pipes,

plugs, and hydrants, and to do the complete work, furnishing everything, excavating and restoring streets, etc., to their proper condition, and handing over the work with the insurance of its successful operation for thirty days, for the sum of $90,875. A. H. McNeal, of Burlington, N. J., stipulated on the foregoing contract with Allen & Co. to furnish the iron, and accepted an order on the water company from Allen & Co. in payment thereof. The work is to be completed by the 1st of May, 1882, and the laborers employed are as far as practicable to be residents of the county. The pipes are twelve inches diameter instead of ten inches as at first intended, and are to be laid along the Hagerstown and Smithsburg turnpike.

This increase in the diameter of pipe will secure fifty per cent. of an increase in the volume of water supplied, and will involve an additional expenditure of about twelve thousand dollars. This increase in expenditure and capacity of the pipe was incurred after great deliberation by the company, and after it had been ascertained to be the almost universal wish of the stockholders and others interested who desired to supply a sufficiency of water-power for the rapid development of the manufacturing interests of the town. The entire cost of the works when completed is not expected to exceed $100,000. The work of laying pipes, constructing the necessary works at the reservoir, etc., is being carried forward with all possible speed.

Hotels and Early Inns.—Hagerstown has long been noted for the excellence of its hotels and taverns, or inns. Situated on the great national highway from the North and East to the West and South, it was at one time an important stopping place for politicians, office seekers, etc., on their way to and from the national capital. Some of its early taverns attained a wide spread celebrity, such, for instance, as the Globe, the Indian King, the General Washington, and many others. The Globe was the great rendezvous for the huge wagons in which in those days the produce of the surrounding country was transported. It occupied the site of the present Baldwin, formerly the Washington, House, and was kept for many years by George Beltzhoover, brother of Daniel Beltzhoover, the proprietor of the Fountain Inn, Baltimore. Beltzhoover was succeeded in turn by Daniel Snively, John Cline, and John Young.

The Indian King Tavern was one of the oldest in Hagerstown, and its hospitalities were dispensed by many different landlords during the long term of its existence. On the 28th of October, 1797, John Ragan, who had kept this noted tavern for some time, sold out, and [illegible] In 1799 we find John Ragan again in charge. On the 31st of October in that year he announced that having resumed his old stand, at the sign of the Indian King, on the Main Street leading from the court-house to Bath and the Western country, he was prepared to entertain travelers in the best manner, etc. In 1812, under the proprietorship of Samuel Bayly, the name was changed to the Hagerstown Hotel. It was then the principal tavern in the town. In 1818 the old name had been restored, and Christopher Griffith was proprietor.

In 1797, Melchior Beltzhoover was proprietor of a tavern on the corner of the public square, near the court-house. In 1798, George Scholl kept a tavern at the sign of the Black Bear. This house was situated at the corner of Walnut and Franklin Streets, on the present site of the Eyler House. In 1799, H. Peck announced that he would open a house of entertainment in his gardens, near Col. Rochester's, in Hagerstown. In the same year he was landlord of the Columbian Inn, in Baltimore. In 1818, George Witmer was proprietor of the White Swan, and George Brumet of the Black Horse. The Bell Tavern, now the Newcomer House, stood nearly opposite the court-house in 1821, and was owned by Wm. Hammond. In that year John McIlhenny was proprietor of the Eagle Tavern on the public square, George Beltzhoover was landlord of the Globe, opposite the bank, formerly kept by O. H. W. Stull, and John Schleigh kept the Swan Tavern on Potomac Street, formerly kept by Ridenour and by George C. Hamilton. In 1827, Thomas H. Rench took charge of the hotel on North Potomac Street, Hagerstown, formerly kept by Martin Newcomer. In the same year Daniel H. Schnebly announced that he had rented the Bell Tavern, opposite the Hagerstown court-house, where he intended opening a house of entertainment.

Another popular hostelry was the Swan Tavern, on North Potomac Street, near the public square, now owned by Philip Wingert, and occupied with stores. Contemporaneous with it was Enstein's General Washington Inn, situated near the present Hoover House, which is on the corner of Franklin and Potomac Streets. Nearly opposite the General Washington Inn was a tavern kept by Mr. Cook, a famous resort in its day. Stover's tavern, kept for many years by Frederick Stover, is now the Mansion House, kept by John Riley, opposite the depot of the Cumberland Valley Railroad. It has recently been refitted and enlarged. At the corner of Baltimore and South Potomac Streets was another well known tavern, kept by Michael Treiber, which is now used as a private dwelling [illegible] le Tavern was

located on the present site of the Hagerstown *Mail* office, at the corner of Washington Street and the public square In this building Henry Clay was married to Letitia, daughter of Col Thomas Hart, of Hagerstown, uncle of Thomas Hart Benton, the famous Western senator

At present the leading hotels of Hagerstown are the Baldwin, the Franklin, the Newcomer, the Antietam, the Mansion, and the Hoover House The Baldwin is a handsome brick structure, and is one of the largest and finest hotels in Maryland outside the city of Baltimore It is situated on Washington Street, near Potomac, and is managed by Messrs McLaughlin and Herbert Its site is that of the Washington House, which was burned on the 29th of May, 1879 The construction of the Baldwin was commenced on the 1st of November, 1879, and it was finished and opened to guests on the 1st of September, 1880 During the year ending September, 1881, it entertained 16,176 persons The arrivals by months were as follows September, 1880, 1680, October, 1460, November, 1175, December, 1126, January, 1881, 964, February, 1132, March, 1221, April, 1311, May, 1618, June, 1440, July 1318, August, 1731 Total for the year, 16,176 Its principal owners are C C Baldwin, president of the Louisville and Nashville Railroad, who represents the heirs of the late James Dixon Roman, one of the leading proprietors of the Washington House, E W Mealey, Dr Josiah G Smith, David C Hammond, and William T Hamilton Originally the site of the Baldwin House was occupied by the famous Globe Tavern. James I Hurley and Mrs Harbine bought the property from Dr Frederick Dorsey, and sold it to a company of which the directors were J Dixon Roman, president, Peter Swartzwelder, George W Smith, William B Chaney, James Wilson, and James I Hurley The new management tore down the old structure and erected a large brick hotel, which they named the Washington House The new hotel was kept at first by a Mr Stitson, then by Joseph P Mong, who was followed by Henry Yingling The latter was succeeded by a Mr Wiles, afterwards proprietor of the Howard House in Baltimore, who in turn was followed by John Anderson, Stanhope & McLaughlin, and George Middlekauff On the death of the latter his widow undertook the management of the property, and was in charge when the fire broke out

The origin of the fire has never been discovered The alarm was given by a guest, who was awakened by the smoke, and the local fire companies repaired at once to the scene. In the mean time, however, the flames had made [illegible] to rescue some of the inmates Of those in the house at the time, J C Taylor, of Adams, Buck & Co, Baltimore, escaped with slight bruises, Wm Middleton, of New York, uninjured, J F Stine, Philadelphia, uninjured, Mrs Melville Patterson, daughter, and nurse, of Baltimore, and Miss Josephine Gerry, of Portland, Me, rescued by S H Dorsey and Wm Stake, C F Manning, uninjured, T J Wallace, of York, Pa, uninjured, Judge Geo A Pearre uninjured, also Henry Swartzwelder, of Cumberland, Md, Walter Bray, of Philadelphia, J W Showaker, of Baltimore, and T J Kyle, of Baltimore Isaac Wyman, of New York, engaged in the flour, grain, and commission business, escaped down the main stairway to the office, thence to the veranda and thence to the pavement He was badly, but not seriously, burned A Mr Little of Philadelphia, escaped by the back stairway, as did also R J Stewart, of Oneida, N Y Edward Watts and his son, Edward C Watts, also succeeded in escaping Edward C Watts, however, returned and extricated Mr Exline, of Hancock, who was in imminent danger

The following also escaped Wm K. Benner, Middletown, Pa, Henry B Keiper, Lancaster, Pa, C L Jackson, Baltimore, George and Henry Rinker and John Rippon, Cumberland, Md, M Shannon and C Hoenicka, of Cumberland, badly hurt, Solomon Jenkins and J H Exline, of Hancock, Col E Ames, A O Dillingham, agent of the Singer Sewing-Machine Company, Mr and Mrs Hill and two children, August Tabler, Charles M Valentine, W G Haller, and Joseph Hughes, Geo A Davis, J M Landis, severely burnt about the head and on the hands, J H Hannis, of Renovo, Pa, D S Wolfinger, F F Burgess, of Baltimore, Wm Gibson, J W Yost, H Hillbrunner, of Philadelphia, Col D Bruce, of Cumberland, W H Zorns, of Philadelphia, S Jacques, William Stake, R H Groverman, of Baltimore, Wm M Price and Jesse Korns, of Cumberland, W T Barth, of Baltimore, Mr and Mrs T B. Cushwa, J M Knodle, A B Almony, and Dr W Macgill, of Cumberland J E Troxell, of Hancock, who occupied room No 25, was fatally burned F B Snively, of Shady Grove, Pa, was terribly burned and died a few hours later J H Exline and Solomon Jenkins were both severely, but not seriously, injured A number of other persons were more or less severely hurt The building was insured for twenty one thousand dollars Immediately after the fire a stock company was formed for the erection of a new hotel, and the result is the Baldwin,—a carefully constructed edifice, with ele- [illegible] of a first-

class hotel in one of the larger cities Attached to the Baldwin House proper, in the same building, is the Academy of Music, located on the site of Christian Winters' restaurant, a noted establishment in its day The length of the Baldwin House is one hundred and fifteen feet, and its depth one hundred and fifty feet It is seventy feet in height, is furnished throughout with solid walnut furniture of one pattern, and handsome Brussels carpets, and is supplied with hot and cold water and gas throughout There are in all one hundred and ten rooms, of which eighty eight are sleeping apartments Besides the Academy of Music, which seats eight hundred persons, the building contains the offices of the Adams Express Company, Baltimore and Ohio Express, and the American Union Telegraph Company The rooms of the Baldwin House are spacious and well appointed, and the general appearance of the establishment, as well as the food and service, does full justice to the business activity and enterprise of the progressive and thriving community in which it is situated Messrs McLaughlin & Herbert, the present courteous and enterprising proprietors, have had long experience in hotel management, and to their tact, good judgment, energy, and unfailing politeness to their guests, the remarkable success of the Baldwin House is chiefly due Their staff of employes was selected with great care, and is diligently kept up to the original standard, while all the appointments of the house are of the best description

The Franklin House, which now ranks next to the Baldwin, was known for many years as Wright's Hotel It is owned and managed by Philip Yahn, and has recently been enlarged and improved It stands on North Potomac Street, near the public square

The Antietam House, situated at the corner of Washington and Jonathan Streets is one of the oldest landmarks in the town Many years ago it was a tavern, kept by Benjamin Light, who was succeeded by Martin Newcomer and a number of others At one time it was known as the "Southern and Western Hotel," and as such was kept by a Mr Pollard, who was afterwards a contractor for the construction of the Cumberland Valley (then the Franklin) Railroad Subsequently, during the management of Mr Powers, its name was changed to the "City Hotel," and afterwards to the "Antietam House," kept by Wm E Doyle Its present manager is John Cretin, and the proprietors are Wm T Hamilton, Dr N B Scott, Z S Claggett, and James I Hurley The Antietam House is believed to be at least one hundred years old, [illegible]

ern property in Hagerstown Part of the lot on which it stands was occupied during the official term of its first president, Col Nathaniel Rochester, by the old Hagerstown Bank

The Newcomer House, formerly the Bell Tavern, is now owned by Dr N B Scott, and managed by Jonathan Newcomer Alfred Cline, a noted character in Hagerstown, was at one time proprietor of the Newcomer House

Paving.—By the act of Assembly, November session of 1791, Thos Hart, Ludwig Young, Wm Lee, John Shyrock, John Geiger, Peter Heighfly, and Baltzer Goll were made commissioners to improve and repair the streets in Hagerstown, and April 28, 1801, John Heddinger, clerk of the market, "by order of the commissioners," gave notice "to the inhabitants of Elizabeth Town" that, "whereas it was ordered by the commissioners in the month of May, 1791, and public notice thereof given, that the ditch from the public spring to the foot of Frederick Brentlinger's lot should be made three feet wide and two feet deep, and the sides of the said ditch done with stone or logs by the owners of each lot through which the water runs," and that "at the same it was ordered that the inhabitants of Elizabeth Town should have their footways paved and posted, and whereas little attention has been given to the above orders," the commissioners gave notice that unless these orders are obeyed by the 1st of September, they will employ workmen at the expense of the owners, and complete the work of ditching and paving On the following 5th of April, 1802, the same commissioners, by their clerk, issued the following notice

"To the Inhabitants of Elizabeth Town

"Whereas, notice has heretofore been given by the commissioners of Elizabeth Town to the inhabitants of the town to have their footways paved and posted, this is therefore to give notice that the commissioners will meet at the court house on Monday next, the 12th inst, when they are determined to make such arrangements as will compel the inhabitants aforesaid to post and pave the footways of the said town, agreeably to law, and will appoint some day when they are to commence Any of the inhabitants who have not as yet complied with the former notice of the commissioners are requested to attend at their next meeting, at the time above appointed, when they shall receive the necessary instructions Those persons who own lots which the water from the public spring runs through are requested to attend

"By order of the commissioners

"John Heddinger,
"April 5, 1802 *Clerk of the market*"

The work of paving the streets was resumed the following year, Feb 16, 1803, when by an act of Assembly Nathaniel Rochester Adam Ott, Otho Holland W[illegible] William Heyser

were appointed commissioners for a scheme or schemes of a lottery for raising a sum of money not exceeding two thousand dollars, to be used in improving the streets of Hagerstown, in Washington County Under this authority the following advertisement from the *Hagerstown Herald*, Feb 16, 1803, offered fortunes and footways to the good people of Hagerstown

"STREET LOTTERY

"Authorized by law to raise two thousand dollars for improving the streets in Elizabeth (Hager's) Town, in Washington County, Maryland

"All Prizes

"*Scheme*

"1 prize of	400	dollars	$400
2 prizes of	100	"	200
4 "	50	"	200
8 "	25	"	200
40 "	10	"	400
104 "	5	"	520
1 "	4	"	4
3170 "	$2\frac{1}{2}$	"	7925
3 last drawn of $50 each			150
3333 tickets at $3			$9999

"All prizes subject to a deduction of twenty per cent, will be paid immediately after drawing by Jacob Harry and William Heyser, with whom the money arising from the sale of tickets will be lodged for the purpose

"Those prizes not demanded within six months after drawing will be considered as relinquished for the benefit of the streets

"The lottery will be drawn as soon as the tickets are disposed of, and public notice given of the time and place of drawing

"Tickets at $3 each ($1 only to be paid at the time of purchase) are to be had of the following commissioners

"N ROCHESTER, JACOB HARRY,
"ADAM OTT, WILLIAM HEYSER"
"O H WILLIAMS,

The people of Hagerstown were actively engaged in paving and improving the streets, and from April, 1814, to March, 1815, there was expended on streets $692 20

The Telegraph.—On the 3d of May, 1854, I Dixon Roman organized a company for the construction of a telegraph between Hagerstown and Frederick City, of which he was president, with William M Marshall, M S Barber, Peter Swartzwelder, Howard Kennedy, and George W Smith as directors The line was speedily constructed and opened, bringing Hagerstown into connection with the then existing telegraphic communication of the country

Street Lighting.—While it is quite certain that Hagerstown had no street lamps in December, 1827, when the question of light or no light was decided is not very clear Gas-lights were authorized by a vote of the people, Jan 20, 1858, with a majority of 24 votes out of 148 polled The Hagerstown Gas-Light Company was organized and chartered in the summer of 1854 The [illegible] was man[illegible] by [illegible] McKee, H K Tice, and Thomas G Robertson, whose object at the start was to have gas furnished to light up only the stores, hotels, and business rooms generally, between the square and the court house, on West Washington Street The projectors had no hope at the time of securing the co operation of citizens living or doing business outside of these limits to an extent that would justify the erection of works of sufficient capacity to furnish gas for any considerable portion of the town As soon, however, as it became manifest that these gentlemen, with a large proportion of the business men in their district, were determined to carry out their purpose, a number of those outside, first from one section, then from another, proposed to subscribe for an additional amount of stock necessary to build works of sufficient capacity to supply their respective portions of the town These propositions were accepted, and the company was organized by the election of James Dixon Roman as president, who was re-elected every succeeding year until 1859, when George Kealhofer succeeded him, with an entire new board of directors

The amount of capital was fixed for the present at $6000, with the privilege of increasing it to $10,000 A contract was entered into with the "Maryland Portable Gas Light Company" for the building of the works, at a cost of two thousand dollars, and for laying down all main pipes at a cost of 80 cents, $1 35, and $1 65 per foot for two inch, three inch, and four-inch pipes respectively The works were erected in the rear of Lyceum Hall, and were constructed to manufacture gas from rosin oil, under Longbottom's patent The result of the first year's operation was unsatisfactory, having fallen far short of the Baltimore company's guarantee, and at the end of three years it was discovered that the company had not paid expenses The Baltimore company then proposed to build new works to manufacture gas from coal The capital stock was increased to $15,000, with the privilege of a further increase to $25,000 The new works were built on South Locust Street, and gas was made from coal, and at the end of the year 1859, notwithstanding the company charged five dollars per thousand feet of gas, its receipts were far short of its expenses A meeting of the stockholders was held, when the president and directors all resigned, and a new board was elected The Baltimore company, at the same time, proposed to lease the works for ten years, and pay the stockholders five per cent per annum for the first five years, and six per cent per annum for the next five years, which was readily accepted, as hitherto they had received nothing, and [illegible] the debt that

CPSIA information can be obtained at www.ICGtesting.com
Printed in the USA
LVOW130454161211

259557LV00001B/54/P

9 781172 097722